THE HANDBOOK OF MARITIME ECONOMICS AND BUSINESS

About the Editor

Costas Th. Grammenos, OBE, DSc, President of IAME since 1997, is Deputy Dean of the City University Cass Business School, City of London, and Pro Vice-Chancellor of City University, where he founded the Centre for Shipping Trade and Finance in 1983. The Centre carries out research through members of its staff and PhD students and international dialogue is cultivated by formal and informal meetings. He designed and directed two world-class Master's of Science: Shipping, Trade and Finance, introduced in 1984; and Logistics, Trade and Finance, introduced in 1997. In 1977, he introduced credit analysis and policy of bank shipping finance which has been applied by many international banks; and, in 1978, published the book *Bank Finance for Ship Purchase* (University of Wales Press), which formed the key principles in shipping finance. His research interests are in Bank Shipping Finance, and Capital Markets.

He was appointed OBE in 1994 for his contribution to international shipping and finance; and was 1998 Seatrade Personality of the Year for his contribution to international maritime studies. He is a member of the Board of Directors of the Alexander S Onassis Public Benefit Foundation; Member of the American Bureau of Shipping; Member of the Editorial Board of the International Journal of Maritime Economics; Founder and Chairman of the City of London Biennial Meetings; a Founding Trustee of the Institute of Marine Engineers Memorial Fund; and Liveryman of the Worshipful Company of Shipwrights.

THE HANDBOOK OF MARITIME ECONOMICS AND BUSINESS

COSTAS TH. GRAMMENOS

EDITOR

LONDON HONG KONG

2002

Informa Professional
(a trading division of
Informa UK Ltd)
Informa House
30–32 Mortimer Street
London W1W 7RE
professional.enquiries@informa.com

EAST ASIA
Informa Asia Publishing
Suite 1802, The Centrium
60 Wyndham Street
Central
Hong Kong
informa.asia@informa.com

© Costas Th. Grammenos and contributors, 2002

Reprinted 2003

British Library Cataloguing in Publication Data
A catalogue record
for this book is available
from the British Library

ISBN 1-84311-195-0

All rights reserved. No part of this publication may be reproduced, stored in a retrieval system, or transmitted, in any form or by any means, electronic, mechanical, photocopying, recording or otherwise, without the prior written permission of Informa Professional.

Whilst every effort has been made to ensure that the information contained in this book is correct, neither the authors nor Informa Professional can accept any responsibility for any errors or omissions or for any consequences resulting therefrom.

Text set in 10/12pt Postscript Plantin
by Tony Lansbury
Printed in Great Britain by
MPG Books Ltd, Bodmin, Cornwall

To Anna and Theophilos

PREFACE

In the late 1960s, when I started focusing on shipping finance, there were only a limited number of publications on Maritime Economics which mainly analysed the broader theoretical topics. Now, after almost thirty-five years, this unique volume is published, covering for the first time a wide variety of maritime issues and sectors, written by fifty-one members of the International Association of Maritime Economists (IAME). Over forty of the contributors are well-known academics, with the remaining younger ones already showing recognisable academic presence, all teaching and conducting research at thirty universities, in seventeen countries.

IAME was established in 1992 with an aim to promote the development of maritime economics as a distinct discipline, to encourage rational and reasoned discussion within it, and to facilitate the international exchange of ideas and research. Throughout this decade, IAME has worked towards these aims most successfully, and here one should mention the organisation of international conferences, on an annual basis; this year (on its tenth anniversary), members will meet in Panama.

The Handbook of Maritime Economics and Business contains thirty-nine refereed chapters which are, primarily, based on research carried out over a number of years, covering eleven broad areas of Maritime Economics, *viz*:

Maritime Economics and Globalisation; International Seaborne Trade; Economics of Shipping Markets and Cycles; Economics of Shipping Sectors; Issues in Liner Shipping; Maritime Safety and Labour Markets; National and International Shipping Policies; Aspects of Shipping Management and Operations; Shipping Investment and Finance; Port Economics and Management; and Aspects of International Logistics.

As I was studying these chapters, not only did I recall the questions that arose when I was collecting data for my study in Bank Shipping Finance, all those years ago, when so many answers were not readily available in published paper form or any other publication, I also found myself smiling many times, with great satisfaction, as I measured the width and depth of research presented here, in the wider spectrum of Maritime Economics. Indeed, *The Handbook of Maritime Economics and Business* is unique as it demonstrates the immeasurable progress, since the 1960s, in this area of research and teaching.

PREFACE

Because of its high quality output and its relevance to real life business, it will serve as a very valuable instrument for the stakeholders of the broader maritime world, including: university undergraduate and postgraduate students; shipowners; shipbrokers; shipmanagers and operators; bankers; underwriters; lawyers; shipping consultants; international logistics companies; port authorities; governmental maritime agencies; and official international organisations.

Over the last six months, I have worked closely with all the contributors and I thank them *de profundis* for the spontaneous acceptance of my invitation and the prompt delivery of what they promised. I am also grateful to them for agreeing, like myself, to waive their royalties in favour of IAME. My sincere thanks go to David Gilbertson, Chief Executive of Informa Group, who from the early days has strongly supported the idea of this volume; also to the LLP editorial and printing staff, in particular Vanessa Larkin and Tony Lansbury, for their co-operation and patience in meeting the tight deadlines. Finally, I thank very warmly two members of my staff: Dr Amir Alizadeh, also a contributor to this volume, and my Personal Assistant, Mrs Gladys Parish, for their enthusiasm and valuable assistance in the preparation of this *Handbook*.

Costas Th. Grammenos
London, September 2002.

TABLE OF CONTENTS

Preface vii
List of Contributors xiii

Part One: Shipping Economics and Maritime Nexus

Chapter 1 The Future of Maritime Economics
           RICHARD O GOSS   3

Chapter 2 Maritime Business During the 20th Century:
           Continuity and Change
           GELINA HARLAFTIS & JOHN THEOTOKAS   9

Chapter 3 Globalisation: The Maritime Nexus
           SHASHI KUMAR & JAN HOFFMANN   35

Part Two: International Seaborne Trade

Chapter 4 Patterns of International Ocean Trade
           DOUGLAS K FLEMING   65

Chapter 5 International Trade in Manufactured Goods
           MARY R BROOKS   90

Chapter 6 Energy Economics and Trade
           MICHAEL N TAMVAKIS   105

Chapter 7 Establishment of Europe-Wide Maritime Trade
           Flows by Origin/Destination
           MANFRED ZACHCIAL   147

Part Three: Economics of Shipping Markets and Shipping Cycles

Chapter 8 The Economics of Shipping Freight Markets
           PATRICK M ALDERTON & MERVYN ROWLINSON   157

Chapter 9 Economics of the Markets for Ships
           SIRI PETTERSEN STRANDENES   186

Chapter 10 Shipping Markets Cycles
           MARTIN STOPFORD   203

Part Four: Economics of Shipping Sectors

Chapter 11 The Dry Bulk Shipping Market
           AMIR H ALIZADEH & NIKOS K NOMIKOS   227

TABLE OF CONTENTS

Chapter 12	The Tanker Market: Current Structure and Economic Analysis DAVID GLEN & BRENDAN MARTIN	251
Chapter 13	Economics of Shortsea Shipping ENRICO MUSSO & UGO MARCHESE	280

Part Five: Issues in Liner Shipping

Chapter 14	Liner Shipping: Modelling Competition and Collusion WILLIAM SJOSTROM	307
Chapter 15	The Economic Regulation of Liner Shipping: the Impact of US and EU Regulation in US Trades BERNARD GARDNER, PETER MARLOW & RAWINDARAN NAIR	327
Chapter 16	The Role of Liner Shipping Co-operation in Business Strategy and the Impact of the Financial Crisis on Korean Liner Shipping Companies DONG-KEUN RYOO & TAE-WOO LEE	346
Chapter 17	Supply Chain and Logistics Management: Implications for Liner Shipping TREVOR D HEAVER	375

Part Six: Economics of Maritime Safety and the Seafaring Labour Market

Chapter 18	Economics of Maritime Safety and Environment Regulations SHUO MA	399
Chapter 19	Maritime Safety and Accident Analysis WAYNE K TALLEY	426
Chapter 20	The Economics of the Seafaring Labour Market HEATHER LEGGATE & JAMES MCCONVILLE	443

Part Seven: National and International Shipping Policies

Chapter 21	The Rise and Fall of National Shipping Policies GUNNAR K SLETMO	471
Chapter 22	Shipping Policy in the Globalisation Era: the Inter-relationship between International, Supra-national and National Shipping Policies MICHAEL ROE	495
Chapter 23	Ships, Flags and Taxes PETER MARLOW	512
Chapter 24	Government Policies and the Shipbuilding Industry JOON-SOO JON	530

Part Eight: Aspects of Shipping Management and Operations

Chapter 25	Marketing Strategies in Shipping A GÜLDEM CERIT	553

TABLE OF CONTENTS

Chapter 26	Fleet Operations Optimisation and Fleet Deployment ANASTASSIOS N PERAKIS	580
Chapter 27	Consolidation, Mergers and Acquisitions in the Shipping Industry PHOTIS M PANAYIDES & STEPHEN X H GONG	598

Part Nine: Shipping Investment and Finance

Chapter 28	Investing in Ships: An Essay on Constraints, Risk and Attitudes HELEN A THANOPOULOU	623
Chapter 29	Valuing Maritime Investments Using Real Options Analysis HELEN BENDALL	642
Chapter 30	Business Risk Measurement and Management in the Cargo Carrying Sector of the Shipping Industry MANOLIS G KAVUSSANOS	661
Chapter 31	Risk Management in the Shipping Industry: Theory and Practice NIKOS K NOMIKOS & AMIR H ALIZADEH	693
Chapter 32	Credit Risk, Analysis and Policy in Bank Shipping Finance COSTAS TH GRAMMENOS	731

Part Ten: Port Economics and Management

Chapter 33	Port Management, Operation and Competition: A Focus on North Europe HILDE MEERSMAN & EDDY VAN DE VOORDE	765
Chapter 34	Port Pricing HERCULES E HARALAMBIDES & ALBERT W VEENSTRA	782
Chapter 35	The Productivity and Efficiency of Ports and Terminals: Methods and Applications KEVIN CULLINANE	803
Chapter 36	The Economics of Transhipment ALFRED J BAIRD	832

Part Eleven: Aspects of International Logistics

Chapter 37	International Logistics and Modal Choice KUNIO MIYASHITA	863
Chapter 38	The Economics of International Trade Logistics and Shipping Transactions ERNST G FRANKEL	877
Chapter 39	IT in Logistics and Maritime Business LAURI M OJALA & DAVID A MENACHOF	898

Index   915

LIST OF CONTRIBUTORS

PROFESSOR PATRICK M ALDERTON

Born in 1931 and educated for the usual period, though left the sixth form to run away to sea in 1948 in BTC (later known as BP Tankers). Later in 1959, after trying most types of ships, he obtained his Extra Masters Certificate and lectured in one of the two navigation schools in London that in the late 1960s were amalgamated into the City of London Polytechnic. In the 1970s he moved to the Transport Department of the CLP and worked on his MPhil which he obtained in 1973. In 1989 he joined the World Maritime University as Professor of Ports and Shipping where he remained until he retired in 1995. Since then he has been a visiting professor at the London Metropolitan University. Publications include *Sea Transport – Operations & Economics* (4th ed) in 1995 and *Port Management and Operations* in 1999, plus over 100 papers, articles and chapters in various books.

DR AMIR H ALIZADEH

Amir Alizadeh is a research fellow in shipping investment and economics at City University Cass Business School, City of London. He has a first degree in Nautical Studies from Iran where he worked as a ship's officer for a short time. He then joined City University Cass Business School where he gained an MSc in Shipping, Trade and Finance and consequently studied for a PhD in Finance. Currently he is lecturing in Quantitative Methods, Shipping Economics, Economic Modelling and Maritime Business. His research interests include modelling freight markets and markets for ships, derivatives and risk management in financial and commodity markets, and forecasting. He has published in several academic journals in the area of transportation, finance and economics.

DR ALFRED J BAIRD

Alfred Baird is Head of the TRi Maritime Research Group at Napier University in Edinburgh, Scotland. Before embarking on an academic career, he worked for a liner shipping company, followed by a position as shipping manager in a manufacturing company. His doctoral study investigated the subject of strategic management in the global container shipping industry, and was carried out in collaboration with Sea-Land Service. He has acted as Specialist Adviser to both UK Parliament and Northern Ireland Assembly Select Committees during investigations into shipping matters. He has also acted as Technical Adviser to Scottish Government Agencies in assessing and selecting shipping services and in promoting seaport developments. He has researched and published in a number of areas in maritime transport, including port competition and privatisation, strategic management in liner shipping, market analysis in the ferry industry, shipping cost modelling, and assessing the feasibility of new shipping services and associated port developments.

LIST OF CONTRIBUTORS

PROFESSOR HELEN BENDALL

Helen Bendall specialises in International Financial Management in the Finance and Economics School at the University of Technology, Sydney, Australia. She is well known for cross-disciplinary financial analysis to shipping and maritime investment problems. Her PhD on the economics of technological change in shipping included an innovative approach to measuring ship and cargo handling productivity across several ship types. Many of her subsequent publications have analysed applications of new shipping technology such as advanced algorithms to solve complex fast ship scheduling problems. Recently her research has focused on fast and high speed vessels with the application of real options analysis to develop and evaluate the financial viability of new ship technology. Professor Bendall is a popular guest speaker on shipping investment and technological change in industry conferences and is an advisor to several peak industry and policy councils, having taken an active role in recent IMO working parties.

PROFESSOR MARY R BROOKS

Mary Brooks is the William A Black Chair of Commerce at Dalhousie University, Halifax, Canada. She was Membership Secretary and Treasurer of the International Association of Maritime Economists from 1994–98 and currently chairs the Committee on International Trade and Transportation, Transportation Research Board, Washington DC. She is a Member of the Chartered Institute of Transport and a Director of the Halifax International Airport Authority. Dr Brooks received her undergraduate degree from McGill University (1971), her MBA from Dalhousie University (1979) and her PhD in Maritime Studies from the University of Wales in 1983.

PROFESSOR A GÜLDEM CERIT

Güldem Cerit received her BSc degree in Engineering and completed her MBA and PhD in Marketing. She worked for the private industry for nine years and joined Dokuz Eylul University School of Maritime Business and Management as an Assistant Professor. She received her Associate Professor degree in Shipping and has been serving as the director of her School since 1997. She lectures at BSc, MSc and PhD programmes and her research concentrates on marketing in shipping. Her studies are published in journals and edited books. She was the winner of a Fulbright grant and the Maritime Prize at the 8th WCTR.

PROFESSOR KEVIN CULLINANE

Kevin Cullinane is Professor of Maritime and Transport Economics in the Department of Shipping & Transport Logistics at the Hong Kong Polytechnic University and former Head of the Department of Maritime Studies (since renamed Department of Shipping & Transport Logistics). He is a fellow of the Chartered Institute of Logistics & Transport, a member of the Chartered Institute of Purchasing & Supply and a science adviser in transportation to the government of Hong Kong. He also undertook projects for the UK government's Overseas Development Administration, Dar-al-Handasah Engineering and the Egyptian National Institute of Transport. He holds visiting Professorships at a number of institutions and has recently been appointed to an Honorary Professorship at the University of Hong Kong. His major research interests include: freight mode choice modelling, the measurement of economic efficiency and the development of mathematical models of financial and shipping markets.

LIST OF CONTRIBUTORS

PROFESSOR DOUGLAS K FLEMING

Douglas Fleming is a transportation geographer and professor emeritus at University of Washington, Seattle. He earned an undergraduate degree in Geology at Princeton in 1943 and a PhD in Geography at Seattle in 1965. He served at sea in the US Navy from 1944 to 1946 and with a commercial steamship line in various capacities from 1946 to 1961 in New York, Houston and Seattle. From 1965 to the present he has taught various classes in geography and marine affairs. He has contributed numerous articles to American and European journals and has served periodically on editorial boards in Europe.

PROFESSOR ERNST G FRANKEL

Ernst Frankel served in the Royal Navy and later as Chief Engineer on commercial vessels. He holds doctorates in Transport Economics as well as in Operations Research. He is Professor Emeritus of both Ocean Systems and of Management at MIT. He has served as Technical Director of Litton Industry; advisor for Port, Shipping, and Aviation at the World Bank; Chairman of American President Lines; Director of NOL, American Eagle Tankers, and APL Ltd.; Director of Ocean Futures Foundation; and Project Manager for over 62 major projects. He is the author of 14 books, 212 refereed articles, and holds 17 patents. He currently does research on transaction costs in intermodal supply chains and continues to teach project and risk management.

DR BERNARD GARDNER

Bernard Gardner is currently a reader in the Cardiff Business School. He is a former deck rating and ship's officer. In 1970 he graduated in economics from the University of Lancaster and joined the UK Government Economic Service. In 1973, he became a senior research associate at Cardiff University. While on study leave from Cardiff in 1986/87 he contributed to the FMC's Section 18 Study on the impact of the 1984 Shipping Act. He has over 70 publications in the maritime transport field including a number of articles relating to the economics of liner shipping and its regulation.

DR DAVID GLEN

David Glen is Reader in Transport at the Centre for International Transport Management, London Metropolitan University. He has published articles in a number of leading academic journals, including the *Journal of Transport Economics and Policy*, and *Maritime Policy and Management*. His research interests include tanker market economics and the market for seafarers. He is also involved in research work for UK government agencies and City organisations.

MR STEPHEN X H GONG

Stephen X H Gong is Lecturer in Finance at the Department of Shipping and Transport Logistics of the Hong Kong Polytechnic University. His research interests include finance, maritime and transport economics, industrial organization and logistics revenue/cost analysis. He has contributed to international refereed journals, government consultancy, professional magazines and academic conferences in the areas of shipping finance and management. Prior to joining the University, he had several years overseas work experience in international trade and logistics. He has studied at the City University Cass Business School, City of London, the London School of Economics, and the Hong Kong Polytechnic University.

LIST OF CONTRIBUTORS

PROFESSOR RICHARD O GOSS

Richard Goss trained on HMS *Worcester* and served at sea 1947–55. He became a Master Mariner and then took an economics degree at Cambridge. After working for the New Zealand Shipping Co he was appointed Economic Advisor on Shipping, Shipbuilding and Ports, to the Minister of Transport. He then spent 17 years in the Civil Services, serving as Economic Advisor to Lord Rochdale's Committee of Inquiry into British Shipping and rising to be Under-Secretary. In 1980 he moved to Cardiff University as Professor of Maritime Economics. He retired from this post in 1995. He has published papers in journals related to transport and maritime economics.

PROFESSOR HERCULES E HARALAMBIDES

Hercules Haralambides is Professor of Maritime Economics and Logistics at Erasmus University Rotterdam and Head of the Erasmus Center for Maritime Economics and Logistics (*www.maritimeeconomics.com*). He is also Editor of the International Journal of Maritime Economics (IJME) (*www.palgrave-journals.com/ijme*) and Chairman of the Special Interest Group (SIG) on Maritime Transport and Ports of the World Conference on Transport Research. Among a number of consultative and advisory functions at the national and international level, he is expert of the European Commission, OECD, ILO and IBRD/IFC and one of the Founding Members of the International Association of Maritime Economists (IAME).

PROFESSOR GELINA HARLAFTIS

Gelina Harlaftis graduated from the University of Athens (BSc)and has completed her post graduate studies at the Universities of Cambridge (MPhil) and Oxford (DPhil). She is Associate Professor, Department of History, Ionian University, Corfu. She is author of a large number of articles and books, among which *Greek Shipowners and Greece 1945–1975* (1993), *A History of Greek-owned Shipping* (1996) (that was honoured with the Runciman Award 1997), with David Starkey (eds), *Global Markets: The Internationalization of Sea Transport Industries since 1850s* (1998), and, in Greek, *Shipping and History, 16th–20th centuries* (2001). She has been a visiting professor at universities in Canada and the UK and is Vice-president of the International Association of Maritime History.

PROFESSOR TREVOR D HEAVER

Trevor Heaver is Professor Emeritus, University of British Columbia, and Visiting Professor, University of Antwerp. He is a Fellow of the Chartered Institute of Transport, Past-President of the International Association of Maritime Economists and a Past-Chairman of the World Conference on Transport Research. He has served on various advisory committees and consulted for governments and corporations. His most recent papers and publications have dealt mainly with international shipping and logistics.

DR JAN HOFFMANN

Jan Hoffmann works as international transport analyst for the United Nations' Economic Commission for Latin America and the Caribbean (ECLAC), Chile, since 1997. He specializes in port reforms, liner shipping, and international transport costs. His work has resulted in numerous publications and technical missions to more than thirty countries as well as ECLAC's Internet "Maritime Profile" and "International Transport Data Base". Previously, he spent two years with the International Maritime

Organization. He studied in Bath, Barcelona, and Hamburg, where he obtained his doctorate degree. Parallel work included assistant professor, export agent, and seafarer for a tramp shipping company.

PROFESSOR JOON-SOO JON

Joon-Soo Jon began his academic life with a first degree in English Literature at Sogang University, and went on to obtain a master's degree in Transport Management at SUNY in USA and a doctorate in Maritime Studies at the University of Wales in Cardiff. Currently he is a professor at Sogang University in Seoul. While he is teaching and researching in the maritime sector, he has been involved in policy making as an adviser to various Korean Government Agencies such as the Ministry of Maritime Affairs, the Ministry of Industry and the Ministry of Foreign Affairs. He has very extensive research works and publications. His current research interests focus upon the development of logistics systems in the Far Eastern Countries.

PROFESSOR MANOLIS G KAVUSSANOS

Manolis Kavussanos works at the Athens University of Economics and Business, Greece, elected since 2001. He holds a BSc and MSc (Economics), from the University of London; and a PhD (Applied Economics) from City University Cass Business School, City of London, where he was Director of the MSc in Trade, Transport and Finance, from its inception in 1997, until 2001, and has held posts including Visiting Professor at Erasmus University (Rotterdam); expert evaluator and consultant in financial economics, econometrics and transportation issues, for organisations such as the Community of the European Commission and private companies. He is the author of numerous pieces of academic work published in top international refereed journals and has presented in international conferences around the world, gaining awards for the quality of his work.

DR HEATHER LEGGATE

Heather Leggate is the Director of the Centre for International Transport Management, London Metropolitan University. She pursued a professional and industrial career with Price Warehouse Coopers and as Financial Analyst with IBM. Fellow of the Institute of Chartered Accountants in England and Wales. Studied Economics at Lancaster University, followed by a master's degree in Finance and a PhD in risk management in the maritime industry; an academic career which includes research and publication interests in the maritime industry primarily in finance, currency risk management and economic and commercial exposure; more recently an interest in the global seafaring labour force with a series of major studies commissioned by the International Labour Organisation (UN).

PROFESSOR UGO MARCHESE

Professor emeritus, University of Genoa. President, Istituto Internazionale delle Comunicazioni, Genoa. Former full professor of Shipping and Transport Economics, Political Economy, Regional Economics, International Economics, university of Genoa. Author and/or editor of more than 20 books and more than 200 scientific articles. President, Italian Society of Transportation Economists, 1995–99. Member, Board of Directors of scientific reviews *Trasporti* and *Quaderni Regionali*. Member, Editorial Committee, *International Journal of Maritime Economics*. Expert for Italian General Transport Plan 1984–90. President, Committee for Maritime and Port Planning, 1988–89.

LIST OF CONTRIBUTORS

DR PETER MARLOW

Peter Marlow has over 25 years experience in academia and research work and is the author of more than 60 published works. He is currently the Head of Logistics and Operations Management at the Cardiff Business School and is a transport economist with considerable expertise in maritime and land transport as well as logistics. He is External Advisor to the Research Committee of the UK Maritime and Coastguard Agency and is an expert on the fiscal treatment of shipping and the choice of flag in international shipping. Other research interests include short sea shipping, port economics and logistics, and inter-modal transport.

MR BRENDAN MARTIN

Brendan Martin is a director of the British shipbroking house E. A. Gibson Shipbrokers Ltd. He is reponsible for the company's research, data and consultancy services. Since joining Gibsons in 1985, he has worked on a number of the company's developments and travelled extensively lecturing and making presentations in his specialist area – the economics of the tanker market and oil production. He has authored numerous studies relating to the tanker market, both for clients on a consultancy basis and for various industry forums. Before joining Gibsons, he worked in various branches of shipping after graduating with a master's degree in transport planning and management in 1978. These included being the planning manager of Cunard's cargo shipping division, a consultant in container and fleet development, and providing analysis of the importance of the flags of convenience in European shipping for the then EEC Commission in Brussels.

PROFESSOR JAMES MCCONVILLE

James McConville is Professor Emeritus of the London School of Foreign Trade, at the London Metropolitan University. He was educated at Oxford, Hull and Warwick universities following a career at sea. A distinguished academic career including pioneering research on manpower and labour issues. Specialist advisor to the House of Commons Select Committee on Transport for a number of years with inquiries into Shipping, Ports, Inland Waterways and HM Coastguard. Visiting Professor and Consultant to a number of leading institutions worldwide. An extensive list of publications including the definitive maritime economics textbook *The Economics of Maritime Transport: Theory and Practice*. Editor of the IAME journal *Maritime Policy and Management*.

PROFESSOR HILDE MEERSMAN

Hilde Meersman is a full-time professor at the Faculty of Applied Economics at the University of Antwerp. She is a member of the directorate of, and professor at, the Institute for Transport and Maritime Management Antwerp (ITMMA). She chaired the Local Organising Committee of the 8th World Conference on Transportation Research (12–17 July 1998, Antwerp) and is at present chairing the International Scientific Committee of the WCTR-S. From 1994 until 1998 she was the head of the Centre for Economic and Social Research (SESO) at UFSIA which had research in port and transportation economics as one of its major activities. She is involved, directly or indirectly, in a large number of research projects on a.o. international investment, modelling and forecasting commodity transportation, empirical analysis of port competition, inland navigation, mode choice, sustainable mobility, etc.

DR DAVID A MENACHOF

David Menachof is Lecturer in International Logistics and Distribution and Director of the MSc in Logistics, Trade and Finance degree at City University Cass Business

School, City of London. Dr Menachof received his doctorate from the University of Tennessee, and was the recipient of the Council of Logistics Management's Doctoral Dissertation Award in 1993. He has previously taught at the University of Charleston, South Carolina, and the University of Plymouth, England. In addition, he is a Fulbright Scholar, having spent an academic year in Odessa, Ukraine, as part of the grant. His research interests include Logistics and Distribution, Supply Chain Management and Modelling, e-commerce and Information Technology.

PROFESSOR KUNIO MIYASHITA

Kunio Miyashita is the Professor of International Logistics and Transportation at the Graduate School of Business Administration, Kobe University and holds the PhD from this University. He is the author of 6 books, the first of which is *Market Behaviors in Competitive Shipping Markets* (published by the Institute of Shipping Economics, Bremen, 1977) and the last of which is *Global Competition of Japanese Logistics Industry* (published by Chikura Shobo, Tokyo, 2002, in Japanese). He is the President of the Japan Society of Shipping Economics and the Research Advisory Committee Member of the Japan Maritime Research Institute.

PROFESSOR ENRICO MUSSO

Full professor in Applied Economics; head, section of Transport Economics and Economic Geography, department of Economics, University of Genoa. Coordinator, doctoral program in Transport Economics, University of Genoa. Former visiting scholar/professor in the universities of Nice, Cambridge, Rome "La Sapienza", Tavrida (Ukraine). Member, Steering Committee of SIG-2 (Maritime Transport and Ports), World Conference on Transport Research Society. Regional Editor for South Europe/Middle East and member of the editorial board of the *International Journal of Maritime Economics*. Author of eight volumes and about 100 scientific articles. Member, Authority for Public Utilities, City of Genoa.

DR RAWINDARAN NAIR

Rawindaran Nair graduated from the University of Malaya with a degree in economics in1970 and joined the Malaysian Civil Service. He served as Trade Commissioner in Paris and Stockholm until 1978 and later in the Ministry of Finance in Kuala Lumpur. In 1986 he graduated with a Master's degree in maritime studies from the University of Wales. Subsequently he obtained a degree in law from the University of London. In 1997, he obtained a Master's degree in legal aspects of marine affairs from the University of Wales and recently obtained his doctorate from the same University whilst studying at Cardiff.

DR NIKOS K NOMIKOS

Nikos Nomikos holds a first degree in Economics from Athens University of Economics and Business. On completing his MSc in Shipping, Trade and Finance, at City University Cass Busines School, City of London, where he graduated with distinction, he commenced working at the Department of Shipping, Trade & Finance as a researcher and doctoral candidate. After completing his PhD thesis, he worked at the Baltic Exchange as Senior Market Analyst, being in charge of the freight indices and risk management section. Since November 2001, he has been with the Faculty of Finance as a Lecturer in Shipping Risk Management at the Cass Business School. His current research interests include risk management and risk analysis in shipping, commodity and financial futures markets. His research papers have been published in international finance journals and have been presented in conferences worldwide. He also acts as a consultant on issues of risk management for the Baltic Exchange and provides consulting services on a number of other shipping and financial institutions.

PROFESSOR LAURI M OJALA

Lauri Ojala is professor of logistics at the Turku School of Economics and Business Administration, Finland. His previous positions include Linköping University and Abo Akademi University. He has also worked as a short term consultant for the World Bank on several occasions. His research interest include logistics, shipping economics and transport markets. He has published in journals such as *The International Journal of Physical Distribution and Logistics Management*, *The International Journal of Logistics Management*, and *Maritime Policy and Management*.

DR PHOTIS M PANAYIDES

Photis Panayides is Assistant Professor in Strategic Marketing at the Department of Shipping and Transport Logistics of the Hong Kong Polytechnic University. His research interests include marketing and strategy, foreign direct investment, multinational corporations and industrial organisation. He has published in the *International Journal of Maritime Economics*, *Maritime Policy and Management*, *Transport Reviews* and *The Service Industries Journal* and has contributed to numerous international refereed conferences. He is also the author of *Recent Developments in International Shipping Finance* (Informa, 2002), *Professional Ship Management: Marketing and Strategy* (Ashgate, 2001) and *International Ship Management: Market Analysis and Strategic Opportunities* (IIR Publications, 1999).

PROFESSOR ANASTASSIOS N PERAKIS

Anastassios Perakis obtained his first degree from NTU Athens (NA&ME), and his Master's (Ocean Eng/Operations research), PhD and MBA, from MIT. Tenured faculty of Department of NA&ME, University of Michigan. Sponsored research: fleet deployment, logistics, routing/scheduling, reliability/safety, environmental policy, probabilistic modeling, optimisation, decision analysis for marine systems. Published a book, two chapters in books, and over 120 refereed journal, conference proceedings, reports, etc. Visiting Professor, Technical University Berlin (twice), NTU Athens, Institute of Water Resources (USA), Fellow IESET (University of Michigan). Chaired four graduated (and one current) PhD students, three also professors, several academic "grandchildren" and "great-grandchildren". Member SNAME, INFORMS, WTCR, IAME.

PROFESSOR MICHAEL ROE

Michael Roe holds the Chair of Maritime Policy at the University of Plymouth and previously worked at the Universities of Aston, Coventry and London Guildhall. Graduating in Geography, and Transport Planning and Engineering with a Doctorate in Transport Policy, he has authored over 40 journal papers and 12 books. Frequently visiting East Europe he has worked closely with universities in Gdansk, Szczecin, Klaipeda, Riga, Budapest, Bucharest, Constantza and Varna. His wife, Liz, provides moral and intellectual support whilst his two children, Joe and Siân, provide entertainment and expenses. He has interests in modern European literature, the work of Patti Smith and the exploits of Charlton Athletic.

LIST OF CONTRIBUTORS

DR MERVYN ROWLINSON

Mervyn Rowlinson is a Senior Lecturer in Shipping and Transport at London Metropolitan University, where he has special responsibilities as Course Manager of the Institute of Chartered Shipbrokers' Courses. He has 20 years teaching experience, including the Merchant Navy College and Warsash Maritime Centre, Southampton; and 9 years' industrial experience, including tankers and tugs. His research interests are: Shortsea Shipping, Towage, Intermodal Operations.

DR DONG-KEUN RYOO

Dong-Keun Ryoo received a PhD in the field of maritime transport at Cardiff University in 1999 and currently holds a position as a lecturer in Korea Maritime University, teaching subjects such as maritime transport, shipping management, maritime economics, shipping policy, port policy and management, and logistics management. He is a member of the International Association of Maritime Economics, of the Korean Association of Shipping Studies, and of the Korean Society of Transportation. He acts as an external advisor to the Ministry of Maritime Affairs and Fisheries, and Busan Metropolitan City, Korea. He also acts as a referee of the *Journal of the Korean Association of Shipping Studies* and *Journal of International Maritime Affairs*. The research areas in which he is interested are alliance strategy and management in the shipping industry, business strategy of shipping companies, maritime e-commerce, port policy and management, logistics management in maritime transport, and maritime economics.

PROFESSOR SHASHI KUMAR

Shashi Kumar is the founding chair and professor of International Business and Logistics at the Loeb-Sullivan School, Maine Maritime Academy, Castine, Maine, USA. He earned his PhD from the University of Wales, Cardiff, Wales, UK and a MS in Maritime (Business) Management at Maine Maritime Academy. He did his undergraduate work at the University of Bombay, India, and also at the Indian Maritime Academy (T S Rajendra). He is a licensed Master Mariner (UK). He serves on the editorial board of the *International Journal of Maritime Economists*, the *IAMU (International Association of Maritime Universities) Journal* and the *Marine Transport Policy Journal*, and as the current Treasurer of IAME.

PROFESSOR SHUO MA

Shuo Ma is a professor of shipping management and port management at World Maritime University in Malmö, Sweden. He is also holding, currently, the position of Vice-Rector and Academic Dean. Dr Ma is active as a researcher and consultant in the area of shipping and port economics and management. He served from 1996 to 2000 as an IAME Council member. He has a Master's degree in transport and distribution and a PhD in economics from the University of Paris.

DR WILLIAM SJOSTROM

William Sjostrom received his PhD in 1986 at the University of Washington, supervised by Keith Leffler, a specialist in competition policy, and Douglas Fleming, a maritime geographer. He taught at Northern Illinois University and currently is senior lecturer in economics at the National University of Ireland, Cork, where he also served as dean of the Faculty of Commerce. He serves on the editorial board of the *International Journal of Maritime Economics*. His maritime research focuses on competition policy in liner shipping, but also on maritime safety. He has also published papers on crime, unemployment, and oligopoly in the lumber industry.

PROFESSOR GUNNAR K SLETMO

Gunnar Sletmo recently retired from l'Ecole des Hautes Etudes Commerciales (HEC), Montreal. He previously held academic positions at Columbia University, New York and at the Norwegian School of Economics and Business Administration, Norway. He served the Canadian Minister of Transport as Chairman of the Federal Task Force on Deep-Sea Shipping (1984–85) and was Maritime Policy Advisor to CIDA (the Canadian International Development Agency) as well as to the Federal Maritime Commission (Washington DC) He was Chairman of the Cotonou Round Table of the Transport Ministers of West and Central Africa (Benin 1992), organised in the context of the Sub-Saharan Africa Transport Policy Program and represented Canada at the Second Cotonou Round Table (Benin 1997). Professor Sletmo has published extensively on shipping policy and on Asian economies.

PROFESSOR MARTIN STOPFORD

Martin Stopford is a graduate of Oxford University and holds a PhD in International Economics from London University. During his 30 year career in the Maritime Industry he has held positions as Director of Business Development with British Shipbuilders, Global Shipping Economist with Chase Manhattan Bank NA, Chief Executive of Lloyds Maritime Information Services and currently Managing Director of Clarkson Research. He is a Visiting Professor at City University Cass Business School, City of London, and is a regular lecturer and course leader at Cambridge Academy of Transport. His publications include *Maritime Economics*, the widely used shipping text, and many published papers on shipping economics and ship finance.

PROFESSOR SIRI PETTERSEN STRANDENES

Siri Pettersen Strandenes is professor at the Centre for International Economics and Shipping, Department of Economics, Norwegian School of Economics and Business Administration (NHH). She has worked at NHH since 1989. Her fields of research are transport and market analysis focusing on the maritime and the airline industries. She has published in international research journals and is member of the editorial board of the *International Journal of Maritime Economics*. She teaches graduate level courses in shipping, transport and logistics, international economics and international finance. She is member of the board of Maritime Research Programme, Research Council of Norway.

PROFESSOR TAE-WOO LEE

Tae-Woo Lee holds a PhD from Cardiff University in the UK. Having been Visiting Professor at the Faculty of Economics and Politics in Cambridge, IMS at University of Plymouth and others, he is head of the Division of Maritime Transportation Science at Korea Maritime University. He has served as a council member of the International Association of Maritime Economists, including a secretarial job. He has also contributed in the maritime arena, as guest editor of *Maritime Policy and Management*, columnist for *Lloyd's List*, a member of the Regulatory and Reform Committee and advisor at the Ministry of Maritime Affairs and Fisheries, Korea, and keynote speaker at international conferences.

PROFESSOR WAYNE K TALLEY

Wayne Talley is Professor of Economics at Old Dominion University, Norfolk, Virginia, USA, where he is the Executive Director of the International Maritime, Ports and Logistics Management Institute and holds the designations of Eminent Scholar and the

LIST OF CONTRIBUTORS

Frederick W Beazley Professor of Economics. He has published four transportation books and over 120 papers. He has held visiting domestic positions at the Woods Hole Oceanographic Institution (Woods Hole, Massachusetts), the US Department of Transportation (Cambridge, Massachusetts), the Interstate Commerce Commission (Washington DC), and the National Aeronautics and Space Administration (Langley, Virginia) and international positions at other universities around the world. He is the Editor-in-Chief of *Transportation Research Part E: Logistics and Transportation Review*, and a member of the editorial boards of three other transportation journals. He has served on several standing and study committees of the US National Research Council and is a member of the Council of the International Association of Maritime Economists.

DR MICHAEL N TAMVAKIS

After he graduated with a BSc in Economics from the Economic University of Athens he attended the MSc course in Shipping, Trade and Finance in 1988–89 at City University Cass Busines School, where he also received his PhD. He joined the staff of the Centre for Shipping, Trade and Finance as an ESRC Management Teaching Fellow in 1989, at the Cass Business School and was then appointed lecturer in International Commodity Trade. He was appointed Director of the MSc in Shipping, Trade and Finance in January 1998 and became a Senior Lecturer in Commodity Trade and Finance in April 2001. His research interests are in the areas of commodity risk management and bulk shipping economics, among other. He has published in academic journals and has addressed conferences in Antwerp, Bangkok, London, Oslo, Piraeus and Vancouver. He is a member of the Education and Training Committee of the Institute of Chartered Shipbrokers.

DR HELEN A THANOPOULOU

Helen Thanopoulou was born in Athens, Greece, in 1958 and studied at the University of Athens and at the University of Paris I, Pantheon-Sorbonne. She obtained her PhD from the University of Piraeus where she taught in the early 1990s. In 1995 she joined Cardiff University. She is currently a Senior Lecturer in the Cardiff Business School and the Programme Director for MSc International Transport, MSc Marine Policy and the Diploma in Port and Shipping Administration. She has published extensively in English; her book on *International and Greek Shipping* was published in Greece in 1994.

DR JOHN THEOTOKAS

John Theotokas has received a BA in economics and a PhD in Shipping Management from the University of Piraeus. He is a Lecturer at the Department of Shipping, Trade and Transport of the University of the Aegean. His research and publications have focused on the evolution of Management and Organization of Greek-owned Shipping Companies, on Organizational Culture and on Strategies of Shipping Companies.

PROFESSOR EDDY VAN DE VOORDE

Eddy Van de Voorde teaches at the University of Antwerp (UFSIA-RUCA and ITMMA). His work deals with Maritime Economics, Port Economics and Air Transport Economics. He is responsible for several new research projects, financed by a number of Belgian and international government institutions and private companies. Extensive research in the field of modelling in the sector of freight transport has resulted in a large number of academic publications. He is a member of the editorial boards of a number of international transport journals such as *Maritime Policy and Management* and *Transportation Research E*. He also is a Visiting Professor at several Belgian and foreign universities. In July 1998, he acted as Vice-President of the 8th World Conference on Transport Research (8th WCTR). In the period 1995–2001 he was Vice-Chairman of the international scientific committee of the WCTRS. Next to this, he acts as Vice-President of the International Association of Maritime Economists (IAME) and Chairman of BIVEC/GIBET, the Benelux Interuniversity Group of Transport Economists. Being one of the founding fathers of ITMMA, he is Vice-Chairman of the Executive Board of the Institute.

DR ALBERT WILLEM VEENSTRA

Albert Veenstra is Programme Director at the Erasmus University Centre for Contract Research and Business Support (ERBS) BV, for research programmes in Transport, Infrastructure and Logistics, and Supply Chain Management. He obtained his PhD from the Erasmus University Rotterdam where, from 1994 to 1999, he lectured in maritime and port economics at the department of Regional, Transport and Port Economics. He has written papers that were presented at international conferences and published in books and academic journals. His research interests include: forecasting shipping variables, modelling shipping markets, topics in port economics and supply chain management, and transport education and training.

PROFESSOR DR MANFRED ZACHCIAL

Manfred Zachcial belongs to the Board of Directors of the Institute of Shipping Economics and Logistics (ISL), Bremen, and has a chair of economics and statistics at Bremen University. Manfred Zachcial has been working on economics, land and maritime transport projects since 1972. He is a leading authority on shipping economics, statistics, transport planning, logistics and maritime information systems. In addition to his academic responsibilities, Professor Zachcial advises governments and international agencies on transportation strategies, port and shipping, and on the feasibility of various transport infrastructure developments. His wide ranging research activities have resulted in numerous published works on modelling in both land and maritime transport, including transhipments at European sea ports. One of his major research activities is the analysis and forecast of world container shipping along the whole transport chains including hinterland transports and their determinants.

PART ONE

SHIPPING ECONOMICS AND MARITIME NEXUS

CHAPTER 1

THE FUTURE OF MARITIME ECONOMICS

Richard O. Goss

Professor Emeritus, University of Cardiff, Wales, UK (retired).
E-mail: *rogoss@weirgardens.demon.co.uk*

INTRODUCTION

Another paper[1] has recently recorded and discussed the history of maritime economics, noting that it has developed into a recognised subject, mainly within the last four decades, that it is now being taught, usually as a part of other courses, in many institutions around the world, and that its literature now seems to appear in two parts. The first of these concerns economic aspects of ship design and is addressed mainly to naval architects. The second is addressed to a more general audience including those who supply and consume maritime transport services and those who develop public policies concerning them. It is therefore appropriate to speculate how the subject may develop in the future and this paper does so under those two headings, offering some suggestions for future studies. We should not be surprised, however, that the relationships between economic theory and policy are, however, becoming increasingly obvious in each of them.

THE ECONOMICS OF SHIP DESIGN AND SAFETY

It was originally considered that the optimum ship was simply the most profitable one and that, in the long run, competitive markets would ensure that this would be that with the lowest costs. Discounted cash flow models were therefore developed for comparing and improving alternative ship designs[2] and others compared the long run average total cost of carrying cargo, e.g., for ships of different sizes,[3] on various bases. Such methods have been taught to potential ship designers in such universities as Michigan in the USA and at Newcastle-upon-Tyne in Britain and used by shipbuilders and ship operators (i.e., owners, managers and charterers) in increasingly sophisticated forms.

In maritime transport, as elsewhere, however, there has been an increasing concern with the protection of the environment. Following numbers of well-publicised maritime disasters, however, this economic approach has been extended to maritime safety in general. This was accelerated by a Report from a Select Committee of the House of Lords[4] which concluded (p. 67) that:

"modern science and technology are not being adequately applied in many of the fields which affect the safety of ships, the lives of those who travel in them, and the marine environment; that the systems which have evolved over the last two centuries to enhance safety at sea are not conducted on a scientific basis; and that there are new developments in marine technology affecting the design, construction and operation of ships which the regulators constantly struggle to keep up with and constantly fall behind as technology develops."

These and other, equally trenchant, criticisms (including comments on the absence of any comprehensive figures for deaths and injuries comparable to those for civil aviation) were widely reported and led Britain's Marine Safety Agency[5] to seek and obtain some £3/4m of additional research funds.[6] These were put to good use in developing and adapting what is now termed Formal Safety Assessment (FSA), involving a systematic consideration of the relevant hazards, the various ways in which they might be overcome, the costs and benefits of each proposal and thus leading to the modern scientific decision-making approach whose absence the Carver Committee had so deplored. With the UK government taking the lead, and producing a fully worked example involving high speed catamaran ferries, this was adopted by the International Maritime Organisation (IMO). Though there were one or two countries which expressed doubts about using such "non-technical" approaches, most countries supported the move. This has led to a general realisation that such a disciplined approach is the only way of securing a rational basis for the formulation of international regulations for the design and operation of ships. As far as the British studies were concerned it was notable that representatives of trade associations like the Chamber of Shipping and trade unions like the National Union of Maritime, Aviation and Sea Transport Officers and the Rail and Maritime Trade Union worked together and with officials without any friction.

The cost-benefit stage of FSA clearly involves obtaining, and using, values for ships, for their cargoes, for the lives of those travelling on them and for the effects that actual or potential maritime casualties may have on the environment. Since most such casualties involve damage to ships (sometimes people and cargoes as well) rather than total losses, it follows that typical costs of repairs and of the resultant delays to passengers and cargoes will also need to be established, as will the extent and duration of environmental effects. Many of these aspects of cost-benefit analysis will therefore require a good deal of original research in which it will be necessary to integrate the work of engineers and environmental scientists with that of economists. No doubt some of this will, in the near future, develop into the familiar iteration between those responsible for developing the models and those who provide the quantitative information necessary to make them work.

It therefore seems likely that, for the first time, this process of integration will lead to a much needed improvement in the quality of the statistics of maritime casualties, probably involving the answers to such physical and qualitative questions as what happens?, to such quantitative ones as how often does it happen? or how much of it happens? and only then proceeding to such economic questions as what is it worth? It is, of course, important that the approaches to all three types of question actually are integrated, and that maritime economists are involved throughout, since otherwise the earlier stages may produce data which is not useful in the final one.

Most maritime economists have experienced frustration with the standard maritime statistics; many of these appear to be laboriously collected as by-products of statutory procedures but with purposes that are both ancient and obscure. Gross and net tonnages of ships are amongst the obvious examples. Amongst the more important current omissions are the necessary details of ships lost and damaged, the delays to the latter, of cargoes lost, damaged and delayed and of seafarers killed and injured. Since historical data will sometimes need to be revised for price-changes, it will also be useful to have appropriate price-indexes. A useful start might lie in producing some maritime equivalent of Dawson's 1971 study on road accidents.[7]

In due course there may be room for a major text-book, possibly on FSA in general but certainly covering the cost-benefit part of it, and drawing on a wide range of ideas both from within the maritime world and from outside it. A possible model would be the work of the Flood Hazard Research Centre at Middlesex University.[8]

MARITIME ECONOMICS AND POLICIES GENERALLY

1. Protectionism

As Sturmey[9] and the Rochdale Committee[10] argued, protectionism in shipping has been minimal in recent years, subsidised fleets like that of the USA being small and declining whilst flag discrimination affected only a small proportion of world trade. Nevertheless, recent years have seen a welcome reduction, with the European Union and Mercosul reducing cabotage in Europe and South America respectively and the USA subsidising fewer international liner services – though, for the time being, maintaining comprehensive cabotage under the Jones Act of 1920. Newly independent countries seem to have become disillusioned with the results of supporting national lines, possibly because academic studies have shown that such a capital-intensive industry has quite the wrong ratio for economies with surplus labour; and that such lines did not justify the investment, did little to enhance gross domestic product, employment, the balance of payments, countervailing power, national security or national prestige and that, in general, the gains had been less than the opportunity costs of the resources involved.[11] In contrast to the ideas promoted by the Shipping Secretariat of UNCTAD,[12] such countries as the Philippines and China have specialised in supplying crews to ships owned elsewhere and to their great advantage. Similarly, we hear less of spurious ideas about shipping creating special balance of payments effects and being useful for defence purposes,[13] whether from newly-independent countries or any others.

Whilst all this must be welcome to the majority of economists there is more to be done, especially in the field of cabotage. For example, it would be good to see a thorough study of the effects of opening the domestic trades of Canada and the USA to international competition. There can be no doubt that this would lead to lower costs and freight rates, to the great benefit of consumers in both countries. Similarly, though other forms of financial assistance for shipping still seem to be popular with Congress, a continued winding-down of these would benefit American producers and consumers as well as taxpayers.

2. Competition policy

The activities of shipping conferences also attract rather less attention than hitherto, as multi-modal container services involve far fewer lines, whether in consortia, mergers or "alliances", with such arrangements changing more frequently and with regulatory authorities insisting that any derogation from the usual arrangements of competition policy can apply only to the strictly maritime component. Since the essence of many such services is the availability of a door-to-door service for a single charge, this tends to make conventional agreements on maritime freight rates otiose. Indeed, some observers feel that shipping conferences are either undergoing fundamental changes or on the way out. Consistently with the pattern observed in other industries following the removal of restrictive practices, there are no observations of price-instability, let alone anything resembling chaos. However, as mergers are likely to prove more efficient than the looser arrangements currently known as alliances it may be that some new and international competition policy measures will come to be needed in the future.

3. Flags of convenience

The doctrine that any international legal person (e.g., a state, or the United Nations itself) may register ships on whatever terms it pleases, and whether it has the capacity to administer international conventions on safety or not, has led to the proliferation of flags of convenience who operate registers primarily in order to attract revenues. These provide opportunities for the less responsible operators to register ships which achieve low costs by failing to comply with many safety requirements and switching flags whenever an administration show signs of becoming more active. (Examples of unsafe practices include inadequate maintenance, especially of life-saving and fire-fighting equipment, unqualified officers and, on some tankers, using the cargo to fuel the boilers.) Some of these countries are, in effect, kleptocracies.[14] The competition which these provide for more responsible operators is, to a limited but increasing extent, constrained by a sample of ships being inspected, and sometimes detained, under Port State Control measures. There remain, however, far too many examples of ships which are still operating, whilst continuing to be unsafe in respect of their design, maintenance or operation. Crew fatigue is an example frequently commented upon[15] and is the subject of work in progress at the Seafarers' International Research Centre in the University of Cardiff. It might be thought that a free market in marine insurance would penalise the less-safe operators but this has not taken place, partly because they can change their names and re-enter the market. There is, therefore, a need for economic studies aimed at quantifying the effects of reduced safety, in terms of increased risks and lower costs, and it might be hoped that insurance markets would either commission such studies or participate in them. It would also be interesting to have studies of ways in which the insurance market might exert more discipline on those who operate high-risk ships.

4. Market models

Claims that the average rate of return on ship investments is fairly low necessarily suppress a fairly wide range, e.g. between ships of different types, ages and levels of efficiency. Since both freight rates and ship prices fluctuate markedly it is obviously helpful to develop models of the markets for, e.g., ordering, operating and scrapping various types and sizes of ships. These models may then have a variety of assumptions inserted so as to provide forecasts. Some good work has already been done on this but there is a rich field waiting for econometricians. Once again, we may expect a fruitful iteration between those who develop the models and those who provide the raw data they need.

5. Seaport economics

From its very beginning the term "Maritime Economics" has been defined so as to include the economics of seaports and such specialist journals as *The International Journal of Maritime Economics* and *Maritime Policy and Management* frequently contain papers on port pricing, organisation and privatisation. In particular, there is a great need to reform the traditional methods of charging for port services, so as to avoid the extensive cross-subsidisation that these involve. Other examples include the relative virtues of "hub and spoke" container services, with much transhipment, larger ships for the trunk hauls and longer transit times against a greater number of direct services. Since each system must have its own virtues in different circumstances it may be appropriate to examine the margin between them.

SUMMARY AND CONCLUSIONS

We may therefore expect to see much good work being done, in the context of FSA, on the development and application of cost-benefit analysis as well as in the other fields described above. For the future, maritime economics seems to be firmly-established in teaching, research, publication and in conferences like those organised, in various parts of the world, by the International Association of Maritime Economists. As indicated above, there are many opportunities for good research in this field, probably more by way of practical application, comparison and examples of "best practices" than by the development of new theory. A good deal of future effort may well turn out to consist of gaining acceptance amongst those who operate maritime services, in ships and ports, for ideas which are already common ground within the profession. Port charges are an example.

This is appropriate since maritime economics is essentially an application of the general body of economic theories to the maritime world. Certainly the future will involve the application of scientific methods to a wide variety of maritime problems and an end to the isolation of the maritime world on which Lord Carver's Committee commented, i.e. the idea that "shipping is different", needing special institutions and ideas. This is likely to involve using a variety of social and physical sciences, of which economics is only one.

ENDNOTES

1. "A history of Maritime Economics", *Intl. Jour. Maritime Economics* (forthcoming).
2. I.L. Buxton, *Engineering Economics and Ship Design* (BMT, 1987) is a well-developed example.
3. E.g., Goss, R.O., and Jones, C.D. (1982): *The Economies of Size in Dry Bulk Carriers*, Govt. Economic Service Occasional Papers (HMSO, 1971), reprinted in R.O. Goss (ed.) *Advances in Maritime Economics* (Cambridge University Press).
4. House of Lords, Select Committee on Science and Technology: *Safety Aspects of Ship Design and Technology*, HL Paper 30-I (HMSO, 1992) (Carver Report).
5. Now the Marine and Coastguard Agency.
6. We still have no firm data on deaths and injuries. The latest estimates are contained in Li, K.X., and Wonham, J. (2001): *The Role of States in Maritime Employment and Safety: A Legal and Economic Study* (Dalian Maritime University Press).
7. Dawson, R.F.F. (1971): *Current costs of Road Accidents in Britain*, Road Research Laboratory Report No. LR 396.
8. See, e.g., Penning-Rowsell, Green, Thompson, Coker, Tunstall, Richards and Parker (1992): *The Economics of Coastal Zone Management: A Manual of Benefit Assessment Techniques* (Belhaven).
9. Sturmey, S.G. (1962): *British Shipping and World Competition* (London, Athlone Press).
10. *Report of the Committee of Inquiry into Shipping* (Rochdale Report), Cmnd 4337 (HMSO, 1970).
11. See, e.g., Jon, Joon-Soo (1986): *Development of shipping in Korea in the containerisation era*, PhD thesis (Cardiff); Mobereola, A.E. (1987): *The establishment of a national shipping line – an asset or a liability? The case of Nigeria*, PhD thesis (Cardiff); and Kim, Gil-Soo (1991): *Shipping investment and allocative efficiency in Korea*, PhD thesis (Cardiff). These and other references are reviewed in Goss, R.O., and Marlow, P.B. (1992): "Internationalism, Protectionism and Interventionism in Shipping", Gwilliam, K.W. (ed.), *Current Issues in Maritime Economics* (Kluwer), which also criticises the UNCTAD doctrines.
12. E.g., in *The establishment or expansion of merchant marines for developing countries* (UNCTAD Secretariat Report, 1976).
13. Short wars seem to require specialised merchant ships to be available quickly. Moreover, any admiral offered the choice between devoting resources to supporting merchant ships and getting warships invariably opts for the latter.
14. A kleptocracy is, of course, a government of thieves.
15. E.g., in various issues of the *Safety Digest* issued by the Marine Accident Investigation Branch, Southampton.

CHAPTER 2

MARITIME BUSINESS DURING THE 20th CENTURY: CONTINUITY AND CHANGE

Gelina Harlaftis* and John Theotokas†

* Department of History, Ionian University, Corfu, Greece. E-mail: *gelina@ionio.gr*
† Department of Shipping, Trade and Transport, University of the Aegean, Chios, Greece. E-mail: *gtheotokas@aegean.gr*

1. INTRODUCTION

The historical process is dynamic, and the changes that occurred during the course of world shipping in the past century, embedded some of the structures of the 19th century. The methodological tools of a historian and an economist will be used in this chapter, tracing continuity and change in the 20th century shipping by examining maritime business at a macro- and micro-level. At the core of the analysis lies the shipping firm, the micro-level, which far from being a "black box" will be a "transparent box" that reveals and helps us understand the changes in world shipping, the macro-level.

The shipping firm functions in a specific market, and the shipping market can only be understood as an international market, in a multiethnic environment. The first part of this chapter follows the developments in world shipping, analysing briefly the main fleets, the routes and cargoes carried, the ships and the main technological innovations. The second part provides an insight on the main structural changes in the shipping markets by focusing on the division of liner and tramp shipping. The third part enters the "black box" and reveals from inside the shipowning structure and its changes in time in the main 20th century fleets: the British, the Norwegian, the Greek and the Japanese; it is remarkable how similar their organisation and structure proves to be. Maritime business has always been an internationalised business. In the last five centuries of capitalist development, European colonial expansion was only made possible with the sea and ships; the sea being but a route of communication and strength rather than of isolation and weakness. Wasn't it Sir Walter Raleigh in the late 16th century, one of Elizabeth's main consultants who had set some of the first rules for the British expansion? "He who commands the sea commands the trade routes of the world. He who commands the trade routes, commands the trade. He who commands the trade, commands the riches of the world, and hence the world itself." The real truths are tested in history and time.

2. DEVELOPMENTS IN WORLD SHIPPING

There were two main developments in the 19th century that pre-determined the path of the world economies: an incredible industrialisation of the West and its dominance in the rest of the world. During that period the world witnessed an unprecedented boom in world exchange of goods and services, an unprecedented boom of international sea-trade. The basis of the world trade system of the 20th century was consolidated in the 19th century: it was the flow of industrial goods from Europe to the rest of the world and the flow of raw materials to Europe from the rest of the world. In this way, deep-sea going trade became increasingly dominated by a small number of bulk commodities in all the world's oceans and seas; in the last third of the 19th century, grain, cotton and coal were the main bulk cargoes that filled the holds of the world fleet. At the same time, the transition from sail to steam, apart from increasing the availability of cargo space at sea, caused a revolutionary decline in freight rates. Europe, however, remained at the core of the world sea-trade system: until the eve of the First World War, three quarters of world exports in value and almost two thirds of world imports concerned the old continent.[1]

It does not come as a surprise then, that European countries owned the largest part of the world fleet. Due to technological innovations, the international merchant fleet was able to carry an increasing volume of cargoes between continents with greater speed and lower cost. By the turn of the 20th century Great Britain was still the undisputable world maritime power owning 45% of the world fleet, followed by the United States, Germany, Norway, France and Japan (see Table 1). Over 95% of the world fleet belonged to 15 countries that formed the so-called "Atlantic economy"; what is today called the "developed" nations of the OECD countries. Meanwhile, at the rival Pacific Ocean, Japan was preparing to be the rising star in the world shipping of the 20th century.

Pax Brittanica and the incredible increase of world economic prosperity of more than one hundred years closed abruptly with the beginning of World War One. The main cause was the conflict of the big industrial European nations for the expansion of their economic and political influence in the non-European world. It was the result of the competition of western European nations for new markets and raw materials that determined the 19th century and peaked in the beginning of the 20th century as the influence of the industrialization of western European nations became more distinct. At the beginning of the 20th century almost all Asia and Africa were in one way or another under European colonial control.

The factors that created the international economy of the previous century proved detrimental during the two world destructive wars by multiplying their effects. Firstly, the formation of gigantic national enterprises in Europe and the United States and their concentration in vast industrial complexes with continuous amalgamations of small and medium companies resulted in an exponential increase of world production. Secondly, the search for markets beyond Europe that would absorb the excessive industrial production, resulted in the fierce competition of British, German, French and American capital in international capital investments worldwide. The result was the creation of multinational companies and banks that led in the development of monopolies on a national and international level. Within this framework, the great expansion of the United States and German fleets took place, along with the multiple mergers

Table 1: The largest fleets of the 20th century

Country	1914 grt	1914 %	1937 grt	1937 %	1963 grt	1963 %	1992 Real ownership including all flags dwt	1992 %
Great Britain	21.0	43%	20.6	31%	21.6	15%	23.6	3.4
Germany	5.5	11%	3.9	6%	5.0		16.9	2.4
U.S.A.	5.4	11%	12.4	18%	23.1	16%	59.1	8.5
Norway	2.5	5%	4.3	6%	13.7	9%	54.1	7.8
France	2.3	5%	2.8	4%		4%	7.0	1
Japan	1.7	4%	4.5	7%		7%	90.2	12.3
Italy	1.7	3%	3.2	5%	5.6	4%	11.7	1.7
Holland	1.5	3%	2.6	4%	5.2	4%		
Sweden	1.1	2%	1.5	2%	4.2		12.2	0.3
Austro-Hungary	1.0	2%	–	–	–	–	–	–
Russia-U.S.S.R.	1.0	2%	1.3	2%	5.4	4%	19.2	2.8
Spain	0.9	2%	1.0	1%	2.0		5.1	0.7
Greece	0.8	2%	1.9	3%	15.0*	10%*	100.6	14.5
Hong-Kong			0.3		0.8		31.6	4.5
China			0.6		0.5		27.5	3.9
South Korea					0.1		18.2	2.6
Total of 10 largest fleets					108.3	74%	441	63%
World total	49.1	100%	66.7	100%	145.9	100%	694.6 (444.3 grt)	

Sources: Lloyd's Register of Shipping 1914, Lloyd's Statistical Tables 1990, 1992 and Gelina Harlaftis, *A History of Greek-owned shipping, 1830 to the present day* (Routledge 1993), Table 6.3.

and acquisitions in the northern European liner shipping business and the gradual destruction of small tramp shipping companies, particularly in Great Britain.

The interwar economy never recovered from the shock of World War One that influenced the whole structure of the international economy with result of the worst economic crisis that the industrial world had seen in 1929. During the interwar period world shipping faced severe problems stemming from a contracting world sea-trade, decreasing world immigration and increasing protectionism. The impact on Britain was particularly felt. This is the period of the economic downhill of mighty old Albion. It was World War One that weakened Britain and allowed competitors to challenge its maritime hegemony. The withdrawal of British ships from trades not directly related to the Allied cause opened the Pacific trades to the Japanese. Moreover, both Norway and Greece were neutrals, which meant that their fleets were able to profit from high wartime freight rates (Greece entered the war in 1917). Norwegian and Greek ships were able to trade at market rates for three years while most of the British fleet was requisitioned and forced to work for low, fixed remunerations. Freight rates in the free market remained high until 1920, after which they plummeted;

while there was a brief recovery in the mid-1920s, the nadir was reached in the early 1930s.

Table 1 records the development of the world fleets of the main maritime nations from 1914 to 1937. During this period the world fleet increased at one third of its pre-war size. The British fleet remained at the same level with a slight decrease but its percentage of the ownership of the world fleet decreased from 43% to 31% due to the increase of the fleets of other nations. The interwar period was characterised by the unsuccessful attempt of the United States to keep a large national fleet with large and costly subsidies to shipping entrepreneurs. Most of the increase of the world fleet in the interwar period apart from the US was due to the Japanese, the Norwegians and the Greeks, that proved the owners of the most dynamic fleets of the century. Their growth was interconnected with the carriage of energy sources. The most important change in the world trade of the interwar period was the gradual decrease of the coal trade and the growing importance of oil trade.

The main coal producer (and exporter) in 1900 was the UK, with 225 million metric tons or 51% of Europe's production. By 1937 Britain was still Europe's main producing country with 42% of European output. In 1870 the production of oil was less than one million tons and in 1900 oil was still an insignificant source of energy; world production of 20 million tons met only 2.5% of world energy consumption. Because production was so limited there was little need for specialized vessels; tankers, mostly owned by Europeans, accounted for a tiny 1.5% of world merchant tonnage. But all this changed in the interwar period: by 1938 oil production had increased more than 15 times; it was 273 million tons and accounted for 26% of world energy consumption.[2] The tanker fleet had grown to 16% of world tonnage, and although it was mostly state-owned, independent tanker owners started to appear in the 1920s. The largest independent owners of the interwar period were the Norwegians.[3]

Technological innovations continued in the 20th century; the choices and exploitation of technological advances by shipping entrepreneurs determined the path of world shipping. The first half of the 20th century was characterised on the one hand by the use of diesel engines and the replacement of steam engines and on the other, by the massive standard shipbuilding projects during the two world wars. Diesel engines that appeared in 1890 were only used in a more massive scale on motor ships during the interwar period particularly in Germany and the Scandinavian countries; the cost of fuel being 30% to 50% lower than that of the steam engines. Standardization and shipbuilding programmes were introduced in World War One when Germans sunk the allied fleets in an unprecedented submarine war. The world had not yet realised what industrialisation and massive production of weapons for destruction could do. The convoy system had been abandoned and naval battleships with their complex weapons were ready to confront the enemy. But it was the allied merchant steamships that were the artery of the war, transporting war supplies. And this armless merchant fleet became an easy target to the new menace of the seas: the German submarines. From 1914 to 1918, 5,861 ships or 50% of the allied fleet was sunk.

Replacement of the sunken fleet took place between 1918 to 1921 in U.S. and British shipyards. It was for the first time that standard types of cargo ships, the "standards" as they came to be called, were built on a large scale. The "standard" ships became the main type of cargo ship during the interwar period; they were steamships of 5,500 grt. It was these "standard" ships that Greeks, Japanese and Norwegian tramp operators purchased *en masse* from the British second hand market and expanded their fleets amongst the world economic crises. For similar reasons during World War Two the United States and Canada launched the most massive shipbuilding programmes the world had known, using new and by far quicker methods of building ships: welding. During four years they managed to build 3,000 ships, the well-known Liberty ships, that formed the standard dry-bulk cargo vessel for the next 25 years.[4] Greek, Norwegian, British and Japanese tramp operators all came to own Liberty ships, in one way or another up to the late 1960s.

The second half of the 20th century was characterised by an incredible increase of world trade that towards the end of the century was described as the globalization of the world economy. The period of acceleration was up to 1970s; world trade from about 500 million metric tons in the 1940s climbed up to more than three billion metric tons in the mid-1970s. If the history of world maritime transport in the first half of the 20th century was written by coal and tramp ships, in the second half the main players were oil and tankers. During this period, sea-trade was divided into two categories: liquid and dry cargo. Almost 60% of the exponential growth of world sea trade was due to the incredible growth of the carriage of liquid cargo at sea, oil and oil products. Impressive was also the growth of the five main bulk cargoes: ore, bauxite, coal, phosphates and grain. To carry the enormous volumes required to feed the industries of the West and East Asia, the size of ships carrying liquid and dry cargoes had to be increased. The second half of the 20th century was characterised by the gigantic sizes of ships and their specialisation according to the type of cargoes. The last third of the century was marked by the introduction of container ships. The new "ugly" ships revolutionised the carriage of industrial goods, world transport and port system.

Up to the 1960s the main carriers of the world fleet remained the same with the US and Britain continuing to hold their decreasing shares in world shipping, followed by the continually rising Greece, Japan and Norway (Table 1). Flags of convenience were used informally by all maritime nations but in the immediate post-war years more extensively by Greek and American shipowners. Flags of convenience that were later to be called open registries became a key manifestation of the American maritime policy and a determining feature of post war shipping that guaranteed economical bulk shipping.[5] After the repetitive freight rates crises of the 1980s they were extensively used by all western and eastern maritime nations.

The 1970s marked a new era: this period was characterised by the final loss of the pre-dominance of European maritime nations, with the exception of the Greeks that continue to keep their first position to the present day, and of the Norwegians that despite the great slump of the 1980s, kept their share of the

Figure 1: Shipping markets, 1870s–1970s

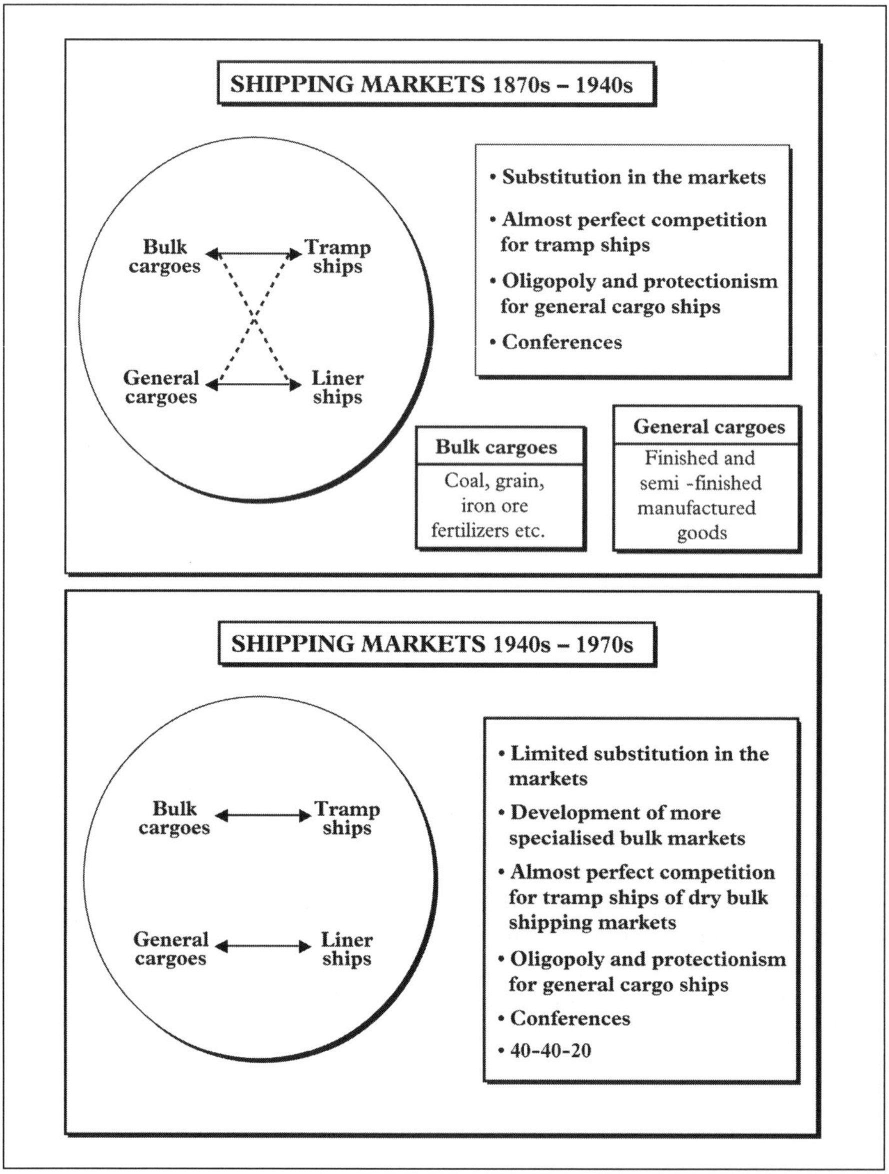

SHIPPING MARKETS 1870s – 1940s

Bulk cargoes ↔ Tramp ships
General cargoes ↔ Liner ships

- Substitution in the markets
- Almost perfect competition for tramp ships
- Oligopoly and protectionism for general cargo ships
- Conferences

Bulk cargoes: Coal, grain, iron ore, fertilizers etc.

General cargoes: Finished and semi-finished manufactured goods

SHIPPING MARKETS 1940s – 1970s

Bulk cargoes ↔ Tramp ships
General cargoes ↔ Liner ships

- Limited substitution in the markets
- Development of more specialised bulk markets
- Almost perfect competition for tramp ships of dry bulk shipping markets
- Oligopoly and protectionism for general cargo ships
- Conferences
- 40-40-20

market in the 1990s. During the last third of the 20th century the increase of the size of the world fleet shipping continued but slowed down. The United States has kept, mostly under flags of convenience, a much lower percentage, while Japan remains steadily in the second position (Table 1). The rise of new maritime nations from Asia was evident; by 1992 China owned more tonnage than Great Britain, while South Korea was close. The world division of labour in world shipping had changed dramatically.[6]

3. SHIPPING MARKETS

Following world shipping developments, the shipping markets had taken its 20th century form since the last third of the 19th century. Before the 1870s the shipping market was unified. By the last third of the nineteenth century the distinction of the shipping market into two categories, liner and tramp shipping started gradually to adapt. Liner ships carried general cargoes (finished or semi-finished manufactured goods) and tramp shipping carried bulk cargoes (like coal, ore, grain, fertilizers, etc.) For the next one hundred years, until the 1970s liner and tramp shipping markets continued more or less on the same lines. This one century of shipping operations can be distinguished into two sub-periods (see Figure 1).

During the first period, from the 1870s to the 1940s, the cargoes carried by liner and tramp shipping were not always clearly defined: liner ships could carry tramp cargoes and vice-versa. Although there was substitution between the two distinct markets, the main structures of each one were diametrically different: oligopoly and protectionism for liner market with the formation of the shipping cartels from the 1880s, the conferences, and almost perfect competition for tramp ships.

The unprecedented increase of world production and trade in the first post-World War Two era brought more distinct changes in the structure of the markets that led to a gradual decrease of substitution between the markets.[7] In tramp/bulk shipping, the introduction of new liquid bulk cargoes on a massive scale, like oil, and of the main dry bulk cargoes as mentioned above (coal, ore, fertilisers and grain) led to specialisation of function: to the creation of specialised bulk markets and to the building of ships to carry specific cargoes (Figure 1). The liner market continued along the same lines of oligopoly but witnessed increased competition into their protected markets from competitors from developing and socialist countries.

The 1970s were the landmark decade for the liner industry; unitization of the cargoes, called also containerization, brought a revolution in the transport of liner cargoes (Figure 2). Containerisation included radically new designs for vessels and cargo-handling facilities, global door-to-door traffic, early use of information technology, and structural change of the industry through the formation of consortia, alliances and international mega-mergers.[8] The above led to a total transformation of the liner shipping companies that became the archetype of a globalised multinational shipping company. This transformation was further provoked by the continuous trend to globalisation. Liner companies ought to serve the transport needs of their customer on a global basis. Thus, they were enforced to establish global networks in order to meet their customers' needs. The enlargement of the companies' size through mergers and acquisitions and the formation of global alliances were the necessary steps toward this. For example, the biggest privately-owned shipping company of the world, Danish Maersk, acquired Sealand, the biggest liner American shipping company, actually the first company in the world that introduced the innovative technology of containers. The new shipping giant employs 10,000 people, holds

Figure 2: Shipping markets, 1970s–2000s

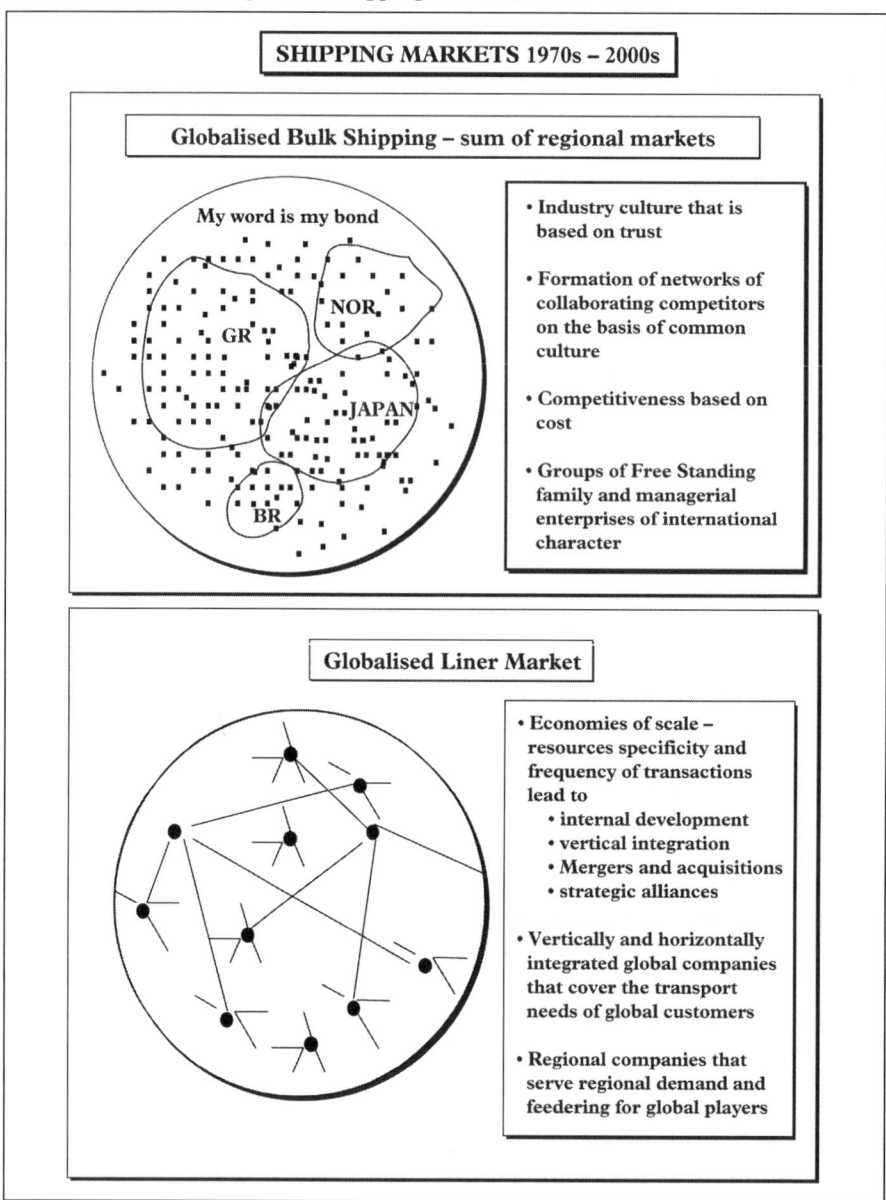

SHIPPING MARKETS 1970s – 2000s

Globalised Bulk Shipping – sum of regional markets

My word is my bond

NOR.
GR
JAPAN
BR

- Industry culture that is based on trust
- Formation of networks of collaborating competitors on the basis of common culture
- Competitiveness based on cost
- Groups of Free Standing family and managerial enterprises of international character

Globalised Liner Market

- Economies of scale – resources specificity and frequency of transactions lead to
  - internal development
  - vertical integration
  - Mergers and acquisitions
  - strategic alliances
- Vertically and horizontally integrated global companies that cover the transport needs of global customers
- Regional companies that serve regional demand and feedering for global players

325 offices in one hundred different countries, operates 25 container terminals world-wide and a fleet of 250 ships (of 600,000 TEU) that make 20,000 approaches to ports per year. Out of the fleet that Maersk operates, 110 ships are owned by Maersk-Sealand and the rest are time-chartered from independent owners. It is thus evident that such a multinational company is a global network by itself and offers global services to its clients. This kind of development brought a total re-structuring in the port systems of the various regions and

brought the need of minor shipping lines to serve regional transport needs or offer feedering services for global liner companies. For example, Maersk-Sealand approaches main international ports, described as gateways/entrepots from which minor shipping lines through the so-called feedering services distribute the products to the so-called hubs, primate ports and jetty ports.[9] These two groups of companies, the big and minor container companies are not competitive to each other but complement each other.

On the contrary, the development of tramp shipping did not involve such innovative technological developments and no dramatic changes in the organization and structure of markets took place. Gradual adaptation to the demand needs were internalized, and the "tramp" ship was replaced by specialised ships that were built according to the bulk cargoes and the specialized bulk shipping markets. The general pattern, has not changed over the last 130 years. However, since 1970s we are not talking of tramp shipping and tramp ships, but of bulk shipping since the type of the ship does not characterise the market anymore, but instead the cargoes that are transported. Globalised bulk shipping even to the present day is an industry based on trust. Companies form networks of collaborating competitors on the basis of common national cultures of traditional maritime nations such as Britain, Greece, Norway and Japan (Figure 2). Even members of the same network compete with each other and competitiveness is based on cost. During the twentieth century size has not played an important role to the competitiveness of the company.[10] Bulk shipping consists of companies of various sizes, that vary from large companies of more than 50 large ships to single-ship companies that directly compete each other. For example in 1970, the Greek-owned shipping company of Stavros Niarchos and the Norwegian shipping company of Wilhem Wilhelmsen operating more than 60 ships co-existed and competed with the British Turnballs that operated 5 ships and the various Bergen-based small companies that operated ships of similar characteristics. Tramp shipping was mainly formed by groups of family enterprises that retained many characteristics of a multinational entreprise.[11]

4. SHIPPING COMPANIES

Overall analysis of the main trends in world shipping fleets and their markets throughout the 20th century does not provide us with an understanding of the structure of the maritime industry. The core of the economy is the firm; the core of the maritime industry is the shipping company. In this section we will examine more closely the actual players, the shipping companies of the four main 20th century nations: the British, the Norwegians, the Greeks and the Japanese. In the first three European nations, we can distinguish similar patterns of organization and structure in the shipping companies worldwide that concerned both liner and tramp shipping. The first important aspect of shipping companies was their connection with a specific home port, the second one was the ownership and management of the company by distinct families for multiple generations, the third one was the use of a regional network for drawing investment funds, the fourth was the existence of an international network of overseas agencies that collaborated closely with trading houses on a particular oceanic region, or on a particular commodity trade.[12]

4.1 The British

British commercial and shipping business in the nineteenth century developed along the lines of its colonial empire, and the inter-Empire and British external trade that was operated by close-knit business networks. Britain, despite the decreasing share, remained world's maritime leader up to the1960s.

The regional dimension in maritime Britain has played an important role in the organization of both tramp and liner business. The main poles of liner shipping have traditionally been Liverpool and London followed by Glasgow and Hull. The newly emerging liner shipping companies from the mid-nineteenth century onwards were very strongly connected with a big home port, like London, Liverpool, Glasgow and Hull, where strong shipping elites were formed. For example, the Peninsular and Oriental (P&O), based in London, was established by Wilcox and Anderson in 1837 and specialised in carrying the trade of India and Australia; the Cunard Company, established by Samuel Cunard, Burns and the MacIvers in 1839 specialised in the north Atlantic; the British India (BI) shipping company, based in Glasgow, was established in 1856 by the MacKinnon shipping group and specialised in the Indian ocean; the Ocean Steam Ship Company known as the Blue Funnel Line, based in Liverpool, was established by the Holt family in 1865 and specialised in the trade with southeastern Asia. The Union-Castle Line, was established in the 1850s and by the 1870s run by Donald Currie, was specialised in South Africa; the Elder-Dempster based in Liverpool, was formed by Alexander Elder and John Dempster in 1868 and specialised in the African trade; Lleyland, Moss, McIver and Papayanni, all based in Liverpool, were established in the 1840s and 1850s and were involved in the Mediterranean trade. Hull was the home port of the Wilson Line, established by the Wilson family – "Wilson's are Hull and Hull is Wilson's" – that traded in all oceans and seas.[13] In 1910 there were 65 liner companies that owned 45% of the British fleet. And all, during the previous thirty years, had organised themselves in closed cartels of the sea, the conferences, according to the oceanic region they traded, securing their share in the world market.[14]

Among the five largest liner companies in 1910 were British India, White Star Line, Blue Funnel Line, Peninsular & Oriental and Elder Dempster (see Table 2). Low freight rates and a widespread depression in the late 1910s led to intense competition and a wave of mergers that produced giant lines in the five years before World War One. The most notorious example is the Royal Mail Steam Packet Co that from 1903 to 1931 was led by Owen Philipps (later Lord Kylsant). Within thirty years Royal Mail reached the peak, by owning 11% of British fleet, and the nadir in 1931 when it was liquidified producing a major crisis in British shipping business circles. In a remarkable series of acquisitions Royal Mail acquired Elder Dempster in 1910, Pacific Steam in 1910, Glen Line and Lamport Holt in 1911 and Union –Castle in 1912.[15] Equally, another giant emerged just before the war, when Peninsular and Oriental apart from Blue Anchor Line, acquired British India Steam Navigation and its extensive shipping and trading interests in India. P&O continued its acquisitions and mergers throughout the interwar period and in contrast to Royal Mail, remained throughout the 20th century the largest British shipping concern.

Mergers and amalgamations of lines into groups under common ownership continued in the interwar period and changed the structure of British liner shipping.[16] The economic crisis of the 1930s hit hard British shipping. The contraction of the tramp shipping sector that was lost to Norwegians and Greeks, and the concentration to fewer liner companies was evident: in 1939 the number of British liner companies had dropped to 43 companies that owned 61% of the fleet. The demolition of Royal Mail, and the intervention of the British banking system to save Britain's largest liner concerns, brought a re-structure of liner ownership in the 1930s that defined its path in the second half of the 20th century.

As Table 2 indicates, in 1939 P& O, Ellerman group of companies, Cunard, Blue Funnel and Furness Lines appear in the top five positions. P& O by consecutive mergers and amalgamations became the indisputable queen of the Indian Ocean and Pacific routes; apart from British India steam Navigation in 1914, it acquired in 1917 and 1919 another seven lines that serviced those routes. In the 1960s and 1970s the P&O remained the largest shipping group of the world; after the 1970s it adjusted in the container revolution, adopted a globalised ownership and diversified also in the bulk sector. Ellerman acquired a number of smaller Liverpool lines that traded in the Mediterranean before World War One and its biggest acquisition was in 1916 when it amalgamated with Wilson Line; its importance contracted in the post-World War Two period. Cunard, another giant of the "big five" of British shipping traditionally engaged in the Atlantic passenger services since 1840s, had acquired three or four lines during the second and third decade of the 20th century. It profited largely from the demolition of Royal Mail when it acquired White Star Line in 1934. Persisting in passenger shipping, however, it eventually lost its importance in the post-war period.

Blue Funnel (Ocean Steam Ship Company) group of companies owned by the Holt family exemplified family capitalism in liner shipping. Based in Liverpool and specialized in the far eastern trades, it also profited from the demolition of Royal Mail and amalgamated with Elder Dempster that hold the African trades. It has continued its business with vigor well into the second half of the 20th century. The Cayzer family from Glasgow that formed in 1890 the Clan Line, established in 1956 the British and Commowealth group by amalgamating with the Union-Castle Line, another line that had belonged to the disintegrated Royal Mail group; it continued its business throughout the 20th century. The Furness group until the beginning of the 20th century was one of the main British tramp shipping operators, that later diversified into liner shipping. By taking part in the acquisitions and amalgamations and exploiting the demolition of Royal Mail of which it acquired a fair share, proved, along with P&O, one of of the most important shipping groups of the 20th century; it has

Table 2: The largest British shipowning groups of the 20th century (in thousand grt)

Tramp/Bulk Shipping

1910			1939		1960		1970		1998		
Name	Nrt		Name	Grt	Name	Grt	Name	Grt	Name	Grt	Dwt
Furness Withy	179		British Tanker Co.	595	British Petroleum	1383	BP Tanker Co. Ltd	2439	BP Shipping Ltd		2823
Usmar John Henry (Anglo-American Oil Co)	108		Anglo-Saxon Petroleum	376	Runciman (United Molasses)	361	Trident Tanker Ltd	985	P&O Bulk Carriers Ltd		2654
Ropner R.	93		Ropner Group of Companies	243	Hunting Group		Denholm (Mgmt) Ltd	801	Trader Navigation Agencies Ltd		1381
Hain Edward & Sons	93		Eagle Oil Shipping	229	Watts, Watts & Co.	187	Common Brothers (Mgmt) Ltd	707	Ocean Agencies Ltd		797
Burrell & Son	79		Hain steamship	159	Denholm Co.	160	Maritime Overseas Corp.	436			

Liner Shipping

British India Steam	304		P&O Group (British India Steam Navigation)	663	P&O Group	2369	Ocean Steam Ship Co. Ltd	755			
Ismay Imrie (White Star Line)	232		Ellerman Group of companies	651	Furness group	1420	Cayzer, Irvine & Co. Ltd	610			
Holt A. (Blue Funnel Lines)	219		Holt A. (Blue Funnel Lines)	562	Blue Funnel Group	971	P & O Steam Navigation Co.	396			
Peninsular & Oriental	203		Cunard Group of Companies	461	Cunard group	947	Houlder Brothers & Co. Ltd	366			
Elder Dempster Group of Companies	202		Furness Lines	426	British and Commonwealth	872					

Note: For the years 1914 and 1939 ships above 500 grt, for the years 1970 and 1998 ships above 1000 grt.
Sources: Processed data from *Lloyd's Register of Shipping*, 1910, 1939, 1970, *Shipwatch Directory*, 1998. For 1960 data from Stanley Sturmey, *British Shipping and World Competition*, Athlone Press, 1962, Table 50.

been also the first among the British liner groups to continue operating in tramp/bulk shipping.

Liner shipping companies form the most known and the most glorious part of British shipping. Liner companies owned the most famous, luxurious steamships of the latest technology. British liner steamships that carried millions of passengers, became widely known, the proud manifestation of power of the mighty British Empire that ruled the waves. Most of the owners of British liner companies, among Britain's most powerful capitalists, were commoners that became Lords or were knighted: Lord Kylsant of Royal Mail, Lord Inchcape of British India, Sir Alfred Jones of Elder Dempster, to mention only a few. British historians have said the stories of the main British liner business.[17] But liner shipping throughout the 19th and 20th century formed less than half of the large British fleet.

In fact, it was the less glorious ships of less technological achievements that formed more than half of the British fleet that fed the industries of the Empire. Tramp shipping formed the largest part of the British mercantile marine up to the Great War with 462 companies owning 55% of the fleet. The Industrial revolution determined the areas in which British tramp operators developed in close connection with deep-sea export coal trade: The Northeast ports and Wales became the main hubs of British tramp-operators in combination with those of the Clyde in Scotland who were traditionally connected with the trading world-wide networks of the Scottish merchants.

In 1910 the shipping companies of the northeast ports, namely Newcastle, Sunderland, Hartlepool, Middlesborough, Whitby, Scarborough and Hull handled almost one third of the British tramp shipping tonnage.[18] Some of the most powerful British shipping families that continued to the end of the twentieth century came from this area: the Furnesses, Turnballs, Ropners and Runcimans. The next most dynamic group in tramp shipping were Scottish tramp operators that handled 18% of British tramp shipping in 1910. Some of the most known Scottish tramp shipowning families were the Burrells and the Hogarths. Wales also emerged as a generator of tramp companies. Wales drew human capital from the West Country as well, and shipping companies established in Wales operated 9% of the British tramp fleet in 1910. With Cardiff as the central port, tramp shipping thrived in the Welsh ports from Chester to Llanelli.[19] Known Cardiff tramp operators were the Hains, Morells, Tatems and Corys. London and Liverpool drew branch offices from almost all the above tramp operators and both cities handled 42% of the British tramp fleet in 1910.

Table 2 indicates the evident importance of tankers and the distinct inexistence of independent tanker owners; one of the great failures of British tramp owners was that they did not enter the tanker business. The main big tanker owners remain the petroleum companies like the Anglo-American Oil Co in 1910, British Tanker Co and Anglo-Saxon Petroleum in 1939 and British Petroleum in the post-World War Two period. The new structure in the organisation of tramp/bulk shipping, are the management companies under which one finds some of the traditional British tramp owners. Denholm Management is a good example of a management company. In 1970 it managed 38 ships of 17 shipping companies including the Turnbull Scott Shipping.[20]

Contrary to the beliefs that want family capitalism to belong only to the Mediterranean, family was important in both British liner and tramp maritime business. Big liner companies might have been joint-stock companies, but the ownership was spread usually in a select circle of family and friends; families like the Cayzers, Ellermans, Brocklebanks, Holts and Furnesses retained their command over major British lines. The case was stronger in British tramp companies, that were family-owned companies that kept ownership and management of the companies and used intermarriages to expand and keep the business within closed circles. From the most prominent ones like the Runcimans, the Turnbulls, the Ropners, to the medium and smaller ones, kept business in the family for several generations. One of the great handicaps of British shipping, however, has been the loss of the importance of the regional dimension of maritime Britain; regions and ports that reproduced shipping entrepreneurship.

4.2 The Norwegians

Norway is considered as a leading maritime nation not only due to the high percentage of owned tonnage since the 19th century, but also because shipping was and still is a vital activity of many areas and ports of the country. Norwegians have traditionally carried bulk cargoes, lumber, grain and fish along the Northern European and Atlantic routes.[21] Shipowing has been an important business in all ports of Norway's extensive coastline. The regions of Oslo and Oslofjord, the South Coast, the Western and Northern Norway included almost 60 ports active in shipping and shipowning activities, most of whom were engaged in tramp shipping. More importantly, shipping absorbed a large portion of investment and labour of the country.

With a developed expertise in wooden and later metallic sailing ships that continued well into the 20th century some areas, closely connected to the traditional shipbuilding industry failed to make the transition from sail to steam. The region of Adger in the South Coast of Norway for example, during the years prior to the First World War, owned between 55% and 58% of the Norwegian iron and steel sailing ship tonnage, but failed to invest successfully into steam shipping.[22]

The structural transformations of Norwegian shipping differentiated the relative importance of each port to its development, without however changing the regional pattern. Shipping companies continued to be located in specific ports throughout the 20th century. While the majority of shipping companies are in our days established in Oslo, ports like Bergen, Grimstad, Stavanger, Arendal and Kristiansand still remain important maritime centres.

As Norway's external trade could not support the development of a competitive shipping industry, Norwegian shipowners, like the Greeks, based their expansion to their ability to produce cost effective shipping services and to serve the needs of international trade. Equally, they exploited their competence in managing ships and the abundance of low cost and high quality Norwegian seamen and became at the last third of the 19th century and the first half of the

20th century, the main cross trader fleet of the world. Their involvement in liner shipping was limited and with the exception of the interwar period, when a percentage between 25% and 30% was engaged in liner trades, the corresponding figures for the whole of 20th century has not surpassed 15% of the fleet.[23] Norwegians invested heavily in bulk shipping and especially in tankers and since 1920s became major players in this sector. This business strategy however proved to be a source of strength as well as of weakness. They prospered during the expansion of the tanker market until the 1970s and were hit hard during the crisis of 1973.[24] Their massive orders for supertankers along with their low ratio of liquid to fixed asset made them highly vulnerable.[25] Despite their diversification to offshore activities and their exploitation of the know-how in managing ships to enter the market of third party ship management, they remain a major power of the bulk shipping industry and the leading players of many specialised bulk shipping markers like those of gas, and the chemicals, where they can be considered as the leading group[26] or this of open hatch bulk carriers.[27]

Although the co-operative character continued to be a major trait of the Norwegian shipping during the 20th century, the role of families to the establishment and development of shipping companies was crucial. Various families, tied to particular ports, established their companies during the end of the 19th century or the first decades of the 20th century, and most of them continue to be active to the present days. Bergesen, Olsen, Knutsen, Naess, Reksten, Odfjell, Rasmussen, Wilhelmsen, Stolt Nielsen, Fredriksen, Westfal-Larsen, Hoegh and Uglands are only a few of the families that run the leading companies of the Norwegian shipping during the 20th century. Representative cases of family businesses with a long tradition in shipping are Wilh. Wilhemsen and Bergesen d.y, as both remained at the forefront of world shipping for the whole of their history.

The company of Wilh. Wilhemsen was founded in 1861 in Tonsberg by Morten Wilhelm Wilhelmsen, who was also a successful shipbroker. As early as 1870 he started to invest in steamships acquiring shares in various ships and in 1887 he made his first steamship purchase.[28] By 1910, when the founder of the company died, the fleet consisted of 31 steamships. It was in 1911 that the company, after several years of scepticism, finally entered the liner trades in co-operation with Fearnley and Eger operating the Norwegian Africa and the Australia Line. At approximately the same time Wilhelmsen entered the tanker market. In 1912 the first two tankers were ordered and a fleet of this type of ships was created. In the forthcoming years Wilhelmsen's involvement in liner trades became stronger while the tanker operation was abandoned. After World War Two, Wilhelmsen focused again on tanker business and in expanding in the liner trades. Today, the Wilhelmsen group is involved in many sectors of international shipping. Although it is still active in the bulk sector, its core activity is in the liner and it is considered as the leader of the Ro-Ro and Car Carriers sector.[29] In 1999 the Wilhelmsen Lines merged with the Swedish Wallenius Lines creating a world-wide network and a fleet of about 60 vessels. The Group is also active in the third party management sector as well as in agency services. After more than 140 years, Wilhelmsen is still a dynamic globalised shipping group, which remains family controlled.

Sig. Bergesen d.y., was established in 1935 when the youngest son of Sigval Bergesen left the family company to create his own business. A second generation shipowner, of a shipowning family whose maritime activities can be traced back in the 19th century. Sig. Bergesen d.y. started his own business by contracting tankers without his father's consent.[30] Tankers turned out to be a totally successful choice. The years after World War Two, Bergesen built a fleet of tankers, either in his own shipyard Rosenberg Verft or in other yards, and became Norway's largest shipowner. Bergesen's successful path, especially during the crises of the 70s, has been attributed to his decision to secure the deployment of his ships with long-term charters to oil majors. In addition, he diversified his fleet by investing in combination and bulk carriers. In 1976 the founder of the company gave up the control of the company to his grandchildren. Diversification was further intensified in late 70s when the company entered into gas transportation. Today, Bergesen is the world's largest owner and operator of gas carriers and one the largest owners of large crude oil carriers. Furthermore, building on its competencies and utilizing its tanker expertise Bergesen expanded to offshore businesses. By 1986 Bergesen became a public listed company with shares listed on the Oslo and London stock exchanges, while in 1998 Bergesen family members, who are still the largest shareholders, gave up the daily management of the company and retained their position on the Board of Directors. Following the trend towards consolidation, Bergesen merged with Havtor ASA, acquired Scantank Offshore and entered a pool alliance with A.P. Moller.[31]

Norwegian saga consists also of leading entrepreneurs like E.D. Naess and H. Reksten, whose lives turned to be a myth that was to be repetitively compared with the Greeks Onassis and Niarchos. The Norwegian US citizen Erling Dekke Naess became active in shipping after having studied and worked in the U.K. After having invested extensively in whaling in the 1920s, in the 1930s he entered dynamically in the tanker business. With the outbreak of World War Two Naess moved to New York and there he became head of Nortrashp, the governmental organization that administered Norway's requisitioned merchant fleet to the Allies. Naess became one of the major shipping factors in the newly emerging America's economic capital New York. His relations with American oil companies and his involvement in the tanker business and flags of convenience made him among world's largest cosmopolitan shipowners. Involved both in dry and liquid bulk shipping, like his Greek counterparts, he turned since the 1950s to the cheap and efficient Japanese shipyards to order his bulk carriers and tankers. Using Bermuda as his official base, he really administered his fleet from London with his Anglo-American Shipping company, that eventually became Anglo-Norness and collaborated closely with the British P&O.

But it was his decision to sell his fleet for $208 million a few months before the first oil boom and the great depression of the tanker freight markets that made him known as the shipowner who predicted the oncoming crisis. Naess attributed this decision to his study of the business cycles.[32] It is very probable, however, that at that point in time Naess was not the owner of "his" fleet that belonged to the company Zapata Norness but was only "an honorary chairman of the board" as it is reported that he had already sold his fleet at a much lower price in the 1960s.[33] Whatever the truth, his exodus remained glamorous, and he never stopped his interests in shipowning. In collaboration with the Greek tanker owners he establishes the Intertanko in the mid-1970s of which he became President, while in the early 80s Naess returned to business again. His use of various nationalities to shelter his companies, of various flags on his ships, and of crews of various nationalities make most Norwegian analysts not regard him as a Norwegian shipowner, and not to include his ships in the Norwegian fleet. A nation that prided itself on its maritime infrastructure only accepted the term Norwegian-owned after the 1980s crisis and the formation of NIS.

Hilmar Reksten followed a path similar to that of Naess, his ending however was different, as he was hardly hit by the depressed freight rates of the 70s. In his case, the strong involvement in tanker business functioned both as strength and weakness in the different phases of the downfalls and upheavals in the shipping business. Reksten ordered his first tanker in 1938 and expanded in tanker sector after the World War Two. He was convinced for the high profits of the tankers, so he focused on the market for oil transport, created a fleet of large tankers and operated them in the spot market.[34] This strategy proved extremely successful in the period before 1973, when the freight rates were continuously rising and Reksten became one of the biggest tanker owners worldwide, but it proved unsuccessful for the depressed freight markets of the period after 1974 and was finally led to the bankruptcy in the late 70s.

But Norway is a maritime nation, and apart form the above mentioned well-known shipowning families, the backbone of the fleet still rests in the hundreds of small shipping companies active in shipping for shorter or longer periods, which although not as innovative and dynamic as the larger companies, have contributed in making Norway remain among the top maritime nations worldwide.

4.3 The Greeks

If at the north-east tip of Europe lies one of the most dynamic European nations, at the south-east tip of Europe lies another dynamic maritime nation that became world's leader in the maritime business in the last thirty years. Greek-owned shipping developed since the 19th century as an international cross trader almost exclusively involved into tramp shipping. It carried bulk cargoes, particularly grain from the Black Sea and coal from north western Europe, along the routes of Mediterranean waters establishing commercial and maritime networks along the main ports from the south to the north. Before the First World War and during the interwar period, Greek shipping companies were established in London, and Piraeus-London remained the axis around which Greek-owned shipping developed during the 20th century. Greek shipping, like Norwegian shipping, developed in close connection to the British maritime industry.

Family capitalism has prevailed in the structure of Greek-owned maritime business. At the beginning of the 20th century there were about 200 families, all specialised in shipping, running 250 shipping firms and at the end of the twentieth century about 700 families running more than 1000 shipping firms. After a short interval in New York, in the 1940s and 1950s, by the last third of the twentieth century the Greek-owned fleet had the same operational centres (Piraeus and London) as at its beginning, but now the Greek entrepreneurial network was not confined to European waters but extended to all oceans of the world.[35]

The management, and all the branch offices of Greek shipping companies throughout the twentieth century continued to be in the hands of members of the same family or co-islanders. In this way kinship, island and ethnic ties ensured the cohesion of the international Greek maritime network. The unofficial but exclusive international "club" was extremely important for their economic survival. It provided access to all the expertise of shipping: market information, chartering, sales and purchase, shipbuilding, repairing, scrapping, financing, insurance and P&I clubs. It also provided consultancy from older and wiser members and information about the activities of the most successful members of the group. Imitation proved an extremely useful `rule-of-thumb'. The main strength of the Greeks then, has been the formation of an exclusive «Greek» transnational network of family enterprises that interacted with local, national and international shipping networks and organisations, local, national and international financial institutions and organisations.

The regional dimension has also proved extremely important in Greek-owned shipping. During the first two thirds of the 20th century the so-called traditional shipping families, all involved for multiple generations in shipping activities, predominate and came from the islands of the Ionian and the Aegean. On the eve of World War One the biggest shipowning groups came almost exclusively from the islands of the Ionian sea, as a continuity of the entrepreneurial networks of the 19th century. Apart from the Embiricos family that originated from the Aegean island of Andros, and formed the most powerful shipowning group of the first third of the century, the rest, Dracoulis Bros, Stathatos, Lykiardopoulos, Yannoulatos and Vaglianos came from the Ionian islands of Cephalonia and Ithaca (see Table 3). The importance of shipowners from Chios did not begin but later; in 1914 only the shipowning groups of Scaramanga and Michalinos stem from Chios.

If the Ionian Sea dominates in the first third of the century, in the last two thirds the Aegean took over. It is in the interwar period that the family groups of the maritime islands of the Ionian were replaced by the family groups of the Aegean islands. In this way, the five brothers of Ioannis Goulandris from Andros, the five sons of Elias G. Kulukundis from Kasos, the numerous sons of the Embiricos from Andros, the five sons of George Livanos, the two sons of the Ioannis Chandris and those of the large family of Laimos, all from Chios, served as officers on their fathers' steamships and eventually became directors in the offices in Piraeus and London and shipowners themselves. For more than sixty years, as Table 3 indicates, we distinguish the same names of the above mentioned families figuring in the top ten positions of Greek shipping. The only "foreigners" that broke the tightly-knit shipowning circle and conquered its peak were Aristotle Onassis and Stavros Niarchos, both of whom, however, followed the rules. They married within the traditional shipowning circle, the daughters of Stavros Livanos. The importance of the old traditional families, most of them active for at least three generations, started to apparently fade and give way to new shipowners; the new blood in Greek-owned shipping came from masters, first engineers and employees of shipping companies. In the list of the top shipowners of 1999 as it appears in Table 3, only three, A. & S. Polemis, P.G. Livanos and E.G. Embiricos came from traditional families. The rest are new, post-war shipowners: Martinos bros, Prokopiou, Tsakos, Alafouzos, Karnessis, Frangos, Moundreas and Angelicoussis. The strength of Greek-owned shipping was that it managed to reproduce itself and provide new and dynamic entrepreneurs that enlarged the fleet to unprecedented size at the beginning of the 21st century. And as in the Norwegian case, apart from those found in the top, it is the hundreds medium- and small-scale shipowning companies that form the backbone and the seedbed for the expansion of Greek-owned shipping.

4.4 The Japanese

Japan's unique seclusion from the world trade for more than two centuries, makes its maritime history of the last hundred years quite extraordinary. The Japanese could not escape from the integration to the world economic system; the United States that needed bases for their merchant fleets were able to persuade Japan to open up to the "barbarians" in 1853. The demand for modernization brought the end of the old feudal system and the shogun. Japanese business, its dominance in the world economy of the 20th century has attracted the attention of a number of economists and historians; the incredible "otherness" however, combined with the language barriers, still means that its maritime business history remains, for many, a *terra incognita*.[36] For the purpose of this paper we will limit ourselves to a short analysis of the continuity and change of Japanese maritime business, which remains highly comparable to that of its European counterparts.

It was really following the Meiji (the enlightened power) Restoration in 1868 and the nation's industrialization that Japan's shipping showed a remarkable expansion: in the middle-19th century Japan did not own a single ocean going vessel, sixty years later it figured in the third position of world maritime powers. The rapid development of Japanese shipping was the product of a combination of government initiative and active enterpreneurship. Japanese shipping developed, like the British, serving the country's external trade and has been equally divided between liner and tramp. It was in the 1880s that two large companies with government support were formed. The first one was the Nippon Yusen Kaisha (NYK, Japan Mail Steamship Company Ltd), a joint stock company that has remained the largest Japanese shipping company ever since. Based in Tokyo, it was meant as a liner company from the beginning. The other company emerged from Japan's private businessmen and in that con-

Table 3: The largest Greek shipowning groups of the 20th century (in thousands)

Name 1914	Nrt	Name 1938	Grt	Name 1958	Grt	Name 1975	Grt	Name 1999	Dwt
Embiricos Group	92.5	Kulukundis Group	145.3	Goulandris P. sons	1.176	Goulandris P. sons	2.578	Livanos P.G. Group (Ceres)	4.797
Scaramanga Bros	24.2	Goulandris Bros	74.5	Onassis A.	1.098	Onassis A.	2.562	Martinos D.	3.985
Stathatos	24.1	Livanos S.G. (Theofano)	57	Niarchos Stavros	1.033	Lemos C.M.	2.274	Polemis A.&S.	3.458
Dracoulis Bros	20.4	Nomikos Petros	39.9	Livanos S.G.	785	Niarchos Stavros	1.786	Prokopiou G.	3.391
Michalinos	19.3	Chandris I.D.	37.7	Kulukundis Group	730	Kolokotronis M.	1.581	Tsakos P.	3.238
Vagliano A.S.	18.1	Lykiardopoulos N.D.	36.3	Goulandris N.G. sons	420	Goulandris N. sons	1.333	Alafouzos A.	3.236
Panellinios Atmoploia	17.8	Kassos Navigation (Rethymnis, Pneumaticos)	35.4	Lemos C.M.	530	Livanos G.S.	1.219	Karnessis A.&S.	3.074
Lykiardopoulos	14.4	Nikolaou	34.7	Goulandris Bros	320	Coulouthros N.	817	Embirikos E.G.	3.028
Greek Transatlantic Steamship Co.	12.8	Yannoulatos Bros (ELMES)	31.7	Embiricos S.G.	280	Chandris Bros	791	Frangos N. & Moundreas N.	2.401
Yannoulatos Bros	11.9	Embirikos S.G.	27.6	Chandris Bros	200	Kulukundis Bros	712	Angelikoussis A.	2.250
Total of ten companies	255.5		520.1		6.572		15.653		32.858
Total of Greek-owned fleet	822.9		1.889		10.425		45.392		139.255
Share of ten largest	31%		28%		53%		34.5%		23.6%

Source: Gelina Harlaftis, *A History of Greek-owned Shipping, 19-20th centuries* (Nefeli, Athens, 2001), Table 11.5 (in Greek).

trasted the formation of NYK. Based in Osaka, Osaka Shosen Kaisha (OSK, Osaka Mercantile Steamship Co) emerged in the 1880s from the combined forces of Osaka's leading 55 shipowners and merchants.

Since these two large shipping companies were distinguished from all others in terms of their size, type of operation and government subsidy, their ships were called *shasen* (company ships), while all the others were called *shaigasen* (non-company ships). These terms were used to indicate owner or operator, and they roughly indicated the difference between liner and tramp shipping. There were numerous *shaigasen* firms that stemmed from the traditional shipowners or operators that traded in the coastal trade and Japanese seas. They were tramp operators that particularly during and after World War One extended their activities in overseas trade to Korean and Chinese coasts. World War One provided enormous profits to Japanese shipping as the increased demands of belligerent nations the Asian markets looked upon Japanese products.

In the interwar period, Japanese shipping expanded and it was then that the Japanese network of routes was extended to all regions of Southeast Asian, to India, Africa and South America. NYK and OSK were able to become part of the British system of conferences and opened their path to the City of London and the Baltic Exchange. During the shipping boom of World War I a large number of capitalists invested in ships and the tonnage of *shaigasen* companies increased impressively. Most of the *shaigasen* shipowners were not operators themselves but they rather chartered their ships to foreign and Japanese trading companies as well as to the NYK and OSK. In the 1930s five large-scale shaigasen operators, Yamashita, Mitsui, Kawasaki, Kokusai and Daido came to dominate Japanese shipping along with the NYK and OSK. Yamashita, based in Kobe, specialized in long-distance ocean going shipping, while Kawasaki profited from its connection with its production in its shipyards. All shaigasen Japanese companies had access in the London maritime market and were involved in the British second-hand sales and purchase market.

The third forerunner of Japan's steam shipping, and different from the above started from the Mitsui family, that had prospered in Japan as merchants and financiers since the late 17th century, and as the prime financiers of the new Meiji government. They established in 1876 the Mitsui Bussan Kaisha (MBK, Mitsui Trading Co) that with branch offices in Shanghai, Hong Kong, Paris, New York, London and Singapore was oriented in *sogoshosha*, that is in foreign trade, dealing with both bulk trade (coal, rice, cotton) and general manufactured goods.[37] This company proved to be the pioneer in the eventual expansion of Japanese firms on a global basis. In the post war era, the company expanded and eventually became the main competitor of NYK by merging with OSK, what came to be called MOL (Mitsui-OSK Lines).[38]

In a way, the role of the *shaigasen* was exactly the same as that of the British tramp ships; they carried Japanese coal to Argentina, Australia and Java and brought back wheat, wool and sugar. The Japanese imitated successfully the British path, as prime coal exporters on the other side of the globe in the first third of the century, and in the second third of the 20th century became world's main shipbuilders. In a global co-operation, Greek and Norwegian shipowners were among the prime and largest clients of Japanese shipyards from the 1950s to the 1970s.

5. CONTINUITY AND CHANGE

The analysis of the shipping industry and of the main markets has revealed the structural transformations and changes that occurred during the 20th century. The hierarchy of maritime powers changed, as new maritime nations emerged and most traditional maritime countries lost their competitiveness and decreased their market share. The changing patterns of development in the international trade along with the technological advances determined the path of the industry. Shipping markets have followed the path to globalization and specialization has become the drive for their development.

In this context, shipping companies have moved towards the necessary organizational adaptations. Liner shipping companies expanded to the newly developed markets and served almost any destination worldwide. The need for efficiency and effectiveness led them to adapt to unitization investing in containerships and terminals and gradually turned to become transport providers that cover the needs of their customers in a global basis. Conferences are still present but the drive for the achievement of both the critical size and the global coverage are new forms of co-operation that is, the consortia and the strategic alliances. Either through cooperation, internal development or mergers and acquisitions, liner operators strive to become the global players of a global market. In a rather playful game of fate, the beginning and the end of the 20th century were marked by the same trends.

Bulk shipping continues to be a sum of markets that are organized along the needs of the cargoes they transport. Contrary to the liner sector, bulk shipping continues to be characterized by volatility, which increased the risk for the companies. Decisions regarding the choice of the type of ship, the timing of investment and chartering determine the long-term survival of the companies. Information remains one of the most critical factors for success. Dry, liquid and specialized markets like gas and chemicals create a mosaic that incorporates many distinct organizational forms. For the more recently created specialized markets, concentration of tonnage and consolidation of companies were the means for companies that seek to cover the transport needs of global customers. For the dry and liquid markets on the other hand, the tramp character continued to exist throughout the past century, although certain transformations have diminished its presence.

Structural changes on the demand side have provoked the introduction and disparity of cooperation of the commercial side of their operation, mainly through the formation of pools. Trust continues to be at the core of the business: for the main players it is the factor that allows the formation of networks of collaborating competitors. Bulk shipping has traditionally been a sector that rewarded the entrepreneurial spirit, adaptation and flexibility. The business environment for bulk shipping companies during the past century became more regulated and shipping operation more formalized. To a certain extent however, these changes diminished the entrepreneurial character and created the need to balance between the necessity to conform to the business's environment requirements and the necessity to adapt for competitiveness. Still, the beginning and the end of the past century saw the largest part of world's main tramp operators work more or less on similar lines.

ENDNOTES

1. Fischer, L.R., and Nordvik, H.W. (1986): "Maritime Transport and the Integration of the North Atlantic Economy, 1850-1914", Wolfram Fischer, R. Marvin McInnis and Jurgen Schneider (eds.), *The Emergence of a World Economy, 1500-1914* (Wiesbaden, Franz Steiner Verlag). See also Harlaftis, G., and Kardasis, V. (2000): "International bulk trade and shipping in the Eastern Mediterranean and the Black Sea", Williamson, J., and Pamuk, S. (eds.), *The Mediterranean Response to Globalization* (Routledge).
2. Eden, R., and Posner, M. (1981): *Energy Economics* (New York); Harley, C.K. (1989): "Coal Exports and British Shipping, 1850-1913", *Explorations in Economic History*, XXVI.
3. Sturmey, S.G. (1962): *British Shipping and World Competition* (The Athlone Press), pp. 75–79.
4. More on the subject and for further bibliography see Harlaftis, G. (1996): *A History of Greek-owned Shipping, 1830 to the present day* (Routledge), chapters 6 and 8.
5. For an insightful analysis see Cafruny, A.W. (1987): *Ruling the Waves. The Political Economy of International Shipping* (University of California Press). For a classic on flags of convenience, see Metaxas, B.N. (1985): *Flags of Convenience* (London, Gower Press). For the resort of the Greeks to flags of convenience see "Greek Shipowners and State Intervention in the 1940s: A Formal Justification for the Resort to Flags-of-Convenience?", *International Journal of Maritime History*, Vol. I, No. 2, December 1989, pp. 37–63.
6. See Thanopoulou, H. (1995): "The Growth of Fleets Registered in the Newly-emerging Maritime Countries and Maritime Crises", *Maritime Policy and Management*, Vol. 22, No. 1, pp. 51–62.
7. More on the substitution relationship of the tramp with the liner see Metaxas, B.N. (1981): *The Economics of Tramp Shipping* (2nd ed.) (London, Athlone Press), pp. 111–116.
8. See the excellent analysis of Broeze, F., *The Globalisation of the Oceans. Containerisation from the 1950s to the present* (forthcoming 2003).
9. Broeze, F. (1996): "The ports and port system of the Asian Seas: an overview with historical perspective from the 1750", *The Great Circle*, Vol. 18, No. 2, pp. 73–96.
10. However, regulations imposed to the shipping industry during the 90s are among the factors that have contributed to the increase of the importance of the company size to the competitiveness of bulk shipping companies. More on the subject see Theotokas, I.N., and Katarelos, E.D., "Strategic choices for small bulk shipping companies in the post ISM Code period", *Proceedings of WCTR 2001*, Seoul, Korea.
11. Carvounis, C.C. (1979): "Efficiency contradictions of multinational activity: the case of Greek shipping", unpublished Ph.D. thesis (New School of Social Research), p. 81.
12. Harlaftis, G., and Theotokas, G., "'Multinationals' of a Family Character: the European tramp shipping companies of the 20th century", *Business History*, forthcoming.
13. Starkey, D.J. (1996): "Ownership Structures in the British Shipping Industry: the Case of Hull, 1820–1916", *International Journal of Maritime History*, Vol. VIII, No. 2, December, pp. 71–95.

14. More on conferences in also Sturmey, S.G. (1962): *British Shipping and World Competition* (London, The Athlone Press) and Cafruny, A.W. (1987): *Ruling the Waves. The Political Economy of International Shipping* (University of California Press).
15. For the story of Royal Mail see Green. E., and Moss, M.S. (1982): *A Business of National Importance. The Royal Mail Shipping Group, 1902–1937* (London, Methuen).
16. See also Sturmey, S.G. (1962): *British Shipping and World Competition* (London, The Athlone Press), chap. IVX; and Boyce, G. (1995): *Information, Mediation and Institutional Development. The Rise of Large-scale Enterprise in British Shipping, 1870–1919* (Manchester University Press).
17. There is a large bibliography on the liner shipping companies; the leading role was played by the so-called "Liverpool School" founded by Professor Francis Hyde, main factor also in the creation of *Business History*. See Hyde, F.E. (1956): *Blue Funnel: A History of Alfred Holt & Company of Liverpool, 1865–1914* (Liverpool); Hyde, F.E. (1967): *Shipping Enterprise and Management, 1830–1939: Harrisons of Liverpool* (Liverpool); Marriner, S., and Hyde, F.E. (1967): *The Senior: John Samuel Swire 1825-98. Management in Far Eastern Shipping Trades* (Liverpool); Hyde, F.E. (1975): *Cunard and the North Atlantic, 1840–1914* (Liverpool); Davies, P.N. (1973): *The Trade Markets: Elder Dempster in West Africa* (London), *Sir Alfred Jones: Shipping Entrepreneur par Excellence* (London, 1978). For P&O see Cable, B. (1937): *A Hundred Year History of the P&O 1837–1937* (London); Howarth, D., and Howarth, S. (1986): *The Story of P&O* (London), and Rabson, S., and O'Donoghue, K. (1988): *P&O. A Fleet History* (Kendal); Napier, C.J. (1997): "Allies or Subsidiaries? Inter-Company Relations in the P&O Group, 1914–39", *Business History*, Vol. 39, pp. 67–93. For British India (BI) see Forbes Munro, J. (1988): "Scottish Overseas Enterprise and the Lure of London: The Mackinnon Shipping Group, 1847–1893", *Scottish Economic and Social History*, Vol. 8, pp. 73–87. "Sir William Mackinnon" in Slaven, A., and Chekland, S.G. (eds.), *Scottish Dictionary of Business Biography* (Glasgow, 1990), Vol. 2, pp. 279–301; "Suez and the Shipowner: The Response of the Mackinnon Shipping Group to the Opening of the Canal, 1869-84", Fischer & Nordvik, *Shipping & Trade* (1990), pp. 97–118.
18. Harlaftis, G., and Theotokas, G., "'Multinationals' of a Family Character: the European Tramp Shipping Companies of the 20th century", *Business History*, forthcoming.
19. There has been remarkably little research on other than British liner shipping in the last 25 years with an important exception being Gordon Boyce in his *Information, Mediation and Institutional Development. The rise of large-scale enterprise in British Shipping, 1870–1919* (Manchester University Press. 1995), and Forbes Munro, J., and Slaven, T. (2001): "Networks and Markets in Clyde Shipping: The Donaldsons and the Hogarths, 1870–1939", *Business History*, Vol. 43, No. 2, April, pp. 19–50. But it has been the work of the path-breaking maritime historian Robin Craig that has revealed the main aspects of tramp shipping. See Craig, R. (1980): *The Ship. Steam Tramps and Cargo Liners, 1850–1950* (London, HMSO); (1973) "Shipowning in the South-West in its national context, 1800–1914", Fisher, H.E.S., and Minchinton, W.E. (eds.), *Transport and Shipowning in the Westcountry* (University of Exeter); (1970) "Capital formation in Shipping", Higgins, J.P.P., and Pollard, S., *Aspects of Capital Investment in Great Britain (1750–1850)* (Methuen); (1986): "Trade and Shipping in South Wales – The Radcliffe Company, 1882–1921", Baber, C., and Williams, L.J. (eds.), *Modern South Wales: Essays in Economic History* (Cardiff, University of Wales Press), pp. 171–191.
20. *Lloyd's Register of Shipping*, 1970.
21. Nordvik, H.W. (1985): "The Shipping Industries of the Scandinavian Countries, 1850–1914", in Fischer, L.R., and Panting, G.E. (eds.), *Change and Adaptation in Maritime History, the North Atlantic Fleets in the Nineteenth Century* (St. John's, Newfoundland, Maritime History Group), pp. 117–148.

22. Johnsen, B.E. (2001): "Cooperation Across the North Sea: the Strategy Behind the Purchase of Second-hand British Iron and Steel Sailing Ships by Norwegian Ship owners, 1875-1925", paper presented in the International Conference "Maritime History: Visions of shore and sea", Fremantle, Australia, December.
23. Tenold, S. (2000): *The shipping Crisis of the 1970s: Causes, Effects and Implications for Norwegian shipping* (Bergen, Norwegian School of Economics and Business Administration), p. 29.
24. For an analysis of the Norwegian shipping during the crisis of the 1970s see Stig Tenold, *op. cit.*
25. Drury, C., and Stokes, P. (1983): *Ship Finance: The Credit Crisis – Can the Debt/equity Balance Be Restored?* (London, Lloyd's of London Press), p. 37.
26. Ostensjo, P. ((1992): *A Competitive Norway: Chemical Shipping* (Bergen, SNF, NHH).
27. Stokseth, B. (1992): *A Competitive Norway: Open-Hatch Bulk Shipping* (Bergen, SNF, NHH).
28. Bland, A.L., and Crowdy, M. (1961): *Wilh. Wilhelmsen, 1861-1961. The Firm and the Fleet* (Kendal, World Ship Society).
29. Wil. Wilhelmsen ASA, *Annual Report 2000*.
30. For a short analysis of the company see, Stig Tenold, *ibid.*, pp. 247-255.
31. For more on the Bergesen's facts, see Bergesen d.y. ASA, *Annual Report*, 2001.
32. Naess, E.D. (1990): *Autobiography of a Shipping Man*, Colchester, 1977; "61 years in the shipping business", Strandenes, S.P., Svendsen, A.S., and Wergeland, T., *Shipping Strategies and Bulk Shipping in the 1990s* (Institute for Shipping Research, Center for International Business), p. 1.
33. Stig Tenold, *op. cit.*, p. 15.
34. *Op.cit.*, pp. 231-232.
35. For English-speaking bibliography on Greek shipping, see Metaxas, B. (1981): *The Economics of Tramp Shipping* (2nd ed.) (London, Athlone Press); (1985): *Flags of Convenience* (London, Gower Press); Harlaftis, G. (1993): *Greek Shipowners and Greece, 1945-75. From Separate Development to Mutual Interdependence* (London, Athlone Press); (1996) *A History of Greek-owned Shipping. An International Tramp Fleet from 1830 to the Present Day* (Routledge); Theotokas, J. (1998): "Organisational and Managerial Patterns of Greek-Owned Shipping Enterprises and the Internationalization Process from the Interwar Period to 1990", Starkey, D., and Harlaftis, G. (eds.), *Global Markets: The Internationalization of the Sea Transport Industries since 1850*, Research in Maritime History no. 14, I.M.E.H.A. (St. John's, Newfoundland); Serafetinides, M., Serafetinides, G., Lambrinides, M., and Demathas, Z. (1981): "The development of Greek Shipping Capital and its Implications for the Political Economy of Greece", *Cambridge Journal of Economics*, September; Carvounis, C. (1979): "Efficiency and contradictions of multinational activity: the case of Greek shipping", PhD thesis (New School for Social Research).
36. Bibliography in English on Japanese maritime business is rather limited with the exception of its two main shipping companies. An exception to this rule are: Yui, T. (1985): "Introduction", Yui, T., and Nakagawa, K. (eds.), *Business History of Shipping, Proceedings of the Fuji Conference* (University of Tokyo Press); Nagakawa, K. (1985): "Japanese Shipping in the Nineteenth and Twentieth Centuries: Strategies and Organization in Tsunehiko Yui and Keiichiro Nakagawa (eds.), *Business History of Shipping, Proceedings of the Fuji Conference* (University of Tokyo Press); Miwa, R. (1985): "Maritime Policy in Japan: 1868-1937",Yui, T., and Nakagawa, K. (eds.), *Business History of Shipping, Proceedings of the Fuji Conference* (University of Tokyo Press). Otherwise, there is extensive bibliography on the leading companies. See Wray, W.D. (1984): *Mitsubishi and the NYK, 1870-1914: Business Strategy in the Japanese Shipping Industry* (Cambridge, MA); "NYK and the Commercial Diplomacy of the Far Eastern Freight Conference, 1896-1956", Yui and Nakagawa, *Business History of Shipping*; (1990): "The Mitsui Fight", Fischer & Nordvik,

Shipping & Trade 1750–1950 (Lofthouse Publications); Wray, W.D. (1993): "The NYK and the World War I: Patterns of Discrimination in Freight Rates and Cargo Space Allocation", *International Journal of Maritime History*, Vol. 5, No. 1, pp. 41–63; Goto, S. (1998): "Globalization and International Competitiveness – An Historical Perspective of Globalization of Japanese Merchant Shipping", Starkey, D.J., and Harlaftis, G. (eds*.), Global Markets: The Internationalization of the Sea Transport Industries since 1850*, RIMH no. 12 (St. John's, Newfoundland). On shipbuilding, invaluable is Chida, T., and Davies, P.N. (1990): *The Japanese Shipping and Shipbuilding Industries. A History of their Modern Growth* (London, The Athlone Press).
37. Nagakawa, K. (1985): "Japanese Shipping in the Nineteenth and Twentieth Centuries: Strategies and Organization", Yui, T., and Nakagawa, K. (eds.), *Business History of Shipping, Proceedings of the Fuji Conference* (University of Tokyo Press), p. 5.
38. Japan Business History Institute (1985): *The First Century of Mitsui OSK Lines Ltd* (Osaka).

CHAPTER 3

GLOBALISATION: THE MARITIME NEXUS

Shashi Kumar* and Jan Hoffmann†

* Loeb-Sullivan School, Maine Maritime Academy,
Castine, USA. E-mail: *Skumar@mma.edu*
† United Nations' Economic Commission for Latin America and
the Caribbean (ECLAC), Chile. E-mail: *JHoffmann@eclac.cl*

1. INTRODUCTION

Trade in merchandise and unfinished goods increases faster than the world's GDP, and so does the demand for maritime transport services. These services form part of the global logistics chain that determine a good's competitiveness. At the same time, the maritime business is itself strongly affected by globalisation. Trade in maritime services is one of the most liberalised industries, and its "components", such as vessels, flag registration, class inspections, insurance and the work of seafarers, are purchased globally.

As mainstream economists attempt to tackle the causes and impacts of globalisation, international transport is re-entering the debate on trade models and development theories. This chapter attempts to contribute to this debate. It analyses the mutual relationships between trade and its maritime transport, including the specialisation of countries in different shipping sectors, the determinants of transport costs and their relation to trade volumes, and the externalities of growing trade and maritime transport.

2. GLOBALISED BUSINESS IN A GLOBALISED ECONOMY

"Globalisation" means different things to different people. For some, it is the culprit of poverty and war, for others, globalisation is a requirement to economic development for a growing world population. Even "when did globalisation begin" (O'Rourke and Williamson 2000) is a disputed topic. For us, in this brief chapter about maritime economics, it is simply a concept that describes a trend in international trade: It means a) that trade is growing faster than the world's GDP, and b) that this trade is not only in finished goods and services, but increasingly in components and services that are used within globalized production processes (ECLAC 2002a). Maritime transport is growing because it is required to move traded goods and components, and trade in maritime services is itself also taking place on an ever more global scale.

Transport is one of the four cornerstones of globalisation. Together with telecommunications, trade liberalisation and international standardisation, the increased efficiency of port and shipping services has made it ever easier to buy and sell merchandise goods, raw materials and components almost anywhere in the world. International standards and homogenous products foster global competition. Trade liberalisation allows the efficient international allocation of resources. Finally, telecommunication and transportation are the necessary tools to transfer information and goods. "Despite all the headlines and political bluster surrounding the World Trade Organization, NAFTA and other trade pacts, the real driving force behind globalisation is something far less visible: the declining costs of international transport" (*The Journal of Commerce*, 15 April 1997).

At the same time, maritime business itself is probably the most globalised industry. Most maritime transport is provided between two or more countries, and the service providers no longer need to be nationals of the same countries whose cargo they move. In fact, a simple commercial transaction may easily involve people and property from a dozen different countries: A Greek owned vessel, built in Korea, may be chartered to a Danish operator, who employs Philippine seafarers via a Cypriot crewing agent, is registered in Panama, insured in the UK, and transports German made cargo in the name of a Swiss freight forwarder from a Dutch port to Argentina, through terminals that are concessioned to port operators from Hong Kong and Australia. International standardisation, an important component of globalisation in general, also affects shipping. Thanks to containerisation, any liner shipping company from anywhere in the world can now easily enter new markets and provide its services globally. Equivalently, international operators are now in a position to take a concession of a container terminal in any port of the world, suppliers of port and ship equipment produce and sell globally, and ISO's and IMO's standards concerning quality, safety and training apply equally on all international waters.

The remainder of this chapter will look at the mutual relationship between maritime business and globalisation. Section II discusses how trends in international maritime transport affect globalisation, and section III looks at the same relationship, but from the opposite direction, i.e. how the maritime business is affected by globalisation.

3. MARITIME TRANSPORT AND ITS RELEVANCE FOR GLOBALISATION

3.1 Global trade, and how it is being moved

Shipping continues to be the dominant mode of transport, accounting for almost two thirds of world trade (metric tons). World seaborne trade has grown almost continuously since World War II, increasing more than two-fold since 1970 (UNCTAD 2001). The Asia Pacific region accounts for one third of this trade. Industrialised countries have a trade deficit in terms of weight (in metric tons), whereas the exporters of commodities in developing countries have a surplus (Table 1).

Figure 1 illustrates the growth of global trade, and its modal split into air, seaborne and other modes of transport. The latter include pipelines, rail, and trucking, which has grown particularly within Europe. Air cargo, albeit starting

GLOBALISATION: THE MARITIME NEXUS

Table 1: World seaborne trade, by region, 2000, in metric tons

	Exports	Imports	Total
Asia Pacific	1,395,048,612	2,106,116,904	3,501,165,517
Europe	673,405,518	1,421,793,751	2,095,199,269
North America	536,183,767	910,728,180	1,446,911,947
Latin America and the Caribbean	948,292,825	313,012,648	1,261,305,473
Persian Gulf	832,325,214	76,224,353	908,549,566
Other	829,195,627	386,575,726	1,215,771,353
Total	**5,214,451,562**	**5,214,451,562**	

Source: Authors, based on DRI-Wefa, August 2001.

from a very low base, has the highest growth rate. During the eight years covered in Figure 1, it grew by almost 63%, compared to 57% for sea and 58% for other. Air cargo has particularly grown on intercontinental routes, where it competes mainly with maritime transport. This relative increase reflects the globalisation of markets and production processes; higher valued products with shorter life cycles and components used for Just-In-Time delivery require faster (air-) transport. The growth of air transport on intercontinental routes is somewhat offset by the growth of intraregional trade, such as intra-EU, intra-NAFTA or intra-MERCOSUR, which has gained relevance compared to intercontinental trade, and which is mainly moved by trucks.

For the same period, between 1994 and 2002, containerisation of seaborne trade has increased from 8.8% to 10.1%, if measured as percent of all seaborne trade, and from 17.2% to 18.1% if measured as a proportion of dry cargo only

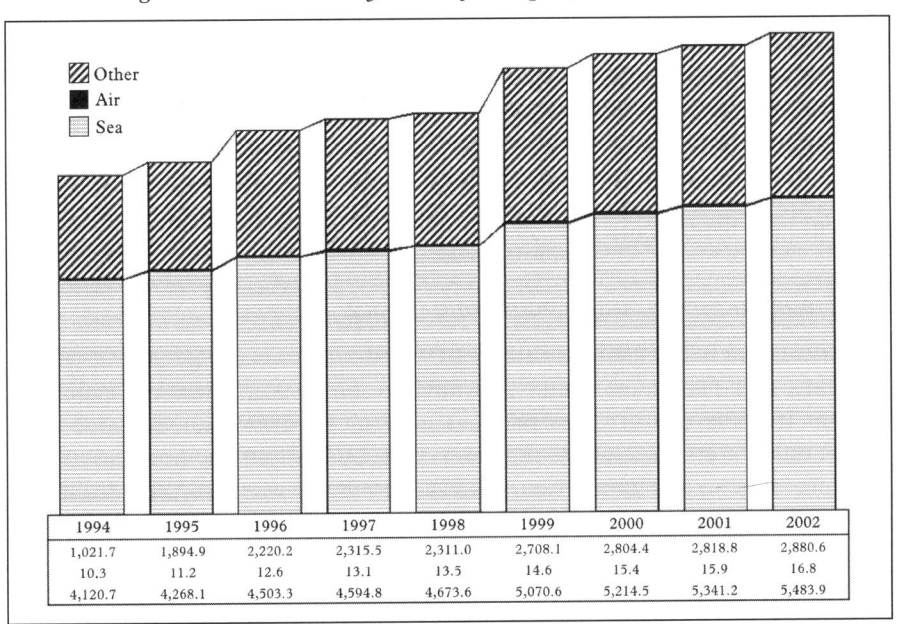

Figure 1: World trade by mode of transport, million metric tons

	1994	1995	1996	1997	1998	1999	2000	2001	2002
Other	1,021.7	1,894.9	2,220.2	2,315.5	2,311.0	2,708.1	2,804.4	2,818.8	2,880.6
Air	10.3	11.2	12.6	13.1	13.5	14.6	15.4	15.9	16.8
Sea	4,120.7	4,268.1	4,503.3	4,594.8	4,673.6	5,070.6	5,214.5	5,341.2	5,483.9

Source: DRI-Wefa, August 2001.

(Figure 2). Container vessels have increased their share of the world fleet from 8% to 8.6% between 1999 and 2000. During the same year, ton-miles have grown by +4.6% (UNCTAD 2001).

Figure 2: World trade by type of transport service, forecast 2002, % of metric tons

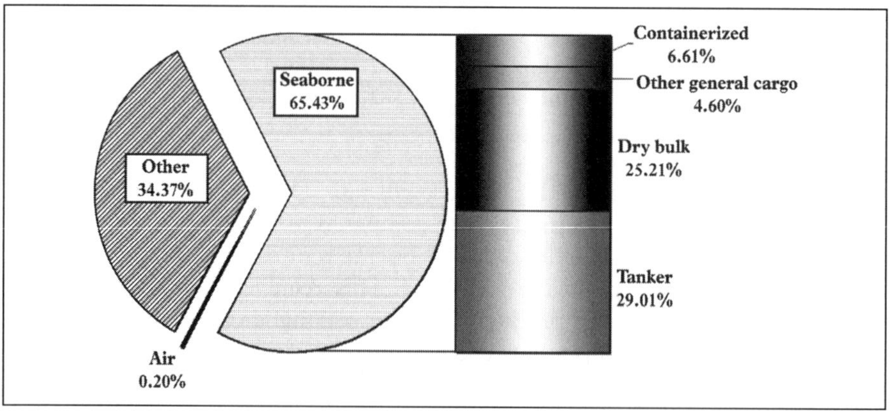

- Seaborne 65.43%
- Other 34.37%
- Air 0.20%
- Containerized 6.61%
- Other general cargo 4.60%
- Dry bulk 25.21%
- Tanker 29.01%

Source: Authors, based on data from DRI-Wefa, August 2001.

The relative importance of airborne cargo becomes clearer if the value of trade rather than its volume is analysed (Table 2). Data for Latin American countries clearly confirms that it is the higher valued goods that are moved by air, whereas cargo with a lower value per ton tends to be transported on ships.

In terms of weight (metric tons) air transport accounts for only 0.1 to 0.6% of Latin American foreign trade, whereas in terms of value (USD) air cargo represents between 8 and 21% of Latin American imports and exports. Table 2 also illustrates that sea and air transport are for obvious reasons the preferred mode of transport for inter-continental trade. Most South American imports and exports from and to more industrialized countries simply cannot be moved otherwise. Mexico, on the other hand, predominantly trades with the United States, using mainly trucks and also some rail and pipelines. Also Uruguay has relevant land based trade with neighbouring Argentina and Brazil.

3.2 Trade and transport in economic theory
International trade and economic growth

Allowing and facilitating trade has obvious positive impacts on economic growth. If Chile can produce bananas only under glass, and Ecuador grow grapes only on an inaccessible highland, then both countries' populations can eat more bananas and grapes (i.e., achieve measurable economic growth) if they specialise and trade – as long as the shipping services are less expensive than the savings in production costs.

Going a step further, even if one country could produce both commodities with less land or manpower than the other country, according to David Ricardo's (1817) theory of the comparative advantage, it still makes sense for both coun-

Table 2: Modal split of foreign trade of Latin American countries, 2000

	Waterborne	Airborne	Other	% water	% air
Metric tons					
Argentina	93,957,510	682,415	20,111,550	81.9%	0.6%
Brazil	324,991,224	694,280	12,138,087	96.2%	0.2%
Chile	88,924,018	514,559	9,690,672	89.7%	0.5%
Colombia	76,028,013	431,106	2,985,532	95.7%	0.5%
Mexico	198,857,095	1,031,833	885,890,600	18.3%	0.1%
Peru	25,376,372	153,151	699,142	96.8%	0.6%
Uruguay	6,121,614	20,962	2,330,273	72.2%	0.2%
USD					
Argentina	30,803,450,978	6,610,214,390	12,847,589,316	61.3%	13.2%
Brazil	77,131,549,173	20,737,749,036	13,279,384,005	69.4%	18.7%
Chile	25,121,557,671	4,060,155,106	4,407,174,136	74.8%	12.1%
Colombia	16,320,897,681	5,004,128,509	2,573,655,568	68.3%	20.9%
Mexico	53,293,421,982	27,744,495,395	259,642,986,404	15.6%	8.1%
Peru	10,567,412,782	2,731,755,335	409,752,032	77.1%	19.9%
Uruguay	2,980,842,542	636,039,812	1,954,864,886	53.5%	11.4%
USD per metric ton					
Argentina	328	9,687	639		
Brazil	237	29,869	1,094		
Chile	283	7,891	455		
Colombia	215	11,608	862		
Mexico	268	26,889	293		
Peru	416	17,837	586		
Uruguay	487	30,343	839		

Source: Authors, based on ECLAC, *www.eclac.cl/transporte/perfil* (April 2002).

tries to specialise and trade. Ricardo's example uses the production of cloth and wine, where Portugal has an absolute advantage concerning both: It needs 80 man-months to produce X litres of wine and 90 man-months to produce Y metres of cloth, whereas England needs 120 and 100 man-months respectively. England has a comparative advantage concerning cloth, and a rational decision of Portugal and England will imply that the first specialises in growing wine and the latter in producing cloth, consequently leading to English exports of cloth to Portugal and Portuguese exports of wine to England. This type of specialisation, and thus also the resulting trade, can partly be explained by the "Factor Proportions Model", which was developed by Eli Heckscher and Bertil Ohlin in the 1920s (Ohlin 1933). This model expands Ricardo's basic version by including differences in the endowment of resources. Linking both models thus allows to explain trade flows by differences in available technology, capital, manpower and natural resources.

Today, the academic discussion on why and how much countries trade with each other is far developed. The impetus for new trade theories came from the limitations of the classical models because of their relatively simplistic assumptions and also their empirical weaknesses. This was illustrated by the Leontief Paradox (1953) when the Factor Proportions Model, discussed earlier, was applied to the US. The empirical analysis did not support the theory's prediction that a nation's abundance in a particular factor of production would dominate its exports. New contributions in the post-WWII era include Vernon's product life-cycle theory of the mid-1960s, the new trade theory of the 1980s (Krugman 1981, Lancaster 1980) and Porter's (1990) national competitive advantage trade theory. The product life cycle theory explained the international trade patterns of the 1960s when the US dominated the global economy and most new products originated in that country (Vernon and Wells 1986). As demand for the product increased gradually in other developed nations, it was initially met through US exports until the production itself moved to those countries because of higher US labour costs. Furthermore, once the product became standardised, US production was typically replaced with exports from other developed nations first and, in the long-run, exports from developing countries. However, the limitations of this theory are far too many in the contemporary global economy where production is dispersed to different parts of the world simultaneously and no one particular nation is in a position to claim hegemony in international trade.

The new trade theory is based on the increasing returns to specialisation that arise in an industry when it is characterised by high economies of scale. The presence of such economies of scale in production would lead to the existence of only a limited number of global players in the market. Those firms that are first-movers may benefit from their early entry and establish themselves, erecting entry barriers for others. It has been argued that to be successful in such an environment, in addition to the firm being lucky, entrepreneurial, and innovative, the nation itself must have a strategic, proactive trade policy that facilitates first-mover advantage in key and newly emerging industries (Hill 2000). Porter's national competitive advantage theory postulates the existence of a diamond that consists of factor endowments, demand conditions, related and supporting industries, and firm strategy, structure and rivalry. The diamond will be favourable when the four components are in place along with an element of luck and favourable government policies as was the case for the Japanese automobile industry in the 1980s (Porter 1990).

In practice, the different theories of international trade obviously complement each other and make their own contributions. They apply as much to trade in goods as to trade in services – including maritime transport services: Flag registries, for example, surely benefit from economies of scale, shipyards require an endowment of capital and labour, and London was a "first mover" concerning insurance and finance. Later on, we will look in more detail at this specialization in different maritime sectors.

And what does trade mean for economic growth and well-being? Under almost any model, it is "potentially possible to find a free trade consumption point and an appropriate lump-sum compensation scheme such that everyone is at least as well-off with trade as they had been in autarky" (Suranovic 2002). And, accordingly, "international economic integration yields large potential welfare effects" (Anderson and Wincoop 2001). The posterior distribution of these benefits within society is a different matter, beyond the scope of this chapter.

Mainstream economics and its consideration of transport
How does transport fit into this analysis of trade and economic development? Standard Economics text books, if they include it at all, do so by considering it as part of the overall transaction or arbitrage costs. Trade will take place if price differences between two countries are higher than the total transaction costs.

Until the early 1970s, transport and transport related infrastructure played an important role in location theories and development economics, including the lending policies of the World Bank and bilateral technical co-operation. It was assumed that by simply providing for infrastructure such as ports, roads and bridges, developing countries would soon become more competitive and catch up with the industrialised nations. This changed for two main reasons: first, as transport costs declined and connectivity and efficiency improved, it was assumed that further improvements in transport were no longer relevant for trade and development. Second, the relationship between transport and economic growth is quite complex, and impacts of changes were – and still are – difficult to measure. Some of the measurable results of infrastructure investments were actually disappointing or even contrary to the expected and desired impact. For example, if imports suddenly became more competitive, port investments actually led to a closure of local industries (Pedersen 2001, Hilling 1996, Simon 1996).

Very few Nobel Memorial Prizes in Economics have so far been given to authors who worked – partly – on transport related topics. One was in 1993, when the prize was won by Robert Fogel and Douglass North. Fogel's main contributions included research on the role of the railways for the development of the national economy in the United States. Douglass North worked, inter alia, on the economic development in Europe and the United States before and in connection with the industrial revolution, including the roles of sea transport and changes in the pattern of regional specialization and interregional trade.

Nowadays, most trade models include transport costs or some related variables, such as distance and common borders, to explain the geographical distribution of international trade flows. In empirical research, measurable reductions in transport costs are taken as a given exogenous trend, driven by technological advances, that obviously promotes trade. O'Rourke and Williamson (1999), for example, analyze how in different historical periods trade grew as a result of reductions in freight rates.

Yet still, "there isn't nearly as much trade as standard trade models suggest that there should be. Formal trade barriers such as tariffs and quotas are far too low to account for much of the missing trade while changes in tariffs and quotas in the last 50 years explain too little of the growth in trade. Transport costs help explain the missing trade, but distance and other location variables are far too important in their trade suppressing effects to be accounted for by the effect of distance and measurable transport costs. Measured transport costs do not fall so cannot explain the growth in trade. These anomalies have until recently been ignored by the profession" (Anderson 1999).

Whether transport costs have fallen or not is surely debatable and we shall briefly discuss this question later on. What is true, however, is that by considering only transport costs and not other aspects such as connectivity, safety, security, reliability, speed, or port facilitation, many trade analysts have not been too impressed with the advances in the field of transport and their impact on trade growth. And what has apparently been ignored altogether is how increased trade, i.e. demand, influences transport costs, i.e. the supply of transport services.

3.3 Trade and its transport: a mutual relationship

Rediscovering transport

As mentioned above, the question of "why do nations trade (so little)" (Anderson 1999) is not answered satisfactorily. Perhaps – we hope – this is about to change. Since the late 1990s, in the context of globalisation and the analysis of its causes and impacts, transport is slowly moving back to the mainstream of Economics and related sciences. Thompson (2000), from the World Bank, writes he is "delighted to see the general economics profession rediscovering the importance of transportation costs and geography in international trade considerations", and Pedersen (2001) explains that "during the 1990 transport and communication appear slowly to be on their way into the mainstream again, but now transformed into a much broader concept of logistics, which has become an increasingly important element in the organisation and restructuring of the globalizing economy. From being an external factor, transport has become an integrated part of the production and distribution system".

Recent empirical research which incorporates transport into trade and economic policy analysis includes Limao and Venables (1999), who conclude that "halving transport costs increases the volume of trade by a factor of five". In a related paper (Venables and Limao 1999), the same authors highlight that a "theory of trade that ignores transport costs will yield systematically incorrect predictions about trade patterns, industrial structure, and factor incomes".

What are the determinants of international maritime transport costs?

Limao, Venables, and also Radelet and Sachs (1998) not only use transport cost data to explain trade, but also undertake regressions to explain transport costs. The explanatory variables used in their analysis are basically related to distance and connectivity, such as if countries are land locked, or if trading partners are neighbours, and to country characteristics such as GDP per capita. García Menéndez et al. (2002) investigate the determinants of maritime transport costs and the role they play in allocating trade across countries for the case of the ceramic sector (tiles). They include a discussion on the sensitivity of trade flows and transportation costs to the existence of back hauling, and suggest that higher distance and poor partner infrastructure increases transport costs notably. Inclusion of infrastructure measures improves the fit of the regression, corroborating the importance of infrastructure in determining transport costs. Higher transport costs significantly deter trade, and distance does not appear to be a good proxy for transport costs, at least not in the ceramic sector. For Latin America, continuing work by Micco and Pérez (2001), Sanchez et al. (2002)

analyze the impact of port reform on transport costs, and also possible determinants of the port reforms themselves. Hummels (1999a, 1999b, and 2000) discusses if "international transport costs have declined", and he introduces "time as a trade barrier". One of his conclusions is that that "each day saved in shipping time is worth 0.5% ad-valorem, approximately 30 times greater than costs associated with pure inventory holding" (Hummels, 2000). Fink *et al.* (2001) analyse how liberalisation in trade in transport services leads to further reductions in transport costs, which in turn lead to a further promotion of trade in goods. Although criticised in its methodology and specific conclusions concerning liner shipping's anti trust immunity (World Shipping Council 2001), there is no doubt that the liberalisation and globalisation of the maritime business (see section 3 of this chapter), have led to a reduction of transport costs, which is contributing to the globalisation of trade and global production.

What appears to be missing in the reviewed literature is a more thorough consideration of the mutual relationship between trade volumes, transport costs, and the quality of transport services. Some preliminary research for intra Latin American trade suggests that higher quality of service implies higher transport costs, yet also promotes trade. Economies of scale from high trade volumes have a strong negative (i.e., decreasing) impact on transport costs. Therefore, it appears very likely that the strong relation between trade and transport costs detected by Limao and Venables (1999) quoted above (see page 42) does not only reflect the elasticity of trade towards transport costs, but also almost certainly reflects the economies of scale through which higher volumes lead to lower costs of transport.

For the case of Intra-Latin American trade, ongoing research of ECLAC analyses the impact of a number of factors on transport costs. The results suggest a number of interesting conclusions. For example, the unit value of traded goods and economies of scale appear to have a stronger impact on transport costs than distance (Table 3).

The regression results can be interpreted as follows:
- As expected, more expensive goods also require higher transport and insurance costs.
- Moving a higher volume reduces transport costs thanks to economies of scale.
- A longer distance obviously increases transport costs, albeit by far not with a linear relationship.
- "More services" are closely related to the transport system's overall economies of scale and may also be an indicator of the intensity of competition.
- When shipping competes with land transport, maritime transport costs tend to be slightly lower (4.2%), which may reflect competition from truckers, and also the fact that goods that are particularly difficult to handle by waterborne transport are taken onto trucks – an option that exists between, say, Peru and Ecuador, but not between Peru and Mexico.
- Advances in port privatisation do, as expected, reduce transport costs. Not only may ports operate less expensively, but above all reduced waiting times and risk also lead to lower shipping freight rates.

Table 3: Determinants of international maritime transport costs for intra-Latin American trade, containerisable commodities and general cargo, 2000

Variable (Logarithm)	Estimated parameter (t-value)	Standardised coefficient	Partial correlation, zero-order	Partial correlation, zero-order
Constant	1.114 (21.400)			
Unit fob value of transported cargo per transaction (US$ per ton)	0.340 (138.476)	0.480	0.631	0.513
Volume of transported cargo per transaction (tons)	−0.127 (−102.931)	−0.353	−0.586	−0.406
Distance between both countries' main ports (km)	0.237 (37.480)	0.190	0.149	0.160
Liner shipping services between both countries (number of services per month)	−0.094 (−22.713)	−0.116	−0.135	−0.097
Land transport connection between both countries (Dummy variable: "1" if countries are connected by road transport; "0" otherwise)	−0.048 (−5.820)	−0.020	0.003	−0.025
Successful advances in port privatisation of the exporting country (qualitative variable from a poll, values between 1 and 10)	−0.167 (−13.546)	−0.044	−0.079	−0.058
Bilateral trade balance of containerisable cargo (tons, exports divided by imports)	−0.042 (−23.732)	−0.073	−0.082	−0.102
Speed of liner shipping services between both countries (km per day of fastest available service between both countries)	0.051 (6.669)	0.024	0.022	0.029

Dependent variable: International transport costs (maritime freight and insurance) per individual commercial transaction (US$ per ton). Trade in containerisable commodities between 15 exporting and 6 importing Latin American countries.
Number of observations 53,770
Adjusted R^2 0.564

Source: Authors, based on regressions undertaken by ECLAC.[1]

Explanatory notes: The estimated parameter reflects an elasticity, e.g. a 1% increase in the distance leads to an increase of transport costs per ton of 0.237%. The "t-value" is a division of the estimated coefficient by its standard deviation, and a value above approximately 2 or below −2 indicates that the estimated parameter is "significant" at the 95% level (i.e., all estimated parameters in our regression are highly significant). The standardised coefficient is equivalent to the estimated parameter, but based on deviations from the mean. The partial correlation coefficient, zero-order, is independent of the regression and varies between 1 and −1. The partial correlation coefficient in the regression reflects each variable's contribution to the explained variance of the transport costs; e.g., although the estimated parameter for distance is higher than that for transaction volume, the fact that distance varies far less than the transaction volume has the effect that the latter has a bigger contribution to the explanation of the variance of transport costs.

- If exports exceed imports, the latter tend to be less expensive because empty transport capacity is required for the exports.
- Higher speed implies fewer stopovers and thus possibly loss of business opportunities, plus additional fuel consumption.

In sum, econometric regressions confirm basic assumptions about the determinants of maritime transport costs. Above all, they strongly suggest that transport costs cannot be taken as fixed or exogenous in trade analysis.

Transport and regional integration

If it is true that international transport (unit-) costs are declining, and distance has a decreasing impact on these transport costs, why then apparently regional trade is growing (even) faster than inter-regional trade? Intra-Asian container traffic is growing faster than global container traffic. Intra-European or intra-MERCOSUR trade has been increasing at a higher rate than trade between these two regional blocks.

Some of the intra-regional trade growth certainly has less to do with transport but rather with language barriers, historical trends, trade facilitation at common borders, and lower intra-regional tariffs. But some of the reasons do have a relation with transport costs and options: as shown above, due to larger traded volumes, unit transport costs decline (economies of scale) and frequencies and even possibly speed increases. Also, on a regional level, more options (road, rail) are available. This in turn reduces delivery times, allows for more Just-In-Time delivery, and thus increases the demand for goods and components. In other words, more trade leads to better and less expensive transport services, which in turn again lead to more intra-regional trade.

The impact of better and less expensive transport on trade is equivalent to the impact of lower tariffs, and the relatively faster growth of intra-regional trade does not contradict the previous statement that goods and components are increasingly purchased globally. A large part of the growth of intra-regional trade replaces previous national "trade", i.e. between counties or regions of the same country, and is not a diversion of imports or exports that would otherwise be bought from or sold to countries outside the region. Just as "most analyses of most Free Trade Agreements, including most importantly by far the European Union, conclude that trade creation has dominated trade diversion" (Bergsten 1997), improved transport costs and services on a regional level are to be seen as a result and a component of the entire process of globalisation.

Just as in the relation between globalisation and international transport, the relation between regional integration and regional transport is also two-fold: Less expensive and better intra-regional transport services lead to further regional integration, and at the same time regional integration also affects the markets for transport services. Within the European Union, maritime cabotage services are liberalised for European registered vessels, trucks from all Member Countries have liberty to move national cargo in all other countries, and common standards help to create not only a common market for goods, but also a common market for transport services.

3.4 Outlook

Trade, and its transport, will continue to shape the world's economic development. Historically, when transport costs were prohibitive for most products, each country, or even town, would produce its own goods. Most countries made their own toys, furniture, watches and even cars. Then came the international economy; as transport costs went down and delivery times and reliability improved, many national industries died out and production became concentrated in a few, specialised places, from where world markets were being served. Cars, and car parts, were made in Detroit; watches, and batteries, in Switzerland; furniture, and the required wood, were made in Sweden.

At present, we are observing how the international economy gives rise to globalisation. As transport costs decrease even further, and delivery times and reliability continue to improve, production is again becoming less concentrated, albeit in a different manner: cars may still be designed in Detroit, yet car parts may be made in Mexico and assembly takes place in Malaysia; watches may still be marketed as "Swiss", yet most components are likely to be imported; and a Swedish producer of furniture will franchise his name and design, to produce local furniture with imported materials and components from wherever these are provided at the best price and quality.

The same applies to shipping. A ship may be registered in Antigua and Barbuda, but its owner can be German, and the "components" of the shipping service, such as insurance, equipment, the work of seafarers, or certificates of classifications societies, are very likely to have been purchased in many different countries. "The claim that 'trade follows the flag', often used in the past to justify support for national fleets, has become primarily an argument of special interest groups seeking support for maritime sector enterprises. It is agreed that access to efficient maritime transport is a key variable in economic development. This does not necessarily imply fleet ownership or government control" (Audigé, 1995). The next section will look in more detail at how globalisation affects maritime business.

4. GLOBALISATION AND ITS RELEVANCE FOR MARITIME BUSINESS

4.1 The global supply chain
Global supply chain management
Although globalisation is sometimes referred to as being Janus-faced for its inequitable distribution of benefits among nations of the world, the perceptible impact that it has had on international production and marketing are beyond cynicism. Porter (1985) thinks of the firm as a value chain composed of a series of value creation activities, some of them (such as production and marketing) being primary activities and the others (such as logistics services that include shipping movements) being support activities. As firms tend to focus more on their core competencies and maintain their competitive advantage in the global marketplace, the orientation towards procuring raw materials and sub-assemblies from sources all over the world, based on optimal purchasing arrangements, becomes even more crucial. This, along with the reduction in numerous trade barriers (because of the role of the World Trade Organisation) and the apparent diminution of ideological conflicts between leading nations of the world have led to greater levels of outsourcing and thus, the diffusion of the value chain across the oceans, and hence, the evolution of global supply chains.

Mentzer et al. (2001) argue that firms must have a supply chain orientation to effectively manage the supply chain that could result in lower costs, increased customer value and satisfaction, and competitive advantage. Leading edge logistics firms have recognised that it is the supply chain of a firm that is in competition with that of its competitors rather than the firms themselves (Christopher 1992). The establishment of such a supply chain requires the formation of strategic alliances with channel members that include transportation service providers such as shipping companies. Integration of transport activities is essential for the success of a supply chain and a well-integrated transportation system's contributions to the supply chain could include time compression, reliability, standardisation, Just-In-Time delivery, information systems support, flexibility and customisation (Morash and Clinton 1997). Although the emphasis on building supply chain partnerships is a relatively new trend in corporate strategy, it is not a novel concept in the maritime business, two early examples being the evolution of the open registry concept and that of the ship management industry.

The objective of outsourcing non-core activities in search of efficiency and adding value to the end customer is potentially advantageous and adds to societal welfare – as long as the functions are being performed at acceptable levels of quality which in today's lexicon for product standards is one of "zero defects". The ship owner's effort to create a "least cost system" in the maritime business is tantamount to designing a global supply chain based only on least cost channel members.

Whereas this may lead to a loss of market share and corporate profits for the channel members of a supply chain, deficiencies of the least cost maritime system could have more drastic consequences, ranging from loss of life to environmental degradation that impacts society at large besides the more traditional commercial losses of the business enterprise. Hence, while the temptations of using the cheapest crew and registering the ship in a lax ship registry might be appealing to the business acumen, the likely catastrophic magnitude of a mishap would make the ship owner think hard before making such choices. Globalisation and its underlying market forces appear to provide some guidance in this regard as there are perceptible specialised markets for virtually any aspect of the maritime business today that parallel the developments in specialisation in a broader context.

Specialisation in maritime business

Readily observable examples of specialisation exist in ship construction, technical management of ships, ship repairs and dry-docking, ship registration, crewing, shipping finance, ship chartering and brokering, and marine insurance. Analogous to the economic philosophy driving the new trade theory in international business, some areas of specialisation in shipping are an outcome of proactive trade policies in combination with luck, entrepreneurship and innovation that created a new breed of first-movers in areas like open registries, and ship construction and repairs. However, the socio-economic conditions of the leading nations (in specific areas of maritime specialisation) have also contributed toward their evolution as global leaders.

Examples of this include small service economies that have specialised in open registries (such as Panama, Cyprus, Bahamas, or Bermuda), and large populous Asian nations that provide seafarers (such as the Philippines, India, Indonesia and China). Norway, combining tradition and financing from its oil exports, is strong in shipping finance. London is a leading supplier of insurance and brokering services in general, including shipping. Korea and Japan are highly industrialised countries that build most of the world's shipping tonnage. There appears to exist a close relation between a country's endowment of resources and general specialisation in services or industrial production and its specialisation in specific maritime sectors, whereas the relation between the different maritime sectors themselves appears to be increasingly weak.

The other side of that same coin is of course "concentration"; as countries spccialise, the market share of the major players is increasing (Hoffmann 1998). Between January 2001 and 2002, Panama's share of the world fleet (Gross Tons, GT) has further grown from 21 to 22% (ECLAC 2002b). Maersk-Sealand now controls 11% of the world's container carrying capacity (*www.alphaliner.com*), up from around 6% for Maersk only in 1997. Four Asian nationalities provided around 40% of the world's seafaring personnel in 2000, forecasted to grow to 48% by 2005.

If the world were still divided into "maritime nations" and others, non-maritime nations that do not participate in the maritime business, then the same countries where carriers are based would also build and register the ships and provide the seafarers. A cross country comparison based on indicators for these maritime activities would produce very high correlation coefficients. The reality under globalisation, however, is quite different, as the following example of Latin America and the Caribbean illustrates.

Specialisation and clustering: The case of Latin America and the Caribbean

For Latin American and Caribbean countries, a clustering and principal component analysis of main maritime sectors confirms that, today, the countries that provide seafarers to the industry are very different from those that provide the registries or the ship building. On a per-capita basis, some positive correlation remains between carriers and registries. Other positive correlations appear to be rather a coincidence; the same small countries in the Caribbean with a long coastline per capita are also home to transhipment ports, and some provide open registries. It should also become clear that foreign trade is hardly related to most maritime business, i.e., a statement such as "trade follows the flag" is not supported by empirical evidence (Table 4 and Figure 3).

In what maritime sectors do countries specialise (Figure 4)? Antigua & Barbuda and Panama are specialising in services and provide open registries. Honduras has a very low income and exports the highest number of seafarers per capita. Chile, Brazil and Argentina are home to the region's main shipping companies, and they are also among the few countries that have maintained some ship building during the last five years. In the latest edition of *Fairplay*

Newbuildings (March 2002), these three are the only Latin American and Caribbean countries at all with any vessels on order in their national shipyards.

Except for GDP per capita, the statistical comparison that underlies Figure 4 only contains maritime indicators. Nevertheless, it appears that the grouping of countries coincides with other common characteristics of the countries in the same group. Chile, Brazil and Argentina are also among the more industrialised countries of the region; Antigua & Barbuda and Panama are service economies;

Table 4: Correlation coefficients between different maritime sectors in Latin America and the Caribbean

Per capita indicator	Coast	Port	Flag	Carriers	Shipyard	Seafarer	Trade	GDP
Coast, km	1.00							
Port moves, TEU	0.68	1.00						
Flag registration, GT	0.74	0.85	1.00					
Carriers, GT	0.26	0.66	0.56	1.00				
Naval construction, GT	-0.09	-0.15	-0.10	0.31	1.00			
Seafarers, persons	-0.02	0.08	0.07	0.21	-0.07	1.00		
Trade, US$	-0.03	0.42	0.18	0.36	-0.22	0.34	1.00	
GDP, US$	0.45	0.30	0.34	0.19	0.39	-0.21	-0.36	1.00

Source: Authors, based on per capita indicators for 27 Latin American and Caribbean countries from *www.eclac.cl/transporte/perfil*

Figure 3: Clustering of maritime industries in Latin America and the Caribbean

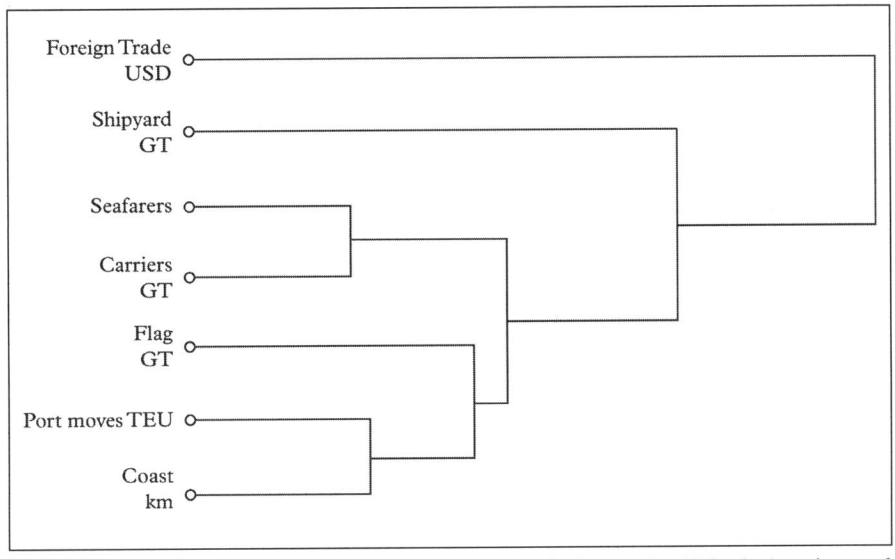

Source: Authors, based on normalized industry per capita indicators for 27 Latin American and Caribbean countries from *www.eclac.cl/transporte/perfil*. Clustering with software xlstat.

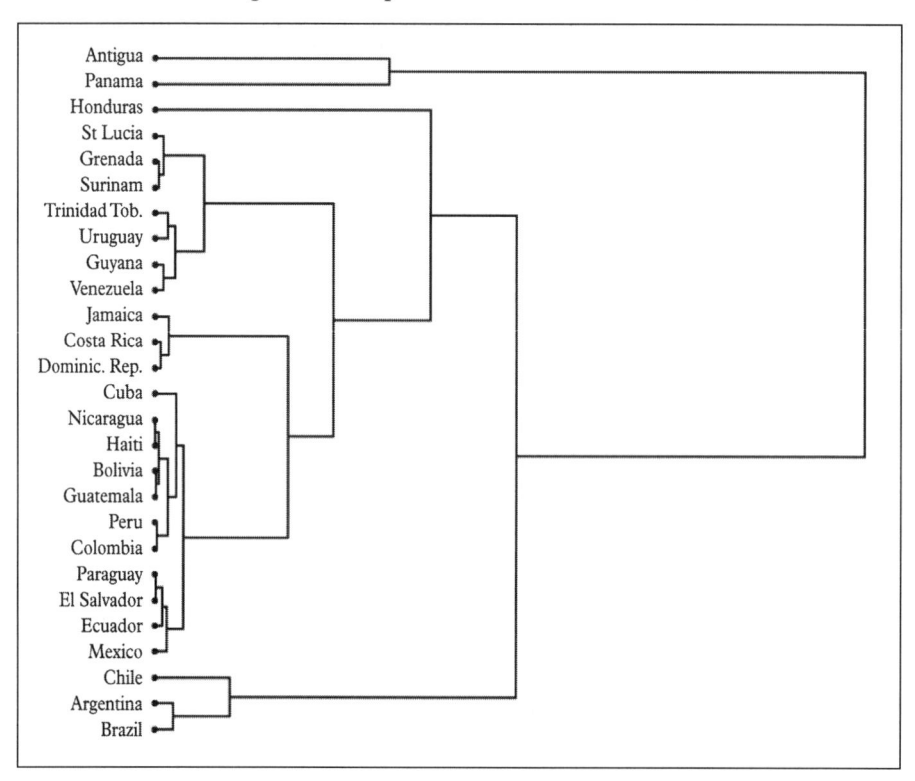

Figure 4: Grouping of Latin American and Caribbean countries according to similar specialisation in maritime industries

```
Antigua
Panama
Honduras
St Lucia
Grenada
Surinam
Trinidad Tob.
Uruguay
Guyana
Venezuela
Jamaica
Costa Rica
Dominic. Rep.
Cuba
Nicaragua
Haiti
Bolivia
Guatemala
Peru
Colombia
Paraguay
El Salvador
Ecuador
Mexico
Chile
Argentina
Brazil
```

Source: Authors, based on data from *www.eclac.cl/transporte/perfil*. Clustering undertaken with normalised per capita indicators, utilising software xlstat. To request the underlying data in xls format, contact *jhoffmann@eclac.cl*

and Suriname, Grenada and St Lucia are among the smallest economies of the continent. In other words, the specialisation in exports of particular maritime services has ever less to do with other maritime businesses, but rather with geographic location, natural resources and other comparative advantages – just as trade in any other good or service in a globalised economy.

As globalisation in maritime business has led to increasing levels of specialisation in the industry, this has had varying impacts on nations. Along with the traditional maritime nations, a number of new maritime players have evolved, some of which have very little maritime history or even a coastline. A good example is Switzerland, a land-locked nation, which is home to the world's largest freight forwarder and to Mediterranean Shipping Company, one of the top five liner shipping companies in the world. According to UNCTAD (2001), there are 246 Swiss ships – 13 flying the national flag and the rest open-registry – that constitute 0.92% of the world fleet. The following subsection discusses salient policy developments in traditional maritime nations as well as newcomers that have shaped the course of maritime business.

4.2 Policy issues

The decline of traditional maritime nations

The globalised economy and the relatively invisible role played by the maritime sector in facilitating it have led to predictable outcomes for the sector in general. No one attaches the same prominence to shipping today as Sir Walter Raleigh did in the early 1600s when he linked the command of the sea to the possession of the riches of the new world. The irony is that the relative decline of the maritime political power is partly because of the sophistication of contemporary shipping operations wherein a cargo movement from Argentina to Zimbabwe or Mumbai to Marseilles is as predictable as a commute to the suburbs. Thus, shipping operations have become literally invisible in the global chain of commerce, albeit still important and unavoidable. Accordingly, the declining importance given to maritime issues is understandable.

Lovett (1996) provides an excellent discussion of the rise and fall of various maritime empires, from the Greeks and Phoenicians (480 BC) to the British, West European and the US merchant fleet as of the early 1990s, and makes a strong argument for a resurgence of maritime policy-making in the United States. Maritime economists have offered remedial measures to stem the flow of maritime business interests of developed nations like the US (e.g., Kumar 1994). However, two powerful forces, in combination, have solidified the ongoing decline of traditional maritime nations. One is the power of the market forces driving the global economy and specialisation in general, discussed earlier, and the other, the political reality at the bargaining table.

The political reality in the developed economies today is such that shipping-related issues are subservient to the trade needs of those nations. The balance of power has swung visibly in favour of the cargo owners from that of the transportation service providers (Kumar 1987). This has impacted current transport policy-making, in the maritime sector as well as in other modes. Sletmo (2001) captures the contemporary maritime policy-making trend by emphatically placing the supremacy of global trade perspectives over maritime issues. Accordingly, mode-specific transportation policy has become a doctrine of the past in developed market economies, most of who were the most important maritime nations of the past. Although one could argue that air movements are still an exception because of the extensive use of bilateral negotiations involved in air transportation, major developed nations today advocate a transport policy that favours seamless multimodal freight movements in general.

These nations have thus assumed a more holistic approach in national transportation policy-making that is conducive to the facilitation of a seamless movement of its commerce. Accordingly, the emphasis today in many developed nations is not in the size of their fleet or their tonnage, but on eradicating the barriers to the through movement of cargoes. An excellent example of this is the United States, the world's largest importer and exporter, and the home of many prestigious shipping firms of the past. Today, it is left with relatively very little presence in the deep-sea fleet, in spite of the Jones Act

Table 5: Maritime engagement of traditional maritime nations, end 2000

Country	Percent value share of world trade generated	Percent share of world fleet in dwt
United States	15.7	7.87
Germany	8.1	4.11
Japan	6.6	12.74
United Kingdom	4.7	3.76
France	4.6	1.48
Italy	3.6	1.84
Netherlands	3.1	0.85
Belgium-Luxembourg	2.9	0.99
Spain	2.0	0.71
Russia	1.1	2.09
Norway	0.7	10.90

Source: UNCTAD, *Review of Maritime Transport, 2001*, Table 30.

and other protectionist measures that oblige carriers to use US flagged, built and manned vessels for cabotage services.

Table 5 shows the maritime engagement of traditional maritime nations as of end 2000. It is to be noted that among the nations listed, only Japan, the Russian Federation and Norway have a greater percentage share of world fleet in deadweight than their share of world trade in value. Figure 5 shows the precipitous decline in the shipping fleet registered in developed market economy nations, most of who also fall under the traditional maritime countries category. The decline in the fleet of these nations during the past 30 years is in direct contrast to the gains made by fleets registered in open registry nations and developing countries. Presently, almost two out of every three ships are registered either under an open registry flag or in a developing country.

The rise of a new order in maritime business

While the traditional maritime nations in general are losing their supremacy in the business, a new group of nations have proactively enacted maritime policies that favour their shipping base. A 1996 attempt to classify nations based on their attitude towards shipping in general listed these new centres of maritime business as shipping-friendly whereas the policies of many of the traditional maritime nations were listed under the shipping-hostile category (Lovett 1996). Examples of the shipping-friendly category include nations such as South Korea, Taiwan and Singapore. The ascendancy of these nations is usually focused on specific aspects of the shipping business, such as ship operation and construction in South Korea, or ship registration in smaller service economies.

Some, such as Singapore or Brazil, do apparently pursue all-out efforts to build the entire shipping milieu. A recent announcement from the Ministry of Maritime Affairs and Fisheries, South Korea is another example. Coincidentally, the day this segment was written, the Journal of Commerce reported the South Korean government initiative to establish a ship-registration site in the southern island of Cheju to complement the international logistics centres being planned for Pusan and Kwangyang in South Korea. Reportedly,

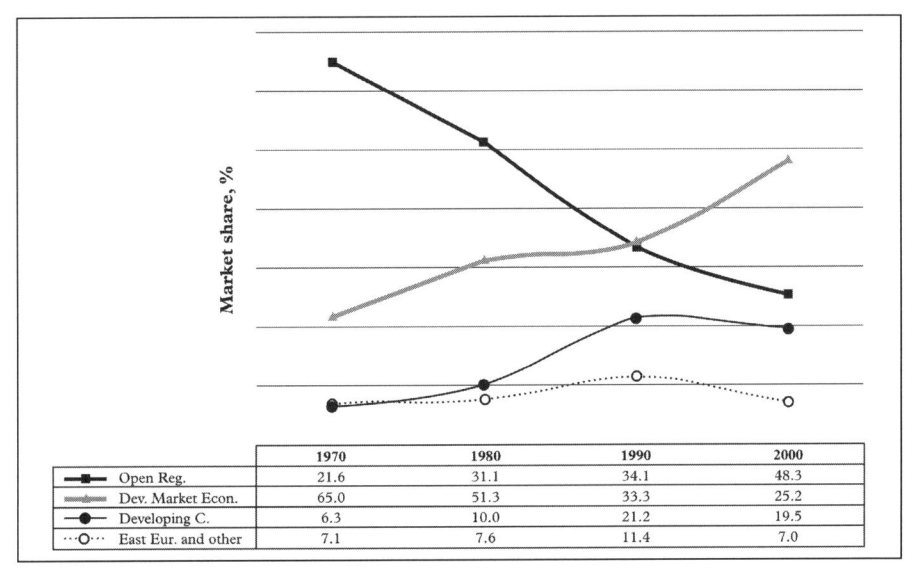

Figure 5: Ship registration trends

	1970	1980	1990	2000
Open Reg.	21.6	31.1	34.1	48.3
Dev. Market Econ.	65.0	51.3	33.3	25.2
Developing C.	6.3	10.0	21.2	19.5
East Eur. and other	7.1	7.6	11.4	7.0

Source: UNCTAD, *Review of Maritime Transport, 2001*, Table 29.

the new plan is to provide various incentives to lure ship owners to the Korean registry and make it the fifth largest in the world (*www.joc.com*, 15 April 2002). In a similar move, Jamaica, two years ago, tried to establish its own open registry, in an attempt to generate synergies between its transhipment business and other maritime activities. So far (January 2002), only five ships have made use of this registry, three more than in January 2000 (ECLAC 2002b). In Brazil, the aim to maintain a broad spectrum of maritime industries has been achieved more successfully, albeit at a cost to users; "the Brazilian model of support to maritime industry implies net economic benefit transfer from the Brazilian importers to private maritime investors and shipbuilding domestic input suppliers" (Pires 2001).

Even in countries that are strong (per capita) trading nations and have a high market share in shipping services, these two situations usually have very little to do with each other. By way of example, the Chilean carrier CSAV generates 82.7% of its freight income from outside Chile, and moves just 5.9% of Chilean foreign trade. Hardly any of this foreign trade (0.1%) is transported under the Chilean flag. Concerning ownership of vessels, 86 000 TEU of a total of 91 000 TEU operated by CSAV are chartered capacity, i.e. the ships are not even owned by CSAV (Hoffmann 2001). In other words, whereas CSAV historically depended on Chile's foreign trade, today, as a result of globalisation, the company depends far less on this traditional basis, and, at the same time, its host country relies increasingly on foreign carriers and flag registries for its own foreign trade.

It is noteworthy that despite the efforts by shipping and seafarer organisations from some traditional maritime nations, the open registry fleet has continued its spectacular growth during the last two decades (see Figure 5). Furthermore, the open registry nations have also contended with increasing competition from some traditional maritime nations like Norway that have established international ship registers to stem the outflow of their domestic tonnage to foreign registries if not attract some of the previously lost tonnage back to the national fleet. An attempt to control the growth of open registry fleet through a United Nations Convention on Conditions for Registration of Ships introduced in 1986 (that emphasises the existence of a genuine link between the ship and its flag of registration) has so far received the support of only eleven contracting states, none of which have any significant maritime clout. It is to be expected that the open registry fleet will continue to surge ahead in future years.

Governmental interference in shipping has a long history (Farthing 1993). Ever since the British enacted their restrictive Navigation Acts in the mid-1600s the global maritime business has never operated in so liberal a commercial environment as it exists today. A rational justification for this new wave of liberalism is the impact of globalisation. As maritime policies have become subservient to the overall trade policies of major trading nations, the crux of the issue is not the flag of registration but the overall fit of the shipping services in the global supply chain. Under such circumstances, the specialisation referred to earlier has led to a new breed of maritime players where nationality is once again irrelevant. As an example, the concept of giving away one's flag to a ship owned by a foreign entity (although not *pro bono*) and staffed by foreign crew is an illustration of high shipping liberalism.

A cursory examination of the current breed of ship owners will show relatively few of the historic shipping families but more so of investment firms, pension funds and business conglomerates, none of which have any shipping heritage typically. Thus, it is ironical that globalisation has led to a certain loss of identity and respectability for the industry. A perfect example of this irony is the high public attention that the industry receives when there is a shipping accident but the total lack of coverage that it receives from the media when it performs normally. The average citizen today is more aware of the mistakes made by the maritime industry rather than its contributions to the global commerce because of the extreme negativity it receives from the press. The following sub-section examines issues related to safety at sea and employment conditions. It suggests that the neo-liberalism in shipping policies has not meant a decline in operating standards but on the contrary, a general improvement in the safety of ships and the environment.

4.3 Safety and employment: the victims of globalisation?

Safety at sea

The increasing environmental awareness of the global community is vividly marked in all aspects of life today including maritime business. Given the inherent operating environment of merchant ships and their propensity to be a major environmental polluter, the increasing safety regulations imposed on the industry are only to be expected. A number of major shipping accidents in certain locations and the subsequent investigations, such as the *Ships of Shame* Inquiry (House of Representatives 1992) in Australia, have also provided further momentum for an increase in maritime safety regulations.

The International Maritime Organisation (IMO), established under the auspices of the United Nations to promote safety standards in shipping and cleaner seas, has a number of provisions aimed toward these objectives. Although some of these conventions date back to the 1960s and 1970s, they have been amended extensively to enhance the overall safety standards in a globalized operating environment. Two recent developments are particularly noteworthy, those being the *ISM (International Safety Management) Code Amendment to the Safety of Life at Sea Convention* and the *Amendments to the STCW (Standardisation of Training, Certification and Watchkeeping) Convention*. The ISM Code for the Safe Operation of Ships and Pollution Prevention extends the scrutiny of shipping operations and management to the shore office and the decision-makers therein. This is a drastic change from prior efforts and aims to establish an all-encompassing safety management system in compliance with legislative and company requirements. The recent amendments to the STCW Convention introduced globally accepted minimum standards for maritime training, evaluation criteria and assessment mechanisms. Given the diversity in national origin of seafarers today and their varying levels of skill and proficiency, the new amendments have been propitious and timely.

There is a concerted multilateral effort now for ongoing scrutiny of the hardware and software of the maritime business. Some multilateral efforts originated as a unilateral initiative to enhance safety and prevent pollution (such as the US Oil Pollution Act of 1990 that made double-hulls mandatory for oil tankers and certain other ships calling the US ports and was subsequently matched by the IMO through Amendments to the multilateral *MARPOL Convention*). Aside from these, individual nations have signed agreements to enforce safety standards by inspecting the ships that call their ports. Such Port State Control agreements cover all major ship operating areas today and the respective national enforcement authorities arrest ships that do not meet the accepted minimum safety standards. As a further embarrassment (and incentive to scrap unsafe ships), some national authorities (e.g., the UK) publish the list of "rogue" ships in the trade media. Equasis (*www.equasis.org*) publishes inspection results from many P&I Clubs, classification societies, and port state control organisations on a global level (an unfortunate exception is the Latin American "Viña del Mar Agreement", which does not share the results of its port state control inspections with Equasis).

Along with the governmental agencies, a number of non-governmental agencies such as labour organisations (e.g., the International Transport Workers' Federation), ship owners' association, ship charterers, classification societies, marine insurance firms and others have also raised the barriers and discourage the operation of sub-standard ships. The overall effect of these multi-pronged initiatives is visible in the following figure (Figure 6) that shows the trend in maritime casualties, both ships lost (actual or constructive total loss) as well as lives lost. Despite the increase in global shipping tonnage and maritime activities in general, and despite the diffusion of ship registration (in the neo-liberal maritime environment) to open registry and developing nations, the safety record of the industry is laudable. Even one life lost at sea is one too many, and the authors are not arguing that the current level of lives lost at sea is acceptable, but quite the contrary. However, all numbers strongly suggest that the overall trend in safety at sea is optimistic, that is especially if we consider the growing volumes of trade (Figure 1, page 37), the decline in the number of lives lost (Figure 6) must be viewed as a positive trend.

The seafarer dilemma

Any discussion of the impact of globalisation on maritime business will be incomplete if the human element is not included. Various technological advances have helped reduce the number of crew required on board a ship compared to the period before the 1980s. This has by no means diminished the role of seafarers in the maritime business; on the contrary, crewing costs still constitute a major component of the operating cost of a ship, and crew-related issues remain relatively complex (IMO – *Globalization and the Role of the Seafarer 2001*). The impacts of globalisation on seafaring serve as excellent illustrations of the pros and cons of globalisation in general.

Seafaring is a glorious profession and has no room for error or negligence. Indeed the education of a young sailor is incomplete if it does not include indoctrination for facing calamities at sea or ashore. Successful seafarers are unique individuals. The uniqueness comes not from the possession of any extraordinary intellectual capacity but from the possession of simple common-

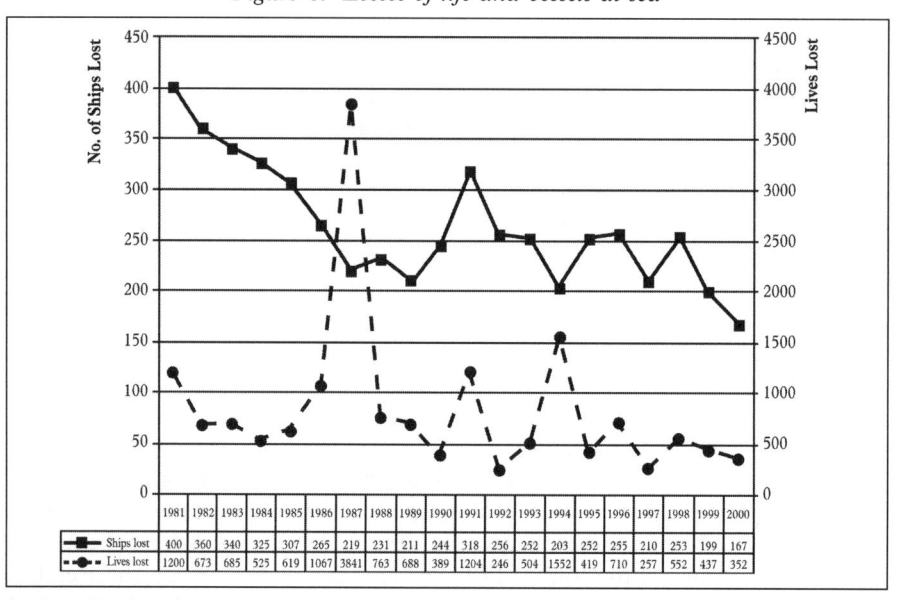

Figure 6: Losses of life and vessels at sea

	1981	1982	1983	1984	1985	1986	1987	1988	1989	1990	1991	1992	1993	1994	1995	1996	1997	1998	1999	2000
Ships lost	400	360	340	325	307	265	219	231	211	244	318	256	252	203	252	255	210	253	199	167
Lives lost	1200	673	685	525	619	1067	3841	763	688	389	1204	246	504	1552	419	710	257	552	437	352

Source: *World Casualty Statistics*, Lloyd's Register, various annual issues.

sense (euphemistically referred at sea as behaving in a "seamanlike manner") and from the willingness to subject oneself to the rigors of self-discipline of the highest order and separation from near and dear ones for prolonged periods of sailing. It also comes from the individual's mental and physical aptitude to face the unknown, be that hurricane force winds at sea, pirates, or militant stevedores trying to pilfer cargo in port. The sea is certainly no place for incompetence, negligence or complacency for it can be tranquil one day, and ruthless the other. The only way a seafarer can gain respect from fellow shipmates is by knowing his/her job and carrying it out in the most professional manner. These skills are by no means restricted to any particular nationality, race, religion or creed. On the contrary, well-trained seafarers from a poor country can do the same job as effectively as their well trained, colleagues from a developed nation at drastically reduced cost to the ship owner. Herein lies the dilemma – globalisation has opened up avenues of opportunity for seafarers from developing countries at the expense of those from traditional maritime countries such as the North European nations, the United States and Japan. Today's labour market for seafarers is perhaps the most globalised; standards and minimum wages are agreed globally, as for example in the "Geneva Accord" (ILO 2001), where "Representatives of shipowners and seafarers... adopt a historic accord on the future development of labour standards in the international shipping industry".

This has created a schism and ruptured the historic common bondage among seafarers of the world, built over the years based on their professional pride and their wider view of the world that their land-based colleagues often did not fathom. We live in an era today where seafarer organisations in developed nations look upon those from poorer nations as a potential threat to their livelihood, and as a result, lobby for protectionist policy measures that restrict the mobility of foreign crew members within their national borders.

During the last few decades, we have witnessed a tarnishing of the image of some seafarers, in particular those from less developed countries who crew a majority of the open registry and international registry vessels (*Ships of Shame 1992*). However, it is important to differentiate the cause and the symptom. How many seafarers truly want to go to sea and work on board an unsafe ship without the expectation of coming back to their near and dear ones? So, the fault does not lie with the seafarers who crew substandard vessels, but with those responsible for putting them on such ships without adequate training and proper quality control in the first place. Furthermore, the argument that seafarers from developing countries are responsible for all maritime disasters does not appear to be true as a number of the recent maritime casualties involved ships that were crewed by seafarers from developed nations (an example being the grounding of the *Exxon Valdez* off Alaska in the US).

Another dilemma facing the global seafarer, especially those working on board open registry vessels, can be attributed to the declining number of traditional ship owners discussed earlier. As ship ownership and operation shift from traditional ship owners to pension funds and conglomerates that seek instant gain from the sale and purchase market (for ships) or from certain tax exemption loopholes, the seafarers' roles and functions have been marginalised and their loyalty made meaningless. With the increasing number of open registry vessels and the outsourcing of ship and crew management (discussed earlier), the relationship between the management entity and the ships' crew hardly exceeds the length of a contract today unlike the life-long relationship of the bygone pre-globalisation era. Furthermore, ship managers providing the crew for open registry vessels as well as other fleets often find themselves in a highly competitive market where there is little room for the ongoing training of seafarers, especially given the tendency of some of their principals to switch their management companies frequently. This is truly an irony as the challenges of seafaring have never been more than what they are now, despite all the technological advances made by humankind.

4.4 Outlook

The conflicting nature of public arguments regarding the impact of globalisation in general was mentioned earlier. There is a strong sentiment in the media that multinationals and their home nations (typically, developed countries) would benefit more than the developing countries who are likely to suffer from the abuses of globalisation ranging from exploitation to cultural degradation. It is remarkable that the arguments are quite the contrary when one looks at the impact of globalisation on maritime business. The traditional maritime nations appear to be on the losing end in terms of national tonnage and loss of shipping-related jobs, and perceive the new centres of shipping business (and specialisation) as potential threats to their maritime interests. Developing and newly industrialised nations, on the contrary, appear to be the winners with increasing number of ships under their control and better career opportunities for their seafarers. This trend will continue in the neo-liberal era of maritime policies and business environment.[2]

The most encouraging outlook from our perspective is the increasing level of safety at sea which we hope will continue to improve. This means that, so far, the improvements in the quality, frequencies, reliability and costs of maritime transport have not implied an increase in negative externalities. The challenge for policy makers will be to observe and monitor potential future monopolistic abuses in a concentrating industry, and to assure adequate standards of training, working conditions and pay levels for seafarers, the pioneers on the world's most globalised labour market.

5. SUMMARY AND CONCLUSIONS

As trade in merchandise and unfinished goods increases, so does demand for maritime transport services. These services form part of the global logistics chain that determines a good's competitiveness.

At the same time, the maritime business is itself strongly affected by globalisation. Trade in maritime services is one of the most liberalised industries, and its "components" such as vessels, flag registration, class inspections, insurance and the work of seafarers are purchased globally.

The results of these two trends are manifold, and some may even appear to be contradictory:
- The market for maritime transport services is growing. Nevertheless the specialisation of countries in certain maritime areas has implied that today there are fewer remaining players in individual maritime sectors.
- A county's national shipping business has ever less to do with its national external trade. Whereas in the past, for historic reasons and due to protectionist cargo reservation regimes, foreign trade was mainly moved by vessels registered and owned by companies of the trading partners themselves, who employed national seafarers and nationally constructed vessels, today most carriers earn their income transporting other countries' trade, and the trade of most countries is largely moved by foreign shipping companies.
- We observe increased concentration in the maritime industry, yet at the same time the intensity of competition has not declined. This does not mean that fewer suppliers are per se good for competition, but the impact of globalisation leads to both – fewer suppliers and more competition.
- Transport unit costs decline, and yet the incidence of maritime transport costs in the final value of a good increases. The value of the final good not only includes its transport costs from origin to destination, but also the transport costs of all the components that have been purchased internationally.
- Lower transport costs are closely related to more trade. This is partly because lower prices (freight rates) obviously encourage demand, and also because economies of scale lead to lower unit transport costs.
- Ever more cargo is being moved across the oceans, benefiting from better maritime transport services and lower costs. This has generally not been at the cost of safety at sea, but, on the contrary, the globalisation of standards by IMO and ILO help to reduce the negative externalities of shipping.

"Transport undoubtedly belongs to the most complicated, and therewith fascinating economic sectors" (Verhoef *et al.*, 1997). As mainstream economists attempt to tackle the causes and impacts of globalization, international transport is re-entering the debate on trade models and development theories. As maritime transport is the true nexus between all trading nations, the role for maritime economists (and IAME) in this ongoing debate is clear and beyond doubt.

ENDNOTES

1. In an ongoing research project, the Transport of the United Nations Economic Commission for Latin America and the Caribbean (ECLAC) is analysing trade flows between 15 exporting Latin American countries into 6 importing Latin American countries, i.e. 120 trade flows: the correlation between trade volumes, modal split, and transport costs. For information about the database, see *www.eclac.cl/transporte/perfil/bti.asp*. For further information about the research project, contact Gordon Wilmsmeier (*Wilmsmeier@aol.com*) and Jan Hoffmann (*JHoffmann@eclac.cl*). Sources of data: Trade flows, volumes, trade balances, values

and transport costs: International Transport data Base (BTI) *www.eclac.cl/transporte/perfil*. Distances: Fairplay ports guide. Liner shipping services: *www.ci-online.co.uk*. Advances in Port Privatization: IJME 2001, 3, p. 226. The regressions were undertaken with SPSS 10.

2. In order to keep to the assigned limits, the authors had to make a conscious decision to stay away from certain other potential impacts of globalisation on maritime business such as the structural changes in the industry (particularly in the tanker and liner markets), the relative commoditisation of the liner market, and piracy and terrorism issues.

REFERENCES

Anderson, J.E. (1999): *Why do Nations Trade (So Little)?*, mimeo, Boston College.

Anderson, J.E., and van Wincoop, E. (2001): *Border, Trade and Welfare*, NBER Working Paper 8515, Cambridge, October.

Audigé, M. (1995): *Maritime Transport Serving West and Central African Countries: Trends and Issues* (The World Bank), SSATP Working Paper No. 16.

Bergsten, F. (1997): *Open Regionalism, Institute for International Economics*, Working Paper 97-3.

Christopher, M.L. (1992): *Logistics and Supply Chain Management* (Pitman Publishing).

DRI/WEFA (2001) Data from DRI/WEFA (*www.dri-wefa.com*) obtained by e-mail from *robert.west@dri-wefa.com*.

ECLAC (2002a): Globalization and Development, United Nations Economic Commission for Latin America and the Caribbean, LC/G.2157 (SES.29/3)/I, Santiago de Chile.

ECLAC (2002b): Maritime Profile of Latin America and the Caribbean, United Nations Economic Commission for Latin America and the Caribbean, LC/W.001, *www.eclac.cl/transporte/perfil*, April.

Fairplay Newbuildings (March 2002): Supplement to *Fairplay International Shipping Weekly* (London).

Farthing, B. (1993): *International Shipping: An Introduction to the Policies, Politics and Institutions* (2nd ed.) (London, Lloyd's of London Press).

Fink, C., Mattoo, A., and Neagu, I.C. (2001): *Trade in International Maritime Services: How much does Policy Matter?* (World Bank Development Research Group DECRG, Washington), January.

García Menéndez, L., Martínez-Zarzoso, I., and Suárez Burguet, C. (2002): *Maritime Transport Costs And Port Infrastructures: Do They Influence Exports?*, Conference proceedings, IAME annual meeting and conference, Panama, November (forthcoming).

Hill, Charles, W.L. (2000): *International Business: Competing in the Global Marketplace* (3rd ed.) (Irwin, McGraw-Hill).

Hilling, David (1996): *Transport and Developing Countries* (London, Routledge).

Hoffmann, Jan (1998): *Concentration in Liner Shipping* (United Nations), LC/G.2027, Santiago de Chile.

Hoffmann, Jan (2001): *Transporte marítimo regional y de cabotaje en América Latina y el Caribe: el caso de Chile*, Serie de la CEPAL DRNI 32, Santiago de Chile

House of Representatives, Standing Committee on Transport, Australia (1992): *Inquiry into Ship Safety: Report from the House of Representatives Standing Committee on Transport, Communications and Infrastructure* (Australian Government Publishing Service).

Hummels, David (1999a): *Toward a Geography of Trade Costs* (University of Chicago, January).

Hummels, David (1999b): *Have International Transportation Costs Declined?* (University of Chicago), November.

Hummels, David (2000): *Time as a Trade barrier* (Purdue University), October.

ILO (2001): Press release 01/05, 26 January, *www.ilo.org/public/english/bureau/inf/pr/2001/05.htm*, Geneva.
IMO (2001): IMO – *Globalisation and the Role of the Seafarer*, mimeo, IMO.
Krugman, P. (1981): "Intra-Industry Specialisation and the Gains from Trade", *Journal of Political Economy* 89 (Oct. 1981), pp. 959–973.
Kumar, Shashi (1987) *The US Shipping Act of 1984: A Scrutiny of Controversial Provisions* (Castine, Maine Maritime Press).
Kumar, Shashi (1994): "Comparative Maritime Policies: A US Dilemma", *Transportation Journal*, 34.1, pp. 32–38.
Lancaster, K. (1980): "Intra-Industry Trade Under Perfect Monopolistic Competition", *Journal of International Economics*, 10 (May 1980), pp. 151–175.
Leontief, W. (1953) "Domestic Production and Foreign Trade: The American Capital Position Re-Examined", *Proceedings of the American Philosophical Society* 97, pp. 331–349.
Limao, Nuno, and Venables, Anthony J. (1999) *Infrastructure, Geographical disadvantage, and Transport Costs*, World Bank Working Paper 2257, December.
Lovett, William A. (ed.), (1996) *United States Shipping Policies and the World Market* (Westport, CT, Quorum Books).
Mentzer, John T., DeWitt, William, Keebler, James S., Min, Soonhong, Nix, Nancy W., Smith, Carlo D., and Zacharia, Zach G. (2001): "Defining Supply Chain Management", *Journal of Business Logistics* 22.2.
Micco, Alejandro, and Pérez, Natalia (2001): *Maritime Transport Costs and Port Efficiency* (Washington, Inter-American Development Bank), February.
Morash, Edward A., and Clinton, Steven R. (1997): "The Role of Transportation Capabilities in International Supply Chain Management", *Transportation Journal* 37.1.
Ohlin, Bertil Gotthard (1933): *Interregional and International Trade*, monograph.
O'Rourke, Kevin H. and Williamson, Jeffrey G. (1999): *The Heckscher-Ohlin Model Between 1400 and 2000: When it explained factor price convergence, when it did not, and why*, NPER Working Paper 7411 (Cambridge), November.
O'Rourke, Kevin H., and Williamson, Jeffrey G. (2000): *When did Globalisation Begin?*, NPER Working Paper 7632 (Cambridge), April.
Pedersen, Poul Ove (2001): "Freight transport under globalisation and its impact on Africa", *Journal of Transport Geography* 9, No. 2 (2001) p. 85.
Pires, Floriano C. M. (2001): "Shipbuilding and shipping industries: net economic benefit cross-transfers", *Maritime Policy and Management*, 2001, Vol. 28, No. 2, pp. 157–174.
Porter, Michael E. (1985): *Competitive Advantage* (Free Press).
Porter, Michael E. (1990): *The Competitive Advantage of Nations* (Free Press).
Radelet, Steven, and Jeffrey Sachs (1998) *Shipping Costs, Manufactured Exports, and Economic Growth* (Harvard Institute for International Development), January.
Ricardo, David (1817) *Principles of Political Economy and Taxation* (London).
Sánchez, Ricardo J., Hoffmann, Jan, Micco, Alejandro, Pizzolitto, Georgina, and Sgut, Martín (2002): *Port Efficiency And International Trade*, Conference proceedings, IAME annual meeting and conference (Panama), November (forthcoming).
Simon, David (1996): *Transport and Development in the Third World* (Routledge), London.
Sletmo, G.K. (2001): "The End of National Shipping Policy? A Historical Perspective on Shipping Policy in a Global Economy", *International Journal of Maritime Economics* 4.3, pp. 333–350.
Suranovic, Stephen (2002): *International Trade Theory and Policy Analysis*, "e-text" *http://internationalecon.com/v1.0/*
Thompson, Robert (2000): "The Role of Transportation in the Global Food System", William Coyle and Nicole Ballenger (eds.), *Technological Changes in the Transportation Sector – Effects on US Food and Agricultural Trade* (United States Department of Agriculture), Miscellaneous Publication Number 1566.
UNCTAD (2001) *Review of Maritime Transport, 2001* (United Nations, Geneva).

Venables, Anthony J., and Limao, Nuno (1999): *Geographical disadvantage: a Heckscher-Ohlin-von Thunen model of international specialisation* (Washington, World Bank), December.

Verhoef, E.T., Nijkamp, P., Rietveld, P., and Lakshmanan, T.R. (1997): *Benefits and Costs of Transport* (Amsterdam).

Vernon, R., and Wells, L.T. (1986): *The Economic Environment of International Business* (4th ed.) (Prentice).

World Shipping Council (2001): *A Review of "Trade in International Maritime Services"*, a Paper by World Bank Researchers, May.

PART TWO

INTERNATIONAL SEABORNE TRADE

CHAPTER 4

PATTERNS OF INTERNATIONAL OCEAN TRADE

Douglas K. Fleming
University of Washington, Seattle, USA
E-mail: *dkf@u.washington.edu*

1. INTRODUCTION

In the first year of this millennium nearly five and a third billion metric tons of goods were shipped in commercial ocean-borne trade. The ocean transport task for this movement in the year 2000 translates to more than twenty two trillion ton-miles.[1] Roughly 60% of the total cargo volume moved in bulk. These impressive dimensions of world seaborne trade leave unrecorded a huge amount of empty space and deadweight, the cargo capacity of merchant ships steaming in ballast towards their next loading range or leaving their loading range only partly full of revenue cargo. Empty cargo space, like empty seats on passenger airplanes, reflects something lost forever, while vessel operating costs continue inexorably. This lost potential, to an extent inevitable because of basic global patterns and geographic separation of commodity production and commodity consumption, will be a recurring theme in this chapter.

The opening section of this study contains a few reflections on centuries-old trading patterns for ships under sail. Today's bulk commodity trades, which generate each year millions of miles of ballast steaming, will then be examined. Possibilities for combining different bulk trades in some sort of logical geographic sequence will be considered. The general cargo trades, with particular focus on container line service, will be investigated. The directional imbalances of cargo flow on the main liner routes will be noted and possible network adjustments and service scenarios to cope with the empty space problem will be presented for consideration. Finally, prospects for the twenty first century, with special focus on the efficiency of ocean trading patterns, will be briefly outlined.

2. EARLY PATTERNS UNDER SAIL

Thirty years ago A.D. Couper's *The Geography of Sea Transport* appeared on the bookshelves of students interested in ocean trade and transport (Couper, 1972). Professor Couper, master mariner, geographer and head of the Department of Maritime Studies at the University of Wales Institute of Science and Technology (UWIST), was an expert on ocean trade patterns. In his book there is a thought-provoking map entitled "World Wind Systems (January) and ocean routes of European sailing vessels". It is drawn to a cylindrical projection, stretching apart meridians of longitude, as does Mercator's projection. It covers a "world and a quarter" so that the Pacific, Atlantic and Indian Oceans can be seen in uninterrupted form. On it are depicted, with sweeping arrows, the major wind systems encountered at sea in January, and five historic trade routes in the sailing ship era – the Guinea trade triangle, the Dutch East India Co. route between Amsterdam and the East Indies, the clipper ship route between Europe and Australia, the transatlantic Anglo-American colonial route and the transpacific Acapulco-Manila Spanish galleon route.[2]

The correlation between the favouring winds and the chosen tracks for the trading vessels stands out clearly on Couper's map. One knows that the chosen tracks shift seasonally as the prevailing winds shift. By summertime, for example, southwest monsoons replace northeast monsoons in the Indian Ocean.

Basically this is a pre-industrialisation, pre-liner service picture. To it one might add many other Portuguese, Spanish, French, Dutch and British "imperial routes" connecting mother countries with their colonies. And many of the routes were controlled by state-franchised trading companies. To be sure, most of these old transoceanic paths of commerce have been displayed in historical atlases,[3] usually in the form of simple lines curving around continents and across oceans, joining points of origin and points of destination with no attention to precise tracks, much less to seasonal variations in ocean tracks. Couper's map suggests much more. Removing his winds, removing the Guinea trade triangle and simplifying his continental forms we have the graphic image reflected in Figure 1.

These old trading patterns were "round voyages", with outbound and homeward legs of the voyage quite often following very different paths, not only

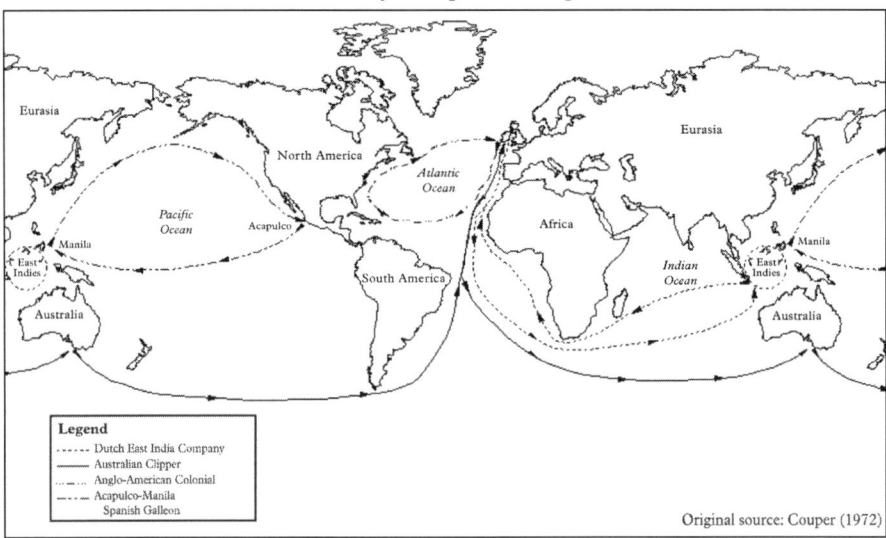

Figure 1: World wind systems (January) and ocean routes of European sailing vessels

because of prevailing winds and weather but also, in the case of the Anglo–American colonial route, to pick up and deposit cargo en route, e.g. in the Caribbean and heading north along the American east coast. Generally, two-way cargo flows were available on the Spanish-controlled Acapulco–Manila route, the Dutch controlled East Indies route and the British-controlled Australian route. However, in cargo volume terms, there could be large directional imbalances and seasonal variations. The ships engaged in these trades were, by modern standards, very small and often the cargoes were valuable goods – silver, gold, silks, spices, for instance – that took up little cargo space but generated high freight revenues when rates were ad valorem-based. And the "organized" nature of the trade routes mentioned above, since they were controlled by the imperial state or by a powerful state-franchised trading company, meant that the ships serving the trades had fair assurance of onward or homeward cargoes. Empty space on long ballast voyages was not the important consideration it was to become in the late 19th and 20th centuries. It should be noted that these were, by modern definition, at least, tramp trades, however well organized, served by relatively small, multi-purpose sailing vessels adaptable to various cargo types, not excluding human cargoes, slaves or emigrants.

Unfortunately the mercantilist philosophy that was fashionable in Europe in 17th, 18th and part of the 19th centuries led to highly protected trades in which mother countries paired off with their own colonies, enacted navigation laws which favored ships of their own flag and often used high tariffs against imports from rival empires. Merchant fleets were really armed merchant navies, commanded to serve the state. When one views these mercantilist systems in global perspective, it is clear that they led to geographically inefficient networks in the form of many shuttle services within imperial frames and relatively little "cross-trading" that could have reduced the amount of empty cargo space sailing unproductively across the oceans. Ironically these shuttle service patterns between imperial home ports and distant overseas colonies were somewhat analogous to the much more recent UNCTAD 40-40-20 scheme for splitting cargo allotments and ocean transport privileges 40-40 between trade partners (e.g. a developed and a developing nation) and leaving only 20% for "cross-traders". Of course the political, social and general economic motivations for the two sets of shuttle service patterns were vastly different. Yet the fact remains that the general back-and-forth route configurations were quite alike and there was a consequent accentuation of the empty cargo space problem when there were striking differences in the volumes of cargo flowing in either direction, as there almost always were.

A final glimpse at Figure 1 reveals the remarkable clipper ship route in the Australian trade in the 1850s, outbound from Britain via Cape of Good Hope and homeward via Cape Horn. From a point in the South Atlantic, usually closer to South America than Africa, these very fast, fine-lined sailing ships swooped south of Cape of Good Hope into the "roaring forties" zone of westerlies and along a looping approximation of the great circle route to the southern coast of Australia. Homeward bound in an easterly direction, the ships again dipped far into the Southern Ocean, again with following westerlies, and again approximating a great circle track past Cape Horn. These were ships, both American and British-owned, at the dawn of the free trade era in the 1850s, that took maximum advantage of the winds, currents, navigational aids of the time, and the cargo potentials, to turn profits for their owners.

3. BRITISH IMPACT ON OCEAN TRADING NETWORKS

As the world's front-runner in massive industrialisation, Britain by mid 19th century seemed to have the world of commerce by its tail. Having abandoned the mercantilist doctrines of the past for the principles and practices of free trade, Britain was a leader in seaborne trade, equipped with what became the world's largest steam-powered merchant fleet and the world's most highly developed banking, chartering, insuring, shipping and other trade related services concentrated in the old City of London.

The curious thing about Britain's spectacular and, to some extent, unilateral movement toward freer trade was that it took place in the imperial frame, in an empire that spread over the globe. Perhaps it made practical sense to be a free-trading imperialist when you led the world in the production of goods and services. Not to say that Britain traded only within the imperial frame, but the latter certainly had an impact on the networks of ocean trade, reinforcing the radial patterns emanating from home base that were handed down from the sailing ship era. If one added the radial patterns of the French and other European powers to the British hub and spoke pattern and put the whole in global perspective it gave a pronounced Eurocentric impression of world commerce in the latter part of the 19th century. And it was not really a false impression. Western Europe *was* the hub of world commerce. However, this set of Europe-based radial networks did not necessarily reflect the most efficient transportation system. Network analysts in the modern era have noted that pure hub and spoke networks have minimal connectivity. There is only one path from any one spoke end to any other and that is via the hub.

A.J. Sargent, British commercial geographer, recognized this network connectivity problem long ago in his unusually perceptive study, *Seaways of the Empire*. From early 20th century data he traced movements of British shipping in South African, Indian, Australian and other commonwealth trades, finding that ships "disappeared" from one trade and "reappeared" in another. In between was a "hidden" ballast voyage or half empty intermediate voyages moving ships to other trade routes. Of course this is common tramp shipping behavior and not infrequent liner behavior, and it shows that British steamship lines before World War I had ways of coping with the radial networks and ways of coping with directional imbalances of trade volumes on specific routes. It reminds us, too, that, for British shipowners then, and most shipowners today, "ocean lines are not worked for purposes of philanthropy but to pay dividends" (Sargent, 1930, p. 15).

Although we may have heard more about their spectacular passenger liners, the British merchant fleet in the two decades prior to World War I contained a large number of multi-purpose freighters in the 7,000 to 8,000 deadweight tonnage range. These could be used either in tramp or liner service. Quite often there would be outbound cargoes of coal from Britain to coaling stations around the globe and return cargoes of the various products of the colonies or other overseas areas the British lines were willing to and allowed to serve. The versatility of most of these vessels was an important attribute, enabling the steamship lines to adjust to directional imbalances on trade routes, ballast to other trades, if necessary, and, in general, minimise the empty cargo space problem by reducing the amount of non-paying ballast steaming. These British coal-burners were the forerunners of the thousands of World War II – built oil-burning "10,000 tonners", the Liberty, Victory, and C2 types which had the built-in flexibility and adaptability for the carriage of various bulk and break-bulk cargoes in various trades. The prototype of the amazingly serviceable American Liberty ship was, by the way, British-designed. Sixty of them were contracted to be built in American yards for the British early in World War II (Gibson & Donovan, 2000, p. 166).

Altogether, the British, with such a large portion of the world's merchant fleet, had a remarkable impact on the patterns of 19th and early 20th century ocean shipping. Americans are obliged to concede, too, that it was the British who selected New York as the main distribution point for goods that had accumulated during the War of 1812 awaiting entry into the American market. This gave New York's port its great leap forward (Albion, 1939, chap. 1). It was a small group of expatriate British textile merchants, originally from Yorkshire, who formed Black Ball Line to provide the very first transatlantic liner service between New York and Liverpool. Black Ball booked baled cotton diverted to New York from southern US ports for their eastbound transatlantic voyages and lined up Yorkshire and Lancashire textile goods for their westbound voyages (Albion, 1939, pp. 99–100). It was the British, again, who propelled world shipping into the use of iron-hulled, propeller-driven steamships. And it was Britain that gave the world the theories and, especially from 1850 to 1875, the practices of free international trade (Ellsworth, 1958, chap. 4).

4. BULK COMMODITY TRADES: 2000

A.J. Sargent remarked, long ago, "The ultimate determining element in the employment of shipping lies in the sum of the geographical conditions of each region in relation to those of other regions of the world, though the effect of such conditions may be modified greatly by economic or political policy on the part of individuals or Governments" (Sargent, 1931, p. 25). Sargent's comment pertained to *any* seaborne commodity trade. It certainly would apply to bulk commodity shipping today, perhaps with the insertion of "or corporations" between "individuals" and "Governments".

The tonnage imbalances between exports and imports for regions of the world and for individual ports are most striking in the bulk commodity trades. Very seldom are there two way cargo flows between regions for the bulk movement of oil, coal, iron ore or grain, even though these four broad commodity categories contain different sub-types and grades. However, there *are* two-way movements of the ships that carry these materials. One way they are laden with cargo. The other way they are ballasting, very often returning to the original loading range, signifying that half the voyage steaming is in ballast, a regrettable but seemingly inevitable waste of cargo space. This, of course, reflects the basic commercial geographic reality that raw material supply sources and the markets for these materials are often separated by large transoceanic mileages. It also suggests that both shippers and carriers are somewhat resigned to shuttle service itineraries.

Over the past half century the rise of proprietary carrier fleets – oil companies owning, or controlling by long term charters, fleets of tankers; steel making enterprises controlling dry bulk carrier fleets for the movement of their inputs of coking coal, iron ores, etc. – seems to accentuate the long ballast voyage problem. The ships engaged in these proprietary carrier trades are often very large and specially built for the carriage of one commodity type. There is a built-in inflexibility when such vessels are employed. Their operations may be confined to a back-and-forth shuttle service. The primary purpose of the fleet is to serve the transport needs of the corporation; therefore the emphasis is on timing and cost, in other words on the production function. The focus, understandably, is not on revenues from shipping since shipping is viewed by the firm as an "in house" and "at cost" service. Unless the normal intra-firm movements of materials are in some way disrupted, the proprietary carrier fleet is not inclined to move from one trade route to another. It stays in the trade for which it was designed and built, or for which it was chartered.

On the other hand, the independent tramp operator of the past and a dwindling number of owners of multi-purpose or combined carrier fleets, today, might be inclined to move from one trade route to another, seeking efficient geographic patterns that maximise their rate of utilisation on paying cargo and minimise ballast steaming.[4] Whether this results in profit, assuming profits are desirable, depends also, of course, on the revenue side of the equation.

4.1 Market locations

In the last half of the 20th century many scholars in a variety of social sciences became enamoured with concepts of "cores and peripheries". Geographers struggled to define, in precise and mappable terms, the core industrial regions of the world. The unevenness of industrial development in the spatial sense makes this difficult. Very often the available statistical data pertained to the nation, not to the regions within it. And, as one famous historian observed, "*All* advanced economies have their 'black holes'", their local pockets of backwardness (Braudel, 1984, p. 42). Economists identified the processes and stages of economic growth, the leading sectors in specific countries, the industrial concentrations and industrial linkages. They even assigned time frames to the stages of growth (Rostow, 1962, chap. 13) but they were not particularly concerned with the precise geographic dimensions.

PATTERNS OF INTERNATIONAL OCEAN TRADE

It is clear, and well supported statistically, that the world's most massive industrial developments over the past two and a half centuries took place in western Europe, eastern North America and eastern Asia, setting a pattern that profoundly shaped ocean trade patterns. To conform to today's realities, one could expand those three economically-advanced and populous regions to include all of Europe, all of North America and an East Asia that extends from Vladivostok to Singapore and includes the islands and archipelagoes of Southeast Asia. This, of course, amounts to a gross geographic generalization, but it does identify three core areas, albeit with many "black holes" inside, that generate a huge portion of world trade. These industrial cores experienced rapid growth of the manufacturing sector, originally fueled by coal and given great economic momentum by ferrous metallurgy and metal-using industries. They contain, today, the world's largest markets for seaborne bulk shipments of oil, iron ore, coal and grain.

It is noteworthy that a relatively small number of very large oil companies and mining and steel-making interests have a great deal to do with three of the four major bulk commodity trades.

4.2 Crude oil

Crude oil seaborne shipments exceed those of any other bulk material, constituting nearly 30 percent of total world seaborne shipments.[5] Figure 2 depicts origins and destinations and directions of movement of approximately 70 percent of the seaborne crude oil shipments in 2000.

The major destinations for these crude oil shipments are the oil refineries of eastern Asia, western and Mediterranean Europe and eastern North America. The largest importer is the United States, far ahead of second ranked Japan, but it is worth noting that the 15-member European Union, if considered a bloc, is the greatest crude oil importer.[6] The Middle East is the primary source of supply for these crude oil shipments but the Caribbean (Venezuelan and Mexican sources especially) and both West African and North African supply sources are important too. Compared to these major sources, southeast Asian oilfields, the North Sea offshore fields, oil piped to Near East terminals on the Mediterranean coast for tanker shipment onward, and Russian oil piped to Black Sea terminals generate minor, but regionally significant, tanker trades.

Tanker itineraries depend in part on the size and loaded draft of the vessels. The ultra large crude carriers (ULCC) cannot transit the Suez Canal or the Malacca and Singapore Straits, fully loaded, and must round the Cape of Good Hope on their laden voyages to Europe, or the Lombok and Makassar Straits on their laden voyages to northeast Asian destinations.

Both the United States and Russia are important crude oil producers as well as consumers. The US, once self-sufficient, has become the world's largest net importer of crude oil, while Russia is a net exporter, via pipeline to eastern and central Europe and via ocean transport from Black Sea termini to other parts of Europe.

Not depicted on Figure 2 is the sizeable crude oil flow from Valdez, Alaska by tanker to western US termini and refineries. This is a domestic, "protected"

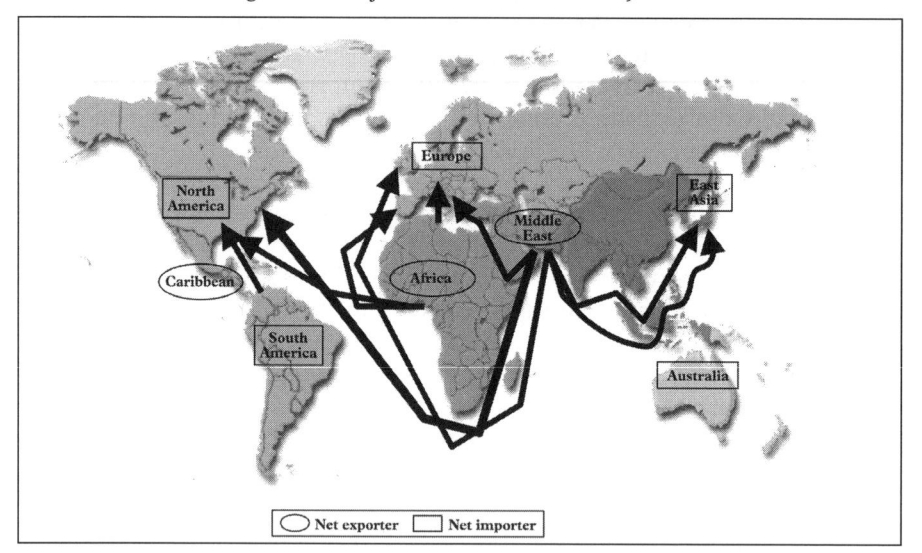

Figure 2: Major crude oil trade routes, 2000

trade. Also not depicted are the refined products shipped in smaller tankers, usually on shorter voyages, for instance from Caribbean refineries to US Gulf coast and US east coast markets; and from Southeast Asian refineries to East Asian markets. The total tonnage of the oceanborne refined products trade amounted to slightly over a quarter of the tonnage of crude oil ocean shipments in 2000.

4.3 Iron ore

Iron ore in crude, sintered or pelletised form is shipped by sea transport from sources on all the world's inhabited continents to metallurgical regions which have been located predominantly in the northern hemisphere.

The arrowed lines of Figure 3 depict origins, destinations and directions of movement of the main oceanborne flows of bulk iron ore in 2000, representing major high volume routes and seventy percent of total seaborne shipments in that year. Clearly, Western Europe and East Asia are the big recipients. In recent years the two countries producing the most abundant iron ore for export have been Australia and Brazil. The former is a big supplier for Japanese steelworks, especially, while the latter ships large tonnages to European, Japanese and other East Asian (e.g., South Korean, Taiwanese and Chinese) market destinations. There are numerous iron ore sources in Africa but, in total, they generate comparatively small volumes for export to European and East Asian markets. Canadian and Swedish mines produce quite impressive volumes of iron ore for export usually in rather short-distance seaborne trades to near neighbours such as the US, Germany, UK, etc.

The size of the dry bulk vessels carrying the ore affects the exact itineraries and limits the ports that can be used in the ore trades, although not quite as remarkably as in the crude oil trades. It should be noted that long-distance ore trades, as on the Brazil–Far East routes, generate large annual ton-mile totals.

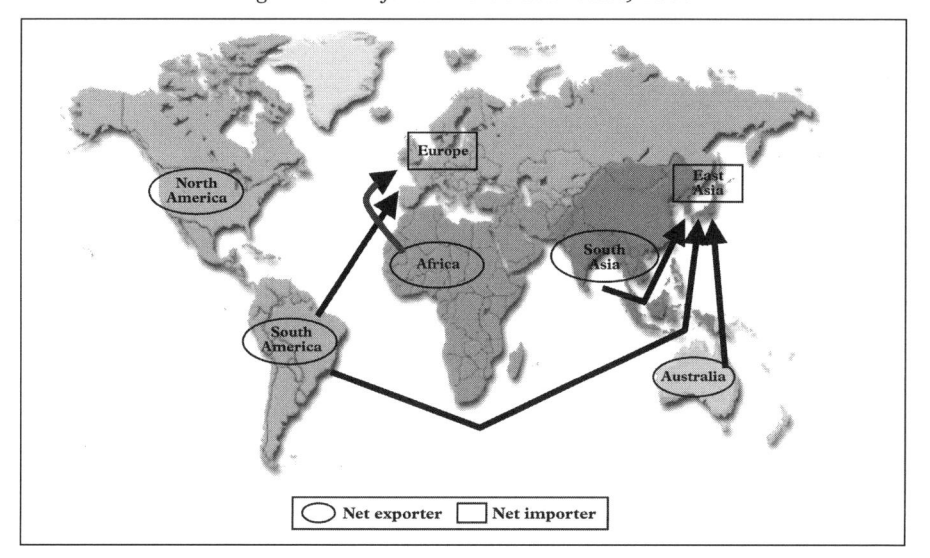

Figure 3: Major iron ore trade routes, 2000

Very large ore carriers, some of more than 300,000 deadweight tons, perform well on these routes.

Metallurgical enterprises in the three great core regions have drawn for a long time on their own iron ore deposits as well as on imported ores. Three of the world's five largest steel producers – China, Russia, US – are large iron ore producers. Japan and Germany are much more reliant on ore imports. In all five countries the 21st century scale of steel production will require supplementing the old and, in some cases, depleted or uneconomically low grade, northern hemispheric sources of iron ore supply. The southern hemisphere now possesses the richer and more abundant supply sources.

4.4 Coal

"Hard coal" includes steam coal, an important industrial and thermal power plant fuel and the somewhat higher grade coking coal, heavily used in its beneficiated form (i.e. coke) as blast furnace fuel in iron and steel works. These were the primary energy resources of the Industrial Revolution. There were abundant coal deposits in the European and North American industrial regions, fueling their rapid 19th and 20th century growth. In more recent times north Chinese coal mining spurred massive Chinese development of heavy industry. Today China is both the world's largest producer and the largest consumer of hard coal.

Figure 4 depicts the major routes accounting for nearly 70% of the total seaborne movement of hard coal in year 2000. Close to two thirds of seaborne coal shipments are steam coal; therefore only one third, the coking coal, is directly dependent on the state of the iron and steel industry.

Australia, today, outstrips all other coal exporters and the Japanese market has been particularly important to them. Chinese and Indonesian steam coal exports have recently cut into Australia's East Asian markets, however. South

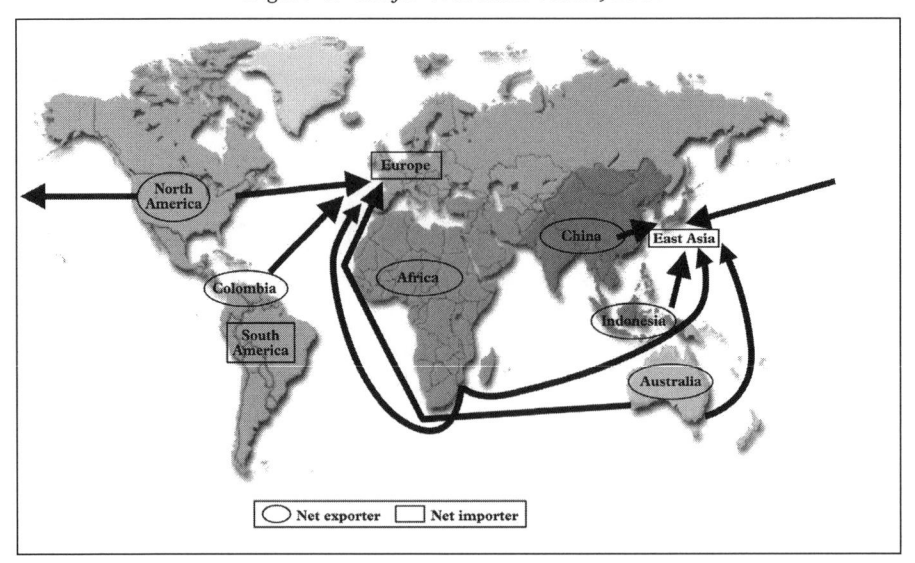

Figure 4: Major coal trade routes, 2000

African coal exports to Europe and Asia have been strong. For quite a few years, now, there has been an interesting shipping pattern that combines US coal exports from Hampton Roads with South African exports to the East Asian market. The coal has been loaded to the maximum allowable vessel draft on large bulk carriers at Hampton Roads and the carriers "top off" with coal in South Africa proceeding on to Japanese or other destinations. Other notable sources for coal exports include Colombia which favours the European market, western Canada which directs its shipments toward East Asia and Poland which mainly serves European markets on short-distance shipping routes to north-western and Mediterranean Europe.

US coal exports which were so prominent in early post World War II times and vital to the rebuilding of European and Japanese industrial economies have dropped off noticeably in the last decade. However, the US, Russia and China remain huge coal producers and consumers, and still have a net surplus for export.

4.5 Grain

Grain shipments including wheat, barley, rye, oats, maize, sorghum and soyabeans make up the most inconstant patterns of the four major bulk commodity trades.[7] There have been large seasonal and year-to-year fluctuations in the volumes and directions of the oceanborne grain trade. Even so, grain shipments have been a significant component of world seaborne commerce since ancient times. The grain trade typically attracts tramp shipping which can adjust to the inherent variability. Nevertheless there have been very large grain companies such as Cargill, Continental Grain, Bunge, etc, that have a large influence on trading patterns (Morgan, 1979).

Despite the variability of tonnage and directions of the grain trade, there are source countries that, year after year, are net exporters. These include the US, Canada, Argentina and Australia. The North American continent generates by far the largest volume of oceanborne grain exports.

Figure 5 shows the major grain trade routes on which nearly 70% of the oceanborne shipments moved in year 2000. Intercontinental flows of grain are complex and, as mentioned, vary from year-to-year. Parts of Europe, e.g., France, are net exporters; other parts, e.g., several East European countries, have often been net importers. The northern countries of South America are net importers whereas parts of Brazil, Uruguay and Argentina are exporters.

The markets are different in different countries for different types of grains, some of which are domestically produced; others of which are not.

East Asia, notably including Japan, South Korea, China and Taiwan, with their large populations and, in some cases, relatively limited available arable land, exerts the strongest market demand for imported grains. To a certain extent, the "green revolution" has rescued parts of South Asia, especially India, from what had become an overdependence on grain imports. Other parts of the developing world have not been as fortunate. Africa, for example, has some alarming agricultural problems ranging from desertification and drought, to the dreadful impacts of civil wars on farming, to ruinously low, artificially-set crop prices, to the chaotic land-holding "reforms" in Zimbabwe, once a land of great grain-producing potential. Africa, with these problems and its fast-growing population, has been forced to become a rather large grain importer. The grain shipments are often, of necessity, enabled by foreign aid and relief programs.

Despite variations from year to year in the grain production of each of the major supply sources, and variations also in market procurement programs, the total annual volume of the seaborne grain trade has remained remarkably

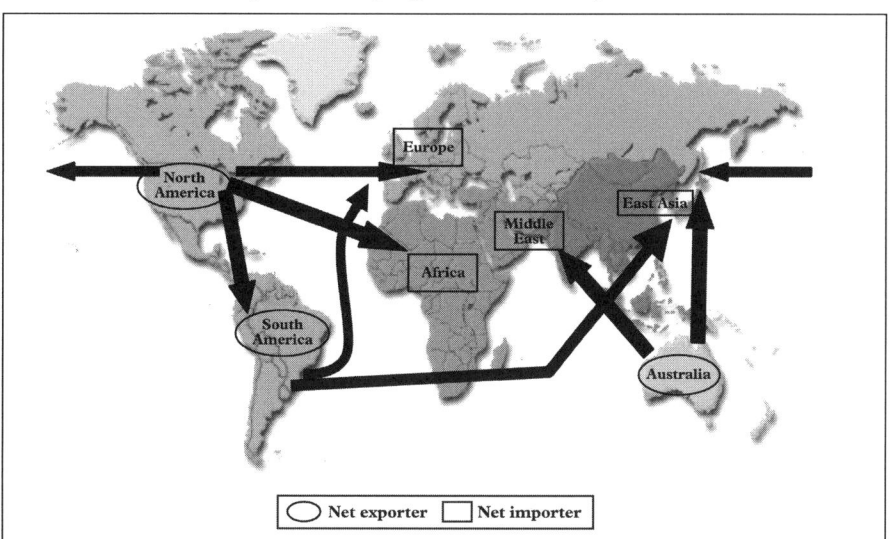

Figure 5: Major grain trade routes, 2000

steady at an approximate 200 million ton level over the past decade.[8] Actually the percentage of world grain production that enters ocean shipping channels is comparatively small. Most of the world's largest grain producers, for instance Russia, China, India and the United States, consume domestically a large proportion if not all of their annual grain production.

4.6 A composite picture

Visualising the four major bulk commodity ocean trades in geographical perspective, as rather crudely sketched in Figure 6, a composite picture, one recognises immediately that a large portion of the cargo flow is aimed at the three northern latitude industrial core regions – East Asia, Europe and North America. Europe and East Asia are the two greatest bulk commodity importing regions; however, North America, in an enviable position as a net exporter of coal and grain, is the recipient of huge quantities of crude oil from Latin America, Africa, the Middle East and lesser sources. A sizeable portion of the coal and grain trades is between North America and Europe and between North America and East Asia, trades entirely within the northern hemisphere.

The world's greatest oil producing region, the Middle East, is also in the northern hemisphere and practically athwart the main ocean shipping corridor from East Asia across the Indian Ocean, through the Red Sea and Suez Canal, to the Mediterranean and Western Europe. The largest tankers, however, must dip into the southern hemisphere rounding the southern tip of Africa to perform their transport task of carrying oil to Europe or to the US. (Figure 6 takes graphic liberties by assuming that the main volumes of bulk commodity ocean trade are not shipped via either the Suez or Panama Canals.) The southern hemisphere is not "neglected" by bulk carriers because South American, African and Australian supply sources are a very significant factor in bulk commodity ocean trade.

When one considers Venezuelan oil, Brazilian iron ore, Colombian coal and Argentine grain, not the mention other somewhat smaller supply sources, South America is an important contemporary exporter of all four major bulk commodities entering ocean trade. Australia, with its remarkably abundant mineral reserves and productive grain fields, is a significant supplier of three of the four main bulk commodities – all except oil. The commercial ties between Australia and Japan, enabling the shipments, have been consolidated by long term contracts on purchases and shipments and Japanese participation in infrastructure developments to facilitate these trades (Manners, 1971, p. 317).

Figure 6 depicts origins, destinations and directions of movement for only seventy percent of the total volume of these four bulk commodity trades. There is no visual expression in Figure 6 of comparative tonnages of cargo flow on the various routes, nor is there a precise picture of ocean tracks taken by the carriers. Suez and Panama transits have been "assumed away", whereas, in fact, these canals are on the itineraries of many smaller-size bulk carriers and figure importantly on ballast voyages.

The composite picture is essentially a "laden voyage" picture. That is to say, ballast voyage segments are not shown and, of course, ships in ballast add

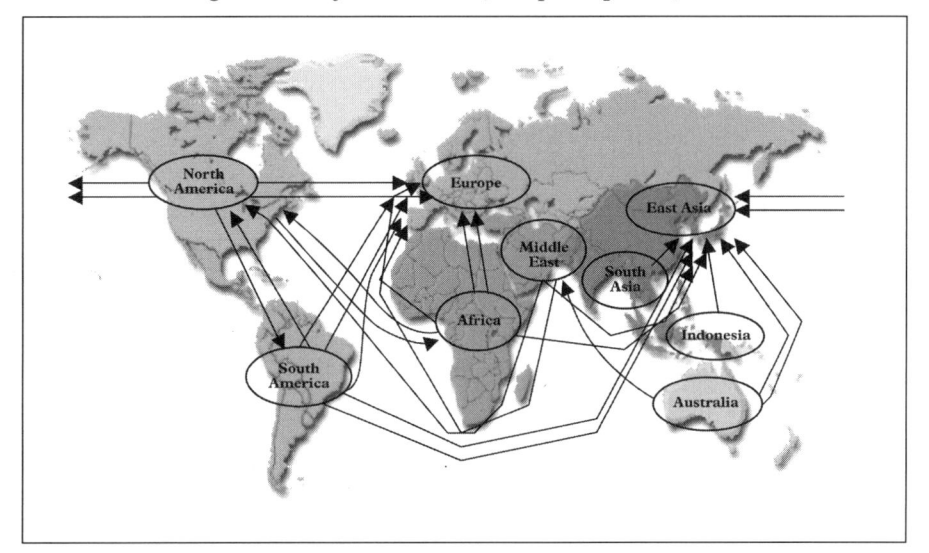

Figure 6: *Major bulk trades, composite picture, 2000*

almost as much to congested waters and to the incidence of accidents at sea as fully laden ships, although the latter are more of an environmental hazard if accidents do take place. One can deduce from available traffic data, much of which has been used above in composing the picture,[9] that the approaches to western Europe, Japan and the eastern coast of the US are very heavily trafficked by ships, full or empty, serving the three great core industrial regions that generate so much of the oceanborne bulk trade. One can deduce, also, that there are traffic convergences at straits such as Malacca, Lombok, Hormuz, Gibraltar and Dover. One can imagine that there are convergences of full and empty ships rounding Cape of Good Hope and other promontories where the dangers of "hugging the coast" to shorten voyages can never be completely removed by traffic separation schemes.

The rough tracings of global bulk commodity trades reinforce the impression that the northern core industrial regions have been the main focus of market demand. And this might also reinforce the impressions conveyed by dependency theorists a few decades ago and voiced by the UNCTAD Committee on Shipping in the 1970's and 1980s, suggesting that not only the control of world merchant fleets, under whatever flag, but also the relevant supply and demand elasticities for the products exported favour the developed nations in the industrial core regions. As Alexander Yeats wrote twenty years ago: "The incidence (that is, the question of who pays transport costs in a trading transaction) of freight rates depends on the relative elasticities of supply and demand for the goods transported. Theoretical analyses show that the relevant elasticities are such that developing countries bear a major portion of increased transport costs for both exports and imports" (Yeats, 1981, p. 2).

The patterns graphically presented in Figures 2, 3, 4, 5 and 6 suggest that there is a great deal of empty space on ships steaming about the oceans, fully manned, consuming fuel, as they ballast to their next loading range. There may be no way to eradicate this problem, but the next section of the chapter explores possible strategies by independent shipowners to ameliorate it.

5. FEASIBILITY OF COMBINING BULK TRADES

In the late 1970's, when the world energy crisis was acute, Deeds (1978) and Fleming (1978) both addressed the issue of reducing ballast steaming as a percentage of total voyage steaming. Both considered patterns in the bulk commodity trades. The use of combination carriers (e.g., OBOs) offered a flexibility that allowed the accommodation of any of the four main oceanborne bulk commodities. The ballast leg, in Deeds' words, "ties together many of the world's shipping routes in a world where complete reciprocal specific complementarity does not exist" (Deeds, 1978, p. 87). In other words there are regional imbalances and ballasting becomes a necessity. Careful routeing can reduce the percentage of ballast steaming if an OBO, for instance, can move from one commodity trade to another. Deeds examined the regional imbalances in some detail and experimented with different combinations, alternatives and scenarios, arriving at a routeing model, using OBOs, that would reduce ballast steaming, vastly reduce annual fuel oil consumption for the fleet, increase the rates of vessel utilisation and annual work capacity of each vessel, thereby reducing the necessary size of the bulk carrier fleet.

Deeds constructed his final model using recorded bulk commodity trade data at a high level of geographical generalisation. Fleming's model that combined four different bulk commodity trades in logical geographic sequence was even more abstract. A comparison of the four trades using specialized bulk carriers in back-and-forth shuttle service on each route with an OBO fleet moving progressively from one bulk trade to the next showed the theoretical cost and efficiency benefits of combining the trades. Both researchers were impressed by the potential of the modern-day combined carrier but both were skeptical that the geographic configurations of global bulk commodity shipments would ever match their idealised models.

What has prevented the combined carrier from catching on? It was recently reported that "A ninth consecutive year of decline has reduced the total combined carrier fleet to less than half its level a decade ago. The end-2001 fleet amounts to 13.9 million deadweight tons compared with 29.7 million at the end of 1991... In fact, this was the lowest end-year fleet since 1969" (SSY 2002, p. 10). One might begin by asking who controls the oil, ore, coal and grain trades. Obviously the big oil, steel, and grain trading companies have huge shipping influence and often have had large proprietary fleets of vessels under their ownership or firm control. Understandably, these companies have been primarily interested in their own basic raw materials or energy resources. Tying together diverse commodity trades has not been their first priority although the flexibility inherent in the combined carrier may have had some appeal when their own trade was in the doldrums. In normal times, however, the industrial carrier, controlling and securing the transport function for the firm, serves the production and marketing divisions of the larger corporation and tries to provide an efficient, reliable, timely, transportation service. Routeing efficiency and low fuel consumption are not likely to be ruling considerations, although annual work capacity of the fleet is a significant long term concern.

Proprietary carriers, especially in the oil trades, have been wooed by the dramatic economies of scale derived from mega-ship transport despite the inflexibility in routeing that large size adds to the inherent inflexibility of specialized single-purpose vessels. Extremely low costs per ton mile seem to magnify the advantages of the supertanker, for example, and "microfy" the disadvantages of longer-distance voyages. (One sometimes forgets that the cost per ton of carrying a bulk commodity in a ship of given size and specifications is always going to be higher on a long voyage than on a short voyage.) The costs per deadweight ton of capacity of building a combined carrier are, to be sure, considerably higher than the costs of building a single purpose vessel of the same cargo carrying capacity. Admittedly, also, scheduling ships on back-and-forth shuttle service between the company's own terminal facilities, as is the case on many of the oil company trade routes, is far easier than arranging more elaborate and time-consuming itineraries that combine different trades and different commodities. Moreover, there are "time economies" that come from ballasting straight home for the next outbound voyage.

When governments or government agencies develop industrial or shipping policies that allow them to intrude in the development of shipping networks and merchant fleets, the complexion of the issues, objectives and priorities, with respect to the transport function, may change. The careful bulk commodity routeing strategies of BISCORE when British Steel was a nationalised venture, and in the 1960s the use of combined carriers by SIDERMAR, the shipping wing of Finsider, the Italian state-owned steel combine, are cases in point. Perhaps there was less attention to the immediate "bottom line" of the bulk commodity shipping operation, but more attention to longer-term planning of voyages and voyage combinations, usually resulting in a more efficient and productive use of the fleet. SIDERMAR, for a while, combined coking coal cargoes eastbound from the US to Italian steelworks with iron ore cargoes westbound from West Africa to the US, the westbound shipments for the account of an *American* steel company (Fleming, 1968, p. 31). The government agencies in such cases had a proprietary interest in the transport function. One supposes that, beyond their transportation service to the national steel company, certain general principles of fuel conservation, environmental safety and even the implementation of national political objectives could come into play.

There is another major component in bulk commodity ocean trading and that is the independent shipowner, or the modern version of the tramp shipping operator. Some of these shipowners, whose names have become legendary in shipping circles, have built enormous fleets of tankers or dry bulk carriers. Also, many of the owners have been serious students of the patterns and trends of the bulk commodity trades. Most of their vessels are "ships for hire." Their fleets are fixed on charters of various durations, from spot voyage charters to long term bareboat charters. Quite often the long term charterers are "big oil" or "big steel" or "big mining" concerns and, for all intents and purposes, the ships become part of the proprietary carrier fleet.

One of the most successful steamship operators of the 20th century was Erling Naess, a Norwegian who pioneered the financing, building and operating, under charter contracts, of fleets of OBOs and other versatile bulk carriers. In Naess' own words, "For owners of large bulk carriers the secret of operating a profitable shipping business is to a large extent one of arranging trading patterns in such a way that the time at sea in loaded condition exceeds the time at sea in ballast condition." and, later, "I spent much of my time dreaming up 'combination trades' in which the individual market rates might appear uneconomic but in combination with return trades a satisfactory return might be secured." And, still later, "I was strongly in favour of 'combination carriers', later known as OBOs, which could carry liquid or alternatively dry cargo"(Naess, 1973, p. 191). By clever choices of trading patterns Naess was able to reduce ballast steaming dramatically. On an 89-day voyage, for instance, loading coal at Norfolk for Japan via the Panama Canal, ballasting to the Persian Gulf, loading crude oil for Portland, Maine and ballasting back to Norfolk he calculated only 19 days in ballast or 25% of the total steaming days (Naess, 1977, p. 150).[10]

One concludes that it is not necessary to have official government collaboration in the shipping programs or even official agreements between the different commodity trades to make combination trades work. The independent steamship operator with a fleet of combined carriers can discover the efficient geographic patterns, latch on to them for as long as the commodity flows last and the transport service is providing mutual benefit to carrier and shipper, and retain the flexibility to move all or part of the fleet elsewhere when contracts expire. *Theoretically*, it's appealing.

To be realistic, contemporary evidence suggests that neither combined carriers nor combined bulk commodity trades have caught on with the big shippers or with proprietary carrier fleets. It is the independent shipowner component that might still make the combinations work in the future. There are a multitude of smaller bulk trades and trade routes that do not appear on Figures 2–6. There are many possible combinations and there are many tramp operations of modest size that involve much more than one bulk commodity trade on one trade route. It is not unrealistic to suppose that combinations of trades do more than accommodate "demand for spot transit of bulk commodities" and go beyond the "derived and marginal character of the demand for tramp shipping services", therefore beyond some of the usual theoretical explanations of the rationale for these services (Metaxas, 1971, pp. 4, 41, 230).

One could hardly expect the tramp operator to adopt highly idealistic policies of ballast reduction to help the world in an energy crisis, or of combining trades for the sake of international good will. However, more efficient patterns of movement can be more profitable patterns of movement and *that* should appeal to most tramp operators and independent shipowners.

6. GENERAL CARGO TRADES: 2000

The cargo flows in the bulk commodity trade are obviously unidirectional, as depicted graphically in Figures 2, 3, 4, 5 and 6. This creates a ballasting necessity, either to return to the original loading range or to move "onward" to a different trade route and, perhaps, a different commodity to carry. General cargo trades, those served by container lines, for example, nearly always have bidirectional cargo movements. The need for ballast legs without *any* paying cargo aboard is not an important concern for liner shipping on the major general cargo routes.

Yet there remains a problem that cannot be eliminated. Seldom are the liner trades directionally in balance in size of cargo flows. This means that a container ship very often has a high load factor, in percentage of slots filled with revenue-paying containers, in one direction and a low load factor in the opposite direction, with many slots filled with empty containers being "positioned" for the heavier flow direction. Furthermore, the directional imbalances can vary for many different reasons, economic and political. One of the big challenges for the liner operator is to cope with these imbalances that create unused cargo space if the vessels are used in simple bidirectional shuttle service.

6.1 Network strategies

As in the bulk trades, one of the ways to cope with empty space involves routeing strategies that discover the most appropriate itineraries, port sequences, transhipment junctions and methods of tying one liner route to another so that vessels can avoid the weak cargo flow direction of one liner route by slipping into an adjoining liner route with stronger cargo prospects. In attempts to handle the directional imbalance problem and elevate the achieved load factors (or capacity utilisation percentage) for the extended voyage, some of the major container lines, Evergreen, for instance, have constructed elaborate globe – encircling network systems, choosing strategically located hubs for transhipment purposes as they coordinate schedules of main line and feeder services, but, more importantly, choosing ports of call with the most powerful cargo-generating local and regional hinterlands.

Many other container lines have developed pendulum systems which allow them to serve all three of the major industrial core regions leaving out one ocean: Atlantic or Pacific or Indian, and using coordinated intermodal connections, overland, to penetrate or sometimes cross large landmasses like North America.

Both the round-the-world and the pendulum networks and itineraries, mentioned above, need to be flexible enough, and the size of the container line fleet needs to be adjustable enough to adapt to changing market conditions in a competitive environment.

Doctoring a liner network for maximum operating efficiency needs to be a constant consideration, but doctoring it for maximum freight revenue generation is very important too. And the two types of doctoring are not necessarily the same. In recent years the container lines, having rushed headlong into the acquisition of mega-ships, schedule these vessels on long voyages on the heavy-volume *inter-core* routes calling at relatively few ports, transhipping frequently to extend their market reach. Some have gravitated towards hub-and-spoke systems. The latter offer strong market-penetrating potential but one should remember that pure hub-and-spoke systems, are, in graph theoretical terms, networks of minimal connectivity. This means that there is only one path, and no alternatives, between any two points in the system, and that path is either to or through the hub. This translates, in fact, to lower rates of vessel utilisation and lower annual work capacities for the fleet if both main line and feeder services are under the same corporate roof. It could also amplify the directional imbalance problem by shifting it to the feeder services. However, both the network connectivity problem and the directional imbalance problem are not without solutions if the large container line shifts focus from main line to feeder line and does the necessary network-doctoring.[11]

The arguments for hub-and-spoke networks are much stronger on the revenue side of the voyage proforma than on the cost side. Andrew Goetz, in a recent article on the US airline industry, commented, "The widespread adoption of hub-and-spoke networks conferred tremendous economies of scope to airlines, as the costs of adding each additional spoke to a hub are generally quite small in comparison to the benefits of increased traffic feed" (Goetz, 2002, p. 3). Are there parallels to this in the container trades? Generally speaking, yes. The carriers are willing to incur the cost inefficiencies inherent in hub-and-spoke operations if the "traffic feed" to and from their main line service is sufficiently enhanced. Remember, however, that hub-and-spoke operations entail transhipments, and potential cargo can be lost to competitors who offer direct port calls rather than transhipment service.

6.2 Northern latitudes

The impact of the three industrial core regions on general cargo trades and, more specifically, on container trades is even more spectacular than their impact, largely as a market destination, on bulk commodity oceanborne shipping. More than 70% of global seaborne container trade is "inter-core"[12] (see Figure 7).

Container lines have not abandoned the rest of the world but there is no doubt that they have found most of their freight in northern latitudes. In the developed nations of the north and neighbouring rapidly developing economies it is estimated that more than three quarters of the containerisable general cargo is now being containerized. The world's largest container lines with the world's largest container ships have gravitated to the heavy volume east-west inter-core routes. They have transatlantic, transpacific and Asia-Europe via Indian Ocean services, all north of the equator. These are heavy volume routes that, together, ring the globe with cargo flows in both directions, east-west and west-east. The traditional all-water routes via the Panama Canal and Suez Canal have been supplemented by continental overland bridge routes (sketched in Figure 7), notably in and across North America.

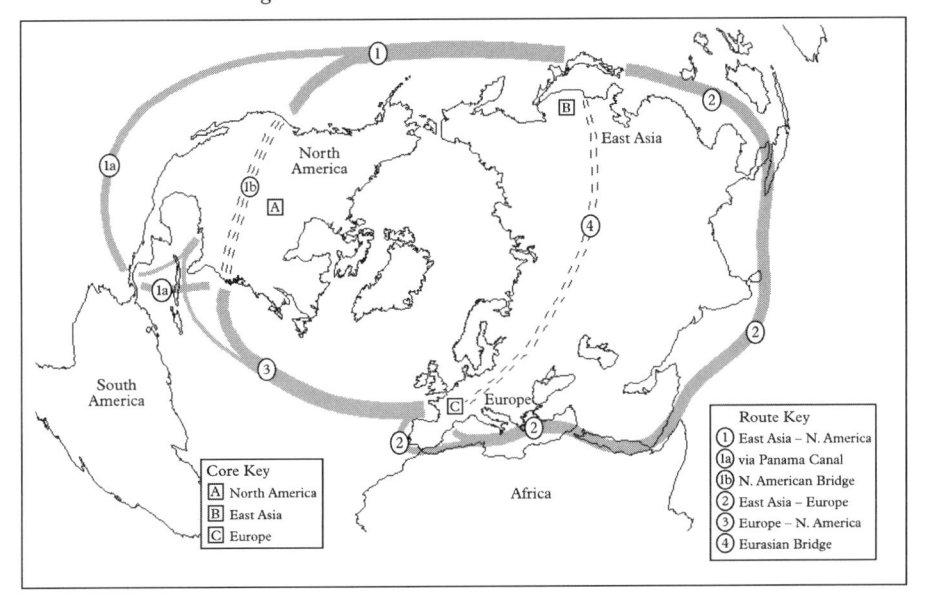

Figure 7: Global inter-core container trade

The three major transoceanic routes attract feeder traffic from the southern hemisphere at strategically located points such as Singapore, Algeciras, Freeport (Bahamas) and at transhipment terminals at either end of the Panama Canal. At these points the container transfer is often between medium-sized container ships on medium-volume trade routes and the giant 6000 TEU (plus or minus) vessels that are seen more and more frequently on the ring of mainline routes connecting the three industrial core regions. The economies of scale measured by (low) slot costs of the mega-ships need to be matched by economies of scope increasing traffic feed, thereby increasing the percentage of slots filled with revenue-paying containers.

Large container lines operating large container ships need to have a carefully designed global intermodal strategy. To begin with, there are certain clearly defined physical geographic constraints. A vessel with sufficient beam to load more than 13 containers abreast is too wide for the Panama Canal locks and this generally means vessels of more than about 4200 TEU capacity cannot get through. Moreover, there are many ports without adequate water depth to accommodate fully-loaded container ships in the 5 or 6 thousand TEU capacity range; and these large ships require terminal cranes with enough reach to handle containers lined up on the ship 16 or 17 abreast.

A second area of concern is the directional imbalance of cargo flow on virtually all container routes. The large container lines, with large ships in their fleets, need to be especially sensitive to "weak directions" and "weak segments" in their extensive networks. Periodic adjustments need to be made to respond to changes in market demand: adjustments of network configuration, itineraries, schedules, alliances, fleet capacity, vessel sizes, not to mention freight rate adjustments. This is part of a global strategy that each line constructs and modifies.

6.3 Directional imbalances

In year 2000 the container trade on inter-core routes 1,2 and 3, depicted on Figure 7, was tallied as shown in Table 1.

Table 1: Inter-core route container traffic in year 2000

	TEU	Load Factor Est.
Route 1 North America–East Asia (westbound)	3,249,809	58
Route 1 East Asia–North America (eastbound)	5,589,968	100
Route 2 East Asia–Europe (westbound)	3,893,219	100
Route 2 Europe–East Asia (eastbound)	2,709,931	70
Route 3 Europe–North America (westbound)	2,944,063	100
Route 3 North America–Europe (eastbound)	2,192,503	74

Notes:
(1) North America includes Canada, US, Mexico
Europe includes all European coasts
East Asia includes northeast and southeast Asia
(2) Route 2 totals do not include en route cargo generated in South Asia and Middle East and carried on vessels not providing end-to-end East Asia-Europe service.
(3) The estimated load factors are simply based on the premise that they are proportional to comparative directional traffic densities. The highest volume direction of each of the three routes is assigned a load factor of 100.
Source of TEU traffic data: *Containerisation International*, February, 2002, p. 18.

From Table 1 one can construct three general scenarios for container line service:

Scenario 1: Shuttle services

- Container lines offer back-and-forth shuttle services on Routes 1, 2 and 3.
- There are no special physical geographic constraints except on Route 1 where only Pacific Coast North American ports can be used for megaships.
- The least empty space and the best directional balance in year 2000 occurred on Route 3 (transatlantic).
- The highest total TEU traffic occurred on Route 1 (transpacific).

Scenario 2: Round-the-world (RTW) services

- RTW services offered in both directions.
- Complete RTW all-water service limits vessel size to about 4200 TEU capacity enabling Panama Canal transit.
- Eastbound direction of Routes 1,2,3 accounted for 10,492,402 TEU, all types of services included; westbound directions accounted for 10,087,091 TEU, suggesting a fairly even total traffic potential in either direction.

Scenario 3: Pendulum services

- Container lines can construct three types of pendulum service, one centered on Europe, one centered on East Asia and one on North America.

PATTERNS OF INTERNATIONAL OCEAN TRADE

Notes:
(1) TEUs in millions
(2) Load factors in parentheses

3a. 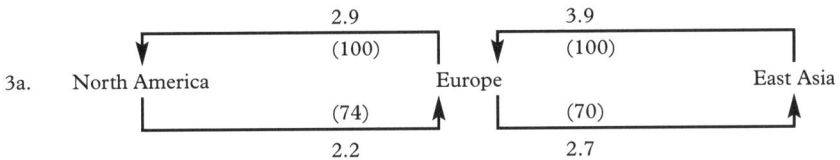 North America — Europe — East Asia

- North America → Europe: 2.9 (100); Europe → North America: 2.2 (74)
- Europe → East Asia: 3.9 (100); East Asia → Europe: 2.7 (70)

- No special constraint on vessel size; mega-ships use east coast North America ports.
- The least empty space of the pendulum services: highest average load factors.
- Lowest total traffic potential.

3b. 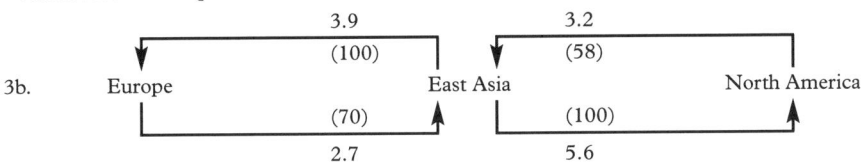 Europe — East Asia — North America

- Europe → East Asia: 3.9 (100); East Asia → Europe: 2.7 (70)
- East Asia → North America: 3.2 (58); North America → East Asia: 5.6 (100)

- No special constraint on vessel size.
- The most empty space of pendulum services: lowest average load factor.
- Heaviest total traffic potential.
- Presence on heaviest volume route: transpacific eastbound.

3c. 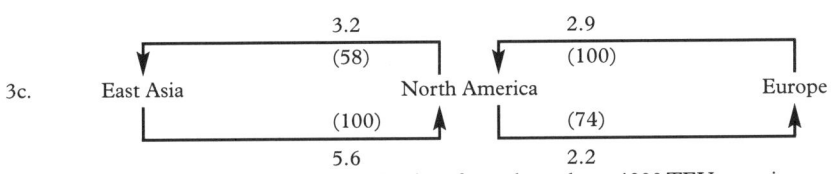 East Asia — North America — Europe

- East Asia → North America: 3.2 (58); North America → East Asia: 5.6 (100)
- North America → Europe: 2.9 (100); Europe → North America: 2.2 (74)

- All water service via Panama Canal limits size of vessels to about 4200 TEU capacity.
- Average load factors almost as low as 3b.
- Presence on heaviest volume route: transpacific eastbound.
- Most comprehensive access to North American intermodal system.

These scenarios suggest some of the general geographical factors of network structure, traffic densities and favoured directions of movement that enter into the container line's thinking as global strategies are constructed. It should be emphasised that there are many other factors in the decision equation, for instance the revenue yields per filled slot which vary from one route to another, the break-even load factors for ships of different sizes on different routes, the degree of competition on the various routes, the amount of traffic feed that might be expected at well-chosen transhipment hubs, and so forth.

There is no fail-safe scenario. Each requires reevaluation as market conditions change, for the better or the worse. The empty space problem engendered by "weak directions" and weak route segments can sometimes be softened by moving from one scenario, or form of service, to another. Every one of the big container lines has used shuttle services and pendulum services in the past. A few of the largest lines have tried RTW services, some like US Lines in the 1980s very unsuccessfully (Lim, 1996).[13] Recently, Evergreen, the huge Taiwanese carrier, whose competition really precipitated US Lines demise, announced the cessation of their RTW services, replacing them with pendulum services, one centered on North America using 4200 TEU vessels and Panama Canal transit, and the other centered on East Asia using new 5600 TEU vessels.[14] The need to accommodate mega-ships has become a vital consideration in current network decisions. Apparently the promise of low slot costs outweighs the fears of overcapacity, leading to cut throat competition, low yields per slot and the inherent inflexibility in the operation of these huge vessels.

7. SUMMARY AND PROSPECTS

Analysing the empty-space phenomenon, whether from bulk carriers in ballast or from container ships with low achieved load factors, one can certainly find flaws in some of the network efficiencies. However, much of the empty space problem for the world merchant fleets, in aggregate, stems from unavoidable commercial geographic realities, namely the spatial separation – by oceans – of regions of production and regions of consumption and the directional imbalances of cargo flows on each trade route. "Overbuilding" in the 1990s adds to the problem. There is very little prospect of correcting the flaws in global network efficiencies by any sort of comprehensive governmental "edict".

There is every reason to hope, however, that individual steamship operators in both bulk and liner trades will use their own ingenuity to fashion networks and patterns of operation that will enhance their capacity utilisation, annual fleet work capacity, and, on the revenue side, annual fleet yields. There is no general prescription for success; however, each carrier, serving a geographical domain that is somewhat unique in its specifics, with a fleet that is somewhat unique in vessel sizes and specifications, should be able to differentiate itself from its competitors in some "attractive" way. Yet there have been many recent indications of "copy-cat behavior" in the liner trades – not a good sign, perhaps, if it leads to indiscriminately competitive efforts, overbuilding, overcapacity, bankruptcies, emergency mergers, and the like.

The trend towards using mega-ships in both bulk and liner trades complicates network strategies and, unless market demand is really robust, compounds the empty space problem. There is, as mentioned, an inherent inflexibility from large size although, of course, the owners count on this being outweighed by scale economies, measured in unit costs of transport.

Unfortunately the combined carrier for bulk trades, while conceptually appealing, has not lived up to its former promise or, in Erling Naess' case, its former success. (Naess, 1977, chap. 21). Many operators have complained that dry and liquid bulk commodity trades just do not mix, not only because of expensive vessel design, cleaning costs when shifting trades, etc., but also because of difficulties coordinating trades between two or more "masters," each absorbed with own-company needs. Many of the remaining combined carriers still in operation have reverted to the carriage of one commodity type, liquid or dry. So much for flexibility!

There is little doubt that the 21st century will bring more development of southern hemispheric trade routes, especially for container lines. It has been estimated that only 50% of the containerisable commodities in the developing economies are, in fact, containerised for ocean transport whereas the percentage in the developed economies approaches 90. It is predictable that as trade itself grows, and as the infrastructure for container handling and intermodalism develops, the volumes of containerised cargo in all parts of the world will increase.

China and India are special cases, both with enormous growth potential in the container trades. It was recently estimated that 55% of North American imports in the container trade and nearly 30% of exports involve China and this can only increase as more and larger vessels offer direct calls in China.[15] China and India, however, are on the main pathway from East Asia to Europe, so their burgeoning ocean transport needs will probably accentuate the east-west northern hemispheric ring of inter-core trade routes. Incidentally, the data that appears in Table 1 for year 2000 traffic on the East Asia – Europe route do not include the sizeable "intermediate" movements, for instance South Asia and Middle Eastern containers westbound to Europe (639,260 TEU) and European containers eastbound to the Middle East and South Asia (884,852).[16] This en route traffic potential is all the more reason for the use of mega-ships on the East Asia – Europe inter-core route and the development of en route transhipment terminals.

There is much reason to expect the filling-out of networks to and in the southern hemisphere, especially if the South American and African economies rise to their true potential. However, it is unlikely that the dominant inter-core pattern in northern latitudes will disappear. It is too firmly etched on the mercantile maps of the globe.

A final prediction relates specifically to the container trades of the future. There has been much talk of intermodality, total logistics chains, seamless movement of containers, electronic data interchange, and so forth. These are good ideas but not ideas that have yet been fully and successfully implemented. There always seem to be weak, often time-consuming, links in the chain. One trend, however, that has been notably strong and growing stronger in recent years has been the service contracting between carriers and shippers based on time-volume freight rates. On American container trade routes, the North America – East Asia route, for instance, a large proportion of the total trade falls under these service contracts. The latter seem to reflect a true partnership between shipper and carrier unlike the more confrontational shipping arrangements of the past. It is hoped that the partnership philosophy based on perceived mutual benefit will prevail in the 21st century.

8. CONCLUSION

As mentioned at the beginning of this chapter, an important focus was to be on empty cargo space steaming across the oceans. In the bulk commodity trades very often there are shuttle services with half the steaming time for the round voyage in ballast. This can be perceived as lost cargo lifting potential but there are, of course, extenuating circumstances such as the unavailability of return cargoes, and, on a more positive note, the time economies of a ballast run compared to time expended on a slow voyage in a nearby trade at a low freight rate.[17]

Tramp operators undoubtedly search the globe for efficient and profitable patterns of operation and there are ways that they can improve on engaging in shuttle services if they have a fleet of versatile multi-purpose bulk carriers. As mentioned, however, the combined carriers have not been an unqualified success in an age when vessel size and single purpose specialization offer the cost benefits most appreciated by the proprietary carriers.

In the container trades we have noted the most important trade routes and the directional imbalances of cargo flow on those routes. A few strategies were mentioned, including moving back and forth from shuttle services to pendulum services to round-the-world services, or vice versa, to tailor the supply of vessel space more evenly to the demand for it when market conditions change. Of course, this requires a certain amount of operational flexibility. And the carrier's flexibility needs to be weighed against the shippers' usual need for reliable and uninterrupted service.

All told, "flexibility" enters the picture of both tramp and liner shipping in many different shades and colours. It can be a general characteristic and expectation of tramp shipping operations. It is a built-in quality of a steamship line's network that interlocks various trade routes and services. Its opposite, inflexibility, can be inherent in the operations of single purpose mega-ships.

Flexibility can relate also to a philosophy or grand strategy of company operations which favours a thoughtful adaptability to market conditions and customer needs.

ENDNOTES

1. SS&Y, *Monthly Shipping Review*, February, 2002; *Fearnleys Review*, 1999 and 2000.
2. Actually, there is a span of almost three centuries between the first Spanish galleon trans-pacific round trip, Acapulco to Manila and return, and the mid 19th century US-built clipper ships plying the Australia–Britain route.
3. See, for instance, the three "flow maps" depicting colonial trades, circa 1775, on pp. 198–199 of *The Times Atlas of World History*.
4. Despite the potential for shifting from one trade to another and despite the fact that the OBOs were designed for that very purpose, the combined carriers, today, tend to stick exclusively to one type of bulk commodity trade.
5. As calculated from *Fearnleys* and SS&Y data records.
6. See SS&Y *Monthly Shipping Review*, February, 2002. Most of the statistics that are the basis for the analysis in this chapter of the liquid and dry bulk trades come from this source.
7. Rice is not included in the data on which this analysis of the grain trade is based. Soyabeans, technically not a grain, are included, however.
8. *Fearnleys Review*, 1999, p. 46.
9. SS&Y provided most of the data.
10. Of course, the Panamax-size, or smaller OBO vessels used in these earlier days (mid-1960s) were easier to route; shifting trades was easier, too.
11. In fact, some of the feeder line carriers move progressively from one "spoke-end" port to another, adding connectivity to the network. Some of the ports in these "loops" are favoured with faster cargo-transit times than others.

12. *Containerisation International Yearbook*, 2001.
13. Lim's article gives interesting explanations of US Lines' downfall.
14. *Containerisation International*, January, 2002, p. 14.
15. J. Fossey (2002), "Trans-Pacific Outlook", *Jo C Week*, March 25–31, 2002, p. 38.
16. *Containerisation International*, January, 2002, p. 7.
17. Assume that a combined carrier is fixed on a dry bulk 30 day voyage, laden outward, ballast return, promising a net profit of $150,000 or $5,000 daily. That might appeal more to the operator than combining the dry bulk trade with a ballast-reducing oil trade back to the original loading range if the combination of the two trades results in a 50-day total voyage and a net profit of $200,000 or $4,000 daily. The daily profit is, in a sense, the "running bottom line".

REFERENCES

Albion, R.G. (1939): *The Rise of New York Port, 1815–1860* (New York, Charles Scribner's Sons).
Barraclough, G. (ed.) (1978): *The Times Atlas of World History* (London, Times Books Ltd).
Braudel, F. (1984): *The Perspective of the World*, Vol. III of *Civilization and Capitalism 15th–18th Century*, translation by Siân Reynolds (New York, Harper & Row).
Couper, A.D. (1972): *The Geography of Sea Transport* (London, Hutchinson Univ. Library).
Deeds, C.L. (1978): "Fuel conservation as a regulation of vessel routeing", *Maritime Policy & Management*, 5, pp. 75–88.
Ellsworth, P.T. (1958): *The International Economy* (2nd ed.) (New York, The Macmillan Co.).
Fleming, D.K. (1968): "The independent transport carrier in ocean tramp trades", *Economic Geography*, 44, pp. 21–36.
Fleming, D.K. (1978): "A concept of flexibility", *Geo. Journal*, 2, pp. 111–116.
Fossey, J. (2002): "Trans-Pacific Outlook", *Jo C Week*, March 25–31, p. 38.
Gibson, A. and Donovan, A. (2000): *The Abandoned Ocean, A History of United States Maritime Policy* (Columbia, SC, Univ. of South Carolina Press).
Goetz, A.R. (2002): "Deregulation, competition and antitrust implications in the US airline industry", *Journal of Transport Geography*, 10, pp. 1–19.
Lim, S.M. (1996): "Round-the-world service: The rise of Evergreen and the fall of US Lines", *Maritime Policy & Management*, 23, pp. 119–144.
Manners, G. (1971): *The Changing World Market for Iron Ore, 1950–1980, An Economic Geography* (Baltimore, The Johns Hopkins Press).
Metaxas, B.N. (1971): *The Economics of Tramp Shipping* (London, The Athlone Press).
Morgan, D. (1979): *Merchants of Grain* (New York, The Viking Press).
Naess, E.D. (1977): *Autobiography of a Shipping Man* (Colchester, Seatrade Publications Ltd).
Rostow, W.W. (1962): *The Process of Economic Growth* (2nd ed.) (New York, The Norton Library).
Sargent, A.J. (1930): *Seaways of the Empire* (2nd ed.) (London, A. & C. Black Ltd.).
Yeats, A.J. (1981): *Shipping and Development Policy, An Integrated Assessment* (New York, Praeger).

CHAPTER 5

INTERNATIONAL TRADE IN MANUFACTURED GOODS

Mary R. Brooks
Dalhousie University, Halifax, Canada
E-mail: *mbrooks@mgmt.dal.ca*

INTRODUCTION

To most maritime economists, it appears that the largest proportion of international freight moves by water. As will be seen, however, this is not a definitive conclusion. Over the past century, world trade patterns have become more complex and trade, particularly for manufactured goods, has relied on inexpensive ocean-going transport systems.

Cargo transported by ship falls into two broad categories – bulk and unitised cargo. The former usually travels via tramp vessels and includes both liquid and dry bulk, the latter including iron ore, grain and coal. Based on ton-miles, crude oil, oil products and dry bulk commodities are the most important trades in ocean shipping (Figure 1). Unitised cargo (predominantly containers, and included in Other in Figure 1) is not dominant in terms of ton-miles demanded; unitised cargo accounts for between 25% and 28% of ton-mile demand in the 1990s, up from 19.9% in 1970 (UNCTAD, 1987, 2002). However, shipping demand in ton-miles is only one measure of importance. In value terms, trade in manufactured goods drives world prosperity.

This chapter provides an overview of world trade in manufactured goods, the primary user of containerised liner shipping. It begins by identifying the key manufactured goods traded worldwide, the leading trading nations, and the accompanying trade flows. As air cargo is the principal competitor to maritime transport for inter-regional trade in manufactured goods, the incursion of air cargo is examined in order to understand the likely short-term future for the transport of manufactured goods by sea. Canada's modal split for non-US international trade is used to illustrate the variation in the air-water modal split. To complete the picture, the trader's view is discussed and conclusions drawn about what the future may hold for the transport of manufactured goods.

THE KEY MANUFACTURED GOODS TRADED GLOBALLY

The world in the early days of general cargo shipping looked nothing like the world of trade today. The heyday of trade in tea and silk financed by opium sales to China is long gone. By 1900, China's imports had become more diversified,

INTERNATIONAL TRADE IN MANUFACTURED GOODS

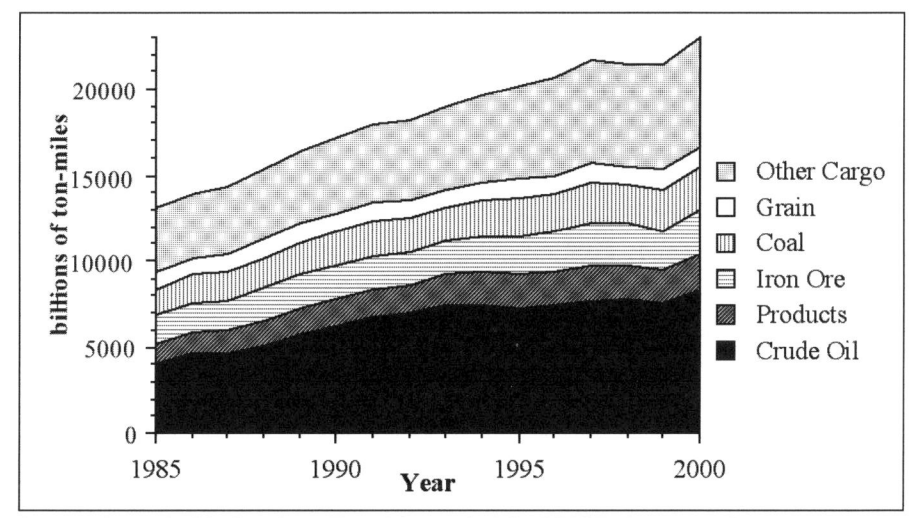

Figure 1: World seaborne trade, 1985–2000

[Stacked area chart showing billions of ton-miles from 1985 to 2000, with categories: Other Cargo, Grain, Coal, Iron Ore, Products, Crude Oil]

Source: Created with data from Fearnleys as cited by UNCTAD (2002), *Review of Maritime Transport 2001*, Table 5, p. 15 and equivalent tables from prior years.

with cotton goods and yarn replacing opium. While tea and silk may have been China's key exports to Europe in 1870, by 1890 they too had diversified, giving way to shipments of seeds, oil, beans, hides and "all other items" on the westbound leg from Asia (Jennings, 1980).

Many of the manufactured goods critical to business success today, such as personal computers and mobile phones, had barely been contemplated by product development departments 30 years ago. However, post-war consumerism was well established and, with the advent of containerisation in the 1960s, the transport of manufactured goods and the world economy entered a new era. Asia continued to be at the heart of the manufactured goods trading sector. From 1985 to 1990, the average annual growth in containerisable trade on North America/Far East and Far East/Europe trade legs exhibited double-digit rates and, after a brief slowdown in the early 1990s, growth in trade production in many Asian nations resumed its former pace.

From 1990 to 2000, the rate of growth in merchandise trade outstripped the rate of growth in world GDP and commodity output (WTO, 2002). Over the same period, the demand for waterborne trade of other cargo in ton-miles grew by 42% (UNCTAD, 2002); from 1993 to 1999, world exports of goods in billions of US dollars grew by 68% (International Monetary Fund, 2001:74). The additional growth was largely in higher value goods—component parts, semi-finished and finished goods, the type of goods carried in containers.

According to the World Trade Organization's latest statistics (WTO, 2002), trade in manufactured goods accounted for 74.9% of all merchandise exports in 2000 (Figure 2). This figure was significantly higher than the 70.5% recorded in 1990. It included iron and steel, and chemicals, both of which may be carried as bulk commodities, although the latter makes up a significant component

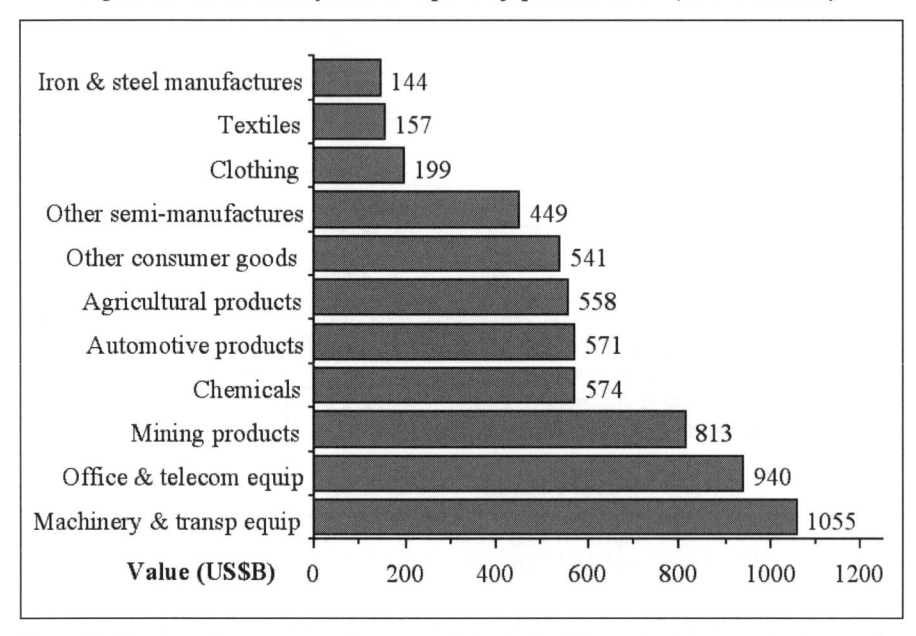

Figure 2: World manufactured exports by product 2000 (in US$billions)

Product	Value (US$B)
Iron & steel manufactures	144
Textiles	157
Clothing	199
Other semi-manufactures	449
Other consumer goods	541
Agricultural products	558
Automotive products	571
Chemicals	574
Mining products	813
Office & telecom equip	940
Machinery & transp equip	1055

Note: Machinery and transport equipment excludes both office and telecommunications equipment and automotive products.
Created from data provided by World Trade Organization (2002), *International Trade Statistics 2001*, Table IV.1, p. 95.

of containerised trade. If these two categories of manufactured goods are discounted, the remaining manufactured goods still account for 63.3% of merchandise exports by value. By far the largest category of manufactured products is machinery and transportation equipment, even after the highly visible automotive category is extracted.

The World Trade Organization (2002) notes that, in 2000, growth was 6% in manufactured goods, 14.5% in manufacturing exports and only 4% in world GDP. Much of this growth has been driven by enhanced labour productivity. However, growth in global sales for office equipment and production machinery will slow, if not stagnate, when interest rates rise and the current technology revolution completes its restructuring of both the office environment and the shop floor. There are signs in the US that interest rates have bottomed. Once business investment in office and production technology slows, demand for transport equipment will too.

Looking forward, the world is moving towards a service economy and, in general, service economies do not use sea transport. Demographers report that there are no new jobs to be had worldwide in manufacturing and agri-business. The new job growth is in economies and industries that do not contribute to shipping ton-miles—software, pharmaceuticals, education, bio-technology, tourism, recreation and business services.

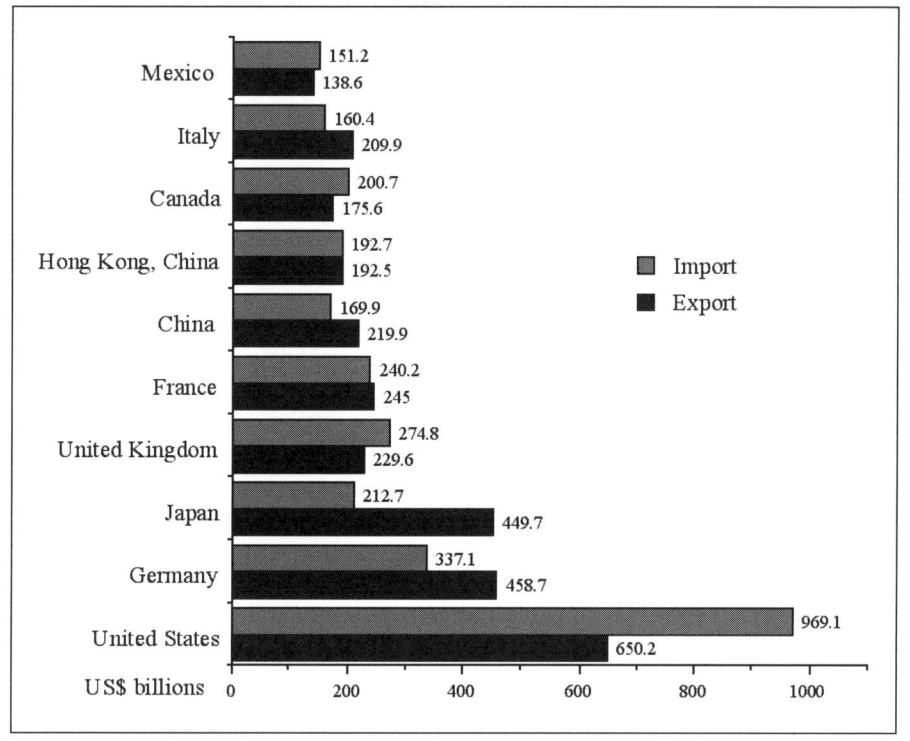

Figure 3: Leading traders of manufactured goods in 2000

Country	Import	Export
Mexico	151.2	138.6
Italy	160.4	209.9
Canada	200.7	175.6
Hong Kong, China	192.7	192.5
China	169.9	219.9
France	240.2	245
United Kingdom	274.8	229.6
Japan	212.7	449.7
Germany	337.1	458.7
United States	969.1	650.2

US$ billions

Created from data provided by World Trade Organization (2002), *International Trade Statistics 2001*, Table IV.30, p. 115.

WHO ARE THE LEADING TRADERS?

As already noted, export growth has been phenomenal in Asia. North American trade is not growing at a rate approaching that of Western Europe, let alone Japan and the developing countries of Asia. As Figure 3 illustrates, the top 10 world traders in manufactured goods are all, with the exception of China and Hong Kong, members of the Organisation for Economic Co-operation and Development.[1] Most of the manufactured goods exported from Hong Kong are re-exports, reflecting its role as a key transhipment hub. Not far behind these 10 are Belgium and its neighbour the Netherlands, key gateways for Europe's trade in manufactured goods.

Before drawing any conclusions about geographic interests in the trade in manufactured goods, and what that might mean for those with an interest in shipping, it is important to examine the major trade flows of manufactured goods and how much of that trade is intra-regional. After all, in addition to trade liberalization and the development of the World Trade Organization, the last two decades bore witness to an explosion of regional trade agreements. The European Single Market and the subsequent broadening of the European Union; the Canada US Trade Agreement and later the North American Free

Table 1: Top ten trade flows of manufactured goods in 2000

Origin	Destination	Value (US$B)
Western Europe	Western Europe	1,290.0
Asia	Asia	626.0
Asia	North America	396.0
North America	North America	313.8
Asia	Western Europe	249.4
Western Europe	North America	224.9
North America	Asia	178.4
Western Europe	Asia	172.6
Latin America	North America	163.7
North America	Western Europe	161.2
Top 10 Total		3,775.9

Created from data provided by World Trade Organization (2002), *International Trade Statistics 2001*, Table IV.28, p. 113.

Trade Agreement; Mercosur in South America and numerous others encouraged intra-regional trade growth. The impact of regional trade integration on world trade in manufactured goods should not be underestimated.

The top 10 trade flows of world exports in manufactured goods (Table 1) total 82.2% of all exports in value terms. However, when examining the trade flows in detail, it becomes quite clear that intra-regional flows are quite significant. The intra-regional flows of the three largest trade blocs (Europe, Asia and North America) account for about 48.2% of all trade in manufactured goods and all intra-regional flows worldwide account for half of world exports of manufactured goods. Should the trend of trade integration continue along its current path, a prospect not unlikely given US preoccupation with homeland security, how much trade growth will be available for ocean transport? The likely answer is a smaller share of this growing trade than is now available.

In order to illustrate the significant impact of the longer-term trend of regional trade integration on the availability of cargo for marine carriage, it is useful to examine intra-North American trade in greater detail. In a tri-national examination of transport and trade, Brooks (2001) found that only 2.4% of Canada's 1998 exports to the US (in dollar terms) moved by water (4.4% by air); US exports to Canada used water transport even less (1.5% by water and 9.2% by air). While Canada-Mexico water transport fared better, with 44.1% of Canada's traffic to Mexico moving by water, the volume was extremely small and there was very little backhaul cargo. Coastal or shortsea shipping is not widely used in North America, although Dibner (1993) suggested prospects for shortsea shipping are better in the broader Latin America/Caribbean Basin region.

Returning to Figure 3, it is important to note the dominant position the US holds as both lead exporter and importer. Indeed, its imports exceed those of Germany by three times and are slightly less than the combined imports of Germany, the United Kingdom, France and Italy. Table 1 suggests that the impact of American and European consumption patterns will be particularly critical for extra-regional transport demand as they are the two most significant extra-regional trade flows. Which modes will get the business and what share will they acquire?

HOW ARE MANUFACTURED GOODS CARRIED?

In some measure, the choice of transport mode for manufactured goods is dictated by shipment characteristics—the value to weight ratio, the value to volume ratio and the size of the shipment. However, it is not quite this simple.

For many years, such ratios indicated when breakbulk and general cargoes would continue to be carried by tramp vessels and when they would likely be converted to a container "format." Some growth in container volumes is attributable to such conversion, or penetration of containerisation. However, future growth is unlikely to come from this source. The Port of Hamburg has noted that 93% of its general cargo now moves in containers (Journal of Commerce, 2001d). Worldwide, we see commodities like scrap and specialty grains making the switch to containers from breakbulk or dry bulk vessels, but the value to density ratio of most general cargoes not yet containerised means prospects are poor for further penetration. This means of acquiring traffic growth for liner companies has simply run its course.

It has already been noted that significant trade in manufactured goods is intra-regional in nature, and therefore is a potential target for switching to land transport options away from ocean carriage. For many regional trade flows, shortsea shipping is an option, but one with an image problem. There are very good land-based transport systems in place, particularly within Western Europe, North America and the Eastern Europe/Baltic States and Eastern Europe/Scandinavia groupings. Although severe congestion in road transport is a widespread problem, shortsea or tug/barge transport options are not viewed as positive solutions. A number of studies have examined the potential for sea routings to take traffic away from surface-based alternatives. Dibner (1993) concludes that this is more likely to happen in Europe than in North America, but that it is most likely to happen in product sectors that are not competitive over the longer term. Van Willigenburg and Hollander (1993) argue that shortsea shipping has difficulty responding to shippers' need for just-in-time systems, and Zachial (1993) notes that the usual evaluative criteria of transit times, departure frequencies and costs will continue to drive the choices made, often in favour of land routings.

In finished goods trade, a very small percentage of the delivered value of the goods is attributed to transport. A dated Canadian study notes that, in 1986, transport costs consumed only 2-3% of the export sales value of furniture and fixtures, and motor vehicles, but accounted for 45% of the export sales value of coal (NTA, 1992). A 1983 US study put the transport cost component at 4% for electronic machinery and instruments, 8% for transportation equipment, 12% for furniture and fixtures, but 24% for petroleum products (Anderson, 1983). A UK study of manufacturing and services industries reported transport costs at 3-6% of production costs (Diamond and Spence, 1989). More recently, TACA (2001) drew attention to the relatively insignificant role that transport costs can play in some finished goods trade, citing these shipping prices on the North Atlantic westbound route:

French wine to New York	11.5 cents/bottle
European beer to New York	5 cents/bottle
UK whiskey to New York	14 cents/bottle
European mineral water to New York	9 cents per litre bottle

Therefore, as the value of the goods rises, the importance of transport cost as a function of delivered price diminishes but the value of transport time rises. Because of this, high value goods of low density and small shipment volumes become targets for air cargo providers. In recent years, companies like Northwest have targeted specific trades through density incentives, which seek to induce modal switching and enhance plane utilisation (Anonymous, 1999).

It is difficult to allocate various commodities to the type of transport they will demand. The trade statistics, while indicating the relative value of flows between countries, provide very little indication of what moves by what mode of transport. In the world of increasing proprietary data, only a superficial assessment is possible. Figures 4 and 5 indicate that modal split is not common across markets, using Canada's international modal split to illustrate.

Figure 4 depicts the ratio of airborne to waterborne exports for Canada's 10 largest export markets. The representation of modal split is quite accurate; the remainder of traffic moves by surface transport (road, rail, or pipeline), and is strictly continental in nature. On the other hand, the accuracy of Figure 5 is very suspect; many importers only know the origin of the goods, not how they

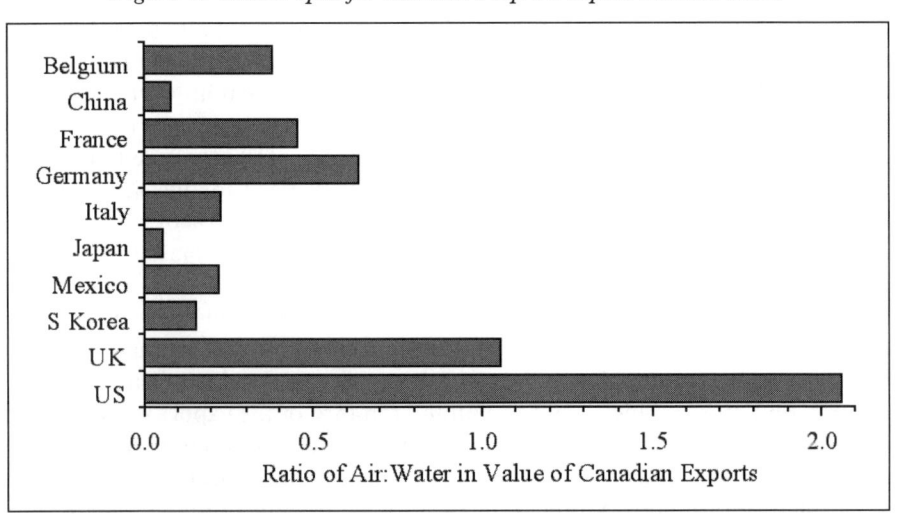

Figure 4: Modal split for Canada's top 10 export markets 2000

Countries are in alphabetical order.
Created from data found in Statistics Canada (2001), *Exports Merchandise Trade 2000 (65-202)*, Ottawa: Statistics Canada, Table 3.

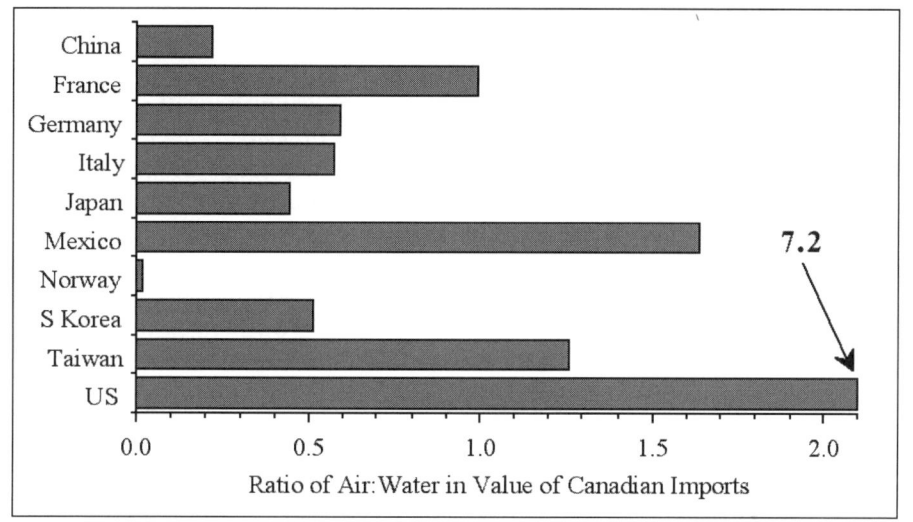

Figure 5: Modal split for Canada's top 10 import countries 2000

Country	Ratio of Air:Water in Value of Canadian Imports
China	~0.2
France	~1.0
Germany	~0.55
Italy	~0.55
Japan	~0.45
Mexico	~1.65
Norway	~0.02
S Korea	~0.5
Taiwan	~1.25
US	7.2 (~2.1 shown, arrow indicates 7.2)

Countries are in alphabetical order.
Created from data found in Statistics Canada (2001), *Imports Merchandise Trade 2000 (65-203)*, Ottawa: Statistics Canada, Table 5.

were transported to their destination. To cite the most obvious data errors as examples, the value of goods from Italy, China, or Japan arriving by truck exceeded the imports from that respective country by air! Perhaps such a land-bridge is wishful thinking, but really reflects the use of truck for the local delivery of a water or air shipment. In the case of the US trade with Canada, however, the preference for air cargo services over water in both directions is clear, but neither mode is able to compete with the greater than 80% of traffic that travels by road.

In conclusion, modal splits are more likely based on the product characteristics and seller/consignee preferences for fast transit time and time-definite delivery. As noted by Foster (1999), shippers are now more willing than ever to trade-off higher transport costs to reduce risk in making and holding inventory. Time-based competition is the new logistics watchword. The inroads made by air cargo on some trade routes should be of concern to shipping companies.

HOW GREAT IS THE THREAT POSED BY AIR TRANSPORT?

In the early 1980s, interest rates and the cost of capital increased the likelihood of traders evaluating the carrying costs associated with in-transit inventory in assessing transport options; efforts to address these costs contributed to tremendous growth in the air cargo industry. Air's share of total trade moved in 1985 was 13.7% and was forecast by Sclar and Blond (1991) to be 18.2% by the year 2000. Much of growth was expected to come at the expense of ocean transport, and it did. The combination of a low cost supply chain and just-in-time delivery has resulted in the demand for time-definite shipment options, something ocean shipping has been hard-pressed to deliver when in competition with air or truck-air combinations.

Air cargo companies compete intensely for a growing share of the trade in high quality manufactured goods. In its *World Air Cargo Forecast 2000/01*, Boeing (2000) predicted the long-term growth of air cargo traffic in freight tonne-kilometres to be at an annual rate of 6.4%, an increase from the 6.2% it averaged over the previous decade. These projections were based on a scenario of world GDP growth of 3% annually through 2019.

Boeing expected the biggest growth to come in the Asia/North America and intra-Asian markets, particularly given their 1999 growth rates of 13.4 and 13.0% respectively. The forecast for Europe/North America eastbound is still a respectable 6.8%, 7.0% westbound, through to 2019. With double-digit growth in air freighter fleet capacity in 1999, the air cargo industry has its sights clearly set on increasing its share of finished goods transported internationally. While some of that growth in air transport is expected to come at the expense of long-haul trucking in continental markets, ocean transport is a definite target.

Since the publication of the Boeing forecast, the air cargo sector has been severely tested by the collapse of the technology sector (*Air Cargo Yearbook 2002*). With 20–25% of air cargo being high-technology or information technology products, there was a significant decline in the volume of air cargo prior to the World Trade Center tragedy and its subsequent chilling effect on consumer spending. Analysts at *Air Cargo Yearbook 2002* expect only a short-term dip in traffic and do not intend to scale back their agreement with Boeing's long-term forecasts. It is expected that when the global economy recovers, air freight will benefit to a greater level than other forms of freight transport (Putzger, 2001).

Moreover, the International Air Transport Association released its Special Edition freight forecast in March of 2002, and predicted an early recovery with market growth in 2002. The growth forecast for total international air freight has been revised downward from 3.9% in the original 2001 forecast to 2% for 2001. Recovery will be quick on the transpacific route; it is predicted to have an average annual growth rate of 6.3% over the period 2002-05, and growth in excess of 7% from 2003 onwards. By 2005, 20.8 million tonnes are projected to be carried by air (IATA, 2002).

The difficulty of some airlines post-September 11 made headlines. Did this affect the provision of air cargo services? As Figure 6 reveals, the largest air cargo providers are well-established airlines, none of which was immediately threatened by the financial crisis the airline industry faced in the immediate aftermath. With the excellent service provided by air cargo operators to trading interests, a greater percentage of world trade is likely to move by air cargo because this is a reliable form of transport for those decision-makers worried about cargo damage, just-in-time delivery and cargo security. It is expected that air cargo will continue to erode the cargo base for ocean carriers by extracting more of the higher value cargoes from ocean boxes.

INTERNATIONAL TRADE IN MANUFACTURED GOODS

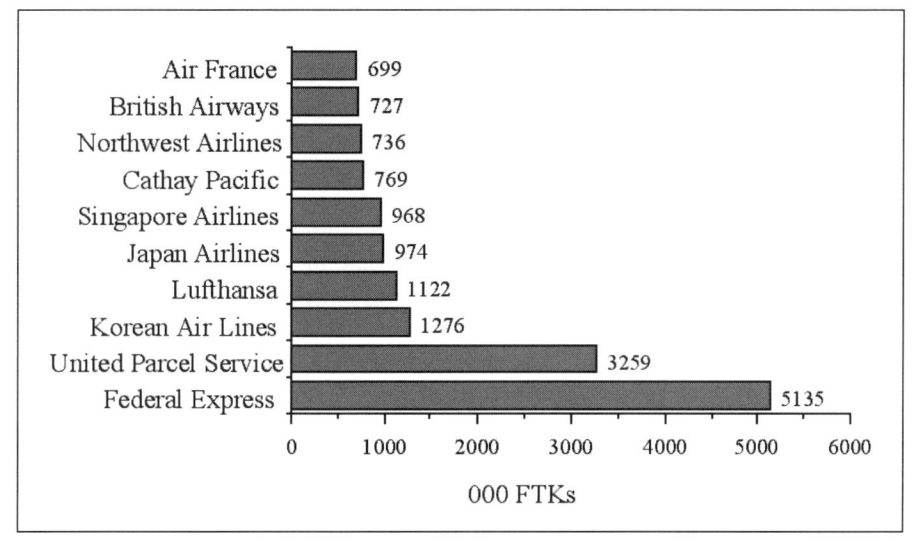

Figure 6: Top ten air cargo carriers 2000

Carrier	000 FTKs
Air France	699
British Airways	727
Northwest Airlines	736
Cathay Pacific	769
Singapore Airlines	968
Japan Airlines	974
Lufthansa	1122
Korean Air Lines	1276
United Parcel Service	3259
Federal Express	5135

Created from data provided by IATA and cited by the *Air Cargo Yearbook 2002*, p. 23.
(FTK = scheduled freight tonne-kilometre flown).

The US market provides a good illustration of air cargo taking market share from liner shipping. In dollar terms, US exports using ocean as a ratio to using air was 58:42 in 1990. By 2000, that ratio was 26:74. On the other hand, water transport was holding its own on the import side, with a ratio in 2000 of 63:37 (Journal of Commerce, 2001b). While some of that export air cargo growth can be ascribed to the rising value of goods at the top end, much of it is clearly attributable to the growth in product sectors like pharmaceuticals, electronics (office and telecom products in particular) and automotive parts. These products have a high value to weight ratio, tend to be more time-sensitive and favour air as a mode of transport. Furthermore, the just-in-time nature of time-managed manufacturing and the slimming of retail inventories to the barest necessary has enhanced the shift to air cargo overall; the consumer's desire for mass customised products requires the speed and agility that ocean transport is often incapable of delivering.

While shipping will never compete with air cargo in the emergency goods market because the consequential loss suffered by the delay of a critical input, be it assembly line parts or parts for human transplant, these are not products shipping targeted in the first place. The problem for shipping is that many high-value low-density manufactured goods are the core business of shipping lines and quite easily switched to air cargo. This is particularly true if just-in-time systems have reduced the shipment size to less than the weight restrictions faced by the air carrier. The existence of the air cargo option has the ability to keep transport prices for high value goods depressed; without sufficient cross-subsidisation potential, lower-value high-density product volumes will be of less interest to the shipping lines and the total volume traded will be less.

THE TRADER'S VIEW

Today's trading perspective can be traced to the post-war rise in consumer demand. By the 1960s, trade in manufactured goods had reached new heights. The dramatic increase in oil prices in the 1970s, however, brought unacceptable rises in interest rates. As a result, traders turned their attention to extracting inventory-carrying costs from the system. Those selling the goods sought new ways to ship that improved transit time and restructured their operations to diminish time-to-purchase at retail. They also began to reconsider where they produced goods, expanding their horizons to include servicing more than just domestic markets. The seeds of the globalisation of production and distribution were planted.

By now it should be evident that the future transport of manufactured goods by sea is dependent on a pro-marine modal split decision by traders. Clearly for some high-value, low-density products, the choice will continue to be air cargo. At the other end of the continuum, for awkward, bulky, and unconventional machinery, there will also be no choice but non-unitised ocean transport. In the middle lies the largest share of manufactured goods. For these, renewed focus on regional trade may encourage defection to surface modes. For the remainder, will the transport mode of choice be air or ocean container? The answer depends on which meets the customer's needs better.

Research has shown that traders' transport decisions are multi-criteria ones. They take into account product and customer requirements and specific attributes deemed desirable in making route- and product-specific decisions. Brooks (1985, 1990, 1995) examined this decision-making process for the liner industry, identifying a number of key purchase determinants for a liner company's services. The research series illustrated that different criteria can be identified for different customer segments but that these criteria are dynamic over time. As the industry evolved, emphasis on price diminished and other factors like transit time grew in importance. Brooks (1995) concluded that shippers, consignees, and freight forwarders all have significantly different decision criteria when it comes to choosing a carrier; these factors are also distinct geographically. Furthermore, some customers clearly buy a package of attributes for the rate paid while others evaluate individual attributes separately. Finally, Brooks (1995) confirmed the move away from transaction-specific carrier decisions towards relationship building and agreements with carriers and logistical service suppliers. The heavy use of professional logistics firms and the outsourcing of these functions are two directions traders moved towards in the 1990s, both serving to concentrate decision-making power in fewer hands.

The 2001 "peak" shipping season serves as a useful illustration of the ramifications of traders' decision-making on ocean carriers. The growth in trade in manufactured goods is partly driven by consumer demand for holiday gifts, particularly in North America and Europe. As large retailers tie up shipping capacity in the period of August to November each year on the Asia/North America eastbound and Asia/Europe westbound routes, the full impact on all manufactured goods trade capacity is felt. The 2001 peak season was particularly interesting to watch. A slowdown in the US economy through the early summer months meant many US retailers delayed placing orders for Christmas merchandise for as long as possible; this, coupled with increasing supply from vessel deliveries over the year, resulted in severe difficulties for carriers with capacity well in excess of demand. Add the tragedy of September 11, 2001, to the mix, and consumer demand plummeted. The impact on available ocean capacity and transport prices was immediate, devastating, and exacerbated further by those who took advantage of excess air cargo capacity to cover any shortfall. The economic slowdown could have been predicted, although not far enough in advance to address the additional vessel capacity being delivered, but the tragedy could not.

As was seen in Figure 2, the automotive sector is ranked fifth in terms of dollar value in world trade in manufactured goods. The sector is a heavy user of both maritime and air transport, and provides a second illustration of the impact of trader choices on shipping. A special segment, car carriers, services the delivery requirements for the global manufacturers of these finished goods. However, this niche sector is under increasing pressure on two fronts. First, while sales of finished cars have grown steadily in recent years, there has been a consistent move by the industry to locate production plants for newer models closer to the market. This raises questions about the future shipping capacity that will be needed to service the car transport demand (Journal of Commerce, 2001a), by both air and ocean. Second, in an economic downturn, there is a tendency for the industry to switch from air cargo or air charter to slower modes such as ocean and time-definite trucking for automotive parts (Journal of Commerce, 2001c). If the two trends are combined, it may be that ocean transport for the automotive sector loses market share to truck rather than air (or perhaps to the Fastship technology still being touted for the North Atlantic).

LOOKING FORWARD

Over the past decade, the nature of transport of manufactured goods has changed as many consumer products sectors have globalised. Manufacturers can buy components in many places, distribute somewhere else for assembly and the final products end up in a third location to be sold. Sometimes some component parts have been moved seven or eight times in the process of getting on the retail shelf or to the automotive showroom. According to Meersman and Van de Voorde (2001:69), declining real transport costs, increasing value of goods transported, a declining weight to volume ratio, along with diminishing telecommunications and computing costs all encourage a concentration of specialized production. However, companies producing products requiring customisation have moved the customisation location as close as possible to the end-market. All this means, in an era of supply chain management, that these multiple moves are dependent on continuous improvement activities, regular and frequent performance monitoring and re-evaluation of the network of manufacturing and distribution partners. With a global perspective, the conclusion for container shipping is one where large volume routes will continue to dominate but, at the level of the trader, the product mix and route will be less predictable. Direct delivery, via air cargo, is now the norm for many high value-to-weight segments, such as personal computers, particularly those where products are customised to order.

Furthermore, with the trend to mega-retailers in North America and Europe, and the use of fewer and fewer distribution points, the network for warehousing and distribution has become very dynamic. Companies now have the capacity for creating just-in-time systems of distribution and that has been accompanied by an intense focus on performance monitoring. Constant re-evaluation of the entire supply chain has mean frequent changes to the network as continuous performance improvements are sought. If system performance does not measure up, not only can manufacturers choose to re-route the traffic, but they may decide to relocate their production or assembly facilities, thus shifting trade flows. The mergers and acquisitions trend of the 1990s led to industry consolidation in many sectors; the result is fewer, larger production facilities and those "relocation" decisions are now in the hands of fewer and fewer "global" shippers.

In the developed world, consumer fascination with high technology products appears to continue to grow unabated. In the case of the telecom sector, the waiting time for the installation of a land-line is sufficiently long in many countries that mobile phones have leapfrogged the local network to become the de facto standard. However, recent stagnation in mobile phone sales for industry giant Nokia may be a harbinger of the maturing of this high volume trade.

Will world trade in manufactured goods continue to grow? There will be some growth attributed to rising population, and significant growth due to the expanding middle class in many of the world's more populated countries. As already noted, growth in container transport demand arising from the penetration of containerisation is less probable, as containerisation will soon reach maximum penetration except on low volume routes. Furthermore, the incursion of air cargo into traditional ocean shipment markets is likely as manufacturers continue to squeeze buffer time out of the transport chain and to favour time-definite transport over the vagaries of weather-influenced shipping. Most important is the issue of whether or not the growth of the past decade resulting from manufacturing supply chain management and national economic specialisation has run its course. Most industrial sectors have undergone a decade of consolidation; the accompanying strategic merger and acquisition activities were intended to prepare surviving companies for global reach in defined niches or global domination. It is likely that industrial restructuring is nearing completion, given the slowdown of international merger and acquisition activity experienced at the end of the 1990s (Brooks and Rosson, 2001).

CONCLUSIONS

In the months since the September 11 tragedy, economists have grappled with the impact of this event on global trade, national finances, transport companies, and industry sectors relying on strong consumer and business confidence. It is quite clear that some sectors, like the electronics and semiconductor industry, were in difficulty long before this date. The economic slowdown in the US led to reduced demand for transport before the chill on consumer confidence reached its peak in late September 2001. The recession had already spread into non-electronics products and tourism, and many manufacturing companies, faced with growing inventories, slowed production. Likewise, retailers, unsure of holiday demand, postponed peak season deliveries further depressing the demand for transport of manufactured goods and component parts. Most countries responded with lower interest rates intended to encourage consumer and business spending. Now everyone from the consumer to business to government is re-evaluating the situation in light of the greater economic uncertainty posed by the catastrophic events of that day. The recovery of trade in manufactured goods will depend in large measure on how quickly the US, and consequently its trading partners, move from the current state of introspection and, once again, encourage trade growth. The International Monetary Fund (2001:66) notes that the situation remains subject to considerable uncertainty but argues that completion of the inventory corrections begun in early 2001 will improve demand and that the stronger economic fundamentals of many countries will give them greater resiliency in dealing with this external shock. Whether ocean or air transport gains remains to be seen.

ENDNOTES

1. The Organisation for Economic Co-operation and Development is a multilateral grouping of developed economies comprising the countries of Western Europe, North America, Australia, New Zealand, Japan and more recently Korea, Mexico and some of the Eastern European economies.

REFERENCES

Air Cargo Yearbook 2002 (London, Air Transport Publications Limited).
Anderson, D.L. (1983): "Your Company's Logistic Management: An Asset or a Liability?", *Transportation Review*, Winter, pp. 111–125.
Anonymous (1999): "Northwest Restructures Cargo Rates", *Transportation and Distribution*, 40, 3, p. 7.
Boeing (2000): *World Air Cargo Forecast 2000/01*, Seattle: Boeing Commercial Airplanes Group.
Brooks, Mary R. (1985): "An Alternative Theoretical Approach to the Evaluation of Liner Shipping, Part II. Choice Criteria", *Maritime Policy and Management*, 12, 2, pp. 145–155.
Brooks, Mary R. (1990): "Ocean Carrier Selection Criteria in a New Environment", *The Logistics and Transportation Review*, 26, 4, pp. 339–356.
Brooks, Mary R. (1995): "Understanding the Ocean Container Carrier Market—A Seven Country Study", *Maritime Policy and Management*, 22, 1, pp. 39–50.
Brooks, Mary R. (2001): "NAFTA and Transportation: A Canadian Scorecard", *Transportation Research Record 1763*, pp. 35–41.
Brooks, Mary R. and Philip J. Rosson (2001): "Mergers & Acquisitions: The Corporate Visual Identity Dilemma", Douglas Mackay Lecture Series, Dalhousie University, November 30.

Diamond, D. and N. Spence (1989): *Infrastructure and Industrial Costs in British Industry* (London, Her Majesty's Stationery Office).
Dibner, Brent (1993): "Shortsea Shipping in Europe and the Americas: Status and Prospects", *European Shortsea Shipping: Proceedings from the First European Research Roundtable Conference on Shortsea Shipping*, N. Wijnolst, C. Peeters and P. Liebman (eds.) (London, Lloyd's of London Press), pp. 289–300.
Foster, Thomas A. (1999): "Air Freight Weathers the Storm", *Logistics Management and Distribution Report*, 38,5, pp. 55–60.
International Air Transport Association (2002): *Freight Forecast 2001-2005 Special Interim Edition*, 19 March. (*www.iata.org*)
International Monetary Fund (2001): *World Economic Outlook: The Global Economy After September 11*, Washington, DC: International Monetary Fund, December. (*www.imf.org*)
Jennings, E. (1980): *Cargoes: A Centenary Story of the Far Eastern Freight Conference* (Singapore, Meridian Communications (South-east Asia) Pte Ltd).
Journal of Commerce (2001a): "Keeping an Even Keel", *Journal of Commerce Week*, July 16-22, pp. 20–24.
Journal of Commerce (2001b): "Air Over Water", *Journal of Commerce Week*, August 20–26, p. 15.
Journal of Commerce (2001c): "No Longer Flying High", *Journal of Commerce Week*, September 3–9, pp. 16–17.
Journal of Commerce (2001d): "Four Years, Many Changes", *Journal of Commerce Week*, September 3–9, p. 26.
Meersman, Hilde and Eddy Van de Voorde (2001): "International Logistics: A Continuous Search for Competitiveness", *Handbook of Logistics and Supply Chain Management*, A.M. Brewer, K.J. Button and D.A. Hensher (eds.) (Oxford, Pergamon Press), pp. 61–77.
NTA (1992): *An Integrated and Competitive Transportation System: Meeting Shipper and Traveller Needs* (Ottawa, National Transportation Agency of Canada), March.
Putzger, Ian (2001): "It's All About Speed", *Traffic World*, 265, 40, L16–18.
Sclar, M.L. and D.L. Blond (1991): "Air Cargo vs. Sea Cargo Trends", DRI/McGraw-Hill Conference *World Sea Trade Outlook*, London, 25 September.
Statistics Canada (2001): *Exports Merchandise Trade 2000* (65-202), Ottawa: Statistics Canada
Statistics Canada (2001): *Imports Merchandise Trade 2000* (65-203), Ottawa: Statistics Canada
TACA (2001): *Submission of the Trans-Atlantic Conference Agreement ("TACA") Before the Organisation for Economic Cooperation and Development in the Matter of OECD Discussion Paper on Regulatory Reform in International Maritime Transport* (*www.oecd.org*).
UNCTAD (1987): *Review of Maritime Transport 1986* (New York, United Nations).
UNCTAD (2002): *Review of Maritime Transport 2001* (New York, United Nations).
Van Willigenburg, J. R. and S. Hollander (1993): "Coastal Shipping Opportunities in a Changing Market", *European Shortsea Shipping: Proceedings from the First European Research Roundtable Conference on Shortsea Shipping*, N. Wijnolst, C. Peeters and P. Liebman (eds.) (London, Lloyd's of London Press), pp. 184–192.
World Trade Organization (2002): *International Trade Statistics 2001*, *www.wto.org/english/res_e/statis_e/its2001_e/its2001_overview_e.htm*
Zachial, Manfred (1993): "Assessment of Land/Sea Feeder Traffic Flows in Europe", *European Shortsea Shipping: Proceedings from the First European Research Roundtable Conference on Shortsea Shipping*, N. Wijnolst, C. Peeters and P. Liebman (eds.) (London, Lloyd's of London Press), pp. 316–327.

CHAPTER 6

ENERGY ECONOMICS AND TRADE

Michael Tamvakis
City University Cass Business School, City of London, UK.
E-mail: *m.tamvakis@city.ac.uk*

1. INTRODUCTION

It is a well known fact that the international maritime industry is driven by the movement of goods and people. Maritime economists have long established that the demand for shipping services is one derived from the demand for international trade and awareness of what drives the latter is the aim of this chapter.

Within the space and scope of the next few pages, it is impossible to encompass all trades and factors that affect demand for maritime services. We will focus, instead, on the economics and major trade patterns of the most important commodity group, energy, which encompasses three very important commodities: crude oil and products, gas and coal.

2. ENERGY

2.1 Demand for energy

Energy is what drives modern economic development and for the last couple of centuries at least, human societies have relied on hydrocarbons for the supply of that energy. Despite continuous research and development into renewable, sustainable and ecologically friendly energy resources, we very much rely on three major forms of hydrocarbons – oil, coal and gas – for effectively 90% of the world's primary energy consumption (see Figure 1).

In principle, a country's economy becomes more demanding in raw materials and energy resources, as it grows and then stabilises its economic development. On an aggregate basis, it is reasonable to assume that energy consumption is directly related to the level of gross domestic product (GDP). Figure 2 shows the development of world GDP and primary energy consumption since 1974. Notice the fundamental change in the relationship between the two indices after 1980. For comparison, the price of oil is also plotted on the same chart, and highlights the effect of a major price shock on energy consumption.

The notion of a straightforward relationship between energy consumption and GDP is quite appealing, but rather simplistic. One has to look at the disaggregated picture of energy consumption to get a more accurate idea of the underlying demand parameters. Primary energy consumption is usually classified into four broad categories: domestic or residential; industrial; transport;

106   INTERNATIONAL SEABORNE TRADE

Figure 1: World primary energy production

Source: BP Statistical Review of World Energy, 2000.

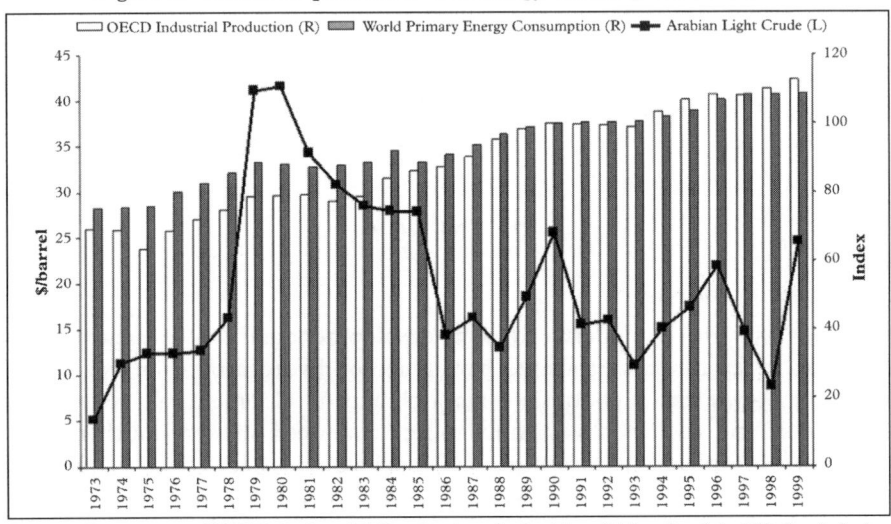

Figure 2: Industrial production and energy consumption in OECD

Source: Datastream (OECD Industrial Production & Arabian Light Crude); BP Statistical Review of World Energy (World Primary Energy Consumption).

and a fourth category encompassing all other uses that are not covered by the aforementioned three. Figure 3 shows an example of energy usage in OECD countries in 1996.

2.1.1 Residential consumption

Like for any other good, demand for energy depends on the price of the commodity and the total disposable income of households. Any change in the price of the commodity will affect the quantity purchased by consumers. For example, if the price of oil falls, its consumption is expected to increase *ceteris paribus*. The total change in consumption is usually split between the *income* and the

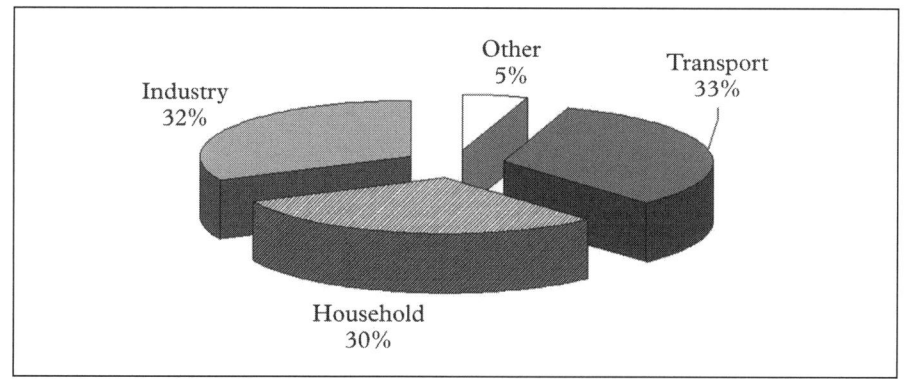

Figure 3: Energy consumption by sector

[Pie chart showing: Industry 32%, Other 5%, Transport 33%, Household 30%]

Source: IEA, World Energy Outlook, 1996.

substitution effects. The first is attributed to the fact that with the new, lower price the same amount of income will buy more units of the commodity; the second effect is due to the switch from other, more expensive substitutes to the lower-priced commodity.

When analysing the demand for specific energy commodities, it is always useful to know their responsiveness to changes in their own price, changes in disposable income and changes in the price of substitutes. This responsiveness is measured by the own price – or demand – elasticity, the income elasticity, and the cross-price elasticity. The usefulness of these three parameters was eminently demonstrated during the two oil price shocks in 1973 and 1979. While the first shock put pressure on household incomes, which had to accommodate a larger expenditure for energy, it did not tamper demand for oil substantially. This was not the case with the second oil price shock, however, when income and price elasticities of oil experienced a structural change and led to a dramatically reduced demand for oil.

2.1.2 Industrial consumption

The production cost of an industrial process depends – in the short to medium term – on the cost of its inputs and a set of fixed costs; in the long term, of course, all costs are variable. The production cost function can be formally written as $C = f(X_1 \ldots X_n, E, FC)$, where $X_1 \ldots X_n$ are production inputs, E is energy and FC is fixed cost. This function represents a slight deviation from the usual norm of depicting production costs as a function of capital and labour, and is more suitable for our needs.

The total demand for industrial energy can be viewed as an aggregation of all production cost functions like the one given above. The effects of price changes on energy demand will depend on the *rate of technical substitution*, which represents the rate at which one input of production can be replaced by another, in order to achieve the same cost.

In practical terms the rate of technical substitution shows how easily energy can be replaced by other input factors, and how easily different sources of energy can substitute one another in the same production process. Once again, a suitable example can be taken from the two oil price crises. The first price shock took industry by surprise, as no cost-effective alternatives to oil were available. The second shock, however, came after considerable restructuring in energy usage and efficiency had been implemented, with the result that total energy requirements were reduced and alternative sources of energy – predominantly coal, but also natural gas and nuclear power – replaced oil.

2.1.3 Transport consumption

Energy consumption in transport is dominated by oil, which displaced coal earlier or later in the history of different transport means. In the car industry, for example, gasoline was used since the very beginning, as it was the most appropriate fuel for the internal combustion engine. At sea, coal was dominant until after the end of the first World War, but was rapidly replaced by oil afterwards. On land, coal persisted slightly more as a source of energy for locomotives, but eventually had to give in to oil's undisputed superiority.

Today, oil is used in transport almost exclusively; perhaps the only notable exception is that of Brazil, which has promoted the extensive use of gasohol, and a few other countries that promote the use of natural gas.

Because oil has virtually no – commercially viable – substitutes in transport, demand for it depends very much on income and efficiency of use. The latter is probably more important, as is shown in Figure 4, which graphs the development of passenger car efficiency in the United States. Three indicators are used: the rate of fuel consumption expressed in miles per gallon; the mileage expressed in miles per car, which effectively shows the average use of cars; and the average fuel consumption expressed in gallons per car. As one can see, mileage was not affected substantially; it was the marked increase in fuel efficiency that accounted for the decrease in fuel consumption per car.

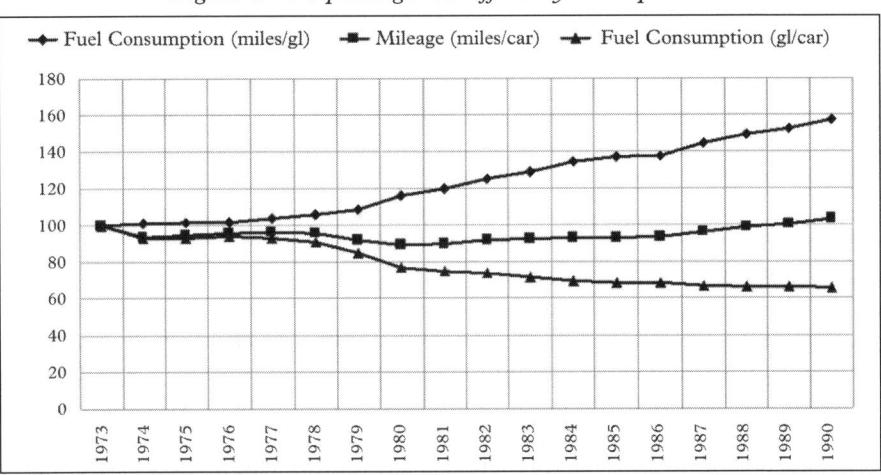

Figure 4: US passenger car efficiency development

Source: IEA, World Energy Outlook, 1996.

2.1.4 Other consumption

This category encompasses all the remaining sectors of the economy, primarily energy consumption for agricultural use. This category is by no means small; as one can see in Figure 3, it accounted for almost 5% of energy consumption in the whole of OECD. Parameters affecting this segment of consumption include fuel efficiency and the degree of mechanisation of agriculture.

2.2 Supply of energy

Energy can be generated by both exhaustible and renewable sources. Although the latter have amassed considerable scientific attention and certainly have ample potential, currently they cannot be considered as serious alternatives to exhaustible resources, with the exception of hydroelectric power, perhaps. In this chapter we are going to concentrate on three of the most important energy commodities: oil and its products; natural gas; and, later on, coal.

Like other minerals, energy commodities fall in the category of exhaustible resources. Available reserves, rates of extraction and economic rents are some of the parameters governing the usage of exhaustible resources. The theory behind this was explored as early as 1929 by Hotelling who built a basic economic framework for the exploitation of non-renewable natural resources.

Basic economic theory anticipates that each additional unit (the "marginal" unit) of a natural resource will be extracted as long as the economic cost of extraction – which includes marginal[1] cost and user[2] cost – is lower or equal to the price[3] paid for the resource plus the marginal utility of present consumption.[4] Like in most production processes, extractive firms benefit initially from increasing returns to scale, then their average total cost curve stays flat for some time after reaching the minimum efficient scale, and if they decide to increase output further they are usually faced with decreasing returns to scale. In the long-run, production tends to stabilise along the bottom of their long-run average total cost curve.

The theory, as it stands, implies that high-cost producers – which usually also have limited reserves – should be the first to be squeezed out of the market when energy prices fall and operating costs are not covered. It also implies that large low-cost producers should be relatively immune to price downswings, and continue to produce under all – but the most extreme – market conditions.

Alas, real life is not as clear-cut as this model suggests. To take yet another example from the oil industry; although Gulf OPEC countries are indisputably the lowest-cost producers, it is high-cost producers that seem to be operating at full capacity, while low-cost competitors seem to play the role of "swing" producer balancing demand and supply.

The picture becomes even more complicated when government economic policies are taken into account. Energy supplies are of strategic importance to every government world-wide. If they are in abundance, they will be used to cover domestic needs and the balance will probably be exported; if they are in short supply, the government will resort to imports and a certain amount of stockpiling for security reasons. If security of supplies is a major issue on the

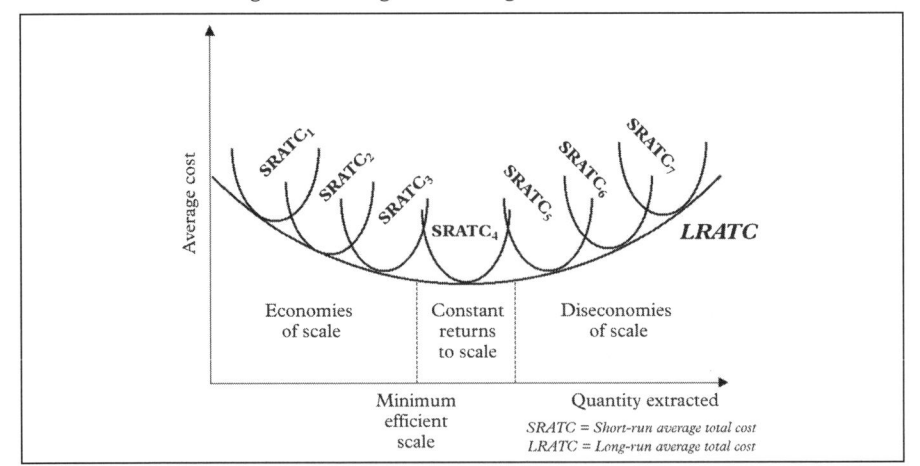

Figure 5: Long-run average total cost curve

[Figure 5: Long-run average total cost curve showing SRATC₁ through SRATC₇ curves forming the LRATC envelope, with regions labeled Economies of scale, Constant returns to scale, and Diseconomies of scale. The x-axis is Quantity extracted with Minimum efficient scale marked; y-axis is Average cost. SRATC = Short-run average total cost; LRATC = Long-run average total cost]

energy agenda, demand will tend to be biased towards certain (perhaps low-cost) producers, and "secure" (perhaps high-cost) suppliers will realise this and step up their production. Finally, if financial flows from exports and/or export taxes are considered as well, national fiscal and monetary policies may distort the picture even further.

In any project for the extraction of mineral resources there are three main stages: exploration, development, and production. Exploration may last a few years, until proper geological surveys point with high probability to the existence of reserves. Several exploratory wells/shafts may have to be drilled in order to assess the quality and extent of the deposits. Costs at this stage can be substantial and are sunk. The development stage involves extensive drilling in the case of oil and gas, and construction of an open pit or underground mine in the case of coal. Again, costs at this stage are sunk, and further costs might have to be incurred at later stages of a project, in order to improve and/or extend capacity.

At the production stage, most of the costs are operating costs, which tend to increase as reserves are being depleted and more effort is required to extract them. This is particularly true for coal, especially when underground mining is the method of production.

Energy projects use capital quite intensively and embody a substantial amount of risk. Even when adequate reserves are found, the high rate of discount applied to such projects makes the extraction of the commodity more desirable sooner rather than later. This argument is often used to explain the intensive exploitation of high-cost oil reserves like the ones in Alaska or the North Sea, in order to maximise oil recovery as quickly as possible.

Another important characteristic of the energy sector – and the mineral sector in general – is the large extent of heterogeneity in production costs. Depending on the geomorphy of the field and local climatic conditions costs can vary considerably from one region to the next. In the oil sector, for instance, capital expenditure for field development may range from "low-cost" to "frontier areas".

3. OIL

With a share of 40% in world primary energy consumption, oil is currently the leading energy commodity, and has been so for at least the past three decades. Oil reserves currently amount to just over one trillion barrels, over half of which are located in the Middle East. Latin America is the second largest reserve holder, with deposits mainly in Mexico and Venezuela. The FSU is also rich in oil reserves, although gas is the most abundant energy resource there.

What is remarkable about the oil sector is its imbalance in terms of reserves. It has to be noted, however, that production by different countries has never been proportional to their reserves, as technology, investment capital, and finance are not freely available to all producers, and political conditions have often distorted economic principles of production.

3.1 Geology and extraction[5]

Oil is one of a number of hydrocarbon compounds that can be found in the earth's crust. In fact four-fifths of the world's sedimentary basins provide suitable geological conditions for the formation of crude oil. On several occasions, parts of the earth's crust move against each other to form an *anticline*, which creates a *reservoir* of impervious rock, where organic material is trapped and broken down by enzymes over a period of several million years. A reservoir usually contains several oil *fields*, some of them grouped together in *provinces*. The organic material contained in the fields is a mixture of oil, water and gas. Oil floats on top of the water, while gas provides pressure in the field, which is invaluable for the extraction of the precious fuel.

Oil exploration is the part of the oil industry that has always caught the imagination of the masses, as it contained a huge element of risk, but offering the possibility of extremely good returns. Modern oil exploration does not rely that much on luck any more. A number of scientific methods are used for the location of possible oil reservoirs and the estimation of their reserves. These are usually grouped in three main categories: geophysical analyses; geophysical surveys; and drilling and well logging.

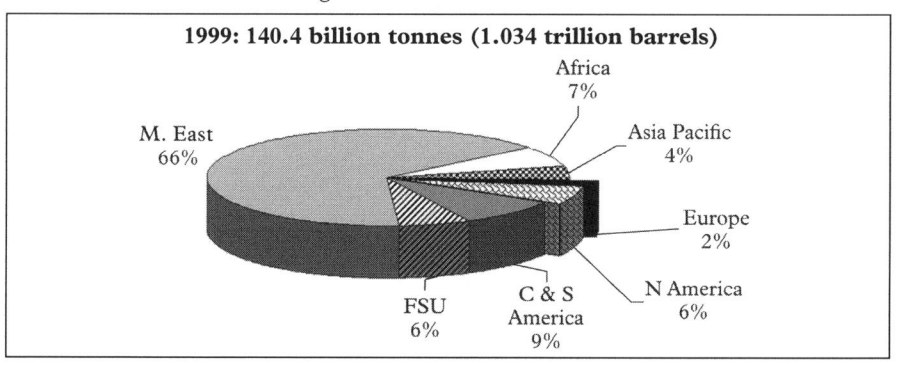

Figure 6: Proven oil reserves

1999: 140.4 billion tonnes (1.034 trillion barrels)

- M. East 66%
- Africa 7%
- Asia Pacific 4%
- Europe 2%
- N America 6%
- C & S America 9%
- FSU 6%

Source: BP Statistical Review of World Energy, 2000.

Geological analysis includes a number of alternative – and often complementary – methods, ranging from traditional field geology (examining surface rocks), to the use of orbiting satellites. Geochemical analysis is also used, in order to establish the presence of suitable material for the formation of oil deposits. The aim of all the above techniques, is to understand the geological structure and history of an area, and decide whether it is worthwhile to spend more money on exploring it.

The main geophysical technique used nowadays is the seismic survey, although gravimetric and magnetic surveys can also be used to identify underlying structures that are possibly oil-bearing. Seismic surveys involve the artificial generation of shock waves, using a variety of techniques, like controlled explosions, dropping of weights and vibration generators. The aim is to record the reflections of those waves by the various geological strata. The data are recorded by geophones, which are similar to seismographs, and then transmitted and recorded on tape.

The *recording* stage is followed by the *processing* of the data collected, which involves their enhancement by computers. Finally, the results are *interpreted* by experts, who build an image of the underground formations and the likely location of deposits. All three stages (recording, processing and interpretation) have been immensely improved by the use of enhanced computer technology. The latter has allowed the advance from 2D to 3D seismic surveys, which use a lot more signal recorders and provide a far more accurate picture of underground formations. A traditional 2D seismic survey, until a few years ago, was shot along individual lines, at varying distances, producing "pictures" of vertical sections of the underground formations. A 3D seismic survey, on the other hand, is shot in a closely spaced grid pattern – like the one reproduced in Figure 7 – and gives a complete, more accurate, picture of the subsurface.

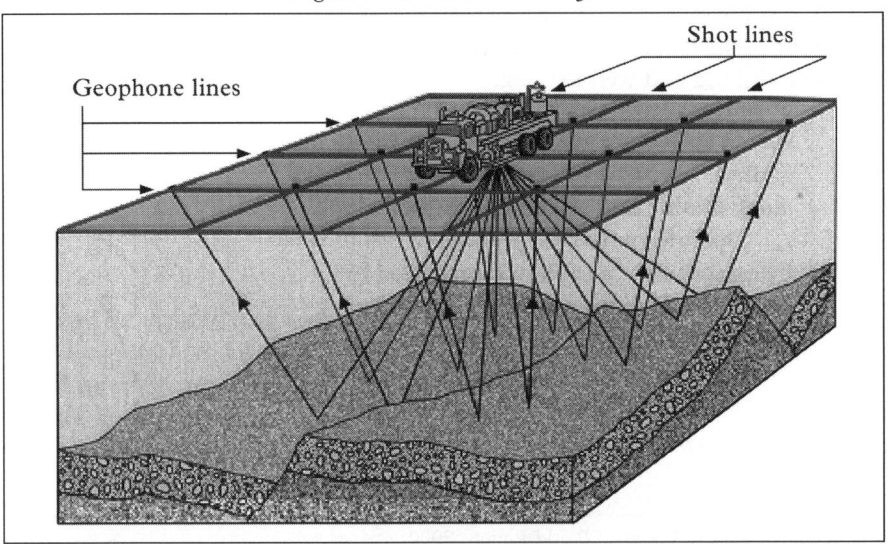

Figure 7: 3D seismic survey

The next stage in oil exploration is well drilling. To collect more accurate survey data, *boreholes* are drilled on top of the area suspected to contain oil reserves. Many of these *wildcat* drills end up as dry holes. The purpose of the boreholes is not only to extract the oil. For the purposes of *well logging*, rock cuttings, core samples and geophysical data are extracted from boreholes, giving scientists an idea of the local geological structure and, if any oil does exist, the history, nature and extent of the reservoir.

The boreholes that are successful eventually become oil *wells*. To date, there are over 30,000 known oil wells. Of these, 330 produce just over 50% of the world's oil output, while just 17 of them produce just over 30% of the same. Some of the wells are classified as giants – each holding over 0.5 billion barrels of reserves – while the biggest of wells are also known as *elephants*. The largest of all, Ghawar, is located in Saudi Arabia, and is estimated to hold over 83 billion barrels of oil reserves.

The discovery of oil deposits and the drilling of oil producing wells is not, of course, the end of the story. The entire production process has to be organised properly. This involves a detailed reservoir management plan; the well layout and design; design of production and evacuation facilities; and an implementation schedule covering the drilling of wells and construction and installation of facilities.

The next step is to ensure that oil can be extracted in the most efficient way. The reservoir's own pressure is usually sufficient, at least initially, to drive the oil or gas to the surface. When recovery levels are low, however, secondary recovery enhancements can be used, whereby the reservoir's natural drive is supplemented with the injection of water or gas. Finally, where both natural drive and secondary recovery are not producing the desired production levels,

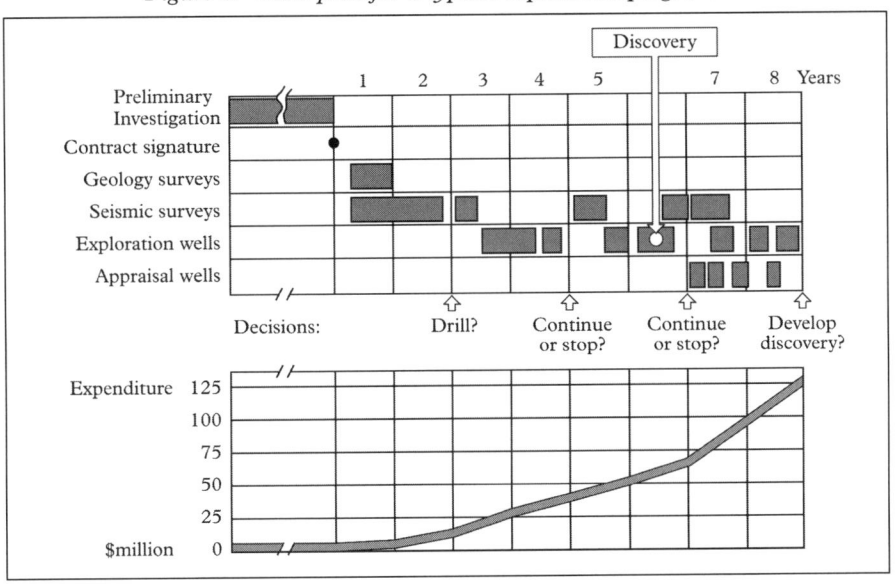

Figure 8: Time plan for a typical exploration programme

enhanced oil recovery (EOR) methods can be used. These techniques are considerably more expensive and must be justified by oil market conditions. EOR methods include: the heating of oil by injecting hot water and/or steam, in order to increase its viscosity and flow; mixture of oil with a suitable gas or liquid solvent to reduce or eliminate residual oil trapped in the displacement process; and use of chemical additives, which modify the properties of the water that displaces the oil and which change the way water and oil flow through the reservoir rock.

Oil is not the only fuel produced by oil wells. Natural gas liquids (NGLs) are by-products of oil extraction. NGLs include: a type of light oil called *natural gasoline*; a mixture of petroleum – or "wet" – gases, like butane, propane and ethane; and sometimes natural – or "dry" – gas, which is methane.

There are also 'non-conventional' sources of oil. These include: kerogen, which consists of hydrocarbons not yet developed into oil; tar sands, which are impregnated with oil; and synthetic petroleum, which can be produced – rather expensively – from coal.

3.2 Physical characteristics

Oil has three physical characteristics which have significant economic importance. The first one is specific gravity. Crude oils are classified as: light, or paraffinic; medium, or mixed-base; and heavy, or asphaltic. Light crudes have lower specific gravity and are easier to refine. Specific gravity is measured in 'degrees API', which were introduced by the American Petroleum Institute. The lighter the oil, the more degrees API attributed to it. The baseline is the specific gravity of water, which is 10° API. Crudes below 22° API are considered heavy, while those above 40° API are considered light.

The second characteristic is viscosity, which is sometimes measured in centistokes. The less centistokes, the more viscous the crude, and the easier it is to burn. Two common grades of crude oil, typically used for vessel bunkers, have viscosities of 180 CST (intermediate fuel oil - IFO) and 380 CST (heavy fuel oil – HFO).

Finally, a crude's quality also depends on its content in sulphur. Crudes with high sulphur content are known as "sour" crudes, while the rest are known as "sweet".

3.3 Reserves

As with any non-renewable natural resource, it is important to be able to establish the stock of reserves available for future extraction. The total reserves world-wide are known as *ultimate* reserves, but their estimation is of little practical use. It is more interesting to estimate the amount of *oil-in-place*, which is an indication of recoverable reserves. Reserves, for which there is conservatively reasonable certainty of production under existing economic and operational conditions, are called *proved* reserves. In contrast, *probable* reserves are those whose production would be achievable as a result of further exploration and development, or changed economic and operating conditions.

Frequently, the *reserves:production ratio* is used as an indicator of the future life of existing reserves. The ratio shows the number of years that reserves will last, if production continues at the current rate. The R:P ratio, however, only offers a view of the future, extrapolated from the present, and assuming that technology and prices remain unchanged.

3.4 Trade in Crude Oil

From a total of nearly 3,500 million tons (about 74 million barrels per day) of crude oil and distillates produced in 2000, over 2,000 million tons (over 40 million barrels per day) were traded internationally. Of these, over 75% was carried by sea. Throughout oil's turbulent history, international trade has played an important role. In fact, one of the biggest integrated oil companies – Royal Dutch Shell – started life as a trade and transport company.

The fortunes of the tanker market have been driven by the economics and politics of the oil market. It makes sense, therefore, to understand the development and current situation of international trade in crude oil and its products.

3.4.1 Initially: Trade in products

Trade in oil was initiated from the early days of the industry, near the end of the 19th century. Before the First World War, international trade was almost exclusively in products. Carrying crude was quite uneconomical, due to its low value in comparison with its transport cost. Refineries were also located at the production sites, so that the final products only were shipped to the end-users. Most of the world trade in oil products was structured around the United States, which was the leading producer and exporter of oil. Standard Oil had a strong foothold in Europe and controlled most of the fleet carrying its oil from the United States. In Europe, in the meantime, Russian production became exportable with the completion of the trans-Caucasian railway. Subsequently, Russia dominated the markets of the Near East and a small share of the European market. The Bolshevik revolution in 1917 disrupted Russian output, but both production and exports were resumed in 1920.

At about the same time, crude oil started being traded internationally, even though it was carried on short-haul routes. The main crude oil exporters were Mexico and later Venezuela, with United States being the recipient. With the gradual expansion of Middle East and Southeast Asian oil production, crude oil trade increased in importance; there was little scope for local refining, and the majority of refining capacity was now located in the consuming markets.

World oil production and exports from 1939 to 1945 reflected very much the energy needs of the Second World War. Oil for the Allied Forces was flowing in from the United States with increasing difficulty, due to the submarine war. On the other hand, the Allies managed to secure control over the oil reserves of the Middle East, whose contribution in oil production increased substantially during the war. The military importance of the area was highlighted towards the end of the war, with the construction of the big oil refinery and terminal in Ras Tanura.

3.4.2 Switch to Crude Oil Trade

After the end of the Second World War, Europe had increased needs for energy resources in order to proceed with its reconstruction. A large part of those needs were covered by the Middle East, which became the world's leading oil exporting region, especially after production of the large Kuwaiti fields came in line. During the same period, the United States turned into a net oil importer, with most of its imports coming from Venezuela, although some crude imports had already originated from the Middle East in the late 1940s. The old adversary of the US in the European market, Soviet Union, resumed exports in the late 1940s, with most of them being directed to other countries in the communist bloc.

At the same time as Europe, Japan also embarked on its reconstruction programme. With energy resources virtually non-existent domestically, Japan had to turn to oil imports, in order to fuel its rapidly growing economy. In its quest to secure crude oil supplies, Japan turned initially to Indonesia (the former Netherlands East Indies), and even the Soviet Union. As Middle East continued its rally to world domination of oil production, the Japanese eventually entered agreements with both Saudi Arabia and Kuwait, in the late 1950s. The Japanese involvement in the Middle East was very low-profile from the beginning; even their exploration company was discreetly named "Arabian Oil Company". Their venture in the Middle East provided the Japanese with an independent – i.e., non-oil major – source of oil, supplying about 15% of their needs.[6]

The major characteristic of this period (roughly between 1945 and 1960) was the substantial increase of international movements of oil, and the rising in importance of the trade in crude oil. The period, however, was not devoid of turmoil. In 1956 the Suez Canal was closed, causing a major disruption in the trade and distribution of crude oil from the Middle East, and sending the tanker market sky-high overnight. Although the effects were not lasting, the whole incident amply demonstrated the role politics were going to play in the post-war order in the oil industry.

3.4.3 Rise and rise of the Middle East

The 1960s was an era of growth: of oil trade, and crude oil in particular; of the export expansion of the Middle East; and of the size of tankers used to carry oil internationally. Western Europe, Japan and the United States experienced high levels of growth during the decade, with a resultant augmentation of their energy requirements.

At the same time, refinery capacity and throughputs increased immensely in all the major importing regions. Within the span of 10 years, world refining throughputs increased from 21,000 bpd to almost 45,000 bpd. Most were accounted for by West Europe and Japan. Within a decade, from 1960 to 1970, the volume of crude oil exports almost tripled, from just over 9 Mbpd to just over 25 Mbpd. In both cases, the Middle East accounted for about half of the world's crude oil exports, half of which were directed to Western Europe.

At the same time, Venezuela also became a prominent crude oil supplier, with total exports in 1970 amounting to just under 3.5 Mbpd, two-thirds of which were exported to the United States. The vision of Pérez Alfonso, the Venezuelan Minister of Mines and Hydrocarbons back in the late 1950s, of oil producing countries being able to command higher rents for their natural resources, could now become a reality; the economic fundamentals were in place at the end of the decade. The three first years of the 1970s, however, were anything but ominous: GDP growth rates were buoyant, industrial production and energy production had strong forecasts attached to them, and the future of crude oil trade looked better than ever. The rush of shipowners to order new tanker tonnage could only be compared to the oil rush of the 1860s in Pennsylvania; the anti-climax would be equally harsh.

3.4.4 Turbulent years

While world economic growth had been providing the necessary impetus for an upward movement of oil prices, increasing supply from old and new producers prevented the possibility of any demand squeeze. In fact, during the 1960s, prices had been rather slack and oil companies had repeatedly readjusted their posted prices downwards, much to the frustration of host governments, who saw their oil revenues being undercut.

The beginning of the 1970s, however, witnessed a demand rally – particularly in the United States, with a combined fall in domestic production and a surge in demand. As a result, crude oil import requirements had to be revised upwards and had to be covered mostly by the Middle East.

Despite the tight demand/supply balance, the oil price regime did not look particularly threatened. It was a political event once again – the Yom Kippur War, and the subsequent Arab oil embargo on exports to the US – that created a tremendous price rally, and gave oil producers the chance to test their strength. The result was an approximately fivefold increase of the price of crude oil, which jumped from about $2/bbl to over $15/bbl, with some extreme cases of bids over $20.

The new developments took everyone by surprise, including oil producers themselves, but there was no question of curtailing oil consumption. Even the embargo itself did not last for long. The blacklisted countries soon started procuring their crude oil requirements from other countries importing from the Middle East. It was now evident that the new price levels were there to stay.

The interruption of world economic growth, because of the first oil price shock, was quite short-lived. Economic growth resumed in 1974, although at lower levels; so did oil consumption and the demand for oil imports. In fact, during the 1970s dependence on the Middle East increased.

In 1974 the United States procured some 16.7% of its total imports from the area; in 1978 that proportion had gone up to 28%. In a similar fashion, in 1978, W.Europe imported about 8.7 Mbpd of crude oil from the Middle East, representing some 66.3% of its total oil imports that year. For comparison, the contribution of the Middle East in world oil exports for 1978 was about 19.7 Mbpd, or approximately 58%.

Middle East, of course, was not the only OPEC producer. Venezuela had a substantial share of the American market, while Indonesia was an important oil supplier to the Japanese market. In the western world there were no substantial oil producers, or at least not large enough to substitute the Middle East as a prime source of oil imports. USSR was a substantial producer and exporter, although not to the American market.

The increase in oil prices, however, was not detrimental to the western world only. Awareness about the security of oil supplies became widespread, resulting in the foundation of the International Energy Agency by the country-members of the OECD. At the same time, oil's high price provided the incentive for oil exploration in "politically safe" regions, the most notable being the North Sea.

Although the existence of oil reserves in the North Sea was known since the 1960s, their exploitation was uneconomical. But with an international oil price high enough to cover the increased costs of offshore oil exploration, crude production in the North Sea covered a substantial part of the consumption requirements of the producing countries (UK, Norway, Netherlands and Denmark) and allowed modest exports.

In the United States, oil companies had been exploring in Alaska since the late 1960s, following the Suez Canal crisis in 1956. Their attempts had been largely unsuccessful, until Boxing Day 1967, when the ARCO-Humble venture struck a massive oil field at Prudhoe Bay. A few more drills confirmed that the deposit was of world class; in fact it ranked third, behind Saudi Arabia's Ghawar and Kuwait's Burgan. Despite the massive discovery, plans to extract the crude and transport it to the mainland were delayed for the remaining of the 1960s. The cost of extracting the oil under arctic weather conditions was not economically justifiable and, what was more, the whole plan stumbled on protests by environmental groups opposing any plans for the construction of a Trans-Alaskan pipeline, which would damage irreparably the arctic flora and fauna. After the rude awakening of the first oil shock, most environmental considerations were brushed aside and the Alaskan project progressed at a much faster pace. Proposals for alternative pipeline routes through Canada had been considered but, in the end, the pipeline from Prudhoe Bay to Valdez was favoured.

During the 1970s, the new jigsaw of the world energy markets was being painstakingly put together. OPEC countries rose to prominence, with the Middle East at the forefront. Western producers sought new secure sources of oil and, at the same time, stability in their relationship with the Middle East. The USSR edged its way into the international oil market, taking advantage of the high prices to replenish its hard currency reserves. High energy consumption and broad dependence on oil, however, meant increased production costs and inevitable inflationary pressures. In fact, most of the oil producers' incomes were being severely eroded by the explosive world inflation of the late 1970s. The bubble was again ready to burst; the Iranian Revolution kindly obliged.

3.4.5 OPEC in turmoil

The reaction to the second oil price shock was markedly different from that to the first. A number of important adjustments changed the structure of energy

consumption. More specifically:
- Renewed emphasis was put on energy conservation and oil substitution, with the result that the non-communist world's oil consumption went into steady decline after 1979.
- There was a switch to politically safer sources of oil, boosting the production of non-OPEC countries, while dependence on OPEC oil fell considerably during the first half of the 1980s.
- The switch to new supply sources resulted in higher utilisation of heavier and sourer crudes; this urged many refiners to upgrade an increasing proportion of their facilities in order to improve the yield of lighter products from heavier crudes.

The new price increase boosted immensely the fortunes of new, high-cost suppliers, like the UK, Alaska and Canada. In the UK alone, a brand new industry was created almost overnight, giving a tremendous boost to the local and national economies. The combination of changed demand and supply patterns resulted in a radical structural readjustment of the international oil trade. The share of OPEC in oil production fell by 45% between 1979 and 1985, while that of non-OPEC producers increased by 26% in the same period. The share of Middle East in world oil trade fell from 58.3% in 1978, to 42.5% in 1983; the US alone decreased its imports from the Middle East and West Africa by almost 75%, although its imports from Venezuela fell by less than 20%.

3.4.6 Balance restored

Faced with decreasing world demand for oil, and increasing competition from non-OPEC producers, the OPEC countries attempted to redress market conditions by reducing official prices, and by introducing quotas with a view to establishing some order among member countries. Following the radical change of the fortunes of OPEC producers, many of them had to compete in order to secure market share, thus resorting to price undercutting all too often. With tension among OPEC members increasing, due to poor market conditions, Saudi Arabia played the role of the "swing" producer, decreasing its production to accommodate the needs of other members. In the end, however, even the Saudis could not restore order in OPEC circles, and resorted themselves to quoting netback prices, pulling world oil markets to prices around $10/bbl.

The new situation was not desirable for oil producers, OPEC and non-OPEC alike. Market prices eventually recovered in 1987, and the new level of about $15-$18/bbl made oil popular once more, and led to a steady growth of oil imports, from about 24.5 Mbpd in 1985, to 40 Mbpd in 1998. In terms of price fluctuations, of course, the situation remained as "interesting" as ever. For most of the 1990s, the price fluctuated between $15 and $20 dollars per barrel (using Brent crude as a benchmark). Then in 1998 prices collapsed at below $15 to remain around $12/bbl for most of the year. Although this was good news to consumers around the world, the protracted price squeeze far from pleased state oil producers and oil companies alike. As a result, 1999 witnessed major restructuring in the oil sector, with extensive M&A activity which culminated in the creation of Exxon-Mobil and BPAmoco. At the same time, a regenerated OPEC managed to instil some discipline among its members, which adhered to their quotas, forcing the oil price to above $25/bbl in the space of a few weeks only.

3.4.7 Current situation

Despite the political uncertainty associated with the region, the Middle East remains the world's top oil exporter, supplying approximately 45% of the world's crude oil exports. The vast majority of flows are directed towards three main areas: North America, Northwest Europe and Asia Pacific. These flows coincide very much with the main trade routes for VLCCs and some of the larger-size tanker tonnage. Following Middle East, Africa and Latin America come a distant second and third. Western (mainly Nigeria) and North (mainly Libya and Algeria) Africa are very important suppliers to the European union and Nigerian crude is also very competitive in transatlantic trades to the USA.

Latin America (mainly Venezuela and Mexico) are the most important short-haul suppliers to the USA and Canada and are the first recourse for short term demand upsurges (e.g., due to cold weather). The rest of the demand generated in these two large developed economies is satisfied either by medium-haul (West Africa and North Sea), long-haul (Arabian Gulf) or domestic (Alaska) supplies. Pacific Rim countries are still largely dependent on the Middle East for their imports, although some of their demand is satisfied by regionally produced crudes in Indonesia, Australia and Vietnam. Finally, another increasingly important supplier is the Former Soviet Union, especially Russia and Kazakhstan, who channel substantial quantities of crude oil from the Caspian Sea to the Mediterranean and to Northwest Europe.

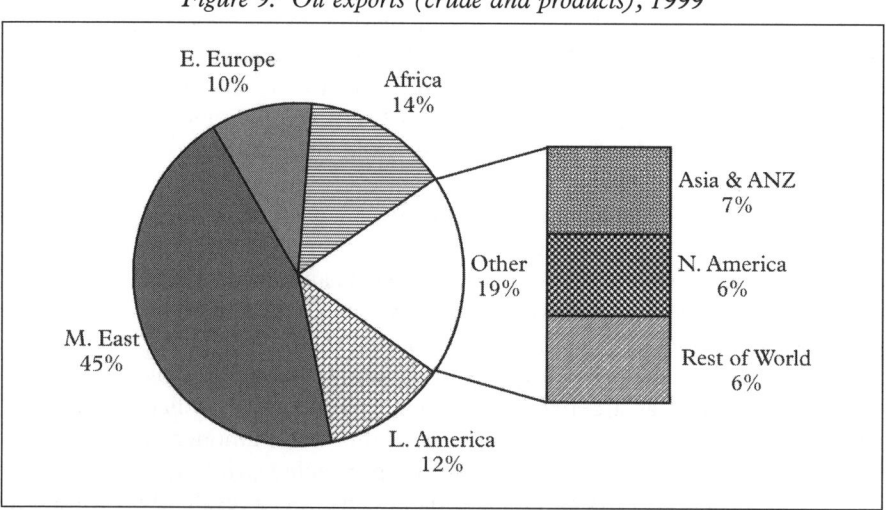

Figure 9: Oil exports (crude and products), 1999

Source: BP Statistical Review of World Energy, 2000.

4. OIL PRODUCTS

Much of the discussion up to now has dealt primarily with crude oil, although trade figures referred to both crude and products. In this section, we will begin with a brief description of the refining process, continue with the main categories of refined products and, finally, discuss production, consumption and trade patterns for major regions, like the United States, Western Europe and South East Asia.

4.1 Refining process

Although much of the economics of the oil industry revolves around crude oil, it is the final products that are used by the end-consumers. Crude oil is rarely usable and has to be refined and broken down into products adequate for final consumption.

The fundamental principle on which oil refining is based has not changed since the 19th century: crude oil is heated until it is vaporised and then the vapours are condensed separately, according to the boiling points of their constituent molecules; the procedure is called distillation. Crude oil is stored into large tanks and from there it is pumped continuously through a series of steel tubes into a furnace. From there it is pumped to the bottom of a tall cylindrical tower, usually 8–24 feet in diameter and 100–150 feet in height. This is called a "fractioning" tower, as it is divided into "floors", with perforated trays, which allow vapours to pass from lower to higher floors. The hydrocarbon vapours with highest boiling points condense first, on the bottom floors, and those with the lowest boiling points condense last, higher up the tower. The most volatile product – petrol – comes off at the top of the tower and is then condensed separately.

This simple distillation procedure yields about 20% light distilates from an average crude, and usually falls short of the commercial needs for petrol. At the same time, the process yields heavier products in quantities that exceed consumption requirements. To redress this imbalance, some of the heavier oil distillates are further processed, using methods such as *thermal cracking* and *catalytic cracking*. Both these procedures allow enhanced recovery yields of petrol from crude: the first procedure used high temperature and pressure to 'crack' the large hydrocarbon molecules of heavier products into smaller molecules of petrol and petroleum gas; the second process uses catalysts to facilitate cracking under milder and more easily controlled conditions. Reverse procedures are also available, which reform lighter gas molecules into heavier products, such as petrol. Finally, several of the gases are used as feedstocks for the petrochemicals industry.

The outputs of the refining process are classified into three broad categories: *light*, *middle*, and *heavy* distillates. Light distillates – also known as *white* or *top-end* cuts – include ethane, propane, butane, naphtha (all used as feedstock for petrochemicals), aviation turbine fuel (ATF), kerosene, petrol and other industrial spirits. Middle distillate (or middle cuts) include gas oil, diesel, marine diesel, and medium and high grade fuels. Finally, heavy distillates – also known

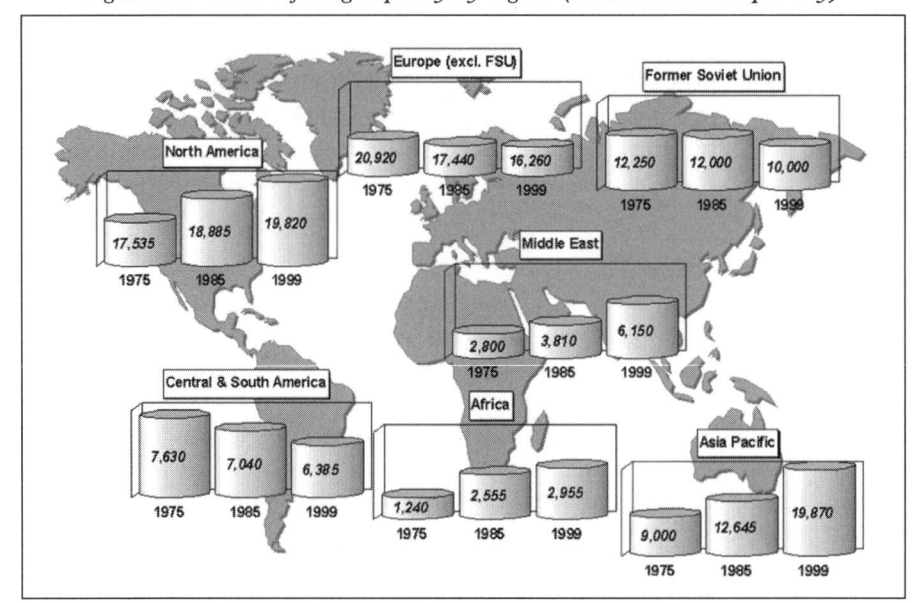

Figure 10: World refining capacity by region (thousand barrels per day)

Region	1975	1985	1999
North America	17,535	18,885	19,820
Europe (excl. FSU)	20,920	17,440	16,260
Former Soviet Union	12,250	12,000	10,000
Middle East	2,800	3,810	6,150
Central & South America	7,630	7,040	6,385
Africa	1,240	2,555	2,955
Asia Pacific	9,000	12,645	19,870

Source: BP Statistical Review of World Energy, 2000.

as *black* or *bottom-end* cuts – include heavy fuels, paraffins, lubricating waxes and greases.

4.1.1 Refining: capacities and throughputs

The supply of oil products is very much dependent on the available refining capacity around the world. In fact, refining capacity sets the upper limit to the supply of distillates. What is more interesting in terms of production, however, is the refinery *throughput*, i.e. the quantity of oil being processed by refineries per annum. This also allows the calculation of refinery utilisation rates, a figure most important for the profitability of a refiner. Figure 10 shows the development of refining capacity through the 1970s, 1980s and 1990s. Taking a closer look, one can see that North America – and this is mainly the United States – is head and shoulders above the other two important refining regions: Western Europe, and Asia Pacific. However, Asia Pacific is now fast catching up, a trend which is particularly evident in 1999. These three regions are top in the league of refinery throughputs as well. In 1999, United States alone produced almost 15 Mbpd of oil products, with Europe (excl. FSU) standing at just above 15 Mbpd, and Asia Pacific just over 16 Mbpd. Within the latter region, the largest refiner by far is Japan, now closely followed by China and then by Singapore.

Refinery throughputs and consumption of oil products give a broad framework for the study of patterns in international trade in oil products. As we are going to see later, however, trade flows are much more complicated, and there is often exchange of similar products between countries which produce all distillates, but in varying proportions.

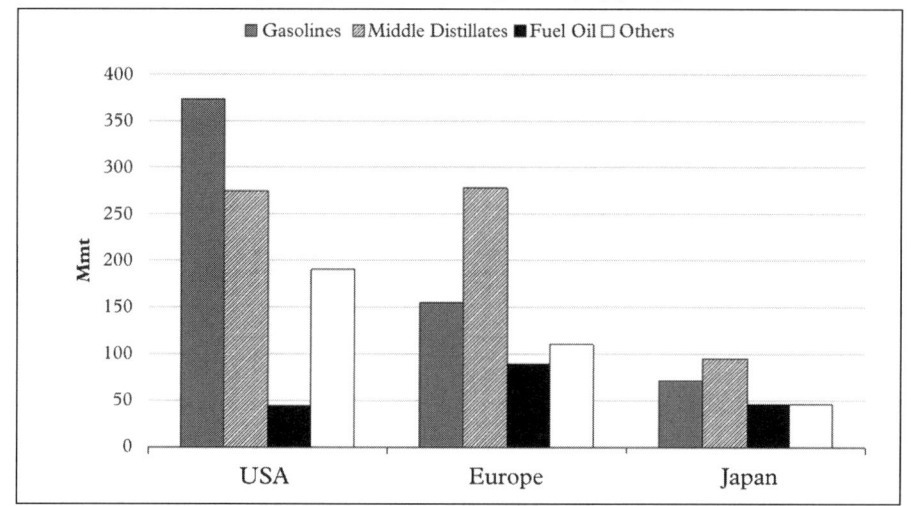

Figure 11: Regional products consumption, by type of product, 1999

Source: BP Statistical Review of World Energy, 2000.

4.2 Consumption patterns

It is consumption patterns, of course, that influence both the short and the long-term balance of the market. Different regions have different tastes for oil products, depending on their economic activities, climatic conditions and other consumption habits. Although refinery yields can change to match demand, imbalances do arise, and trade flows are generated in order to cover them. Figure 11 shows consumption patterns in 1999. United States is a heavy consumer, with the emphasis on gasolines. Western Europe is the second largest

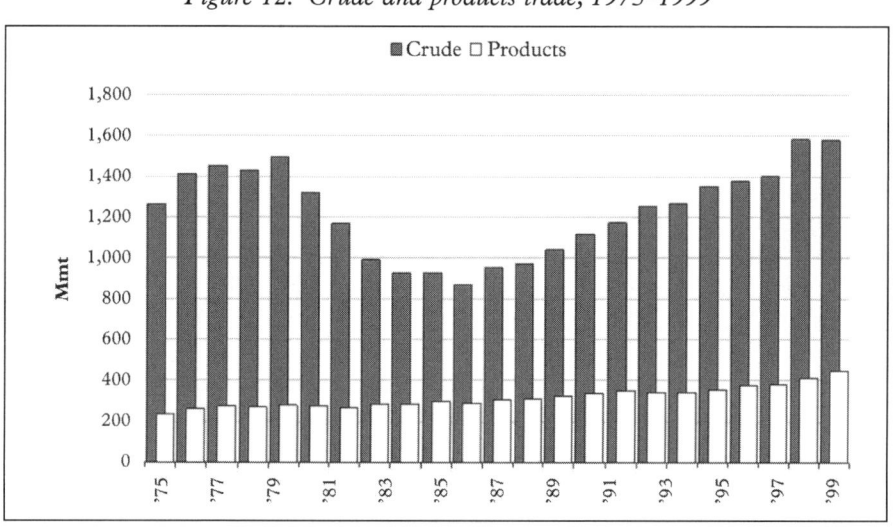

Figure 12: Crude and products trade, 1975–1999

Source: BP Statistical Review of World Energy, 2000.

consumption area, with the emphasis on middle distillates, while Japan shows a slightly more balanced picture.

4.3 Trade in products

Trade in oil products is older than trade in crude, but with increasing scale economies in the transportation of crude oil, products trade has shrank to about a quarter of total trade in oil.

Figure 12 depicts the development of crude and products trade since 1975. As one can see, products have fluctuated a lot less than crude oil trade, with the result that in 1983 products trade peaked as a proportion of total oil trade (31%).

Figure 13 shows the importing and exporting activity of major regions worldwide, and their relative deficit or surplus positions. In terms of regional patterns, United States, Western Europe and Japan, are once more the most active exporters and importers of oil distillates. Another important group of countries comes under the title "Other Asia", which includes NICs and emerging economies in South East Asia; Singapore is probably the most important single country in this group.

South East Asia is a major growth area for trade – almost exlcusively seaborne – of oil products. The region is a net importer of both crude and products, primarily from the Middle East. In terms of refining, large capacities exist in Japan, Singapore and South Korea, and expansions are planned in Indonesia, China and other emerging economies. The problem with some of these refineries is their technology; as regional demand increases pressures for the "whitening of the barrel", more sophisticated refineries will be needed in order to achieve higher yields in gasolines and middle distillates.

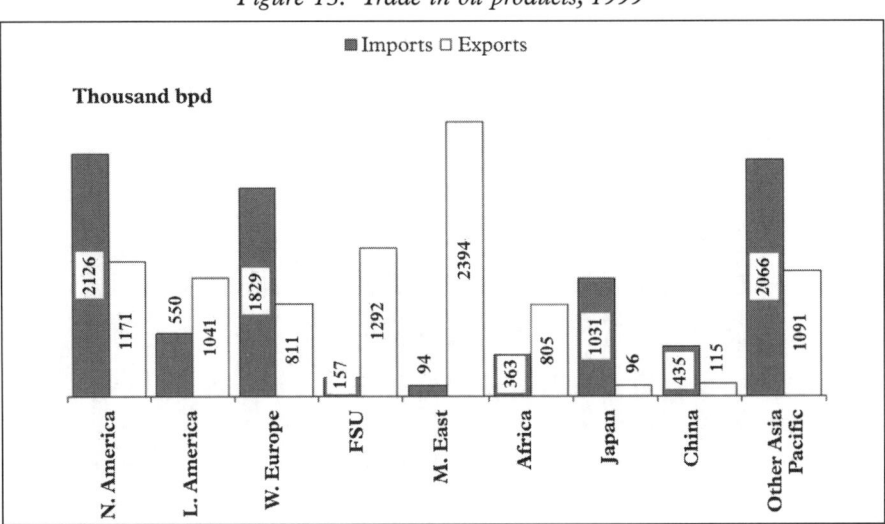

Figure 13: Trade in oil products, 1999

Region	Imports	Exports
N. America	2126	1171
L. America	550	1041
W. Europe	1829	811
FSU	157	1292
M. East	94	2394
Africa	363	805
Japan	1031	96
China	435	115
Other Asia Pacific	2066	1091

Source: BP Statistical Review of World Energy, 2000.

The combination of factors that were discussed earlier, makes the international trade in oil products fairly complicated, and its study long enough to be the subject of a separate treatise. Partly due to this complexity, there is a very active market in oil products, both on the floor of major commodities' exchanges, and over the counter.

5. BRENT CRUDE AND OIL PRICING

There is a large variety of crude oils and oil products available in the open market, many of which are priced on a purely competitive basis. One such market which developed and matured in the 1980s is the market for Brent crude, which is extracted in the UK sector of North Sea. The presence of Brent crude prices in the pricing formulae of several crudes around the world, emphasises its international character and importance.

Brent is named after one of fields, whose output is used to create a standard blend. In fact, there are two distinct pipeline systems – Brent and Ninian – which contribute towards the production. In 1976 the first consignments of Brent crude were loaded at Brent Spar, and in 1979 the terminal at Sullom Voe became operational. Brent blend is denominated as a light, sweet crude, with a specific gravity of 38° API. Its constituent crudes, however, have a specific gravity in the range of 30°–40° API, and a sulphur content of 0.2–1%. Standard quality is of course important, since market participants expect at least some security in terms of the blend's properties.

Brent is very much an international crude, with about three quarters of it being exported. It is mainly, though, an Atlantic basin crude, with most of the exports to the United States, Canada and Germany. Flows to the US are primarily received in Gulf ports, where Brent's main competitor is Nigerian crude, which has similar physical characteristics, and other domestic sweet, light crudes.

In addition to being an important pricing benchmark for a number of internationally traded crude oils, Brent really drives a multi-layer market, consisting of a number of derivative instruments, traded both on exchange floors and over the counter.

5.1 Price reporting

With the collapse of OPEC prices in the mid-1980s, there was a move towards market related pricing. This trend was already evident due to the introduction of Brent crude in the world markets, and was accentuated with the resort of some OPEC countries to netback pricing, which made the availability of reliable and up to date spot prices crucial. As the market for financial oil derivatives also took off, the need for reliable and transparent price setting and reporting became crucial.

Today there are several oil price reporting agencies, which are used worldwide for pricing spot and derivatives deals. One of the most well known is probably Platt's. The agency was founded very early, in 1924, and originally concentrated on products. It started reporting crude prices in 1983 and is currently owned by McGraw-Hill. Petroleum Argus is another well known reporting agency, which was the first to start quoting crude oil prices in 1979. LOR-ICIS started in 1978 as London Oil Reports, publishing a weekly newsletter with price assessments. In 1985 it merged with Independent Chemical Information Services which provided price quotations for chemicals and petrochemicals. There is also a number of screen services, which provide up-to-date prices, such as Telerate, Reuters, Global Alert, Bloomberg and Knight Ridder.

Prices are quoted on a minute-by-minute basis for Brent and most other crudes. Sometimes agencies report high/low price assessments, but they mostly tend to quote bid/ask ranges, which show the difference between the highest offer to buy (bid) and the lowest offer to sell (ask). Figure 14 reproduces an

Figure 14: Crude oil price quotations

```
PLATT'S CRUDE OIL MARKETWIRE                                    January XX 19XX

BRENT (FEB)      +14.49-15.00+   DUBAI (FE)      13.77-13.81-    WTI (MAR)     15.50-15.52
BRENT (MAR)      +14.42-14.46+   DUBAI(MA)       13.52-13.56-    WTI(APR)      15.49-15.51
BRENT(APR)        14.23-14.29+   DUBAI (AP)     -13.27-13.36-    P-PLUS         +1.51-1.53
BRENT (DTD)      +15.01-15.08+   OMAN (FEB)     -14.07-14.12-    WTI (MID)    +15.55-15.60+
FORTIES          +15.14-15.21+   MAR "MPM"        0.05-0.06      WTS          +14.55-14.62+
EKOFISK          +15.31-15.38+   URAL           +14.45-14.54+    EUGENE I      14.70-14.79+
STATFJORD        +15.28-15.35+   ILT (SIDI)     +14.45-14.54+    LLS           15.78-15.82
OSEBERG          +15.32-15.41+   IHVY (SIDI)    +13.82-13.91+    HLS           15.55-15.60
FLOTTA           +14.51-14.58+   SUEZ BLEND     +12.71-12.78     WYO SWT       15.50-15.52
BQ               +15.80-15.89+   ES SIDER       +14.81-14.88+    ANS (FEB)    +14.15-14.17+
FORCADOS         +15.67-15.77+   CABINDA        +14.12-14.22+    ANS (MAR)    +14.15-14.17+
CANO LIMON       +13.90-13.92+

CALIFORNIA CRUDE ASSESSMENTS
ANS/LOMG BEACH    +12.95-12.97
LINE 63/HYNES     +12.60-12.62+
THUMS/LONG BEACH   +9.56-9.61+
KERN RIVER         +8.38-8.43+

PACIFIC RIM SPOT CRUDE ASSESSMENTS        SPREAD VS ICP
TAPIS                16.65-16.70   MINAS      +14.90-14.95+   + -0.35- -0.30+
PAP.TAPIS (FEB)      16.50-16.55   ATTAKA      15.80-15.90      -0.15- -0.05
PAP.TAPIS (MAR)      16.57-16.62   ARUN        15.45-15.55       0.00-  0.00
LABUAN               16.75-16.80   ARDJUNA     15.55-15.65       0.10-  0.25
MIRI                 16.45-16.50   HANDIL      14.55-14.60      -0.60- -0.50
GIPPSLAND            15.70-15.75   CINTA       14.05-14.15      -0.55- -0.50
JABIRU               16.65-16.70   DURI        11.98-12.05       0.05-  0.10
SALADIN              16.65-16.70   WIDURI      13.92-14.00      -0.10-  0.00
KUTUBU               15.40-15.55   BELIDA      15.75-15.85       0.15-  0.20
DAQING              +14.20-14.25+
SHENGLI              12.15-12.20

CANADIAN CRUDE ASSESSMENTS
                   CD/CM            USD/BBL
PAR CRUDE        114.75-116.75   -13.78-14.02-
MIXED LT SR       93.27-35.27    -11.20-11.44-
BOW RV/HDSTY      84.05-86.05    -10.09-10.33-
```

Source: Platt's Crude Oil Marketwire, McGraw-Hill Inc.

excerpt from "Platt's Crude Oil Marketwire", with some of the most commonly quoted crudes. Price quotations are also *time stamped*, especially when they are near the opening and closing times of the markets. Naturally, the most interesting price quotation is at the closing of a market, since closing prices are often used for settlement of contracts.

Although individual crudes have their own quotations, it is not uncommon that these prices are calculated as differentials from a few *benchmark* crudes. Brent and WTI (West Texas Intermediate) are such *marker* crudes and are used extensively around the world. As far as Brent and WTI are concerned, the most liquid forward month is usually assessed first; then quotations for other forward months and from dated deals are also used to compile the daily settlement price. Once this process is completed, other crudes are priced on a differential basis and so are inter-crude spreads and inter-month spreads for other crudes. Differentials themselves are not *ad hoc* stable; in fact, they do fluctuate, but markedly less than absolute prices.

5.2 Other crude markets

Despite the market liquidity and importance for pricing of crudes around the world, one should also bear in mind that Brent is only a small fraction of the world crude oil production and exports (less than 4%). The bulk of oil exports comes from countries which have their own pricing formulas, but look to the Brent market in order to assess the true supply and demand situation. Some of the other available crudes and their main characteristics are discussed in the following paragraphs.

5.2.1 North Sea

Brent is one of a number of crude oils produced in the North Sea. In the UK sector blends from the Forties and Flotta sectors are also competing for export shares, although they are prices as Brent spreads. Of the two, Forties seems more likely to take Brent's place as an international crude, when the latter is exhausted.

In the Norwegian sector, the most prominent fields are Ekofisk, Oseberg, Statfjord and Gullfaks. All of them enter the international market, as most of the Norwegian production is exported. Most of these crudes are priced against Brent, although there is a small proportion priced against WTI.

5.2.2 United States

The most prominent crude in the United States is West Texas Intermediate. Like Brent, it is a blend of several crudes with specific gravities between 34°-45° API and sulphur content below 0.5%. The par grade is 40° API and has 0.4% sulphur content, which is slightly lighter and can be slightly sweeter than Brent. The physical base consists of crude deliveries at the end of the pipeline at Cushing, Oklahoma. Shipments are usually 50,000 or 100,000 bbls.

Like Brent, WTI has a very active forward market, where the trading lot is 1,000 bbls, and there are 22 months ahead open for trading. The futures market is even more active and forward looking, with months open until the year

2000 (in 1995). WTI contracts are more flexible than Brent contracts, in that they allow a considerable number of alternative crudes to be delivered. More specifically, acceptable deliveries include one of seven domestic grades (low sweet mix, mid continent sweet, New Mexico sweet, North Texas sweet, Oklahoma sweet, South Texas sweet, or WTI), or one of three imported grades (Bonny light, Brent, or Oseberg).

Another important US crude is that produced in Alaska. Alaskan North Slope (ANS) is extracted from the fields at Prudhoe Bay and then carried by the Trans-Alaskan pipeline to Valdez. From there, it is shipped by tankers to US West Coast and US Gulf. There is also a forward market on ANS, but it is primarily priced as a spread on WTI.

Other US crudes include: West Texas Sour and Light Louisiana Sweet, both of which are priced as differentials of WTI. West Texas Sour is also linked to the sour crude contract traded on NYMEX, since it is accepted as one of the deliverable grades. The others are: ANS, Dubai, Flotta, Iranian light, Oman, Oriente, and New Mexico sour.

5.2.3 West Africa

A substantial amount of international oil trade is generated from the west cost of Africa, where the producer countries are Nigera, Angola, Gabon, Congo, and Cameroon. Their target markets are primarily transatlantic, notably the US. There are several types of crude, but three are the most commonly known: Bonny light; Forcados; and BBQ, a blend of Brass River, Bonny light and Qua Iboe. All of the above crudes use mainly Brent as a marker crude, but pricing on WTI is not uncommon.

5.2.4 Middle East and Mediterranean

Middle East is the biggest exporter of crude in the world and plays, therefore, a key role in regulating the supply side of oil trade. The role of the Middle East was extensively discussed in the previous chapter and was recently reaffirmed during the Gulf Crisis.

One of the commonly quoted crudes for many years was Arab light, and it is still used as a benchmark for Middle East OPEC members. A relatively newer entrant in the market is Dubai Fateh. This is a medium crude of 31° API and containing up to 2% sulphur. It is often considered as the equivalent of Brent in the Middle East. It has, however, a physical base smaller than Brent and its forward market is certainly less liquid. Production averages 400,000 bpd, with a total of about 20 cargoes per month. The equity holders are Conoco, CFP, Repsol, Texaco, Sun and Wintershall; a relatively diverse base, but not as diverse as Brent's. There is no equivalent of the 15-day nominations, with the choice of loading dates at the buyer's discretion, primarily, but usually agreed jointly with the seller, subsequently.

In the Middle East Gulf area, Dubai-Fateh seems to dominate the spot market. Oman and UAE are two very active participants in the spot crude market, but their grades are relatively sour. Pricing formulas in the region are quite complicated, often involving retroactive pricing. Some of the often quoted prices are OSP, and MPM or PDO[7]; the latter, however, seems to be priced as a spread of Dubai.

In the Mediterranean the main producers participating in the spot market are Libya, Egypt, Syria, and Algeria. Iran and Russia are also active; the former from Sidi Kerir and the later from the Black Sea. Libya has the disadvantage of the US embargo, but has considerable transactions with other Mediterranean countries, Italy in particular. Spot prices are quoted for most of these crudes, and a sample of these prices is given in Figure 14. Brent and Dubai prices are often involved, directly or indirectly, in the pricing formulas of Mediterranean crudes.

5.2.5 Far East

The situation in the Far East is far from clear-cut. There are several crude grades available, coming primarily from Indonesia and Malaysia, but also from Australia, China and Vietnam. There are, however, essentially only two prices: APPI and ICP.[8] The first is assessed weekly by a panel of traders, producers and refiners. The second is assessed monthly and is based on a basket of crudes, including Oman, Dubai Fateh, Gippsland (Australia), Minas (Indonesia), and Tapis (Malaysia). Both pricing system have been criticised as non-representative of real market conditions, and as too slow in responding to changing circumstances.

5.2.6 Products

Up to now we have concentrated exclusively on crude oil. The fact is, however, that there are active spot markets for products as well, which have been in existence well before the spot market for crude. The products market tends to concentrate around several main areas. Three of them, Rotterdam, Houston, and Singapore, have considerable refining, storage and shipment facilities, and usually offer the most competitively priced products. Other areas include the Mediterranean, Caribbean, and New York harbour.

Prices are quoted for a wide array of products, including gasoil, marine bunkers, jet fuel, diesel, unleaded gasoline, and naphtha, among others. Products in the A-R-A[9] range are commonly quoted as "barges f.o.b. Rotterdam" and are usually quoted on an f.o.b. export basis. Parcel sizes of up to 5,000 mt

Table 1: Product futures

Contract	Size	Quote	Tick
NYMEX			
Heating Oil #2	42,000 US gallons	$/gl	$0.01/gl = $4.2/contract
Unleaded Regular Gas	42,000 US gallons	$/gl	$0.01/gl = $4.2/contract
IPE			
Gasoil	100 metric tonnes	$/mt	$0.25/mt = $25/contract
Unleaded Gas	100 metric tonnes	$/mt	$0.25/mt = $25/contract
SIMEX			
Fuel Oil	100 metric tonnes	$/mt	$0.10/mt = $10/contract

are common for gasoline and jet fuel, while other products are bundled in consignments of 25-35,000 mt.

Some fundamental products also have an active futures market operating alongside the spot market. The products contracts traded on NYMEX, IPE and SIMEX are shown in Table 1, together with their sizes, price quotation and minimum fluctuation per contract. Heating oil has been trading on NYMEX since 1979, and is the second most active energy contract after crude oil. Gasoline contracts are more recent and have not yet established a market as deep and wide as that for crude oil.

6. NATURAL GAS

Natural gas is an entirely separate source of energy. Although it is often a by-product of oil production, much of the world production comes from dedicated gas fields. Natural gas is a rising power in energy consumption internationally, and although not a serious threat to oil yet, it certainly is a weighty contender, and the most promising source of energy due to its excellent burning properties.

It is a "dry" gas, as opposed to the "wet" gas – or petroleum gas – that comes as a by-product of oil extraction. Natural gas is primarily methane and propane. It is usually carried in two ways: by pipeline; and in liquefied form by specially built LNG carriers.

The largest consumers and producers of gas are by far Eastern Europe and North America, followed by Asia and Australasia, and Western Europe. In terms of reserves, the FSU is the undisputed leader with 40% of the world's total gas reserves, followed by the Middle East, which holds nearly a third of them.

Natural gas consumption has experienced remarkable growth, doubling from 900 Mtoe in 1970 to over 2,000 Mtoe in 2000. Reserves have shown an even more spectacular growth, from 45 trillion cu.m. in 1970 to just over 145 trillion cu.m. in 2000.

Gas was first marketed in the United States, in the late 19th century. It was not until the 1930s, however, when technological improvements made possible the laying of high pressure pipes over long distances, that it was extensively traded.

The United States were rather an exception to the common practice among producers to flare natural gas at extraction, or at best use it to increase pressure in the oil deposit. In 1966, OPEC producers flared 65% of their gas production, with 22% being re-injected into wells, 11% used for domestic consumption, and less than 1% being exported. Twenty years later, the situation was markedly different. Only 16% of gas was flared, 28% was re-injected, and the rest was marketed either domestically or in export markets.

Gas provides about a quarter of the USA's energy consumption requirements, with industry and households sharing it almost equally.

In Europe gas was discovered in small quantities at Lacq (France) and the Po Valley (Italy) in the 1950s. The first substantial discovery came about in 1959 at Groningen in the Netherlands, while Britain made the first commercially

Figure 15: Natural gas proven resources

1999: 5,172 Trillion cu. ft. (146.4 trillion cu. m.)

- M. East 34%
- N. America 5%
- C & S America 4%
- Europe 4%
- Africa 8%
- Asia Pacific 7%
- FSU 38%
- Other 26%

Source: BP Statistical Review of World Energy, 2000.

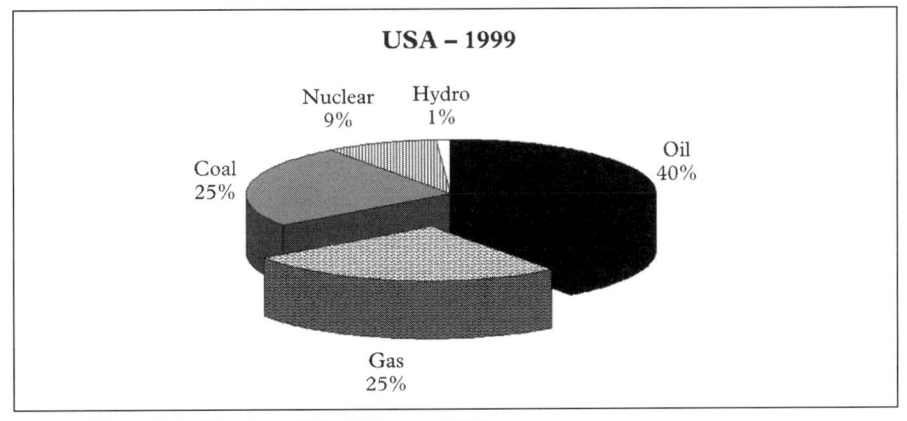

Figure 16: Gas use in the USA

USA – 1999

- Oil 40%
- Gas 25%
- Coal 25%
- Nuclear 9%
- Hydro 1%

Source: BP Statistical Review of World Energy, 2000.

exploitable discoveries in its sector of the North Sea in 1965. Since then gas has had a predominant position in domestic consumption.

The big player in Europe, however, is the Former Soviet Union, which is sitting on the largest proven gas reserves in the world. A considerable pipeline network is in place – although its condition might be questionable – which was created to link the FSU with countries in Eastern Europe. The same network was then used for exports of Russian gas to West European countries, as well.

In Japan natural gas contributes over 10% of the country's primary consumption. Although lower than USA and Europe, this market share is set to expand, as Japan has been showing increased interest in expanding the role of gas in its primary energy consumption. Japan is the single largest importer of gas in liquefied form (LNG), importing from countries in the Pacific Rim, as well as from the Middle East.

132 INTERNATIONAL SEABORNE TRADE

Figure 17: Gas use in Europe

FSU – 1999

- Nuclear 6%
- Hydro 2%
- Oil 20%
- Coal 19%
- Gas 53%

Europe (excl. FSU) – 1999

- Nuclear 14%
- Hydro 3%
- Oil 42%
- Coal 19%
- Gas 22%

Source: BP Statistical Review of World Energy, 2000.

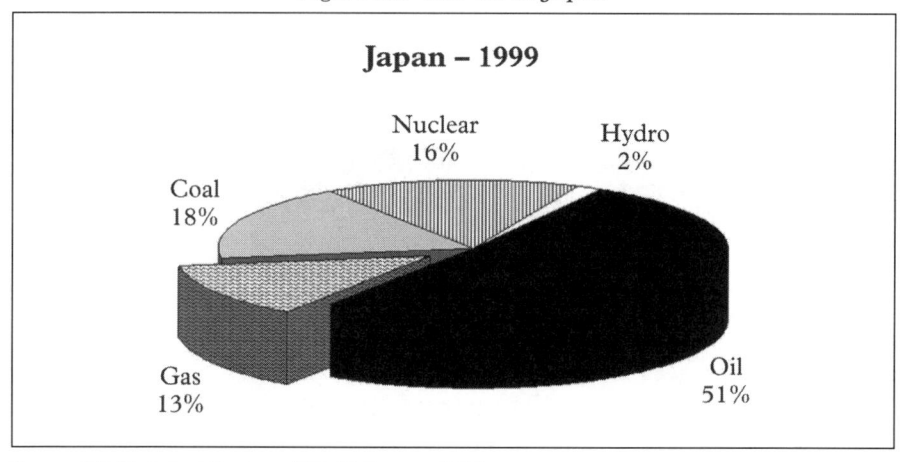

Figure 18: Gas use in Japan

Japan – 1999

- Nuclear 16%
- Hydro 2%
- Coal 18%
- Gas 13%
- Oil 51%

Source: BP Statistical Review of World Energy, 2000.

6.1 Trade in natural gas

Natural gas is not as extensively traded as oil and coal. Its physical characteristics make it more difficult to handle and its high flammability makes precision and care imperative. In 2000, just 20% of the world production entered international trade. As can be seen from Figure 19, 80% of gas was consumed domestically, with the remaining 20% being exported by pipeline and in liquefied form. Pipeline exports are predominant between Canada and the United States and from FSU to the rest of Eastern and Western Europe.

LNG trade accounted for only 5% of world natural gas production and is rather small compared to trade flows of other energy commodities; but because of the complexity of its transport logistics, LNG flows have been meticulously

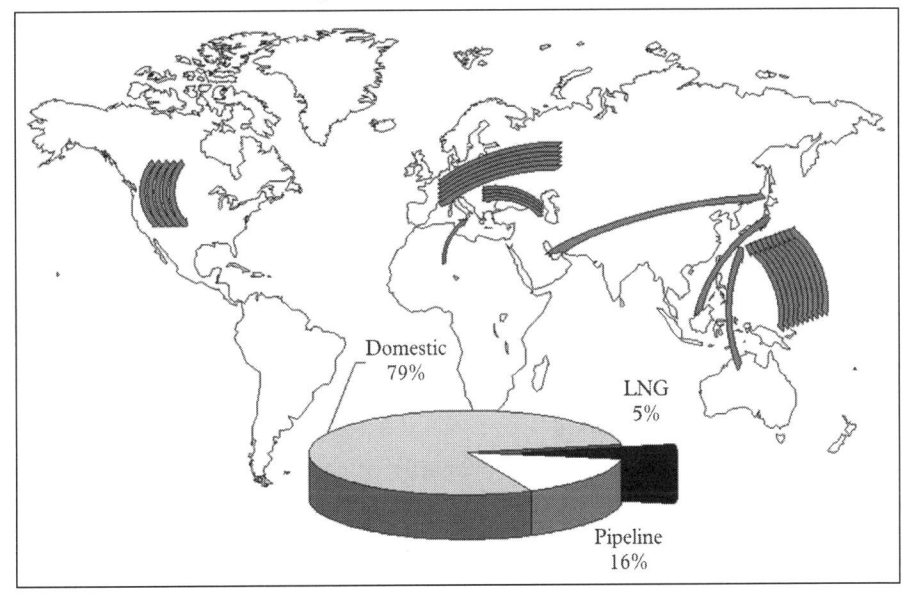

Figure 19: World usage of gas

Domestic 79%
LNG 5%
Pipeline 16%

Source: BP Statistical Review of World Energy, 2000.

documented on a voyage to voyage basis, since the very beginning in the 1960s. The carriage of the liquid itself is only one of several steps of a carefully planned procedure, which includes carriage of gas from the point of production to the port liquefaction facility; loading; regasification at the port of destination; and transport to the point of consumption. LNG contracts have been extensively documented and are being regularly quoted in special publications by Cedigaz and BP. Examples of existing contracts are given in the two following tables, which record long term contracts in the Western hemisphere and the Far East. As we mentioned earlier, natural gas entered international trade in a very modest way in the 1960s. The first experimental voyages with LNG carriers were carried out in the 1950s, but the first commercial trip was in 1964, between Algeria and the UK. A year later LNG cargoes began flowing from Algeria to France, while in 1969, trade between Alaska and Japan was initiated.

In the 1970s gas entering world trade increased to 13% of total production and new countries appeared in the scene, like Netherlands, Norway, Soviet Union, Iran and Mexico. The 1980s saw the opening of the submarine pipeline between Tunisia and Italy, the beginning of trade between Malaysia and Japan and the expansion of Soviet gas exports. The most challenging issue for the economics of the industry in that decade was the relation of gas and oil prices. Traditionally, gas prices were determined on the basis of its calorific equivalence to oil. The 1986 oil price collapse increased pressure for a reassessment of gas pricing formulae, and many countries resorted to hybrid pricing mechanisms, often incorporating one or more petroleum products, like gas oil or gasoline.

7. COAL

Last in the discussion we have coal. This was deliberate, due to coal's dual role both as a source of energy and as an input to steel production. We will discuss the supply and demand characteristics of coal, its important role as one of the major bulk commodities traded internationally, and the specifics of marketing, procuring and pricing coal.

Coal has two distinct markets – one for energy and another for steel production. Although we could easily analyse the two separately, we will look at them simultaneously, in order to contrast their differences. We will start with a description of the coal's main physical characteristics, and then continue with a discussion of supply and demand determinants, marketing, and trading of the commodity.

7.1 Physical characteristics

Coal is a solid mineral, composed primarily of carbon; other components of coal are volatile hydrocarbons, sulphur and nitrogen, and the minerals that remain as ash when the coal is burned.

Most of the coal in the earth's crust was formed during the Carboniferous period – between 280 to 345 million years ago. At that time much of the world was covered with luxuriant vegetation growing in swamps. Many of these plants were types of ferns, some as large as trees. This vegetation died and became submerged under water, where it gradually decomposed. As decomposition took place, the vegetable matter lost oxygen and hydrogen atoms, leaving a deposit with a high percentage of carbon. As time passed, layers of sand and mud settled from the water over some of the carboniferous deposits. The pressure of these overlying layers, as well as movements of the earth's crust and sometimes volcanic heat, acted to compress and harden the deposits, thus producing coal.

Coal is classified in several sub-types, primarily according to its carbon content. Peat, the first stage in the formation of coal, has a low fixed carbon content and a high moisture content, but it does not have the same uses as commercial coal.

Commercial coal is usually classified in two broad categories – brown and hard. The first category includes lignite – the lowest rank of coal – and sub-bituminous coal. Both of these types are invariably used for power generation and, because of their low quality, they are consumed in domestic markets. Lignite is usually brownish-black in colour and often shows a distinct fibrous or woody structure. Lignite is inferior in calorific value to ordinary coal because of its high (43.4%) water content and low (37.8%) carbon content; the high (18.8%) content of volatile matter causes the lignite to disintegrate rapidly upon exposure to air.

The term "hard coal" comprises all the remaining high-quality types of coal, from bituminous coal to graphite. Bituminous coal has more carbon than lignite and a correspondingly higher heating value. It is primarily used for generating power, although coals closer to anthracite are suitable for further processing into coke for steel production.

Anthracite is a hard coal with the highest fixed-carbon content and the lowest amount of volatile material of all types of coal. It contains approximately 87.1% carbon, 9.3% ash, and 3.6% volatile matter. Anthracite is glossy black, with a crystal structure; although harder to ignite than other coals, anthracite releases a great deal of energy when burned and gives off little smoke and soot. Anthracite is ideal for reduction into coke, which is then used to fire iron ore in order to produce molten iron.

Coke is a very important input in the steelmaking process. Coke is the name given to the hard, porous residue left after the destructive distillation of coal; it is blackish-grey, has a metallic lustre and is composed largely of carbon – usually about 92%. It has excellent burning properties, with a heating value of 13,800 Btu/lb, which makes it appropriate for use as a reducing agent in the smelting of pig iron.

Coke was first produced as a by-product in the manufacture of illuminating gas. The growth of the steel industry, however, produced a rising demand for metallurgical coke, making it inevitable that coke should be manufactured as a chief product rather than as a by-product.

Coal normally contains a number of other compounds, mainly sulphur and metallic elements, which form the ash. When burnt, coal generates a number of undesirable by-products, which have largely contributed to the image of coal as a 'dirty' source of energy. Carbon reacts with oxygen to produce carbon monoxide (CO) and dioxide (CO_2). Increased emissions of these two gases are thought to produce the so-called greenhouse effect on the earth's atmosphere, with detrimental long-term consequences for global climate. When burnt, the sulphur contained in coal reacts with oxygen to form sulphur dioxide (SO_2), a gas which has several useful industrial applications. If the gas is released in the atmosphere, however, it mixes with water (H_2O) in a lethal combination – sulphuric acid (H_2SO_4) – which returns to earth as acid rain. Finally, coal burning also produces a number of nitrogen oxides (NO_X), which also have detrimental effects on earth's atmosphere.

As the coal industry is trying to improve the image of the commodity, several attempts have been made to improve its combustion, with the aim to reduce emission of impurities, such as sulphur and nitrogen oxides, and increase the efficiency of energy production. Clean coal technologies (CCTs) are a new generation of advanced coal utilisation processes, some of which may be commercially viable early in the 21st century. In general, these technologies are cleaner, more efficient, and less costly than conventional coal-using processes. A wide variety of CCTs exist, but all of them alter the basic structure of coal before, during, or after combustion. CCTs include: improved methods of cleaning coal; fluidised bed combustion; integrated gasification combined cycle; furnace sorbent injection; and advanced flue-gas desulphurisation.

7.2 Supply characteristics

The supply determinants of coal have been discussed earlier in this chapter, together with other energy commodities. One definite advantage of coal over all other fossil fuels is its sheer abundance. World coal reserves were estimated at over one trillion tonnes at the end of 1999, with an R/P ration of 235 years. With R/P ratios of 66 years for natural gas, and 43 years for oil, coal seems likely to dominate the energy market in the distant future. Another very interesting statistic is that while just over 10% of oil and natural gas reserves are located in OECD countries, well over 40% of coal reserves are located in the OECD area, which makes coal a "politically safe" source of energy.

With such obvious advantages then, why is coal not the most popular source of energy in most countries around the world? The answer lies very much in the economics of coal mining and the challenge to coal by the 'new' fuels – oil and natural gas.

As in any project for the extraction of mineral resources there are three main stages in coal recovery: exploration, development, and production. Exploration may last a few years, until proper geological surveys point with high probability to the existence of reserves. Several exploratory shafts may have to be constructed in order to assess the quality and extent of the deposits. Costs at this stage can be substantial and are sunk. The development stage involves the construction of an open pit (if the developer is lucky enough to find coal near the ground surface) or the digging of an underground mine. Again, costs at this stage are sunk, and further costs might have to be incurred at later stages of a project in order to improve and/or extend capacity.

At the production stage, most of the costs are operating costs, which tend to increase as reserves are being depleted and more effort is required to extract them. This is particularly true when underground mining is the method of production. Another important difference of coal mining from oil and gas extraction is that coal has to be moved at every stage, whereas oil and gas flow naturally; coal requires a lot more effort to break and extract, while oil simply requires a steady pressure which will keep it flowing out of the well, naturally.

Another important characteristic of the coal industry, which is also evident throughout the mineral sector, is the large extent of heterogeneity in production costs. Depending on the geomorphy of the field and local climatic conditions, costs can vary considerably from one region to the next. Indonesia, South Africa and Colombia, for example, are low to medium-cost producers, while countries like Germany, UK and France produce coal at such high costs that it is often cheaper to import the commodity from distant, low-cost exporters.

Apart from regional differences, one should also expect different production costs between surface and underground coal mines. Intuitively, one would anticipate lower production costs for open pit mines; this, however, is not always so. Underground mining does suffer from increased costs for tunnelling, roof and wall supports, adequate ventilation, and a transport system to move coal to the surface. However, because of the extent of these costs, many high-cost producers – particularly European mines – have developed increasingly mechanised, and more cost-efficient, ways of extracting coal. These technologies have been largely adopted by medium-cost producers – like US mines, for instance – resulting in lower costs for underground mines and increased competitiveness with surface mines.

ENERGY ECONOMICS AND TRADE

On the other hand, surface mines can do little to improve their earth-moving equipment, except perhaps by using a continuous transport system, like a conveyor belt. No matter how efficient the movement of coal is, however, it cannot compensate for the fact that there is a lot of waste material that has to be moved as well. The overall effect is, of course, that the cost per tonne of coal increases, often making surface mines more expensive than underground mines.

Although capital and land are the most important contributors to extraction costs, one should not underestimate the role of labour in coal production. Taking into account the fact that coal is largely produced in OECD countries,

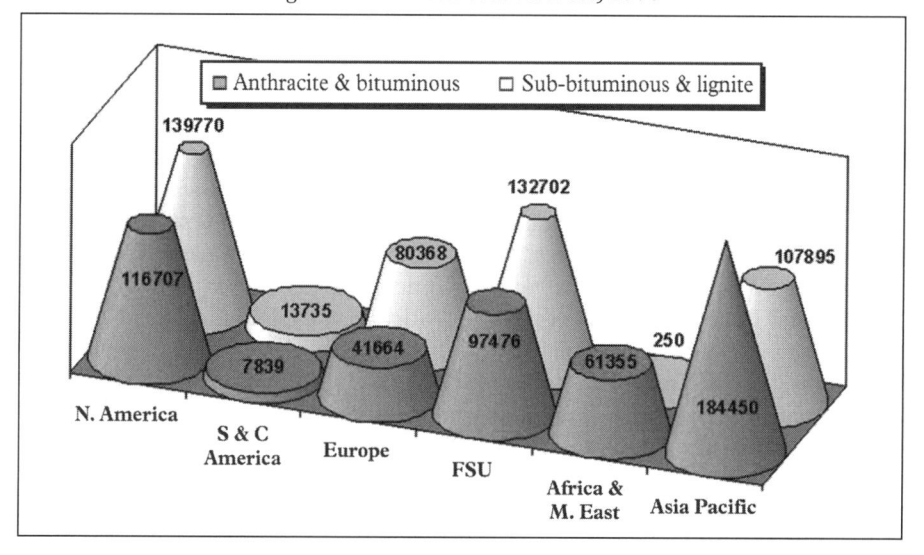

Figure 20: Proved coal reserves, 1999

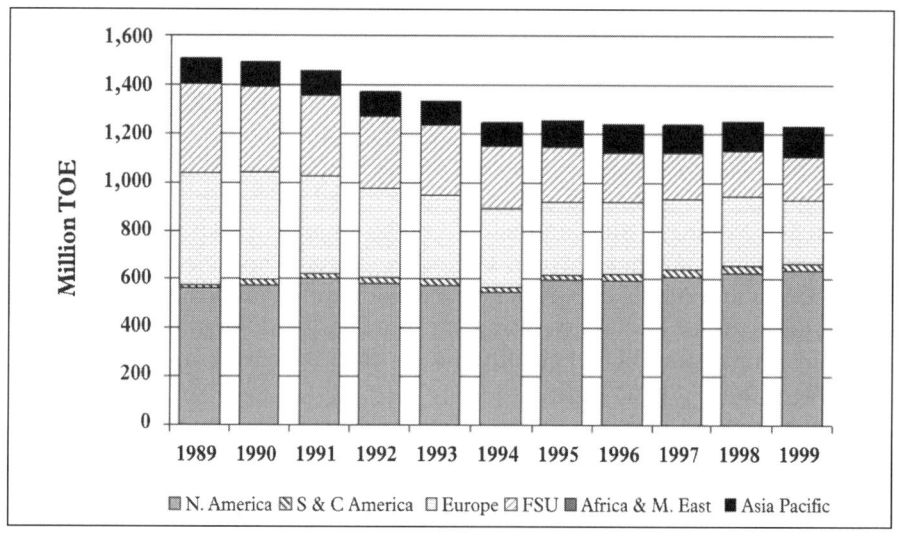

Figure 21: Coal production

labour costs become quite sizeable, and labour relations are central to the uninterrupted running of a coal mine; one has only to recall the huge disruption caused, in the UK economy, by the long strike of coal miners at the beginning of the 1980s.

7.2.1 Reserves and production

Coal is found in nearly every region of the world, but deposits of present commercial importance are confined to Europe, Asia, Australia, and North America. Great Britain, which led the world in coal production until the 20th century, has deposits in southern Scotland, England, and Wales. In western Europe, coalfields are found throughout the Alsace region of France, in Belgium, and in the Saar and Ruhr valleys in Germany. The French and Belgian production is rather small, with the latter disappearing altogether, after 1993. Germany is still the most important Western European producer, but its production has been falling steadily for the last 10 years. Most of Germany's deposits contain brown and sub-bituminous coal, which are of lower calorific value and, hence, decrease total German production in oil equivalent terms.

Eastern European deposits include those of Poland, the Czech Republic, Romania, Bulgaria, and Hungary. The most extensive and valuable coalfield in the former Soviet Union is that of the Donets Basin between the Dnepr and Don Rivers; large deposits have also recently been exploited in the Kuznetsk Coal Basin in Western Siberia. The former Soviet Union holds the world's largest reserves of coal, with some 241 Bmt in 1999, which was marginally higher than US deposits. The most important producers among the new republics are Russia, Ukraine and Kazakhstan. As in Western Europe, however, Soviet production has also been experiencing a declining trend in coal production, in the last 10 years. Unlike Germany, the former Soviet republics – especially Ukraine and Kazakhstan – produce primarily hard coal.

The coal reserves of the United States are divided into six major regions. Only three of these regions, however, are mined extensively. The most productive region is the Appalachian field, which includes parts of Pennsylvania, West Virginia, Kentucky, Tennessee, Ohio, and Alabama. In the Midwest one large field covers most of Illinois and sections of Indiana and Kentucky. A thick field extends from Iowa through Missouri, Kansas, and Oklahoma. These three regions produce a majority of the coal mined in the United States. There are large deposits of lignite and sub-bituminous coal in North Dakota, South Dakota, and Montana. Sub-bituminous and bituminous coal deposits are scattered throughout Wyoming, Utah, Colorado, Arizona, and New Mexico. The Pacific Coast and Alaska have small reserves of bituminous coal. Almost all the anthracite in the United States is in a small area around Scranton and Wilkes-Barre, in Pennsylvania. The best bituminous coal, for coking purposes, comes from the Middle Atlantic states.

Canada does not have the massive coal reserves of the United States, but it produces very good quality anthracite, large quantities of which it exports to Japan, as well as Western Europe. Most of Australia's coal reserves are located in Western Australia, close to the large iron ore reserves. Australia is a substan-

Figure 22: Coal shares

1999: 4.73 billion mt
- Lignite 18%
- Anthracite 8%
- Bituminous 74%

tial producer, and a very important exporter, of coal, particularly in the Pacific Rim.

The coalfields of north-western China, among the largest in the world, were little developed until the 20th century. Today, however, China is the world's largest coal producer, although its reserves are only about half those located in the United States; the Chinese economy is a very intensive user of the commodity.

Finally, the most important producer in Africa and the Middle East is South Africa, with reserves of over 55 Bmt. The country is essentially the only significant producer of coal in the African continent, with a production of 103.5 Mtoe in 1994, all of which was hard coal.

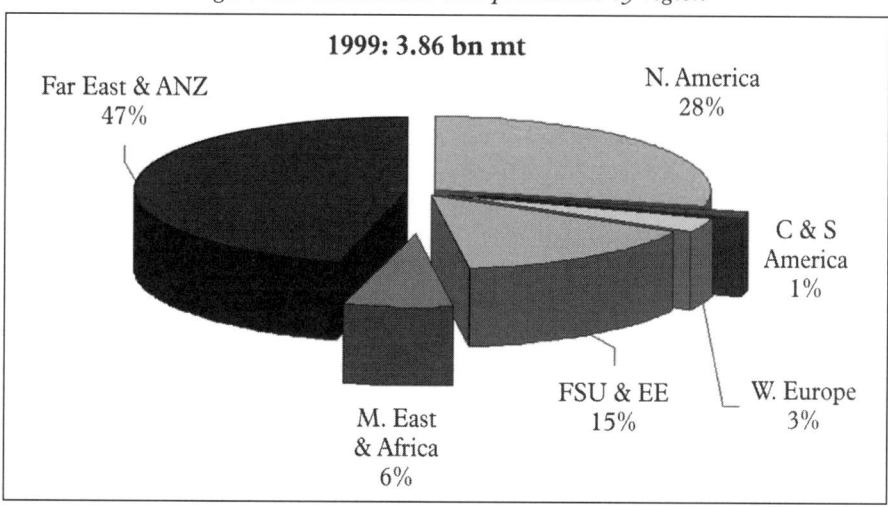

Figure 23: Bituminous coal production by region

1999: 3.86 bn mt
- Far East & ANZ 47%
- N. America 28%
- C & S America 1%
- W. Europe 3%
- FSU & EE 15%
- M. East & Africa 6%

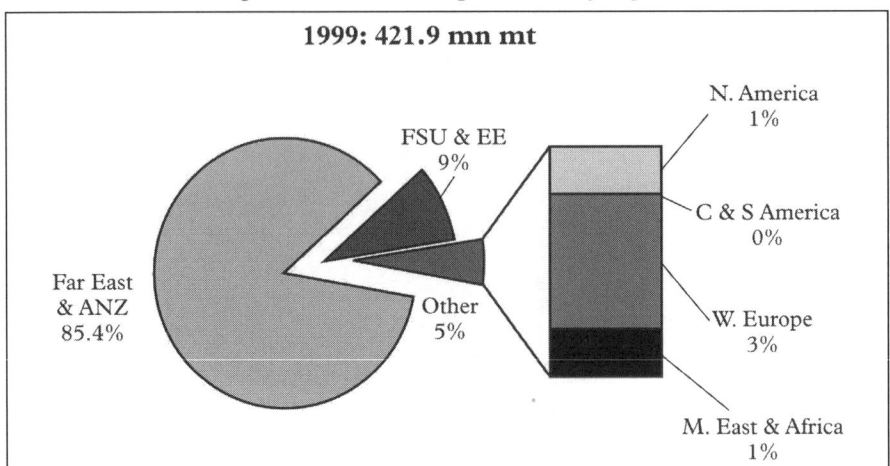

Figure 24: Anthracite production by region

1999: 421.9 mn mt

- Far East & ANZ 85.4%
- FSU & EE 9%
- Other 5%
- N. America 1%
- C & S America 0%
- W. Europe 3%
- M. East & Africa 1%

Figure 25: Lignite production by region

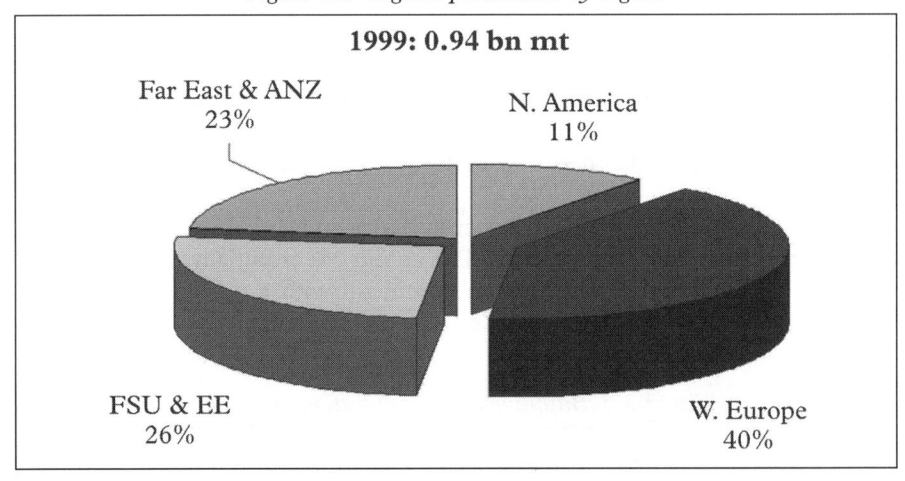

1999: 0.94 bn mt

- Far East & ANZ 23%
- N. America 11%
- FSU & EE 26%
- W. Europe 40%

7.3 Demand characteristics

All types of coal have some value; as an old saying in the coal industry goes: "anything pale brown will burn". This, of course, does not necessarily mean that it will burn efficiently. Although peat is frequently used as a fuel in rural communities and, more recently, peat and lignite have been made into briquettes for burning in furnaces, it is brown and hard coals that are consumed extensively; and, of these two, only hard coal is traded internationally.

If one were to point at a single factor that has tremendously affected the fortunes of the coal industry, this would be its cross-substitutability with oil and natural gas. We saw that energy is needed for residential, industrial, transport, and "other", consumption. Although oil fits very well into all types of consumption, this is no longer the case for coal. Coal has been substituted by oil and natural gas in domestic consumption; in transport, coal burns inefficiently and is quite bulky to carry around; in industry, however, it is still used extensively.

Coal has two main uses – power generation, and as a fuel in the production of other industrial materials. Coal is used extensively in power plants with coal-fired electricity generators, as well as in other industrial processes that use coal-fired generators. In industry, coal is used in the production of steel and cement. For the latter, coal is mixed with limestone and other materials, and fired to produced clinker – the raw material which is pulverised to become cement. In steelmaking, the procedure is not that simple; coal has to be carbonised – i.e. purified – in special furnaces, in order to produce coke, a coal of a quality very close to that of graphite. Coke is then mixed with iron ore and a flux, and fired in a blast furnace, to yield pig iron.

Only anthracite and high-quality bituminous coal can be used for coking; coal with such attributes is known as coking coal. All other coal is used for power generation, and is known as steam coal. These two new groupings of coal should not be confused with brown and hard coal. By definition, all lignite and sub-bituminous coal is steam coal, and so is the lower-quality bituminous coal; anything of higher quality is suitable for coking.

Steam coal is a very important input in power generation, accounting for about 80% of the variable cost of producing coal-fired electricity. Demand for steam coal depends on the price of the commodity itself, the price of other substitutes – like oil and natural gas – and the ease with which a power plant can switch between different fuels. After the first oil price shock, although coal became affordable, it was rather difficult for coal to capture a large market share, because most power generators were geared to use oil as fuel. During the 1970s, it became evident that oil was getting too expensive and too unsafe to be relied upon; the result was increased popularity for coal, which was readily

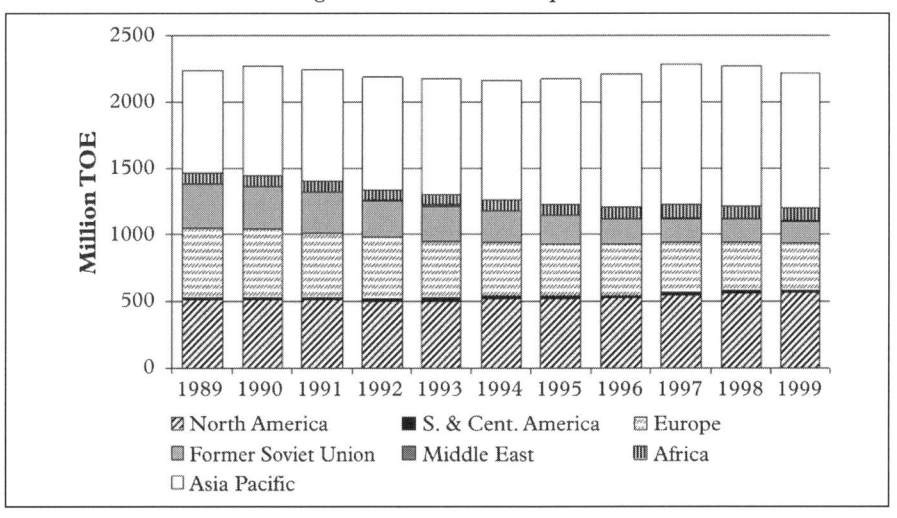

Figure 26: Coal consumption

available from politically safe areas. With electricity companies and other industries changing their generators to accommodate coal, it was little surprise to see a massive boost in coal consumption and trade, after the second oil price shock.

While steam coal is by far the most important cost contributor in electricity generation, this is not the case with coking – or metallurgical – coal, which is estimated to account about 10% of the finished cost of steel. There is no substitute for coal in blast-furnace steel production; instead, the whole steelmaking process has to be replaced with an electric arc furnace. The increased popularity of EAF's has curtailed the share of blast furnaces in crude steel production and has, therefore, undermined the demand for coking coal, as well. While this is true, however, new smelting reduction techniques for making steel utilise coal[10] once again and, thus, increase the demand of coal.

Power generation steelmaking and cement production, are not the only uses of coal, however. Coal was also used, from the early 19th century to the World War II era, for the production of fuel gas, just as coal liquefaction techniques were used to produce liquid oil products. In the 1980s, several industrialised nations showed interest in developing CCTs, but the popularity of the environmentally-friendlier natural gas and the availability of cheaper oil after the mid-1980s has hampered the rapid development of such technologies.

7.4 Marketing and trade

Not all coal that is produced, is marketed internationally. Brown coal has a high humidity content, which makes it susceptible to spontaneous combustion and, therefore, difficult to transport. Moreover, its low carbon content makes brown coal uneconomical to export.

Hard coal, however, is quite actively traded, and a total of about 505 Mmt of coal were traded in 1999. Hard coal traded is made up of steam coal and metallurgical coal. Steam coal trade is usually the larger of the two, but metallurgical coal is actually the most actively traded.[11]

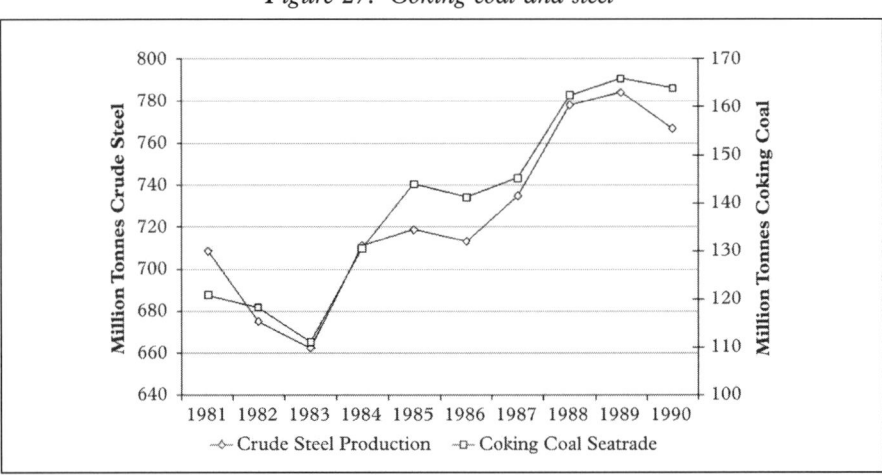

Figure 27: Coking coal and steel

ENERGY ECONOMICS AND TRADE

The list of top exporters of coal differs somewhat from that of top producers. Some of the most important producers of coal use it domestically; the case of China is an extreme example, whereby only a tiny portion of the country's production is exported. At the other extreme, Australia channels most of its production in the export market, while the United States presents a mixed picture, with substantial quantities of coal disappearing through domestic demand.

Overall, the most prominent exporter of coal is Australia, controlling over one quarter of exports of steam coal, and over 40% of exports of coking coal. Other important exporters of coal include the United States, South Africa, Canada, Poland, Colombia, Indonesia, the CIS, and China.

Focusing on steam coal trade now, Australia and South Africa are the largest exporters, followed by the United States, and then by Indonesia, Colombia, China, the FSU, and Poland, all with shares not exceeding 10%. The direction of most steam coal trade flows is Western Europe, which receives over 40% of world imports. Japan is the single most important importer of steam coal, absorbing over 20% of world trade.

The situation in metallurgical coal is quite different. Both exports and imports are dominated by a few large players. Coking coal is not abundant, and there are only a few countries that have adequate reserves. Australia, the United States, and Canada, are the three most important exporters of coking coal, accounting for a staggering 85% of total trade. Other exporters include Poland, South Africa, and the FSU.

Coking coal imports are directed primarily to Western Europe and Japan. Once again, Japan is the largest single importer of coking coal, sourcing most of its needs from Australia. Because of this interdependence, it is no surprise that both Japanese steel mills (JSMs) and Australian coal producers enter negotiations every year, in order to determine quantities and prices for coking coal exports. These negotiations parallel those for iron ore, and they usually involve the same companies.

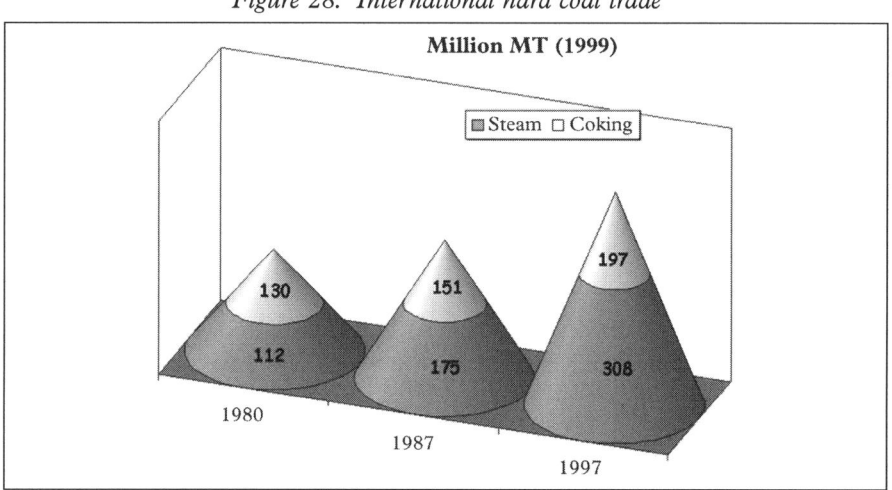

Figure 28: International hard coal trade

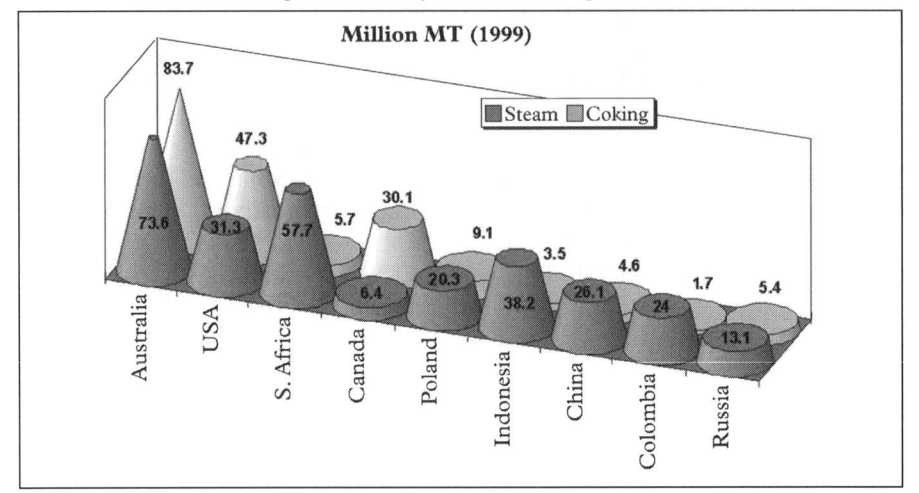

Figure 29: Major hard coal exporters

Million MT (1999)

Country	Steam	Coking
Australia	73.6	83.7
USA	31.3	47.3
S. Africa	57.7	5.7
Canada	6.4	30.1
Poland	20.3	9.1
Indonesia	38.2	3.5
China	26.1	4.6
Colombia	24	1.7
Russia	13.1	5.4

The steam coal market is not as concentrated as the market for coking coal. There are several suppliers of coal in each of the large producers: in Australia BHP, CRA and MIM Holdings are the most important producers; Amcoa, Randcoal and Trans-Natal are the main producers in South Africa; and in the United States there are many producers with an exporting capacity of about 2–4 Mmt per annum, making the US one of the most competitive markets in the world.

Like steel producers, power plants need reliable supplies of adequate quality of coal that will make electricity generation as efficient as possible. Power plants usually enter their own negotiations with coal mines and/or traders, and any respectable procurement manager of a power plant concentrates on four main aspects of the negotiations:
– physical characteristics of the coal;
– the reliability of the supplier;
– contract specification; and
– pricing.

Coal quality is determined by a number of parameters, like its calorific value (measured in kcal/kg), percent content of volatile matter, moisture, ash, and sulphur; hargrove; and initial deformation point. Coal quality is important, because low-quality coal results in: energy losses; excessive waste material that has to be disposed of; increased corrosion and, hence, increased maintenance costs; and increased expenses for desulphurisation.

As far as the supplier is concerned, a power plant needs a counterpart with adequate infrastructure, in an area of relative political stability, with a healthy financial position, a long-term attitude to doing business, and commitment to quality development, and cost control. Moreover, the supplier should preferably have prior export experience, which will help overcome any difficulties that may arise.

The contract is, of course, the most important part of the agreement, and should be fair and equitable, which will keep both partners happy throughout

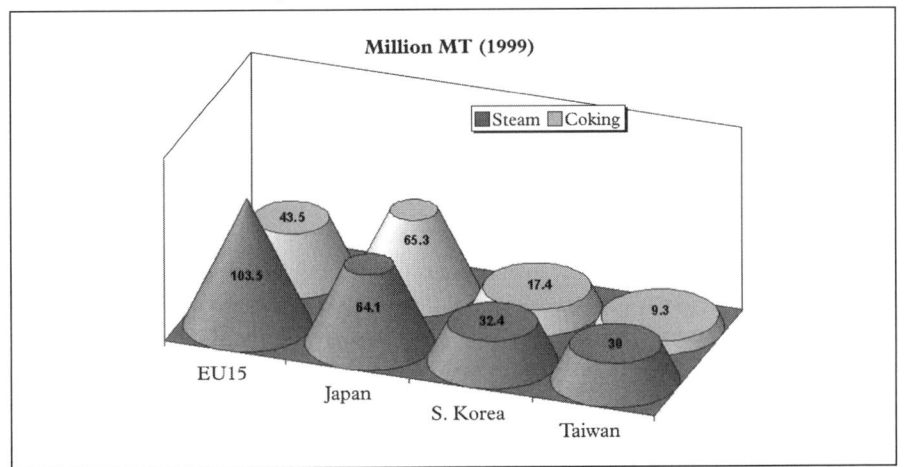

Figure 30: Major hard coal importers

Million MT (1999) — Steam, Coking

- EU15: 103.5 (steam), 43.5 (coking)
- Japan: 64.1 (steam), 65.3 (coking)
- S. Korea: 32.4 (steam), 17.4 (coking)
- Taiwan: 30 (steam), 9.3 (coking)

its duration. After all, the contract provides security of supplies for the buyer, while income security is the main benefit for the coal producer, together with the ability to use the contract as a loan collateral. Although contracts usually include long lists of clauses for every eventuality, it is always preferable to keep them simple, since arbitration is expensive and time consuming. Finally, contracts also make proper arrangement for the transportation of coal from source to destination. More than 90% of the world trade in coal is carried by sea; coal is in fact – with iron ore – the largest seaborne dry bulk commodity, providing employment for all sizes of dry bulk carriers, but particularly for capesize and panamax vessels.

Pricing is the last stage of the agreement between buyer and seller. Prices are usually set every year, in a process that is called annual price nomination, and are usually based on the average cost of operations plus a profit component. This method is called cost-plus and is the most popular – but not unique. Another, very similar method uses a base price, which is estimated from the cost-plus price, and an escalation term is attached to it. Finally, market prices can also be used although, due to the large heterogeneity of the commodity, such prices are quite difficult to determine. Coal prices reflect, of course, the conditions in the energy and steel markets. An increase in the price of oil (like the ones in 1973 and 1979) will increase demand for oil substitutes – like coal – and will, thus, push prices upwards.

8. CONCLUSION

Concluding the discussion on energy commodities, we focused first on the history and current situation of crude oil, oil products and natural gas economics, trade and pricing internationally. After the oil price collapse of the mid-1980s, the world witnessed a notable switch to open market pricing. This led to the emergence of some crudes, like Brent and WTI, as marker crudes. Although not commanding an important part of world production or trade, the markets (spot, forward and futures) of these crude grades provide competitiveness and transparency, and are used for two very important activities in commodity trading: price discovery and hedging. Natural gas is the new contender in the energy industry, with a massive increase in the last 10–15 years of reserves and production. Natural gas markets are also very exciting as they increasingly become liberalised and a host of derivative instruments is being developed to help the many new market participants to manage the risks associated with the new opportunities created in this market.

We also discussed the supply and demand economics of coal. One distinction that should be made when studying coal, is of that between steam and metallurgical coal. Demand for the former is driven by demand for other energy commodities, while the latter depends on the fortunes of the steel industry.

Coal is considered a "safe" commodity, because it is largely located in OECD countries; it also suffers from the negative image of the "dirty" fuel, which is always lagging behind oil – and sometimes even behind natural gas – and is favoured only in case supply of the other energy substitutes becomes troublesome.

Despite all the above, coal is still one of the most heavily traded commodities, and the largest dry bulk commodity traded by sea.

ENDNOTES

1. Marginal cost is the cost of extracting one additional unit of the commodity. This often includes the operating cost, a fixed cost element, and possibly an allowance for the cost of capital investment required to achieve extra production.
2. User cost is usually defined as "the present value of the resource foregone when a unit of the commodity is produced today rather than tomorrow". Although a more "academic" concept of cost, it becomes quite relevant when environmental concerns become of substance.
3. The price may also include a "normal" rate of return on the investment undertaken.
4. The utility/satisfaction gained by bringing production forward, i.e. producing an additional unit today rather than tomorrow.
5. Parts of this section were compiled with material from the *Institute of Petroleum and Shell Briefing Service*.
6. Yergin, D. (1991): *The Prize: The Epic Quest for Oil, Money and Power* (Simon & Schuster), p. 507.
7. OSP stands for Official Selling Price; both MPM and PDO are acronyms for official Omani prices.
8. APPI stands for Asian Petroleum Price Index; ICP stands for Indonesian Crude Price.
9. Amsterdam–Rotterdam–Antwerp.
10. Coal is substituted for coke in these techniques.
11. It is estimated that about 30% of coking coal is traded, whereas only 7–8% of steam coal production reaches the international market.

CHAPTER 7

ESTABLISHMENT OF EUROPE-WIDE MARITIME TRADE FLOWS BY ORIGIN/DESTINATION

Manfred Zachcial

Institute of Shipping Economics and Logistics (ISL), University of Bremen, Germany. E-mail: *Zachcial@isl.org*

1. INTRODUCTION

This chapter presents a summary of various Institute of Shipping Economics and Logistics (ISL) activities in relation to the establishment of the European maritime and land/sea trade and traffic flows matrices. There is an urgent need to set-up such databases as inputs for comprehensive and valid policy advice regarding the promotion of European short-sea shipping. The major topics of this chapter are therefore: the integration of foreign trade and transit flows as well as maritime transport; a review of a pilot study on international origin/destination matrices; and an approach to the assessment of model split functions concerning intermodal transport as an alternative to pure land transport.

2. ESTABLISHMENT OF LAND/SEA TRADE AND TRAFFIC FLOWS DATA

As stated during a speech on the "Third European Research Roundtable Conference on Shortsea Shipping"[1] there is a substantial need for valid data concerning freight flows information along the whole transport chain including mixed/combined land/sea movements. This also includes the wide variety of ferry and ro/ro traffic from/to the Continent. Several attempts have been undertaken to create consistent data on this topic. In most cases, individual trading areas have been analysed. A full-scale consistent approach, however, does not yet exist. For several reasons the use of these data causes substantial methodological problems.

In order to evaluate the seaborne trade potential and the loaded/unloaded seaborne transport potentials of EU member countries it is necessary to expose foreign trade transit and warehouse traffic as well. Transit and warehouse traffic is in almost all cases excluded from the external statistics.

It should be mentioned that the port of transit which passes through a country without transhipment is ignored due to the fact that it is neither part of the country's international trade nor does it belong to the cargo traffic which is loaded or unloaded in the country in question.

The EU external trade statistics include, as far as the mode "sea" is concerned, only seaborne trade directed via national ports (direct seaborne foreign trade). In order to determine the total foreign trade of the various countries under review it is necessary to include the transit/transhipment volumes via transit countries as well. These "indirect" seaborne trade volumes are mainly attributed to Belgium and the Netherlands and, to a lower extent, to Germany, France, Spain and Italy.[2]

The attempt to figure out freight traffic flows along the whole transport chains in Europe can only be reasonably successful if sea and land trades as well as the coastal areas of loading/unloading can be identified. Given the difficulties of data quality and of different procedures it is very hard to set-up a full-scale pattern or even several patterns for individual commodity groups or loading categories such as dry bulk, liquid bulk, general cargo/breakbulk, the latter further disaggregated by conventional cargo, container and ro/ro.

3. INTEGRATION OF FOREIGN TRADE FLOWS AND SHIPPING

A puristic approach based upon NST-R-2 digits (= 24 commodity sections) causes substantial problems when trying to solve the wide range of irregularities involved in the various origin/destination flows and hence in the various loading/unloading pairs. In order to get a better insight into the data quality, the results for the 24 commodity section matrices (multiplied by 2 directions and 2 concepts = foreign trade and loaded/unloaded) should always be controlled by very thorough individual analyses for the major commodity groups, such as iron ore, coal, grain and other dry and liquid bulk, especially crude oil and petroleum products. The remaining quantities of general cargo/breakbulk should be treated as one major loading category which can better be balanced out concerning discrepancies in the cargo flows compared to a number of more than 15 individual – partly very small – commodity sections. The adjusted matrices for this summarised loading category can then be distributed down to the level of commodity groups by using balancing procedures based upon FRATAR/gravity models.

For transport policy issues it seems to be sufficient to show the trends and structures of European land/sea trade and transport for major dry and liquid bulks and general cargo/breakbulk by loading categories, namely, conventional general cargo, containers and ro/ro cargo.

This chapter focuses on the separation of freight flows into land and sea components. It does not show the split of land transport into road, rail, inland waterways and pipeline transportation which is a topic of additional research.

Looking at the transport structures within Europe it is evident that, except for the United Kingdom (before the opening of the Channel Tunnel) and Ireland, various transport modes can be used for foreign trade movements. Problems arise when foreign trade comprises several transport movements with various means of transport. As mentioned above, the overall transport chain information cannot directly be derived from the external trade statistics or any other statistical information. In other words, the modal split for a country-to-country relationship is different for the importing and the exporting (reporter) country due to various modes included in the total transport.

Modal split assumptions are mainly based on EU foreign trade data supplemented by seaborne transit data. These splits exposing the seaborne foreign trade per origin/destination and commodity group are related to the OECD foreign trade data.

Figure 1 shows the basic idea on setting up the choice of route by using direct and indirect traffic by mode as well as transhipment flows. Purely land transport must be separated from total transport in order to identify the following sea transport related components.

In reality, there are several cases of manifold transit flows. To give an example: a container from Austria goes by truck via Germany, then crosses the Netherlands, there loaded onboard at the Port of Rotterdam and transported to a port on the US East coast from where it is transhipped to Mexico.

4. PILOT STUDY ON INTERREGIONAL ORIGIN/DESTINATION MATRICES

ISL's empirical works is – among other topics – related to land/sea freight flows and found that:

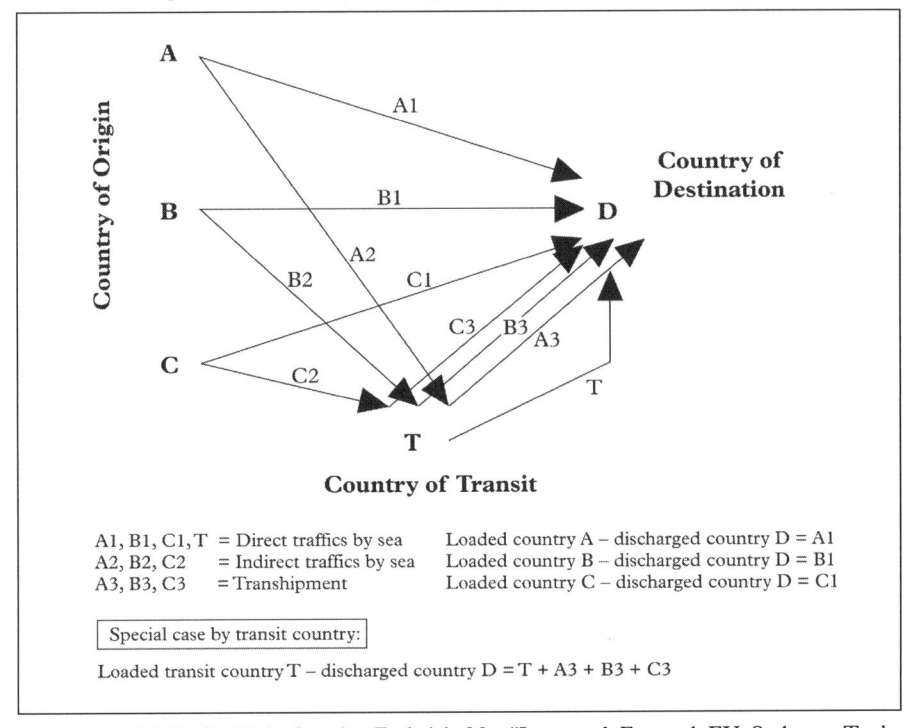

Figure 1: Choice of route by using direct and indirect traffic

```
A1, B1, C1, T  = Direct traffics by sea      Loaded country A – discharged country D = A1
A2, B2, C2     = Indirect traffics by sea    Loaded country B – discharged country D = B1
A3, B3, C3     = Transhipment                Loaded country C – discharged country D = C1
```

Special case by transit country:

Loaded transit country T – discharged country D = T + A3 + B3 + C3

Source: Heideloff, C., Hübscher A., Zachcial, M., "Intra and External EU Seaborne Trade. Methodological Paper on the Demand Side", unpublished (Bremen, 1996).

- full-scale interregional cargo flows information within Europe are generally not available and very difficult to be obtained and/or estimated;
- international freight flow information on a country-to-country level are in many cases not sufficient to solve specific sea/land transport planning problems;
- the process of establishing interregional freight flow matrices has to be carried out in combining various statistical sources and estimation algorithms;
- the procedures of coming into force are only possible by individual analyses, beginning with those countries that have the reputation to provide rather reliable data.

4.1 Former applications for Germany

About six years ago a rough description of an adequately seeming methodology had been presented based upon German international trade and transport data. This approach has been used in recent projects such as a study about a possible Fehmarnbelt fixed link. The basic ideas are here summarised.

Since the beginning of the '90s the German government has been trying to find possibilities of shifting cargo from road to sea.[3] The objective was and is to find traffic corridors crossing the German highway network over long distances (for example between Scandinavia and coastal areas in Germany, but also in neighbouring countries or in third countries such as Spain, Portugal, Italy, Greece, Turkey etc.) which might be interesting for shifting cargo from road to sea.

In order to identify such corridors it is necessary to have a good insight into the long-distance origin/destination flows by mode of transport and by route, differentiated by commodity groups or at least by loading categories (as mentioned in Section 2 of this paper).

In an earlier study on behalf of the Federal Ministry of Transport[4] it could be shown that the approach generally can be solved for Germany as one important country within the centre of Europe. Similar approaches have been made by the Netherlands and Scandinavian countries, but merely on national level. The same is true for studies conducted by Transmodal with relation to container transport.[5]

Based upon a comprehensive modelling procedure it could be proved that fairly complete and reliable data about traffic flows along the transport chains can be made available by commodity groups and origin/destination pairs (80 regional units in Germany and 20 of surrounding countries multiplied by 36 countries/country groups in Europe/overseas).

4.2 Brief description of the compilation process

There are three main types of data used for compiling the O/D flows by mode and route:
- German foreign trade and transit data as defined in Section 1;
- German freight movement data and additional information of several surrounding countries (especially the Netherlands, Belgium etc.);
- German maritime transport statistics including port and ferry statistics, assisted by port and transit statistics of the Netherlands and Belgium.

ESTABLISHMENT OF EUROPE-WIDE TRADE FLOWS

An example of how to use the various sources of information is contained in an earlier contribution. This example was related to imports of consumer goods from the USA to Germany/Bundesland Bavaria by modes of transport, border sections, and ports when more that one port can be reached via border section and vice versa.

Step 1: Total import volumes of consumer goods of Bavaria from USA, by border section.
Step 2: Split of import volumes into direct and indirect seaborne trade.
Step 3: Modal split pattern by border section relevant for indirect seaborne trade.
Step 4: Modal split pattern in Germany seaports' hinterland traffic.
Step 5: Split of mode-specific freight flows by traffic zones in Bavaria and by border sections.
Step 6: Further split of indirect seaborne trade into ports related to relevant border section(s).
Step 7: Assignment of port traffic to border section by mode of transport.
Step 8: Derivation of a full-scale matrix of Bavarian imports from the USA by traffic zones, modes of transport, border sections and ports.

5. ASSESSMENT OF "ROAD TO SEA" SPLIT FUNCTIONS

Until now, the system-immanent disadvantages of intermodal transport including maritime transport compared to direct trucking have not been quantified in monetary terms. There are only certain tentative estimations available assuming advantages of transport cost of 15–30 % in favour of sea transport to be necessary to shift a certain amount of cargo from road to sea.

5.1 Modelling approach

Since a number of determinants of mode choice is not possible to be quantified and expressed in monetary terms, ISL has applied a modal split model which estimates system-immanent disadvantage of intermodal transport compared to pure road haulage. In concrete words, the freight flows between Lisbon and the centres of the German countries have been used for modelling purposes.

It has been assumed to have C_1 and C_2 as the known parts of transport cost (better of generalised cost) for each mode and origin/destination pair. Provided there is valid information about the portions choosing each mode (sea and road haulage) for each (ij) pair within the research areas. The following modal split model has been defined.

The ratio of the proportions or transport shares of both modes yields:

$$\frac{P_1}{1-P_1} = \frac{1}{\exp\{-\lambda(C_2+\delta-C_1)\}} = \exp\{\lambda(C_2+\delta-C_1)\}$$

The various components of the formula mean the following:

P_{ij} = market shares of O/D pairs
λ = dispersion parameter
δ = modal disadvantage (penalty)

Linearisation of using logarithms results in the following formula which is used later for linear regression:

$$\ln\left\{\frac{P_1}{(1-P_1)}\right\} = \lambda(C_2 - C_1) + \lambda\delta$$

The values of λ and δ as the regression's unknown parameters have been calibrated by regression analysis with

$$\left\{\frac{P_1}{(1-P_1)}\right\}$$

acting as dependent is variable and (C_2-C_1) as the independent one. The term $\lambda\delta$ equals the regression's constant and λ the slope of the function. δ equals $\lambda\delta/\lambda$.

The theoretical modal split function implies that both modes will have 50% market share of the difference between total cost including all relevant qualitative factors.

5.2 Results

By applying the modelling approach on empirical data for Germany/Portugal trades,[6] the following linear regression function resulted:

$$y = \ln\left(\frac{P_1}{1-P_1}\right) = 0{,}0095(C_2 - C_1) - 7{,}4826$$

$$(5{,}402) \qquad\qquad (-5{,}689)$$

Figure 2: Theoretical modal split function

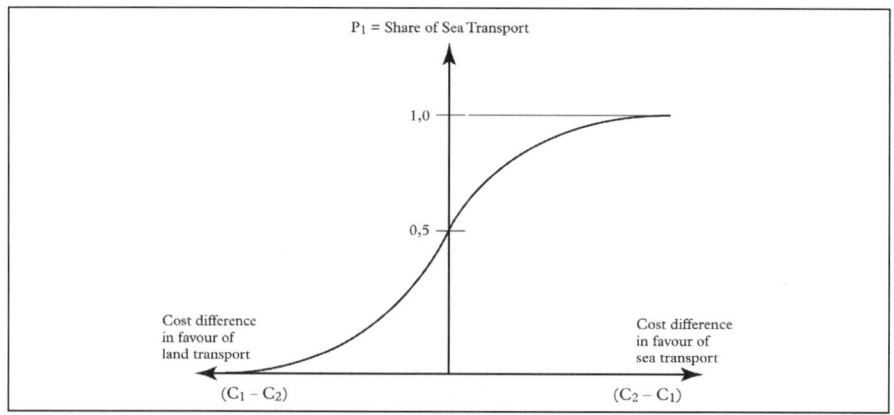

C_1: cost of mode sea; C_2: cost of mode road

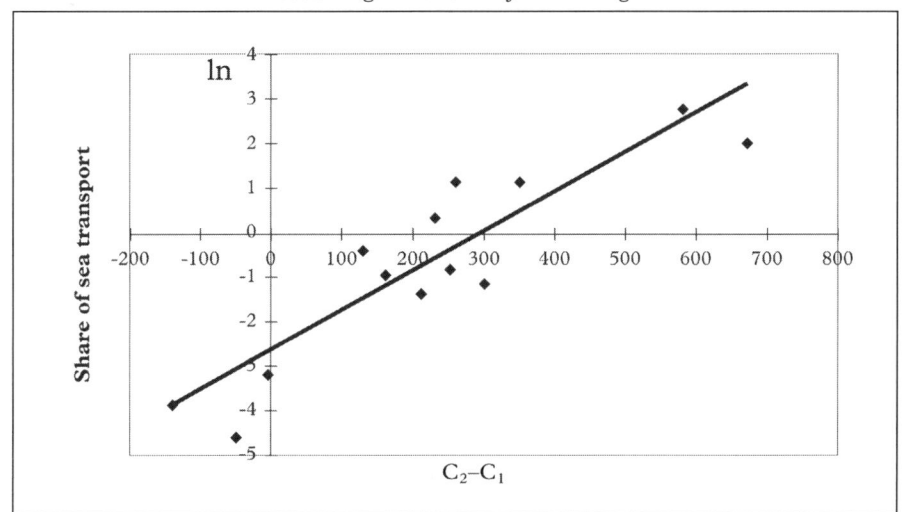

Figure 3: Linearised regression line of mode choice assuming 0.90 €/km for trucking

[Figure: Scatter plot with regression line. Y-axis: "Share of sea transport" (ln, range -5 to 4). X-axis: C_2-C_1 (range -200 to 800).]

The function is very satisfactory from statistics' point of view with a rate of determination of $R_2 = 81\%$ and the values for the t-statistics (number in brackets below the regression coefficients). This holds for the fact that the regression has been calculated based upon cross section data (not time series).

The numerical result can be interpreted as follows: the regression line crosses x-axis at about €134. This means that with regard to this transport relation (Lisbon-Germany cities) sea transport achieves 50 % of the market if the pure transport price (including port handling) is by €134 – cheaper than trucking (as average). If the price differential is zero or even negative, the share of intermodal land/sea transport is zero or close to it.

This means also that the market share of intermodal transport could be increased if on a certain route the price difference could be increased (for example by lower handling cost or lower freight rates by using economies of scale) or the qualitative disadvantage of shipping including time cost, capital binding cost and others would be reduced. Our Institute continues to analyse interesting routes to improve the knowledge on the market shares and competitive situation between trucking and intermodal transport by sea.

6. CONCLUSIONS

For several years, the Institute of Shipping Economics and Logistics (ISL) has dealt with the problem of establishing reliable and valid data sources concerning origin/destination flows. In the meantime one may state that substantial progress in this direction could be achieved. For several areas of origin/destination flows of cargo differentiated by loading categories and major commodity groups, respective data files could be generated. Based upon these data, modal split models for land/sea traffic flows with respect to the "From Road to Sea" discussion have been elaborated and tested. The respective empirical results may be used to develop price/quality strategies in order to improve the competitiveness of European coastal shipping.

ENDNOTES

1. Zachcial, M. (1996): "Land/Sea Transport Flows in Europe", *Building European Shortsea Networks Conference* (Bergen, Norway), 20 June.
2. In most cases, detailed commodity-specific data are not avaiable in transit traffic. Almost total quantities moved or containerised are shown, if any. The approach is more complex as can be described here since the country-specific information have to be harmonised (gross/net weight of cargo etc.).
3. ISL/Bremen–IWW/Kiel–PLANCO/Hamburg: Contribution of Shortsea Shipping to Cope with Traffic Problems of Europe – Federal Ministry of Transport, Bonn 1991.
4. Zachcial, M., *et al.* (1996): *Data Processing of Land/Sea Traffic in Germany* (Bremen).
5. *MDS Transmodal: Containers Inland* (Chester, 1994).
6. Market shares for sea transport between 2% (Stuttgart–Lisbon) and 94% Hamburg/Lisbon.

PART THREE

ECONOMICS OF SHIPPING MARKETS AND SHIPPING CYCLES

CHAPTER 8

THE ECONOMICS OF SHIPPING FREIGHT MARKETS

Patrick Alderton and Merv Rowlinson
Centre for International Transport Management, London Metropolitan
University, London, UK. E-mail: *alderton@lgu.ac.uk* and *rowlinsn@lgu.ac.uk*

INTRODUCTION

The purpose of this chapter is to provide analysis of the many economic changes that have occurred in freight markets in recent decades. Whereas great technological leaps in container, bulker, tanker and ro-ro shipping were already well in train by the 1970s , the three decades since have witnessed less evident, but equally forcible changes in the shape and composition of freight market supply and demand. The intention here is to build on the solid theoretical foundations of freight markets that the blossoming discipline of maritime economics had already provided by the 1970s. From this position, the critical changes that occurred in freight markets will be discussed and their impact on freight markets analysed. Additionally, the intention is to focus on the new trends already taking place in the freight market.

The freight market can be defined as the place where the buyers and sellers of shipping services come together to strike a deal. Categorisation may be made in a number of ways. The charter market can be divided up into the following four main sectors: First, the *Voyage Charter Market*; under this type of contract the charterer hires the ship to carry his cargo for usually an agreed rate per ton. Most of the problems are for the shipowners with the major points of negotiation being the freight rate and the laytime (the time the charterer wants for cargo handling). For obvious economic reasons charterers will opt for this market when freight rates are high and when the expectations are that they will fall and when the demand of the commodity markets seems unstable. Second, *The Contract of Affreightment Market* (C.O.A.); this is a variation of consecutive voyage chartering or in other words a contract between owner and charterer to move so much cargo on a regular basis. No ship is named, which is an advantage to owners with large fleets or with owners who are members of a "pool". Third, *Time Charter Market*; this market can be split into short, medium and long period of times. Prior to 1970 many tramp owners would have a good percentage of their fleet under long-term (say 15-year) charters. This gave stability to their business as they could estimate their income for long periods of time. However when many accepted long term charters in the boom year of 1970 they suffered financially in the period of inflation that followed in 1973. Since then the majority of the market has been in short and medium charters. In this type of contract the charterer becomes the disponent owner and has to accept many of the problems that might arise, so the negotiations will usually be more complex. Finally, *Bareboat Charter Market*; under this contract the shipowner will lease the bare ship to the charterer who for practical purposes will operate the vessel as his own. However, in this market often standard contract forms are seldom used so the actual conditions will vary, though they can be for a long period of time, often for the life of the ship. It can be used as a way of financing a ship, particularly in a period when shipowning enjoys certain tax advantages, as in such situations financiers can enjoy the benefits of shipowning without the problems of having to operate the vessel. In addition to the charter market manufacturers and traders with significant annual volumes to move may express a preference for directly owned, vertically integrated tonnage.

The plan of work provided here outlines the nature and composition of shipping freight markets in the 1970s and the theoretical framework constructed by the new school of maritime economists in this era. The dramatic technological and operational changes to freight markets in the 1970s were well in train. Oil markets were becoming a dominant force in global shipping as the seemingly insatiable oil demand by developed industrial nations was accelerated by uninterrupted world growth (up until the late 1970s), post World War Two. The increased demand, coupled with increasing tonne-mile factors brought about by growth in long-haul oil trades, proved conducive to radical developments in vessel size. Economies of scale were the economic *zeitgeist* of this period as tanker and bulker sizes soared upwards. Equally dramatic changes were occurring in the cargo liner sector, with capital intensive fully cellular and Ro-Ro vessels replacing the traditional labour intensive cargo liner. During this period the dominance of North America and Europe in world trades was being supplemented by the dynamic industrial growth of Japan, with Korean industry beginning to register as a world force.

Building on the theoretical framework which was well established in the 1960-80s era by the burgeoning school of maritime economists, this chapter considers new developments in freight markets. Whereas great technological leaps in design – containerisation, massively increased sizes in the tanker and dry-bulk and tanker sectors, Ro-Ro shipping – accompanied by a revolution in operational practice, occurred in the decade post 1960, later decades have been much less dramatic. However a number of areas in the freight market have undergone significant change. The intention is to explain the change process by analysing the shifts in the demand and supply of shipping within the context of freight market changes.

This is followed by a statistically based analysis of the principal changes to aggregate freight markets in the past three decades. The fundamentals of derived is revisited within the context of these changes. Whilst it is not proposed to challenge the main precepts of demand, it is important to recognise that important new developments have affected specific freight markets. Trends of industrialisation and de-industrialisation have wrought changes to the pattern of demand. Additionally unforeseen events shaping the global political economy have impacted on the freight market

THE ECONOMICS OF SHIPPING FREIGHT MARKETS 159

Finally, the concept of "green shipping" is discussed within the context of increased environmental concern during the last three decades. The intention is to explain the change process via the utilization of a broad-based range of economic and organisational theory. This should not only contribute to the understanding of change but also endorse the value of theory which will deepen analysis of the dynamics of restructuring and strategy in the industrial transition process.

THE THEORETICAL FRAMEWORK

The key determinants of demand for sea transport were clearly defined by Chrzanowski.[1] These are:
(1) the volume and quantity of cargoes to be transported;
(2) the distance of transport.

The basic tools for meeting this demand were met by a mixture of charter market and directly owned tonnage. The essential question this raises is what type of allocative process was best suited to meeting these demands. The market mechanism was clearly favoured by leading maritime economists. By the 1970s the economic principles determining freight markets had been rigorously defined by the new wave of maritime economists. From this period a strong tradition of neo-classical economic analysis has been maintained in maritime economics. With the emphasis on cost competitiveness in open freight markets, maritime economists have argued for the efficacy of market forces. Svendsen's 1958 work[2] provided a seminal analysis of the neo-classical micro economics of freight markets, stressing the essential comparative costs of shipping and their importance in attaining competitiveness in the global market. Thorburn[3] effectively employed supply and demand analysis to develop a detailed model of shipping freight markets, identifying some thirty six supply and twenty four demand conditions to be found in the working marketplace. Goss[4] reflected the emerging macro factors which were beginning to affect shipping markets by the late 1960s. The changes in the world political order during this period led to the market model of open freight markets being challenged. The once colony nations were beginning to pressurise for more economic independence which included the ownership and management of merchant shipping. Additionally, open registry tonnage was becoming a major force in the world fleet. Both trends were to prove difficult for traditional owners in the USA and in Northern Europe. Protectionism in the freight market was seen as an effective response to these difficult conditions. Goss was to question the efficacy of resorting to protectionism, particularly where it negated the benefits of the competitive markets.[5] Goss' position on the open market has been a consistent feature of the maritime literature. In 1993, he was to counter calls for intervention in the freight market:

"International shipping services are commonly bought and sold in competitive markets which lead to the survival of those with the lowest private costs...the relevant principle is that of comparative advantage."[6]

Gilman[7] heralds the great leap in technology and innovation that facilitated the container revolution. Focusing on such major liner routes as the North Atlantic and Transpacific, Gilman credits the great economic gains of containerisation on the competitive process which ensured that leading lines would strive for ever increasing efficiency. Jansson and Schneerson[8] identified the benefits of a rigorously competitive shipping liner industry, one optimises the most economic use of the global supplies of capital and labour:

"The best division of labour in international sea transport is obtained when the most efficient operators become price leaders."[9]

CHANGES IN FREIGHT MARKETS

World Trade from 1840 to 2000

World trade in the form we know it today started in the middle of the 19th century as global communications developed. Before that what the ship brought back from her voyage depended on the commercial ability of the master or the discretion of the owners agent. As London became the communication centre of the world it became the trading centre of the world.

Figure 1 shows that although world trade has faltered from time to time it has continued to grow. Note also how after World War II from the mid-1950s in growth in demand dramatically increases and the modern trend of maritime transport can be considered to have started.

Figure 1 also shows the general increase in world trade since World War II apart from a plateau in the 1980s caused by a slight decline in the oil trades in that period. Since then the growth has followed the same buoyant trend established in the 1960s.

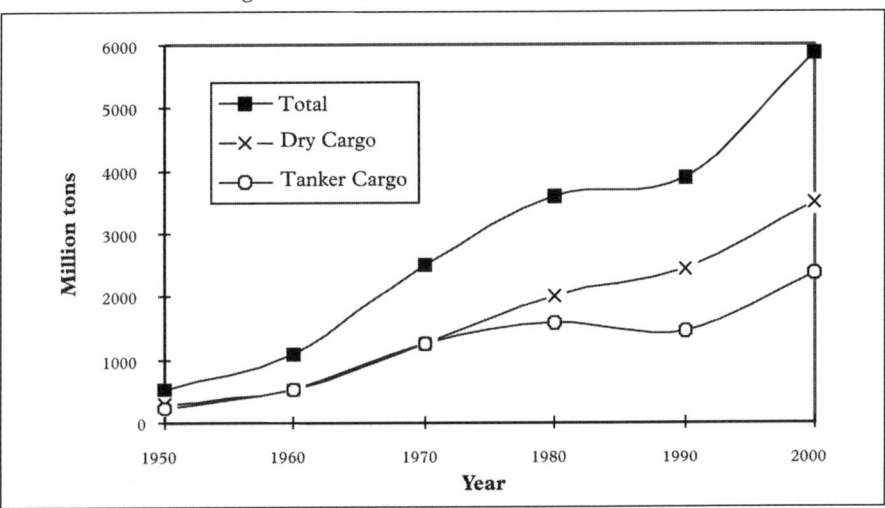

Figure 1: Growth in world seaborne trade

THE ECONOMICS OF SHIPPING FREIGHT MARKETS 161

Main specific markets post 1970s

Figure 2 shows the growth in the world container traffic from 1970–1995 and illustrates that although the global growth has been consistently increasing the growth has varied in the three main trading regions. In 2000 World Container Ports handling increased by 8.7% but in South-East Asia and South America the growth would be nearer 25%. Note that some 20% of container traffic is in empty containers. ISL predicts an annual growth rate of 7.5% for world container port throughput between 2000–2005.

Figure 3 indicates the percentage of general cargo that is containerised in the global situation. At many of the major ports in the developed countries that percentage may be well into the 90s.

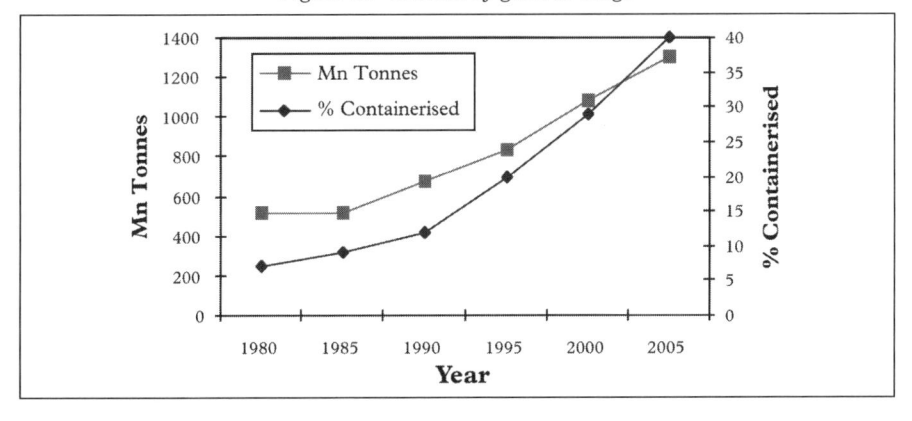

The dry bulk trades

In 1937 total seaborne trade of all mineral ores was 25m tons. Demand due to post war reconstruction boomed during the 1950s helped by re-armament

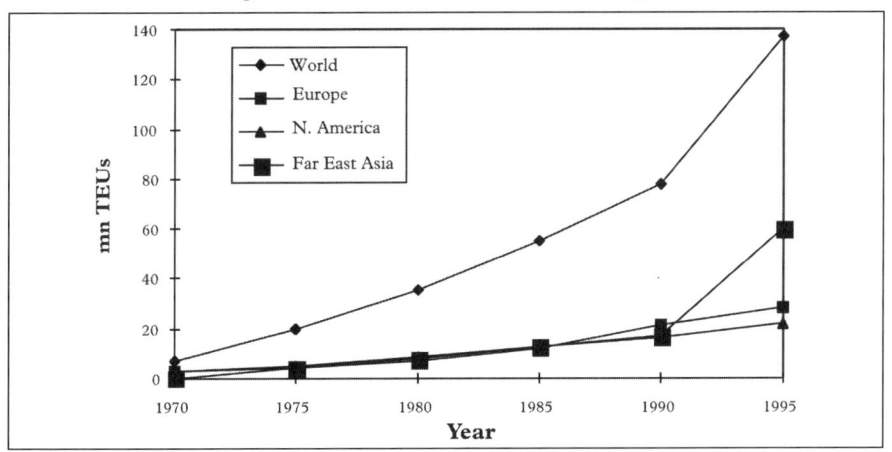

Figure 2: Growth in world container traffic

Figure 3: Growth of general cargo

Table 1: World dry bulk trade

World dry bulk trade in million tonnes					
Year	Iron Ore	Coal	Grain	Bauxite & Alumina	Main Bulk Commodities
1913	30	91.3	39.7		
1929	30	93	47		
1937	30	71	42		
1950	35	45	37		125
1960	101(31%)	46(6.5%)	46(2%)	17	228 (2%)
1960–69	**12.5%**	**8.8%**		Average growth per annum in tonnes	
1960–69	**27.5%**	**19.5%**		Average growth per annum in tonne/miles	
1970	247	101	73	34	500
1980	314	188	198	48	796
1990	347	342	192	49	968
1997	423	453	203		
1975–97	**1.7%**	**6%**	**1.8%**	Average growth per annum in tonnes	
1975–97	**2.3%**	**6.1%**	**2.1%**	Average growth per annum in tonne/miles	
2000	420	490	210		1200

Figures in parentheses indicate the percentage of that cargo carried in bulk carriers.

Figure 4: World crude oil production

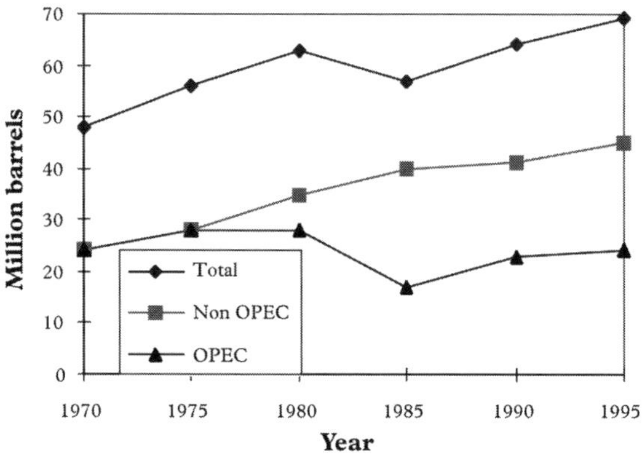

(Korean war) and increased consumer demand, in particular by the motor car industry. During the 1960s the bulk carrier fleet increased from 7 to 70m dwt. During the last few years iron ore, coal and grain have accounted for some 65% of seaborne dry bulk cargo movements. Other important bulk cargoes include bauxite, sugar, wood, wood pulp, wood chips, fertilisers and cars. (full cargoes such as cars and packaged lumber are sometimes referred to as neo-bulks.)

THE ECONOMICS OF SHIPPING FREIGHT MARKETS

Table 2

Year	Million tonnes oil cargo	Tonne/miles x 1000
1976	1,950	11,463
1985	1,198	5,440
1991	1,523	8,000

Tanker cargo

Following the 1973 oil price rise it became economic to develop indigenous sources of supply which is reflected in Table 2, which shows how the distance the oil is carried reduces at a faster percentage rate than the amount of cargo carried.

If India and China increase their energy per capita to only half that of say Europe or Japan the demand in this sector will be tremendous.

Freight costs as a factor in trade demand

Figure 5, comparing the growth of world maritime trade against the reduction of the cost per ton mile (cptm) in pence in 2000 real values, does suggest an inverse correlation between the values. (It does in fact give an $R^2 > 0.9$.)

To what extent do the high freight costs in, say, Africa impede demand?

Table 3: Oil consumption at the end of the 20th century

Country	Energy (bbls per capita)	Oil consumption (bbls per capita)
India	2	0.8
China	4.4	1.3
Korea	28.5	17.2
Japan	29	16.4
UK	27.6	10.7
Germany	29.1	12.6
USA	58.6	24.6

Source: Poten & Partners.

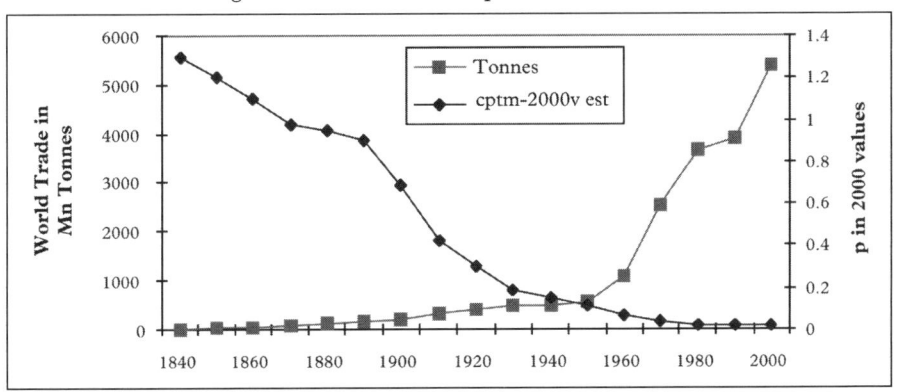

Figure 5: World trade v. cptm in 2000 values

Table 4: Freight costs as a percentage of import values

Country group	Freight costs as a percentage of import values		
	1980	1990	2000
World Total	6.64	5.22	5.06
Developed Countries	5.49	4.4	4.07
Developing Countries	10.44	8.6	8.06
of which in:			
Africa	13.42	11.05	
America	8.85	8.17	
Asia	10.41	8.19	
Europe	8.23	8.96	
Oceana	12.84	12.26	

Source: UNCTAD Review of Maritime Transport.

Derived demand revisited

The intention now is to consider some of the specific demand factors that have altered the freight market in recent decades. The concept of derived demand serves to define and predict the nature and pattern of demand for shipping. Key determinants of demand have been clearly identified by maritime economists. These include: the level and location of economic activity, distance factors, population levels and trend factors. In the last three decades derived demand has been affected by the pattern of deindustrialisation in the mature economies. This has been reflected by changes in such staple trades as coal, iron ore and steel. The run down of the coal mining industry in Northern Europe has created a heavy demand for the deep-sea carriage of steam coal. Australian, Chinese, Columbian, South African and North American coal exports have benefited by the new international division of labour. The economics of such long haul trades are facilitated by the comparative costs of sea transport. Table 5 illustrates the competitiveness of sea transport over long distances. The assumptions made here are based on representative cost between the three transport modes:

(1) Imported South African Coal: Voyage Chartered Capesize Vessel, 180,000 dwt Richards Bay-Clyde, >6000 nautical miles.
(2) UK Mined Coal: Rail Central Scotland-Central England Merry-go-round train. 15 trucks, 200 miles approx. Payload 45 tonnes per truck
(3) UK Mined Coal: Road Central Scotland-Central England Tipper Truck, 200 miles approx. Payload 25 tonnes.

Developments in the inland German Port of Duisburg clearly reflect the deindustrialisation process. The run down of the giant Krupp steel complex not only reduced demand for regionally produced coal but also the import of iron ore via the ports of Rotterdam and Antwerp. The transformation of Duisburg into a centre of logistics now emphasises the growth of container flows through the port.

The switch of heavy industry to the Far East has also had a similar impact on the demand for coking coal.

Table 5: Comparative tonne-mile costs

Mode	Sea	Rail	Road
Rate per tonne	$6.5	$7.7	$9.0
Rate per ton-mile	.001	.002	.007

Source: UNCTAD Review of Maritime Transport.

The impact of changes in the political economy

Freight markets have also been affected by unforeseen changes in the political economy. The impact of the ending of the Cold War, the welcoming of South Africa back into the world trade network and the inexplicable decline of the industrial giants of Japan and Korea.

In the 1970s the growth of the Soviet bloc fleet posed some concern for Western Defence strategists. Fearful that the low cost of the socialist ships would enable them to penetrate crucially important freight markets. It was argued that the socialist ship-managers did not have to pay insurance charges and benefited from low cost East European labour and fuel supplies. On some key liner routes socialist ships were charging rates up to 65% lower than conference rates.[10] The rapid collapse of Communism following the periods of Glasnost and Perestroiksa in the late 1980s has led to a drastic reduction of consumer power as the ex-command economy struggled to achieve a market mechanism. An obvious casualty has been the market for North American grain imports. The normal shortfalls in the Soviet wheat harvest provided a sizeable market for American and Canadian grain. The impoverishment of the economy means that there is little consumer purchasing power and that the state lacks the hard currency to make large scale bulk purchases, regardless of the poor state of the nation's diet.

Another unanticipated outcome of the collapse of the ex-Soviet economy has been the relinquishment of large volumes of merchant shipping into world trade routes. Additionally, the collapse of the Soviet bloc economies in the late 1980s saw large amounts of ageing tonnage and low cost crews entering into the European market. Particularly noticeable has been the incursions of the Russian Volga barges into the trades. These vessels usually named Lagoda were originally intended for the calmer waters of the Volga these vessels can now be seen in the less clement waters of the North Sea, the Irish Sea and the Bay of Biscay. Whilst the Eastern bloc seamen had hitherto enjoyed a sound worldwide reputation for professionalism, the substandard conditions and ships they now find themselves on has diluted their craft status. Typical of the plight of these seamen in British waters was the case of the 2,317 gt Maltese flagged coastal vessel, *Black Sea Star*, which ended up under arrest in the Port of Immingham in summer 2001. It became evident to Mission to Seamen Chaplain, Rev David Craig, that the Georgian crew were in a distressed condition; they had existed on a diet of potato soup for three weeks and some had not received any pay for over a year.[11]

The impact of changes in the international political economy is currently being felt in the Far East, particularly the impact of China's trade liberalisation

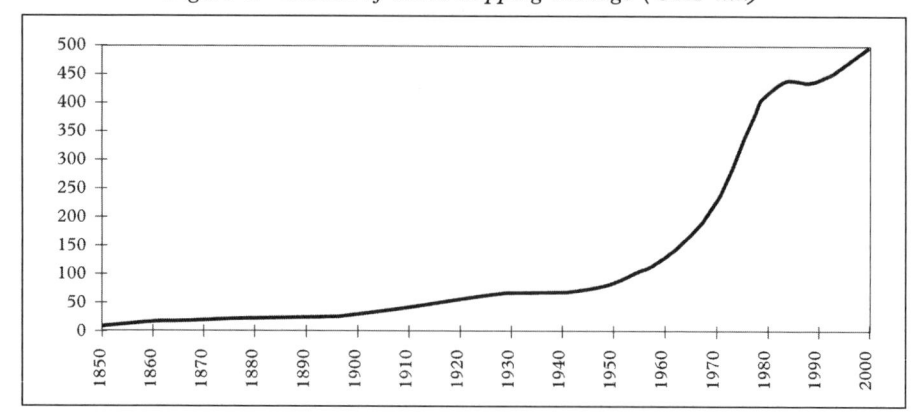

Figure 6: Growth of world shipping tonnage (GRT mn)

and the transfer of Hong Kong to the Peoples' Republic of China as a Special Economic Region.

Supply. The supply of shipping is made up of the carrying capacity of ships to move cargo. This is made up of four main factors.

The first factor is ships. Ships have consistently grown bigger over the last century. The growth was slow from 1880 to 1955 but from 1955 to 1975 the growth was spectacular, as owners realised the possibilities of new technologies and trade routes. 1975 was the time when the last of the ships ordered before the oil crisis ended the boom of the early seventies, were being constructed. Since then the situation has stabilised – tankers, for instance, have not grown any bigger but ferries have. The number of ships: over the last century the number of *ships which carry things* has declined but the total tonnage of ships has greatly increased. The reason for this is *the size*.

Figure 7 indicates that the depth of water was not a major issue until the 1960s. Even in 1950 Rotterdam still had only ten meters. In 1970 there were only eight ports in Europe which could accept the new class of VLCC tankers and there were no ports with sufficient depth of water on the east coast of North America. By 1975, following a period of energetic dredging there were 22 ports in north-west Europe which could accept such ships. Dredging is a very expensive activity and the question facing port managers is: "Will ships continue to get bigger?" Figure 7, showing average ship size since 1850, does indicate a levelling off in average ship size after 1980. If the average of the five largest tankers are considered for each year it can be seen tanker size peaked around 1975. If the same exercise is considered for dry bulk carriers their size seems to have peaked around 1985–1989. If so, should one dredge the old channel or develop a new terminal in an area which enjoys deeper water?

The second factor is Port Time. The less time ships spend in port the more cargo they can carry in a year – hence reducing port time increases the supply of ships.

Another factor is speed – increasing speed obviously increases the supply of ships and vice versa. This is the only way supply can be adjusted in the short

THE ECONOMICS OF SHIPPING FREIGHT MARKETS 167

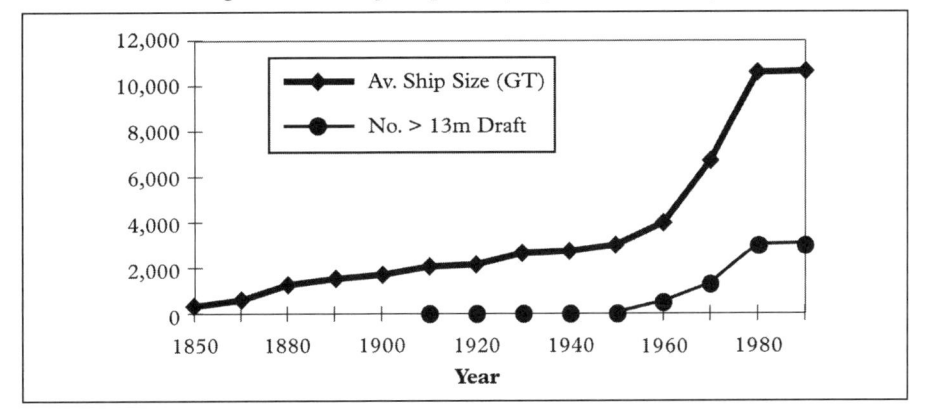

Figure 7: Average ship size (GT)/No.>13m draft

term – apart from laying ships up and reactivating them. Few marine engines allow wide variations of speeds but reducing speed two or three knots can show significant economies, so "slow steaming" can be a valid strategy in the attempt to balance supply and demand or to reduce propulsion costs in periods of high bunker costs, as seen in the late 1970s and early 1980s.

Perhaps a more useful analysis is to consider the supply from the different types of vessels.

Cruise vessels

Originally cruise ships tended to be relatively small catering for say less than 500 passengers as they needed to be able to manoeuvre in and out of the smaller historical and romantic ports on the "traditional" cruise itinerary.

General cargo and container ships

In 1998 there were some 36 container ships with drafts greater than 14 metres. From the 3,000-box ship of 1972 container ship size did not increase any fur-

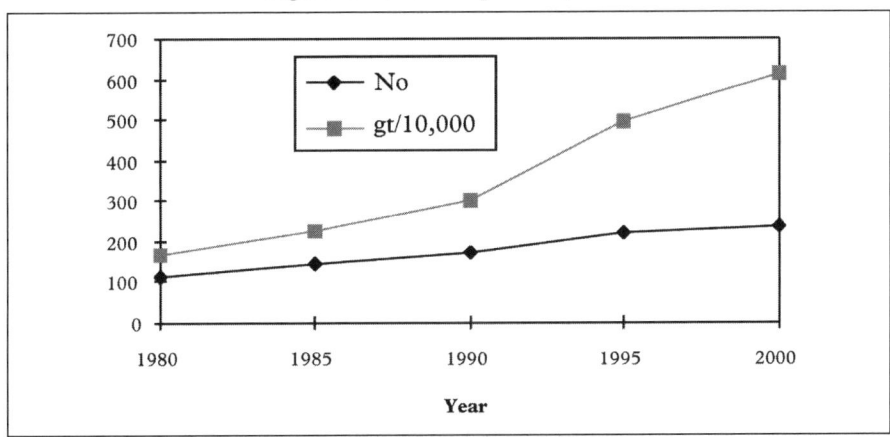

Figure 8: Cruise ship development

Table 6: Dry cargo fleets, 1970–2000

Ship Type	1970 No.	GT mn	1980 No.	GT mn	2000 No.	GT mn	Age	dwt mn
General cargo	22,366	72.4	22,676	81.3	16,755	54.9	22	78
Container	167	1.9	662	11.3	2,590	60.2	10	69.1

Source: UNCTAD Review of Maritime Transport.

Table 7: The increasing size of the container ship

Date	Generation	No. of TEUs	Speed	Length (m) Draft (m)	No. – 1999
1960–1970	1st	<1,000	16	200 9	831
1970–1980	2nd	1,000–2,999	23	275 10	1,136
1987	3rd	3,000–4,000	23	290 11.5	222
Start of post Panamax v/ls: Max. size for the Panama Canal = 289.5m Loa, 32.3m beam 12.04m.					
1988	4th	4,000–6,000	23	320 14.3	172
1996	5th	6,000–8,000	23	310 –42.8b 14.5	22
	6th	8,000 +	23	338 46b 13m draft	

6th Generation – see *Lloyd's List*, July 1998, on proposed new Maersk tonnage.

ther until 1982 when the 4000-box was introduced. From there another size plateau was sustained until the early 1990s when the 6,500-box ship appeared. McLellan's[13] analysis of this growth in container ship size concludes that one serious constraint on building a 6000+ box vessel was the lack of an engine that could generate the necessary 90,000 bhp capable of driving such a vessel at 24.5 knots on a single screw. However, the development of the Sulzer 12RTA96C and the MAN B & W 12K98MC-C reduced this problem. As ships' beams increase, cranes must also increase in size. This involves increase in weight and there comes a point when the terminal cannot take the extra load without considerable civil engineering expense. As ships' drafts increase, depth of water in ports becomes a problem. Virtually all major ports have 10 metres but few can offer over 15 metres.

For large ships to maintain the same schedules as their smaller brethren cargo-handling speeds will have to be increased. From this it follows that the terminal area will need to be increased and the inland distribution facilities improved. Increasing the size of ships may well also increase the peaking factor which can be a serious cost problem for a centre hub port.

Table 9 shows the numbers of vessels in the accepted commercial sector classification. As can be seen the number of feeder vessels and their TEU capacity is quite small but so is the average length of their round voyage compared with the post Panamax vessels which will be used on the longer routes.

The term "Ro/Ro" can cover a variety of ships such as car ferries, specialist vehicle carriers, of which over 50% are owned by the Japanese, and general cargo ships which are described as having Ro/Ro capability. These Ro/Ro ships

Table 8: Container ship sizes

Ship Size	No of Tiers Underdeck	No. of Tiers on Deck	No. of Rows across Deck
2,000 TEUs	7	4	13
3,000 TEUs	7/8	4/5	13
4,000 TEUs	8/9	5/6	13
5,000 TEUs	9	5/6	16
6,000 TEUs	9	5/6/7	17
15,000 TEUs*	10/11	6/7	28

* Hypothetical vessel.
Source: McLellan (1997).[12]

Table 9: World container fleet in operational categories in 2000

Sector	TEU Range	No of v/s	% of Vessels	% of TEU capacity
Feeder	100–499	376	15	2
Feedermax	500–999	482	19	7
Handy	1000–1999	801	32	25
Sub-Panamax	2000–2999	399	16	21
Panamax	3000–3999	230	9	17
Post Panamax	4000–4999	157	6	15
Post Panamax	5000–5999	60	2	7
Post Panamax	6000+	32	1	4

are expensive; a 15,000 dwt size would be about twice the price of a conventional ship of this size and the "wasted space" can be considerable but their productivity is very high and their extreme flexibility – virtually anything can be rolled on, containers, heavy loads, large objects, etc. – makes them attractive to operate. These ships have also been referred to as STO/ROs in cases where the cargo is rolled on board by fork lift trucks which stow and handle the cargo as in a warehouse. Ro/Ros have also proved very useful in areas where congestion has occurred.

It was originally considered that Ro/Ro was only suitable for short distances but many such ships have been operating for years between Europe and Australia and across the Pacific – there are also ships which are part cellular containership and part Ro/Ro.

The oil tanker market

As can be seen from Figure 9 there has been a considerable correlation between tanker supply and demand, though after the oil price rise in 1973 there was, in the short term, a reduction in demand which left, for that period, an excess of supply.

Table 10: Ro/Ro fleets, 1993–2000

	1993		2000			
Ship Type	No.	GT mn	No.	GT mn	Age	dwt mn
Ro/Ro cargo	1,494	14.4	1,882	27.1	17	13.7
Ro/Pax	2,125	8.4	2,574	13.1	21	3.8

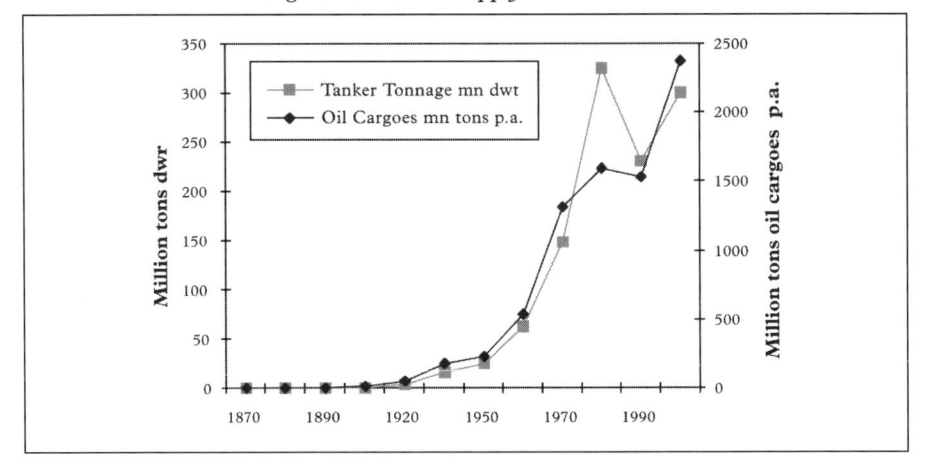

Figure 9: Tanker supply and demand

The dry bulk carrier

A bulk carrier is a large single deck ship, say >10,000 dwt which carries unpackaged cargo. Statistics concerning bulk carriers may not be always consistent as different authors and different times will arbitrarily determine at what size a single decked vessel will classed as a bulk carrier. The term bulk cargo is however simply unpackaged cargo that can be poured, tipped or pumped into the holds or tanks of the ship.

Although there have been colliers for centuries carrying bulk coal and grain and various ores have also a long history of bulk carriage, the modern concept of a variety of bulk cargoes being loaded and discharged quickly into single deck "open hatch" dry cargo ships from modern terminals equipped for handling bulk cargoes, dates only from the mid 1950s.

Shipping textbooks written in the 1940s and early 1950s refer to bulkers but these seemed to have been on the Great Lakes or part of a vertically integrated operation. Like container ships they were born of economic necessity. Tramp freight rates were very depressed though demand was increasing after the Korean war, so a cheaper means of carrying bulk cargoes had to be found. Also technically it was not possible to build open hatch ships much before this date In 1962 there were only 21 bulk carriers over 40,000 dwt and the world total of bulk carriers was only 611.

The particular design features of a bulk carrier are the single deck, a large hatchway and wing tanks. The upper wing tanks are shaped to give a conical transverse section to the hatch, so that when bulk cargo is being poured in the amount of "trimming" is reduced as the cargo is being loaded. When loading bulk cargoes the danger has always been that the upper corners of the hold would be left empty with the consequent danger of the cargo shifting in bad weather

The large bulk carriers usually trade between special terminals and therefore seldom have any derricks or lifting gear. Smaller bulk carriers have to be prepared to discharge anywhere so will usually have their own gear.

THE ECONOMICS OF SHIPPING FREIGHT MARKETS

Table 11: Types of tankers

Ship Type	1970 No.	1970 GT mn	1980 No.	1980 GT mn	1995 No.	1995 GT mn	2000 No.	2000 GT mn	% GT all v/ls	Age
Oil	6,103	86.1	7,112	175	6,761	144	7,009	156	29.4	16
Liquefied Gas	288	1.4	631	7.4	986	14.9	1126	19.7	3.7	14
Chemical	216	0.5	649	2.2	2,077	12.1	2,534	17.5	3.3	14
0/0 and OBOs	207	8.31	424	26.2	226	14.1	205	8.6	1.6	17
Other liquids			120	0.2	316	0.4	345	0.5	0.1	23

The most popular sizes are:
- 10,000–25,000 tons dead-weight – these are some times referred to as "handysize" as they can trade to most ports in the world though 20,000 is about the largest size that can use the St Lawrence Seaway. There were some 77.4 million dwt in this class in 2000.
- Handymax 35,000–50,000. There were some 45.5 million dwt in this class in 2000.
- Panamax class, which is the largest size that can use the Panama Canal. This is about 65,000 dwt as the limiting lock width is just over 32 metres

Table 12: Bulk carriers

1852	John Bowes – worlds first successful collier – precursor of the bulk carrier 750 dwt. Previous sail colliers c 280 tons
1873	A Royal Commission on Unseaworthy Ships – witness asserted grain the most dangerous of all bulk cargoes. However, the encouragement of the Commission did little good to improve the situation. In 1880 there was an effort to reduce the problem of grain shifting. The MSA of 1894 set the standard from then until 1914
1883	Mechanical handling of iron ore used in the Great Lakes
1892	Great Lakes had a specialised self unloader *Samuel Mitchell*. 1916 converted to self unloading cement carrier. Still in service in 1981.
1894	The 1894 Merchant Shipping Acts have provisions concerning the carriage of bulk grain.
1900	Iron ore carriers
1900	Associated Portland Cement Manufacturers (Blue Circle) had its first bulk cement vessel
1904	Stag line has a bulk carrier fleet in 1904 (firm founded in 1846)
1909	Hulett unloaders with 15 ton grabs could discharge a 12,000 ore carrier in 1 shift
1910	steel hatch covers fitted in large colliers and ore carriers
1929	Ore loading plant Durban Source Lloyds List (LL) 1/6/29
1935	Ore discharging plant Rotterdam Source LL
1944	Ore carrier with own belt unloading system
1949	First ship arrives in London with 5,073 tons bulk sugar (the *Bara Haig*)
1954	a paper on *The Development of Ore Carriers*
1954	May 27 LR assigned a class for ore carriers
1956	New design for all purpose bulk carrier
1964	Carlton claimed to be the 1st Universal Bulk Carrier
1965	*Naess Norsemam* of 71,183 dwt possibly the first OBO

Table 13: Development in the size and tonnage of bulk carriers

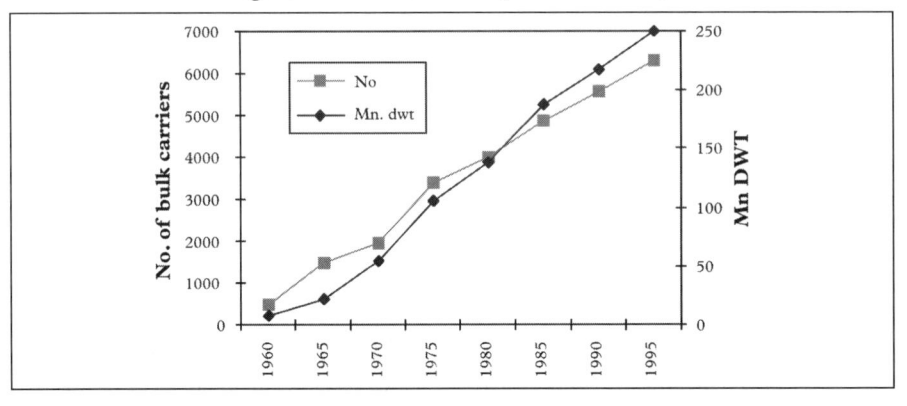

Year	No	Mn dwt	GT mn tons	Age	Self discharging	No. O/O +OBO
1938		4				
1948		2.8				
1952		2.9				
1960		7				
1965	1493	22	18.8			87–3.4gt mn
1970	1964	55.1	38.3			212–8gt mn
1980	4020	137.7	83.4			406–26gt mn
1995	4316	214.0	121.1	14	154–2.8gt mn	244–15.2gt mn
2000	4886	255.0	142.7	14	165–3.2gt mn	205–8.6gt mn

Figure 10: Bulk carriers (No. v. mn dwt)

and with a maximum LOA of 289.5 metres This class is important as much of the ore trade is through the Panama Canal. There were some 70.5 million dwt in this class in 2000.
- Capesize bulkers which are 100,000–180,000 dwt and are used mainly for ore and coal on specific routes between well equipped terminals. There were some 86.6 million dwt in this class in 2000.
- VLBC Bulkers greater than 180,000 of which most are trading between Australia & Japan.

During the period between 1969–1970 they proved to be one of the most lucrative ships to operate and have been one of the largest growing types of ship outside the tanker fleets. In 1972 bulk carriers made up 17% of world GT. In 1995 bulk carriers represent 32% of the world shipping tonnage, i.e. there were about 4,600 bulk carriers with a total dwt tonnage of over 200 million. Liberia, Panama, were the main countries of registry.

Type variations

Combos – that is, dry and wet bulkers. Experiments had been tried in the 1920s but it was not until the 1950s that the combination types became built in any numbers and Universal Bulk Carriers (UBCs) were developed but by the 1980s this type had largely disappeared being superseded by O/Os (early 1950s) and

OBOs (1965). Around 1970 the Conbulker was introduced which are bulkers fitted for carrying containers, packaged timber and/or bulk cargo.

The equilibrium

As Figure 11 illustrates, supply and demand in the shipping world are seldom in balance. In the early 1970s they were close, which was why these were profitable years for shipowners. In 1973 demand exceeded supply and this was a very profitable year but in October 1973 came the oil price rise following the Arab Israeli war and there has been surplus tonnage ever since with the inevitable lowering of freight rates. The surplus does not have to be large. If there are 10 shiploads and 9 ships the shipowner can be a price maker but if there are 10 shiploads and 11 ships the shipowner will be a price taker and can be beaten down to the break even cost of the cheapest operator.

If the shipping market was a genuinely *free* market one would expect supply and demand to remain in step but the shipping market has problems; Ships take a long time to build. There will be a rush of ordering during periods of high freight rates and it may be several years before they are actually delivered. The new owners will be reluctant to sell as prices will probably be also low and the new owners will also not wish to "lay up" as they will usually have to make monthly payments to a financier. Many of the new shipowners enticed into shipowning following the very high rates of 1973 were state enterprises , many in developing countries, who thought they had found a solution to their hard currency problems. When the freight rates started to fall many received the advice to "hang on" as the market will recover in a few months. Governments were therefore encouraged to intervene with subsidies and financial help and therefore the surplus increased.

Note that the graph in Figure 11 is a global one and the actual situation has been different in each market. For instance the dry cargo market has never actually seen a decrease in demand but since 1973 the supply has outstripped it.

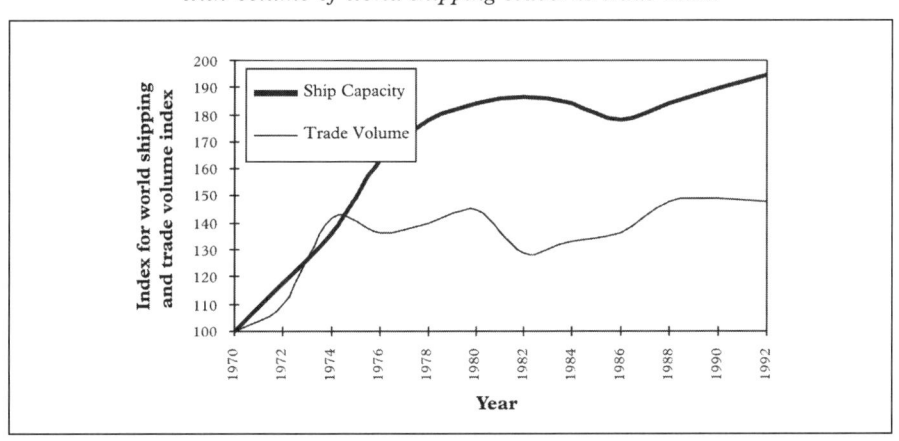

Figure 11: Comparison of world shipping capacity index with volume of world shipping seaborne trade index

Over-capacity in the liner freight market

Despite the enduring problems of the dry bulk and tanker sectors in recent decades, the liner sector has maintained a position close to the equilibrium. This contrast was typically explained by maritime economists as the difference between low and high entry barriers. The relatively low technology, low capital cost of a bulk carrier or a crude oil tanker posed few barriers to entry. By way of contrast, the high capital costs of vessels and their container suites, plus the need to set up a reputable quality door-to-door service, militated against market entry of all but the most determined and resourceful shipping line. Furthermore the protection placed by the liner conference ensured that over-capacity resulting from to many carriers was avoided. Critical mass is an important factor in entering the major conferences. This would entail at least six $100m, state-of-the-art, 25 knot post-panamax container ships as an entry ticket to Transpacific or Europe-Far East conferences. In addition, the administrative infrastructure of a global logistics provider is vital.

With the emphasis on service and a large asset portfolio, the focus has always been on quality) rather than unbridled price competition.[14] Well this was the story up until the late 1990s and into the new millennium. This era was to witness a period of over-capacity in the liner trades – a economic phenomena new to the sector.

The shock of over-capacity and its resulting impact on liner freight tariffs has been hard felt in the industry. Following a decade of continuous investment in new, large vessels, the major carriers found themselves not in the stable, regulated market as envisaged by the original founders of the conference.

Porter's *Five Forces*[15] are used as a benchmark of competitive structure. These are composed of:

(1) the threat of new entrants;
(2) the threat of substitute products or services;
(3) the bargaining power of suppliers;
(4) the bargaining power of buyers;
(5) rivalry among existing competitors.

During the early years of containerisation, new entrant companies from the Asian Tiger nations added to the supply of tonnage. Taiwan's Evergreen Line, Singapore's Neptune Orient Line (NOL) and Hong Kong's Overseas Ocean Container Line (OOCL) were all challengers to the status quo, hitherto dominated by US, Japanese and European Liner companies. In recent decades, however, these new entrants have become assimilated into the liner status quo.

With limited threat from substitute products and services the liner operators enjoy a predominance over alternative types of shipping. The bargaining power of suppliers is also diminished. Shipbuilders in Korea, China and Japan have all reduced rates post 1995 in their desperate bids for new business. The global manifold supply of ships' crews ensures that there is always cost and quality competition between labour forces. The bargaining power of the buyers of liner services may be seen as represented by liner conference participation. However, this has been partly off-set by trends towards merger and concentration in liner ownership. Large groupings – Maersk-Sealand, P&O-Nedlloyd, APL-NOL have ostensibly strengthened the bargaining power of the owners. The paradox of these trends, however, is that the liner freight market has suffered not from any disadvantages accruing from an oligopoly position but from an enduring over-capacity and correspondingly depressed freight rates. The figure above describes problem on the premier transpacific trade lane.

The greening of freight markets

A major change in freight markets in the last three decades has been the intensifying focus on maritime safety and environmental factors. Whereas earlier attention had been focused on the dynamics of the market mechanism, it is now impossible to extricate the normal economic transactions of the freight market from environmental standards, particularly in the tanker sector.

Major environmental advances have occurred in the international maritime regime in recent decades. These include, the prevention of waste dumping waste dumping into the sea, the outlawing of oil tank slops dumping, double hull regulations for oil tankers, segregated ballast water systems and toxic anti-fouling hull protection chemicals. These factors have become an essential part of the freight market as charterers, owners and operators struggle to come to terms with the new environmental imperative. The imposition of global standards via the IMO undoubtedly leads to an increase in the private costs of shipping. This is at odds with the traditional and enduring concept of "The Freedom of the Seas", which has been held as an essential component of the free market in shipping.[16] The resilience of this concept is clearly demonstrated by the battles to regulate the safe passage of shipping in one of the world's busiest seaways, the Dover Straits. From the 1880s onwards calls for increased regulation have been resisted by shipowners and their principals on the grounds

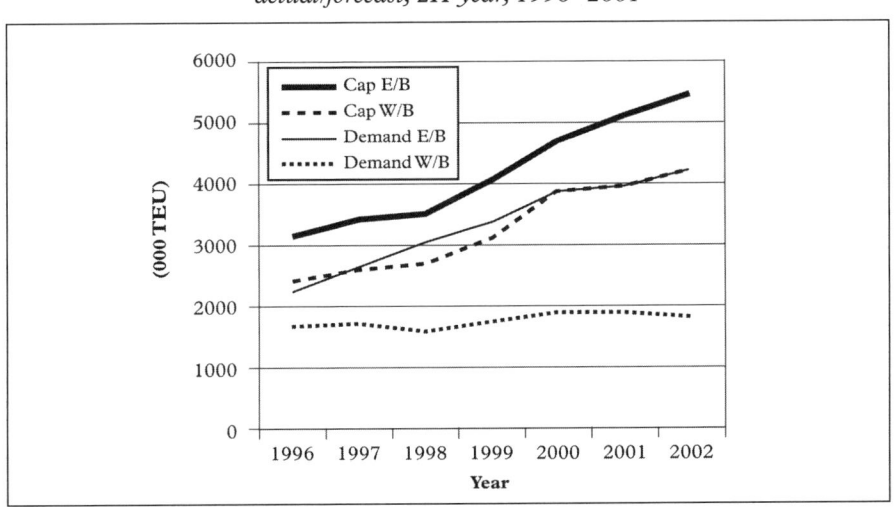

Figure 12: Transpacific container demand and supply, actual/forecast, 2H year, 1996–2001

that there was a need to retain a free market.[17] The market failure – loss of life, pollution, vessel damage, trade disruption – resulting from shipping's failure to manage its own safety in such critical conditions was to prove untenable.

The upsurge in vessel traffic, in conjunction with increases in vessel size, began to manifest as causes of rising trends in serious English Channel collisions and groundings in the 1960s and 1970s. The following sequence of tragic events demonstrates not only the traffic intensity of the Dover Straits but also the positive impact of traffic regulation. Things came very much to a head in 1971 with the serious collision between the Panamanian flag tanker, *Texaco Caribbean* and the Cypriot flag dry cargo vessel, *Paracas*, in the Dover Straits on January 11th. The tanker exploded, broke into two sections and eight crewmen were lost. The disaster was compounded the following day when the German vessel, *Brandenburg*, struck a section of the tanker at full speed and within 2 miles capsized and sank with the loss of 21 crewmen. The final part of this catalystic sequence came on February 27th when the Norwegian tanker, *Hebris*, reported a vessel sinking ahead. This proved to be the Greek cargo vessel, *Niki*, which had run into one the sunken hulls; another 22 lives were lost as a result. The resulting loss of life (51 seafarers in total) wreck of ships and catastrophic oil pollution focused attention on the anarchic practice of navigation in such confined and congested waters. The resulting Vessel Traffic Regulation System brought all vessels under the surveillance of the French and British Traffic centres, Cap Gris Nez and Dover Langdon Battery. Clearly defined Traffic Separation Schemes (TSS) had been first introduced in 1967, however "rogue" vessels straying outside of their allotted track still averaged 20–30 per day in 1972.[18] Gradually, however, intensified monitoring using radar and computer screen plotting of vessel headings has led to illegal incidents declining. By the 1990s "rogues" were down to around four per day.[19] High profile prosecution by the Dover Magistrates and their Normandy equivalents have helped to enforce TSS.

The management of safety

The question over shipping's environmental performance is inextricably linked with quality. The manner in which the vessel is crewed, maintained and operated is a function of management. This was established in a leading Admiralty case involving the management of coastal shipping operations. Case law was provided by the *Lady Gwendolen*. In 1965[20] the vessel was directly owned by the Dublin brewer, Arthur Guinness, and was engaged on the important Dublin-Manchester stout beer trade. In order to keep to the schedule the master, Captain Meredith, adopted the practice of navigating at full speed, relying on radar observation, even in the frequently foggy conditions of the Irish Sea and River Mersey. The unfortunate outcome of this practice in November 1961 was collision and sinking of the coastal vessel, *Freshfield*, which was anchored fog-bound in the approaches to Liverpool. Although the recklessness of the Master was found to be a contributory factor in the accident, the owners, Arthur Guinness were deemed negligent in not adequately monitoring the way the *Lady Gwendolen* was operated. Lord Justice Sellers summarised:

"A primary concern of a shipowner must be the safety of life at sea. That involves a seaworthy ship, properly manned but also requires safe navigation. Excessive speed in fog is a grave breach of duty, and shipowners should use all their influence to prevent it."[21]

Although there was no evidence to suggest that the master was under pressure from the owners to maintain schedules in poor weather conditions, the case does illustrate the balance between shipping efficiency and operational safety.

A more serious accident which did bring condemnation of the shoreside management was that of the *Herald of Free Enterprise* disaster in 1987. The loss of the ferry in Zeebrugge Harbour with the loss of 189 passenger and crew. Following the lengthy investigation into the disaster management systems failures were identified as a principal cause. The vessel attempted to leave Zeebrugge without securing her bow doors. The resulting water ingress (from the bow wave) as the vessel picked up speed quickly led to the vessel entering into an irretrievable list situation. The dichotomy between commercial considerations and basic seafaring safety was highlighted by the report. In evidence it became apparent that vessel's leaving port on intensive Channel routes was not an uncommon practice. Several Masters of the ferries had requested a double check system which assured them that the doors were secured before sailing. This request was denied by a disdainful management. The same management were later to be thoroughly criticised for their failure to manage safety competently.[22]

Such cases emphasise the duties of the shipowner. Increasingly this responsibility is becoming a feature of the freight market. The aftermath of the *Exxon Valdez* oil pollution disaster in 1989 and the resulting US Oil Pollution Act (OPA 90), intensified the trend towards corporate liability. In June 1990 *Fairplay* expressed the dilemma facing oil majors trading to US waters:

"It is quickly becoming impossible to put a cost on trading tankers to the US. And that means it is unattractive, ultimately unacceptable business."[23]

Costs and competition

The dichotomy between cost competition and the quality of operational standards is a feature of modern freight markets. This is evident in low value bulk markets such as scrap, aggregates and animal feeds. In such highly competitive freight markets costs are trimmed to the narrowest of margins. The enduring concerns over bulk carrier safety have been a feature of the last three decades. The Derbyshire disaster prompted concerns over bulk carrier safety. Foy's study of bulker losses in the 18 month period up until June 1987 revealed 11 founderings in the steel/scrap/iron ore sectors.[24] The North European container feeder sector is another example of this. Feeder rates are driven down by three powerful factors:
 – the extent of the competition from many small operators of chartered tonnage;
 – the alternatives of road and rail haulage to coastal/shortsea shipping;
 – the buying (oligopsony) power of the large liner groupings.

The problem was highlighted by the total loss of the container feeder ship, *Cita*, in 1997.[25] In this instance the fatigue factor was a very real component of the vessel's grounding. One way of reducing operational costs, introduced in the early 1990s, was the One Man Bridge Operation (OMBO). International Regulations stipulate that in the hours of darkness and also poor daytime visibility, two watchkeepers will carry out bridge duties. Primarily this is to limit the risk of watchkeepers falling asleep and to provide extra look out capabilities – a particularly welcome support in confined and congested waters. The OMBO system was devised as a labour saving device in that it facilitated one watchkeeper operation. Integral to the system is the anti-sleep alarm which ensures that the watchkeeper does not fall asleep. The need to respond to the alarm at frequent intervals, however, may be seen as an irksome task by the irritated officer. Unfortunately this has led to irresponsible behaviour with officers switching off the system. Invariably this leads to sleeping watchkeepers and ensuing near misses, collisions and groundings. The fate of the *Cita* was sealed when the Chief Officer switched off the system on a voyage between Southampton and Belfast. The inevitable happened, the Chief Officer fell asleep, and the vessel grounded on St Mary's Isle (Scilly Isles) at full speed. As well as the vessel being condemned as a constructive total loss along with her container cargo.[26]

The incident revealed the gruelling schedule that such coastal feeder vessels have to adhere to (outlined in Table 14).

Table 14: Feeder service schedule (Netherlands–UK–Eire)

Day	Depart	Arrive
Sunday pm	Rotterdam	
Monday noon		Southampton
Monday pm	Southampton	
Wednesday noon		Belfast
Wednesday pm	Belfast	
Thursday am		Dublin
Thursday pm	Dublin	
Saturday am		Southampton
Saturday pm	Southampton	
Sunday am		Rotterdam

Source: MAIB.

An identical case to the *Cita* loss was that of the *Coastal Bay*. It was established that the vessel was operated by just two watch keeping officers, with the Master and the Chief Officer working a fatiguing rotating watch on watch system. Lloyd's List's reporting of the incident referred to:

"The seven day overnight cycle for months on end. The mate was on a four month contract and had been operating for 84 days non-stop under a regime which never permitted either he or the master ever to enjoy a six hour period of real sleep."[27]

Blame was diverted from the watchkeepers: the MAIB targeted the vessel managers, imposing a $29,481 fine plus $8,844 costs.[28] Such cases not only demonstrate the economic pressures placed upon operators and their crews but also the growing determination of the authorities to rectify the imbalance between cost and quality operations.

The waste issue

Cultural change in the disposal of waste has occurred in recent decades. The clean seas strategy of the International Maritime Organisation (IMO) has led to an enhanced ethical attitude towards waste. Nautical Institute Secretary, Julian Parker succinctly summarised the previous "over the wall" culture: "... all the main trade routes could be identified by from beer cans on the bottom of the ocean".[29] In European waters the problem of tank washing and its overside disposal was evident from coastline pollution. Main tanker routes generated oil trails with disastrous impact on the coastline environment. Partly the change in behaviour has been as a result of the encouragement of such proactive strategies such as the "Green Award". Tanker terminals such as Sullom Voe and Rotterdam make the award to vessels which attain high environmental standards and entitles the owners to rebates on port dues.

Up until the impact of environmental concern and sensitivity of the late 20th Century much of the vessel's waste went "over the wall" (into the sea). This would include oily rags, empty oil drums, beer and food cans and food waste. Concerns over the amount of carbon soaked and plastic based wastes finding their way into the ocean from ships has led to a 1995 amendment of the International Convention for the Prevention of Pollution from Ships (Marpol 73/78). This stipulates that all vessels over 400 gt are required to have a garbage management plan and record book. A 2000 study into the efficiency of waste disposal at sea by Captain Patraiko of the Nautical Institute has found that a contrasting pattern of how the plans were initiated.[30] Clearly, the evidence of the study found that advances were being made in the education of crews and the development of a waste management culture. Examples of waste segregation was found in 70% of vessels surveyed. Also, the practice of incinerating wastes such as plastic and oil was well advanced.

A problem area identified was that poor waste reception facilities in come ports. Examples of positive crew attitudes to waste recycling being undermined by inadequate port reception systems. These include simply amassing the carefully segregated waste into one single container. Likewise, the efforts of the crew to achieve efficient waste disposal standards were undermined by poor information on port facilities and in some cases bureaucratic non-user friendly procedures. In coastal vessels everything thrown into "the big green bin" was prevalent.[31] Overall, the evidence is of a positive change in waste disposal behaviour with ship's crews and port management increasingly adopting an environmentally friendly response.

The fuel emissions issue

It has been demonstrated that shipping exhaust emissions are in average terms much lower per tonne-miles than road equivalents. European Commission (EC) concerns have focused on the impact of air pollution from ships' exhausts, in particular where heavy concentrations of shipping affected local communities in port city and areas of coastal residential spread. Marpol Annex VI – yet to be fully ratified – places a sulphur cap of 1.5% for ships passing through North Sea and Baltic territorial waters. The International Bunker Industry Association (IBIA), has expressed concern over the impact on voyage costs. In 2002, the IBIA outlined the example of a voyage from Gothenburg to Belfast which under proposed EC rules would require a continuous use of 0.2 sulphur fuel as it consisted of a 100% EC voyage. The IBIA estimated that vessels bunkering in European waters could face an additional $20 per tonne premium.[32] The question facing shipowners and operators is whether such increased cost can be passed onto the shipper, ultimately the consumer. Again it can be seen how environmental factors are increasingly impacting on freight markets.

Environmental standards in the tanker freight market

Tanker design has been held up to a great deal of scrutiny following well publicised disasters such as the *Exxon Valdez*, *Braer*, *Sea Empress* and *Erika*. In addition to the potential for devastating large volume spills of crude and black oils, there is also the problem the release of volatile organic compounds into the atmosphere during loading operations. Partly this can be seen as a result of the relocation of the oil extraction regions from the Persian Gulf to the environmentally (thus politically) sensitive US (Alaska) and Europe (North Sea) fields. This sensitivity places a high premium on safety standards in the oil market, as shuttle tankers replace long-haul VLCC and ULCC operations.

The evidence on double hull shuttle tankers in the North Sea points to a big risk reduction compared to single hull tankers. A 1998 study[33] by US oil offshore oil specialist, Amerada Hess, in conjunction with Lloyd's Register, has concluded shuttle tanker were more at risk than deepsea trading tankers because of their frequent port calls and passages through confined waters, including the loading location zones. Three particular areas of risk were identified – collision, contact (objects other than ships) and grounding. Risk is specifically acute when tankers are manoeuvring close to loading platforms in the North Sea.[34] The Amerada Hess study has found that double hull tankers would reduce spillage from the three risk areas identified by 75%.[35] The demand of North Sea loading operations, frequently in adverse weather conditions, places great stress on skill and managerial systems. The study found that almost all reportable incidents were attributable to human error. Although the shuttle tankers are fitted with dynamic positioning devices this manoeuvring aid needs the utmost level of skill and concentration. A 1999 study by the International Marine Contractors Association has concluded that better training is required in order that vessel operators understand the limitations of their vessels under the strained circumstances of platform manoeuvring; it was also found that they need the courage and management support to disconnect as soon as unacceptable positional instability occurs.[36]

The 1999 new building, *Navion Britannia*, for the Norwegian state owned Statoil Group and its joint venture partner, Rasmussen, was the first of a trio of advanced, environmentally focused, 120,00dwt shuttle tankers. The trio were greeted as providers of "A new era in shuttles" by *Lloyd's Tanker Focus* in October 1998.[37] Built by the state owned Spanish yard, Astilleros Espanoles, Astilleros Sestao, for the crude oil trades of the Norwegian field these vessels operate effectively as coasting vessels and can be found trading to at such British oil refinery ports as Southampton (Fawley Marine Terminal) and Milford Haven. The environmental interest is protected by a number of design features. Loading tanks are designed in order to reduce VOCs when loading. The prime propulsion system is provided by two symmetrical but independent engine rooms, divided by a fire-resistant, watertight bulkhead. The advantages of this are that in the event of a breakdown in one of the engines, the Master is still able to control the vessels on one engine. Manoeuvrability is a critical safety factor in the off-shore trades and this is aided by twin bow thrusters, a stern thruster, twin rudders and propellers. The vessels loading capability is greatly aided by a dynamic positioning system. The vessels 18 cargo tanks and fuel oil tanks are encompassed in a double hull arrangement which reduces the risk of oil leakage in the event of a collision or grounding.

Naval architects Armstrong Technology have identified tanker risks, including a 0.2% cargo loss equaling 200 tonnes of crude in a typical 100,000 dwt shuttle tanker loading operation.[38] The result of this emission is that lower order hydrocarbons (non-methane VOCs) react in sunlight with nitrous oxides (Nox) and contribute to ground level ozone. Armstrong's safety case is built around the following key design features:

- double hull construction in excess of Marpol rule 13f;
- all bunker and ready use fuel tanks protected by double hull;
- a volatile organic compounds (voc) recovery system;
- designed for ballast water exchange at sea;
- reliability assessment of hull girder structure;
- designed structural connections to have a fatigue life with
- a minimum factor of safety equal to twice the operating life;
- diesel-electric propulsion which ensure machinery operates at it most efficient loading.[39]

The *Erika* shock

The history of oil freight markets has been punctuated by a number of serious, defining accidents. The 1967 *Torrey Canyon* grounding on Seven Stones reef was instrumental in promoting the English Channel vessel traffic scheme. Similarly the large scale pollution following the grounding of the *Exxon Valdez*, the *Braer* and the *Sea Empress*.

The shock of the 1999 *Erika* break up and sinking had implications for the industry stretching into the new millennium. Ostensibly, the tanker on passage between Dunkerque and Livorno with 25,000 tonnes of heavy fuel oil was a tangible example of the coastal highway at work. 25,000 tonnes of oil represents the equivalent more than 800 road tanker journeys across the Alps. However, the combination of Gale force weather conditions and an ageing, metal corroded, vessel was to prove an environmental disaster for the French coastline and its ecology. It has been estimated that compensation payments will be in the region of €300m.[40] For the chartering oil major, Total-Elf, the result was not only heavy financial penalties but also the loss of corporate reputation. However, the immediate aftermath of the Erika and similar tanker disasters has led to more stringent state intervention in the market.

(1) Large chartering companies, particularly the oil majors need to be targeted as a deterrent to sub-standard operations.
(2) In Europe the environmental sensitivity of large stretches of coastline has focused attention on qualitative factors, including the charterers vetting of ships.
(3) Safety standards such as ISO 9000 and the International Safety Management (ISM) Code have placed emphasis on the management systems of not only the operators but also the charterers.
(4) It is also evident that public opinion in Europe nations will no longer tolerate the environmental costs of substandard operations.

The reality of shipping supply and demand is that in many markets, many shipowners compete for the business of much fewer buyers of shipping services, the shippers. The role of the charterer is crucial to improving standards of ships in this oligopsonistic market which bestows market power on the buyer of shipping services. Leading UK shortsea operator, Michael Everard, has argued that "Charterers should take responsibility for the ships they charter".[41]

Six principles of maritime safety within the European Union were outlined Transport Commissioner, Neil Kinnock, in 1996:

(1) promotion of IMO regulations on flag administrations responsible for ship registration and control;
(2) definition of common registration principles within the EU;
(3) adoption of a code of conduct on maritime trade;
(4) encouragement of owners to achieve high standards of operational quality;
(5) legislative and financial penalties imposed on shippers employing substandard vessels;
(6) introduction of compulsory third party insurance for vessels trading in the EU.[42]

Environmental concerns are to the forefront in the North Sea oil shuttle trades. The NKr 1.7b 1998 order of three 120,000 dwt twin screw tankers for the Norwegian Government's Statoil fleet featured attention to safety attributes. These include double hulls, tank design which provides increased control of the production and emission of volatile compounds and improved vessel manoeuvring aids.[43] The double hull facility strengthens the integrity of the cargo holds. This is of particular importance in vessel grounding accident situations and was a key talking point in the *Sea Empress* Milford Haven environmental disaster. Loading tanks are arranged with three per section – with two longitudinal bulkheads instead of one – to reduce the release of volatile organic compounds which build up during the loading process. The high degree of manoeuvrability is of special value in the confined North Sea waters, particularly in the oil rig zones. In addition to twin propellers the vessels are assisted by two bow thrusts and a stern thrust.

Table 15: Comparative external cost modelling, Southampton–Livorno

	Sea	**Road**	**Rail**
Trip length(km)	3713	1731	1774
No. equivalent vehicles	1 Ro-Ro ship *Grande Europa* Class	1000 trailers (300 car transporters and 700 heavy duty vehicles	40 trains (600 wagons)
Tonnes moved	14,500	14,500	14,500
Traffic (million tonnes x kilometres)	53.9	25.1	25.7
External costs(Euro)	319,000	1,246.000	1,223.000
External specific costs	5.9m Euro/tkm	49.7 Euro/tkm	48.6 Euro/tkm

Source: "Maritime Transport Scientifically Proven to be the Leading Transport Mode", in *Grimaldinaples News*, The Quarterly Publication of the Grimaldi Group, Issue 8 (July–September 2000), p. 13.

The sustainable freight market?

The debate on sustainable transport has focused on the question of externalities. Comparative analysis between modes seeks to identify the external cost generated per mile or per tonne. Shipping, despite the adverse press resulting from major maritime environmental disasters such as *Exxon Valdez*, is now well positioned to claim its position as a sustainable source of transport. The lessons of the Brent Spar oil rig disposal in the mid 1990s demonstrated not only the sensitivity of marine environmental issues but also negative consumer reaction towards perceived abusers of the environment. The progressive Italian liner grouping. Grimaldi Line, has been quick to turn such "green" concerns to market advantage. Evidence from a 1999 comparative study by the Italian environmental pressure group, Amici delia Terra, points to shipping having far lower external costs than road and rail haulage. The research was based upon freight shipments between Southampton and Livorno. Utilising data from the fixed day, weekly, Euro-Med service as operated by Grimaldi Line, the *Grande Europa* class of vessel was used for the modelling and a cargo totalling 14,500 tonnes was assumed.

Despite the sealeg distance being more than double the overland distance the external costs of the shipping option are estimated to be eight times lower than those of land transport.

CONCLUSIONS

Throughout this chapter we have tried to trace the changes in technology, changes in economic pressures, changes in commercial practice, changes in global pressures regarding the environment, changes in cultural expectations and changes in political attempts to regulate and control the maritime industry and hope the basic conclusions are in or implied in the text. One general observation however is clear, is that although the changes since the early 1970s has been greater than the previous century the speed of change has not been uniform in all sectors, with the most pressing problems facing the industries' decision makers having fluctuated wildly. Even in 1970 few maritime economists wrote about the environment. Since September 11th 2001 security has arisen as a major factor to be considered in the economics of the industry though it may be some time before the impact of this relatively new factor is realised and understood.

Maritime economics is a relatively new area of academic study. If one looks at most areas of academic theories it seems that theory often lacks behind practice. Let us hope that the new generation of maritime economists can keep pace with this fast changing industry.

ENDNOTES

1. Chrzanowski, I.(1985): *An Introduction to Shipping Economics* (London, Fairplay) p. 17.
2. Svendsen, A.S., *Sea Transport and Shipping Economics* (Bremen, ISL).
3. Thorburn, T. (1960): *The Supply and Demand of Water Transport* (Stockholm, Stockholm School of Economics).
4. Goss, R.O. (1968): *Studies in Maritime Economics* (Cambridge, CUP).
5. *Ibid.*, p. 48.
6. Goss, R.O. (1993): "The Decline of British Shipping: A Case for Action? A Comment on the Decline of the UK Merchant Fleet: An Assessment of Government Policy in Recent Years", *Maritime Policy and Management*, Vol. 20, No. 2 (1993), pp. 93–100.
7. Gilman, S. (1983): *The Competitive Dynamics of Container Shipping* (Aldershot, Gower).
8. Jansson, J.O., & Shneerson, D. (1987): *Liner Shipping Economics* (New York, Chapman and Hall).
9. *Ibid.*, p. 288.
10. Of course, the Panamax-size, or smaller OBO vessels used in these earlier days (mid-1960s) were easier to route; shifting trades was easier, too.
11. In fact, some of the feeder line carriers move progressively from one "spoke-end" port to another, adding connectivity to the network. Some of the ports in these "loops" are favoured with faster cargo-transit times than others.
12. McLellan, R.G. (1997): "Bigger vessels: How big is too big", *Maritime Policy & Management*, Vol. 24, No. 2 (April–June 1997), pp. 193–211.
13. *Loc. cit.*
14. Goss, R.O. (1968): *Studies in Maritime Economics*. Cambridge: CUP. pp. 14–20.
15. Porter. M.E. (1990): *The Competitive Advantage of Nations* (London, Macmillan), pp. 34–36.
16. Farthing, B. (1987): *International Shipping: An Introduction to the Policies, Politics and Institutions of the Maritime World* (London, LLP).
17. *Loc. cit.*
18. Source: Dover Coast Guard.
19. *Loc. cit.*
20. Grimes, R. (1989): *Shipping Law* (London, Sweet and Maxwell), p. 183.
21. Cockcroft, A. (1990): *Collision Avoidance Rules* (London, Newnes), p. 142.
22. Department of Transport (1987): *The Merchant Shipping Act 1984: MV Herald of Free Enterprise, Report of Court No. 8094, Formal Investigation* (London, Department of Trade).
23. "Shell Shocked", *Fairplay International Shipping Weekly*, 21.6.90, pp. 2–3.

24. Foy, D. (1990): "Bulk carrier Losses – Unanswered Questions", *Seaways* (May, 1990), pp. 21–22.
25. Marine Accident Investigation Branch (MAIB) Report 3/98 (1998), *Report of the Inspectors' Inquiry into the Grounding of the Feeder Container Vessel, Cita off Newfoundland, Isle of Scilly*, 26.3.97 (Southampton, MAIB).
26. "Mate slept as Ship heads for Island", *Shipping Today and Yesterday* (December, 1988).
27. "No mystery of the seas", in *Lloyd's List*, 13.3.01, p. 6.
28. "Lean manned ships should be targeted", *Lloyd's List*, 13.3.01, p. 17.
29. Parker, J. (2000): "Environmentally friendly ship operations: risk and reward", *Seaways: The International Journal of the Nautical Institute* (June, 2000), pp. 11–13.
30. Patraiko, D. (2000): "Managing shipboard waste: A Nautical Institute study", *Seaways: The International Journal of the Nautical Institute* (August, 2000), pp. 7–10.
31. *Op. cit.*, p. 8.
32. Fields, C. (2002): "IBIA backs BP trading system on emissions", *Lloyd's List*, 25.4.02, p. 4.
33. Reported in "Double hulls are safer, says study", *Lloyd's Tanker Focus* (October, 1998), p. 21.
34. "Shuttle tanker misses highlighted by new report", *Lloyd's List*, 1.3.99,, p. 1.
35. Reported in "Double hulls are safer, says study", *Lloyd's Tanker Focus* (October, 1998), p. 21.
36. Reported in "Shuttle tanker misses highlighted by new report", *Lloyd's List*, 1.3.99, p. 1.
37. "A new era in shuttles", *Lloyd's Tanker Focus* (October, 1998), pp. 20–21.
38. "Balancing safety and economy: A safety case approach to a green tanker", *Fairplay*, 3.8.00.
39. *Loc. cit.*
40. *Commission of the European Communities, Communication from the Commission to the European Parliament and the Council on a Second Set of Measures on Maritime Safety following the Sinking of the Oil Tanker, Erika*. COM (2000) 802 final (Brussels, 6.12.2000), p. 6.
41. Everard, M. (1995): "Rogue Ships a Shipowner's View", *Maritime Policy and Management*, Vol. 22, No. 3, pp. 179–199.
42. Kinnock, N.(1996): "Developments in EU Maritime Policy", *Bimco Review* (1996), pp. 61–65.
43. "Environmentally friendly shuttle tanker leads trio of twin screw ships", *Lloyd's List*, 25.8.98, p. 10.

CHAPTER 9

ECONOMICS OF THE MARKETS FOR SHIPS

*Siri Pettersen Strandenes**

Centre for International Economics and Shipping, Department of Economics,
Norwegian School of Economics and Business Administration, Bergen, Norway.
E-mail: *siri.strandenes@nhh.no*

1. INTRODUCTION

Vessels are sold and purchased in several markets. New vessels are contracted and sold in the newbuilding market, whereas the scrapping market balances scrapping volumes and prices. In the second-hand markets vessels are sold and purchased for further trading. Activities in the newbuilding and scrapping markets set the total transport capacities available to seaborne trade and passenger transport worldwide. In this they resemble other markets for capital equipment for use in production of goods or services. Transactions in the second-hand market on the other hand, do not change the available transport capacity world-wide, but only shifts the existing transport capacity between the different shipowners or shipping companies. Therefore, the second-hand markets are kinds of auxiliary markets. (See Eriksen and Norman[1] and Wijnolst and Wergeland.[2])

In this chapter we will discuss the elements and the functioning of the markets for ships. In the next section we describe characteristics and differences of the markets in more detail. Thereafter we comment the structure of the markets for ships before we discuss pricing and ship values in the last section. The points put forward are illustrated in several places by graphs from the *Platou Report*,[3] published by R S Platou Shipbrokers a.s. on the web. We are thankful to Platou for making their report available on the Internet.

2. MAIN CHARACTERISTICS OF THE MARKETS FOR SHIPS

The markets for ships fulfil several of the requirements needed for well functioning markets. Generally there are few limits to entry into these markets. It also is fairly easy for shipowners to stay informed on the activities and developments in the markets compared to the situation in most other world-wide markets. The cost of exiting the markets varies somewhat, but they tend to be fairly low, as we shall point out below. Shipbrokers operate in markets for ships and they collect relevant information and allocate it to the decision makers in the shipping industry. All these characteristics indicate that well functioning markets for ships exist.

Table 1: Real and auxiliary markets for vessels

	Real markets	Auxiliary markets
Freight markets	Spot freight market	Time charter market
Markets for ships	Newbuilding market Scrapping market	Second-hand market
	Determination of transport capacity	**Trading risk**

Source: Eriksen and Norman[1]; also shown in Wijnolst and Wergeland.[2]

Demand for ships is derived from demand for transport services. This has implications for the markets for ships as it links the development in these markets directly to the conditions in the world economy and international trade. Since trade flows fluctuate, so do the activities in the markets for ships. Deliveries and deletions of bulk carriers in the last 10 years may illustrate the degree of fluctuations. Figure 1 shows a wide variation in deliveries and even stronger shifts in deletions over the last 10 years. Such variations make timing more important for profits, but also more challenging to the decision makers in shipping.

In addition to these general characteristics on entry and exit and the availability of information, the markets for ships feature some specific characteristics. They function as the market place both for shipowners seeking ships to fulfil transport assignments and for asset players who focus on the potential rise in ship values, when they decide whether to enter the market. Hence, variations in prices and activities in the markets for ships attract investors that enter mainly to exploit such price variations. These players' activities are positive in that they increase the liquidity of the markets for ships and thus ensure better allocation of vessels among ship owners servicing international trade. As long as the asset players make rational decisions, their activity also contribute by dampening price fluctuations and thus reduce the risk for shipowners who enter mainly to secure transport capacity for seaborne trade.

Similar to deep-sea shipping, the ships are traded in world-wide markets where agents from all over the world meet to trade. Ships thus are traded

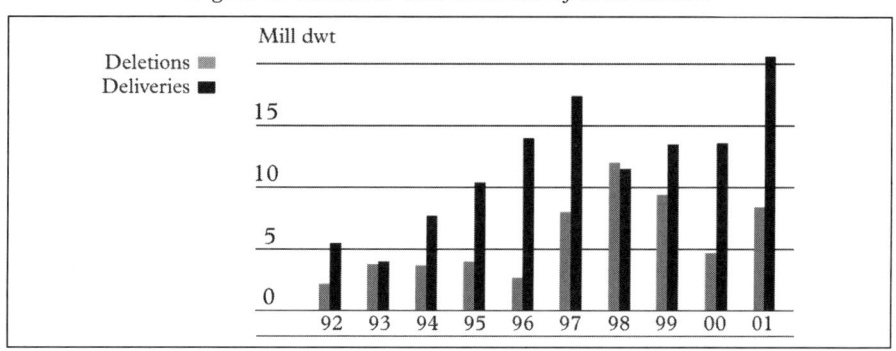

Figure 1: Deletions and deliveries of bulk carriers

Source: *The Platou Report 2002*, p. 20.

among owners in geographically separate parts of the world. Shipowners do contract and scrap vessels abroad and far away from their home country. The bulk of scrapping activity, for example, takes place in Asia. Asian countries also dominate shipbuilding for large groups of vessels.

Irrespective of the worldwide character of these markets, the activities are not evenly spread around the world. The industry has experienced a geographic shift as more and more of the newbuilding capacity moved eastward, first to Japan and later to South Korea. Now there also is strong competition within Asia where China is an upcoming supplier in the market for new vessels. This move eastwards has left Europe and USA with excess shipbuilding capacity. Capacity partly has been closed down and partly converted to other uses, for example to making offshore equipment. Some yards switched toward building specialised ships. By specialised ships we mean research ships, naval ships and vessels tailor made for a specific trade or route. In this process, subsidies have been used to try to halt the downsizing of newbuilding capacities in traditional shipbuilding nations in the west.

Quality assessment and quality requirements are challenges to the functioning of and the activity in the other markets for ships, the second-hand and the scrapping market. There is a long tradition for securing quality in the newbuilding markets stemming back to the introduction of ship classification in the 19th century. Classification societies have inspectors at the site to oversee the construction of the new vessels they are going to class. The uncertainty about the quality of vessels being traded poses a problem affecting the decision makers' information and therefore influences both pricing and the number of vessels traded. Quality is currently assessed mainly by numerous inspections of vessels. In addition to inspections performed by class societies, cargo owners, ports and creditors require inspections to assess the vessel. This is both costly and time consuming as commented for example in Fairplay.[4] Introducing incentive contracts and signalling to induce operators to focus on quality may reduce the number of inspections. A preliminary discussion of the possibility for such schemes in the freight markets is found in Strandenes.[5] Problems of assessing quality of vessels represent important imperfections in the second-hand market and influence the functioning of that market.

Quality assessments have other effects for the conditions in the scrapping market. When quality requirements increase, there will typically be a rise in the activity level in the scrapping market. Similarly, whenever policy decisions to phase out low quality vessels materialise, this will increase the volume of tonnage sold for scrapping.

2.1 Characteristics specific for the newbuilding market

Here we concentrate on how the other markets influence activities in the newbuilding market. By the other markets we mean the two other markets for ships and the freight or passenger markets. For more thorough discussions of the supply side in the newbuilding market and the shipbuilding industry (see Wijnolst and Wergland[2]).

Ideally, demand for new vessels reflects the need for transport capacity in the different vessel categories or types. It takes time, usually one to one and a half years, but sometimes up to four years, from ordering a vessel until the vessel is delivered and starts operating in the market. Since freight markets are volatile this implies that vessels often are delivered into markets with freight rate levels that differ much from the market conditions prevailing when the vessels were ordered. A decision to order a vessel should reflect the expected future freight rates or correspondingly the future income level over the economic life of the new vessel. Hence, a short-term dip in the freight rates upon delivery is of limited significance to the return from the investment. During the time it takes to build the vessels the long-term prospects for the freight markets may also change and especially so if the time for delivery is long. This means that shipowners sometimes may prefer to cancel an order or to convert the vessel into another size or kind of ship to adjust to the change in expected future demand for transport services.

The large variation in the volume of new vessels ordered is one effect of such uncertainty about the future income for the vessels and the fluctuations in the freight markets. See, for example, Figure 2 on orders for new vessels as a percentage of the fleet over the last ten-year period. Figure 2 also illustrates the variations that exist among the different vessel types when it comes to fluctuation in deliveries.

2.2 Characteristics specific for the scrapping market

One might expect a synchronisation of the activity levels in the newbuilding and scrapping market. This would be the case if the economic and technical life of vessels were constant and similar across vessel types. We know that this is not the case and Figure 1 above nicely illustrates that the variations in the volume of new transport capacity delivered are not linked directly to the volume scrapped.

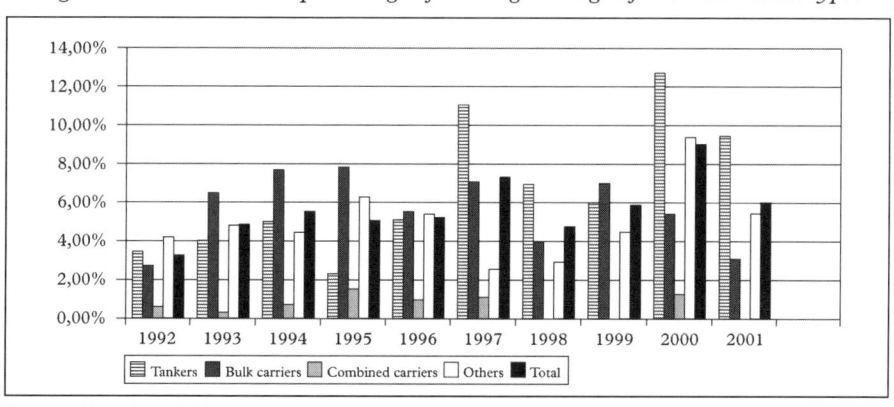

Figure 2: Order book in percentage of existing tonnage of the main vessel types

Source: Based on Tables 1 and 3 in *The Platou Report 2002*, pp. 34–35.

The activity level in the scrapping markets fluctuates, as do the freight level and conditions in the freight markets. Even though reactions are lagged this indicate that the economic life of a vessel is linked to the freight level and the income expected over the rest of the vessels technical life.

Scrapping volumes furthermore reflect political decisions on phasing out of vessels that do not fulfil the stricter requirements on environmental and safety standards being introduced. This means that the phasing out plan for single hull tankers set by International Maritime Organisation (IMO) ought to be reflected in the scrapping volumes. If markets are weak in the years ahead, the old tankers that were built in the 1970s and first part of the 1980s may be phased out for economic reasons even ahead of the planned phasing out, however. If so, the link between scrapping volume and the IMO decision becomes less apparent.

Fluctuations indicate that the capacity level in the scrapping industry should be flexible. As stated above entry into the market has hitherto been fairly easy. To set up a new scrapping site one needs a beach and labour. This has been available mainly in the Asian countries with China, Bangladesh, Pakistan and India as the important locations. Environmental concerns have set focus on scrapping activity both following from the potential spills into the waters surrounding the scrapping site and the health problems faced by workers in the scrapping industry. A change in requirements will influence the costs of entry and exit in the scrapping industry and thus the flexibility in capacity. In the future we may therefore experience higher fluctuations in scrapping prices than those we currently experience. The effects on pricing will be discussed in more detail below.

2.3 Characteristics specific for the second-hand markets

As pointed out in the introduction to this chapter the second-hand markets differ from newbuilding and scrapping markets by being auxiliary markets in the sense that they do not change the number of vessels or the transport capacity offered in the markets. This contrasts with the other markets for ships, which have expansion or contraction of transport capacity as their main function. The purpose of a second-hand market is to reallocate vessels among operators and thereby to increase the efficiency in markets for transport services. By doing so, second-hand markets support efficient use of capital equipment in the shipping industry and contributes to reducing transport costs in world trade.

Transactions performed in the second-hand markets also contribute to the efficiency in seaborne transport in another way. When shipowners can sell the bulk of their real capital in a liquid second-hand market, their exit costs are pushed down. Similarly the existence of second-hand markets facilitates entry into shipping, since potential suppliers may buy an existing vessel and enter the transport market on short notice. Both aspects affect competition in the freight markets in a positive way. In addition shipowners may use the flexibility to switch markets or restructure their fleet in line with changes in demand.

Viable second-hand markets do not eliminate the exit costs, however. Ship values fluctuate with freight market conditions as is illustrated by figure 3.

Hence, the value of the vessel may be low when the owner wishes to sell and exit. Therefore second-hand markets reduce, but do not eliminate, costs of exit compared to an alternative setting were shipowners had to scrap their capital equipment to exit.

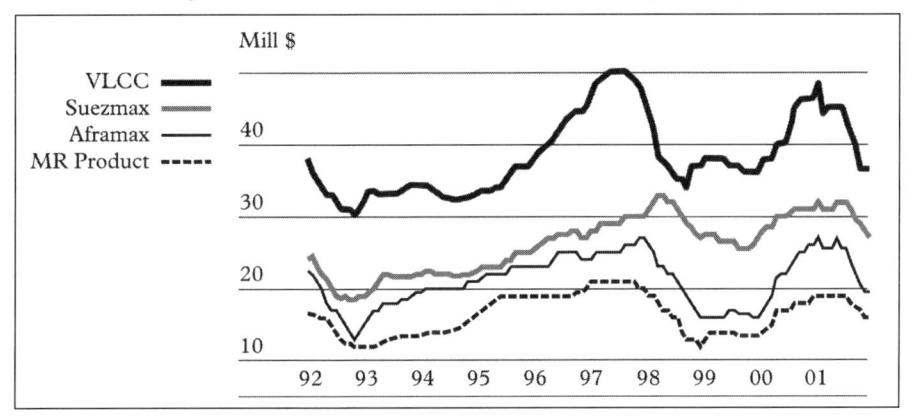

Figure 3: Second-hand values of tankers (10 years old)

Source: *The Platou Report 2002*, p. 13.

Not only shipowners who operate vessels in the freight market, but also investors who purchase and sell vessels in an asset play, enter the second-hand market. Their activities increase the liquidity of the second-hand market and contribute to at better functioning market and thus to a more efficient allocation of capital equipment in the freight market. Asset play may increase the volatility in ship values, if the players do not act rationally or have correct information. This increases profit opportunities, but also the risk of investing in a vessel.

2.4 Characteristics of markets for different vessel types

In the above comments on the different markets for ships we have indicated that the situation differs somewhat among vessel types. In the newbuilding market some suppliers specialise on building a restricted number of types. There are for example, yards that specialise on cruise vessels. Most European shipbuilders concentrate on specialised vessels either cruise vessels, ferries, fast vessels or supply or research vessels. Producing these vessels with high labour costs is more profitable than producing standardised tankers or dry bulk carriers under similar cost conditions. Thus, a main difference in supply of different ships in the newbuilding market is the location of the yards and thereby the cost level for labour. There is however currently an eastward move also for specialised vessels, similar to the one experienced earlier by contractors of standard wet and dry bulk vessels.

In the scrapping market there is little differentiation on vessel type. The environmental concern is also similar irrespective of type of vessel, since all vessels contain materials that are potentially harmful to the local environment.

The second-hand markets feature the clearest difference in market conditions for different ships. The differences reflect whether the vessel is suitable for more than one trade or transport service. Standard vessels such as most tankers and bulk carriers are suitable for operating in several trades. Hence, they can operate for a number of shipping firms and fulfil these firms diverse transport obligations. Container vessels may be somewhat less flexible across trades, but the standardised types may still be used in several markets. In addition to the effect of higher flexibility and transferability among trades enjoyed by standardised vessels, the number of vessels that compete in the tanker and dry bulk markets is high. This implies more frequent transactions in the second-hand market involving these vessel types. As a result the second-hand market is more liquid for these vessels than for specialised vessels. At the same time we know that the liquidity in the second-hand market is important for efficient allocation of vessels to their best use.

3. ALTERNATIVES TO INVESTING IN VESSELS: RENTING AND LEASING

Operators may choose not to invest in vessels and instead concentrate on the commercial operations in the markets for transport services. There are several options open to operators. They may rent vessels for a shorter or longer duration. An operator, either an intermediator in international trade or a cargo owner, may rent vessels for specific trips in the spot charter markets or for longer duration in the time charter markets. Time charters may be available for periods of some months and up to most of the economic lifetime of the vessel.

The possibility to rent instead of investing in vessels increases the flexibility in seaborne transport further and rises the efficiency of the markets. There are, however, interdependencies between the time charter rates and ship values. The similarities in developments in market values and time charter rates are indicated by figure 4 panel A and B. The possibility to avoid high prices by postponing the investment and instead hiring a vessel in the time charter markets is therefore limited. Even so hiring poses an advantage since the operator may use this to postpone the investment in a vessel and may thus avoid tying capital into a vessel until he has acquired further information on the conditions in the shipping markets. Decisions on whether to hire now and purchase later or correspondingly to let your vessel now in order to sell it later, are similar to buying a real option to purchase or sell a vessel. Real option analysis and ship pricing is discussed in Chapter 29 by Bendal.

Leasing offers another opportunity for acquiring transport capacity. Leasing has little effect on the capacity offered or the operations in the transport markets, but has bearing for the way shipowners acquire capital to invest in transport capacity. By leasing vessels the shipowner engages in off-balance operations and may secure more favourable financing than ordinary debt or equity financing. Leasing may also have bearings on the tax position of the shipowning firm and thereby reduce or postpone tax payments.

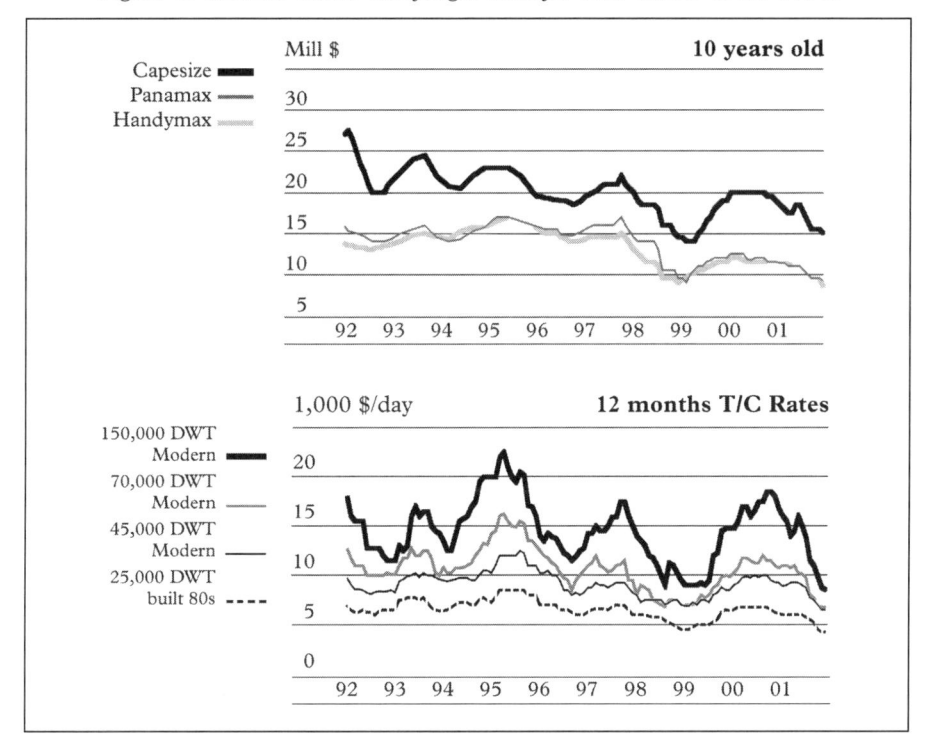

Figure 4: Market values and freight rates for bulk cariers in the 1990s

Source: *The Platou Report 2002*, pp. 18 and 19.

Leasing may influence demand in the markets for ships and the corresponding price level or ship values, if it increases the investment opportunities open to shipowners. It may increase the efficiency of the markets for vessels by lifting a potential restriction on demand stemming from lack of capital at acceptable cost. Leasing of vessels is discussed in more detail in Part 9 of this volume. Here we only want to point out that by facilitating demand, the option to lease also influences the activity level and thus the liquidity in the market for ships in a positive way.

4. MARKET STRUCTURE AND COMPETITION

Above we have made some comments on the effects on market efficiency of the characteristics in the different markets for ships. In this section we will discuss market structure and the implications in more detail.

We found that in general markets for ships fulfil important requirements for efficient markets. These requirements are; low cost entry and exit; relevant information on market conditions and transactions; and high liquidity in the market resulting from a fairly high number of agents demanding or offering ships for sale. Even though markets for ships in general are competitive and efficient markets posting prices that reflect future income to the owner, there are several particulars that differ among the markets. In this section we will point at and discuss such special elements of the market structure for the newbuilding, scrapping and second-hand markets for the main types of vessels.

4.1 Market structure in newbuilding market

The market structure in the newbuilding market carries several characteristics of a competitive market. There are a number of yards in different parts of the world and several independent shipowners looking for attractive offers to build vessels. New sites are constructed and others convert from constructing vessels to building other capital equipment, for example for offshore oil production. Thus, entry into and exit out of the newbuilding markets takes place.

The existing order book split on yards and types of ships offers information to the agents in this market. This means that shipowners have information that may induce them to postpone ordering new vessels from yards with high demand or consider switching to types of vessels in lower demand at the time. By doing this shipowners induce a more efficient use of the total shipbuilding capacity with more similar time for delivery and backlog of orders across yards and vessel types. This levelling out of differences is not perfect, however, because the different vessel types are not perfectly interchangeable whether in operation nor in building requirements.

Since transport markets fluctuate and the information on the order book is frequently updated, shipowners may get information that make them decide to cancel contracts or to convert an order from one type of vessel to another, if for example they find that there will be delivered too many vessels of a specific type. Cancellation or conversion is prevalent in periods with big changes in expectations. Cancellations represent a cost for the shipowner and the yard, but may result in a lower cost than the expected cost of going on with the investment after conditions have changed. Hence it opens up for correcting earlier decisions, when conditions in the transport market changes. This also contributes to a higher efficiency in the markets for ships by dampening potentially distorting effects of the fluctuations in demand for seaborne trade on the market for new vessels compared to what would be the situation if cancelling or conversions were not accepted.

Traditionally labour unions have been strong in shipbuilding. This has led to lower flexibility in the labour market. Such imperfections in a factor market affect newbuilding. The result has been a setting where nations compete to keep their shipbuilding industry to avoid layoffs. This competition has been visible and often more influential than competition between individual shipbuilding firms. Changes in relative labour costs induced a movement eastward for shipbuilding capacity, especially for standard vessels. For such vessels costs competition is more important than special designs or qualities that otherwise may make the shipowner willing and capable to pay higher prices. When demand facing traditional shipbuilders in Western Europe and USA contracted, the authorities in both areas answered by offering economic support to the shipbuilding industry in order to reduce the need for restructuring. Later, when the industry in the upcoming shipbuilding nations in Asia matured, they also faced rising labour costs and competition from other Asian countries that entered into a period of industrial growth later. Thus, Japan met strong competition from South Korea and more recently they both face growing competition from emerging Chinese shipbuilders. Governmental policies support the shipbuilding industries also in the Asian countries. The result is a world-wide subsidy competition that presses prices and increases demand for new vessels. In order to limit the politically induced subsidisation policy OECD regulated the maximum subsidisation allowed in the industry. For several years subsidisation was limited to yard credits for a maximum of 80% of the newbuilding costs at 8% yearly interest for $8\frac{1}{2}$ years. There was a movement to curb subsidies by 1996. This failed, however, and there still are subsidies open to shipbuilding in several nations. The general trend of falling interest rates in financial markets worldwide has reduced the subsidisation element in such yard credits, however. For a further discussion on the subsidisation in the newbuilding industry, see Chapter 24 of this volume by Joon-Soo Jon.

What interests us here is the effect of such policies on ship values and the functioning of the newbuilding market. By offering vessels at subsidised prices demand for new vessels increases other things being equal and so do transport capacities when these vessels eventually are delivered. Subsidisation implies that new vessels are sold at a lower than optimal price, that is at a lower price than the value of the resources going into building the vessel. This favours investments in new relative to buying an operating vessel in the second-hand market and thus results in a higher supply of transport capacity. The result may be a pressure downward on the freight rates. A rising level of subsidisation thus may reduce the return on investment also for all existing vessels. This introduces a distortion into the markets for ships. Limiting subsidisation in the newbuilding market therefore contributes to a more proper functioning of the markets and the relative values of new versus existing vessels.

If subsidisation presses ship values strongly, there will also tend to be higher scrapping activity with vessels being scrapped at younger ages than would be the case without such subsidisation. The value of all vessels fall following the pressure on freight rates and depending on scrapping prices, the reduction in value may push the market value of the oldest or less valuable vessels below their scrapping value. If this link between higher delivery of new vessels and correspondingly higher scrapping is strong, we may still end with a close to optimal capacity of transport services. Subsidisation in this case mainly results in a shortening of the economic life of the vessels. This implies a premature destruction of capital invested in shipping, but do no rise the total volume of transport capacity above the level needed in international seaborne trade. There is little reason to believe, however, that the effects of subsidisation are totally absorbed in this way. If not, subsidisation also induces a cost in the market for transport services. We may conclude that the newbuilding market has been characterised by competition between shipbuilding nations and not only by competition among shipbuilding firms. The resulting subsidisation has influence markets for ships and ship values.

4.2 Market structure in scrapping market

Above we saw that also the scrapping market carries several characteristics of competitive markets. First and foremost it is fairly easy to enter into the scrapping market. "Green field" scrapping capacity can be installed at a low cost and at short notice. The labour requirement is high, but no special qualifications are asked for. There are also few differences in the work or methods needed for scrapping vessels of different type. This flexibility in expanding scrapping capacity is especially important since demand for scrapping varies greatly and in correspondence with the variations in freight rates for operating vessels, see Figure 4 above. Above we also argued that more intense subsidisation of new vessels may induce a shift in the volume scrapped. This increase is not sudden, however, and poses fewer problems for capacity utilisation.

As long as demand for scrap steel is high there will also be economic reasons for the scrapping industry to increase capacities. Demand for scrap steel varies with economic activities, but scrap steel from vessels does not represent the marginal supply in the scrap steel market. Hence, variations in demand are smaller for scrap steel from ships than for scrap from other sources. But changes in the conditions in the shipping markets of course induce changes to the scrapping industry. See Figure 5 on variations in scrapping volumes.

Similarly the phasing out of vessels caused by changes in regulations such as the IMO agreement on single hull tankers, pose fewer problems to the scrapping markets as long as the capacity adjustment is flexible. Scrapping prices may be depressed for some time since the owners of those vessels do not have further trading as an alternative. If the markets for second-hand vessels are well functioning this should be anticipated in the values for single hull tankers, at last when the agreement was reached by IMO and thus represent a sunk cost to the owners of these vessels.

Under normal conditions the shipowner can choose between scrapping and selling the vessel for further trading. The decision should reflect the relative

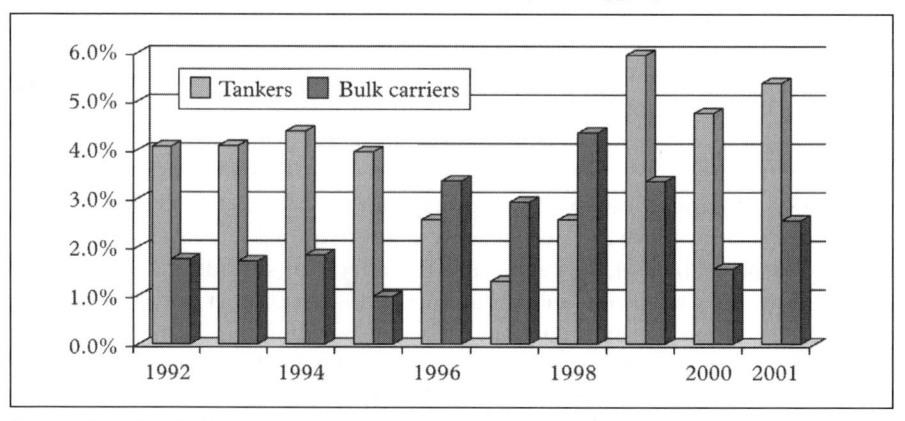

Figure 5: Tankers and bulk cariers sold for scrapping 1992–2000

Source: Based on Tables 11 and 17 in *The Platou Report 2002*, pp. 38 and 40.

costs of the two alternatives. This links the scrapping and second-hand market. The option to alternatively sell the vessel for further trading may vary with the type of vessel, however. For standard tankers and dry bulk carries and standard container vessels sale for further trading may be a viable alternative. Specialised vessels on the other hand, may have low value in alternative uses. If so, scrapping is the main alternative open to the shipowner. Since there are several firms offering scrapping services, the shipowner still is not captive to that market. No scrapping firm can operate as monopsonist and dictate the scrapping value.

Conditions and market structure in the scrapping market may change in the near future, however. The relative ease of setting up a new scrapping site is an important element in securing well functioning and fairly competitive scrapping markets. Environmental concerns may limit this by requiring more secure and costly disposal of environmentally dangerous materials from scrapping. This will increase the cost of scrapping and reduce scrapping values. Even more important, these requirements will reduce flexibility in the scrapping capacity and may increase the market power of approved scrapping firms. It is of less importance whether the shipowner or the scrapping firm are made liable for environmental protection against dangerous material. The will be effects on the functioning of the scrapping market irrespective of who gets to be ultimately responsible.

We may conclude that the scrapping market is fairly competitive and has remained so for a long time. There may be changes ahead, however, since environmental concerns may increase the requirements for entering into this market.

4.3 Market structure in the second-hand market

Above we argued that the second-hand markets for standard vessels have the characteristics of well functioning markets. The shipbrokers network handles information and financing is catered for by a series of international shipping banks or shipping departments in the larger international banks, in leasing markets and by equity financing.

The main function of the second-hand market is to secure efficient exploitation of the existing capital equipment, i.e. the vessels serving seaborne trade. Being what we called an auxiliary market since it does not alter the transport capacity supplied, one important function of the second-hand market is to open up for trade in risk exposure linked to investing in shipping. By opening up for sale of existing vessels for further trade, these markets reduced the risk of lock in to an investor. It does not eliminate all risks, however, since the ship values vary in accordance with the expected future return from investing in the vessel. Hence, a general reduction in the market expectations has to be borne by the current owner even though he has the option to leave the market by selling his vessel as a sale is only possible at a depressed price when expectations are low. He may curb future losses by selling, but will also forego any upside that might result from being in the market when conditions better. Thus, the second-hand market reduces, but does not eliminate the risk from investing in standard or tradable vessels.

The shipowners alternatives to selling a vessel for further trading are to let the vessel on a time charter or to scrap it. Even if he does not see satisfactory income opportunities from operating the vessel in the transport market himself, he may let the vessel for shorter or longer duration against a fixed time charter rate. By doing this he may postpone or avoid selling the vessel, if he expect to gain by operating the vessel in the future. This link between the second-hand and the time charter market implies, however, that a reduction in the second-hand values follow a fall in time charter freight rates. Again the opportunity to let the vessel in the time charter market reduces the risk from investing, but does not eliminate the risk for a reduced return on the investment.

As discussed above investments in specialised vessels are relatively illiquid compared to the situation when investing in standard vessels. The second-hand market may be illiquid or even non-existent for specialised vessels. If the vessel can operate in standard trades, this may represent a sales opportunity at a lower price that do not reflect the costs of the special equipment carried by the vessel. Similarly, the opportunity to let the vessel in the time charter market will be limited by the fact that the vessel is best suited for operations in one or a few trades only.

We may conclude that the market structure and competitive situation in the second-hand markets varies with ship type from competitive for standard vessels to fairly illiquid and close to monopsony for specialised ones. These differences have bearings on the efficiency of the second-hand market in reducing the risk from investing in vessels. The allocative function of the second-hand markets that secure that vessels are engaged in their best employment, is less hurt, however, since specialised vessels by definition have fewer alternative uses than standard vessels.

5. PRICING AND SHIP VALUES

The expected future return from operating the vessel is the basis for ship values and thus for pricing in the markets for ships. In other words pricing in markets for ships is similar to pricing in other markets for real capital. The existence of viable second-hand markets is fairly common for transport equipment like aircraft, cars or ships. This said, it should be pointed out that the existence of viable second-hand markets implies that ship values are quoted on a regular basis only for the vessel types often traded in the market. Hence, for standard vessels the markets valuation is reported daily. The main difference between ships regularly quoted in second-hand markets and more specialised vessels with few alternative uses, is that owners of the first type of ships get regularly updated information on the market assessment of the ships' value. Specialised vessels with no or few alternative uses to the trade they have been built for, will not be quoted in a second-hand market and therefore the information on the current market value will not always be available.

The basis for the market prices in efficient second-hand markets thus is the expected future return from purchasing and operating the vessel. The challenge to shipowners and insurance or finance institutions thus is to assess the *expectations on future income* for the vessels. For older vessels the assessment must also include an evaluation of its *remaining economic life*. This reflects the quality and maintenance of the vessel in addition to whether new technologies are expected that will reduce the value of existing vessels with old technologies.

5.1 Expectations on future income

Extrapolative, rational and semi-rational expectations have been used, when analysing expected return in shipping. Norman[6] and Beenstock and Vergottis[7] are examples of studies using rational expectations, whereas Strandenes [8, 9] assumes semi-rational expectations. Under extrapolative expectations assumptions on future prices are based on the historical development of prices and values for the individual vessel type. One example of extrapolative expectations is when the future price is assumed to be a linear function of the current price. Assuming rational expectations on future price formation on the other hand implies that shipowners and other market agents have an economic assessment of the future developments. In this case we assume that a dynamic model of the development in the market finds the expected future price or ship value. In other words agents then are expected to have an opinion both on the long-term equilibrium price level and the time path to be followed by the current prices to reach that equilibrium. When using semi-rational expectations, we assume that shipowners can assess the future equilibrium conditions in the markets, but that they have no theoretical basis for evaluating what time path prices will follow towards long-term equilibrium. In later studies semi-rational expectations was introduced to the term structure theory.

The common assumption of the term structure theory is that agents expect freight rates to fall when current short-term rates are high. Conversely they expect the short-term freight rates or spot rates, to rise in the future in periods when the current spot rates are low. When the spot freight rates are close to the long-term equilibrium level the curve depicting the expected development in freight rates is flat. No large adjustment is needed for the freight rates to reach long-term equilibrium. The term structure theory is an example of a theory that may handle semi-rational expectations. Originally the term structure theory was applied to the structure of interest rates for assets with different maturities. In the first versions rational expectations were assumed.

Prices or ship values for vessels of different age, that is vessels with different remaining economic life may be "read" from the curves signifying the paths towards equilibrium. Older vessels resemble short-term investments, whereas newer vessels are investments that are to be recouped over several years. Accordingly when the spot market is expected to rise, newer vessels have a higher market value than older vessels both since they will earn an income for more years and from changing market conditions if they are expected to improve in the future. Currently new vessels will still operate in the now future markets, whereas the current older vessels then have been scrapped. If the market expects the values to fall in some years time and to remain low for a longer period, the value of the older vessels may be relatively high compared to values for newer vessels. They will enjoy a better return on the capital invested for the rest of their economic life compared to newer vessels that may face several years in a depressed market before their economic life expires. If the currents freight rates are very high, and the markets furthermore are expected to fall to a low level even before newly contracted vessels can be delivered; the values of existing vessels may lie above the costs of building a new vessel. The market then assumes that the freight rates have fallen when the newly contracted vessels are delivered and start operating. Thus, they loose out on the income opportunities in the high markets because they are delivered only after the market conditions have normalised.

Strandenes[8] analysed term structure in ship values for tankers and bulk carriers in the 1970s. The analysis of the components of ship values indicated that for panamax bulk carriers and for medium sized tankers the long-term equilibrium freight level was more important to the value than the current spot freight rate. For large tankers the results indicated, however, that the current spot freight rates were of great importance to the values for these ships. Never studies of the term structure in shipping markets indicate that the results must be corrected for shipowners' differences in assessing the risk. Kavussanos' and Alizadet's[10] results on the term structure for time charter rates indicate that shipowners have time varying risk perceptions. This distorts the term structure of freight rates of different durations found by the older studies, where risk assessment was assumed to be stable over time. Hence, the expectations on future income and also the evaluation of ship values have several components, risk assessment and expected income in the freight markets for the rest of the economic life of the vessel being the main elements. The prevailing expectations are difficult to model and assess, however, because there seem to be no pattern in risk assessment over contracts of different durations and thus over vessels of different age. Real option analysis may increase the understanding of assessment of ship prices. For a discussion of real option analysis see Chapter 29 by Bendal.

5.2 Economic life of a vessel

The relevance of term structure theory to ship values follow from the difference in the remaining economic life of the vessel. It is important to assess the length of the remaining active life of the vessel. This includes assessing both the chance of technological obsoleteness, political decisions that may render the vessel obsolete and gaining knowledge on what influences decisions on when to scrap the vessel as it approaches the end of its economic life.

The situation in the newbuilding market will influence the decision to scrap a vessel. In high markets the existence of limited shipbuilding capacity and thus extended time for delivery, may induce shipowners to postpone the demolition of old vessels. In extreme periods such as in the early 1970s when the time for delivery reached four years, existing vessels obtained higher values than new contracts since they were able to take advantage of the very high spot freight levels. The market did not expect these freight levels to remain until the new vessels were delivered and correspondingly these vessels would not be in for the extraordinary profits offered in that period. For that particular period these expectations turned out to be right and several shipowners lost large amounts on their new orders.

6. CONCLUDING COMMENTS

In this chapter we have focused on the markets for ships and discussed characteristics of each type of market and pointed at the differences among them. We explained that there are both real and auxiliary markets for ships. Transactions in the real markets; the newbuilding and scrapping markets, change the number and types of ships available and thus the transport capacity. The auxiliary markets or the second-hand markets, do not change the total transport capacity. Transactions in these markets re-allocate ships among shipowners and contribute thereby to a more efficient use of the available capacity.

There are several agents in the markets for ships and no individual shipping company, yard or scrapping firm can dominate the markets. Entry and exit are possible. Information on the activities in these market is readily available, especially so because shipbrokers function as intermediaries and collectors of market information.

There are differences among the markets, however. In the newbuilding markets governments have engaged to halt restructuring that induced shifts in the geographic localisation. Subsidisation has influences price setting and thus contracting. The scrapping markets have functioned fairly efficient. In the future they may be controlled more strongly by governments, who are becoming concerned by spill of dangerous materials at the scrapping sites. This may reduce the flexibility that we have observed for available scrapping capacity and may result in stronger fluctuations in scrapping prices in the future. We argued that the second-hand markets are efficient for standard vessels. For these ships the markets are liquid and prices are quoted regularly. The second-hand markets are not equally liquid for specialised vessels. Thus, owners of such specialised vessels may face larger exit cost.

Ship values ideally reflect the expected future profit gained from operating the vessel for the rest of its economic life. We pointed out that the term structure theory may help in assessing ship values and differences in values for new and existing vessels from differences in the remaining economic life of the individual vessels. Newer studies have revealed, however, that shipowner's time dependent risk assessments complicate the analyses of ship values. We pointed out that real options analysis if used in shipping markets might contribute to assessment of ship values.

ENDNOTES

1. Eriksen, Ib. E., and Norman, Victor D. (1976): *ECOTANK – en modell for analyse av tankmarkedenes virkemåte* (ECOTANK – Econometric Model for Tanker Companies), Report (Institute for Shipping Research, Bergen).
2. Wijnolst, N. and Wergeland, T. (1997): *Shipping* (Delft, The Netherlands, Delft University Press).

3. *The Platou Report 2002*, 2002 (Norway, R S Platou Shipbrokers a.s. Oslo), http://www.platou.com
4. Anonymous (2002): "Vetting again and again", *Fairplay International*, February 28.
5. Strandenes, Siri Pettersen (2001): "Quality incentives payoff?", *Proceedings on CD from the 9th World Conferences on Transport Research* (July, Seoul).
6. Norman, Victor D. (1981): "Shipping strategies", *Studies in shipping economics : in honour of Professor Arnljot Strømme Svendsen*, Einar Hope (Ed.) (Oslo, Norway, Bedriftsøkonomens forlag).
7. Beenstock, Michael, and Vergottis, Andreas (1993): *Modeling the World Shipping Markets* (London, Chapman and Hall); and Beenstock, Michael (1985): "A Theory of Ship Prices", in *Maritime Policy and Management*, pp. 215–225.
8. Strandenes, Siri Pettersen (1984): *Price determination in the time charter and second-hand market*, Working paper (Centre for Applied Research, Bergen).
9. Strandenes, Siri Pettersen (1999): "Is there a potential for a two-tier tanker market?", *Maritime Policy and Management*, Vol. 26, 3, pp. 249–264.
10. Kavussanos, Mannolis G., and Alizadeh, Amir H. (2001): "The expectations hypothesis of the term structure and risk premia in the dry bulk shipping freight markets", *Proceedings on CD from the 9th World Conferences on Transport Research* (July, Seoul).

CHAPTER 10

SHIPPING MARKET CYCLES

Dr Martin Stopford
Clarkson Research, H. Clarkson & Co.Ltd., London, UK.
E-mail: *mstopford@clarksons.co.uk*

1. INTRODUCTION

Shipping cycles create endless problems for shipping investors and analysts alike. If the shipping industry, like Sisyphus, the mythological character condemned to pushing a stone up a hill, only for it to roll own again, is caught in an endless sequence of cycles over which it has no real control, why bother to issue warnings?[1] How would Sisyphus have felt if each time he was half way up the hill some smart economist was standing there to warn him that the stone would soon be on its way down again? Shipowners feel the same way about the killjoy analysts intent on spoiling their bit of fun during the all too brief freight booms.

It is not just modern shipping executives who feel this sense of frustration. A century ago in his 1894 annual report, a London shipbroker spoke for all of us when he wrote:

"The philanthropy of this great body of traders, the shipowners, is evidently inexhaustible, for after five years of unprofitable work, their energy is as unflagging as ever, and the amount of tonnage under construction and on order guarantees a long continuance of present low freight rates, and an effectual check against increased cost of overseas carriage."[2]

This masterpiece of understatement precisely captures the sense of dedication, purpose and *déjà vu* that characterises shipping cycles today, as it obviously did a century ago. It also leaves shipping economists with a legitimate question about what they can really contribute to the commercial shipping industry as it beats its way through these cycles. Warnings aside, what have we to say?

In this chapter we study these cycles, or waves, in the shipping market. There are three main aims. Firstly to look at some of the general characteristics of shipping cycles and discuss how they fit into the economics of the shipping market. Secondly we will study the historical pattern of cycles (if we decide they are cycles), so that we get an idea of the many different economic forces which contribute to their progress. We might call this "cyclical recognition". Thirdly we will discuss the causes of cycles and focus more closely on the economic mechanisms which control them.

2. THE ROLE OF CYCLES IN SHIPPING ECONOMICS

Market cycles are the primary driving force behind shipping investment and chartering. They are the heartbeat of the shipping market, pumping cash in and out of the business and by forcing companies to compete with each other for a share of this wealth, the market lures them in the direction needed to give the most efficient use of resources. In fact the "cycles" are so much a part of the culture of the industry, that it seems hardly necessary to define them. However it is worth spending a little time discussing what the industry generally means by a cycle, and what impact the cycles have. This will help to give perspective.

2.1 The characteristics of shipping cycles

Strictly speaking a cycle is "an interval of time during which one sequence of a regularly recurring sequence of events is completed".[3] The cycle in Figure 1 is defined by its amplitude (A), which is the distance from peak to trough, and its frequency (F), which is the distance between peaks (or troughs) in the cycle. Viewed in this way a shape of a regular cycle C can be defined in terms of the values of A and F.

$$C_{t_{1-n}} = f(A, F)$$

Figure 1: A generic "cycle" showing frequency and amplitude

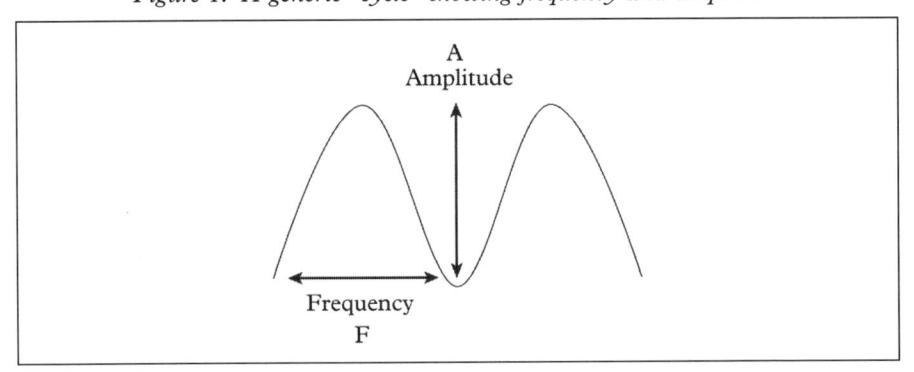

Of course nobody expects shipping cycles to be this regular. There is a widely held "rule of thumb" that they last seven years, but even a cursory examination of the tanker and bulk carrier market cycles in Figure 2 confirms that in the real world the periods of feast and famine bear little relationship to the stylised cycles in Figure 1.

The fact that the cycles are not regular makes it even more important to understand them, at least from the viewpoint of the shipping analyst. The practical importance of cycles cannot be understated. In 1999 a 280,000 dwt tanker was earning $9,000 a day, but just nine months later in 2000 it was earning up to $90,000 a day. This volatility in earnings has a tremendous impact on the way everyone involved in the commercial operation of shipping views the business. For shipowners it offers an incentive to "play the cycle", earning premi-

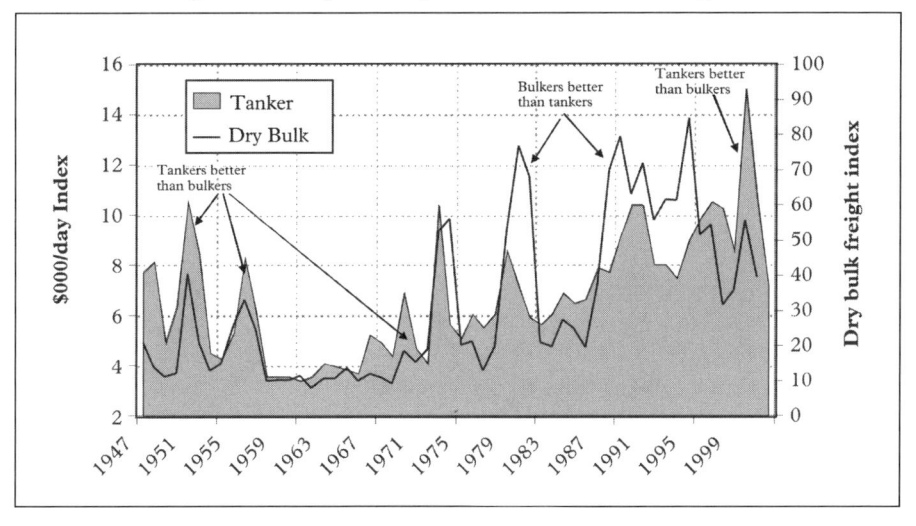

Figure 2: Comparison of tanker and bulk carrier cycles

um revenue when the market is high and, in an ideal world, fixing the ships on time charter just before the market moves in to a trough.

Another feature of the shipping cycle illustrated by Figure 2 is the correlation between cycles in different segments of the market. Between 1950 and 1974, peaks and troughs in the tanker and bulk carrier markets occurred at roughly the same time. However, the correlation is not perfect and during the next 25 years the markets started to behave differently. In 1980 the bulk carrier peak was much stronger than tankers and in the 1990s when the tanker market was in recession, dry bulk rates were relatively high. Then in 1997 the tanker market enjoyed a peak, during a rather bleak year for the bulk carrier market. If nothing else this demonstrates that we cannot generalise about cycles, without reference to particular market sector. It also suggests that different shipping segments are, to some extent at least, isolated from each other.

Even more prominent is the opportunity for "asset play", the term often used to describe speculating on the sale and purchase of ships. Every shipping investor's ambition is to buy in at the bottom of the cycle and sell at the peak. Historically this has always been an important part of shipowners' revenues, especially during periods of inflation. The 1980s provided one of the most spectacular opportunities ever. A VLCC could be purchased in the mid-1980s for about $3 million, but by 1989 its price had gone up to almost $30 million, a tenfold increase in just 5 years. Of course the fact that the cycles are so irregular makes this a tricky game to play, but with so much at stake financially, who would expect it to be simple?

Figure 3 illustrates the link between cycles is earnings and asset values by comparing the one year Time Charter rate for a five year-old Aframax Tanker (left axis) with its market value (right axis). The correlation coefficient of 0.87 is very close, with peaks and troughs following the same cyclical pattern, confirming the common sense expectation that the asset's price will be correlated with its earning capacity. With such high volatility it is no wonder that shipowners spend so much time considering how to take advantage of this volatility by buying low and selling high.

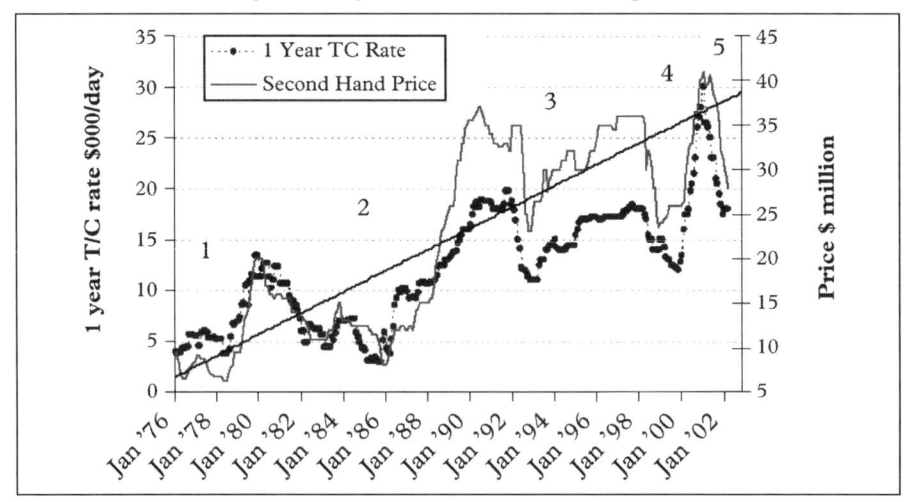

Figure 3: Cycles in revenue and asset price

In fact the causal mechanism underlying the cycles is simple enough. They are generated by changes in the delicate balance of supply and demand for ships. When demand increases faster than supply, freight rates and second hand prices move up to a peak. Conversely when supply exceeds demand, freight rates are driven down by competition, and in many cases fall to the operating cost of the ship. But like many "simple" economic mechanisms, in practice it can develop in a host of different ways. In the next section (3) of this chapter we will study the way cycles have behaved over 120 years of modern shipping. This provides some practical insights into the many different permutations of factors which can drive the supply and demand sides of the market. We will then look more closely at the cyclical mechanism and in particular the dynamics of the market cycle, in an effort to understand the economic framework itself.

3. A BRIEF HISTORY OF SHIPPING CYCLES, 1869–2002

A dry freight index covering the 133 year period from 1869 to 2002 is shown in Figure 4. Identifying the start and finish of each cycle is not always easy. Some cycles are clearly defined, but others leave room for doubt. Does a minor improvement in a single year, as happened in 1877, 1894 or 1986, count as a cycle? There are several of these "mini-cycles" where the freight rates moved slightly above trend. However, careful examination of the statistics and other information suggests that taking 1869 as the starting point,[4] there were 15 dry cargo freight cycles during the 130 year period covered by the graph. For the purposes of discussion in this chapter we will divide this sequence of 15 cycles into four periods, which are marked in Figure 4. The first of these, period 1,

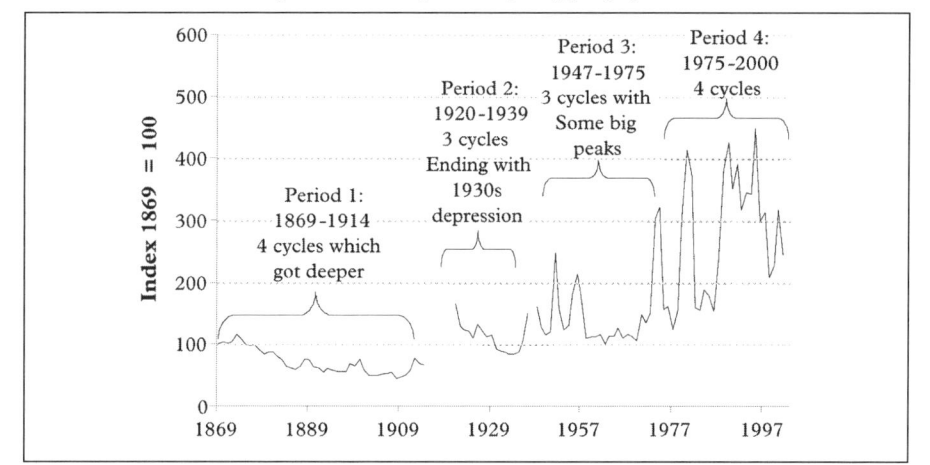

Figure 4: Four periods of shipping cycles

[Chart showing Index 1869 = 100 on y-axis (0-600) and years on x-axis (1869-1997), with four periods labelled:
- Period 1: 1869-1914, 4 cycles which got deeper
- Period 2: 1920-1939, 3 cycles Ending with 1930s depression
- Period 3: 1947-1975, 3 cycles with Some big peaks
- Period 4: 1975-2000, 4 cycles]

covers one of the most exciting periods of modern shipping history, when much of the basic technology used by the industry today was developed. Period 2 covers a much more difficult phase between the first world war and the second world war, and of course it includes the Great Depression of the 1930s. Period 3 encompasses the second great era of expansion between the end of the second world war and the first oil crisis in 1973. In a very different way this was another period when the shipping industry was adopting new technology in response to rapid trade growth. Finally period 4 covers the quarter-century from the first oil crisis through to the end of the 20th century. It includes the second great shipping depression in the 1980s.

In the following sections we will review each of these periods, with two main aims. The first is to establish the general economic conditions which existed on the supply and demand sides of the shipping market during each period, to give us an idea of the overall tone of the market. Secondly we will look at the course the cycles took and try to get some sense of how the industry saw them at the time. In this way we can identify the turning points, marking the beginning and end of each cycle and the length of each trough. Finally we will examine the impact the cycles have had on shipping over the last century. Statistics give no sense of the real events underlying these cycles. For example the brief dips in the index during the 1930s and 1980s give no sense of the desperation and financial hardship which shipowners suffered during these periods. So if we are to obtain a better insight into the nature cycles, and their causes we must focus more closely at what was going on in each period.

Period 1: Shipping cycles 1869–1914

The forty five years before 1914 provides an example of the tight interplay between short term cycles and long term supply/demand fundamentals. The freight index in Figure 5 shows a long term downward trend fell from 100 in 1869 to 45 in 1908. To put this into cash terms, we can take the example of the freight rate for coal from South Wales to Singapore. In 1869 the freight was 27 shillings/ton, but by 1908 it had fallen to a low of 10 shillings.[5] Onto this long term trend was superimposed the series of four shorter cycles of about ten years in length.

This was a period of great activity on both the demand and supply sides of the shipping market. Driven by industrialisation and the expansion of the European empires, trade grew rapidly. Continuous advances in technology on the supply side of the shipping market helped the whole process, not least by reducing transport costs. Ships were becoming bigger and more efficient. In 1871 the largest transatlantic liner was the *Oceanic*, a 3,800 gt vessel with a 3,000 horsepower engine capable of 14.75 knots. It completed the transatlantic voyage in 9? days. By 1913 the largest vessel was the 47,000 gt *Aquatanai*. Its 60,000 horsepower engines drove it at 23 knots. The transatlantic voyage time had fallen to under five days. These vessels were comparable in length with a 280,000 dwt tanker and vastly more complex in terms of mechanical and outfitting structure.

Perhaps the most important technical improvement was in the efficiency of steam engines. With the introduction of the triple expansion system and higher pressure boilers the cargo payload of steamships increased rapidly. The early steam engines had worked at 6lbs/in pressure and consumed 10lbs of coal/horsepower hour. They could carry little but bunker coal. By 1914, pressures had increased to 165lbs/in and coal consumption had fallen to 1½lbs/horsepower hour, giving the steamer a decisive economic advantage, despite its high capital costs. The economic advantage of steam ships was compounded by economies of scale. As a result, the world fleet doubled from 16.7 million grt in 1870 to 34.6 million grt in 1910 and the continuous running battle between the new and old technologies dominated market economics as each generation of more efficient steamers pushed out the previous generation of obsolete vessels. The first to come under pressure were the sailing ships, which

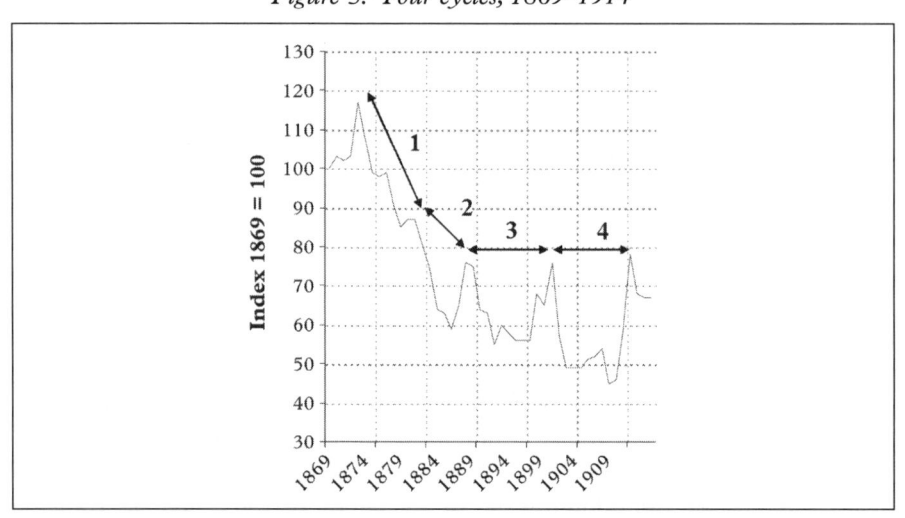

Figure 5: Four cycles, 1869–1914

were replaced by steamers. In 1870 steamers accounted for only 15% of the tonnage but by 1910 they accounted for 75% of the world merchant fleet.[6] The growth in demand was matched by equally rapid growth in supply. As shipyards gained confidence in steel shipbuilding, production grew rapidly. Between 1868 and 1912 shipbuilding output of the shipyards on the Wear, trebled from 100,000 grt to 320,000 grt. Change is never easy and the market used a series of cycles to alternately draw in new ships and drive out old ones. The cycles can be clearly seen in Figure 4, which shows peaks in 1871, 1881, 1889 and 1900.

Cycle 1 started in 1871, and lasted 10 years until 1881. During this period rates fell steadily, as a new generation of steamers competed with the sailing ships which continued to offer low-cost freight carriage. There was a slight recovery of rates in the second half of 1873, the year when Mr Plimsoll published *Our Seamen*, and started his campaign which led to the introduction of the Plimsoll line on ships. From there it was downhill all the way, with rates hitting a trough in 1879, driven by the "excessive and ever increasing supply of tonnage". However, in 1880 the market started to pick up and 1881, the peak of a business cycle in the United Kingdom, saw "in almost every trade a fair amount of business". This good start led to a second excellent year in 1882, described by brokers as being "exceedingly satisfactory"; a sure sign that a great deal of money was made.

Cycle 2 started almost immediately and rates fell through 1883 to a new trough in 1884. Brokers reported that rates were unprofitable for steamers, and even in the better months insufficient to provide for depreciation. The next three years from 1885 through to 1887 were still dull and highly competitive, with relatively low rates. By this time the newly founded liner business was working hard to establish conferences that would protect them. However, things improved in 1887 and by 1888 brokers were reporting the year as "a remarkable one in the history of shipping. A transformation of the whole trade from abject depression to revival and prosperity." Again we find that this coincided with a peak in the world trade cycle. The good times continued through 1889.

Cycle 3 commenced in earnest in 1890 when freight rates slumped, driven down by heavy deliveries which greatly exceeded the previous peak in the early 1880s. By 1892 the market was in severe depression and rates remained very depressed through 1894, and 1895. By 1896 the balance seems to have been partly restored and brokers report fluctuating rates which gave way to a much firmer market in 1898. This upward trend continued and the market moved to a peak in 1900 which was reported to be a memorable one for the shipping industry. Brokers reported "vast trade done and large profits safely housed". This concluded the third cycle, which had lasted the greater part of the decade and was the worst so far.

Cycle 4 turned out to be another long recession. In 1901 the market crashed, leading to a series of very depressed years. This did not let up until 1909 when the market started to believe that the worst was over. For once they were right and 1910 was an excellent year. Once again the explanation of the long recession, at least as reported by the contemporary brokers, was a recession in trade which followed the great boom of 1900 and over-production of ships.

So what was driving these "short" cycles? On the demand side, rapidly growing trade was dominated by the world business cycle, whose cyclical peaks in 1872, 1883, 1892 and 1903 roughly correspond to the peaks in the shipping cycles.[7] On the supply side shipbuilding production amplified the demand instability by overshooting during the booms. This combination laid the foundations for a sequence of cycles which got steadily longer, with the last one stretching out for the best part of a decade.

Looking back over the period, one lesson is that trade growth and technical development do not necessarily lead to easy profits. Many fortunes were made during this period, but across the market competition was cut-throat. Shipbrokers' reports painted a dismal picture of long recessions during which marginal tonnage struggled for survival against a continuous stream of more cost effective new vessels. There were only a handful of years that did not warrant a complaint about the state of the market. As time progresses the complaints about over-building intensified. A comment on 1884 is typical "This state of things was brought about by the large over-production of tonnage during the three previous years, fostered by reckless credit given by the banks and builders and over-speculation by the irresponsible and inexperienced owners".[8] Fleets were growing, but there were no easy profits.

Period 2: Shipping cycles, 1919–1938

The period between the First and Second World Wars was another very difficult period for shipowners, featuring three cycles, numbers 5, 6 and 7, shown in Figure 6.

By 1920 the sailing ships had been driven from the seas, the rate of technical innovation had slowed and the tone was set for a period dominated by a general misalignment of fundamentals. Jones (1957) comments "For most of the period between the wars it appears from the statistics of laid up tonnage that the world was over-stocked with shipping". To begin with in the 1920s trade grew rapidly at about 5% per annum. The problem was on the supply side where there was acute overcapacity in the shipbuilding industry, due to the massive expansion during the war and new entrants to the market. This ensured a weak market. The result was a gradual erosion of freight rates. The freight chart shown in Figure 6 shows freight peaks in 1921 and 1926. From there the trend was downwards towards the recession of the 1930s.

Cycle 5 started with a peak of freight rates in 1921. This was one of the highest levels of earnings experienced for many years, and was the result of an acute shortage of merchant shipping tonnage following the Great War which ended in 1918. During the closing years of this war German U-boat activity had greatly depleted the merchant fleet, and the shipyards had worked flat out to fill the gap. The extent of the shortage ships can be judged from the fact that according to Fairplay the second hand price of a steamer increased from £71,000 in 1915 to £258,000 in 1920. The rapid expansion of shipyard capacity coincided with a peak in the world business cycle in 1920, producing the peak in freight rates shown in the chart.

SHIPPING MARKET CYCLES

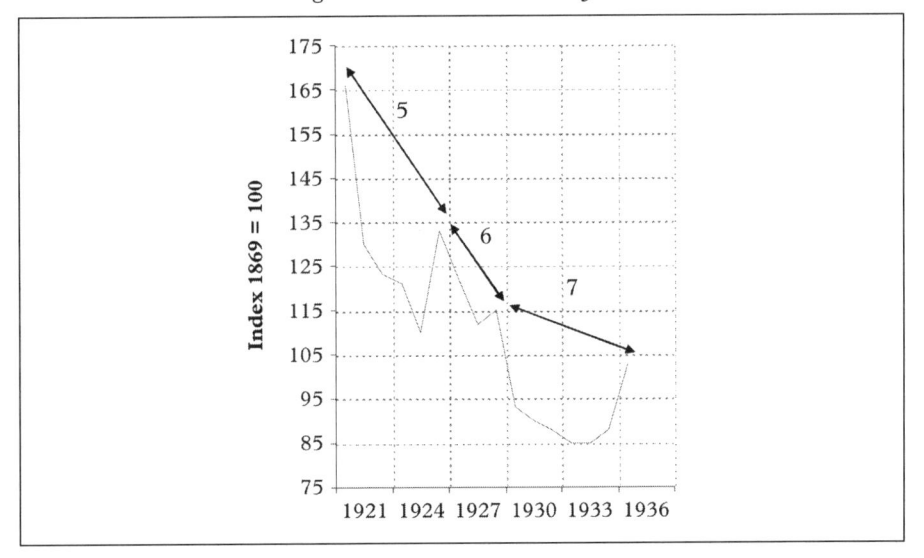

Figure 6: Three inter-war cycles

Cycle 6 commenced with the downturn in the world economy in 1922 and freight rates fell sharply to a trough in 1925, by which time the second hand price of a steamer had collapsed to £60,000, one quarter of the price paid five years earlier. There was a brief recovery in freight rates during 1926. Cycle 7 was short and not severe. Trade grew rapidly between 1928 and 1930, but heavy production of new ships continued to depress the market and rates fell slightly in 1927. By 1929 the shipping industry was anticipating a full recovery next year, but this expectation was not fulfilled.

Cycle 7 started in 1931 as the shipping industry moved into the Great Depression of the 1930s. The Freight Index slumped from 115 in 1929 to a trough of 85 in 1933, the lowest ever recorded. This recession was driven by an unprecedented collapse in the volume of seaborne trade which fell by it 25% between 1931 and 1934. The freight index fell by 30% to operating costs and stayed there for five years from 1930 to 1935. However the best indicator of the severity of the recession is second hand prices. Between 1933 to 1935 good quality second hand ships were sold at distress prices 80–90% below their previous peak, singling this out as a depression rather than a recession. However, shipyard production responded very quickly, and by 1936 the market was moving back towards recovery.

Period 3: Shipping cycles, 1945–1975

The first twenty five years after the Second World War saw an extraordinary growth in sea trade, which increased from 500 million tons in 1950 to 3.2 billion tons in 1973. Once again this was a period of great technical change in the shipping industry. This time the change was not in the technology of shipbuilding, but in the way the industry was organised. This was the era when the liner and bulk shipping industries applied the principles of mechanisation which were being adopted so effectively in manufacturing production on land. Major shippers in the energy and raw materials took the initiative in developing integrated transport operations designed to reduce their transport costs. The trend towards specialisation and economies of scale was continuous and pervasive.

Against a background of rapidly expanding demand, it was the shipbuilding industry which set the commercial tone for the period. For the first decade from 1945-56 there was a shortage of shipbuilding capacity, due to the destruction of the Japanese and German yards during the war. The result was a decade of prosperity (see freight chart in Figure 7). *Cycles 8* and *9*, which occurred between 1945 and 1956, illustrate the cyclical mechanism at its most favorable. There were two cyclical peaks, the first in 1952 which coincided with the Korean War and the second in 1956 which was amplified by the closure of the Suez Canal, greatly increasing the voyage time to the East from Europe. Unusually both peaks lasted longer than the preceding trough, making this a golden age for shipping, at least compared with the depression of the 1930s and the four deep cycles before 1914. Once the shipyards in Japan and Europe got going in the late 1950s this changed and the cycles became longer and less profitable.

Cycle 10, which lasted from 1957 to 1966, probably ranks third in severity behind the 1980s recession and the 1930s recession. It was triggered by an extreme combination of supply and demand developments. On the demand side, the world economy had a severe downturn in 1957 (see Figure 11), and this resulted in a reduction in the volume of seaborne trade, just as the world shipyards were expanding to meet the massive investment demand placed during the 1956 Suez boom. The recession was very severe in the late 1950s, and

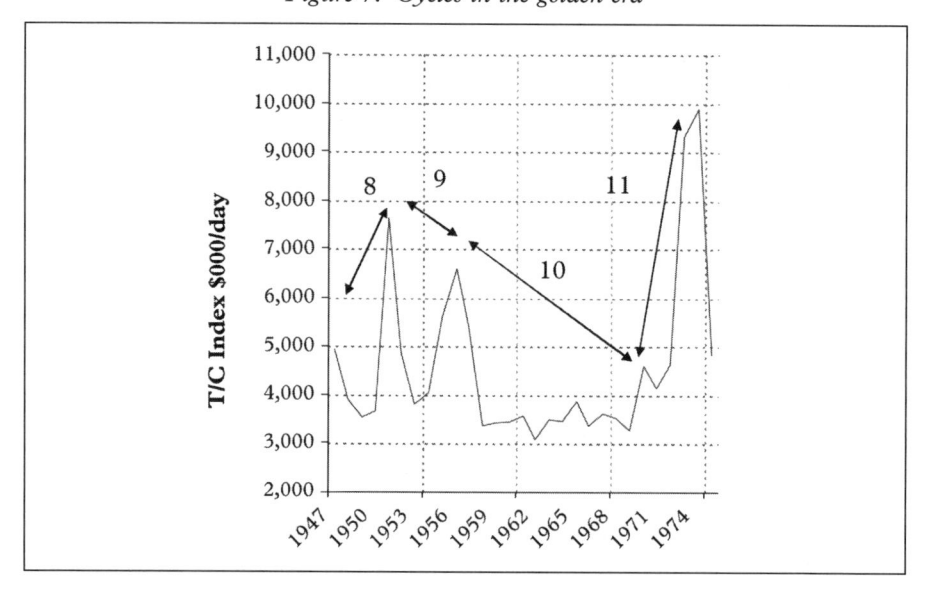

Figure 7: Cycles in the golden era

only started to show sign of recovery in the early 1960s. Freight rates slumped to a low-level and stayed there for almost a decade. However this low level of earnings is not a reliable guide to the cashflow of the shipping industry. During the 1960s shippers placed many long-term time charters for bulk carriers and tankers. These were generally negotiated at levels which gave an adequate return on capital, so the majority of shipowners had a firm cashflow, and only marginal vessels were traded on the spot market, receiving the low rates reported here. It was really an extended period of weak rates.

Cycle 11 was short and not very deep. The market finally peaked moderately in 1970 (the tanker market had a much stronger peak). Cycle 12 was even shorter. The market slumped in 1971, and with a very large orderbook analysts were predicting that the market would not recover until 1976, proving once again how wrong forecasts can be. In 1973 the market moved into one of the best peaks in its history.

By the end of this period shipbuilding output was geared to high growth, making the market very sensitive to any small downturn. There were profits to be made by those who judged the cycles correctly, but this was a very competitive period.

Period 4: Shipping cycles, 1975–2002

In the mid 1970s, following the 1973 oil crisis, the shipping environment changed again. The final section of our review brings a sequence of four cycles shown in Figure 8, each of which had a very different character. After two decades of continuous growth there was a fall in sea trade in the mid 1970s, followed by a major dip in the early 1980s. The scale of this downturn in trade rivaled the 1930s in its severity. In the tanker market the sprint for size lost momentum and the fleet, which had previously been young and dynamic, grew old and sluggish. Shippers became less confident about their future transport requirements, and the role of tanker owners as subcontractors gave way to an enlarged role as risk takers trading on the "spot" market.

Cycle 12 started in the spring of 1975 when the dry cargo market collapsed after the remarkable boom of 1974. The bigger sizes of vessels had already started to move into recession during the second half of 1974, but in 1975 even the small bulk carriers were affected. This downturn was triggered by a deep recession in the world economy, which followed the 1973 oil crisis. The steel industry was very depressed, with 20% to 30% over capacity, and the chronic over tonnage in the tanker market forced combined carriers into dry cargo, increasing the oversupply. In 1976 the market remained depressed, though the trade volume was busy, and many owners were beginning to face liquidity problems. About 5 million deadweight of dry cargo ships and 6 million deadweight combos were in lay-up (Figure 9). By 1977 the market had started to edge upwards, with an improvement in the steel industry and the thermal coal trade which was benefiting from a high oil prices. However the real recovery came in 1979, driven by a seven per cent growth in the major bulks and supply growth of only two and a half percent, due to the run-down of the order book. Finally the boom reached a peak in 1980, driven by a strong steel industry and heavy congestion in continental ore discharging ports and the coal ports in the United States.

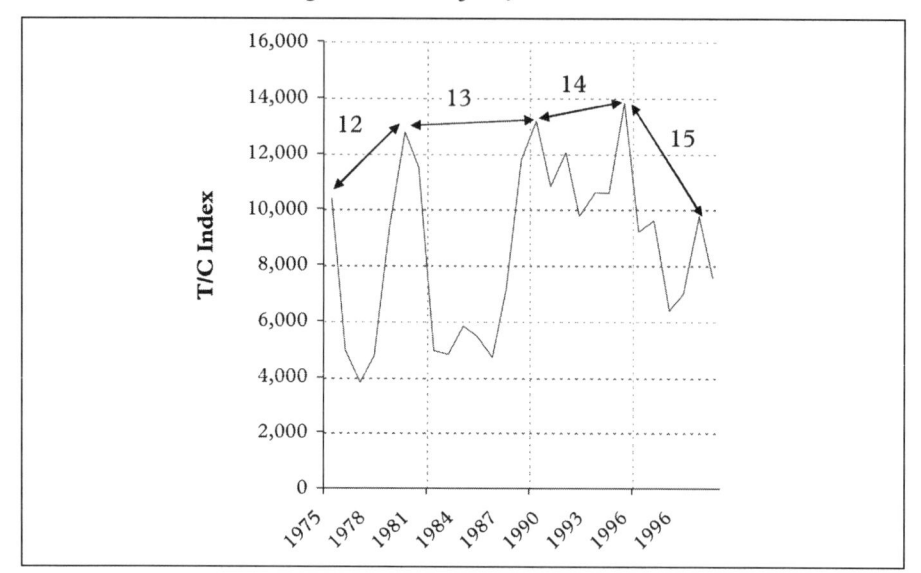

Figure 8: Four cycles, 1975–2002

This strong bull market with 1 year time charter rates lasted until March 1981 when it started to collapse.

Cycle 13 certainly turned out to be unlucky for the dry bulk shipping industry. Rates fell steadily during 1982 and the deep recession in the world economy had a major impact on the movement of dry cargo. By 1983 the one-year Time Charter rate for a Panamax bulk carrier was down to $4,700 a day. However investors remained liquid from the high profits earned during the previous three years and this triggered heavy counter cyclical investment in the "cheap" new bulk carriers being offered by the shipyards. The surge of deliveries which followed completely swamped the recovery in the world economy which happened in 1985–1986. Defaults on time charters, and a long period when freight rates left owners with little cash beyond the level required to pay operating expenses created a serious liquidity crisis in the industry. As one broker's report put it "the equity was drained out of the industry". By the summer of 1986 the financial distress was so great that a Panamax bulk carrier which had recently been delivered for a price in excess of $25 million could be purchased for $8 million. Bankers found that their customers could not even meet interest payments, and the collateral value of the ships had shrunk to a fraction of their market value when the finance had been put in place. Some bankers withdrew from the industry, foreclosing on loans and taking heavy write-offs. However, like all recessions, eventually supply and demand adjusted, and by 1989 rates were back to the level of 1980.

Cycle 14 started off with a boom very much like the one experienced in 1979 and 1980. However the following years were quite different. Although there was a recession in the world economy, bulk carrier investors had by now become so conservative in their ordering activity that deliveries fell to a very low level in

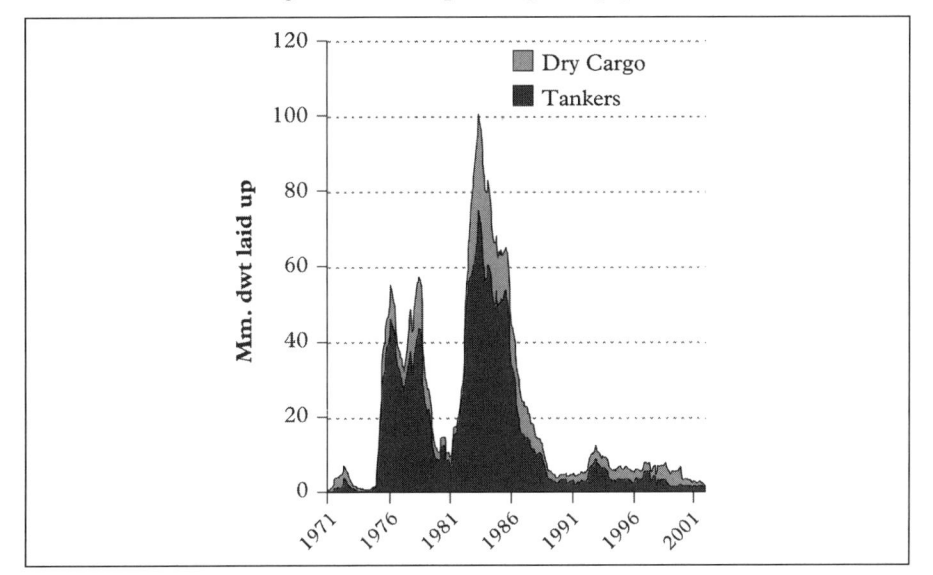

Figure 9: Laid-up tonnage – big cycles

the early 1990s. This meant that cycle 14 was unusually shallow, as is clearly apparent in Figure 8. Rates fell briefly to $10,000 a day in 1992, after which they recovered, reaching a new peak in 1995. This proved to be an exceptionally firm market, with an acute shortage of handy bulk carriers in the Pacific during the summer of that year.

Cycle 15 started in 1995. By the middle of the 1990s the conservative investment policy followed by the dry bulk market had evaporated, and bulk carrier deliveries, which had fallen to 4m dwt p.a. earlier in the decade, increased to 15 to 20 million deadweight per annum. The most extraordinary example of investment optimism came in the autumn of 1999 when, two years after the Asia crisis and after three years of depressed freight rates, bulk carrier owners ordered 25 million deadweight tons of new bulk carriers. The rationale was that the vessels were cheap and would be delivered into an upswing. However, the surge of deliveries ensured that the bulk market remains relatively weak during 2000 went the tanker market was booming. Another practical demonstration of the difficulty of tactical ordering.

The length of cycles and volatility

If we look at the statistics of the cycles we discussed in the previous section, we find that between 1872 and 2000, the average shipping cycle had a frequency of 7.1 years from peak to peak (Table 1). The average cycle length of 6.6 years over the period 1947–2000 was 17% less than the 7.6 years average between 1872 and 1936. This certainly gives credibility to the shipping folk law that shipping cycles last seven years.

However, none of the cycles actually lasted seven years. The longest cycle was 11 years (from 1889 to 1900), one lasted ten years, three lasted nine years, two five years and one lasted six years. In other words half the cycles were 3/4 years longer than the others. A very big difference to a business struggling to survive, so as a predictive device this analysis is not much help!

Another aspect of the cycle which it is useful to analyse is the variation in the frequency of cycles F. This can be estimated by using the standard deviation of the cycle length, measured from peak to peak. This statistic is shown at the bottom of Table 1, for three periods. Firstly the average for the whole period 1872 to 2000; secondly the average for the first period 1872-1937; and finally the average for the second period 1947 to 2000. Over the whole period the standard deviation is 2.3 years. However, cycles in the earlier period had at standard deviation of 2.5 years, whilst the later period had a standard deviation of 2.1 years.

This is an interesting result. We know that provided the underlying data distribution is normal, the length of a cycle is 95% certain to fall within a range plus or minus two standard deviations of the mean. On the basis of the last 50 years, we would expect cycles to last between 2.6 years and 10.6 years. This confirms the volatility of the shipping market and offers a warning to anyone interested in the future of the shipping market. It is comforting to predict that the market will improve next year (the famous "hockey stick" forecasting model), but this analysis demonstrates that rapid recoveries are not typical, though they do happen. This makes it all the more important to study each cycle as a unique event, examine the fundamentals and determine what factors will drive the next cycle.

Table 1: Cycles, 1869–2000

Cycle No.	Start peak	End peak	Length (f) years
1	1873	1888	8
2	1881	1889	8
3	1889	1900	11
4	1900	1910	10
War	1913	1919	
5	1921	1926	5
6	1926	1930	4
7	1930	1937	7
War	1939	1945	
8	1945	1951	6
9	1952	1957	5
10	1957	1966	9
11	1966	1975	9
12	1975	1980	5
13	1980	1989	9
14	1989	1995	6
15	1996	2000	4

Statistical analysis
1872–2000: Average 7.1   Standard deviation 2.3
1872–1937: Average 7.6   Standard deviation 2.5
1947–2000: Average 6.6   Standard deviation 2.1

4. CYCLICAL MECHANISMS AND THE CAUSES OF CYCLES

The supply/demand model

So, having established that the shipping market is cyclical, albeit in an irregular way, we now need to explain what causes them. If we can do that it offers the hope that we can use analysis to narrow down the statistical uncertainty about the length of cycles discussed in the previous section.

The usual way to analyse this process is the supply/demand model. Most economists accept that the shipping market is driven by a competitive process in which supply and demand interact to determine freight rates (see Figure 10). A change in the relative demand and supply of ships leads to a shortage or surplus of tonnage, which in turn triggers an increase or a reduction in freight rates. When demand exceeds supply it drives freight rates up and the market responds by investing in more new ships, which have now become very profitable. Conversely when supply outstrips demand, competition drives freight rates down and owners start to scrap uneconomic ships. Shipping cycles can usually be explained by this supply demand model, and indeed we saw plenty of evidence of this mechanism at work in the preceding discussion of the freight cycles. It is useful to distinguish exogenous and endogenous factors. An *endogenous* factor is an event or mechanism within the shipping market which triggers or accentuates a cycle, whilst an *exogenous* factor is some external event such as a business cycle in the world economy which triggers a cyclical pattern. Both are important.

Demand factors contributing to the shipping cycle

Starting with the demand side of the model, by far the most important cause of shipping cycles is the business cycle in the world economy. This injects a cyclical pattern into the demand for ships which works through into sea trade. Historically there has been a close relationship between cycles in world industrial production and cycles in seaborne trade. This is illustrated in Figure 11 which compares the percentage change in seaborne trade with the percentage change in industrial production from 1953 to 2001. Although the correlation is far from perfect, it certainly exists, especially during extreme fluctuations in the world economy. During the major economic crisis of 1957, 1973 (first oil crisis), 1981 (second oil crisis) and 1997 (Asia crisis) the correlation was particularly clear. In other years it was less marked, but still visible. Common sense tells us that this is precisely what we should expect. When world industry goes into recession the steel mills use less raw materials, energy consumption drops, power stations import less coal and motorists drive less, so the oil trade reduces. Cumulatively this drags down the demand for sea transport. When the world economy recovers the whole process reverses and the demand for seaborne imports escalates. In fact the majority of freight "booms" shown in Figure 2 coincided with peaks in the economic cycle.

Why does the world economy have cycles? There has been much academic study of these short cycles in the world economy, which were identified by

Figure 10

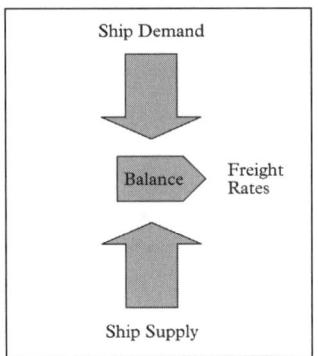

J. Kitchin (1923).[9] He suggested that these cycles were due to businesses over estimating inventory requirements during cyclical upswings, and then cutting back too much during recessions. This injected volatility into their purchasing activity, which tended to accentuate the downswing of the cycle and emphasise the upswing. Whilst this explanation does not demonstrate the original cause of the fluctuations, it suggests that once the economy starts to "vibrate" this endogenous mechanism will tend to emphasise the "vibrations" making them more clearly identifiable as cycles.

Another mechanism which contributes to the business cycle is the multiplier and accelerator. This mechanism leads to cycles because when the economy picks up and an increase in investment occurs, it raises income by a larger amount (the investment multiplier), which in turn may produce an increase in demand for the product (the income accelerator) generating demand for more investment goods, so that the economic system expands rapidly. Eventually labor and capital become fully utilized and the expansion is sharply halted, throwing the whole process into reverse. This creates a basic instability in the economic 'machine'.

Investigation of this type of cycle in the 19th century was carried out by Juglar[10] who studied cycles in France, the United States and England, and from

Figure 11

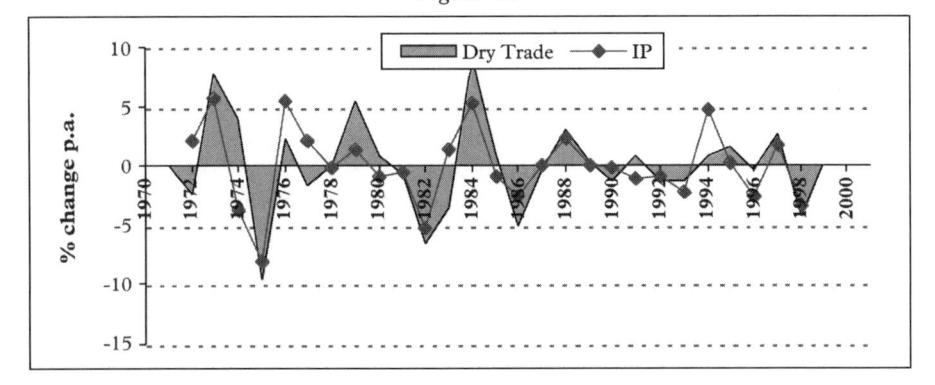

this concluded that be there is a longer cycle of about seven to 12 years driven by investment. The basic mechanism is similar to the Kitchin cycle in that it is built around systematic under correction and over correction, but in this case the variable at work is investment. During the upswing there is a tendency to invest heavily in plant and machinery, but once the peak is reached and capacity is more than sufficient to meet demand, investment activity slows sharply and less works back into the economy through a multiplier effect to generate a sharp downswing.

Another major factor influencing the demand for ships are economic shocks which suddenly change the demand for sea transport. Shock factors from recent years include the oil crises of 1973 and 1979, the Asia Crisis in 1997 and the Gulf war in 1990/91. By their nature these events are unpredictable, but that does not reduce their importance.

Supply factors contributing to shipping cycles

The main cyclical force on the supply side of the shipping market is the investment cycle. A major component of this is the time lag between ordering a new ship and taking delivery. Depending on the state of the shipyard orderbook and the type of ship being ordered, this can be anything from 18 months to three years, and during this period ship demand may have changed. For example shipowners often place large numbers of orders during the peak of the market cycle when freight rates are high and second-hand ships look expensive compared with new buildings. If the freight market peak is driven by a world business cycle, by the time the ships are delivered it is quite likely that the world economy will have plunged into recession, dragging down freight rates. As a result, the new ships arrive in the market just at the time when they are least needed, driving down freight rates even further. Naturally this discourages shipowners from ordering new ships, and the whole process is thrown into reverse. Few orders are placed, so when the world economy recovers a few years later, few new ships are being ordered and this reinforces the upward trend in freight rates.

The historical review of freight cycles in section 3 of this chapter provides plenty of evidence that this time lag mechanism has been a great part of the shipping cycle for at least the last 120 years. Surely shipowners should by now have learnt their lesson and developed a strategy of counter cyclical ordering? In fact there are numerous examples of precisely this happening. For example in the early 1980s shipowners ordered many small bulk carriers at the trough of the recession, and the same thing happened in 1999 after the Asia crisis. They argued that the ships were cheap and they would take delivery into the upswing. Unfortunately it is difficult to beat the market. On both occasions when the world economy recovered, heavy deliveries of new ships kept freight rates down. Counter-cyclical ordering just meant that the shipping market missed out on its "boom", demonstrating that shipowners need to be quite clever to "beat the cycle".

In fact it raises one of the most important factors driving at the shipping cycle, namely market sentiment. The delays between economic decisions and their implementation can make cyclical fluctuations more extreme. Many years ago Professor Pigou put forward the theory of "non-compensated errors".[11] If people act independently, their errors cancel out, but if they act in an imitative manner a particular trend will build up to a level where they can affect the whole economic system. Thus periods of optimism or pessimism become self-fulfilling through the medium of stock exchanges, financial booms and the behavior of investors.

Secular trends and structural factors impacting on cycles

Finally there are long term structural factors to consider. It was clear from the review of cycles in section 3 that during some periods the shipping industry faced very different characteristics from others. For example 1870–1914 and 1950–1973 were periods of exceptional demand growth. The shipping cycles were clearly influenced by these currents in the economic fundamentals of supply and demand, and contributed significantly to the "market tone" over extended periods. Table 2 shows my assessment of these factors during the period under review, ranked by the relative prosperity of the shipping industry. We can briefly summarise the impact which the alignment of the fundamentals had on market conditions in the following terms:

1. *Prosperity*: Top of the list was the prosperous 1950s when rapidly growing demand coincided with a shortage of shipbuilding capacity.
2. *Competitive*: There were three periods of intensely competitive activity characterized by growing trade and shipbuilding capacity that expanded fast enough to keep up with demand.
3. *Weak*: There was a weak market in the 1920's when growing demand was damped by over-capacity in the shipbuilding market
4. *Depression*: There were two depressions, in the 1930s and the 1980s when falling trade coincided with shipbuilding over-capacity

Analysis of these long term cycles in supply and demand is an area where maritime economists do have something to say. The challenge is to help the shipping industry remember the past and anticipate the future. To do this models can be used to improve the clarity of the analysis message with better information, improved analysis, clearer presentation and greater relevance to the decisions made in the commercial shipping market.

5. THE DYNAMICS OF SHIPPING CYCLES

So far in this chapter we have concentrated on the dynamics of the shipping supply/demand model. The freight market analysis suggests that there is a cyclical component in the shipping market generated by business cycles in the world economy and reinforced by the time-lag taken to adjust supply to demand and the frequent miscalculation by shipowners of the future level of demand. We now need to ask two questions: first, "How do business cycles feed through into

Table 2: Shipping fundamental trends

	Demand tendency	Supply tendency	Market tone
1945–1956	Very fast	Shortage	Prosperous
1869–1914	Fast	Expanding	Competitive
1956–1973	Very fast	Expanding	Competitive
1988–2000	Slow	Expanding	Competitive
1920–1930	Fast	Over-capacity	Weak
1930–1939	Falling	Over-capacity	Depressed
1973–1989	Falling	Over-capacity	Depressed

the key variables in which the shipowner is interested – freight rates and prices?" and, secondly, "Are the cycles predictable?".

Do business cycles affect freight rates?

The simplest way to deal with the first question, is statistical analysis comparing the historic pattern of cycles in the world economy, seaborne trade and freight rates. To make such an analysis it is necessary to analyse these variables into a form in which they are directly comparable. The technique used is to take a five-year moving average for the basic statistical series and compute the deviation of the actual observation from the five-year trend. When the variable moves above zero this indicates a cyclical upswing or 'boom' and when the variable swings below zero it indicates a depression. The analysis for the dry cargo trade in Figure 11 indicates the remarkable degree to which the world business cycle has influenced dry cargo trade since 1970. There has been a series of alternating peaks and troughs, with particularly severe troughs which followed the 1973 and 1979 oil crises and the 1999 Asia crisis. It is worth making the point that the use of OECD industrial production to represent world economic activity is a statistical convenience that becomes less valid as the Third World takes a larger share of world economic activity. The problem in carrying out an analysis of this type is the difficulty of obtaining a long, but up-to-date, time series for world industrial output.

Turning to the financial variables, Figure 12 shows the relationship between dry cargo cycles and cycles in the dry cargo freight rate. The correlation is remarkably close, with freight market booms coinciding with trade booms in 1974, 1980 and 1989 and 1995. This indicates that in the dry cargo market the growth rate of seaborne trade has, in the past been an excellent indicator of freight rate movements, though not a precise one. It is, however, necessary to be cautious in extrapolating this relationship into the future, since determination of freight rates depends upon supply as well as demand. During the period covered by this analysis the supply of dry cargo vessels was broadly in line with the demand on a trend basis. As a result, peaks in trade caused a shortage of shipping capacity, so that freight rates rose, whilst recession in sea trade caused a surplus of shipping capacity and freight rates fell. This pattern will not occur if there is a permanent miss-alignment between supply and demand, as happened in the tanker market.

6. ARE BUSINESS CYCLES PREDICTABLE?

Our analysis of the shipping market has raised several warning flags about the dangers of relying on simple "rules of thumb" about the cyclical nature of the shipping market, but it has also shown the importance of the industrial business cycle in determining the underlying performance of seaborne trade and freight rates. Inevitably this raises the question of whether business cycles are predictable.

The statistical analysis discussed earlier in the chapter offered convincing evidence that the concept of a regular seven-year cycle has little merit as a way of predicting the future of market. In reality the cycles may be three years or 10 years in length. From a practical business perspective that is much too wide a range to be acceptable, so we must look elsewhere.

Our analysis of supply demand models suggested that this might be a fruitful avenue. Although there are far too many variables at work to hope to predict cycles accurately, at least analysis of world economy and the shipping investment cycle can help to narrow down the possibilities which lie ahead, and give decision-makers some idea of the risks which they are of taking. Indeed one of the most useful applications of the supply demand model is to examine the impact of the shipping investment cycle. One lesson which is all too apparent from the historical analysis of shipping cycles is the extent to which the market is driven by supply-side factors, and in particular the ordering activity of shipowners. Analysts often deplore the fact that shipowners order at the top of a cycle, but when they try "counter-cyclical" ordering at the bottom of the cycle, the result can be equally disastrous.

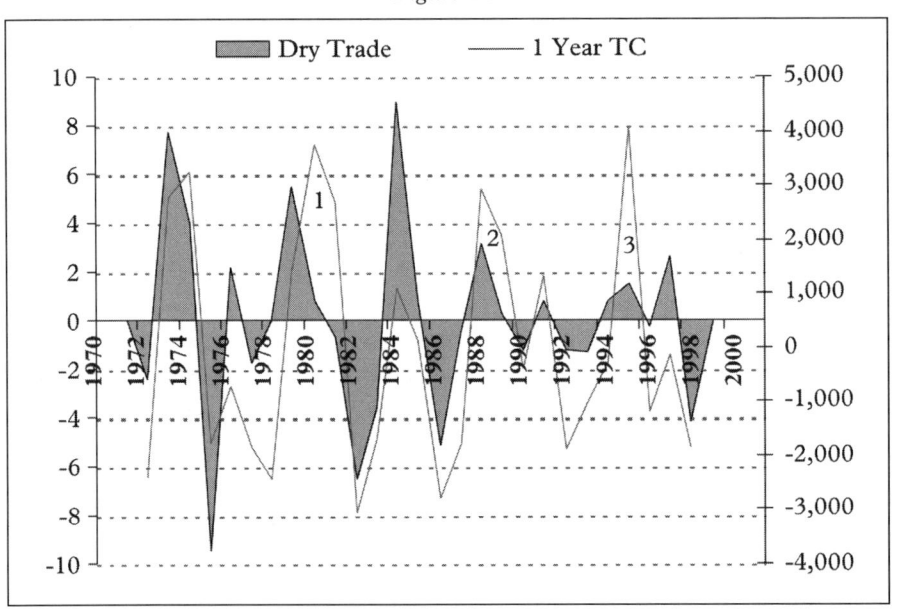

Figure 12

On the demand side of the market, business cycles are clearly a dominant force, though one which can be very difficult to predict. However the historical analysis suggests that it is vital to be aware of the possibility of serious recessions in demand. The two really serious depressions in the shipping industry both coincided with a major depression be in the world economy (in 1931 and 1983), so provided we can obtain some forewarning of these factors that can be very helpful. Statisticians have, over the years, developed leading indicators that give an advance indication of turning points in the economy. For example, the OECD publishes a leading indicators index, which is based on orders, stocks, the amount of overtime worked, the number of workers laid off, in addition to financial statistics such as money supply, company profits and stock market prices. It is suggested that the turning point in the lead index will anticipate a similar turning point in the industrial production index by about six months. To the analyst of short-term market trends such information is extremely valuable.

In conclusion, whilst we can usefully employ the concept of a "cycle" to discuss fluctuations in seaborne trade, most experts would warn against the assumption that cyclical peaks and troughs will follow in an orderly progression. As the graphs show, seaborne trade generally recovers from each trough, but it is difficult to say in which year this will occur or how strong the recovery will be. We must take many other factors into account before drawing such a conclusion.

7. SUMMARY

In this chapter we started by observing that the shipping market can change very quickly and that decisions by shipowners about the sale, purchase and chartering of vessels depend crucially upon timing. In the space of a few months the market value of a vessel may change by millions of dollars. The cycles are certainly not regular, appearing as fluctuations in revenue of variable length. Different market segments, especially tankers and bulk carriers have exhibited similar cyclical patterns during some periods, but in others they have diverged significantly, suggesting that each segment of the shipping market must be treated separately. We also noted that cycles in shipping revenue work through into cycles in the price of second-hand assets.

A cycle was defined as an interval of time during which one sequence of a regularly recurring sequence of events is completed. In section 3 we set about reviewing the sequence of fluctuations in freight rates which have occurred during the period 1869 to 2002. A total of 15 cycles were identified, with an average length of 7.1 years and a standard deviation of 2.3 years. Although this confirms the "rule-of-thumb" that shipping cycles last seven years, the standard deviation suggests that this specific outcome is not particularly likely. At a 95 per cent confidence level we can expect shipping cycles to last between 2.6 years and 10.6 years.

In the absence of regularity, the best approach to analyzing cycles is to understand their causes, and this was discussed in Section 4. Shipping cycles are a manifestation of fluctuations in supply and demand and freight rates are highly sensitive to quite small movements in either of these variables. On the demand side of the market the main driving force is the world business cycle, and reference was made to the short business cycles identified a by Kitchen and the longer investment cycles identified by Juglar. These introduce volatility into the demand side of the market, though random economic shocks such as the 1973 oil crisis or the closure of the Suez Canal in 1956.

On the supply side of the market the outstanding influence is the investment cycle, as shipowners struggle to match investment to the essentially unpredictable demand cycles. The genuine uncertainty which triggers these supply-side fluctuations is reinforced by a market sentiment which Professor Pigou first identified as "non compensatory errors".

Finally, we noted the long-term secular trends which set the tone for the shipping market over periods of the 20 or 30 years. These trends are characterized by differences in the underlying growth rate of seaborne trade, due to economic developments in the world economy, and the level of shipbuilding capacity.

In view of their lack of regularity, the best hope of predicting business cycles is to analyse the underlying causes and project them forward. Many analysts use computer models for this purpose, and although the forecasts may not always be accurate, they help to narrow down uncertainty and give decision-makers a better feel for the way things might develop.

ENDNOTES

1. According to Greek mythology, Sisyphus was condemned to roll a stone up a hill, only to have it continuously roll down again.
2. J.C. Gould, Angier & Co, *Market Report*, 31 December 1894.
3. According to *Websters Dictionary* the word is derived from the Greek word *kilos* – a ring, circle or wheel.
4. This was the date when global freight rate statistics first became available. It also coincided with the introduction of steamships and an international communications system which allowed a global shipping industry to evolve from the regionally fragmented business which existed during the era of sail.
5. Before decimalization in 1972, the English pound (£) was divided into 20 shillings. Thus 27 shillings was equivalent to £1.35.
6. These fleet figures understate the true growth of shipping supplies. According to contemporary estimates, the productivity of a steamer was four times as high as a sailing ship, so in real terms the available sea transport capacity increased by 460%. No doubt much of this was absorbed by increasing ton-miles as more distant trades were opened up, though unfortunately no ton-mile statistics were collected at this time.
7. Tylecore, Andrew (1991): *The Long Wave in the World Economy* (London, Routledge), Table 9.1.
8. From Angier (1921).
9. J Kitchin (1923): "Cycles and trends in economic factors", *Review of Economic Statistics*, 5, pp. 10–16.
10. C. Juglar in (1862): *Des Crises commerciales et leur retour periodique en France, Angleterre et aux Etats Unis.*
11. Pigou (1927).

PART FOUR

ECONOMICS OF SHIPPING SECTORS

CHAPTER 11

THE DRY BULK SHIPPING MARKET

Amir H. Alizadeh and Nikos K. Nomikos
City University Cass Business School, City of London, UK.
E-mail: *a.alizadeh@city.ac.uk* and *n.nomikos@city.ac.uk*

1. INTRODUCTION

Dry Bulk shipping was developed as a result of the need to reduce transportation costs when cargo sizes became large enough to be carried in shiploads, and economies of scale were apparent. This goes back to the 19th century when small wooden ships, fully laden with coal, were employed to meet the increasing demand for coal transportation in the coal trade between North England and London. Nowadays, the number of commodities carried on a "one ship, one cargo" basis has increased, thanks to the increasing demand for raw materials and energy commodities, liberalisation in international trade, trans-nationalisation of industrial processes as well as technological advances in shipbuilding and design.

The growth in international trade led to a corresponding expansion of the bulk shipping fleet to match the requirements of seaborne bulk trade. Today, the world's dry bulk fleet constitutes one third of the total world fleet, with 6000 ships providing 260 million dwt of cargo carrying capacity.[1] In 1998, total world seaborne trade in dry bulk commodities reached 1,882 million metric tons (mmt), of which 1,172 mmt represented movements in the so called "major" dry bulk commodities; iron ore (426 mmt), coal (452 mmt), grain (208 mmt) and bauxite, alumina and phosphate rock (86 mmt).[2]

Additionally, technological developments led to more sophisticated and larger ship designs, aiming not only to realise the economies of scale but also to match specific cargo and trading route requirements. The latter depend very much on commodity trade patterns and industrial production processes in the world economy. As a result, dry bulk shipping may be broadly divided into four different sectors according to the cargo carrying capacity of the vessels. These are handysize (30,000 dwt), handymax (45,000 dwt), panamax (65,000 dwt) and capesize (120,000 dwt and over) markets.

The purpose of this chapter is to provide a description of the dry-bulk shipping markets, and discuss current issues and developments in this area. In particular, we discuss the segmentation of the dry bulk shipping markets in different sub-sectors which arises, due to different physical and economic factors such as commodity parcel size, the underlying shipping routes, the physical characteristics of the loading and discharge ports as well as the vessel's design features. We also present the structure of the shipping markets as well as the theory for the determination of freight rates. Additionally, we also present empirical evidence on issues relating to the properties of the dry bulk shipping freight rates. These issues include the seasonal behaviour of the freight market; testing the dynamic interrelationships between freight rate levels and volatilities for different size vessels in the spot, and period markets; testing the expectations hypothesis of the term structure and modelling time-varying risk premia in the formation of long term rates, and finally, investigating the existence of time-varying risk premia in the market for newbuilding and second-hand vessels.

The structure of this chapter is as follows. The next two sections describe the structure of the dry bulk market and its contribution to the world economy by connecting the sources of supply and demand for raw materials; section 4 presents the seasonal properties of international freight rates; section 5 investigates the efficient market hypothesis in dry bulk shipping markets; section 6 describes the interrelationships between freight rate levels and volatilities; and section 7 investigates the relationship between new-building and second-hand prices in the market. Finally, section 8 presents some conclusions.

2. MARKET SEGMENTATION OF THE DRY BULK SHIPPING INDUSTRY

The enormous growth in international seaborne commodity trade along with developments in the shipbuilding industry in the past forty years or so, are a manifestation of the liberalisation in international trade and the inherent economies of scale existent in seaborne commodity transportation. This has encouraged the construction of specialised ships of various sizes, which can be employed in the transportation of certain types of commodities over certain trading routes. Therefore, different sub-markets within the dry and the liquid bulk sectors with distinguishing characteristics in terms of supply and demand features, operations, risk and profitability have developed. Generally speaking, the decision to hire a certain type of vessel for ocean transportation of a certain commodity depends on three main factors; first, the type of the commodity to be transported; second, the parcel size, and third, the trade route and the physical characteristics and infrastructure at the loading and discharge ports.

Different types of commodities, are generally distinguished for the purposes of shipping operations, market analysis and research; these are classified as follows: liquid bulk, dry bulk, general cargo and unitised (containers). There are also specialised cargoes such as natural gas, refrigerated cargoes, automobiles, forest products and live-stocks, which require special types of ships for transportation. Since it is the type of commodity that determines which type of ship the charterer (cargo owner or shipper) requires for the transportation of his/her cargo, any change in the trade pattern for that commodity is reflected in the demand and freight rates for different types of vessels. For example, industrial developments in the Far East, especially South Korea and China, in the past two decades have increased the demand for capesize vessels in that region. As another example, the demand for capesize vessels in the Atlantic has been reduced in recent years due to an increase in the European Union's (EU) grain

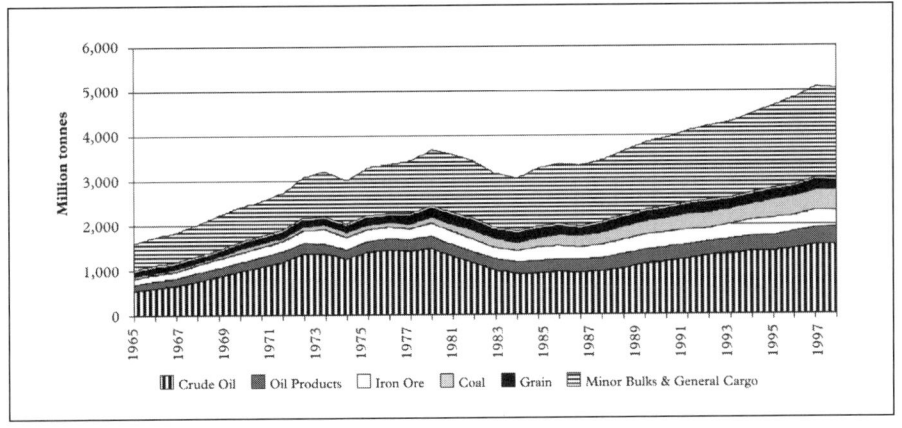

Figure 1: Pattern of international seaborne trade in major commodities

Source: Fearnleys.

production and a corresponding decline in EU's grain imports from the United States after the 1980's. Figure 1 illustrates the evolution of seaborne trade in major dry and liquid bulk commodities between 1963 to 1998. We can note that the volume of international seaborne trade in bulk commodities has doubled since the 1960's.

The second factor that a charterer should bear in mind before taking any decision to hire a vessel is the conventional shipment size of each commodity, generally known as the "commodity parcel size". This is defined as the amount of cargo, in tons, that can be carried by sea considering the economies of scale and associated transportation and storage costs for that commodity. The commodity parcel size also depends on the economics of the industrial process or consumption of such commodities as raw materials for industrial goods and other finished products. For certain commodities such as iron ore, crude oil and coal, the economies of scale in sea transportation have reduced the transportation costs to such an extent that it is most economical to hire large vessels for their carriage by sea. Therefore, parcel sizes for those commodities are quite large (e.g., for iron ore 80,000 to 300,000 tons). On the other hand, agricultural commodities are carried in smaller shipments, for example from 12,000 to 60,000 tons, again depending on the type of cargo transported. This is mainly because of the perishable nature of those commodities and the fact that they need specialised storage facilities (e.g., special storage silos). Therefore, traders prefer smaller shipments as it enables them to store and market these products in time. In addition, the higher storage and inventory costs of agricultural commodities and oil products, compared to lower value goods such as iron ore and coal, suggest that it is more economical to transport these commodities in smaller consignments.

Finally, when the shipper is deciding which size vessel to hire, he must consider factors such as the trading route, the physical characteristics of ports of loading and discharge, such as berth size and draught, as well as the existence of cargo handling facilities at the ports. The draught factor is important because

Table 1: Different size vessels with their respective cargo and routes

Class of Bulk Carriers	Commodities (percentage of total shipments)			
	Iron ore	Coal	Grain	Bauxite & Alumina	Phosphate Rock
Capesize	70%	45%	7%	–	–
Panamax	22%	40%	43%	45%	20%
Handymax and Handysize	8%	15%	50%	55%	80%

Class of Bulk Carriers	Major Routes				
	Iron ore	Coal	Grain	Bauxite & Alumina	Phosphate Rock
Capesize (120,000 dwt and over)	• Brazil to West Europe & Japan • W. Australia to West Europe & Japan	• Australia to Far East, Japan & West Europe • South Africa to West Europe and Far East	• Argentina and River Plate to Near East, & East Europe		
Panamax (65,000 dwt)	• Brazil to West Europe & Japan • Australia to W. Europe & Japan	• N. America to Japan & W. Europe • Australia to Far East, Japan & West Europe	• N. America to Far East, W. Europe & Near East		
Handymax & Handysize (45,000 dwt) & (30,000 dwt)	• India to Japan & Korea • Canada to USA & Japan • Liberia & Mauritania to West Europe	• S. Africa to Far East & Europe	• Australia to Far Japan & Middle East • N. America to Africa & West Europe	• Caribbean to North America & W. Europe • West Africa to W. Europe & Japan • Australia to Japan & West Europe	• Morocco to W. Europe • Russia to W. Europe • The US to Japan & West Europe

large ships with deep draughts cannot approach ports with shallow harbours and the costs of lightening them at the anchorage should be compared against the capacity loss when using smaller vessels. In ports where cargo-handling facilities are lacking, small and geared vessels are needed. In general, shippers try to minimise the associated transportation costs by hiring an optimal size vessel after considering all the above named factors.

These costs and size optimisations bring up the idea that there must be a close relationship between certain types of commodities and vessel sizes, i.e. certain classes of vessels are employed in the transportation of particular commodities on specific routes. In fact, Table 1 summarises the three broad categories of vessels distinguished in the dry bulk sector and the associated cargo types and routes that these vessels trade in. Handysize (30,000 dwt) and Handymax (45,000 dwt) vessels are mainly engaged in the transportation of grain commodities from North and South America and Australia to Europe and Asia, and minor dry bulk commodities such as bauxite and alumina, fertilisers, rice, sugar, steel and scrap around the world. Due to their small size, shallow draught and cargo handling gears, these vessels are quite flexible in terms of the trading routes and ports that they can serve. Panamax vessels (65,000 dwt) are used primarily in coal, grain and to some extent in iron ore transportation, from North America and Australia to Japan and West Europe. These vessels are not equipped with cargo handling gears and have deeper draught, therefore they are engaged in the transportation of fewer commodities than handysize bulk carriers, since they are not as flexible. The majority of the capesize (120,000dwt and over) fleet is engaged in the transportation of iron ore from South America and Australia to Japan, West Europe and North America and also in coal transportation from Australia and North America to Japan and West Europe. Due to their deep draught and limited number of commodities that they transport, the operation of these vessels in terms of trading routes and ports they can approach is restricted.

It has also been argued in the literature that the risk/return characteristics of dry bulk carriers vary across vessel sizes. In particular, Kavussanos[3,4] shows that freight rate volatilities and second-hand ship price volatilities are higher for larger vessels compared to smaller ones and relates such differences to operational flexibility and trading restrictions of larger vessels. Such strong contrast in risk/return and operational profitability among different size of dry bulk carriers stems from differences in their supply, demand, freight rate and price determination factors which reflect their trading and operational flexibility. This in turn implies a high degree of disaggregation in this shipping sector.

3. MARKET CONDITIONS IN THE DRY BULK FREIGHT MARKET

One of the most important features of any market, is the degree of competition prevailing in that market. On the one extreme, we can identify those markets in which there is perfect competition and no individual seller can influence the market price. On the other extreme the market might be monopolistic, in which case the price is set by the monopolist by taking account of a downward sloping demand curve and production costs. In between these two extremes, there are oligopolistic market conditions under which a group of sellers might be able to collude and set prices.

In markets where perfect competition exists, sellers and buyers always search for the best offer, through a range of offers. The price at which contracts are settled at each point in time, the equilibrium price, is determined through the interaction between supply and demand. For perfect competition to exist certain conditions must be satisfied. In the case of tramp shipping markets these conditions are; ease of entry into and exit from the market, a large number of participants (sellers and buyers), homogeneity of the product (service), the mobility of assets and services which the owners provide and efficient information dissemination. The following sections discuss the nature and importance of these conditions with respect to competition in dry bulk shipping markets.

3.1 No barriers to entry and exit

In the shipping business, it is relatively easy to enter into the market, as long as the investor can afford the initial investment required for purchasing a vessel. This is especially evident from the expansion of the industry during the past 50 years. During this period many private investors have been attracted to the shipping business, especially the dry bulk sector, due to the profitability of this market, which, at least at certain times, has been higher compared to other sectors of the economy (see Stopford,[5] page 71). Availability of special and lenient financing terms on newbuilding or second-hand vessels for potential investors through banks and financial institutions shows that it is not very difficult to enter into shipping operations. Moreover, operational simplicity and the existence of management companies allows investors to participate in the market without any particular prior knowledge of shipping operations. At the same time, there are no barriers for investors to exit the industry by liquidating the company or selling off their vessels and leaving the business after even a short period of involvement.

The argument of ease of entry and exit is also true for operating or switching between different routes, when each route is considered as a separate market. There are no barriers to restrict owners or operators to enter into a particular trade or switch between trading routes. This is in contrast to liner shipping where oligopolistic market conditions exist. Ease of entry and exit also allows owners and operators in the market to search and operate in routes which offer higher returns. As a result, any opportunity for making excess profit in a particular route may be eliminated in a relatively short period.

It can also be argued that there are not any complications to prevent shipowners and charterers from switching between contracts with different times to maturity; namely, spot and time-charter contracts in order to maximise their profits or minimise their costs. The only problem is that once a time-charter contract is agreed upon, both parties must fulfil their obligations until the terminal date of the contract. However, for short term time-charter contracts, say

6 to 12 months, flexibility and ease of switching between different charter markets ensures perfect competition in both spot and period markets.

3.2 Number of market participants

It is well known that in markets where the number of participants is limited, there is always the possibility that prices may be affected by a small group or even by only one participant. In such markets, as in the case of the liner shipping industry, few buyers or sellers control a large share of demand or supply. Therefore, they may virtually control the pricing mechanism of the market by timing their entry or exit.

The large number of participants (owners and charterers) in the dry bulk market is a necessary condition for the existence of perfect competition. On the one hand, the large number of private shipowners and shipping companies as well as state owned companies prevents any single company or a group of them to influence the supply for freight services and hence, freight rates. On the other hand, the number of charterers, in the form of private importers, government agencies and trading companies, is large enough to prevent demand being influenced by a single agent or a group of them.

3.3 The homogeneity of the product (shipping services)

An important condition, which should be satisfied for perfect competition to prevail in a market, is that products offered and demanded in that market must be homogeneous. In other words, there should not be any diversity in terms of product quality and price. In contrast to the liner shipping industry, in which services offered may vary according to quality, speed and price, the services offered by shipowners and demanded by charterers in the dry bulk market are believed to be homogeneous; that is, there is no product differentiation in this market. For instance, the product (services) offered by bulk shipowners cannot be distinguished through advertising, trademarks, branding or even reputation and relationships. In fact, it is the standard nature of the product offered by shipowners and demanded by shippers that prevents any single participant, or a group of participants, in the market to take advantage and over price the product or depress the market.

The main reason behind this is that commodities transported in the bulk shipping sector are relatively low value cargoes and can be shipped on the basis of "one commodity, one ship". Therefore, as long as there is a large number of participants in the market, shippers generally look for the lowest freight rate offered in the market to fulfil their requirements and shipowners do not offer any tonnage at a lower rate than that pertaining in the freight market.

3.4 Efficient information dissemination

Efficient information dissemination is a necessary condition for the existence of perfect competition in a market. This is because access to up to date information prevents any owner or group of owners from taking any opportunity to influence a trading route or market. In fact, this is due to the existence of institutions such as the Baltic Exchange, the Lloyd's Maritime Information Services and Lloyd's Register of Shipping as well as brokers and chartering firms around the world which are involved in collecting shipping information and publishing reports on a regular basis. Recent advances in information technology have improved information dissemination in the industry and enabled many owners, brokers, and charterers, not only to keep track of the market, but also to look for the best offer and fix the best available contract. Apart from a vast number of periodicals and publications reporting current market conditions, recent fixtures and future forecasts, there are also online information networks, such as, Bloomberg, Reuters, Shipping Intelligence Network, etc., connecting brokers and agents around the world. Such networks enable agents to obtain up to date information about market conditions, supply, demand and fixtures in different routes and trades.

3.5 Mobility of ships and competition

As Zannetos[6] mentions, an important factor which contributes to the existence of perfect competition conditions in international shipping, is the fact that the assets that provide the service in the market (i.e. the ships) are mobile. Mobility of shipping services allows owners to take advantage of freight rate differential and relocate their vessel(s) to those areas, which are expected to generate higher revenues. This, in turn generates a higher supply in the region and eliminates any extra profit making opportunity. Therefore, it is the mobility of ships and shipping services that prevents a small number of market participants influencing the market in a region or trading route.

The preceding discussion, indicates that shipping market satisfy all the conditions that characterise a perfectly competitive market. In the following section, we now analyse the characteristics and statistical properties of dry bulk shipping freight rates.

4. SEASONAL BEHAVIOUR OF DRY BULK FREIGHT RATES

In the shipping industry fluctuations in ship prices and freight rates are considerable compared to rates and prices in other sectors of the world economy. Unexpected changes and sharp movements in freight rates, over short periods of time, hinder the decision making process whilst, at the same time, provide the opportunity for substantial gains or losses for those involved. Therefore, comprehending and analysing these movements in the market is an essential first step for any decision maker in the shipping industry.

Shipping freight rates reflect the supply-demand balance for freight services. The demand for shipping services is a derived demand, which depends on the following factors. First, the economics of the commodities transported by sea; that is, the level of production and consumption for the commodity to be transported. Second, the global economic conditions and world economic activity, and finally related macroeconomic variables of major economies (Stopford,[5] page 238). These macroeconomic variables are shown elsewhere to have random variations as well as deterministic seasonal components in most cases

(Beaulieu and Miron,[7] Dickey[8] and Canova and Hansen[9]). Trade figures in several commodities are also shown to be seasonal; for instance, there are seasonal variations in the grain trade (Stopford,[5] pages 238–239). Therefore, it is possible that those seasonalities are transmitted to shipping freight rates and prices; see for instance, Denning et al.,[10] on the seasonality of the Baltic Freight Index, BFI.[11]

Investigating the seasonal behaviour of shipping freight rates is important and has both economic and econometric implications. From the economic point of view, revealing the nature and true behaviour of seasonal fluctuations in freight rates can be of interest to shipowners and charterers in their chartering strategies, tactical operations and budgeting. From the econometric point of view, it is important to investigate the existence of seasonal behaviour in the freight rates for the purposes of modelling and forecasting these series. Kavussanos and Alizadeh[12] examine the seasonal behaviour of dry bulk freight rates and compare them (a) across different size vessels, (b) across freight contracts with different maturities, and (c) under different market condition. The first two issues are investigated through the following equation, over the period January 1980 to December 1996:

$$\Delta X_t = \beta_0 + \sum_{i=2}^{12} \beta_i Q_{i,t} + \varepsilon_t \quad , \quad \varepsilon \sim \text{iid}(0, \sigma^2) \quad (1)$$

Where ΔX_t represents the growth rate of the underlying series (either spot, one-year time-charter or three-year time-charter freight rates for handysize, panamax and capesize vessels), $Q_{i,t}$, i = 2,...,s, are relative seasonal dummies, β_i are the parameters of interest and ε_t is a white noise error term. The significance of each seasonal dummy indicates the existence of deterministic seasonality in the respective period; that is, a significant change in the dependent variable compared to its long-run mean, β_0.

The results are shown in graphical form in Figures 2–4. An asterisk (*) above or below a bar indicates a significant, at the 10% level, increase or decrease, in monthly changes in freight rates at a particular month compared to the average over the sample period.

We can note for instance, that spot rates for capesize bulk carriers increase significantly during April. Similarly, panamax spot rates increase in March, while there is a significant seasonal increase in handysize spot rates in both March and April. The rise in the level of dry bulk spot rates in those months could be explained by the surge in demand from Japanese importers for all commodities (grain, coal, iron ore, etc.) because of the end of the fiscal (tax) year in Japan at the end of March.[13] Also, the harvest season in the Southern Hemisphere (February to March in Australia and Argentina) increases the demand for handysize and panamax dry bulk carriers (during March and April). Due to the shortage of storage facilities and the port structure in these countries grains harvested are exported immediately using mostly smaller vessels that can approach these shallow ports. In contrast, large inventories of grains are held during the year in the Northern Hemisphere. These stock levels are reduced during March and April to make way for storage space required for the forthcoming harvest. Thus, the increase in demand for freight services in the Handysize and Panamax sizes affect rates positively. Capesize freight rates are also influenced by the shift of the handysize and panamax tonnage to grain transportation. This, in turn, causes an under-supply of these types of vessels in transportation of other major and/or minor dry bulk commodities.

Panamax spot rates also show a combined increase of almost 15% during October and November. This may reflect the seasonal increase in US grain exports (harvested between June and October) during this period as well as the increase in the demand for coal to stock up for the winter requirements. The results also show a seasonal decline in rates during June and July across all the three sizes of vessels. This decline is more pronounced in July compared to June and in larger vessels compared to smaller ones. The significant seasonal decline in the dry bulk spot markets at mid summer is caused by the start of the summer holidays and a drop in the industrial output of the industrialised countries.[14]

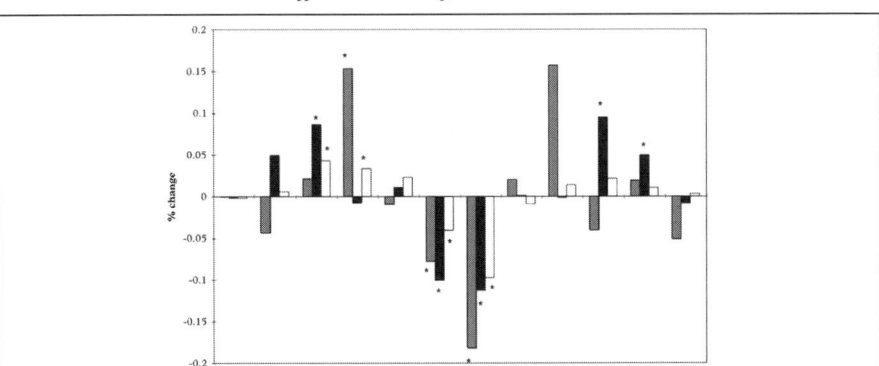

Figure 2: Comparison of seasonal changes in spot rates for different size dry bulk carriers

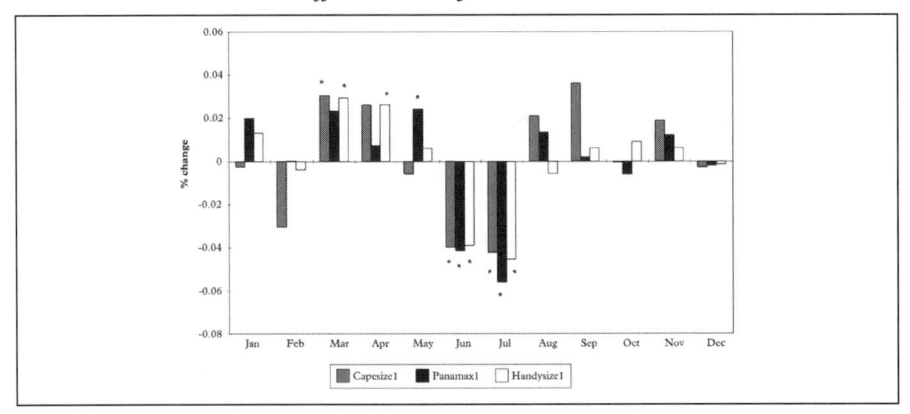

Figure 3: Comparison of seasonal changes in one-year TC rates for different size dry bulk carriers

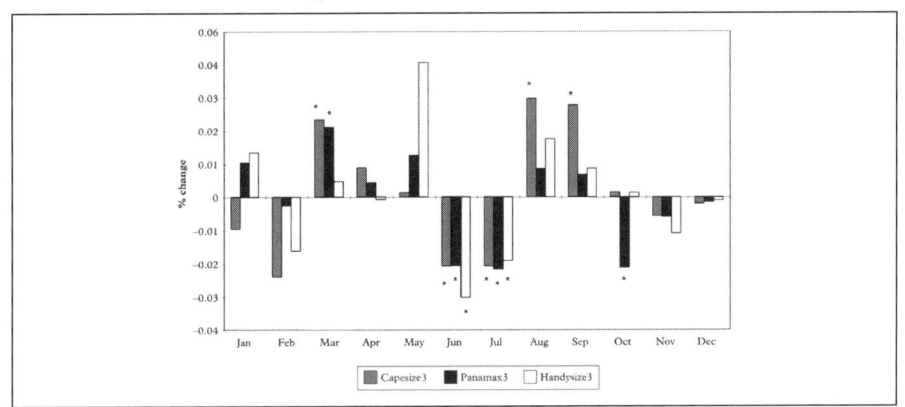

Figure 4: Comparison of seasonal changes in 3-year TC rates for different size dry bulk carriers

The weaker seasonal increase or decline in average freight rates for smaller size vessels may be attributed to their flexibility, which enables them to switch between trades and routes more easily compared to larger ships. In addition, most capesize vessels are mainly engaged in long term charter contracts leaving relatively fewer tonnage to trade in the spot market. As a result "shocks" to spot rates have a much greater effect on capesize rates compared to smaller vessels.

Turning next to the one-year time-charter rates in Figure 3, we can note that rates for handysize vessels show a significant rise during March and April, while the rates for panamax and capesize vessels show a significant increase in May and March, respectively. In line with the spot market, there is a significant decline during June and July. This may be due to two reasons; the reduction in the level of industrial production and trade in mid summer or switch of spot operators to time-charter operation after the end of the Japanese and harvest led spring upsurge, which causes an over-supply in the time-charter market. Also, since time-charter rates are linked to the current and expected spot rates, a drop in the spot market is transmitted to the time-charter market accordingly. Also in line with spot markets, the net seasonal effect on 1-year time-charter rates is negative for each sector; the summer fall in rates is higher than the corresponding spring rises.

The pattern of the three-year time-charter rates, in Figure 4, is similar to that of one-year rates. That is, there is a significant seasonal increase during spring for capesize and panamaxes and a decline in rates for all the sizes during June and July. However, both the increase and the decline in three-year time-charter rates are less pronounced compared to one-year rates. There is also a significant increase in the freight rates for capesize bulk carriers during August and September. This is thought to reflect the fact that during this period the Japanese and Korean steel mills negotiate (or re-negotiate) and renew their long term imports (iron ore and coal) and the associated charter contracts.

Overall, the seasonal movement of dry bulk time-charter rates suggests that, on average, the levels of freight rates increase in certain months (March and

April) and drop in others (June and July). Shipowners (and charterers) can base tactical operations on such movements, in order to maximise their revenue (minimise their transportation costs). For example, the best time for a shipowner to fix (renew) a dry bulk time-charter contract or switch from spot to time-charter operation might be March and April. Taking such opportunity, he may well be able to "ride the seasonal cycle" until the next year. On the other hand, the best time for a charterer to fix a dry bulk vessel for one year is June and July. Also, these regular seasonal movements in dry bulk rates suggest that, if cleaning and repositioning costs permit, shipowners operating combined carriers might be able to switch between sectors (tanker and dry bulk) in order to exploit these short-run fluctuations.

Finally, another point worth noting is that the degree of seasonal fluctuation of shipping freight rates varies across vessel sizes and duration of contract. For instance, the impact of seasonal fluctuations is more pronounced for the spot rates and declines as we move to the one-year and three-year time-charters, across all types of vessels. This is because one-year time-charter rates, say, are formed as the expected future spot rates over the year (see e.g. Beenstock and Vergottis[15]). Therefore, one would expect that one-year time-charter rates would have already incorporated expected future seasonal variations and are smoother than spot rates. In addition, spot rate seasonalities are expected to be higher than time-charter rate ones to incorporate possible periods of unemployment.[16] As a consequence differences in freight rate seasonalities between sectors are eliminated since they depend less on the idiosyncratic factors influencing rates in sub-markets and more on the length (type) of the contract involved. These arguments extend to longer term contracts, e.g. 3-year time-charters.

The higher seasonal fluctuations of spot rates compared to time charter rates may be further explained by the chartering strategies of industrial charterers (e.g., power stations and still mills). These types of charterers use long term charter contracts not only to fulfil their long term requirements in terms of supply of raw materials, but also to secure and maintain their transportation cost at a relatively fixed level over a long period. They use the spot market then in order to meet their seasonal or cyclical requirements. Therefore, they may enter the spot market at certain seasons, which leads to an increase in demand in the spot market and consequently the freight rates at those periods.

4.1 Seasonality under different market conditions

It is well established in the literature that the elasticity of shipping supply, in a market equilibrium framework, depends on the state of the market. This implies that a change in the demand function during a market expansion, when the supply curve is inelastic, has a greater impact on freight rates compared to periods of market downturn, when the supply function is elastic, as in Figure 5.

This property of the shipping supply curve is also examined by Kavussanos and Alizadeh[12] who distinguish between different market conditions (market expansion and market contraction) and compare the seasonal fluctuations of freight rates under these two market conditions. They use the following equa-

THE DRY BULK SHIPPING MARKET

tion threshold switching model to investigate the possibility that seasonal pattern in freight rates differ under different market conditions.

$$\Delta X_t = \beta_{1,0} d_{1,t} + \sum_{i=2}^{12} \beta_{1,i}(d_{1,t}Q_{1,t}) + \beta_{2,0} d_{2,t} + \sum_{i=2}^{12} \beta_{2,i}(d_{2,t}Q_{i,t}) + \varepsilon_t \, , \quad \varepsilon_t \sim \text{iid}(0,\sigma^2)$$

where state dummies $d_{1,t}$ and $d_{2,t}$ are
$$\begin{cases} d_{1,t} = 1 \text{ and } d_{2,t} = 0 & \text{if } \dfrac{1}{12}\sum_{j=-6}^{5}\Delta X_{t+j} > 0 \quad \text{upturn} \\[2mm] d_{1,t} = 0 \text{ and } d_{2,t} = 1 & \text{if } \dfrac{1}{12}\sum_{j=-6}^{5}\Delta X_{t+j} \leq 0 \quad \text{downturn} \end{cases}$$
(2)

In the above threshold switching seasonal model, two dummy variables, $d_{1,t}$ and $d_{2,t}$, allow estimation of different seasonal coefficients according to the prevailing market conditions. Estimation results of the threshold switching seasonal models for spot, one and three-year time-charter rates indicate that the seasonal fluctuations (positive or negative) are stronger for periods of market expansion as opposed to periods of market contraction. However, such differences become smaller as the duration of the contract increases. For three-year contracts it seems that seasonality is mainly attributable to periods of expansion, with the majority of seasonal coefficients becoming insignificant in depressed markets. This points to the conclusion that the supply for shipping services schedule is less and less steep (more and more elastic) at the top end of the curve as the contract duration rises. For instance, the supply curve is almost flat for three-year time-charter rates in "bad" markets, as in Figure 5. This is an important issue in the cyclical shipping freight markets since the elasticity of supply is high during troughs and low in peaks of the shipping business cycle. As a result, changes in demand during the recovery period in the

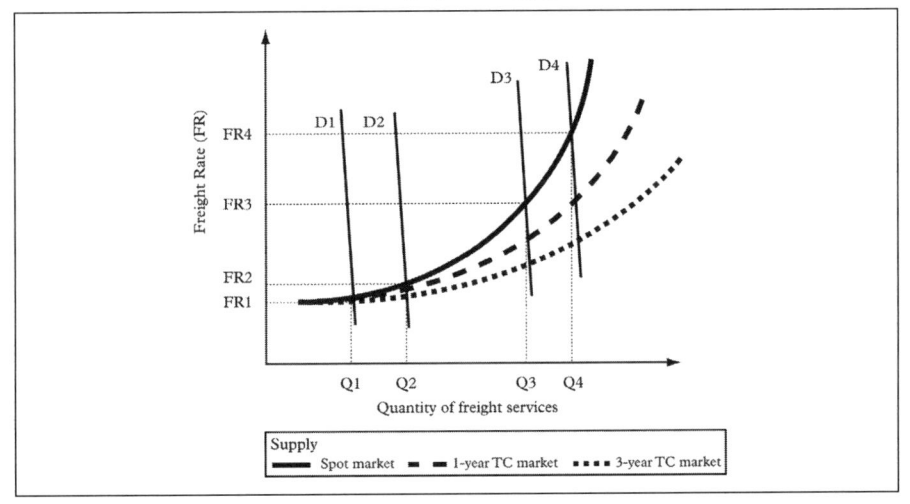

Figure 5: Seasonal changes under different market condition and elasticity of the supply curve

cycle produce seasonal reactions in freight rates, which are higher compared to the low reactions in market downturns.

In general, the results for the dry bulk shipping sector indicate the existence of seasonal fluctuations in freight rates. These fluctuations seem to be different across the size of vessels, the duration of the charter contract as well as the market conditions. More specifically: (1) the levels of freight rates for different sizes of dry bulk carriers increase during the spring and autumn months and drop sharply in June and July, (2) seasonal changes are asymmetric, in that rises (during spring and autumn) are less pronounced over all sectors compared to falls (in the summer), (3) spot rate seasonality seems to be more pronounced for freight rates of larger tonnage than smaller ones, (4) differences in seasonality amongst sectors are broadly eliminated as the duration of contract increases indicating less curvature in the supply function of longer duration contracts, and (5) seasonal movements in dry bulk freight series are also found to be asymmetric under different market conditions; that is, seasonal variations are more pronounced during market expansions than under market contractions. However, the degree of asymmetry decreases as the duration of contract increases.

5. THE EFFICIENT MARKET HYPOTHESIS IN DRY BULK FREIGHT MARKETS

The relationship between spot and period (time-charter) rates has always been a pivotal issue in modelling shipping freight markets. Several studies in the literature are devoted to examining this relationship utilising different theories, methodologies and various data sets. The studies on the relationship between long and short term rates can be classified into two categories. On the one hand, there are attempts to model long term rates assuming that some form of expectations mechanism relates long term to short term rates and the efficient market hypothesis holds (e.g., Zannetos,[6] Beenstock and Vergottis,[15,17] Glen et al.[18] and Strandenes[19]). On the other hand, a number of studies test the efficient market hypothesis and investigate the validity of the expectations hypothesis in the relationship between short and long term rates (e.g., Hale and Vanags[20] and Veenstra[21]).

The notable work of Zannetos[6] was the first attempt to study the relationship between long- and short-term tanker rates. He provides comprehensive theoretical arguments and analyses to establish the theoretical relationship between long and short term tanker freight rates during the 1950s. Zannetos points out the similarities between money markets and freight markets and argues that period rates should represent a weighted average of future spot rates. He also proposes the "elastic expectations" theory in the formation of long term rates, but fails to provide supporting evidence.

Glen et al.[18] propose a present value model for the relationship between spot and time-charter rates in the tanker market, and transform the relationship to estimate an autoregressive distributed lag model which relates period rates to lagged spot rates. They find a different lag structure to that proposed by

Zannetos, and conclude that the expectations in the formation of period rates may not be elastic.

Strandenes[19] argues that period rates are formed through agents' "semi-rational expectations". She finds that current spot and long run equilibrium rates are both important determinants of time-charter rates for panamax dry bulk carriers, and medium and large tankers. However, her estimation results show that current spot and long run equilibrium rates have different impacts on the formation of long term rates across different types of vessels; that is, results are not consistent across sizes.

Beenstock and Vergottis[15,17] assume that Rational Expectations (RE) and the Efficient Market Hypothesis (EMH) in the formation of time-charter rates are valid and base their integrated shipping industry model on these assumptions. They find that current and expected spot rates are significant determinants of time-charter rates. However, they do not attempt to investigate the validity of EMH and rational expectations in the formation of period rates.

Hale and Vanags[20] test the EMH and RE in the formation of freight rates using disaggregated dry bulk market series and find no support for the theory. Recently, Veenstra[21] reports further results on the expectations hypothesis and the term structure relationship of dry bulk voyage and time-charter rates. Although his study suffers from methodological issues (see Kavussanos and Alizadeh[22]), he concludes that the results support the expectations hypothesis of the term structure for three different size dry bulk carriers.

More recently, Kavussanos and Alizadeh,[22] use the present value relationship between long term and short term rates and modify a series of tests, proposed initially by Campbell and Shiller[23,24] for the bond market, to investigate the relationship between short and long term freight rates in the dry bulk shipping sector and test for the validity of the Expectations Hypothesis of the Term Structure (EHTS) in the formation of long term rates for three different size dry bulk carriers. Tests employed include; the perfect foresight spread test, restrictions on the Vector Autoregressive (VAR) model, variance ratio and cointegration tests. These tests are more robust than those that had been employed previously in studies of shipping freight rates, as they directly take into account the stochastic properties of freight rate series, which is strongly recommended in the literature in order to avoid several statistical problems.[25]

More specifically, the EHTS is tested by Kavussanos and Alizadeh[22] using the following present value relationship between the spot and period time-charter rates

$$\sum_{i=0}^{k-1} \frac{TC_t^n}{(1+r)^i} = \sum_{i=0}^{k-1} \frac{E_t(FR_{t+i}^m)}{(1+r)^i} \qquad k = n/m \qquad (3)$$

where TC_t^n and FR_t^m are n and m period spot and time charter contracts, respectively, k is an integer, r is the discount rate, and E_t is the expectations operator. The EMH in the formation of long term rates (or the relationship between long term rates and expected spot rates) implies that the above equation should be empirically valid. Kavussanos and Alizadeh[22] use different transformations of the above model for one-year and three-year time-charter rates for three different size dry bulk carrier. Based on a series of tests, they find that the EMH is rejected.

They then propose a model which relates spot and long term time-charter rates and takes into account the risks associated with the spot market. This model uses an Exponential Generalised Autoregressive Heteroskedasticity in the Mean, (EGARCH-M) (Nelson[26]) framework.[27] They find that the coefficient of time-varying risk premium, which relates long term and short term freight contracts is negative. In other words, shipowners are prepared to offer a discount, which varies over time, in order to fix charter contracts with longer terms to maturity (time-charters) compared to when they operate in the spot market.

The argument that they put forward for the existence of such negative risk premia is based on the fact that shipowners operating in the spot markets are generally exposed to four types of risk, in comparison to those operating in time-charter markets. First, spot rates show higher fluctuations compared to time-charter rates; risk-averse shipowners may thus respond to this by fixing their vessels in the period market. Second, for a shipowner operating in spot markets there is always a chance that he may not be able to fix a contract for a period of time (unemployment risk) even when operations and chartering is well planned. Thirdly, there are cases when the owner has to relocate a vessel from one port to another for a new spot charter contract; depending on the occasion this may take some time and involve substantial costs. Finally, if voyage spot rates (rather than trip-charter spot rates) are compared to time-charter rates, shipowners are also exposed to voyage (mainly bunker) cost fluctuations.[28] Thus, shipowners operating in the time-charter market are prepared to offer a discount to cover the risk, which they are exposed to when operating in the spot market. It seems that the magnitude of this discount is time dependent and reflects the degree of uncertainty in the market.

Furthermore, the sentiment of the banks and lenders in shipping finance might be another important factor influencing shipowners' decision to operate in the spot or the time-charter market. Financiers view differently clients (shipowners) who are committed to long term shipping contracts when financing a ship purchase or newbuilding, since this ensures a relatively more secure stream of income for the shipowner and reduces the probability of loan default. Thus, shipowners may be prepared to offer a discount when fixing their vessel on a long term contract, as opposed to short term ones, in order to fulfil the lender's requirements for the loan. This argument can be quite important during periods of market uncertainty, supporting further the existence of time-varying risk premia in shipping freight markets.

The fact that time charter rates can deviate from their theoretical values for considerable time periods has an important implication as risk neutral or risk prone operators can make excess profits by hiring vessels in the time-charter market, when time-charter rates are under priced, and operating them in the spot market. Agents involved in freight carriage can utilise the difference between actual and theoretical time-charter rates as an indicator of which contract to choose at any point in time. Thus, risk neutral shipowners may choose to operate in the spot market when actual time-charter rates are below their theoretical values and switch to the time-charter market when actual time-charter rates are greater than their theoretical values.

6. INTERRELATIONSHIPS AND SPILLOVER EFFECTS BETWEEN FREIGHT RATE LEVELS AND VOLATILITIES

It has been argued earlier, as well as in the literature (e.g., Stopford,[5] Kavussanos[3,4]), that the dry bulk market is disaggregated by size, and each size vessel is involved in the transportation of certain commodities with a low degree of substitution between vessels of different sizes. This implies a degree of segregation in the behaviour of freight rate levels and volatilities. However, sometimes vessels of adjacent size categories are used as substitutes; for instance, panamax instead of handysize, capesize instead of panamax and vice versa. Such substitutions become more significant when the demand in one market is relatively higher than in the other market and is enough to attract, say, larger vessels to accept part cargoes and make a profit. On the other hand, there might be occasions when charterers prefer to hire smaller vessels for the transportation of commodities, which are conventionally carried by larger vessels; for example by splitting the large consignment into two or three shipments. This is usually the case when importers prefer or switch to "just in time" inventory management techniques, or try to top up their seasonal requirements, which might be less than a large shipment.

The above argument suggests that although different size dry bulk carriers are not perfect substitutes, they may overlap in their cargo transportation capabilities or even be linked through intermediate size vessels. Therefore, one would expect that shocks to any sub-sector might be transmitted to other sub-sectors. For instance, if there is an increase in demand and subsequently freight rates for handysize vessels, other size categories such as panamax vessels may react by participating in the handysize market and accepting part cargoes, if this is found to be more profitable. This shift from one market to the other will cause an over supply in the handysize market and a shortage of supply in the panamax market, and, as a result, handysize rates will drop and panamax rates will rise. This process will continue until both markets stabilise; that is, until supply equals demand in each market and there is no opportunity to make extra profit by switching between markets.

Investigating the interrelationships among these sub-markets in shipping can shed light to important issues such as the degree of substitutability between different dry bulk sub-sectors and the speed of stabilisation of freight rates in each market. Beenstock and Vergottis[29] investigated the spillover effects between tanker and dry bulk markets. They trace the spillover effects between the markets through the market for combined carriers, shipbuilding and scrapping markets using dynamic econometric models and simulation techniques. Alizadeh[30] extends the findings of this study, by investigating the spillover effects between different segments within the dry bulk sector of the shipping industry. He employs recently developed time series techniques such as VAR, cointegration, and impulse response analysis instead of dynamic structural models. Analyses are carried out on charter contracts with different terms to maturity, i.e. spot, one-year and three-year time-charter rates, and comparisons are made to highlight differences in spillover effects within spot markets in comparison to those of time-charter markets.

Additionally, the same study also investigates the existence of volatility spillovers from one sub-sector to other sub-sectors within the spot and time-charter markets. This is done by using a multivariate vector error correction model (VECM) in the mean with a multivariate generalised autoregressive conditional heteroskedasticity (GARCH) specification, in what is termed a VECM-GARCH model. These types of models have been used in the financial economics literature to assess the integration as well as the transmission of information between the capital, interest rates or commodity markets worldwide (see for instance, Koutmos and Booth,[31] Koutmos and Tucker[32] and Kavussanos and Nomikos[33]).

In total, three different systems (for spot, one-year and three-year time-charter rates) of VECM and VECM-GARCH models for freight rates for three size vessels have been estimated over the period January 1980 to August 1997 for the purposes of this analysis. Impulse response analyses on the estimated models reveal that the interaction between freight rates for different size vessels are higher in the spot market compared to the one-year and three-year time-charter markets. This might be due to the difference between the charterers' decision making process on hiring vessels in the spot market and time-charter markets. Decisions on hiring vessels in the spot market are thought to be more instantaneous, based on short terms and sometimes urgent transportation requirements. In contrast to the spot market, decisions made by charterers to hire vessels in the period market are in general based on detailed analysis of costs and transportation needs. Furthermore, there might be situations where owners operating in the spot market find that even a part cargo is better than waiting for a full load. They may even accept a part cargo on a back haul voyage rather than returning to the loading area in ballast. Such decisions by owners in the spot market increase the competition between vessels of different sizes for cargo and consequently increase the interaction between their freight rates. As a result, shocks to freight rates for any size vessel in the spot market are transmitted across to freight rates for other size categories faster than shocks in the period charter markets.

Analysis of spillover effects between volatilities of freight rates for different size vessels in the spot and period markets reveal that volatilities of freight rates for capesize vessels affect volatilities of freight rates for smaller vessels across the contract maturity spectrum. More specifically, shocks to the capesize market are transmitted to the market for smaller vessels without any feedback effects. The unidirectional volatility spillovers from capesize market to the market for smaller vessels can be explained by the fact that the market for larger vessels is more sensitive to news than the market for smaller size vessels. This is because small vessels are more flexible than capesize vessels in terms of operational flexibility. As a result, shocks to freight rates for smaller vessels, due to changes in the demand for transportation of certain types of commodities over a particular route, may be absorbed by employment of those vessels in other trading routes. On the other hand, the number of routes and trades at which large vessels operate is limited. As a result, unexpected changes in the market for those vessels may have a greater impact on the whole dry bulk market compared to the effect of unexpected events the market for smaller vessels.

In addition, the carrying capacity of larger vessels compared to smaller ones and the agents' expectations about movements of vessels between markets might be an important factor in causing volatility spillovers. Given that the carrying capacity of a capesize vessel is two times that of a panamax vessel (three times that of a handysize vessel), shift of one capesize vessel to the panamax market, during the capesize market downturn or a relatively good panamax market, may satisfy the demand for two panamax vessels. In an opposite situation, two panamax vessels are required to satisfy the demand for one capesize vessel. This suggests that shifts of larger vessels to markets for smaller vessels may have greater impact on the supply and demand balance in markets for smaller vessels compared to the impact caused by shifts of smaller vessels to the market for large vessels.

Another interesting finding of this study is that levels of time-varying volatilities of freight rates in each of the spot and period (one-year and three-year) markets are directly related to vessel size; that is, the level of time-varying volatility is higher for larger vessels compared to smaller ones. Results also indicate that the level of time-varying volatilities for each size vessel are also related to the duration of contract; that is, the longer the duration of contract, the lower the level of time-varying volatility. This is because time-charter rates reflect the weighted average of expected future spot rates and therefore sharp changes in spot rates are smoothened when time-charter rates are formed. Also, spot rates are more influenced by current market conditions and news, whereas period rates depend on agents' expectations about the future market conditions over a period of time.

7. EFFICIENCY OF NEWBUILDING AND SECOND-HAND MARKETS FOR DRY BULK CARRIERS

One of the most important and interesting areas in the shipping economics literature is the determination of ship prices. Many studies have been devoted to modelling, evaluating and forecasting ship prices and their volatilities in the past, among these are: Strandenes,[19] Beenstock,[34] Beenstock and Vergottis,[15,17] Charmeza and Gronicki,[35] and Kavussanos.[3,4] Studies on the determination of ship prices, e.g., Strandenes[19] and Beenstock and Vergottis,[15,17] consider ships as capital assets and share the same theoretical framework. Present value models, which posit that the price of an asset should reflect the discounted present value of expected income that the asset may generate over its life, are used extensively in modelling ship prices. The major difference among the studies on ship price determination, is the way they deal with the expectations about the future income generated by ships. More precisely, they assume that the EMH is valid and utilise different forms of expectations hypothesis in their pricing models. For example, Strandenes[19] assumes that expectations are semi-rational, while Beenstock[34] and Beenstock and Vergottis[15,17] assume rational expectations in price formation.

Hale and Vanags[36] dispute the assumption of rational expectations and the EMH in models for ship prices, and argue that such assumptions should be investigated and their validity must be verified prior to any modelling and forecasting. This is because rejection of these hypotheses may have serious consequences on the ensuing empirical results. They argue that for the EMH to be valid, prices for different size vessels should incorporate all the available information; that is, given past prices, no other information should improve the predictability of prices. They propose a test based on the cointegration approach and Granger-causality between prices for the three sizes of bulk carriers. They find that not only there are cointegrating relationships between the price series, but also prices Granger-cause each other. They conclude that their results cast doubt on the validity of the EMH and RE in price formation in the dry bulk sector. Glen[37] re-examines the informational efficiency in dry bulk carriers price determination using Johansen's[38] multivariate cointegration test, which is more powerful compared to the test employed in Hale and Vanags,[36] although his findings are similar. However, he attributes the link between prices for different size vessels to the existence of common stochastic trends rather than the failure of the EMH.

Wright[39] attempts to examine different forms of expectations in the formation of second hand prices for small dry bulk carriers for the period 1980 to 1990 using quarterly data. He tests three different hypotheses, namely, rational, static and adaptive expectations hypotheses. Apart from statistical issues, such as the direct use of non-stationary variables, his tests also suffer from theoretical shortcomings, so not much reliance can be placed on these results. Nevertheless, for the sake of completeness, we report here that he finds mixed results and concludes that ship prices are formed under a mixture of expectations depending on market conditions.

More recently, Kavussanos and Alizadeh[40] employ cointegration and nonlinear tests on the VAR model proposed by Campbell and Shiller[23] to examine the present value model and the EMH in the determination of newbuilding and second-hand prices in the dry bulk sector. One advantage of the VAR approach is that stochastic properties of variables are explicitly considered. In addition, the bivariate model of Campbell and Shiller[23] is extended to a trivariate model, which incorporates the residual (scrap) values as the third variable in the model.

They employ the following present value model, which relates the price of a ship (either newbuilding or second-hand) to the discounted present value of expected profits, generated through chartering operations plus the discounted present value of her expected residual value as follows:

$$P_t = \sum_{i=0}^{n-1}\left(\prod_{j=0}^{i}(1 + E_t R_{t+j+1})^{-1}\right) E_t \Pi_{t+1+i} + \left(\prod_{j=0}^{n-1}(1 + E_t R_{t+j+1})^{-1}\right) E_t P_{t+n}^{SC} \qquad (4)$$

where P_t is the price of the vessel, E_t is the expectations operator (expectations formed at time t), $E_t\Pi_{t+i}$ represents expected profit in period t+i, $E_t R_{t+j}$ is the expected discount rate and $E_t P_{t+n}^{SC}$ is the expected terminal value of the vessel. Variables in (4) are found to be nonstationary, a fact which would invalidate direct tests for EMH. As a result, the Campbell and Shiller[23] transformation is used to re-parameterise (4) and hence, obtain a model with stationary variables.

Two distinct cases are considered for testing the price efficiency of newbuilding vessels. In the first case, it is assumed that the vessel operates for five years and her value after five years reflects the price of a five-year old second-hand vessel; the second-hand price is then used as her terminal value. In the second case, it is assumed that the newbuilding will be used for her entire economic life and, as a result, the residual value is her scrap price. A limited economic life of 20 years is assumed for a newbuilding and 15 years for a five-year old second-hand vessel.

Kavussanos and Alizadeh[40] also investigate another implication of the EMH, which requires the unpredictability of excess (or abnormal) one period returns, that is returns on shipping investments over the market return. The EMH implies that one period excess returns should be independent of information available at time t. In other words, in an efficient market abnormal returns should be unpredictable, otherwise, excess profit making opportunities may be identified and exploited by a group of investors.

Empirical results from tests, based on equation (4), reject the EMH in the market for newbuilding and second-hand dry bulk vessels. In addition, it is found that excess returns on shipping investments (second-hand vessels) over LIBOR are highly predictable, which is again against the notion of informational efficiency in the market for second-hand dry bulk ships. These findings can be explained by the fact that investors in the shipping industry are characterised by heterogeneous behaviour and different investment objectives and horizons and hence may use different pricing models, discount factors or weights depending on their investment objectives and horizons. This seems to be a very important point since the EMH requires homogeneous investment behaviour and pricing formulas across all the investors.

8. CONCLUSIONS

The aim of this chapter was to provide a description of the dry-bulk shipping markets and discuss current issues and developments in this area. In particular the segmentation of the dry bulk markets in different sub-sectors, which is due to the different physical and economic factors which determine supply and demand conditions in these sectors, is discussed and the factors which contribute to this segmentation are identified and analysed. These factors include, among others, the commodity parcel size, the nature of the underlying shipping routes, the physical characteristics of the loading and discharge ports as well as the vessel's design features. Furthermore, the conditions under which the dry bulk market can be categorised as a perfect market are highlighted and discussed.

Additionally, this chapter also presents recent empirical evidence on issues relating to the properties of the dry bulk shipping freight rates, such as the seasonal behaviour of freight rates. The magnitude and pattern of seasonal fluctuations is measured and compared across freight rates for different size vessels as well as contract durations. Moreover, the seasonal behaviour of freight rates is examined and compared under different market conditions.

Empirical evidence on the term structure relationship between long and short term rates for different sizes of dry bulk carriers is also presented. Recent studies in the literature[22] have employed a variety of testing methods to test the validity of the expectations hypothesis. Their results indicate rejection of the expectations hypothesis of the term structure which may be due to the time-varying perception of risk by the agents involved in the market. The interrelationships between freight rate levels and spillover effects between freight rate volatilities for different size dry bulk carriers within the spot, one-year and three-year time-charter markets, are also analysed. Finally, results from recent studies on the existence of time-varying risk premia in the market for new-building and second-hand vessels, are also presented.

ENDNOTES

1. Source: Fearnleys.
2. Source: Clarksons Research Studies.
3. Kavussanos, M.G. (1996a): "Comparisons of volatility in the dry-cargo ship sector: Spot versus time charters, and small versus larger vessels", *Journal of Transport Economics and Policy*, January, pp. 67–82.
4. Kavussanos, M.G. (1997): "The dynamics of time-varying volatilities in different size second-hand ship prices of the dry-cargo sector", *Applied Economics*, Vol. 29, pp. 433–444.
5. Stopford, M. (1997): *Maritime Economics* (London, Unwin Hyman).
6. Zannetos, Z.S. (1966): *The theory of oil tank shipping rates* (Massachusetts, MIT Press).
7. Beaulieu, J.J., and Miron, J.A. (1992): "A cross- country comparison of seasonal cycles and business cycles", *Economic Journal*, 102, pp. 772–788.
8. Dickey, D.A. (1993): "Discussion: Seasonal unit roots in aggregate US data", in *Journal of Econometrics*, 55, pp. 329–331.
9. Canova, F, and Hansen, B.E. (1995): "Are seasonal patterns constant over time? A test for seasonal stability", *Journal of Business & Economics Statistics*, Vol. 13, pp. 237–252.
10. Denning, K.C., Riley, W.B., and Delooze, J.P. (1994): "Baltic Freight Futures: Random walk or seasonally predictable?", *International Review of Economics and Finance*, Vol. 3, pp. 399–428.
11. Nomikos, N., and Alizadeh, A., "Risk management in the shipping industry: Theory and practice", chapter 31 in this volume, provide a detailed description of BFI.
12. Kavussanos, M.G. and Alizadeh, A.H. (2001): "Seasonality patterns in the dry bulk shipping spot and time-charter rates", forthcoming in *Transportation Research – Part E; Logistics and Transportation Review*.

13. Japanese importers try to stock up their inventories (inputs in production) before the end of the year so as to show them as expenses in their books.
14. The decrease in the level of industrial output in North America during June and July is documented by Beaulieu, J.J., and Miron, J.A. (1991): "The Seasonal Cycle in US Manufacturing", *Economic Letters*, 37, pp. 115–118, among others.
15. Beenstock, M. and A. Vergottis (1989a): "An econometric model of the world market for dry cargo freight and shipping", *Applied Economics*, 21, pp. 339–356.
16. For a more formal analysis of the factors driving the relationship between short and long term charter contracts see Kavussanos, M.G., and Alizadeh, A.H. (2000): "The expectations hypothesis of term structure and risk premia in dry bulk shipping freight markets: An EGARCH-M approach", paper presented at the 13th Australasian Banking and Finance Conference, 18–20 December 2000, Sydney, Australia.
17. Beenstock, M., and Vergottis, A. (1989b): "An econometric model of world tanker market", *Journal of Transport Economics and Policy*, 23, pp. 263–280.
18. Glen, D., Owen, M., and Van der Meer, R. (1981): "Spot and time charter rates for tankers, 1970-1977", *Journal of Transport Economics and Policy*, No. 1, pp. 45–58.
19. Strandenes, S.P. (1984): "Price determination in the time-charter and second-hand markets", Working paper No. 06, Centre for Applied Research, Norwegian School of Economics and Business Administration.
20. Hale, C., and Vanags, A. (1989): "Spot and period rates in the dry bulk market: some tests for the period 1980–1986", *Journal of Transport Economics and Policy*, pp. 281–291.
21. Veenstra, W. A. (1999): "The term structure of ocean freight rates", *Maritime Policy and Management*, Vol. 26, pp. 279–293.
22. Kavussanos, M.G., and Alizadeh, A.H. (2002a): "The expectations hypothesis of term structure and risk premia in the dry bulk shipping freight markets", *Journal of Transport Economics and Policy*, vol. 36, pp. 267–304.
23. Campbell, J.Y,. and Shiller, R.J. (1987): "Cointegration and test of present value models", *Journal of Political Economy*, 95, pp. 1062–1088.
24. Campbell, J.Y., and Shiller, R.J. (1991): "Yield spread and interest rate movements: a bird's eye view", *Review of Economic Studies*, Vol. 58, pp. 495–514.
25. See Campbell and Shiller (notes 23 and 24) for more details on associated statistical issues in testing the expectations hypothesis of the term structure in the bond market, and Kavussanos and Alizadeh (2002) for the freight markets.
26. Nelson, D.B. (1991): "Conditional Heteroskedasticity in asset returns: A new approach", *Econometrica*, Vol. 59, pp. 347–370.
27. More details of ARCH, GARCH and EGARCH-M models see Bera, A.K., and Higgins, M.L. (1993): "ARCH models: Properties, estimation and testing", in *Journal of Economic Surveys*, Vol. 7, No. 4, pp. 305–366; and Bollerslev, T., Chou, R.Y., and Kroner, K.F. (1992): " ARCH modelling in finance: A review of theory and empirical evidence", *Journal of Econometrics*, 52, pp. 5–59.
28. These types of risk can be eliminated to some extent through hedging tools; for more on this see Nomikos, N., and Alizadeh, A., "Risk management in the shipping industry: Theory and practice", chapter 31 in this volume.
29. Beenstock, M., and Vergottis, A. (1993): "The interdependence between the dry cargo and tanker markets", *Logistics and Transportation Review*, Vol. 29/1, pp. 3–38.
30. Alizadeh, A. (2001): "An econometric analysis of the dry bulk shipping industry; Seasonality, efficiency and risk premia", unpublished PhD Thesis, City University Business School, London, UK.
31. Koutmos, G., And Booth, G.G. (1995): "Asymmetric volatility transmission in international stock markets", *Journal of International Money and Finance*, Vol. 14, pp. 747–762.
32. Koutmos, G., And Tucker, M. (1996): "Temporal relationships and dynamic interactions between spot and future stock markets", *The Journal of Future Markets*, Vol. 16, No. 1, pp. 55–69.

33. Kavussanos, M.G., and Nomikos, N. (2000b): "Hedging in the freight futures market", *Journal of Derivatives*, Vol. 8, Fall 2000, pp. 41–58.
34. Beenstock, M. (1985): "A theory of ship prices", *Maritime Policy and Management*, Vol. 12/3, pp. 215–225.
35. Charemza, W., and Gronicki, M. (1981): "An Econometric Model of World Shipping and Shipbuilding", *Maritime Policy and Management*, Vol. 8, pp. 21–30
36. Hale, C. and Vanags, A. (1992): "The market for second-hand ships: some results on efficiency using cointegration", *Maritime Policy and Management*, Vol. 19/1, pp. 31–140.
37. Glen, D. (1997): "The market for second-hand ships: Further results on efficiency using cointegration analysis", *Maritime Policy and Management*, vol. 24, pp. 245–260.
38. Johansen, S. (1988): "Statistical analysis of cointegration vectors", *Journal of Economic Dynamics and Control*, Vol. 12, pp. 231–254.
39. Wright, G. (1993). "Expectations in the shipping sector", *International Journal of Transport Economics*, Vol. 20, No. 1, pp. 67–76.
40. Kavussanos, M.G., and Alizadeh, A. (2002b): "Efficient Pricing of Ships in the Dry Bulk Sector of the Shipping Industry", *Maritime Policy and Management*, forthcoming.

CHAPTER 12

THE TANKER MARKET: CURRENT STRUCTURE AND ECONOMIC ANALYSIS

David Glen* and Brendan Martin[†]

*Centre for International Transport Management, London Metropolitan University, London, UK. E-mail: *glen@lgu.ac.uk*
[†] E. A. Gibson Shipbrokers Ltd, London, UK. E-mail: *btmartin@btinternet.com*

1. INTRODUCTION

What is a tanker? A tanker is defined as a vessel that is designed specifically to carry liquid cargoes. Refined oil products and crude oil are the most common types of cargo carried in such vessels, but tankers also transport chemicals, wine, vegetable and other food oils. The market for crude oil tankers is by far the largest. The markets for crude oil and refined products are often referred to as the tanker trades. This chapter reviews the world tanker market as it stands in 2001.

It has two objectives:
(1) to provide the reader with an outline of events that have shaped the present tanker market, and
(2) to review economic theories of tanker market dynamics.

2. THE SHAPING OF THE PRESENT TANKER MARKET

As of February 2002, the world tanker fleet (measured in terms of carrying capacity, the deadweight ton) stood at 290mn dwt.[1] The world fleet consists of around 3,328 vessels of 10,000 dwt. or more, all engaged in activities related to the extraction, storage, and distribution of both crude oil and its refined products.[2] One might assume that this level of activity has been reached by a steady, continuous expansion of the industry, but this is far from the case. In fact, the 1990's can be viewed as the decade of "recovery" of the industry from shocks that affected it in the early 1970's, and which led to record deadweight tonnage capacity by the early 1980's.

Indeed, the story does not start in the tanker market at all. Its behaviour can only be understood by knowing something of the economic development of the oil industry itself. The reason for this is simple. The great bulk of oil is transported from its production areas to the main consumption areas by sea. Some is transported by pipeline, and road and rail transport are used as well for intra country movements; but approximately 95% of the inter-area oil movements are seaborne. In 2000, approximately 2 billion tonnes of crude and products was exported, from a total production level of 3.6 billion tonnes.[3] Thus sixty per cent of the world's total oil production in 2000 was moved across the world by sea, generating the source of demand for oil transportation services, and creating the demand for oil tanker services.[4]

The major oil consumption regions happen to be net importers of oil, so their demand creates a need to move oil safely and efficiently from its various sources. The oil tanker, which emerged as a specialised vessel during the 1940s and 1950s, was developed to meet that need.

Oil transportation can be viewed as a productive input, a part of the process that turns crude oil extracted from the ground or from under the sea, into a variety of refined products, from petrol for cars, heating oil, marine diesel fuel, feedstock for the chemical and plastics industry. The capital investment required to develop the industry was very large, with significant expenditure required to develop oilfields, construct refineries, and develop distribution systems for the products in the rapidly growing markets of the United States and Western Europe. The industry evolved as a "vertically integrated" structure, with several very large multi-national companies dominating all aspects of exploration, extraction, storage, distribution and refining of the product. Investment in tankers is on-going, with approximately five per cent of the fleet delivered annually by the world's shipyards. In addition, there is an active market in the buying and selling of existing tankers for continued trading. Whilst this does not represent new capacity, it does indicate that there are relatively few barriers for new entrants wishing to join the industry.

This economic arrangement, whilst efficient, meant that the principal owners of oil tankers, and of course, their principal users, were the oil majors. By the late 1960s, the seven oil majors that dominated the global industry became known as the "Seven Sisters". The industry was highly integrated and very concentrated. The dominant players at the time included Esso, BP, Shell, Mobil, Texaco, and Gulf. In addition, many European countries had one state owned oil company "champion"; Italy had ENI, France had Elf and Total. In other parts of the world, state owned companies were significant local players; for example, Petrobras in Brazil. The very largest companies had large departments whose function was to manage each of the segments of the oil production process. Oil transportation was one of those segments.

The domination of the "Seven Sisters" of the retail side of the oil industry has declined from its peak of the late 1960s. One reason for this was the emergence of a spot market for lots of refined petrol from Rotterdam, the result of refinery overcapacity. New companies entered the retail market, and put competitive pressure on the incumbents. The world of a regulated market was finally destroyed by the Arab–Israeli war of October 1973, and the resulting embargo of oil exports to certain European countries including The Netherlands, along with a dramatic rise in the oil price, from $1.90 per barrel to nearly $40 during 1973–1980.[5]

The dramatic rise in the world crude oil price, coupled with the nationalisation of American and European oil interests in the Middle East and Libya, led to a transformation of world economic growth prospects and a shift in the balance of economic power towards OPEC (Organisation of Petroleum Exporting

Countries).[6] A major, and permanent slowdown in world economic growth occurred, and a new era for the oil industry began.

Much of the present structure of the tanker market has been created by these events. Indeed, the 1990's could be argued to be the first decade in which the tanker market was primarily driven by economic and environmental issues, rather than politics. Political events of course, are always of potential consequence – they are woven into the history of both the industry and the tanker market.

3. OIL CONSUMPTION

The world's demand for oil is large, and growing at around 2% per annum. Figure 1 shows the trend in world oil consumption over the past 35 years. Demand declined after 1973, recovered, peaked in 1979–1980, and then fell until 1985. In fact, world oil consumption peaked at around 3,100mn tonnes in 1979, and declined by approximately 10%, to 2,801mn tonnes in 1985. The 1979 peak is not surpassed until 1990; and even in 1995 it has only reached 3,200mn tonnes, rising to 3,500mn tonnes in 2000.[7]

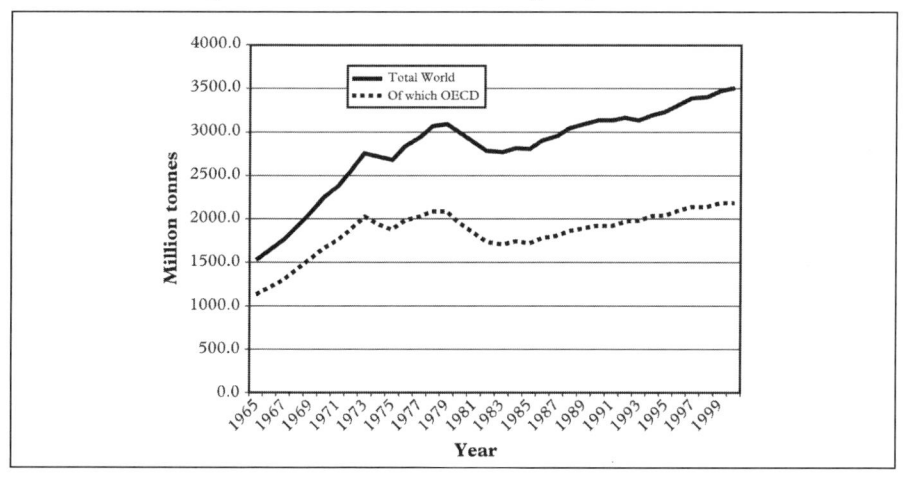

Figure 1: Total world oil consumption, 1965–2000

Table 1 shows that the trend growth in oil consumption over the past ten years is 1.1% per annum. The International Energy Agency (IEA) forecasts, which are conditional on assumptions about the behaviour of the price of crude oil, projects growth at around 1.4% per annum for the next few years.

The composition of oil consumption has also altered over the period, and will continue to alter in the future. Figure 1 shows the oil consumption of the OECD countries for 1965–2000. It is clear from visual inspection that the share of non-OECD members has increased over the past two decades. Despite its declining share (74% in 1965; 65% in 1980; 62% in 2000), the economic performance of the OECD countries is central to the growth in demand for oil. By far the most significant player in this sector is the USA. In 2000 it alone

Table 1: Regional consumption patterns, 2000

	Mn Tonnes	Annual Growth 1990–2000	Share
North America	1064.6	1.4%	30.4%
S & Cent America	218.7	2.7%	6.2%
Europe	752.6	0.6%	21.4%
Former Soviet Union	173.1	-8.8%	5.0%
Middle East	209.0	2.4%	5.9%
Africa	116.7	2.1%	3.3%
Asia Pacific	968.9	3.9%	27.8%
Total	**3503.6**	**1.1%**	**100.0%**

Source: Derived from *BP Statistical Review of World Energy, 2001*.

accounted for nearly 900mn tonnes of oil (an all time high), or just under 25% of the world's consumption. The whole of Europe accounts for 700mn tonnes, whilst Asia accounts for around 900mn tonnes. Japan, Asia's wealthiest economy, (which has not exhibited its former growth pattern and that of the other countries in the South East/Pacific Asian economies), consumed 254mn tonnes, in 2000, approximately the same as it consumed in 1976. The present pattern of regional consumption is shown in Table 1.

A number of points are worthy of note. First, the decline in consumption in the economies that constitute the Former Soviet Union has been very marked. This reflects, at least in part, the well known problems affecting these economies since1989. Oil consumption in this region is now lower than that in the Middle East. Secondly, the highest consumption growth rate occurred in Asia, but even this must be tempered with knowledge of the economic problems that have affected some of the economies in this region since 1997. For example, South Korea, Japan and Thailand all have peak consumption in 1996 or 1997. Indeed, the Far East has become the most important market for oil from the Middle East Gulf.

4. ECONOMIC DRIVERS OF OIL CONSUMPTION

Having briefly outlined the present profile of oil consumption and its regional pattern, attention is now turned to addressing the question as the principal factors driving oil consumption. The standard set of economic factors are; Incomes, the price of crude oil and its refined products; the price of substitute products; the price of complementary products, Tastes; Political factors, and Expectations. The exposition is necessarily short.

The relationship between Incomes or Gross Domestic Product (GDP) and oil consumption or its constituent components has been extensively studied. Professor Dahl has published a survey of 100 econometric studies of the relationship between gdp and petrol demand.[8] She concluded that the income elasticity of demand was greater than unity, which implies that gasoline consumption will grow faster than the economy under examination. The survey reports estimates of between 0.80 and 1.38 for the long run response.[9] The short run response was much lower however, between 0.4 and 0.5.

The second key element in the behaviour of oil consumption is the reaction of consumers to changes in the real price. Dahl reports estimated values of –0.22 to –0.31 for short run values, and –0.58 to –1.02 for long run values derived from the 100 studies surveyed. These figures are indeed inelastic (the proportionate fall in demand is significantly less than the proportionate rise in the price), but they relate to just gasoline demand, which constitutes around 30% of world oil consumption.[10]

Figure 2 shows the time path of nominal price of Arabian Light oil from 1972 to 2000, in annual average form. The data shows tremendous variations, from $1.90 per barrel in 1972, to $10.41 in 1974, peaking at $35.69 in 1980, declining to $12.95 in 1986, before peaking again at $20.50 in 1990, declining to a low of around $8.00 in the late 1990's, before rising in the boom of 2000, following the introduction of production quotas by OPEC members in the second quarter of 1999. At the time of writing, the price of Brent Oil, which is highly correlated with Arabian Light, had reached $30 per barrel in 2002. It should be noted that Arabian Light is not traded as such, but is subject to "netback pricing" – a notional crude price based on the value of constituent products from a barrel of oil on the Rotterdam market, after deducting refining and sea transportation costs The chart clearly shows that many of the peaks in the oil price are associated with Middle-East wars or other globally significant economic events. The only item that might need further explanation is the apparent change in direction in the nominal price before and after 1979–1980. The primary causes were the world recession of 1979–1982, and the accelerating substitution of oil by coal for power generation, along with initiatives to reduce energy consumption in the principal consuming areas. It has been argued that

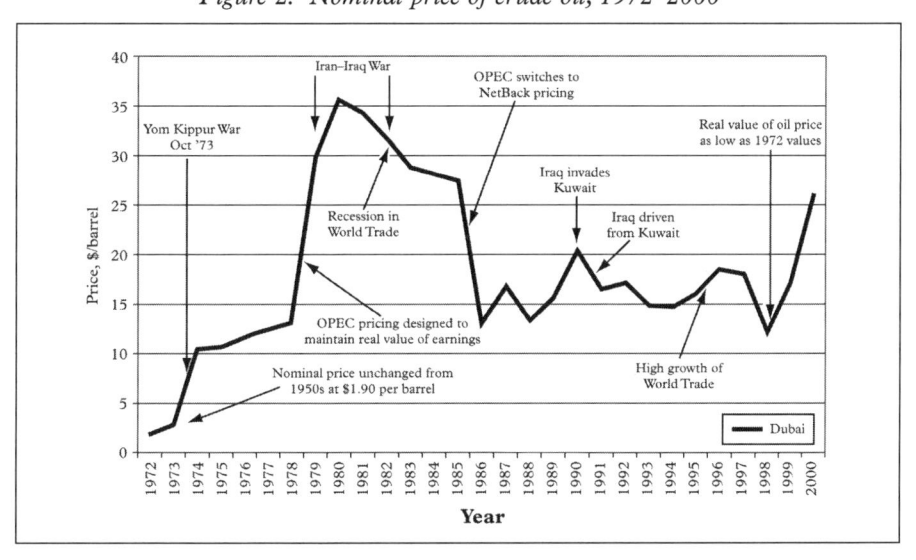

Figure 2: Nominal price of crude oil, 1972–2000

the eventual abrupt relinquishment of the high price oil strategy in April 1986 was the result of joint undertakings between the world's largest consuming nation and the OPEC's largest producer.

The second reason relates to the changing pricing policy of OPEC members themselves. By the mid 1980's, after five years of oil prices between $25 and $20, oil production from the North Sea, and Alaska provided competition from Non-OPEC suppliers; and OPEC, watching the decline in oil demand, dramatically altered its policy on oil pricing. Prior to the change, OPEC would try to maintain the real value of its earnings in nominal dollar terms. Whenever the dollar fell in value, (as it did in the 1970's), the nominal price of oil was raised to offset the fall. In the mid-1980's, OPEC members changed their policy, switching to "netback pricing". This change, in response to declining market share as Mexican and North Sea production became more important, meant that the real price of crude oil was no longer being maintained. OPEC was under the impression that the marginal cost of Non-OPEC crude was $21/barrel, and tacitly applied an $18 "benchmark" price for the basket of OPEC crudes. In fact, the real price of crude oil fell to its lowest value since the early 1970's, following the 1986 watershed. The history of oil pricing since 1990 has been one of high volatility and subject to prolonged stock-building as more Non-OPEC oil came on stream. In addition, there has been periodic weakness in demand, before its recovery in the late 1990's.

A noteworthy element of the surveys by Dahl[11] is the *absence*, in many of the econometric studies, of cross-price effects. There may be two reasons for this. Firstly, the investigations ignored the effects by failing to include any cross price elements in their model. For example, it could be argued that the demand for petrol will be negatively influenced by downward changes in the price of public transport, where it is available. Thus cross price effects may influence oil consumption. Secondly, the investigators may have tried such factors, and discarded them, when they prove to be statistically unimportant. Indeed, given the low own price elasticities of demand, it would not be surprising if cross-price elasticities were negligible. Economic theory implies that the smaller the degree of substitutability between goods or services, the lower the level of cross price elasticity. For many uses, oil products have few, if any substitutes.

Oil demand can be affected by changes in the price of complementary products. For gasoline consumption a vehicle is required. For fuel oil, a power station. In many cases the price of the oil product is extremely small as a proportion of the overall costs of deriving the service that it generates. It is true, however, that two of the key drivers of the growth in oil consumption in the 20th century were the rise of the motor vehicle, and the switch to oil as a source for power generation, away from coal. The former is an example of complementarity; the latter an example of price substitution.

Shifts in tastes can influence demand. The rise of the motor car has been a major event in the western economies, and appears to be happening in the developing economies too. Until the 1970s, little or no regard was being paid to the negative effects of this expansion; namely the rise in carbon dioxide emissions, the growing evidence of the damage that lead additives to petrol caused, and the rising levels of environmental damage caused by the exploitation of the word's resources. Environmental awareness has been raised significantly over the past 25 years, and this has had an impact on the oil industry. Energy conservation has become a key issue, although the more cynical observer is more likely to point to the oil price increase of 1973 as being the event that forced many governments to develop such policies. In addition, a number of significant oil pollution incidents led to successively tighter regulatory frameworks governing the production, distribution and transportation of oil.[12]

Since the end of the Second World War, oil has been a strategic resource. The fact that significant shares of the world's oil resources are located in the Middle East and the Soviet Union meant that Western Europe was particularly vulnerable to disruption of oil supplies. The USA switched from being self sufficient in oil to becoming increasingly dependent on oil, in particular from North Africa, the Middle East, Venezuela and West Africa. Major political crises punctuate the history of the oil industry, and have identifiable effects on the tanker market. The UK French attempt to occupy the Suez Canal, following its nationalisation by Egypt, and the nationalisation of US oil interests in Libya, created tensions in the Near- and Middle East, which focused on the conflict between Israel and the Palestinians. The Egypt Israeli war of 1967 caused the closure of the Suez Canal for eight years, and led to another clash in 1973. This was the event that precipitated a major shift in the economic balance of oil, as OPEC exercised its economic power, and raised the price of crude oil by 400% in the space of a few months. Political instability remains a theme at the present time. The 1981–1989 Iran-Iraq war, the 1990 invasion of Kuwait by Iraq, and the recent increase in the level of conflict between Israel and the Palestinians shows that oil is still a strategic product. However, a very significant change has occurred which makes it likely that embargoes will be less likely – there has been a significant shift in OPEC's pricing strategy.

The demand for oil is also affected by players' *expectations* of future events. Oil prices are volatile; nowadays some of the risk volatility can be hedged against by taking out forwards or futures contracts on the International Petroleum Exchange. Whether or not all of the risk can be hedged depends on the efficiency of the markets and the nature of the contracts available. Nevertheless, the presence of these markets allows oil companies to hedge some of the risk of current price volatility by "taking a position" on the paper markets to offset some of the risk.

The existence of such markets can also generate forward prices, which can be viewed as the market's guess as to the future path of present (spot) prices. In some recent economic theories, current prices for a commodity or financial asset are viewed as being entirely determined by the expected price. In other words, today's price is determined by the today's expectation of tomorrow's price. When political uncertainty increases, market expectations are for a shortage of oil in the future, and this leads to a sharp increase in the present price of oil. Thus expectations may play a key role in understanding market dynamics.

It has been shown that the demand is very insensitive to own price, but quite sensitive to economic growth. The sharp change in conditions in 1973 led to permanently lower growth trends for oil demand, and a significant incentive to lower the intensity of oil use. Both of these effects led to decline in oil consumption until 1985-6, with 1975 levels reappearing only recently.[13]

5. WORLD OIL PRODUCTION TRENDS

Not surprisingly, world oil production tends to track demand very well. There is an important element that "gets in the way" of this relationship however – oil is produced in regions were there is little demand, and traded. The time taken to move the oil to its region of consumption means that there is inventory, either in the form of oil on ships or in storage tanks at oilfields, oil terminals and refineries. In addition, since 1973 many countries have instituted strategic reserves of oil, in the event of any oil export embargo repeating itself. One estimate of the OECD countries' crude and product inventory puts it at 2,612mn barrels, or 355 mn tonnes, roughly two months supply at 2000 consumption levels.[14]

Production can therefore be divorced from consumption to a certain extent, and there will be periods when demand exceeds current production and vice versa. But over the longer period, it is consumption that drives production. Comparison of the average annual growth rate over the past ten years of world oil consumption and production yields figures of 1.26 and 1.11% respectively.

5.1 Regional production patterns

Examination of regional patterns yields a different story (Table 2). North American production has declined slightly over the past decade, and there have been significant falls in production in the economies of the former Soviet Union (FSU). Elsewhere Europe and South America have experienced the largest growth in production. However, it is the Middle East that still dominates world production, with 31% of the world share in 2000. Whilst this is lower than at some points in the past, it is also higher than at other times, particularly in the early 1980s.

Table 2: Regional consumption patterns, 2000

	Mn Tonnes	Annual Growth 1990–2000	Share
North America	651.9	-0.1%	18.1%
S & Cent America	348.2	4.2%	9.7%
Europe	329.0	4.1%	9.2%
Former Soviet Union	394.4	-3.7%	11.0%
Middle East	1112.4	2.7%	31.0%
Africa	373.2	1.5%	10.4%
Asia Pacific	380.5	1.6%	10.6%
Total	3589.6	1.3%	100.0%

Source: Derived from *BP Statistical Review of World Energy, 2001.*

Putting the two tables of production and consumption together leads to the generation of a crude estimate of the need to move oil between one region and others; this generates a "derived demand" for oil tanker services. BP's estimates of inter-area oil movements are shown in Table 3.

These figures will not correspond to the volumes of oil traded by sea, because the data includes other modes of transport, but they give a general indication of the major directions that oil is traded. In fact, many of the movements shown in the Table will be entirely by sea; for example, exports from West Africa to the USA and Europe, exports for the Middle East to Japan. The trade data emphasises the importance of Middle East exports in the oil trade; nearly 50% of the world's oil was exported from that region in 2000.

6. TANKER DEMAND

It is clear from inspection of the chart, that the need to service consumption from the major oil production centres leads to a demand for the transportation of oil, either in its crude (unrefined) form, or in the form of refined products.

6.1 Derived demand

Maritime economists define this demand for this service as a *derived* demand. That is, the need to move oil is not demanded for its own sake, as there is no intrinsic value or utility in so doing. The movement is made to "add-value" to the commodity, by selling it in a market where the marginal utility to the consumer is much higher than it is at the point of production. The process of moving the cargo is not directly determined by the consumer, as it is a part of the "supply-chain" process, and is best viewed as part of the production process. This means that the act of transporting oil is in effect, a factor input, and the laws that apply to factor demand apply to oil. There are four "Marshallian rules"[15] of factor demand.

These rules are useful in indicating, from first principles, just what the likely demand responsiveness is for oil movements. The rules are as follows:

Table 3: Regional flows of oil, 2000

From:	To: North America	South & C. America	Europe	Africa	Asia Pacific	Total
North America	170.2	16.4	20.8	0.5	8.5	216.4
South & C America	134.3	0.0	12.5	0.6	4.4	151.8
Europe	72.2	1.4	12.7	8.4	10.0	104.7
Former Soviet Union	3.2	8.1	167.4	0.5	12.3	191.5
Middle East	130.6	21.3	192.5	34.9	559.8	939.1
Africa	88.2	7.6	132.5	5.7	68.4	302.4
Asia Pacific	14.1	0.3	1.5	0.2	102.7	118.8
Total	612.8	55.1	539.9	50.8	766.1	2024.7

Source: Derived from the InterArea Trade Trade Flows in *BP Statistical Review of World Energy, 2001*.

(1) The elasticity of demand for the factor input (oil transportation) will be higher (lower), the higher (lower) the elasticity of demand for the final product (petrol, fuel oil, feedstock, heating oil, etc)
(2) The elasticity of demand for the factor input will be higher (lower), the higher (lower) the degree of substitutability between the factor and other factor inputs in the production process.
(3) The elasticity of demand for the factor input will be higher (lower) the higher (lower) the share that the input takes of the overall costs the consumer of the final product.
(4) The elasticity of demand for the factor input will be higher, the higher the elasticity of supply of the factor input.

Having already discussed some of the evidence of the income and price elasticities of demand for the final product, it is easy to realise that the above rules imply that the elasticity of demand for oil transportation with respect to changes in the cost of transporting it (the freight rate, in the case of shipping) is very likely to be extremely small, if not zero. The reason for this is to be found in rules 1 to 3. Rule 1 implies that the freight rate elasticity of demand will be proportional to the own price elasticities of demand for the final good, which has been, at the most optimistic, been estimated at –1, with most studies in the short run yielding –0.4. Rule 2 implies that this elasticity will be lower, the lower the degree of substitutability. Whilst oil pipeline transportation can and does, have a significant role in certain parts of the world, the fact remains that the overwhelming majority of oil has to be moved by sea, or not at all. Rule 3 implies that the smaller the share of the input cost as a proportion of the final landed price to the consumer, the lower the freight rate elasticity. In the UK, it is estimated that the freight cost component in the retail price of petrol is between 0.5 and 1p on a current price of around 74p a litre; large variations in the freight rate will have almost no noticeable effect on the retail price in the UK.

The conclusion from the combination of empirical evidence and economic theory is that oil transportation demand will be highly price inelastic in most situations, but elastic with respect to changes in economic activity. Where substitute transportation forms exist however, such as major oil pipelines, cross price elasticities may be considerable.

6.2 Demand measurement

It has been demonstrated that large volumes of oil are annually transported from region to region. This provides *one* indicator of the derived demand for oil movements. Transportation is a non-storable *service*; it requires the movement of the oil cargo between two geographical points for that service to be performed. Oil demand has to be measured in two ways. Firstly, in terms of the tonnes of oil being moved per time period; and secondly, in terms of the *tonne miles* being demanded per time period. Transportation service demand is a flow demand, and it is the product of cargo volume and distance travelled per time period that generates overall demand.[16] Average voyage length is thus a proxy for route structure, since changes in that structure, say a significant shift to short haul trades, will reduce tonne mile demand even if oil volume demand is unchanged. A shift towards long haul routes does the opposite.

6.3 Tanker demand trends

Table 4 gives some information on the trends in tanker demand, in terms of tonnes of cargo carried and tonne miles performed per year, for the period 1990–2000. It is worth noting that the average haul of crude and products movements is around 5,000 miles over this period. Whilst this appears to be relatively constant, it has not always been thus. In 1967 the average haul was 4,775 miles; in 1977, 6,651 miles. The closure of the Suez Canal between 1967 and 1975 clearly divorced tonne miles demand from tonnes demand. Over the period 1968–1973 tonne mile demand grew at an annual average of 21.4% per annum, whereas tonnage demand grew at 13.6% per annum; for the period 1978-1983 tonnage demand fell by 5.6% per annum, whilst tonne mile demand declined by 9.0% per annum.[17] For the tanker markets, the main reasons for discrepancies between tonne mile demand and tonne demand are the closure of strategic routes, such as the Suez Canal, and the changing structure of oil demand patterns, towards or away from long haul trades. The early 1970s also saw the rise of the 200,000 tonne-plus tanker, or Very Large Crude Carrier (VLCC), which became dominant on long haul crude oil movements, essentially from the Middle east, to Europe and the Far East. The size and draft of these vessels made laden transit of the Suez Canal impossible, but the new technology provided sufficient scale economies to make the "distance" considerations irrelevant.

Table 4 shows clearly that the volume of oil transported has grown over the past ten years. The chart of oil movements shows that there is a wide variation in the volume of cargoes being moved on the principal oil trade routes, whose structure has remained relatively stable, but which can change in response to new oilfield developments, interruptions of existing supplies, and changing patterns of oil consumption.

6.4 Cyclical features

The data so far presented might suggest to the reader that demand trends are rather long term and gentle. In fact, there are very marked cycles of economic activity in the shipping markets, and the tanker industry is no different. In fact,

Table 4: Trends in oil transportation demand, 1990–2000

	1990	1995	2000
World Production (Mn Tonnes)	3,164	3,269	3,589
Seaborne Trade			
Mn Tonnes	1,526	1,808	2,119
Bn Tonne Miles	7,821	9,320	10,420
Average Haul (Miles)	5,125	5,155	4,917
Seaborne Trade Share of Production	48%	56%	59%

Source: *BP Statistical Review of World Energy*; *OECD Maritime Transport Review*, various issues.

it could be argued that the most recent tanker boom, which peaked in 2001, is the first for many years that has not been triggered by an external shock, such as a middle-east war. The marked cyclical nature of the industry can be seen in the Figure 3, which shows the behaviour of one year time charter[18] rates for three different crude tanker sizes.

The two identifiable peaks in hire rates, in 1997–1998 and in 2001, are quite marked, especially the most recent one. These periods do not correspond to external events, and are a sign that the tanker market has escaped the legacy of the 1970s and 1980s. Whilst every player in the tanker industry is aware that their business is cyclical, no-one has been able to develop a successful method of consistently forecasting the points at which the cycle switches from one phase to another. The cyclical behaviour of rates reflect the cyclical growth in demand, and supply, neither of which change at a constant rate.

7. TANKER SUPPLY

7.1 The structure and composition of tanker supply

The tanker supply situation has become increasingly fragmented over the past thirty years. Analysts and industry observers now segment the supply side into a number of different categories. Whilst overall macroeconomic conditions will drive all segments, each component of the market has its own characteristics. After reviewing fleet developments in broad terms, these segments will be examined in more detail.

7.2 Tanker fleet development

The world tanker fleet is defined as all those vessels that are classified as being dedicated to the movement of crude oil or refined products. It constitutes

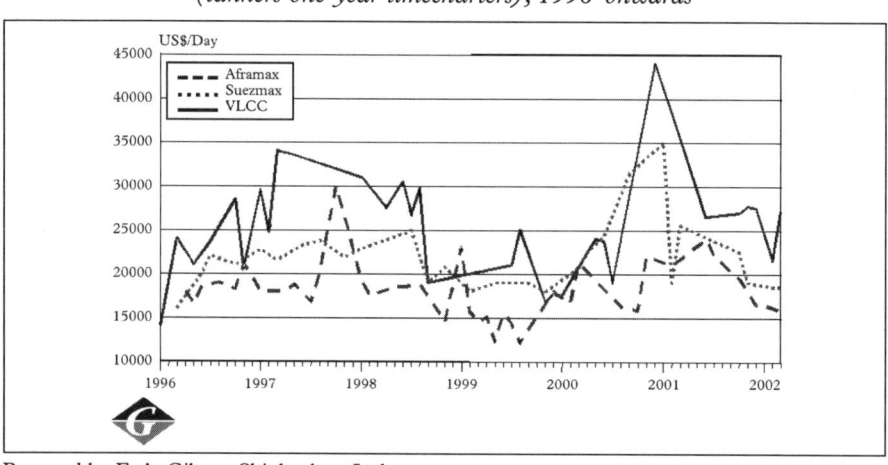

Figure 3: Monthly average timecharter rates (tankers one-year timecharters), 1996–onwards

Prepared by E. A. Gibson Shipbrokers Ltd.

approximately 40% of the world's merchant fleet. Conventional analysis defines the smallest as 10,000 dwt, a convention adopted here. In addition, a number of vessels were designed and built to operate in both the oil and dry bulk cargo trades. These are called combination carriers, and can be used to carry either iron ore, or bulk, or crude oil. In 1999 there were 159 such vessels, or 16.0mn dwt. This contrasts with the 3,307 tankers, or 287.4mn dwt. The potential oil carrying fleet includes both of these types. Table 5 provides some summary statistics for the tanker fleet itself.

Table 5: World tanker fleet, 1990–2000

	1990	1995	2000
World Tanker Fleet (Mn dwt)	257.4	263.0	298
(% of World Shipping Fleet)	40	39.7	41
Tanker Productivity			
(Tonnes Cargo moved per dwt per year)	6.2	6.8	7.0

Source: *UNCTAD Maritime Review*, various issues, Paris; Fearnleys, Oslo.

7.3 Structure of tanker supply

The world's tanker fleet is segmented into various submarkets. The segmentation is by size and by product type. Analysts distinguish between the markets for products tankers and crude oil tankers, and between a number of important size ranges of both of these segments.

The distinction between crude and products is an important one. The small products tankers have segmented (parcel) tanks. The current fleet of products carriers includes vessels over 120,000dwt, all of which have tank coatings and more complex cargo pipe work and pumping arrangements to protect the vessel against its highly corrosive and volatile cargo, whilst also maintaining and protecting the cargoes specification. Generally, product carriers are significantly smaller in size than crude tankers. Both construction and operating costs are higher for product vessels. The increasing concerns over product contamination has led to these ship types limiting their trading to clean or white petroleum products. Whilst it is possible to carry "dirty cargoes" in these vessels, the consequent contamination risk to future cargoes means that switching back would be difficult, and owners incur cleaning costs for the removal of residues, before their vessel becomes acceptable to potential charterers for the carriage of clean products again. No crude vessel is used to carry products, so there is a significant degree of segmentation between these market components.

More problematic is the segmentation of the crude oil market by ship size. The main workhorses of the tanker industry are now the Very Large and Ultra Large Crude Carriers, (VLCC/ULCC), defined broadly as vessels of 175,000 dwt or above; vessels of 120<175,000 dwt, which can transit the Suez Canal (Suezmax[19]), the Aframax Tanker, of around 80,000–120,000dwt, and the Panamax tanker, 60-80,000dwt. Products tankers tend to be smaller (25–50,000dwt), although there are some quite large vessels (100,000dwt) in this category. Essentially, the wide variation in draft/beam specification in vessels means that there is considerable potential overlap between these segments, but it is the case that the different ship sizes are generally found on different routes, reflecting the underlying economic drivers.

The VLCC/ULCC market is the one that has suffered the most in the past. Vessels of 170,000dwt or more did not become significant in numbers until the mid-1970's, at the time of economic slowdown. For some years in the early 1980's, no-one placed any orders at all for this size of vessel. Thus from a rapidly increasing, young fleet, the VLCC sector became a story of weak trading conditions and an ageing fleet.

The Oil Pollution Act, OPA90, which followed from the *Exxon Valdez* oil pollution incident in 1989, has had a great impact on the structure of the fleet. Good trading conditions, particularly after 1995 have also had an influence. 91mn dwt of the 126mn dwt that constitute the 200,000+ dwt sector are aged 15 years or less, and 74mn dwt is aged 10 years or less.[20] At December 2001, only 7 VLCC's were inactive – awaiting repairs rather than laid-up or withdrawn from service, approximately 1% of the fleet. Analysis of vessel deployment by Gibsons reveals that most of the older VLCCs are employed trading crude oil from Iraq, a somewhat ironic point given the numerous Iraqi one month oil export embargoes and the high expectation of an attack on Iraq in the near future. The recent high levels of ordering for this size of tanker imply that, if the demand were to remain unchanged, the loss of such vessels will already have been compensated for.

The primary routes for these vessels are long haul, mainly from the Middle-East, to Japan and the Far East. Trading into the North American east coast is restricted by port and draft limitations, although vessels can call at LOOP.[21] Significant increases in VLCC activity can thus raise tonne mile output significantly, because of the combination of ship size and voyage distance. Trading to Europe is the other primary route. In 2002, there were 439 vessels of 128mn dwt, and an orderbook for a further 50 more to be delivered 2002-2004.[22]

The Suezmax tanker trades on more specific routes. In the mid 1990's, half of the Suezmax fleet was deployed on the trade from Nigeria and other West African loading terminals to the USA and Europe,[23] with trading being generally restricted to the Atlantic basin. The fleet has an age profile which is very similar in structure to the VLCC's. This means that IMO 13G could impact this segment in the same way as the VLCC sector; recent high levels of orders will more than compensate for present scrapping needs. There were 260 vessels, or 38mn dwt, in this sector in 2002.

The age profile of the Aframax fleet is noticeably different from the larger tankers. This sector has a much more even age distribution for it's fleet, with recent order levels again compensating for required phase out under IMO 13G. Analysts do not sees any significant impact on the fleet from IMO 13G until 2015. There were 467 vessels of 45mn dwt as at February 2002. The Panamax sector is a rather small segment of the market, with 160 vessels totalling 10mn dwt. The Panamax fleet expected to expand as crude oil exports from the west coast of South America increase and find their way to the US Gulf refineries.

At the same time, the increasing number of products carrier movements from the US Gulf and Venezuela to the US west coast will necessitate more coated tankers to transit the Panama Canal, and therefore subject to the canal's 32.3 metre beam restriction.

Products tankers' load factors are much higher than for crude vessels and long balancing ballast voyages usually only apply to the large products carriers, and they tend to operate on shorter haul routes. However, the cubic capacity tends to be the main limiting factor for products carriers. The clean products tend to be lighter, having lower specific gravities, than those for dirty products and crude oil. In fact, vessels carrying full cargoes of clean products do not attain their maximum deadweight draft. An important trade is moving refined products from the Caribbean refineries to the US east coast. This is a market that has been effectively ignored by academic economists when analysing shipping market dynamics.

7.4 Tanker ownership structures

The tanker market has undergone a significant change in the composition of ownership over the past 25 years. Three key elements can be identified in this process. First, the emergence of significant refinery overcapacity in Europe. In the period 1965–1971, capacity increased by 50%.[24] This process created a 'spot market' for oil and oil products in Rotterdam, and helped to alter the structure of the UK's market for petrol. Secondly, the collapse in tanker demand in the 1970s led to many oil companies changing their tanker strategy. Analysis of data provided by Gibsons shows significant changes in the proportions of the tanker fleet that were employed by the oil majors in terms of owned vessels, the proportion hired on long term (5–10 years) time charters, or employed on a "spot" basis. The transformation from a highly controlled structure, where oil companies relied on spot market transactions for only 10% of their needs, to a situation where they take approximately 60% of tanker capacity from the spot market, was greatly accelerated by the drop in demand in the 1970s, which was accompanied by a severe oversupply of tonnage, especially in the VLCC segment.

The third element that helped to transform the structure of ownership has been the significant shift in attitudes to environmental pollution, mentioned earlier. In 1989, the *Exxon Valdez* struck a submerged reef whilst sailing in the Prince William Sound, Alaska, laden with crude oil. The vessel struck rocks, and lost 37,000 tons of crude oil through her single hull into the sea. Whilst not a large spill by historic standards,[25] the political reaction in the USA had ramifications that are still felt today. The ratification of the Oil Pollution Act of 1990 led to many major oil corporations deliberately reducing their direct ownership of oil tonnage, in an attempt to reduce their exposure to liability in the event of future incidents.[26] The decline in the apparent role of the major oil companies, and the rise of the so-called "independent" tanker owners, means that in economic terms, the market has become more competitive than it was.

The standard method of examining the degree of dominance of specific companies in an industry is to measure its degree of industrial concentration. The

Table 6: Ten largest tanker fleets, 2002

Oil Companies	Mn dwt	Independents	Mn dwt
Vela	5.6	Frontline	14.7
Petrobras	3.7	Mitsui OSK	9.5
NITC	3.7	NYK	7.9
KOTC	3.2	World-Wide	7.0
ExxonMobil	2.3	TeeKay	6.5
Idemitsu	2.1	Ofer	5.8
Chevron Texaco	1.7	OSG	5.4
Nisseki-Mitsubishi	1.6	Bergesen	5.3
Vamina	1.6	Moller	5.1
CPC	1.5	Astro Tankers	3.6
Top Ten	**27.0**	**Top Ten**	**70.8**

Source: E. A. Gibson Shipbrokers Ltd.

simplest way is to measure the share of the industry total accounted for by the five largest or 10 largest companies. Whilst this method has weaknesses, it is simple and easy to understand. Table 6 provides data on the tanker fleets owned by the 5 largest oil companies and the five largest independent tanker owners. In 2002, the largest oil company fleet was Vela, of Saudi Arabia, which owned 5.9mn dwt. They were followed by Petrobras (Brazil) and NITC (Iran) with 3.7mn dwt each. ExxonMobil was fifth largest with 2.3mn dwt, and the total for the five largest oil companies was 27mn dwt. The five largest independents owned 70.8mn dwt, and the smallest of these, Astro tankers, would rank fourth, if it was an oil company. The five largest companies would account for 15% of the world's tanker fleet in 2002, whilst the ten largest companies would account for 25%. These figures are very small compared to many industrial market structures. They imply that acting singly the very largest tanker owners have no potential to influence market behaviour. Even if the five largest companies got together to try to influence rates, they would not have sufficient market power to do so.

The tanker market has become more fragmented than it was in the past. In the 1960s, the oil companies owned significantly more tonnage, and contracted a very large share of independent owner's vessels as well. With 90% of oil company needs being met from the spot market, it is clear that they do not have the potential to influence rates. Whether this composition remains the same for the next decade is difficult to surmise. There is a possibility that the oil companies may, as market conditions get tighter, review their long term strategy, and raise the share of tonnage they control on long term charter.

7.6 Impact of external regulation on tanker supply: the environmental dimension

The present structure and future transformation of the tanker industry has been directly affected by regulatory changes brought in by the US Government and the IMO. Both of these changes were triggered by oil pollution caused by the grounding or loss of oil tankers at sea. The first incident, the *Exxon Valdez* incident in 1989, has already been referred to. The passing of the Oil Pollution Act in 1990 by the US Congress had two effects on the world's tanker markets.

First, it led to the decision, by the IMO, to introduce double-hull tanker technology embodied in Regulation 13F, which came into effect in 1992. This required all new tankers over 20,000 dwt to be double hulled. Tankers of specific size and vintage had to comply with OPA requirements which phased in the double hull specification over time. Vessels not complying with the rules would not be permitted to trade in US waters. The IMO was also spurred into the adoption of a phase-out programme for existing single-hulled tankers, regulation 13G, which was based on the OPA90 legislation. OPA90 also required that all owners trading into the US should have a certificate of financial responsibility, in effect a providing a guarantee that they would be able to pay for the costs of any accident shown to be their responsibility. Furthermore, if the owners were shown to be grossly negligent, their liability to damages is unlimited.

The choice of double-hull technology to improve the safety of crude oil transportation has not been unchallenged. Indeed, its worthiness on the basis of economic costs and benefits has also been questioned.[27] At the time of its introduction, other forms of increasing safety were being discussed, including the use of hydrostatic balancing. Under this alternative, single hull vessels would not have their cargo tanks fully loaded. Instead, they would be loaded until the point sea pressure from the outside of the tank wall would be greater than the pressure of the oil. This meant that any rupture would mean that sea water would ingress rather than oil escape. There would be a loss of cargo carrying potential of around 15%. Whilst this is a feasible solution in principle,[28] the market rejected it. The major oil charterers refused to accept single-hulled vessels certificated for this process, and, in consequence, double-hull has become the standard.

An important effect of the OPA law should be noted. The legal liability under the OPA regulation was laid squarely at the feet of the owner of the vessel, not the *charterer*. Oil companies noted this, and Exxon, who owned the *Exxon Valdez*, and who thus were liable for the claims resulting, began to reduce its fleet of owned tankers. It was a deliberate strategy, because any future oil pollution incident would appear to be focused upon the owner, rather than the charterer. The fewer the ships that they directly owned, the smaller the risk exposure.

The second event which has affected the market is the loss of the *Erika*. The *Erika* was a 24-year-old single-hulled 37,000dwt tanker which literally split in two and sank in the Bay of Biscay, carrying 30,000 tonnes of heavy fuel oil from Dunkerque to Livorno in Italy.[29] Both sections sank on 13th December 1999. During her life the vessel had changed names seven times and been classed by four different classification societies. She was owned by a Maltese registered company, The vessel had apparently passed its recent classification survey, and had been chartered from an Italian shipowner. The oil washed up on the Brittany coast at a crucial time for tourism, causing significant loss of business to French fishing and tourism industries, as well as significant clean-up costs. The French authorities reacted by arresting the Total-Fina managers responsible for chartering the vessel, as well as those directly responsible for the ship's operation. The implication of this action is that not only is the shipowner liable in the event of an oil pollution incident, the charterer themselves may also be liable when the judicial process is completed.

Charterers for oil tankers re-appraised their policies as a consequence of this action. Tanker brokers reported the first signs of significant price premiums for new tonnage, as owners of old tonnage suddenly found that the charterers had begun to discriminate by age.[30] As a direct consequence of this incident, the EU has proposed that the phase-out of single-hulled tankers, agreed at the IMO after the US unilateral action in OPA90, should be accelerated.[31] The accelerated phase-out was adopted by the IMO in 2001. This action has further accentuated the increased acceptance in the industry that old tonnage is likely to be a greater pollution risk, and given that charterers may now be liable, a greater degree of discrimination is evident.

It is unsurprising, but perhaps disappointing, to note that the two major legislative changes affecting the operation of the tanker industry *per se* in the past decade have both been a result of a *reaction* by governments and international organisations to the political pressures created as a result of a well publicised environmental accident.[32]

8. THE ECONOMICS OF TANKER MARKETS

8.1 Freight rate and ship price behaviour

Tanker freight rates and asset prices display marked features. Freight rates are expressed in either $/tonne, a dollar lump sum amount, or in WorldScale. The WorldScale system is well established, replacing its predecessor, IntaScale. It in turn originated in World War II, when the UK's ministry of transport set up a set of common scales to be used to reimburse tanker owners for the use of their requisitioned assets. Expressing rates in dollars per tonne of cargo delivered was felt to be uninformative when trying to make comparisons of the relative revenues being charged for across different routes. This is because the voyage fixture cost will be affected by fuel prices in the region, the voyage distance, the port dues being charged, and of course the vessel size. The WorldScale system in effect tries to provide a "standard", a reference marker, to allow some comparison to be made across routes. It is based on setting up a Reference rate, "WorldScale Flat", which is to be charged for the carriage of one tonne of cargo between any two ports. The absolute value of the Flat rate depends on an assumed bunker price, and is based on a 75,000dwt tanker with specific fuel consumption and speed. Port and cargo discharge dues are surveyed annually at every port, and the fuel costs for the voyage are estimated. In addition, a fixed notional daily hire charge is included. WorldScale Flat is then arrived at. The WorldScale Association calculates these flat rates between for thousands of voyage possibilities. The rate is based on a round voyage and allows a standard 48 hours for both loading and discharging. WorldScale flat rates are updated annually; from the mid-1970s they were updated twice a year, because of high inflation rates. In 1989, WorldScale reverted to an annual review and update of the Flat Rate, as inflation rates stabilised.

THE TANKER MARKET: CURRENT STRUCTURE 269

Any spot voyage fixture that takes place on the market is then translated from the $/tonne cargo into a WorldScale equivalent. Given the cost structure of ships, even if a 250,000dwt vessel were to earn the same net revenue as the reference 75,000dwt vessel, its rate would be well below WS100, the reference value. Norman[33] states that the advantages of a scale system are; the simplification of communication, the simplification of charter parties for option fixtures by the replacement of alternative freight rates by one scale reference, the simplification of charter parties for consecutive voyage agreements, and the simplification of the comparability of earning opportunity, because differences due to voyage length and port costs have been embodied in the flat rate itself. Norman demonstrated that the ability to make comparisons across routes was more to do with the high correlation and limited variation of bunker fuel prices around the world than the reference system itself. The existence of WorldScale does cause a second problem. Whilst freight rates are often quoted in WorldScale, (strictly, nominal WorldScale), time charter rates are quoted in $ per day, and the prices of ships, both new and second-hand, are also quoted in $. To match spot earnings to time charter hire rates therefore requires a transformation – and time charter rates are sometimes quoted as World Scale Equivalent. Similarly, owners convert their prospective revenues, less commission, and the particular voyage related costs, to produce a time charter equivalent daily rate. This is the first stage in the voyage budgeting and accounting process.

The pattern of tanker freight rates has not changed in any significant way in the 1990s. Spot rates are quoted for the various size segments discussed briefly above. The behaviour of tanker spot rates over the past is illustrated in Figure 4.

Figure 4: Spot rates for crude and clean products by route and size, 1996–2000

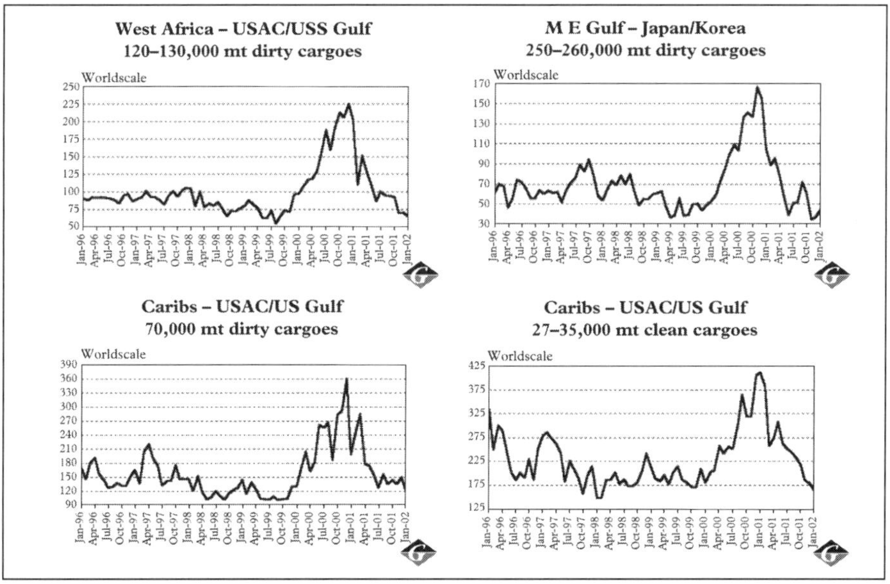

Source: E. A. Gibson Shipbrokers Ltd.

The chart illustrates two basic points. One is the great volatility of rates; on the Middle-East to Japan route, spot rates reached WS165 at the end of 2000; but four months later, they had fallen to WS30. This peak can be observed across all the routes and oil cargoes shown, which illustrates the second feature, the very high correlation of rates across all routes. Similar patterns exist for all sizes.

The behaviour of both the new and second-hand price of ships is also of interest. It is well known that both of these prices fluctuate over time, reflecting changing conditions in the freight market. The relationship between the relative prices of different tanker sizes is not constant over time; nor is the relationship between the second hand price of a vessel and the newbuild and scrap prices of a similar type.

The relationship between the asset price and freight earnings has been the central focus of recent econometric studies of the tanker market, as will be discerned in the following sections.

8.2 The demand and supply approach

The standard approach to analysing the tanker market has been to use the static competitive model. This approach can be split into two interrelated segments – the modelling of demand and supply for oil tanker services, i.e. transport demand and supply; and the modelling of the change in the stock of tankers that provide the services, i.e. the newbuilding, second-hand tankers, and scrapping markets.

It has already been established that the industry structure is very fragmented. It has also been shown that the derived demand for tanker services is extremely inelastic with respect to the freight rate. How does tanker supply respond?

The conventional answer to this question is to employ the argument that the tanker supply side is determined by competitive conditions. The standard economic model of perfect competition requires four principal assumptions to be made before it can be applied. They are:

(a) The presence of a large number of buyers. In the tanker market, the buyer is the charterer of the tanker service. There are indeed, hundreds, if not thousands, of individual companies who hire tankers.

(b) The presence of a large number of sellers. It has already been established that the largest owners of oil tankers control only a very small percentage of the tanker fleet, and this percentage has, if anything, declined in the last 30 years. There are hundreds of tanker owners.

(c) Free entry and exit. An important feature of a competitive market is the ability for new entrants to win business without being impeded by existing companies, or suffering from a significant cost disadvantage when they enter.

(d) Homogeneous product. In order to ensure that buyers view each supplier's service as identical, the product offered must be very similar. The "product" in this case is the safe and reliable transportation of the cargo, as specified by the contract. Providing that tanker owners ensure that their vessels' can comply with this condition, the only criteria for choosing between competing suppliers is the freight rate.[34]

THE TANKER MARKET: CURRENT STRUCTURE 271

(e) Full Information. The market is extremely well served by the specialised shipbroking companies who keep in constant contact with both owners and charterers on a 24 hour basis all round the world. These companies have offices in strategic points all round the world to offer this service. The role of London is crucial, because it is located in a timezone that allows trade with the Far East and New York in the same trading day. This unique position makes London the ideal base for such companies. In addition, there are many specialist companies offering consultancy services to companies. All this activity means that charterers and owners are continuously informed of recent events and prices. Many shipping fixtures are publicly reported, with all salient details available. This makes the provision of market information relatively cheap and very efficient.

Overall then it would appear that all of the fundamental assumptions of perfect competition are fulfilled when one examines the tanker market. This means that modelling its behaviour using demand and supply analysis can thus be justified.

8.2.1 Explaining the freight rate

The nature of supply differs between the short run period, defined as the period in which the tanker fleet is unchanged in size, and the long run, in which the tanker fleet is allowed to contract or expand. Contraction occurs if the rate of scrapping of tankers exceeds the rate of newbuilding deliveries; expansion when newbuilding deliveries exceed scrapping.[35]

The short run supply schedule for the market as a whole is assumed to have a "reverse L" shape, which is very elastic (flat) when there is a low demand for tanker services relative to the existing fleet size, but which becomes very inelastic (vertical) as demand approaches full capacity of the existing fleet (Figure 5). The "flat" range of the supply curve is created by the ability to 'mothball' tanker tonnage by placing the vessel in layup when trading conditions are poor, and freight earnings are low. As demand approaches the potential maximum productive capacity of the present fleet, all lay ups are brought into use, and the ability to further expand supply becomes very limited. This explains the vertical section of the short run supply curve.[36] The position of the short run cost

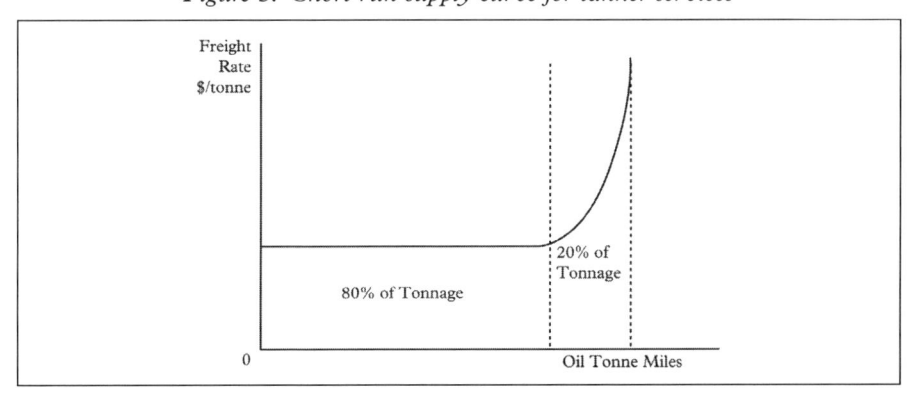

Figure 5: Short run supply curve for tanker services

curve is also indicative of the overall level of marginal cost. One very important determinant of this is the assumed value of factor input prices. In the case of ships, the most significant of these in the short run is the price of bunker fuel, since most of the short run variable costs are related to voyage activity. The position of the short run costs curve will shift upwards if bunker price rise significantly, and shift downwards if they fall.

The 80:20 split is based on the analysis by Platou[37] of tanker rate volatility - they argue that practically all of the variations that are observed in the tanker market are observed when the utilisation of the fleet was in the last 20% – this is consistent with the shape of the supply curve above – elastic over the 80% range, but becoming less and less elastic until full capacity utilisation was achieved.

It is important to remember that this is a model for the short run supply of shipping. The assumption is being made that the stock of tankers is unchanged; variations in tonne miles produced are generated by variations in lay-ups, storage, and speed.

Putting the very inelastic demand schedule together with the varying elasticity supply schedule generates a model of the equilibrium spot freight rate for tanker services. as shown below, in Figure 6. The important feature to note about this figure is the asymmetric response of the freight rate to shifts in the position of the demand curve. When demand increases from D0 to D1, a large shift in demand, there is little effect on the market freight rate, because of the presence of unemployed or underemployed vessels. The equilibrium freight rate moves from P1 to P2, whilst tonne miles increase from Q1 to Q2. When demand shifts again, from D1 to D2, which is a smaller shift in demand, spare capacity is less readily available, so the result is larger increase in rate. The freight rate rises from P2 to P3, and tonne miles increase from Q2 to Q3. Finally, when demand shifts from D2 to D3, tanker supply is perfectly inelas-

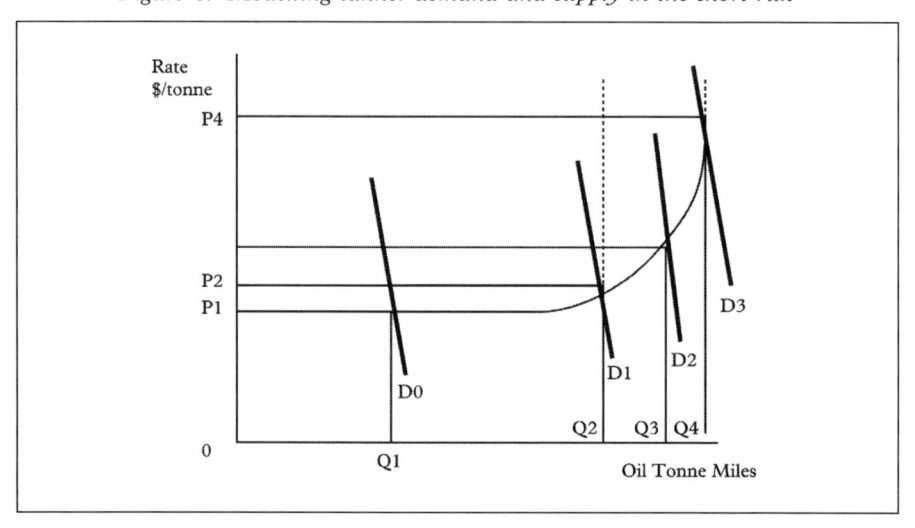

Figure 6: Modelling tanker demand and supply in the short run

THE TANKER MARKET: CURRENT STRUCTURE 273

tic, and small shifts in demand generate large increases in rates. In this case, the freight rate rises rapidly from P3 to P4 but tonne miles performed rise only slightly from Q3 to Q4.

The long run supply of tanker services is found by allowing the short run supply schedule to shift its position over time. As the total fleet expands, the curve will shift down (slightly) and to the right, reflecting two elements. Firstly, new tankers tend to be more efficient than old ones. The long economic life means that technical change will be embodied in the new vessels, particularly in terms of the fuel consumption of new engines, levels of automation, and days off-hire for servicing and repair will be lower. So a similar size vessel, when replaced with its modern equivalent, will be have a lower short run marginal cost per tonne mile. This change is gradual, but its cumulative effect is important. Secondly, owners do not necessarily replace same sized vessels with their modern equivalent. As trade volumes change, the optimal vessel size for a specific trade route will alter. When demand grows in volume, average tanker sizes will increase. Because of the scale economies inherent in ship size, irrespective of type, larger vessels will tend to mean lower short run marginal costs. It is important to note however if the fleet is doubled in size, the same basic short run supply relationship will still exist. There will always be a finite productive capacity whatever the size of the fleet, and hence, with sufficient demand volume, a limit on short run output. But this is not true of long run supply. In principle, the long run supply will expand in line with demand. Indeed, the efficient allocation of resources requires that the capital embodied in the tanker companies should be sufficient to meet long term demand needs, but no more. It is expected then, that over time, the growth in the tanker fleet should be in proportion to the growth in the level of tonne mile demand.

The application of this model helps to explain the short-run fluctuations in freight rates observed in the market, which are viewed as the result of the interaction of the short run supply schedule with the shifting demand schedule. The long term trend will appear as demand trends assert themselves, and supply adjusts through the expansion or contraction of the fleet. It is thus possible to explain both short run volatility of freight rates and profits, and at the same time, explain the long term trend decline in the real costs of transporting oil, brought about by the use of larger and more technically efficient ships. Given that demand responds primarily to the balance between economic activity and the prevailing level of tanker supply (the fleet), whilst costs are directly affected by the behaviour of bunker prices, it is not surprising to find that these three variables are regularly employed as explanatory factors in the econometric modelling of the tanker freight rate.

8.2.2 Freight rates and profitability by tanker size

The above analysis has taken for granted that the market for all tankers is the same – the market for 50,000dwt crude is identical to the market for 350,000dwt crude vessels. But one or two authors have suggested that the changes that occurred in the 1970s have made that assumption incorrect. The different size classifications of tankers has already been outlined. The key question is: do these different segments behave differently, in economic terms, or are they all so highly correlated that it is still valid to analyse the market as if it were a single entity? Earlier research suggested that there are indeed sufficient differences to warrant separate analysis, which has been confirmed more recently by others. Svendsen showed that different tanker sizes had different own-price and cross-price elasticities of demand with respect to freight rates. This implies some degree of differentiation in the market. Glen,[38] in a study of tanker profitability in the 1970s, showed that the gross profit margins varied widely between sizes, and that large tankers had significantly greater variability in those margins. If the tankers were all in the same market, the variability should have been the same. More recently, Kavussanos showed that there are significant differences in the volatility of tanker freight rates by size, and therefore, significant differences in the level of risk associated with owning different sizes of tankers. This implies that, viewed as a financial asset, they are distinct. This result has been confirmed by Glen & Martin.[39]

The question arises, does this mean that the segments of the tanker market can be viewed as independent of each other? The answer to this is a resounding no, because although the segments within the tanker market may have become more distinct, allowing them to behave differently in the short run, it does not follow that they are unrelated in the long run. This is because shipowners have the choice of investing in all of these segments – none is closed to them. Thus free entry and exit exists in all parts, so that market imbalances may exist for a few years, but will be self corrected by different rates of entry and exit in the sectors. Thus, if the market for VLCC's is badly hit, this sector will have very high lay-ups, higher than average scrapping rates, and few new orders - owners will be concentrating on the sectors that are relatively more profitable- until the excess supply problem is resolved. In the long run then, one would expect to see the same common factors driving each of these sectors, and common trends appearing.

8.2.3 Term structure relations

The simple demand supply explains the determination of the spot rate, but does not directly help analyse the behaviour of time charter rates. One way of exploring the relationship between these two is to note the similarity between the term structure of interest rates, whereby long term rates on interest are explained in terms of short term rates, and the tanker market, in which the period rate which is return to the owner, is expected to be equivalent to the sum of the expected discounted returns earned by the owner if they operated their tanker on the spot market over the same time horizon as the relevant period charter. In an efficient market, the only difference between these two should be a liquidity premium, normally assumed to be negative, because by hiring the vessel for a longer period, the owner has transferred some of the risk of ownership to the charterer. The hypothesised relationship can be written as

$$(1) \quad TC_t^{(n)} = \varpi^{(n)} \Sigma \delta^{(i)} E_t V_{t+1} + \lambda$$

which states that a time charter equivalent of n period duration will be equal to the present value of the expected returns obtained from trading in the spot market (V). The last term in the expression can be positive or negative as it reflects the liquidity cost or benefit from being in the spot market, which depends on present market conditions. In rising markets the owner would prefer to be trading in the voyage market, but if the market is declining, fixing a period charter is preferable, and the "liquidity premium" is reversed.[40] This relationship can be transformed, in terms of the "spread" or the difference between the time charter rate of a given period and the appropriate spot rate. It can be shown that the spread is a function of the expected future changes in the corresponding spot rate. Veenstra, using modern econometric methods, has tested this model, and argues that it is a valid representation of the relationship between spot and time charter rates, with the exception of that for the VLCC market.[41]

This so-called "present value" relationship is very important, as it also appears when the determinants of the price of ships are examined.

8.2.4 The price of ships

The price of second-hand ships correlates very well with movements of spot and timecharter rates. When market conditions are very good, second hand prices are high, and in some extreme cases have risen close to, and even above, the newbuilding price of an equivalent sized tanker. On the other hand, when market conditions are poor, the second hand price may be closet the value implies if the vessel were to scrapped; its value determined by the prevailing price of scrap. Both of these situations have been observed in the past. In the poor market conditions of the early 1980's, second-hand prices were at the scrap price "floor". In 2001, some second hand tankers were being sold at newbuild prices.

The key to understanding this lies in the present value relation introduced in the previous section. This time, the relationship is between the ship price, (the asset), and the stream of earnings it is expected to generated to the owner whilst they trade it. This is best defined in present value terms.

$$(2) \quad P_t = \Sigma \beta^i \Pi_{t+i} + \beta^{t+n} D_{t+n}$$

where the second hand price, P_t, is determined by the expected future profits earned by trading the vessel, plus any income, discounted back to the present, obtained when it is disposed of D_{t+n}. This last term represents either the price received from another shipowner if the vessel is sold on for further trading, or the scrap value. The former is determined by the expected future second hand price of the vessel, the latter, the expected price of scrap. Since the expected future price of a second-hand ship depends on earnings, the relationship implies very high levels of correlation between freight rates, bunker costs, scrap prices and the second-hand price.

Putting these elements together provides a model of tanker market behaviour. Freight rates are determined by the joint interaction of the supply of, and demand for tanker services. The latter is very insensitive to the freight rate itself; it has been shown to be highly price inelastic. But demand is sensitive to changes in expectations about the future, and to political and other external events that can impact on it. The reaction of the freight rate to shifts in demand will depend in part, on the level of utilisation of the existing fleet. At high levels of employment, shifts in demand will create large movements in the freight rate; but when there are significant numbers of vessels laid up, supply is more elastic and freight rates will tend to be less volatile.

Because of the fact that second-hand tanker prices are driven by expected future earnings, high levels of freight rates will lead to greater expected profits and an immediate rise in second-hand prices. The variation in the price of tankers is thus highly correlated with events in the spot market. High profits mean increasing orders, and an increased level of tanker deliveries in the near future. If demand growth declines, or fails to grow as anticipated, the increased level of deliveries will lead to a lowering of spot rates in the future as the newbuildings are delivered. In addition, at high levels of demand, older vessels, which might have been scrapped, are traded for longer. This reduces the supply of tankers for scrap and raises the scrap price. At the same time, the pressure of owners on yards increases, and newbuilding prices will tend to rise. Thus freight rates, second hand prices, scrap prices and newbuild prices will tend to move together in a cyclical fashion. This process is driven by the interaction of many owners, charterers, shipbuilders and shipbrokers, none of whom have any significant control over their environment.

9. SUMMARY AND CONCLUSIONS

The tanker market is a fascinating sector of the shipping industry. It has played a pivotal role in the transportation of oil from the major production centres to the major consuming ones. The industry is dynamic, and very sensitive to political and environmental issues.

The tanker market has proved to be a fruitful sector for applied economic research, ranging from modelling of rate and price behaviour, to measuring the economic impact of oil pollution on the environment. Whilst the composition of the individual players has changed considerably over the past 30 years, it is still a very good example of a competitive industry. It exhibits many of the behavioural traits that are associated with fierce competition, and will no doubt continue to do so in the future.

This chapter has
1. Outlined developments in the oil industry. The market for tanker services is derived from the movement of oil, and an understanding of the tanker market is not possible without an understanding of the structure of the oil industry. It was shown that some 60% of the world's oil is traded across regional boundaries. The oil tanker market directly serves this trade.
2. Examined the demand for tankers. It was shown that demand is derived, and this characteristic means that the demand for tankers is essentially perfectly inelastic with respect to the cost of transporting it.

THE TANKER MARKET: CURRENT STRUCTURE

3. Explored the supply of tanker services. The low degree of industrial concentration was discussed, and the structure of tanker supply was explained. The impact of oil pollution on future tanker supply was discussed
4. Reviewed the economics of the tanker market. Section 8 discussed the determination of freight rates, and the interaction between the freight market and the market for new and second-hand tankers. These relationships have formed the focus of research efforts in this area in the past decade.

ENDNOTES

1. Source: *Monthly Shipping Review*, March 2002 (London, SSY Consultancy & Research).
2. The data provided in this chapter concentrates on crude and dirty products. The combination carrier, a vessel that can carry bulk cargoes and crude oil simultaneously, has been ignored. Whilst important in the past, their numbers are declining, and their trading patterns tend to be based either in dry cargo or in the crude oil trades. Empirical evidence suggests that their potential to link the dry and wet sectors of shipping, through shifting their capacity, and hence supply, is very slight in practice. A fuller analysis of supply would of course allow for the combination carrier tonnage employed in the oil trades.
3. All data quoted are from the *BP Statistical review of World Energy, 2001*, available at *www.bp-amoco.co.uk*
4. See Table 3 for details.
5. The Annual average price of Brent Light was $36.83 for 1980. Source: *BP Statistical review of World Energy, 2001*, available at *www.bp-amoco.co.uk*
6. The Organisation of Petroleum Exporting Countries. Formed in 1960, its first real exercise of economic power came in October 1973 with the oil price rise and an embargo on oil exports to the USA and the Netherlands.
7. *Ibid.*, n. 3.
8. Dahl, C., & Sterner, T. (1991): "Analyzing gasoline demand elasticities: a survey", *Energy Economics*, 13, pp. 203–210.
9. See Dahl, C., & Sterner, T., *op.cit.*, Table 2, p. 210.
10. According to 2000 data, world oil consumption split 21% gasoline, 40% Middle distillates, 23% Fuel oil, and 16% others. North American oil consumption is 41% gasoline, 31% Middle distillates, 8% Fuel Oil, 20% Other. Source: *BP Statistical Review of World Energy, 2001*.
11. Dahl, C. (1993): "A survey of oil demand elasticities for developing countries", *OPEC Review*, XVII, pp. 399–419; and Dahl, C. (1994): "A survey of oil product demand elasticities for developing countries", *OPEC Review*, XVIII, pp. 47–86.
12. Some significant tanker disasters are the *Torrey Canyon*, 1967, the *Amoco Cadiz*, the *Exxon Valdez*, 1989, and the *Erika*, 1997, all of which led to change in the oil industry.
13. It should be noted that the prevailing oil demand forecasts of the early 1970s were totally unsustainable in terms of the rationale underlying the demand projection; the notion that supply, or oil discoveries and production, could continue to expand exponentially, and of course without political and environmental resistance. Could output actually have reached the projected 200 million barrels a day by year 2000? (Actual consumption was almost 75M b/d.)
14. *Maritime Group Tanker Industry Overview* (2001), Table 3, p. 5 (New York, Jefferies & Co. Inc.).

15. Named after the economist, Alfred Marshall, who first developed them.
16. The distinction may not make a lot of difference in a market with a constant route structure, because average voyage length may remain constant over time. If there is a dramatic change in voyage length, the demand for shipping services can be significantly affected even if tonnage movements are constant. For example, the average voyage length for oil rose dramatically in 1967 with the closure of the Suez Canal, from 4,775 to 6,540 miles in 1974. Demand for tanker services, measured in tonne miles, rose in proportion to this, assuming that oil volume demand remained constant.
17. Figures calculated by the authors from *OECD Review of Maritime Transport*, various issues (Paris, OECD).
18. The time charter rate is the daily rate, in thousands of dollars, that is paid to hire a vessel by a charterer from its owner or present operator. The rate is a charge for the use of the vessel, complete with crew, insurance and other costs, except for those related to voyages, i.e. fuel, food, port and cargo dues. The most extreme form of charter, the bare-boat charter, for 25 years, would give the charterer the use of the vessel for that lifetime. The charterer would then pay the entire costs of operating the vessel, including manning and insurance. A bare-boat charter is in effect, a rent to the owner for the use of the capital tied up in the vessel.
19. These vessels are sometimes called "one million barrel" tankers. There are approximately 7 barrels to one tonne of crude oil, so this translates into 130,000 tonnes. The measure is a convenient parcel size for transporting, storing, and trading.
20. Source: *www.gibsons.com*
21. Louisiana Offshore Oil Port. The alternative is transhipment at sea, but increased environmental pressure mean that these activities are not desirable. The US Coastguard has designated areas suitable for transhipment and lightering operations.
22. Gibsons 2002, *Tanker Book 2002* (London, E. A. Gibson Shipbrokers Ltd).
23. Tusiani, M. (1996): *The Petroleum Shipping Industry*, Vol. I, p. 179 (Tulsa, Oklahoma, Pennwell Publishing).
24. See *BP Statistical Review of World Energy, 2001*.
25. The *Atlantic Empress* lost 287,000 tons of crude oil off Tobago in 1979; the *Amoco Cadiz* lost 223,000 tons off Brittany in 1978. See Tusiani, 1996, vol. 1, p. 225.
26. For a discussion of the *Exxon Valdez* incident, see Tusiani, (1996) vol. 1, pp. 227–251.
27. It has been argued that the void space between the two hulls will become corroded by sulphuric acid created by cargo fumes and moisture interacting. Inspection of the void space may be difficult. See Brown, R., & Savage, I., 1996: "The economics of double-hulled tankers", *Maritime Policy and Management*, 23, pp. 167–175, for an assessment of the economic arguments for double-hull technology.
28. Indeed, a tanker that operates under HBL is exempted from the revised phase out dates. See, for example, ABS, 2001, *Oil Tanker Outlook: Assessing the Impact of the Revised IMO MARPOL 13G Phase Out*, ABS at *www.eagle.org/index.html*
29. Details of the incident can be found in Annex 1A of Commission of the European Communities, 2000, *Proposal for a Directive of the European Parliament and of the Council amending 95/21/EC, 94/57/Ec and accelerating phasing of double-hull or equivalent design requirements for single hull tankers.* COM(2000) 142 final 121pp, and in OECD, 2001, *The Cost to Users of Substandard Shipping*, 45pp. Paper prepared by SSY Consultancy and Research Ltd. Both available from *www.oecd.org*
30. Tamvakis, in a study of rate differentials on fixtures for vessels trading to the USA post OPA'90, could not find strong evidence to support the idea that there would be a premium for better quality vessels. See Tamvakis, M. (1995): "An investigation into the existence of a two-tier spot freight market for crude oil carriers", *Maritime Policy and Management*, 22, pp. 81–90. For an analysis based on simulation, see Strandenes, S. (1999): "Is there a potential for a two-tier tanker market?", *Maritime Policy and Management*, 26, pp. 249–264.

31. The regulation is 13G, adopted in August 2001.
32. It would be nice to be able to comment on a proactive industry decision to raise standards without such pressures – but we can't think of one.
33. Norman, V. (1977): *An Assessment of the WorldScale System*, paper presented to INTERTANKO annual meeting, Italy.
34. It is possible, under certain local conditions, for owners to be able to charge a premium; if for example, only one vessel is open for cargoes at a particular terminal at a particular time. This will not last long however; the mobility of tankers ensures that such premia rapidly disappear.
35. This corresponds to the notion that capital, at least that tied up in the tanker, is the fixed factor of production. In economics, the short run is defined as the time period in which the firm cannot vary the employment of at least one factor of production.
36. For a discussion of a model constructed for tankers on this basis, see Wijnolst, N. & Wergeland, T. (1996): *Shipping* (Delft, Delft University Press). The principle is to estimate the short run marginal costs of tankers, and then rank in increasing order of cost, until all vessels are included. The result is the short run supply curve, and it looks similar to the one used in the text.
37. Platou, M. (1996): *Platou Market Report*, Platou, Oslo.
38. Glen, D. (1990): "The emergence of differentiation in the oil tanker market, 1970-78", *Maritime Policy and Management*, 17, pp. 289–312.
39. See Kavussanos, M. (1996): "Price Risk Modelling of Different Size Vessels in the Tanker Industry", *Logistics and Transportation Review*, 32, pp. 161–176, and Glen, D., & Martin, B. (1998): "Conditional Modelling of tanker market risk using route specific freight rates", *Maritime Policy and Management*, 25, pp. 117–28.
40. This relationship was first formulated by Zannetos, Z. (1966): *The Theory of Oil Tankship Rates* (Boston, USA, MIT Press). See also Glen, D., Owen, M., & Van der Meer (1981): "Spot and Time Charter Rates for Tankers, 1970–1977", *Journal of Transport Economics and Policy*, XV, pp. 45–58; and Veenstra, A. (1999): *Quantitative Analysis of Shipping Markets* (Delft, Holland, Delft University Press). For a modern analysis of the tanker market, see Beenstock, M., and Vergottis, A. (1993): *An Econometric Model of World Shipping* (London, Chapman & Hall).
41. See Veenstra, 1999, pp. 201–206.

REFERENCES

BP (2001) *Statistical Review of World Energy* (BP, London, UK).
Beenstock, M., and Vergottis, A. (1993): *An Econometric Model of World Shipping* (London, Chapman & Hall).
Gibsons (2002) *Tanker Book 2002* (London, E. A. Gibson Shipbrokers Ltd).
McConville, J. (1999): *Maritime Economics: Theory and Practice* (London, Witherbys).
Newton, J. (2002): *A Century of Tankers* (Oslo, Norway, Intertanko).
Tusiani, M. (1996): *The Petroleum Shipping Industry* (Tulsa, Oklahoma, Pennwell Publishing).
Wijnolst, N., & Wergelend, T. (1996): *Shipping* (Delft, Delft University Press).
Veenstra, A. (1999): *Quantitative Analysis of Shipping Markets* (Delft, Delft University Press).
Zannetos, Z. (1966): *The Theory of Oil Tankship Rates* (MIT, Boston, USA, MIT Press).

CHAPTER 13

ECONOMICS OF SHORTSEA SHIPPING

*Enrico Musso** and Ugo Marchese[†]
*Department of Economics, University of Genoa, Genoa, Italy.
E-mail: *musso@economia.unige.it*
†University of Genoa, Genoa, Italy. E-mail: *marchese@economia.unige.it*

1. INTRODUCTION

1.1 Purpose

It is often claimed that developing Short-Sea Shipping (from now on: SSS) is crucial in the issue of enhancing land-sea intermodality, thus pursuing (i) environmental benefits, since it reduces pollution and accidents of road transport, and (ii) economic benefits, since it reduces congestion on transport networks, reduces investments in transport infrastructure and increases competitiveness of port hinterlands on the international markets.[1]

SSS has been growing significantly over the past 10-20 years – although mainly in South East Asia and Europe – due to the growth of infra-regional trade and the boost of hub-and-spoke maritime transport. Yet, there seems to be a gap between present growth rate and the goals of policy makers, namely in the European Union (EU). So far, the growth seems limited to captive markets, such as connections with islands, or on feeder traffic for Deep-Sea Shipping (DSS), while SSS does not appear as a real alternative to land transport, namely to road haulage.

This chapter aims at:

- outlining the development of SSS, types of ships and cargoes involved, traffic volumes, modal split between short-sea and land transport (section 2);
- proposing a simple conceptual framework in order to resume and coordinate geographic and transport/economic conditions that make SSS viable and competitive; and to point out the key issues for successful policies (sections 3-4);
- listing different pros and cons of SSS, and wondering on the actual advisability of its enhancement (section 5);
- pointing out the different policies to be implemented (section 6), those outlined so far, namely by the EU (section 7), and trying to assess their potential effectiveness (section 8).

1.2 A definition of short-sea shipping

Despite many efforts, we actually still lack an unambiguous definition of SSS, as Van de Voorde and Viegas (1995), Marlow *et al.* (1997) point out.[2] Some consider it as a synonymous for cabotage, i.e., all seaborne traffic between ports of the same country, sometimes including frontier ports of adjacent countries.[3] To other authors the relevant point is that alternative land transport must be available.[4]

Some authors choose "tailored" definitions suitable for specific situations: Marlow *et al.* (1997) define SSS as seaborne flows of all kinds of freight performed by vessels of any flag, from a EU member country to whichever destination within the territory embracing Europe, the Mediterranean and Black Sea non-European countries.[5] Actually there are many "regional-based" (often European-based) definitions.[6]

Some authors propose a very pragmatic definition. Stopford (1997) states that SSS is normally a maritime transport within a region, essentially serving port-to-port feeder traffic, and can be in competition with land transport.[7] While according to Bjornland (1993) SSS is "seaborne goods transport which does not cross oceans".[8] Sometimes pragmatism turns to tautology: for some authors, SSS includes any services which are not considered to be DSS, or "SSS refers to relatively short distances".[9]

Some authors focus on ships' characteristics. Crilley and Dean (1993) report that "Short-sea ships have often been defined as sea-going cargo-carrying ships (including passenger carriers) of less than 5,000 gt" (ships of less than 100 gt, non-propelled vessels and harbour or inland waterways services being not included).[10]

Van de Voorde and Viegas (1995) suggest that it would be better to define SSS in terms of trading patterns instead than ships characteristics, since a 100% exclusive use of ships for SSS or DSS is not practicable. Besides, they follow Linde (1993) on the idea that SSS "as a global phenomenon, means to a very large degree SSS in particular; in other words, coastal shipping in the larger European area, managed by European shipping companies".[11] While coastal shipping is defined by Bagchups and Kuipers (1993) as all forms of maritime transport within Europe and between Europe and adjacent regions, irrespective of whether it involves small ocean-going vessels, large ocean-going vessels or coasters.[12]

The European Commission (1992) defines "cabotage" as (a) carriage of passengers and goods by sea between ports situated on the mainland of one member state without call at islands (mainland cabotage), (b) offshore supply services, (c) services between ports of one member state where one or more ports are situated on islands (island cabotage).[13]

The European Conference of Ministers of Transport (ECMT, 2001) considers as SSS maritime transport which does not imply the crossing of a deep sea, coastal navigation and connection with island, and as cabotage international traffic where origin and destination ports are European, and European parts of transoceanic routes.[14]

These definitions involve further ambiguity, since SSS clearly has a broader meaning than cabotage, which seems to have a merely juridical meaning (based on state borders) instead of an economic one (potential competition between sea and land transport). So, we can conclude that so far there is no generally accepted definition of SSS. The reason for ambiguity is that different criteria are used for defining it, namely:

- geographical criteria (based on the length of maritime leg);
- supply criteria (based on type/size of vessels, or on being part of a longer journey);
- demand or commercial criteria (competition with land transport; distinction between feeder or intra-regional traffic; nature of cargo);
- juridical criteria (ports belonging to the same state).

Moreover, some definitions are tailored for a certain geographical space, or for a certain time and correspondent level of technical progress.[15]

1.3 The field of analysis

Unfortunately, the number and ambiguity of definitions imply non homogeneity of the (few) available data and statistics, that refer to one of the definitions. The number of definitions also implies some confusion in the scientific and technical debate. As Wijnolst et al. (1993) point out, statistics are often neither reliable nor consistent, since flows vary considerably according to the definition considered; definitions of import and export may also vary; and differences exist also in goods classification criteria.[16] Thus it seems quite useless choosing one existing definition or proposing an additional one, while it seems more useful to outline which are the two key points underlying the definition efforts.

One is certainly whether land transport is possible or sea transport has no alternatives (one or both ports being located in an island without tunnels or bridges connecting them). In this case we have a captive market with no or very little competition from other modes (air transport for passengers or some rich goods; pipelines for liquid bulks). If a land alternative exists, this sets a structural difference compared to DSS as for market organisation and "competition between substitutes" issues. The framework proposed in section 3 addresses this situation. The case for SSS competing with land transport is thus the most interesting for theoretical issues and for policies and future development.

The second key question is whether SSS is the main leg of a regional intermodal traffic, or the feeder traffic of a hub-and-spoke cycle based on DSS. While in infra-regional transport SSS introduces an intermodal option competing with land transport, in feeder traffic it is normally the opposite: the maritime hub-and-spoke cycle is a monomodal solution where SSS competes with land transport feeders (rail or road) which would set an intermodal transport. Most remarks proposed in this chapter apply to both cases. Yet the current debate and policy issues mainly refer to the opportunities of enhancing intermodality based on a SSS leg, while less interest is shown for SSS as a feeder traffic to DSS, unless this traffic can be alternatively supplied by SSS or by land transport.

2. FLEETS AND TRAFFIC: AN OVERVIEW

2.1 Fleets, cargoes, and the market organisation

The high number of journeys (of normally less than four days) makes management and organisation costs of SSS comparatively high, although cost structure is very different for feeder and intra-regional markets. In the first case costs are mainly vessel related: capital (or charter), operating and voyage costs. Overhead and administration costs are relatively small. As a consequence, feeder carrier rely mostly upon chartered vessels (with the exception of a few Asian carriers).[17] On the other side, the carrier involved in intra-regional intermodal SSS will bear high costs for handling cargo and providing land transport. Administrative overhead costs will also be higher.

Short-sea ships are normally much smaller than deep-sea ones (usually from 400 to 6000 dwt).[18] Ships are small since (i) demand is normally weak for SSS routes, and (ii) the high number of short journeys requires smaller ships in order not to spend too much time in port calls. Cargoes include bulk (generally dry), general cargo (container, wheeled vehicles, other), passengers. Multipurpose ships are about 67–72% of those used in SSS, and confirm a strong need for higher flexibility.

According to Hoogerbeets and Melissen (1993), European SSS can be divided into three main categories: the traditional single-deck bulk carriers, the container-feeder vessels and the ferries.[19] As Marlow *et al.* (1997) point out, SSS fleet is normally identifiable as a number of carriers with similar characteristics (SSS is usually performed by vessels up to a certain size and conversely vessels up to a certain size are usually deployed in SSS). Even if these parameters are likely to change significantly over time, they estimate that SSS include:

– tankers and bulk carriers up to 13,000 gt and/or 20,000 dwt;
– general cargo and break bulk carriers up to 10,000 gt and/or 10,000 dwt;
– combined passenger/cargo ships and RoRo between 1,000 gt and/or 500 dwt and 30,000 gt and/or 15,000 dwt.[20]

The ratio of dwt to gt shows, when below 1, that the fleet is mainly formed by passenger/cargo ferry and roro, what means a more domestic-oriented fleet. When above 1, it reveals a prevalence of tankers and dry cargo, and the fleet is oriented to international or coastal trade.

Market is mainly monomodal for bulk and intermodal for general cargo, usually with feeder traffic based on tonnage charters with one or more shippers, plus a certain spot demand.

Most markets are characterised by strong competition, given the contestability of each geographical segment of SSS, both between operators (within maritime transport) and between transport modes (with land and namely road transport).

Figures reported by ECMT[21] on ships which are supposed to be employed in SSS show that on a worldwide basis there seems to be a quite constant share of ships employed in SSS, as well as in terms of gt and dwt. A 1995 survey[22] estimates the 1992 SSS fleet as including 68.5% of the ships (57.3% in the European Union), 9.6% of gt (7.9% in the EU), 8.9% of dwt (6.7% in the EU), and an average gt of 1,319 (1,654 in the EU). The same survey shows for EU SSS fleet a prevalence of general cargo and, among specialised units, of liquid bulk carriers.

In the EU, in 1998, fleet "potentially employed in cabotage" (in practice: ships of less than 10,000 dwt) is:

- for the North European member states: 2,091 ships, 8,529 gt and 11,349 dwt;
- for the South European member states: 1,428 ships, 6,570 gt, 6,772 dwt.[23]

2.2 Some trends in traffic flows

Statistics do not allow the same level of information for all markets. Most data refer to containerised traffic, and namely to Asia and Europe. Yet a look at some data will help to better understand the market.

In the world market, SSS increased its importance over (at least) the last decade, due to a number of reason: the growth of feeder traffic as a result of growing deep-sea transport and of reducing port calls of DSS. So far, Asia and Europe have been the most relevant markets, but feeder trade will obviously follow developments in transhipment hubs, which are rapidly involving the Caribbean, Middle East and South America.

In container shipping, SSS is reported to be one of the most dynamic markets of the shipping industry, both in feeder traffic and intra-regional trade. In 1996, world container SSS traffic of over 15 million TEUs in feeder traffic, and 16 million TEUs in intra-regional trade, was reported. It was then expected to grow (at an average annual growth rate of 9.4% and 5.4%, respectively) to over 24 million TEUs and 21 million TEUs, in 2001.[24]

Since feeder traffic is a function of containerised trade *and* of transhipment, a growth of 800% from 1980 to 1996 has been estimated.[25] The geographical dispersion of origins and destinations for feeder flows is likely to cause different growth patterns in DSS (mainly based on the increase in ship size) and SSS (mainly based on the increase in number of ships, although their size is also increasing in most important regional markets). In 1996, intra-regional container traffic represented about one third of the total for SSS (18% Asia, 11% Europe, 3% North America, 1% Others). Asia and Europe market shares, respectively of 50.7% and 27.9% in 1996, were estimated at 52.6% and 25.4% for 2001.[26]

It is important to note that the relevant differences in the market size bring about relevant differences in the size of vessels and thus in costs, both for the economies of scale of the vessel and for the impact on average overhead costs.

In the European Union 70% of external trade and 30% of internal trade goes by sea. With the relevant exception of Greek islands, the internal market has been liberalised since Jan.1st, 1999.[27]

In Europe there is a stronger competition with land transport, both for feeder and intra-regional traffic. Channel ports are facing overcapacity due to competition by the Channel Tunnel, while the opening of road haulage to Eastern European firms provides low cost alternatives to both shipping and railways. This resulted in a fall of freight rates squeezing profitability of SSS industry. Negative trends mainly concern traffic to/from British Islands, while the Baltic Area and especially the Mediterranean market are still experiencing a significant growth. Bremerhaven and Hamburg concentrate major transhipment flows and feeder traffic from Scandinavian and Baltic countries (which also are experiencing a growth in international trade due to the transition to market economy). Mediterranean takes advantage of the growing traffic in major transhipment hubs (transhipment has almost reached the volumes of Northern Europe – around 6 millions TEUs, while it was half of Northern Europe in early '90s).

In Asia the fast growth and low elasticity of demand due to scarce or no competition from land transport explains the fast growth of SSS namely in the container sector, based on big hubs such as Singapore, Port Klang, Hong Kong and Pusan, and recently Kaohsiung.

2.3 Short sea shipping and modal split

An analysis of market shares for SSS and land transport makes sense in the European arena, as competition with land transport is higher due to geographical reasons and to the comparatively highly developed land transport infrastructure. The geographical and economic conditions for this competition are modelled in section 3.

Both SSS and road transport have been expanding over the last 30 years. Yet, as traffic flows constantly increase (a 37% growth of freight transport within EU is expected from 1995 to 2010[28]), the share of road transport is growing, while investments in infrastructure do not.

In terms of tonne-kms, market shares intra-EU traffic are similar (sea: 40.4%; road: 44.5%), but they were respectively 35.3% and 30.8% in 1970. In international traffic SSS has by far the largest share (69% against 18%), since average journeys are much longer in SSS (1,385 km, against 100 km for road), but only 6% of total tonnes transported in the EU are carried by SSS, while road transport carries over 80%, mostly over short distances.[29]

Also, SSS grows less than road transport (in tonne-kms, +30% from 1990 to 1999, at an average annual rate of +2.9%, against +41% in road transport, at an average annual rate of +3.9%[30]). Growth in SSS is mainly due to increasing containerised cargo: +44% over the years 1993-1997, against a 16% average growth of SSS.[31]

Obviously, the share of maritime transport is higher in traffic between EU and adjacent regions: in import, 61% from EFTA countries, 47% from other European countries, 74% from North Africa (in export 40%, 76% and 91% respectively).[32] While at the whole European level, 1995 internal traffic is estimated at 908 millions tonnes, with shares of sea, road and rail at 30%, 41% and 6% respectively.[33]

As for competition with land transport, it seems that Lo-Lo container traffic has the major potential, since it allows low vessels costs per unit, although with possible higher terminal costs and/or times.

The considerable difference between the average distances of a tonne carried by SSS (1,385 km) and by road (100 km)[34] leads to the conclusion that markets for SSS and road are partly separate. Since about 90% of freights are transported on short distances and usually within national borders, the potential for SSS seems to be not so high unless the threshold for competitiveness with road transport is considerably shortened. This issue represents one of the critical issues in recent EU transport policy, as also the 2001 White Paper points out.[35]

3. GEOGRAPHIC AND ECONOMIC CONDITIONS FOR DEVELOPING SHORT SEA SHIPPING: A THEORETICAL FRAMEWORK

3.1 Introduction

Maritime transport is normally part of a transport cycle involving other transport modes. The maritime leg can also be a complex cycle, when organised on a hub-and-spoke basis, involving ships of different size in order to attain economies of scale/density on some routes. Since the goal is to attain the cheapest, fastest and most reliable transport conditions (i.e., to minimise the generalised cost), the demand for sea transport is related to the generalised cost of the whole transport cycle.

The framework proposed here considers jointly geographic and economic conditions involved in the mode choice, and identifies the critical thresholds in land/sea distances and land/sea generalised costs which determine a potential competitiveness for SSS. In a microeconomic approach, we consider generalised costs, and the result explains the user's choice; while in a macroecomic approach, total costs (including infrastructure and external costs) are considered, and the results will be in terms of general utility.

3.2 The rationale

The framework applies either to the case of a SSS intermodal chain competing with land transport, or to feeder traffic for DSS. If SSS replaces a part of a journey otherwise performed by a single vehicle, the additional modal change implies higher generalised costs. Total time increases, while reliability, punctuality and safety are jeopardised by bottlenecks, congestion, mistakes, damages. These costs are compensated by savings that different modes/vehicles allow in the different part of the journey, because of changing cargo volumes and economies of scale/density. SSS is chosen when the optimisation of modes/vehicles on the different legs generates benefits higher than the additional transhipment costs.

The boost of intermodality over the last 30 years is due both to increasing benefits and decreasing transhipment costs, as:

- the growth of world trade allowed economies of scale not conceivable before, also because production functions are more capital intensive and involve relevant fixed costs;
- new handling techniques reduced costs, times and risks of transhipment.

3.3 Conditions for SSS and critical thresholds

In both key areas (feeder traffic and intermodal traffic competing with land transport) a simple cycle is replaced by a complex one. Unlike SSS captive markets, where there is no user's choice and the goal is to minimise generalised costs of modal change, here SSS is chosen if it allows generalised benefits higher than the generalised costs of additional transhipments.

An approach à la Hoover[36] accounts for different terminal and haulage costs of different modes, which cause different costs per mile. Thus, different modes have a different competitiveness for different distances, and therefore different markets. Road transport has low terminal costs but relatively high line haul costs, sea transport has high (generalised) terminal costs but comparatively lower transport costs. Rail has intermediate levels for both terminal and transport costs. Since terminal costs do not vary with distance, road transport will be cheaper on shorter journeys, and sea transport on the longer ones. Such a framework points out conditions for competitiveness of SSS. We now consider the case of SSS as main leg of an intra-regional transport, competing with land transport. The approach is similar if we consider feeder traffic.

In Figure 1 a journey OD is considered, where in the central leg AB both road and sea transport are available, while only road transport is available in OA and BD. The function a shows total transport cost if only road haulage is chosen.

Figure 1

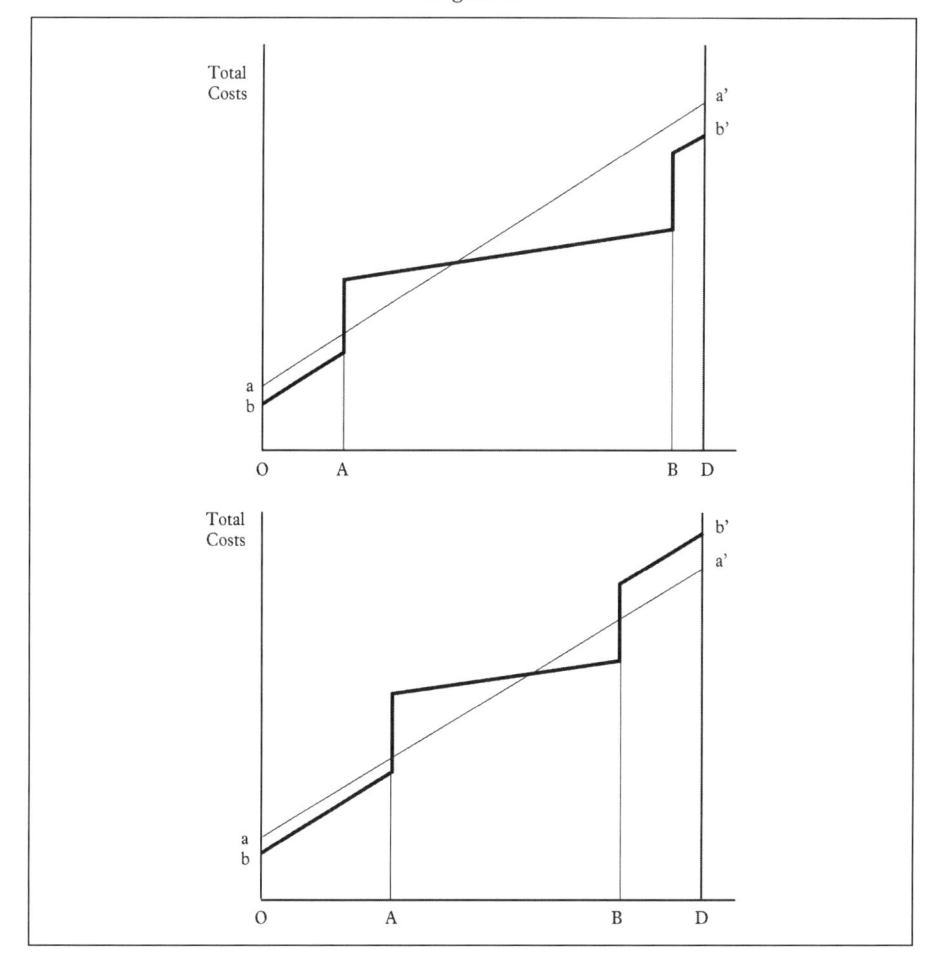

The function b shows the cost of transport using SSS in the central leg. While modal change costs are added in A and in B, a lower cost is paid on the leg AB. SSS is then advantageous when AB is long enough to compensate higher terminal costs.

Unless O, A, B and D are aligned, Figure 1 only accounts for economic conditions, not for geographic conditions for competition. To find out the combination of economic (transport and terminal costs) and geographic variables (land and intermodal distances) which jointly account for SSS competitiveness, we compare a land transport OD by mode m_1 (e.g., road haulage) and an alternative $OABD$ based on mode m_1 for OA and BD and on SSS indicated as mode m_2 for AB. Ports A and B are not aligned with OD.

If T is the transhipment generalised cost in ports; t_{m_1}, t_{m_2} transport rates per mile of a given cargo unit; and C and S terminal costs in O and D; then total transport costs are

$$C + t_{m_1} \cdot OD + S \qquad (1)$$

for road transport OD, and

$$C + t_{m_1} \cdot OA + T + t_{m_2} \cdot AB + T + t_{m_1} \cdot BD + S \qquad (2)$$

for intermodal transport $OABD$. The competitiveness of the latter is then given by **(1) > (2)**:

$$t_{m_1} \cdot (OD - OA - BD) - t_{m_2} \cdot AB - 2T > 0 \qquad (3)$$

If x is the maritime distance between ports A and B, and y is the difference between road distance OD and feeder road legs OA and BD of SSS transport, equation **(3)** can be written as:

$$y > \frac{t_{m_2}}{t_{m_1}} \cdot x + \frac{2T}{t_{m_1}} \qquad (4)$$

setting the combination of geographic and economic conditions for competitiveness of SSS, as in Figure 2. Each journey OD identify a set of (x, y) satisfying or not the condition in equation **(4)**, according to transhipment costs, and rates per mile in m_2 and m_1. Obviously the competitiveness increases by reducing T or t_{m_2}, or by increasing t_{m_1}.

A key point is that if m_2 allows more relevant economies of scale than m_1, as is normally the case for short-sea compared to road transport, the increase in traffic flows reduces the slope of equation **(4)**, thus increasing competitiveness of the former.

This is just a joint representation of geographic and economic conditions which make viable a SSS-based alternative to land transport. The approach *à la* Hoover allows to find out the "economic distance" of each transport mode, since:
 – terminal and transport costs weight differently in different modes;
 – costs in different modes are a function of cargoes and cargo units characteristics;
 – reducing terminal costs in ports lowers the threshold distance for SSS, as it moves downwards in equation **(4)**;
 – higher returns to scale in SSS cause a growth in traffic to reduce SSS threshold distance, by a rotation of equation **(4)**.

ECONOMICS OF SHORTSEA SHIPPING

Figure 2

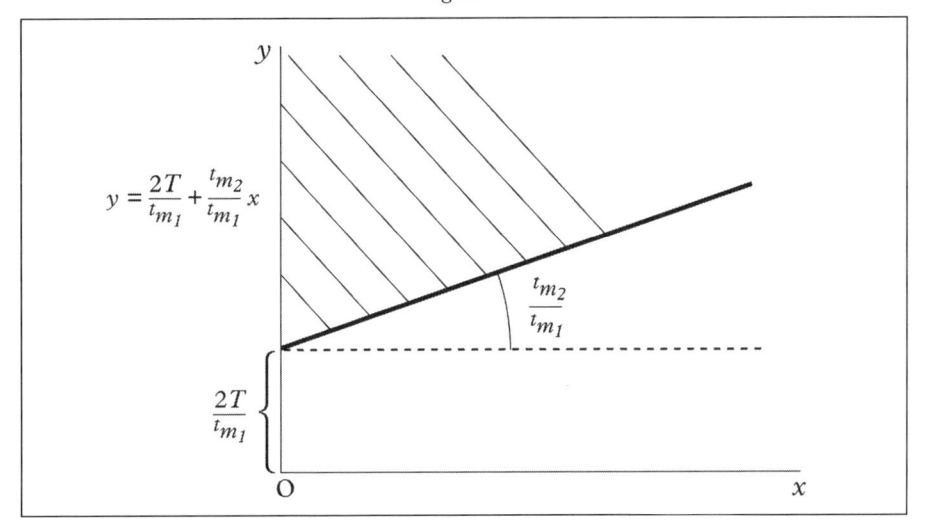

$$y = \frac{2T}{t_{m_1}} + \frac{t_{m_2}}{t_{m_1}} x$$

$\frac{t_{m_2}}{t_{m_1}}$

$\frac{2T}{t_{m_1}}$

Thus, the economic competitiveness of SSS rely upon the contemporaneous occurrence of the following conditions:
(1) cargo volumes involved cause "pure" transport costs for sea transport lower than for road transport;
(2) different origins and/or destinations don't allow to employ the sole maritime transport (cargo volumes don't fulfil the condition 1);
(3) distances involved are longer than the threshold distances for sea transport;
(4) origins/destinations of single shipments allow the unification of parcels on some legs in order to satisfy condition 1;
(5) lower generalised costs of using the best transport mode on each leg are higher than additional generalised costs deriving from transhipment.

When referred to SSS as feeder traffic, different returns to scale account for the hub-and-spoke organisation. Limits to economies of scale are now on the demand side, and increasing returns to scale can be pursued only by grouping cargoes on the main leg. Volumes and costs per mile being equal, the longest is the main leg *AB*, the most competitive is the hub-and-spoke solution using SSS. Conditions 1, 2 and 5 will be here referred to thresholds for ships of different sizes. Condition 5 will refer to transhipment from SSS to DSS.

As for competition between SSS and road transport for the feeder service, since a haulage feeder service is normally needed for the final part of the journey, the comparison is between savings allowed by maritime feeder and costs of an additional transhipment (from the feeder to the deep-sea ship), that is

$$(t_{m_1} - t_{m_2}) \cdot OA - T > 0 \qquad (5)$$

The same conditions apply, since there are combined effects of economic distance, size of shipments and location of origins/destinations. This approach outlines the conditions that make SSS competitive, even when not forced by geographical (or, in the short run, infrastructural) constraints. The same framework applies to both main current strategic areas of SSS: an intermodal transport competing with land transport, or a feeder traffic competing with road/rail feeders.

As already noted, this framework allows both a microeconomic and a macroeconomic approach, with different implications. In the former, short term generalised cost (given the infrastructure) account for behaviour of transport operators and consequent modal split. In the latter, total direct and external long run costs (including infrastructure and energy) account for a macroeconomic comparison, resulting in a cost-benefit assessment which pursues a higher welfare.

3.4 A remark on generalised costs

In its microeconomic approach, the proposed framework refers to generalised, not to out-of-pocket costs. Generalised costs correspond to production costs only in perfect competition. In freight transport, shippers happen not to decide transport mode nor route, and multimodal transport operators (MTOs) are likely to choose modes/routes according to *their* convenience. Monopoly, or collusion between providers (e.g., due to horizontal and vertical integration of the supply chain) can cause a substitution between time and cost, reducing costs and increasing times without (or with little) reduction of prices for shippers.

The case for passenger transport is different, since users directly choose the mix of modes by comparing the generalised cost of each solution. Their preference will thus account for their choice. It is probably no accident that intermodality is barely chosen unless forced by geographical constraints or by huge savings in monetary costs, or unless other options are totally congested or restricted.

In other words, intermodality allows increasing productivity, but may cause a decreasing quality (for the cargo, not necessarily for the vehicle) with higher time and lower reliability, punctuality and safety. If there is not a high level of competition this trade off may encompass a transfer of costs from the producer to the consumer. The market organisation is then crucial for the benefits to spread on the demand side, allowing higher accessibility of regional markets, specialisation of production, and cumulative growth of regions involved.

4. FACTORS INFLUENCING THE COMPETITIVENESS OF SSS

According to section 3, the more SSS will be competitive:
(1) the more substantial reduction in generalised port costs is attained;
(2) the longer is the maritime leg with respect to the total length of the journey;
(3) the higher is the ratio of y to x in **(4)**;
(4) the bigger are cargo volumes;
(5) the higher is the ratio of land transport generalised costs to sea transport ones.

Besides these key issues, some additional remarks are worthwhile.

First, the growing importance of ports and their performance/efficiency involves not only efficient modal change and handling, but also efficient logistic and distribution functions. Choices concerning number and location of ports and logistic platforms on which the SSS network will hinge are strategic, since they pursue the optimal trade off between economies of density, pushing for concentration of flows which reduce the ratio t_{m_2}/t_{m_1} in equation (4); and minimisation of road feeders, pushing for dispersion of flows which cause higher values of y and positively affects equation (4). Case-by-case search for optimal equilibrium is a major operational research issue, and a key issue for SSS development strategies.

It is notable that virtually all issues highlighted – threshold distances, demand volumes and their origin/destinations, returns to scale in competing modes, number and location of intermodal nodes, etc. – have been addressed so far in a largely empirical way, frustrating most of the potential of SSS. There has been no strategy at all, and SSS nodes have followed, at best, strategies of big transport operators.

Another point implicit in condition (4) is that implementing SSS should not result in fragmentation and complications of relations between shippers and transport operators, difficulties in organising and controlling the logistic chain, problems arising from liabilities, damages or losses, etc.. This means that implementing SSS requires the integrated management of the entire SSS-based logistic chain. Risk is, on one side, that economies of scale/scope related to the management of the whole logistic cycle can set relevant barriers to entry, issue of alliances and co-operation strategies. On the other side, if the control of the chain is taken up outside the maritime link, this may squeeze profitability and limit operational control of SSS operator, who faces, in a door-to-door cycle, relevant fixed costs, and does not enjoy any spatial "protection" of its market, thus coupling high competition and low profitability. Moreover, by operating on one link of the chain, there is no influence/control on the quality of the door-to-door service, and no control on key factors influencing the demand, since comparison between SSS and competing modes requires that the whole cycles are compared.

The above mentioned factors, although not explicitly modelled in the proposed approach, are likely to influence deeply the cost elements of the (4), which can vary with high levels of uncertainty, not proportionally to distance, and change rapidly over time.

5. IMPLEMENTING SHORT SEA SHIPPING: PROS AND CONS

Any further development of SSS will necessarily rely upon its possible microeconomic competitiveness (in terms of generalised costs), more than upon its macroeconomic desirability. Yet, since most researcher and policy makers agree on the need of enhancing SSS, it is useful to resume a checklist of main benefits and costs from the macroeconomic and political viewpoint.

Benefits can be summarised as follows:
- low environmental costs: it generates much less emissions per tonne-km than road and rail transport, as shown in Table 1.

Table 1: Polluting emissions (grams for tonne/km)

Polluting emission	Road	Rail	Sea
Carbon monoxide CO	0.5	0.2	0.04
Carbon dioxide[37] CO_2	98	28	15
Hydrocarbon HC	0.2	0.1	0.01
Nitrogen oxide NO_x	1	0.5	0.3
Sulphur dioxide SO_2	0.03	0.04	0.3
Particulate	0.08	0.03	0.006

Source: Eurostat Trends Project

- less accidents, namely for human life safety: 96% of all transport fatalities occur in road accidents; in EU there are 40,000 losses of life per year due to road accidents, 115 in rail transport, 140 in maritime transport (the world average being of 709 per year). The death rate in sea transport (including crew) is 1.4 deaths per 100 millions passenger-kms (against 100 for road and 40 for rail)[38];
- lowering congestion of land transport networks;
- low energy consumption;
- larger economies of scale;
- higher flexibility of transport costs to shifts in demand, and low need for new infrastructure;
- more competitive environment than for (rather monopolistic) land transport networks;
- advantages for maritime economy and namely for shipyards;
- development of peripherals and isolated regions (of difficult or impossible access with other transport modes), and enhanced competitiveness of hinterlands economies facing international markets.

On the minus side, the development of SSS also brings about some disadvantages, such as:
- partial increase of pollution: unlike other emissions, sulphur dioxide (SO_2) emissions are much higher than in other modes (see above);
- partial increase of accidents, namely with major environmental damages;
- congestion in port nodes;
- negative impact on other transport sectors, as well as on the industry of infrastructure construction and related sectors;
- low flexibility in service times, due to larger unit capacity and consequent lower frequency of service for any O/D link;
- lower reliability of scheduled departure and arrival times (mainly due to weather conditions);
- higher risk of damages and loss.

It is not certain *a priori* that the comparison between costs and benefits is always positive, even if most policy makers consider costs largely exceeded by benefits. Nevertheless, some points should be highlighted:

(1) As for environmental effects, the balance is likely to be positive, since SO_2 higher emissions can be reduced (see section 6). Nevertheless, nobody can extrapolate this statement on a long term, as no forecasts on future levels of polluting emissions are highly reliable, namely for land transport, where a major research effort is being done to attain environmentally friendly propulsion systems;

(2) As for congestion of transport infrastructure, the congestion of land transport network is clearly more damaging and less remediable, for the economy as a whole, than the congestion of existing port nodes.

(3) Under the point of view of economic effects, namely in total production costs of transport, clearly the lower flexibility of land transport costs is replaced by a lower flexibility in transit times and a lower punctuality; there is a trade off between quality and cost, and the effects on demand are likely to be different for different segments of the market (as for types of cargoes and cargo units), due to different values of price-elasticity and time-elasticity.

(4) As for macroeconomic "keynesian" impact, the replacement of a demand in land transport and infrastructure construction with a demand in maritime transport, shipyards and port infrastructure construction, needs to be carefully investigated and quantified; yet it does not appear a reason to stop a possible change if otherwise desirable.

Even if case-by-case assessments and surveys can lead to results sometimes different, it seems acceptable that in a macroeconomic vision SSS should develop further, and that policies aiming at implementing it are consequently well founded.

6. SOME POSSIBLE POLICIES

If previous paragraphs showed that some conditions influencing SSS are given (on the geographical side, land and sea distances; as for demand, the nature of cargoes, and, to some extent, their volumes), most other elements influencing competitiveness of SSS can be changed through suitable policies.

Nevertheless, it must be clear that what jeopardises the competitiveness of SSS is the "unfair competition" played by land transport, namely road haulage, in terms of much higher environmental costs, and much higher public financing of infrastructure. Strictly speaking, equalising environmental and fiscal externalities of all transport modes should be the ultimate goal of any policy aiming at a fair modal split (and not simply at the growth of SSS, which might well be not desirable). As a consequence, first best policies "for SSS" do not concern necessarily SSS, but should focus on internalising major external costs of land transport.

Remembering that, we can look at the framework outlined in sections 3–4 in order to find out actions aiming at enhancing SSS, which can apply to different areas. First, ports are a key node for the effectiveness of SSS, since port costs reach up to 70% of SSS total costs.[39] Actions listed afterwards should increase fluidity of transit in ports, reliability and on time delivery, by minimising quality components of generalised cost.

Secondly, comparisons between transport rates highlight two areas where positive actions can be deployed: internalising all costs following the "user pays" principle, or at least equalise the level of external costs. These actions, namely if they involve infrastructure, turn to land use/planning policies, developed either for optimising transport performance, or for reinforcing the cohesion and economic proximity of different regional economies.

Finally, policies can involve the transport industry and providers of transport services, by inducing changes both into the market and technical/industrial organisation, and on cargoes and shippers' organisation. Policies and actions appear to fall into six main strategic areas:

1. Infrastructure policies: addressing both planning/construction and location of infrastructure influencing competitiveness of SSS. Main actions are:

- improvement of ports to the needs of SSS, namely widening space for SSS traffic (most present terminals would be inadequate if SSS attracted relevant traffic flows), and implementation of dedicated terminals/areas;
- improvement of handling plants in ports, namely through a further diffusion of containerisation in SSS;
- enhancement of port accessibility and connections between ports and land networks (road and rail); since competition between road and rail has been estimated around 170-250 km,[40] connections with rail networks are crucial for expanding ports' market areas;
- development of inland waterways and promotion of a better balanced modal split between land transport and inland waterways, whose integration with SSS is easier and more efficient than for land transport.

2. Law and regulations: aiming at enhancing competition to increase the efficiency and attract further investment; and at eliminating distortions caused by excess of regulations for SSS, and lack of environmental regulations (or of their enforcement) on road transport. Main action should include measures aiming at:

- liberalising access to market, namely abolishing flag reservations on domestic traffic;
- integrating bureaucratic (customs/administrative) procedures in order to simplify/reduce difficulties and times;
- equalising external costs;
- integrating different contracts and liabilities;
- regulating port services and their input, thus allowing a higher efficiency of port operations.

3. Commercial actions: addressing the perception of SSS as an obsolete, not transparent, and not suitable for present needs of production and logistics, with low flexibility, reliability, frequency, speed. Measures needed include:

- restoring the image of SSS from that of an old-fashioned, slow and complex transport mode to a modern element in the logistic chain, characterised by high speed, reliability, flexibility, regularity, frequency, and cargo safety;

- information aimed at restoring trust; logistic operators and shipowners should fight *for* market transparency and to promote information on conditions of supply[41];
- specific information on safety (see section 6) helping to promote a positive image.

4. *Organisational actions and policies*: involving either the industrial or the technical organisation in the aim of reorganising SSS-related operators. Such actions should:

- reorganise and allow a better modal integration to fulfil requirements of just-in-time and compensate the additional breaks of bulk; frequency and reliability of scheduled times are the key issues, so 24/7 port services are needed, as well as a better organisation of storage/distribution areas;
- stimulate co-operation of SSS operators with shippers and forwarders in order to supply comprehensive networks and door-to-door services at competitive prices, thus integrating the strengths of different modes into seamless customer-oriented services. Either SSS operators need partners to carry out the land legs of intermodal chain, or land operators must be ready to use SSS for a relevant part of their journeys;
- concentrate SSS flows on a limited number of ports, in order to achieve higher economies of density and provide more frequent services; possibly locate them close to major metropolitan areas in order to be more competitive in delivery times;
- promote specialisation of terminals and alliances between port operators;
- promote concentration in road haulage industry, in order to incentive road-SSS intermodal journeys which are more competitive for non accompanied trailers;
- promote standardisation of cargo units (e.g., "europallets" do not allow a standard ISO1 maritime container to be filled with two rows of pallets) in order to reduce costs of modal change;
- locate value-added services (VAS) in SSS ports, in order to better integrate port functions with logistical service provided by forwarders and MTOs.

5. *Pricing policies*: since quality component of generalised cost is comparatively high, SSS must be cheaper in monetary costs.[42] Some possible price-based actions are:

- compensating lower quality (higher times for ships and cargoes) by lower prices; Pettersen Strandenes and Marlow (2000) suggest a two-parts port tariff partly related to port stay and waiting time: prices inversely related to quality should enhance competitiveness of SSS and incentive port operators to improve quality[43];
- pricing policies promoting fair competition between transport modes by: charging for the cost of building infrastructure in all modes (the "user pays" principle); harmonising financing and pricing policies in different ports; internalising external costs, particularly in road haulage;

- lowering port taxes (which, unlike pricing for using infrastructure, does not correspond to a real recovery of production cost) in order to attain indirectly the same results.

6. *Technological actions*: age and the low specialisation of SSS ships are consequences, rather than causes, of low profitability. Higher investments in new ships and R&D, and generally in technological advance, are needed. Some useful action can be:

- development of high speed ships, to reduce the gap with road in terms of time; even if competition between faster and more expensive road haulage and a slower and cheaper SSS rely solely on the value of time for the user;
- new vessels and advanced flexible ship designs to better integrate SSS (namely with high speed ships) within logistic chains;
- harmonisation of standards for information and communication technologies (ICT) and development of "community systems" to reduce costs of information input;
- harmonisation of standards concerning cargo units (see above), to achieve higher occupancy rates and highly or fully automated handling techniques;
- research reducing polluting emissions of ships, like SO_2, namely by lowering the sulphur content in bunker fuel oils or equipping the ships with exhaust gas cleaning systems.[44]

7. POLICIES: THE CASE OF EUROPE

Bearing in mind what we said at the beginning of section 6, it must be stressed that, so far, little or no effective policies have been implemented, in order to establish fair competition between transport modes.

Although not really effective so far, some important documents providing guidelines, as well as minor policies concerning development of SSS have been produced mainly by the European Union, or by individual EU member states.

Europe is geographically suitable for SSS, although infrastructure networks are pretty much developed. In recent years the EU Commission set out a strategy to restore competitiveness of EU fleets. As an environmentally friendlier alternative to road transport, SSS must be integrated into the logistic chain, its links with other modes must be improved, the quality of service must be closer to the customer's needs. Port installations should be organised such that they can match better the requirements of SSS. In June 1999 the Commission adopted a communication[45] stating that SSS needs to become a "genuine intermodal door-to-door concept", an essential element in its development being the integration in European logistic chains. It must fulfil the users' requirements and be perceived, through a new dynamic image, to fulfil them.

The reasons for enhancing SSS in the EU are:
- promoting the general sustainability and safety of transport, by providing an alternative to congested road transport, also in order to reach CO_2 target under the Kyoto Protocol;

- strengthening the cohesion of the community, facilitating connections between member states and European regions, and revitalising peripherals regions;
- increasing the efficiency of transport in order to meet current and future demand arising from economic growth.

According to the Commission, firms should integrate SSS into door-to-door services, and networks with other modes and parties in the supply chain should be created to attract cargo. Actions towards standardisation/simplification in administrative procedures of member states are needed, and ports are encouraged to promote SSS within their commercial strategies.

Within EU policy guidelines, some general transport policies have consequences on SSS, while other policies are specifically oriented to implementing SSS. Among the former (*transport policies*), the liberalisation of domestic transport markets,[46] which allows free access to EU operators in cabotage transport of all member states (apart from Greece until 2004) is the most relevant concrete action, and caused higher competition at lower prices.

Among general transport policies, other guidelines are potentially relevant to SSS:
- infrastructure planning: the Trans European Transport Network (TEN-T) approved in 1996[47] are a tool to enhance the domestic market and perspectives of enlargement of EU: ports, originally not included in the TEN-T framework, have been subsequently integrated[48];
- harmonisation/liberalisation processes: they should increase the efficiency in all transport modes, proportionally more for those less liberalised so far (such as rail and sea transport), compared to road haulage;
- inland waterways liberalisation: it should help SSS as a link of the intermodal chain;
- equitable behaviours in the field of environment and safety;
- regulations on infrastructure financing and pricing: they should limit distortions favouring road transport and push for a fair competition between transport modes.

Some also argue that policies enhancing rail transport can help intermodalism based on SSS. Actually, it seems that once rail transport is improved, either by opening access to railways systems (according EU Directive n.440/1991, which is now being implemented in most member states), or by developing policies which harmonise technical standards and simplify administrative/custom procedures (the case of the 17 "rail freeways" recommended by the Commission in the 1996 White Paper,[49] which moreover are established on port-to-port routes, such as Rotterdam-Gioia Tauro, or North Germany – East Italy), the new potential for railway traffic will directly compete with SSS in intermodal transport. Since a final road haulage feeding is likely to be necessary, it seems that in very few cases, on a European geographical scale, there might be the conditions for developing an intermodal cycle based both on rail *and* maritime transport.

But as a matter of fact rail intermodalism is probably the most difficult to enhance, at least for unitised freight, since it requires high investments, an extensive commercial organisation, and harmonisation between different technical standards. It can be noted that, after German reunification, former DDR rail traffic shifted significantly to road, showing that in terms of market competition, and given present regulations on external costs, road haulage fits better to the shippers' requirements. On the other side, other political and environmental options, such as the goal of reducing road congestion and external costs of road haulage, are clearly able to positively influence the market for SSS.

As for *maritime transport and/or ports policies*, the need for developing SSS is already stated in 1992 White Paper on "the future development of the common transport policy",[50] while 1995 Commission Communication on "Short Sea Shipping in Europe – a dynamic alternative in a sustainable transport chain"[51] highlights the need for port policies concerning infrastructure, information/communication technologies, and their inclusion in the TEN-T.

The 1997 Green Paper on ports and maritime infrastructure[52] also urges for links between ports and TEN-T, enhancement of ports' role in the intermodal chain, development of SSS, transparency of prices, and states a strategy based on the "user pays" principle. In 1999 the second two-yearly progress report on 1995 Communication[53] underlines that turnaround delays, infrastructure constraints and non-transparent charges are a relevant problem for SSS. It also suggests that:
- ports should consider to set up dedicated short-sea terminals in larger ports and providing other specialised services to SSS;
- obligations in some ports to use separate pilots could be re-examined where the ship's master is certified to carry out the pilotage on his own;
- administrative procedures should be standardised and simplified, since documentation required in SSS is more than for road transport; improvements are possible namely in a uniform acceptance of IMO FAL forms, delegation of tasks to one authority or to a third part, permission to start unloading ships before reporting procedures have been finalised, increased use of Electronic Data Interchange;
- incentives to research aiming at reducing polluting emissions of ships are recommended.

Finally, the entire strategy underlying 2001 White Paper "European transport policy for 2010: time to decide"[54] is based on the need of "shifting the balance between modes" since the growth of road transport caused high congestion and environmental costs. A specific chapter is dedicated to "Developing 'motorways of the sea'", where it is stressed once more that SSS is a real alternative to land transport, and that:
- certain shipping links, providing a way around major bottlenecks in land transport networks, should be made part of the TEN-T;
- regulated competition in ports must be implemented, through clearer rules for access to the port service market[55];
- rules governing operation of ports must be simplified;
- "one-stop shops" should be created to bring together all links in the logistics chain (consignors, shipowners, shipping, road, rail and inland waterways operators);

– advanced telematic services in ports should be developed in order to improve operational reliability and safety.

Also the European Council of Ministers of Transport (ECMT) underlines the well-known and already mentioned problems in developing SSS (costs and times of ports nodes, inadequate intermodal integration, complexity of procedures, costs of the additional breaks of bulks, lack of transparency, inadequacy to requirements of just-in-time). SSS is regarded as a key factor of European economic cohesion[56] and proximity between regions, namely between West and East Europe. ECMT highlights the importance of setting rules for a fair competition between transport modes, through infrastructure pricing and financing, and internalisation of external costs.[57]

8. CONCLUDING REMARKS

Short-sea shipping has reached a high development in the world, namely in South East Asia and Europe. A significant share of traffic is concentrated around internal seas (Baltic, Mediterranean/Black Sea, South-East Asia, Gulf of Mexico). Its growth is mainly related to captive markets caused by geographic/infrastructure constraints, or by feeder traffic for hub-and-spoke deep-sea transport. SSS can hardly compete with land transport, namely road haulage, when both land and sea links are available between origin and destination.

Nevertheless, this business area is precisely the most important one for policy makers facing the problems of growing congestion and high environmental and infrastructure costs of land transport. Thus, a wide interest rises about critical factors in competition between SSS and land transport. As shown in sections 3–4, low competitiveness is sometimes due to geographic characteristics (too short distances between origin and destination, a bad ratio of maritime distance to land transport distance) or to demand characteristics (types of goods, volumes, etc.). Yet, low competitiveness is often due to "supply" factors – concerning either SSS or competing modes – on which it is possible and desirable to intervene, since they do not come from a fair competition between modes, rather from imbalances in costs of different modes, namely:
– external costs;
– infrastructure costs, pricing and subsidisation;
– transaction costs due to conditions outside the market (e.g., administrative/custom regulations, etc.).

Thus, actions are being planned by a few states, where the domestic market is more relevant, or by international organisations (like EU), and efforts are being undertaken by experts and policy makers, in order to remove distortions to fair competition between modes, or at least to attain a more balanced modal split. Proposed measures range within those outlined in section 6, including infrastructural, organisational, pricing, commercial, regulatory and technological guidelines aiming at:
– ensure fluid transit of goods in ports;

- integrate SSS in the intermodal logistic chain;
- draw generalised costs as near as possible to the real cost of transport (including external costs, energy and infrastructure), equalising the level of cost externalisation in the different modes, through both internalisation of environmental costs and financing of infrastructure.

Yet, so far, researchers and policy makers just agreed, with little exceptions, that developing SSS is desirable. But effective actions are still far from been implemented.

A few further remarks about changing scenarios might be useful to assess the potential effectiveness of future policies.

(1) The huge outsourcing of logistic functions shows that logistics, while remaining highly strategic for firms, become more and more specialised. Its complexity in the era of globalisation requires higher quality and efficiency in transport activities. The need for distribution networks and the consequent, relevant scale/networks economies should be favourable to SSS only if it is able to fulfil higher and higher requirements in terms of quality standards (speed, punctuality, reliability). Otherwise, the need for speedy door-to-door, just-in-time services will be better matched by road haulage, despite higher transport costs per unit. Transport monetary costs are just a (small) part of the overall logistic cost, what makes it difficult to attract traffic flows on a low price basis.[58] The strategic role of logistics implies that the quality elasticity of the demand (for logistic/transport services) is much higher than price elasticity. The outsourcing of logistic functions can be for SSS either an opportunity or a threat.

(2) In the global market, control of logistic flows has become a crucial competitive advantage. Transport is part of a set of services that must match the logistic needs of the shippers. Network economies influence the geographic organisation of logistic operators. This means that potential for SSS is also related to the ability of ports to act not only as transhipment sites but as nodes of value-added services and logistic functions. The integration of a port within a (infrastructure and service) network becomes more important than the traditional concept of port hinterland. A proactive role of ports in integrating different links of logistic chains clearly becomes a key issue for SSS.

(3) With fair competition between modes, there would be opportunities for a further growth of SSS, since its overall costs are comparatively low. The goal must be internalising both environmental and infrastructure costs in the prices paid by the users ("user pays" principle).

Higher care for environment may lead to policies on road transport which will make the ratio of costs for users more favourable to maritime transport, so that relevant flows would shift from road to sea, starting from dangerous goods. Yet, the ongoing research is producing significant results in reducing pollution and noise and increasing safety of road transport. It is then not sure that road transport will still be so little sustainable as it has been so far.

Dire straits in public finance of most developed countries (which normally have both a developed infrastructure network, *and* high levels of public expenditure for social/welfare issues) should result in lower public aids to infrastructure financing. Besides, improving land networks becomes more and more difficult also for territorial and environmental problems. The growing rigidity and cost of transport infrastructure is thus a major opportunity for developing SSS (apart for the need of increasing port capacity). Regulations on infrastructure public financing and pricing should limit present inequalities.

(4) Too much attention may have been paid on competitiveness of SSS compared to road haulage. In the next future not only SSS-based intermodality will compete with road transport, but also rail-based intermodality, namely with the development of high-speed railways. So that SSS and rail could be direct competitors, unlike today where low competitiveness of rail is due to technologic and managerial backwardness. Also, international integration, namely in the EU context, could promote easier procedures and techniques in land transport (harmonisation of railways technologies and standards, development of rail freeways). It may be meaningful that among new intermodal technologies which are being developed in order to reduce costs and times of transit in intermodal nodes, most are tailored on road-rail intermodality (swapbodies, piggyback, bimodalism) and only a few ones can help SSS-based intermodality (e.g., palletwide containers).

(5) It has been shown that contestability of SSS market is crucial. Strictly speaking, the market appears to be contestable since there are no barriers to entry or to exit, and incursions are possible from new entrants operating on other SSS routes (less from DSS because of different ships' size). Thus, liberalisation should be desirable. Yet within logistic networks contestability can be jeopardised by operators with dominant position on the whole chain.[59] Big maritime carriers influence more and more intermodal networks, ports and logistic platforms at the regional/continental level. Vertical integration may give, namely in the feeder traffic, a low level of competition, which could spread on the infra-regional SSS market, because of probable economies of scope. Also, vertical integration of supply chains will require alliances/mergers between SSS operators and other carrier or terminal operators.

(6) It is presently highly uncertain if the elasticity of transport demand to GDP will still be so high in the next future. The potential for a revival of regional development/trade patterns is presently investigated, namely after that (i) some excess of globalisation bring about relevant externalities and inequalities, and (ii) diffusion of economic growth make it more and more difficult to exploit cheap inputs, and firms' requirements are shifting from cheap inputs to efficient infrastructure and public utilities, technological skills, legal and political reliability, etc. A possible revival of infra-regional growth and trade patterns would be an opportunity for SSS.

It is very difficult to forecast whether SSS opportunities will overcome the threats, and if policy guidelines will be effective and helpful. The potential for SSS will depend both on the growth of transport and on the possible modal shift from land transport, which is in turn a function of a number of elements which are restraining its uninterrupted growth, like congestion and long run capacity limits.

Once developed beyond some relevant thresholds, the growth of SSS is likely to develop cumulative effects since average costs should decrease more than in land transport. As stated in section 6, the key issue in ensuring a "fair" level of development for SSS is to neutralise the effect on modal shift of different levels of market failures, namely in the fields of external costs, public expenditure on a natural monopoly such as infrastructure networks, and oligopoly/monopoly within the maritime transport industry.

Consequently, a paramount role of economic policy has to be developed by states, unions of states and international organisations, not only in ensuring fair competition and free access to the market of SSS, but also in order to equalise the level of cost externalisation in different modes. Thus, there should be three major guidelines on the agenda of policy makers:
- to ensure fair competition within sea transport, through liberalising access to the market and harmonising regulations;
- to ensure fair competition between transport modes, through the harmonisation of regulations concerning public aids to transport (namely in financing infrastructure);
- to ensure fair competition between transport modes, through the internalisation of external costs of transport.

ENDNOTES

1. See *ECMT* (2001), *Short Sea Shipping in Europe*, OECD/ECMT.
2. Van de Voorde E., Viegas J. (1995): "Trans-European Networks: Short-Sea Shipping", in Banister D., Capello R., Nijkamp P. (eds.), *European Transport and Communication Networks: Policy Evolution and Change*, John Wiley and Sons Ltd; Marlow P.B., Petitt S.J., Scorza A.D. (1997): *Short Sea Shipping in Europe: Analysis of the UK and Italian Markets* (Dept of Maritime Studies and International Transport, University of Wales, Cardiff).
3. Balduini G. (1982): "Short-Sea Shipping in the economy of inland transport in Europe: Italy" (paper presented at the ECMT, Gothenburg, 1–2 April).
4. Williamson M. (1982): "Short-Sea Shipping in the economy of inland transport in Europe: Sweden" (paper presented at the ECMT, Gothenburg, 1–2 April).
5. Marlow P.B., Petitt S.J., Scorza A.D. (1997): "Short Sea Shipping in Europe: Analysis of the UK and Italian Markets" (Dept. of Maritime Studies and International Transport, University of Wales, Cardiff).
6. Peeters C., Verbeke A., Declercq E., Wijnolst N. (1995): *Analysis of the competitive position of short sea shipping* (Delft University Press).
7. Stopford M. (1997): *Maritime Economics* (Routledge).
8. Bjornland D. (1993): "The importance of short sea shipping in European transport", *ECMT, Short Sea Shipping*, Economic Research Centre, pp. 59–93.
9. Respectively: Rich C.A .(1982): "Short-Sea Shipping in the economy of inland transport in Europe: United Kingdom" (paper presented at the ECMT, Gothenburg, 1st–2nd April); Wijnolst N., Sjobris A., Peeters C., Verbeke A., Declercq E., Schmitter T.J.N. (1994): *Multimodal shortsea transport. Coastal superhighway* (Delft University Press).
10. Crilley J., Dean C.J. (1993): "Shortsea shipping and the world cargo carrying fleet – a statistical summary", in Wijnolst N., Peeters C., Liebman P. (eds.), *European Shortsea Shipping* (Lloyd's of London Press), pp. 1–21.
11. Van de Voorde E., Viegas J. (1995), *op. cit.*; Linde H. (1993): "Status and perspectives of technological development in European shortsea shipping", in Wijnolst N., Peeters C., Liebman P. (eds.), *op. cit.*, pp. 107–124.

12. Bagchus R.C., Kuipers B. (1993): "Autostrada del mare", in Wijnolst N., Peeters C., Liebman P. (eds.), *op. cit.*, pp. 52–65.
13. European Commission (1992), Council Regulation (EEC) No.3577/1992, applying the principle of freedom to provide services to maritime transport within Member States (maritime cabotage), OJ No L 364.
14. *ECMT* (2001), *Short Sea Shipping in Europe*, OECD/ECMT
15. E.g. size: see Øvrebø, S. (1969): *Short sea and coastal tramp shipping in Europe* (Bergen, Institute for Shipping Research).
16. Wijnolst N., Peeters C., Liebman P. (eds.) (1993): *European Shortsea Shipping* (Lloyd's of London Press).
17. Drewry (1997): *Short Sea Container Markets – The Feeder and Regional Trade Dynamo* (Drewry Shipping Consultants Ltd).
18. Stopford (1997), *op. cit.*
19. Hoogerbeets J., Melissen P. (1993): "Facilitation of shortsea shipping: improvement in the sea/land interface (the Dutch case)", in Wijnolst N., Peeters C., Liebman P. (eds.), *op. cit.*, pp. 346–350.
20. Marlow P.B., Petitt S.J., Scorza A.D. (1997), *op.cit.*
21. *ECMT* (2001), *op. cit.*
22. By Policy Research Corporation, Antwerp: quoted in Peeters C., Verbeke A., Declercq E., Wijnolst N. (1995), *op. cit.*
23. Source: COM(2000)99 final – EU Commission (1999), *3rd Report on the implementation of council regulation 3577/1992 applying the principle of freedom to provide services to maritime cabotage.*
24. Drewry (1997), *op. cit.*
25. Drewry (1997), *op. cit.*
26. Drewry (1996): *Global Container Markets: Prospects and Profitability in a High Growth Era* (Drewry Shipping Consultants Ltd), quoted in Stopford (1997), *op. cit*, p. 367.
27. Regulation (EEC)3577/1992.
28. *ECMT* (2001), *op. cit.*, p. 10
29. Source: *Eurostat*.
30. Source: *Eurostat*.
31. Source: COM(99)317 final.
32. Source: *Eurostat*, quoted by Marlow P.B., Petitt S.J. and Scorza A.D. (1997), *op. cit.*
33. Source: ISL and *Eurostat*, quoted by *ECMT* (2001), *op. cit.*
34. COM(1999)317 final.
35. European Commission (2001), White Paper "European transport policy for 2010: time to decide" COM(2001)370 final.
36. Hoover E.M. (1948): *The Location of Economic Activity* (New York).
37. It is estimated that transports are responsible for 25% of world CO_2 emissions, shared as follows: road 75%, air: 12%; sea: 7%; other 6% (ECMT, 2001, *op. cit.*, p. 46).
38. European Transport Safety Council, quoted in ECMT (2001), *op. cit.*, p. 69.
39. *ECMT* (1993): *Short Sea Shipping*, Round Table 89, ECMT, quoted in Van de Voorde E., Viegas J. (1995), *op. cit.*
40. Schiffer E. (1996): "Competition between European ports and the effect on intermodal development", *Transportation Research Circular*, No. 459.
41. Zachcial (2001): "Short Sea Shipping and Intermodal Transport", *ECMT* (2001), *op. cit.*
42. ISL, quoted by Zachcial (2001), *op. cit.*, estimated in 1996 that on the route Lisbona–Germany a reduction of 267DM would have obtained 50% of the market.
43. Pettersen Strandenes S., Marlow P.B. (2000): "Port pricing and competitiveness in short sea shipping", *International Journal of Transport Economics*, XXVII, 3, pp. 315–334.
44. As suggested in Commission Communication on Short Sea Shipping (COM(99)317 final).

45. COM(1999)317 final.
46. Regulations 4055/1986 and 3577/1992.
47. Decision 1692/1996/CE.
48. Decision 1346/2001/CE.
49. COM(1996)421.
50. Commission Communication COM(92)494 final.
51. COM(95)317 final.
52. COM(97)678 final.
53. COM(99)317 final.
54. COM(2001)370 final.
55. Object of a proposal of Directive in May 2001 (GUCE C154 E, May 29th, 2001).
56. See Psaraftis H.N. (1995): *Short Sea Shipping: Key to European Cohesion*.
57. *ECMT* (2001): *Short Sea Shipping in Europe*, OECD/ECMT.
58. Van de Voorde E., Viegas J. (1995), *op. cit.*; Stuchtey R.W., Zachcial M. (1993): "Perspectives and trends of the European short-sea shipping industry", in Gwilliam (ed.), *Current Issues in Maritime Economics* (Kluwer Academic Publishers).
59. Van de Voorde and Viegas (1995), *op. cit.*

PART FIVE

ISSUES IN LINER SHIPPING

CHAPTER 14

LINER SHIPPING: MODELLING COMPETITION AND COLLUSION

William Sjostrom

National University of Ireland, Cork, Ireland
E-mail: *W.Sjostrom@ucc.ie*

1. INTRODUCTION

International liner shipping has long been dominated by collusive agreements called shipping conferences. Conferences have been used since at least the 1870s, when the industry was being established. In recent years, these agreements have been supplemented by other kinds of agreements such as consortia and alliances. The focus of this chapter is on explaining the economic models of competition used to analyse shipping conferences for purposes of competition policy. The underlying principles of liner shipping are discussed in Chapter 16, and the legal issues are discussed in Chapter 15.

Conferences are organisations of shipping lines operating on a particular route. At different times, subject to various regulations, they have set tariffs, employing policing agencies to check on adherence to the tariff. Members have been fined out of the membership bonds they post.[1] They may also allocate output among their members, by either cargo quotas or more commonly sailing quotas. If ships always sailed at the same capacity, which they do not, cargo and sailing quotas would be identical. Sailing quotas are, however, probably easier to enforce. They may also pool revenues and allocate particular ports on a given route.[2] All of these practices have been used by conferences throughout their history. For example, in the late nineteenth century and into the beginning of the twentieth century, as part of the Calcutta Conference, the P&O, the B.I., and the Hansa line had an agreement about the number of sailings each would make out of Hamburg.[3]

Beginning in the 1970s, liners consortia and alliances were formed by conference members as a supplementary means of conference enforcement.[4] They are essentially a system of common agency. Only recently have economists begun to examine them.[5]

An understanding of conferences, especially for purposes of competition policy, requires confronting two of their features: their longevity and their (at least partial) popularity with their customers.

The instability of cartels is a standard feature of elementary economic theory.[6] We do not ordinarily expect cartels to survive for great lengths of time. Moreover, ships are particularly movable capital, so entry into a particular market would seem easy. How then do we explain the success of shipping conferences?

There is evidence that a substantial portion of their customers approves of them[7] (a phenomenon not confined to ocean shipping[8]). There is evidence that larger shippers tend to oppose conferences whereas small shippers favour them. This appeared in US disputes over regulatory changes in the 1990s,[9] at the Royal Commission on Shipping Rings (1906-1909),[10] and in the pre-WWI West Africa Conference,[11] where opposition to conferences came from large shippers who had to charter through the conference, whereas small shippers, who would not be able to profitably charter a ship in any event, favoured the conferences.[12]

2. HISTORICAL ORIGINS

Because sailing ships are subject to the vagaries of the wind, liner shipping offering regular scheduled service had to wait for the arrival of the steam vessel.[13] Steam did not begin to be a competitor to the sailing ship until the development of the compound engine in the late 1860s and the triple expansion engine in the early 1880s.[14] These developments substantially improved fuel economy and increased speed to about 10–12 knots. The compound engine cut fuel consumption by over half compared to a single cylinder steam engine. Essentially, it involved adding additional cylinders to the steam engine, each additional cylinder reusing steam before it cooled. The increase in fuel economy also expanded the space available for cargo. Steam vessels began to offer regular, scheduled service, i.e., liner service. It is in liner shipping that conferences have thrived.

Curiously, sailing vessels belonged to conferences operating on the UK-Australia route and the Germany-South America route,[15] and there were early British coastal conferences involving sailing vessels as well.[16] By and large, however, these were exceptions.

The UK-Calcutta conference is usually described as the first conference, and is certainly the first modern conference. It started in 1875, consisting of five carriers: the P&O (Peninsular and Oriental Steam Navigation Co.), the B.I. (British India), and the City, Clan, and Anchor Lines. Within a decade or so, the conference extended its coverage of ports of origin from only the UK to the rest of northern Europe. There was, however, a conference from 1850 to 1856 on the North Atlantic involving the British and North American Steam Packet Company (the Cunard Line) and the New York and Liverpool United States Mail Steamship Company (the Collins Line).[17] Glasgow ship owners may have fixed rates with a conference system in the 1860s.[18] In addition, the Transatlantic Shipping Conference was formed in 1868. It was concerned, however, with issues such as uniform bills of lading and improving methods for inspecting cargo, and did not become involved in rate setting until 1902.[19] Although conferences are generally associated with international shipping, there were precursors in British coastal shipping as early as the 1830s.[20]

It is commonly assumed by historians of shipping conferences that they were formed in response to excess capacity, typically based on documents produced by participants in the trade.[21] A common version of this argument is that the opening of the Suez Canal, by shortening the distance between Europe and Asia, created excess capacity, but this version is not supported by the evidence.[22] Sailing vessels could not use the Canal. Existing steamships had been built for short routes through the Mediterranean Sea or the Red Sea, and most of them were scrapped after the opening of the Canal. Moreover, after the opening of the Canal, there were increases in net steamship production, which increased later in the 1870s with the introduction of the double expansion engine. The continued steamship production is inconsistent with excess capacity.

In the thirty years following the formation of the UK-Calcutta conference, conferences were formed on most of the major trade routes out of the UK and northern Europe. The Australia conference was started in 1884, the South African conference in 1886, the West African and northern Brazil conferences in 1895, the River Plate conference in 1896, the west coast of South America conference in 1904, and a conference covering the North Atlantic trade around 1900.[23] Most of these conferences covered the outbound trade from Europe, leaving the inbound trades of mostly bulk commodities to tramp vessels.[24]

One alternative to conferences would be merger. Merger is generally a substitute for collusion, but not a perfect substitute because merger increases agency costs.[25] The only known attempt to replace a conference with a merger was the largely unsuccessful International Mercantile Marine Company.[26]

3. ALTERNATIVE MODELS OF AGREEMENTS

3.1 Introduction

Most work on shipping conferences has involved four kinds of models: monopolistic cartels, contestable markets, destructive competitive, and empty cores.[27] The argument that conferences are monopolistic cartels is at least as old as Alfred Marshall,[28] who argued that conferences could act as monopolists because there were substantial scale economies in the industry that led to a small number of firms. (Both Lenin and the Marxist historian J.A. Hobson described shipping conferences as vivid examples of the tendency toward the concentration of capital.[29]) The other explanations arose largely as responses to the cartel model. Destructive competition and its modern variant, the empty core, are alternative explanations of why conferences exist. Contestable markets have been used to criticise the proposition that conferences can usefully be described as monopolistic cartels. This matters for competition policy, because if conferences are not monopolising cartels, then competition policy need not address them.

3.2 Measuring markets and competition

Models of competition within markets have been applied to conferences and other agreements in liner shipping for two reasons: to explain what the agreements are doing, and to show what they cannot be doing. The first reason is important for making sense of the role agreements play in liner shipping, and seeing whether those insights can be generalised to other industry. The second reason is important for competition policy. Assuming that competition authorities are attempting to increase competition,[30] it is important to establish whether a particular practice reduces competition rather than having an alternative purpose. If it can be established that a practice does not reduce competition, it needs no further analysis for purposes of competition policy.

Modelling competition requires at least a brief glance at two questions: what is a market, and what does it mean for a market to be more or less competitive.

The standard definition of a market,[31] frequently called an economic or trading market, is the area in which prices tend towards uniformity, allowing for transport costs. For purposes of competition policy, however, a distinction is made between an economic market and an antitrust market. An antitrust market can be larger or smaller than an economic market. First, to the extent there are capacity constraints, some members of an economic market may not be effective members of an antitrust market. For example, if conferences raise prices, an outsider may not provide much of an alternative if cannot increase its output. Second, the size of economic markets is influenced by market power of participants. A seller with market power will raise price until its rivals' products are good substitutes. (It will raise price until marginal cost equals marginal revenue. Positive marginal cost implies positive marginal revenue, and positive marginal revenue implies an elastic demand.) The frequent assertion that conferences cannot be monopolies because they face too many good substitutes[32] may be the opposite: they face good substitutes because they act monopolistically.

The size of liner markets remains a steady debate. On the one hand, ships are often specialised to some degree to particular routes, if only because of their size or the cargo they can carry. On the other hand, ships are movable capital, which implies that individual routes are part of a larger market. In 1903, Sir Thomas Sutherland, the chairman of the P&O, told stockholders, commented on low rates at the time[33]:

"It is the world's tonnage at large, the cargo-carrying tonnage of the world at large, which dictates, or rather determines the current rates of freight both by cargo steamers and by mail steamers, and we are simply dragged into the wake of that great movement."

The term "competition" is routinely used vaguely, with differing and sometimes inconsistent meanings. Sometimes it is used simply to mean the number of sellers (both as a measure of concentration and as a measure of how far to the right the supply curve lies). Sometimes it is used to mean low measured profitability,[34] which is taken to mean the absence of monopoly and monopoly profit. Sometimes it is used to mean that buyers have good substitutes; sometimes it is used simply to mean that the seller faces a downward sloping, rather than perfectly inelastic demand curve.

Rather than getting absorbed in a semantic debate, it is simpler to think about competition by the outcome: the price-cost margin (or Lerner index), measured as the mark-up of price over marginal cost, relative to price. Measuring

LINER SHIPPING: COMPETITION AND COLLUSION

the difference between price and marginal cost allows for an estimate of the elasticity of demand as perceived by sellers. Conventionally, price-cost margins were measured using accounting data, but these have always been unreliable. Methods developed since the 1980s, and known as the New Industrial Organisation,[35] allow the price-cost margin to be inferred.

The approach can be seen in Figures 1 and 2. In models of monopoly and of perfect competition, an increase in demand raises price and output, and a decrease in demand lowers both, as shown in Figure 1. Therefore, the consequences of a rise or fall in demand cannot separate the two models. Suppose instead that the demand rotates (becoming steeper or flatter). In a model of perfect competition, this does not raise or lower price or output. In a model of monopoly, however, flattening the demand curve raises marginal revenue relative to demand, thereby lowering price and raising output. Making demand steeper lowers marginal revenue relative to demand, thereby raising price and lowering output. This can be seen in Figure 2.

Figure 1

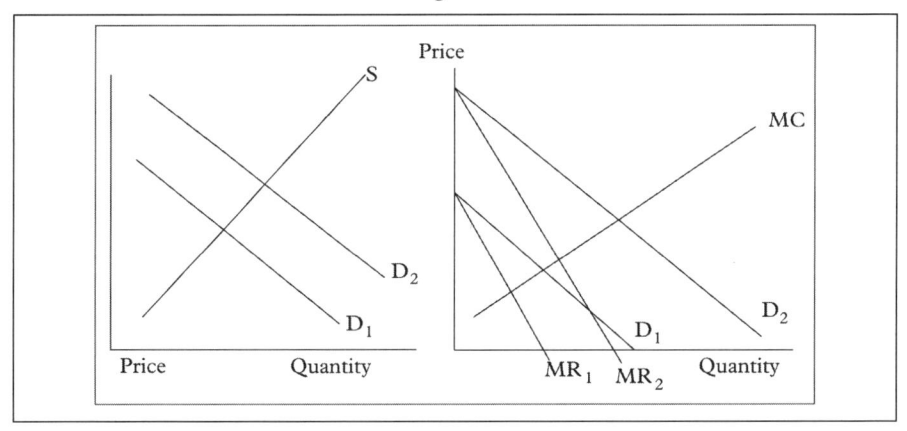

Figure 2

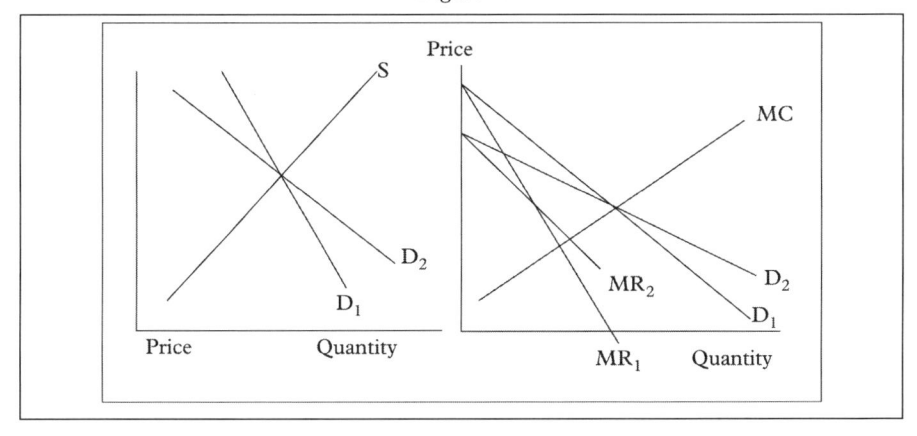

Start by writing the market demand curve as $P(Q)$, so that price depends on quantity sold. The slope of the demand curve is $\Delta P/\Delta Q$. Marginal revenue is $P + (\Delta P/\Delta Q)Q$. Equating marginal revenue to marginal cost gives $P + (\Delta P/\Delta Q)Q = MC$, which can be rewritten as

(1) $\qquad P = MC - (\Delta P/\Delta Q)Q$

Because $(\Delta P/\Delta Q) < 0$, the second term on the right hand side, $-(\Delta P/\Delta Q)Q$, is the mark-up of price over marginal cost charged by a monopolist in the industry. Modify equation (1) slightly to

(2) $\qquad P = MC - (\Delta P/\Delta Q)Q\theta$

If $\theta = 1$, equation (2) gives the monopoly solution in equation (1). If $\theta = 0$, there is no mark-up of price over marginal cost, so $\theta = 0$ corresponds to perfect competition. In a Cournot model with n identical firms, $\theta = 1/n$. Measuring θ means measuring how much of the difference in the market between price and marginal revenue is perceived by individual sellers. These techniques allow both a measure of the extent of competition in the market and a way to test alternative theories of markets.

3.3 Non-cooperative game-theoretic models of collusion: cartel enforcement

It is easy to get involved in pointless and unproductive discussions about what it "really" means to be a cartel. It is simpler to simply define a cartel, following the conventional practice of economists, as an agreement that attempts to get its members to act jointly as a monopolist. Agreements that serve other purposes, such as preventing destructive competition, reducing risk, or trade promotion, should simply be referred to as such.

In perfect competition, output allocation is simple and automatic. Each seller produces an output such that its marginal cost is equal to the market price. In a cartel, prices are increased, but output must be reduced. Therefore, each firm's output must be centrally directed. Each firm produces an output such that marginal cost is less than the price, giving each firm an incentive to raise output and upset the cartel arrangement. The primary problem for any monopolising cartel is therefore enforcement. Enforcement means that output increases must be punished,[36] but first they must be detected.[37]

The last decade has seen a substantial amount of work testing whether shipping conferences can be explained by cartel models. Three attempt have been made to measure whether conferences have market power. Nancy Fox measured the effect of the number of firms in a conference and a conference's market share on freight rates.[38] She finds that freight rates fall when the conference market share falls. She also finds that as the number of conference members rises, freight rates also fall, which is consistent with Stigler's theory of oligopoly,[39] specifically that increased numbers in a cartel increase the cost of coordination.

Fox also looked at the provision in the US Shipping Act of 1984 that allows conference members to deviate from conference rates on ten days notice.[40]

A cartel model would predict that allowing independent action, even though it is public rather than secret price cutting, should undercut conferences because it makes enforcing the conference tariff more difficult. She fails, however, to find evidence that the Act made any difference at all to conferences.

Paul Clyde and James Reitzes, in an ingenious study, distinguished between increased freight rates because of increased conference market share and because of increased market concentration.[41] They find statistically significant but economically insignificant effects of increased market concentration on freight rates, but, contrary to the results in Fox, no effect of increased conference market share on freight rates.

It is worth emphasis that focusing on price can be misleading. Conferences can raise price because they restrict output (making shippers worse off) or because they add value, thereby raising demand and raising output. A better test would be to focus on the effect of conferences on output.

The most recent study took a historical approach, using a sample of 47 pre-World War I conferences.[42] It looked for reasons why a cartel might be easier to negotiate and enforce, arguing that a cartel can then successfully impose stricter, less flexible terms on its members. Enforcement is easier if there is multi-market contact. The basic intuition is that punishment for deviations from a cartel agreement in one market can be carried out in several markets.[43] It also argues that enforcement is also easier if one or more of the firms has a large global market share. In that case, it is easier for the large firm to transfer ships to a market to carry out punishment. Agreements are easier to negotiate if there are a small number of firms and if there is heterogeneity in size, allowing a large firm to dominate the agreement. A strict, inflexible agreement is also more sustainable if entry is less likely.

3.4 Non-cooperative game-theoretic models of collusion: contestable markets

The theory of contestable markets focuses heavily on sunk costs. It draws on the insight that potential competitors are a constraint on pricing behaviour as much as actual competitors. Suppose in a market there are no sunk costs and incumbent firms do not respond to entry by lowering prices. Then entry is costless in the sense that all costs of entry can be recovered on exit. Entry is therefore riskless. Moreover, the entrant can make its entry decision without regard to strategic decisions by the incumbent.

Suppose a market had only one seller. The seller could not act as a monopolist because an entrant would undercut it. If entry is costless, schemes to exclude entry do not work because the entrant cannot be threatened with losses on entry. Should the entrant face the prospect of losses, it can always costlessly depart until the problem goes away.

John Davies has focused attention on the degree to which liner firms face sunk costs, and the risks of retaliatory price-cutting.[44] He has provided evidence that sunk costs are low, and that retaliation is slow. That is, he has shown that the assumptions of contestability are roughly satisfied by the liner market. If the liner market is contestable, then conferences may have difficulty acting like monopolising cartels. Whatever service they provide, they must do so at (economic) cost, lest they are uncut by entry.

An important, unresolved difficulty is how sensitive contestable markets are to deviations from the assumptions of zero fixed costs and no retaliatory pricing. There are theoretical grounds for believing that very small deviations from these assumptions can have large consequences for contestability,[45] but little effort has been made to quantify the problem.

3.5 Destructive competition

Destructive competition arguments come in two forms. The usual form among maritime economists focuses on high sunk costs, inelastic demand, and the risks to carriers of "overtonnaging" or excess capacity. (The next section discusses another version, the theory of the core.) Daniel Marx is the primary early exponent,[46] and the argument has been made by industry practitioners.[47] Maritime historians have tended to favour this argument as well.[48] In this argument, because a large proportion of costs is sunk, it follows that price would have to fall substantially before sellers would leave the market. Therefore the short run market supply curve will tend to be inelastic. In addition, it is usually asserted that the demand for liner shipping services is highly inelastic, although there is very little systematic evidence for this. The combination of inelastic supply and demand leads to a highly unstable price. Therefore, carriers are exposed to increased risk of losses, and shippers face substantial uncertainty about freight rates. On this explanation, conferences offer reduced risk to both carriers and shippers.

This explanation suffers from two serious flaws.[49] First, if fluctuating prices lead to periods of losses, then they must also lead to periods of offsetting gains. Carriers will not enter unless the risk-adjusted present value of profits is positive. If long run changes in the market occur such that the present value of profits is negative, firms will (efficiently) leave the market, and the losses are their signal to do so. Second, if shippers valued rate stability, they could write forward contracts.

3.6 Cooperative game-theoretic models of collusion: the empty core

A more recent and theoretically coherent revival of the idea of destructive competition is the theory of the core,[50] which has been applied several times to conferences[51] and alliances.[52]

The theory of the core focuses on avoidable fixed costs and the integer problem (the number of firms in an industry must be an integer). With avoidable fixed costs and rising marginal cost, the relevant average cost curve is U-shaped. No output will be produced at any price below minimum average cost. When price rises to a firm's minimum average cost ($p^\star$), that firm will enter at the output $q^\star$ where average cost is minimised. The firm will produce $q \geq q^\star$ if $p \geq p^\star$. Under perfect competition, the firm's output will therefore be either 0 or $q \geq q^\star$. Suppose firms are identical. Then at $p^\star$, industry output must be an integer multiple of $q^\star$ (the integer problem). It would be only by chance that demand at $p^\star$ would be an integer multiple of $q^\star$. It is therefore possible that demand and supply would not intersect. The problem would go away if a firm were willing to produce a fraction of q*, but avoidable fixed costs mean that no firm could profitably do so.

If inventories were inexpensive, a firm could produce only part of the time and provide a fraction of q* with inventories. In transportation industries especially, however, output is cargo or passenger space. Once the ship or airplane leaves, empty space is gone, so inventories are impossible.[53] The only way to create inventories is to have excess capacity, which can lead to an empty core.

The integer problem does not necessarily lead to an empty core, but is likely to under some circumstances. Consider an example attributable to George Bittlingmayer.[54] Suppose taxis can carry at most two passengers, and that the cost of a taxi trip is independent of whether there are zero, one, or two passengers. Admittedly, these assumptions are likely to be factually inaccurate. Most taxis can squeeze in an extra passenger in a pinch, and extra passengers reduce mileage. These assumptions, however, capture the same points that a more realistic but also more complex model would. First, there are some scale economies: once a taxi carries one passenger, the marginal cost of a second is less than the average cost. Second, there are capacity constraints: marginal cost exceeds average cost beyond some output.

Assume each taxi's cost of a trip to the airport is £5, and that there are no sunk costs, so the competitive supply of taxi trips is constant at £5 per trip. Assume as well, for simplicity, that each possible passenger is willing to pay £10 for a taxi trip, so a taxi trip is efficient (relative to no trip) even if there is only one passenger. Suppose four people want to make a trip to the airport. They will take two cabs, each with two passengers, and each pair of passengers will pay £5. How they divide the £5 cost between them is irrelevant to the problem.

Suppose instead that only three people, imaginatively named A, B, and C, want to make the trip. The efficient solution is for the three to take two taxis, generating a surplus of 3 x £10 − 2 x £5 = £20. In this case, however, the problem of dividing the £10 cost of the two taxis eliminates the possibility of a competitive equilibrium. One possibility is that A and B travel together, pay £2.50 each, and let C travel alone and pay £5. C, however, could offer to let A travel with him if A pays £1. C is better off, paying only £4 instead of £5, and A is better off, paying only £1 instead of £2.50. B is left, however, paying £5 instead of £2.50, leaving B in the same position as C was originally, to upset the allocation.

An equilibrium allocation has to ensure that no coalition (A, B, or C alone, pairs of A and B, A and C, or B and C, or the grand coalition of A, B, and C) can do better by upsetting the existing allocation. If X_i is the surplus to customer i, i = A, B, C, then an equilibrium allocation has to satisfy the following constraints:

$$X_A + X_B \geq £15; X_A + X_C \geq £15; X_B + X_C \geq £15$$
$$\Sigma X_i = X_A + X_B + X_C \leq £20$$

The first constraint states that any two passengers travelling together can get a combined surplus of £15. The second constraint states that the best all three passengers can get is the surplus from the efficient solution of travelling in two taxis. Summing all three terms in the first constraint implies that $\Sigma X_i \geq £22.50$, which is inconsistent with the second constraint. There is no equilibrium allocation. In this example, $q^*=2$, and if demand is not a multiple of two, there is no equilibrium.

The absence of equilibrium in market exchange poses a problem for the participants in the market, both buyers and sellers, because it necessarily raises the costs of contracting. Sellers will try to protect themselves from the consequences of the integer problem by selecting technology with lower capacity and higher costs.[55] It is therefore in the mutual interests of buyers and sellers to find a way to achieve an allocation through non-market means. It remains true that an individual buyer or seller has an incentive to disrupt the allocation, just as in a cartel model. Unlike a cartel model, however, buyers as a group do not have an incentive to assist the deviating party.

The example suggests two of the more interesting implications of the model of the empty core. First, it is worth noting that there are ways of resolving the problem. For example, if the three passengers were friends, they might simply split the cost three ways because an attempt by two of them to exclude the third would result in the loss of a valuable friendship. Alternatively, there might be a social custom, the violation of which would result in being ostracised, dictating that in such cases there be some fair division of the cost. It is important, however, to recognise that these methods of resolving the problem are not market solutions. This implies that collusion may be a means of resolving the problem of an empty core, although merger and vertical integration may be alternatives.

Second, suppose there were sunk entry costs. Then the necessity of earning a return on the initial sunk investment, aggravated by the prospect of facing the costs of an empty core, would limit entry. In the example, suppose there are only three taxis. Then there is an empty core if demand is three or five, but not otherwise. If demand were seven or greater, because capacity is only six, competition would drive the price up to the reservation price of £10, and only six passengers would travel. The empty core would only occur when demand was low, for example if the industry were in decline or if demand were a low draw from a high variance distribution.

Two systematic tests of the empty core model have been made. Sjostrom[56] focused primarily on demand conditions. Two important results are that increased conference market share raises output and that conferences are more dominant when demand is more variable, both consistent with an empty core and contrary to a monopoly model. Sjostrom does not specify the precise mechanism whereby increased share increases output. Given the results in the study by Clyde and Reitzes[57] that increased market share has trivially positive effect on freight rates, the increased output presumably comes from less costly contracting and more efficient production.

Pirrong[58] focuses on measuring the assumptions of the model, providing evidence of rising marginal cost and U-shaped average cost curves (implying fixed costs). With cost data from the routes to Europe from the North and South Atlantic ports of the US, he estimates alternative cost functions. Of particular interest is his successful use of the semi-logarithmic cost function, with the form (simplifying from Pirrong) $\ln C = \beta_0 + \beta_1 Q$, where C is total cost and Q is output. With $\beta_1 > 0$, the marginal cost function is rising ($\partial^2 C/\partial Q^2 = \beta_1^2 C > 0$) and the average cost function is U-shaped [$\partial(C/Q)/\partial Q = (C/Q)(\beta_1 Q-1) < 0$ if $Q < 1/\beta_1$]. Pirrong's empirical results imply falling average cost over a substantial range of output, which in turn implies that the integer problem is significant. He also discusses why the model implies the absence of conferences in tramp shipping, which is consistent with only two attempts, both unsuccessful, to form conferences in tramp shipping.[59]

4. CONFERENCE PRACTICES

Three conference practices have generated some controversy. Predatory pricing and loyalty contracts are ways in which conferences may have controlled the problem of entry. The effect of price discrimination on cartel stability is more problematic. In a cartel model, it is destabilising because it attracts entry. In an empty core model, it is a way of increasing output when there are falling average costs.

4.1 Predatory pricing

The most common allegation of predatory pricing revolved around the use of "fighting ships". The conference would, in response to an entrant, lower the rates on one of its vessels to compete with the entrant until the entrant lost money and left the market. John McGee casts doubt on the use of fighting ships,[60] describing them as instances of normal competition, but Basil Yamey[61] cites the opinion in the 1891 decision by the law lords in the House of Lords in the case of Mogul Steamship Co. v. McGregor, Gow & Co. *et al.*[62] for an example of the use of fighting ships.[63] It is not clear, however, from Yamey's discussion whether predatory pricing was successful in this instance. When, in 1885, Mogul sent two ships to Hankow, an inland port on the Yang-tse River (another non-conference firm sent a ship as well), the China conference responded by sending ships to Hankow, inducing a fall in rates, which the Court in Mogul described as unprofitable. On the other hand, the two Mogul ships and the third independent ship sailed sufficiently full that they did not have to carry ballast (effectively garbage carried to stabilise the ship when there is too little cargo), whereas some of the conference ships sailed empty. Although Mogul was not admitted to the China conference, it was given some landing rights on the Yang-tse.

Two recent contributions have improved our understanding of the ways in which conferences may have used predatory pricing to control entry. Fiona Scott Morton, studying pre-World War I conferences, finds evidence supporting the "long purse" theory of predation, whereby firms can profitably engage in predation if their financial resources are large relative to the prey.[64] A long purse theory requires that capital markets are sufficiently costly that the prey cannot gain access to capital to survive the price war, whereas the predator can, most likely because the predator already owns larger liquid assets before the war starts.[65]

In a later study with the sociologist Joel Podolny,[66] Scott Morton extended her earlier results primarily by finding that entrants with high social status were less likely to be preyed upon. The social status of an entrant is used as a measure of the extent to which an entrant could be relied upon to cooperate with the conference. They also show that the effect of social status declined with the age of the entering firm. This is consistent with the idea that information about a firm becomes more public over time and therefore the conference had less need to rely on social status as a proxy.

These results are consistent with Gordon Boyce's discussion[67] of the International Mercantile Marine (IMM), a combination of five transatlantic lines sponsored by J.P. Morgan and formed in the period 1900–1902. The IMM had alliances with two German lines, Norddeutscher Lloyd (NDL) and the Hamburg Amerika Line (HAPAG), with whom it had a ten year route allocation agreement. Boyce argued that IMM's connection to Morgan gave it access to "abundant capital".

4.2 Loyalty contracts

Conferences use two kinds of loyalty contracts: the deferred rebate and the dual rate contract (sometimes called contract rates). Under a dual rate system, the shipper signs an agreement to deal exclusively with the conference, and in turn receives a discount on the freight rate. If the shipper uses a non-conference carrier, the conference imposes a fine. Under a deferred rebate system, if the shipper deals exclusively with the conference for, say, six months (the typically length of time), and then deals exclusively with the conference for next six months, the shipper receives a rebate of an agreed proportion of his freight bill from the first six months. The deferred rebate was a novel contract first introduced successfully by the UK-Calcutta Conference in 1877[68] after being proposed in 1873 on the Yang-tse River trade.[69] The deferred rebate system was prohibited in U.S. trades by the 1916 Shipping Act.

There are two important distinctions between the two systems. First, under the deferred rebate system, the shipper loses interest on the price cut. Second, the conference incurs lower enforcement costs with the deferred rebate because it does not have to enforce the fine by going to court.[70] Perhaps because of these differences, discounts under deferred rebates tended to be larger than under dual rate contracts, typically double the size.[71] Under both systems, the conference must incur the costs of determining whether the contract has been broken, giving rise to estimates of violations of the loyalty agreements of 5–15% of shippers.[72] In a recent study, however, Pedro Marín and Richard Sicotte used the event study technique to show that loyalty agreements made significant contributions to profitability.[73]

Whichever system a conference used, deferred rebate and dual rate systems usually applied to only certain commodities. For example, the Far East Conference introduced the deferred rebate when it was formed in 1879, but certain bulk commodities such as rice and silk were excluded from the loyalty arrangement.[74] Moreover, the loyalty requirement was typically waived if the conference were unable to provide sufficient capacity within a reasonable time.[75]

Loyalty contracts are designed to encourage customers to use a particular seller exclusively. The shipper is charged a lower price in exchange for dealing exclusively with the conference. One question is whether they serve to exclude new entry, or whether they serve to reduce costs by gaining economies of regularity, such as easier planning. A second question is, assuming they serve to exclude entry, whether such exclusion is efficient.

Under constant marginal costs, loyalty contracts are an unprofitable method of deterring entry. Moreover, the customers who are most deterred from dealing with the entrant are those the conference least wants to deter, i.e., those owed the largest rebate.[76] Nevertheless, they can efficiently exclude an entrant constrained in its ability to offer a service of sufficiently high frequency to satisfy shipper demand.[77] Loyalty contracts reduce uncertainty for conference members by ensuring them a less variable flow of cargo, which is particularly valuable given the cost structure that makes full ships particularly attractive.[78] These arguments are consistent with evidence that shippers were favourable to dual rate contracts.[79] The pre-WWI West Africa Conference used a deferred rebate system, which small shippers favoured but large shippers opposed.[80]

4.3 Price discrimination

Conference freight tariffs have for a long time been detailed and lengthy documents, with different freight rates for each commodity shipped. An important issue of contention is the extent to which those differing rates are the consequence of cost differences or price discrimination. Differences in cost could arise from, *inter alia*, differences in density (called the stowage factor), difficulties in handling the cargo, insurance, and the need for refrigeration. Differences in transport demand elasticities could arise from differences in the costs of waiting: more valuable and more readily perishable goods would bear a higher freight rate for quick service. Even after the widespread use of containers, which have made cargoes more homogeneous, these tariffs have remained in effect.

Allegations that conferences price discriminate by charging higher freight rates to higher valued commodities are of long standing. One claim is that they are simply attempts to extract additional profits from a monopoly position.[81] The alternative view is that conferences price discriminate because the large element of fixed common costs requires price discrimination to cover costs.[82]

On the monopoly interpretation, price discrimination is destabilising for the conference. Price discrimination makes entry more attractive because entrants are encouraged to focus on the high priced end of the market. The conference sacrifices stability and durability in exchange for higher profits now. Besides entry, price discrimination is endangered by the prospects for resale, but resale is difficult in any service industry, and in transport it is possible only if the shipper can successfully deceive the carrier about the contents of the shipment.

On the common cost interpretation, price discrimination increases the stability and durability of the conference because it allows the conference to expand output and therefore is in the joint interests of the conference and shippers as a form of Ramsey pricing.[83]

An important difficulty is that Ramsey pricing is necessary only if marginal cost prices do not cover costs, which means that firms are operating under falling average costs. This seems inconsistent with several firms in a conference. Having several firms all operating in the region of falling average costs may be consistent with efficiency, although not with perfect competition. With U-shaped average cost curves, in general it is efficient to add an additional producer at a level of demand lower than that level necessary to bring the additional producer into the market under competition.[84]

It is perhaps easy to see this with a simple numerical example. Suppose each firm has a fixed cost of 8 and variable costs of $½Q^2$, implying a marginal cost of Q. Under competition, the firm's supply curve is given by the solution to $\max_Q \pi = PQ - ½Q^2 - 8$, which is $Q = P$ (i.e., the supply curve for all prices at least equal to average cost). The minimum price that allows the firm to cover the fixed cost of 8 is given by substituting the supply curve into the profit function and equating it to zero to get $\pi_{max} = P^2 - ½P^2 - 8 = 0$, which implies $P = 4$.

Suppose there are three firms, so that market supply is $3P$ ($P \geq 4$). Suppose further that demand is $Q = 16 - P$. The solution to this problem is $P = 4$, and therefore competition supports exactly three firms, which is also the efficient solution. Suppose that demand is only $Q = 15 - P$. Competition will support only two firms. It is efficient, however, to have three firms in the market. The trade-off to be resolved is that when reducing from three to two firms, the fixed cost of the exiting firm is saved, but the remaining two firms produce output at higher marginal cost. In this case, the demand function $Q = 15 - P$ implies the total valuation function is $V = 15Q - ½Q^2$. The minimum industry cost function with two firms is $(1/4)Q^2 + 16$ and with three firms is $(1/6)Q^2 + 24$. Although the fixed cost is higher with three firms, the marginal cost is lower at $(1/3)Q$ rather than $(1/2)Q$. Total surplus (total value less total cost) is 60.375 with three firms and only 59 with two firms. At the efficient solution, each firm produces an output of 3.75, with a marginal cost of 3.75 and an average cost of 4.008. The slope of each firm's average cost curve is approximately –0.07. The efficient solution is therefore unsustainable with marginal cost prices.

A number of attempts have been made to find out whether conferences practice price discrimination, and the answer remains mostly that we do not know.[85] A number of attempts have been made to measure price discrimination by regressing the freight rate for different commodities against the price of the commodity and a group of variables intended to capture differences in transport costs. The fundamental difficulty is identifying variables that capture differences in demand elasticities without also identifying differences in costs. A statistically significant regression coefficient on commodity price is usually asserted to be evidence of price discrimination. Unfortunately, higher priced goods usually carry higher insurance costs and frequently require more delicate handling. To identify price discrimination, we would have to know the (unknown) coefficient implied by these higher costs and look for evidence of a higher coefficient. The cost variables, moreover, might include price discrimination elements. For example, refrigerated goods usually carry a higher freight rate. The higher rate may the result of the extra costs of refrigeration, or the result of the less elastic demand implied by the perishability of the goods. To complicate matters, it could easily include both elements.

Clyde and Reitzes[86] have made an innovative attempt to separate the effects of market power from cost differences by using panel data (different commodities on fourteen routes over four years) in a fixed effects model. By using dummy variables for each commodity, they effectively control for cost differences. The relevant part of their regression is $r_{ij} = \beta_1 s_j + \beta_2 s_j p_{ij}$, where r_{ij} is the freight rate for commodity i on route j, s_j is the conference market share on route j, and p_{ij} is the price of commodity i on route j. It follows that $\partial r_{ij}/\partial s_j = \beta_1 + \beta_2 p_{ij}$. If conferences are price discriminating, then a drop in competition from independent carriers (an increase in s_j) will not only raise freight rates ($\beta_1 > 0$), but will raise them more for higher valued commodities ($\beta_2 > 0$). Clyde and Reitzes find no evidence for discriminatory pricing.

5. CONCLUDING REMARKS

Far more is known about shipping conferences than only a decade ago. The dispute over whether conferences are cartels or institutions to prevent destructive competition remains. Nevertheless, the theoretical arguments are much clearer than in the past, and are being addressed with more systematic evidence than ever before.

We also know more about the ways in which conferences remain stable by controlling entry. Recent studies have systematically addressed the problem of predatory pricing years, and ways have finally been found of sorting out whether conferences price discriminate. Loyalty contracts have unfortunately remained an object of largely theoretical interest; the difficulty of obtaining data has inhibited much systematic study of their effects.

ENDNOTES

1. Jansson, J.O. and Shneerson, D. (1987): *Liner Shipping Economics* (London, Chapman and Hall). For historical evidence on this point, see also Greenhill, R. (1977): "Shipping, 1850-1914", *Business Imperialism, 1840-1930: An Inquiry Based on British Experience in Latin America*, edited by D.C.M. Platt (Oxford, Oxford University Press).
2. Bennathan, E. and Walters, A.A. (1969): *The Economics of Ocean Freight Rates* (New York, Praeger); Jansson, J.O. and Shneerson, D. (1987): *Liner Shipping Economics* (London, Chapman and Hall).
3. Smith, J.R. (1906): "Ocean freight rates and their control by line carriers", *Journal of Political Economy*, 14, pp. 525–541. The range of detail in conference agreements is described in Deltas, G., Serfes, K., and Sicotte, R. (1999): "American shipping cartels in the pre-World War I era", *Research in Economic History*, 16, pp. 1–38.
4. Farthing, B. (1993): *International Shipping* (2nd ed.) (London, Lloyd's of London Press); Clarke, R.L. (1997): "An analysis of the international ocean shipping conferences system", *Transportation Journal*, 36, pp. 17–29.

5. Ryoo, D.-K., and Thanopoulou, H.A. (1999): "Liner alliances in the globalisation era: a strategic tool for Asian container carriers", *Maritime Policy and Management*, 26, pp. 349–367; Thanopoulou, H.A., Ryoo, D.-K., and Lee, T.-W. (1999): "Korean liner shipping in the era of global alliances", *Maritime Policy and Management*, 26, pp. 209–229; Midoro, R. and Pitto, A. (2000): "A critical evaluation of strategic alliances in liner shipping", *Maritime Policy and Management*, 27, pp. 31–40.
6. Carlton, D.W., and Perloff, J.M. (2000): *Modern Industrial Organization* (3rd ed.) (Reading, Massachusetts, Addison-Wesley), especially chapter 5.
7. McGee, J.S. (1960): "Ocean freight conferences and American merchant marine", *University of Chicago Law Review*, 27, pp. 191–314; Marriner, S., and Hyde, F.E. (1967): *The Senior: John Samuel Swire, 1825-1898, Management in Far Eastern Shipping Trades* (Liverpool, Liverpool University Press); Ludwick, E.M. (1983): *Shipping conferences: survey of users' views* (Ottawa, Consumer and Corporate Affairs Canada); Beargie, T. (1987): "Shippers Evenly Divided", *American Shipper*, August; US Federal Maritime Commission, 1989, Section 18 report on the Shipping Act of 1984; Heaver, T. (1993): "Workable competition, politics, and competition policy in liner shipping", *Current Issues in Maritime Economics*, edited by K.M. Gwilliam (Dordrecht, Kluwer Academic), pp. 68–84; Productivity Commission, 1999, *International liner cargo shipping: a review of Part X of the Trade Practices Act 1974*, Report no. 9.
8. Bittlingmayer, G. (1982): "Decreasing average cost and competition: a new look at the Addyston Pipe case", in *Journal of Law and Economics*, 25, pp. 201–230, offers evidence of customer support for cartels in the late nineteenth century US cast iron pipe industry.
9. Clarke, R.L. (1997): "An analysis of the international ocean shipping conferences system", in *Transportation Journal*, 36, pp. 17–29.
10. Leubuscher, C. (1963): *The West African Shipping Trade: 1909-1959* (Leyden, A.W. Sythoff).
11. Davies, P.N. (1973): *The Trade Makers: Elder Dempster in West Africa* (London, George Allen & Unwin).
12. In principle, a group of small shippers could have collectively chartered a ship. They would have had to agree on a departure date, however, and differences in the value of quick departure would have reduced the group's willingness to pay for a chartered vessel.
13. Boyce, G.H. (1995): *Information, Mediation and Institutional Development: The Rise of Large-Scale Enterprise in British Shipping, 1870-1919* (Manchester, Manchester University Press).
14. Harley, C.K. (1971): "The shift from sailing ships to steamships, 1850-1890: a study in technological change and its diffusion", *Essays on a Mature Economy: Britain after 1840*, edited by D.N. McCloskey (Princeton, Princeton University Press).
15. Burley, K. (1968): *British Shipping and Australia, 1920-1939* (Cambridge, Cambridge University Press).
16. Armstrong, J. (1991): "Conferences in British nineteenth-century coastal shipping", *Mariner's Mirror*, 77, pp. 55–65.
17. Sloan, E.W. (1998): "The first (and very secret) international steamship cartel, 1850-1856", *Research in Maritime History*, 14, pp. 29–52.
18. Dyos, H.J. and Aldcroft, D.H. (1969): *British Transport: An Economic Survey from the Seventeenth Century to Twentieth* (Leicester, Leicester University Press).
19. Smith, J.R. (1906): "Ocean freight rates and their control through combinations", *Political Science Quarterly*, 21, pp. 237–263.
20. Armstrong, J. (1991): "Conferences in British nineteenth-century coastal shipping", *Mariner's Mirror*, 77, pp. 55–65.
21. Greenhill, R. (1998): "Competition or co-operation in the global shipping industry: the origins and impact of the conference system for British ship owners before 1914", *Research in Maritime History*, 14, pp. 53–80.

22. Sjostrom, W. (1989): "On the origin of shipping conferences: excess capacity and the opening of the Suez Canal", *International Journal of Transport Economics*, 16, pp. 329–335.
23. Kirkaldy, A. (1914): *British Shipping* (London, Kegan Paul, Trench, Trubner); Dyos, H.J. and Aldcroft, D.H. (1969): *British Transport: An Economic Survey from the Seventeenth Century to Twentieth* (Leicester, Leicester University Press).
24. Marx, D. (1953): *International Shipping Cartels* (Princeton, Princeton University Press); Dyos, H.J. and Aldcroft, D.H. (1969): *British Transport: An Economic Survey from the Seventeenth Century to Twentieth* (Leicester, Leicester University Press).
25. Bittlingmayer, G. (1985): "Did antitrust policy cause the great merger wave?", *Journal of Law and Economics*, 28, pp. 77–118.
26. Livermore, S. (1935): "The success of industrial mergers", *Quarterly Journal of Economics*, 50, pp. 68–96; Navin, T., and Sears. M. (1954): "A study in merger: formation of the International Mercantile Marine Company", *Business History Review*, 28, pp. 291–328; Boyce, G.H. (1995): *Information, Mediation and Institutional Development: The Rise of Large-Scale Enterprise in British Shipping, 1870-1919* (Manchester, Manchester University Press).
27. An innovative attempt was made to apply monopolistic competition models to conferences, but was not followed up. See Officer, L. (1971): "Monopoly and monopolistic competition in the international transportation industry", *Western Economic Journal*, 9, pp. 134–156.
28. Marshall, A. (1921): *Industry and Trade* (London, Macmillan).
29. Cafruny, A.W. (1987): *Ruling the Waves: The Political Economy of International Shipping* (Berkeley, University of California Press).
30. A point disputed with respect to both the US and Europe in McChesney, F.S., and Shughart, W.F. (1995): *The Causes and Consequences of Antitrust: the Public-Choice Perspective* (Chicago, University of Chicago Press) and Sjostrom, W. (1998): "Competition law in the European Union and the United States", *The New Palgrave Dictionary of Economics and the Law*, volume 1, edited by P. Newman (London, Macmillan).
31. For a good recent survey, see Geroski, P. (1998): "Thinking creatively about markets", *International Journal of Industrial Organization*, 16, pp. 677–695.
32. Sletmo, G., and Williams, E. (1981): *Liner Conferences in the Container Age: US Policy at Sea* (New York, Macmillan).
33. Smith, J.R. (1906): "Ocean freight rates and their control through combinations", *Political Science Quarterly*, 21, pp. 237–263.
34. Productivity Commission (1999): *International liner cargo shipping: a review of Part X of the Trade Practices Act 1974*. Report No. 9 (Canberra, Australia: AusInfo).
35. For a detailed survey covering both the theoretical and econometric issues, see Bresnahan, T.F. (1989): "Empirical studies of industries with market power", *Handbook of Industrial Organization*, Volume II, edited by R. Schmalensee and R.D. Willig (Amsterdam, North-Holland), pp. 1011–1057.
36. The basic models of punishment are Green, E.J., and Porter, R.H. (1984): "Noncooperative collusion under imperfect price information", *Econometrica*, 52, pp. 87–100, and Rotemberg, J.J., and Saloner, G. (1986): "A supergame-theoretic model of price wars during booms", *American Economic Review*, 76, pp. 390–407.
37. Stigler, G.J. (1964): "A Theory of oligopoly", *Journal of Political Economy*, 72, pp. 41–61.
38. Fox, N.R. (1992): "An empirical analysis of ocean liner shipping", *International Journal of Transportation Economics*, 19, pp. 205–225.
39. Stigler, G.J. (1964): "A Theory of oligopoly", *Journal of Political Economy*, 72, pp. 44–61.
40. Fox, N.R. (1995): "Some effects of the U.S. Shipping Act of 1984 on ocean liner shipping conferences", *Journal of Maritime Law and Commerce*, 26, pp. 531–544.
41. Clyde, P.S., and Reitzes, J.D. (1998): "Market power and collusion in the ocean shipping industry: is a bigger cartel a better cartel?", *Economic Inquiry*, 36, pp. 292–304.

42. Deltas, G., Serfes, K., and Sicotte, R. (1999): "American shipping cartels in the pre-World War I era", *Research in Economic History*, 16, pp. 1–38.
43. Their argument should not be confused with the idea that a firm operating in multiple markets can cross-subsidise predatory pricing to prevent destabilising entry. Gordon Boyce argues that because the International Mercantile Marine (a combination of five transatlantic lines sponsored by J.P. Morgan formed in the period 1900–1902) ran diversified lines from the UK to Canada, the US, and Australasia, it could use cross-subsidisation to harm smaller, single route firms. See Boyce, G.H. (1995): *Information, Mediation and Institutional Development: The Rise of Large-Scale Enterprise in British Shipping, 1870-1919* (Manchester, Manchester University Press). This sort of argument assumes inefficient capital markets. See McGee, J.S. (1980): "Predatory pricing revisited", *Journal of Law and Economics*, 23, pp. 289–330.
44. Davies, J.E. (1983): *Pricing in the liner shipping industry: a survey of conceptual models*, Canadian Transport Commission, Report No. 1983/04E; Davies, J.E. (1989): "Impediments to contestability in liner markets", *Logistics and Transportation Review*, 25, pp. 325–342.
45. Farrell, J. (1986): "How effective is potential competition?", *Economics Letters*, 20, pp. 67–70.
46. Marx, D. (1953): *International Shipping Cartels* (Princeton, Princeton University Press).
47. Graham, M.G. (1998): "Stability and competition in intermodal container shipping: finding a balance", *Maritime Policy and Management*, 25, pp. 129–147.
48. Hyde, F.E. (1967): *Shipping Enterprise and Management 1830-1939* (Liverpool, Liverpool University Press).
49. McGee, J.S. (1960): "Ocean freight conferences and American merchant marine", *University of Chicago Law Review*, 27, pp. 191–314; Bennathan, E., and Walters, A.A. (1969): *The Economics of Ocean Freight Rates* (New York, Praeger); Officer, L. (1971): "Monopoly and monopolistic competition in the international transportation industry", *Western Economic Journal*, 9, pp. 134–156.
50. Surveyed in Telser, L. (1994): "The usefulness of core theory in economics", *Journal of Economic Perspectives*, 8, pp. 151–164.
51. Sjostrom, W. (1989): "Collusion in ocean shipping: a test of monopoly and empty core models", *Journal of Political Economy*, 97, pp. 1160–1179; Pirrong, S.C. (1992): "An application of core theory to the analysis of ocean shipping markets", *Journal of Law and Economics*, 35, pp. 89–131; Sjostrom, W. (1993): "Antitrust immunity for shipping conferences: an empty core approach", *Antitrust Bulletin*, 38, pp. 419–423; Davies, J., Pirrong, C., Sjostrom, W., and Yarrow, G. (1995): *Stability and related problems in liner shipping: an economic overview*, Hearings before the Committee on Commerce, Science, and Transportation. US Senate, 104th Congress, first session.
52. Button, K. (1999): *Shipping alliances: Are they at the "core" of solving instability problems in shipping? Liner Shipping: What's Next*, Proceedings of the 1999 Halifax Conference, International Association of Maritime Economists, Halifax, Canada, September, pp. 58–88.
53. The accounts in Smith, T.K. (1995): "Why air travel doesn't work", *Fortune*, 3 April, of conversations with airline executives are similar to the views routinely expressed by people in the liner shipping business, particularly the problem that inventories are extremely expensive.
54. Bittlingmayer, G. (1989): "The economic problem of fixed costs and what legal research can contribute", *Law and Social Inquiry*, 14, pp. 739–762.
55. On this point, see Telser, L. (1978): *Economic Theory and the Core* (Chicago, University of Chicago Press), especially chapter 3, and McWilliams, A. (1990): "Rethinking horizontal market restrictions: in defense of cooperation in empty core markets", *Quarterly Review of Economics and Business*, 30, pp. 3–14.
56. Sjostrom, W. (1989): "Collusion in ocean shipping: a test of monopoly and empty core models", *Journal of Political Economy*, 97, pp. 1160–1179.

57. Clyde, P.S., and Reitzes, J.D. (1998): "Market power and collusion in the ocean shipping industry: is a bigger cartel a better cartel?", *Economic Inquiry*, 36, pp. 292–304.
58. Pirrong, S.C. (1992): "An application of core theory to the analysis of ocean shipping markets", *Journal of Law and Economics*, 35, pp. 89–131.
59. McGee, J.S. (1960): "Ocean freight conferences and American merchant marine", *University of Chicago Law Review*, 27, pp. 191–314; Abrahamsson, B.J. (1980): *International Ocean Shipping: Current Concepts and Principles* (Boulder, Colorado, Westview).
60. McGee, J.S. (1960): "Ocean freight conferences and American merchant marine", *University of Chicago Law Review*, 27, pp. 191–314.
61. Yamey, B.S. (1972): "Predatory price cutting: notes and comments", *Journal of Law and Economics*, 15, pp. 129–142.
62. [1892] App. Cas. 25.
63. Mogul Steamship Co. is the most well known instance of a claim of predatory pricing in liner shipping. Useful discussions can be found in Letwin, W. (1965): *Law and Economic Policy in America: The Evolution of the Sherman Antitrust Act* (Chicago, University of Chicago Press) and Yamey, B.S. (1972): "Predatory price cutting: notes and comments", *Journal of Law and Economics*, 15, pp. 129–142. Its legal fame rests on the Court's decision that under common law, agreements in restraint of trade (which the Court judged the conference to be) are unenforceable but not actionable.
64. Scott Morton, F. (1979): "Entry and predation: British shipping cartels, 1879–1929", *Journal of Economics and Management Strategy*, 6, pp. 679–724.
65. McGee, J.S. (1960): "Ocean freight conferences and American merchant marine", *University of Chicago Law Review*, 27, pp. 191–314; Bork, R.H. (1980): *The Antitrust Paradox* (New York, Basic Books).
66. Podolny, J.M., and Scott Morton, F.M. (1999): "Social status, entry, and predation: the case of British shipping cartels 1879–1929", *Journal of Industrial Economics*, 47, pp. 41–67.
67. Boyce, G.H. (1995): *Information, Mediation and Institutional Development: The Rise of Large-Scale Enterprise in British Shipping, 1870–1919* (Manchester, Manchester University Press).
68. Marshall, A. (1921): *Industry and Trade* (London, Macmillan); Marx, D. (1953): *International Shipping Cartels* (Princeton, Princeton University Press).
69. Marriner, S., and Hyde, F.E. (1967): *The Senior: John Samuel Swire, 1825-1898, Management in the Far Eastern Shipping Trades* (Liverpool, Liverpool University Press).
70. McGee, J.S. (1960): "Ocean freight conferences and American merchant marine", *University of Chicago Law Review*, 27, pp. 191–314
71. Marx, D. (1953): *International Shipping Cartels* (Princeton, Princeton University Press).
72. Grossman, W.L. (1956): *Ocean Freight Rates* (Cambridge, Cornell Maritime Press).
73. Marín, P.L., and Sicotte, R. (2001): *Exclusive contracts and market power: evidence from ocean shipping*, Centre for Economic Policy Research Working Paper 2828.
74. Hyde, F.E. (1957): *Blue Funnel: A History of Alfred Holt and Company of Liverpool from 1865 to 1914* (Liverpool, Liverpool University Press).
75. Marx, D. (1953): *International Shipping Cartels* (Princeton, Princeton University Press).
76. Bork, R.H. (1980): *The Antitrust Paradox* (New York, Basic Books).
77. Sjostrom, W. (1988): "Monopoly exclusion of lower cost entry: loyalty contracts in ocean shipping conferences", *Journal of Transport Economics and Policy*, 22, pp. 339–344.
78. Lewis, W.A. (1949): *Overhead Costs: Some Essays in Economic Analysis* (New York, Rinehart); Boyce, G.H. (1995): *Information, Mediation and Institutional Development:*

The Rise of Large-Scale Enterprise in British Shipping, 1870–1919 (Manchester, Manchester University Press).
79. Gordon, J.S. (1969): "Shipping regulation and the Federal Maritime Commission, Part 1", *University of Chicago Law Review*, 37, pp. 90–158.
80. Davies, P.N. (1973): *The Trade Makers: Elder Dempster in West Africa* (London, George Allen & Unwin).
81. McGee, J.S. (1960): "Ocean freight conferences and American merchant marine", *University of Chicago Law Review*, 27, pp. 191–314; Bennathan, E., and Walters, A.A. (1969): *The Economics of Ocean Freight Rates* (New York, Praeger).
82. Jansson, J.O., and Shneerson, D. (1987): *Liner Shipping Economics* (London, Chapman and Hall); Sjostrom, W. (1992): "Price discrimination by shipping conferences", *Logistics and Transportation Review*, 28, pp. 207–215.
83. For a detailed description of Ramsey pricing, see Brown, S.J., and Sibley, D.S. (1986): *The Theory of Public Utility Pricing* (Cambridge, Cambridge University Press).
84. Telser, L. (1978): *Economic Theory and the Core* (Chicago, University of Chicago Press).
85. Sjostrom, W. (1992): "Price discrimination by shipping conferences", *Logistics and Transportation Review*, 28, pp. 207–215..
86. Clyde, P.S., and Reitzes, J.D. (1998): "Market power and collusion in the ocean shipping industry: is a bigger cartel a better cartel?", *Economic Inquiry*, 36, pp. 292–304.

CHAPTER 15

THE ECONOMIC REGULATION OF LINER SHIPPING: THE IMPACT OF US AND EU REGULATION IN US TRADES

Bernard Gardner, Peter Marlow and Rawindaran Nair
Cardiff Business School, University of Cardiff, Wales, UK.
E-mail: *Gardner@Cardiff.ac.uk, Marlow@Cardiff.ac.uk* and *nairR1@yahoo.com*

1. INTRODUCTION

Liner services were developed in the second half of the nineteenth century when reliable steam power made it possible for the first time for shipping companies to provide regular scheduled services. The provision of scheduled services created a problem for shipping companies, since the failure to co-ordinate such services often led to bunching of arrivals in ports, and competition for cargo among rival firms proved destructive owing to the predominance of fixed costs in liner shipping operations. The problem was solved by self-regulation through the creation of cartels known as shipping conferences. Liner shipping conferences were among the earliest forms of cartels in international trade. They were widespread by the turn of the 20th century and covered most international trade routes by then.[1]

A liner shipping conference agreement is an agreement among scheduled carriers on a particular trade route to restrict competition among themselves by setting mutually agreed freight rates and conditions of service. The anti-competitive practices of conferences during the early years of their operation were a cause of concern to shippers, particularly the use of deferred rebates and fighting ships. In the United Kingdom, a Commission, the Royal Commission on Shipping Rings, was set up in 1906 to investigate these practices. The Commission's report was published in 1909. It contained both a Majority report and a Minority report. The Majority report stressed the importance of the benefits of conferences, such as regularity of sailings and the improved quality of ships, that were made possible by the greater security which conferences afforded capital invested in steamship businesses. It concluded that there were no serious defects in the conference system, despite noting that there existed pressure from large shippers which might lead to preferential contracts or discriminatory rates. The Minority report, on the other hand, was not so keen to give the system a clean bill of health. It considered there were serious defects in the system and, moreover, that the advantages stressed by the Majority report had been exaggerated. It did not, however, favour a legislative solution. Instead, it recommended that a system should be established for consultation and conciliation between conferences and shippers. It suggested, *inter alia*, that the Board of Trade could perhaps take the initiative by recognising trade associations as representing shippers.[2]

This chapter is concerned with competition policy in shipping and in particular the economic regulation of liner shipping in US trades, where conferences have been subject to regulatory oversight since 1916, first by the United States Shipping Board, then by the Federal Maritime Board (FMB), and currently by the Federal Maritime Commission (FMC). The chapter is divided into seven sections. Section 2 briefly considers the relevance of the United States antitrust laws. Sections 3 and 4 discuss the evolution of economic regulation in the United States. Section 5 discusses the more recent development of EU regulation. Section 6 discusses the impact of the current US regulatory regime on liner shipping considering its impact in US/EU trades where carriers have also to comply with EU regulation as well as its broader impact. Section 7 draws some conclusions.

2. UNITED STATES ANTITRUST LAWS

Competition policy may be defined as the economic regulation of the marketplace in order to encourage and enhance the competitive process. It originated in the United States where it is referred to as antitrust policy. The term "antitrust" was coined to describe the measures put in place to curb a particular anti-competitive business practice that had become commonplace in the United States by the end of the 19th century, namely, that of placing the stock of a large number of competing firms in an industry into the hands of trustees who were then able to restrict competition in that industry.[3] The antitrust laws were designed to prevent such potentially abusive business structures and practices from manifesting themselves and are based on the concept that a competitive marketplace is desirable as it promotes the most efficient use of society's scarce resources. The laws were passed, therefore, to preserve competition through the control of anti-competitive behaviour in the marketplace.[4] The Sherman Act of 1890,[5] the principal antitrust law, condemns in uncompromising terms such practices:

"Every contract, combination in the form of trust or otherwise, or conspiracy, in restraint of trade ... is declared ... illegal. Every person who shall monopolise, or attempt to monopolise ... any part of the trade or commerce [of the United States] shall be deemed guilty of a felony."[6]

Such practices became criminal with the passing of the Act. The Act, initially, proved unworkable as it caught in its net a wide range of business practices besides those that were clearly anti-competitive. Interpretations by the Supreme Court of the United States eventually provided a workable *modus operandi* by introducing "the rule of reason". Under this rule, certain forms of business behaviour that were considered *prima facie* to be harmless could be judged, not only by their form, but also by their effects or by the intent of the parties concerned. Price fixing agreements and market sharing and numerous other business practices, considered to be clearly anti-competitive, continued,however, to be deemed illegal *per se*. Proof of their existence is thus sufficient to gain a conviction under the Act. Consequently, no defence based on their effects is allowable.[7]

The Clayton Act of 1914 supplemented the antitrust provisions of the Sherman Act. Among the practices made unlawful were four types of specific business behaviour: price discrimination, exclusive dealing and tying-in contracts, acquisition of competing firms, and interlocking directorships. Illegality, in each case, is subject to the condition that the purpose and effect of the practice would be substantially to lessen competition. In 1936, the section in the Clayton Act dealing with price discrimination was amended by the Robinson-Patman Act making it unlawful to discriminate in price between purchasers of goods of similar technical specification where the effect would be substantially to lessen competition, and in 1950 the Act was further amended to prohibit mergers that would also substantially lessen competition. Offences, under the Clayton Act and its amendments, however, are not criminal, unlike those under the Sherman Act.[8]

3. EVOLUTION OF ECONOMIC REGULATION IN THE UNITED STATES: 1911 TO 1984

3.1 Events foreshadowing the Shipping Act of 1916

Collusive agreements among liner shipping companies are clearly in conflict with the provisions of antitrust laws and thus would be unlawful unless given immunity under other legislation. It is not surprising, therefore, that the US Department of Justice (DOJ), in 1911, brought a suit against three conferences, charging violations of the Sherman Act through agreements and practices in restraint of trade.[9] The suit was brought because of shippers' complaints about rate discrimination and other arbitrary action by shipping conferences and their use of anti-competitive devices such as fighting ships and deferred rebates. The outbreak of the First World War in 1914 disrupted the court proceedings, which had not reached a conclusion by then. The Supreme Court held in the three cases that the questions were moot and dismissed the charges without prejudice to the government.[10]

The issues raised in the above cases, however, stimulated wider public debate about the anti-competitive practices of shipping conferences. In response to this, the US House of Representatives in 1912 directed its Committee on Merchant Marine and Fisheries (the Alexander Committee), chaired by Representative Joshua W. Alexander of Missouri, to investigate shipping combinations and their practices. The Alexander Committee published its findings in 1914. The Committee reported in favour of the continuation of the conference system in US trades because it considered that the system provided benefits such as improved service and greater stability of rates. These were, in its opinion, essential for the sound development of trade. Nevertheless, it was unhappy about granting a blanket exemption from the antitrust laws without governmental oversight.[11]

It, therefore, recommended that:
- the Interstate Commerce Commission (ICC) regulate carriers' rates and contracts between carriers;
- conference agreements be filed with the ICC and approved by it, with the ICC having the power to deny the agreements if found to be discriminatory or unjust;
- the ICC have the power to investigate rates determined to be unreasonable;
- rebates and other discriminatory practices against shippers to be made illegal; and
- fighting ships and deferred rates be made illegal and carriers prohibited from retaliating against shippers for any reason.[12]

Following the publication of his report, Congressman Alexander in 1916 introduced a bill, H.R. 15455, in the first session of the 64th Congress. This bill reflected many of the recommendations contained in the report and eventually became the Shipping Act of 1916 on 8 September after the bill was signed by the President.[13]

3.2 US Shipping Act of 1916 and its aftermath

The Act did not expand the role of the ICC but instead established a separate agency to oversee the ocean shipping industry, namely, the United States Shipping Board. The Act prohibited fighting ships and deferred rebates. It required common carriers to file their agreements with the Shipping Board and agreements filed with the Board were sheltered from the antitrust laws. While conferences were permitted to fix rates under their agreements, the 1916 Act subjected them to numerous restrictions designed to limit their potential for monopolistic abuse.[14]

With their ability to rationalise constrained and deferred rebates made illegal, in the years following the enactment of the 1916 Act, conferences sought to establish a stable market for themselves by offering lower rates to shippers who agreed to patronise their members exclusively. In 1958, the Supreme Court ruled in an action taken by the FMB against Isbrandtsen Co.[15] that such "dual rate" contracts were unlawful. Congress, in reaction to the Supreme Court ruling in this case, adopted a series of amendments to the Shipping Act of 1916. This was the result of a review by Congress of the conference system and its use of dual rate contracts, which took place between 1958 and 1961. The review was conducted by the House Merchant Marine and Fisheries Committee under the chairmanship of H.C. Bonner and the Antitrust Sub-Committee of the House Judiciary Committee under the chairmanship of E. Celler. These amendments, Public Law 87-346, the "1961 Amendments", legislatively reversed the Isbrandtsen ruling and authorised the use of dual rate contracts, while providing additional safeguards to shippers.[16]

3.3 Public Law 87–346 ("1961 Amendments") and its aftermath

Under the 1961 Amendments, a conference could not constitute a dual rate contract until it had been approved by the FMC, the agency that replaced the FMB. However, the FMC could not approve if it found the contract:

- detrimental to the commerce of the US;
- contrary to the public interest; or
- unjustly discriminatory or unfair as between shippers, exporters, importers or ports, or between exporters from the US and their foreign competitors.[17]

In addition, there was a list of conditions governing the specific terms of the contract, which had to be complied with if it were to be approved. The 1961 Amendments also modified section 15 of the 1916 Act to provide that:
- inter-conference agreements would be approved only if conference members retained the right of independent action;
- conferences were required to remain open to all qualified carriers, which were also free to exit without penalty; and
- agreements contrary to the public interest would not be approved.[18]

In the years following the 1961 Amendments dissatisfaction with the regulatory procedures led to calls for further reform. Carriers complained about delays in the FMC's approval process for conference agreements, application of vague standards for approval, and loss of predictability in regulatory decision making. Carriers also complained that the regulatory procedures severely hampered their ability to secure timely approval for conference agreements. Rate-making agreements, intermodal arrangements, pooling agreements, joint ventures, and rationalisation agreements were affected. Discussion agreements and inter-conference agreements were also affected by delay. Moreover, many carriers complained that even if approval of discussion agreements and inter-conference agreements were obtained, fear of prosecution under the antitrust laws remained.[19]

Most of the dissatisfaction with the regulatory procedures following the 1961 Amendments centred on the FMC's administration of section 15 and related to the "public interest" standard. The FMC held that an agreement that was a *per se* violation of the antitrust laws was *prima facie* contrary to the public interest. The FMC thus required that such agreements had to be shown, by the parties concerned, to meet a serious transportation need, be necessary to secure important public benefits, or serve a valid regulatory purpose to be approved. The FMC's test was approved by the Supreme Court ruling in a test case, *FMC v Aktiebolaget Svenska Amerika Linien*.[20] This test became known as the "Svenska" standard.

Carriers and conferences complained that this standard was too vague and placed an unfair burden on them. Moreover, carriers also took the view that there was a need for the antitrust immunity, given under section 15 of the 1916 Act, to be expanded and its scope clarified if the benefits of intermodalism were to be achieved.[21]

4. EVOLUTION OF ECONOMIC REGULATION IN THE UNITED STATES: 1984 ONWARDS

4.1 US Shipping Act of 1984

The US Shipping Act of 1984, which repealed the 1916 Act, was enacted by Congress and signed into law by the President on 20 March 1984.[22] This Act which, subject to the amendments contained in the Ocean Shipping Reform

Act of 1998 (OSRA), defines the US regulatory regime operative today, addressed the concerns of carriers over antitrust immunity and the Svenska standard.

Section 6(g) of the Act provides that the FMC may, at any time after the filing or effective date of an agreement, seek an injunction in a district court against any such agreement if it finds that it is likely, "by a reduction in competition, to produce an unreasonable reduction in transportation service or an unreasonable increase in transportation cost". In such an action, the burden of proof is on the FMC, thereby reversing the position in the Svenska standard where the burden was on the parties to the agreement.

Carriers may be subject to prosecution by the Department of Justice (DOJ) for concerted action taken pursuant to an agreement that has not been filed, but under section 7(a) they are immunised for conduct for which they have a reasonable basis to conclude is covered by a filed agreement. In addition, in section 7(c), the Act provides that no person may recover damages under the antitrust laws for conduct, which is prohibited under the 1984 Act. This provision has eliminated much of the uncertainty that existed under the 1961 Amendments to the 1916 Act. So, antitrust exposure is now limited to DOJ actions; treble damages and injunctive relief are not available to private litigants.

In order to balance the concessions to carriers, the Act extended the scope of the independent action to all agreements. Independent action became mandatory on any rate or service item for all conference agreements, except for service contracts where the conference needed to provide for such action, since section 4(a) gave conferences the authority to regulate or prohibit their use of such contracts. The notice period was not more than ten days (section 5(b)(8)).

An important procedural change introduced by the Act was in section 6(c) which provided that the agreements become effective "on the 45th day after filing, or on the 30th day after notice of the filing is published in the Federal Register, whichever day is later".

The statutory tariff filing system that was established by the 1961 Amendments was preserved. While retaining this provision, the Act also provided for the filing of through rates covering routes between US and/or foreign inland points.

Section 8(c) permitted carriers or conferences to enter into service contracts, which are the functional equivalent of time/volume contracts, with shippers. It required them to file such contracts confidentially with the FMC. Moreover, they also had to file a concise statement of the essential terms of such contacts with the FMC and make them available to the general public in tariff format. The essential terms, according to the Act, are:
- the origin and destination port ranges in the case of port to port movements, and the origin and destination geographic area in the case of through intermodal movements;
- the commodity or commodities involved;
- the minimum volume;
- the line-haul rate;
- the duration;

– service commitment; and
– the liquidated damages for non-performance, if any.

The Act required that the essential terms be made available to all shippers similarly situated, thus retaining the principle of common carriage. This provision became known as the "me-too" provision.

Section 4(a)(1) clarifies conference authority to set intermodal rates, and section 10(c)(4) makes it clear that a conference can agree on the inland portion of such rates. However, this section prohibited a conference from negotiating with inland carriers (for example, truck or rail operators) on any matters relating to rates or services within the United States; only individual members were permitted to do this.

The Act also prohibited the use of loyalty, presumably dual rate, contracts by conferences (section 10(b)(9)), and confirmed that conferences must be open to any qualified common carrier willing to serve the trade (section 5(b)(2)).

4.2 The Advisory Commission on Conferences in Ocean Shipping

Under section 18 of the 1984 Act, the FMC was mandated to collect and analyse data concerning the impact of the Act on the international ocean shipping industry for a period of five years following its enactment. Within six months of completing this study the FMC had to submit its findings to Congress, to the Advisory Commission on Conferences in Ocean Shipping (ACCOS), and to the Department of Transportation (DOT), the Department of Justice (DOJ) and the Federal Trade Commission (FTC). The latter three agencies were also required to assess the impact of the Act and report their findings to Congress and to ACCOS.[23] ACCOS was a temporary body that was set up five-and-half years after the enactment of the Act, also under section 18, to conduct a study of, and make recommendations concerning, conferences to the President and Congress. In particular, it was set up to advise whether the United States would be best served by prohibiting conferences, or by closed or open conferences. Despite the comprehensiveness of its study, ACCOS was unable to reach a consensus about these issues, perhaps because of its composition. Commissioners represented a wide spectrum of interested parties, including shippers, carriers, port authorities and non-vessel operating common carriers as well as members of Congress. It thus felt unable to make any recommendations, and no proposals were made for regulatory change when it reported its findings in April 1992.[24]

4.3 Pressure for change in the 1990s

During the 1990s, however, pressure for further change in the regulatory regime emerged from large shippers. In 1994, there was a proposal for reform of the Act, which came from the National Industrial Transportation League (NIT League), which represented the interests of such shippers. The NIT League, as a shippers' body, was sceptical of the pro-carrier attitude of the FMC and pressed for total deregulation of the industry through removal of its antitrust immunity.[25] Its initial proposal included the following suggested amendments:

- removing carriers' antitrust immunity altogether;
- terminating the requirements for public filing of tariffs and service contracts with the FMC;
- abolition of the FMC; and
- shifting the regulation of carrier consortia to the DOJ and licensing and bonding of forwarders to the DOT.

As the above proposal was clearly a threat to carriers' interests, there were objections to it from carriers. However, in July 1995 when the NIT League decided to drop its objection to carriers' antitrust immunity, there was a change in the attitude among major US flag carriers to the proposal. This led to a revised legislative proposal that would retain carriers' antitrust immunity but which would abolish the FMC and permit confidential service contracts. A bill containing these reforms was passed by the House of Representatives in September 1995, but ran into opposition early in 1996 when it reached the Senate floor, where the Senate Majority Leader opposed the abolition of the FMC. This led the Clinton Administration to reconsider its earlier support for the bill. A new compromise bill was introduced in November 1997. This bill retained the FMC as the regulatory agency and antitrust immunity for carriers' agreements. The House passed the bill in August 1998 and the Senate approved its final version on 1 October 1998, which was then signed by the President.[26] This Act, which amended the Shipping Act of 1984, is known as the Ocean Shipping Reform Act of 1998 (OSRA) and came into force on 1 May 1999.

4.4 US Ocean Shipping Reform Act of 1998

The Ocean Shipping Reform Act (OSRA)[27] made some fundamental amendments to the Shipping of 1984.

Under section 8(a)(1), carriers are no longer required to file their tariffs with the FMC. They are, however, required to publish their tariffs electronically, and under section 8(a)(2) to make them available to the public in an automated system with appropriate access from remote locations.

The provision of the period of notice for independent action under the 1984 Act is reduced from 10 days to five days (section 5(b)(8)).

The provisions on service contracts that were first introduced under the 1984 Act have been amended extensively. In the first place, other agreements among ocean common carriers, besides conferences, may enter into such a contract with shippers (section 8(c)(1)).

Secondly, confidentiality aspects of such contracts have been redefined. Under section 8(c)(2) it is provided that while certain essential terms should continue to be filed together with the service contract with the FMC, the terms that deal with the strategic component of service contracts now remain confidential. These terms are:
- the origin and destination geographic areas in the case of through intermodal movements;
- the line-haul rate;
- the service commitments; and
- the liquidated damages for non-performance, if any.

THE ECONOMIC REGULATION OF LINER SHIPPING 335

The provision under section 8(c) of the 1984 Act, which required that "those essential terms shall be available to all shippers similarly situated", or the so called "me-too" right has been removed.

Thirdly, under section 5(c) conferences and other ocean common carrier agreements may not:
- prohibit a member or members of the agreement from engaging in negotiations for service contracts with one or more shippers;
- require a member or members to disclose a negotiation on a service contract, or the terms and conditions of such a contract, except those terms that are published under section 8(c)(3); or
- adopt mandatory rules or requirements affecting the right of a member or members to negotiate or enter into service contracts.

These provisions are strengthened by the removal of the provisions in section 4(7) of the 1984 Act, which allowed conferences to regulate or prohibit their use of service contracts.

Finally, an agreement may provide authority to adopt voluntary guidelines that relate to the terms and procedures of an agreement member's or members' service contract, provided such guidelines explicitly state that members have the right not to follow them. These guidelines must be confidentially submitted to the FMC (section 5(c)(3)).

Freight forwarders and non-vessel operating common carriers (NVOCCs) are defined as ocean intermediaries (OTIs) under section 3(17). Since NVOCCs do not operate vessels, they are also defined as shippers (section 3(17)(B) in their relationship with vessel operating common carriers (VOCCs) and are not allowed to enter into service contracts with other shippers. As a common carrier, however, they are required to publish their tariffs in the same way as VOCCs.

The scope of intermodal authority provided in the 1984 Act is extended under OSRA. The prohibition concerning the negotiation of matters relating to rates or services within the United States involving conferences and inland carriers in the 1984 Act is relaxed. The negotiation of such matters involving these parties is now permissible, provided that such negotiation and any resulting agreement does not infringe the antitrust laws and is consistent with the purposes of OSRA (section 10(c)(4)). This relaxation permits conferences to operate as a single entity inland in their negotiations and in their agreements for inland transportation.[28]

5. DEVELOPMENT OF ECONOMIC REGULATION IN THE EUROPEAN UNION

5.1 The competition rules of the Treaty

In the European Union (EU), the rules on competition are contained in Articles 81 and 82 of the European Community Treaty (formerly Articles 85 and 86 of the Treaty of Rome, which have been renumbered under the Treaty of Amsterdam with effect from May 1999).[29]

Article 81 prohibits all agreements between undertakings, decisions of associations of undertakings and concerted practices which may affect trade between Member States and which have as their object or effect the prevention, restriction or distortion of competition within the common market. There is a provision under Article 81(3) for exemption under certain strictly defined conditions. Such exemption can either be on an individual basis or by category of agreement. The former is known as an individual exemption and the latter as a block exemption. Agreements within the scope of a block exemption and which meet its conditions are automatically exempt; they do not need, therefore, be notified to the European Commission (EC).[30]

Article 82 provides that any abuse by one or more undertakings of a dominant position within the common market or in a substantial part of it shall be prohibited as incompatible with the common market in so far as it may affect trade between Member States. There is no possibility of an exemption from prohibition under Article 82.[31]

5.2 Applying the competition rules to transport

It took almost three decades after the European Community Treaty was signed in Rome in 1957 by the founder members of the Community before the EU competition policy was applied to maritime transport.[32] The first regulation applying the rules on competition, Regulation 17, adopted in 1962[33] gave the European Commission (EC) powers to enforce the Articles 81 and 82 of the European Community Treaty (the Treaty). Transport was, however, excluded from the application of this regulation through an amending regulation. Regulation 141/62, issued on 26 November 1962, provided that Regulation 17/62 was not to be applied to agreements within the transport sector. On 19 July 1968, Regulation 1017/68,[34] which applied the rules on competition to transport by rail, road and inland water transport, was adopted by the Council of Ministers of the European Communities (Council of Ministers), but maritime transport had to wait a further eighteen years before being brought within the EU regulatory net.

The need for specific regulations for the sea and air transport was, however, made clear after a judgment of the European Court of Justice (ECJ) at Luxembourg in 1974, which concluded that the general rules of the Treaty applied to these modes.[35] In a subsequent case, the ECJ confirmed, moreover, that the general rules include the competition rules contained in Articles 81 and 82 of the Treaty.[36] No real progress in applying the competition rules to maritime transport, though, was made until 1984 when the EC published a Memorandum on Maritime Transport laying down the main lines of action for a Community shipping policy. Soon after, in 1985, the EC addressed a communication to the Council entitled "Progress towards a Common Transport Policy (maritime transport)".[37] The policy was based on four elements: freedom to provide services; a competition regime; a system of protection against unfair trade practices; and the implementation of the United Nations Code of Conduct for Liner Conferences.

THE ECONOMIC REGULATION OF LINER SHIPPING 337

5.3 Regulations applying to liner shipping

In December 1986 the Council of Ministers adopted the "1986 maritime package" with four regulations. It constituted the first phase of the development of the Community's maritime policy and was intended to give legal force to the flexible approach outlined in the EC Memorandum. It came into force on 1 July 1987.[38] One of these regulations, namely Council Regulation 4056/86, lays down detailed rules for applying the competition principles embodied in Articles 81 and 82 of the Treaty to maritime transport.[39]

In June 1990 the EC made a proposal to the Council of Ministers in favour of a new block exemption for consortia agreements,[40] so as to increase the range of regulatory instruments available to it. The Council adopted enabling Regulation (EEC) No. 479/92 on 25 February 1992.[41] Following this enabling regulation, the EC adopted Commission Regulation No. 870/95[42] to provide a block exemption for consortia agreements. Commission regulations are subject to periodic review every five years. Hence, this regulation expired in April 2000 and has been replaced by a revised consortia regulation, Commission Regulation 823/2000.[43] Council regulations have no time limit.

5.4 Scope and effect of EU regulations

The scope and effect of Regulation 4056/86 can be ascertained from how the EC has interpreted its provisions in decisions adopted relating to a number of landmark cases.[44] The interpretations contained in these decisions have determined what conferences are, and what they can and cannot do in the context of their agreement to fix prices when providing services to and from EU ports. The Treaty, however, provides that decisions of the EC can be appealed, firstly to the European Court of First Instance (CFI) and then to the European Court of Justice (ECJ). The CFI hears appeals concerning decisions on points of fact and law. Thereafter, a further appeal may be made to the ECJ on a point of law. The task of the ECJ under Article 220 of the Treaty is to "ensure that in the interpretation and application of the Treaty, the law is observed".[45]

Although this appeal procedure is provided for in the Treaty, it is recognised that some of the principal issues raised in these landmark cases and thus the scope of Regulation 4056/86 have not yet been fully resolved. This is because in some of these landmark cases referred to below, the appeal process to the European Courts has not been exhausted, although the decisions of the EC have been delivered. As a result, the interpretation given by the EC in these cases and to the extent that, they have been affirmed, by the European Courts remains the current state of the law. The interpretation given to the regulation in the decisions adopted by the EC in these cases and the judgement on them in so far as they have been given by the CFI and ECJ are now outlined.

The scope of the provision in Article 1(3)(b) of Regulation 4056/86, which defines a "liner conference", has been clarified in a decision of the EC. This decision of the EC has been upheld in an appeal of the same case by the CFI. The EC decision on the Trans-Atlantic Agreement (TAA),[46] made on 19 October 1994 implies that a "liner conference" within this article, excludes discussion agreements. This definition of a "liner conference"[47] has been affirmed in the judgement of the CFI delivered on 28 February 2002.

The rules that apply to joint service contracts entered into by conferences are contained in the EC decision in the case of the Trans-Atlantic Conference Agreement (TACA)[48] made on 18 September 1998. According to that decision, while individual service contracts in which only one carrier is a party do not fall within the scope of Article 81(1), conferences that enter into joint service contracts have to seek individual exemption under Article 81(3) from the EC. This, the EC decided, was because the group exemption for liner conferences contained in Regulation 4056/86 does not authorise joint service contracts.

The EC also decided that liner conferences entering into joint service contracts cannot authorise:
- a prohibition on individual service contracts;
- a restriction, whether binding or non-binding, on the contents of such contracts; and
- a prohibition of independent action on joint service contracts.

The EC in that decision stated, further, that since these contracts are the outcome of business relations among carriers and shippers their contents need not be shared either with other carriers in the conference or with other shippers.

The EC decided in the case of the Far Eastern Freight Conference (FEFC)[49] on 21 December 1994 that:
- Regulation 4056/86 does not provide block exemption to a "liner conference" for intermodal authority; and
- Regulation 1017/68 is the appropriate regulation to consider such authority.

This decision has been upheld by the judgment of the CFI delivered on 28 February 2002.[50]

The EC, however, has in the case of the TACA, agreed to the provision in its agreement that its members should not charge less than "out of pocket" expenses when supplying inland transport within the European Union as part of an intermodal service.[51] According to the EC, members of TACA are only permitted to implement a capacity regulation programme under which a co-ordinated capacity withdrawal is permissible where such withdrawal is necessary in order to cope with a short-term fluctuation in demand. Any other co-ordinated capacity withdrawal is not compatible with the provisions of Article 81(3) of the Treaty.[52]

Finally, in the Associated Central West Africa Lines (CEWAL) case,[53] the first concerning the application of Regulation 4056/86 to have been decided by the Community judicature, the ECJ confirmed that the same practice may simultaneously give rise to an infringement both of Article 81(1) and Article 82 of the Treaty. In this regard, the Court found that a liner conference as defined by the regulation, by its very nature and in the light of its objectives, could be described as a collective entity presenting itself as such on the market. In view of that, a liner conference was therefore capable of holding a dominant position within the meaning of Article 82 of the Treaty.[54]

6. IMPACT OF OSRA

There is no doubt that OSRA has contributed to the restructuring of the liner shipping industry that has taken place over the past few years. The recently published FMC study on its impact provides ample evidence of this.[55]

Many of the key reforms under OSRA relate to service contracting. Redefining the confidentiality aspects of such contracts so that certain commercially sensitive terms, such as line-haul rates and service commitments, are no longer disclosed publicly, eliminating the "me-too" requirement for similarly situated shippers, removing the right of conferences to prohibit their members from individually engaging in negotiations for service contracts, and permitting independent action on conference service contracts have fostered a marked shift towards contract carriage in US trades.

According to the FMC, since OSRA came effective on 1 May 1999, there has been a 200 per cent rise in the number of service contracts and amendments filed. The FMC also found in an industry survey, which it conducted as part of its impact study, that service contracts were being used to ship a far greater volume of cargo as a result of OSRA. In certain major US trades some shippers reported that they were moving nearly 100 per cent of their cargo under service contracts; and in several trades carriers reported that the volume of cargo moving under such contracts was in excess of 80 per cent.[56] In a random sample survey of service contracts filed with it, involving a sample of 1,000 contracts, the FMC found, moreover, that 98 per cent of contracts filed were individual, indicating a marked preference by shippers for individual contracting with carriers over multicarrier or agreement contracting.[57]

The marked shift towards contract carriage and the increase in individual service contracting resulting from the OSRA reforms has been a significant factor in altering the structure of the liner industry in US trades, as it has led to the termination or suspension of major conference agreements in many trades. This is because where only a small volume of cargo in a trade moves under tariff rates or conference service contracts, there is little incentive for carriers to belong to a conference if a discussion agreement that covers the trade exists or could be established.[58]

Discussion agreements are non-binding ratemaking agreements and thus the rates established under such agreements are not subject to enforcement or policing as under a conference agreement where the ratemaking is binding. They are the product of overtonnaging that had become endemic in the main east/west arterial liner trades by the mid-1980s. They were initially established in the transatlantic trade and the US inbound Far East trades, where the Eurocorde Discussion Agreement covered the former trade and the Transpacific Stabilisation Agreement (TSA) the latter trade.[59]

Discussion agreements were the means by which conference carriers were able to induce strong independent carriers in these trades that were unwilling to engage in binding ratemaking, required by conference membership, to enter into a voluntary ratemaking agreement designed to mitigate rate competition between the two types of carrier.[60] These agreements spread to other US trades, including the US/South American, the US/Caribbean and other Pacific trades. As in the case of the TSA, which introduced a capacity management programme when it was established in 1989, their members soon realised that where overtonnaging existed it was necessary to exert control over supply in order to maintain rate stability and prevent destructive competition.[61] Consequently, managing capacity also became a feature of discussion agreements. However, the TSA withdrew its formal capacity management programme in 1995 in the face of a potential legal challenge by the FMC.[62] Since then, although discussion agreement members in US trades are still concerned about managing capacity and would consider the possibility of reducing it where circumstances dictate, such reductions are not co-ordinated. Hence, cuts when required are made independently by individual lines or alliances withdrawing capacity, as to do otherwise would invite a legal challenge from the FMC.[63]

The Eurocorde Discussion Agreement was established in the transatlantic in 1985. When, in 1992 the members of the two conferences the trade, the USA North Europe Rate Agreement (USANERA) and the North Europe USA Rate Agreement (NEUSARA) amalgamated their agreements to form a single conference in the trade, the Trans-Atlantic Agreement, they also tried to induce the independent carrier members of Eurocorde to join the new conference agreement by having a multi-tier tariff as well as a formal capacity management programme as part of the agreement. This proved successful as most of the non-conference members of Eurocorde joined the TAA.[64] In a letter to the TAA's lawyers in June 1992, the EC's Competition Directorate, however, expressed the view that the agreement fell outside the scope of the block exemption for liner conferences as provided for in Article 3 of Regulation 4056/86. Moreover, even if the TAA were a liner conference that fell within the scope of the block exemption, it was the Directorate's opinion that its capacity management programme would not be covered by the exemption. The letter emphasised that "under [the Community's] competition law, simultaneous multilateral price fixing and capacity reductions have never been tolerated by the Commission [and that Article 3] must if possible be interpreted in a manner consistent with the well established principles of Community competition law".[65] On 19 October 1994, the EC decided to adopt a decision to prohibit the TAA as it was held to violate EU competition law. One of the reasons given for its decision was the TAA's multi-tier price and capacity management agreements infringed Article 81(1) of the Treaty. The decision also clarified the scope of Article 1(3)(b) of Regulation 4056/86 and implies that a "liner conference" as defined within this article excludes discussion agreements (see above). Hence such agreements do not enjoy the benefit of the block exemption under the regulation and are unlawful in EU trades.

With recent demise of conferences in many US trades, discussion agreements have become the only forum where carriers can share commercial information about rates and capacity and formulate pricing policy. Currently there are only four discussion agreements that include a conference as a member, whereas in June 2000 there were eighteen such agreements.[66] In the transatlantic trade, on the other hand, where carriers must comply with the EU regulatory regime, too, traditional conference carriers have found it necessary to retain the conference, namely TACA (formerly TAA), because it is the only forum they have for sharing such information and formulating pricing policy (albeit only on a very restricted basis), as discussion agreements are prohibited.[67]

On 29 January 1999, the members of TACA submitted to the European Commission an application in respect of a revised version of the agreement. Under this revised version, TACA has amended its service contract provisions to comply with OSRA and with the EC decision of 16 September 1998. Consequently, TACA members are able to enter into individual service contracts, but they cannot discuss the contents of these contracts among themselves and may not collectively gather information to be shared.[68] Under EU law, moreover, conferences cannot issue voluntary guidelines on matters relating to non-conference service contracts, which is permissible under OSRA. They are, however, able to establish a model conference service contract and rate matrices, provided such information is publicly available, and their members may refer to and adopt such rates in their individual contract negotiations.[69]

Before the EC decision on TACA and the OSRA reforms came into effect, a major portion of the trade's cargo moved under conference service contracts. In 1998, TACA filed 596 conference service contracts with the FMC. In 1999, however, with OSRA becoming effective and following the EC decision, TACA members actively entered into individual service contracts.[70] By the end of 1999, according to the information that TACA provided in response to the FMC's industry survey, upwards of 80% of the conference's cargo was moving under individual service contracts, and now only about 10% of the cargo carried by members moves under conference rates. Of over 1000 service contracts entered into by the members in 1999, only 30 were conference contracts. In 2000, TACA entered into only three conference service contracts. This indicates a marked decline in TACA's direct authority over its members' service contracts and, consequently, over its binding ratemaking authority, which may be attributed to the OSRA reforms and to the EC decision. When the TAA/TACA conference was formed in 1992, it had, initially a market share close to 80%; today its market share is approximately 50%. In terms of membership, participation by carriers has fallen from a high of seventeen to the present low of seven carriers.[71]

In the US/Mediterranean trade, which is also to subject to EU as well as US regulatory oversight, the situation in the trade is similar to that in the transatlantic. The conference, the United States South Europe Conference (USSEC), with three members, has been retained but the combined effect of EU and US regulation has weakened the pricing authority that it can exercise over the cargo moved by its members. According to information provided to the FMC in its impact study, USSEC members, since the enactment of OSRA, have substantially increased their use of individual service contracts. As of the first half of 2001, the conference had a market share of less than 50%.[72]

The FMC in its industry survey, found widespread general satisfaction with most aspects of the current US regulatory framework. But it also found that

NVOCCs consider themselves "at a competitive disadvantage in relation to VOCCs because they must make all their rate information publicly available, [whereas] VOCCs are free to enter into confidential service contracts with their shipper customers".[73]

7. CONCLUSIONS

This chapter has provided an account of how economic regulation of liner shipping developed in the United States and the European Union. It has also discussed the impact of the recent OSRA reforms and how these reforms have been modified in US/EU trades by the EU regulatory regime. There are a number of interesting conclusions that may be drawn from the discussion, some that are obvious and some perhaps less so. They are:
- Achieving a major change in the US regulatory regime for liner shipping is a lengthy process. This is partly because the window of opportunity is small as the effective life of a Congress is less than two years and bills often run out of time before passing all stages of the legislative process (and have to be reintroduced in the next Congress); and partly because to be successful a bill needs the support of all major interested parties. In the past that has meant, besides having the support of the relevant government agencies, a compromise has had to be reached between the major US carriers and big shippers. This may not be the case in the future, since consolidation in the industry has left the US without any major carriers at present.
- The principle of common carriage, which was enshrined in all previous US legislation concerning the economic regulation of liner shipping has been undermined by the OSRA reforms relating to service contracts, which have resulted in a marked shift towards contract carriage and an almost universal preference for individual contracting among shippers who use such contracts.
- The OSRA reforms have led to the suspension or termination of conference agreements in many US trades, leaving discussion agreements as the only forum where carriers can share commercial information about rates and capacity and formulate pricing policy.
- Conferences have been retained by their members in the transatlantic and US/Mediterranean trades because discussion agreements are not an option in EU trades as they have been prohibited under EU law since the TAA decision of October 1994.
- Even if the experiment in the early 1990s by traditional conference carriers in the transatlantic trade to establish a novel type of conference agreement that was also attractive to major independent carriers had not been squashed by the EC's TAA decision in October 1994, and this conference had become the model for other conferences in US trades, it is clear that the impact of the OSRA reforms relating to service contracts would have emasculated the binding ratemaking authority of the new type of conference.

- The removal of antitrust immunity for carrier agreements in US trades would expose them to the full force of the antitrust laws. However, efficiency agreements such as slot sharing agreements, vessel sharing agreements and multi-trade lane alliances would probably be protected by the "rule of reason". On the other hand, pricing agreements, even those where ratemaking is non-binding, would not receive such protection. So, discussion agreements would be prohibited. This could have an indirect detrimental effect on efficiency agreements if, which seems probable, the prohibition of discussion agreements were to open the door to destructive competition that plagued the liner shipping industry in its early history before the conference system evolved, since bankruptcies among major carriers would place a severe strain on the working of such agreements and in particular the major global alliances.

ENDNOTES

1. Gardner, B.M. (1997): "EU competition policy and liner shipping conferences", *Journal of Transport Economics and Policy*, 31, pp. 317–324.
2. Marx, Jr. D. (1953): *International Shipping Cartels* (Princeton, New Jersey, Princeton University Press).
3. Gardner, N. (2000): *A Guide to United Kingdom and European Union Competition Policy* (Basingstoke, Macmillan).
4. Vitharana, A.J. (1982): "The Influence of Competition and Regulation on the Development of Modern Transportation – A comparison of the Laws and Policies of the United States with those of her 'major' trading partners", PhD thesis, University of Southampton; See also Davies, J.E. (1980): "The Regulation of Liner Shipping: A study of motives and consequences", Ph.D. Thesis, Wales.
5. The Sherman Act of 1890, 26 Stat 209 (1890) as amended, 15 USCA. The Act was signed into law by President Harrison on 2 July 1890.
6. This paragraph quotes sections 1 and 2 of the Sherman Act of 1890.
7. Gardner, N. (2000), *op. cit.*
8. *Ibid.*
9. *US v Hamburg-American SS Line*, 216 Fed. 917 (SDNY 1914); *US v Prince Line Lte.*, 220 Fed. 230 (SDNY 1915); *US v America-Asiatic SS Co.*, 220 Fed. 230 (SDNY 1915).
10. Vitharana, A.J. (1982), *op. cit.*
11. Federal Maritime Commission (FMC) (1989): *Section 18 Report of the Shipping Act of 1984* (Washington DC, FMC).
12. *Ibid.*
13. *Ibid.*
14. *Ibid.*
15. See *Federal Maritime Board v Isbrandsten Co.*, 356 US 481 (1958) at p. 499.
16. FMC (1989), *op. cit.*
17. *Ibid.*
18. *Ibid.*
19. *Ibid.*
20. 390 US 238 (1968).
21. FMC (1989), *op. cit.*
22. Pub. Law 98-237, 98 Stat 67.46 USCA 1701-1720, March 20, 1984. An Act to Improve the International Ocean Commerce Transportation System of the US. All references to individual sections in subsection 4.1 refer to the relevant sections of the Act.

23. FMC (1989), *op. cit.*
24. Advisory Commission on Conferences in Ocean Shipping (ACCOS) (1992): *Report to the President and the Congress of the Advisory Commission on Conferences in Ocean Shipping* (Washington DC, The Commission).
25. Drewry Shipping Consultants (1996): *Global Container Markets: Prospects and Profitability in a High Growth Era.*
26. Beargie, T. (1994): "NIT League Files Complaint Against TAA", *American Shipper*, February 1994; (1995): "NITL Submits Its Proposals for Deregulation," *American Shipper*, February 1995; (1995): "Is NITL Drive Losing Steam?", *American Shipper*, May 1995; (1995): "Ocean Shipping Reform Act of 1995", *American Shipper*, August 1995; Shashikumar, N. (1999): "The US Ocean Shipping Reform Act of 1998: An analysis of its economic impact on carriers, shippers and third parties", *Proceedings of the Conference of the International Association of Maritime Economists* (Halifax, Nova Scotia), September 13–14, 1999 (Centre for International Business Studies at Dalhousie University).
27. Ocean Shipping Reform Act of 1998, Public Law 105-258, 14 October 1998. All references to individual sections in subsection 4.4 refer to the relevant sections of the Act.
28. Weil, R.T. (1999): "US Ocean Shipping Reform Act of 1998, OSRA: A step forward or away from an international consensus on the regulation of ocean liner shipping", *Proceedings of the 1999 Conference of the International Association of Maritime Economists* (Halifax, Nova Scotia, Canada), 13 and 14 September 1999 (Centre for International Business Studies Dalhousie University).
29. Wesseling, R. (2000): *The Modernisation of EC Antitrust Law* (Oxford, Hart Publishing); Greaves, R. (1996): "EC's Maritime Transport Policy: A retrospective view", *The Proceedings of the EC Shipping Policy – The 17th Nordic Maritime Law Conference*, September (Oslo, Juridisk, Forlag.); Van der Ziel (1994): "Competition policy in liner shipping: policy options", *Proceedings from a conference organised by the International Association of Maritime Economists (IAME) and the University of Antwerp* (Antwerp, University of Antwerp).
30. Gardner, B.M. (1997), *op. cit.*
31. *Ibid.*
32. Van der Ziel (1994), *op. cit.*
33. Council Regulation 17 of 6 February 1962, *Official Journal of the European Communities* (OJ). 204/62; [1962] OJ Soec. Ed. 87.
34. OJ No. L 175, 23 July 1968, p. 1.
35. *EC Commission v France*: Case 167/173,[1974} ECR 359; [1974] 2 CMLR 216.
36. *Ministere public v Lucas Asjes et al.* [1986] ECR 1425.
37. Greaves, R. (1966), *op. cit.*; see also COM(84) 668 final; COM(85) 90 final – OJ 1985 C212.
38. Gardner, B.M. (1997), *op. cit.*; See also Greaves (1996), *op. cit.*
39. CEC (1986): "Council Regulation (EEC) No. 4056/86 of 22 December 1986". OJ No. L 378/4, 3112.86, Brussels.
40. Greaves, R. (1996), *ibid.*
41. OJ No. L 55, 29 February 1992, p. 3.
42. OJ No. L 89, 21 April 1995, p. 7.
43. OJ No. L 100, 20 April 2000, on the application of Article 81(3) of the Treaty to certain categories of agreements, decisions and concerted practices between liner shipping companies (consortia).
44. Fitzgerald, E. (1999): "EC Competition Policy and Liner Shipping", Paper presented at the Transasia '99 Conference, Hong Kong, 25–27 August 1999.
45. Barry, J.R., and MacCulloh, A. (2001): *Competition Law and Policy in the European Community and United Kingdom* (London, Cavendish Publishing Ltd.); Whish, R. (2001): *Competition Law* (London, Butterworth); Furse, M. (2000): *Competition Law of the UK and EC* (London, Blackstone Press Ltd).

46. European Commission (EC) Decision of 19 October 1994, OJ No. L 376 Case IV/34.446 – Trans-Atlantic Agreement, 31 December 1994.
47. *Ibid.*
48. European Commission Decision of 16 September 1998 relating to a proceeding pursuant to Articles 85 and 86 of the EC Treaty on Case No. IV/35.134 – Trans Atlantic Conference Agreement.
49. European Commission Decision 94/985 of 21 December 1994 on the Far Eastern Freight Conference (FEFC).
50. Judgment of the Court of First Instance (Third Chamber) on 28 December 2002 in Case T-86/95.
51. Porter, J. (1999): "Shipper accuses EC over TACA", *Lloyds' List*, 1 December 1999.
52. Commission Notice concerning Case COMP/37.396 Revised Transatlantic Conference Agreement in OJ C335/12 dated 29 November 2001.
53. Associated Central West Africa Lines is regarded as a shipping conference whose secretariat is in Antwerp; see Joined Cases T-24/93, T-25/93, T-26/93 and T-28/93 *Compagnie Maritime Belge SA and Others*; see also Joined Cases C-395/96P and C-396P *Compagnie maritime belge de transports and Others v Commission* [2000] ECR I-1365, paragraph 48.
54. Judgment of 16.3.2000 in Joined Cases C-395/96 P and 396/96 P, Compagnie *Maritime Belge Transport and Others v Commission* [2000] ECR I-1365. See also Pons, J.F., "Competition in the maritime transport sector: a new era", *Competition Policy Newsletter*, Number 1, February 2002 (Brussels, European Commission).
55. Federal Maritime Commission (2001): *The Impact of the Ocean Shipping Reform Act of 1998* (Washington DC, FMC).
56. *Ibid.*
57. *Ibid*
58. *Ibid.*
59. *Ibid.*
60. *Ibid.*
61. *Ibid.*
62. Federal Maritime Commission (2000): *The Ocean Shipping Reform Act: An Interim Status Report* (Washington DC, FMC).
63. See *American Shipper*, January, 2002: "Pacific lines ponder rate increases: Struggling ocean carriers talk tough, but provide no specifics on planned increase."
64. EC Decision, 19 October 1994, *op. cit.*
65. Dean J.B. (1992): "Shipper's Perspective", *American Shipper*, 34, pp. 28–30.
66. FMC (2000), *op. cit.*
67. *Ibid.*
68. OJ No. C 335/03 of 29 November 2001.
69. FMC (2001), *op. cit.*
70. *Ibid.*
71. *Ibid.*
72. *Ibid.*
73. *Ibid.*

CHAPTER 16

THE ROLE OF LINER SHIPPING CO-OPERATION IN BUSINESS STRATEGY AND THE IMPACT OF THE FINANCIAL CRISIS ON KOREAN LINER SHIPPING COMPANIES

Dong-Keun Ryoo* and Tae-Woo Lee[†]

*Division of Shipping Management, Korea Maritime University, Pusan, Korea.
E-mail: dkryoo@hanara.kmaritime.ac.kr
†Division of Maritime Transportation Science, Korea Maritime University, Pusan, Korea.
E-mail: tlee@hanara.kmaritime.ac.kr

1. INTRODUCTION

One of the most notable trends during the last decade has been the growth in the number of alliances between competitors in many industries. A recent figure from the *Economist* in 1998 shows that 32,000 alliances have been created since 1995, and three quarters of these consist of agreements between partner companies of different nationality.[1] The use of cooperative agreements has thus become an important phenomenon in international business.

Currently, container liner shipping companies are actively involved in co-operation of one form or another. Strategic advantages as well as economic necessity have combined to make partnership a dominant pattern in the container shipping industry. Leaving aside a price setting co-operation such as conferences, introduced in liner shipping over one hundred years ago, various operational co-operation forms such as slot charters, joint services, consortia, joint ventures and pooling agreements have proliferated since containerisation. Most notably, the industry is moving into an era of global alliances.[2] Among the top twenty liner carriers, fourteen carriers are members of the five major alliances.

This paper thus examines the role of liner shipping co-operation in business strategy. The paper focuses on theoretical and practical perspectives of liner shipping co-operation with a view to draw out ideas for choosing the right co-operation form in terms of business strategy. This is investigated through three research questions: (1) What motivates liner shipping firms to form co-operation?; (2) do the motives for co-operation formation vary with the form of liner shipping co-operation?; (3) to what extent does the business strategy of liner shipping companies influence their choice of co-operation form? In so doing, it is also concerned with the impacts of financial crisis on Korean liner shipping companies in Korea.

2. LITERATURE REVIEW

2.1 Definitions of alliances

Modern literature pertaining to co-operation employs a variety of terms and definitions to describe interorganisational relationships. Some of the terms employed in this context include "cooperative agreement", "coalition", "collaborative arrangement", "strategic alliance", "co-operation" and "partnership".

In a recent study conducted by Das and Teng (1997), strategic alliances are defined along similar lines as "interfirm co-operative arrangements aimed at pursuing mutual strategic goals". Alliance forms included in their definition are joint ventures, joint R&D, product swap, equity investment and sharing, and licensing.[3]

In the liner shipping industry, a global alliance is a distinct form of collaboration, although alliances in the general literature are used to describe a large range of collaborative agreements.[4] Thanopoulou et al. (1999) pointed out that in the 1970s and 1980s, pools and consortia were the prevailing forms of co-operation in the container shipping industry, by means of which container carriers increased their service frequency and optimised fleet deployment under the pressure of the high investment costs containerisation entailed. As the era of consortia came, however, to a close in the early 1990s, global alliances were ultimately born as a result of a major reshuffling of co-operation agreements and of the globalisation of the production process on the demand side.

2.2 Forms of liner shipping co-operation

Liner shipping co-operation forms can be divided into two groups in terms of the nature of the co-operation: co-operation on rates and operational co-operation. Co-operation between liner shipping firms is not new. Historically, many liner firms have become widely involved in either price setting agreements, such as shipping conferences, or operational co-operation forms, such as slot charters, poolings, joint services, consortia and joint ventures. However, what is new in the latter part of the 1990s is the extent to which some firms have become involved with other firms as part of their liner business strategy, and the range and types of co-operation that are taking place. The types of cooperative agreements are listed in Appendix A, together with a brief description of the nature of each type of co-operation agreements taken from the literature related to the liner shipping industry.

2.3 Competitive business strategies in the liner shipping industry

The competitive pressures and the market recession of the past decades, as well as the changing shippers' demands in liner shipping, have prompted a re-examination of competitive business strategy by most container shipping companies. There has been a growing need for container operators to find ways to secure a competitive advantage. Several authors have suggested a firm-specific competitive advantage and explored the competitive business strategy of container shipping companies by applying Porter's (1980) generic strategies to the container shipping industry (Williams (1991); Brooks et al. (1993); Moon (1996); and Lu (1997)). The competitive strategies suggested for exploiting competitive advantage have included cost leadership, differentiation and focus strategies.

2.3.1 *Generic strategies*

2.3.1.1 Cost leadership in container shipping

Cost leadership refers to the ability of a firm to establish a clear cost advantage relative to its competitors. Due to a lower cost structure, the cost leader can either set a lower price than competitors and still make the same profit, or use the same price as its competitors but achieve higher levels of profit.[5] If firms are to sustain cost leadership successfully across their range of activities they must be clear as to how this is to be achieved through the various elements of the value chain. For example, a company may gain cost advantage through its access to low cost sources of raw materials or within its own operations because of its special skills, technologies or systems, or high levels of capacity utilisation.[6]

Container shipping companies can achieve cost advantage by rationalising their ports of call and utilising their assets, both in terms of vessel and container equipment. Brooks *et al.* (1993) points out that the use of slot charters and equipment sharing arrangements is one method whereby container carriers may reduce slot and equipment costs, and thus cut overall capital cost commitments to their container operation.

2.3.1.2 Differentiation as a generic container shipping strategy

Differentiation means the creation of perceived differences from other firms that offer similar products or services. Such differentiation may occur through design, technology, brand image, customer service and service network. Firms successfully performing this strategy will be able to earn above-average returns in an industry and to command customer loyalty and consequently higher prices. Achieving a differentiation strategy, however, requires as a rule a trade-off with cost position and specific activities such as intensive customer service.[7]

Williams (1991) notes that more differentiated service offerings have become a key successful business strategy in the container shipping industry.[8] There have been several studies examining service attributes in liner shipping (Brooks *et al.* (1993); and Lu (1997)). These have attempted to find important service attributes either from the shippers' or carriers' perspective, or both. Although significant variations in the service attributes were shown in these studies, nevertheless, frequently used attributes perceived to be more important from a shipper's perspective included frequency of services, directness of sailings, port coverage, door-to-door service, intermodal service, cost of service, transit times, reliability of delivery, logistics service and information technology.

2.3.1.3 Focus strategy in container shipping

The third generic strategy, focus, means that the business focuses on one or more narrow market segments rather than going after the whole market. By concentrating on a particular group of customers or geographic markets, firms are able to serve their narrow strategic target more effectively or efficiently than competitors who are competing more broadly.[9] From the container shipping companies' point of view, some companies may prefer to provide container services in regional trades rather than global trades. They thus become niche liner carriers.

2.3.2 Beyond classic generic strategies

2.3.2.1 Globalisation strategy in container shipping

Apart from the generic strategies applicable to the container shipping industry, as in other industries, there are alternative strategic options available to container shipping companies to cope with the structural changes in the container shipping business. One of the options is a globalisation strategy. Moon (1996) notes that a container carrier needs to pursue a globalisation strategy in order to meet a fast changing international shipping environment and thus occupy the competitive edge prior to any other carrier. To implement a global strategy, a container shipping firm needs to establish global service networks and a through intermodal system for worldwide big shippers. At the same time, it has to localise its overseas marketing network and secure overseas logistics centres in major regions to build up a global logistics service system. As the primary method of globalisation strategy, forming a global alliance between larger container carriers is a very useful device for establishing a global network composed of three trunk routes. In addition, a global alliance makes partner container carriers lighten the financial burden involved in building up a global network.[10]

2.3.2.2 Market stabilisation as an *ad hoc* strategy

The major objective of a market stabilisation strategy is to avoid competition and to stabilise the market condition within which a company operates. In the liner shipping industry companies can choose between several alternative methods by which the market stabilisation strategy is to be developed. The most frequent method which liner carriers choose is a shipping conference with an aim to control a given freight market by limiting both internal and external competition.[11] However, from a geographical point of view, the scope of activity of a shipping conference is limited; most conferences serve definite trade routes, generally in one direction. Nonetheless, the conference system is powerful due to the number of conferences themselves, and the existing links between the conferences.[12]

Conferences have, however, lost the advantage that they possessed due to the penetration of independent carriers based on their low cost operation and high quality of service.[13] For example, conferences previously held dominant market positions – more than 90% on many trade routes – before the containerisation era, but the advent of unitisation has progressively reduced this to around 50% on the main east-west trades.[14] Furthermore, co-operation on a global basis, especially through alliances, has shaken the role of conferences in that today's alliances created by mixing conference and non-conference lines may prove to be the most alarming threat to the future of conferences as a powerful alliance straddling the major conferences may well acquire sufficient monopoly power so as to assume to itself the price-setting role.[15]

2.3.2.3 Market development strategy

A market development strategy aims at capturing a larger market share in a saturated or growing market, or developing new markets for current products or services.[16] In the liner shipping industry, this can be translated into increased market share in the liner market or the introduction of container vessels on new trade routes.[17]

3. RESEARCH QUESTIONS AND HYPOTHESES

The first research question primarily addresses the motivating factors for co-operation formation and the relative importance of each motive for specific strategic co-operation forms. There is a lack of discussion in the existing literature regarding the choice of types of co-operation, and no prior discussion of how strategic motives might vary between different forms of co-operation in the container shipping industry. However, literature related to strategic co-operation in other industries has suggested that fundamental motivating forces differ between different co-operation forms, with one set of motives being more prevalent for one type of co-operation than another (Forrest (1989); and Stiles (1994)). This reasoning has led to the formulation of the first hypothesis:

Hypothesis 1: *The relative importance of the strategic motivation for co-operation formation varies with the form of liner shipping co-operation.*

The second research question focuses on choice of co-operation form in the context of the specific business strategy of a liner shipping company. It is assumed in the literature that if firms participate in strategic co-operation, that co-operation formation is part of the business strategy of the participant firms (Porter and Fuller (1986); Ghemawat et al. (1986); Doz (1986); Forrest ((1989); Bronder and Pritzl (1992); and Yoshino and Rangan (1995)). This has subsequently led to the second hypothesis:

Hypothesis 2: *The business strategy of liner shipping companies influences their choice of co-operation form.*

4. METHODOLOGY

The research involves a sample of Korean liner shipping companies. Information relating to the research objective was collected via a postal questionnaire. An important aspect of methodology is the sample design. Churchill (1991) categorised sampling procedures into two broad types: probability (derived through random selection) and non-probability (based on personal judgment).[18] Non-probability samples are particularly effective when certain explicit criteria are necessary in a sample. The focus of this research on co-operation between container liner shipping firms required that sample companies should have some form of co-operation defined in this study. The selected firms were chosen because the research could draw upon their experiences resulting from their co-operation involvement. The presence of this requirement therefore made non-probability sampling the most appropriate sampling technique for this research.

Companies were identified from the co-operation database created on the basis of data in the *Containerisation International Yearbook*, the leading publication in the container shipping industry which includes data on co-operation agreements from which their forms may be deducted. Co-operation forms contained in *Containerisation International Yearbook* are slot charters, joint services, joint ventures, consortia, global alliances, merger and acquisition. However, additional information regarding Korean companies which were involved in pooling agreements, conferences and stabilisation agreements was needed. It was possible to obtain such information through the Ministry of Maritime Affairs and Fisheries (MOMAF) in Korea. Thus, of a total of fifteen Korean liner shipping companies, fourteen were identified suitable for the postal questionnaire survey.

Respondents were asked to identify whether strategic co-operation was an explicit part of their liner shipping business strategy. They were also asked to indicate the reasons why firms had established strategic co-operation and to qualify the reasons in terms of their importance on a scale from 1 to 3: 1 = not important at all; 2 = important; 3 = very important. Twenty-one reasons were listed; these had been identified as important reasons from the general literature on alliances in various industries and from the literature related to the container shipping industry.

Three copies of the questionnaire were sent to each company in the sample seeking to obtain information from more than one company executive. As the research objectives were to investigate cooperative strategy, it was vital to have responses from both decision-makers on cooperative strategy and other members of staff in each company rather than just one response from each company in the sample. The use of multiple respondents at multiple organisational levels was intended to provide greater reliability and validity of data (Kidder and Judd, 1986).

The questionnaire data were analysed using the Statistical Package for the Social Sciences (SPSS) 6.1. Given the small sample size the best tests for this type of data are non-parametric tests which make no assumptions concerning the population parameters, or the shape of the distribution.[19] Such tests require limited distribution assumptions about the data and are useful for categorical, ordinal, interval, or ratio data.[20] The data obtained were analysed in terms of frequency distributions, sample means and standard deviations.

5. ANALYSIS

5.1 Characteristics of responses

The return rate for valid responses was 100%. One principal reason for this excellent response rate was due to the fact that questionnaires were delivered to the sample companies through the Ministry of Maritime Affairs and

Fisheries(MOMAF) which possesses a direct communication channel to them. In co-operation with the MOMAF, the researcher was thus able to obtain a very high response rate.

The respondents had a wide range of positions in the companies selected, from assistant manager to director. 81% of the respondents from the sample had the title of manager or higher. 36% of respondents had the title of general manager, while 14% had the title of director. The reliability of information could thus be deemed to be good, at least as far as the position of respondents allowed as they were all in positions to possess a global picture of their companies' activities.

In terms of the size of responding firms' TEU capacity operated in 1997, eight companies out of the total 14 sample companies surveyed, operated between 10,000 TEUs and 100,000 TEUs in 1997. Six companies in the sample operated 100,000 TEUs or more in the same year.

5.2 Comparison of motives for the different types of co-operation

The survey results of the motives for the different types of liner shipping co-operation are shown in Appendix B. To analyse the results Appendix B was transformed into two XY scatter charts (see Appendix C and D). Appendix C shows a comparison of motives for forming two different types of co-operation on rates, and Appendix D presents a comparison of motives for entering into seven different types of operational co-operation. The X-axis for each Figure represents the motivations for co-operation formation and the Y-axis indicates mean values on a scale of 1.00 (= not important at all) to 3.00 (= very important).

It can be seen in Appendix C that respondents had, to some extent, similar views on motives for forming freight rate co-operation. Among the twenty-one motives, two motives, "to stabilise freight rates" and "to limit external competition" were identified as most important reasons for both conferences and stabilisation agreements. Although the overall mean values of importance of the motives for conference formation were relatively higher than those for stabilisation agreements, the mean scores of two motives – "to rationalise service routes" and "to share the risks of providing new liner services" – were comparatively higher for stabilisation agreements. However, "to develop a liner service for specific market niches" was identified as the prime strategic purpose for entering into conference agreements.

Appendix D shows a comparison of motives for forming different types of operational co-operation, which included alliances, consortia, joint services, joint ventures, pooling agreements, slot charters, and mergers and acquisitions. As can be seen in Appendix D, the level of importance of motives was found to be comparatively different across the different types of co-operation. Global alliances, pooling agreements, and consortia were identified as the most important co-operation forms with a view to stabilising freight rates and limiting external competition, while joint services, joint ventures, slot charters, and mergers and acquisitions were shown to be relatively less important co-operation forms for stabilising freight rates and limiting external competition.

Among other operational co-operation forms, M&A and global alliances were identified as comparatively more important co-operation forms in terms of increasing market share, gaining economies of scale, maximising operational synergy, rationalising service routes, increasing the utilisation of container boxes, and linking into partner's marketing network. Respondents further identified global alliances as the most suitable form of co-operation to provide intermodal and total container logistics services.

Slot charters were found to be the most efficient co-operation forms in cases where liner companies wanted to extend service coverage, develop a liner service for specific market niches, and share the risks of providing new liner services.

Respondents identified almost all operational co-operation forms as suitable for reducing firms' capital cost of purchasing or supplying ships, and reducing the financial burden of equipment investment. The sample companies considered joint services as the most suitable co-operation form for providing more frequent sailings.

As shown in both Appendix C and D, the mean value for each individual motive is comparatively different across the different types of co-operation. Consequently, there is reasonable support for hypothesis 1 (H1).

5.3 Role of co-operation in the business strategy of liner shipping firms

The previous section examined the importance of each motive for the different types of liner shipping co-operation. However, the motives for co-operation can be best analysed by focussing on the role of co-operation in the business strategy of the firm. It has been argued in the literature that if firms participate in any form of co-operation, that co-operation formation must be part of the overall strategy of the firm (Harrigan (1985); Porter and Fuller (1986); Ghemawat et al. (1986); Doz (1986); Forrest (1989); Bronder and Pritzl (1992); and Yoshino and Rangan (1995)). Accordingly, the respondents to the questionnaire were asked if strategic co-operation was an explicit part of their liner shipping business strategy. All respondents answered in the affirmative. The involvement in strategic co-operation was thus considered to be part of the business strategy of the sample companies.

To analyse further the extent to which Korean container shipping firms formed co-operation as part of their liner shipping business strategy it was deemed appropriate to group the co-operation motives used in the questionnaire survey into specific categories. The motives were classified into four business strategy groups: those which formed part of the firm's market stabilisation strategy, those which were part of the firm's service differentiation strategy, those which formed part of the firm's cost reduction strategy, and those which contributed to the firm's market development strategy (see Table 1).

It was assumed that if the mean values of the motives for specific types of co-operation exceeded or were equal to the median measure (2.00), co-operation forms were regarded as important in terms of the business strategy focus into which the motives were classified. Based on this assumption, motives which exceeded or were equal to the median value (2.00) were extracted from the survey results in Appendix B. As a result, the mean values of the motives for each co-operation type are tabulated in Appendix E, indicating the relative importance of co-operation forms in terms of business strategy focus. As can be seen in Appendix E, there is a degree of variation in the mean values of importance of the motives across the different types of co-operation, after these have been narrowed down and classified according to type of business strategy.

Table 1: Categorisation of co-operation motives according to business strategy focus

Business strategy	Co-operation motive
Market Stabilisation Strategy	• Stabilise freight rates • Limit external competition
Service Differentiation Strategy	• Extend service coverage • Provide more frequent sailings • Provide intermodal service • Provide total container logistics service
Cost Reduction Strategy	• Benefit from economies of scale • Maximise financial synergy • Maximise operational synergy • Rationalise service routes • Increase the utilisation of container boxes • Share the risks of providing new liner services • Reduce capital cost of purchasing or supplying ships • Reduce firm's financial burden of equipment investment
Market Development Strategy	• Increase market share • Develop a liner service for specific market niches • Fast entry to new trade routes • Link into partner's established marketing network

Figure 1: Co-operation forms focused on market stabilisation strategy

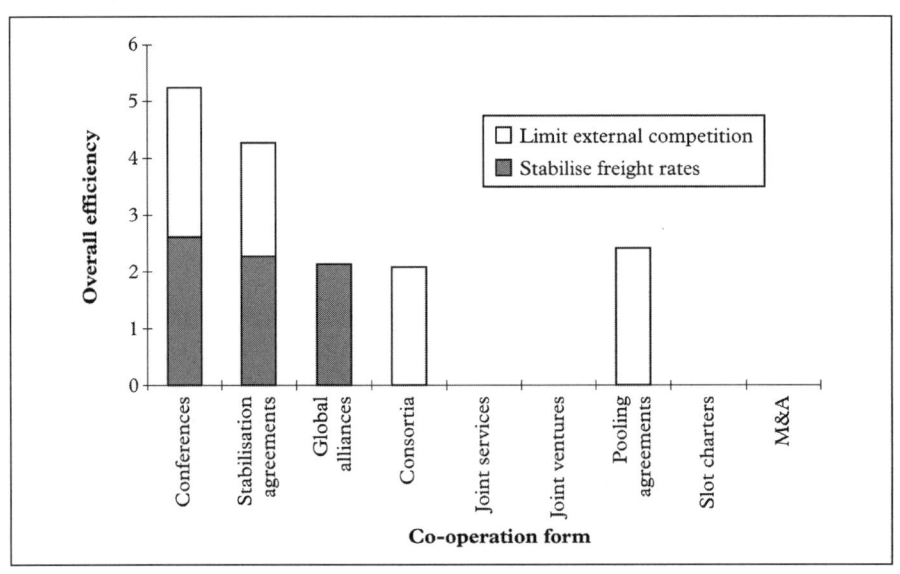

Note: Y-axis measures aggregate means as in Appendix E.

5.3.1 Market stabilisation strategy

Conferences were identified as the most important form of co-operation achieving market stabilisation strategy, with the two motives, "to stabilise freight rates" and "to limit external competition" achieving the highest mean values for co-operation motive. Stabilisation agreements were identified as the second most important co-operation form in terms of stabilising freight rates, while pooling agreements were the second most important co-operation form for limiting external competition. Based on the mean values of each co-operation form from a market stabilisation perspective, and taking into account results regarding both components, conferences were found to be the most efficient form of co-operation for fulfilling overall market stabilisation strategy (see Figure 1).

5.3.2 Service differentiation strategy

Co-operation forms which the surveyed companies entered into to achieve their service differentiation purpose included slot charters, joint services, consortia, global alliances and M&A. Of these forms, slot charters were found to be the most important co-operation forms in terms of extending service coverage and providing more frequent sailings. Joint services were identified as the second most important co-operation form for achieving these strategy purposes, followed by consortia, global alliances and M&A (see Figure 2).

5.3.3 Cost reduction strategy

Korean liner companies surveyed utilised, principally, six co-operation forms in order to achieve their cost reduction purposes. The forms included M&A, consortia, global alliances, joint services, joint ventures and slot charters. Of these

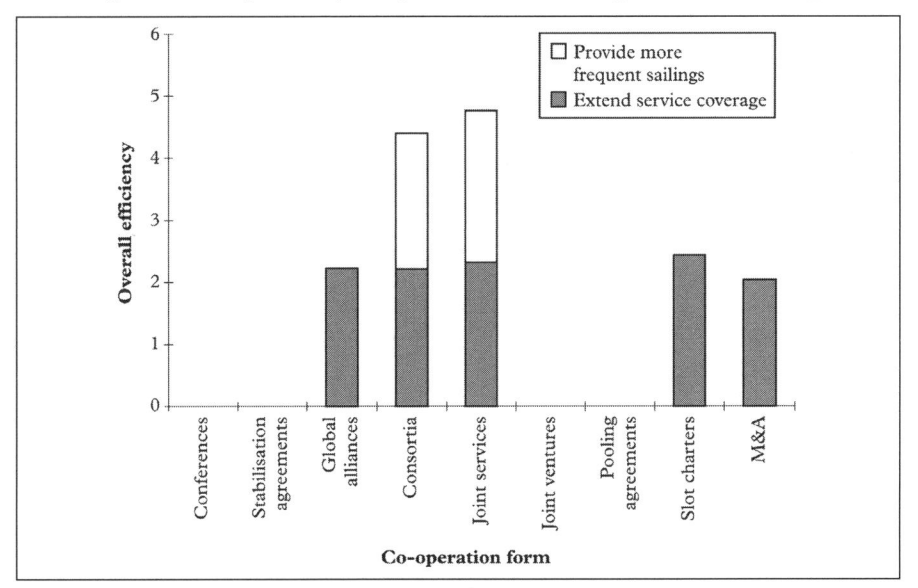

Figure 2: Co-operation forms focused on service differentiation strategy

Note: Y-axis measures aggregate means as in Appendix E.

forms, M&A was identified as the most efficient form for gaining economies of scale and maximising financial and operational synergy. Global alliances were formed primarily to rationalise service routes and to increase the utilisation of container boxes. Slot charters were utilised primarily to share the risks of providing new liner services. To reduce the capital cost of ships and the financial burden of equipment investment, results showed that companies opted most commonly for joint ventures and consortia.

When considering the overall efficiency of each co-operation form in terms of achieving cost reduction purposes, M&A emerged as the most efficient form of co-operation, followed by consortia, global alliances, joint services, joint ventures and slot charters (see Figure 3).

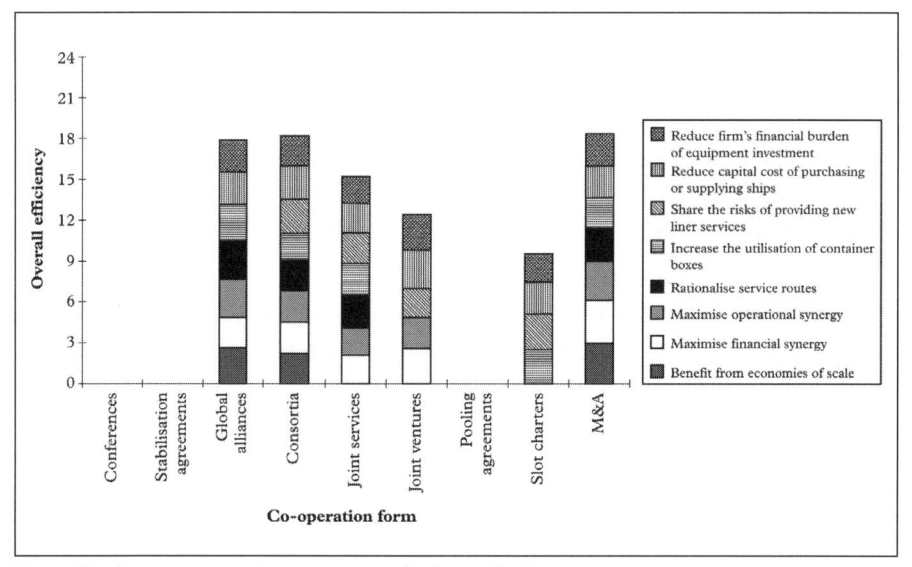

Figure 3: Co-operation forms focused on cost reduction strategy

Note: Y-axis measures aggregate means as in Appendix E.

5.3.4 Market development strategy

With regard to market development strategy, Korean liner operators used all operational co-operation forms. Of the forms, M&A was identified as the most important co-operation form for increasing market share, entering new trade routes and linking into partner's established marketing network, while slot charters were formed primarily to develop a liner service for specific market niches.

The overall efficiency of each co-operation form in terms of achieving market development strategy is shown in Figure 4. M&A was found to be the most efficient co-operation form for market development strategy, followed by global alliances, slot charters, pooling agreements, joint services, consortia and joint ventures.

The findings of the role of co-operation in the business strategy of the firm. indicated that some co-operation forms seemed to be important for more than

THE ROLE OF LINER SHIPPING CO-OPERATION 357

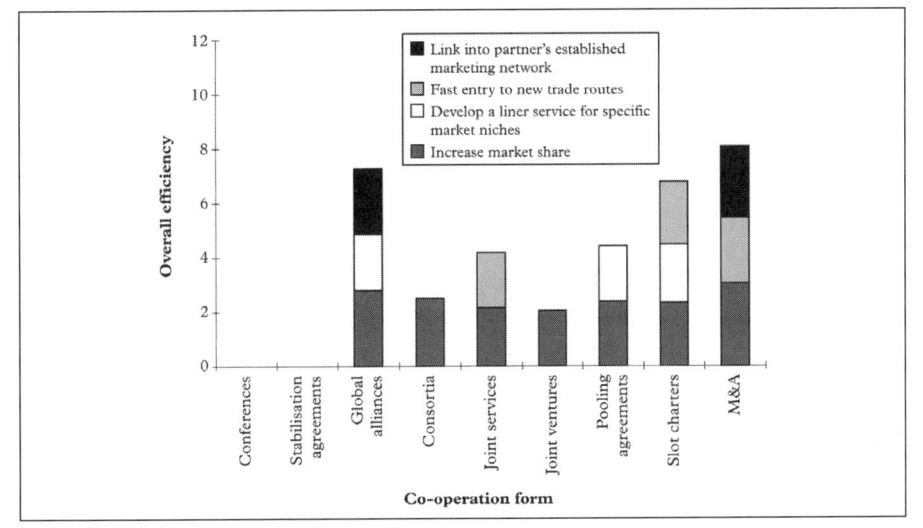

Figure 4: Co-operation forms focused on market development strategy

[Bar chart showing overall efficiency across co-operation forms: Conferences, Stabilisation agreements, Global alliances, Consortia, Joint services, Joint ventures, Pooling agreements, Slot charters, M&A. Legend: Link into partner's established marketing network; Fast entry to new trade routes; Develop a liner service for specific market niches; Increase market share.]

Note: Y-axis measures aggregate means as in Appendix E.

one type of business strategy because of their multi-purpose nature. There was, however, a clear distinction between co-operation on rates and operational co-operation according to strategy focus. While co-operation on rates, such as conferences and stabilisation agreements, contributed only to the firm's market stabilisation strategy, operational co-operation forms fitted into more than one business strategy. Two forms of co-operation emerged as the most versatile, namely, global alliances and consortia, which were identified as the most suitable co-operation forms for the four business strategy groups previously outlined.

It is interesting to note that the newly created co-operation form of global alliances fulfils and complies with all types of business strategy. This supports Thanopoulou's *et al.* (1999) study on the rationale behind global alliance formation. They noted that global alliances were formed between major global liner carriers in response to the globalisation of the production process on the demand side and the challenges of competition on major trade routes. The need for the provision of multimodal and logistics services, and frequent services on a global scale as part of the firm's service differentiation strategy, was one of the prime reasons for the creation of global alliances. Through alliances, partner carriers could gain operational and financial synergies, and increase market share. Most importantly, alliances might well acquire sufficient monopoly power as to assume themselves the price-setting role. Nevertheless it is noticeable in this respect that alliances have also included combinations of conference and non-conference members (Thanopoulou *et al.* (1999)).

Drawing on the findings with regard to Korean container shipping, Appendix F links liner shipping co-operation and business strategy. The most important co-operation forms which were entered into as part of market stabilisation strategy were conferences and stabilisation agreements. To achieve a successful service differentiation strategy, Korean operators made more use of slot charters and joint services, whereas M&A and consortia were the most important co-operation options for cost reduction strategy. The study of Korean liner operators showed that M&A and global alliances were primarily used for market development. On the basis of these findings it may be assumed that there is a certain degree of support for hypothesis 2 (H2).

6. THE IMPACTS OF THE FINANCIAL CRISIS ON THE LINER SHIPPING COMPANIES IN KOREA

6.1 Brief review of overcoming the Korean financial crisis

President Kim Dae-jung is the first-ever Korean opposition leader to take power, ending decades of domination by the same ruling group. His government, called "The People's Government", started on 25th February 1998 promising the simultaneous development of democracy and free competition to the domestic market. He has been trying to restore international confidence in Korea by pledging to honor the retrenchment terms of the IMF in return for massive bailout loans since his election on 18th December 1997. A key economic policy of the new government focused on economic recovery and free economic activities in the market-driven economy through across-the-board innovations and reform of chaebols. This can be found in President Kim's inaugural address.

As far as his speech on the economic policies of the new government is concerned, the five reforms under the principle of market economy include commodity price stabilisation, sweeping reforms of chaebols and active support for small businesses, export increases and improvements in the current account balance, inducements of foreign capital, and increases in incomes of farmers and fishermen. President Kim attributed the economic crisis mainly to government-controlled banks and chaebols that have spawned a slew of uncompetitive subsidiaries with heavy borrowings. In reference to the chaebol policy, he said: "To help the national economy make another leap forward, businesses should engage in transparent management, stop cross-guaranteeing debt payments, concentrate on building a sound financial structure, and limit the number of their key businesses."

The Korean government launched its rigorous efforts to restructure the economy from the time the crisis hit. The reforms can be broadly classified into the four sectors: corporate sector, labor market, financial sector, and market liberalization (see Table 2). Most notable things in the progress Korea has made are reforms in the chaebols and the financial sector.[21] As a result, with the exit of non-viable financial institutions and the injection of fiscal resources, Korean banks were able to obtain a clean bank status with BIS ratios of 10 to 13%. These efforts have greatly helped Korea its credit in the global economy.

Thanks to the government's efforts, just as the crisis came unexpectedly and proved to be sharper than initially envisaged, the recovery has generally come

Table 2: *Major contents of reforms in the Korean economy*

Sector	Contents
Corporate Sector	• Adopted combined financial statements • Banned additional mutual loan guarantees between • Downsized chaebol by big deal • Allowed M&A, including hostile takeovers • Achieved agreements between banks and firms to improve their capital structure • Expanded the rights of small investors(shareholders) • Liberalised the rules on equity issue
Labor Market	• Set up the Tripartite Commission of labor, business, and government leaders • Enhanced labor market flexibility • Expanded unemployment insurance • Implemented comprehensive unemployment policy • Strengthened and privatised job placement services
Financial Sector	• Suspended operation of insolvent non-bank financial institutions • Increased funds for non-performing asset disposal and deposit insurance • Deregulated internal bank management • Launched Consolidated Financial Supervisory Commission
Market Liberalisation	• Opened long- and short-term financial markets • Abolished the ceilings on stock holding • Deregulated the use of commercial loans by foreign-owned firms • Abolished limits on foreign ownership of real estate • Extended the list of industries open to foreign investment

Source: Oh-Seok Hyun, "Korea's Corporate Governance System: Applying New Remedies", in *Proceedings of Conference on Corporate Governance in Asia: A Comparative Perspective*, organised by OECD and KDI, 3–5 March, 1998.

more quickly – and more strongly – than expected. Seen in the larger context of Asia's long-term growth performance, the Korean financial crisis could almost be seen as a temporary dent in Asia's sustained economic growthxxii. Whether or not this is the case will depend on how strongly the present recovery can be carried forward in the coming years.

Sound macroeconomic management has been crucial to help stabilise the financial markets in Korea and support an early return to growth(see Table 3). There can be no doubt that safeguarding and entrenching macroeconomic stability will remain essential.

However, by itself, it will not be sufficient to restore vibrant economy in Korea. A much stronger emphasis on structural, institutional, and other governance-related reforms is needed to sustain stable growth. In other words, the unfinished structural agenda in Korea will dominate the economic policy discussions over the next years.[23] There are at least three important areas that call for further action:

– financial sector reforms to restore a sound banking system and attract foreign investment;

Table 3: *Selected economic indicators in Korea*

Year Indicator	1995	1996	1997	1998	1999
Real GDP	8.9	6.8	5.0	-5.8	9.0
Private consumption	9.6	7.1	3.5	-9.6	10.0
Public consumption	0.8	8.2	1.5	-0.1	-1.1
Gross fixed investment	11.9	7.3	-2.2	-21.1	3.7
Net foreign balance	0.2	-1.1	5.7	12.2	-0.6
Exports	24.6	11.2	21.4	13.3	18.1
Imports	22.4	14.2	3.2	-22.0	31.0
GDP deflator	7.1	3.9	3.1	5.3	0.9
CPI (period average)	4.5	4.9	4.4	7.5	0.9
Unemployment rate (period average)	2.0	2.0	2.6	6.8	6.6
Industrial production (period average)	11.9	8.7	5.3	-7.3	21.7
Current account balance					
- Billion of US$	-8.5	-23.0	-8.2	40.0	25.2
Percent of GDP	-1.7	-4.4	-1.7	12.5	6.1
Yield on corporate bonds (period average)	13.8	11.9	13.4	15.1	8.9
Exchange rate Won/dollar rate (period average)	771	804	951	1,402	1,190

Source: IMF (2000).

- corporate restructuring to strengthen international competitive edge of enterprises; and
- legal and regulatory reforms to back up the two above.

6.2 Challenges for the Korean Liner Shipping Companies

To look into the challenges for the Korean shipping industry, more specifically major shipping lines, let's make two assumptions:
- the government tackles successfully the unfinished structural agenda over its whole range during the coming years; and
- global economic developments remain favorable.

The second assumption is based on the IMF forecast in this direction: while growth in the US economy will inevitably slow down at some stage, the impact on world growth could be more than offset by stronger growth in Europe and in Japan. World growth, which rose from some 2% to 3% last year, is expected to further accelerate to close to 4% this year. A correction in the US stock market has been widely expected and, were it to occur, there is every reason to believe that it could take place without a general loss of confidence and a major disruption in financial markets.

With regard to the first assumption, on policy performance, we have to wait and see how vigorously the government will continue their present reform course, and whether they will avoid reform fatigue and complacency. If they are successful and at the same time the second assumption remains valid, we can be confident about the future of Korean major shipping lines, and we can look at a scenario where the Korean financial crisis marks only a temporary interruption of their growth.

However, the continuing volatile rise in oil prices, if sustained, would pose significant adverse implications for the shipping industry. It is critical for the industry to increase operating costs to unsustainable levels.

Meanwhile, today, technology revolutionises traditional operation process in all business contexts. Shipping business, in particular in container shipping is no exception. Having said that, the challenge to management in this respect is how to motivate people to adapt themselves to the infrastructure developments accelerated by IT. In addition, we have to be concerned with the fact that the gap between the skill sets required for shore and sea staff is getting wider due to the changing structure of ship-shore relationship. Furthermore, management of shipping companies are required to maximise value creation in the business process, applying the following strategies to exploit that value to full extent[24]:
– customer relationship management strategy
– knowledge management strategy
– strategy of re-aligning and enhancing core values

The last part of the previous section was concerned with the unfinished structural agenda over its whole range during the coming years in Korea.

Bearing that in mind, corporate restructuring in Korea is the other side of the coin of bank restructuring and thus closely related to international competitive edge of shipping companies.

According to the government's harsh guideline of debt-reduction on chaebols, the top five chaebols in terms of assets had to lower their debt-to-equity ratios below 200% by the end of last year, not through asset reevaluation, but through self-rescue efforts such as sell-off or attraction of foreign capital. This is being monitored by the Financial Supervisory Commission (FSS) in association with chaebols' main creditor banks and financial authorities planned to intensify the workout process throughout the first half of this year. Eligible for workout plans are those companies whose cash flow has deteriorated prominently, sales are short of debt, or making insufficient progress in keeping accords with creditors to improve their financial structure while recording net losses for the past three consecutive year. Furthermore, cross debt guarantees between subsidiaries of a chaebol was eliminated by March 2000.

Meanwhile, the FSS reviewed the consolidated and combined financial statements for 1999 and thereafter will do on a regular basis. They will provide useful new information for assessing the overall financial structure of the top five chaebols. Creditor financial institutions will additionally consider the statements when they classify loans to affiliates of the top chaebols. Compliance of these consolidated and combined financial statements with the revised and upgraded Korean accounting and auditing standards will be reviewed and available remedies pursued against companies and auditors found to be in non-compliance.

Having said that, Korean shipping companies are currently suffering from the shortage of operational fund due to their highly geared financial structure.

This explains the reason why Hanjin Shipping Co., Ltd. sold 26 container ships, with ranging from 768 to 2,700teu, 2 Panamax and 1 handy size bulk carrier in 1998 and raised US$457 million from the sales of the above ships (see Table 4). In association with issuance of new stocks, it has led to improve their debt-to-equity ratios (see Table 5). They were mostly sold with charter back condition in order to keep shipping services. As a result, it has been reported that Hanjin posted a net profit last year.

Table 4: Ships sold by Hanjin Shipping Co. Ltd

Ship type	Capacity	Number of ships	Sale condition
Container	768TEU	1	Straight Sale: 1
	1200TEU	6	T/C Back: 5
			Straight Sale: 1
	1600TEU	1	Straight Sale: 1
	2700TEU	18	T/C Back: 14
			Straight Sale: 4
Bulk carrier	Handy Size (25K)	1	Straight Sale: 1
	Panamax (61K)	2	T/C Back: 1
			Straight Sale: 1
Total number of ship sales		29	T/C Back: 20
			Straight Sale: 9
Total Sales Amount		US$ 457 million	

Source: Hanjin Shipping Co. Ltd (1999).

Table 5: Debt-to-equity ratios of HSC and HMM

Name	Hanjin Shipping Co. Ltd (HSC)			Hyundai Merchant Marine Co. Ltd (HMM)		
	Year			Year		
Item	1997	1998	1999	1997	1998	1999
Total assets	4,598,773	4,402,100	4,757,411	3,861,356	5,963,903	7,157,382
Total debt	4,256,961	4,060,844	3,907,193	3,456,434	4,303,103	4,615,184
Total equity	341,812	341,256	850,248	404,922	1,660,800	2,542,198
Total assets & debt	4,598,773	4,402,100	4,757,411	3,861,356	5,963,903	7,157,382
Debt-to-equity ratios	1,245%	1,190%	459%	853%	259%	181%

Source: Hanjin Shipping Co. Ltd (2000) and Hyundai Merchant Marine Co. Ltd (2000).

To finance the renewed growth in output, corporations need credit, and the restructured banks should be in a position to lend again. But to make damaged corporations credit worthy, their balance sheets have first to be cleaned up through debt restructuring, debt write-offs, and conversion of debt to equity. This will bring down the high debt-to-equity ratio. However, broader corporate restructuring is also needed to restore efficiency, competitiveness, and profitability. The measures include changes in management structure, closure of non-profitable assets, elimination of excess capacity, concentration on core activities, sale of affiliates, and mergers. In particular, major shipping lines in Korea are needed to improve the environment for private investment, especially to attract new investments from the financial markets, building sound institution to give reliable signals to financiers, national and international. That is one of key sectors and also an essential part of the agenda in the aftermath of the financial crisis. It may lead to underpin the forward movement that is needed in corporate restructuring.

Korean major shipping lines need a variety of measures to increase their cost saving and efficiency through further expansion of foreign crew employment. Deregulation of foreign crew employment remains on the agenda for negotiation in the circle of the government, shipowner and labor union. In the process of negotiations, it has to be carefully implemented and have to go hand-in-hand with the strengthening of the cost competitiveness.

There are other important structural areas unsolved yet. Liberalisation of the labor market at container terminals is, among others, urgent for the more advanced operators. It allows the government to proceed with needed structural reforms, without causing service interruptions that inevitably lead to deteriorate international competitiveness of shipping lines.

Another challenging are the questions raised by mega-shipping alliances, among others, Maersk-Sea Land alliance, with a plan to build mega-carriers, apparently excessive movements in the container shipping history. The trend has rapidly developed over the last five years.[25] It may enable Korean major carriers to consider the development in terms of the current imbalance in growth rates among major alliances and the need to adapt themselves to rebalance supply growth. But this is only part of the story, for it is of great importance for Korean terminal operators. This will be an area that requires further urgent examination.

The Korean shipping industry and the skills of Korean seafarers have been a crucial part of Korean success as a shipping and shipbuilding country. This success has never been achieved without the competent and able crew.[26] But an estimation and statistics report that there has been a heavy decline in the number of seafarers, in particular officers with careers longer than seven years at sea. It implies that this has potentially serious consequences for the continued strength of the shipping and shore-based industries in the near future, e.g. shipbuilding, ship repairing, ship broking, maritime law and arbitration, marine insurance, ship classification, and ship survey. Increasing the number of skilled seafarers, particular officers, is a key aim of those who seek to keep the shipping industry stable growth. That cannot be achieved without cost. This makes it vital to have regard to the fiscal regime if we want to maintain a successful shipping industry.

Last but by no means least, the urgent armory in the battle for success of Korean shipowners includes a virtually tax-exempt fiscal regime. The regime may have to be comprehensive to grant special tax breaks in the context of vigorous revision of the current International Vessel Register Act in Korea, which deregulates restriction in employing foreign crew on Korean flagged ships. In this regard, we may take some lessons from "tonnage tax" regimes in some European countries, such as UK, German, Norway, and The Netherlands.[27]

7. CONCLUSION

Korean liner shipping firms were minor players in liner shipping in the 1970s, but have since become major carriers in the world. In line with the ongoing success of Korean liner shipping, Korean liner operators have greatly benefited from involvement in different types of co-operation. The success of Korean liner shipping exemplifies the potential cooperative strategies. The present examination of the Korean liner shipping industry provides a general foundation for theory development and an extension to the existing body of knowledge in the area of strategic partnerships.

The findings revealed that Korean liner shipping firms had multiple motives for forming specific co-operation forms, and the level of importance of each individual motive was different across the different forms of liner shipping co-operation. Additionally, the research showed that the rationale behind the formation of specific co-operation varied according to the firm's business strategy. This research provides a general framework for the identification of suitable co-operation forms based upon liner shipping firms' business strategies.

The findings from this research, as in all research, must be tempered by the limitations of the study. The focus of this research was the motives for strategic co-operation and the role of co-operation in the business strategy of liner shipping firms. The research setting for this study was limited in two ways: (1) it focused on one industry only – the container liner shipping industry, and (2) it was limited to container liner shipping firms in Korea. As data were collected from container liner shipping companies only in Korea, caution must be exercised when making any broad generalisations based on this study. The empirical evidence included in this research was conclusive only in relation to the current perception of co-operation and the benefits of co-operation participation of Korean container shipping companies. Nevertheless, the methodology used for this study can be deemed as one valid option for expanding future research.

Appendices A to F follow. For Endnotes and References see page 371.

APPENDIX A: TYPES AND NATURE OF LINER SHIPPING CO-OPERATION

	Type	Author	Nature of co-operation
Co-operation on rates	Conference	Frankel (1985), Gardner (1997)	an agreement reached by shipping companies operating liner services for the purpose of regulating or restricting competition with the objectives of a relative stability of rates, regularity and realising reasonable frequency of sailings while maintaining services to less remunerative ports.
	Stabilisation agreement	Canna (1992)	a voluntary agreement to reduce the level of overcapacity in order, eventually, to increase unremunerative rate levels.
Operational Co-operation	Slot charter	Jon (1986)	an agreement by which a liner service operator leases part of the slot on another's ships and markets that slot as his own.
	Pooling agreement	Frankel (1985)	an agreement between shipping companies in order to increase the pool's share of the market, provide an equitable distribution of benefits among members, limit service competition and rationalise operations.
	Joint service	Frankel (1985), Gardiner (1994)	an agreement which establishes a new and separate line or service to be operated jointly by partner companies. The service fixes its own rates, publishes its own tariffs, issues its own bills of lading, and acts generally as a single carrier.
	Consortium	Koch (1975), Bras (1991)	a cooperative venture of varying degree of closeness in which shipping companies involved operate under one name by pooling all or some of their activities in a particular trade.
	Joint venture	Koch (1975), Frankel (1985)	an agreement in which each party has a share of ownership as shareholders, in one separate and legally autonomous venture and the participants jointly own or lease vessels, equipment, and terminals. The venture has its own management.
	Global alliance	Thanopoulou *et al.* (1997)	an agreement between container shipping companies co-operating on a global trade route basis involving usually the provision of multimodal and logistics services as well.
	Merger and acquisition	Jones (1982)	a fusion of two companies. The assets become vested in and under the control of one company.

Source: Ryoo, D.K. (1999) *Co-operation Forms and Business Strategies: the Case of Korean Liner Shipping*, dissertation presented for PhD in UWC.

APPENDIX B: MOTIVES FOR FORMING LINER SHIPPING CO-OPERATION

| Co-operation motives | Freight rate co-operation ||||| Operational co-operation ||||||||||
| | CONF || SA || ALL || CONS || JSA || JV || PA || SC || MA ||
	M	SD	M	SD	M	SD	M	SD	M	SD	M	SD	M	SD	M	SD	M	SD
1. Stabilise freight rates	2.63	.60	2.25	.89	2.11	.78	1.38	.77	1.04	.20	1.17	.41	1.95	.97	1.00	.00	1.00	.00
2. Limit external competition	2.58	.61	2.00	.76	1.89	.60	2.08	.76	1.29	.55	1.17	.41	2.42	.77	1.03	.17	1.00	.00
3. Increase market share	1.74	.73	1.25	.71	2.78	.44	2.46	.78	2.04	.75	2.00	.63	2.37	.76	2.26	.70	3.00	.00
4. Benefit from economies of scale	1.11	.32	1.00	.00	2.67	.50	2.31	.85	1.87	.80	1.83	.75	1.42	.61	1.26	.61	3.00	.00
5. Maximise financial synergy	1.16	.37	1.00	.00	2.11	.78	2.15	.69	2.00	.83	2.50	.55	1.58	.77	1.26	.51	3.00	.00
6. Maximise operational synergy	1.05	.23	1.13	.35	2.89	.33	2.31	.75	2.04	.81	2.33	.52	1.42	.51	1.49	.70	3.00	.00
7. Rationalise service routes	1.42	.77	1.88	.83	2.78	.44	2.23	.73	2.33	.64	1.67	.52	1.74	.65	1.60	.77	2.33	.58
8. Increase the utilisation of container boxes	1.37	.68	1.38	.52	2.78	.44	2.15	.80	2.67	.56	1.50	.55	1.58	.61	2.63	.65	2.33	.58
9. Extend service coverage	1.42	.51	1.25	.71	2.22	.67	2.23	.73	2.33	.70	1.67	.52	1.37	.60	2.43	.74	2.00	1.00
10. Develop a liner service for specific market niches	1.84	.69	1.00	.00	2.11	.60	1.92	.76	1.83	.56	1.83	.98	2.00	.88	2.20	.68	1.67	.58
11. Fast entry to new trade routes	1.47	.70	1.25	.46	1.78	.67	1.92	.64	2.08	.78	1.83	.98	1.47	.70	2.31	.68	2.33	1.15
12. Link into partner's established marketing network	1.11	.32	1.13	.35	2.33	.50	1.54	.52	1.50	.78	1.50	.55	1.44	.62	1.56	.75	2.67	.58
13. Share the risks of providing new liner services	1.47	.61	1.75	.89	1.89	.78	2.38	.65	2.04	.81	2.17	.75	1.53	.77	2.51	.61	1.00	.00
14. Reduce capital cost of purchasing or supplying ships	1.32	.75	1.00	.00	2.33	.71	2.54	.52	2.17	.82	2.83	.41	1.26	.56	2.31	.68	2.33	1.15
15. Reduce firm's financial burden on equipment investment	1.21	.54	1.00	.00	2.33	.71	2.15	.69	2.00	.78	2.50	.55	1.26	.56	2.06	.64	2.33	1.15
16. Provide more frequent sailings	1.37	.76	1.00	.00	1.78	.83	2.15	.69	2.42	.65	1.17	.41	1.26	.56	2.40	.74	1.67	.58
17. Provide intermodal service	1.05	.23	1.00	.00	1.78	.67	1.46	.52	1.13	.45	1.17	.41	1.05	.23	1.06	.24	1.33	.58
18. Provide total container logistics service	1.05	.23	1.00	.00	1.78	.44	1.38	.65	1.04	.20	1.33	.82	1.05	.23	1.03	.17	1.33	.58
19. Gain access to general management skills	1.11	.32	1.00	.00	1.22	.44	1.23	.44	1.33	.76	1.83	.41	1.21	.42	1.03	.17	1.67	.58
20. Conform to shipping policy of national government	1.21	.54	1.00	.00	1.00	.00	1.00	.00	1.04	.20	1.17	.41	1.26	.45	1.00	.00	1.00	.00
21. Conform to shipping policy of foreign government(s)	1.32	.67	1.00	.00	1.00	.00	1.23	.60	1.08	.41	1.17	.41	1.37	.60	1.00	.00	1.00	.00

Valid Number	CONF	SA	ALL	CONS	JSA	JV	PA	SC	MA
	19	8	9	13	24	6	19	35	3

* Respondents ranked motives from 1 (not important at all) to 3 (very important). CONF: Conference, SA: Stabilisation agreement, ALL: Global alliance, CONS: Consortium, JSA: Joint service agreement, JV: Joint venture, PA: Pooling agreement, SC: Slot charter, MA: Merger and acquisition. M: Mean; SD: Standard Deviation

THE ROLE OF LINER SHIPPING CO-OPERATION 367

APPENDIX C: COMPARISON OF MOTIVES FOR FORMING CO-OPERATION ON RATES

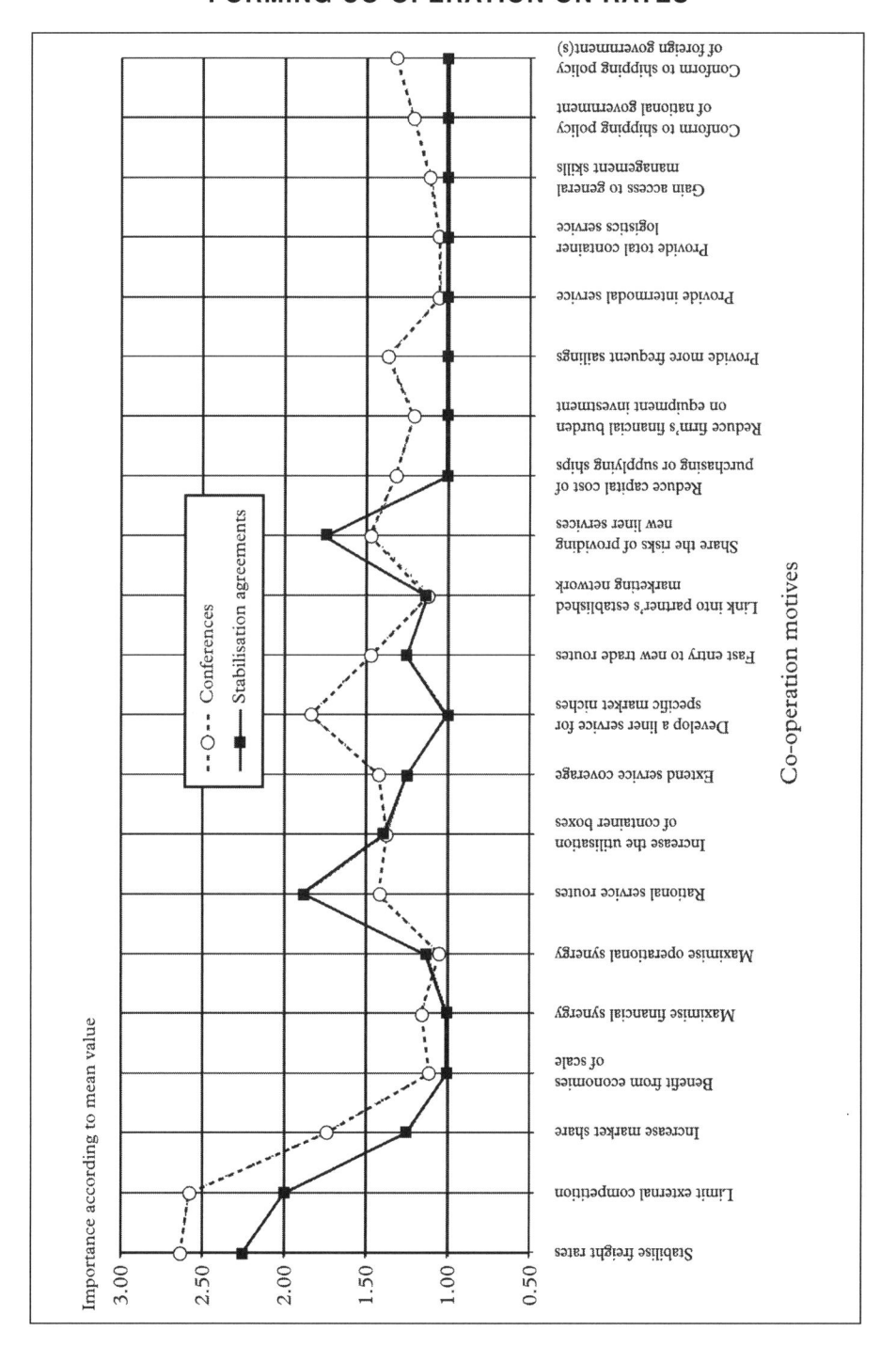

368 ISSUES IN LINER SHIPPING

APPENDIX D: COMPARISON OF MOTIVES FOR FORMING OPERATIONAL CO-OPERATION

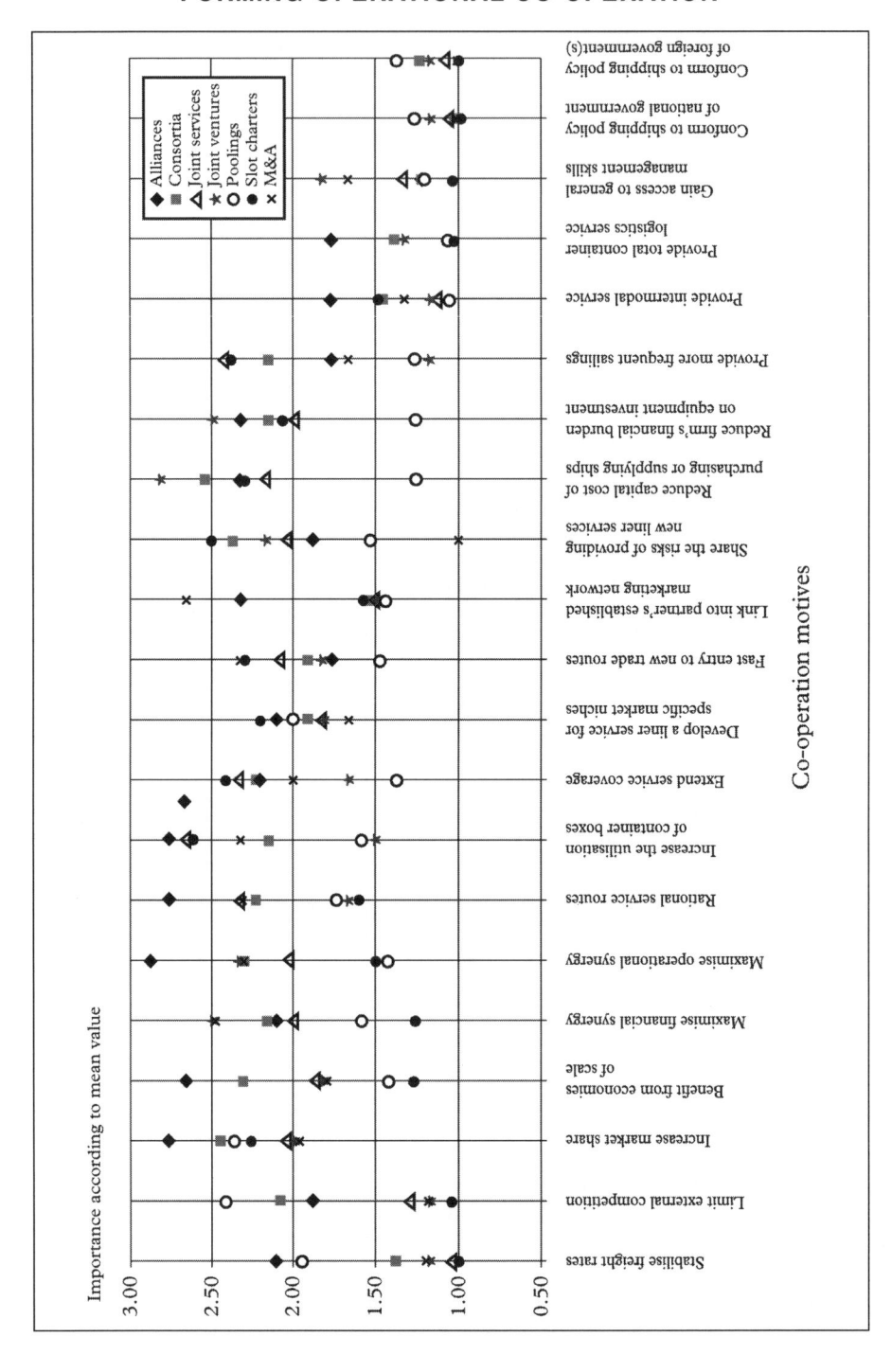

APPENDIX E: CO-OPERATION FORMS IN TERMS OF BUSINESS STRATEGIES

BUSINESS STRATEGY	Co-operation on rates CONF	Co-operation on rates SA	Operational co-operation ALL	CONS	JSA	JV	PA	SC	MA
Market stabilisation strategy					Mean				
Stabilise freight rates	2.63	2.25	2.11	–	–	–	–	–	–
Limit external competition	2.58	2.00	–	2.08	–	–	2.42	–	–
Service differentiation strategy					Mean				
Extend service coverage	–	–	2.22	2.23	2.33	–	–	2.43	2.00
Provide more frequent sailings	–	–	–	2.15	2.42	–	–	2.40	–
Cost reduction strategy					Mean				
Benefit from economies of scale	–	–	2.67	2.31	–	–	–	–	3.00
Maximise financial synergy	–	–	2.11	2.15	2.00	2.50	–	–	3.00
Maximise operational synergy	–	–	2.89	2.31	2.04	2.33	–	–	3.00
Rationalise service routes	–	–	2.78	2.23	2.33	–	–	–	2.33
Increase the utilisation of container boxes	–	–	2.78	2.15	2.67	–	–	2.63	2.33
Share the risks of providing new liner services	–	–	–	2.38	2.04	2.17	–	2.51	–
Reduce capital cost of purchasing or supplying ships	–	–	2.33	2.54	2.17	2.83	–	2.31	2.33
Reduce firm's financial burden on equipment investment	–	–	2.33	2.15	2.00	2.50	–	2.06	2.33
Market development strategy					Mean				
Increase market share	–	–	2.78	2.46	2.04	2.00	2.37	2.26	3.00
Develop a liner service for specific market niches	–	–	2.11	–	–	–	2.00	2.20	–
Fast entry to new trade routes	–	–	–	–	2.08	–	–	2.31	2.33
Link into partner's established marketing network	–	–	2.33	–	–	–	–	–	2.67

* CONF: Conference, SA: Stabilisation Agreement, ALL: Global Alliance, CONS: Consortium, JSA: Joint Service Agreement, JV: Joint Venture, PA: Pooling Agreement, SC: Slot Charter, MA: Merger & Acquisition. * The mean is the average on a scale of 1 (= not important at all) to 3 (= very important).

APPENDIX F: IMPORTANCE OF CO-OPERATION FORMS IN TERMS OF BUSINESS STRATEGIES

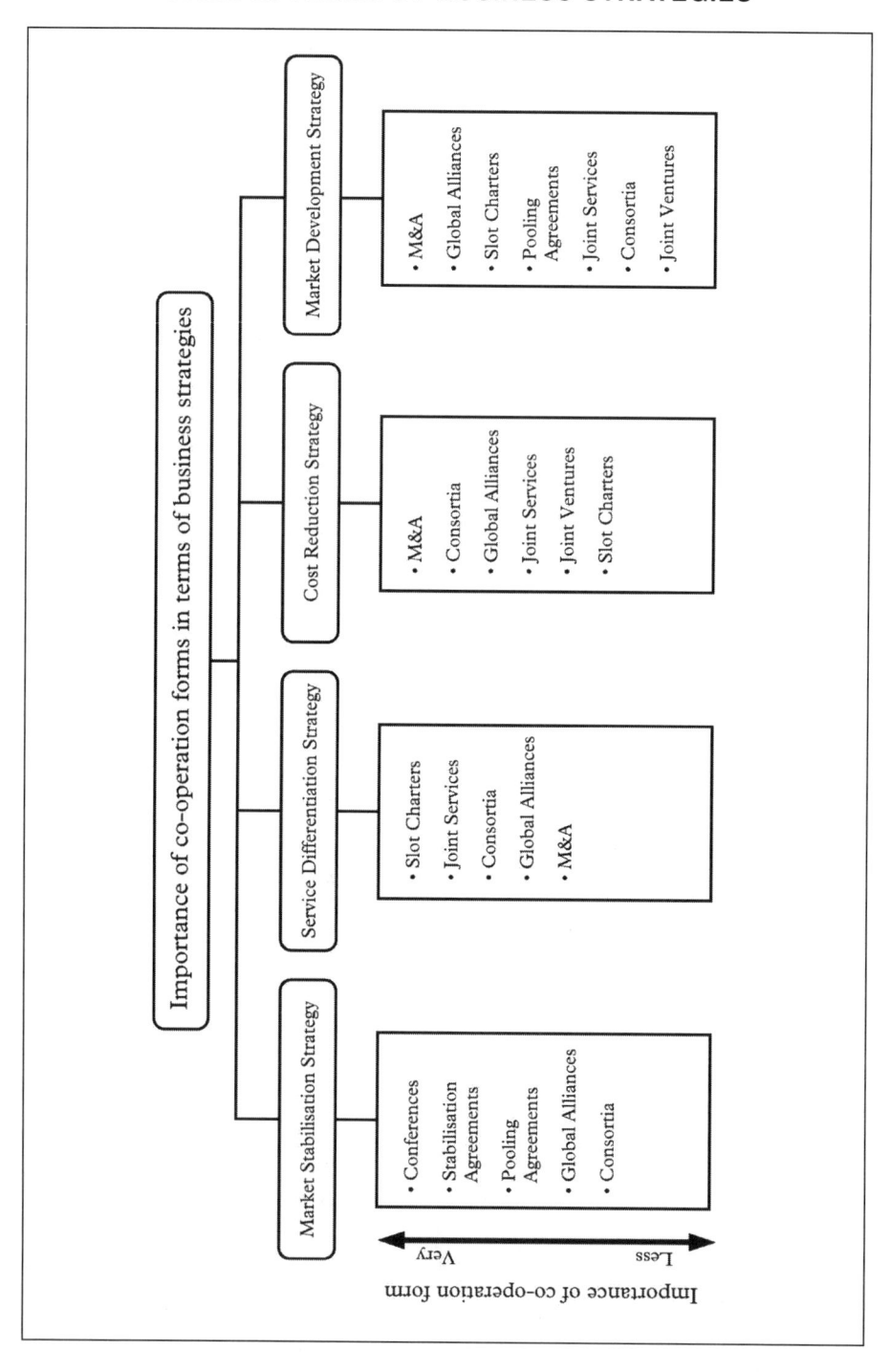

Importance of co-operation forms in terms of business strategies

Market Stabilisation Strategy
- Conferences
- Stabilisation Agreements
- Pooling Agreements
- Global Alliances
- Consortia

Service Differentiation Strategy
- Slot Charters
- Joint Services
- Consortia
- Global Alliances
- M&A

Cost Reduction Strategy
- M&A
- Consortia
- Global Alliances
- Joint Services
- Joint Ventures
- Slot Charters

Market Development Strategy
- M&A
- Global Alliances
- Slot Charters
- Pooling Agreements
- Joint Services
- Consortia
- Joint Ventures

Importance of co-operation form: Very ← → Less

ACKNOWLEDGEMENTS

The authors wish to express appreciation to Dr Helen A. Thanopoulou for her valuable advice and suggestions during the preparation of this paper.

ENDNOTES

1. *The Economist*, April 4, 91, 1998.
2. Thanopoulou, H. A., Ryoo, D. K., and Lee, T. W., "Korean Liner Shipping in the Era of Global Alliances", *Journal of Maritime Policy and Management* (1999) Vol 26, No. 3, pp. 209–229.
3. Das, T. K., and Teng, B. S., "Sustaining Strategic Alliances: Options and Guidelines", *Journal of General Management* (1997) Vol. 22, No. 4, pp. 49–64.
4. Ryoo, D. K., and Thanopoulou, H. A., "Liner Alliances in the Globalisation Era: A Strategic Tool for Asian Container Carriers", *Journal of Maritime Policy and Management* (1999) Vol 26, No. 4, pp. 349–367.
5. Porter, M. E. (1980): *Competitive Strategy* (New York, Free Press).
6. Johnson, G., and Scholes, K. (1999): *Exploring Corporate Strategy* (5th ed.) (London, Prentice Hall Europe).
7. Porter, M. E., *op. cit.*, 1980.
8. Williams, E. C., "Evolving Competitive Strategies of Ocean Container Operators: A Preliminary Analysis", *Journal of Global Marketing* (1991) Vol. 4, No. 2, pp. 93–107.
9. Porter, M. E., *op. cit.*, 1980.
10. Moon, I. S. (1996): "Structural Changes Going on inside the Container Shipping Industry and the Competitive Strategies of the Major Carrier", in Korea Maritime Institute (ed.), *The Globalisation of Logistics Management and the Restructuring of Shipping and Port Industries* (Seoul, Korea Maritime Institute).
11. Heaver, T. D. (1973): "A Theory of Shipping Conference Pricing and Policies", *Maritime Policy and Management*, Vol. 1, pp. 17–30.
12. Chrzanowski, I. (1985): *An Introduction to Shipping Economics* (London, Fairplay Publications).
13. Thanopoulou, *et al.*, *op. cit.*, 1999.
14. Drewry Shipping Consultants (1999): *Strategy and Profitability in Global Container Shipping* (London, Drewry Shipping Consultants Ltd).
15. Thanopoulou *et al.*, *op. cit.*, 1999.
16. Hunger, D. J. and Wheelen, T. L. (1996): *Strategic Management* (5th ed.) (USA, Addison-Wesley Publishing Co.).
17. Rich, C. A. (1978): "Corporate Planning in Shipping: relating theory to practice", *Maritime Policy and Management*, Vol. 5, pp. 39–50.
18. Churchill, G. A., Jr. (1991): *Marketing Research: Methodological Foundations* (5th ed.) (Chicago, The Dryden Press,).
19. Hopkins, K. D., Hopkins, B. R., and Glass, G. V. (1996): *Basic Statistics for the Behavioral Sciences* (3rd ed.) (USA, Allyn & Bacon).
20. Bryman, A., and Cramer, D. (1997): *Quantitative Data Analysis with SPSS for Windows* (London, Routledge).
21. Michael Backman (1999): *Asian Eclipse: Exposing the dark side of business in Asia* (New York, John Wiley & Sons); E. Borensztein and Jong-Wha Lee (2000): "Financial Crisis and Credit Crunch in Korea: evidence from firm-level data", IMF Working Paper WP/00/25; Dominic Casserley *et al.* (1999): *Banking in Asia: The end of entitlement* (New York, John Wiley & Sons); F. Philippe Delhaise (1998): *Asia in Crisis: The implosion of the banking and finance systems* (New York, John Wiley & Sons); Oh-Seok Hyun (1998): "Korea's Corporate Governance System: Applying New Remedies", *Proceedings of Conference on Corporate Governance in Asia: A Comparative Perspective*, organised by OECD and KDI, Korea, 3–5 March.

22. Michael Camdessus (2000): *From the Crises of the 1990s to the New Millennium* (IMF); Hubert Neiss (2000): "The Unfinished Reform Agenda in Asia: How much does it matter in the context of renewed growth?", IMF Media Seminar, Singapore.
23. Philip Kotler and Hermawan Kartajaya (2000): *Repositioning Asia from Bubble to Sustainable Economy* (New York, John Wiley & Sons).
24. R. Bajpaee (2000): "The Evolution and Development of Ship Management", *Journal of the Korea Marine Transport Policy Foundation*, Vol. 24, pp. 85–101.
25. A. Helen Thanopoulou, Dong-Keun Ryoo, and Tae-Woo Lee (1999): "Korean liner shipping in the era of global alliances", *Maritime Policy and Management*, Vol. 26, No. 3, pp. 209–229; Luc Cuyvers (2000): "Sea Changes: The Challenge of the Ocean in the 21st Century", *The Journal of the Korean Association of Shipping Studies*, Vol. 31, pp. 17–27; Kunio Miyashita (2000): "Global Management Problem of Container Shipping", *The Journal of the Korean Association of Shipping Studies*, Vol. 31, pp. 29–44.
26. Tae-Woo Lee (1996): *Shipping Developments in Far East Asia: The Korean Experience* (London, Avebury).
27. Department of the Environment, Transport and the Regions, UK (1998): *British Shipping: Charting a new course*(London, DETR); Lord Alexander of Weedon QC (1999): Independent Enquiry into a Tonnage Tax (London, HM Treasury).

REFERENCES

Backman, Michael (1999): *Asian Eclipse: Exposing the dark side of business in Asia* (New York, John Wiley & Sons).

Bajpaee, R. (2000): "The Evolution and Development of Ship Management", *Journal of the Korea Marine Transport Policy Foundation*, Vol. 24, pp. 85–101.

Borensztein, E., and Jong-Wha Lee (2000): "Financial Crisis and Credit Crunch in Korea: evidence from firm-level data", IMF Working Paper WP/00/25.

Bronder, C., and Pritzl, R. (1992): "Developing Strategic Alliances: A Conceptual Framework for Successful Co-operation", *European Management Journal*, Vol. 10, No. 4, pp. 412–421.

Brooks, M. R., Blunden, R. G., and Bidgood, C. I. (1993): "Strategic Alliances in the Global Container Transport Industry", in Culpan, R. (ed.), *Multinational Strategic Alliances* (London, International Business Press).

Bryman, A., and Cramer, D. (1997): *Quantitative Data Analysis with SPSS for Windows* (London, Routledge).

Camdessus, Michael (2000): *From the Crises of the 1990s to the New Millennium* (IMF).

Casserley, Dominic et al. (1999): *Banking in Asia: The end of entitlement* (New York, John Wiley & Sons).

Chrzanowski, I. (1985): *An Introduction to Shipping Economics* (London, Fairplay Publications).

Churchill, G. A., Jr.(1991): *Marketing Research: Methodological Foundations* (5th ed.) (Chicago, The Dryden Press).

Cuyvers, L. (2000): "Sea Changes: The Challenge of the Ocean in the 21st Century", *The Journal of the Korean Association of Shipping Studies*, Vol. 31, pp. 17–27.

Das, T. K., and Teng, B. S. (1997): "Sustaining Strategic Alliances: Options and Guidelines", *Journal of General Management*, Vol. 22, No. 4, pp. 49–64.

Delhaise, F. P. (1998): *Asia in Crisis: The implosion of the banking and finance systems* (New York, John Wiley & Sons).

Doz, Y. (1986): "Technology Partnerships between Large and Small Firms: Issues and Pitfalls", presented at the Conference on Strategic Alliances (Rutgers University, Brunswick, N J, October 24–26).

Drewry Shipping Consultants(1999): *Strategy and Profitability in Global Container Shipping* (London, Drewry Shipping Consultants Ltd).

Economist, The (1998), April 4.
Flynn, Matthew (1998): "South Korean yards begin to lose out as won gains strength", *Lloyd's List*, 8 February.
Forrest, J. E. (1989): "The Management of Technological Innovation: Strategic Alliances in the New Biotechnical Industry", dissertation presented for PhD in UWCC.
Furman, Jason and Joseph Stiglitz (1998): "Economic Crises: Evidence and Insights from East Asia", *Brookings Papers on Economic Activity*, pp. 1–123.
Ghemawat, P., Porter, M. E., and Rawlinson, R. A. (1986): "Patterns of International Coalition Activity", in Porter, M. E. (ed), *Competition in Global Industries* (Cambridge, MA, Harvard University Press), pp. 345–365.
Goldstein, Morris (1998): "The Asian Financial Crisis: Causes, Cures, and Systemic Implications", *Policy Analyses in International Economics*, Vol. 55 (Institute for International Economics), June.
Hanjin Shipping Co. Ltd (1999), Internal Data.
Hanjin Shipping Co. (2000) and Hyundai Merchant Marine(2000), Internal Data.
Heaver, T.D. (1973): "A Theory of Shipping Conference Pricing and Policies", *Maritime Policy and Management*, Vol. 1, pp. 17–30.
Hopkins, K.D., Hopkins, B.R., and Glass, G.V. (1996): *Basic Statistics for the Behavioral Sciences* (3rd ed.), Allyn & Bacon.
Hunger, D.J., and Wheelen, T. L. (1996): *Strategic Management* (5th ed.) (New York, Addison-Wesley Publishing Co.).
Hyun, Oh-Seok (1998): "Korea's Corporate Governance System: Applying New Remedies", *Proceedings of Conference on Corporate Governance in Asia: A Comparative Perspective*, organised by OECD and KDI, 3–5 March.
Johnson, G., and Scholes, K. (1999): *Exploring Corporate Strategy* (5th ed.) (London, Prentice Hall Europe).
Kidder, L.H., and Judd, C. M. (1986): *Research Methods in Social Relations* (5th ed.) (New York, CBS College Publishing).
Kotler, Philip, and Hermawan Kartajaya (2000): *Repositioning Asia from Bubble to Sustainable Economy* (New York, John Wiley & Sons).
Lee, Tae-Woo (1996): *Shipping Developments in Far East Asia: The Korean Experience* (London, Ashgate).
Lee, Tae-Woo (1997): "IMF bailout could bring difficult times", *Lloyd's List*, 2 December.
Lee, Tae-Woo (1998): "Chaebol dilemmas", *Lloyd's Shipping Economist*, Vol. 20, No. 4, April.
Lee, Tae-Woo (1999): "Restructuring the economy and impacts of the financial crisis on the maritime industry in Korea", *Maritime Policy and Management*, Vol. 26, No. 4, pp. 310–323.
Lu, C. S. (1997): "Strategic Groups and Logistics Strategy in the Taiwanese Liner Shipping Industry", dissertation presented for PhD in UWC.
Miyashita, Kunio (2000): "Global Management Problem of Container Shipping", *The Journal of the Korean Association of Shipping Studies*, Vol. 31, pp. 29–44.
Moon, I.S. (1996): "Structural Changes Going on inside the Container Shipping Industry and the Competitive Strategies of the Major Carrier", in Korea Maritime Institute (ed.), *The Globalisation of Logistics Management and the Restructuring of Shipping and Port Industries* (Seoul, Korea Maritime Institute).
Neiss, Hubert (2000): "The Unfinished Reform Agenda in Asia: How much does it matter in the context of renewed growth?" (Singapore), IMF Media Seminar.
Porter, M.E. (1980): *Competitive Strategy* (New York, Free Press).
Porter, M.E., and Fuller, M. B. (1986): "Coalitions and Global Strategies", in Porter, M.E. (ed), *Competition in Global Industries* (Cambridge, MA, Harvard University Press), pp. 315–343.
Radelet, Steven, and D. Jeffrey Sachs (1998): "The Onset of the East Asian Financial Crisis", Working Paper (Harvard Institute for International Development).

Ryoo, D.K., and Thanopoulou, H. A. (1999): "Liner Alliances in the Globalisation Era: A Strategic Tool for Asian Container Carriers", *Maritime Policy and Management*, Vol. 26, No. 4, pp. 349–367.

Stiles, J. (1994): "Strategic Alliances: Making Them Work", *Long Range Planning*, Vol. 27, No. 4, pp. 133–137.

Thanopoulou, H.A., Ryoo, D.K., and Lee, T.W (1999): "Korean Liner Shipping in the Era of Global Alliances", *Journal of Maritime Policy and Management*, Vol. 26, No. 3, pp. 209–229.

Williams, E.C. (1991): "Evolving Competitive Strategies of Ocean Container Operators: A Preliminary Analysis", *Journal of Global Marketing*, Vol. 4, No. 2, pp. 93–107.

Yoshino, M.Y., and Rangan, U.S. (1995): *Strategic Alliances: An Entrepreneurial Approach to Globalization* (Boston, Harvard Business School Press).

CHAPTER 17

SUPPLY CHAIN AND LOGISTICS MANAGEMENT: IMPLICATIONS FOR LINER SHIPPING

Trevor D. Heaver
University of British Columbia, Vancouver, Canada.
E-mail: *tdheaver@hotmail.com*

1. INTRODUCTION

The purpose of this chapter is to interpret developments in liner shipping in the light of developments in concepts and practices associated with supply chain and logistics management. In particular, the shift in management philosophy away from managing individual functions to integrating activities into key supply chain business processes (Lambert[1]) has implications for the expectations of shippers and the service decisions of shipping companies. Shippers seek service suppliers able to offer them better integrated service packages than in the past. However, the extent and forms of integration that that are efficient for service suppliers and that are seen as beneficial by customers remain uncertain.

Change in the liner shipping industry has been characterised by increased horizontal and vertical integration. The former has been the result of mergers and acquisitions and of the on-going evolution of alliances. The latter has been achieved through shipping companies or the corporations of which they are a part extending their services through internal growth and acquisitions in three main areas. They are the management of container terminals, the provision of intermodal services and the provision of logistics services. The relationship of each of these services with the shipping activities deserves individual attention. In general, the level of corporate integration with shipping is greater in the terminal and intermodal activities than in logistics. Major shippers are not interested in negotiating rate and service conditions in shipping and logistics as a single process. This is contrary to the interests of some shipowners who believe it would be mutually beneficial for shippers to negotiate ocean transportation and logistics services together (Damas[2]). At issue is whether the position of shippers is a transitory stage in the evolution of logistics management or reflects conditions that are likely to persist.

The approach adopted in this chapter is to commence by reviewing the evolving conditions in supply chain management and logistics. This sets the stage to review the responses of lines. Both the horizontal and vertical restructuring of lines are covered but the emphasis is on the latter. This part of the chapter draws, in particular, on Evangelista *et al.*[3] and Heaver.[4] Interpretation of the patterns of relationships draws on the literature dealing with supply chain management, out-sourcing and transaction cost economics. The evolving organisational relationship between the shipping and logistics services of lines is explored in the concluding part of the chapter. The interests and conduct of shippers in the allocation of traffic among lines and in the negotiation of liner rates and services appear vital to the levels and processes of integration of shipping with logistics services.

2. EVOLVING CONDITIONS IN SUPPLY CHAIN MANAGEMENT AND LOGISTICS

Liner shipping is but one of the myriads of service and product activities that are necessary for the delivery of the goods and services required by consumers. The opportunities and challenges faced by the lines are affected by the network environment in which they operate. As the environment changes under technological, economic and political conditions, so the lines have opportunities to follow strategies that give them an advantage in serving customers needs. These strategies may involve and certainly have implications for the organisational structure of the industry, as anticipated by Chandler.[5] This section of the chapter explores the influence of supply chain and logistics management concepts and practices for the shipping industry. It starts by defining the concepts and then proceeds to examine the implications of customer needs and the associated challenges and opportunities for shipping. It concludes by describing some of the changes in the logistics industry that affect the position of liner shipping companies.

2.1 The definition of supply chain management and logistics management

The advance of more integrated approaches to the management of intra-corporate and inter-corporate relationships is well documented (Hall and Braithwaite[6]). Although the progress of types of practices and of the terminology to be applied to them have been erratic, the interpretation of supply chain management and logistics management has become standardised widely. Even though Hall and Braithwaite suggest "there is little point in seeking to document a perfect definition for supply chain management", a definition that captures the extent of application of the integration concept is useful. Mentzer *et al.*[7] define supply chain management as "the systematic, strategic coordination of the traditional business functions and the tactics across these business functions within a particular company and across businesses within the supply chain, for the purposes of improving the long-term performance of the individual companies and the supply chain as a whole". That the "chains" referred to are more likely "networks" of private and public goods and services providers distributed globally is one of the possible shifts in the terminology that is generally treated, fortunately, as too esoteric to worry about.

Supply chain management is the wide framework within which logistics functions. The definition of logistics by the US Council of Logistics Management reflects this. The definition is: "Logistics is that part of the supply chain process that plans, implements, and controls the efficient, effective flow and storage of goods, services, and related information from the point-of-origin to the point-of-consumption in order to meet customers' requirements." It recognizes that logistics management is only a part of the supply chain.

2.2 Customer needs and the challenges and opportunities for liner shipping

Global improvements in logistics performance have contributed to and been required by increased competition in product markets. The reduction of tariff and other trade barriers, improvements in the efficiency of transport services and the increased value and reduced weight of many products have all contributed to the ability of products from distant locations to compete locally. Multi-national firms that used to be organised with regional marketing and production divisions have switched to product-based supply chains that source and market globally. Spatial competition (the competition in common markets for products from far away) is more important now than ever before.

Increased competition heightens pressures for the redesign of supply chains and logistics systems. The competition drives the need to reduce costs while, at the same time, maintaining or improving service levels. Actions taken to reduce costs and to improve service work concurrently and dynamically, although descriptions of them often focus on specific effects. Such actions are considered next, prior to considering their implications for shipping lines.

2.2.1 Developments in logistics

Four strategies provide examples of the central role for logistics in improving supply chain performance. They are: sourcing in low-cost locations; just-in-time delivery; postponement; and improving supply chain visibility. While these strategies are not strictly separate, it is convenient to deal with them individually.

Sourcing in low-cost locations
Industries have always made trade-offs among locations based on the benefits of locating close to low cost resource inputs compared with the benefits of proximity to markets. Typically, industries in which labour costs are high gravitate to low wage-cost locations. The ability of firms to do this is dependent on efficient logistics services to get products to where they are needed. Examples of the pull of low cost production are the shift of manufacturing textile, footwear, automobile, electronic and toy products to Asia. However, the attractiveness of shifting to low-cost production locations has decreased recently if logistics conditions in those locations have not been compatible with the operation of manufacturing and retailing with low inventories. For example, the changing pattern of activities in the hard disk drive industry in Asia has been affected by various aspects of time responsiveness, including transit and order cycle times (McKendrick et al.[8]). Similarly, the location and role of facilities of the Taiwanese computer manufacturer Acer reflects the trade off between costs of manufacture and assembly in Asia and the time of delivering product to consumers (Nemoto and Kawashima[9]).

Just-in-time and postponement
Reducing the costs of logistics and improving service to customers by shortening time cycles is important in the design of supply chains. The successful use of the kanban system in the Japanese automobile industry has had a major influence on all industries around the world as they have shifted to new delivery systems. Just-in-time (JIT) is just one approach to reducing inventories in supply chains through frequent, small quantity and highly reliable deliveries. These deliveries are timed to respond to immediate user needs; the products are pulled through the supply chain by demand. This is a major difference to the time when goods were produced in long, low-cost runs based on forecasts well ahead of demand. When manufacturers are the immediate recipients of goods, terms such as lean manufacturing are used to describe the new environment. When the recipients are retailers, the term lean retailing may be used.

The strategy of postponement involves the delay of processes. Manufacture of products may be delayed until a customer places an order; this is most likely when product manufacture or assembly can be done quickly. More frequently, undifferentiated products are held in a centralized inventory, thereby reducing the total inventory held and the costs built into it. When more information is obtained about demand, differentiating processes can be performed whether the final manufacture of a product, the labelling to national market requirements or simply shipping to one market rather than another.

For products with highly uncertain demand, the ability to defer production until as much as possible is known about demand is especially advantageous. Thus, the geographical shifts of manufacturing in the textile industry reflect the predictability of particular product groups. For example, increased manufacture of fashion textiles has taken place in the Caribbean and Central America at the expense of Asia as time to North American customer has assumed greater importance (Abernathy *et al.*[10]). Similarly, the efforts of the automobile industry to provide individual car buyers with the style, colour and options they desire within ever-shorter times and at reasonable cost requires a supply chain with more responsive logistics than previously. An example illustrates the situation.

Car seats are usually assembled close to the auto assembly plants, for the obvious reason that their bulk makes them expensive to transport. However, the manufacture of components of seats may be more widely distributed. An example is the manufacture of leather seat covers. This can be labour intensive. As a result, production is found in Asia often using imported materials. The finished covers are shipped back by sea container. Products of good quality have been produced in systems that have had long though precise round-trip cycles. However, the pressures to give car buyers choice and fast delivery, at reasonable cost, require changes to the system. To achieve the responsiveness to meet variable demands without excessive inventory close to auto markets requires a much more flexible logistics system. In the absence of forecasts of demand long enough in advance, some seat covers, at least, have to be sent by airfreight. The difference in costs between sea and airfreight is such that the viability of exports from Asia is threatened. The challenge increases the competitiveness of alternate locations with low labour costs closer to the major markets, for example, Eastern Europe for Western Europe and Mexico or the Caribbean for North America. A general consequence for consumers if effective supply solutions are not found is that the range of options available in short times becomes limited.

Supply chain visibility
Reductions in the order cycle and delivery lead times have been achieved through many changes in the design and operation of supply chains and logistics systems. Vital contributions to the changes have been made by the developments in information and communications technologies (ICT). Notable has been the transfer of data and other information resulting in enhanced supply chain visibility.

Firms are striving to achieve better visibility, forwards and backwards, along their supply chains. Forward information reveals point of sale information from bar code scanning, shared real time or frequently through automatic electronic transmission. This allows members of supply chains to make quick and consistent decisions (with different levels of sophistication among supply chains) about replenishment based on common information. It enables the use of cost-effective methods such as Manufacturing Resource Planning or Continuous Replenishment Planning and avoids the violent fluctuations of inventories associated with sequential and delayed information provided along disjointed supply chains (Forrester[11]). Visibility backward along supply chains enables receivers to be fully aware of the status of orders so that early actions can be taken to minimize costs associated with delays in supplies or with changes in requirements. The visibility of the status of purchase orders from the time they are placed until goods are delivered is one of the competitive services offered by major logistics service companies. It also lies at the heart of increasingly sophisticated supply chain software.

2.2.2 Challenges and opportunities for liner shipping

Each of the strategies described above is associated with a range of changes in the characteristics of supply chains and logistics systems. These create challenges and opportunities for shipping lines.

Relationships among supply chain participants tend to be closer. To achieve this there are fewer suppliers of particular goods and services. For shipping lines and other carriers, this means that shares of shippers' business are larger but go to fewer firms. One of the attributes desired by shippers as they develop closer relationships with fewer lines is that those lines have an extensive service network able, therefore, to serve them in various trade lanes. The pressure on lines is to develop more extensive service networks (Evangelista et al.[3]).

The reduction of time is becoming a more important logistics strategy to reduce costs and to improve customer service. Hummels estimates that for manufactured goods imported into the US each day of travel is worth an average of 0.8 percent of the value of the good and that each day in transit reduces the probability of a country as a source by 1.5% (Hummels[12]). The related feature is the greater attention to reliability of products and processes. The costs of "disruptions", whether associated with variations in demand, logistics or supplier performance warrant close attention (Levy[13]). The effects of disruptions are particularly great when lead times are long, even with good information systems. Greater recognition of the costs of disruptions encourages the design of shorter, faster supply chains. This encourages local sourcing, the use of improved IT and of expedited logistics services. The liner shipping industry faces prospects of a diminishing role in international trade and competitive advantages accruing to lines offering short reliable transit times. These are lines on short routes, with fast ships and with related services that ensure fast and reliable door-to-door service. Whether the heightened value of short transit times is sufficient to create a market to support new fast ships in ocean services remains to be seen.

In pricing their services, lines face heightened competitive conditions. The increased competition for market share is heightened by the traffic allocation strategies of shippers, the legislative weakening of conferences and the rapid increase in capacity resulting from the new generations of larger ships. Also, shippers have available to them a widening range of manufacturing locations and logistics strategies that place limits on the rates chargeable by lines on particular routes.

These changed conditions create opportunities for the lines that respond well. Notably, the strategies of lines to ensure faster, more reliable services are resulting in on-going shifts in the span of activities in which the shipping lines are engaged. Striving to provide enhanced customer service is taking lines into additional service areas and redefining relationships in international logistics service, consistent with Chandler's hypothesis. Before examining the position of shipping companies in other services, it is appropriate to examine developments in the logistics services sector.

2.3 Changes in the logistics industry

It has long been customary for firms with small volumes of international traffic destined for or originating in a foreign country to use a freight forwarder. Freight forwarders have long been specialists in arranging the transportation, storage and handling of goods along with associated documentation activities between and within countries.[14] They manage the activities through their own offices and through those of partners. They may act as agents in arranging transportation or act as a non-vessel owning common carrier (NVOCC) co-loading freight onto a shipping line's vessel and issuing their own bill of lading. In the trade of countries with highly specialised logistics and transportation conditions, even large firms with substantial volumes of trade into the country have traditionally sought the assistance of such specialists.

The increased demand for logistics services in the last fifteen years has resulted in substantial changes in the freight forwarding industry. The growth of the logistics services industry has been marked by structural trends. They are: the enhancement of existing and the development of new global networks; the development of domestic and contract logistics capabilities; the provision of more sophisticated services; and the integration of transportation and logistics services.

The major freight forwarders had a wide international presence for most of the twentieth century. They were present in most continents but had varied intensities and relied on partners in some countries. However, in the last two decades they have increased the number of countries in which they have a direct presence and have increased the intensity of their presence in most countries. They have generally done this by acquisitions and mergers. Examples are the acquisition of Royal Cargo Corporation of the Philippines by Danzas and the acquisition by the Swiss-based Kuehne & Nagel (KNI) of the American USCO Logistics and a majority interest in Virtual Integration Associates of Canada, a leading supplier of supply chain management and vendor-managed inventory programs for the electronics industry.[15] KNI also entered a strategic alliance with SembCorp Logistics of Singapore to increase its presence in Asia.[16] These developments are a part of KNI's strategy to become a global contract logistics player.

The development of logistics services has been marked, also, by the expansion of services not to deal just with the challenges of international trade but to deal with the challenges of logistics management in demanding domestic supply chain contexts. Contract logistics suppliers have developed to take advantage of the interests of some large companies to out-source logistics activities. The best examples of these new third party logistics providers in the US are Schneider Logistics and Ryder Logistics both of which expanded into logistics from trucking operations. In the US, the contract logistics business is estimated to have grown in one year by over 20 percent to a total of $56.4 billion in 2000 (Armstrong and Associates[17]). European contract logistics firms, such as Exel, have been more aggressive than those in the US in going international.

To meet the needs of shippers, firms in the logistics services business have had to shift their strategies from being asset driven to being knowledge driven. An essential component of the knowledge base is built around ICT. Traditional freight forwarders have generally lagged behind new logistics service companies in the use of ICT technologies. However, increasingly, all logistics companies are introducing web-based capabilities so that shippers can perform activities on line and can access information about the status of their shipments, now by purchase order. In addition to the benefits for shippers of being able to track their shipments, the resulting database becomes an integral tool for them to plan, budget, forecast, negotiate, and manage their businesses. The capabilities are being provided through proprietary systems and through shared portals. The trade literature is replete with logistics companies adding to their ICT capabilities, often through the acquisition of or partnerships with specialised software companies.

A major shift that has taken place in the logistics services industry is the entry of carriers. Responding to the interests of shippers to deal with fewer suppliers and to outsource logistics activities, carriers in many developed countries have added logistics services. The import of manufactured goods from Asia gave rise to specialised needs. Importers of Asian goods felt the need for better assistance in managing the flow of imports. The value of imports from Asia was increasing and the interest of shipping lines in extending their range of services to customers was developing. The result was the development of consolidation services, most notably initially by Maersk, known as Mercantile, American President Lines (APL), known as American Consolidation Services (ACS) and by Sea-Land, known as Buyers. The services differed in some important respects from those offered by freight forwarders. They were focused on the needs of importers for monitoring the movement of goods to consolidation points, managing the consolidation of goods and shipping according to the specifications of the buyers. The companies were aided in the development of these services by existing familiarity with the buyers' needs through their shipping services. They were able to offer consolidation services with high visibility by utilising their existing links with the shipping lines' documentation processes.

The characteristics of the logistics services offered by logistics companies vary among geographic and commodity markets. Also, the relationships between carriers' transportation and logistics services vary among the modes and among carriers. These variations will be explored later.

3. THE HORIZONTAL AND VERTICAL RESTRUCTURING OF LINES

Shipping lines have faced pressures in the changing market place to expand their services geographically and to widen the range of services offered (Heaver[18]). The response of lines has differed depending on their views of market opportunities, their resource base in terms of their financial resources, the initial geographical extent of their services, the range and level of supporting services, especially in information technology, and the depth and breadth of their human resources.

3.1 The horizontal restructuring of liner shipping

As large shippers have followed supply chain strategies involving the use of fewer suppliers, they have placed heightened value on the extent of the network of services offered by liner companies. This is the primary reason given by American President Line (APL) in 1995 for the introduction of its first service from Asia to Europe through a slot-charter agreement. The new service was a significant shift in APL's policy as up to that time it had a Pacific-only service strategy. It is the dominant reason for the increased concentration in liner shipping which is one of the prominent features of the industry.

The strategies of lines in extending the network of their services have been covered extensively in the literature (Brooks et al.[19]; Gardiner[20]; Evangelista and Morvillo[21]; Brooks[22]) and feature prominently in this book in the chapter by Lee. The addition of routes by lines has been dominantly by slot charter, alliance and merger or acquisition rather than the extension of own services. These methods limit the need for new investments while extending route networks and avoid reductions in the density of traffic in relation to infrastructure costs by route, an important consideration in network industries.

There has been speculation that the growth of global carriers will lead to the development of global contracting for services by major shippers. However, while shippers have a preference for dealing with fewer carriers and, therefore, with carriers with large networks, global contracts appear not to be common. Contracts still appear to be related mainly to traffic volumes and service conditions by route. This is not to say that in negotiations, traffic volumes and conditions across routes are not relevant. Simply, there is no evidence so far that the more global orientation of logistics is having a major effect on shipping beyond encouraging the geographical expansion of companies' services. The effects of logistics on the vertical structure of the industry are more prominent.

3.2 The vertical restructuring of liner shipping

The vertical structure of liner shipping has been affected by developments in logistics in a number of ways. The interests of shippers in dealing with fewer suppliers have influenced lines to extend the vertical reach of their services. The interests of shippers in faster and more reliable services have not only affected the design of shipping services but also the relationship among the services necessary to deliver value to shippers, for example, by door-to-door services. The interests of shippers in outsourcing logistics services have created an opportunity for shipping lines (and others) to expand their third-party logistics services. The expansion of lines into services beyond shipping has lead to greater vertical integration in the industry but the organisational relationships vary with the nature of activities and the interests of shippers in those activities. The added services common in shipping are divided into three. They are terminal operations, intermodal services and logistics services.

3.2.1 Involvement in terminal management

Container terminals are providing mainly intermediate services in international logistics. They are designed to ensure the fast and efficient transfer of containers at hub terminals in shipping networks and at throughput terminals for transfer to inland carriers.[23] On-dock cargo-handling services that might be requested by shippers are becoming an insignificant part of the modern terminal business. The terminals view their main customers as the shipping lines as the contracts with them are the single largest determinant of their business volume. However, in the long run, the success of terminals is dependent not only on how efficiently they serve the ships but also the efficiency of the closely related on-dock operations and the connections with inland carriers. Efficient terminal operation is measured by the speed and reliability with which containers can be moved through terminals at a competitive cost in order to meet the logistics needs of shippers. Terminals must have levels of performance compatible with the same-day-of-the-week services of shipping lines.

Traditionally, the port authority or a stevedoring company local to the port or region managed port terminals. However, starting with the introduction of containerisation and the focus on customer service by Malcolm McLean of

Sea-Land Services in the US in the 1970s, the interest of large lines in dedicated terminals has increased. For companies with a sufficient volume of traffic, dedicated terminals can provide better opportunities to integrate the operating philosophy and day-to-day operations of vessels, terminals and inland transportation.[24] Dedicated terminals have been common in the US since the start of container services.

In most other countries, concerns of governments and public port authorities about the effects on competition of allowing dedicated terminals and the limited opportunities for lines to ensure effective intermodal services inhibited dedicated terminals. In the 1990s, the shortage of capital available to port authorities, the general increase in privatisation and greater interest in intermodal developments, have resulted in an increase in the number of dedicated terminals and in the number of countries accepting them. Recent examples are Evergreen in Taranto, Italy, Maersk Sealand in Rotterdam and the Port of Tanjung Pelepas, Malaysia, and Hanjin in South Korea. Dedicated terminals are now commonplace.

Given the importance of close operating philosophy and practices between a line and its terminal, it is not surprising that lines with dedicated terminals have often managed those terminals as units integrated with the shipping line. However, some lines have contracted with specialised terminal management companies for the management of terminals leased long-term from port authorities.

The relationship of terminal management and line management is complicated by the rapid growth of specialised terminal management companies. The growth has been concurrent with the worldwide need for more capital investment in ports creating new opportunities in port businesses. Two types of firms are found in this burgeoning business. First, there are firms that have no ownership link with lines, such as the Port of Singapore Authority, Hutchison Port Holdings of Hutchison Wampoa and Stevedoring Services of America. Second, there are firms linked with corporations involved in shipping. They are P&O Ports owned by P&O Steam Navigation Co., which has a 50% interest in P&O Nedlloyd, and Orient Overseas International Ltd. (OOIL), which owns Orient Overseas Container Line (OOCL). OOIL manages four ports through a Terminal Investment unit (the terminals are in Vancouver, New Jersey, New York and Venice) and has two container terminals operated as a part of and for OOCL. These are in Kaohsiung and Long Beach.

The ownership pattern, then, was that the dedicated terminals were linked with the shipping business while terminals for other lines were managed separately. This is consistent with the case for integration where the volume of traffic and the interest of lines in the advanced integration of services exists and the avoidance of conflicts of interest where a common user terminal is being operated. However, A.P. Moller is making its Maersk Ports, which was the terminal operating company for the dedicated terminals of Maersk Sealand, a standalone unit known as APM Terminals (Economics Intelligence Unit, 2001). The Maersk unit already has investments in ports such as Malaysia's Tanjung Pelepas where it has a 30% stake, and Oman's Port Salalah where it is a 49% shareholder. The objective of APM Terminals is "to strive for excellence in terminal management while actively seeking new opportunities in port and terminal development" (Economics Intelligence Unit, 2001). AP Moller sees its terminal management business as having a scale warranting a standalone status and it anticipates that its substantial business with Maersk Sealand (now 90% of its throughput) will not jeopardise its position with other lines.

3.2.2 Involvement in intermodal services

Traditionally, the business of shipping lines was the movement of cargo on a port-to-port basis. This may still true of smaller lines competing on a low-cost strategy and is necessary for most or all lines in regions in which intermodal movements are impractical. However, in Europe and in North America all the major lines now offer door-to-door service. The door-to-door services are designed to make available to shippers reliable fast service through a single supplier.

The integration of shipping with inland services has largely been achieved through shipping lines managing the purchase of inland transport. It has been done mainly through a combination of long-term contracts and short-term purchases. However, some lines have maintained ownership of some trucking. Intermodal services are arranged through units of the shipping lines such as CP Logistics within CP Ships, which is comparable to Maersk Intermodal in Maersk Sealand.[25]

Shipping lines were leaders in the development of rail intermodal services in North America and are now playing leading roles in Europe and China because they have been in a better position than freight forwarders to commit for the volume of traffic necessary to make dedicated rail service viable under long-term contracts. However, achieving efficient utilisation of rail intermodal capacity has been challenging. In the US, APL marketed its container capacity for domestic traffic within the Intermodal Marketing Services unit (IMS). IMS was involved in the development of stack-train services but was sold to Pacer Stacktrain in 1999.

Thus the extension of shipping lines into intermodal services was consistent with the logistics needs of shippers and facilitated by the transaction economies enjoyed by the lines and the effectiveness for integrating operations. Shippers remain free to select the port-to-port or the door-to-door service.

3.2.3 Involvement in logistics services

Unlike dedicated terminals and intermodal services, which are managed within the shipping business, the conduct of logistics services is largely done in independent business units, although these are now frequently being re-branded to carry the group name, for example, Mercantile and Buyers have been joined in Maersk Logistics and ACS is now APL Logistics. Other companies are starting such units, for example Cosco Logistics. Also, unlike intermodal services, not all of the top 20 container lines in the world have such units. For example, Evergreen and CP Ships are currently focusing their efforts on excellence in meeting shippers' requirements through their shipping and door-to-door service capabilities. (However, in June 2002, Evergreen announced that it would invest in forwarding and logistics in Asia and South America.)

The development of logistics services by lines was in locations in which the lines had particular knowledge. For P&O, Nedlloyd and Maersk, services were developed to serve mainly European shippers, for APL and Sea-Land the needs of US shippers. Now, however, the lines see value-added services in logistics as offering faster growth and better profitability than shipping. Developments at APL, P&O Nedlloyd and Maersk Sealand are cited as evidence. The interests of these lines in logistics are the largest of the maritime enterprises but still have modest size compared with the major global freight forwarding companies.

Following its acquisition of APL, NOL reorganised its logistics services into APL Logistics (APLL) to advance its strategy of rapid growth in the logistics area. APLL has experienced double digit growth each year, the fastest-growing business unit in the NOL Group. Its growth in 2001 was 72% reflecting the acquisition of GATX Logistics, the second largest warehouse-based contract logistics company in the US. The acquisition enables APLL to serve customers more effectively through the primary (importing) and secondary (national) distribution phases of the supply chain. Flemming Jacobs, the President of NOL, has stated that he wants "the logistics business to challenge the Liner business as a major breadwinner of the Group" (NOL News Release, 19 June, 2000). In 2001, liner revenues were US$3.6 billion, logistics revenues were US$723 million (NOL News Release, 27 March, 2002).

With the acquisition of Sea-Land, A. P. Moller also re-branded its logistics services into Maersk Logistics (ML) while leaving it independent of the shipping line. ML's mission statement is that it "is an independent organisation operating world wide through locally incorporated companies and is engaged in satisfying customers' expectations in respect of competitive, international export and import management services" (*www.Maersk-logistics.com*).[26] It is largely a non-asset-owning company managing its quality through the careful selection of subcontractors. It has offices in more than 70 countries. ML acts as a full-service freight forwarder and logistics provider fully independent of the shipping line. It is in markets that are dominated by traditional freight forwarding requirements as well as those in which large clients such as large retail chains have special needs for more integrated services.

The A. P. Moller Group is less open than NOL about the role expected of ML within the Group. However, Soren Brandt, the head of ML, has noted, "the logistics activity could grow to outperform those of the liner, but it will take a while" (Le Lloyd[27]). He also characterised the shipping and logistics businesses "as distinct businesses". ML made a number of acquisitions during 2001 of which the largest was the US-based Distribution Services Limited (DSL) which had offices in 60 countries and 1500 employees, compared with ML's 3500 employees. Wal-Mart was one of DSL's major clients (Maersk Logistics[26]).

The structure of logistics in P&O Steam Navigation Co. (P&O), the senior company that holds the 50% interest in P&O Nedlloyd, is complex. This may be the result of the particular interests of P&O and Nedlloyd at the time of the merger.[28] Most of the logistics services of P&O are in different businesses from P&O Nedlloyd but one is integral to the shipping business. When P&O Nedlloyd was created by the merger, it brought together the previously separately identified Global Logistics and a variety of logistics services that had evolved as ancillary to shipping activities. The new group was named Value Added Services. It was intended to work with P&O Nedlloyd customers in providing advanced logistics or supply chain management services. Intermodal transport arrangements were not the responsibility of VAS; they were managed within shipping services. P&O Nedlloyd was attempting to bridge the gaps of different personnel skills and backgrounds among its own employees in shipping and VAS. It had one sales force, which it hoped would develop effective contact levels with clients to deal with shipping and logistics interests. It expected to identify effectively those clients for whom an integrated approach of a line with its logistics service was practical and attractive.

P&O did not follow this model only. It has three other logistics service groups that operate quite separately from the shipping services. Damco is a separate but wholly-owned subsidiary of P&O Nedlloyd engaged in freight forwarding with its own offices in nine countries in N.W. Europe and the Far East and represented through partnerships with local forwarding agents in a further 40 countries. This is a typical organisation structure for a modest-sized freight forwarder. P&O also owns P&O Trans European, a European-based logistics service company, and Cold Logistics, which specialises in serving the cold-product sector globally. The Chairman of P&O in his message to shareholders in the 1999 Annual Report notes that the company's logistics services are "high growth, high return businesses" and that "the ongoing P&O would focus on its high return logistics activities". Growth and profitability were maintained during 2001.

With the exception of VAS, the logistics businesses of these companies are organised as corporate units quite separate from shipping. A major reason for this is the expectation of shippers that logistics service providers (LSPs) act independently of interests in carriers when choosing modes of transport and carriers to meet shippers' logistics needs. Thus, even though logistics units may be re-branded with the name of the shipping corporation, their executives point to the independence of those units in selecting carriers.

There are also operating conditions relevant to the level of integration. There are substantial differences in the skills required in the design and management of trucking, shipping, warehousing and supply chain management functions. Further, the points of interface of these services with clients – consignors or consignees – differ and the knowledge and skills of sales and service personnel need to reflect this. While the differences may be lessening as shippers and carriers develop more sophisticated approaches to logistics management, the differences are still significant.[29]

In spite of the organisation of logistics units as separate structures, the actual level and ways of sharing resources and information between the business units remains uncertain. The utilisation of common information systems provides economies. However, it is in the sharing of market intelligence that uncertainty about relationships exists. For example, NOL has been trying for some time to increase the awareness of its sales forces to the service range of its companies.

The relationship between shipping and logistics services has been put in the spotlight by comments from shipping executives concerned with the focus of shippers on rates in their dealings with the lines. In 2001, the president of NOL, Flemming Jacobs, is quoted as having said that "Shippers and ocean carriers are 'confused' when they focus on narrow yearly negotiations on freight rates, instead of looking for opportunities to increase overall supply chain efficiencies".[30] He went on: "I am going to give a wake-up call to those who still get their kicks from yearly, or even more frequent, fights over freight rates with their ocean carriers – those who just cannot wait for the 1st of May to come around and who derive the greatest satisfaction from succeeding in squeezing another $50 from the carriers, even though in the process they miss tons of opportunities in the total supply chain." In March 2002, C.C. Tung, the chief executive office of OOCL, expressed concern about competition among "commoditised" shipping services as contributing to the reduction of rates. To avoid "over-commoditisation" he urged "offering value-added products".[31]

Uncertainty about the appropriate relationship between shipping and logistics services exists. Is it appropriate for some lines to avoid investment in logistics services? Is the current relationship between logistics and shipping where corporations control both merely a transitional stage in the development of the services. Is it appropriate for shippers to retain control of the negotiation of rates with lines? Examining the bases for the organisation structures described above may provide insights into these questions.

4. ASSESSMENT OF THE ORGANISATIONAL STRUCTURE

Examination of the attributes of the relationships of shipping with each of the three further services described above provides insights into the probable future of the organisational structures. The structure of each of the services is considered in turn. The examination considers the relationships in terms of their economic attributes and their attributes related to arguments for outsourcing in supply chain management.

4.1 The organisation structure for terminal management

There are strong arguments for the operation of a container terminal on a dedicated basis by a line when the line has a sufficient volume of traffic to achieve an economic utilisation of the terminal capacity and the line has a network of routes and terminals to achieve economies of scale and proficiency in terminal management. Alternatively, a line may contract a terminal management company to operate its dedicated terminal. Port terminal operations influence the service and cost characteristics of the through transportation service by the design and conduct of operations. For example, a line may prefer more labour intensive handling equipment to automated container terminal handling because of the greater versatility in the handling rate of the former. This provides flexibility to retain service standards during peaks in throughput.[32]

Some lines have preferred to operate terminals using chassis for container storage for the greater ease of movement on and off the dock even though it results in a much lower density of containers in the yard. The development of well-integrated information and communication systems (ICT) has been facilitated through dedicated terminals although this advantage should become less as ICT capability generally increases. In these ways, the integration of vessel schedules, terminal handling and land access can be better integrated to provide value to customers efficiently.

Concerns that have existed in some countries about dedicated terminals have been based largely on their potential effects on competition. Those concerns have diminished as the competition among lines and routings have increased, in part because of the improved throughput capabilities to which dedicated terminals have contributed.

Dedicated terminals are consistent with greater integration in supply chains without raising any conflicts with the interests of shippers. The services are intermediate services in the process of moving goods from terminal to terminal at which point the choice of shippers for alternate transport arrangements arises.

The case for dedicated terminals does not necessarily mean that the terminal needs to be operated by the shipping line or a closely related company. Given the growth of specialised terminal management companies, such a company might be used. This might arise if a line's resources make expansion into managing another terminal difficult or if a port authority has difficulty (likely political) allowing management and exclusive use of a terminal to a (foreign) line. However, such an arrangement would add a layer of relationships; contracts would exist between a port authority and the terminal operator and the latter and the shipping line.

4.2 The organisation structure for intermodal services

The case for the close involvement of a shipping line in intermodal services is comparable to that for terminals, except for two factors. First, the diversity of traffic flows and modes would make it difficult for a single agent to invest in, contract for and arrange all inland moves. The business is heterogeneous so that control of all inland movements by lines is impractical. Second, the diversity of shipper interests in the nature of inland transport arrangements means that the right of choice is important for shippers to ensure that the right mix of service, control and cost are preserved. Whether the efficient integration of the inland transportation into the supply chain processes is achieved best by use of intermodal service arranged by a line or a service arranged by the shipper or his agent (a "traditional" freight forwarding function) is best left to the shipper.

However, shipping lines can have an advantage over shippers and freight forwarders in arranging intermodal transport services when the ability to commit volumes of traffic is important to the viability of a service. This has been the case with the introduction of dedicated trains and certain barge services where reliable volume commitments are important. These are situations in which there are economies of scale.

4.3 The organisation structure for logistics services

The organisation structure appropriate to the relationships among shippers, LSPs and shipping lines involves more issues than the relationships considered so far. The range and scale of logistics functions are large. Therefore, the issues go well beyond effects to the efficiency of transport processes. Increasingly shippers have been willing to outsource more aspects of logistics so that a third major player is often involved. The LSPs may be relatively new to the logistics business, as are some of the new "independents", or they may be linked to transportation companies or they may have a long history in freight forwarding.[33] When shippers use LSPs, what levels of responsibility are they likely given in their dealing with carriers? Do they negotiate rates and traffic allocations or do shippers retain those functions?

There are many factors that influence the answers to these questions. They work concurrently and in diverse conditions. In general, shippers retain the negotiation of rates and the allocation of traffic. Although there are undoubtedly exceptions to this, they appear to be very infrequent. Answers to the questions are based on discussions with a few shippers, carriers and writers on the liner shipping business. Consequently, the arguments presented are speculative. They are presented under three headings and are considered in relation to all modes of transport not just shipping in order to help identify the particular features affecting shipping. The headings are: the nature of the service, the importance of the function and the effectiveness of process performance.

4.3.1 The nature of the service

The elements of a logistics service may be conceived of in different ways. Differences may be a result of different types of business and processes or they may be product of different visions, histories and preferences. The particular expertise, size, resources and needs of a shipper influence the merits of outsourcing functions such as transport and logistics. Whether the functions or their management are outsourced separately or as a package is also a choice.

In order for transportation and logistics price and service conditions to be negotiated as a single package, they need to be seen and function in a highly integrated way. The product needs to be "delivery" under tightly prescribed conditions, not "transportation and logistics services". Two examples of integrated services follow. The first example is the just-in-time delivery of automobile parts to an assembly plant involving trucking and parts management. The second example is the international delivery and inventory management of computer components by a courier company. In these cases, conditions enable the design of separate functions into an integrated service, the business equivalent of the creation of a mixture in chemistry. The characteristics of the mixture can be varied to serve particular purposes but it may be attractive to acquire the mixture rather than the component parts.

In the case of the delivery of time sensitive products, the linkage of transport and logistics services may be close enough that on occasion it is beneficial to package them under a management and to price them together. In some cases for expedited services and inventory management, a service provider may essentially be expected to do all or nothing. This is most unlikely in cases involving liner services.

The shipping function by its nature is not as tightly bound to other logistics activities, as may be trucking or air transport. The length and uncertainty of time involved in the movement of goods by sea prevents such tight integration of transport and logistics operations. A result is that shipping by a particular company is a readily separable and substitutable part of the overall service. Certainly, the growth of logistics services by shipping lines was to enhance supply chain visibility and integration of foreign sourcing through consolidation facilities. In conjunction with shipping services, the logistics services such as Mercantile and ACS advanced primary logistics capabilities. As these companies developed, they have acquired logistics and distribution companies in destination countries to enhance their secondary (national) distribution capabilities. However, a liner service between ports or extending to services between inland cities may be as readily provided by one line as another. Indeed, in this sense, the service is commoditised although this is not to deny the existence of important differences in service attributes among lines. Consequently, shippers are unlikely to bundle the design and pricing of logistics and shipping services together in the way that is done for more time-sensitive services.

4.3.2 The importance of the function

Shippers' interests in outsourcing are affected by the importance of the good or service to their businesses. There are various dimensions affecting importance among which are the strategic significance of the goods or services and the value of the transactions involved. Given argument for the substitutability among (major) shipping companies, it cannot be argued that the selection of a carrier has substantial strategic importance to the characteristics of a service with a region. However, strategic decisions about which logistics service suppliers and lines to use in which regions can be made with more flexibility if the selection and pricing of lines and logistics providers are kept separate. Further, for large companies, liner contracts are very valuable and complex so that shippers may view these periodic activities as essential for them. The subsequent on-going administration of the logistics activities, cargo tracking from the time of purchase order, maintaining cargo allocations among lines and monitoring freight charges may not be strategic and may well be contracted out.

4.3.3 The effectiveness of process performance

The effectiveness with which processes can be performed in-house or contracted out is a crucial consideration in out-sourcing. At issue is the likely effectiveness of traffic allocation among lines and the associated rate and service conditions depending on whether this is done by a shipper or its LSP. Three factors are relevant. First, it has been argued above that the negotiation of the shipping and logistics arrangements are readily separable. Second, it is most unlikely that a logistics supplier, which is a company, related to a line, even if a standalone business, is going to be entrusted with the negotiation of traffic allocations and rates. There is too much uncertainty about the role of the logistics company as a supplier of traffic to the sister shipping company. Third, there are issues associated with the nature of the negotiating function and the likely proficiency of the shipper and an independent LSP.

The negotiation of liner rates has and is changing greatly under the influence of government policy changes and economic conditions. The single most important policy development has been the requirement in the US Ocean Shipping Reform Act, 1998 that liner conferences allow confidential independent contracts to be made between their members and shippers. The result has been a huge shift of traffic to confidential rates and the weakening or demise of conferences. The weakening of rate agreements has been advanced by economic conditions of excess capacity associated with new large vessels being delivered during a market downturn. The surplus capacity is temporary although some of the market structure and behavioural results may not be.

In spite of the changes in shipping markets, the negotiation of shipping rates by large shippers is likely to remain more attractive for them than outsourcing that function to logistics providers. This conclusion rests on the nature of the negotiation process. Controlling a large volume of traffic is important, especially when surplus shipping capacity exists. It is for this reason that, for small shippers, the rates offered by freight forwarders (now LSPs) have been and will remain attractive. However, for large shippers, the potential advantage of a LSP because of the total volume of traffic they control is less. Large shippers are likely to have potential arguments involving volume on multiple routes as well as LSPs. On the other hand, LSPs are at a disadvantage in that as agents their interests are not likely to be seen as sufficiently aligned with the interests of their clients. The other disadvantage of LSPs is that that they are not going to have the intimate knowledge of a shipper's business and the negotiating positions that are associated with the variety of competitive pressures and logistical alternatives that a shipper may have or expect to face. A shipper may be aware of the possibility of a new plant or a sourcing or marketing alternative that may shift traffic from one region to another and from one carrier to another or diminish the amount of ocean shipping needed in total. For example, a new chemical plant may be located close to one source material or another or close to market rather than resources. A textile manufacture may be moved from Asia to a place closer to market to achieve a short and more responsive supply chain. The pressures created by such actual or potential moves by some firms affect their ability and willingness to pay certain freight rates and, in the long run would affect the position of their competitors too. While such general conditions become widely known by managers in the international transport and logistics businesses, shippers have more intimate knowledge of such potential developments and can be more effective in the use of such confidential information than LSPs.

The negotiation of rate and service conditions by a shipper is usually the responsibility of a specialised management group. Such an internal organisation structure tends to preserve the negotiation role with shippers, but it appears to do so for good reason and not just resistance to change.

The discussion focuses on freight rates but a variety of service conditions are important. The extent to which responsibility for maintaining product flows in the face of vessel delays is accepted in contracts is one of the types of development under confidential contracts. Maintenance of leverage by shippers is reflected in the importance that they attach to the allocation of traffic both on routes and among routes.

4.3.4 Conclusions on the organisation structure for logistics services

The extension of corporations in the liner business into logistics services took place in standalone companies from the lines and with the exception of the VAS services of P&O Nedlloyd, since re-organised into P&O Nedlloyd Logistics. The separation has remained in spite of re-branding the businesses with the identifiable shipping lines' name. As LSPs, it is necessary for these companies to maintain independence in the allocation of traffic to modes and companies.

Although new dimensions of service have become important in confidential rate contracts between lines and shippers, the negotiation of shipping rates and services by shippers has been conducted separately from the negotiation of logistics services. The separability and substitutability of shipping services, the importance attached to the negotiations by shippers and the advantages that shippers have over LSPs in the negotiating process indicate that this structure is likely to persist.

5. OVERVIEW OF RESPONSES OF LINES TO SUPPLY CHAIN MANAGEMENT

The relationships discussed in this chapter are evolving as lines respond to the challenges and opportunities associated with the growth of trade and greater emphasis on SCM. Greater horizontal integration in the industry is one of the major developments in liner shipping, discussed in some detail in the chapter by Lee. This chapter deals with the addition of added value services by lines or their parent companies.

The advantages of integrating terminal management closely with shipping services arise from the essential close operating relationship that needs to exist between the functions. Terminal operations are one of the intermediate services needed to deliver goods to shippers. There is no direct conflict for shippers in closer relationship of terminal management with the lines. Shippers do have an interest in making sure that the terminal management business continues to operate in a competitive environment.

It is necessary to distinguish between the management of terminals dedicated to a line. These are often managed by a unit closely related to the line or may be managed by a contracted terminal operating company. P&O, OOIL and, more recently, AP Moller are corporations with shipping lines and standalone terminal management companies.

The development of intermodal transport capability is one of the inherent advantages introduced with containerisation. The advantages of lines in their ability to commit volumes of traffic to warrant specialised inland rail and water services has been important to the success of intermodal services. Two features of the services because they are integral parts of the service package offered to shippers by lines. First, it is the shipping lines themselves that arrange and market the services for importers and exporters. Second, they are available to shippers as an option to port-to-port service. The inland services themselves are provided largely through contracts although lines participate in the ownership of some trucking.

Development of logistics services by corporations with shipping lines is an important but more complex and controversial development. Some shipping lines commenced their consolidation services during the early days of containerisation and these have expanded through internal growth and acquisitions to be substantial LSPs. They are operated mainly as standalone business units. They are growing much more rapidly than the liner business but are far from matching the size of the liner operations or of the LSPs that have expanded from freight forwarder origins.[34] The relationship of lines with their related LSPs is somewhat controversial. The LSPs operate as competitors with a major customer group, the independent international LSPs. They have enjoyed an advantage in the integration of their ICT capability with that of their related line, but this advantage appears to be diminishing with the general development of ICT capabilities. On the other hand, the line-related LSPs have been at a disadvantage in that some shippers are concerned about a possible bias to the related shipping line. Large shippers have preferred to negotiate liner rates and traffic volumes quite separately from logistics services, no matter who the LSP. Small shippers benefit from the rates offered by LSPs and NVOCCs. The position of large shippers appears rational in the light of the separability of the shipping service from logistics services and the substitutability among shipping lines. Further, large shippers are likely to regard the negotiation of rates and traffic allocations as of a size and character to be of strategic importance. They are unlikely to see the interests of LSPs sufficiently aligned with their own and they have better and sometimes confidential grounds for the negotiation of rate and service conditions. It is likely then, that in spite of the interests of some lines to incorporate more service conditions into the negotiation of liner rates, the current situation will persist.

ENDNOTES

1. Lambert, Douglas M. (2001): "The Supply Chain Management and Logistics Controversy", *Handbook of Logistics and Supply-Chain Management*, A.M. Brewer, K.J. Button and D.A. Hensher (eds.) (London, Pergamon Press).
2. Damas, Philip (2001): Jacobs: "Put 'service' in contracts", *American Shipper*, April 6–8.
3. Evangelista, P., Heaver, T.D., and Morvillo, A. (2001): "Liner Shipping Strategies for Supply Chain Management," a paper to be presented to the World Conference on Transport Research, Seoul, July, 19pp.
4. Heaver, Trevor D. (2002): "The evolving roles of shipping lines in international logistics", *International Journal of Maritime Economics*, 4,3, pp. 210–230.

5. Chandler, Alfred D., Jr. (1962): *Strategy and Structure: Chapters in the History of Industrial Enterprise* (Cambridge, MIT Press.). Chandler's thesis is also presented in Muris *et al.* (1996): "Strategy and transaction costs: the organization of distribution in the carbonated soft drink industry," *Case Studies in Contracting and Organization*, Scott E. Masten (ed.) (Oxford, Oxford Univeristy Press).
6. Hall, Darren, and Braithwaite, Alan (2001): "The development of thinking in supply chain and logistics management", *Handbook of Logistics and Supply-Chain Management*, A.M. Brewer, K.J. Button and D.A. Hensher (eds.) (London, Pergamon Press).
7. Menzter, John E., *et al.* (2001): "Defining Supply Chain Management", *Journal of Business Logistics*, 22, 2, pp. 1–25.
8. McKendrick, David G., Doner, Richard F., Haggard, Stephan (2000): *From Silicon Valley To Singapore* (Stanford, Stanford University Press).
9. Nemoto, Toshinori and Kawashima, Hironao (eds.) (2000): *Logistics Integration in the Asia-Pacific Region*, Report Prepared by The OECD TRILOG Asia-Pacific Task Force (Tokyo, Institute of Highway Economics), 122pp.
10. Abernathy, Frederic H. *et al.* (2001), *Globalization in the Apparel and textile Industries: What is New and What is Not* (Harvard University, Center for Textile and Apparel Research), mimeo.
11. Forrester, Jay W. (1958): "Industrial Dynamics: A Major Breakthrough for Decision Makers", *Harvard Business Review*, 36:4, pp. 37–66.
12. Hummels, David (2001): *Time as a trade barrier* (Purdue University, Department of Economics), Mimeo, 27pp.
13. Levy, David (1995): "International Sourcing and Supply Chain Stability", *Journal of International Business Studies*, 26:2, pp. 343–360.
14. Freight forwarders formed to serve growing nineteenth century trade among European countries that was faced with the problems of many border crossings. The leading European forwarders went on to become the major international firms, for example, Danzas, Kuehne & Nagel, Panalpina and Schenker.
15. Danzas, Press Release, 2 October 2001; Kuehne & Nagel, News Release, 5 September 2001.
16. SembCorp Logistics (2000): Proposed Acquisition of 20 Per Cent Interest in the Enlarged Issued Share Capital of Kuehne & Nagel International AG (KNI), Announcements, 27 November, *http://www.Semblog.com/home_frame.htm*
17. Armstrong and Associates (2001) at *http://www.3plogistics.com/logmkt.htm*
18. Heaver, T. (1996): "The opportunities and challenges for shipping lines in international logistics", paper given at the *1st World Logistics Conference*, Ramada Hotel, London Heathrow, UK.
19. Brooks, M.R., Blundel, R.G., and Bidgood, C.I. (1993): "Strategic alliances in the global container transport industry", in Refick, R. (ed.) *Mulinational Strategic Alliances* (London, International Business Press).
20. Gardiner P. (1997): *The Liner Market 1997/1998 – New Alliances and The New Era*, (London, Lloyd's Shipping Economist).
21. Evangelista P., Morvillo A. (2000): "Cooperative strategies in international and Italian liner shipping", *International Journal of Maritime Economics*, 2 :1, pp. 1–16.
22. Brooks M. R. (2000): *Sea Change in Liner Shipping* (Oxford, Elsevier Science).
23. The global networks of carriers and increases in the volume of container traffic are making hub ports for the transfer of cargo between routes more important in liner shipping networks.
24. Dedicated terminals are intended to serve the vessels of a parent company. However, when surplus capacity exists (berth time slots and on-dock capacity) other lines may be served. In the case of Maersk Ports, which handled over 13 million TEUs in 2000, 90% of containers handled were for Maersk Sealand.
25. CP Logistics does not arrange other logistics services beyond a minimal amount of warehousing as may be requested by shippers.

26. Maersk Logistics (2001), *Maersk Logistics bolsters market position*, Press Release, 1 August. *http://www.maersk.com/press_releases.asp?nav=5&subnav=51&press_id=172&year=2001*
27. Le Lloyd (2001): "Expanding Maersk lifts its profile in Central America", Feb. 15, p. 4.
28. In addition to its interest in P&O Nedlloyd, P&O pursues three business sectors. They are ports, logistics and ferries.
29. In a News Release of 24 June 2002, P&O Nedlloyd announced the reorganisation of VAS into P&O Nedlloyd Logistics (PONL) apparently to develop and deepen logistics services by integrating primary overseas sourcing with secondary delivery and distribution. Later, as a part of PONL's strategy to develop a worldwide network it acquired "The Gilbert Companies" in the US (News Release, 10 July 2002). This was "to meet the increasing demand from global customers requiring integrated supply chain management facilities for goods sourced both internationally and domestically". However, the reorganisation of VAS shows that all the major lines now believe that the form of "integration" required is achieved best with separate shipping and logistics divisions! The possible sale of P&O Trans European's Contract Logistics business by P&O, announced on 15 May 2002, appears consistent with the P&O Group's commitment of resources to global logistics.
30. *American Shipper* (2001): "APL's Jacobs calls for wider, long-term logistics contracts", *Shipper Newswire, ShippersNewsWire@shippers.com*, 8 March.
31. *American Shipper* (2002): "OOCL's Tung warns against 'consolidation and commoditization'", *Shipper Newswire, ShippersNewsWire@shippers.com*, 7 March.
32. This may have been a factor in the desire of Maersk Sealand for a dedicated terminal in Rotterdam.
33. Some of the lines' logistics operations trace their services back to the mid-1970s. The evolution of companies such as Exel is more recent although some of the companies that have been acquired by them may have long histories. The "traditional" freight forwarding companies have their origins well over 100 years ago.
34. In 1991, for example, the revenue of APL Logistics was US$723 million, of APL Liner was US$3.6 billion, of Kuehne & Nagel was US$ 5.9 billion. (Danzas is larger but includes the large German postal service.)

PART SIX

ECONOMICS OF MARITIME SAFETY AND THE SEAFARING LABOUR MARKET

CHAPTER 18

ECONOMICS OF MARITIME SAFETY AND ENVIRONMENT REGULATIONS

Shuo Ma[1]

World Maritime Univeristy, Malmo, Sweden. E-mail: *Shuo.Ma@wmu.se*

1. INTRODUCTION

Quality shipping can generally be referred to as a ship or ship operation that is in accordance with the applicable international standards of the day (Quality Shipping, 2000, pp. 1–3). Such international standards, in turn, can be broadly divided into three categories: economic, social, and safety and environment. Economic standards are mainly concerned with good commercial practices, social standards are basically concerned with the well-being and treatment of seafarers, while safety and environment standards deal primarily with the technical and operational aspects of a ship or shipping company. It is on this last aspect, concerning safety and environment standards that the discussions in this chapter will concentrate.

Safety and environment standards in maritime transport, as well as in other sectors, are normally subject to specific rules and regulations. In addition, these rules and regulations are mostly made by national or international governmental organisations rather than by the industries themselves or any other professional bodies. Today, few people would disagree that safety is important for maritime transport and environment protection is essential for quality shipping. However, not many share the same opinion with regard to questions such as: Are rules and regulations the proper way to achieve safety and environmental objectives? How much should governmental bodies be involved? Is maritime safety and environment an economic issue? What are the appropriate types and levels of such regulations and how can they be determined? These are the key questions that the economics of maritime safety and environment regulations should address and answer. The economics of maritime safety and environment specialises in studying the relationship between the economic system and the maritime safety and environment system and the way the two systems interact. Such a study aims at achieving a balance between the objectives of the two systems.

The rest of this chapter is structured as follows: Section 2 presents an overview of the general economics of safety and environment: its development, its special features and its application in the maritime sector; Section 3 discusses the economic methods used in the analysis and valuation of regulation, especially the cost-benefit analysis and stakeholder analysis; In Section 4, different methods of measuring the costs and benefits of safety and environment regulations are examined along with their application in maritime transport. Section 5 is the conclusion.

2. THE ECONOMICS OF MARITIME SAFETY AND ENVIRONMENT: AN OVERVIEW

2.1 Maritime safety and environment is an economic issue

Economics can be briefly defined as a study of *choices* among people's "unlimited" wishes given "limited" financial and natural resources. Clearly, such a definition implies the conflicting nature among various wishes or objectives and, subsequently, one has to choose. Is maritime safety and environment a matter of choice? The answer to this question is the key in understanding the economics of maritime safety and environment and it is also the root source for some arguments, which deny an economic treatment of safety and environment issues (McBurney, 1990, pp. 47–73; Sandel, 2000) or advocate that economy should be shaped by the principle of ecology rather than the market (Brown, 2001).

Some general discussions show that occupational safety and environmental issues cannot be separated from economic activities simply because the latter is the origin of the former (Coase, 1969; Pearce *et al.*, 1990, p. 36). Taking the environment as an example, it is threatened by pollution coming from the waste generated in an economic system. The economic system is certainly not alone in generating pollution, the natural system creates waste too, e.g. gas emitted from an active volcano, dead wood and leaves in a forest or waste from animals, but the natural system tends to recycle its waste. The economic system, however, has no such built-in tendency to recycle. The economic activities of man obtain the energy and materials needed from either the global ecosystem or the solar ecosystem and an economic activity is, by nature, human intervention in the surrounding environment. The first law of thermodynamics[2] implies that there can be no such thing as a pollution-free product and seldom, if at all, a non-polluting service. Ecology and economics can therefore be seen as two conflicting systems.

Similar principles apply to occupational safety problems too. In the maritime sector, for instance, safety-risk-free transportation does not exist. In any given technical and operational setting, the number of accidents threatening the safety to people or property is proportional to the scale of production. As the environment (or safety) system and economic system are "conflicting" systems, one cannot optimise *simultaneously* the objectives of both systems. The gain of the one is the loss of the other. The environment system interacts with the economic system and the whole issue becomes a matter of choice: either more A at the expense of B, or more B at the cost of A (Simpson, 1998).

It is said, therefore, that safety and environment questions fall within the sphere of economic analysis; and the economics of safety and environment specialises in studying the relationship between the two systems. Such a study in general aims at achieving *a balance between the objectives of the two systems*. If the only way to alleviate the poverty of some people is to allocate more resources to them in terms of housing, water, energy and food, etc. it can inevitably only be done at the expense of the environment. Similarly, if the only way to *eliminate* the safety risks to seafarers' lives is *not* to put men on board ships, it will clearly be only achievable to the detriment of economies. The choice here signifies a balance. The economic study of "choices" is to define the objectives, to select the means and to measure the consequences and effects. As such, the economics of safety and environment provides people with a set of principles and analytical tools to achieve the required balance.

2.2 Special features of the economics of maritime safety and environment

Although an economic issue, the problems associated with safety and environment cannot be completely tackled by using the traditional approaches of economics. In other words, the economics of safety and environment is different from general economics.

The core of neo-classical economic theories and approaches is market mechanism. The market is believed to function in making economic choices by allocating resources efficiently. However, in practice, markets fail to deliver efficiency as far as safety and environment is concerned. Some economists suggest a market solution to a problem caused by market failure would be, for example, to put a polluter and a sufferer at a bargaining table and get each to compensate the other according to who has the property rights (Coase, 1960; Smith, 1993). The problem is that the property rights of safety and environment goods are in most cases not identifiable. Critiques are also made (Fullerton and Stavins, 1998) concerning most of the assumptions used by economists, under which, they declare, markets will function efficiently to solve safety and environment problems. Those assumptions include, for example, that there are no public goods, no externalities, no monopoly, no common property, no transaction cost, etc. However, these assumptions and conditions do not usually hold true in the real world, not simultaneously at least. Another critique is the use of market price to measure the value and change of safety and environment, despite the fact that many safety and environment phenomena, problems and solutions are not sold and bought in a market and therefore cannot be priced accurately.

One of the cornerstones of the market economy is the clearly defined *property rights*, which are exclusive, transferable and protected (Asafu-Adjaye, 2000). In the absence of such property rights, markets will fail. This is the case of safety and environment. Safety and environment goods (i.e., safety and environment products and services) have the characteristics of public goods. For example, there is no individual person who can be identified as the exclusive beneficiary of a cleaner sea. Contrary to exclusive property rights, which imply a private and individual ownership, public goods are characterised as non-exclusive and non-rival in consumption. This means that the consumption of the goods by one does not reduce the amount available to others. A seaman's benefit of being on a safer ship does not exclude another seaman from taking the same amount of benefit. Expressed in another economic concept, safety and environment goods have zero marginal cost, which means an extra unit of consumption, for example having one more person to enjoy cleaner air does not incur any additional cost to the system. Such weak or absence of property rights results in an inefficient allocation of resources and a failure in achieving safety and environment objectives, as there is a lack of any incentive for a rational person to make an investment since he cannot own (and transfer) the full benefits.

The public-goods nature of safety and environment reveals another important feature: *externalities*. The market economic system is a "closed" system (Asafu-Adjaye, 2000) or a "linear" system (Pearce and Turner, 1990) in the sense that it does not take into account its relationship with, and its impact on, the surrounding environment. A closed economic system considers only the production, consumption and exchange between economic agents within the system. It ignores the flow of materials and energy that cross the boundaries. Unpriced activities and resources have no value in a closed economic system.

An externality is said to exist when an activity by one agent causes a loss of welfare to another agent. For example a ship disposes illegally waste into the water incurring financial or recreational losses to other people who have no economic relationship with the polluter. One reason for which externalities occur is the failure of the market to price the effects caused by one person on another person with such a failure leaving the affected person uncompensated. Another reason is the lack of property rights, as mentioned above, which makes the sufferer unable to demand the externality to be reduced or ask for compensation. The high transaction costs associated with the settlement of the externalities between the parties is another major cause of externalities.

Externalities are not necessarily always negative. For instance many public goods have a built-in positive externality. A ship uses an engine with higher fuel efficiency not only to save fuel costs, but also to create, at the same time, positive externality to the environment. The nature of externality varies with different persons or different time. For example, if I enjoy the music played by my neighbour the externality is positive, whereas if the music bothers another person the externality is negative for that person. When an externality is negative and not compensated for, it is said to have an external cost. If such an external cost is paid for, in the form of compensation, we then say that the externality is internalised.

Maritime transport does cause negative externalities, mainly in relation to the pollution of the environment and the safety threat to the health and/or life of seafarers and dockworkers. Environment-related externalities include oil spills from ships related to accidents, ship operations, terminal operations and drydocking. Although oil is the most well-known source of marine pollution, other materials such as garbage and sewage from ships and many chemicals carried by sea may be as dangerous as, or even more dangerous than, oil to the marine environment. For example, externality caused by pollution in the atmosphere from emission from ships is also becoming an increasing concern.

Problems related to occupational safety in maritime transport are also a main source of externality. To see how externality occurs, the safety and health related costs should be divided into economic costs and non-economic costs or pri-

MARITIME SAFETY AND ENVIRONMENT REGULATIONS

vate costs and social costs or direct costs and indirect costs (Dorman, 2000). When the economic costs in the case of injury or illness are covered, non-economic costs still exist in the form of pain, worry, fear, etc. suffered by the victims and their families. Such costs may persist for a long time and are difficult to evaluate and compensate for.

The safety-related externality in the form of social costs is more complex. For example, let us say that at a port the high accident rate with a particular item of equipment forces the company to pay an extra USD300,000 a year in medical, indemnity and replacement costs. Further the consequent injuries and illnesses incur another USD400,000 for the victims, families, insurance and social security system. Thus, a new safety device may solve the problem. However, if the company pursues only a financial interest, its decision to invest or not in the new device will depend on whether it costs more or less than USD300,000 per annum. If the device costs USD500,000 each year, there may not be sufficient incentive for the company to make the investment. Spending USD500,000 to save a total of USD700,000 is a good deal for society, but not for the company. Such externality leads to an inefficient allocation of resources for society.

Using the above example as an illustration as in Figure 1, we have the demand curve for the port service as represented by D, which is also the curve for marginal revenue in the case of a competitive market. MC_P is the marginal cost for the port company and MC_S is the marginal social cost. In this case MC_S is always higher than MC_P since the externality is negative and society bears both the costs of production and the other safety related costs resulting from the production. However, with unpriced safety costs, the company considers only its direct marginal cost to maximise its surplus by keeping the port production at Q. Such a production level will incur a direct production cost at P and a total social cost at P_T, creating a net externality cost (P to P_T). In the

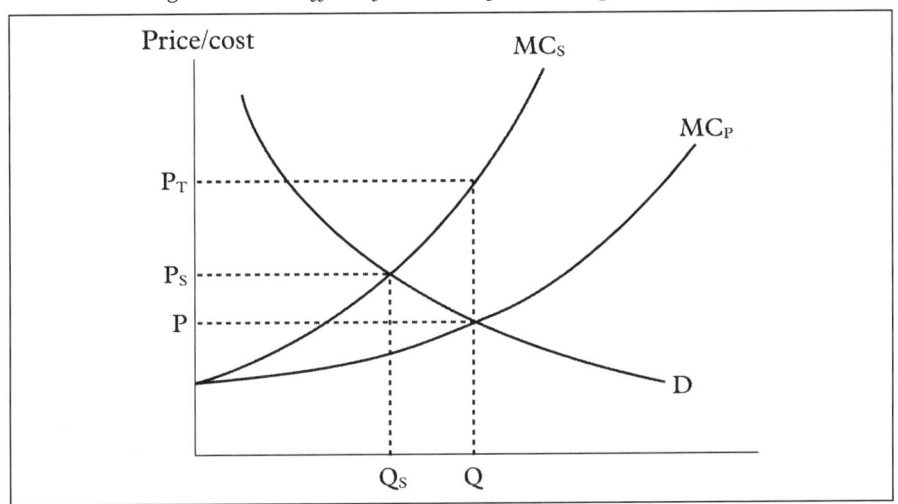

Figure 1: The effect of externality in a competitive market

above case such external costs are therefore paid by the victims, their families, insurance and the social security system. Figure 1 indicates further that if such externality is internalised, i.e. the company is made to cover the total cost P_T, then the producer will reduce the production to arrive at a new demand-supply equilibrium. The production is therefore reduced to Q_S, at which point the company has to raise the price, which is based on marginal social cost curve, to P_S. Also at this reduced production level, the external cost diminishes and the total cost decreases too, to P_S.

2.3 Maritime safety and environment regulations

According to the above discussions that due to the conflict nature of the economic system and safety and environment system, right choices need to be made to allow the overall long-term surplus for a society to be maximised. The economics of safety and environment is for the purpose to study how these two conflicting systems interact and how the scarce resources can be allocated to balance the objectives of the two systems for the maximum benefits of the society. However, due to the special characteristics of safety and environment problems markets fail to find solutions and ensure an efficient allocation of resources. Different economic approaches have to be developed to tackle the particular issues, especially those in relation to the lack of property rights and the existence of negative externalities. As a result of these special features, the total costs of production are not totally paid by the producers. Therefore safety and environment suffer. The efficient allocation of resources cannot be left to the markets.

Three main approaches have been suggested to deal with externality problems. The first is the market solution. This, as described briefly above, allows free market systems to solve the problems through bargaining between those who create the externality and those who suffer from it (Coase, 1960). The advantage of the method is in its minimum requirement for government intervention. However, the major shortcomings are that the key assumptions, such as zero transaction cost, perfect competition, and no income effects are quasi-absent in the real world. So the method has little practical value.

The second approach is to rely on self-discipline. Take maritime safety and environment for example. It has been suggested that up-grading safety and preventing pollution is a question of having the right mentality. Shipowners should be honest and improve safety and environment until it is no longer economically feasible (Korteland, 1998). This is certainly the noblest approach; the major advantage being its simplicity and low cost. However, it is not a proven method and early experience has shown it to be either not effective or not sustainable. This is due to the fact that it depends so much on the social and cultural environment, which, in shipping, a highly open and global sector, is greatly diversified.

The third method is by means of government intervention through rules and regulations. The advantage of this approach is the applicability: it is feasible and a proven method. The main deficiencies of the approach are the accuracy of the regulations resulting from subjective judgement, bureaucracy and political influence. A major goal of economics of safety and environment is, therefore, to study various aspects of government regulations with the aim to enhance accuracy and effectiveness.

As far as maritime safety and environment is concerned, government regulation is nothing new. Although the first items of shipping related regulation and law can be traced back to as early as the 15th century (Farthing, 1997, pp. 6–10), the real development and expansion of maritime regulation is something remarkably recent. In the area of maritime safety, for example, the first government regulation is perhaps the British Merchant Shipping Act of 1872 through which an office of Registrar General of Shipping was established with the main responsibilities of collecting official log books, confirming that merchant ships obeyed applicable laws, and recording deaths, accidents and casualties. Further, a series of marine safety provisions, such as the 1875 requirement for ships to be marked with loadlines, were incorporated into Britain's Merchant Shipping Act of 1894 (Drewry, 1998, p. 17).

Compared to that on maritime safety, the first pieces of regulations on environmental problems related to maritime transport came much later. According to Farthing (1997, p. 212), it was not until 1954 that the first International Convention for the Prevention of Oil Pollution from Merchant Ships was adopted at the Second International Conference on this subject. Although the convention was very limited, as it covered only operational pollution not accidental, it was the first international agreement ever on environmental issues related to ships.

Maritime safety and environment related regulations are made at national and international levels. Individual countries set their own rules and norms in connection to the various technical aspects of ships and navigation in order to enhance safety and environment standards. A country that regulates ships under its registration is a flag state. The flag state has the responsibility and obligation to "exercise its jurisdiction and control in administrative, technical and social matters over ships flying its flag, these include maintaining a register of ships, their masters, officers and crews and taking the necessary steps to ensure safety at sea, including regular surveys". Flag states should "ensure compliance of their vessels with international rules and standards, through adoption of the necessary implementing legislation and effective enforcement irrespective of where a violation occurs" (UN Convention on the Law of the Sea 1982).

A country the ports of which vessels, regardless of their flags, are calling is called a port state. Many international conventions (e.g., SOLAS) require inspections to be exercised by officers authorised by the port state in order to verify that the necessary certificates and documentation are on board, complete and valid. Whenever there is clear evidence to believe that such certificates and documentation are incomplete, invalid or the conditions of the ship or its equipment are not adequate in accordance with the certificates and documentation, the officers have the power to prevent the ship from sailing until it can do so without endangering persons, property and the environment. This is also called *Port State Control*. Regional efforts have been made to coordinate the actions of port state control of individual countries such as in Europe (Paris

MOU – Memorandum of Understanding on Port State Control), Asia (Tokyo MOU), the Mediterranean region, and the Caribbean region.

In the course of the last century, maritime safety and environment regulations have been introduced at high speed at the international level. There are a number of intergovernmental organisations involved in formulating regulations in the areas of maritime safety and environment. The most important of all is IMO (International Maritime Organisation). Other relevant organisations, which cover not only maritime transport, are ILO (International Labour Organisation – for the safety, health and the well-being of seafarers and dockworkers) and ISO (International Organisation for Standardisation – for equipment, e.g. containers and quality standards).

3. ECONOMIC ANALYSIS OF REGULATION OPTIONS

3.1 Aims of safety and environment regulations

Safety and environment regulations are for the purpose of achieving a balance between the objectives of the economic system on the one hand, the social, safety and environment system on the other and also a balance between the needs of the current and future generations. If the word "society" is employed to embrace the entire beneficiary interests of such balances, the ultimate goal of the regulations should then be to maximise a society's total surplus. The basic economic principles tell us that when marginal cost equals marginal revenue, surplus is maximised and the corresponding quantity produced is at its optimal level. In the context of maritime safety and marine environment regulations, marginal costs indicate the costs incurred by an individual or a company or a society at large to comply with the requirements of the regulations concerned. This means, in practice, the costs relating to safety control or to pollution abatement. As far as marginal revenue is concerned, it signifies the benefits received by an individual, a company or the entire society resulting from enhanced safety standards or reduced pollution levels. In the real world, such benefits include the cost savings from reduced safety accidents or pollution and also the improvement in the quality of life.

The economics of safety and environment regulations and the introduction of external costs highlight the fact that the physical presence of pollution does not necessarily mean that economic pollution exists (no third party interests affected). Discharging limited amounts of oil into the high sea does create physical pollution but it does not necessarily generate a cost to a third party if the level of discharge is well within nature's assimilation capacity. Hence, it is not seen as economic pollution, but more like the discharge of waste by the natural system. Another notable feature is that even if economic pollution or dangers to safety do exist, it may not be the case that they should be eliminated.

As illustrated in Figure 2, the level of pollution (P), take for example the amount of waste discharged (equally applicable if it is replaced by the level of safety risk), is shown on the horizontal axis, whereas the cost and benefit levels are shown on the vertical axis. MB represents the "marginal benefit" of the polluting activity and MEC refers to the "marginal external costs" generated by the pollution to society.

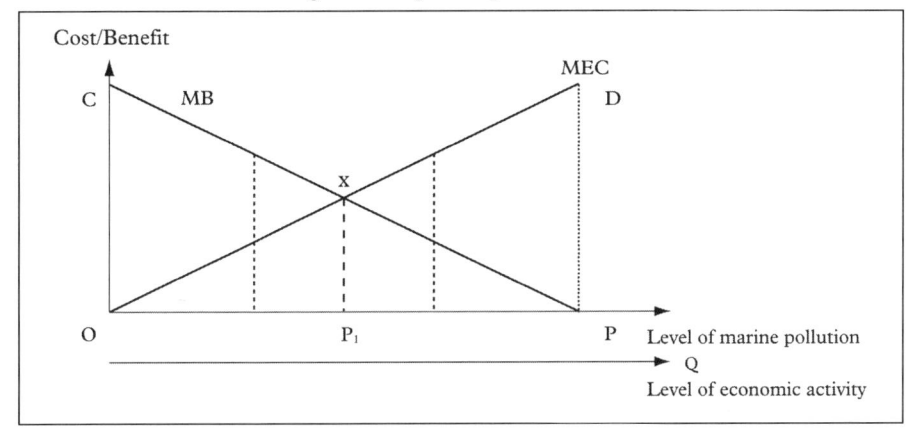

Figure 2: Optimal pollution level

```
Cost/Benefit
    ▲
    │                                    MEC
  C │╲          MB                      ╱ D
    │ ╲                               ╱
    │  ╲                            ╱
    │   ╲                         ╱
    │    ╲                      ╱
    │     ╲                   ╱
    │      ╲                ╱
    │       ╲            X
    │        ╲         ╱
    │         ╲      ╱
    │          ╲   ╱
    │           ╲╱
    │          ╱ ╲
    │        ╱    ╲
    │      ╱       ╲
    │    ╱          ╲
  O └───────────┴──────────────┴──────────▶
                P₁              P    Level of marine pollution
    ────────────────────────────────────▶ Q
                                         Level of economic activity
```

As maritime transport activities give rise to pollution and/or safety risks, with other conditions remaining constant, the more one produces, e.g. ship transports, the higher the level of marine pollution and/or the risks of safety and environmental accidents will be. Following the rule of declining rate of return, from a certain moment as the level of pollution increases, the marginal benefit of the polluting activity will slide down. The higher the pollution level, the more difficult it is for nature to assimilate and the more costly the clean up operations will be.

As MB and MEC are marginal curves, the area under CPO is the total benefits and the area under DPO is the total external costs. As the aim of the safety and environment policy is to maximise the total benefits minus the total costs, the optimal level of pollution (or safety risk exposure) will be at P_1.

However, such an optimal pollution level and optimal safety risk exposure at P_1 is not automatically achieved in a free market system. As described in the earlier section, the existence of (negative) externalities always leads the actual pollution and risk exposure to be at a higher level than the optimum. Therefore, the aims of maritime safety and environment regulations are to correct such deficiencies by controlling the pollution and safety risk at the optimal level.

3.2 Cost-benefit analysis for optimal regulations

Most economists would argue that economic efficiency, measured as the difference between benefits and costs, ought to be one of the fundamental criteria for evaluating proposed environmental, health, and safety regulations (Arrow et al., 1996). Any regulations once implemented will inevitably have positive effects and negative effects on the broad interests of the society. As mentioned above, the positive effects are called benefits and the negative effects are known as costs. In economic terms, the benefits are an outcome, which result in an increase in the aggregated utility of the society, whereas the costs are an outcome, which result in a decrease in such a utility. Therefore, in selecting the optimal safety and environment regulations, one should find a way to identify, quantify, compile and evaluate all the consequent benefits and costs.

Cost-benefit analysis, CBA, provides a useful tool to carry out such a task. It provides a model for consistent and rational decision-making. As defined by Dorfman (1993), CBA is used to enumerate all the ways in which a proposed regulation would impinge on society, to estimate how great each of these effects would be and finally to aggregate all these benefits and costs into a total effect of the policy on society. The CBA consists of several steps starting from building a framework, then tracking the effects, converting those effects into monetary terms and finally aggregating the benefits and costs into an estimate of the effect of the regulation under scrutiny.

CBA is a standard method being used to evaluate decision choices among alternatives in a variety of areas including agriculture, business, health, natural resource, transportation and many others. There are a number of areas that need to be considered in the process of conducting a CBA (Dorfman, 1993; John, 1994; Spiro *et al.*, 1995; Asafu-Adjaye, 2000). Essentially they are the following:

(1) Define the scope of the regulation and objectives.
(2) Identify all possible alternatives.
(3) Specify all the costs and benefits for each alternative.
(4) Calculate, and discount cash flows if necessary, costs and benefits in monetary terms.
(5) Weigh the costs against the benefits and rank the alternatives in order of preference.
(6) Conduct a sensitivity analysis and/or a risk analysis of the preferred alternative(s).
(7) Make recommendations for decision making.

These steps are explained as follows:
- Every regulation must have clearly and unambiguously stated objectives. For example, a regulation may be formulated for the objective of improving the environmental impact of used-machinery scraping by introducing a cost-sharing formula regarding the treatment of polluting materials.
- A comprehensive list of all possible alternative ways to achieve the objectives must be made. Knowledge and experience are extremely important at this stage for the quality of the alternatives. The list should be scrutinised to eliminate the obviously unrealistic suggestions. "Doing nothing" should also be an option for two purposes: one is to serve as a benchmark in the measurement of the costs, especially the benefits of the regulation; then, it is an important starting point to estimate the long-term effects of the regulation by projecting the future impact of the current development, should nothing be done.
- As defined above that benefits are gains in social utility and costs are losses in social utility. The CBA cares only for the marginal changes in costs and benefit as a result of the regulation. In other words what CBA consid-

MARITIME SAFETY AND ENVIRONMENT REGULATIONS 409

ers is the difference between the costs and benefits *with* the regulation implemented and those *without* the regulation being implemented. The costs and benefits to be computed should include both direct and indirect costs and benefits. The indirect costs and benefits are from activities that are triggered by the regulation in question.
- After all possible costs and benefits have been identified, they should be converted in meaningful value terms for analysis and comparison at a later stage. Indirect costs are sometimes hard to specify and quantify and the tendency is that they are estimated higher than that in reality. To avoid the possible exaggeration of indirect costs and benefits the opportunity cost method could be used by asking, for example: what would have been the alternative use of the resources concerned?
- When comparing the cost and benefit aggregates of the alternative regulation options, risk elements need to be taken into account. Also the difference between the short term and long term effects should be taken into account using discounting techniques. The benefit-to-cost ratio of each alternative is then calculated and those with a benefit-to-cost ratio smaller than 1 are eliminated and the rest ranked in order of preference.
- In the cost and benefit aggregates there are inputs, which are the estimates with possible impact of uncertainty. If a small change in one or several variables leads to major changes in the final outcome, the CBA result is said to be unstable (or sensitive). So a sensitivity analysis highlights the critical factors that affect the regulation's viability. There are two purposes for such an analysis: one is to pinpoint the areas where special attention is required during the implementation stage; the other is to indicate the need for further scrutiny and eventually an alternative regulation.
- The final step is to present the recommended regulation(s) with the main conclusions of the analysis.

3.3 Variations of and complementary methods to cost-benefit analysis

Although CBA is the most widely utilised method to assist evaluating regulation measures for decision makers, it has frequently proved to be inapplicable in many circumstances. Many costs, and especially benefit elements, are not possible to be quantified in monetary terms. In this case, CBA cannot be employed. The question to ask then is whether there is a cheaper way to achieve the objective. Based on the same principle of economic efficiency, a method called *cost efficiency analysis* (CEA) can answer the question. This concerns finding the least costly alternative for achieving the specific physical or social goals. (Tietenberg, 2000, pp. 379–380; Dorfman, 1993, p. 306). Obviously, CEA can also be a useful tool when two or more regulation options have a similar or very close economic benefit level.

The CBA approach is an effective tool to identify the optimal regulation, which has the highest cost-to-benefit ratio. When the benefits cannot be quantified, the CEA approach is to be utilised instead. Both methods are designed to find economic efficiency by finding optimal points of the economic aggregates. An important omission of these methods is that the receiver's identity and the magnitude of the costs and benefits for each receiver are totally ignored. Maritime transport offers the same examples in this regard: if the costs of a regulation are to be born by a single entity in a very concentrated way, it is the same in a CBA (or CEA) as if the costs are born by a big number of entities. However, the results of the regulation implementation can be entirely different. The individual interest is not considered in a standard CBA system. Therefore the best regulation chosen according to the CBA may be the one whereby a terribly uneven distribution of costs and benefits exists between various stakeholders; for example most costs are born by one group while the benefits are harvested by another group. Such a lack of fairness and social justice is believed to be one of the keys for the failure of many safety and environment regulation implementation attempts.

An impact analysis, or especially a *stakeholder analysis* (SHA) is a relevant method to correct the above deficiencies of the CBA approach. SHA is designed to identify the key players of a project, or all affected parties of a regulation, to assess their interests and the way these interests affect the viability, effectiveness and risks of a project (Mitchell, Agle and Wood, 1997; Freeman, R.E., 1984; MacArthur, 1997). The stakeholders include individual persons, groups, communities, companies, government agencies and non-governmental organizations. This approach is meant to scrutinise safety and environment regulation initiatives by analysing and answering questions such as: who are the key stakeholders? What are their interests in the regulation? What are the power differentials between them and on the implementation of the regulation? A systematic analysis of this information can sensibly enhance the quality of the regulations and the effectiveness of their implementation.

A number of proposals have been made with regard to the procedure of making a SHA. The following illustration is the World Bank's suggested formula, which consists of four steps (World Bank, 2001):

Step 1 – Identifying key stakeholders
This is to short-list, among many more affecting or affected parties, the key stakeholders whose involvement should be sought.

Step 2 – Determining stakeholder interests
This is not a straightforward process to find out the stakeholders' exact expectations, or benefits or resource commitment in relation to the regulation concerned. Some stakeholder interests are more obvious than others. In this respect, some types of social study and analysis can be helpful.

Step 3 – Determining stakeholder power and influence
This is to identify the effect stakeholders can have on the regulation. Stakeholders' interrelationships are as important as their individual relationship with the regulation.

Step 4 – Formulating a strategy
In view of the interests, influence and power of the key stakeholders, a strategy is to be made in order to deal with the expected positive and negative responses. Some stakeholders should be involved in the regulation formula-

tion and implementation process. At the end of a SHA, the following questions should have been properly answered: What stakeholder role is realistically assumed for the success of the regulation? What are the positive responses expected? What would happen if such positive responses are not materialised? What are the negative responses expected and what are the impacts? What can be done to encourage stakeholder support and to mitigate negative responses?

3.4 Alternative ways to regulate

The way safety is regulated is generally referred to as the command-and-control approach (the opposite is the market approach). This is different when compared with environment regulations. Both command-and-control and market-based approaches are alternative methods to regulate the environment. They are also referred to as quantity instrument and price instrument. The first, like safety regulations, is designed to set a limit, such as maximum pollution, and to control that such a limit is respected. The second approach is to fix a price or a tax, which is levied in proportion to the amount of pollution. The Weitzman (1974) theorem suggests that under the condition of certainty concerning the cost of pollution abatement, quantity or price instruments are equally efficient. However, in the presence of uncertainty, the choice between the two approaches depends on the relative slopes of the marginal costs and marginal benefit of environment control measures.

When the marginal cost and marginal benefit regarding pollution abatement are known, or under the condition of certainty, the marginal cost of pollution reduction is expressed in the form of a Marginal Cost (MC) curve and the marginal benefit or damage caused by the pollution is represented by a Marginal Benefit (MB – benefit from pollution abatement) curve, as demonstrated in Figure 3, where the horizontal axis represents the pollution level.

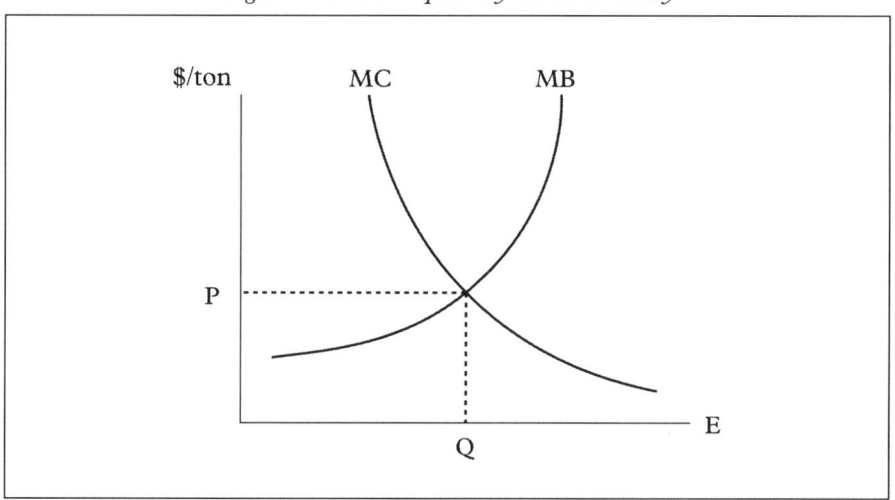

Figure 3: Price or quantity under certainty

Under the condition of certainty, the placement of the curves in price and quantity coordinate is known. The intersection of the curves is the optimal level of control and such objectives are achieved equally well by either limiting the pollution at Q or by levying a tax at P.

When the marginal cost and marginal benefit are not known with certainty, one method is better than the other depending on the rates at which the costs rise and benefits fall as the pollution level reduces. Consider, for instance, that the marginal cost curve is steep and that the marginal benefit curve is flat. In this case, the price instrument is preferable because in order to reduce the pollution level, the marginal cost in absolute value is much greater than the rate of increase in marginal benefits (or pollution damage cost), which is represented by a flatter curve. In other words, the price instrument will be effective to control the pollution. In contrast, should quantity regulations be used in this situation, they would yield a marginal cost far higher than the marginal benefit under the same level of control. This is shown in Figure 4a. To keep the pollution at its optimal level Q, for example a regulator, with incomplete information, uses the price instrument to fix the tax at P. Assuming that the true marginal pollution control cost is later revealed to be MC_H, the resulting pollution would be at D, relatively close to Q_H – the level of control when the uncertainty is resolved. If instead, the quantity regulation (at Q) was employed, in this case it would yield a marginal cost $P_H(Q)$ far higher than the marginal benefit at this level of pollution control.

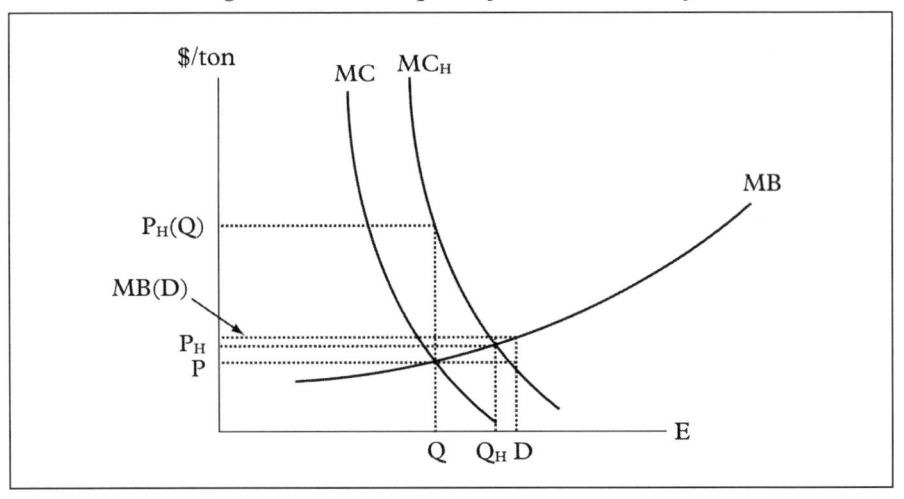

Figure 4a: Price or quantity under uncertainty

Similarly, when the marginal benefit curve is steep and the marginal cost curve flat, as shown in Figure 4b, quantity based regulations should be applied. This is because every additional pollution unit causes more damage, in absolute value, than the savings in abatement cost. So, to fix the level of damage (pollution level) it is more efficient to achieve the optimal point. If, instead, a tax option was adopted in the same situation and the true costs of pollution con-

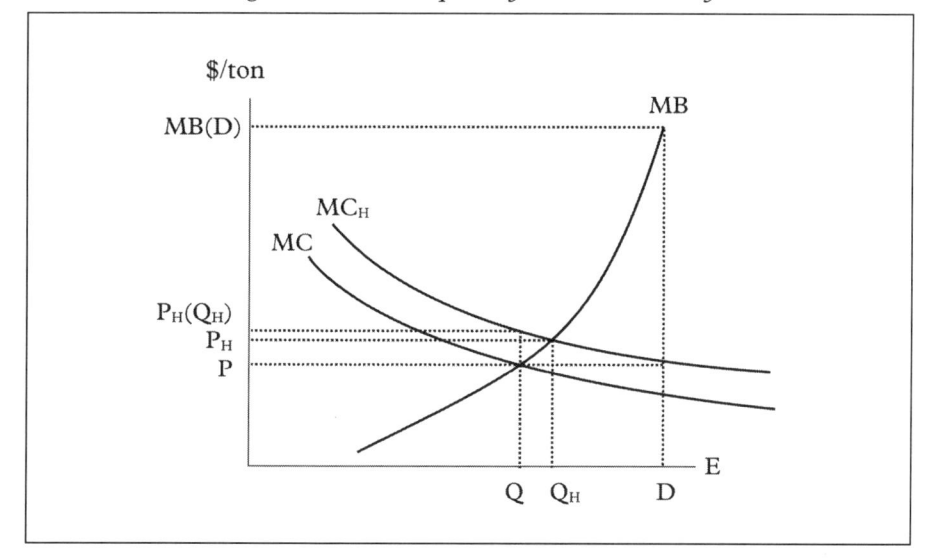

Figure 4b: Price or quantity under uncertainty

trol were underestimated, pollution might exceed largely the acceptable level at D, resulting in very high social costs at MB(D).

The above discussion about the conditions under which each of the regulation approaches is to be chosen instead of the others does not preclude the possibilities to use the quantity and price instruments together. Some recent research indicates that by combining the two approaches better results can be expected. In a proposal to reduce the greenhouse gas emission for example, a "safety value" was suggested to be used together with quantity regulations. In such a way, should the costs of control increase too sharply to a trigger price, the quantity level will be adjusted (Morgestern, 2002, pp. 2–5; Jacoby and Ellerman, 2002).

To conclude this section, it can be said that the optimal regulation is the one, which dictates the pollution or safety risk level to the point where the consequent marginal cost and the marginal benefit to the entire society are equal. At such a point the society's surplus is maximised. As the direct result of the regulation is to internalise the externalities, a too relaxed regulation would lead to part of the externalities not being paid for and a pollution or safety level higher than the optimum. On the other hand, a too stringent regulation will do the opposite. A cost-benefit analysis provides a systematic approach to identify a regulation that gives the best cost-to-benefit ratio. Supplementing the CBA, a shareholder analysis should be used to examine how the costs and benefits are distributed among the main parties involved. Not only the aggregates of costs and benefits are important, it is also essential to know the slope of the marginal cost and marginal benefit change when the level of pollution or safety risk change, because, under the conditions of uncertainty, which is mostly the case in maritime transport, such knowledge will help determine the type of regulation to employ.

4. MEASURING THE COST AND BENEFIT OF SAFETY AND ENVIRONMENT REGULATIONS

4.1 Overview of valuation methods

From the above discussions, we see that measuring costs and benefits in monetary value is a critical step in the process of regulation making. The value quantification of market goods is relatively straightforward and can be determined with fairly good accuracy. For example, one may have a clear idea how much an accident affecting safety costs a ship. However, as mentioned earlier, part of safety and environmental goods (costs and benefits) are not market goods: they are un-priced and are not sold and bought in a market place and thus they are externalities. These goods are called non-market goods. It is a real challenge to calculate this part of cost and benefit. The methods to determine the monetary values for these goods can basically be placed into two categories: revealed-preference and stated-preference methods (Freeman, 1993; Daniel and Hensher, 2000, p. 193).

Revealed-preference method (RPM)

The hedonic price approach is a typical revealed-preference method (Pearce, 1990 pp. 143–148, Adamowicz et al., 1994). An oil spill from a ship on the beach will directly affect the value of the beach: for instance fishery output, tourism income and residential property price are the most obvious values affected. The RPM measures the values for safety or environmental goods or service using the information regarding the market price of the close substitutes. In view of the fact that different locations have diversified environmental and/or safety attributes, this leads to differences in property values. With the aim to identify how much of a property differential is due to a particular environmental difference, the RPM uses a specific mathematical function where the property price is determined by various attributes, among which are the environment (or safety) attributes. For example, the emission from ships into the atmosphere in the harbour area is becoming a main source of environmental concern. Such pollution has an effect on the property price of the harbour area. Using RPM, the following equation is estimated:

$$PP = f(PROP, NHOOD, ACCESS, ENV)$$

where the property price is a function of property variables (PROP – such as demand and supply market), neighbourhood variables (NHOOD – such as security, schooling, etc.), accessibility variables (ACCESS – such as transport and other services) and environmental variables (ENV – such as green space, atmosphere quality). Using multiple regression techniques, the above equation can be estimated. The effect of pollution ENV can be singled out and measured. Subsequently the negative correlation between property price and the amount of ships (horsepower) can be calculated.

A similar equation can also be made to determine the effect of safety standards. An airline with a good safety reputation can expect to get a reward by

MARITIME SAFETY AND ENVIRONMENT REGULATIONS 415

having more passengers willing to pay a higher price. Similarly a shipping company with a poor safety record will find it difficult, or will have to pay more, to attract good seafarers and have good insurance conditions. Using HPM, the effect of a safety standard on the ship's operating cost can be identified.

Stated-preference method (SPM)

The cornerstone of an economic analysis of non-market goods is to place a monetary value on the consequences of safety incidents and pollution discharge. The revealed-preference method is used to achieve such an objective. However, in many cases, it is difficult to use this method due to a lack of suitable substitutes, for example, for the value of reducing the risk of seamen's illness or death. Another method that has been developed to deal with such situations is called the state-preference method (SPM). The basic idea is straightforward: as one cannot obtain value from the market, one should obtain it from individuals by simply asking them to place values on safety and environment goods. The dominant approach in the state-preference method is called the contingent valuation method (CVM). Although CVM was first proposed a long time ago, it was not until the 1980's that the approach began to draw more public attention and be considered in regulation making procedures (Hanemann, 1994; Smith, 1993).

In conducting CVM, the most commonly used approach is to ask individuals the maximum amount of money they are willing to pay (WTP) for having a good service. Or, alternatively, the question asked can concern the minimum amount of money they are willing to accept in compensation (WTA) to forgo a given safety or environmentally good service. Typically a CVM survey consists of the following steps (Portney, 1994):
– It should first describe a scenario of a policy or a regulation on which the respondent is asked to value. The expected impact of the proposed policy or regulation should be clearly described.

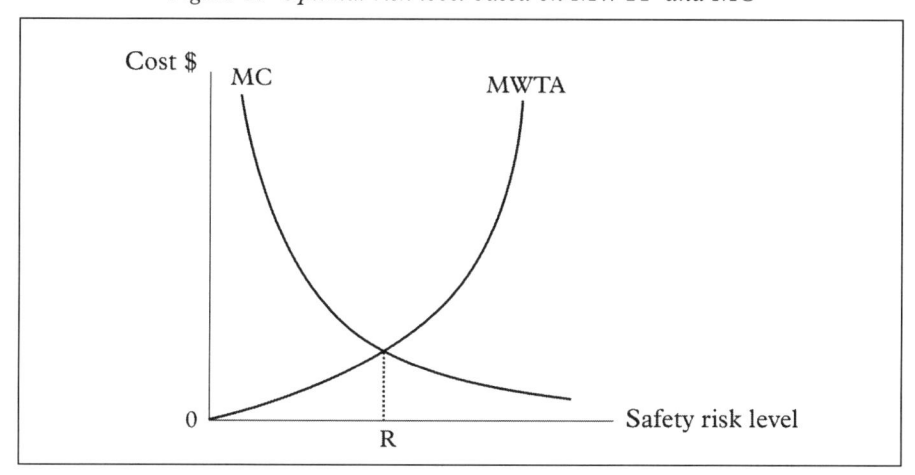

Figure 5: Optimal risk level based on MWTP and MC

- The following step in the survey is to obtain the bids by asking the questions through questionnaires or face-to-face interviews. The questions can be in various forms, such as open-ended (asking for the maximum payment, for example) or bidding games (progressively increasing the amount until it reaches the maximum).
- The next step is to consider the socio-economic conditions of the respondents (such as age, income, education, etc.)
- The last step is to estimate the mean value and the curve of WTP or WTA.

This is shown in Figure 5 (MC – marginal cost, MWTA – marginal willingness to accept).

WTA is a concept, which is correct in theory but not straightforward to apply in practice. Various economists have tried to find the most suitable methods for the measurement of WTA, but none has been totally satisfactory, or without noticeable bias (Hanemann, 1994, Diamond and Hausman, 1994, Pearce and Turner, 1990 p. 97; Daniels and Hensher pp. 190–195). However, if the attempt is not to obtain a mathematically precise calculation of WTA for any particular marine pollution incident, but to get an overall feel on some reasonable and economically correct principles for the evaluation of maritime environment regulations, then we may have possibilities to derive more merits and relevant indications from the WTA concept. As a matter of fact, it may not be difficult to see that in real life, whether they realize it not, people do apply WTA principles whenever they have a free decision to make on pollution related matters.

4.2 Maritime safety, marine environment and their relationship with economics

The principles of safety and environment economics apply certainly in maritime transport. Due to the international nature of sea transportation, safety and environmental problems in relation to maritime transport have for a long time been a major preoccupation of the international community. Subsequently, a specialised international instrument dealing with maritime safety and environmental issues was created in 1948, which is the origin of today's IMO – International Maritime Organisation. Since then, especially from the 1960's, a good number of international rules and regulations have been made by the IMO in the areas of maritime safety and ship-sourced pollution (O'Neil, 1996). These regulations, supplemented by national legislations, have led to an explosive growth in maritime regulations. A rough estimate indicates that the level of regulatory control in maritime safety in 2000 is twice as much as the level in 1980, or three times as much as that in 1960 and five times as much as the level in 1900 (Drewry, 1998). Many of these regulations are criticized to be too accident-driven (Sasamura, 1996) and politically motivated. However, when proposing and adopting new rules, O'Neil (1996, p. 18) indicates, "maritime authorities and politicians, who are under pressure from the public to do something about shipping safety and environmental protection, are unlikely to be sympathetic to the complaints from the industry which caused the problem in the first place". It has been proposed that a systematic approach consisting of an economic analysis of regulations should be introduced in the process of formulating maritime safety and environment rules and regulations (Riding, 1997).

Maritime transport related pollution problems distinguish themselves from those in many other sectors in the sense that they are not only operation generated (such as fuel oil, sewage, ballast water, etc.) but a substantial amount of pollution is related to *accidents* (such as oil spills). The same characteristic is certainly also found in maritime safety problems and frequently both safety and environmental consequences originate from the same accidents. It is argued that maritime safety is the prevention of damage to people, the environment, the ship and the cargo (Korteland, 1996, p. 68), and in this sense, marine pollution from ships is a maritime safety problem. Maritime safety and environmental managements should not be separated. Due to such "accidental nature", the "emission permit" system, which applies to the situation of normal, acceptable and voluntary pollution, has only limited application[3] in maritime regulations and because of its international features, the tradable permit approach is not meaningful. Subsequently, instead of discussing how much pollution should be allowed, the real issue is the appropriate level of *risks* that should be accepted.

Risk comes from the uncertainty of the occurrence of various events and it is a function of the frequency and consequences of the incidents. A risk assessment estimates the probabilities for such an occurrence. Experience and historical data are often used to make a risk estimation. In maritime transport, historical data such as casualty reports and pollution accident statistics are generally accessible, although they are perceived to be not in sufficient detail for more useful analysis (Dobler, 1994). Such data normally gives a certain kind of indication with regard to the frequency of accidents and their tendency. Based on such data, mathematical models can be used to calculate the probability of the occurrence of projected events.

Risk management is to reduce the risk. In maritime transport, this is sometimes left to market mechanisms such as marine insurance, through which the risk is reduced by balancing the aggregated risks against the total premium income (Donnellan, 1995). However, as explained above, due to the externalities generated by maritime safety and environment incidents, the markets alone cannot achieve the efficient allocation of resources and regulations are therefore needed. Using economic analysis, it is hoped that the risks can be kept at an appropriate level when the surplus for the whole society is maximised.

As far as the optimal risk level is concerned, pollution is sometimes perceived differently to safety. As far as the environment is concerned, the risks should be regulated to the extent that the pollution level is reversible and well within nature's assimilative capability and at the same time without generating economic cost (Ma, 1995). However, when it comes to the risk level of safety, especially the safety of life at sea, opinions are more divided with regard to the optimal risk level. While many economists see the level of safety risk as a question of *choice* based on economic optimisation, others have different views. Goulielmos (1996) argues that marine accidents that lead to loss of life should be distinguished from those leading to sea pollution as the former are irreversible and an absolute quality should be aimed at, which is a severe condition meaning *zero* marine accidents involving loss of human life. In another illustration from 1997, the Swedish parliament decided that the Vision Zero, i.e. *zero* dead and severe casualties in the traffic environment, should be a goal for traffic policy makers (Andersson, 2001). Such extreme objectives of zero risk are of course politically meaningful and socially understandable, but they are economically irrational and statistically incorrect.

The above divergence of opinions concerning the risk level of the safety of life deserves more clarification before analysing economically the appropriate safety regulations. It is certainly difficult to disagree with the statements like: Human lives cannot be traded or exchanged for any financial gain; or it is never too expensive to save lives as, it is often said, the life saved may be your own. When discussing the value of life, an important distinction has to be made between the *value of a particular life* to him/herself and the *value of a statistical life* (Schelling, 1992; Haight, 1994). And it is the latter – the value of statistical life – that maritime regulation makers should be concerned with. Or in other words, the relevant studies to make are about whether or not, and to what extent, a regulation should be formulated to reduce the *probability* of injuries and loss of life – or the statistical frequency of them – within an identifiable group of people.

In this respect, two methods are normally used to value life: one is called *human capital* (HC) and the other is *willingness to pay* (WTP) (Landefeld et al., 1982). The HC approach measures the value of a human being to society in terms of future production potential by calculating the net present value of expected earnings. It is the discounted amount of value the individual will create in her/his lifetime minus her/his total consumption. The WTP approach measures the aggregated individuals "willingness to pay" (or accept as compensation) for a change that would reduce (or increase) the probability of injury or death in the population. Asking a group of 10,000 people how much each is willing to pay for the implementation of a programme, which would reduce the probability of death from 0.0004 to 0.0003, assuming the WTP is USD10, then the implied value per life saved is USD100,000. Both methods are not without major deficiencies. It is, however, not our purpose to discuss and assess these methods. The real message we are interested in is that there is an economic choice to make as life can be valued.

4.3 Evaluation of maritime safety and environment benefits and costs

All preventive regulations regarding maritime transport (including most IMO conventions) are for the purpose of improving a ship's safety and environment standards by reducing the risk or probability of an accident. What regulations are needed? How much of them are enough? Or in other words, should they be general or specific, broad or narrow, severe or more relaxed? The economics of maritime regulations answers these questions by applying a cost-benefit analysis. The key element in this regard is the measurement of benefits and costs of the regulations. The revealed-preference method (RPM), rather than stated-preference method (SPM), is often employed in maritime transport related cost-benefit analysis.

Let us first look at the cost and benefits of the entire maritime safety and environment regulations for the shipping industry. A study made by OECD (1996) reveals that it will cost a shipowner operating a 30,000 DWT bulk carrier some USD500/day to up-grade his substandard and barely operational ship to the level in compliance with the basic international safety regulations. Such a cost represents about 13% of the annual running cost for this vessel type at the common practice level. So the total costs for such a shipowner operating the above type of ship in compliance with international safety regulations should be in the region of USD162,500 per year. The total benefits of such safety regulation compliance are more difficult to quantify. Although classification societies and insurance companies can provide some sort of accident probabilities based on different ship ages and types, the level of maintenance and equipment, as well as the kind of accidents that might be encountered, remain as variables. However, one way of measuring the benefit is perhaps in the area of ship detentions in ports. The probability of being detained by the Port State Control (PSC) is easier to obtain. For example, if both the Tokyo and Paris Memoranda of Understanding on Port State Control have the policy to inspect 25% of all ships calling at their ports in a year, and assuming that the above ship will have to call at the ports in these regions, then the probability of being detained can be calculated. As estimated by OECD the financial loss during the detention period is USD16,000 per day, in which case the total benefit of compliance with safety regulations can be quite significant as 1 day's detention is equal to 32 days' benefit. Should the PSC be seriously implemented and extended to cover all ports, the cost-benefit analysis suggests that it would be too expensive to operate sub-standard ships.

The double-hull tanker case offers another example whereby applying CBA to shipping regulations leads to interesting results. In the wake of the tanker *Exxon Valdez* running aground in Alaska on 24 March 1989 spilling 10 million gallons of crude oil, a special National Research Council committee was established. It was concluded that the most cost-effective design for the prevention of major oil spills was a double-skinned hull for tanker ships. Subsequently, in the USA a requirement was included in the Oil Pollution Act of 1990 that by the year 2015 all tankers operating in US waters would have to have a double hull. Subsequently, a similar regulation was introduced in 1992 into the IMO's MARPOL Convention. Further, a more stringent amendment was adopted at the IMO to accelerate the phasing out of single-hull tankers following another major oil spill from the tanker ship *Erika* in 1999 off the French coast.

Double-hull tankers are expected to reduce the probability of oil spills in the case of grounding and collision. However, this type of ship is also more expensive in terms of higher capital cost, operating cost and cost associated with the loss of carrying capacity. In one study (Kit-Powell *et al.*, 1997), it is suggested that double-hulls are expected to reduce oil spills in the event of an accident by 40% in small tankers and 70 per cent in large tankers. Using the average annual total amount of accidental spill in the USA and the higher end of the cleanup/remediation cost per ton of spill, the total benefit of double-hull tankers in preventing oil pollution damage per annum would be USD370 million. The total cost of double-hulled tankers carrying the above cargo is estimated at USD1.6 billion. This leads to negative expected net benefits of double-hull requirement with a benefit/cost ratio of 0.23 (or 23%). A similar conclusion is also drawn in another study (Brown *et al.*, 1996) where it is found that based on a 20-year vessel life, a cost-benefit analysis suggests that the expected benefits of double-hull tankers are only 20% of the expected costs.

As far as the costs of safety and environment regulations are concerned, some attempts have been made to allocate indicative costs related to the compliance of some selected safety and environmental regulations to various types of ships (Drewry, 1998, p. 87). It is revealed that to comply with SOLAS (an IMO convention on Safety of Life at Sea) including the ISM Code and the STCW-95 requirements, the cost per ship varies from USD51,000 per annum for a 10-year old, 2000-teu container vessel, to USD66,000 per year for a 12-year old Suezmax tanker, or USD88,000 per year for 10-year old Panamax bulk carrier and to USD 160,000 for a 10,000 dwt and 14-year old Ro/Ro passenger/vehicle ferry ship.

It is certainly more difficult to measure the benefits that one can expect from the implementation of safety and environment regulations. It has been observed that the predominant cause for marine accidents is related to the "human factor". Some studies reveal that over 60% of maritime accidents are attributable to human error, others estimate such a proportion to be as high as 90 per cent (Havold, 2000). It is generally believed that 80% of all marine accidents are caused by human error (Perrow, 1984). Therefore, it is logical to believe that a regulation dealing with human elements hits more precisely at the heart of the safety problems than those tackling technical issues. That is why a North-West European project on safety of passenger/Ro-Ro vessels (Mathiesen *et al.*, 1996) reveals that the ISM Code is the most effective regulation in reducing maritime fatality rates with more than 90 per cent fatalities expected to be avoided. This is followed by regulations on collision avoidance, damage stability, etc. whilst the benefits from implementing SOLAS II-1D (electrical equipment) are far more limited as this leads to a reduction of the fatality rate by about a mere 2%.

To accurately quantify the costs and benefits related to the implementation of safety and environment regulations has proved to be very difficult. The long-term, indirect and induced effects with costs and benefits make it more unrealistic to have exact figures. As explained above, the real purpose of CBA is not to compare with precision the cost and benefit of each regulatory item but rather to have an overall feel for the rightfulness of the regulation concerned and to trade off between the alternative policy programmes (Arrow et al, 1996).

4.4 Introducing economic analysis into the formulation of maritime safety and environment regulations

It is said that all new IMO conventions and any amendments to the existing conventions should not be considered unless a clear and well-documented compelling need is demonstrated (Sasamura, 1996) and such needs are generally presented in the form of proposals made by IMO member states. The economic analysis has been missing in the process of the regulation making (Mathiesen et al, 1996). The disaster-triggered regulations sometimes have to be set up with urgency, which may unfortunately lead to the under, or more often, over-dosing or poor results of implementation. Such reactive or prescriptive regulations, even when fully implemented, have no built-in capabilities to prevent different accidents that may happen in the future. A more scientific and systematic approach is needed. The most widely recommended and applicable method is no doubt the cost-benefit analysis approach.

To incorporate an economic analysis component into safety and environment regulation making is not new. In the USA, the Executive Order 12291 of 1981 requires that benefit-cost analysis be performed for all major environment, safety and health regulations (Cropper *et al.*, 1992). In the maritime sector, the cost-benefit analysis (CBA) has been introduced in a framework called the *Formal Safety Assessment* (FSA) approach. FSA is "a rational and systematic process for assessing the risks associated with shipping activity and for evaluating the costs and benefits of IMO's options for reducing these risks" (IMO, 2002). It was first presented to IMO's Maritime Safety Committee in 1993. Then at the 65th meeting of the Maritime Safety Committee in 1995, the FSA was considered favourably. Interim guidelines were adopted in 1997 and it is now being applied to the IMO rule making process such as for the regulations concerning bulk carrier safety (IMO, 2002). The FSA approach comprises five steps:

1. *Identification of hazards (or "what might go wrong?")*
This step consists of collecting all data about the accident under study, then identify all hazards that might impair the functions of the generic ship type used in FSA. The hazards are finally screened and ranked using historical data and an expert system.

2. *Assessment of risks associated with those hazards (or "how bad and how likely?")*
This is to evaluate the probability or frequency of each accident type and its severity or consequence. This step can be completed by examining (e.g., using a Risk Contribution Tree) the risk contributors and quantifying the risks in terms of probability and consequence of outcome.

3. *Consideration of alternative ways of managing those risks (or "can matters be improved?")*
This is to list all the possible measures of risk control with the attributes attached, which indicate the nature of each measure (e.g. whether the measure is preventive or mitigating, engineering or procedural.)

4. *Cost benefit assessment of alternative risk management options (or "what would it cost and how much better would it be?")*
The standard CBA techniques are applied to each option to determine the economic costs and benefits in net present value terms.

5. *Decision on which option to select (or "what actions should be taken?")*
Actually FSA does not give a ready-to-use decision, it provides a framework with more complete and systematically collected and presented information, which is necessary for the decision-making.

FSA aims at a quality decision based on cost-effectiveness for the whole maritime sector. It also takes into account the stakeholder principles by examining the effect on all parties of interest involved in the risk under scrutiny. It provides regulators with better information on the full implications of their decisions and indicates whether or not the benefits obtained from the regulations or their amendments overweigh the costs entailed. Having a full picture and the knowledge of the entire scope of the risks encountered, as well of the possible ways of reducing the risks, will help create a safety culture.

5. CONCLUSION

Although the need for regulations is, to a large extent, due to market failure, the establishment of maritime safety and environment regulations is not only a technical issue but also an economic problem. This is because there is always a choice to make in terms of the policy programme options and of the optimal regulatory level. Economic analysis provides tools and a systematic approach to define the risks associated with shipping activities and to measure the optimal risk level, which is expected to be achievable with the help of appropriate regulations. Relevant economic methods ought to be incorporated into the regulation making process. Risk assessment, cost-benefit analysis and stakeholder analysis are some main and proven economic analytical tools applicable to regulation formulation. There are limitations to the economic analysis of the regulations mainly due to the difficulties in valuating safety and environmental goods as most of them are not market-priced goods. Therefore, despite various techniques developed in this regard, the results are still not stable and accurate. However, if the ultimate purpose is to ascertain whether the programme is on the right track or not, rather than to calculate with precision the exact numbers, the existing economic methods are adequate to achieve the objective.

It has never been clear whether maritime safety and environment protection problems are technical or economic or political matters. Such kinds of ambiguity also affect the quality of regulations in the area. The situation so far seems to suggest that the problems are *technical* when looking at their nature, *economic* when looking at the consequences and *political* when looking at the solutions. This is unfortunate, as the solutions do not always address the real problems. Recognizing that it is an absolute necessity that appropriate regulations be scrutinized through economic analysis is of significant importance. Such an analysis can correct from the root the deficiencies of the prescriptive approaches currently used by regulators and instead open up the way for a more scientific and systematic approach to be employed. A recent development of introducing the *formal safety assessment* system into the maritime regulation making process is a good move in this direction. One has every reason to expect that quality, in terms of the effectiveness of maritime safety and environment regulations, can noticeably be improved.

ENDNOTES

1. Shuo Ma, PhD in economics (University of Paris), is a professor of Shipping and Port Management at World Maritime University and currently also the University's Vice Rector and Academic Dean. Address: *sm@wmu.se*, phone: +46 40 356 369, fax: +46 40 128 442, PO Box 500, S-20124 Malmö, Sweden.
2. First Law of Thermodynamics is briefly described as follows: energy and matter cannot be created or destroyed, it can only be converted and dissipated. In other words, the used up resources must end up, as waste, within the environmental system.
3. One of the few examples in this aspect is that a limited amount of oil is allowed to be discharged into the open sea (a maximum rate of 30 liters per nautical mile according to MARPOL 73/78).

REFERENCES

Adamowicz, W.L., Louviere, J., Williams, M. (1994): "Combining Revealed and Stated Preference Methods for Valuing Environmental Amenities", in *Journal of Environmental Economics and Management*, 26, pp. 423–429.

Andersson, H. (2001): *Essays on the Economics of Traffic Safety – Methods for Estimating the Value of Safety*. Research proposal (Sweden, Department of Technology and Society, Lund Institute of Technology, Lund University).

Arrow, K.J., Cropper, M.L., Eads, G.C., Hahn, R.W., Lave, L.B., Noll R.G., Portney P.R., Russell, M., Schmalensee, R., Smith, V.K., Swavins, R.N. (1996): "Is There a Role for Benefit-Cost Analysis in Environmental, Health, and Safety Regulations", *Science*, 272, April 1996, pp221–222.

Asafu-Adjaye, J. (2000): *Environmental Economics for Non-Economists* (Singapore, World Scientific Publishing Co.) pp. 14, 65–98, 131–173.

Brown, L.R. (2001): *Eco-Economy: Building an Economy for the Earth* (W.W. Norton & Co. Ltd) pp. 26–72.

Brown, R.S.; Savage, I. (1996): "The Economics of Double-hulled Tankers", *Maritime Policy and Management*, Vol. 23, No. 2, pp. 167–175.

Coase, R. (1960): "The Problem of Social Cost", *The Journal of Law and Economics*, October 1960.

Cropper, M.L. and Oates, W.E. (1992): "Environment Economics: A Survey", *Journal of Economic Literature*, June 1992, pp. 675–740.

Daniel, R.F., and Hensher, D.A. (2000): "Valuation of Environmental Impact of Transport Projects: The Challenge of Self-Interest Proximity", *Journal of Transport Economics and Policy*, Vol. 34, Part 2, January 2000, pp. 189–214.

Diamond, P.A., and Hausman, J.A. (1994): "Contingent Valuation: Is Some Number Better than No Number?", *Journal of Economic Perspectives*, 8(4) 1994, pp. 45–64.

Dobler, Jean-Pierre (1994): "The Requirement for the Publication of Detailed Global Marine Casualties Statistics", *Maritime Policy and Management*, 1994, Vol. 21, No.1, pp. 45–60.

Donnellan, P. (1995): "Safer Ships, Cleaner Seas", *Maritime Policy and Management*, 1995, Vol. 22, No. 3, pp. 209–312.

Dorfman, R. (1993): "An Introduction to Benefit-Cost Analysis", in Stavins, R.N. (ed.) *Economics of the Environment – Selected Readings* (3rd ed.) (W.W. Norton & Co. Ltd), pp. 297–322.

Dorman, P. (2000): "The Economics of Safety, Health, and Well-Being at Work: An Overview", *InFocus Program on SafeWork* (ILO), May 2000, pp. 13–15, 29–31.

Drewry Shipping Consultant Ltd (1998): *Cost of Quality Shipping – The Financial Implications of the Current Regulatory Environment* (Drewry Shipping Consultant Report) Nov. 1998, pp.17–22, 40–42, 59–87, 86–87.

Farthing, B., and Brownrigg, M. (1997): *Farthing on International Shipping* (3rd ed.) (London, Lloyds of London Press), pp. 6–21.

Freeman, A.M. (1993): *The Measurement of Environmental and Resource Values: Theory and Methods* (Washington DC, Resource for the Future).

Freeman, R.E. (1984): *Strategic Management: A Stakeholder Approach* (Boston, Pitman, 1984).

Fullerton, D., Stavins, R.N. (1998): "How Economists See the Environment", *Nature*, 395: p. 6701.

Goulielmos, A.M. (1996): "The Human Factor and Its Role in Quality Shipping", in Haralambides, H. (ed.), *Quality Shipping – Market Mechanisms for Safer Shipping and Cleaner Oceans* (Erasmus Publishing), pp. 173–186.

Haight, F.A. (1994): "Problems in Estimating Comparative Cost of Safety and Mobility", *Journal of Transport Economics and Policy*, January 1994, pp. 7–36.

Hanemann, W.M. (1994): "Valuing the Environment Through Contingent Value", *Journal of Economic Perspectives*, 8(4) 1994, pp. 19–43.

Havold, J.I. (2000): "Culture in Maritime Safety", *Maritime Policy and Management*, 2000, Vol. 27, No. 1. pp. 79–88.

IMO (2002): *Safety Assessment*, at http://www.imo.org/newsroom/contents.asp?doc_id=648&topic_id=227

Jacoby, H.D., and Ellerman, A.D. (2002): *The "Safety Value" and Climate Policy*, MIT Joint Program on the Science and Policy of Global Change, Report No. 83 (February 2002), pp. 6–8,

John, M. (1994): "The Case for Using Cost Benefit Analysis to Evaluate the Supply of Public Goods in the Maritime Industry", *Maritime Policy and Management*, Vol. 21, No. 1, pp. 3–13.

Kite-Powell, H.L., Jin, D. & Farrow, S. (1997): "Expected Safety Benefits of Electronic Charts and Integrated Navigation Systems", *Journal of Transport Economics and Policy*, May 1997, pp. 147–162.

Korteland, A. (1998): "Setting the Scene: Market Forces and Participants' Responsibility; The Shipowner's Perspective", in Haralambides, H. (ed.), *Quality Shipping – Market Mechanisms for Safer Shipping and Cleaner Oceans* (Erasmus Publishing), pp. 65–76.

Landefeld, J.S., & Seskin, E.P. (1982): "The Economic Value of Life: Linking Theory to Practice", in Dorfman, R., & Dorfman, N.S. (eds.), *Economics of the Environment 1992* (W.W. Norton & Co. Ltd), pp. 377–387.

Ma, S. (1995): Economics of Ocean Environmental Management – Optimal Pollution Level and Environmental Regulations, IAME Conference, MIT 1995.

MacArthur, John (1997): "Stakeholder Analysis in Project planning: Origins, Applications and Refinements of the Method", *Project Appraisal*, 12 (4), pp. 251–264.

Mathiesen, T.C., & Skjong, R. (1996): "Towards A Retional Approach to Marine Safety and Environmental Regulations?", in Haralambides, H. (ed.), *Quality Shipping – Market Mechanisms for Safer Shipping and Cleaner Oceans* (Erasmus Publishing), pp. 259–276.

McBurney, S. (1990): *Ecology into Economics Won't Go*. (Devon, UK, Green Books), pp. 47–73.

Mitchell, R.K., Agle, B.R., & Wood, D.J. (1997): "Towards a theory of stakeholder identification: defining the principle of who and what really counts," *Academy of Management Review*, 22(4), pp. 853–884.

Morgenstern, R.D. (2002): "Reducing Carbon Emission and Limited Costs", discussion paper in *Resource For the Future* (February 2002), pp. 2–7.

OECD (1996): *Competitive Advantages Obtained by Some Shipowners As A Result of Non-observance of Applicable International Rules and Standards* (OECD/GD(96)4).

O'Neil, W.A. (1996): "Keynote Address", in Haralambides, H. (ed.), *Quality Shipping – Market Mechanisms for Safer Shipping and Cleaner Oceans* (Erasmus Publishing), pp. 17–22.

Pearce, D.W., & Turner, R.K. (1990): *Economics of Natural Resources and the Environment* (London, UK, Harvester Wheatsheaf), pp. 35–42.
Perrow, C. (1984): *Normal Accidents – Living with High-Risk Technologies* (New York, Basic Books, 1984), p. 224.
Portney, P.R. (1994): "The Contingent Valuation Debate: Why Economists Should Care", *Journal of Economic Perspectives*, 8(4), 1994, pp. 3–17.
Riding, J.F. (1997): "Formal Safety Assessment (FSA) – Putting Risk into Marine Regulations", *International Maritime Technology*, Volume 109, Part 2 (The Institute of Marine Engineering Science and Technology), pp. 185–192.
Sandel, M J. (1997): "It's Immoral to Buy the Right to Pollute", in Stavins, R.N. (ed.) *Economics of the Environment 2000* (W.W. Norton & Co. Ltd), pp. 449–451.
Sasamura, Y. (1996): "Development of International Regulations on Maritime Safety and Pollution Prevention", in Haralambides, H. (ed.), *Quality Shipping – Market Mechanisms for Safer Shipping and Cleaner Oceans* (Erasmus Publishing), pp. 293–303.
Schelling, Thomas C. (1992): "The Life You Save May Be Your Own", in Dorfman, R., & Dorfman, N.S. (eds), *Economics of the Environment 1992* (W.W. Norton & Co. Ltd), pp. 388–408.
Simpson, R.D. (1998): "Economic Analysis and Ecosystems: Some Concepts and Issues", in Stavins, R.N. (ed.), *Economics of the Environment 2000* (W.W. Norton & Co. Ltd), pp. 529–541.
Smith, V.K. (1993): "Nonmarket Valuation of Environmental Resources: An Interpretive Appraisal", in Stavins, R.N. (ed.), *Economics of the Environment 2000* (W.W. Norton & Co. Ltd), pp. 219–252.
Spiro, E., & Parfitt, A. (1995): "Applying Cost-Benefit Analysis to Marine Safety Measures", *Maritime Policy and Management*, Vol. 22, 3, pp. 215–224.
Summary conclusions of the *Quality Shipping Seminar*, March 2000, Singapore, pp. 1–3.
Tietenberg, T.H. (2000): "Economic Instruments for Environmental Regulations", in Stavins, R.N. (ed.), *Economics of the Environment* (4th ed.) (W.W. Norton & Co. Ltd), pp. 378–393.
Weitzman, M.L. (1974): "Prices vs. Quantities", *Review of Economic Studies*, October 1974, pp. 477–491..
World Bank (2001): *Stakeholder Analysis*, see "Social Assessment" under "Social Development" (World Bank).

CHAPTER 19

MARITIME SAFETY AND ACCIDENT ANALYSIS

Wayne K. Talley
Old Dominion University, Virginia, USA.
E-mail: *wktalley@odu.edu*

1. INTRODUCTION

Maritime safety consists of vessel safety and safety in the operation of a vessel. Vessel safety is concerned with whether a vessel adheres to technical, design or construction standards and therefore is seaworthy. Given the difficulty of directly observing safety in the operation of a vessel, proxies for improvements or reductions in vessel operation safety have been used. Both input and outcome proxies have been used. Input proxies represent actions by shipping lines, ports, and government to decrease the probability of unsafe vessel operation; outcome proxies represent unsafe outcomes of vessel operation. Vessel maintenance and operator training expenditures are examples of input proxies; ship accidents, fatalities, and injuries are examples of outcome proxies. Since little is known of the extent to which safety inputs translate into vessel operation safety, outcome rather than input proxies may be more reliable proxies for vessel operation safety.

A vessel accident is an unintended happening. A vessel accident may be described as a: (1) collision – vessel struck or was struck by another vessel on the water surface or vessel struck a stationary object, not another vessel; (2) grounding – vessel is in contact with the sea bottom or a bottom obstacle, struck object on the sea floor, or struck or touched the bottom; (3) fire/explosion – the fire and/or explosion is the initiating event reported, except where the first event is a hull/machinery failure leading to the fire/explosion; or (4) a material/equipment failure – hull/machinery damage.

A vessel accident may or may not result in damage to the vessel nor crew and passenger injuries. The probability of a vessel sustaining damage in an accident is the product of two probabilities: (1) the probability of involvement in an accident (event probability) and (2) the probability of vessel damage given that an accident has occurred (damage conditional probability). Similarly, the probability of an injury in a vessel accident is the product of the event probability and the probability of an injury given that an accident has occurred (injury conditional probability). The severity of an accident may vary from: no vessel damage to the loss of the vessel, no injuries to fatalities, and no cargo damage to loss of cargo. A vessel may remain seaworthy following an accident or may be non-seaworthy.

The remainder of the chapter is structured as follows: Section 2 presents a discussion of maritime safety concerns, followed by vessel accident statistics and a discussion thereof in Section 3. Causes of vessel accidents and injuries are presented in Section 4 and vessel accident costs are classified in Section 5. Determinants of vessel accident property damage costs, fatalities and injuries, and seaworthiness are discussed in Sections 6, 7 and 8, respectively. A summary of the above discussion is found in Section 9.

2. MARITIME SAFETY CONCERNS

Prior to World War I the need for uniform international vessel safety rules and their enforcement became evident. Since every vessel must have a country of registry, that is, fly its flag and obey its laws, flag states were asked to adopt and enforce internationally agreed upon rules. Multilateral enforcement of multilateral vessel safety rules worked well until the adoption of "flags of convenience" (FOCs) – the registration of vessels in countries other than those of its citizen owners (Goss, 1994). Prior to the 1950s, FOCs were insignificant in number. By 1996 over one-half of the world's shipping fleet was under FOCs, raising concern for enforcement of international safety rules, given that some FOCs confine their interests to collecting registration dues, having no interest in adopting or enforcing rules, and can not be compelled to do so as sovereign powers.

Some countries have addressed the ineffective enforcement of international vessel safety rules by FOCs by establishing port state control (PSC) systems, i.e., systems that unilaterally enforce such rules (Payoyo, 1994). In 1982 twelve European countries signed the Paris PSC Memorandum of Understanding, arranging to inspect safety and other certificates carried by vessels of all flags (including each other's) visiting their ports, and to insist, by detention if necessary, on deficiencies being rectified. In 1995 member countries inspected 8,834 vessels, of which almost half had deficiencies; vessels were detained in port when deficiencies were regarded as so serious that the vessel or those on board were in danger, or where the marine environment could be threatened (Porter, 1996). In Britain approximately 60% of inspected vessels have some type of deficiency and 6% have such serious defects to prevent, until rectified, their sailing (Goss, 1994, p. 103). Although PSC systems are also found in Australia, Canada, United States, and elsewhere, much of the world remains unaffected by PSC.

In addition to FOCs, doubts also exist about the vessel safety enforcement performance of classification societies. Classification societies inspect vessels to ensure that they are seaworthy, meet national-flag requirements and conform to international safety standards. Since vessel insurers must be confident that vessels are seaworthy, they will insure only classed vessels. Classification societies, numbering more than 50 worldwide and some dating back more than 200 years, also produce vessel specification rules and supervise the design and construction of vessels to see whether these rules are being followed. Classification societies have an insoluble conflict of interest between themselves and vessel owners which arises when hired by vessel owners to class their vessels. In a competitive environment for vessel owner clients, and when vessel owners themselves are facing stiff competition, societies are under pressure to reduce their safety demands, possibly classing non-seaworthy vessels.

Criticisms of classification societies by vessel insurers include (Boisson, 1994): (1) extreme variations recorded in the quality of services provided; (2) difficulty in obtaining vessel inspection reports given the contractual links between societies and vessel owner clients; (3) unwarranted extensions of classification of older vessels; and (4) safety rules which do not consider operational aspects of safety on board (e.g., crew quality and operating standards). The UK P&I Club, responding to its concern that classification societies could no longer provide an accurate evaluation of vessel quality, has established its own vessel appraisal system. Protection and indemnity clubs are vessel owners' organisations that provide liability insurance for the same vessel owners. In 1990, the UK P&I Club inspected more than 1500 vessels, revealing serious safety failings, some aboard classed vessels.

Vessel charters and bankers have also been critical of classification societies. The response of large oil companies has been to use in-house surveyors to inspect tankers for charter; some companies inspecting more than 800 tankers a year. The inspections are then used to determine which tankers are to be chartered. Bankers who require reliable vessel-condition information for making vessel investment decisions have sought the creation of a general data-bank on vessel conditions. Major classification societies have responded to their critics by establishing the International Association of Classification Societies (IACS), having the objectives of promoting the highest standards in vessel safety and preventing marine pollution. IACS members are bound to satisfy Quality System Certification Scheme (QSCS) standards.

Shrinking crew sizes are also a safety concern, since fewer crew members may be available for watch duties and on-board maintenance chores. Opponents (e.g., labor organisations) of smaller crew sizes argue that safety has deteriorated with smaller crews, i.e., increased fatigue from longer working hours, poor vessel maintenance practices and less time for on-the-job training. They further note that crew fatigue was cited as a major contributing factor to the *Exxon Valdez* (major) oil spill in Alaska. Proponents (e.g., vessel operators) argue that smaller crews are more safety conscious and are better trained to operate automated systems. One study (National Research Council, 1990) that investigated the issue concludes that available information shows no link between crew size and commercial vessel safety. However, if crew sizes continue to shrink, they may fall below safety threshold levels; if so, vessel operation safety will deteriorate.

Vessel maintenance and construction also pose safety concerns. As discussed above, vessel maintenance may deteriorate for older vessels as well as for vessels with relatively small crew sizes. Also, vessel maintenance may deteriorate as vessel time in port declines. In a competitive environment, vessel operators are under pressure to cut port time, the time vessels are in port collecting and disbursing cargo and passengers. With less time in port, vessel maintenance that is ordinarily done in port is expected to decline. New vessels are often constructed with lightweight high-tensile steel, which is thinner than plain steel, and thus more likely to crack and suffer dangerous stresses.

Nearly 80% of vessel accidents are caused by human error, a human action or omission identifiable as the immediate cause of the event from which the liability arises, including blame worthy behavior from simple mistakes in arithmetic, judgement, and deliberate risk-taking (Goss, 1994). However, the focus of the vessel safety regulation has been the vessel rather than human actions aboard the vessel. This focus, however, is shifting: The International Safety Management Code which became mandatory for many vessels in 1998 requires shipping lines to document their management procedures for detecting and eliminating unsafe human behavior. "This code is at the heart of the industry's plan to switch toward regulating human factors instead of physical ones" (Abrams, May 2, 1996, p. 8B). The motivation for the shift toward regulating human actions aboard a vessel has been attributed to the fact that vessel accident insurance claims are often attributed to human error and it is less expensive to change human behavior than it is to redesign vessels for safety.

The ageing of the world's fleet of bulk (dry-cargo) vessels is also a safety concern. The overloading and the use of 30-ton buckets, pneumatic hammers, and bulldozers to unload cargoes have weakened the structures of older bulk vessels. Inspections of older coal vessels, for example, reveal that corrosion of side shells is common; moisture in coal vaporises and recondenses against side shells. The majority of the 97 bulk vessels that were lost worldwide between 1990 and 1994 were over 15 years old and vessel structural damage was the primary cause (Porter, 1995). Other safety concerns that relate to all older vessels include the future availability of experienced crew to man older vessels (the current generation of seafarers and new recruits have been trained to man relatively new vessels) and vessel repairmen with the skills to maintain or repair older vessels.

Safety concerns for ferry vessels include insufficient fire protection and their instability. Roll-on roll-off ferries have giant holes that allow for the loading (roll on) and the unloading (roll off) of automobiles and other cargoes and preclude vertical watertight bulkheads that are standard features on most vessels. If water gets in and causes a pronounced list, the vessel will capsize and sink. If their loading doors are breached, they can sink without warning – approximately 60% of roll-on roll-off ferries involved in accidents sink within ten minutes (Barnard, 1987). In Belgium in March 1987, 191 passengers drowned when the roll-on roll-off ferry, the *Herald of Free Enterprise*, capsized when it departed port with its bow doors open, taking on water and becoming unstable. Lock design flaws and a slow response by the crew were instrumental in the deaths of 852 people from the sinking of the Estonia ferry during a Baltic Sea storm in September 1994. It was Europe's worst maritime passenger disaster since World War II.

3. VESSEL ACCIDENT STATISTICS

Statistics for world vessel accidents that resulted in lost vessels are quite accurate; accident statistics for which vessels are not lost are less accurate – the non-reporting of the latter is more difficult to detect. For vessels 500 gross tons and larger, the statistics in Table 1 show that the number of vessels lost worldwide were higher for the years, 1992 and 1993, than for recent years, suggesting a declining time trend in lost vessels. Also, vessel losses measured in lost vessel gross tons were higher for the 1992-94 time period than for recent years.

Table 1: World accident vessel losses (500 gross ton vessels and larger)

Year	Number	Gross tons
1992	136	1,111,157
1993	140	891,098
1994	103	1,237,196
1995	95	693,433
1996	112	699,668
1997	93	788,749
1998	102	860,527

Source: *Lloyd's Nautical Year Book* (London, Lloyd's of London Press), various years.

In Table 2 statistics for world tanker losses reveal that the highest number, 12 losses, occurred in 1996, followed by 11 losses in 1994 and 1997, suggesting no time trend in the number of tanker losses. The greatest tanker losses measured in vessel gross tons, 472,054 gross tons, occurred in 1994, followed by 288,152 tons lost in 1997, suggesting a declining time trend in gross-ton losses. The highest average age for lost tankers, 26.3 years, was for the year 1996, followed by 24.8 years for 1998. The highest number of deaths, 70 deaths, attributed to tanker losses occurred in 1994, followed by 27 deaths in 1996.

Table 2: World accident tanker losses (500 gross ton vessels and larger)

Year	Number	Gross tons	Average yearly age	Deaths
1994	11	472,054	20.4	70
1995	5	167,518	18.2	1
1996	12	53,553	26.3	27
1997	11	288,152	21.0	16
1998	4	27,838	24.8	9

Source: *Lloyd's Nautical Year Book* (London, Lloyd's of London Press), various years.

One of the largest tankers to be lost in 1994 was the 138,765 gross-ton *Stolidi* which sustained extensive damage from fire and an explosion in the Arabian Sea; 20 crewmen died. In 1995 the 144,567 gross-ton *Sea Prince* was driven aground off the coast of South Korea during a typhoon and subsequently sank while in tow. In 1996 the 8,471 gross-ton *Lido* sustained damage from a fire and explosion and sank: six of 24 crewmen died. Japan's worst ever coastal oil spillage occurred on January 2, 1997 when the 13,157 gross-ton *Nakhodka* broke in two during a storm near the Oki Islands, Sea of Japan; one crewmen died. The largest tanker lost in 1998 was the 14,697 gross-ton *Lancer* which sustained an explosion, killing two crewmen.

In Table 3 statistics for world bulk vessel losses reveal that the highest number, 15, occurred in 1994, followed by 14 losses in 1998, suggesting little or no time trend in the number of bulk vessel losses. The greatest bulk vessel losses measured in vessel gross tons, 508,286 gross tons, occurred in 1994, followed by 261,236 tons lost in 1995, suggesting a declining time trend in gross-ton losses. The highest average age for lost bulk vessels, 23.2 years, was for the year 1998, followed by 21.0 years for 1996. The highest number of deaths, 147 deaths, attributed to bulk vessel losses occurred in 1994, followed by 102 deaths in 1998.

Table 3: *World accident bulk vessel losses (500 gross ton vessels and larger)*

Year	Number	Gross tons	Average yearly age	Deaths
1994	15	508,286	20.8	147
1995	6	261,236	14.2	84
1996	12	239,699	21.0	49
1997	6	137,421	20.8	76
1998	14	191,804	23.2	102

Source: *Lloyd's Nautical Year Book* (London, Lloyd's of London Press), various years.

The largest bulk vessel to be lost in 1994 was the 81,263 gross-ton *Marika* which sank during a storm about 935 miles off the east coast of Newfoundland; all 36 crewmen died. In 1995 the 87,709 gross-ton *Mineral Dampier* sank quickly following a collision in heavy fog with another vessel in the East China Sea; all 27 crewmen died. The largest bulk vessel to be lost in 1996 was the 74,278 gross-ton *Iolcos Victory* which sank after taking water in several holds and flooding during bad weather conditions in the Indian Ocean near Cape St Francis, South Africa; four crewmen died. In 1997 the 40,269 gross-ton *Anafi* sustained extensive fire damage while moored in Piraeus Roads. In 1998 the 18,793 gross-ton *Sea Prospect* capsized and sank south-west of Okinawa, Japan; ten crewmen died.

4. VESSEL ACCIDENT AND INJURY CAUSES

Causes of vessel accidents have been classified into human, environmental, and vessel causes. Human causes as defined by the US Coast Guard include stress, fatigue, carelessness, operator error, calculated risk, improper loading, lack of training, error in judgement, lack of knowledge, physical impairment, improper cargo stowage, inadequate supervision, improper mooring/towing, design criteria exceeded, psychological impairment, intoxication, failed to yield right of way, improper safety precautions, failed to keep proper lookout, and failed to proceed at safe speed. US Coast Guard environmental causes include debris, shoaling, lightning, adverse weather, submerged object, channel not maintained, unmarked channel hazard, hazardous bridge/dock/pier, and adverse current/sea condition. Vessel causes include corrosion, cargo shift, dragging anchor, stress fracture, brittle fracture, fouled propeller, improper welding, steering failure, propulsion failure, static electricity, temperature stress, inadequate controls/displays/lighting, inadequate horsepower, inadequate lubrication, and auxiliary power failure.

A vessel accident seldom has a single unambiguous cause. Causes are often a sequence of causes (or events). For example, adverse weather, the initial (environmental) cause of an accident, may in turn contribute to operator error, a secondary (human) cause of accident. However, if a single accident cause is to be selected, the suggestions include either the initial cause or the last cause (beyond the initial cause) in the sequence of causes at which the accident could have been prevented (Oster and Zorn, 1989).

The market environment in which shipping lines (or water carriers) operate can also affect maritime safety. The profit-safety argument (Loeb, Talley and Zlatoper, 1994) states that there is a positive relationship between profitability and safety in the shipping line industry. That is to say, adverse financial conditions in the industry are expected to lead to an increase in vessel accidents. The profit-safety argument opposes market forces for promoting vessel safety and thus favors regulation and more stringent public-sector enforcement for such promotion.

An underlying argument of the profit-safety argument is that a positive relationship exists between shipping line profits and safety expenditures (e.g., vessel maintenance) and these expenditures, in turn, have a positive influence on vessel safety – i.e., a decrease in profits will lead to a decrease in safety expenditures which, in turn, will reduce vessel safety, thereby resulting in an increase in vessel accidents. An investigation of this linkage for the airline industry is found in Talley (1993). A highly statistically significant positive relationship was found between airline operating margins, i.e., one minus operating costs/operating revenue, and relative maintenance expenditures (i.e., the ratio of maintenance expenditures to total operating costs) – thus implying that a decrease in profits will result in a decrease in maintenance expenditures. However, a statistically insignificant relationship was found between relative maintenance expenditures and aircraft accidents. Thus, the profit-safety argument is only supported in part. A liberal interpretation of these results is that lower profits lower the safety margin (e.g., maintenance expenditures) of airlines but the lower safety margin may not lead to more aircraft accidents.

Market forces may also promote maritime safety. The market-response argument (Loeb, Talley and Zlatoper, 1994) states that shipping lines anticipating a deterioration in their financial condition following a vessel accident will take safety precautions in a market environment. Shipping lines that are near bankruptcy might choose to reduce safety expenditures, thereby reducing costs and avoiding bankruptcy, but increasing the risk of vessel accidents. If vessel accidents increase as a consequence, the goodwill of these lines, however, will erode and their value to potential acquirers is likely to be lower. The market-response argument thus favors less regulation and public-sector enforcement for promoting maritime safety.

A test of the market-response argument for the airline industry is found in Mitchell and Maloney (1989). Specifically, Mitchell and Maloney (1989, p. 329) address the following question: "Are consumers reluctant to fly with airlines that have poor safety records or do they treat crashes merely as random events that bear no reflection on the quality of the airline?" If the former is true, the goodwill (or the value of the brand name) of the airline will decline, having an adverse effect on the performance of the airline's stock; if the latter is true, a crash will not affect the performance of the stock. The authors investigated the abnormal stock market performance of airlines immediately following a crash. Two groups of crashes were considered – those caused by pilot error and those in which the airline was judged not to be at fault. Fifty-six such crashes between 1964 and 1987 were examined. For crashes caused by pilot error, the airline experienced statistically significant negative stock returns; for crashes for which the airline was not at fault, there was no stock market reaction. Mitchell and Maloney (1989, p. 355) conclude: "Since our results suggest the market is quite efficient at punishing airlines for at-fault crashes, the need for increased airline safety regulation is not apparent."

Alcohol consumption by and intoxication of a vessel's crew may not only cause the vessel to have an accident, resulting in crew injuries and deaths, but may also result in crew injuries and deaths without a vessel accident occurring. For passenger vessels, passenger intoxication can have similar results. It is well known that alcohol affects human performance. Specifically, alcohol affects human balance, increases risk-taking behavior, increases choice reaction time (the time a person needs to decide which of two responses is correct), has a detrimental effect on hand-eye coordination, and reduces one's ability to make precise positioning movements of limbs (US Department of Transportation, 1988). Since alcohol affects balance, intoxicated crewmen and passengers are more likely to fall overboard than when sober. Further, given that water compounds the effects of alcohol on human performance, intoxicated crewmen and passengers are thus less likely to recover from falling overboard than when sober.

When crew or passengers fall overboard, water may interact with alcohol and compound alcohol's effects on human performance. Specifically, alcohol can magnify the effects of caloric labyrinthitis – becoming disoriented, nauseous, or both, when water different from normal body temperature enters one's ears. An intoxicated person whose head is immersed may become so disoriented as to swim down to death instead of up to safety. Cold water can affect muscle control (peripheral hypothermia) and thus compound alcohol's effects on physical coordination, further impairing a swimmer's abilities. Also, cold water may further impair an intoxicated swimmer's air supply. The combination of inhalation (or gasp) response when suddenly placed in cold water and alcohol induced hyperventilation can result in aspiration of water and rapid drowning.

5. CLASSIFYING VESSEL ACCIDENT COSTS

When a vessel incurs an accident, not only may the vessel be damaged, but also its cargo and nearby properties (e.g., waterfront facilities and pier structures). Also, society may incur environmental costs (e.g., from oil spills) and cargo shippers and/or receivers may incur logistics costs (e.g., an increase in inventory costs from the delay in the delivery of shipments). Vessel and near-by-property damage costs are the costs (e.g., material and labour) of restoring damaged vessels and nearby property to their service conditions that existed prior to a vessel accident.

A vessel accident may also result in the responsible party incurring liability and legal costs. In March 1989 the tanker vessel, the *Exxon Valdez*, ran aground in Alaska, spilling nearly 11 million gallons of oil into Prince William Sound. This spill was the largest vessel oil spill ever in US waters. The oil-polluted waters lead to major losses in fisheries and wages to fisherman and business firms. The responsible party, the shipowner Exxon, has expended $2.2 billion for cleanup, $1 billion to settle state and federal lawsuits, and $300 million for lost wages to 11,000 fisherman and business firms. In 1994 an Alaska jury awarded an additional $5.3 billion in punitive and compensatory damages to those hurt by the *Exxon Valdez* oil spill. Exxon appealed, but its appeal was rejected by an Alaska appeals court in March 2000.

Vessel insurance rates on the vessel involved in the accident and/or those for the responsible party will also likely increase. There are two major types of commercial vessel insurance: protection and indemnity insurance which protects vessel owners if their vessels incur liabilities (e.g., personal injury claims by seamen) and hull insurance which protects vessel owners if their vessels are damaged or lost. In recent years hull insurers have questioned whether expected insurance claims upon which they base insurance rates are correct. They have been highly critical of classification societies which inspect and class vessels to be seaworthy but subsequently are found to be non-seaworthy, resulting in higher than expected hull insurance claims. As a consequence, hull insurers now routinely order their own vessel inspections which are then used with those of classification societies to determine hull insurance rates for particular vessels.

Do hull insurance rates reflect the accident vessel damage cost differentials among types of vessels? If not, the rate payments by owners of one type of vessel may be cross-subsidising the rate payments by owners of other types of vessels. Cross-subsidisation among insurance payees occurs when rate payments in excess of insurance claims by one group of payees are used to cover rate payment deficits (where rate payments are less than insurance claims) of another group. For example, are container and bulk vessel hull insurance rates such that the payees of the former cross-subsidise the payees of the latter?

Other related vessel accident costs include reduced demand (i.e., prospective losses) for the transport services of the vessel that incurred the accident and those of its owner or shipping line. Further, the builder of the vessel may experience the costs of lost sales (or reduced demand) for newly constructed vessels. The approach typically adopted in the literature for investigating reduced-demand accident-related costs borne by both carriers and vehicle manufacturers is to investigate the reaction of the stock market, i.e., to investigate the decline in the stock market value of carriers and vehicle manufacturers following an accident.

6. DETERMINANTS OF VESSEL ACCIDENT PROPERTY DAMAGE COSTS

Hypothesized determinants of the vessel damage cost to a vessel involved in an accident (VESSEL-DAM) include the type of accident (TA), cause of accident (CA), operating conditions (OC), and vessel characteristics (VC), i.e.,

VESSEL-DAM = f(TA,CA,OC,VC)   (1)

The type of accident, as discussed previously, includes a collision, a fire/explosion, a material/equipment failure, or a grounding accident. Also, the accident may involve two or more vessels or a single vessel. A collision is expected to result in greater vessel damage severity than a grounding accident. Greater vessel damage is also expected for a fire/explosion accident, especially if the vessel's cargo (e.g., oil) could contribute to the fire and/or explosion. The relationships between VESSEL-DAM and the remaining types of accidents, material/equipment failure and multi-vessels versus a single vessel involved, are unclear. The cause of an accident, as discussed previously, may be due to either a human, a vessel, or an environmental cause. It is unclear, however, which cause will result in greater vessel damage.

Operating conditions describe the environment in which a vessel was operating at the time of an accident: type of waterway where the accident occurred, weather/visibility characteristics, and phase of vessel operation. The type of waterway includes an inland (river, harbour, lake, or a bay), a coastal, or an ocean waterway. For collisions and groundings, it is likely that vessel damage severity will be less in inland than in a coastal or ocean waterways, since vessels often travel at lower speeds in the former.

Weather/visibility characteristics include the presence of fog, precipitation, wind speed, and whether the accident occurred at nighttime versus daytime. Although adverse weather and visibility conditions are likely to increase the risk of a vessel accident, their impact on vessel damage severity is unclear.

The phase of vessel operation includes whether the vessel was underway, docked/moored, or adrift at the time of the accident. For collisions, the expected relationship between VESSEL-DAM and underway is positive – as speed increases, greater the force of impact and greater should be the vessel damage severity of an accident. The relationship involving fire/explosion, material/equipment failure, and grounding accidents is unclear.

Vessel characteristics include a vessel's age and size and its safety regulation and enforcement. The expected relationship between VESSEL-DAM and vessel age is positive, since vessel structural failure is expected to increase with age. The relationship for vessel size is unclear. On the one hand, larger vessels may sustain less damage in collisions and groundings, but on the other hand, may sustain greater damage in fire/explosion and material/equipment failure accidents. Greater the number of safety regulations for a vessel and greater the enforcement of these regulations (e.g., from vessel inspections), less will be VESSEL-DAM, especially from material/equipment failure accidents.

Hypothesised determinants of the damage cost to the cargo of a vessel involved in an accident (CARGO-DAM) include type of accident (TA), cause of accident (CA), operating conditions (OC), vessel characteristics (VC), and vessel damage cost (VESSEL-DAM), i.e.,

CARGO-DAM = g(TA,CA,OC,VC,VESSEL-DAM)   (2)

The expected signs of the relationships for the TA, CA, and OC variables with respect to CARGO-DAM are the same as in equation (1). Regarding the vessel characteristic, vessel size, larger vessels are generally more seaworthy, less susceptible to hazardous weather and waterway conditions and thus should incur less accident cargo damage costs than smaller vessels. Alternatively, a positive relationship is expected between CARGO-DAM and vessel age. Since a damaged vessel does not necessarily result in cargo damage, a non-negative relationship is expected between VESSEL-DAM and CARGO-DAM.

Hypothesised determinants of the damage cost to other property (other than vessel and cargo) of a vessel involved in an accident (OTHER-DAM) include type of accident (TA), cause of accident (CA), operating conditions (OC), vessel characteristics (VC), vessel damage cost (VESSEL-DAM), and cargo damage cost (CARGO-DAM), i.e.,

OTHER-DAM = h(TA,CA,OC,VC,VESSEL-DAM,CARGO-DAM) (3)

The expected signs of the relationships for the TA, CA, and OC variables with respect to OTHER-DAM are the same as in equation (1) The relationship between OTHER-DAM and the vessel characteristic, vessel size, is unclear: On the one hand, larger the size of the vessel, greater the expected damage from an accident on surrounding property. On the other hand, greater water depths required of larger vessels will restrict the accessibility of these vessels to surrounding property. The expected sign of the relationship between OTHER-DAM and vessel age is unclear. A non-negative relationship is expected between OTHER-DAM and VESSEL-DAM as well as with respect to CARGO-DAM. That is to say, a vessel and its cargo may be damaged in an accident without causing damage to other property.

Support for (or lack thereof) for the above hypothesised determinants of vessel, cargo, and other-property damage costs of bulk barge, tank barge, and tanker accidents are found in studies by Talley (2001a, 2000, 1999a). Specifically, these studies estimate the above three-equation model using detailed data of individual bulk barge, tank barge, and tanker accidents that were investigated by the US Coast Guard. The barge accidents are US flag barge accidents that occurred in US inland waterways. The tanker accidents are non-US flag tanker accidents that occurred in US waters and US flag tanker accidents that occurred in both US and non-US waterways. All three studies utilized accident data for the 1981–91 time period. The costs are measured in real costs, i.e., damage costs were adjusted for inflation.

Statistically significant estimation results for the three-equation model for bulk barge accidents (Talley, 2001a) suggest that: 1) vessel damage cost is less, but other-property damage cost is greater, when a bulk barge is involved in a multi-vessel accident; 2) vessel damage cost increases, but other-property damage cost decreases, with vessel age for fire/explosions, groundings, and material/equipment failures; and 3) vessel damage cost increases, but cargo and other-property damage costs decrease with barge size. Further, vessel damage cost is greater for collision, fire/explosion, and material/equipment failure accidents than for groundings and greater when the accident occurs in rivers, harbors, and lakes than in bays. Both vessel and cargo damage costs are greater when the accident occurs at night. Cargo damage cost is greater when the barge is docked or moored than when underway.

Among types of bulk barge accidents, collision and multi-vessel accidents result in the greatest average vessel damage cost ($21,874) and other-property damage cost ($148,260), respectively. Vessel (other-property) damage cost increases (decreases) by $499 ($1,432) per year of barge age for fire/explosions and groundings. Vessel damage cost is $25,137 greater if the accident occurs in a harbor than in a bay. Cargo damage cost is $1,230 greater when the barge is docked or moored than when underway. Cargo and other-property damage costs decrease by $.38 and $4.76 per gross ton of barge size, respectively. A dollar of vessel damage cost increases other-property damage cost by $1.38, while a dollar of cargo damage cost increases this cost by $6.90.

Statistically significant estimation results for the three-equation model for tank barge accidents (Talley, 2000) suggest that: (1) oil spillage and vessel damage costs are less but other-property damage cost is greater when a tank barge is involved in a multi-vessel accident; (2) oil spillage is less but vessel damage is greater for precipitation weather; (3) other-property damage cost decreases but vessel damage cost increases with vessel size; (4) vessel damage and other-property damage costs are greater for collision, fire/explosion, and material/equipment failure accidents than for groundings; (5) oil spillage is greater for collision and material/equipment failure accidents than for fire/explosions and groundings; (6) vessel damage and other-property damage costs are greater if the initial cause of the accident is a human rather than an environmental or vessel factor; and (7) oil spillage is greater if the accident occurs in a river, as opposed to other inland waterways, and increases with tank barge age.

Among types of tank barge accidents, a collision results in the largest average vessel damage cost ($27,983) as well as the largest average oil spillage cost ($863), whereas a fire/explosion accident results in the largest average other-property damage cost ($125,950). Further, a dollar of oil spillage results in greater other-property damage cost than a dollar of vessel damage cost, i.e., $9.13 in other-property damage cost for the former and $0.51 for the latter.

Statistically significant estimation results for the three-equation model for tanker accidents (Talley, 1999a) suggest that: (1) vessel damage (oil spillage) cost is greater (less) for collision, fire/explosion, and material/equipment failure accidents than for groundings; (2) vessel damage cost is less in inland waterways and if the tanker is underway, but greater if a vessel cause and if precipitation weather exist; (3) oil spillage cost is less for a US flag tanker, but increases with accident vessel damage; and (4) other-property damage cost is positively related to vessel damage and oil spillage costs of the accident.

Among types of tanker accidents, a fire/explosion results in the largest average unit (vessel gross ton) vessel damage cost ($117), but the smallest unit oil cargo spillage cost ($1.22). Alternatively, grounding accidents incur the smallest vessel damage costs, but the largest oil cargo spillage costs, reflecting the difficulty of controlling oil cargo spillage subsequent to such accidents. A dollar of oil spillage results in greater other-property damage cost than a dollar of vessel damage cost, i.e., $1.55 in other-property damage cost for the former and $0.06 for the latter.

7. DETERMINANTS OF VESSEL ACCIDENT FATALITIES AND INJURIES

Hypothesized determinants of the crew injured (fatal and non-fatal) in a vessel accident (NUMINJ) include the number of crew on board (COBD) and the accident damage cost to the vessel (VESSEL-DAM), i.e.,

NUMINJ = i(COBD, VESSEL-DAM)   (4)

A positive relationship is expected between COBD and NUMINJ, i.e., as the number of crew on board increases greater the likelihood that a member of the crew will be injured in a vessel accident. Vessel damage cost should have a non-negative effect on NUMINJ, given that a damaged vessel does not necessarily result in injuries. COBD, in turn, may be expressed as a function of vessel characteristics (VC) such as vessel size and age, i.e.,

COBD = j(VC)   (5)

Vessel size should have a non-negative effect on COBD, since a larger-sized vessel does not necessarily require a larger crew. A positive relationship is expected between COBD and vessel age, since older vessels tend to be more crew labor intensive than newer ones. Substituting equation (5) for COBD and equation (1) for VESSEL-DAM and rewriting, the reduced form equation for NUMINJ becomes:

NUMINJ = k(VC, TA, CA, OC)   (6)

Separate estimates of equation (6) for fatal and non-fatal crew injuries in vessel accidents are found in a study by Talley (1999b). Since several types of vessels were considered in each estimation, type of vessel was also included as an hypothesized determinant of accident injuries in equation (6). Specifically, detailed 1981–91 data of individual container, tanker, and bulk vessel accidents that were investigated by the US Coast Guard were used in each estimation. The vessel accidents are non-US FLAG vessel accidents that occurred in US waters and US flag vessel accidents that occurred in both US and non-US waterways.

Statistically significant estimation results for fatal injuries suggest that the number of fatal crew injuries are greater: (1) for tanker than for container or bulk vessels; (2) if the accident cause is human rather than environmental or vessel related; (3) for fire/explosion than for collision, material/equipment failure or grounding accidents; and (4) for multi- than for single-vessel accidents. Statistically significant estimation results for non-fatal injuries suggest that the number of non-fatal crew injuries are greater: (1) if the accident cause is human rather than environmental or vessel related; (2) for fire/explosion and material/equipment failure than for collision or grounding accidents; and (3) for multi- than for single-vessel accidents.

The results provide strong evidence of a positive relationship between crew injuries and human causes of vessel accidents, thereby providing support for the current shift in safety focus toward regulating human actions aboard vessels as opposed to just the condition of vessels. Further, they predict that vessel human-action regulations will reduce (if they are effective in reducing human causes of ship accidents) the number of both fatal and non-fatal crew injuries. The results also suggest that policies that reduce fire/explosion and multiple-ship accidents are likely to be efficacious in reducing crew injuries.

Separate estimates of equation (6) for fatal and non-fatal crew and passenger injuries in ferry vessel accidents are found in a study by Talley (2001b). Detailed 1981–91 data of individual ferry vessel accidents that were investigated by the US Coast Guard were used in each estimation. Statistically significant estimation results indicate that the average number of fatal injuries are 3.35% higher for fire/explosion than for collision, material/equipment failure or grounding accidents and 3.31% higher for multi-vessel than for single-vessel accidents. The average number of non-fatal injuries are 3.60% and 4.46% higher for collisions and fire/explosions than for material/equipment failure or grounding accidents and 3.38% higher for multi-vessel than for single-vessel accidents. Unlike the fatal injury results, non-fatal injuries are higher when the weather is foggy and less at night and older the ferry.

Among types of ferry accidents, a fire/explosion results in the greatest number of fatal and non-fatal injuries: Every 100 fire/explosions accidents are expected to result in 6.1 fatal injuries, while each fire/explosion accident is expected to result in approximately one non-fatal injury. The results suggest that policies that reduce fire/explosion accidents are likely to be efficacious in reducing both fatal and non-fatal ferry injuries.

8. DETERMINANTS OF VESSEL ACCIDENT SEAWORTHINESS

An alternative approach to investigating determinants of the damage to a vessel involved in an accident is to investigate determinants of its seaworthiness following an accident. Vessel seaworthiness is the ability of a vessel to adhere to intended operation requirements. The literature also refers to vessel seaworthiness as the trustworthiness of a vessel (see Boisson, 1994, p. 368). In a study by Talley (1999c) hypothesised determinants of the seaworthiness of a vessel following an accident (SEAWORTHY) include the type of accident (TA), cause of accident (CA), operating conditions (OC), vessel characteristics (VC), and type of vessel (TV), i.e.,

SEAWORTHY = m(TA,CA,OC,VC,TV)   (7)

Type of vessel includes container, tanker, and bulk vessels. Detailed 1981-91 data of individual container, tanker, and bulk vessel accidents that were investigated by the US Coast Guard were used in each estimation. The vessel accidents are non-US FLAG vessel accidents that occurred in US waters and US flag vessel accidents that occurred in both US and non-US waterways. In the data the seaworthiness of a vessel following an accident was described as seaworthiness not affected, vessel is not a total loss but seaworthiness is negatively affected, or the vessel is a total loss. Consequently, in the estimation of equation (7) SEAWORTHY was measured by an ordinal scale, i.e., equals to 2 if seaworthiness is not affected, equals to 1 if vessel is not a total loss but seaworthiness is negatively affected, and equals to 0 if vessel is a total loss.

Statistically significant estimation results suggest that the seaworthiness of a vessel involved in an accident: (1) increases with vessel size; (2) is greater if the vessel is manned by a licensed operator; (3) is less for a tanker than a container or bulk vessel; (4) is less for collision, fire/explosion and material/equipment failure accidents than for groundings; (5) is less if the weather is foggy; (6) decreases with wind speed; (7) is less when the vessel is underway but greater if the accident occurs in a harbor than in open waterways ; and (8) is less if the vessel is involved in a multi-vessel accident.

The probability that a vessel will be a total lost from an accident decreases by 0.0053 if manned by a licensed operator. For an accident where seaworthiness is negatively affected but the vessel is not a total loss, the probability declines by 0.0841. If a vessel is involved in fire/explosion and material/equipment failure accidents, the probability that the vessel will be a total loss increases by 0.0231 and 0.0206, respectively; the probability that the vessel's seaworthiness is negatively affected but the vessel is not a total loss increases by 0.3680 and 0.3278, respectively. The results suggest that policies that reduce fire/explosion and material/equipment failure accidents and increase the manning of ships by licensed operators are likely to be efficacious in improving vessel accident seaworthiness.

9. SUMMARY

Maritime safety involves vessel safety and safety in the operation of a vessel. Is a vessel seaworthy, i.e., will it adhere to intended operation requirements? Does it operate safely? Maritime safety concerns include ineffective enforcement of international vessel safety rules by FOCs and classification societies, shrinking crew sizes, the decline in vessel maintenance in a competitive shipping environment, the use of lightweight high-tensile steel in vessel construction, the aging of the world's fleet of bulk vessels, and insufficient fire protection for and the instability of ferry vessels.

For vessels 500 gross tons and larger, world accident vessel losses in number and in gross tons have a declining trend over the 1992–98 period. However, there is no apparent time trend in the number of tanker losses. Causes of vessel accidents have been classified into human, environmental, and vessel causes. However, a vessel accident seldom has a single unambiguous cause. Often there is a sequence of causes. The market environment in which shipping lines operate can also affect maritime safety. Adverse financial conditions for the shipping industry may lead to an increase in vessel accidents (the profit-safety argument). Alternatively, shipping lines anticipating a deterioration in their financial condition following a vessel accident may take safety precautions in a market environment (the market-response argument).

The costs of a vessel accident may include damage costs to the vessel, its cargo, and near-by properties as well as environmental and logistics costs. The responsible party may also incur liability and legal costs. Hypothesised determinants of the damage costs, number of injuries, and vessel seaworthiness of vessel accidents include the type of accident (e.g., a collision and a grounding), cause of accident (e.g., human and environmental), operating conditions (e.g., weather/visibility characteristics and phase of vessel operation), and vessel characteristics (e.g., age and size). For bulk and tank barges, statistically significant results from estimated vessel accident damage cost equations suggest that vessel damage costs: (1) are less but other-property damage costs are greater when a barge is involved in a multi-vessel accident and (2) increase, but other-property damage costs decrease with barge size. For tankers, the vessel damage (oil spillage) cost is greater (less) for collision, fire/explosion and material/equipment failure accidents than for groundings.

For container, tanker, and bulk vessel accidents, the number of fatal and non-fatal crew injuries is greater if the accident cause is human rather than environmental or vessel related and for multi- than for single-vessel accidents. For ferry vessel accidents, a fire/explosion results in the greatest number of fatal and non-fatal injuries. For container, tanker, and bulk vessel accidents, the seaworthiness of the vessel is greater for larger-sized vessels and if the vessel is manned by a licensed operator.

REFERENCES

Abrams, A. (1996): "New Rules Put Focus on Human Factors", *Journal of Commerce*, May 2, p. 8B.
Barnard, B. (1987): "Ferry Loss Raises Questions: Concept of Roll-On Vessels Faces Spotlight Again", *Journal of Commerce*, March 10, p. 16A.
Boisson, P. (1994): "Classification Societies and Safety at Sea", *Marine Policy*, Vol. 18, No. 5, pp. 363–377.
Goss, R. (1994): "Safety in Sea Transport", *Journal of Transport Economics and Policy*, Vol. 28, No. 1, January, pp. 99–110.
Lloyd's Nautical Year Book (London, Lloyd's of London Press), various years.
Loeb, P.D., Talley, W.K., and Zlatoper, T.J. (1994): *Causes and Deterrents of Transportation Accidents: An Analysis by Mode* (Westport, Connecticut, Quorum Books).
Mitchell, M.L., and Maloney, M.T. (1989): "Crisis in the Cockpit? The Role of Market Forces in Promoting Air Travel Safety", *Journal of Law and Economics*, Vol. 32, pp. 329–355.
National Research Council (1990): *Crew Size and Maritime Safety* (Washington, DC, National Academy Press).
National Research Council (1994): *Minding the Helm: Marine Navigation and Piloting* (Washington, DC, National Academy Press).
Oster, C.V., Jr., and Zorn, C.K. (1989): "Aviation Safety: The Experience of General Aviation", *Journal of the Transportation Research Forum*, Vol. 30, pp. 187–194.
Payoyo, P.B. (1994): "Implementation of International Conventions Through Port State Control: An Assessment", *Marine Policy*, Vol. 18, No. 5, pp. 379–392.

Porter, J. (1995): "Bulk Carrier, Ferry Safety Discussed", *Business Weekly: The Virginian-Pilot*, May 15, p. 10.
Porter, J. (1996): "Majority of Ships Detained in Asia in '95 Were Bulkers", *Journal of Commerce*, October 13, p. 8B.
Talley, W.K. (1993): "The Impact of Deregulation on Airline Safety: Profit-Safety and Market-Response Arguments", *Privatization and Deregulation in Passenger Transportation*, M. Beesley, D. Hensher and A. Talvitie (eds.) (Forssa, Finland, Auranen Ltd), pp. 205–211.
Talley, W.K. (1999a): "Determinants of the Property Damage Costs of Tanker Accidents", *Transportation Research Part D: Transport and Environment*, Vol. 4, pp. 413–426.
Talley, W.K. (1999b): "The Safety of Sea Transport: Determinants of Crew Injuries", *Applied Economics*, Vol. 31, pp. 1365–1372.
Talley, W.K. (1999c): "Determinants of Ship Accident Seaworthiness," 8th World Conference on Transport Research: Special Interest Group on Maritime and Ports, M. Kavussanos and H. Thanopoulou (eds.), a special issue of the journal *International Journal of Maritime Economics*, Vol. 1, No. 2 (October-December), pp. 1–14.
Talley, W.K. (2000): "Oil Spillage and Damage Costs: US Inland Waterway Tank Barge Accidents", *International Journal of Maritime Economics*, Vol. 2, No. 3 (July-September), pp. 217–234.
Talley, W.K. (2001a): "Determinants of the Property Damage Costs of Bulk Barge Accidents", *Maritime Policy and Management*, Vol. 28, No. 2 (April–June), pp. 175–186.
Talley, W.K. (2001b): "The Safety of Ferries: An Accident Injury Perspective", *Conference Proceedings: The International Association of Maritime Economists Annual Conference 2001* (July), pp. 835–847.
US Department of Transportation (1988): *Alcohol in Fatal Recreational Boating Accidents* (Washington, DC, US Government Printing Office).

CHAPTER 20

THE ECONOMICS OF THE SEAFARING LABOUR MARKET

Heather Leggate and James McConville
Centre for International Transport Management, London Metropolitan University, London, UK. E-mail: *Leggate@lgu.ac.uk* and *Mcconvil@lgu.ac.uk*

1. INTRODUCTION

The chapter aims to undertake the intriguing task of applying the methods of labour economic analysis to the complex problems of seafarers in the maritime industry. Labour is primary factor of production, being the collective name given to any productive service using human physical effort, skill or intellectual power. Labour economics is a branch of applied economics, which can be seen broadly as the study of the pricing and allocation relationships to the factor of production labour. From a slightly different perspective, it is a study of those institutions and mechanisms through which purchase and sale of seafaring labour are arranged. Labour economics uses many of the standard techniques of economic analysis but is also challenged by a number of distinct characteristics, which cause it to be radically different from other productive factors. It is these distinct and occasionally unique differences, which justify its inclusion as a specific branch of the wider economic discipline.

Within this framework there is an absence of work on seafaring labour markets, or for that matter, on the essential part played by seafarers in the operation of the maritime industry. This chapter explores the theoretical and empirical issues as applied to seafarers through an examination of the market and its imperfections.

Labour theory will be applied to the international seafaring labour market using the results of a survey commissioned by the International Labour Organisation (ILO)[1] distributed to government departments, shipowners associations and unions worldwide during 2001. Responses were obtained from 60 different states.[2] The survey was constructed within a comparatively simple explanatory framework concentrated on living and working conditions of seafarers under different flag state regimes. These results are further supplemented with detail from a number of case studies of maritime countries.[3]

Initially this chapter discusses the theoretical issues of demand and supply which jointly determine the structure of the seafaring labour market. It further considers the specific characteristics of mobility and migration and the barriers to free movement of labour. Such barriers create separation and, on occasions, monopsony in the seafaring markets which make discrimination possible and probable.

2. THEORY OF LABOUR ECONOMICS

One of the central problems in labour market theory is the pricing of labour. In common with other goods and services, the price of labour services is seen as being determined by the interaction of the forces of demand and supply in their market. The neo-classic economist treats such a labour market as a close approximation to a perfect market as described in any of the basic economic textbooks as exemplified by commodity, international finance and the stock markets. Within such a theoretical structure, the labour market is an elaboration of the profit maximising theory of the firm, specifically in the process of hiring labour. This approach necessitates the use of a number of assumptions or simplifications, namely that labour is homogeneous, information and mobility are costless and atomistic competition prevails. Such a structure of atomistic firms will of course be incapable of having a wage policy. In the construction of a traditional model, allowances for friction in their operation are generally made. The existence and the extent of such friction casts doubt over any attempt to create some traditional form of matrix of a short run perfectly competitive market classified by occupation and or geographic location. In the present discussion it is the substantial underestimation of the importance of this friction or tension and the extent of the degree of control employers typically exercise which will come under scrutiny.

The function of any market is that it brings buyers and sellers in close touch with one another. In the fulfilment of this function labour markets have never been more than imperfect or partial. This is directly due to the special characteristics of labour as a productive factor which requires some special considerations. These distinctive differences can initially be briefly summarised thus. Firstly, the seafaring labour force is not a single homogeneous entity, but a complexity of associated individuals with different education, training and other characteristics and capabilities. Secondly, the labour market and specifically the supply of seafarers is influenced substantially by national and international institutions and social factors which are absent in other factor markets. Thirdly, the price of seafaring labour, the wage, is a special type of price with a multiplicity of characteristics of its own. These ideas are explored in this chapter, following a discussion of the forces of demand, supply and the seafaring labour market itself.

2.1 Demand for seafarers

Shipping firms or companies combine varying factors of production, mainly capital and labour to produce maritime transport services that are generally sold on the freight market. To simplify the analysis the term markets, that is the freight rate for the movement of commodities, will refer to open markets. The firm is the economic unit producing the service, the function of which is to transform factors of production into that service. The total output will be dependent on three factors, the demand for the service, the amount of labour and capital that can be acquired at a given freight rate, and the choice of technology. What must also be made explicit is in discussing firms, only large enti-

THE ECONOMICS OF THE SEAFARING LABOUR MARKET 445

ties are considered, not single vessel companies. Further, because of the structure of the industry and its labour force, the use of seafaring or industrial labour market can be seen as synonymous.

The firms' demand for seafarers is a derived demand from the consumer of the final product. This means that the demand for seafarers depends or draws on the demand for the service they help to produce. Seafaring labour is firstly demanded not because the work done is desired *per se*, but because it is to be used in the production of some other commodity which the final consumer directly demands. It is derived from the demand for shipping services which, in turn, are derived from the demand for the products being shipped. But this must not be allowed to overshadow the fact that derived demand for seafarers is dependent fundamentally on the firms' or sectors of the industry, success in anticipating and satisfying the final consumer in the market place.

As previously stated, the basic theory of the demand for labour is built on the neo-classical perfectly competitive structure, assuming the profit maximising firm will hire labour up to the point where the value of output produced by the last units of labour equals the unit cost of hiring it. This is more formally known as the marginal productivity theory, which is part of the theory of distribution and attempts to explain the share of total output relating to labour and other factors. Briefly, the firm will equate its marginal cost (the wage) with its marginal revenue product of labour, e.g., the marginal physical product multiplied by the marginal revenue of the firm. Applied to contemporary shipping this theory has a number of problems associated with it, for it over-simplifies the objective function of such a business and underestimates the difficulties posed by the lack of information in an uncertain commercial environment.[4] Such difficulties are explained in the following sections which demonstrate the imperfections of the market.

2.2 Supply of seafaring labour force

As far as the aggregate supply of labour is concerned, there is firstly the decision by the individual whether to seek work and for how long to work each month or year. This is the central argument in the participation rate, that is the proportion of the total population who constitute the active labour force, those working or seeking work. Secondly the individual will attempt to decide on the type of work; this is the determinate factor in the supply of labour to specific occupations. Finally, an important element in the supply of labour to a particular firm is the decision to want to work. The complexity of labour supply carries with it the implications that the worker has to make a number of separate decisions about the supply of labour, depending for example on his age, marital status, family and domestic commitments and other employment opportunities. The total supply of labour is thus dependent on the individual decisions of all those who are eligible to seek employment. Obviously for economic reasons, the vast majority of workers have little or no choice about whether or not to enter the labour force.

Moving to the present context of the maritime industry, the decision is not simply one of entry but is combined with the essential eligibility criteria.

Seafaring labour is not merely a quantitative matter (the number of participants) but a qualitative one in terms of standards of experience and skill that serve to create eligibility. Skills are required either through experience or education, achieved by informal training on the job or formal education. On the basis of this process the theory of human capital investment is postulated. This refers to the competencies possessed by individuals, which facilitate the earning of income. There are also other forms of investment in human capital that can include expenditure on health, time used acquiring information about job opportunities and the expense of mobility or migration to other sectors or labour markets where presumably employment rewards and opportunities are greater. Such a list of criteria questions any assumption of a homogeneous labour force, which will be addressed later in this chapter. Here the concentration is solely on education and training necessitating the acquisition of skills and professional qualifications.

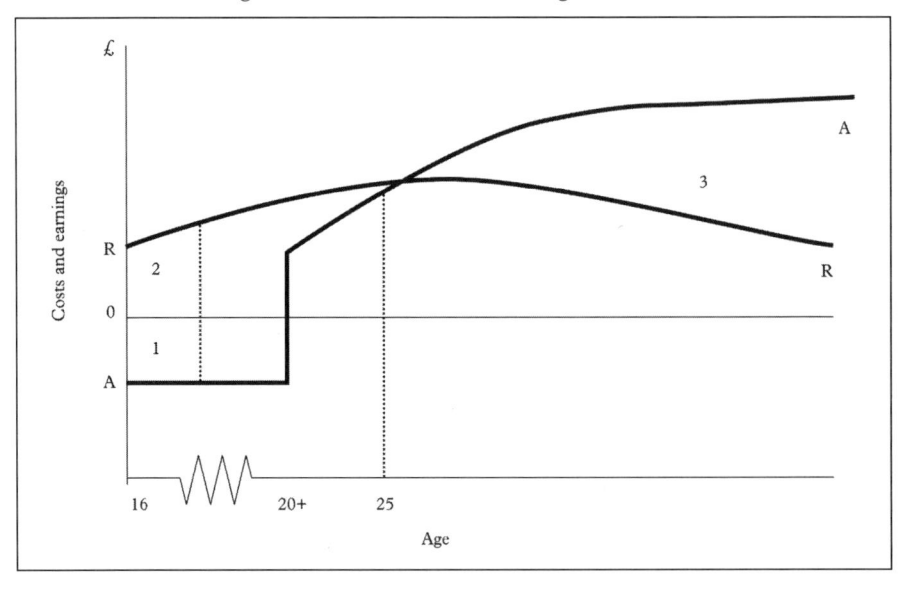

Figure 1: Education and training investment

The analysis considers the investment necessary to the acquisition of qualifications by the individual, supported by his family and the wider society. It will also begin to assist in the understanding of the sources or causes of income differentiation. The intention here is to consider education as an investment or occupationally specific investment. Within the maritime industry such investment can be considered mainly as being in full-time employment and on-the-job sea experience. The notion of human capital analysis is based on the assumed choice between alternative income and consumption streams. This is illustrated in a stylised version in Figure 1, which shows the age entry profile based on the individual's choice between two alternative routes.

The total money income and the costs of education are measured on the vertical Y-axis, with age being measured on the horizontal X-axis. Here the potential working life of a seafarer begins on completion of (compulsory) schooling, and ends at the standard retirement age. All workers possess zero investment in human capital at the end of their schooling and are regarded as unskilled. The case of ratings is indicated by the curve RR. They enter the industry at the age of 16, following a short induction-training period, and will receive some on-the-job training and sea time experience. The curve (RR) generally profiles the earning path through their seafaring career, with earning rising in the first few years with training and experience and tailing off in the latter years possibly due a preference for more leisure time.

The individuals' decision not to enter the labour market at 16 years of age but to continue in full-time education and training will be dependent largely on social class, levels of education and family income. Such individuals are presented with the opportunity to allocate a period of what is potentially their working life to the acquisition of education and training as a means of enhancing the investment in their own human capital. This decision presents the profile of the seafaring officer who will incur two forms of private costs. These are the "out-of-pocket" costs of education, tuition fees, books etc. (direct costs), and the earning forgone during the education period (opportunity costs). Similarly, there are usually the wider costs of state provision or subsidised support for such education as a form of social investment. Occasionally shipping firms contribute finance or other support but it is more generally borne by the individual user.

The officer profile is illustrated by curve AA. This shows a position below zero on the vertical axis, where Area 1 represents the costs of education etc. Area 2 shows income forgone, which is received by ratings due to their early entry into the industry, which means that they have total income well in excess of cadets or apprentices. However, by around the age of 25 the officers' income exceeds that of the ratings, a situation, which persists throughout the remainder of both groups working life, as indicated by Area 3. Two additional points can be usefully made about this figure. Firstly, the dotted line A_1 illustrates the position where officer trainees, usually from developing countries are unable, for reasons of shortage of funds, to continue the necessary course, and opt to become ratings, possibly with the ambition of becoming officers at some later date. Secondly the officers curve (AA) is extremely stylised. It should, throughout much of the early career be a stepped function rather than a smooth curve. Such steps indicate sea time experience and successful completion of additional certificates of competency. What this step system emphasises is that for cadets "the measure of achievement is the acquisition of certificates of competency, a system which can be termed 'status' rather than 'performance' driven. Competency in the performance of the job, satisfying the employers' needs, will tend to be less important to the trainee (or junior officer for that matter) than the acquisition of certificates and endorsements."[5] It has been argued that this widely used method of status versus performance may be contributing to the shortage of officers, particularly in developed countries, by denying entry to a range of people of all ages who may be able to do the job but do not hold the nationally and internationally required certification.

With reference to the theory of investment of human capital, it can be argued that seafarers make individual decisions with regard to forgoing initial earnings and bearing direct costs of education, in expectation of a higher level of future earnings. Such decisions to invest are a means of raising the level of skill, which increases the effectiveness of labour from the employers' point of view.

What has been argued, and will be further developed is that the problem of seafaring labour supply is multidimensional. Seafarers are not a single undifferentiated labour resource, but a complexity of individuals with different capabilities closely allied to levels of training and qualification. Hence the seafaring labour force is greatly influenced by national and international institutional factors which impact on their labour market.

2.3 Labour markets

The traditional neo-classical theory exaggerates the ability of the labour market to match workers and jobs. Such a theory presents the view that the market forces reacting to the price of labour will automatically bring the necessary adjustments to the amount supplied. In reality, a range of organisational and other influences interact to drive labour markets into relatively self-contained sectors, the relation to the industry being a substantial demander of a specific occupational group, seafarers. Furthermore, the industry, as distinct from the individual companies it is made up of, is large and influential enough to be capable of effecting the supply price of seafarers. By using its own hiring activities, it follows that the wage rates are largely determined by the interaction of supply and demand in the usual way. What is obvious is that both demand and supply become increasingly complex. In other words, the assumptions which underpin the traditional theory and the process of wage determination and adjustment will be challenged from an empirical standpoint. Empahsis will be placed on the importance of international and other influences on the seafaring labour market.

What are being highlighted are the problems of the occupation or skill activities within this labour market. The supply of labour to firms will vary according to the occupational structure of labour that they utilise. Within labour economics a distinction is made between skill and occupation. Skill may be defined as the capability of an individual using hand or mind to perform a particular task. An occupation is a combination of skill sets contributing to the production of a particular good or service. Some skills only relate to one occupation and are the principle requirement if that occupation is to be followed. There are both occupational and skill requirements necessary for a seafarer.

An interesting fact about the seafaring labour market is that the controlling and regulating institutions, both national and international, function outside the industry. These regulators establish the criteria for the professional standards for the industry. The essential point here, as argued, is that professional qualifications for officers is the basis of their promotion within the industry, whereas the level of their efficiency or employers' opinions, generally take an insignificant role. This illustrates the way in which international, national and government bodies interfere with the concepts of a competitive labour market, since the securing of professional certificates (or licences) is an essential element to employment, without which it is illegal to practice. Despite this, it must be remembered that the vast majority of seafarers and particularly ratings were always considered to be casual workers. The contemporary situation is one where both the employer, the manning agency, and the ratings themselves, perceive ratings as casual employees. Though superficially the seafarer may be seen as an industrial worker, he or she is in fact participating in an occupational labour market.

The additional factor in the belief of seafaring as an occupational market is the geographical dimension. The changing geographical distribution of the labour force is a function of many separate economic and social phenomena. Much of this movement within the geographical market constitutes net additions and subtractions to and from sub-markets for seafaring labour between the regions. This geographically structured labour market is specifically occupational and based on the free dissemination of information and uninhibited mobility. The inclusion of this geographical dimension brings in the important issues of mobility and migration (discussed in section 3).

The seafarer is the archetypal international worker, employed on board vessels registered under differing flags, owned and operated by citizens of many countries. The international structure of the industry is further reflected in the numerous nationalities of the seafarers themselves. The BIMCO/ISF manpower update estimates the worldwide supply of seafarers at 1,227,0000, comprising 404,000 officers and 823,000 ratings,[6] with the vast majority of seafarers concentrated in just a few countries.[7] Such a geographically diverse industry is dependent on international regulation to establish and ensure adherence to acceptable standards and conditions of employment.

Over recent decades, changes in economic and commercial activities have been fundamental in the restructuring of the international seafaring labour force. This has been combined with changes in the structure of seafarer employment. At its simplest there has been a relentless decline in the number of seafarers coming from developed countries, due to an appreciable reduction in recruitment and retention. This negative growth has created a progressively older age structure. The lack of suitable seafarers from developed countries, coupled with a desire to reduce labour unit costs, has created an increasing demand for seafarers from developing countries. These are the main elements which have gradually created a remarkable new concept, that of the seafarer labour supply country, the majority of which have, what can be termed, no maritime tradition. Initially the vast majority of seafarers from these countries were ratings, but there is now a growing supply of officers both for deck and engine room.

A recent report by the International Commission on Shipping[8] listed the ten top labour supplying countries (see Table 1).

These top 10 countries provided 56% of all seafarers in 2000 (the total supply being 1,227,000). Of this 56%, some 87% came from the Far East, the Indian subcontinent and Eastern Europe. As can be seen from Table 1, there is a slight contraction in the total numbers and some minor redistribution between 1995 and 2000. The primary and obvious point to make is that

Table 1: Top ten labour supplying countries

Country	Officers	Ratings	Total in 2000	Total in 1995
The Philippines	50,000	180,000	230,000[9]	244,782
Indonesia	15,500	68,000	83,500	83,500
Turkey	14,303	48,144	62,447	80,000
China	34,197	47,820	82,017	76,482
India	11,700	43,000	54,700	53,000
Russia	21,680	34,000	55,680	47,688
Japan	18,813	12,200	31,013	42,537
Greece	17,000	15,500	32,500	40,000
Ukraine	14,000	23,000	37,000	38,000
Italy	9,500	14,000	23,500	32,300
Totals	206,693	485,664	692,357	738,109

Source: BIMCO/ISF *Manpower Update 2000* and Couper et al., 1999.

Filipino seafarers represent some 19%, by far the largest source of supply. China has marginally increased while all the developed countries listed show some contraction.

The above discussion demonstrates that seafarers possess skills that are especially scarce in relation to contemporary demand, a fact that requires them to migrate from largely non-traditional regions.

3. MOBILITY AND MIGRATION

Labour mobility and migration are two closely interwoven concepts, for they influence the allocation or reallocation of this important factor, and are a significant channel of competition within the labour market. Of interest in the present context is occupational mobility, which refers to movements between occupational skill level, and spatial or geographical mobility relating to movements between geographical areas or regions. As previously argued, seafarers' employment is regarded in some respects as transitory despite its regularity. Casual labour essentially implies an excess of supply for a given number of job opportunities, often combined with isolated workers and a scattered industry. Further labour costs are viewed as part of the firms' variable costs. Such costs can be reduced by altering labour requirements in response to short-term variations in demand in the open freight market, practices evidenced in the shipping industry. Hence, mobility of the labour force within firms and the industry at national and international level is seen as the norm.

Occupational mobility is influenced strongly by institutions outside the industrial sphere. Professional ships officers secure their position and progress mainly through the gaining of certificates (licences of competency) controlled by departments of governments. Once secured, these qualifications allow the officer mobility, but only within the limitations of the industry. They are generally of only minimal relevance in an alternative occupation. Ratings are semi-skilled experienced workers, capable of mobility between firms across the industry, but as with officers, this horizontal mobility is of marginal relevance to alternative employment.

Pertinent to the present discussion is the phenomenon of migration, the movement between geographical areas as a manifestation of the job search process. The economic and other motive that define the process will form the basis of this analysis. As K G Willis[10] points out, "The genesis of migration lies in dissatisfaction with the contemporary environment. The disparity of opportunity provides the main driving force behind migration, whether this is to enjoy levels of living in terms of income, or the physical or social environment. The importance in migration lies in its capacity to adjust resources and help to equate supply and demand." There are two general components of the redistribution mechanism of migration, these are the relative "push" and "pull" of market forces. The role of the "push" is emphasised by unemployment or a poor economic environment at home, which may be due to technological and structural changes in the economy. The "demand" or "pull" is the response to some buoyant economic conditions at their destination, evidently where labour is in short supply and living standards are higher. That is to say regions in which there is excess labour will be pushing labour out with unemployment and reduced wages, while sectors in which there is excess demand, will be pulling labour in. Here the discussion is not of large scale movement of labour, but rather seafarers responding to economic and perhaps social factors that reflect the attractiveness of alternatives in other countries (sectors of the industry or registry flag). This economic function of migration is the redistribution of labour geographically in accordance with changing demand for specific types of labour.

Having established the generality of migration, it is important to make explicit that seafarers are unquestionably unique migrants (or emigrants) who enter and participate in the country of destinations' workforce (labour market) without entering the country. This is accomplished by working on a vessel whose nationality is indicated by the register and flag and which differs from that of the seafarer's home country. "This place of work is physically isolated from family and from the national and the local community, which the ship represents, frequently for some years at a time. The ship is, on the other hand, Norwegian territory, and certain public functions, e.g. the judicial [sic], are delegated to the captain."[11] By definition, labour migration involves the simultaneous change of employment and residence. Seafarers do not fulfil the latter criteria for their residence remains the same, their home country. Further it would not be viewed as unusual to remain with the same employer whilst changing the nationality of the vessel registry on which the seafarer is employed. This has been the result of the labour market for seafarers becoming increasingly fragmented on a geographical basis.

There is ample evidence of such fragmentation having considerable lineage with Indian seafarers being employed on board British registered vessels since the mid-19th century. But from a more international contemporary situation there are a number of distinct trends, notably the relatively high costs or inability to recruit seafarers in what is termed the "traditional maritime nations" (a proposition not universally accepted). This has been combined with the search by shipowners, particularly since the 1970s for cheaper sources of labour due to their increasing consciousness of variable operating costs. Such a trend is closely related to rapid growth of open registers, the shipowners of which have no allegiance to the country of register, perceiving vessel registration as a simple business arrangement. States providing open register services pay little more than lip service to their own seafarers, if any. Hence what have emerged are states, invariably developing countries, which have become substantial sources of labour to open and international registered companies. Initially they were suppliers of ratings, but now increasingly officers are being trained and recruited.

Thus shipowners are attracted to migrant seafarers that are not only inexpensive, but possess the necessary skills and qualifications, most of them being young men between the ages of 16 and 35 years. In addition, the costs of training have already been incurred in the country of origin by the individual seafarer, their families, the State, or some combination of all three. Such commitment has caused the industry's labour market to contain elements of "crowded" occupations[12] particularly among ratings in labour supplying countries. This is due to the comparatively high income being earned by national rather than international standards. The presence of occupational crowds will, by definition, increase the supply of labour, an outcome from which segregation or discrimination can develop in one form or another.

4. MARKET SEGMENTATION

In the traditional model it is essential that labour mobility and migration progresses smoothly without friction, the premise being that all workers have equal access to all employment opportunities. However, such a premise does not hold for labour markets which are profoundly segregated by national and geographical borders. Further the movement of workers between countries has in recent decades become severely limited by national laws of migration. Even in the unique international seafaring labour market, there is a disparity of opportunity which presents barriers to mobility and migration. The barriers may be direct in the prevention of foreign seafarers on a particular flag or indirect in the terms and conditions offered to the different groups. Other social and cultural barriers also exist such as communication skills and social structures. Such friction discourages the free movement of labour and the employment of any nationality of seafarers on any flag register and serve to create market segmentation.

4.1 Legislative separation

The existence of different legislation in the various flag states causes barriers. This section illustrates the types of legislation implemented by the registers which either directly or indirectly produces these market segments. From the survey of 60 countries it was interesting to note that the majority of flag states operate some kind of restrictive policy with respect to foreign seafarers, partic-

THE ECONOMICS OF THE SEAFARING LABOUR MARKET 453

ularly in the case of the master and senior officer positions. Figure 2 shows that 8.3% or 5 flags require an all national crew: USA (where crew must be US residents), Italy, India, Mexico and Pakistan.

Authorisation for non-nationals is possible in eight countries: Bulgaria, Chile, Papua New Guinea, Peru, The Philippines, Portugal and Yemen (the latter only restricting ratings). There was also a requirement in 16 registers for the officers or senior officers to be nationals.

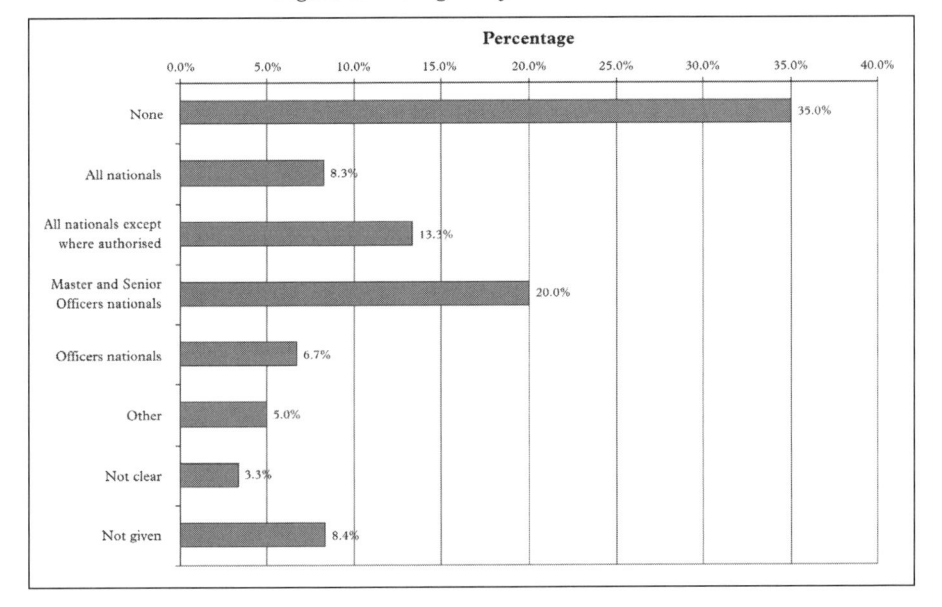

Figure 2: Foreign seafarer restrictions

Category	Percentage
None	35.0%
All nationals	8.3%
All nationals except where authorised	13.2%
Master and Senior Officers nationals	20.0%
Officers nationals	6.7%
Other	5.0%
Not clear	3.3%
Not given	8.4%

Figure 2 illustrates that only 35% of countries have no legal restriction on foreign seafarers, and in some of these, non-nationals are rarely found. This is clearly a major obstacle to free mobility and migration.

Legislation relating to seafarers' terms and conditions of employment create a wide disparity between the flag states further separating the employment markets. From the sample of 60 states, in only 55% of countries where seafarers covered by the normal legislation. Specific seafarer's legislation was evident in only 42% of the sample. Further these laws applied to non-nationals working on a particular flag in only 57% of cases.

In Denmark the national legislation is very prescriptive for the resident Danish seafarers but not for non-nationals. Consequently a framework was established to deal with the employment of non-nationals under different terms and conditions. The agreement applies to collective agreements with foreign trade unions and individual agreements concerning foreign seafarers outside the EEC/EEA. Areas covered are wages, working time, repatriation, service period, illness, disability, grievance procedures, holiday and pension. Thus the legislation in Denmark allows for separation of nationals and non-nationals in terms of working conditions.

The problems in Panama are different from Denmark. Despite new legislation, the Panamanian seafarers feel that they receive a poorer deal than their non-national counterparts. The Decree Law No 8 of 1998 "Whereby work at sea and in navigable waterways is regulated, and other resources are dictated" (February 26, 1998) was drafted in recognition of the need to establish legislation and regulation specific to seafarers both national and international. The decree therefore applies across the fleet regardless of nationality. It regulates recruitment, termination of contract, inspection and procedure regarding disputes. Although it positively discriminates in favour of the Panamanian seafarers, this area of legislation has not been effectively enforced.

Conditions on board ships are an important consideration for the seafarer. Flag states provide regulation and law relating to food, accommodation, welfare and accident prevention. In many states laws require ships on the register to maintain food and catering arrangements designed to secure health and well being of the crews. There are often minimum standards for floor space, berth dimensions, and recreational areas.

In the prevention of accidents on board ship, regulation or laws address structural features, machinery, special safety measurers, loading and unloading, fire prevention, anchor chains, dangerous cargo and ballast, and personal protective equipment for seafarers. In addition, laws guarantee minimum welfare facilities and services provided in port and on board ship.

Table 2: Laws relating to health and welfare

	Percentage of positive respondents
Food	63.3%
Accommodation	63.3%
Accident Prevention	55.0 %
Welfare	48.3%

From the survey, the response to questions relating to health and welfare was good as illustrated by Table 2. Over 63% of countries had laws in place to cover food and accommodation. Accidents and welfare were marginally less positive. The countries, which consistently had no laws relating to these areas of activity were Brazil, Lebanon, Bahrain, Belgium, Pakistan and Venezuela.

Social security is a further issue in determining the working conditions. Seafarers were covered by the national social security system in 73% of cases. The countries where seafarers were outside of the system were Pakistan, Venezuela, Japan, Malaysia, India, Liberia, Nicaragua, the Marshall Islands, and Greece. There were only a limited number of examples (8 cases) of a separate system of benefits, which existed for seafarers. These included Singapore, India, Chile, Portugal, Sweden, France, Japan and Greece. It was not made explicit whether these were state or private provisions. There are clearly some differences in the treatment of nationals and non-nationals in terms of social security benefits obtained. In the sample, 32% of states did not cover non-nationals in their social security system.

The regime of taxation can lead to friction in the market creating separation. In many cases these different tax provisions can dramatically affect the net income received by the seafarers and make foreign flagged vessels a more attractive proposition. Open and international registers tend to provide tax free income to foreign seafarers and, in some cases, national seafarers. Nationals working on a traditional register can often be at a disadvantage in terms of tax liability except where non residency rules can be satisfied.

Denmark is an example of an international register where seafarers effectively receive tax-free income. In addition the shipowners offer an allowance to domiciled seafarers to cover usual tax deductions, notably those for interest on mortgages. They also enjoy all the social security benefits despite the fact that no tax is paid.

Indian seafarers on the Indian flagged vessels do pay tax on their income since they often still qualify as resident under the Income Tax Act 1961. Even if classified as non-resident they receive much of their income in India which is charged to tax in the normal way.

The tax regime can thus lead to a preference for work on foreign flagged vessels particularly the open and international registers where seafarers often enjoy tax-free income.

4.2 Cultural segmentation

A number of cultural differences separate the markets. These are the result of communication skills and social structures which exist in particular states.

Ability to communicate effectively in English is still very much a requirement of the international seafarer particularly when operating within a crew of mixed nationalities. This is one of the reasons why the Philippines remains the highest provider of labour to international fleets. Challenges to its position must come not only in terms of lower unit costs but also on comparable fluency in English. Linguistic ability is often cited as a reason for restricting the use of foreign seafarers. This was certainly the case in India, particularly at officer level.

The age profile of seafarers is indicative of the different social structures and pressures which exist in the various flag states. In the traditional flag states there is a general reluctance to enter the seafaring profession which is leading to an ageing work force. In Denmark, statistics show that many seafaring officers move to land based employment by the age of 40 and only 60% of graduates remain at sea long enough to become masters. Between the ages of 40 and 50 the "drop out" is insignificant but the number of active seamen plummets from around 55% at 50 years to 9% by the age of 65.

Contrary to the situation in many of the OECD countries, seafaring in the developing countries is very much a young person's occupation, particularly for officers. Both the Shipowners and Officers' Union in India recognise a sharp break in employment between 36 and 40 years of age when many officers go ashore to take up other forms of employment. Because of the high turnover, it is possible to become a master by the age of 29. On average the officers' union estimated the senior officer age range to be 40–50 years and the junior officer 25–40 years. The main reasons behind this young "retirement" age are sociological and traditional, based on the importance of extended family commitments. The high earning power during the short sea career enables the officer to accumulate sufficient funds to work ashore, presumably in a less highly paid position. The situation differs on home trade or coastal shipping industry where the age profile is much higher with many seafarers continuing to the age of 60 years. This fits the family argument, since such seafarers would not generally spend excessively long periods away from home.

Indian ratings are thought to have a higher average age, particularly those working on Indian flagged vessels, where the Union estimates a range of 20–60 years. On foreign flagged vessels however, ratings generally retire earlier (at an average age of 44) as a result, it is suggested, of the more arduous working conditions on these vessels. There also appears to be little movement of seafarers between the flags. In other words, there is no evidence of seafarers seeking employment on Indian flagged vessels on reaching the age of 44 years.

In the Philippines, a report from the Scalabrini Migration Centre[13] claimed that the majority of Filipino seafarers are aged between 25 and 44. There appears to be little opportunity for employment beyond 45 years. There are a number of reasons put forward for this phenomenon, such as the higher cost of insurance for seafarers beyond the age of 45. However, social structures are also behind this trend. The family unit is very important in the Philippines and when the costs of schooling children have been met and less money is required, the seafarers may move ashore to less lucrative employment. There is also the suggestion of a shift from overseas (deep sea) to domestic trade vessels at this time.

Thus the cultural differences create different markets of seafarers from which shipowners can choose according to requirements or preferences as to language ability, nationality and age.

This empirical analysis shows a highly segregated seafaring labour market, where there is a multiplicity of active policies aimed at improving the efficiency of the market from the perspective of an individual government or agency. In other words, institutional arrangements are operating in the particular public interest as a method of correcting distortions or friction in the system.

5. DISCRIMINATION

The market separation discussed above opens the door to discriminatory practices, through discrimination shipowners can indulge their preferences for particular groups on the basis of skills, nationality and costs. This latter point highlights the fact that the seafaring labour force is not homogeneous and therefore seafarers are not perfect substitutes for one another. Employers are not indifferent to which seafarer is hired. Even in situations where groups have undergone the same training, their efficiency and even their employers' perception of the efficiency will vary considerably.

Preference to certain groups may be rational or irrational, some shipowners have particular technical requirements relating to the ability to use equipment which requires specific types of labour. Some may prefer different types of crews to others, despite the presence of equal qualifications and skills within the industry. For example, a preference for young ratings rather than old, or officers from developed countries rather than developing countries. In each of these situations this increasing choice is a form of discrimination against those unable to obtain wages or enhanced working conditions achieved by others in the industry.

The following discussion examines various models where discrimination takes place.

5.1 Monopsony

A labour market situation in which there is a single buyer or employer, is called a monopsony. One of several employers of labour is an oligopsonist, for example where a single procurer of labour forms a collusive association. Here there will be no distinction between the cases; they will simply be referred to as firms that possess the power to influence the employment and price of labour.

The market situation of monopsony results from either the existence of specific labour or limitation on its mobility. Primarily monopsonists hire labour which is specialised to meet the needs of a particular firm or industry. In this case, labour possesses uniquely relevant technological knowledge. Where employers offer higher wage rates for special categories of labour, this encourages workers to undergo the necessary education and training. No other industry utilises these particular skills, consequently once trained and holding professional or job qualification, the options facing the worker are to work in the particular industry or move to another where the rewards are significantly lower. There are no alternative job opportunities. The other condition from which monopsony stems is the lack of labour mobility in an economically desirably direction. This is not to say that labour can be immobile, only that mobility out of certain geographical areas is not possible. Various forces may deny labour alternative or attractive employment opportunities or perhaps there is a lack of funds enabling them to seek out these positions. Employers generally discourage workers from "shopping around" for other job opportunities, with offers of employment being made on a "take it or leave it" basis. Similarly, immobility may result from an agreement from the employers not to poach each other's workers. Both criteria, of specialised labour and immobility of resources sit comfortably in the shipping industry. In such a situation the employer will exercise a degree of power at a number of levels, individually or collectively through their own organisations, manning agency or occasionally government influences. This market position is analysed in Figure 3 below.

The vertical Y-axis shows the level of income and the horizontal X-axis shows the number of seafarers employed. The demand curve is denoted by D, and is also the marginal revenue product curve (MRP). The supply curve of labour S is also the average factor cost (AFC) and the average cost of labour. Because the supply curve is positively sloping, the marginal factor curve (MFC), that is the marginal cost of the factor of labour, lies everywhere above the supply curve. The quantity of seafarers hired in a perfectly competitive market would be N at equilibrium E and income level W. The profit maximisation monopsonist will employ seafarers at point N^1, where MFC is equal to MRP. This is because any movement beyond (to the right) of N^1 necessitates hiring more

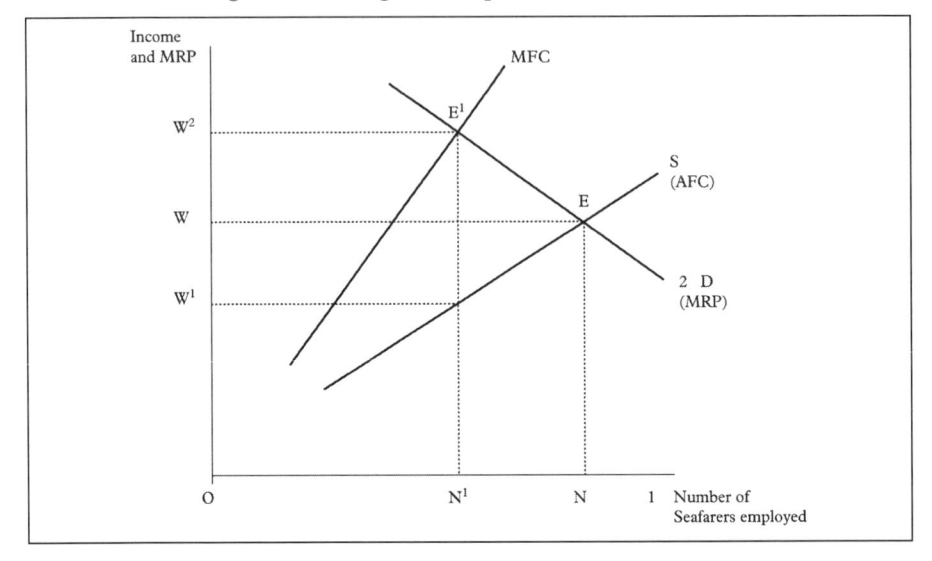

Figure 3: Pricing in monopsonistic labour market

seafarers and profits decrease since MFC exceeds MRP. A movement in the opposite direction, hiring fewer seafarers, would mean once again profits would decrease. The basic rule is that the monopsonist maximises profits by choosing the quantity of labour where marginal factor cost (MFC) is equal to marginal revenue profit (MRP).

5.2 Discriminating monopsony

Thus far there has been a consideration of discrimination of the employment of seafarers and monopsonistic shipowning employers who give all individual seafarers their employment at the same income. Here consideration is made of the situation of the discriminating monopsonist who pays different wages for similar work at the same level of efficiency. This occurs when it is possible to distinguish between two (or more) groups in the seafaring labour force, with differing supply functions. More precisely, the elasticity of supply is different in each market. Further, the seafaring labour market must be distinct and separate, where the supplies of labour in the market cannot transfer their labour to an alternative market or markets. If such conditions hold, a monopsonist will have the ability to discriminate by giving different levels of income in each market. This is achieved by decreasing the level of employment in the more expensive market and substituting the seafarers from the cheaper market where the marginal cost of labour is lower. Assuming two countries A and B, both of which have active seafaring labour markets, the discriminating monopolist will aim at a combination of labour, first from country A and second from country B which will minimise the costs of employing a fixed number of seafarers. This situation is illustrated in Figure 4 where there is a discriminating monopolist who is profit maximising. Countries A and B indicate the level of seafarers supplied and the marginal factor cost MFC function in each individual market.

THE ECONOMICS OF THE SEAFARING LABOUR MARKET 459

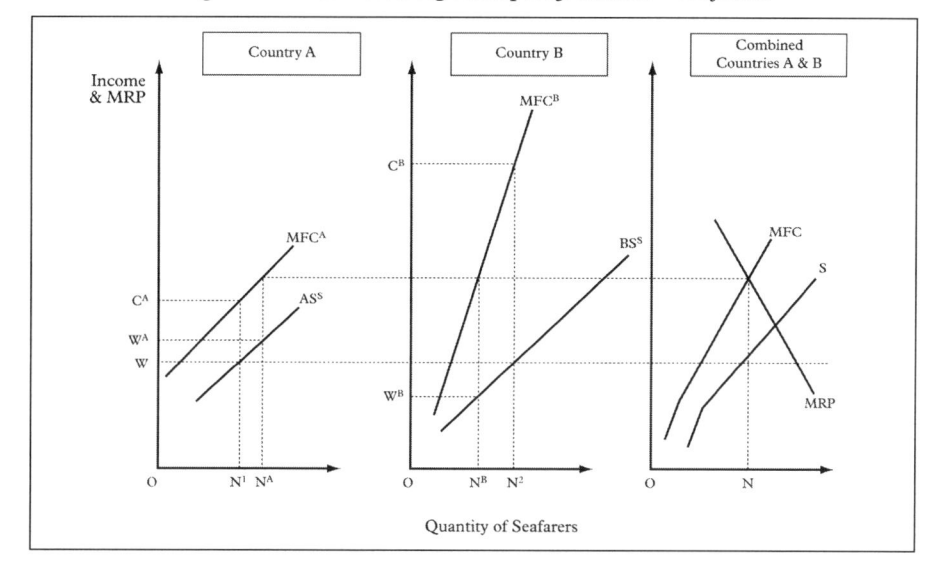

Figure 4: Discriminating monopsony market – seafarers

Section C is obtained by horizontal summation of the respective curves of the sub-markets, MFC and S. If the shipowner is unable to discriminate, he will pay is the same income to each individual seafarer regardless of the market. There is a common income, indicated by wage W in the first country, established at N^1 seafarers and in country B set at N^2.

The discriminating monopsonist would maximise profit by equating MFC and MRP leading to the employment of seafarers at point N. The corresponding income and number of seafarers employed in each sub-market is derived from the MFC in each market. The shipowners' equilibrium level of employment is indicated by NA in country A and NB in country B. It should be noted that the result is the payment of lower wages in markets where the elasticity of labour supply is lower (i.e., country B) as indicated by the slope of the curve.

What is clear is that shipowners require a certain degree of monopsony power if income discrimination is to be promoted. Further the seafaring labour market must be devisable into segments between which transfers are impossible or at least thought to be so.

5.3 Examples of discrimination

The existence of separate markets and separate jurisdictions makes discrimination prevalent in the international seafaring labour market. Such discrimination takes varying forms, some of which have already been discussed such as discriminatory legislation for different nationalities working on the same register. The most widespread form of discrimination however, is shown in terms of wage differentials between different nationalities.

In the survey, response to the request for detailed information on wages for the various ranks over nationalities was only given sporadically. A general question on wage discrimination however, did produce a 55% response and did expose the existence of wage differences between nationals and non-nationals working on the same flag vessels. Only 40% of the total stated that no wage discrimination existed. Where discrimination was practised (in 15% of cases), it took various forms. In Yemen considerably higher rates were paid to non-nationals. Similarly in Peru, non-national seafarers from EU countries and North America secured wages 50% higher than nationals. This practice was reversed in other cases where non-nationals received lower wages, for example in Papua New Guinea, Malaysia and Japan. In the European fleets of Denmark, Italy and Norway, non-nationals or non-EU seafarers were paid less than EU domiciled seafarers.

A more detailed examination of wages in the specific countries of Denmark, India, the Philippines and Panama is presented below.

In Denmark wages are determined by collective agreement between the Danish Shipowners Association and relevant Trade Union for ships registered on the Danish International Ships Register (DIS). Table 3 demonstrates the differences that exist between the wages of nationals and non-nationals due to the fact that wages can be based on rates prevailing in the home country.

Table 3: Monthly wage comparison

As at 1 April 2001	Wages for national seafarers	Wages for non-national/ domiciled seafarers (Filipino)
1st Deck Officer	Dkr.14,648 (US$	US$1,129 (DKr equivalent 8,918)*
1st Engineering Officer	Dkr.14,648	US$1,129 (DKr equivalent 8,918)*
Chief Steward/ Chief Cook	Dkr.16,005	3) US$1,221 (DKr equivalent 9,645)*
A.B.	Dkr.12,908	US$1,100 (DKr equivalent 8,689)*

* Based on exchange rate of US$ against the DKr, 1 April 2001.

The differences between wage levels of Danish and Filipino seafarers illustrate the considerable cost savings that can be made by employing non-Danish crew. A Filipino Deck officer is paid 39% less than the lowest rate of a Danish deck officer, similarly for an engineering officer. The difference in the case of a Chief Steward or Chief Cook is 40%. For an Able Seaman the variation is the least marked at 37% lower than an equivalent Danish rating. Having argued this, the wage levels obtained by Filipinos working on the DIS are substantially higher than those normally obtained under Filipino regulation. The minimum wage for seafarers in the Philippines currently stands at US$385 per month as established the Department of Labour and Employment (DOLE).[14] However, seafarers on domestic flagged vessels, both inter-island and ocean going, do not benefit from the POEA minimum wage and actually receive a fraction of that rate. Typically an AB will only earn the equivalent of US $134 per month.

In Panama, there is an extremely low statutory minimum wage but seafarer wages are generally determined by the contract between the employer and employee. Thus there was little available data on wage rates prevailing on Panamanian registered vessels.

There is a general perception that Indian seafarers are employed at the higher end of the international wage scale, as a reflection of the high quality of the work force. However, on more detailed scrutiny, whilst this may be true in the case of ratings it must be questioned in relation to officers. There is no standard wage for officers and they are known to vary according to the vessel registration. For example, the Maritime Union of India (MUI) estimates differentials as follows for a Master/ Chief Engineer:

Table 4: Officer wages ($ per month)

International Transport Workers Federation (ITF)	$3899
Second Registers	$4030 (NIS)
Indian National Shipowners' Association	$3707 (pre-tax approximately) $2595 (post tax)

Source: Maritime Union of India (MUI) estimates, November 2001.

Table 4 highlights a variation of more than 8% between the INSA and Norwegian International Register (NIS) rate compared to a 3.25% difference between the International Transport Workers Federation (ITF) and NIS. This indicates the two distinct elements in the discussion of officers' salaries. First the lower gross rates for domestic compared to foreign flagged vessels and secondly the tax on that income which can be as high as 30%. Consequently in terms of wages received the differential between highest and lowest becomes a very significant 36%.

However, it should be pointed out that, within the context of the domestic economy, the wage level for a seafaring officer is high relative to that of a comparable professional person in India.

The empirical evidence demonstrates that it is possible to distinguish between groups in the seafaring labour force and to give them differing incomes. This arises due to the existence of separate markets. The monopsonist shipowner is able to reduce seafaring labour costs by decreasing the level of employment in the more expensive market and substituting the seafarers from the cheaper market. The examples of wage levels demonstrate discrimination between different nationalities of seafarers working on the same flag and discrimination between the same nationality on different flags. On the Danish International Register, for example Filipino seafarers are paid up to 40% less than their Danish counterparts. Indian officers receive over 30% less on Indian registered vessels compared to foreign flagged vessels. Filipinos on the domestic trade vessels receive 65% less than the minimum wage set by the government for foreign going seafarers. Given the present and potential competition from other labour supplying countries the variation in labour unit cost is likely to become more marked, particularly as shipowners see this as a vital and perhaps the only flexible element of their operational costs.

6. TRADE UNIONS

Seafarers' trade unions were established in response to the shipowners' domination of an unorganised labour market. They represent an attempt to create a stable organisation to regulate the conditions under which an individual seafarer sells his labour. In this way, they constitute a countervailing power to challenge the shipowners' monopsony. Trade unions are not purely an economic entity, but also a social collective institution with a primary purpose of defending the wide range of members' interest. It is not the aim here to discuss the diverse characteristics of trade unions, but rather to consider the role of seafaring unions in attempting to neutralise the monopsonistic power of the shipowner. The level of trade union strength can be measured by their ability to influence the supply of seafarers. The logical starting point of the analysis is to examine the way the unions have attempted to affect the seafarers labour market to which their membership are suppliers, and in which they, the trade unions, have had varying degrees of success.

The assumption is that the trade unions function as the suppliers of seafarers in the labour market, where there is a single employer (a monopsonist hirer of labour). In such a situation, in principle at least, the union can increase the level of income and employment without the need for the marginal revenue product (MRP) curve, to move to the right. Figure 5 illustrates this situation.

The vertical Y-axis indicates income and marginal revenue product levels, the horizontal X-axis represents the number of seafarers employed. The point where demand is equal to supply is equilibrium E with W income level and N seafarers employed. The monopsonist shipowner will however attempt to restrict employment below the competitive level N in order to maximise profits. The unions will likewise attempt to restrict employment of their members in order to maximise their incomes. If it is assumed that initially the monopsonist shipowner presents the income rates at W^1, the number of seafarers employed would be N^1. With the successful establishment of a trade union, the

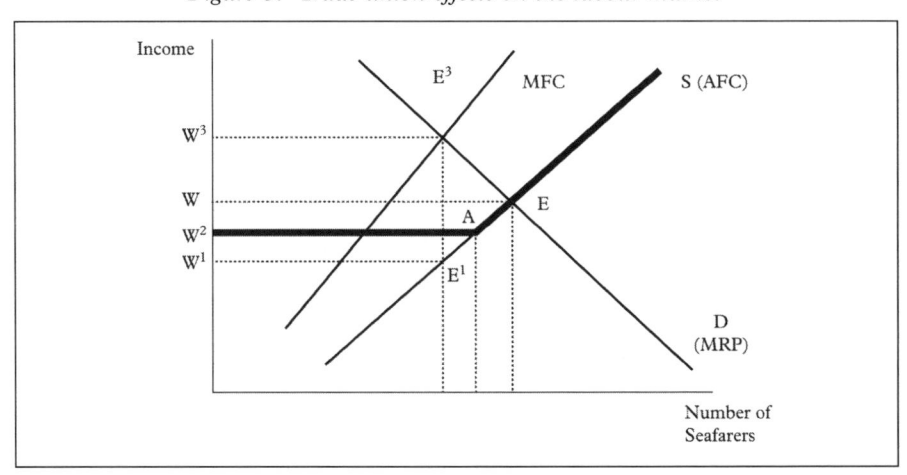

Figure 5: Trade union effects on the labour market

monopsonist is challenged and there is an increase in minimum income levels from W^1 to W^2, and the numbers employed increase to N^2. The important element here is that the minimum income level becomes the supply curve of labour (the thick line). This is perfectly elastic for seafarers up to the point A, N^2. Beyond this point the shipowner will have to offer an increased income to attract greater numbers of seafarers. What the unions have achieved is to increase both the level of income and members' employment compared with the previous situations. The figure further shows that, providing the unions possess the necessary bargaining power, they can raise income beyond W^2 and increase the number of seafarers employed to the point E at income level W and employment level N. If the income is increased beyond W there will be a reduction in employment below N, as shipowners try to protect their position.

What is being discussed here is an imperfect labour market, one in which trade unions may aim at some form of trade-off between higher income and increased numbers of seafarers employed. This is achieved without any reduction in the number of seafarers employment below N^1. The area of such activities known as the "zone of bargaining", is indicated by the area $W^2AE^3W^3$ in Figure 5. In the process of bargaining, the area of monopsonist profit can be diverted away from shipowners to increase the level of income and seafaring employees.

As argued, in the shipping industry the trade unions and federations of trade unions do not in general face a large number of relatively small shipowners, but a monopsony or group monopsony. In such a situation both the shipowners and to a lesser extent unions possess market power. Hence the outcome of wages and other restrictions is indeterminate, and will depend on the bargaining skills of both parties. This can be regarded as typical of any economy, but particularly those of developed countries which have powerful forces on both sides of seafaring labour negotiations.

In the seafaring labour market however, the countervailing power of the trade unions is diluted by the sheer number of unions and agreements negotiated.

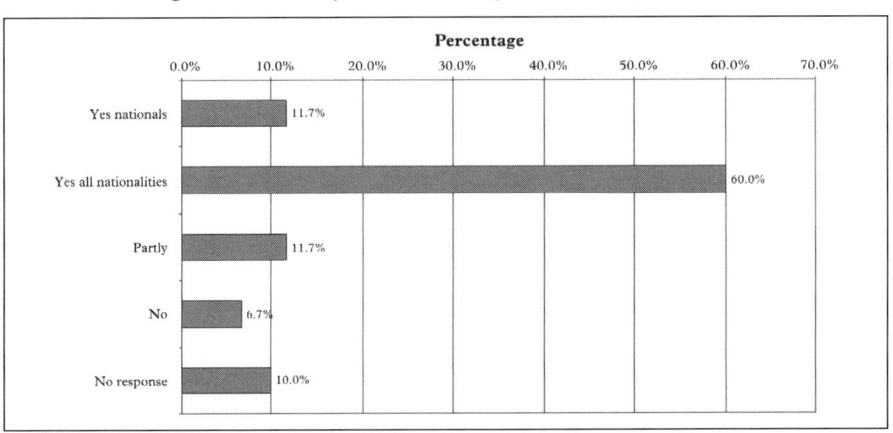

Figure 6: Are seafarers covered by collective agreements?

Category	Percentage
Yes nationals	11.7%
Yes all nationalities	60.0%
Partly	11.7%
No	6.7%
No response	10.0%

The barriers discussed above create separated groups of labour supply which are often represented by separate unions. For example, collective agreements negotiated with shipowners associations or companies apply to all nationalities in only 60% of cases. In 7 cases (Greece, Chile, Netherlands, Finland, Denmark, France and Poland) they only apply to nationals. In some of these countries a separate agreement operates for non-nationals notably in Denmark and in Japan. No collective agreements are in force in Lebanon, Ecuador, United Arab Emirates and Malaysia.

Turning to an examination of the attitudes of trade unions towards recruitment of non-nationals to their membership, only around half (52%) of respondents stated that there were no restrictions whatsoever on such recruitment. Figure 7 shows this in detail.

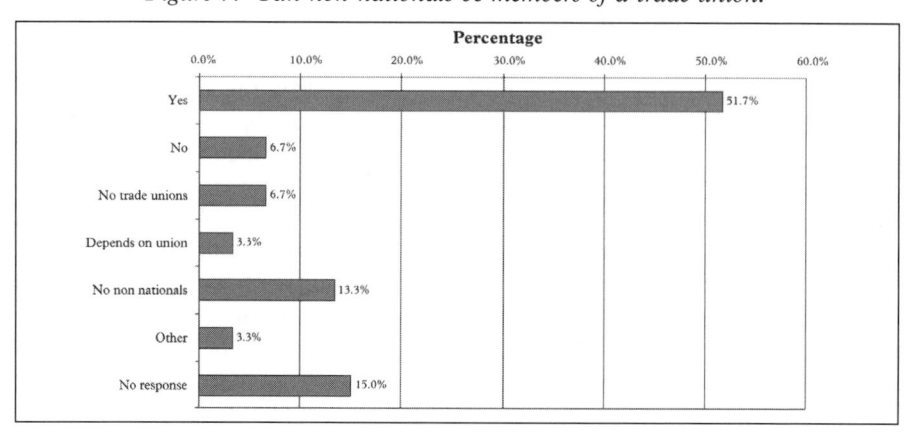

Figure 7: Can non-nationals be members of a trade union?

Category	Percentage
Yes	51.7%
No	6.7%
No trade unions	6.7%
Depends on union	3.3%
No non nationals	13.3%
Other	3.3%
No response	15.0%

A small minority of countries (7%) Canada, Lebanon and Papua New Guinea, and France stated explicitly that non-nationals were prevented from joining national trade unions. Another 13% had no such requirements on the grounds that no non-nationals were employed in their fleet. Similarly 7% did not recruit on the basic premise that no trade unions existed in their countries, namely Malaysia, United Arab Emirates, Vanuatu and Oman. Two countries, Greece and Uruguay (3%) left it to the trade unions themselves stating it was dependent on their attitudes to such recruitment. The final 3% consists of the United States, whose recruitment is limited to seafarers in possession of residential or work permits and Venezuela where there is no regulation in force at present. It is interesting to note that in the case of Denmark, a non- national is allowed to join a Danish trade union but cannot be represented by it in collective bargaining agreements (CBAs).[15] For Filipino seafarers working on Danish registered vessels, CBAs are negotiated with the Manila based Associated Marine Officers' and Seamen's Union of the Philippines (AMOSUP). Other non-nationals are dealt with on an individual basis. Thus non-nationals and Danish seafarers living outside the country but employed on DIS vessels do not experience the same terms and conditions of employment or social rights.

In the case of Panama the decree law no.8 is not prescriptive on collective bargaining and the role of the unions, unlike the Labour Code. This is a contentious issue for their seafaring unions who claim that collective bargaining is no longer a requirement under the new legislation.

India, which only employs Indian seafarers on its vessels, operates a Maritime Board system to determine terms and conditions for ratings. The Board consists of an equal number of members representing Shipowners/ Employers and Ratings' Unions. The Indian National Shipowners' Association nominates nine members of which three are representatives of Foreign Shipowners/Employers using Indian Ratings. These are determined in consultation with the Maritime Association of Shipowners, Shipmanagers and Agents (MASSA).

In the Philippines the largest union is the Associated Marine Officers' and Seamen's Union of the Philippines (AMOSUP) with around 55,000 members. However, it should be noted that this largest single nation of seafarers is the least unionised. In fact only 17% of seafarers belong to a labour union or association.

What has to be made explicit here is that the seafaring labour market is not simple or unified but a diversity of markets cutting across and interacting on one and another in an international environment. In such an environment, the shipowner can act as a monopsonist. Trade unions can counteract the impact of the monopsony power and increase the wage level above what it would otherwise be. The problem for the seafarers is that the trade unions are mostly national organisations trying to fight against international companies and organisations. International representation is therefore needed to provide effective protection in an international arena. To this end there is a heavy reliance upon the International Transport Workers Federation (ITF) agreements and international conventions drafted by the International Labour Organisation (ILO). The ILO set minimum standards for conditions of employment and indeed a minimum wage which certain flag states have ratified. The ITF through their Total Crew Concept (TCC) agreements demand an acceptable standard for many seafarers and provide representation in the event of dispute. Enforcement of these standards and conventions will hopefully improve the position of seafarers worldwide. Although there may be special difficulties in providing an adequate solution for these problems, the problems themselves are basically those familiar from labour economic analysis.

7. CONCLUSIONS

Labour economics must not only be seen as relevant in a purely theoretical sense but in the wider context of economic and social problems. In writing this chapter the aspiration was to clarify the relevant economic issues and to provide a conceptual framework for addressing the complexities of the seafaring labour market. This was viewed from a neo-classical outlook which serves to provide a base of reference for a more realistic analysis. It was argued initially that the construction of a meaningful model of the market for seafarers required more than a bland allowance for market friction. What followed was a concern with the relationships between shipowners and the seafaring labour force both nationally and internationally functioning, as they do, within the maritime economic environment. This analysis of the labour market for seafarers highlights both the heterogeneity of labour and substantial, often monopsonistic, market imperfections. In other words both the assumptions of a competitive theory and its analysis of the problems of labour resource allocation and adjustment are challenged from a practical standpoint.

The empirical analysis demonstrates that the seafaring labour market is profoundly segmented by national boundaries with a multiplicity of barriers both direct and indirect, to free movement of labour within the industry. Numerous flag states overtly restrict the use of foreign seafarers on their vessels. Others use legislation as a indirect deterrent by reducing the level of protection afforded to the seafarer per se and the foreign seafarers in particular. Such barriers combined with the heterogeneity of the labour force serve to create fragmented markets which allow discrimination to take place. This often takes the form of wage discrimination, and differences in conditions of employment. The imperfections in the international seafaring labour market highlight the need for more effective and enforceable national and international legislation for the protection of the labour working within it.

APPENDIX: THE RESPONDENTS

State	Source
Algeria	Permanent Mission
Australia	Ministry
	Union
Bahamas	Bahamas Maritime Authority
Bahrain	Government
Belgium	Union
Belgium	Shipowners' Association
Brazil	Ministry
	Union
Bulgaria	Ministry of Transport
Canada	Government
Chile	Government
Columbia	Ministry of Labour and Social Security
Croatia	Ministry of Social Welfare
	Union
Denmark	Shipowners Association and Ministry Trade and Industry
	Union
Ecuador	Ministry
Egypt	Ministry
Estonia	Ministry of Social Affairs
Finland	Ministry of Labour
France	Government

Appendix continued

State	Source
Georgia	Maritime Administration
Germany	Shipowners and Seafarer Associations
Greece	Government, Shipowners, Union
Honduras	Government
Iceland	Ministry of Social Affairs
India	Ministry of Labour
Israel	Ministry of Transport
Italy	Ministry of Labour and Social Affairs
	Confitarma
Japan	Government
	Union
Korea	Union
Kuwait	Permanent Mission
Lebanon	Ministry of Public Works and Transport
Liberia	Bureau of Maritime Affairs
Lithuania	Ministry of Labour and Social Security
	Union
Malaysia	Ministry of Human Resources
Malta	Government
Marshall Islands	Maritime Administration
Mauritius	Mission to the UN
Mexico	Government
Morocco	Government
Netherlands	Department of International Social Policy and Information
	Union
Nicaragua	Ministry
Norway	Government, Shipowners, Union
Oman	Ministry of Transport and Housing
Pakistan	Ministry of Labour
	Union
Panama	Ministry
Papua New Guinea	Department of Labour and Employment
Peru	Government
Philippines	Maritime Industry Authority, POEA, Maritime Training Council
Poland	Ministry Labour and Social Policy
Portugal	Ministry
Romania	Government
Russia	Union
Singapore	Ministry
Spain	Government
Sweden	Ministry of Industry, Employment and Communications
Ukraine	Ministry of Transport
United Arab Emirates	Ministry of Labour and Social Affairs
Uruguay	Ministry
USA	Government
	US Coastguard
Vanuatu	Maritime Services
Venezuela	Ministry
Yemen	Union

ENDNOTES

1. The authors, due to the extensive nature of the survey, cannot confirm the validity of responses produced.
2. A complete list of these respondents is shown in the Appendix.
3. NB: The authors have completed investigations of seafarers in Denmark, India, and Panama and the Philippines, all of which form ILO case studies.
4. Due to space constraints, there is no discussion of the elasticity of derived demand in this chapter. See McConville, J. (1999): *Economics of Maritime Transport: Theory and Practice* (London, Witherby), Chapter 6.
5. McConville, J., Glen, D., and Dowden, J. (1999): *United Kingdom Seafarers' Analysis 1998*, Marine Society and the Centre for International Transport Management, (London, London Guildhall University).
6. BIMCO/ISF Manpower Update (2000): *The World Demand for and Supply of Seafarers* (Institute for Employment Research, University of Warwick).
7. Li, K.X., and Wonham, J. (1999): "Who Mans the World Fleet. A Follow Up to the BIMCO ISF Manpower Survey", *Maritime Policy and Management*, 26 (3).
8. International Commission on Shipping (2000): *Enquiry into Safety "Ships, Slaves and Competition"*.
9. Published information from other sources indicate that the figure recording the number of Filipino seafarers represents a serious underestimation. Those compiled by the Philippines Overseas Employment Administration (POEA) suggest that the number of Filipino seafarers deployed has in fact increased by almost 20% over the last five years. The number of registered seafarers in 1999 was 472,225, representing an accumulation of new entrants since registration began in 1988.
10. *Problems of Migration* (Farnborough, Saxon House), p. 1.
11. Aubert and Oarner (1969): "The Social Structure of the Ship", reprinted in T. Burns, *Industrial Man* (London, Penguin Education), p. 380. The assumption here is that the seafarer is non-Norwegian.
12. Occupational crowds occur where there is a high density of people wanting to do the same job.
13. *The Need for an International Seafarers Centre in Manila* (Scalabrini, Migration Centre), July 2000.
14. Department Order No. 5, Series of 2000.
15. Leggate, H.K., and McConville, J. (February 2002): *Investigation of Seafarers: Denmark*, Case Study commissioned by the ILO.

PART SEVEN

NATIONAL AND INTERNATIONAL SHIPPING POLICIES

CHAPTER 21

THE RISE AND FALL OF NATIONAL SHIPPING POLICIES

Gunnar K. Sletmo
Ecole des Hautes Etudes Commerciales, Montreal, Canada.
E-mail: *gunnar.sletmo@hec.ca*

1. INTRODUCTION: IS THERE ROOM FOR NATIONAL SHIPPING POLICIES UNDER GLOBALISATION?

Is there any future role for shipping economists in the field of policy? Some would argue that under globalisation there is no room for any form of *national* shipping policy nor for any other form of industrial policy for that matter. Nevertheless national shipping policies remain important in many countries and regions. This chapter explores some of the background for today's policies and discusses possible future trends.

In the past economists considered questions of policy and the business of governing to be at the core of what economists do. Industrial economics was a key discipline and it was taken practically for granted that each industry was unique and in need of specific policy programs and measures. Two sectors for which this was particularly true were agriculture and transportation.

During much of the 20th century, "transportation" was an important field in the United States and elsewhere, not only for academic economists but also for business and economics students who saw the field as an opportunity for interesting careers in the transportation industry and in government. The Interstate Commerce Commission, the Federal Maritime Commission and the Civil Aeronautics Board (all of the United States) were large powerful organisations when this author was an economics graduate student in the 1960s. But by then, the decline of transportation economics related to specific modes approached rapidly.

In the 1970s deregulation became the new byword in transportation economics. Industrial policy in general was declared dead. Norton,[1] in "Industrial Policy and American Renewal" noted that "industrial policy turned out to be an idea with a brief career". He in turn quotes Robert Reich to the effect that "industrial policy is one of those rare ideas that has moved swiftly from obscurity to meaninglessness without any intervening period of coherence".[2] In 1985 the Civil Aeronautics Board closed its doors, following the major deregulation of the airline industry that started in 1978. The mighty Interstate Commerce Commission closed its doors in 1995 after more than a century of proud and powerful service. But interestingly, the Federal Maritime Commission is still alive. So maybe shipping is different?

In this paper "shipping policy" is used broadly, referring to a range of policy tools and regulations applied to the maritime sector. It is important to distinguish between those policies, which are national in scope and intent as opposed to international agreements and treaties that are based on *common interests* among nations. *National shipping policies* are normally intended to promote national flag fleets through various forms of preferential treatment such as fiscal advantages, direct subsidy of operations and construction, and through overtly protectionist measures such as reserving part of or even all cargo for national flag vessels. *International agreements* in general are oriented towards areas such as environmental protection, safety and also rules for manning and conditions for seamen and officers. International agreements are less developed when it comes to economic regulation, although several attempts have been made at setting up a regulatory economic framework also on a multilateral basis. It will be seen later that these two kinds of policies, national versus international, may have very different futures.

A student of maritime economics may do well to reflect on the nature of shipping policy and to have at least some knowledge of the long and fascinating history of maritime policy and politics.[3] In this case there may be at least a grain of truth in the old adage that those who ignore the lessons of history are bound to repeat its errors.

This chapter first reviews the five W's, i.e., the *what, why, when, where,* and *who,* of shipping policy. Then follows a review of three scenarios or models of shipping policy, based on concrete examples from Canada, China and West Africa. Finally, the chapter concludes with a short summary and conclusion.

2. THE FIVE W's OF SHIPPING POLICY

The question of shipping policy is multifaceted and it may be helpful to look at shipping in terms of the following five questions:
  (1) *what* is understood by shipping policy?
  (2) *why* do we have shipping policies?
  (3) *when* did shipping policies come into being and what is their present status?
  (4) *where* does one find shipping policies, by region and by shipping sector?
  (5) *who* are the major players (key agencies and organisations) involved?

2.1 what is maritime policy?

Traditionally, the emphasis has been on *national* shipping policy. Such policies are usually promotional in nature and aim either at promoting a nation's merchant marine or protecting it from competition from fleets of other nations or both. As shipping policy may include promotional as well as regulatory activities, the result may appear outright schizophrenic, with governments on the one hand promoting the freedom of the seas while on the other restricting market access or activities. In fact, shipping policy often becomes the *regulation* of shipping.

Sturmey (1975) has given the following definition of national shipping policy[4]:

"A nation may be said to have a shipping policy when it encourages, permits, or formulates measures to interfere with or control the free play of market forces in regard to the employment of shipping. The interference or control may extend from *ad hoc* measures to a carefully planned and continuous policy."

Stakeholders in today's shipping policies include national and international agencies as well as national and global shipping corporations, their customers, their owners and labor. Some issues may be strictly local in nature while others are international or global. Certain aspects of policy are strongly promoted by or supported by groups far removed from the business of shipping and maritime transport such as prominent environmentalist organisations.

Today's regulatory activities in shipping fall into two broad categories: those that deal with the *rights and obligations of States* and those that directly affect *commercial operations and practices*.[5] Table 1 provides a simple typology of current regulation, in a two-by-two matrix. The classification shows the diversity and variety of existing regulatory framework. It should be noted though that the distinction between state and commercial aspects as well as between national and international is by no means absolute as several regulations actually may touch upon all four categories.

Table 1: A typology of regulations in international shipping

	National	**International**
States' rights & obligations	Labor laws; Cabotage; Competition; Ownership & flag rules	Flag State & Port State Inspections; Law of the Sea; Safety & environmental regulations
Commercial operations & practices	Cargo reservations; Labor laws; Ship registration; Taxation	Cargo liability (e.g., Hamburg Rules); International labor rules; UNCTAD Code for Liner Conferences

Source: Based on OECD (2002), *Regulation Issues In International Maritime Transport.*

Unilateral shipping legislation and regulations are common in many countries. Thus many countries have rules about what flag vessels participating in their foreign trade must fly. Frequently there is a requirement that officers and crew of nationally registered vessels must be citizens of the home country, etc. Many countries reserve cabotage traffic for their own vessels, but note that even the term "cabotage" can be ambiguous. In the English speaking world cabotage usually refers to coastal traffic entirely within the waters of one country, whereas in West Africa the term applies to regional coastal traffic which may involve several countries.

Some countries have competition rules that apply to pricing and agreements among shipping companies, especially in the field of liner shipping. The United States applies such legislation not only to American flag vessels but to all vessels affecting US trades. This may mean that even vessels not directly serving any US port may still be subject to US law if their operations can somehow be said to affect US foreign trade. This is a case where the distinction between national and international is far from clear.

A major difficulty in international shipping is related to the question of cargo and vessel liability, for instance in the case of major oil spills. Who is responsible? The vessel owner, the company that operates the vessel, the oil company? In an attempt to improve safety at sea, there are inspection programs in place both by governments whose flag is used and by the ports where the vessels call. Such inspection programs may be unilateral but more commonly are based on international agreements and standards.

2.2 Why do we have maritime policies?

There was a time when the above question would not even be asked. It seemed obvious that maritime transport constituted an industry of major national importance and that as such, it needed to be protected and promoted by the state. The history of national shipping policies is long and proud and dates back to ancient times when state, trade, and *navie* were closely linked. Even today the concept of "trade follows the flag" is often taken to be self-evident, requiring no further explanation. Such ideas are firmly engraved in the economic and political psyche of many nations.[6]

In the decades following World War II international trade grew at a rate far outpacing world production and foreign trade became an ever-increasing share of the world's gross product, creating new market opportunities for shipping. With the large number of former colonies in Africa and in Asia that won their freedom in the 1960's, a number of "new nations" saw ocean shipping as a field well suited for development. National fleets, it was believed, could be an important source of revenue for these developing economies, providing employment, hard currency income and substantial savings by eliminating the dependence on the fleets of former colonial powers. Inevitably, reality was more complex than dreams, and it gradually became clear than these fledgling fleets would need help to survive. In fact, even with help many if not most of these new shipping lines failed miserably. Decades later, it was the turn of established maritime nations, especially within the OECD, to feel the pressures of competition, and also these industrial countries in many instances went to great length to protect their fleets, again without much success.

Inevitably such measures came under attack from competitors and economists. Goss and Marlow have provided an interesting overview of reasons commonly advanced to defend the reliance on such policies. Their list of theories or arguments which have been put forth to defend or promote maritime policies, includes.[7]

- the infant industry argument (i.e., "young" industries need protection in early stages);
- import substitution in order to develop new industries in developing countries;
- shipping capacity needed to carry trade;
- contribution to balance of payments;
- defence purposes – provide shipping capacity during military conflict;

- need to be present in international organisations in order to participate in international policy decisions.

Although these kinds of partial, ad-hoc arguments may seem outdated and irrelevant in a global economy, they are still alive in many quarters, even in countries generally professing to be freetraders. A sad example of this would be the recently imposed tariffs on steel imports to the United States. In March 2002, President Bush imposed tariffs ranging from 8% to 30% on various kinds of steel, claiming that US producers needed time to "compete on a level playing field" after 50 years of government subsidies to foreign competitors.[8] No nation is a consistent freetrader in the face of well-organised pressure groups.

The items on the Goss-Marlow list of shipping policies still apply in a number of countries, although often in amputated form. Goss and Marlow demonstrate the fallacy of each of these propositions, either through their own research or by ample and convincing references to a number of well-known independent academic studies. They conclude[9]:

"There have been so many errors in so many governments' policies towards shipping, and they have generally combined such high expense with such limited effectiveness, that one must be tempted to fall into the trap of saying that the best policies are those which involve the smallest levels of governmental activity, the lowest levels of public expenditure and the least chance of serious error."

Nevertheless, such policies survive and are being revived at regular intervals, usually by strong interest groups such as maritime labor unions, shipyard workers and politicians wishing to protect local businesses and labor. In short, history and special interest groups play a major role in keeping alive the will to protect and promote national shipping.

Not all measures to regulate shipping are promotional or protectionistic in nature. The problem of *externalities* – factors not adequately or correctly captured by the market mechanism – makes it desirable and frequently necessary, to develop special measures to deal with, e.g., costs associated with accidents such as large oil spills at sea. Other such issues relate to safety for seafarers and vessels. The *Exxon Valdez* grounding on 24 March 1989 is still remembered as a horrible example of the environmental risks inevitably associated with shipping. Following the accident the United States adopted legislation requiring the use of double-hulled vessels in the Alaska trade. This requirement is estimated to have cost about $ 2 billion dollars to implement and is to be paid by the North Slope oil producers.[10] In 1992 MARPOL, a treaty administered by the International Maritime Organisation (IMO) was amended to make it mandatory for tankers larger than 5,000 dwt, ordered after 6 July 1993, to be fitted with double hulls, or an alternative design approved by IMO.

Environmental and safety concerns are universal and require global cooperation. Regulation in these areas is now generally accepted as essential and much work has been done to find solutions. This is undoubtedly one area where "shipping policy" will not only survive but become strengthened over time even if there may be controversy about the nature and scope of regulations required.

In summary, there are many reasons for the existence of national shipping policies, ranging from the belief that national fleets are necessary for the development of trade to the desire to protect maritime jobs and investment as well as a sense that a national fleet contributes significantly to the national interest in the form of prestige and international visibility.

2.3 When did national shipping policies come into being?

Regulation of shipping rooted in antiquity

Gold[11] traces known regulation of shipping back to antiquity, and more particularly to the Phoenicians, the Greeks and the ancient City of Rhodes. As long as there has been international shipping, there appears to have been rules and regulations under which such trade could operate. Gold considers the modern law of the sea to coincide with the great expansion in shipping undertaken by Europeans in the 16th and 17th centuries. A famous jurist often mentioned in this context is Hugo Grotious who in 1606 completed a manuscript entitled *De Jure Praedae Commentaris*. The manuscript was not published till much later, but its third section was published anonymously in 1609 under the title *Mare Liberum*.[12] This became the basis for the freedom of the seas concept, arguing that traffic in international waters should be open and free for all.

Despite the emergence of liberal views on shipping which were to have tremendous influence on future thinking in shipping, the concept of shipping as being of great national significance – and hence worthy of protection – remained strong. A contemporary of Grotius, Hakluyt, a British geographer, recognised the deep-rooted nature of shipping policy – shipping being "the backbone of trade".[13] His monumental *The Principal Navigations, Voyages, Traffiques and Discoveries of the English Nation* (1589–1600) was written to be useful to merchants and entrepreneurs and to influence the direction and nature of public policy. Hakluyt's work demonstrates the extent to which trade ("Traffiques") and shipping ("navigation") were considered inseparable in 16th century England. Hakluyt explored with great enthusiasm British navigation on a global scale, leaving no doubt that the sea and its sailors contain the key to a deeper understanding of the universe! He even quotes the Bible to this effect: "... they which go down to the sea in ships, and occupy by the great waters, they see the works of the Lord and his wonders in the deep ..."[14]

Shipping has always been seen as much more than a means of transport, and has been linked to broader concepts of technology and growth. Francis Bacon (1605) observed in the *Advancement of Learning* "The proficience in navigation and discoveries may plant also an expectation of the further proficience and augmentation of all sciences". Almost three centuries later (1870), Emerson, the American poet and philosopher, expressed similar thoughts: "The most advanced nations are also those who navigate the most."

Maritime power

To this day, the concept that maritime capability equals *power* is reflected in numerous references in books of history and political science. A recent book even suggests that maritime power has significantly affected not only geopolitics on a large scale but also the principles governing world development since the Renaissance.[15] The term *maritime power* can be used to describe the capacity of certain countries to control not only the seas (by military means) but also major trade routes (by commercial means). It can also be used to denote the countries having such power. A *maritime nation* may or may not be a maritime power. This distinction is important. Maritime power is built on a *policy* of creating power – meaning the capacity to influence or control others – through the use of a number of instruments, and of which the merchant marine is but one component. History right up to modern times is replete with examples: The Phoenicians, 19th century USA, the former Soviet Union, and now China.

For many maritime nations, objectives were far more modest. For historical and geographical reasons some nations see the sea as a source of livelihood rather than as a source of "power". They engage in shipping as cross-traders, in fishing and whaling. Some of these nations have indeed become important players in international shipping but they should not be mistaken for "maritime powers". Rather than relying on protectionistic regimes, they tend to pursue liberal policies, favoring free markets and free enterprise. Examples in this group are Greece and Norway.

Important changes took place in shipping in the second half of the 20th century with a major shift in favor of the so-called "open registry" countries, at the expense of the traditional (OECD) maritime countries and the former Soviet Union and its East European allies.[16] In 1914 nine out of the top ten maritime nations were European, the tenth country being the United States. In 1998, four countries were Asian, five European and the United States was still on the list. Clearly, the role of "flag fleets" has declined dramatically and there can be little doubt about the diminished role for national shipping policy on a global scale. Internationalisation and globalisation place severe limits on a country's ability to pursue national policies in global markets.

Continued support for national shipping policies

As more and more countries join the World Trade Organisation and participate actively in the world economy, any serious attempt to maintain, let alone establish new maritime policies with a view towards promoting national shipping seems strangely anachronistic. Logically, shipping policy in its traditional form based on perceived national needs and aimed at maximising the size of national fleets through promotional and protectionistic means, should be dead. Yet, there are still those who aim to revive it. While today most economists would be inclined to scrap all forms of national shipping policy simply on a priori grounds, many political scientists hold a rather different view. Iheduru (1996) writes, "Most international political economy researchers have accordingly recognised the fact that shipping, as a basic infrastructure of international trade, is a key source of influence in world politics".[17] He continues:

"... the maritime sector has ... become a major source of conflict between the North and the South. Shipping is therefore one clear example of the efforts of the weak to change the international system in their favor; and a very important example of why and how poor countries fail in this struggle to achieve their objectives in an international system in which power is unevenly distributed."

Similar ideas can be found in many quarters, including in the United States. In a 1995 talk on "An American Perspective on Maritime Issues", the Maritime Administrator Albert J. Herberger presented a spirited defense of US support to its shipping, domestic and international. His arguments include the following[18]:

"Yes, the American maritime industry has benefited from federal assistance. The maritime industry thus shares common ground with American farmers, who benefit from direct subsidies, price supports and below market financing. It has common ground, too, with the American auto industry, the whole spectrum of defense industries, and others."

The Administrator emphasises that the merchant marine is "vital for national defense". He also has nothing but scorn for those who are critical of the Jones Act (which reserves US cabotage for US vessels):

"... we continue to hear amazing reports of how much the Jones Act costs the economy, and what tremendous growth we would see if only we could eliminate it... Opponents of the domestic shipping industry continue to refer to an old, much repudiated and erroneous study by the International Trade Commission..."

In summary, national shipping policy has always been with us and most likely will remain so in the future although in modified forms.

2.4 Where is the use of shipping policy most prevalent?

Differences by types of service (liner service versus charter)

Not all sectors of shipping are equally affected by policy measures and regulations. There are significant differences by types of services and by region or country. As every student of maritime economics knows, there is a fundamental difference between bulk shipping and general cargo services. Bulk vessels are made up of tankers and dry bulk. In both instances the cargo is generally homogenous and the vessel often carries just one kind of cargo (crude oil, iron ore, wheat, and similar commodities) on a given voyage and that normally for the account of just one customer. The commercial conditions are established by charter contracts.

The general cargo vessel carries a wide variety of cargo on any given voyage. These are usually operated according to a fixed schedule (liner services) and the vessel serves a large numbers of customers. Rates are usually but not always based on rate schedules established by liner companies, often jointly ("conference rates"). Since the late 1960's container vessels have played an ever increasing role in the transportation of finished goods in world trade and constitute the backbone of globalisation, having made it possible to link low labor costs suppliers in developing countries with consumer markets in high income markets.

Shipowners operating in bulk shipping often have no more than one or two vessels and bulk markets are generally seen as very competitive with low barriers to entry. The main regulatory concerns relate to safety and environmental issues. A few countries impose restrictions on the use of foreign flag vessels, even for bulk, usually in the case of "strategic" (such as oil) and military cargoes. Liner services typically require a fleet of vessels (either owned by one company or brought together in an alliance or consortium) and necessitate major land-based infrastructure. As a result, barriers to entry become far more substantial than for bulk shipping. For this and related reasons, liner shipping raises a number of issues of competition and economic regulation.

Table 2 shows the composition of the world merchant marine by vessel type. The category "other" includes, i.e., conventional general cargo vessels (non-containerised), cruise ships and ferries. The table gives an idea of the importance of each vessel type in terms of activities. It does not however indicate the economic importance of each category. Container vessels carry much higher value cargoes that bulk vessels. They are generally much faster and with minimal turn-around time in ports. As a result, their earning power is high. It is therefore not surprising that liner services represent segment of shipping where national policy has been most prevalent.

Table 2: Composition of world fleet as of 1 October 2001 (millions of dwt)

	Tankers	Dry Bulk	Container Vessels	Other	World Total
Deadweight	332	291	74	94	791
Percent	42.0	36.8	9.3	11.9	100.0

Source: MARAD, Washington DC (*www.marad.dot.gov/Marad_StatisticsMarAd*).

Differences by region

The geographic areas where the strongest attempts have been made at imposing protectionist shipping policies are those where trade flows are relatively thin and insufficient to attract aggressive competition. Such trades are largely North–South and some areas of continued battles over national shipping policies include West Africa (this will be illustrated with a case study later in this chapter) and parts of Asia (Pakistan, Malaysia, Indonesia and others). China, which has become a powerful player in international shipping, is actively pursuing nationalistic shipping policies (also reviewed in a case study later in the chapter). Latin America, until the 1990s at least, was also in this category.

Several countries in these regions have gone to great lengths to maintain national control over liner services by means of various promotional and protectionist schemes. In many cases, governments have invested heavily in such companies and may be the actual owner of "national shipping lines". This has been the case in Asia (China, India, Pakistan), Communist Countries (Russia and its satellites), Africa (many national companies set up after independence in the 1960's – most of them now gone) and Latin America (Ecuador, Brazil). It is noteworthy that even the United States maintains a state-owned "National Defense Reserve Fleet", although this fleet does not normally participate in commercial markets. Today, most but by no means all state owned companies, apart from small lines serving domestic markets, have disappeared or exist on paper only.

The dominant East–West trades tend to be much larger than those operating North–South. The world's largest markets for maritime container services involve the trade triangle of US–Europe–Asia (see Figure 1). On these high-density routes there is a considerable amount of competition and limited scope for nationalistic shipping policies. Rather, in recent years the main concerns expressed by governments in these areas relate to competition and the role of consortia and alliances in liner shipping.

Figure 1: Container movements in major liner routes 2000 (million TEU)

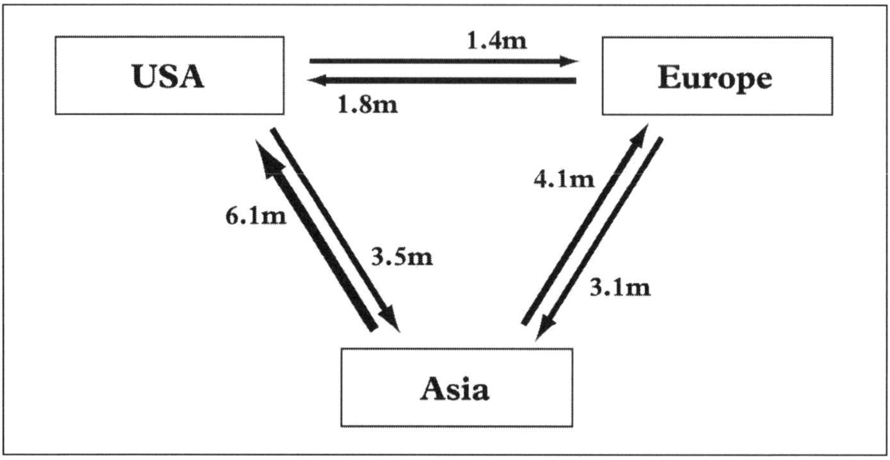

```
                    1.4m
     USA  ←——————————————→  Europe
              1.8m
                                    ↑
                              4.1m /
          ↑                       /
     6.1m  \                     / 
           \    3.5m            / 3.1m
            \                  ↓
                    Asia
```

Source: OECD (2002), *Regulatory Issues in International Maritime Transport*, p. 71.

In summary, national shipping policy has tended to be more prevalent in liner shipping than in bulk markets. Geographically, the major trade routes tend to be highly competitive. Questions of policy arise more in smaller markets, insufficient in size to attract many competitors. Many of these markets concern Africa, Latin America and South Asia. The situation has changed considerably over the last few years as a number of countries have undertaken modest measures of reform, including privatisation of state liner companies. Often these steps have been taken under pressure from markets and other countries, and may not yet truly reflect a sea change towards full deregulation.

2.5 Who are the key players?

Private versus state intervention

Players in the field of shipping policy include an amalgam of private and public entities. Some are national while others are international in scope. Some are active participants in the market while others have a coordinating or regulatory role.

Table 3 gives some examples of the kinds of organisations that may be involved in shipping issues and operations. These organisations are discussed in the following pages. The list is far from complete. A more complete list would include labor agencies (unions and government), special interest groups related to exports and imports, shipbuilding, coast guard and navy, and many more.

THE RISE AND FALL OF NATIONAL SHIPPING POLICIES

Table 3: Some of the key players in the formulation of shipping policy

	National		International	
	Market participant	**Coordination/ regulation**	**Market participant**	**Coordination/ regulation**
Private	shipowners, shippers, forwarders, insurance, etc	shipowners' associations, shippers' councils	consortia and alliances, MNC's logistics departments	international shipowners' associations, international shippers' councils
State	state owned shipping companies, state agencies as buyers of shipping services	ministries of transport, antitrust agencies, environmental agencies	?	IMO OECD MINCONMAR UNCTAD WTO

Table 4: Top 12 merchant fleets by ownership as at 1 October 2001 (millions dwt)

	Tankers	Dry bulk	Container vessels	Other	World total
Greece	64	70	4	8	146
Japan	37	49	5	9	100
Norway	40	12	1	7	60
United States	30	5	1	5	41
China	6	23	4	7	40
Hong Kong	16	17	1	2	36
Germany	5	5	17	6	33
Korea (South)	7	14	3	2	26
Taiwan	3	10	7	1	21
United Kingdom	9	5	4	2	19
Singapore	9	3	3	1	17
Denmark	7	2	6	2	17
Russia	6	2	1	5	13
World	333	291	74	94	791
Top 12 (% of World)	72	74	78	58	72

Source: MARAD, Washington DC (*www.marad.dot.gov/Marad_StatisticsMarAd*).

Of course, shipping policy is first of all associated with the actions of governments. One might perhaps expect that those most actively pursuing national shipping policies would be those with the largest fleets. However, this is not the case today although it certainly was true during much of the 19th and 20th centuries. Table 4 lists the top 12 ship-owning nations in the world. The table is based on actual (beneficial) ownership and is therefore different from the distribution of countries by flag of vessel. Of the 12 nations in Table 4, most are known for their liberal shipping policies. The main exceptions would be the United States and China. Both maintain protectionist measures. The case of the

United States is rather complex though. By ownership the United States is the fourth largest maritime nation in the world, but based on flag it is only number 12. In the year 2002 nearly two-thirds (63%) of its merchant marine was under foreign flag operating under highly competitive conditions. Thus, the United States in fact has two maritime teams: one under US flag and largely dependent upon protective and promotional policies while the other, larger team under foreign flags enjoys nothing less than full freedom from government intervention. Ironically, this team will regularly enlist US government help to fight restrictive national shipping policy in other countries.

Economic versus safety and environmental regulation

In general, we can distinguish between, on the one hand, laws and regulations that are *economic* in nature, dealing with matters such as market access, competition, and subsidies and taxation, and on the other hand, rules and regulations that, while they do have economic implications through their impact on costs, aim primarily at questions of *safety and environmental* impact.

Institutions and agencies involved in economic regulation can be national or international. In the case of foreign trade, some institutions are primarily devoted to the promotion of full liberalisation and free markets, others are more oriented towards coordination and cooperation, while yet others have sought to interfere directly in markets and to redistribute resources by means other than market forces.

Institutions of particular importance to shipping are the United Nations and its specialised agencies, UNCTAD and the International Maritime Organisation (IMO). The Commission of the European Union is becoming an important player in matters relating to international shipping. Another agency, although it represents only a single country, may be included here, namely the Federal Maritime Commission of the United States. The World Trade Organisation (WTO) – a successor to the GATT framework – is a cornerstone in the institutional framework for trade but has yet to arrive at final rules and procedures for shipping.

Table 5: Regulatory levels and institutions involved in shipping policy

Institutional level / Regulatory activity	Coordination	Liberalisation	Redistribution/ promotion
Multilateral	IMO/OECD	OECD/WTO	UNCTAD
National/regional	MINCONMAR	FMC (USA) EU/European Commission	MARAD (USA) MINCONMAR
Industry groups	International Chamber of Commerce (ICC) INTERTANKO/CENSA European Shippers' Council		

THE RISE AND FALL OF NATIONAL SHIPPING POLICIES

Table 5 highlights some of the diversity and contradictions present in shipping policy. The seven content cells are not always mutually exclusive and inevitably represent a gross simplification of a fuzzy reality constantly subjected to change. This is illustrated by certain agencies appearing in more than one column.

In the table regulatory activities have been grouped under three headings: *coordination*, *liberalisation* and *redistribution/promotion*. Coordination refers to the harmonisation of activities undertaken by a larger group. While the coordinating agency may not independently pursue a set of policies, its task is to make sure that the policies and activities of its members or constituent parts are coordinated in such a manner as to maximise the collective impact of these changes.

Some key agencies and their principal roles

IMO, the International Maritime Organisation, a United Nations agency, is charged with improving safety at sea for seafarers and vessels. Its purposes, *inter alia*, are "to provide machinery for cooperation among governments in the field of governmental regulation and practices relating to technical matters of all kinds affecting shipping engaged in international trade, ..."[19]

The OECD, Organisation for Economic Cooperation and Development, produces "internationally agreed instruments, decisions and recommendations to promote rules of the game in areas where multilateral agreement is necessary for individual countries to make progress in a globalised economy".[20] However, the OECD goes beyond mere coordination. It actively promotes liberalisation of shipping through its policies in a Recommendation of its Council, entitled *Common Principles of Shipping Policy*.[21] An additional memorandum, *Understanding of Common Shipping Principles*,[22] signed in 1993 with representatives of the NIS (New Independent States of the former Soviet Union) and the CEECs (Central and Eastern European Countries), further elaborates the Principles and specifically includes multimodal services. Additional negotiations in 1999 with DNMEs (Dynamic Non-member Economies, i.e., Chile, Hong Kong (China), Malaysia, Singapore, Chinese Taipei and Thailand)[23] gave rise to another memorandum extending the principles to a number of countries in Asia and Chile. There are presently discussions going on with China that may lead to the inclusion of China in the "club" of nations professing commitment to liberal shipping policies.

The WTO (World Trade Organisation) is the main institution responsible for global trade. At the heart the WTO framework – known as the multilateral trading system – are the WTO's agreements, negotiated and signed by a large majority of the world's trading nations, and ratified in their parliaments. These agreements are the legal ground-rules for international commerce. Essentially, they are contracts, guaranteeing member countries important trade rights. They also bind governments to keep their trade policies within agreed limits to everybody's benefit.[24]

What makes the WTO different from most other organisations in the international field, is that it binds governments to certain rules and that these rules constitute enforceable contracts. Interestingly, but perhaps not surprisingly, given the ever-present nationalist undercurrent in shipping, WTO has so far not been successful in including shipping in its activities. A number of negotiations have taken place but the lack of success bears clear witness to the reluctance of most countries to accept binding rules for shipping. The inclusion of WTO in Table 5 is therefore provisional, reflecting hope rather than reality.

UNCTAD (The United Nations Conference on Trade and Development) was created in the 1960s at a time when many former colonies achieved their independence and were struggling to develop their fledgling economies, often suffering badly from colonial mismanagement and exploitation. The UNCTAD mandate was to "maximise the trade, investment and development opportunities of developing countries and assist them in their efforts to integrate into the world economy on an equitable basis".[25] At the outset UNCTAD had hoped to create a greater place for developing countries in world markets by a combination of quotas and preferential systems, hence its place in the redistribution/promotion column. In the case study below we shall return to this question and how it applied to shipping.

As we move down Table 5 from the multilateral to the national and regional level, one finds institutions with widely different objectives. MINCONMAR (The Ministerial Conference of West and Central African States on Maritime Transport) provides a legal framework for the promotion of transit and transport efficiency in the region. The organisation played a particularly central role in the organisation of the Cotonou Round Tables referred to in the West African scenario discussed later. MINCONMAR also appears in the right hand column as it has actively argued for and promoted some form of special status for West African shipping.

The European Commission has pursued a relatively aggressive posture in promoting freer competition in shipping and in seeking to apply the full force of anticompetitive legislation to shipping, even in areas where shipping has often been exempted from such legislation.

The United States promotes competition in shipping and has at times attempted to subject liner shipping to the full force of anti-trust legislation.[26] Yet, it also promotes its national flag fleet through various programs administered by the US Maritime Administration[27]: "The overall mission of the Maritime Administration (MARAD) is to promote the development and maintenance of an adequate, well-balanced United States merchant marine, sufficient to carry the Nation's domestic waterborne commerce and a substantial portion of its waterborne foreign commerce, and capable of serving as a naval and military auxiliary in time of war or national emergency."

The last row in Table 5 makes reference to a number of industry organisations that have a strong vested interest in shipping. These groups all share an interest in the efficiency of shipping but at the same time may represent opposing views. These organisations often play an important role as advisors to their governments and international organisations during the formulation of shipping policies.[28]

The above is but a brief review of some of the participants in the diverse and complex process that is shipping policy. While the general trend appears to be towards ever increasing liberalisation, there is no lack of counter arguments.

THE RISE AND FALL OF NATIONAL SHIPPING POLICIES 485

There are several aspects of shipping not covered in Table 5. Of particular importance is the Law of the Sea (UNCLOS) that deals specifically with the right and obligations of flag states.[29]

3. NATIONAL SHIPPING POLICY: THREE COUNTRIES – THREE POLICIES

Policy and circumstance

Policy may be more the result of circumstances than of "rational" analysis. National policies are based on "national interest", which is essentially a polite word for "self-interest". Three cases with which the author has personal experience, may serve to illustrate the interaction between policy and circumstance.

Canada, China and West Africa represent three diverging examples of shipping policy. Canada can be described as a case of *laisser faire*, consistent with globalisation and the trend towards privatisation and reliance on the market place. China pursues a strategy of bilateral (and unilateral) maritime expansion, covering not only shipping, but also ports, shipbuilding, and all aspects of maritime activities. Since they achieved independence in the 1960s, the nations of West and Central Africa have pursued a policy ostensibly of a multilateral nature within the framework of *The UN Code of Conduct for Liner Conferences*. In application, such policies have often been unilateral and arbitrary, imposing heavy penalties on shippers and shipowners alike.

These three examples could in turn be seen as (1) confirming the *death of national shipping policy*; (2) illustrating the *resurgence of traditional maritime power*, actively promoted by the world's most populous nation which is expected to become the world's largest economy within the next twenty years; (3) demonstrating the need for regional approaches to the *difficulties associated with developing efficient multimodal systems in developing countries where limited cargo volume constitute a serious impediment to the development* of efficient, competitive markets. Together, these examples may serve to bring a modicum of *nuance* to the questions surrounding the relevance of national shipping policies in a global marketplace. These examples also suggest that the debate on shipping policy is likely to resurface repeatedly as an important issue in trade disputes in the years ahead.

3.1 Canada: Relying on world markets for its international maritime transport needs

The question: to have a policy or not?

In 1984, the Canadian Minister of Transport, The Hon. Lloyd Axworthy, appointed a Task Force "to evaluate changing conditions in the international shipping market and the possible need for measures to encourage the expansion of the Canadian deep-sea fleet".[30] When the author of this chapter in his capacity as chairman of the Task Force had his first meeting with the Minister, he inquired whether, in the Minister's view, Canada simply did not have any shipping policy, or whether Canada had a policy of *not* having a policy. The Minister's answer was succinct and disarmingly frank: "I was hoping *you* could tell me."

The Task Force had 14 members who represented a cross-section of shipowners, labor, users of shipping services (primarily exporters), and academics. At the outset, it was clear that the majority of the members had a vision of some form of "core fleet" that would show the Maple Leaf in major ports around the world. It was felt by many that such a fleet was important to maintain a labor force skilled in all aspects of navigation and vessel operations, and that vessels were needed to secure Canadian supply lines in the case of armed conflict.

The role of exporters

As the work progressed it quickly became evident that Canadian exporters were determined to prevent any form of national support for a Canadian flag fleet. Their opposition was based on the fear that directly or indirectly, they would be made to bear the cost of any such "promotional" or protectionistic policies. In essence, their argument was: "you may create a few jobs in shipping, but for each job so created, we will lose many more jobs in our exporting industries". While no hard proof for this position was offered, it carried a lot of weight. This was a case where the lobbies of exporters and resource industries by far outweighed the pressures from maritime unions.

The national defence argument

The national defence argument was dispensed with by an Admiral who pointed out two things: First, in wartime, the vessels most needed by Canada would be flexible, manoeuverable vessels such as medium-sized RO-ROs to carry soldiers and their equipment. Generally, these are not the vessels used in Canada's foreign trade. Secondly, he pointed out that in the case of war, Canada's NATO obligation was to supply troops in Northeast Europe, and specifically along the Norwegian coast, and then commented: "Don't you think we could ask the Norwegians to come and get us?" He later "corrected" himself in a written submission, but even so, the message was clear: a merchant marine under Canadian flag would be of no or at best marginal value militarily.

Choice: a "core" fleet or reliance on world shipping markets

The main argument against the creation of a core fleet or any other measure to support a Canadian merchant marine, turned out to be the simple recognition that such a fleet would not be competitive, and would therefore depend on subsidies or various cargo reservation schemes. Secondly, it was concluded that world shipping markets work well and that there is little prospect of any long-term shortage of tonnage. Subsequently, the Task Force's key recommendation was: "... that the federal government not take steps towards the establishment of a core deep-sea fleet under Canadian flag."[31] In so recommending, the Task Force specifically rejected arguments relating to balance of payment, maritime employment, auxiliary industries employment, and strengthened national security. The recommendation to not promote a national fleet was supported by twelve of the fourteen Task Force members, including shipowner representatives. The two who opposed this conclusion were labor representatives.

The Task Force recommendations, in characteristic Canadian fashion, did not give rise to any new *policy*. It is perhaps symptomatic that a Transport Canada document on *National Marine Policy* (1995) makes no reference to *international* activities. It does state that "reflected throughout the National Marine Policy is the principle of commercialisation". National Marine Policy in Canada today is concentrated on (and limited to) "Ports, Seaway (St. Lawrence), Ferries and Pilotage".

There appears to have been one modest, yet important legislative spin-off from the Task Force Report. It contained a recommendation that the government "create a fiscal environment conducive to the establishment and maintenance of international ship management activities in Canada." This was deemed important as many large Canadian exporters were interested in managing vessels from Canada. It was also hoped that certain foreign shipowners might be interested in moving their management activities to Canada. This concept, which at first was strongly resisted by the Canadian Minister of Finance, was later pursued by the Province of British Columbia and various private groups in Vancouver. Eventually these groups were successful in obtaining amendments to the Income Tax Act (December 17, 1991).[32] As a result, there are today at least 25 shipping groups in Canada (International Shipping Corporations or "ISCs") that have taken advantage of the changes in the tax law.

On the surface, the Canadian stance toward international shipping appears to be one of *laisser faire*. In political terms, it may be based more on the structure of the Canadian economy with its heavy reliance on export markets rather than on any profound belief in the market place. Canada does support efforts to modernise and develop efficient infrastructure (such as ports, waterways, pilotage) that facilitate international shipping. But also for infrastructure, the key word is commercialisation. Canada's deep-sea fleet, under Canadian flag, remains marginal and receives no support for its international operations.

3.2 China: A maritime superpower with a future

An expansionist maritime policy

China has joined the league of the top maritime nations in the world. As shown by Table 4 presented earlier in this chapter, as of October 1, 2001 China ranked number 5 in the world among the world's merchant fleets, based on total deadweight tons and beneficial ownership. Its share of world tonnage was an impressive 5 percent. This achievement is the direct result of an expansionist maritime policy.[33]

During more than a century of humiliating foreign dominance, the Chinese had observed the role of shipping as a key element in trade. The communist party was determined to learn from that lesson, and declared maritime self-reliance to be a cornerstone in the development of the new China. The Chinese Minister of Foreign Trade, Mr. Li Chiang, declared in a speech to the United Nations General Assembly in 1975[34] that:

"A country should mainly rely on the strength and wisdom of its own people, *control its own economic lifelines*, make useful use of its own resources, work hard, increase production, practice economy and develop its national economy step by step and in a planned way." (Emphasis added).

To control its shipping lines, the Chinese government's stated policy is to carry all of its domestic waterborne trade and as much of its foreign trade as possible in Chinese-flag vessels. Generally China exports on a CIF basis, while importing at FOB, meaning that China usually is the controlling shipper for both outbound and inbound trade.

Bilateral cargo rights exclude cross-traders

China generally subscribes to the concept that nations have something approaching a legal right to carry "their cargo" and its stated objective is to maximise its share of shipping in its export and import trades. If its trade partner cannot carry its share of the trade, China has sought to take the entire traffic, excluding cross-traders. And it is important to note that China seeks to extend this policy to bulk as well as to liner shipping, having argued for instance that a high foreign market share in one segment should be offset in another. In short, in the Chinese view, cargo sharing and control should apply to total traffic between two countries. As a result, China has expressed a strong desire to work within bilateral agreements. It is worth noting that China has frequently used similar arguments in favor of 'balanced trade" with each of its trade partners.

By 1949 all that remained of ships under Chinese flag prior to 1949, were a handful of oceangoing vessels, totaling a paltry 34,000 tons. (Many vessels had left for Taiwan or Hong Kong where they provided the basis for new merchant marines). The growth of China's merchant marine since then has been remarkable. Heine[35] reports that by the mid-1980s Chinese flag vessels carried over 40% (mid-1980s) of Chinese oceanborne trade, a share far higher than for most other countries. However, given China's tremendous export growth over the last two decades, it seems likely that China has not been able to increase this ratio significantly. The Chinese fleet, after a tremendous spurt in size during the 1970s, slowed its expansion significantly during the 1980s, and even more during the first half of the 1990s. It is important though to note that the Chinese fleet has grown and continues to do so, substantially faster than the world fleet, which has had for result that the Chinese fleet keeps climbing towards the top of key players in world shipping.

In 1982 China's entire container fleet had a total capacity of just 9,800 TEU slot capacity, the equivalent of no more than two modern vessels. By 1995, this had risen to 150,773 TEU slots, equal to 3.4% of world capacity. Presently, COSCON, the container line of COSCO, China's national shipping and logistics company, has a capacity of 230,000 TEUs. And COSCO alone carried about 30% of China's foreign trade during the 1990s.

Greater China: a future maritime superpower?

There is a broader context, which should not be forgotten when considering China's future role in world shipping. Collaboration between Hong Kong, Taiwan and China is increasing in all matters,[36] and the People's Republic considers the first two as integral parts of China. If we consider for a minute the three economies as separate entities in the context of shipping, it is interesting to reflect on their comparative advantage: Hong Kong's management, marketing and financial skills are of world class; the same may be said of Taiwan in the areas of technology and entrepreneurship; for all practical purposes, "mainland" China has an unlimited supply of skilled seamen willing to work at low wages, a strong ship-building industry and in 1996 produced 54% of the world's maritime containers.

Putting *the three maritime Chinas* together, today as an illustrative thought, but possibly a reality in a not too distant future, would yield a super fleet, surpassed only by the flag-of-convenience fleets of Panama and Liberia. In 1996 the world's largest container line, Evergreen - Uniglory was Taiwanese. The fourth largest company was COSCO. OOCL (Hong Kong) was number 15 among the world's company while Yangming of Taiwan was number 14. These four companies together represented 10.8 percent of world TEU slot space as of 1 November 1996 and 12.7 percent of TEU capacity on order.[37]

China's ambitions in maritime shipping continue to cause concern elsewhere and the FMC regularly protests about "the apparent Chinese policy of seeking to control the trade rather than allow market forces to operate. In practice, this policy has been characterised by increasing restrictions imposed unilaterally by the Chinese government on foreign carriers' operations".[38] Some believed that China might wish to liberalise its policies after joining the WTO, but so far this does not appear to be the case. A Chinese decree, "Regulations of the PRC on the International Marine Transportation", became effective on 1 January 2002. As Chinese regulations often are less than transparent, the full impact of this new legislation is not known. The FMC has therefore launched an investigation on its impact.[39]

3.3 West African shipping: a bankrupt new international economic order

What makes the countries of West and Central Africa quite unique in world shipping is the vigor with which the region has pursued protectionist policies aimed at promoting the development of strong national fleets. These policies include the creation of state-owned national lines, the establishment of strong state-controlled or state-sponsored shippers' councils (including "freight bureaux", selling or controlling cargo space) and logistics companies to control cargo flows and the allocation of cargoes to shipping lines, combined with an extensive system of cargo reservation, based on the *UNCTAD Code* cargo sharing formula which African nations take to mean that liner traffic between two countries should be shared on a 40-40-20 basis with a maximum of 20% going to cross-traders, the remainder of the traffic is to be shared between to the trade partners.[40]

A well-intentioned policy that failed

The case of West and Central African shipping is a sad example of a well-intentioned policy that failed miserably and which inflicted high costs not only on shipping companies but also on shippers, hurting exports and imports. In an attempt to alleviate conditions and to remove the root causes of the difficulties associated with shipping in the region, a Round Table was convened in Cotonou, Benin in 1992. The key participants were Members of MINCONMAR (Ministerial Conference of West and Central African States on Maritime Transport), representatives from the World Bank, the European Community, and CIDA (the Canadian International Development Agency). The author of this chapter served as Chairman of the Round Table, a daunting yet highly educational experience.[41]

Although there was no lack of extreme positions at the first Cotonou Round Table, there was also a serious will on the part of many to reach for new approaches. Yet, it quickly became clear that there would be no short-cuts to easy solutions. The World Bank had hoped that the use of *conditionality* – establish criteria to be met before loans would be disbursed – could expedite a transition towards full deregulation of shipping. For most Africans this appeared to be unrealistic and unreasonable, feeling that instead donor countries and agencies had an obligation to help African shipping to survive. The Cotonou experience, part of the Sub-Saharan Trade & Transport Project, turned out to be a long process, not yet finished.

At Cotonou the entrenched protectionistic, "Codist" positions hardly moved, and the general tenor of the Round Table was that ways must be found to save African national fleets through various measures such as capital infusion, creation of regional shipping lines, etc. Recommendations were vague, except for recommending studies to be undertaken, and did not recognise, implicitly or explicitly, the near total failure of West African shipping. The recommended studies were carried out by consultants from Europe and Canada and were presented at Cotonou II five years later.

Cotonou II (June 1997): creeping realism

The five years between the two round tables was a time of continued restructuring and competitive upheaval in international shipping. What was left of truly West African shipping went under with only one significant exception (CAMSHIP). Some companies survived on paper but only as an instrument to collect fees from allocating and selling 'traffic rights'. By the time Cotonou II got under way, the African debate had changed significantly, and the language used had become forward looking.

A new realism is reflected in the final recommendations adopted at Cotonou. A key element in these recommendations is that the MINCONMAR States (West and Central Africa) should aim to join the various conventions dealing with international shipping and trade and that shippers' councils, the main instruments of the existing restrictive policies, should cease their cargo allocation systems and should evolve from state instruments towards genuine user-oriented councils, representing not the interests of the shipping industry, but of exporters and importers.

One of the interesting lessons learnt from Cotonou as well as from the previously discussed Canadian Task Force on Deep-Sea Shipping is that to achieve genuine change in shipping policies takes an exceptionally long time and requires a lot of time-consuming consultation and 'education' of all involved.

Policy making: a slow and lengthy process

A World Bank study of policy reform provides a very useful review of the steps and difficulties involved in transport policy reform. The study (Heggie, 1991) suggests that deregulating transport industries require from 10 to 15 years. The processes involved are identified as follows[42]:

1. Preliminary agreement on the need for reform — 3–5 years
2. Detailed examination of options available — 1–2 years
3. Preliminary consultations with parties likely to be affected — 1 year
4. Attempts to avoid reform through rationalisation — 2–3 years
5. Implementation of reform — 2–3 years
6. Introduction of new policies — 1 year

The Cotonou *process* has taken West African shipping policy through steps 1 and 2 above. The depth of changes having taken place in attitudes and thinking becomes far more evident when one meets privately with businesses, organisations and institutions involved. The language has definitely changed and there is a much greater recognition among mid-level managers and consultants that the international context of shipping has changed irrevocably, that it will continue to change, and that as a result, Africa *must* adjust. As one African expert said in a private conversation: "We understand the need for change but much is at stake for the older generation. Changes *will happen*, but we must do it the African way." The exchange suggested that steps three and four above may already be under way, but also that patience is needed.

Following Cotonou II, the MINCONMAR Ministers of Transport held a meeting in December 1997 in Abuja. At that meeting the Ministers endorsed the recommendations of the second Round Table towards liberalisation of market access and institutional reform. So, the long march towards a new regional and more liberal regime has started. In some countries (Niger and Cameroon) reforms are proceeding rapidly, in others it may take a long while. Structural readjustment is neither a simple nor quick process.

3.4 Lessons from the three scenarios

Canada – like most OECD countries – has no competitive advantage in shipping and has come to accept its need to rely on open markets to supply its shipping services. In so doing it benefits from its integration with the United States logistics systems both within North America and for overseas services. Being part of a large trade system with massive amounts of cargoes, it benefits from aggressive competition among ports, shipping lines and other suppliers of logistics services.

China – benefiting from competitive strength in shipping coupled with a vast "national" freight market – has been able to build up one of the strongest maritime fleets in the world. In order to achieve this position, it has not hesitated to use its market power for leverage.

West Africa – lacking financial resources and having a very thin cargo base – has not been able to build or maintain national fleets despite highly protectionist policies.

4. SUMMARY AND CONCLUSION

In today's global economy shipping is decidedly one of the most international, footloose industries of all. The ever increasing interdependence among nations not only in trade of goods and services, but also in labor and environmental matters, means that traditional national shipping policies, aimed at protecting the "national interest", have lost their *raison-d'être*. Yet, there is an increasing need for international cooperation in a wide range of areas, including labor (such as manning standards, training, minimum social conditions), environment and safety (e.g., double-hull vessels, collusion avoidance systems, classification standards) and competition (including antitrust rules regarding market dominance, cartels, alliances).

It is not only the "national" in national shipping policies that needs to be redefined. Also "shipping" needs to be critically considered. Shipping refers to the technology used and not the needs satisfied in the market. The vessel is but a link in a complex and diversified logistics function. In liner shipping – but also to some extent in bulk operations – a large share of the activities are land based. Vessels are integrated not only into transport chains as in multimodal operations but interact directly with the various functions within the firm using the transport services. Transport choice affects production, financing and marketing strategies. While shipping *per se* may be a commodity, supplying standard products or services, logistics services can be highly differentiated and serve to link firms in highly integrated, idiosyncratic distribution systems, based on transaction cost minimisation.[43] As a result, barriers to entry and exit for every member in the chain may be raised significantly.

While the unit of analysis in traditional shipping policy was the vessel, today the unit of analysis needs to be much broader, oriented towards the logistics chain. At the same time, questions of externalities in areas such as environment and safety need to be specifically considered. Future analysis will need to seek new paths, based on new problem definitions. In many areas data are inadequate or non-existing. There is a great need for developing new measurements and data as well as for institution building and training. The maritime economist of the future will need to develop interdisciplinary skills and to cooperate with researchers from other fields. Most of all perhaps, he will need solid knowledge of the realities not only of his field but of the various links in the larger distribution chain.

ENDNOTES

1. Norton, R.D. (1986): "Industrial Policy and American Renewal", *Journal of Economic Literature*, Vol. XXIV, No. 1, pp. 1–40.
2. Reich, R.B. (1984): "Small State, Big Lesson", *The Boston Observer*, 3 July, No. 7, p. 32. Here quoted from Norton, *ibid.*
3. For a discussion of this point, see Sletmo, G.K. (2001): "The End of National Shipping Policy? A Historical Perspective on Shipping Policy in A Global Economy", *International Journal of Maritime Economics*, Vol. 3, No. 4, pp. 333–350.
4. Sturmey, S.G. (1975): "A consideration of the ends and means of national shipping policies", in S.G. Sturmey, *Shipping Economics – Collected Papers* (London, The Macmillan Press).
5. This distinction is based on OECD (2002): *Regulatory Issues in International Maritime Markets*, Section II, pp. 26–42 (Paris, *www.oecd.org*).
6. Sletmo, G.K. (2001): "The End of National Shipping Policy? A Historical Perspective on Shipping Policy in A Global Economy", *op. cit.*
7. Goss, R.O., and Marlow, P.B. (1993): "Internationalism, Protectionism and Interventionism in Shipping", in Gwilliam, K.M. (ed.) *Current Issues in Maritime Economics* (Dordrecht, Kluwer Academic Publishers), pp. 46–56. Sturmey (1975), *op. cit.*, pp. 180–181, came up with an even longer list, including terms such as "national prestige", "employment for seamen", "counter discriminatory practices by others".
8. *Guardian* (2002): "Today's Issues: Steel Tariffs", March 6.
9. Goss, R.O., and Marlow, P.B. (1993), p. 63.
10. Whitney, D. (1990): "Conferees Ok Double Hulls for Oil Tankers", in *Anchorage Daily News*, 13 July.
11. Gold, E. (1981): *Maritime Transport – The Evolution of International Marine Policy and Shipping Law* (Lexington, Mass., Lexington Books).
12. Gold, E. (1981), *ibid.* p. 45.
13. Sletmo, G.K. (2001), *op. cit.*, p. 339.
14. *The Bible*, 107 Psalm, 23rd and 24th verses.
15. Padfield, P. (2000): *Maritime Supremacy and the Opening of the Western Mind* (New York, The Overlook Press).
16. Sletmo, G.K. (1989): "Shipping's Fourth Wave: Ship management and Vernon's trade cycles", *Maritime Policy & Management*, Vol. 16, No. 4, pp. 293–303. For a further discussion of flags of convenience, see also Sletmo, G.K., and Holste, S. (1993): "Shipping and the competitive advantage of nations: the role of international ship registers", *Maritime Policy & Management*, Vol. 20, No. 3, pp. 243–255.
17. Iheduru, O.C. (1996): *The Political Economy of International Shipping in Developing countries* (Newark, University of Delaware Press), p. 21.
18. Herberger, A.J. (1995): "An American Perspective on Maritime Issues". Remarks before the Connecticut Maritime Association, June 29. Distributed by the Office of the Assistant Secretary for Public Affairs, US Department of Transportation.
19. IMO (2002): "About IMO" (London, *www.imo.org*).
20. OECD (2002B): "About OECD" (Paris, *www.oecd.org*).
21. OECD (2002C): "Recommendation of The Council concerning Common Principles of Shipping Policy" (Paris, *www.oecd.org/pdf/M00001000/M00001994.pdf*).
22. OECD (2002D): "Understanding of Common Shipping Principles" (Consultations with NIS/CEEC 1993) (Paris, *http://www1.oecd.org/dsti/sti/transpor/sea/act/consult.htm*).
23. OECD (2002E): "Understanding of Common Shipping Principles" (Consultations with DNMEs) (Paris, *http://www1.oecd.org/media/release/nw99-110a.htm*).
24. WTO (2002): "WTO in Brief" (Geneva, *http://www.wto.org*).
25. UNCTAD (2002): "UNCTAD in Brief" (Geneva, *http://www.UNCTAD.org*).
26. For a comprehensive discussion of this point, see Sletmo, G.K., and Williams, E.W. (1981): *Liner Conferences in the Container Age* (New York, Macmillan).

494 NATIONAL AND INTERNATIONAL SHIPPING POLICIES

27. MARAD (2002): "Mission Statement" (Washington, DC, *http://www.marad.dot. gov/Offices/mission.html*).
28. The following are the key websites: ICC (2002): "About the ICC", *http://www.iccwbo.org*; European Shippers' Council (2002): "Home Page", *http://www.europeanshippers.com*; Intertanko (2002): "Home page", *http://www.intertanko.com/*; CENSA (Council of European and Japanese Shipowners) does not appear to have an independent website.
29. The following website is dedicated to UNCLOS (2002): "Home page", *http://www.un.org/Depts/los/index.htm*.
30. Sletmo, G.K. (1985): *Task Force on deep-Sea Shipping – Report to the Minister* (Ottawa, Transport Canada), April 1985 (TP 6347E), p. iii.
31. Sletmo, G.K. (1985) p. 51.
32. Seymour, J. (1998): "A Time for Change – An International Competitive Canadian Flag? Pragmatic Reform of the Canada Shipping Act is the Answer", *Canadian Transportation Research Forum: Proceedings of 33rd Annual Conference*, Edmonton, Alberta, May 25–28.
33. See also Sletmo, G.K. and Holste, S. (1989): "China's Open Door and Shipping". *Transport Policy Management & Technology Towards 2001*. Selected Proceedings of the Fifth World Conference on Transport Research (WCTR), Yokohama. Vol. III, pp. 557–571.
34. Heine, I.M. (1989): *China's Rise to Commercial Maritime Power* (Westport, Connecticut, Greenwood Press Inc.), p. 1, and note 1, p. 7.
35. Heine, I.M. (1989), *ibid.*
36. TimesNet Asia (1997) "HK-Taiwan strike flag deal", 1 July; "Cross-straits shipping begins", 1 May; "Shipping's strait-jacket", Oct. (Hong Kong, *http://www.tpl.com.sg/timesnet/indices/cnaship.html*).
37. *Containerisation International Yearbook 1997*, (Annual) (London, Emap Business Communications Limited), Table 2, p. 7.
38. FMC (1998): "Shipping Restrictions, Requirements And Practices Of The People's Republic Of China" (Docket No. 98-14) (Washington, DC).
39. FMC (2002): "Notice Of Inquiry On Restrictive Shipping Practices In People's Republic Of China" (NR 02-04) (Washington, DC).
40. Strictly speaking, the UNCTAD Code should apply only to liner traffic operated within a *conference system*, i.e., pricing agreement among the liner companies. The 40-40-20 scheme is given in the Code as an indication of how traffic can be shared. It is not a firm rule.
41. The following material is drawn from personal notes and summaries prepared by the World Bank (1997): *Trade and Transport in West and Central African States – A New Maritime Policy*, Report on Round Table Cotonou, 3–6 June 1997. Sub-Saharan Africa Transport Policy Program. SSATP Working Paper No. 30 (Washington, DC, Africa Region, The World Bank).
42. Heggie, I.G. (1991): *Designing Major Policy Reform*, World Bank Discussion Paper No. 115, Table 2, p. 12.
43. Williamson, O.E. (1975): *Markets and Hierarchies – Analysis and Antitrust Implications* (New York, The Free Press).

CHAPTER 22

SHIPPING POLICY IN THE GLOBALISATION ERA: THE INTER-RELATIONSHIP BETWEEN INTERNATIONAL, SUPRA-NATIONAL AND NATIONAL SHIPPING POLICIES

Michael Roe

Institute of Marine Studies, University of Plymouth, England, UK.
E-mail: M.Roe@plymouth.ac.uk

1. INTRODUCTION

The shipping industry is characterised by a number of very specific features which make it unlike almost any other. In particular it is inherently mobile – both physically in that ships can be moved with relative ease to a very large number of world locations – and in terms of capital, which involves no physical movement of assets necessarily but a transfer of ownership, registration or other features to wherever makes most financial sense. These two features are intrinsically tied together in that the capital mobility of shipping is enhanced by the physical mobility of the assets which makes any sort of compulsory national association very difficult.

These two features of mobility are also fundamentally important when it comes to the issue of policy, and in this chapter we shall be examining the derivation of shipping policy and in particular the relationship between shipping policies at different levels of imposition and origin – international, supra-national, national, regional and local. The issues of mobility outlined above are the major feature of shipping which drives policy at all levels, although not to the exclusion of a large range of other factors which need to be assessed. This chapter will also place shipping policy in the context of the growth of globalisation and its close relations, foreign direct investment and strategic alliances discussed in the recent works of Frankel,[1] Ryoo and Thanopoulou,[2] Thanopoulou *et al.*,[3] Peters,[4] Randay,[5] Sletmo[6] and Slack, Comtois and McCalla[7] – developments which the shipping industry has experienced often before any other and which are characteristic of the complexities that surround policy relationships in the industry.

This chapter is structured into seven sections. The second outlines the development of research into shipping policy and examines the range of different studies that have taken place across the world and the common themes that have emerged.

The third section provides a model of the major themes that underlie shipping policy today and which are foremost in determining the detailed policy initiatives that have emerged in the late 20th and early 21st centuries. It also incorporates the development of a new model of shipping policy that attempts to represent all the influences that drive and direct policy-making at each level.

Using this new model, the fourth section introduces the concepts of spatial policy levels – international, supra-national, national, regional and local – and provides examples of activities at each level. Here, the specific problems associated with deriving effective and inter-linked policies in the shipping industry begin to become apparent.

Policy can never emerge in any sector without interest groups – government, industry, employees, pressure groups etc. – and shipping is no exception. Section five of the chapter looks at the role of interest groups using the model provided by Aspinwall[8] and other work by Lu[9] and how these affect the inter-relationships between the spatial levels that exist.

Section six follows the work of Ledger and Roe[10] and examines the contextual factors that affect the industry in the derivation of policies; this further illustrates the problems of linking policies in shipping between the spatial levels outlined in section three.

The final section incorporates the role of globalisation and its impact upon shipping industry policies. In particular it focuses upon the problems of reconciling the linkages between the levels of policy that exist and an industry that works outside of many of the constraints that these policy levels imply. The chapter ends with a summary of the issues and conclusions for the future.

2. SHIPPING POLICY RESEARCH – A SPATIAL PERSPECTIVE

Shipping policy is an area of research that has been widely studied over many years focusing on issues from subsidies to safety, the environment to employment, from taxation to inter-modalism and more. The key theme of this chapter is the problems inherent in linking together the different spatial levels of policy-making. The discussion deliberately focuses on the literature on shipping policy at the international, supra-national and national levels as including at this stage the regional and local dimensions and regimes of shipping policy would render the discussion both too specific and complicated; for this reason they are incorporated in the discussion later in the text.

The research publications noted here are not exhaustive but indicative of some of the trends in spatial shipping policy that exist. The reader is advised to read further using these sources as a first step.

The international level of policy-making has been well covered over the years and important works include those by Gold[11] on the international maritime sector in general, Schrier et al.[12] on liberalisation in shipping, Behnam[13] on UNCTAD's role in the shipping sector, Moyer[14] and his analysis of shipping subsidies, Frankel's[15,16,1] works on shipping, logistics and ports, Yannopoulos[17] on shipping policy in general, Ademuni-Odeke's work[18] on protectionism and shipping, Li and Wonham's[19] discussion of the specific policy issues relating to safety, and the earlier seminal work by Goss.[20]

Examples of work at the supra-national level, can be found in the extensive discussion and publication at the European Union level including the seminal works by Bredima-Savopoulou and Tzoannos,[21] Wang,[22] Hart et al.,[23] Peeters et al.[24] and Aspinwall,[8] and the journal articles by Van Der Linden[25] and Paixao and Marlow.[26] In addition, the over-arching supra-national issues and their conflict at national level are discussed in Brooks[27] in terms of liner shipping policies and the relationship between the USA, Canada and the EU. There is also a large number of other publications which dwell on the specifics of policy at the EU level and the complexities of imposing such policies on nation state members who may or may not be willing to co-operate. Aspinwall's work[8] here is especially significant and will be referred to later in some depth.

In East Europe, the work by Ledger and Roe,[10,28] and Roe[29] dominates the discussion of shipping policy issues in a framework where there is no overriding authority (unlike in the European Union) but where regional commonalities are sufficient to suggest that a supra-national consideration of policies and policy implementation is appropriate. The authors stress the difficulties of introducing common-themed policies for the distressed shipping industries of Poland, Romania, Bulgaria, Ukraine, Russia, Latvia and Lithuania in the light of common approaches to EU accession and the need to meet a set of widely applied rules and requirements. is clearly apparent. This is particularly the case where national demands (and even regional and local ones within a country) conflict with the more over-riding needs and demands of a future supra-national authority.

Other pseudo supra-national policy work is typified by that of Hawkins and Gray,[30,31] Sun and Zhang[32] and Hawkins[33] for the Asia-Pacific region which again lacks a supra-national authority to give it coherence and even less so than East Europe, lacks the over-riding driving force of potential EU membership which acts to compel national policies to work with each other and at different levels.

At a national policy-making level the published work is extensive and only a few sources can be noted here. In terms of UK policy much has been produced recently following the introduction of a tonnage tax system – an issue itself that raises conflicting views with respect to the requirements of the EU, relations with neighbouring countries and the international (for example through the effect on flags of convenience) and regional (for example employment) implications. Particularly significant publications include Brownrigg, Dawe and Mann,[34] and broader policy discussions can also be found in Colvin and Marks,[35] Gardner[36] and Gardner, Naim and Obando-Rojas.[37]

Discussion of policies in other countries is sizeable. For example, Poland receives attention from Walenciak, Constantinou and Roe[38] and Wrona and Roe,[39] Taiwan from Lu,[9] the USA from Whitehurst,[40] Iran from Mirmiran,[41] the USA from Sletmo and Williams,[42] Nigeria from Omosun[43] and Nasiru,[44] Japan from Goto,[45] Turkey from Yercan,[46] Yercan and Roe[47] and Barla et al.,[48] China from Flynn[49] and Sun and Zhang,[50] and Korea from Kokuryo,[51] Lee[52,53] and Song, Cullinane and Roe.[54] There are many others for other countries of the world emphasising the significance of the national level of policy-making that exists in shipping and its importance in relationship with other spatial levels.

3. THE FACTORS THAT DRIVE SHIPPING POLICY

Hoyle and Knowles[55] provide a basis for analysing the generic factors that underlie the emergence of transport policy at the end of the twentieth century. These factors can be used as a basis for understanding the development of shipping policy worldwide. From there we can go on to look at the development of shipping policy at different spatial levels before analysing the problems manifest in linking these policy levels together.

The work of Hoyle and Knowles[55] was directed essentially at understanding transport activity from a spatial perspective and for this reason is particularly suited to the discussion here, although they were not considering policy-making and application, nor the shipping sector specifically. Nevertheless, they identified five factors which can be applied to the shipping sector and the emergence of policy:

1. *Historical perspective* – the shipping sector is partly at least, directed by its past, either immediate or more distant. Thus traditional trade routes, port locations and maritime seats of power are all established features of the market place. Shipping policy tends to emerge from, or be associated with, the established network of trade patterns, centres of activity and centres of power. Any policy development – regardless of where it emanates from – has to take this into account as well as any changes to the world maritime scene such as the emergence of new routes, ports or maritime powers.[56]

2. *Nodes, networks and systems* – the shipping sector is essentially a combination of nodes (ports), networks (trading routes) and systems (the organisation and infrastructure that connects the other two items together – including communications, financial agreements, a legal framework, shipbrokers, freight forwarders etc.). Policy making ultimately is about all these elements and the environment it creates for them. This might be to encourage activity in a certain location, trade or at a certain time (e.g., favourable tax regimes in EU member states for shipping), or to control unwanted activity (e.g., sub-standard environmental or safety practices). Policy-makers have to understand the series of inter-linkages that exist if the policies they create are to be specific, meaningful and to achieve what they are aimed to do.

3. *Modal choice, intermodalism and flexibility* – shipping works in a highly competitive environment, not just within the industry itself but also in competition with other modes. In Europe, short-sea shipping faces intense competition from trucking across the whole continent, whilst even international rail services are increasingly competitive, as developments in East European infrastructure continue and new investments such as the Channel Tunnel and the Oresund link have become fully operational. Policy-makers need to have a full view of the choices available to shippers. In addition, the concept of intermodalism continues to expand with the support of the EU, so that shipping is now commonly seen as one link within a complex intermodal chain – including trucks and trailers on ferries, rail ferry operations, containerised services and the multitude of specialist facilities needed to ensure an adequate inter-linkage. Policy making in shipping has much to do here to ensure that developments are co-ordinated and that the shipping industry plays its full role.

4. *Deregulation and privatisation* – both deregulation (the reduction or removal of state control and influence) and privatisation (the partial or complete transfer of ownership from the state to the private sector) have been major

trends world-wide in many economic sectors for some years now. Shipping is no exception. The substantial developments in East Europe (Ledger and Roe[10]) have resulted in many examples of both trends, but elsewhere the privatisation of ports, state shipping companies and ancillary activities coupled with the attempts by the EU to reduce state interference through relaxing cabotage rules and reducing state subsidies have been apparent also. Shipping policies have reflected these trends since the 1980s and will continues to do so although paradoxically, the need for tighter safety and environmental controls and the desire to see reduced state interference has raised government involvement in policing the industry's activities.

5. *Holism* – shipping policies have to recognise that shipping is part of a much wider activity that is closely linked with a multitude of other economic, social, political and technological developments which both influence the shipping environment and are influenced by it. Thus shipping policy-makers have to understand that any changes, for example, in financial policy in the EU will have substantial impact upon the shipping investment climate and may necessitate further action incorporated into shipping policy measures. Shipping is an holistic activity that cannot be separated out from the complexity of the real world but this makes policy-making both difficult and at times, very slow.

4. SHIPPING POLICY – SPATIAL LEVELS OF ORIGIN AND IMPLEMENTATION

Policy in the shipping sector both emerges and is applied to the industry at different spatial levels. These are indicated in Figure 1 which attempts to summarise the shipping policy framework and the factors which influence the policies that emerge and the players involved in its development. They can be divided into five levels – in many ways a convenience as in real life there remains overlap between them – but at the same time there are clear distinguishing features of each which are significant for policy derivation and implementation. These different spatial policy levels and the problems of co-ordinating and making consistent their policy initiatives is the central theme of this chapter and has been identified in earlier work by Cafruny,[57,58,59] and Aspinwall.[8] The following discussion focuses on the relationships between these levels and the difficulties this sometimes presents.

At the highest spatial level there are *international policies* derived by international organisations which should, at least in theory, provide an over-arching structure for the policies derived at lower levels. In the shipping sector, the most prominent international policy-making institutions include the United Nations International Maritime Organisation (IMO), responsible amongst others for policies towards safety and the environment in shipping generally, and the Organisation for Economic Co-operation and Development (OECD), which is made up of the developed countries of the world and which is active particularly in shipbuilding policy world-wide. In each case, there is no compulsory legal requirement to abide by their policies and no direct powers of law-making rest with these

500 NATIONAL AND INTERNATIONAL SHIPPING POLICIES

Figure 1: The context for shipping policy-making

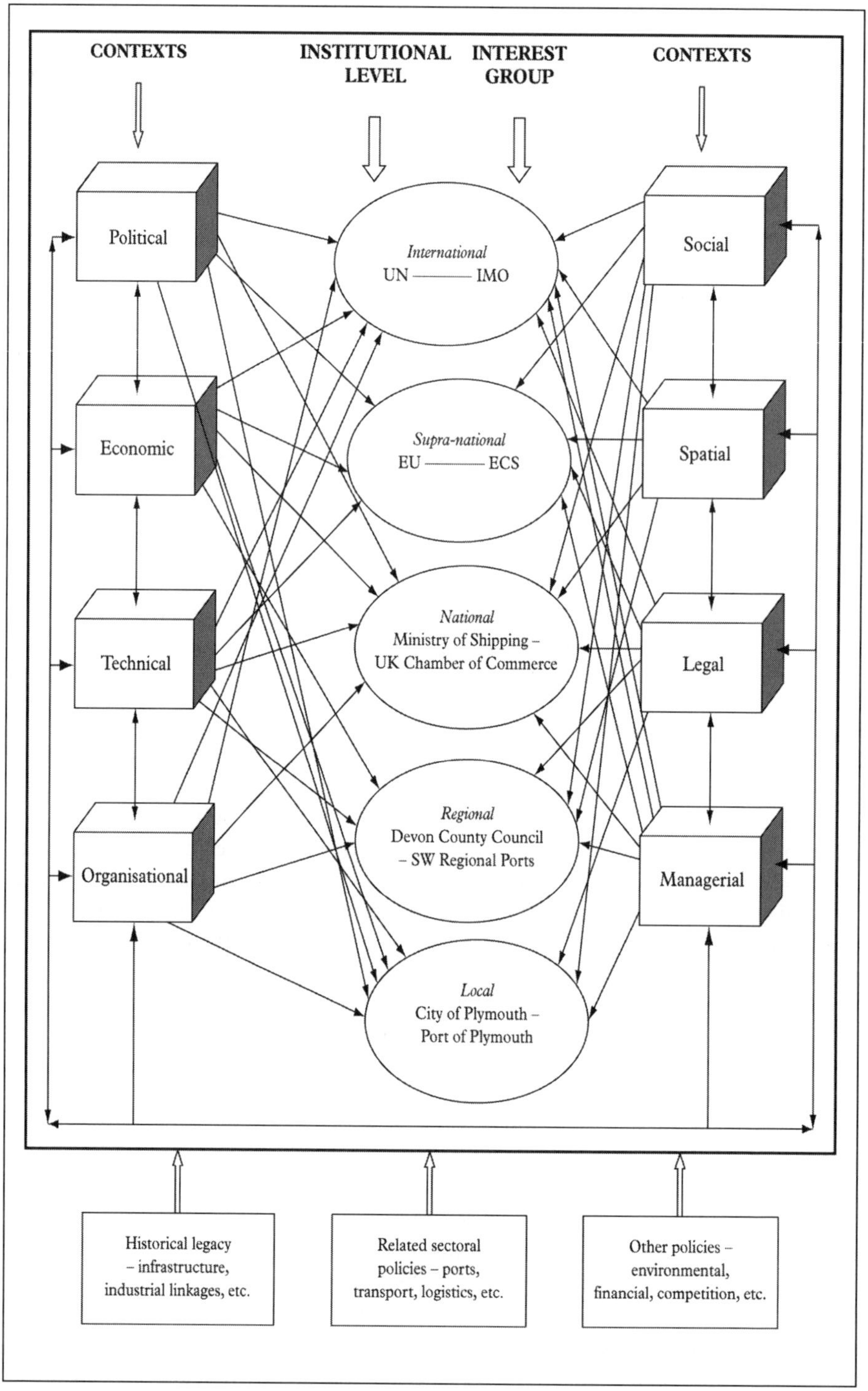

organisations but at the same time, membership by individual (and powerful) nations is extensive and requires that the policies and recommendations are followed. Hence in terms of influence they are most significant organisations.

The policy framework set at the international level provides the general agenda for that at the next level – *supra-national* – which is typified by that of the European Union (EU) which generates policies that are applied to all member states and in the case of the EU, is backed up by laws that are normally superior to national (member state) laws where there may be conflict (Brooks and Button[60]; Kiriazidis and Tzanidakis[61]; Paixao and Marlow[26]).

Alternative supra-national regimes include the North America Free Trade Association (NAFTA) with a series of maritime related policies but no law-making powers,[27] and in historical terms, the Council for Mutual Economic Assistance (CMEA) which represented the countries of the Former Soviet bloc but which again had no legislative powers (although considerable persuasive ones) (Chrzanowski, Krzyzanowski and Luks[62]; Ledger and Roe[63]).

Taking the EU as an example, the policies which emanate from the deliberations of the Commission (DGVII), Council of Transport Ministers and the Parliament are normally designed to inter-act with international policies of (for example) the IMO, so that recent EU legislation on double-hulled tankers and other environmental and safety measures have avoided any conflict between the spatial levels. This may not necessarily be the case where the interests of the EU conflict with those of the wider global framework and it is clear that divergences of policy-making from inter-spatial consistency will produce tensions that are hard to reconcile. The agreement of policy over implementation of the UNCTAD 40/40/20 rule for liner shipping by the EU in 1979 reflected these tensions as the EU's commitment to free trade and liberalisation was tested by UNCTAD's demands for market interference on behalf of developing countries. An agreement was reached but the problems of achieving consistency of policies across spatial boundaries where the agendas were fundamentally different were apparent.

This discussion of supra-national policy-making also needs to refer to the problems of compatibility with national policies, particularly with reference to the EU and the difficulties experienced in reconciling EU policies on (for example) state aids and cabotage with the desires and agendas that exist in individual member states. Aspinwall[8] referred to the prolonged discussion that took place before Greece agreed to the opening up of cabotage markets within the EU to all ships of the European Union, an agreement that eventually contained safeguards for socially vulnerable markets[64] and extended delays in implementation to give the industry time to adapt. These concessions diluted the ambitions of the EU to open all shipping markets to all ships and operators that were both safe and environmentally friendly and reflected a divergence in policy ambitions between supra-national and national interests. Shipping state aids have presented similar difficulties and the EU Commission has compromised on its leading principle of free markets and liberalisation so that some state aid remains in place at a national level, albeit controlled in amount and characteristics.

Figure 1 also notes the existence of two more levels of policy-making in the shipping sector upon which we shall not dwell here but which also play a part in the conflict between spatial levels – *regional and local*. These two levels, typified by regional governments (such as Devon County Council in the UK) and city governments (such as Plymouth in the UK) once again should derive policies that are compatible with the levels above them at national, supra-national and international level as not doing so leads to problems of implementation. Thus a regional authority within the EU might find problems in keeping to EU policies limiting state aid to shipping when the local, dominant ship operator needs regional support to remain financially solvent. Similarly, local city ports need to match their policies with the regions where they are located but at times political differences can interfere with this process.

5. INTEREST GROUPS

The discussion above has focused upon the role of the state at each spatial level in the formation of shipping policy and has emphasised how important but also how difficult it is for these different levels to work together and to ensure that policy created at one level is co-ordinated with that at each of the others to generate meaningful and consistent initiatives.

Figure 1 also includes examples of interest groups that have a significant role to play in the creation and dissemination of shipping policy. These interest groups are those parts of the shipping industry with an active position in the sector and whom are both the generators and those most affected by the policies that are created; examples of them have been noted above. Thus at the international level, the International Maritime Organisation (IMO) is a major interest group which both creates and absorbs international shipping policy measures. At the supra-national level, an organisation such as the European Community Shipowners Association, based in Brussels Belgium, and representing shipowners throughout the EU is a significant interest group that places pressure upon EU and national policy-makers to take account of their views. At a national level, the UK Chamber of Shipping plays a similar role in relation to the UK government, but also in discussion with other interest groups (e.g., the European Shippers Council or the UK seafarers union, NUMAST). Similar relationships exist at local and regional level for port authorities, environmental pressure groups, local truck haulier associations etc. each of whom has a voice feeding into the policy-making process.

These voices act across spatial levels – thus the UK Chamber of Shipping might input policy initiatives directly to DGVII of the EU – and not just to their respective spatial policy-makers (in this case the UK government ministry responsible for shipping – the Department for Local Government, Transport and the Regions). The situation thus gets increasingly complicated as consistency and compatibility vertically up and down policy-making bodies at state level now has also to function horizontally with interest groups and also diagonally with groups at different levels. There is also a very large number of interest groups for each policy level and issue, each inter-relating with each other to a lesser or greater extent either in opposition or collaboration. To add to the complexity, attitude can also vary with the issue concerned.

6. THE CONTEXTS

The final piece of this complex puzzle which makes up the model of shipping policy is provided by the contexts within which all these policy initiatives and relationships must operate and which in turn affect their development, potential and success (or otherwise). A number of these can be identified following the work of Ledger and Roe.[10] They include:

Economic: refers to the impact of economic factors upon the derivation and characteristics of shipping policy for any particular regime (international, supra-national etc.). Thus it might well include the impact of the introduction of the Euro in the 12 EU states, the general condition of the world economy, the specific implications of the state of the scrap market upon the shipping industry, the strength of the US$, economic crises as for example recently in Argentina and the development of free markets in East Europe. It is a significant but wide-ranging context that is difficult to grasp and understand its implications but which is fundamental to decisions upon shipping policy at all levels.

Legal: refers to the legal framework within which the shipping sector has to operate. This will include national laws and regulations as well as those of a supra or international nature – thus shipping operators based within countries within the EU or operating to and from EU ports are required to meet not only the legislation relevant in their home state but also the multitude of EU regulations and directives that are imposed upon the sector. These include, for example, the large number of pieces of legislation referring to safety in the ferry industry, bulk carrier safety, competition rules for liner shipping and rules for cabotage operations. The competition rules for liner shipping are a good example of where different legal regimes apply to the same industrial sector dependent upon the spatial level that is considered. There are domestic laws in, for example, the United Kingdom, that control numerous shipping activities and impacts relating to the local environment (local government pollution controls), port safety (port regulations), seafarer employment (income tax and social security rules) and taxation (UK tonnage tax). The US legal regime will also become relevant for liner shipping companies active in US trades as it regulates various aspects of liner competition. However, at the supra-national EU level there are further regulations that apply to competition between liner operators, agreements through consortia and conferences and the penalties that can be applied by the European Commission (including the infamous 4055-4058/86 Regulations[65]). Meanwhile at an international level, the industry is subject to the rules and recommendations of the IMO in terms of ship safety, seafarer training and environmental protection.

The legal framework is constantly changing at each level as a response to a myriad of social, political and economic pressures and it is within this context that some of the more important failures of co-ordination between levels are evident.

Managerial: refers to the relationship of the internal structure of shipping companies with the policy framework that is imposed. Thus the size and complexity of shipping organisations and the changing range of functions that shipping companies have incorporated has an impact in terms of policy-making and its implementation. The latter point is particularly important as shipping companies increasingly integrate vertically, absorbing logistical functions traditionally carried out by separate organisations but now incorporated within one company structure. Thus Maersk's interests in the full range of logistics from shipping to trucking and agency work to air transport has implications for policy-makers and vice versa in that it is no longer shipping policy which is solely important but a range of policies from competition to industrial, transport to regional development. This increase in the range of functions undertaken by traditional shipping companies adds to the complexities and has also increased pressure on the industry to conform to a wider range of policy initiatives. The problems faced by the TACA operators in liner shipping on the North Atlantic[66] is evidence of this in that they have fallen foul of competition policies of the EU in the area of inland trucking (being accused of being anti-competitive for whole transport journeys and not just shipping links as permitted under Regulation 4056/86 of the EU) rather than any specific shipping offence. It is only whilst the economic and logistical benefits of vertical integration for shipping companies remain greater than the potential complexity that comes with it (and the risks of falling foul of legislation) that this trend will continue.

A further example of complexity that changes within the managerial context can bring includes conflict within the liner industry again on the North Atlantic between the regimes of the EU and the FMC in the USA with their differing views on the permissible nature of liner conferences and also the option of including inland transport within overall conference legislation.[27]

Organisational: refers in particular to the structure and characteristics of the shipping industry as a whole rather than company internal activities and two important trends here stand out in relation to policy-making at all levels – privatisation and globalisation. Following the demise of the Soviet empire (and with it the role of state-owned shipping companies) and combined with the trend of a general divestment of state companies around the world in all sectors, the shipping sector as a whole has seen a considerable move towards private ownership. Thus the significance of state control has lessened as governments become distanced from company decisions, finance and operations. At the same time there has been a consequential increase in supra-national and international policy-making in the sector to control the external effects of the industry as it finds itself released from public sector obligations. This is evidenced in the increased activity in shipping policy-making of the EU, the FMC and the IMO in terms of safety, environment and competition with the objective of protecting public interests in areas where the market has no interest and there is no natural market mechanism to ensure that high levels of safety, low levels of environmental pollution and healthy competition between players in the shipping market are maintained. One problem that emerges here between spatial policy-making levels is that commonly it may be advantageous for competition policy (for example) to be neglected at a national level as this may ensure a strong international presence for a domestic fleet (for example through subsidy in many forms), whilst it is being strictly enforced at a supra-national level – for example at the EU level where subsidies are strictly controlled.

In terms of globalisation, this has changed the characteristics of the shipping industry, which although has always operated at an international level, until recently was much more nationally operated and controlled. Thus, the UK shipping company P&O was a major bulk, ferry and liner operator world-wide for many years but more recently has found it necessary to enter global strategic alliances and to merge its liner operations with Nedlloyd of the Netherlands. Policy-making in the shipping sector is directly affected by such moves particularly at the national level as national policies in the UK and the Netherlands may conflict (for example in terms of subsidy) causing at best, confusion within the sector. In addition the increased impact of flags of convenience and international registers confuses the picture further as nationally based companies have to work more and more within an international framework whilst international and national policies towards training, labour and employment for example, may clearly conflict with the requirements of the international regime.

Political: refers to the political context from which all shipping policies emerge. It is never the case that a single economic, technical or legal framework stimulates and controls shipping policy formulation. In fact, the political acceptability of any particular policy is commonly the most significant context of all. Sizeable political changes (for example those that occurred in Eastern Europe from 1989-1992; the Arab-Israeli conflicts; or the effects of the World Trade Centre incident in 2001) are often of less significance than the political relationships between players within and adjacent to the industry. A fine example, described in some detail by Aspinwall,[8] refers to the political relationship between the European Commission (the executive body of the EU) and the Council of Ministers (the main legislature of the EU) concerning the introduction of Regulation 4056/86. This regulation effectively permitted the existence of liner conferences for shipping operators working into and out of EU ports, something that under the competition rules within the Treaty of Rome should be illegal. The Commission's view was clearly that this should not be permitted but they were ignored by the Council in 1986 who, under pressure from the shipping industry and acting in a political rather than a legal or economic context, legislated to secure their existence. In this example an internal political conflict resulted in policy that conflicts with all other industrial sectors within the EU (none other has such an exemption from competition law) and which has presented a series of difficulties in co-ordinating different policy level initiatives since then. Other political pressures which have been significant at EU level in overtly affecting policy-making include the concessions granted to Greece over the delay in imposing cabotage laws and the continued existence of subsidies for shipping operations against all principles that the EU tries normally to uphold. Such political concessions do nothing to create a consistent and meaningful policy framework for the sector as a whole evidenced in the continuing friction between the European Shippers Council and the European Shipowners

Association over the continued existence of shipping conferences and the maintenance of higher freight rates that the former believe is a consequence.

Social: refers to a multitude of complex relationships between the shipping industry and the society in which it operates. These issues include the significance of maritime employment and policies which promote or reduce it – a major strand within policy-making at local, regional, national and supra-national levels in particular. Much recent debate has focussed within the EU upon the introduction of new tax regimes by nation states for shipping, partly at least aimed at encouraging or sustaining employment levels. In addition there have been widespread policy initiatives concentrating upon seafarer training, conditions of service and the environment all with strong social implications. Certainly at all levels, the social implications of a particular policy have to be noted by politicians when they choose policy initiatives as the relationship between the two is close and the impact can be sizeable.

Spatial: refers to the fact that shipping policy is not only derived at a variety of spatial levels as we have seen – international, supra-national, national, regional and local – but also is affected by a variety of spatial issues. These might include issues relating to peripherality and cohesion – a major theme within the EU – whereby the disadvantage felt by peripherally located regions and states (for example the accession countries of Eastern Europe; or the economically poor area of southern Italy) can be reduced through policies to promote good transport links including those by ship and through ports. By improving these links, the friction caused by a peripheral location can be reduced. Other spatial influences include promotion of short-sea shipping in Europe to reduce dependence upon pollution-generating road transport and various regional policies to improve the lives of island based communities. The latter is evidenced in the EU through the cabotage Regulations which even after the liberalisation of these trades, allow countries to protect some domestic routes for social reasons. A multitude of other spatially related issues are important to shipping – including regional policies to develop economically backward areas and the consequent industrial and commercial impacts, the effects of the emergence of new countries including those of Russia, the Ukraine, and the Baltic States of Latvia, Lithuania and Estonia and their relatively important shipping fleets, and the construction of new port facilities including for example those for oil export in the Baltic which recently has seen new developments in Russia, Latvia and Lithuania all affecting the required geographical focus of policy measures to promote or protect various shipping related activities or impacts.

Technical: refers to the changes in technical facilities and methods which have direct and indirect effects upon the shipping industry. Policies have to take account of these changes and this includes a multitude of new safety and environmental regulations at international, supra-national and national level to accommodate the growth in ship size both in terms of container and bulk vessels. Changes in ferry design and the need for improved technical and safety rules have stimulated further regulation especially within the EU and following the *Herald of Free Enterprise* and *Estonia* disasters. New port facilities and changes in modal choice also have their effect and the continued growth in road transport and the construction of new pipeline facilities have implications for policy-makers in the shipping sector. The EU's continued promotion of intermodalism also has impacted technically upon the shipping policy sector.

These eight major contexts provide the external framework within which all shipping policy – at whatever level – has to be placed; policy-making which ignores their influence has no chance of success. The relative influence of each context will be dependent upon the spatial level and the issue involved as well as a host of other inter-connected issues but undoubtedly in the very large majority of cases, each context has a significant role to play. Some are ever-present and always central – particularly political issues, but also the relevant legal framework and the economic relationships that exist between shipping and its broader setting.

In addition, shipping policy cannot ignore the wider context in which it has to be introduced and implemented. Thus shipping policy at all levels has to accept that there are other policies – including industrial, financial, environmental, competition, infrastructure, energy and so on – with which it must co-ordinate and be aware of. Failure to do so again results in conflict between policy-makers and other players within the shipping sector and therefore ineffective policy-making. In addition, shipping policy makers have to recognise the role of other transport modes and the fact that policies for one mode may conflict with that for another – for example, promotion of road transport through road building and subsidised taxation for trucks has an inevitable impact upon the short-sea shipping industry. Clearly and ideally, the separate modal policies would be integrated into one whole, but this is often made difficult as there remains competition between modal interests and structurally these policies commonly emanate from different government ministries. Finally, shipping policy if it is to be effective, has to be aware of its inheritance in terms of industry structure, ownership, tradition and importance. These in turn will affect its role and potential in terms of policy success.

7. SUMMARY AND CONCLUSIONS

This discussion of shipping policy has focused in particular upon two features – the complexity of the influences that determine both its character and success, and the significance of ensuring that there is compatibility across all spatial levels if policies are to be effective. There is nothing more likely to inhibit the success of shipping policy initiatives than to have conflicting policy ambitions at say, national and supra-national levels – something for example that has characterised the industry in conflicts between Greece and the EU over cabotage trades, and also between the USA's FMC and the EU over liner conferences and their operations on the North Atlantic.

This consistency across levels has to be maintained in the context of policies emerging in other areas as well – for example the environment and economy – or else conflict will again emerge which will effectively prevent the achievement of the objectives that the policies are aimed at. There are many examples of countries promoting both short-sea shipping through tax concessions as well as trucking, both operating within the same markets in competition with each other.

These conflicts of interest that occur regularly within the shipping policy arena have been made more significant and more difficult to resolve with the increased globalisation of markets and the impact that this has had upon the already highly internationalised shipping industry and its increasing moves towards international joint ventures and strategic alliances. In effect, it is now only at an international level that shipping policy can ever be truly effective. Thus the EU may have ambitions to open up markets and insist upon high environmental and safety standards for shipping but is prevented from achieving these ideals and implementing appropriate policies because to do so would destroy EU shipping fleets within a global context – a consequence that would be politically and socially unacceptable. Thus the EU compromises upon issues such as flags of convenience (which in many ways it should welcome as a consequence of a free market) by allowing member states to subsidise their own fleets through low taxation regimes compered with other industries – thus breaking their own Treaty of Rome competition principles. The very international and mobile nature of shipping makes this inevitable. Similar compromises can be seen in terms of liner shipping, cabotage and manning rules. Meanwhile, Port State Control offers an interesting example of where the EU has achieved much of what it wishes to promote within an international framework but at supra-national level: – by enforcing high standards upon ships of all nationalities entering EU ports, safety and environmental standards across the EU are maintained even where the ships concerned are operated under a legal regime outside of the EU. Of course this has little impact upon vessels that never enter EU ports.

At the international level – for example the IMO – it would in theory be possible to achieve agreement across all nations for rules that then could be universally applied at all spatial levels, right down to local. As the analysis in this chapter suggests, due to the complex and often conflicting relationships between the different players in shipping and the various spatial levels of shipping policy, such agreements are difficult (if not impossible) to achieve and conflicts between policies imposed at differing levels remain and will do so whilst nations, ship operators, local interests and others see benefits in imposing their own policy initiatives. The globalisation of a complex and highly mobile industry characterised by excessive international interests and heavily entwined with other sectors – as shipping is – makes policy-making a frustrating and difficult business but one which perhaps more than any other, reflects the complete pattern of commercial interests that exist throughout different areas of the world.

ENDNOTES

1. Frankel, E.G. (1999): "The economics of total trans-ocean supply chain management", *International Journal of Maritime Economics*, 1, 1, pp. 61–70.
2. Ryoo, D.K., and Thanopoulou, H.A. (1999): "Liner alliances in the globalisation era: a strategic tool for Asian container carriers", *Maritime Policy and Management*, 26, 4, pp. 349–368.

3. Thanopoulou, H.A., Ryoo, D.K., and Lee, T. (1999): "Korean liner shipping in the era of global alliances", *Maritime Policy and Management*, 26, 3, pp. 209–230.
4. Peters, H.J. (2001): "Developments in global seatrade and container shipping markets: their effects on the port industry and private sector involvement", *International Journal of Maritime Economics*, 3, 1, pp. 3–26.
5. Randay, T. (2001): "Internationalisation and foreign direct investment in shipping: a study of Norwegian firms", *International Journal of Maritime Economics*, 3, 3, pp. 298–317.
6. Sletmo, G.K. (2001): "The end of national shipping policy? A historical perspective on shipping policy in a global economy", *International Journal of Maritime Economics*, 3, 4, pp. 333–350.
7. Slack, B., Comtois, C., and McCalla, R. (2002): "Strategic alliances in the container shipping industry; a global perspective", *Maritime Policy and Management*, 29, 1, pp. 65–76.
8. Aspinwall, M. (1995): *Moveable feast; pressure group conflict and the European Community shipping policy* (Aldershot, Ashgate).
9. Lu, C.S. (1999): "Strategic groups in Taiwanese liner shipping", *Maritime Policy and Management*, 26, 1, pp. 1–26.
10. Ledger, G.D., and Roe, M.S. (1993): "East European shipping and economic change: a conceptual model", *Maritime Policy and Management*, 20, 3, pp. 229–241.
11. Gold, E. (1981): *The evolution of international marine policy and shipping law* (Mass., USA, Lexington Books).
12. Schrier, E., Nadel, E., and Rifas, B. (1985): *Outlook for the liberalization of maritime transport* (London, Trade Policy Research Centre).
13. Behnam, A. (1994): "The future of the shipping dialogue in UNCTAD", *Maritime Policy and Management*, 21, 1, pp. 15–28.
14. Moyer, R.C. (1977): "Maritime subsidies: problems, alternatives and trade-offs", *Journal of Industrial Economics*, 25, 3.
15. Frankel, E.G. (1989): "Strategic planning applied to shipping and ports", *Maritime Policy and Management*, 16, 2, pp. 123–132.
16. Frankel, E.G. (1992): "Hierarchical logic in shipping policy and decision-making", *Maritime Policy and Management*, 19, 3, pp. 211–221.
17. Yannopoulos, G.N. (1989): *Shipping policies for an open world economy* (London, Routledge).
18. Ademuni-Odeke (1984): *Protectionism and the future of international shipping* (Dordrecht, Kluwer).
19. Li, K.X., and Wonham, J. (2001): "Maritime legislation: new areas for safety of life at sea", *Maritime Policy and Management*, 28, 3, pp. 225–234.
20. Goss, R.O. (ed.) (1982): *Advances in maritime economics* (Cambridge, Cambridge University Press).
21. Bredima-Savopoulou, A., and Tzoannos, J. (1990): *The common shipping policy of the EC* (The Hague, Elsevier).
22. Wang, S. (1993): *European Community shipping competition policy* (UK, University of Plymouth).
23. Hart, P., Ledger, G., Roe, M.S., and Smith, B. (1993): *Shipping policy in the European Community* (Aldershot, Ashgate).
24. Peeters C., Verbeke, A., Declerq, E., and Wijnholst, N. (1995): *Analysis of the competitive position of short sea shipping; development of policy measures* (Delft, Delft University Press).
25. Van der Linden, J. (2001): "The economic impact study of maritime policy issues: application to the German case", *Maritime Policy and Management*, 28, 1, pp. 33–54.
26. Paixao, A., and Marlow, P. (2001): "A review of the European Union shipping policy", *Maritime Policy and Management*, 28, 2, pp. 187–198.
27. Brooks, M.R. (2000): *Sea change in liner shipping* (Oxford, Pergamon).

28. Ledger, G.D., and Roe, M.S. (1995): "Positional change in the Polish liner shipping market", *Maritime Policy and Management*, 22, 4, pp. 295–318.
29. Roe, M.S. (1998): *Commercialisation in Central and East European shipping* (Aldershot, Ashgate).
30. Hawkins, J., and Gray, R. (1999): "Making strategic choices for Asia-Pacific shipping", *International Journal of Maritime Economics*, 1, 2, pp. 57–72.
31. Hawkins, J., and Gray, R. (2000): *Strategies for Asia-Pacific shipping* (Aldershot, Ashgate).
32. Sun, G., and Zhang, S. (2000): "Comment. The APEC future maritime policy and its evaluation", *Maritime Policy and Management*, 27, 2, pp. 209–213.
33. Hawkins, J. (2001): "Quality shipping in the Asia-Pacific region", *International Journal of Maritime Economics*, 3, 1, pp. 79–101.
34. Brownrigg, M., Dawe, G., and Mann, M. (2001): "Developments in UK shipping: the tonnage tax", *Maritime Policy and Management*, 28, 3, pp. 213–224.
35. Colvin, M., and Marks, J. (1984): *British shipping; the right course*, Policy Study 67 (London, Centre for Policy Studies).
36. Gardner, B. (1999): "Investment incentives for British shipping: a further comment", *Maritime Policy and Management*, 26, 2, pp. 195–200.
37. Gardner, B., Naim, M., and Obando-Rojas, B. (2001): "Maintaining the maritime skills base: does the government have a realistic strategy?", *Maritime Policy and Management*, 28, 4, pp. 347–360.
38. Walenciak, A., Constantinou, A., and Roe, M.S. (2001): "Liner shipping between East and West Europe; competitive developments on the Poland-United Kingdom trade", *Maritime Policy and Management*, 28, 4, pp. 323–338.
39. Wrona, A., and Roe, M.S. (2002): "The Polish maritime sector under transition", *Maritime Policy and Management*, 29, 1, pp. 17–43.
40. Whitehurst, C.H. (1983): *The US merchant marine; in search of an enduring maritime policy* (Annapolis, Nautical Institute Press).
41. Mirmiran, S.M.R. (1994): *Iran's national shipping policy* (UK, University of Plymouth).
42. Sletmo, G.K., and Williams, E.W. (1981): *Liner conferences in the container age: US policy* (New York, McMillan).
43. Omosun, A.Y. (1987): *A consideration of the means of attaining the Nigerian shipping policy objectives* (UK, University of Plymouth).
44. Nasiru, I.S. (1994): *The Nigerian national shipping policy; aground or afloat?* (UK, University of Plymouth).
45. Goto, S. (1984): *Japan's shipping policy*, Japan Maritime Research Institute, JAMRI Report 3.
46. Yercan, F. (1999): *Ferry services in Europe* (Aldershot, Ashgate).
47. Yercan, F., and Roe, M.S. (1999): *Shipping in Turkey* (Aldershot, Ashgate).
48. Barla, M.C., Sag, O.K., Roe, M.S., and Gray, R. (eds.) (2001): *Developments in maritime transport and logistics in Turkey* (Aldershot, Ashgate).
49. Flynn, M. (1999): "PRC maritime and the Asian financial crisis", *Maritime Policy and Management*, 26, 4, pp. 337–348.
50. Sun, G., and Zhang, S. (1999): "General review of the Chinese shipping policy for the contemporary era", *Maritime Policy and Management*, 26, 1, pp. 93–99.
51. Kokuryo, H. (1985): *Korean shipping and shipping policy; shipping industry rationalisation plan*, Japan Maritime Research Institute JAMRI Report 8.
52. Lee, T. (1996): *Shipping developments in Far East Asia* (Aldershot, Ashgate).
53. Lee, T. (1999): "Restructuring of the economy and its impacts on the Korean maritime industry", *Maritime Policy and Management*, 26, 4, pp. 311–326.
54. Song, D.-W., Cullinane, K., and Roe, M.S. (2001): *The productive efficiency of container terminals* (Aldershot, Ashgate).
55. Hoyle, B., and Knowles, R. (1998): *Modern transport geography* (London, Wiley).

56. The routes associated with the exploitation of North Sea oil, the development of Port of Fos/Marseille and the rise of China in world shipping are recent examples.
57. Cafruny, A. (1985): "The political economy of international shipping; Europe versus America", *International Organization*, 39, 1, Winter.
58. Cafruny, A. (1987): *Ruling the waves – the political economy of international shipping* (Berkeley, University of California Press).
59. Cafruny, A. (1991): "Toward a maritime policy", in Hurwitz, L., and Lequsne, C. (eds.) *The state of the European Community; policies, institutions and debates in the transition years* (Boulder, Lynne Rienner).
60. Brooks, M.R., and Button, K.J. (1992): "Shipping within the framework of a Single European Market", *Transport Reviews*, 12, 3, pp. 237–252.
61. Kiriazidis, T., and Tzanidakis, G. (1995): "Recent aspects of the EU maritime policy", *Maritime Policy and Management*, 22, 2, pp. 179–186.
62. Chrzanowski, I., Krzyzanowski, M., and Luks, K. (1979): *Shipping economics and policy; a socialist view* (London, Fairplay).
63. Ledger, G.D., and Roe, M.S. (1996): *East European change and shipping policy* (Aldershot, Ashgate).
64. E.g., the Greek Island trade where seasonality of demand could lead to some islands losing shipping services at times of low demand to shipping companies from around Europe "creaming off" the profitable peaks.
65. Regulations 4055–4058/86 were directed at enforcing competition policy within the liner sector but included Regulation 4056/86 which actually allows for the existence of liner conferences which are clearly (at least in part) anti-competitive. The result of a political arrangement at the time involving the Council of Transport Ministers and the ship-owning sector, this Regulation remains infamous as effectively acting in opposition to the Treaty of Rome, to the wishes of the European Commission and to the requirements of shippers in Europe. It is currently under review by the Commission.
66. TACA (Trans Atlantic Conference Agreement) is an attempt by North Atlantic liner operators to stabilise rates in this highly volatile market. The main operators in the trade have achieved this by reaching agreement on rates for entire journeys of containers (including the inland leg) but in so doing have attracted the wrath of the European Commission who successfully fined operators in the Agreement for breaking EU competition law. Exemption from anti-trust under Regulation 4056/86 was deemed to be applicable only to the sea part of such a journey.

CHAPTER 23

SHIPS, FLAGS AND TAXES

Peter Marlow
Cardiff Business School, University of Cardiff, Wales, UK.
E-mail: *Marlow@Cardiff.ac.uk*

1. INTRODUCTION AND BACKGROUND

Most governments of nations possessing merchant fleets, whether state or privately owned, offer some form of assistance to their shipping industry. The stated objective of such measures is to encourage investment in national flag shipping and the incentives can take various forms. The generic name by which such incentives are known is "the fiscal treatment of shipping" and this term embraces both taxation and subsidy aspects of the fiscal arrangements. The taxation of the shipping industry has long been of great interest to shipowners, governments and policy makers, and academics but why should this be so and why is/should the taxation of shipping be any different to the taxation of any other industry? The answer to this question is two fold and relates to the existence of alternative ship registers (the so-called flags of convenience) and to the contribution which shipping makes to the national economy.

It is generally believed that maritime transport can make a major contribution to an economy and in a variety of ways. These economic benefits may be classified under the two broad headings of (a) direct benefits or (b) indirect benefits. The net benefit of domestic ship-owning and operation is really the value added to the economy.[1]

The contribution is thus not necessarily an obvious or direct one, as measured perhaps by the industry's contribution to the balance of payments, and furthermore, the globalisation of shipping, the mobility of the assets (the ships), and the increasingly competitive markets have forced many shipowners to seek to improve their positions by transferring their ships to more financially favourable registers. This raises the questions of where do these benefits arise and to whom (i.e., which country) do they accrue? It is possible that the benefits may follow the flag.

The choice of flag is an interesting decision and one which may give rise to a possible conflict between commercial and national interest. The impact of such a decision may have far-reaching macro-economic consequences which should properly be assessed by means of the input-output multipliers. This assessment will discern the primary and secondary effects of the decision which may lead to the loss of shipping related land based activities and subsequently to a loss of value added and employment opportunities. From such an analysis it is possible to demonstrate that the shipping industry is a vital sector in macro-economic activity and one which can play a pivotal role in economic reconstruction in a global competitive market. Once the value of the industry has been acknowledged and calculated then policy makers can begin to formulate strategies to support its activities and encourage owners and operators to invest in this sector, in the knowledge that the impact of the support/investment will reach beyond the shipping industry and may serve a wider purpose. Input-output analysis will allow policy makers to ask, and to answer, the "what-if" questions and to assess the effects of different forms of support/subsidy inherent in their policies in terms of opportunity cost and value for money.

The existence of open registers, second registers or international registers allows shipowners to register their vessels under whatever flag they choose and, as a consequence, the relationship between shipping and its home country becomes obscured. Equally the value of the shipping industry to the national economy is no longer obvious. Nonetheless it is recognised by governments who then offer support to the industry in order to retain the benefits.

2. INVESTMENT INCENTIVES

Much has been written about the taxation of companies' profits and the offsetting of this taxation by the awarding of tax-related investment incentives designed to reduce their tax liability. In particular it is sometimes felt that a tax related investment incentive is only a relief from taxes that would otherwise be levied and if there were no taxes there would be no need for incentives to offset their effect. It has been stated[2] that "the advantage conferred on investment by an investment incentive is merely an offset to the disadvantages inflicted on it by other parts of the tax system". This somewhat cynical view does not prevent the possibility that these incentives might improve the climate for investment, nor does it explain the existence of non-tax-based investment incentives.

Investment incentives can play some part in stimulating investment both by increasing the profitability after tax of new projects and by reinforcing the cash flow needed to finance those projects. A system of incentives, grants and capital allowances has been developed to encourage investment.

Most governments declare themselves in favour of investment and strive to encourage it through a variety of fiscal and financial incentives, the majority of which have tax consequences. These inducements to invest may try to influence the timing of the investment, its form, or its location; or they may aim solely to increase the gross rate of capital expenditure. Many businessmen feel that, at least for large businesses, the allowances are more in the nature of tax relief than specific incentives but however they are viewed, these incentives improve the climate for investment. There is some debate in the literature as to whether the major effect of incentives is on the profitability of the company or on its liquidity or indeed whether the incentives exert any influence at all on the decision to invest.

Various approaches, e.g., Keynesian, Classical, are discussed and compared in the textbooks and occasionally empirical evidence is stated to support one point of view rather than another. The rate of interest is generally accepted as playing an important role as it measures the cost of funds borrowed to finance the investment expenditure or, in the case of financing from retained earnings, it reflects the opportunity cost of using such funds in this way. The standard textbook diagram portrays an inverse relationship between the quantity of investment and the rate of interest (see Figure 1). An investment will be undertaken provided its internal rate of return (or marginal efficiency of capital) exceeds the prevailing rate of interest. It might be expected that in the absence of capital rationing, investment would be undertaken up to the point at which the internal rate of return (IRR) of the marginal project would be equal to the ruling rate of interest. This implies that the marginal efficiency of capital (MEC) schedule defines the desired capital stock (k*) in terms of the rate of interest as depicted in Figure 2.

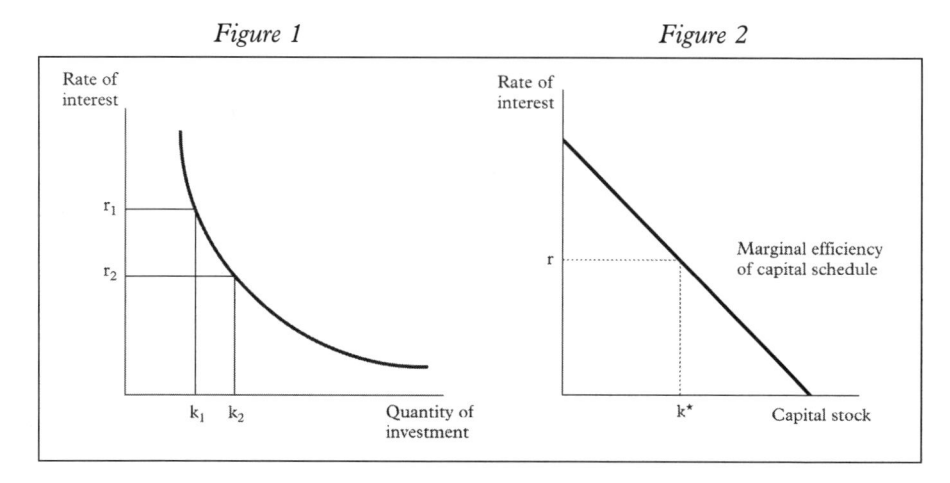

Figure 1

Figure 2

The MEC schedule can be shifted up or down by changes in expectations or the degree of uncertainty felt by the decision maker which will affect the expected rate of return from an investment and hence its IRR. Actual investment decisions resulting from fluctuations in the desired capital stock may appear to be unrelated to changes in the market rate of interest.

In very simple terms an investment is worth undertaking if its revenues exceed its costs. However, revenues usually occur in the future and it is important to consider the time-value of money. Discounting is a means of reducing future sums of money to their present equivalents by multiplying them by discount factors which reflect the length of time involved and the rate at which the future is being discounted. In practice this last is usually derived from the opportunity cost of capital, i.e., the best that could have been obtained elsewhere. It will be seen that a rate of discount is similar, but not identical, to a rate of interest and that discounting is merely a compound interest calculation performed backwards through time.

Hence it is better, and more correct, to consider an investment worth undertaking if the present value of the (discounted) future revenues (*PV*) accruing from it exceeds its (current) acquisition cost (*Co*). We can define *PV* as

$$PV = \sum_{t=1}^{n} R_t/(1 + r)^t$$

where R_t is the expected net return in period t, r is the rate of interest (discount), and n is the life of the investment.

If $PV \geq Co$ then the investment may be undertaken. The internal rate of return is that rate of return (interest, discount) which would make the present value just equal to Co, which accords with what Keynes called the marginal efficiency of capital, as mentioned above.

The effectiveness of investment incentives is often measured by the ratio of additional investment to the cost of the incentives which brought it about. However, assessment in this way has two obvious shortcomings:

(i) the true cost is unclear when it is measured not in the form of cash paid out in subsidies but in the form of notional tax revenue foregone; and

(ii) the approach allows only for investment quantity and not for investment quality as measured by the rate of return on the investment.

Two types of incentive are generally distinguished: tax-based and non-tax-based incentives. On the face of it the former would include, *inter alia*, investment allowances, tax credits and tax-free reserves while the latter would include e.g. investment grants, subsidies and cheap finance. Unfortunately in practice the distinction is not so clear-cut because investment grants, for instance, are tax-related if depreciation allowances are reduced proportionally.

Most lists of possible investment incentives[3] would include the following as the more usual types of incentive:

(a) *Tax (capital) allowances* are any allowances which may be offset against net revenue before tax is assessed. Such allowances will include, *inter alia*, depreciation allowances and investment allowances.

(b) *Accelerated depreciation* which involves the bringing forward in time of the depreciation allowances. This may take the form of initial (i.e., first year) allowances or accelerated allowances (in excess of those deriving from the usual depreciation arrangements) spread over a number of years.

(c) *Initial allowances* are a form of accelerated depreciation used to increase the amount of depreciation allowances which may be taken in the first year of the life of an investment. These initial allowances do not increase the depreciable base of the qualifying asset.

(d) *Advance depreciation* which provides for depreciation allowances to be used once a commitment has been made to the purchase of a qualifying asset and prior to the delivery of that asset.

(e) *Cheap loans* which are offered by many countries to facilitate the purchase of new assets. This is especially true for shipping, and one example of these favourable loan terms were the OECD export credit terms which typically allowed for 80% of the cost of the vessel to be borrowed over a period of eight years at an annual rate of interest of 8%. Domestic credit arrangements may be even more favourable. It is not uncommon for there to be a grace period (or moratorium) of several years before repayment of the loan capital commences.

(f) The governments of some nations (e.g., Italy, Germany) assist their companies to obtain credit at reduced rates of interest by subsidising the interest payments. Such *interest subsidies* are designed to ensure that the rate of interest paid does not exceed some predetermined level (in the case of shipowners this might be the rate prevailing under the OECD Understanding on Export Credit for Ships).

(g) *Investment allowances* are those which increase the depreciable base of an asset before writing down commences e.g. an investment allowance of 40% means that 140% of the cost of the qualifying asset may be written off.

(h) *Investment grants* are a lump sum cash payment of X% of the cost of the asset. Such payments are usually made in arrears (often one year) and often must be deducted from the level of capital allowances available on that asset.

(i) *Investment tax credits* create an incentive by making a part of income exempt from tax. The investment tax credit is an investment allowance at a rate other than the taxpayer's full rate of tax. It is a definite reduction of tax, not merely a tax postponement, and:

(j) *Tax free reserves* are monies set aside in a fund to be used for some specified purpose (e.g., the purchase of new assets or the modification of existing ones) at some future date. Such monies will not be taxed provided they are used in an approved way within the time limit.

(k) *Roll-over relief* allows monies to be put aside for reinvestment in shipping and effectively acts as a first year allowance for new investment as in the case of tax free reserves (see (j) above).

It should be appreciated that all the measures listed above have something in common. They all provide something extra, something additional to the norm. This norm is determined by the method of depreciation in operation to decide the level of writing down (capital) allowances – this method is often either the straight-line or reducing-balance method but, in the United Kingdom, free depreciation was common until 1984 and other methods (e.g., double-declining balance, sum-of-the-years-digits) exist in other countries. It should also be noted that the incentive scheme in operation at any one time may be a composite package of different types of investment incentives and financing arrangements. Under such circumstances it becomes very difficult to assess the impact and significance of any particular component measure in isolation.

Furthermore the disparate nature of the elements of a fiscal regime make comparisons between countries difficult but, as a result of research work started in the government economic service and developed at Cardiff University (see notes[4-11]), a methodology has been developed to achieve such international comparisons.

3. METHODOLOGY

The principles and practices of discounting have been known for several centuries and, after a long period of disuse and re-discovery, are now regarded as standard practice by economists and accountants.[12] It follows that any series of future sums of money may be discounted and added to one another. If they involve an investment, i.e., a negative sum at the start, followed (we hope) by positive net inflows extending over a finite life, then these discounted cash flows can be summed to produce a net present value (NPV). They can also be discounted to a zero NPV when the discount rate thus used is termed the internal rate of return, or yield, as mentioned earlier.

It further follows that any series of payments to, or receipts from a taxing authority such as a local or central government, may also be reduced to a net present value and associated with an investment of any given size (such as £1 million) with a given life (such as 20 years) for any given rates of profit, tax, discount, tax allowance, etc. It may also reflect the form and extent of finance; and with the ready availability of shipbuilding loans from all major shipbuilding countries this is particularly valuable, even though it involves some complexities in the calculations. It is relevant here largely because the interest on such finance is allowed, in most countries, as a deduction from profits before tax is calculated.

In short, given any set of rates of return, discount and inflation (which becomes relevant in the context of ship building loans expressed in money) it is possible to calculate the net present value of the expected flow of payments and receipts which results from any specified fiscal regime and associated financial arrangement. Just as the present values of different ship designs can be systematically compared, so the same may be done for such fiscal regimes and for variations in them.

Such comparisons will, through discounting, reflect the timing as well as the sizes of the payments. With certain aspects of the former UK system, for example, the timing with which the free depreciation allowance available for new ships was used was crucial in deciding whether corporation tax was a genuine burden or not. If the company has sufficient profits from other sources (property, say, or some other activity with low tax allowance) to take full and immediate advantage of it then its present value is much greater than if it were to be postponed. More formally it may be stated that with the marginal investment (i.e., where the internal rate of return equals the chosen rate of discount) and where the ship is not financed by borrowing, the present value of the free depreciation is equal to but opposite in sign from that of the subsequent corporation tax; this remains valid for any credible rate of tax or profit.

Moreover, under any corporate tax regime which seeks to stimulate investment through a system of tax allowances companies may find themselves in different tax positions. A company's specific tax position may be defined in terms of the number of years it will require to write off any available tax allowances it has accumulated, including those on the current investment. A company's tax position affects the net present value of any investment proposal it undertakes. The range of possible values may, however, be determined by calculating the net present value for each of three key tax positions.

4. TAX POSITIONS

These three key tax positions, which together encompass the full range of possibilities are the "no tax", "full tax" and "new entry" positions. They may be defined as follows:

(i) The "no tax" position

A company will be in this tax position if it has accumulated tax allowances from earlier years to an extent that it is now in a position where it is unlikely to have any tax liability for the indefinite future, given the prospective level of aggregate profits.

(ii) The "full tax" position

A company will be in this tax position if it is earning sufficient profits from other sources to take full and immediate advantage of any tax allowances which may be available on the capital cost involved in the investment proposal itself.

(iii) The "new entry" position

A company will be in this tax position if, given the tax allowances available on the capital cost involved in an investment proposal and the level of profit expected to be earned on it, it is neither earning sufficient profits from other sources nor has it accumulated sufficient allowances from earlier years, for either of these factors to have any influence at all on the net present value of the investment proposal. As neither profits from other sources nor accumulated tax allowances enter the calculation of the net present value, this tax position is equivalent to that in which a newly established company would find itself on entering the industry; hence, its name.

Briefly, the relevance of the tax allowances defined above is that a company in the full tax position will obtain the maximum benefit from such allowances by using them as soon as they become available according to the tax regulations. Once the allowances have been fully exploited the company will become liable for tax on all its profits. A company in the no tax position however will not pay any tax at all on its profits from this particular investment as it will possess unused tax allowances from previous investments which it will carry forward and use against the profits from this one. This means that in the past this company had insufficient profits to exhaust completely the tax allowances available to it, either because of the low profitability of its investments or because of generous levels of tax allowances and/or high levels of investment. The discounted value of such unused allowances will obviously fall over time according to the rate of discount and the rate of inflation. Further tax allowances have no value to a company in the no tax position as regards its current investment but they will be useful, though at a reduced value, when carried forward and used against the profits of future investments.

As Brownrigg et al.[13] state "Enhanced first year or writing down allowances, together with roll over relief, are designed to minimise the effective levels of taxation on shipping investment. However, they can, in some circumstances, distort incentives in favour of low return projects and cause the timing of investment and sales to be determined by tax rather than commercial considerations. Enhanced allowances may also deter new entrants to the market." This will be especially true if the new entrants do not already operate within the corporate tax system since they will be unable to make immediate use of the enhanced allowances and hence will be operating at a disadvantage in the market.

One important point about no tax operators is that they have no tax relief on interest payments. This helps to explain why the practice of leasing has been so prevalent in shipping. Leasing companies, or banks, which are in the full tax position can use fully the tax allowances (including interest charges) available on an investment, and shipping companies not in the full tax position can receive through lease arrangements some of the benefits of these tax allowances, which would otherwise be of no value to them. In fact, the leasing market is highly competitive and it is believed that the majority of the tax benefits are passed on to the lessee. It does not follow that a company in the no tax position is better off than one in the full tax position. This argument can be extended to flag of convenience (FOC) operators and it has been shown in the literature[14] that shipowners could be better off, from the fiscal point of view in NPV terms, by registering under a nominally high tax country (e.g., the United Kingdom) with tax allowances than under a flag of convenience regime (e.g., Liberia) which would not charge tax but would not give allowances. Such reasoning does not however consider the operating cost – especially crew cost – advantages afforded by the FOC regimes.

A company in the new entry position will use up capital allowances depending on the profitability of its current investment. Unused allowances will be carried forward at reduced present value, until they have been fully exhausted, and then tax will be paid on all profits over the remaining life of the vessel.

A practical example may help to clarify these points and demonstrate that while the nominal value of allowances, incentives and tax rates are the same for each company in the industry (in the same country) the actual value of those incentives will vary from company to company according to the speed at which they are able to make use of them as determined by their tax position.

Example: A company, operating under a fiscal regime which allows free depreciation and has a corporation tax rate of 50% with no lag in payment, undertakes an investment with a life of 10 years which has a rate of return of 25% per annum. Table 1 shows the timing of the capital allowances used under each of the three key tax positions and also calculates the net present value of these allowances assuming a 10% rate of discount.

Table 1: Timing of capital allowances under the three key tax positions

Year	Full tax	No tax	New entry
0	100	0	0
1	0	25	25
2	0	25	25
3	0	25	25
4	0	25	25
5	0	25	
6	0	25	
7	0	25	
8	0	25	
9	0	25	
10	0	25	

Notes: (i) the full tax company uses profits from other sources to take full use of the 100% first year allowance arising from free depreciation; (ii) the no tax company uses

520 NATIONAL AND INTERNATIONAL SHIPPING POLICIES

its accumulated tax allowances from previous investments to prolong the time stream of annual allowances; (iii) the new entry company can use only the allowances from this investment against its income stream.

The present value of allowances to each company is:

Full Tax = 100.00

No Tax $= \sum_{i=1}^{10} A_i (1+d)^{-i}$ but A_i is constant

$= A \sum_{i=1}^{10} (1+d)^{-i}$

= 25 x 6.144567
= 153.61

New Entry $= \sum_{i=1}^{4} A_i (1+d)^{-i}$

= 25 x 3.169865
= 79.246

It is obvious that the value of the tax regime while nominally the same for each of these companies is, in reality, quite different. A graph may be drawn showing Present Value of Allowances on the Y axis with the number of years before allowances are exhausted on the X axis (see Figure 3).

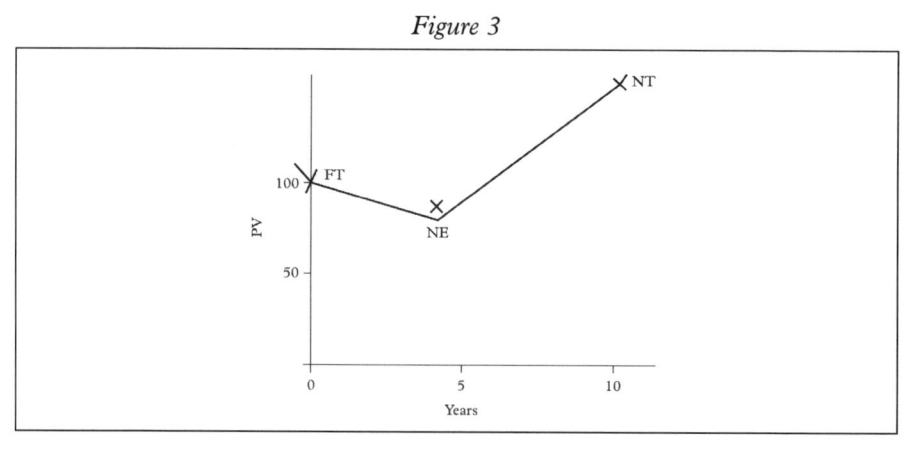

Figure 3

Given that such complexities can arise within countries operating such apparently straightforward systems of taxation imagine the difficulties inherent in trying to compare the treatment of the shipping industry in different countries. Such international comparisons of the fiscal treatment of shipping are only possible by using a model which considers all the disparate components of the whole package in each country, and converts their impact into common units which may be aggregated to produce the net present value of each (say £1 million) investment.

5. THE MODEL

The development of the mathematical form of this model has been described in detail in papers published in the Journal of Industrial Economics,[5,6] and international comparisons arising from the application of the model have also appeared in the Journal of Maritime Policy and Management.[15] The model is based on the present value criterion and in its more sophisticated form is capable of incorporating rates of inflation and shipbuilding loans. The basic form, assuming the vessel is financed from retained earnings is

$$NPV = E\sum_{i=1}^{n} A_i (1 + r)^{-i} + (1 - E) \left\{ \sum_{i=0}^{k} (A_i + P_i)(1 + r)^{-i} + R(1 + r)^{-k-1} \right\}$$

$$+ G_n C_o (1 + r)^{-L} - C_o$$

where $R = (\beta + \gamma) - \sum_{i=0}^{k}(A_i + P_i)$

- β is the value of the tax allowance on the capital cost involved in the investment proposal.
- γ is the value of accumulated tax allowances from other sources which can be set against the profits from the investment proposal.
- P_i is gross profits from other sources.
- G_n is the nominal rate of investment grant (if any). In the more general version of the formula, G_n is redefined as the unlagged percent value of any investment grant or net tax credit.
- C_o is the initial (capital) cost of the investment proposal.
- i is a year in the life of the investment proposal
- n is the economic life of the proposal
- k is the period before tax allowances are finally exhausted if $R \neq 0$ and the period in which tax allowances are exhausted if $R = 0$
- $E = 1 - t(1 + r)^{-L}$
- t is the nominal rate of corporation tax
- L is the lag in receipt of investment grant or tax credit or in payment of corporation tax
- r is the rate of discount per year, and
- A_i is the annual real net cash flow before payment of tax and excluding any investment grant received.

Where Ai and Pi are constant streams the formula can be written as:

$$NPV = EA \left[\frac{1 - (1+r)^{-n}}{r} \right] + (1-E)\left\{ (A + P)\left[\frac{1 - (1+r)^{-k}}{r} \right] + P + R(1+r)^{-k-1} \right\}$$

$$+ G_n C_o (1 + r)^{-L} - C_o$$

In plain language all this simply means is that the net present value of an investment is equal to the present value of the annual cash flows accruing to it (net of tax), plus the present value of any tax allowances used, plus the present value of any grant that may be received, minus its initial capital cost.[16]

It is possible to use one of two different approaches to the calculation of the net present value of a shipping investment. The tabular approach involves a spreadsheet growing from left to right and combining the various columns in some way to arrive at the final column which is then summed to find the NPV of the investment. Such an approach is contained in Evans[9] and Evans and Marlow.[11,17]

The other method is termed the modular approach and this expresses the NPV of the shipping investment as a function of its component (or modules) so that:

NPV = PV (Gross surplus − tax) + PV (tax relief for capital allowances)
 + PV (tax relief on interest) − PV (loan repayments)
 − PV (interest on loan) − PV (equity capital)
 + PV (scrap after tax) + PV (balancing allowance)

A fully worked example using these methods may be found in Chapter 18 of Evans and Marlow.[17]

The output from either of these methods allows the NPV of a shipping investment in any country, under the fiscal conditions relevant to that country, to be calculated and compared. These numerical results may be represented in the form of a bar chart for ease of comparisons. Figures 4 and 5 show a typical example depicting the NPV(£) per £1 million of shipping investment based on 5% rates of return, inflation and discount, and using the relevant credit arrangements in each country.

Such diagrams show very clearly the impact of a change in the fiscal regime of one country compared to others. These diagrams show the effect on UK shipowners of the government decision to replace a system of free depreciation by one of calculating capital allowances under the reducing balance method at

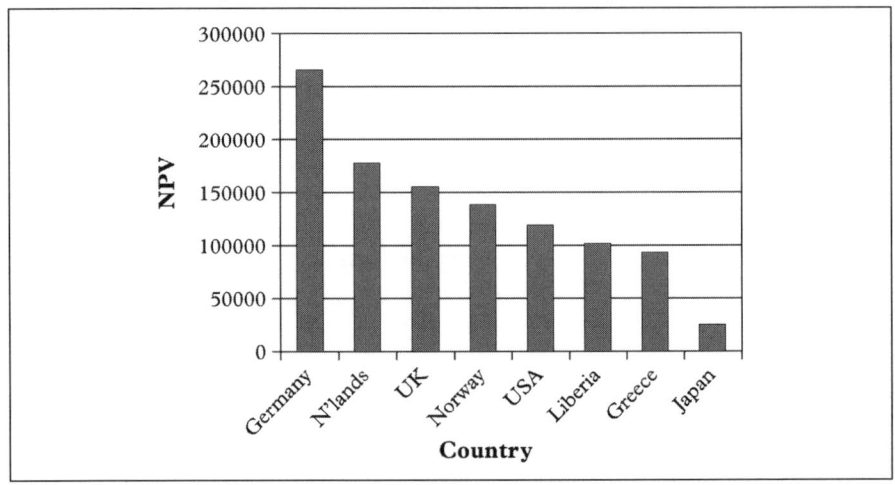

Figure 4: NPV of shipping investment pre-1984

Source: Author.

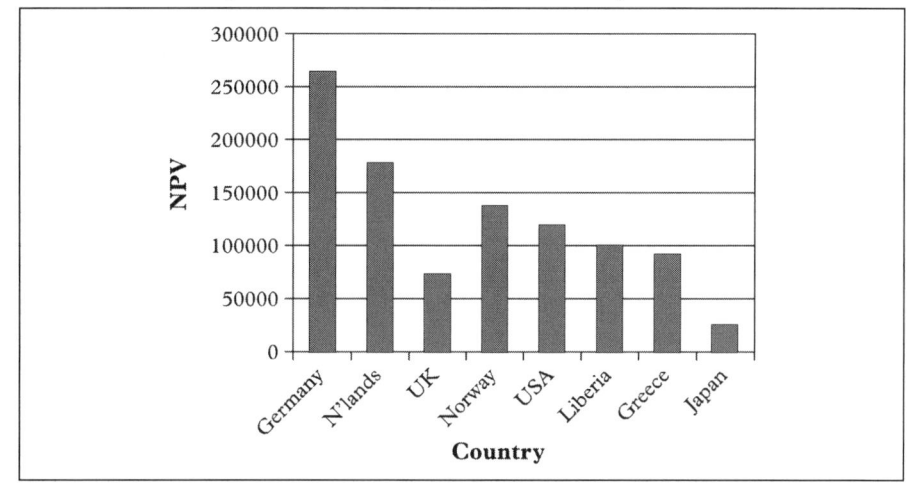

Figure 5: *NPV of shipping investment post-1984*

Source: Author.

a rate of 25% per annum. They illustrate that such a change would be detrimental to UK shipping and might reasonably be expected to lead to an increase in flagging out. Such action might also occur because the returns on an equivalent investment are greater in some countries than in others. In order to obtain a more level playing field shipping companies could choose to leave their national flag and register their vessel under a flag of convenience or open register.

The existence of open registers creates a sort of dualism in the international maritime transport sector splitting the industry into two segments distinguished by operating characteristics peculiar to the two different scenarios and by dissimilar break-even points. The shipowner, like any other entrepreneur, must choose the optimum amount of inputs to obtain the desired service output and strives to have the freedom to do so.[18]

Within the Open Registry fleet Liberia, Panama, Cyprus, the Bahamas and Bermuda used to represent the majority of the FoC tonnage and account for about 90% of the total fleet. However, a number of new registries are rapidly entering the market. The new Open Registries facilities are generally supplied by small states attracted not only by the receipts in foreign currency earnings and source of public revenue, but also by the perceived increase in their degree of political influence. Some examples are: Vanuatu, Gibraltar, Cayman Islands, Malta, Isle of Man, Kerguelen Islands and Maderia Islands; and many more. Moreover, since 1987, a new category of registries have emerged, the so called international registries. Examples of which are: Norwegian International Registry (NIS), Danish International Register (DIS), German International Register (GIS) and the Luxembourg International Register (LIR). These have been established as a more or less successful attempt to avoid en masse flagging out from the related national registry but why should governments be concerned about vessels flagging out?

6. THE IMPORTANCE AND CHOICE OF THE NATIONAL FLAG

There is an argument which says that, from a national economic point of view, the country in which ship owners choose to locate their businesses is more important than the flag they choose to fly for their vessels. Flagging out may mean some loss of tax revenue to the national exchequer but relocating a business to another country will mean further economic losses as well. These losses will include lower contributions to the home country's balance of payments, less direct and indirect employment opportunities for its citizens, a loss of past investment in maritime education and training and, in the medium to long term, a threat to the maintenance of the national maritime infrastructure. This threat can affect a wide range of industries (especially and directly those within the maritime cluster) and is likely to be particularly important in those countries with global centres of shipping expertise. As the shipping industry grows it will support a wide range of related activities, such as shipbuilding, ports, ship brokering, and insurance. This maritime cluster in the UK adds more than £7.5 billion to the economy and includes at least 1200 firms employing more than 110,000 people.[19]

The location of shipping businesses is certainly important. One study[20] has shown that the Dutch flag accounts for only 30% of the value-added by the Dutch shipping sector and the other 70% is created directly and indirectly through management activities ashore. It is felt that ship owners are unlikely to relocate their businesses to other countries if they continue to choose their national flags. They are attracted to working with stable and familiar systems and therefore have a natural affinity with their own flag. The move to open registers usually only occurs if the national flag cannot give them similar benefits or imposes unacceptable penalties. In most cases the decision to flag out is a complex one based on a variety of reasons. The elimination of obstacles and a combination of incentives is likely to be needed to attract them back.

Flagging out is primarily caused by the desire to minimise costs by placing the vessel under a relatively lower cost regime and it is estimated that crew cost differences between selected EU flags and lower-cost open registry vessels range from +22% to +333%.[21] A number of other factors in addition to crew costs can be considered as influencing the shipowners' choice. Bergantino and Marlow[18] suggested that other reasons for choosing a foreign flag might include: the desire for less bureaucratic control, the need to ensure the availability of skilled labour, the high costs of compliance with national flag standards, fiscal considerations, trading routes, and historical reasons. With the evolving of the practice of flagging out the reasons for registering a ship under the flag of a country other than that of the owner have varied, even though the primary reason for flagging out is generally accepted as being the need to reduce overall costs.

Discretionary fiscal regimes have altered the global distribution of ship ownership. The resulting changes of the market has been at the expense of those national fleets which suffer from less favourable tax treatment. For many years the rationale for the decision to flag out was felt to be the detrimental impact of the tax system. However, recent research suggests that it is only one of a plethora of reasons and that the importance of this factor has been diminished since the traditional maritime countries have had a chance to respond to the competition from the FoC countries. The governments of most of the traditional maritime countries have modified their policies to move them closer to the situation created by the legislation of the Open Registry countries. The FoC legislation is used as a benchmark against which to measure the effects of traditional maritime nations' policies. Since tax regimes and maritime subsidies play a crucial role in the competitive position of a shipowner it is felt that, when deciding on flag, the shipowner will evaluate the net impact of subsidies and tax allowances, of corporation/capital gains tax, of personal income tax, and of any other cost or benefit he could incur or receive by remaining under his national flag, when offset against the tonnage taxes and annual registration fees of Open Registry countries, allowing for the facts that profits will still be taxed if/when repatriated.

This relationship can be expressed in the form of a trade-off equation in which the fiscal incentive to flag out is measured by the difference between the discounted value of tax payments and grants/subsidies (A) over the life (n) of the vessel and the present value of tonnage taxes and registration fees (B). We can write:

$$A = \sum_{i=1}^{n} Tax \left[(1+r_p)(1+r_d)\right]^{-i} + Grant \left[(1+r_p)(1+r_d)\right]^{-g\_lag}$$

$$B = RF + \sum_{i=1}^{n} TT \left[(1+r_p)(1+r_d)\right]^{-i}$$

where:
- Tax = effective rate of corporation taxation
- r_p = annual rate of inflation
- r_d = annual rate of discount
- $Grant$ = level of grant
- g_lag = lag in receipt of grant
- RF = Initial Registration Fee
- TT = Annual Tonnage Tax

If $A = B$ the fiscal effect will be neutral. If $A > B$ then the fiscal factors will exert a positive influence on the vessel remaining under its national flag. If $A < B$ then there will be a fiscal incentive to flag out.

7. THE RESPONSE FROM TRADITIONAL MARITIME NATIONS

Whatever the reasons for the decision, flagging out has increased to such an extent that many traditional maritime countries have established their own second registers and in some cases, such as the Netherlands, Norway, Germany and the United Kingdom, have even modified their system of taxation for shipping in an attempt to reverse the trend. The most recent example occurs in the

UK[22] which introduced tonnage – tax for shipping in the year 2000. The regime bears considerable similarity to that of the Netherlands, introduced a few years earlier, and allows a shipping company the option either of remaining under the standard corporate tax regime or to participate in the new tonnage tax regime, under which its taxable profits are derived by reference to the net tonnage of each of the ships it operates whether owned directly or leased.

The shipping company pays corporation tax at the normal rate (currently 30%) on the derived profit. The rates of profit are derived as shown in Table 2.

Table 2: Rates of profit for corporation tax purposes

Net tonnage	Derived profit per 100 net ton per day
1–1000	£0.60
for the excess up to 10,000	£0.45
for the excess up to 25,000	£0.30
25,000 or more	£0.15

This innovation, introduced following the *Independent Enquiry into a Tonnage Tax* report by Lord Alexander of Weedon in August 1999, was justified for a variety of economic reasons, *viz.*:

- Ricardian trade theory states that a country will benefit from deploying its resources in those sectors where it holds a comparative advantage. UK firms hold a comparative advantage in several key sectors of the shipping industry and in many maritime related on-shore activities that provide services to the industry.
- The comparative advantage has been undermined by foreign tax competition and the shipping industry has declined as a result.[23] Without favourable tax treatment the decline of the UK shipping industry would not be arrested let alone be reversed.
- Unless the decline in UK shipping is reversed, the result will be a lack of training opportunities (berths) for UK seafarers and, consequently, the eventual loss of the UK's maritime skills base.
- The loss of the maritime skill base is of concern because the maritime related on-shore sectors of the economy have a requirement for former seafarers to fill certain key jobs. The cut-off of their supply would undermine the comparative advantage presently held by firms in these sectors. A study by Gardner and Pettit[24] in 1996 identified nearly 17000 jobs in more than 25 shore-based sectors which employers would prefer to fill with seafarers. For 70% of these jobs seafaring experience was considered essential. The study further noted that 1200 cadets would need to be recruited annually to meet this demand for trained manpower: the current intake is around 400 cadets each year. Hence there is a worsening shortfall to be rectified.
- Furthermore, support for the shipping industry leading to growth should create a "multiplier" effect spreading economic benefits to the on-shore maritime sectors, since the UK shipping industry provides a market for the output of businesses in these sectors. Thus through such linkages addi-

tional investment in shipping could potentially raise the output, employment and efficiency of the whole maritime cluster.

The estimated cost to the Exchequer of the UK arrangements is reckoned to be less than £40 million per year if the industry remains the same size and perhaps £65 million per year if its size doubles. Since shipping activities currently add around £2 billion to the UK economy each year[13] this cost is well justified. Providing support for one mode of transport raises the possibility of distorting competition between the different modes but the potential for a switch from road to water seems limited given the transport intensity of modern logistics practices. However, any such switch could be considered beneficial on environmental grounds.

This "new" approach is considered to have the advantage over more traditional corporation tax systems in that under the latter the various measures could not effectively be ring fenced and could distort investment decisions determined by tax rather than commercial considerations. Here it is possible to ring fence the shipping activity and hence minimise the risk of tax avoidance. It also provides a level playing field between trans-national partners thereby enabling the centre of gravity of partnership activities to be located in the UK instead of abroad when businesses are merged. Furthermore it addresses the skills shortage and requires companies, if they elect to join, to register for 10 years and to accept a "minimum training obligation". This involves sponsoring or providing the training of one new officer trainee each year for every fifteen deck or engineering officers (of whatever nationality) of their existing sea staff complement.

8. CONCLUSION

Any shipping industry will make a contribution to its national economy in terms of its effect on the balance of payments, the employment opportunities it offers to seafarers and subsequently to shore based management activities, its value to shipping centres such as London or Piraeus, and its backflow to the national government via taxes and value-added. This chapter has considered to what extent this contribution is affected by the choice of flag and, if owners decide to flag out their vessels, whether this will have a negative impact on the macro-economic wellbeing of the country from which the vessels have been moved.

A distinction has been drawn between the immediate and direct effects in terms of balance of payments contributions and the more indirect (longer term) effects on activities within the maritime cluster. Given the value of a national flag fleet to national economies the reasons for government incentives to retain their fleets are clear. Investment in a strong national flag fleet will not only provide immediate benefits in terms of balance of payments contributions and employment opportunities but it will also create wealth in the economy by promoting the shore based ancillary activities associated with the industry. The latter are entirely domestic and hence national in their multiplied impact, and will help to sustain or promote other sectors of the economy which, in their turn, will impact on more sectors. The full effect of this series of inter-relationships can be assessed using input-output analysis, and a consideration of the Leontief multipliers in the UK suggests that shipping (with a multiplier of 1.96) is more helpful than manufacturing (1.79), distribution (1.71) or agriculture (1.94) in this context.[25]

This chapter has suggested that shipping companies make decisions for financial (private) reasons and are not generally concerned with the impact of their decisions on the national economy (public considerations). It has been shown that, provided the macro-economic benefit of retaining vessels under a national flag or second register can be quantified, policy makers have a clear indication of the value of shipping to their national economy and hence some idea of the maximum support it could merit. The model presented allows the value of the package of disparate measures (subsidies, tax allowances, grants, etc.) necessary to persuade ship owners not to flag out, to be calculated. Such a solution would be a national Pareto optimum one in that the gainers (the national economy/government) would in effect be compensating the losers (the ship owners) for not flagging out and both sides would actually benefit from the increased prosperity in their country.

ENDNOTES

1. van Niekerk, H.C. (1997): *Ship registration and tax incentives to promote ship owning in South Africa*. Paper presented at the IAME Conference in London, September 1997.
2. Bracewell-Milnes, B., and Huiskamp, J.C.L. (1977): *Investment incentives*. Number 3 in the International series of the Rotterdam Institute for Fiscal Studies, Erasmus University Rotterdam (The Netherlands, Kluwer).
3. Marlow, P.B. (1991): "Shipping and investment incentives: a trilogy. Part 1 Investment incentives for industry", *Journal of Maritime Policy and Management*, vol 18, no 2, pp. 123–138.
4. Goss, R.O. (1976): *The Economics of Automation in British Shipping*, Transactions of the Royal Institution of Naval Architects, July 1967. Reprinted in *Studies in Maritime Economics* (Cambridge, Cambridge University Press).
5. Gardner, B.M., and Richardson, P.W. (1973): "The fiscal treatment of shipping", *Journal of Industrial Economics*, XXII, 2 December, pp. 95–117. Reprinted in Goss, R.O. (1977): *Advances in Maritime Economics* (Cambridge, Cambridge University Press).
6. Gardner, B.M., and Marlow, P.B. (1983): "An international comparison of the fiscal treatment of shipping", *Journal of Industrial Economics*, XXXI (4), pp. 397–415.
7. Gardner, B.M., Goss, R.O., and Marlow, P.B. (1982): *Ship Finance and Fiscal Policy*. A paper read to the Nautical Institute at the Royal Society of Arts, London, December.
8. Marlow, P.B. (1984): "The effect of the 1984 Budget proposals on the UK Shipping industry", *Maritime Policy and Management*, 11, 2, pp. 75–77.
9. Evans, J.J. (1984): "Some practical aspects of investment appraisal in shipping", *Maritime Policy and Management*, 11, 3 pp. 153–196.
10. Gardner, B.M., Goss, R.O., and Marlow, P.B. (1984): "Ship Finance and Fiscal Policy", *Maritime Policy and Management*, 11 (3), pp. 153–196.

11. Evans, J.J., and Marlow, P.B. (1986): *Quantitative Methods in Maritime Economics* (London, Fairplay Publications).
12. Standard works include Merrett, A.J., and Sykes, A. (1963): *The finance and analysis of capital projects* (Longmans); Merrett, A.J., and Sykes, A. (1973): *Capital budgeting and company finance* (Longmans). In a shipping context references include Goss, R.O. (1968): *Economic criteria for optimal ship designs*, reprinted in *Studies in Maritime Economics* (Cambridge University Press); and Buxton, I. (1976): *Engineering economics and ship design* (2nd ed.) (BSRA).
13. Brownrigg, M., Dawe, G., Mann, M., and Weston, P. (2001): "Developments in UK shipping: the tonnage tax", *Maritime Policy and Management*, Vol. 28, No. 3, pp. 213–223.
14. See notes 5, 6 and 10.
15. See notes 8 and 10, and also Marlow, P.B. (1991): "Shipping and investment incentives: a trilogy. Part 2 Investment incentives for shipping", *Maritime Policy and Management*, Vol. 18, No. 3, pp. 201–216.
16. Marlow, P.B. (1989): "Investment incentives for Shipping", unpublished PhD thesis (Cardiff, University of Wales).
17. Evans, J.J., and Marlow, P.B. (2001): *Quantitative Methods in Maritime Economics* (2nd ed.), reprinted 2001 (Coulsdon, Surrey, Fairplay).
18. Bergantino, A., and Marlow, P.B. (1998): "Factors influencing the choice of flag: empirical evidence", *Maritime Policy and Management*, Vol. 26, No. 2, pp. 157–174.
19. See Brownrigg, M., Dawe, G., Mann, M., and Weston, P. (2001): "Developments in UK shipping: the tonnage tax", *Maritime Policy and Management*, Vol. 28, No. 3, pp. 213–223 at p. 218.
20. Peeters, C., *et al.* (1994): *The future of the Dutch shipping sector* (Delft, Delft University Press).
21. See Bergantino, A., and Marlow, P.B. (1998): "Factors influencing the choice of flag: empirical evidence", *Maritime Policy and Management*, Vol. 26, No. 2, pp. 157–174 at p. 159.
22. Lord Alexander of Weedon, QC (1999): *Independent Enquiry into a Tonnage Tax* (London, HM Treasury).
23. Mayr, T.P., and McGrath, R.H. (1997): "Tramp Shipping: the role of taxation in international resource allocation", *Maritime Policy and Management*, Vol. 24, pp. 261–283.
24. Gardner, B.M., and Pettit, S.J. (1996): *A study of the UK economy's requirements for people with experience of working at sea*, report for the Department of Transport, the Chamber of Shipping and the Maritime Society, contract number DPU – 9/80/1 (Cardiff). See also Gardner, B.M., and Pettit, S.J. (1999): "Seafarers and the land based jobs' market: the present UK situation", *Maritime Policy*, Vol. 23, No. 1, pp. 103–115; and Gardner, B.M., and Pettit, S.J. (1999): "The land based jobs market for seafarers: consequences of market imbalance and policy implications", *Maritime Policy*, Vol. 23, No. 2, pp. 161–175.
25. Marlow, P.B., Pettit, S., and Bergantino, A. (1997): "The decision to flag out and its impact on the national economy", in Misztal, K., and Zurek, J. (eds.) *Maritime Transport and Economic Reconstruction* (Gdansk, Poland).

CHAPTER 24

GOVERNMENT POLICIES AND THE SHIPBUILDING INDUSTRY

Joon Soo Jon
Sogang University, Seoul, Korea. E-mail: *joonsoo@ccs.sogang.ac.kr*

1. INTRODUCTION

The health of the global economy is the most important factor governing the international shipbuilding industry but national economic policies play a crucial role in determining the extent to which a country's shipbuilding industries develop and thrive or, alternatively, decline and possibly disappear. Together, national and international factors can be referred to as the macro economic environment. If the economic climate is unfavourable then industrial organisations, including shipbuilders, will face painful problems and may even have to close their production facilities.

While the macro economic environment sets the conditions that will either allow a shipbuilding industry to thrive, or not, the choices made, decisions taken, by each individual shipbuilding business are crucial to its survival and prosperity. Good decisions at the enterprise level can partially offset an unfavourable macro structural environment.

Government policies in promoting shipbuilding industry are largely implemented through various types of financial assistance such as direct financial aid and or by guaranteeing loans.

Therefore, the main objective of this chapter is to review the historic development of successful shipbuilding countries and provide informative cases for reference in the face of changing national and global circumstances. The structure of this chapter is as follows. The next section focuses on the impact of Government intervention on the shipbuilding industry. The third section considers the global shift in the shipbuilding industry and structural changes in this market. The forth section examines the role of government in developing or supporting the shipbuilding industry. The fifth section explores the impact of recent changes in economic environment on the leading shipbuilding countries such as Japan, South Korea and China. The final section presents the summary and conclusions.

2. THE IMPACT OF GOVERNMENT INTERVENTION ON THE SHIPBUILDING INDUSTRY

2.1 Shipbuilding enterprises

Shipbuilding enterprises can be categorised as falling into two distinct groups; those that engage purely in shipbuilding and those that are diversified enterprises where shipbuilding is only one of a portfolio of interests that may have very little in common. In addition there is also an important distinction to be made between shipbuilders that are private firms and those that are state corporations.

There are strengths and drawbacks associated with being either an independent shipbuilding enterprise or the shipbuilding arm of a conglomerate. Not surprisingly both structures are frequently found within a national shipbuilding industry. Shipbuilders belonging to diversified corporations have the advantage of being able to rely on corporate resources for expansion and support which are independent of the state of the shipbuilding market. Consequently, in periods of shipping recession, the shipbuilding member of the group can call upon reserves acquired in other market areas in order to overcome short-term cash flow difficulties. Moreover, this shipbuilder may be able to use group resources to modernise its production facilities at a time when independent shipbuilding firms are being obliged to cut back their overheads and capacity. This enables the shipbuilding member of the group to boost its competitive position compared to other shipbuilders. The flexibility inherent in within-group transfer of resources to the benefit of shipbuilding operations has been important to the success of Japanese and South Korean shipbuilders.

Access to well organised and funded marketing, and research and development, can be another advantage of being part of a conglomerate. But there is one more, less easily quantifiable but very important, advantage to being in a big group. Conglomerates have political clout. These diversified, large companies command respect and influence in industrial, financial and political circles. This can mean easier access to capital markets and more sympathetic treatment by politicians, than could be expected by a dedicated shipbuilding company. These factors add up to substantial competitive advantage for conglomerate members.

There is, though, a downside to being part of a conglomerate. Although a shipbuilding subsidiary should theoretically benefit from the resources its parent group devotes to R&D and marketing, the bureaucracy surrounding those functions in a large conglomerate may in practice offset any gains.

Unfortunately, a hierarchical, overly-bureaucratic form of organisation can easily lead to inflexible decision-making and rivalry between the managements of member organisations. This can lead to individuals vying for power within the hierarchy of corporate head-office rather than working for the good of the shipbuilding enterprise.

Enterprises solely focused on shipbuilding can, on the other hand, be much more flexible and resilient. As Todd notes:

"They [dedicated shipbuilders] tend to be more loosely organised and more flexible and responsive to changing circumstances in consequence. The independent shipbuilding firm may continue in shipbuilding operations because it simply has no choice – other than closure – whereas the shipbuilding subsidiary may find itself steadily undermined because its corporate parent feels that greater profits can be made by switching assets out of shipbuilding into a more lucrative field. No matter how dedicated the shipbuilding managements of the subsidiary, their subservience to the greater corporate interest takes precedence over their sectoral interests and conceivably, group shipbuilding operations may be phased out not because they are lacking in viability but owing to their low profitability relative to other group interests. It is fair to say that unless the independent shipbuilder can grow to such a position that resources become little or no object, the chances of survival cannot be assured."[1]

2.2 Impact of government intervention

The state is not necessarily, or even usually, a disinterested observer of the shipbuilding scene. Governments often intervene in their shipbuilding industries. Intervention can range from macro economic management to direct intervention at enterprise level.

This chapter looks at two ways governments can intervene to shape the development of a national shipbuilding industry. One way open to the state is to order the building of warships. Through its allocation of naval contracts, the state often appears to be supporting shipbuilding as a kind of implicit regional policy. Awarding warship orders to particular yards can be a way of protecting employment. The balance between ordering motivated by such social factors and objective assessment of national defence needs, seems to vary over time.

The other way is formulating policies to promote the shipbuilding industry in direct and indirect ways. Government role in developing the shipbuilding industry has mainly focused on the financial assistance in various forms.

Governments act as credit guarantors for the construction of ships at their domestic shipyards and often cooperate with shipyards in devising new forms of financial inducement to shipowners to place orders. These can take the form of disguised subsidies to directors. Also a government-sponsored shipbuilding program with favorable financing (in terms of interest rate and repayment period) provides a great impetus to the development of the domestic shipbuilding industry.

3. THE GLOBAL SHIFT OF SHIPBUILDING INDUSTRY

3.1 Structural change in world shipbuilding

In the early1990s South Korean shipbuilders embarked on an ambitious expansion strategy, despite warnings from the rest of the global shipbuilding industry that the move threatened price stability by creating a large excess of capacity compared to supply. The expansion of the South Korean capacity included new building docks at Hyundai Heavy Industry, modifications at Samsung allowing the building of VLCCs and similarly sized vessels and the construction of the large, modern VLCC capable Halla yard at Mokpo.

Japanese shipbuilders responded by booking large numbers of orders at comparatively lower prices. The price competitiveness of the Japanese shipbuilding industry then deteriorated due to a sharp rise in the yen which rose at one time to as high a level as 95 per US dollar. This strengthening of the yen led Japanese yards to buy foreign materials and equipment where possible. Meanwhile the world orderbook increased, mainly due to demand for large-size bulkers and containerships.

GOVERNMENT POLICIES AND SHIPBUILDING 533

Trends of world economy, good or bad, generally begin to produce their effect on shipping with a time lag of around one year, and on shipbuilding one year later than shipping.

3.1.1 Japan

The profitability of the Japanese shipbuilding industry is greatly dependent on exchange rate with the US dollar. Because ship prices are usually denominated in US dollars the sharp appreciation of the yen meant that prices realised by the Japanese yards effectively fell dramatically.

In 1994, the yen rose further to a daunting level of ¥95 per US dollar. Although it then returned to ¥100, these successive surges in the yen caused the shipbuilding industry to become less and less price competitive. However, since the late 1990s the weakening Japanese Yen has once again strengthened the price-competitiveness of Japanese shipbuilders.

3.1.2 South Korea

The OECD shipbuilding working party group considered South Korea's capacity expansion for the first time at a meeting held in January, 1995. A representative of the South Korean government said that the government had no legal basis to impose any restraint on expansion by private firms because a matter of this sort was entirely left to the independent judgment of each private enterprise. While the expansion was happening the gap that had existed between Japan and South Korea in the areas of non-price competitiveness, such as technological skills and quality where Japan claimed to lead, was closing.

South Korea succeeded in achieving a level of quality comparable to that of Japan, at least as far as the hull structure is concerned. This was achieved as result of the large amount of experience gained throughout the 1980s, building diverse types of ships and marine structures. But South Korea still lags behind Japan in such areas as marine engines and ship-related equipment.

3.1.3 Western Europe

Germany has finally stabilised its economy following the economically difficult, reunification of the former East and West Germanys. The country's shipbuilding industry, which had been not been particularly dynamic in the 1980s gradually revived throughout the 1990s with an expanding orderbook.

Orders were at a healthy level during most of the decade, with the national industry especially strong in the container ship and passenger vessel sectors. By the beginning of the 2000s, however, Germany was facing major problems. In 2001 deliveries amounted to 55 ships, totalling just over 1m gt. But very few orders were taken during that year with government-related contracts playing an important part in the survival of many yards. A number of yards also started to look more at conversions and refurbishments to compensate for a lack of newbuilding orders.

Germany had become vulnerable because of its specialistions. Korean shipbuilders were increasingly able to beat German owners on price for container ship orders while the sharp downturn in the cruise industry, exacerbated by the

September 11 terror attacks, hit passenger ship builders like Meyer Werft very hard.

Denmark is another important EU shipbuilding country. Odense Shipyard is by far the country's largest, and is particularly well known for its high productivity attained through sophisticated computerisation and robotics. A large portion of its orderbook comes from A P Moller, one of the biggest ship owners in Europe.

3.1.4 Other countries

China has ranked third largest shipbuilding country, after Japan and South Korea, since 1992. China constructed the New Dalian dockyard, with one building capable of building 250,000 DWT ships in 1995.

Poland built VLCCs back in the 1970s but not in recent years. Since the demise of communism, its yards have been successful in attracting newbuilding orders from Greece and Western Europe. Although existing shipbuilding facilities are old, domestic supplies of marine equipment, including main and auxiliary engines makes the Polish shipbuilding industry largely self-sufficient. This insulates them from currency fluctuations and allows them to book orders at lower prices. An upward trend in the volume of ship construction has become apparent since 1992 as a means to earn foreign currency reserves through ship exports.

Brazil is another country with shipbuilding potential. However its shipbuilding programme has suffered from economic turmoil and shortage of funds. Although Brazil has technological skills comparable with the international standards for building large-size vessels, including DH (double hull) tankers, the real problem lies in its price competitiveness. In an attempt to rectify this Brazil is promoting the rationalization of its yards. In 1995 the merger of ISIBRAS (Ishikawajima do Brasil) Yard and Verolme was the largest merger ever in Brazil.

Structural changes are emerging on a global scale in the shipbuilding industry over the second half of the 1990s and 2000s, while at the same time being affected by structural changes in the shipping industry.

3.2 Demand and ship cycles

Ship costs are strongly affected by the costs of procuring materials and labour in the shipyards. Moreover, shipyard expenses and production costs in general are very sensitive to technological change – a supply factor. Technological change, however, has implications, which extend from supply to demand factors.

Great store was put on the effects of innovation on the competitiveness of industrial organisations.[2] According to this theory, shipbuilders fall into the technological leader category and attract a growing market share as a result of their progressive practices. Those categorised as technological laggards, though, are compelled to react to innovation in order to retain a share of the market.

Obviously, technological change is having a dramatic impact on demand from both perspectives: the lead firms taking away demand from the laggards and they, in turn, being forced to find compensatory demand largely with government help.

It is important to stress, however, that the level of aggregate merchant ship demand is set independently from the actions of either shipbuilders as a whole, or governments intervening to protect national shipbuilding industries. Aggregate demand is, in fact, the outcome of conditions affecting world trade.

The actions of individual shipbuilding enterprises and individual governments may partially regulate the demand for a small component of world shipbuilding, but they will not greatly affect overall demand conditions. In other words, aggregate demand for shipping is very largely an exogenous factor; something outside of the control of the industry or government institutions.

The approach adopted here is one which sets shipping as the derived demand outcome of world trade conditions. It assumes that, derived broadly, it conforms to two categories: a "traditional" ship cycle manifested through the effects of trade on the production of "typical" ships; and a "modern" ship cycle in which trade effects are expressed in varying ways depending on the type of specialised ship.

Warship production, of course, is influenced by different factors. These vessels not only have their own supply requirements which can be quite different from those pertaining to merchant ships, but they also respond to a peculiar form of derived demand that is very different from the ship cycles affecting merchant ships.

Governments intervene in the market for two main reasons order; to bolster the demand for ships and thereby provide support for an otherwise ailing domestic shipbuilding industry. Governments can also intervene in regional economies, which are suffering from depressed conditions in order to bolster regional development and ameliorate the consequences of locally-concentrated unemployment. Ideally, the two objectives complement each other. Ailing shipbuilders receive a boost from government aid, and depressed communities receive a form of employment stabilisation through government support for the job-creation organisations.

Governments are most able to affect demand by ordering warships. Policies using warship procurement as a means of intervening have different effects on shipbuilding than those aimed at stimulating merchant ship demand. This is because demand for commercial vessels is linked to the international trade cycle and is dependent upon the actions of a multitude of mainly private shipping firms. When it comes to warship building, however, national governments are able to control demand, subject to limits on the overall defence budget. Wherever possible government support their national shipbuilding industries by placing orders with local yards as far as possible.

Warship producers are however highly vulnerable to government whims. Overall economic factors also impact on warship building by putting pressure on the national and defence budgets. In practice warship production is, in its own way, as cyclically unstable as commercial shipbuilding. Warship producers can attempt to secure export orders but in general they are highly dependent on a single, very powerful customer – their government.

4. THE ROLE OF GOVERNMENT AND ITS POLICIES TO PROMOTE THE SHIPBUILDING INDUSTRY

4.1 State subsidies, naval shipbuilding

4.1.1 State subsidies

Shipbuilding subsidies have long been, and remain highly controversial. Ship prices are frequently distorted by the effects of state subsidy. One commentary points to the incompatibility of the "heavy over-tonnaging of virtually all types of ships" on the one hand, and the continual scramble to garner newbuilding orders on the other. The motivation for the imbalance between supply and demand is simple and stems from the belief held by all states that their shipbuilders are too important to be allowed to fail. Consequently, "there is great temptation to support ship production beyond 'normal' commercial limits". Whatever form it takes, the end-result is a financial subsidy borne by the state.[3]

In actual fact not all states believe that shipbuilders "are too important to be allowed to fail". Since the late seventies, for example, the UK has generally allowed the decline of its shipbuilding industry to run its course although it did pay subsidies to yards, up to the limit allowed by EU rules.

The conventional subsidy afforded by OECD countries was a credit scheme where 80% of the ship price is funded through a loan repayable over a seven to eight-year period at a fixed interest rate of 7 or 8% per year. However, some states juggled the terms in order to secure a more competitive position for their shipbuilders. This was usually accomplished by either the provision of further subsidies, however described, or through a reduction of the interest rate on the loans advanced.

It is abundantly clear that non-OECD countries offer better concessions in as much as their repayment periods are extended beyond the norm, but, even OECD members manipulate the loan terms to serve their own ends. Japan, for example was marginally extending the loan period to 8.5 years in the case of a bulker ordered for US principals.

The extent and availability of financial concessions of this kind are ultimately determined by overall economic conditions. In other words, there is a tendency to subsidise during periods of downturn in ship cycles and, correspondingly, a tendency to reduce subsidies when conditions signal an upturn in ship cycles.

This generalisation is discernible from the sample of loan schemes applied to bulker newbuildings since 1975. In that year, financial concessions offered by Japanese shipbuilders were relatively modest, covering as little as 50% of ship cost. Such schemes were permissible at that time because of the massive order backlogs held by Japan notwithstanding the disruption caused to the industry as a result of the 1973 oil price rises.

By the end of the decade, however, there had been a significant change: loans were being extended to cover up to 90% of ship prices in a variety of countries including Japan. The change was, of course, in response to heightened competition for increasingly scarce orders.

The level of subsidy declined to the standard of 80% over eight years in the early 1980s by virtue of international agreements among OPEC members on the allowable loan scheme. This level was considerably higher than the mid-1970s level, nevertheless, and reflected the desperation of many nations to secure newbuilding orders at virtually any price.

This behaviour harms shipping, encouraging owners to buy vessels when they would probably hold back if prices were at levels reflecting the true cost of production. It does, however, clearly demonstrates the serious commitment of governments to support their shipbuilding industries.

Government naval procurement programmes are often designed to serve as counter-cyclical measures for shipyard employment stabilisation. It is argued that downturns in merchant shipbuilding demand can be countered by building warships. Without naval orders, the decline in merchant shipbuilding experienced by US shipbuilders would have put most of them out of business. There are, however, problems with using warship building in this way. Naval contracts can end up crowding out commercial orders. Thus, the use of warship orders as a counter-cyclical measure can only be effective if such orders are timed to truly use slack resources and not divert resources from other production. In practice, the timing of defence contracts rarely been truly counter-cyclical may have done more harm than good. Moreover, not all yards can build warships or naval auxiliaries efficiently, limiting the scope of warship construction as a regional development tool.

4.1.2 Naval shipbuilding

Since the Second World War, the USA has been the example of a nation whose shipbuilding has been heavily dependent on defence contracts. At the present time, something in the order of 75% of new ship construction in the USA is destined for the US Navy.

The residual merchant shipbuilding industry is locked into high-costs practices associated with naval construction. According to one official pronouncement, it is owing to generally higher construction costs that the US shipbuilding industry has not, on balance, been an export industry since the days of the clipper ships. In consequence, merchant shipbuilding as well as naval newbuilding is tied to domestic markets: markets which, in turn, rely on an inordinate amount of government regulation.[4] So while US shipbuilding is influenced by the global shipbuilding market, to some extent, domestic circumstances peculiar to the USA shipbuilding are much more important. The USA has established a complex framework of federal policy, statute, and regulation with respect to naval shipbuilding, subsidised commercial shipbuilding, and cabotage, including the well-known Jones Act. Indeed, some observers suggest that without subsidies amounting to up to 35% of construction costs, mercantile newbuilding would be abandoned in the USA.

By its nature, naval shipbuilding is performance-oriented rather than cost-conscious. Navies worry about design details and the fulfilment of target specifications. Ship owners worry about the price of newbuildings and so builders of merchant shipyards are preoccupied with cost efficiency. Consequently shipyards that choose to specialise in warship work largely remove themselves from the discipline of the market. These shipyards may become entirely dependent on a government. to the extent of the state being the sole arbiter of demand, a monopolist in fact. In general governments encourage technical competence in warship suppliers irrespective of production efficiencies.

Warship production when not strictly required to meet defence needs is also justified on strategic grounds. It is argued that defence-production capacity must be maintained in a state of readiness for any national emergency. Governments are also seen as being obliged to purchase products from defence suppliers because the latter have committed so much of their resources to the development of these highly-specialised products which are tailored to specific government requirements.

4.2 Shipbuilding and national economic development

Economic planners and politicians in NICs (Newly Industrialised Countries) have often seen shipbuilding as having an important role in the modernisation process and in national development. Shipbuilding can appear to be an attractive development tool for three reasons. In the first place, it is a medium technology industry, which suits the factor-cost advantages of NICs. Thus, technology does not act as a barrier to entry while the labour intensive nature of shipbuilding favors countries with large, cheap labour forces. Secondly, the market is an international one and thus shipbuilding can be a net earner of foreign exchange. Customers for ships come from all parts of the world. The existence of flag-of-convenience fleets adds to the emphasis on price competitiveness in the market and allows shipowners to circumvent market protection imposed by national governments. A newly emergent producer, capitalising on low factor costs, can offer competitively priced ships, which rapidly find customers in such an open market. Finally, shipbuilding has strong links with other industries. It should, therefore, serve to foster other nascent industries in the NICs.

Not surprisingly, shipbuilding has been singled out by a number of countries in recent years as deserving of special treatment. At one extreme, the state has taken the combined role of planner and shipbuilder. This was the case with command economies such as the China, Poland, and Yugoslavia; and the interventionist economy of India. At the other extreme, the state has encouraged the industry in the name of national development but left the practice of shipbuilding to private enterprise – as is attested by Brazil and South Korea. In between are NICs, such as Spain, which encourage both private and public enterprise in shipbuilding. The case of South Korea is highlighted here – as perhaps the most successful of the NICs engaged in shipbuilding.

4.3 South Korea

The Korean shipbuilding industry in the 1950s had to rely primarily on imported materials, so the cost of building ships domestically exceeded international ship prices. This imposed a heavy burden on cash-strapped Korean shipping companies, and demand for locally built ships declined. The government legislated the Shipbuilding Encouragement Act on 11 March 1958 in an effort to stimulate development of shipbuilding industry as well as to support the shipping industry. About this time, the shipbuilding industry's sphere of influence shifted dramatically. As labor accounts for between 20% and 30% of the total cost of building a ship, shipbuilding activities declined in the U.K. and West Germany, where labor was becoming scarce and expensive. Meanwhile, Japan had emerged as the world's foremost shipbuilding nation as early as 1956, and that country's share of the world market continued to increase, eventually reaching almost 50%. Korea also had a large pool of highly skilled, low-cost labor. The government realized the importance of shipbuilding, but it also understood that private sector companies, which lacked capital, could not be expected to build expensive, large-scale shipyards. Thus, the government put forth a battery of industry development policies and established state-run shipbuilding companies. Korea Shipbuilding & Engineering Corp. was founded in January 1950. Capital for the project came from government US dollar reserves as well as the Agency for International Development (AID).

During the 1960s, the Korean government launched two successive five-year plans which rapidly expanded the scale of the national economy. Fishing companies of all kinds cropped up, causing domestic demand for ships to soar.

However, as Korea was in the early stages of economic development, the overall industrial structure was still weak, so the initial focus was put on light manufacturing. Shipbuilding and the rest of the heavy industrial sector did not see significant progress. The Korean government launched its Second Five-year Plan (1967–1971). In 1967, the government enacted the Shipbuilding Industry Promotion Act and designated the period as a time to modernise facilities and raise technology levels in order to improve national competitiveness. At the same time, a foundation was to be laid for Korea to generate her own ship demand as well as to gradually move towards ship exportation. At the same time, world demand trends pointed to ships of ever-increasing size. However, the government's shipbuilding promotion policy was aimed mainly at expanding the tonnage of small ships for Korean end-users. The policy did help expand total industry output volume, but little was done to develop large-sized ships or shipyards. Demand for ships that could not be built domestically was satisfied through imports, and the domestic shipbuilders only supplied 20% of the total new ships bought by Korean shipping companies.

The Long term Shipbuilding Industry Promotion Plan was announced in March 1973, to promote Korea to be a full-fledged ship exporting nation in the 1980s. Major developments in the Korean shipbuilding industry during the 1970s include the government's establishment of the Planned Shipbuilding Program (PSP) in 1976, which was initiated under a stated goal of "Korean shipyards building Korean ships to carry Korean cargo". Under the aegis of this program, government-financed projects were provided to Korean shipbuilders, with the end-users being selected by the government. The program was institutionalised with basis in Korean law in 1978. In addition, Korea adopted an export credit system in 1972, a move that would have greatly helped domestic shipbuilders to secure new orders. That is between 80% and 90% of the ships built in Korea from 1973 on were for export, and the number of ships purchased by deferred payment increased with each passing year. However, Korean shipyards, which were just becoming established in the world shipbuilding market, were not able to enjoy the same interest rates or repayment periods as the world's leading shipyards could. In the 1970s, the world shipbuilding market was changing rapidly. Soaring world seaborne trade volumes were spurring demand for new ships, and shipowners were interested in buying ships of ever bigger tonnage, in order to lower both the costs of building new ships and transporting cargo. In the mid-1960s, the largest ships being built were 100,000 deadweight tons; the average size was between 30,000 and 50,000 dwt. However, in the early 1970s 200,000dwt vessels were the norm, and the world's shipyards were scrambling to expand facilities. Another big reason for the trend towards larger ships was the rapid increase in the international movement of oil. In the 1960s, oil tankers made up only 21.5% of all ocean-going merchant ships but, by the end of the decade, 75% of the new ship orders were for oil tankers. The huge increase was brought about by the closure of the Suez Canal, which forced ships to travel much longer distances.

To cope with this change, the Korean government encouraged private sector companies to look for an overseas joint venture partner who would transfer the technology, and to find buyers for the ships it was to build. With government encouragement, Hyundai which was the leading pioneer in the Korean shipbuilding industry, approached A&P Appledore and Scott Lithgow in the U.K. and, in September 1971, a contract was made for sales and technical support. Further technical-support arrangement was concluded with Kwasaki Heavy Industries in 1972 and at the same time an order of two 230,000dwt VLCC (Very Large Crude Carrier) was given to Hyundai by the same company. As part of the deal, Kwasaki provided design drawings and trained Hyundai employees.

From the mid-1970s, the principal aspects of the government's policy for advancing the heavy industries: In order to globalise and modernise heavy industrial facilities, the government would provide concentrated support for areas that saved resources, were technology intensive and involved a high degree of local assembly. Korean shipyards continued to increase their output from the early 1970s, but major growth increases began during the Fourth Five-year Plan (1977–1981). During the period, the Korean merchant fleets lacked the tonnage needed to handle the rapidly growing volume of goods being transported to and from Korea. To bolster their fleets, however, Korean shipping companies were mainly buying used ships rather than commissioning the idle domestic shipyards to build new ones. Therefore, steps were urgently needed to help the two industries develop together.

However, a major problem remained: Where would project financing come from? Government provided state-run banks guarantee for those commercial loans secured by private sector companies, from foreign financial institutes.

On the other hand, the government instituted the Planned Shipbuilding Program in 1976. For pre-selected end-users, financial support would be provided for the purchase of domestically-made ships. To help domestic shipyards improve their productivity and design capabilities, it was stipulated that a ship build under PSP have standardised hull forms. At the same time, the program would provide each shipyard with a stable supply of work. The goal was for Korean-owned ships to end up carrying a greater percentage of Korean-made goods and thereby help to improve the international balance of payments. With the establishment of the Export-Import Bank in 1975, Korea also began offering an export financing program for the shipowners to build their ships at the Korean shipyards. According to the Korea Shipbuilders' Association, Korean shipbuilding output was just thirty four ships, totaling 12,000 gross tons in 1973. Five years later, that annual figure had surged to 208 ships, totalling 769,000 gross tons. Korean shipbuilding began to take off in response to growing domestic demand, and it continued to develop in step with the growth of other export-driven Korean industries.

The two Oil Shocks of the 1970s slowed world economy and the shipping volumes were further cut. Faced with the stagnant shipbuilding market, the Korean shipbuilding industry began looking for ways to change form a business based on quantitative growth to one that was more quality oriented. A cost-cutting campaign and Total Quality Control program were vigorously pursued. In addition, the Korean shipbuilding industry geared up for greater diversification into such non-shipbuilding sectors as off-shore and engineering, industrial plants, engines and machinery, robotics and heavy equipment.

It is a typical phenomenon nowadays that international trade volumes do not increase with the low economic growth rates and rising protectionism. To make things worse, as the Korean shipyards had captured one-quarter of the world shipbuilding market and, thus, trade pressure on Korea from the US and EC steadily intensified. In March 1989, the EC nations (now EU) demanded that ship prices be monitored and that market shares be adjusted. Then in June of that year, the Shipbuilders Council of America claimed that government subsidies and tax breaks granted to shipbuilders in Japan, Korea, Germany and Norway, constituted unfair trade practice. The council then filed a complaint against those four countries based on the Super 301 provisions of the US Omnibus Trade and Competitiveness Act. Negotiations dragged on for several years. No more government intervention is the clear policy of the Korean government at a moment.

5. STRUCTURAL CHANGES IN MAJOR SHIPBUILDING COUNTRIES

5.1 Japan

The Japanese shipbuilding industry continually increased its output until the late 1980s. Japan's dominant position as the top shipbuilding country has been threatened by the emergence of South Korea. This development led to significant changes in the structure of Japanese shipbuilding, with both capacity and workforce size cut back considerably.

According to Lloyd's statistics covering ships of 100GT and above, volume of new completions in Japan reached a peak of about 16,991 million GT in

1975, and about 7,206 million GT in the 1990s. In and after 1988, the volume of new completions kept increasing year after year, reaching about 9,263 million GT in 1995, and it went up to about 20,686 GT in 2000. According to the MOT's (Ministry of Transport) shipbuilding statistics covering steel ships of 20GT and above, a substantially similar tendency can be observed.

A review of the ratio of domestic ships to export ships in terms of the number of ships built discloses the fact that the domestic ship's share accounted for 70–80% throughout the past 30 years. In terms of GT basis, however, export ships' share is greater than domestic ships' share because export ships are generally larger in size than domestic ships. This ratio of export ships to domestic ships has undergone a significant change due to the multinationalisation of ships, either owned or controlled, following the globalisation of Japanese shipping firms.

Export ships share increased to 80–90% in the 1990s, and it will rise more in 21st century. This structural change is featured by a decrease in the tonnage of domestic ships due to a drastic decline in the volume of the government-sponsored "planned shipbuilding program".

Table 1: Trend of steel ships built in Japan

Year	Domestic ships No. of ships	Domestic ships Million GT	Domestic ships Billion yen	Export ships No. of ships	Export ships Million GT	Export ships Billion yen	Total No. of ships	Total Million GT	Total Billion yen
1970	2,081	3.95	405.9	222	6.22	392.1	2,303	10.17	797.9
1975	1,010	2.61	432.1	517	12.61	1,403.9	1,527	15.23	1,836.0
1980	1,319	2.78	558.5	273	3.41	643.7	1,592	6.19	1,202.2
1985	817	2.75	486.6	401	6.16	982.4	1,218	8.91	1,469.1
1990	838	1.35	405.9	213	5.12	586.5	1,051	6.48	992.5
1995	593	0.82	293.2	282	7.87	857.2	875	8.68	1,150.4
2000	2,081	3.95	405.9	222	6.22	392.1	2,303	10.17	797.9

Source: Maritime Technology & Safety Bureau, MITI, "Shipbuilding Statistics Summary".[5]

Such decline is attributable to the changes occurred in the pattern of investments in ships as a result of the multinationalisation of ships. The pattern of ownership has changed from domestic owners to foreign ownership in areas or countries of open registry (flag of convenience). For this reason, among export ships, there are a number of foreign-registry ships, which are substantially owned by Japanese shipping firms.

5.1.1 Changes in the composition of major shipbuilders

Japanese major shipbuilders have implemented many restructuring measures, including conversion of shipyards into offshore and construction facilities. As a result the total capacity of major shipbuilders has declined.

These changes also affected medium sized shipbuilders because the large shipbuilders have each been associated with a number of medium size yards. Some of Japan's medium and small sized shipbuilders have increased new-building output greatly over the past 30 years.

A review of the Japan's shipbuilding industry shows that, since the second-half of the 1980s when there were drastic cutbacks of shipbuilding capacity and personnel, the volume of newbuilding output has varied from company to company according to differences in their capacity, and differing management strategies, while market shares of newbuilding output, too, varied depending upon the measures taken by respective companies.

5.2 South Korea

East Asia's financial and currency crises had devastating effects on South Korea, causing drastic structural changes in its economy and industry during the period from the summer of 1997 to middle of 2000. Specifically, the sharp decline in the value of South Korea's currency, the WON, had a severe effect on industries relying on imported commodities whose WON price had soared. The low value of the won did have some positive effects and improved the price competitiveness of its exports. Nevertheless the negative effects of the currency's fall greatly outweighed the positive ones. South Korea's entire economy was forced into a critical situation and there was a desperate attempt to obtain massive amounts of financial assistance from such institutions as IMF.

Because of this situation, South Korea's shipbuilding industry faces a number of tough challenges, such as rationalisation (seen as essential to boosting competitiveness), the rising cost of production, the need to cut out inefficient facilities and to trim the industry's large workforce. A "special retirement program" is underway and the industry has been compelled to carry out drastic structural reforms. Meanwhile, the need to face up to the overcapacity issue will not go away.

5.2.1 Changes in volume of orders received

In 1991, according to Table 2, South Korea's volume of newbuilding orders stood at about 5,433,970 GT in total. In 1993 expansion of capacity by Halla

Table 2: Volume of newbuilding orders in South Korea

	Domestic ships			Export ships			Total		
	Volume of completion		Ship prices	Volume of completion		Ship prices	Volume of completion		Ship prices
Year	No. of ships	GT	$000	No. of ships	GT	$000	No. of ships	GT	$000
1991	10	116,548	195,377	111	5,317,409	5,365,171	121	5,433,957	5,560,548
1992	10	5,070	107,561	41	1,637,584	1,770,610	51	1,642,654	1,878,171
1993	7	16,290	36,927	177	9,490,581	7,289,974	184	9,506,871,	7,326,901
1994	7	4,843	87,441	159	6,366,525	5,794,022	166	6,371,368	5,881,463
1995	2	340	23,438	192	7,132,801	6,768,746	194	7,133,141	6,792,184
1996	2	2,000	29,204	142	6,971,849	7,037,946	144	6,973,849	7,067,150
1997	1	11,800	49,575	200	12,737,616	10,382,531	201	12,749,416	10,432,106
1998	–	–	–	175	9,998,518	7,923,876	175	9,998,518	7,923,876
1999	3	14,800	25,800	224	12,704,309	9,159,620	227	12,719,109	9,185,420
2000	2	23,235	12,647	311	10,378,273	15,146,970	313	10,401,508	15,159,617

Source: The Korean Shipbuilders' Association.[6]

Engineering and Hanjin Shipbuilding pushed Korea to the top position in world shipbuilding, overtaking Japan. However, the economic crisis that hit South Korea in 1997 forced Korean shipbuilders to seek the improvement of productivity that has resulted from drastic restructuring, which, together with relative weakening of the won against the yen, has allowed South Korea to maintain its competitiveness.

5.2.2 Volume of new completions

South Korea's share of the world total of new completions has grown to such a level that it will affect the distribution structure of the world output among shipbuilding countries. According to the Korean Shipbuilders' Association's statistics covering merchant ships of GT, South Korea's volume of new completions increased from 4,429,952 GT in 1991 to 8,212,848 GT in 1999 (Table 3). Completions peaked in 2000 at more than 9 million GT.

A predominant characteristic of South Korea's volume of new completions is that the share of ocean going vessels for export is overwhelmingly greater than that of domestic vessels. This is because the tonnage of the fleet owned by the South Korean shipping industry is still small in world terms.

Table 3: Volume of newbuilding completions in South Korea

	Domestic ships			Export ships			Total		
	Volume of completion		Ship prices	Volume of completion		Ship prices	Volume of completion		Ship prices
Year	No. of ships	GT	$000	No. of ships	GT	$000	No. of ships	GT	$000
1991	22	208,778	325,704	87	4,221,174	3,601,592	109	4,429,952	3,927,296
1992	5	103,998	180,258	89	4,463,441	3,778,170	94	4,567,439	3,958,428
1993	15	64,143	181,549	73	3,318,902	3,226,370	88	3,383,045	3,407,919
1994	8	17,423	41,029	107	5,152,735	4,466,004	115	5,170,158	4,507,033
1995	5	9,546	100,507	135	5,653,231	5,048,896	140	5,662,777	5,149,403
1996	–	–	–	170	7,798,235	6,592,552	170	7,798,235	6,592,552
1997	–	–	–	172	7,449,467	6,944,167	171	7,449,467	6,944,167
1998	2	2,000	29,204	161	8,632,593	7,024,020	163	8,634,593	7,053,224
1999	–	–	–	163	9,481,315	8,212,948	163	9,481,315	8,212,848
2000	2	17,760	18,800	178	6,029,189	9,593,137	180	6,046,949	9,611,937

Source: The Korean Shipbuilders' Association.[7]

5.3 China

The two-digit growth rate of economy experienced by China since the early 1990s has grabbed the world's attention. Growth has been so strong that the Chinese government has had to put a brake on its overheated economy.

5.3.1 Changes in China's economy

In the first half of the 1990s, China further promoted the policy of opening up its economy to the outside world in accordance with its Eighth Five-Year Plan(1990–1995). As a result, its economy grew at the high average annual rate of 12.6% between 1992 and 1994.

The growth of industrial production centering on the steel and heavy machinery industries led to an increase in the production of capital goods and durable consumer goods which are necessary to meet the domestic demand. And, in the economic zones along the southeastern coast around Guangdong and Hong Kong, the production of consumer goods, such as household electrical appliances, textile and foodstuffs as the light industrial products has dramatically increased. Moreover, the mass movement of farmers from the countryside to these coastal regions as an ample source of low wage labour force has significantly contributed to the boosting of China's export industry, thereby allowing it to shift from the exporter of primary goods to that of secondary and finished products.[8]

Thus, China's economy, supported by expanded domestic markets embracing about 1.3 billion population, has structurally changed to assume a more important role in the export and import trades with not only Japan and Southeast Asian countries, but also western countries, including the US, thereby considerably affecting the development of the world economy.

With a huge consumer market supported by enormous domestic demand, China has tremendous potential for growth. So there has been a consistent inflow of foreign capital into China from western as well as Asian countries, including Japan and Korea, aimed at increasing export and import trades. In the medium to long-term, this is likely to continue.

5.3.2 Changes in the shipbuilding industry of China

It was in 1977 that Lloyd's commenced listing China's tonnage data in its statistics covering merchant ships of 100 GT and above. The volume of newbuilding orders received by Chinese yards has kept increasing since the second half of the 1980s. According to *Lloyd's Register*, orders totaled 777,000 GT in 1994 and reached 3, 011, 000 GT in 1999. Chinese yards then accounted for 10.4% of the total world orders (see Table 4).

China publishes the volume of tonnage built in terms of "composite ton" which is essentially the mixed unit of deadweight ton for cargo ships, including non-self-propelling steel ship and displacement ton for others. According to these statistics, volume of tonnage newly built started from almost 1,079,000 GT in 1994 (see Table 5).

Table 4: Volume of newbuilding orders in China

Year	Number of ships	Thousand GT	Per cent of world total
1994	50	777	3.1
1995	85	1,108	4.3
1996	113	1,665	7.1
1997	131	1,461	4.0
1998	96	662	2.5
1999	173	3,011	10.4
2000	172	2,531	5.6

Source: *Lloyd's World Shipbuilding Statistics, 2001.*

Table 5: Volume of newbuilding completions in China

Year	Number of ships	Thousand GT	Per cent of world total
1994	144	1,079	5.5
1995	159	953	4.3
1996	138	1,102	4.3
1997	152	1,479	5.8
1998	154	1,446	5.7
1999	144	1,556	5.6
2000	101	1,484	4.8

Column group header: Volume of newbuilding completions

Source: *Lloyd's World Shipbuilding Statistics, 2001.*

The volume of completions in 1999 reached almost 1,556,000 GT, accounting for 5.6% of the world total.

5.3.3 The Role of China State Shipbuilding Corporation(CSSC)

China State Shipbuilding Corporation is essentially the core of China's shipbuilding industry and it exercises control over large and medium-size shipyards capable of building ocean-going vessels and warships, as well as large-size marine structures. On the other hand, small-size shipyards, engaged in the building medium and small-size steel vessels to be used for inland waterways and for coastal trading, are under the jurisdiction of the Ministry of Communications or regional autonomous bodies.

CSSC is one of the state-owned mammoth enterprises belonging to the Ministry of Machine-Building Industry. With its headquarters located in Beijing, CSSC exercises general control over major shipyards throughout China through nine regional shipbuilding corporations located in Shanghai, Dalian, Tianjin, Guangzhou, etc. CSSC has control over the Merchant Ship Design & Research Institutes which are located in regional centres such as Shanghai and Wuhan.

As for ship design, basic plans are mainly drawn up in Beijing, while detailed plans are worked out by these regional institutes. Depending upon the type of ships ordered, however, there are cases where basic plans are drawn up by regional institutes.

In the early 1990s, a new modernised large yard was constructed within the Dalian Shipyard. This new yard, together with the old one and factories for the production of ship related products, formed the "Dalian Group". This is a sure indication that the manner of the central control by CSSC has become flexible enough to allow certain autonomy to part of the regional institutes.

The case of Guangzhou Shipbuilding Industry Corporation is a typical example of this flexibility. Its corporate name changed to "Guangzhou Shipyard International" with its stocks listed on the stock exchanges in Shanghai and Hongkong. Although this shipyard is still under the jurisdiction of CSSC, it is essentially the advent of an independent shipyard as a stock company with the same form of business organization as those commonly seen in the capitalist economy.

China Shipbuilding Trading Co.(CSTC) became independent of the CSSC in 1987. Since then it has promoted ship exports through collaboration with CSSC.

6. SUMMARY AND CONCLUSION

Shipbuilding enterprises come in two distinct groups; those that engage purely in shipbuilding and those that are diversified enterprises where shipbuilding is only one of a portfolio of interests that may have very little in common.

Shipbuilders belonging to diversified corporations have the advantage of being able to rely on corporate resources for expansion. Consequently, in periods of shipping recession, the shipbuilding member of the group can call upon reserves acquired in other market areas in order to overcome short-term cash flow difficulties and to modernise its production facilities and to avail itself of research and development initiatives sponsored by the group as well. The flexibility inherent in within-group transfer of resources to the benefit of shipbuilding operations has been important to the success of Japanese and South Korean shipbuilders. Also as a member of a large group called "chaebol"[9-11] this type of shipbuilder commands respect in industrial, financial and political circles. This respect may be manifested through easier access to capital markets and more sympathetic treatment of the enterprise by policymakers.

The state actively seeks to regulate the activity levels of whatever portion of the industry falls within its jurisdiction. In this way the government can shape the shipbuilding industry.

Aggregate shipbuilding demand is the outcome of conditions affecting world trade. The actions of individual shipbuilding enterprises and individual governments may partially regulate the demand for a small component of world shipbuilding, but they will not greatly affect overall demand conditions. In other words, aggregate demand for shipping is very largely an exogenous factor; something outside the control of the industry or government institutions.

The health of a country's shipbuilding industry has ramifications for the role of governments on the one hand, and the prosperity of communities and regions within countries on the other. In the first instance, governments can intervene in the market in order to bolster demand for ships and thereby provide support for an otherwise ailing domestic shipbuilding industry. In the second Instance, governments can intervene in regional economies which are suffering from depressed conditions in order to bolster regional development and ameliorate the consequences of locally-concentrated unemployment.

Ship prices are frequently distorted by the effects of state subsidy. The motivation for the imbalance between supply and demand is simple and stems from the belief held by most states that their shipbuilders are too important to be allowed to fail. Consequently, there is great temptation to support ship production beyond "normal" commercial limits. Whatever form it takes, the end-result is a financial subsidy borne by the state. The extent and availability of financial concessions of this kind are ultimately dependent on the conditions prevailing in the economic environment.

Government support for shipbuilding is not confined to loan schemes for newbuildings. It can be manifested through direct forms of demand management. One of the means often resorted to by governments is the formulation of naval programmes such that they serve as counter-cyclical measures for shipyard employment stabilisation.

Shipbuilding has been perceived as a key player in modernisation of society and the furthering of national development which follows from industrialisation. Shipbuilding is an enticing tool of development, it is a medium technology industry which appears to suit the factor-cost advantages of NICs. Also shipbuilding has strong links with other industries. It should, therefore, serve to foster other nascent industries in the NICs.

The Japanese shipbuilding industry has had to adapt to an ever-changing environment. Japan's competitive edge was reduced as South Korea emerged as a major shipbuilding country. Worth noting as the measures that brought about significant changes in the structure and constitution of the Japanese shipbuilding industry were its drastic cutbacks of shipbuilding capacity and mass dismissal of employees through a Special Retirement Program.

East Asia's financial and economic crises had devastating effects for South Korea, causing far-reaching structural changes in its economy and industry since the summer of 1997. Following the decline of its economy, South Korea's shipbuilding industry has faced a number of major challenges, such as rationalisation to enhance competitiveness, the rising cost of production, cutbacks in capacity and employees, and drastic structural reforms. At the same time South Korea is under pressure to find ways deal with overcapacity; an issue which is certain to remain controversial in the 21st century.

China's economy, supported by expanded domestic markets supporting about 1.3 billion people, has changed structurally with exports and imports becoming more important. The volume of newbuilding orders received by Chinese yards has kept increasing since the second half of the 1980s. According to *Lloyd's Register*, orders totalled 777,000 GT in 1994 and reached 3,011,000 GT in 1999. Chinese yards then accounted for 10.4% of the total world orders. China will certainly continue with its ambitious shipbuilding expansion plans.

The shipbuilding industry is simply a player in the commercial market, so any form of subsidy distorts the price and damages free market mechanisms. Government subsidy to shipyards merely undermines the strength of the commercial market for new merchant ships. This has resulted in a situation where the taxpayers of many countries pay substantial sums to support uneconomic national shipbuilding industries.

Artificially low newbuilding prices represent a loss to all in the shipbuilding and shipping markets. In order to improve productivity, it is essential to utilise automated machinery and tools and sophisticated automated systems effectively. Technological competence is equally important. It serves as the basis for the development of design and engineering capabilities. This technological competence coupled with efficient management know-how will determine ultimate productivity. How to achieve the superior productivity will determine the future of a country's shipbuilding industry.

ENDNOTES

1. Todd, D. (1985): *The World Shipping Industry* (Croom Helm Ltd).
2. *Ibid.*, p. 205.
3. *Fairplay*, January 1984, p. 9.
4. National Academy of Sciences (1980): *Personnel Requirements for an advanced Shipyard Technology* (Washington, DC), p. 13.
5. Maritime Technology & Safety Bureau, MITI: *Shipbuilding Statistics Summary*.
6. The Korean Shipbuilders' Association, 2001: *Shipbuilding Statistics*, p. 15.
7. The Korean Shipbuilders' Association, 2002: *Shipbuilding Statistics*, p. 28.
8. JAMRI (1995): *Recent Trends of China's Shipping and Shipbuilding*, JAMRI report, No. 53, November 1995, pp. 4–5.
9. Chaebol: largest conglomerate companies existing in Japan and Korea. They command large influence on policy making and finance.
10. Hyundai heavy industries Co. Ltd. (1999): *Hyundai Shipyard, Yesterday and Today; Traditions of Excellence* (KorCom International Inc.), pp. 202–208.
11. Jon, Joon-Soo: *Over Capacity; Who Is to Blame?*, paper presented at the Plymouth University conference in 1995.

PART EIGHT

ASPECTS OF SHIPPING MANAGEMENT AND OPERATIONS

CHAPTER 25

MARKETING STRATEGIES IN SHIPPING

A. Güldem Cerit
School of Maritime Business, Dokuz Eylul University, Izmir, Turkey.
E-mail: gcerit@turk.net

1. INTRODUCTION

Shipping is a service industry, which performs in an international business market where the demand is derived from international trade and transport. Shipping constitutes the main actor of the supply chains in building the international logistics systems. The markets in shipping diverse among bulk or liner shipping, shorter or longer distance routes, sizes and types of ships, types of goods carried and types of services provided. Shipping provides the customers, namely the shippers, with a transportation service, main sources of differentiation appearing to be the operational and functional aspects of the service and the service quality. Shipping adds value to materials and goods and contributes to international trade in the field of cheaper and more efficient transport services.

Technological developments, rapid growth in liner shipping, upward trends in ship sizes, integration of shipping companies through mergers, alliances and acquisitions and fluctuations in international trade produce pressures on the shipping industry ending in declines in freight rates and affecting the competitive position of the industry negatively. The fierce competitive environment of shipping forces the industry to concentrate on market oriented strategic planning where competitive strategies of cost-leadership, differentiation and focus lie at the centre.

This chapter presents the theoretical background for the terms strategy, strategic planning, market orientation, market oriented strategic planning and competitive strategies. The chapter explains the competitive strategies concentrating on service quality, relationship marketing, marketing public relations and social marketing issues concerning sustainable transport. The chapter provides the analysis of the market environment for shipping and explains the competitive advantage of shipping in international marketing. Through the points reached, the chapter discusses the main marketing strategies for the shipping industry that will create competitive advantage through differentiation.

2. MARKETING AND STRATEGIC PLANNING

Maritime industry, being one of the most internationalised economic sectors, performs under the laws of global competition and the sub-sectors and organisations taking part in the industry need to be strategically oriented in order to survive and to continue growth against the changing market environment of the 21st century.

2.1 Strategy and planning

Strategy is explained as the management of natural competition and a deliberate search for a plan of action that will develop a business's competitive advantage and compound it (Henderson 1989). Within any organisation strategy development occurs at multiple levels – the corporate level, the business level and the functional level (Kerin et al. 1990). Modern business management links strategy with competition and *competitive strategy* is defined as the search for a favorable competitive position in an industry, the aim of competitive strategy given as "establishment of a profitable and sustainable position against the forces that determine industry competition" (Porter 1985). Choice of competitive strategies depends on industry attractiveness and competitive position.

The strategy formulation process involves development of alternative strategies of which competitive strategies are at the centre. Considering global markets, a globally focused firm uses its world-wide system of resources to compete in national markets (Chakravarthy and Perlmutter 1985; Porter 1986; Hout, Porter and Rudden 1994). Industries and companies competing in the global market place have to adopt global strategies which are built on information systems that scan the world business environment to identify opportunities, trends, threats and resources (Keegan and Green 1997).

A *planning system* is a formalised and systematic approach to developing and implementing strategies (Kerin et al. 1990). A *strategic planning process* on the other hand is understood as a management process involving consultation, negotiation, and analysis which is aimed at insuring effective strategic decision making (Dyson 1990). The aim of strategic planning is to shape and reshape the organisation's businesses and products/services so that they yield target profits and/or growth (Kotler 2000). Strategic planning is conceptualised as analysing the current and expected future situation, determining the direction of the firm and developing means for achieving the mission (Weihrich 1990). This process demands a systematic approach for identifying and analysing factors external to the organisation and matching them with the firm's capabilities.

Corporate strategies are affected by both the macro and the micro external environmental factors and the internal environmental factors of the businesses (Kotler 2000; Keegan and Green 1997). *External macro environment* consists of the demographic/economic, technological, natural, social/cultural and political/legal forces. External micro environment actors are grouped as customers, competitors, distribution channels and suppliers. *Internal environmental factors* are related to the business functions of marketing, finance, manufacturing and organisation.

2.2 Market orientation

Market orientation is explained as representing superior skills in understanding and satisfying customers (Day 1994). Its principal features are given in three groups:

(1) A set of beliefs that put the customer's interest first (Deshpande, Farley, and Webster 1993).
(2) The ability of the organisation to generate, disseminate and use superior information about customers and competitors (Kohli and Jaworski 1990).
(3) The coordinated application of interfunctional resources to the creation of superior customer value (Shapiro 1988; Narver and Slater 1990; Slater and Narver 1995).

Empirical evidence has proved that, market orientation is positively associated with superior performance (Deshpande, Farley, and Webster 1993; Jaworski and Kohli 1993; Narver and Slater 1990; Narver and Slater 1994). These points regarding the effects of marketing organisations, customers and competitors are obtained through empirical studies and ended in approaches toward market orientation measures. Studies concentrating on analysis of market orientation through marketing functions, marketing organisations and market orientation measures have been realised in different markets and differing company structures (Baker and Sinkula 1999, Balakrishnan 1996, Barrett and Weinstein 1998, Pelham and Wilson 1996, Pelham 2000, Cadogan *et al.* 1999, Atuahene-Gima 1996, Han *et al.* 1998, Hurley and Hult 1998, Avlonitis and Gounaris 1997). Finally market orientation is described as a business philosophy (Harris 1999).

Regarding the maritime transport field, an empirical comparative study that was performed in the shipbuilding industry concentrated on the effects of marketing organisations over market orientation. The effects on (1) competitive position of a company in the market, and (2) customer choices directed towards the company are searched in order to be able to comment on the market orientation measures with respect to marketing organisations. It is concluded that, shipyards with more developed marketing organisations approach market orientation determinants of modern marketing effectively and effective approach to market orientation measures strengthen competitive position and success in customer choices (Cerit 2002).

As can be noted from the explanations and results of the empirical studies, customer and competitor analysis are the main features of market orientation, accompanied by the effective utilisation of interfunctional resources. Planning system of a market oriented business has to be designed according to the analysis of the customers and the competitors.

2.3 Market oriented strategic planning

Contributions of marketing to strategic management have long been a matter of discussion among researchers. Marketing is a societal process by which individuals and groups obtain what they need and want through creating, offering and freely exchanging products and services of value with others (Kotler 2000). The American Marketing Association defines *marketing management* as the process of planning and executing the conception, pricing, promotion and distribution of ideas, goods, services to create exchanges that satisfy individual and organisational goals (AMA 1995). Marketing perspective is believed to offer a distinctive view to the strategic context in three areas (Day and Wensley 1988):

(1) analysis of competitive market behavior;
(2) defining viable organisation boundaries;
(3) allocating resources.

Since strategy is described as the integrated action in the pursuit of competitive advantage (Day 1990), a business has to successfully steer a strategic course through market turbulence and become proactive in shaping events and competitive behavior to its advantage. The three ingredients that are necessary for this process are summarised as follows (Day 1990): (1) Strategic vision that focuses the energies of all parts of the organisation toward competition, (2) Market orientation in which the beliefs and values of the organisation put the customer first, (3) Process for formulation and choice of the best strategy in light of the issues facing the business. These points emphasise the importance of strategic vision, market orientation through integrated efforts of the whole business, customer focus and strategy formulation.

A market oriented strategic planning process covers the main phases of statement of the corporate mission and corporate objectives; analysis of the environment and assessment of the situation audit and portfolio decisions through the use of the management information systems; determination of the business objectives; generation of competitive strategies; planning alternative programs in the functional areas; planning for implementation and organisation and finally the control phase (Kerin *et al.* 1990; Kotler 2000; Day 1990; Porter 1985). The phases of the market-oriented strategic planning process are given in Figure 1.

Once the *mission statement* and the *corporate objectives* are formulated, corporate management is aware of the related environment. The *external environment analysis* will end in identification of the opportunities and threats facing a major business unit. The business unit should set up a *marketing intelligence system* as a part of the *management information systems* to track trends and important developments. Through *internal environment analysis* each business evaluates its internal strengths and weaknesses. *Situation audit* covers the market segments, the appropriate market targeted and the offer's value positioning. *Portfolio assessment* profiles the organisation's current mix of businesses and their current and anticipated performance ending in *portfolio decisions*. The *business objectives* are established in functional areas and *competitive strategies* are identified among either cost-leadership, or differentiation or focus strategies. Alternative marketing, financial, manufacturing and organisational functional programs are developed. The *organisation* for *implementing* the strategic plans is also settled and finally the *control* phase covers the tracking of the results.

3. MARKET LOGISTICS AND DEALING WITH THE COMPETITION

The rise in world output of goods and services and the rapid growth of world merchandise trade after the 1990s have been readily reflected in the volume of trade. Companies competing in the global marketplace are forced to develop

MARKETING STRATEGIES IN SHIPPING

Figure 1: Market oriented strategic planning model

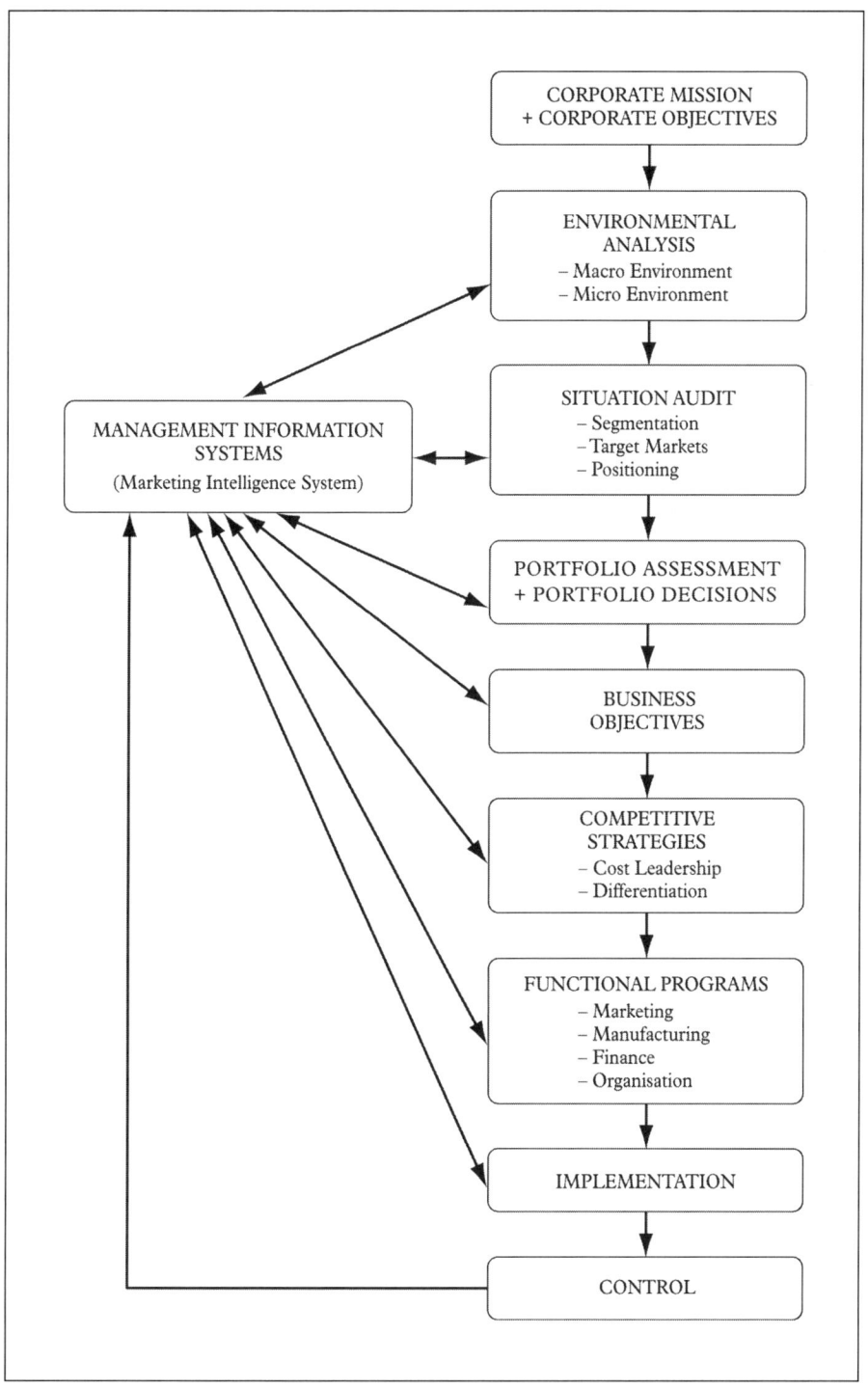

```
                              ┌─────────────────────┐
                              │ CORPORATE MISSION   │
                              │ + CORPORATE         │
                              │   OBJECTIVES        │
                              └─────────┬───────────┘
                                        ▼
                              ┌─────────────────────┐
                              │ ENVIRONMENTAL       │
                              │ ANALYSIS            │
                              │ – Macro Environment │
                              │ – Micro Environment │
                              └─────────┬───────────┘
                                        ▼
    ┌─────────────────────┐    ┌─────────────────────┐
    │ MANAGEMENT          │◄──►│ SITUATION AUDIT     │
    │ INFORMATION         │    │ – Segmentation      │
    │ SYSTEMS             │    │ – Target Markets    │
    │ (Marketing          │    │ – Positioning       │
    │  Intelligence       │    └─────────┬───────────┘
    │  System)            │              ▼
    │                     │    ┌─────────────────────┐
    │                     │◄───│ PORTFOLIO ASSESSMENT│
    │                     │    │ + PORTFOLIO         │
    │                     │    │   DECISIONS         │
    │                     │    └─────────┬───────────┘
    │                     │              ▼
    │                     │    ┌─────────────────────┐
    │                     │◄───│ BUSINESS OBJECTIVES │
    │                     │    └─────────┬───────────┘
    │                     │              ▼
    │                     │    ┌─────────────────────┐
    │                     │◄───│ COMPETITIVE         │
    │                     │    │ STRATEGIES          │
    │                     │    │ – Cost Leadership   │
    │                     │    │ – Differentiation   │
    │                     │    └─────────┬───────────┘
    │                     │              ▼
    │                     │    ┌─────────────────────┐
    │                     │◄───│ FUNCTIONAL PROGRAMS │
    │                     │    │ – Marketing         │
    │                     │    │ – Manufacturing     │
    │                     │    │ – Finance           │
    │                     │    │ – Organisation      │
    │                     │    └─────────┬───────────┘
    │                     │              ▼
    │                     │    ┌─────────────────────┐
    │                     │    │ IMPLEMENTATION      │
    │                     │    └─────────┬───────────┘
    │                     │              ▼
    │                     │    ┌─────────────────────┐
    │                     │◄───│ CONTROL             │
    └─────────────────────┘    └─────────────────────┘
```

international marketing strategies to overcome the challenges in global marketing and international marketing strategies have long become a special area of interest for the marketing scientists (Wind *et al.* 1973; Hulbert *et al.* 1980; Chakravarthy and Perlmutter 1985; Jain 1989; Samiee and Roth 1992; Cavusgil and Zou 1994; Terpstra and Sarathy 1994; Cavusgil 1996; Kotler 2000).

Physical distribution, being a strategy area under global marketing (Terpstra and Sarathy 1994), has also been a major topic of research for the business discipline aiming to contribute to the analysis of the competitive position of the companies (Anderson 2000; Ballou 1992; Aertsen 1993; Bukold 1993; Londe and Masters 1994). The scope of the function has been broadened into *market logistics*, which involves planning, implementing, and controlling the physical flows of materials and final goods from point of origin to points of use to meet customer requirements at a profit (Kotler 2000).

The goal of international marketing is stated as creating and retaining customers in global markets (Terpstra and Sarathy 1994) and global marketing strategy has been investigated by business and marketing scientists since the end of the 1960s.

In terms of marketing mix, distribution has always been considered as one of the most critical decisions in international marketing with respect to (1) market entry decisions (Terpstra and Sarathy 1994), (2) selection of distribution channels (Stern and Sturdivant 1987; Jones *et al.* 1992; Mueller *et al.* 1993; Aertsen 1993), and (3) global logistics (Ballou 1992; Bukold 1993; Londe and Masters 1994). Physical distribution is a major cost of international marketing and profits can be increased through cost reductions in the transportation of the goods (Terpstra and Sarathy 1994).

Transportation as a sub-system of the logistics system has been defined as "the most important single element in logistics costs" (Ballou 1992) and has attracted the attention of the researchers in the transportation business (Wood and Johnson 1996). Research on developments in transportation technology, analysis of the time factor in transportation businesses, transportation costs, and organisation and management of the transportation systems have been the major areas of interest in this context (Wood and Johnson 1996; Casson 1986). For those competing in the international markets, an efficient and inexpensive transportation system contributes to greater competition, greater economies of scale in production and reduced prices for goods (Ballou 1992).

3.1 Competitive strategies

Global strategies contribute to the competitive advantage of the firms competing in international markets (Porter 1990a; Porter 1990b). Competitive strategy aims to establish a profitable and sustainable position against the forces that determine industry competition (Porter 1985) and competitive strategy is defined as deliberately choosing a different set of activities to deliver a unique mix of value (Porter 1996).

Studies on competitive strategies have been based on two groups of competitive factors: industry attractiveness (industry position or external factors) and competitive position (firm resources or internal factors) (Porter 1985; Porter 1987; Barney 1991). External factors cover macro and micro environmental factors (Barney 1991; Cerit *et al.* 1997). Competitive factors concerning firm's resources are based on internal analysis (Barney 1991) and are referred to as organizational functions (Belohlav 1993; Boscheck 1994) or as business functions (Cerit *et al.* 1997).

Porter's approach to external factors is grouping them into five competitive forces that determine industry competition, namely, (1) rivalry among existing competitors, (2) threat of new entrants, (3) threat of substitute products and services, (4) bargaining power of suppliers and (5) bargaining power of buyers (Porter 1985; Porter 1990a).

Porter groups the activities performed in competing in a particular industry in two categories: primary activities and the support activities. Firm infrastructure (e.g., finance, planning), human resource management, technology development and procurement constitute the "support activities" whereas, inbound logistics, operations (manufacturing), outbound logistics, marketing and sales and after-sale service account for the "primary activities" (Porter 1985).

The whole system of activities is referred to as the "value chain" and all these activities in the value chain contribute to buyer value. To gain competitive advantage over its rivals, a firm must either provide comparable buyer value but perform activities at a lower cost, or differentiate and perform activities in a unique way that creates greater buyer value and commands a premium price (Porter 1990).

The two basic types of competitive advantage are lower costs and differentiation. The three generic strategies defined by Porter for superior performance in an industry are grouped as cost leadership, differentiation and focus strategies (Porter 1985).

The theory of competitive advantage is applicable in the same manner for domestic and international markets, considering the characteristics of different markets. The main areas of differentiation strategies for transportation services appear in service quality, relationship marketing, marketing public relations and promotion of environmental considerations.

3.1.1 Service quality

As an element of international marketing, functional aspects of the transportation service cover the operational activities taking place in the transport business according to the special characteristics of each transport mode, namely marine, truck, air, rail or pipeline transport (Wood and Johnson 1996).

Transportation systems are part of the whole international marketing system and are affected by all the external and internal factors surrounding the system. Moreover, the transportation system itself is subject to competitive forces and the other factors of its own dynamics, and the direction of the transportation service with respect to competitive strategies affects the outcomes of the service (see Figure 2).

The *value chain* provides a tool for understanding the sources of cost advantage. Lower transportation costs lower the costs for logistics and hence the primary activities as a total thus assisting the company in gaining a cost advantage. The value chain also exposes the sources of differentiation by meaning a raise in the buyer's performance in ways the buyer cannot match by purchasing from competitors. As a service industry, transportation industry provides the customers with a service, main sources of differentiation appearing to be the operational and functional aspects of the transportation service and the service quality.

Figure 2: Competitive position of transportation in the international marketing system

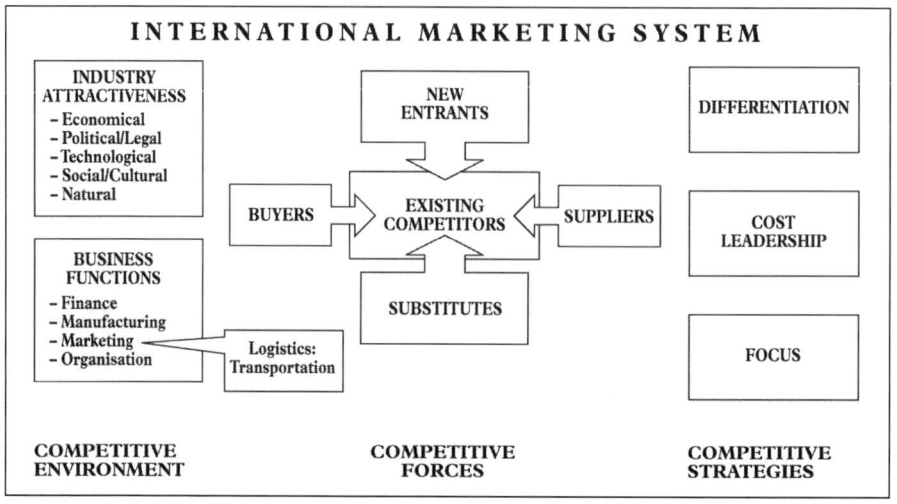

```
                INTERNATIONAL MARKETING SYSTEM

   INDUSTRY
   ATTRACTIVENESS            NEW
   - Economical            ENTRANTS                    DIFFERENTIATION
   - Political/Legal
   - Technological
   - Social/Cultural
   - Natural
                   BUYERS    EXISTING    SUPPLIERS       COST
                            COMPETITORS                LEADERSHIP
   BUSINESS
   FUNCTIONS
   - Finance                SUBSTITUTES
   - Manufacturing
   - Marketing    Logistics:
   - Organisation Transportation                          FOCUS


   COMPETITIVE              COMPETITIVE                COMPETITIVE
   ENVIRONMENT               FORCES                    STRATEGIES
```

Sources: Michael E. Porter (1990): *The Competitive Advantage of Nations* (New York, The Free Press); Jay Barney (1991): "Firm Resources and Sustained Competitive Advantage", in *Journal of Management*, 17(1), 1991, pp. 99–120; A. Güldem Cerit, Hakki Kisi, Okan Tuna and Omur Saatcioglu (1997): "Gümrük Birligi Sürecinde Ege Bolgesi Sanayiine Rekabet Gucu Acisindan Stratejik Bir Yaklasim", in *Verimlilik Kongresi*, 3, 14–16 May 1997 (Ankara, MPM Publications), pp. 177–195; A. Güldem Cerit (2000): "Maritime Transport as an Area of Competitive Advantage in International Marketing", in *International Journal of Maritime Economics*, Vol. 1, No. 3, January–March, pp. 49–67.

3.1.2 Relationship marketing

Relationship marketing is analysed (Morgan and Hunt 1994) as a concept that encompasses relational contracting, relational marketing (Gundlach and Murphy 1993), partnership marketing (Kotler 2000), symbiotic marketing (Varadarajan and Rajaratnam 1986), strategic alliances (Day 1990), co-marketing alliances, and internal marketing (Berry and Parasuraman 1991).

When all the forms of relational exchanges are considered, the definitions appear as "the practice of building long-term satisfying relations with key parties-customers, suppliers, distributors – in order to retain their long-term preference and business" (Kotler 2000) and "all marketing activities directed toward establishing, developing and maintaining successful relational exchanges" (Morgan and Hunt 1994). Focusing on the customer relations, relationship marketing takes the definition as "the task of creating strong customer loyalty" (Kotler 2000).

In the services marketing area, the proposed definitions of relationship marketing are; "concerning attracting, developing and retaining customer relationships" (Berry and Parasuraman 1991); "recognition of the value of current customers and the need to provide continuing service to existing customers so that they will remain loyal" (Lovelock 1996); and "a means by which an organisation seeks to maintain an ongoing relationship between itself and its customers, based on continuous patterns of service delivery, rather than isolated and discrete transactions" (Palmer 1994).

To develop relationships with customers, both the factors governing relationship marketing and the strategies to handle these factors must be considered. When aiming to establish the quality factors between the seller and the buyer, the two main factors that relationship marketing relies on are *ethical foundations and trust*.

Ethics require an individual to behave according to the rules of moral philosophy. (Gundlach and Murphy 1993). Legal rights of exchange parties guide the planning and conduct of exchange through contract relations and negotiations. However, in today's world the development of extensive impersonal relationships has accounted for the gradual replacement of moral governance with contractual governance (Palmer 1997).

Trust is considered as an important means of governing exchange when one party has confidence in an exchange partner's reliability and integrity (Moorman, Deshpande and Zaltman 1993; Morgan and Hunt 1994; Palmer 1997). Although trust is an important element, financial benefits of the customers must also be fulfilled for an ongoing relationship (Palmer 1994).

3.1.3 Marketing public relations

Public relations is defined as the variety of programmes designed to promote and/or protect the image and products/services of a company. Basic public relations functions are stated under the headings, (1) Press relations, (2) Product/service publicity, (3) Corporate communication, (4) Lobbying and (5) Counselling (Kotler 2000).

Marketing public relations assists these programmes to be designed effectively so as to support the marketing strategies of the firm and thus add value to the interactive marketing communications (Harris 1993, Marken 1995). In its marketing support function, public relations are used to achieve a number of objectives. The most important of these are to raise awareness, to inform and educate, to gain understanding, to build trust, to make friends, to give people reasons to buy and finally to create a climate of consumer acceptance (Harris 1993). Public relations is considered as a part of the integrated communication efforts (Miller 1994, Gonring 1994, Wightman 1999, Brody 1994). Depending on this structure the leading functional areas to support marketing appear to be: advertising and contributing to the selection of the message which appeal most likely to succeed with the target audience (Howard 1993, Miller 1994), communicating with and training the sales force (Watson 1997, Howard 1997, Wightman 1999), relationship marketing (Lindenmann 1998), and market positioning (Marken 1997).

3.1.4 Promotion of environmentally friendly transport

Regarding the trends towards the developments of social marketing issues by the beginning of the 21st century, and due to the extensive pollution created by the transport systems, international institutions and governmental bodies have concentrated on prevention of pollution and every company and organisation that is involved in marketing activities has included policies concerning "sustainable development" in their mission statements.

Sustainable transport involves (1) environmentally friendly transport, (2) efficient transport, (3) safe transport, and (4) socially acceptable transport (Blonk 1999a). The following is the definition of Sustainable Transportation accepted by the Center for Sustainable Transport, which is located at Toronto, Canada (*http://www.cstctd.org/*):

"A sustainable transportation system is one that:
- allows the basic access needs of individuals and societies to be met safely and in a manner consistent with human and ecosystem health, and with equity within and between generations;
- is affordable, operates efficiently, offers choice of transport mode, and supports a vibrant economy;
- limits emissions and waste within the planet's ability to absorb them, minimises consumption of non-renewable resources, limits consumption of renewable resources to the sustainable yield level, reuses and recycles its components, and minimises the use of land and the production of noise."

4. MARITIME INDUSTRY AND COMPETITIVE MARKETING STRATEGIES

Maritime industry performs in an international environment where the demand is derived from the international trade. There are driving and restraining forces in global marketing (Keegan and Green 1997). The driving forces are regional economic agreements, converging market needs and wants, technology advances, improvements in communication and transportation technology, pressure to cut costs, pressure to improve quality, global economic growth and opportunities for leverage (Cerit and Guler 1998).

4.1 Environmental analysis of the maritime industry

Macro and micro environmental factors affecting the maritime industry are shown in Figure 3. When the global macro environment of the maritime industry is considered, economic, demographic, technological, natural, social/cultural and political/legal factors affect the development of the industry.

International trade in goods and services has approached 8 trillion dollars (WTO 2001). Internationalisation of the world economy has ended in economic integration and global markets and global competitors have steadily displaced local ones (Drucker 1994). The new realities can be summarised as (1) increased volume of capital movements exceeding the volume of world trade in goods, (2) growth of productivity in manufacturing, exceeding the growth in

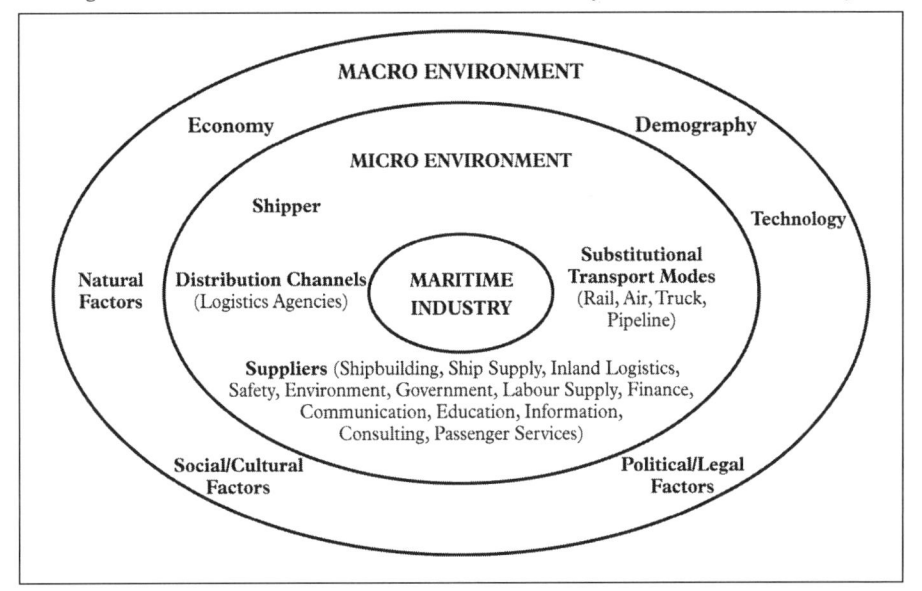

Figure 3: External macro and micro environment for the maritime industry

[Diagram: Nested ovals showing MACRO ENVIRONMENT (outer) containing Economy, Demography, Technology, Political/Legal Factors, Social/Cultural Factors, Natural Factors; MICRO ENVIRONMENT (middle) containing Shipper, Distribution Channels (Logistics Agencies), Substitutional Transport Modes (Rail, Air, Truck, Pipeline), Suppliers (Shipbuilding, Ship Supply, Inland Logistics, Safety, Environment, Government, Labour Supply, Finance, Communication, Education, Information, Consulting, Passenger Services); and MARITIME INDUSTRY at the center]

employment, (3) emergence of the world economy as the dominant economic unit (Keegan and Green 1997).

Globalisation of the world economy has forced nations and businesses to move towards internationalisation of the competition policies and liberalisation. Regional trade blocks such as EU and NAFTA have lowered boundaries to trade within the region. Due to deregulation and privatisation, tremendous market opportunities are being created.

In today's business climate, companies are forced to accept increasing responsibility for the environment. The environmental movement has ended in strict environmental regulations thus raising costs for the related industries.

Technological advances have produced a major impact on world trade. The boom in the communication technology has helped the developments in markets, customers and trade globally. Electronic market places have emerged where a new area of contact has occurred between the customer and the company's sales force. The revolution in transportation technology has affected market logistics measures ending in a decline in costs and reducing the time required for shipment.

Global competition, political and legal requirements and social and cultural developments have forced the industries and companies to improve the quality of their products and services and internationally accepted regulations and standards have been put into action.

As was discussed, for any industry external micro environment actors are grouped as customers, competitors, distribution channels and suppliers.

When shipping industry is considered, participants of the world trade, namely the shippers, are the customers. The competitors are the existing competitors or new entrants. Other transport modes (air, rail, truck, and pipeline) may act as either substitutes or partners in case of an integrated approach of multimodal transport. Main distribution channels of the shipping industry are the logistics agencies. Any industry taking part in the supply function for the maritime industry acts as a supplier for the industry. Shipbuilding industry and the related industries, ship supply industries, organisations involved in the inland logistics, global, regional and local organisations participating in safety and environment issues, governments, labor supply, shipping finance, communication industries, educational institutions, information sources, organisations taking part in research, development and consultancy, and businesses that assist passenger services are the main suppliers of the industry (Cerit and Guler 1998).

External macro environmental factors have an impact on the micro environmental factors. Starting with the 1990s, globalisation of trade and industrial production have affected maritime industry in different ways. It has changed the demand for transport and related services and has forced all transportation companies to adopt the services to render to the trading community. Due to the improvements in communication technologies, and improvements in other technological aspects in shipbuilding, new geographically distant markets opened and locational linkages in production and marketing processes reduced. As far as the maritime transportation is considered, several regional groups of countries formed many regional conventions. Government interventions play an important role in the competitive environment of the maritime industry. In many countries, government subsidies for shipping and ports are among the most important factors that shape the industry (Peters 1990).

4.2 Competitive strategies for the maritime industry

As a transportation mode, maritime transport, which operates in the international markets, is affected by all the environmental factors surrounding international trade and reflects the industrial characteristics of a transport service industry, and related competitive advantages of the businesses stem accordingly.

World seaborne trade has reached 5.88 billion tons in 2000 (UNCTAD 2001) and shipping remains by far the main mode of international transport of goods (*http://www.wto.org*). The main characteristics of maritime transport can be stated as allowing large shipment sizes at low prices. However, the relatively lower speed of the mode causes switches to other transport modes due to competitive reasons.

Regarding the outstanding importance of maritime transport in international trade a special research was accomplished to evaluate the related competitive advantage factors depending on the approaches of the customers, namely exporters. The corresponding results proved the fact that exporters consider the transportation function generally and maritime transportation in particular as very important factors in the creation of competitive advantage (Cerit 2000).

4.2.1 Cost leadership strategy

In economic theory, price is defined as the value of goods expressed in terms of monetary units and it represents the terms on which individuals and businesses voluntarily exchange various commodities (Samuelson and Nordhaus 1992).

For businesses, price is considered as a tool of the marketing function (Kotler 2000) and acts as a factor in providing competitive advantage (Porter 1985; Ramaswamy *et al.* 1994).

Cost leadership strategy requires the firm to be a low-cost producer, thus at equivalent or lower prices than its competitors; a cost-leader's low-cost position will result in higher returns. Pricing decisions stem from competitive strategies. Cost leadership strategies enable application of low prices (Porter 1985; Curry 1985).

In the company level, price is an element of the marketing mix (Kotler 2000). Marketing planning requires formulation of strategies related with the elements of the marketing mix (Kerin *et al.* 1990). Strategies on market segmentation, market targeting and product positioning result in action programs on the elements of the marketing mix, including price.

In *international marketing* internationalised competition, in both the manufacturing and services industries, has ended in global strategies (Porter 1990). Differing market and demand situations, national differences in factor costs, government subsidies in the international market place and the resulting global competition force companies to apply export sales prices lower than domestic prices (Cundiff and Hilger 1988; Terpstra and Sarathy 1994). Especially for the industries where international bidding conditions exist, competitive forces end in creation of advantages either on costs or differentiated products and services.

Industrial markets are classified according to The Standard Industrial Classification (SIC) System (Haas 1989) and shipping is a sub-sector of the Water Transportation Industry (Major Group 44). Basic characteristics of the industrial markets are fewer and larger buyers on a geographically concentrated basis; derived, inelastic and fluctuating demand; professional purchasing where specifications play an important role; emphasised personal selling, physical distribution and scheduling (Kotler 2000; Haas 1989).

Demand for industrial goods and services is derived from the demand for consumer goods. Demand for consumer products and sales trends of consumer goods are directly reflected in the demand for industrial goods, regardless of price. The inelastic demand characteristic for the industrial products is such that, demand for those products is not much affected by price changes (Kotler 2000). Pricing in industrial markets is applied as a result of the marketing strategies (Doyle and Saunders 1985), mainly through negotiations and bidding processes (Haas 1989).

As an international industrial sector, shipping is affected by the demand for international trade (Zeien and Hillmann 1994). However, prices in the industry, namely the freight rates, are not settled only through the levels of demand and the costs, but the pricing policies of the leading international shipping companies affect the prices as well. The increasing capacity of the world fleet and the fierce competition in the shipping industry force marketing departments to concentrate on price competition based on low-cost advantages. This competitive strategy requires high concentration on the costs of the shipping services. The area where the main reason for cost reduction in shipping stems from is the technological environment. Technological developments aiming reduction in operating costs have been primarily reflected in increased vessel sizes. In 1985 only around 15% of the world container capacity were provided by vessels of 2000 TEU or more, however it is predicted that by the year 2010, several 15000 TEU vessels will be in operation on the biggest maritime routes (UNCTAD 2001, Cerit 1997).

4.2.2 Differentiation strategies

Marketing is considered as getting, keeping and growing customers through creating, delivering, and communicating superior customer value (Kotler 2000) and it has already been discussed that creating superior costomer value means offering something more valuable than the competitors do. Marketing's main role in creating this superior value stems from the differentiation strategies developed through the governance of marketing management.

In a differentiation strategy, a company targets to possess some dimensions that are highly valued by the customers and that will keep the company in a unique position in its industry. In international markets, shipping services meet the demand of import/export activities and the service quality produced by shipping for the sake of the customers, namely the shippers, has to meet certain standards for the transportation service to create competitive advantage.

Considering maritime transport industry as a whole, the main differentiation strategies may be created through (1)service quality, (2) relationship marketing, (3) marketing public relations and (4) promoting maritime industry as an environment friendly transport mode.

4.2.2.1 Maintaining service quality in shipping

According to the classification of services process (Lovelock 1996), shipping services can be considered among the "possession processing services category" in which customers ask a service organisation to provide treatment not to themselves but rather to some physical possession, e.g., ships or cargoes owned.

Determinants of service quality have been analysed by those in the marketing discipline and consequently the following ten groups of variables have been reached (Parasuraman *et al.* 1985; Zeithaml *et al.* 1990; Zeithaml *et al.* 1996): reliability, responsiveness, competence, access, courtesy, communication, credibility, security, understanding/knowing the customer, tangibles. With the results of further research on service quality these ten dimensions have been combined and reduced into five dimensions, namely reliability, responsiveness, tangibles, assurance (combination of competence, courtesy, credibility and security) and empathy (combination of access, communication, knowing and understanding the customer) (Zeithmal *et al.* 1990). These determinants may briefly be grouped as tangibles and intangibles and the importance of these differs according to the nature of the industry. Tangibles play a major role in some industries, whereas intangibles are more important in others.

In ports and especially container terminals, tangibles, namely the physical facilities provided by the port, are important dimensions of service quality. Quality of port operations is also related to the physical infrastructure. Analysis of applications of service quality criteria in port services to container transport will present the port with the data necessary for better quality service (Deveci et al 2001).

A recent study on market research for container ports proved that service quality is an important decision parameter for both container lines and shippers (Teurelincx 1998b). Another research completed among shippers involved in export business ended with the results that services of maritime agencies is the most important attribute, and among the highest factor loadings the quality of port services took place (Cerit 2000).

International maritime bodies such as International Maritime Organisation-IMO also emphasises the importance of quality in shipping through the regulations and codes that are presented and mandatory rules for the shipping industry. International Safety Management-ISM Code aims to provide safe practices in ship operation and a safe working environment (IMO 2002). Besides these mandatory requirements, standards aiming at better management systems in the industry, such as the ISO 9000 series of quality system standards and the International Ship Managers Association (ISMA's) ISMA-CSS-Code of Ship Management Standards, all aim at a quality based environment in the shipping industry (LSM 1995).

Developments in the supply chain management services have resulted in the introduction of total logistics providers to the shipping industry. This has provided the shipper with both a reduction in transport logistics costs and moreover an increase in the quality of such services. Increased specialisation in the logistics industry have ended in outsourcing of logistics services towards the third party and even fourth party logistics providers. These developments have forced maritime companies to include total logistics services and subsidiaries in their organisations in order to improve the quality of their services (Ozer and Tuna 2002).

4.2.2.2 Relationship marketing applications in shipping

Performing in the services sector, shipping companies are in a position to consider relationship marketing as the main tool of creating customer loyalty, both in the liner and tramp shipping areas and the port industry.

Through relationship marketing, financial, social and structural bonds are formed by the customers (Berry and Parasuraman 1991:136). *Financial bonds* result in financial benefits to the customer. *Social bonds* cover increasing the social relations with the customers by individualising and personalising the relations. *Structural bonds* include providing special equipment, proprietary software, marketing research, sales training and sales leads to loyal customers.

Main differentiation created by the financial bonds take place in prices lower than those of the competitors. When both financial and social bonds are put into action, both price and personal communication effects take place and a higher level of differentiation is formed. When all three of financial, social and structural bonds are applied, service delivery is supposed to reach the highest degree of differentiation.

Shipping companies make use of all the three types of bonds with the customers. Partnerships, mergers and alliances, vertical and horizontal integrations in the industry allow shipping companies build stronger relations both with the customer and with related companies in the same service area. Price competition ends in several forms of financial bonds. Social bonds of the company with the shippers maintain the continuation of the business relationship. Shipowners provide shippers with special information especially on international markets and the means to reach this information to form closer links with the customers. The rapid developments in e-business and Business-to-Business networks strengthen the relations between the parties and constitute an additional bond mainly through the activities of the sales force.

To develop relationships with customers, shipping companies must establish the quality factors between the seller and the buyer by the two main factors that relationship marketing relies on, which are *ethical foundations* and *trust*.

4.2.3 Marketing public relations for the shipping industry

In industrial marketing the leading role of public relations appears in the development of programs that may contribute to the interactive communication environment between the sales force of the company and the companies and publics that are in contact with the company. The tools used for this purpose are press, public speeches, seminars/congresses/conferences, special exhibitions, annual reports, funds, sponsorships, various publications, state and governmental relations, lobbying and various other activities.

The target groups for public relations of ports are both port users who are the customers and/or potential customers and also the shareholders of the port, administrations, authorities, services, financial institutions, labor unions, political parties, groups of environmentalists and ecologists, students, teachers and instructors, university professors and also all of the people in the region who are sharing the benefits and problems of the port. Leading ports all over the world have established independent port promotion or marketing departments (Willemsens 1992, Port of Hamburg Marketing Association 2001), and these units include representatives of the public and private institutes in the region. Main public relations activities organised by these units are port days, conferences and seminars, open-door days, audio-visual means, exhibitions and fairs, publications, articles and press releases, information and documentation services, instruction and training, promotion of the port logo and annual reports. In addition to these activities, ports make use of advertising through press, radio, TV and billboards (Frankel 1987).

4.2.3.1 Promotion of maritime transport as an environment friendly transport mode

The technological developments in the shipping industries will help meet the higher expectations businesses will demand of transportation services: reliability, timeliness, efficiency, low cost, and damage minimisation. Advances in technology and efforts to improve productivity led the move to intermodal freight shipments. During the past 25 years, motor carriers, railroads, and ports have invested in container facilities as they recognised the efficiency of containerised transport. Growth in container transportation worldwide and associated developments by railroads and ports have resulted in growth in intermodal transportation. The growing demand for intermodal transport has also spurred demand for larger, specialised container ships and enough inter-modal capacity to handle increased landside traffic (USA DOT 1999).

Maritime transport continues to handle more international cargo by value, and substantially more international cargo by weight, than any other mode. However in most developed countries, the largest share of transport activity is by road. Road transport is responsible for over 80% of final energy consumption for transport (OECD 1997).

Road transport is essential to social and economic vitality, especially for employment, but it also entails social and economic costs, such as traffic accidents and impacts on the environment. With 1995 figures, transport accounts for 20% of total CO_2 emissions from fuel combustion in million tonnes, of which 16% comes from road transport (EC Directorate General for Transport 1999). When road accidents are considered, there are annually over 500,000 road traffic deaths and 15 million injuries world-wide, i.e., 1,400 fatalities and 41,000 injuries per day – of which about one quarter and one third, respectively, are in OECD countries (The World Bank 2000, OECD 1997). It is estimated that the economic losses due to accident fatalities, injuries and damage amount to between 1 and 2% of GDP in OECD countries (OECD 1997).

Another measure to be considered is the usage of land and energy. Road transport requires large land areas for more and more highways to be built and this can be accomplished only by making use of land that can be utilised for other resources. When energy is taken into account and when petroleum products consumed in OECD countries by all sectors are considered, about 50% is consumed by road transport (OECD 1997). These data are presented to illustrate that the costs associated with road transport in terms of the loss of human life, the impact on the environment, and the utilisation of non-renewable resources are profound. In this regard all countries share a common interest in finding the means to reduce the high costs associated with road transport. Maritime transport remains advantageous with respect to both transport costs, fatalities in accidents and environmental concerns regarding sustainable transport requirements (Cerit 2001).

Transportation policy operates by taking into account both politics and markets. Because transportation is very expensive and completely vital, governments inevitably intervene to influence transportation markets. Transportation is closely linked to so many private investments, employment, and residential choices, so it is impossible for government alone to control all the key aspects of the transportation system. Industrial organisations, institutes and companies should assist governments in building those policies. The strongest differentiation strategy for maritime transport will be promotion of its environment friendly structure to the stakeholders.

The challenge of transportation policy is to discover the most economically efficient and politically acceptable arrangements for coordinating public and private efforts to improve mobility and to apportion costs and benefits among the many stakeholders (Dunn 1999).

Promotion targeting the service users. Promotion of transport services requires effective political, legal, economic, technological, social, cultural and demographic approaches both for service providers and service users.

Social marketing is explained as the adaptation of commercial marketing technologies to programs designed to influence the voluntary behavior of target audiences to improve their personal welfare and that of the society of which they are a part (Andreasen 1994). In this manner social marketing deals with both structural and behavioral aspects (Wiener and Doescher 1991).

The application of social marketing in transport safety contains distinct elements, namely, focusing on the target user and his/her perceptions and motivation; receiving help from the safety expert, practitioner or policy maker to adapt objectives set to the perceived requirements, costs and benefits of the target group; and encouraging promotion of remedial measures and communication with the public on the anticipated benefits and socio-economic costs to be incurred (OECD 1997).

Promotion targeting the service providers. Due to the concentration and importance of transport industry public-private partnerships are very common in transportation. Two broad categories of public-private partnerships are categorised in transportation, namely, the *policy-level partnerships*, and *project-based partnerships* (Dunn 1999). In the former a set of general rules are put forward for public and private investment, operation, and dispute resolution in a given transport mode, such as railroads, urban transit, highways, inland waterways, and others. The latter is described as focusing on a specific site or circumstance, where often local political leaders promote particular project-based partnerships to achieve a goal that can not be accomplished following the normal rules of an established modal benefits regime.

The types of public-private partnerships that are formed are related to the stages of growth of particular transport modes. Different transportation technologies are often at different stages of their cycle of growth, stability, decline, and renewal, and they need very different types of policy support. Dunn categorizes the steps in policy making in a mode to be dominated successively by *promotion, regulation, protection, and rationalisation* (Dunn 1999).

5. CONCLUSION

Globalisation and developments in the world shipping have produced severe competitive pressures for the maritime industry. The decline in freight rates, the need for investment either to apply new technologies or to improve quality services present the industry with the task of applying competitive strategies. The highly internationalised position of the maritime industry forces the companies to apply market-oriented strategic planning processes in order to gain competitive advantage.

Shipping is a service industry, which performs in an international business market where the demand is derived from international trade. Shipping constitutes the main actor of the supply chains in building the international logistics systems.

Marketing's main role in creating this superior value stems from the differentiation strategies developed through the governance of marketing management. Considering maritime transport industry as a whole, the main differentiation strategies may be created through service quality, relationship marketing, marketing public relations and promoting maritime industry as an environment friendly transport mode.

Developments in international trade have been readily reflected in shipping which is responsible for the vast majority of international trade. Concentration and centralisation of capital in the shipping industry have reached ultimate high point by the beginning of the 21st century and the resulting severe competitive environment has caused companies to apply various strategies in order to be successful in the market place. However, the boundaries of competition have reached a two fold case both as strong as the other: (1) extensive drops in freight rates, (2) aiming quality services by one-stop-shopping, reducing the delivery time and decreasing the number of parties involved in the shipping process.

Marketing's mission of delivering superior value to the customer leads us to start with the market and to put our focus on the customer. The application of this phenomenon in shipping urges us to concentrate on differentiation strategies that lead to (1) service quality, (2) relationship marketing, (3) marketing public relations, and (4) promotion of maritime transport as an environment friendly mode of transport.

The industry has considered these strategies at the highest importance and to obtain competitive advantage, service quality and relationship marketing have been the key factors in building long-term relations with the customers. Shipping industry must also fulfill the macro requirements of the community and the society. Marketing public relations and highlighting the environment friendly nature of the maritime industry will help linking the industry and the society.

REFERENCES

Aertsen, F. (1993): "Contracting out the Physical Distribution Function", *International Journal of Physical Distribution and Logistics Management*, 23-1, pp. 23–39.

AMA-American Marketing Association (1995): *Dictionary of Marketing Terms* (2nd ed.), Bennett, P.D. (ed.) (Chicago, AMA Publications).

Anderson, S.C. (2000): "The Globally Competitive Firm: Functional Integration, Value Chain Logistics, Global Marketing, and Business College Strategic Support", *Competitiveness Review*, Vol. 10(2), pp. 33–45.

Andreasen, A.R. (1994): "Social Marketing: Its Definition and Domain", *Journal of Public Policy & Marketing*, (Spring), Vol. 13(1), pp. 108–114.

Atuahene-Gima, K. (1996): "Market Orientation and Innovation", *Journal of Business Research*, 35, pp. 93–103.

Avlonitis, G.J., and Gounaris, S.P. (1997): "Marketing Orientation and Company Performance", *Industrial Marketing Management*, 26, pp. 385–402.

Badoe, D.A., and Miller, E.J. (2000): "Transportation–Land-Use Interaction: Empirical Findings in North America, and their Implications for Modeling", *Transportation Research Part D: Transport and Environment*, Volume 5(4), July, pp. 235–263.

Baird, A. J. (1999): "Container Vessels in the New Millenium: Implications for Seaports. Liner Shipping: What's Next?", *Proceedings of the IAME 1999 Conference* (Halifax), pp. 141–173.

Ballou, R.H. (1992): *Business Logistics Management* (New Jersey, Prentice Hall Inter'l).
Baker, W., and Sinkula, J.M. (1999): "The Synergistic Effect of Market Orientation and Learning Orientation on Organizational Performance", *Journal of the Academy of Marketing Science*, 27(4), pp. 411–427.
Balakrushnan, S. (1996): "Benefits of Customer and Competitive Orientations in Industrial Markets", *Industrial Marketing Management*, 25, pp. 257–269.
Barney, J., and Zajac, E.J. (1994): "Competitive Organizational Behavior: Toward an Organizationally Based Theory of Competitive Advantage", *Strategic Management Journal*, 15, pp. 5–9.
Barney, J. (1991): "Firm Resources and Sustained Competitive Advantage", *Journal of Management*, 17(1), pp. 99–120.
Barrett, H., and Weinstein, A. (1998): "The Effect of Market Orientation and Organizational Flexibility on Corporate Entrepreneurship", *Entrepreneurship: Theory & Practice*, 23(Fall), pp. 57–70.
Beard, C., and Easingwood, C. (1992): "Sources of Competitive Advantage in the Marketing of Technology Intensive Products and Processes", *European Journal of Marketing*, 26.12, pp. 5–18.
Belohlav, J.A. (1993): "Quality, Strategy and Competitiveness", *California Management Review* (Spring), pp. 55–67.
Berry, L.L., and Parasuraman, A. (1991): *Marketing Services, Competing Through Quality* (New York, The Free Press).
Bishop, W.S., Graham, J.L., and Jones, M.H. (1984): "Volatility of Derived Demand in Industrial Markets and Its Management Implications", *Journal of Marketing*, 48 (Fall), pp. 95–103.
Blonk, Wilhelmus A.G. (1999a): "Policies for Transport and Environment Beyond 2000", Transport Expo '99, April 12–16, Washington DC.
Blonk, Wilhelmus A.G. (1999b): "How Intermodal Transport/Supply Chain Development Can Contribute to Trade Competitiveness", Transport Expo '99, April 12–16, Washington DC.
Boscheck, R. (1994): "Competitive Advantage: Superior Offer or Unfair Dominance?", *California Management Review*, 37(1) (Fall), pp. 132–151.
Boyson S., Corsi, T., Dresner, M., and Rabinovich, E. (1999): "Managing Effective Third Party Logistics Relationships: What Does It Take?", *Journal of Business Logistics*, Vol. 20(1), pp. 73–100.
Brody, E.W. (1994): "PR is to Experience What Marketing is to Expectations", *Public Relations Quarterly*, Vol. 39, Issue 2 (Summer), pp. 20–22.
Bukold, S. (1993) "Logistics by Combined Transport", *International Journal of Physical Distribution and Logistics Management*, 23-4, pp. 24–34.
Cadogan, J.W., Diamantopoulos, A., and Pahud de Mortanges, C. (1999): "A Measure of Export Market Orientation: Scale Development and Cross-cultural Validation", *Journal of International Business Studies*, 30(4), pp. 689–707.
Cavusgil, T.S., and Zou, S. (1994): "Marketing Strategy-Performance Relationship: An Investigation of the Empirical Link in Export Market Ventures", *Journal of Marketing*, 58 (January), pp. 1–21.
Cavusgil, T.S. (1996): "Pricing for Global Markets", *The Columbia Journal of World Business* (Winter), pp. 67–78.
Cerit, A.G. (2000): "Maritime Transport as an Area of Competitive Advantage in International Marketing", *International Journal of Maritime Economics*, Vol. 1, No. 3 (January–March), pp. 49–67.
Cerit, A.G. (2001): "Promotion of Maritime Transport for Domestic Shipping: A Model for Turkey", *Proceedings of the IAME 2001 Conference*, 18–20 July 2001, Hong Kong, pp. 677–696.
Cerit, A.G. (2002): "Market Orientation Measures of the US and Turkish Shipbuilding Industries: A Comparative Study", *Journal of Ship Production*, Vol. 18, No. 1 (February), pp. 19–32.

Cerit, A.G., and Güler, N. (1998): "Maritime Industry and the Market Oriented Strategic Planning Approach", *Proceedings of the IC'98, WSDFC–International Conference on World Shipping and Shipping Market Facing 21st Century*, Jiayuan, Chen, Zan, Yang, and Shenzhen, Zhong Ming (eds.), PR China, 12–15 October 1998, pp. 82–96.

Cerit, A.G., and Önce, G. (1998): "Relationship Marketing in Sales Management of Maritime Agencies", *Proceedings of the International Symposium on Marine Technologies and Management – Technonav 1998* (Constanta, Ovidius University), 21–23 May 1998, Vol. I, pp. 250–259.

Cerit, A.G., and Önce, G. (1997): "Price Element and the Shipbuilding Industry: An Analogical Approach to the Relations of Labor/Material Costs", *Proceedings of the NAV & HSMV 1997 – International Conference on Ship and Marine Research* (Sorrento, Universita di Napoli Federico II), 18–21 March 1997, pp. 1.15–1.29.

Cerit, A.G., Kisi, H., Tuna, O., and Saatcioglu, O. (1997): "Gümrük Birli i Sürecinde Ege Bölgesi Sanayiine Rekabet Gücü Açisindan Stratejik Bir Yaklasim", *3. Verimlilik Kongresi*, 14–16 Mayis 1997 (Ankara, MPM Publications).

Cerit, A.G., Kisi, H., and Tuna, O. (1997): "Strategic Marketing Planning for the Yachting Companies, Marinas and Yacht Builders: An Application for Turkey", *1st International Yachting Technology Conference*, Çesme, 3–10 October 1995, Tekogul, N., Neser, G. (eds.) (Izmir, Piri Reis Foundation for Maritime Research, Development and Education Publication), pp. 175–186.

Chacholiades, M. (1978): *International Trade Theory and Policy* (Singapore, McGraw Hill Inc.).

Chadwin, M.L., Pope, J.A., and Talley, W.K. (1990): *Ocean Container Transportation: An Operational Perspective* (New York, Taylor & Francis Inc.).

Chakravarthy, B.S., and Perlmutter, H.V. (1985): "Strategic Planning for a Global Business", *The Columbia Journal of World Business* (Summer), pp. 3–10.

Chrzanowski, I.H. (1975): *Concentration and Centralization of Capital in Shipping* (Hants, Tinling Ltd).

Clark, T. (1990): "International Marketing and National Character: A Review and Proposal for an Integrative Theory", *Journal of Marketing* (October), pp. 66–79.

Colorni, A., Laniado, E., and Muratori, S. (1999): "Decision Support Systems for Environmental Impact Assessment of Transport Infrastructures", *Transportation Research Part D: Transport and Environment*, Vol. 4(1) (January), pp. 1–11.

Craig, S., and Douglas, S.P. (1996): "Responding to the Challenges of Global Markets", *The Columbia Journal of World Business* (Winter), pp. 6–18.

Cundiff, E., and Hilger, M.T. (1988): *Marketing in the International Environment* (New Jersey, Prentice Hall).

Curry, D.J. (1985): "Measuring Price and Quality Competition", *Journal of Marketing*, 49 (Spring), pp. 106–117.

Curry, D.J., and Riesz, P.C. (1988): "Prices and Price/Quality Relationships: A Longitudinal Analysis", *Journal of Marketing*, 52 (January), pp. 36–51.

Danaher, P.J., and Mattson, J. (1994): "Customer Satisfaction During the Service Delivery Process", *European Journal of Marketing*, 28-5, pp. 5–16.

Day, G.S., and Nedungadi, P. (1994): "Managerial Representations of Competitive Advantage", *Journal of Marketing*, 58 (April), pp. 31–44.

Day, G.S. (1994): "The Capabilities of Market-Driven Organizations", *Journal of Marketing*, 58 (October), pp. 37–52.

Day, G.S. and Nedungadi, P. (1994): "Managerial Representations of Competitive Advantage", *Journal of Marketing*, 58(April), pp. 31–44.

Day, G.S. (1990): *Market Driven Strategy Processes for Creating Value* (New York, The Free Press).

Day, G.S., and Wensley, R. (1988): "Assessing Advantage: A Framework for Diagnosing Competitive Superiority", *Journal of Marketing*, 52 (April), pp. 1–20.

Deligönül, Z.S., and Çavusgil, S.T. (1997): "Does the Comparative advantage Theory of Competition really Replace the Neoclassical Theory of Perfect Competition?", *Journal of Marketing*, 61(October), pp. 65–73.

Deshpande, R., Farley, J.U., and Webster, F. Jr. (1993): "Corporate Culture, Customer Orientation, and Innovativeness in Japanese Firms: A Quadrad Analysis", *Journal of Marketing*, 57 (January), pp. 23–27.

Deveci, D.A., Cerit, A.G., and Sigura, J.H.B. (2001): "Liner Agents and Container Port Service Quality", *Developments in Maritime Transport and Logistics in Turkey*, Barla, M.C., Sag, O.K., Roe, M., and Gray, R. (eds.), Plymouth Studies in Contemporary Shipping and Logistics (Hampshire, Ashgate Publishing Ltd), pp. 184–207.

DeWitt, W., and Clinger, J. (2000): *Intermodal Freight Transportation, Transportation in the New Millennium* (Washington, DC, Transportation Research Board).

Dolan, R.J. (1995): "How Do You Know When the Price is Right?", *Harvard Business Review* (September-October).

Doyle, P., and Saunders, J. (1985): "Market Segmentation and Positioning in Specialized Industrial Markets", *Journal of Marketing*, 49 (Spring), pp. 24–32.

Drucker, P.F. (1994): "Trade Lessons from the World Economy", *Foreign Affairs*, (January–February), pp. 99–108.

Dunn, J.A. Jr. (1999): "Transportation-Policy-Level Partnerships and Project-Based Partnerships", *American Behavioral Scientist* (September), Vol. 43(1), pp. 92–106.

Dyson, R. (1990): *Strategic Planning. Strategic Planning: Models and Analytical Techniques* (New York, John Wiley and Sons), pp. 1–14.

European Commission (1999): *Moving Forward the Achievements of the European Common Transport Policy* (Luxembourg, European Commission).

Flint, D.J., Woodruff, R.B., and Fisher, S.G. (1997): "Customer Value Change in Industrial Marketing Relationships", *Industrial Marketing Management*, 26, pp. 163–175.

Frankel, E.G. (1987): *Port Planning and Development* (New York, John Wiley and Sons).

Goldrein, I.S. (ed.) (1993): *Ship Sale and Purchase* (London, Lloyd's of London Press Ltd).

Gonring, M.P. (1994): "Putting Integrated Marketing Communications to Work Today", *Public Relations Quarterly* (Fall), Vol. 39, Issue 3, pp. 45–48.

Gorton, L., Ihre, R., and Sandevarn, A. (1995): *Shipbrokering and Chartering Practice* (London, Lloyd's of London Press).

Gummesson, E., Lehtinen, U., and Grönroos, C. (1997): Comment on "Nordic Perspectives on Relationship Marketing", *European Journal of Marketing*, Vol. 31, No. 1, pp. 10–16.

Gundlach, G.T., and Murphy, P.E. (1993): "Ethical and Legal Foundations of Relational Marketing Exchanges", *Journal of Marketing*, 57 (October), pp. 35–46.

Haas, R.W. (1989): *Industrial Marketing Management* (Boston, PWS-KENT Publishing Co.).

Han, Jin. K., Kim, N., and Srivastava, R.K. (1998): "Market Orientation and Organizational Performance: Is Innovation a Missing Link?", *Journal of Marketing*, 62 (October), pp. 30–45.

Harris, L.C. (1999): "Barriers to Developing Market Orientation", *Journal of Applied Management Studies*, 8 (1), pp. 85–101.

Harris, T.L. (1993): "How MPR Adds Value to Integrated Marketing Communications", *Public Relations Quarterly* (Summer), Vol. 38, Issue 2, pp. 13–18.

Henderson, B.D. (1989): "The Origin of Strategy", *Harvard Business Review*, November–December, pp. 139–143.

Henderson, B.D. (1983): "The Anatomy of Competition", *Journal of Marketing*, 47, (Spring), pp. 7–11.

Heide, J.B., and John, G. (1992): "Do Norms Matter in Marketing Relationships", *Journal of Marketing*, 56 (April), pp. 32–44.

Hine, J. (2000): "Integration, Integration, Integration … Planning for Sustainable and Integrated Transport Systems in the New Millennium", *Transport Policy*, Vol. 7(3), (July), pp. 175–177.

Hout, T., Porter, M.E., and Rudden, E. (1994): "How Global Companies Win Out. Global Strategies", *Harvard Business Review*, pp. 29–46.
Howard, C.M. (1993): "Five Principles of Integrated Marketing", *Public Relations Quarterly* (Fall), Vol. 38, Issue 3, pp. 35–36.
Hulbert, J.M., Brandt, W.K., and Richers, R. (1980): "Marketing Planning in the Multinational subsidiary: Practices and Problems", *Journal of Marketing*, 44 (Summer), pp. 7–15.
Hunt, D.H., and Morgan, R.M. (1995): "The Comparative Advantage Theory of Competition", *Journal of Marketing*, 59 (April), pp. 1–15.
Hunt, D.H. (1996): "The Resource-Advantage Theory of Competition: Dynamics, Path Dependencies, and Evolutionary Dimensions", *Journal of Marketing*, 60 (October), pp. 107–114.
Hurley, R.F., and Hult, T.M. (1998): "Innovation, Market Orientation, and Organizational Learning: An Integration and Empirical Examination", *Journal of Marketing*, 62 (July), pp. 42–54.
Hutt, M.D., and Speh, T.W. (1984): "The Marketing Strategy Center: Diagnosing the Industrial Marketer's Interdisciplinary Role", *Journal of Marketing*, 48(Fall), pp. 53–61.
IMO (2002): *http://www.imo.org/ismcode/ismcode.htm*
Inoue, S. (2001): *Towards the New Framework of Port Industry for the 21st Century* (Tokyo, International Association of Ports and Harbors).
Jacquemin, A.(1995): "Towards an Internationalization of Competition Policy", *The World Economy*, 18(6) (November), pp. 781–789.
Jain, S.C. (1989): "Standardization of International Marketing Strategy: Some Research Hypotheses", *Journal of Marketing*, 53 (January), pp. 70–79.
Jaworski, B., and Kohli, A. (1993): "Market Orientation: Antecedents and Consequences", *Journal of Marketing*, 57 (July), pp. 53–70.
Jaworski, B., and Kohli, A., and Sahay, A. (2000): "Market-Driven versus Driving Markets", *Journal of the Academy of Marketing Science*, 28(1), pp. 45–54.
Johnson, S., Kotchen, D.T., and Loveman, G. (1995): "How One Polish Shipyard Became a Market Competitor", *Harvard Business Review* (November– December), pp. 53–72.
Jones, M., Wheeler, C., and Young, S. (1992): "European Marketing and Distribution in the 1990s: The Case of the Machine Tool Industry in the UK", *European Journal of Marketing*, 26-7, pp. 17–33.
Keegan, W. J., and Green, M.C. (1997): *Principles of Global Marketing* (New Jersey, Prentice Hall).
Kerin, R.A., Mahajan, V., and Varadarajan, P.R. (1990): *Strategic Market Planning* (Boston, Allyn and Bacon).
King, J. (1997): "Globalization of Logistics Management: Present Status and Prospects", *Maritime Policy and Management*, Vol. 24, No. 4, pp. 381–387.
Kinnear, T., and Taylor, J.R.(1991): *Marketing Research* (New York, McGraw Hill Inc.).
Kirby, H.R., Hutton, B., Mcquaid, R.W., Raeside, R., and Zhang, X. (2000): "Modelling the Effects of Transport Policy Levers on Fuel Efficiency and National Fuel Consumption", *Transportation Research Part D: Transport and Environment*, Volume 5(4), (July), pp. 235–320.
Kohli, A.K., and Jaworski, B.J. (1990): "Market Orientation: The Construct, Research Propositions, and Managerial Implications", *Journal of Marketing*, 54 (April), pp. 1–18.
Kohli, A.K. (1989): "Determinants of Influence in Organizational Buying: A Contingency Approach", *Journal of Marketing*, 53(July), pp. 50–65.
Kotler, P. (2000): *Marketing Management* (New Jersey, Prentice Hall).
Kumar, K., Subramanian, R., and Yauger, C. (1998): "Examining the Market Orientation-Performance Relationship: A Context-Specific Study", *Journal of Management*, 24(2), pp. 201–233.

Kurtulus, K. (1996): Pazarlama Arastirmalari. Istanbul: Isletme Fakültesi Yayin No: 28, Avciol Basim Yayin.
Leigh, T.W., and Rethans, A.J. (1984): "A Script-theoretic Analysis of Industrial Purchasing Behavior", *Journal of Marketing*, 48 (Fall), pp. 22–32.
Lewis, S.L. III (1998): "Land Use and Transportation: Envisioning Regional Sustainability", *Transport Policy*, Vol. 5(3), June, pp. 147–161.
Lindenmann, W.K. (1998): "Measuring Relationships is Key to Successful Public Relations", *Public Relations Quarterly*, (Winter 98/99), Vol. 43, Issue 4, pp. 18–24.
Londe, B.J. La, and Masters, J.M. (1994): "Emerging Logistics Strategies", *International Journal of Physical Distribution and Logistics Management*, 24-7, pp. 35–47.
Lovelock, C. (1996): *Services Marketing* (London, Prentice Hall International Editions).
LSM (1995). October, London.
Marchese, U. (1997): "Intermodality and the Evolution of Competition in Shipping Markets", *Proceedings of the International Conference On Ship and Marine Research, NAV' 97*, University of Naples Federico II, Sorrento, pp. 1.3–1.14.
Marchese, U., Musso, E., and Ferrari, C. (1998): "The Role for Ports in Intermodal Transports and Global Competition: A Survey of Italian Container Terminals", *8th World Conference on Transport Research*, 12–17 July 1999, Antwerp.
Marken, G.A. (1995): "Marketing Public Relations... Lead, Follow or Get out of the Way", *Public Relations Quarterly* (Spring), Vol. 40, Issue 1, pp. 47–48.
Meersman, H., Moglia, F., and Van de Voorde, E. (1999): "Mergers and Alliances in Liner Shipping: What do European Port Authorities have to Fear?", *Liner Shipping: What's Next? Proceedings of the IAME 1999 Conference*, Halifax, pp. 204–220.
Mester, B. (1991): *Marketing from the Port's Point of View*, Bremen, Port Management Textbook, Vol. 3, ISL.
Miller, D.A., and Rose, P.B. (1994): "Integrated Communications: A Look at Reality Instead of Theory", *Public Relations Quarterly* (Spring), Vol. 39, Issue 1, pp. 13–16.
Morgan, R.M., and Hunt, S.D. (1994): "The Commitment-Trust Theory of Relationship Marketing", *Journal of Marketing*, 58 (July), pp. 20–38.
Moorman, C., Deshpande, R., and Zaltman, G. (1993): "Factors Affecting Trust in Market Research Relationships", *Journal of Marketing*, 57 (January), pp. 81–101.
Mueller, R.D., Wenthe, J., and Baron, P. (1993): "Case Note: The Evolution of Distribution Systems", *International Marketing Review*, 10-4, pp. 37–52.
Narver, J.C., and Slater, S.F. (1994): "Does Competitive Environment Moderate the Market Orientation-Performance Relationship?", *Journal of Marketing*, 58 (January), pp. 46–55.
Narver, J.C., and Slater, S.F. (1990): "The Effect of a Market Orientation on Business Profitability", *Journal of Marketing*, 54 (October), pp. 20–35.
Noordewier, T.G., John, G., and Nevin, J.R. (1990): "Performance Outcomes of Purchasing Arrangements in Industrial Buyer-Vendor Relationships", *Journal of Marketing*, 54(October), pp. 80–93.
OECD (Organization for Economic Co-operation and Development) (2001): *Liner Shipping Competition Policy Report*. Paris: 6 November 2001, Document submitted at the Workshop on Competition Policy in Liner Shipping – DSTI/DOT (2001)1. (*http:// www.oecd.org*).
OECD (Organization for Economic Co-operation and Development) (1997): Road Transport and Intermodal Linkages Research Programme. *Outlook 2000, Perspectives 2000* (Paris, OECD Publications).
Önce, G. (1997): *Satis Yönetimi* (Izmir, Onur Ofset).
Ozer, D., and Tuna, O. (2002): *Third Party Logistics Services in Turkey: A Delphi Study*. New Trends in Maritime Transport Sector in Poland and Turkey, Zurek, Janusz, Tuna, Okan, and Yercan, Funda (eds.) (Gdansk, University of Gdansk Publication), pp. 83–106.
Palmer, A. (1994): *Principles of Services Marketing* (London, McGraw-Hill Book Company).

Palmer, A. (1996): "Relationship Marketing: a Universal Paradigm or Management Fad", *The Learning Organization*, Vol. 3, No. 3, pp. 18–25.

Palmer, A. (1997): "Defining Relationship Marketing: an International Perspective", *Management Decision*, 35/4, pp. 319–321.

Parasuraman, A., Berry, L.L., and Zeithaml, V.A. (1985): "A Conceptual Model of Service Quality and its Implications for Future Research", *Journal of Marketing*, 49 (Fall), pp. 41–50.

Parasuraman, A., Berry, L.L., and Zeithaml, V.A. (1991): "Understanding Customer Expectations of Service", *Sloan Management Review*, Spring 1991, pp. 39–48.

Pelham, A.M., and Wilson, D.T. (2000): "Market Orientation and Other Potential Influences on Performance in Small and Medium-Sized Manufacturing Firms", *Journal of Small Business Management* (January), pp. 48–67.

Pelham, A.M., and Wilson, D.T. (1996): "A Longitudinal Study of the Impact of Market Structure, Firm Structure, Strategy, and Market Orientation Culture on Dimensions of Small-Firm Performance", *Journal of the Academy of Marketing Science*, 24(Winter), pp. 27–44.

Peteraf, M.A. (1993): "The Cornerstones of Competitive Advantage: A Resource Based View", *Strategic Management Journal*, 14, pp. 179–191.

Peters, H.J. (1990): *Seatrade, Logistics and Transport* (Washington, DC, The World Bank Publication).

Porter, M.E. (1985): *Competitive Advantage* (New York, The Free Press).

Porter, M.E. (1987): "From Comparative Advantage to Corporate Strategy", *Harvard Business Review*, (May–June), pp. 43–59.

Porter, M.E. (1990a): *The Competitive Advantage of Nations* (New York, The Free Press).

Porter, M.E. (1990b): "The Competitive Advantage of Nations", *Harvard Business Review* (March–April) 1990, pp. 73–93.

Porter, M.E. (1996). "What is Strategy?", *Harvard Business Review* (November–December), pp. 61–89.

Prince, T. (2000): "Onward in the Brave New World of Logistics", *Journal of Commerce*, available at *http://www.joc.com/*, as of August 20.

Ramaswamy, V., Gatignon, H., and Jeibstein, R.D. (1994): "Competitive Marketing Behavior in Industrial Markets", *Journal of Marketing*, 58 (April), pp. 45–55.

Rangan, V.K., Moriarty, R.T., and Swartz, G.S. (1992): "Segmenting Customers in Mature Industrial Markets", *Journal of Marketing*, 56 (October), pp. 72–82.

Samiee, S., and Roth, K. (1992): "The Influence of Global Marketing Standardization on Performance", *Journal of Marketing*, 56 (April), pp. 1–17.

Samuelson, P.A., and Nordhaus, W.D. (1992): *Economics* (14th ed.) (New York, McGraw-Hill, Inc.).

Shapiro, B.S. (1988): "What the Hell is Market Oriented?", *Harvard Business Review*, 66 (November/December), pp. 119–125.

Sjetnan, K.C. (1999): *Cargo Systems, The Future of the Container Shipping Industry* (London, IIR Publications Ltd).

Slater, S.F., and Narver, J.C. (1995): "Market Orientation and the Learning Organization", *Journal of Marketing*, 59 (July), pp. 63–74.

Steinman, C., Deshpandè, R., and Farley, J.U. (2000): "Beyond Market Orientation: When Customers and Suppliers Disagree", *Journal of the Academy of Marketing Science*, 28 (Winter), pp. 109–119.

Stern, L.W., and Sturdivant, F.D. (1987): "Customer-Driven Distribution Systems", *Harvard Business Review* (July-August), pp. 34–43.

Stopford, M. (1997). *Maritime Economics* (2nd ed.) (London and New York, Routledge).

Tek, O. B. (1997): *Pazarlama Ilkeleri* (Istanbul, Duran Ofset).

Tellis, G.J. (1986): "Beyond the Many Faces of Price: An Integration of Pricing Strategies", *Journal of Marketing*, 50 (October), pp. 146–160.

Terpstra, V., and Ravi, S. (1994): *International Marketing* (6th ed.) (Orlando, Dryden Press).

Teurelincx, D. (1998a): "Functional Analysis of Port Performance as a Strategic Tool for Strengthening a Port's Competitive and Economic Potential", *8th World Conference on Transport Research*, Antwerp, 12–17 July 1999.

Teurelincx, D. (1998b): "The use of Market Research and Simulation Techniques in Port Capacity Planning", *8th World Conference on Transport Research*, Antwerp, 12–17 July 1999.

The Centre for Sustainable Transportation (2000): *Enabling Tomorrow's Transportation Professionals to Address Climate Change* (Toronto, The Centre for Sustainable Transportation and Government of Canada) (available at *http://www.cstctd.org*).

The United Nations Development Programme, the United Nations Environment Programme, the World Bank, and the World Resources Institute (2000): *World Resources 2000-2001: People and Ecosystems: The Fraying Web of Life* (Washington DC, The World Bank).

The World Bank (1996): *Sustainable Transport: Priorities for Policy Sector Reform* (Washington DC, The World Bank).

Tsamboulas, D., and Mikroudis, G. (2000): "EFECT – Evaluation Framework Of Environmental Impacts and Costs of Transport Initiatives", *Transportation Research Part D: Transport and Environment*, Vol. 5(4) (July), pp. 283–303.

UNCTAD (2001): *Review of Maritime Transport 2001* (New York and Geneva, UNCTAD Publication).

USA Department of Transportation – DOT, Bureau of Transportation Statistics (2000): *The Changing Face of Transportation* (Washington DC, USA Department of Transportation).

USA Department of Transportation – DOT, Bureau of Transportation Statistics (1999): *An Assessment of the US Marine Transportation System* (Washington DC, USA Department of Transportation Report on US Marine Transportation System to the Congress).

Varadarajan, P. ("Rajan") and Rajaratnam, D. (1986): "Symbiotic Marketing Revisited", *Journal of Marketing*, 50 (January), pp. 7–17.

Watson, T. (1997): "Updating Skills in Marketing Communication", *Advertising Age*, 10/13/97, Vol. 68, Issue 41, p. 26.

Weihrich, H. (1990): "The TOWS Matrix: A Tool for Situational Analysis", *Strategic Planning: Models and Analytical Techniques* (New York, John Wiley and Sons), pp. 17–36.

Wiater, S.J. (1975): *Concentration and Centralization of Capital in Shipping* (Hants, Saxon House, DC Heath Ltd).

Wiener, J.L., and Doescher, T.A. (1991): "A Framework for Promoting Cooperation", *Journal of Marketing* (April), Vol. 55(2), pp. 38–47.

Wightman, Ben (1999): "Integrated Communications: Organization and Education", *Public Relations Quarterly* (Summer), Vol. 44, Issue 2, pp. 18–22

Willemsens, J.F. (1992): *Port Promotion* (Antwerp, Port of Antwerp Promotion Association), ASSIPORT Unpublished Course Material.

Wind, Y., Douglas, S.P., and Perlmutter, P.H. (1973): "Guidelines for Developing International Marketing Strategies", *Journal of Marketing*, 37 (April), pp. 14–23.

Wood, D.F., and Johnson, J.C. (1996): *Contemporary Transportation* (New Jersey, Prentice Hall International).

WTO (World Trade Organisation) (2001): *International Trade Statistics 2001* (Geneva, WTO Publication).

WTO (World Trade Organisation) (1998): *Maritime Transport Services* (Geneva, Background Note by the Secretariat, S/C/W/62) (*http://www.wto.org*).

Zeien, J.J., and Hillmann, J.F. (1994): "The Contribution of Maritime Economics to the Revitalization of the US Marine Industry", *1994 Ship Operations, Management and Economics Symposium* (New York, The Society of Naval Architects and Marine Engineers' Publication), p. 12-112-14.

Zeithaml, V.A., Berry, L.L., and Parasuraman, A. (1996): "The Behavioral

Consequences of Service Quality", *Journal of Marketing*, 60 (April), pp. 31–46.
Zeithaml, Valerie A., Parasuraman, A., and Berry, Leonard L. (1990): *Delivering Quality Service* (New York, The Free Press).
http://www.cstctd.org/

CHAPTER 26

FLEET OPERATIONS OPTIMISATION AND FLEET DEPLOYMENT

Anastassios N. Perakis

Department of Naval Architecture and Marine Engineering, University of Michigan, Michigan, USA. E-mail: *tassos@engin.umich.edu*

1. INTRODUCTION

Optimising the operation (i.e., minimising operating costs, if revenues are fixed) of a merchant ship is not difficult to do and can be achieved with a few simple calculations, which can point out the minimum of the operating cost curve as a function of the speed, for example. Texts such as Stopford[1] can provide useful information on the above. Optimising an entire fleet of generally different ships, however, is not as simple, and requires some minimum levels of computer and mathematical skills, as we will see in the following.

Deployment of merchant shipping fleets covers a wide range of problems, concerned with fleet operations, scheduling, routing, and fleet design. Many use some kind of economic criterion such as profitability, income or costs on which to base decisions (Benford,[2] Marbury,[3] Fischer and Rosenwein,[4] and Perakis[5]). Others use non-economic criteria such as utilisation or service; these are more common in fleet deployment models used in the liner trades.[6] Reviews of various fleet deployment models and problems are given in Ronen,[7] Ronen,[8] and Perakis.[9]

An aspect of fleet deployment not covered extensively in the literature until the early 80s was "slow-steaming" analysis and optimisation. "Slow Steaming" is the practice of operating a ship or fleet of ships at a speed less than design or maximum (sustained) operating speed, in order to take advantage of improved fuel economy and reduced operating costs, but, most importantly, to reduce fleet overcapacity (if done by a large number of ship owners).

Managers of merchant ship fleets, especially bulk carriers and tankers, frequently find themselves with excess transport capacity, and hence must decide which ships to use (and at what speeds) and which to keep idle (or perhaps make available to another fleet by sale or charter). Moreover, if fuel prices become relatively high, excess transport capacity offers the potentially profitable strategy of slow steaming some or all of their ships. Such a strategy not only substantially reduces the operating costs of the fleet, but furthermore reduces the supply of ton-miles of the existing total bulker fleet, thereby improving the depressed freight rates. On the other hand, a sharp drop in fuel prices could make it advisable to "fast-steam" ships built during the expensive fuel era, although this would be limited by their design speed and associated operating margin.

FLEET OPERATIONS OPTIMISATION AND DEPLOYMENT

The remainder of this chapter is organised as follows: Section 2 discusses the correct solution of a simple fleet deployment problem, which has been earlier sub-optimally solved in the literature. It is shown that its correct solution can save over 15% of the annual fleet operating costs, or $7.93m per year, for the same 10-ship fleet of the previously published example. In Section 3, more realistic, single-origin, single-destination, and even multi-origin, multi-destination fleet deployment problems for (liquid or dry) bulk shipping are formulated and solved, using both nonlinear and a series of linear programs. In Section 4, fleet deployment problems for Liner Shipping Fleets are solved, and specific examples are given from the fleet of a major liner company. Section 5 provides a summary and conclusions, as well as recent developments in this area.

2. A SIMPLE FLEET DEPLOYMENT PROBLEM

The ships of a fleet could be assumed to belong to N different groups, each consisting of n(i) sister ships, i = 1, ..., N, of equal cargo carrying capacity, speed and fuel consumption (or in general, operating costs). Design speed, cargo capacity and operating costs will in general be different among different ship groups. This is both an efficient and general model, since the case of no two ships in a fleet being identical is obviously covered by setting n(i) = 1, i = 1, ..., N. The mission of a fleet is assumed, for our purposes, to be the movement of one commodity between two given ports.

A simple (but realistic) bulker fleet deployment problem was defined in Benford.[2] Some of the assumptions inherent in the solution approach, such as no-cost lay-up of unneeded vessels, a contract to move a given quantity of a given commodity between one origin and one destination port, availability of

Table 1

Ship group	Annual transport capacity ($\div 10^6$ tons)	Operating cost per ton	Annual operating cost ($\div 10^6$ ton)
1. A, B, C	4.902	$4.562	$22.36
2. D, E	2.884	$4.546	$13.11
3. F, G, H	3.726	$4.562	$17.00
4. I, J	—	—	—
Total	11.500		$52.47

Table 2

Ship	Annual transport capacity ($\div 10^6$ tons)	Operating cost per ton	Annual operating cost ($\div 10^6$ ton)
1. A, B, C	4.158	$3.531	$14.684
2. D, E	2.450	$3.692	$9.046
3. F, G, H	3.241	$4.023	$13.038
4. I, J	1.651	$4.707	$7.771
Total	11.500		$44.539

more than enough ships (tonnage) suited to the trade, etc., were not unrealistic. However, the method proposed for its solution did not give the optimal answer, primarily because of an artificial constraint that all vessels must be operated at a speed resulting in the same unit cost of operation per ton of cargo delivered, imposed for ease of solution, but not a natural constraint of the problem. Table 1 below presents the approach adopted in Benford[2] and its results.

In Perakis,[5] the problem was correctly solved analytically, without the above equal unit cost constraint, using Lagrange multipliers. The results (see Table 2) showed an improvement of at least 15% over those of Table 1, thus verifying once more that "constraints impair performance". More realistic and complicated versions of the problem solved in that paper were subsequently formulated and solved.

Comparing Tables 1 and 2, we see an annual cost reduction of $7.93 million, or over 15%. This represents a considerable improvement. The difference in costs could be even greater if lay-up charges are levied against ships I and J in the solution presented in Table 1. On the other hand, this difference could possibly be reduced if ships I and J could be chartered or sold to a third party at a particular price.

Perhaps it is now appropriate to clarify that in the above problem, the annual demanded transport capacity is assumed to be a given output (constant). This is the case for vessels operating under relatively long-term charters, which normally specify, among other things, the freight rate and the amount of cargo to be carried annually. In a normal market environment, long-term charters are the overwhelming majority of fixtures, whereas vessels operating in the spot market constitute less than 10% of the available capacity.

The conclusion from the above is that, in contrast to past practices where significant effort has been directed toward the optimisation of the design and operation of individual ships, an owner of a fleet of ships (usually non-uniform in terms of age, size and operating speed) should operate each ship in a manner generally quite different from that dictated by single-ship optimisation. Adoption of the results of this and subsequent research should result in significant cost savings in the operations of several shipping companies.

3. MORE REALISTIC BULK SHIPPING FLEET DEPLOYMENT MODELS

Perakis and Papadakis,[10, 11] and Papadakis and Perakis[12] presented far more realistic and complicated fleet deployment problems and their "optimal" solutions. The problem of single-origin, single-destination fleet deployment was first studied. A computer program was developed to solve the problem and to aid the fleet operator make slow steaming policy decisions. A detailed discussion of the problem solution and a sensitivity analysis are presented in Perakis and Papadakis.[10] Sensitivity analysis provides the user with an understanding of the influence on the total fleet operating cost of its various components. For small to moderate changes of one or more cost components, the user can get a very accurate estimate of his new total operating cost without having to re-run the computer program. Some interesting conclusions were made on the basis of the sensitivity results.

The fleet deployment problem with time-varying cost components was also formulated and solved. A computer program was developed to implement the solution of this problem (Perakis, Papadakis, and Pagoulatos[13]). The relevant algorithms are briefly described in the paper as well. The problem of fleet deployment when the cost coefficients are random variables with known probability density functions was formulated in detail (Perakis and Papadakis[11]), where analytical expressions for the basic probabilistic quantities were presented. A shorter description of the above is included in this presentation.

3.1 Objective Function and Constraints

A fleet, consisting of a given number of ships, is available to move a fixed amount of cargo between two ports, over a given period of time, for a fixed price. Each vessel in the fleet is assumed to have known operating cost characteristics. The problem objective is to determine each vessel's full load and ballast speeds such that the total fleet operating cost is minimised *and* all contracted cargo is transported.

A first constraint imposes upper and lower bounds on the vessel full load and ballast speeds. These speed constraints are necessary to insure a feasible solution to the problem; which is, that each speed is less than or equal to its maximum and greater than or equal to its minimum operating limits. In practice, the minimum speed is non-zero and determined by the lower end of the normal operating region of the vessel's main engine. The minimum speed should also be adequate for purposes of ship safety in maneuverability and control. The equality constraint must be satisfied to insure all contracted cargo is transported.

This formulation is based on the following assumptions, some of which use state-of-the-art empirical formulae taken from published articles (Perakis and Papadakis[10, 14]):

(1) A vessel carries a full load of cargo from load port to unload port.
(2) When the vessel is operating in restricted waters, it has a known and constant restricted speed which is usually the maximum allowable speed in the region in question, hence requiring a known, fixed power and fuel rate.
(3) The number of days a vessel spends in port per round trip is known and constant.
(4) The charges incurred at the load port and unload port per round trip are known and constant.
(5) The amount of fuel burned per day in the load port and unload port is known and constant.
(6) The annual costs of manning, stores, supplies, equipment, capital, administration, maintenance and repair, and make ready for sail are known and constant.
(7) The power of vessel i (in HP) may be expressed by

$P_i = a_i \cdot X_i^{b_i}$ for the full load and by

$P_{bi} = a_{bi} \cdot Y_i^{b_{bi}}$

for the ballast condition, where X_i and Y_i are the full load and ballast speeds of ship i respectively and the rest are appropriate constants.

(8) The all-purpose fuel rate for a fully loaded vessel i may be expressed by

$(R_f)_i = g_i \cdot p_i^2 + s_i \cdot p_i + d_i$ for the full load and by

$(R_f)_{bi} = g_{bi} \cdot p_{bi}^2 + s_{bi} \cdot p_{bi} + d_{bi}$

for the ballast condition where p_i and p_{bi} are the normalised (%) p_i and p_{bi} respectively, and the rest are appropriate constants.

(9) The *total* annual cost of laying up vessel i is known for all i = 1, ..., z.
(10) The number of days per year vessel i is out of service for maintenance and repair is known and constant.
(11) This problem formulation and solution is for a single stage, "one-shot" decision.

In the literature, the number of tons carried per year is assumed to be a linear function of a ship's full load and ballast speeds. In our research, we have shown that this assumption can be quite unrealistic. As Figure 1 indicates, this function is quite nonlinear in nature. A derivation of this function may be found in Perakis and Papadakis.[10]

Operating costs (developed in detail in Perakis and Papadakis (1985a)[14,15]) are considered to fit into one of two categories, those that do not vary with ship speed, or *daily running costs*, and those that vary with ship speed, or *voyage costs*. Typical plots for the total (*not* per ton) operating costs per year for a particular ship, for various ballast speeds, are given in Figure 2.

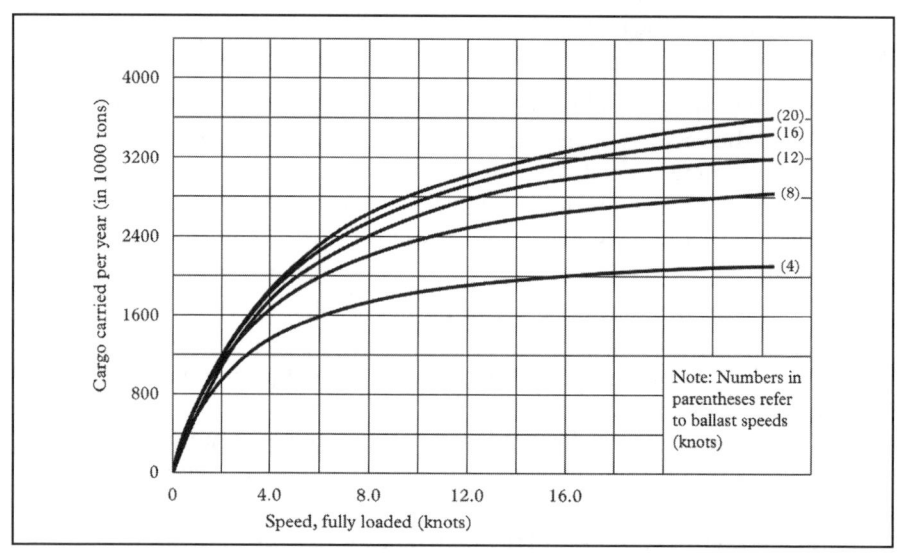

Figure 1: Typical plot of cargo carried per year as a function of ship speeds

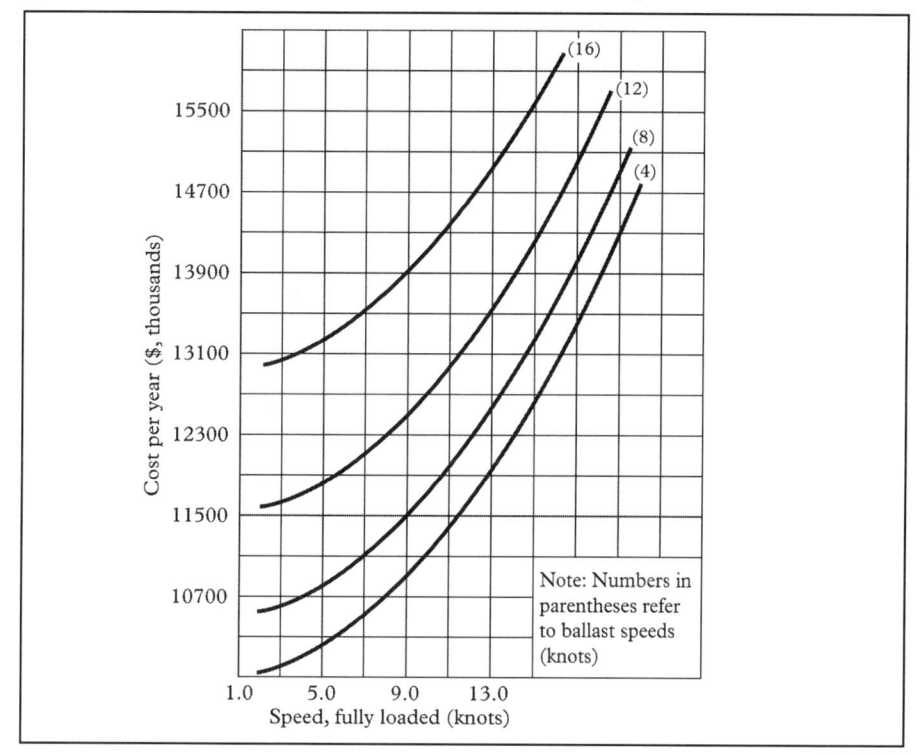

Figure 2: Typical plot for the total operating cost per year as a function of ship full load and ballast speeds

A typical plot of $F(X_i, Y_i)$ is shown in Figure 3, as a function of the full load and ballast speeds. It is seen that F is a smooth convex curve or surface with a single minimum. There is also a finite speed range in which F is not very different from its minimum value, a property which allows approximate solutions to the problem using very different speeds for individual ships to produce total fleet costs very close to one another and to the optimum cost itself. For X_i and/or Y_i going towards either 0 or 8, F approaches infinity. Figures 2 and 3 are for the same ship and for constant route data.

Introducing the linear inequality constraints on the speeds complicates the problem solution considerably. In the first part of this research, an External Penalty Technique (EPT) has been combined with the Nelder and Mead Simplex Search Technique to solve our optimisation problem. The purpose of a penalty function method is to transform a constrained problem into an unconstrained problem which can be solved using the coupled unconstrained technique.

A computer program has been written to solve this problem using the techniques and the formulation mentioned above. The solution returned consists of the ship speeds, for those vessels specified for analysis, that will minimise the total mission operating costs and fulfil the cargo transport obligation.

For the lay-up option, it is shown in the technical report that for even moderate numbers of ships in a fleet, it is rather too time-consuming to use an

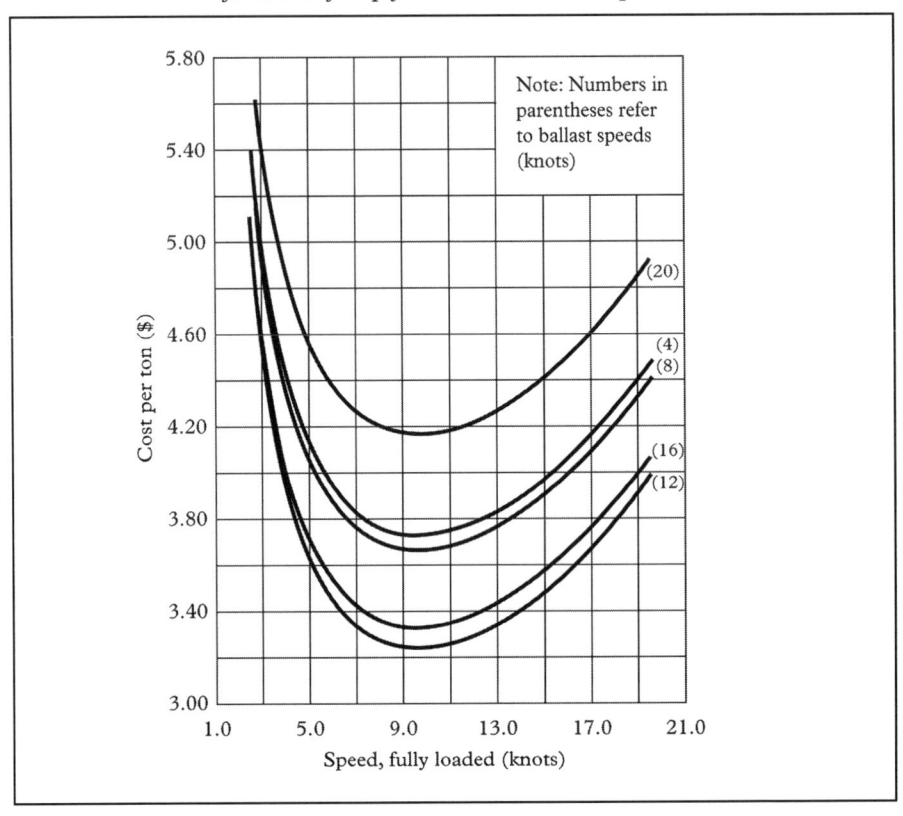

Figure 3: Typical plot for the total cost per ton as a function of ship full load and ballast speeds

[Figure 3: Plot of Cost per ton ($) vs Speed, fully loaded (knots). Y-axis ranges from 3.00 to 5.80; X-axis ranges from 1.0 to 21.0. Curves labeled (20), (4), (8), (16), (12). Note: Numbers in parentheses refer to ballast speeds (knots).]

exhaustive enumeration scheme. Instead, a dynamic programming-like sequential optimisation approach is developed, significantly reducing the computational burden. If Z is the number of ships in the fleet, the maximum number of fleets we will have to examine using this approach is $M_{max} = Z(Z+1)/2 - 1$. The *actual* number of fleets which we will have to consider will be significantly smaller than M_{max}, due to the elimination of several fleets as infeasible and much smaller than the upper limit of total possible cases. The above scheme has been implemented and referred to in the following as the operating cost without rerunning the program. This property holds for a given fleet and not in cases when one or more ships are laid-up or chartered to a third party (on top of the changes in the cost components).

The fleet deployment problem with time-varying cost components was also studied. A time horizon in this formulation is any interval within which cost components are constant but at least one of them is different than its value in another interval. In other words, our cost components are given "staircase" functions of time. In the case of rapidly changing costs, resulting in rather short intervals where these costs are constant, the problem of non-integer number of round trips per interval could be crucial. A heuristic approach was developed

FLEET OPERATIONS OPTIMISATION AND DEPLOYMENT

to find the nearest "integer" solution corresponding to the non-integer solution generally provided by the SIMPLEX algorithm.

Further details may be found in Perakis and Papadakis,[10, 11, 15] and the associated user's documentation (Perakis, Papadakis and Pagoulatos[13]), where a more extensive multi-page flow-chart is presented.

The fleet deployment problem for the case when some of the cost components are random variables with known probability density functions was finally considered (Perakis and Papadakis[11]). We note that the minimum of the possible mean values of the total annual operating costs, C_{min} and the variance of C_{min} can be found relatively "easily". However, this approach has not yet been implemented on a computer and probably will not prove very useful. The inputs to the problem, i.e. the user-supplied probability density functions, can have any particular theoretical or experimental form, thus discouraging the development of any general computer code for this problem.

3.2 The Multi-Origin, Multi-Destination Fleet Deployment Problem

The problem of minimum-cost operation of a fleet of ships which has to carry a specific amount of cargo from several origin ports to several destination ports during a specified time interval was next examined. During the season any vessel can be loaded in any source port (S) and unloaded at any destination port (D) provided that these ports belong to a subset I or J (respectively) of the total set of ports, such that draft and other constraints for the corresponding vessel are satisfied. Under this assumption for each vessel the number of possible routes (number of possible sequences of S-D ports) is quite large. The full load and ballast characteristics of each ship on each route are assumed to be known.

This nonlinear optimisation problem consists of a nonlinear objective function and a set of five linear and two integer constraints. The objective function to be minimised is the total fleet operating cost during the time interval (shipping season) in question. The following constraints have to be satisfied:

(a) for each vessel, the total time spent in loading, traveling from origins to destinations, unloading and traveling from destinations to origins plus the lay-up time has to be equal to the total amount of time available for each ship in the shipping season.
(b) The total amount shipped to a particular destination j must be equal to the amount of cargo to be delivered to j during the shipping season (in tons).
(c) The total amount of cargo loaded from a particular source i must be less or equal to the cargo available at i.
(d) For each ship, the number of trips to destination j must be equal to the number of trips out of j.
(e) Same as (d) for all source ports i.
(f) The full-load and ballast operating speeds have to be between given upper and lower limits.
(g) The numbers of full load and ballast trips for each vessel, origin and destination combination must all be non-negative integers.

The constraints presented above are linear except constraints (a) and (g). The maximum number of unknown variables (if all source and destinations ports are accessible by any ship of the given fleet) is $(4 \cdot I \cdot J + 1) \cdot Z$. The number of the associated constraints is $2Z + (1 + J)(Z + 1) + 4 \cdot I \cdot J \cdot Z$. For a case with $I = 4$, $J = 6$ and $Z = 10$ we have 970 variables and 1090 constraints. Using today's personal computers, it is clear that we cannot use any classical nonlinear optimisation technique, since the expected computation time would be too long.

In the case of the multi-origin, multi-destination fleet deployment problem, it was seen that the linear programming approaches to the literature do not take into account significant nonlinearities of the relevant cost functions and may lead to very suboptimal decisions. The iterative procedure we developed uses a linear programming software in an algorithmic scheme that takes into account these nonlinearities and produces accurate results. This approach is ideally suited for a personal computer due to the reasonable running times of the LP software for almost any practical situation. A second, nonlinear approach to solve the multi-origin, multi-destination problem was also implemented, using the available MINOS nonlinear optimisation package.

In Papadakis and Perakis,[12] the fleet deployment problem for a fleet of vessels operating between a set of *several loading and unloading ports* under certain time and cargo constraints was examined. Full load and ballast voyage costs were treated as nonlinear functions of the ship full load and ballast speeds, respectively. An optimisation model, appropriate for bulk carrier fleets, minimising the total operating cost, was formulated. The existence of a coupling between the optimal speed selection and the optimal vessel allocation on the available routes was demonstrated, and conditions leading to the decoupling of these problems were established. Considerations referring to the structure of the optimal solution resulted in a substantial reduction of the dimensionality of the problem. We found that in cases of low-to-moderate fleet utilisation, linear programming may be applied to derive the optimal solution, while in cases of higher fleet utilisation, use of nonlinear optimisation may become necessary. The potential benefits of our approach were demonstrated by several examples.

Finally, we would like to note that the algorithms and the computer codes, developed for both the one-origin one-destination and for the multi-origin, multi-destination fleet deployment problem can be easily used to find not only the optimal fleet deployment policy within the given time horizon but also to help the fleet operator to make decisions in case unexpected events like strikes or accidents occur. In such a case the programs can be re-run for the remaining time interval and an optimal decision can still be obtained. Other plans, such as renewing or improving a part of the fleet and selling or chartering decisions may also be evaluated.

4. FLEET DEPLOYMENT MODELS FOR LINER SHIPPING

In Perakis and Jaramillo[16] we have reviewed the relevant work on liner shipping deployment and described current industry practices. Our objectives and assumptions were then presented. A model for the optimisation of the deploy-

FLEET OPERATIONS OPTIMISATION AND DEPLOYMENT

ment of a liner fleet composed of both owned and chartered vessels was formulated. The determination of the operating costs of the ships in every one of the routes in which the company operates was carried out by a means of a realistic model, providing the coefficients representing voyage cost and time required for the input of the linear program presented in Jaramillo and Perakis.[17] A method for determining the best speeds and service frequencies was also presented; the fixing of those two groups of variables was required to linearise the deployment problem as formulated there. The overall optimisation method was described in detail, and a real life case study was presented, based on the co-author's company (FMG, Flota Mercante Grancolombiana) operations (Jaramillo and Perakis[17]).

In Powell and Perakis[18] we extended and improved on the above. An Integer Programming (IP) model was developed to minimise the operating and lay-up costs for a fleet of liner ships operating on various routes. The IP model determines the optimal deployment of the existing fleet, given route, service, charter, and compatibility constraints. Two case studies were carried out, with the same as above extensive actual data provided by FMG. The optimal deployment was determined for their existing ship and service frequency requirements.

The inputs to the optimisation model (presented in Powell and Perakis[18]) are based on the existing cost estimation model provided in Perakis and Jaramillo,[16] including ship daily running costs, voyage costs, costs at sea, costs at port, daily lay-up costs.

The optimisation model in Perakis and Jaramillo[16] is given as:

$$\text{Minimise} \left(\sum_{k=1}^{K} \sum_{r=1}^{R} C_{kr} X_{kr} + \sum_{k=1}^{K} Y_k e_k \right)$$

where:

C_{kr} = operating cost per voyage for a type k ship on route r
X_{kr} = number of voyages per year of a type k ship on route r
e_k = lay-up cost for a type k ship
Y_k = number of lay-up days per year for a type k ship

In Perakis and Jaramillo[16] and Jaramillo and Perakis[17] a Linear Programming (LP) approach was used to solve this optimisation problem. Using an LP formulation required the rounding of the number of ships allocated to each route. The rounding led to some variations in targeted service frequencies and to suboptimal results. An Integer Programming formulation is used in Powell and Perakis[18] to eliminate any rounding errors in the previous LP solution.

4.1 Integer Programming Problem Formulation

Decision variables

N_{kr} = the number of a type k ship operating on route r
Y_k = the number of lay-up days per year of a type k ship

for k = 1 to K and r = 1 to R ; K is the number of ship types and R is the number of routes.

Objective function

The objective function in the model minimises the sum of the operating costs and the lay-up costs. The objective function in terms of the decision variables is:

$$\text{Minimise} \left(\sum_{k=1}^{K} \sum_{r=1}^{R} C'_{kr} N_{kr} + \sum_{k=1}^{K} Y_k e_k \right)$$

where

$C'_{kr} = C_{kr} X_{kr}$, are the operating costs of a type k ship operating on route r
e_k = daily lay-up cost for a type k ship

Constraints

Ship availability. The maximum number of ships of type k operating cannot be greater than the maximum number of ships of type k available. Therefore:

$$\sum_{r=1}^{R} N_{kr} \leq N_k^{max} \text{ , for each type k ship}$$

where

N_k^{max} = maximum number of type k ships available

Service frequency. Service frequency is the driving force in liner shipping. With all rates being set by conferences, the main product differentiation is on service. To ensure that minimum service frequencies are met, the following constraint is included:

$$\sum_{k=1}^{K} t'_{kr} N_{kr} \leq M_r \text{ for all r,}$$

where

t'_{kr} = yearly voyages of a type k ship on route r and:
$t'_{kr} = t_{kr}/T_k$
T_k = shipping season for a type k ship
M_r = number of voyages required per year in route r

By finding the highest load level for any given leg of route r and comparing this with given ship capacity, we find the minimum required number of voyages per year for a specific route.

Ship/Route Incompatibility. Some ships may be unable to operate on a given route due to cargo constraints, government regulations, and/or environmental constraints. It is necessary to eliminate these ships from the model. Therefore:

$N_{kr} = 0$, for given (k,r) pairs

Lay-up Time. The lay-up time in our models is equal to the time a ship is not operating during the year. This includes dry-docking and repair time.

$$Y_k = 365 N_k^{max} - T_k \sum_{r=1}^{R} N_{kr} \text{ for all r,}$$

FLEET OPERATIONS OPTIMISATION AND DEPLOYMENT

Non-Negativity. The decision variables N_{kr} must be non-negative.

4.2 Software Application

The software package used to run the above example was "A Mathematical Programming Language" (AMPL) (Holmes,[19] and Fourer, Gay and Kernighan[20]) and OSL, a mathematical program solver. See Powell and Perakis[18] for more details. The output file from AMPL gives the following information:
  (i) optimal value of objective function
  (ii) value of objective function with LP relaxation
  (iii) number of iterations to find solution
  (iv) values of variables at the optimal solution

The values of the Nkr variables will show how many type k ships should be allocated to each route r. The Yk variable will indicate the number of days for which type k ships must be laid-up.

Optimisation examples

The following two examples are for the fleet deployment for FMG. The fleet consists of six types of owned ships and five types of chartered ships (one long-term charter and four short-term charters). The data used to calculate the coefficients for the optimisation model is taken from Jaramillo and Perakis.[17] The cost and time coefficients used are transformed from per voyage units to per ship values.

Example 1: The first example optimises the FMG fleet deployment for their current shipping conditions. This example uses FMG's existing service frequencies and the number of ships available of each type. The current allocation is shown in Table 3.

Table 3: Current ship allocation

Ship Type		Route 1	2	3	4	5	6	7	Total
(Owned)	1	3			3				6
	2						2		2
	3				2		1		3
	4							1	1
	5		1						1
	6			1					1
(Chartered)	7						1		1
	8		1	1					2
	9								0
	10								0
	11					2			2
	Total	3	2	2	5	2	4	1	19

Example 1 results: The IP optimal allocation is given in Table 4. The minimum objective function yields a total operating cost of $91,831,000. This is compared with $93,148,000 for the current allocation. This corresponds to a

592 ASPECTS OF SHIPPING MANAGEMENT & OPERATIONS

reduction in total operating costs of 1.4% (a savings of $1,317,000 per year). Analysing the resulting allocation shows that all owned ships (k = 1 to 6) and the long-term charter (k = 7) are in use for the entire shipping season. This is due to the high lay-up costs associated with these ship types.

None of ship type 9 are allocated. This ship type has the highest operating cost of any of the short-term charters.

Table 4: Resultant ship allocation (Example 1)

	Ship Type	Route 1	2	3	4	5	6	7	Total
(Owned)	1	3			3				6
	2			1				1	2
	3				1		2		3
	4		1						1
	5		1						1
	6						1		1
(Chartered)	7			1			1		2
	8								0
	9								0
	10					2			2
	11				1				1
	Total	3	2	2	5	2	4	1	19

Example 2: Example 2 uses the frequency constraints of the LP model presented in Jaramillo and Perakis.[17] The resultant allocation of the LP model is contained in Table 5. This example compares the results and highlights the advantages of the IP model versus the results of the LP model.

Table 5: Linear programming allocation

	Ship Type	Route 1	2	3	4	5	6	7	Total
(Owned)	1	1			5				6
	2			1				1	2
	3						3		3
	4		1						1
	5		1						1
	6						1		1
(Chartered)	7			1					1
	8								0
	9								0
	10					2			2
	11	2							2
	Total	3	2	2	5	2	4	1	19

Example 2 results: The IP optimal allocation of ships is given in Table 6. The minimum objective function gives a total operating cost of $99,400,000.

FLEET OPERATIONS OPTIMISATION AND DEPLOYMENT

Table 6: Integer programming allocation (Example 2)

	Ship Type		Route 1	2	3	4	5	6	7	Total
(Owned)	1		1			1		4		6
	2					1			1	2
	3					3				3
	4			1						1
	5			1						1
	6		1							1
(Chartered)	7		1			1				2
	8			1						1
	9									0
	10						2			2
	11				2					2
	Total		3	3	2	6	2	4	1	21

The resulting allocation of the IP optimisation model maintains all of the target frequencies. Routes 1, 3, and 5 exactly meet the target frequencies while on routes 2, 4, 6, and 7 the frequency is improved. The improvement ranges from 1.3 days to 3.3 days.

For the LP comparison example presented, the optimal objective function of the IP model is $99,400,000. Although the cost produced by the LP model is substantially smaller, it is important to note that the service frequencies are compromised in the 1991 LP solution, which leads to sub-optimal allocation. Table 7 shows the comparison between service frequencies of the IP optimisation model and the LP model.

Table 7: Comparison of frequencies

	Route 1	2	3	4	5	6	7
Target frequency	14	14	21	15	30	23	35
IP Model	14	10.7	21	12.9	29.2	20.4	33.7
Difference	0.0	−3.3	0.0	−2.1	0.0	−2.6	−1.3
LP Model	14.7	16.1	18.9	16.1	29.2	19.2	33.7
Difference	0.7	2.1	−2.1	1.1	−0.8	−3.8	−1.3

Since service is a priority in liner shipping, it is necessary to meet the target frequencies. The IP optimisation model ensures that all target frequencies are met. The LP model violates the target frequency for routes 1, 2 and 4. This is an average increase in service time of 1.3 days or 9.1%.

Using Integer Programming to solve integer problems always produces the optimal solution for the given constraints. No manipulation of results is necessary. Using Linear Programming to solve IPs requires manipulations of the results to make the decision variables integer numbers. This leads to sub-optimal solutions and constraints being violated.

Substantial savings may be achieved by applying our IP optimisation model for the fleet deployment of a liner shipping company. The first example in [18] compares our IP model against the existing fleet deployment of a liner shipping company.

This example shows a reduction in operating costs of 1.5%. The second example compares our IP model with the LP model contained in Perakis and Jaramillo.[16] The results of the IP model are optimal and meet all service frequency constraints. The LP model violates the service constraints in three routes by an average of 9.1%.

The solution indicates that all owned and long-term charter ship types should be operated for their entire shipping season, due to the high lay-up cost associated with these ship types. Short-term charters should only be used if the owned ships and long-term charters cannot meet the cargo and service frequency constraints.

5. SUMMARY AND CONCLUSIONS

The optimisation of the operations of a fleet of ships is mathematically far more complicated than the optimisation of the operations of a single ship. However, trying to optimise the various full load and ballast speeds of each different ship in the fleet can be even more complicated than that, and necessitate the use of nonlinear programming algorithms and software, as opposed to the largely linear-integer algorithms in cases when the speeds are fixed and not optimised (slow-steaming).

Due to the very different degree of competition in the bulker and liner markets, and also due to the very dissimilar constraints on their respective operations, optimal fleet deployment is quite different for each one. Over the past several years, we have provided "exact" and "approximate" algorithms for realistic, single or multi-origin and destination problems for bulker fleet deployment, including optimal slow-steaming lay-up decisions, under conditions of certainty or uncertainty for the various cost components. We then also solved problems in optimal strategic planning and ship-route allocation for a major liner company, presenting independent models for fixing both the service frequencies in the different routes and the speeds of the ships, using at first linear and integer programming. Several insights from a review and comparative study of the above were presented here, starting from the proper problem definition (constraints artificially imposed have resulted in 15% higher costs in early literature on this problem) and ending with the benefits of optimal integer solutions to the liner fleet deployment problems we studied.

Length limitations prohibit us from discussing our extensive work in other areas of fleet optimisation, such as the operational, day-to-day decisions for a major oil company fleet, which we modeled and solved in Bremer and Perakis[21] and Perakis and Bremer,[22] or go into more details on the research modeling and results we did discuss in this paper. Our work with Bremer was an example of an operational (as opposed to long-term or strategic) optimisation.

We will also not discuss the mathematical details of some recent work of ours (Cho and Perakis[23]), where we were able to re-formulate a complicated bulk cargo ship scheduling problem formulation Ronen,[24] from a non-linear-integer to an equally accurate integer-linear problem, with far fewer variables, using a generalisation of the "capacitated facility location problem", a classic result of optimisation theory. That problem was referring to a single loading port, several unloading ports, and fixed speeds (no slow-steaming allowed.)

For a detailed exposition of liner shipping economics, the textbook by Janson and the late D.S. Schneerson[25] is highly recommended. In the recent liner logistics research,[26, 27] presented nonlinear programming models, aiming to maximise total profit by finding an optimal sequence of ports of call for each ship. For solution methods, they used Lagrangean relaxation[4] and decomposition methods. Their first paper develops only a one-ship model, while their second is rather complicated by its non-linearities in both objective function and constraints. The model of Perakis and Jaramillo,[16] and its subsequent more accurate integer solution[18] is easier to use for a realistic situation, but does not take into account the cargo demand forecasts that arise between pairs of ports in the model.

We have addressed that in Cho and Perakis,[28] where we have suggested two optimisation models. The first is a linear programming model of profit maximisation, providing an optimal routing mix for each ship available and optimal service frequencies for each candidate route. The second is a mixed integer programming model with binary variables, providing not only optimal routing mixes and service frequencies, but also best capital investment alternatives to expand fleet capacity, and is a cost minimisation model. In both models, we have suggested and used the concept of "flow-route incidence matrix", and discuss its usefulness for similar routing and scheduling problems.[28] The most important merit of using the flow-route incidence matrix is that it links various cargo demands to route utilisation in a simple, systematic way. These models can help improve existing network of routes or service frequencies, and their solution can be easily implemented with standard linear or integer programming packages.

Other examples of complicated operational models we have studied in detail are Ship Weather Routing problems, but since we are restricting this chapter to fleet, not individual ship, optimisation, we will not discuss them here. The models described in this chapter are all strategic. However, at the request of the reviewer of this book chapter, we cite a few key recent references in that area.[29, 30, 31]

The results of our research in Fleet Deployment have been cited in graduate courses at Michigan, MIT, and elsewhere in the US, but also in universities around the world, such as in the recent textbook[32] used at the Maritime Studies Dept. in Dalian, China. Further dissemination of these results in this chapter will hopefully result in more students and practitioners being exposed to the significant benefits of proper optimisation and the pitfalls, and their heavy price in higher fleet operating costs, of suboptimal policies.

ACKNOWLEDGEMENTS

The author would like to acknowledge the support of the US Maritime Administration University Research Program, Contract #DTMA-91-83-6-30032 in the early phases of his research on the "Fleet Deployment" problem. That research was also partially supported by an award to the author by The University of Michigan, Horace Rackham School for Graduate Studies. The author also wishes to acknowledge the partial support provided by the Society of Naval Architects and Marine Engineers and Chevron Shipping Company, as well as by FMG Inc. and the help of his graduate research assistant, Mr. Zhiyong Yang, with figure scanning for this chapter.

REFERENCES

1. Stopford, M., (1997): *Maritime Economics* (2nd ed.) (London, Routledge), ISBN 0-415-15310-7.
2. Benford, H. (1981): "A simple approach to fleet deployment", *Maritime Policy and Management*, 8(4), pp. 223–228.
3. Marbury, F. (1982): "The Finer Points of Slow Steaming", *SNAME Ship Cost and Energy Symposium*.
4. Fischer, M.L., and Rosenwein, M.B. (1985): *An Interactive Optimisation System for Bulk Cargo Ship Scheduling*, Dept. of Decision Sciences, Univ. of Pennsylvania, Philadelphia.
5. Perakis, A.N. (1985): "A second look at fleet deployment", *Maritime Policy and Management*, 12(2), pp. 209–214.
6. Appelgren, L.H. (1971): "Integer Programming methods for a Vessel Scheduling problem", *Transp. Science*, 5, pp. 64–78.
7. Ronen, D. (1982): "Cargo ships routing and scheduling: Survey of models and problems", *European Journal of Operational Research*, 12, pp. 119–126.
8. Ronen, D. (1993): "Ship Scheduling: The last decade", *European Journal of Operational Research*, 71, pp. 325–333.
9. Perakis, A.N. (1995): "Optimal Fleet Deployment: Insights from a Decade of Research", paper presented at and included in *Proceedings, 7th World Conference of Transport Research*, Sydney, Australia.
10. Perakis, A.N., and Papadakis, N. (1987a): "Fleet deployment optimisation models, part I", *Maritime Policy and Management*, 14, pp. 127–144.
11. Perakis, A.N., and Papadakis, N. (1987b): "Fleet deployment optimisation models, part II", *Maritime Policy and Management*, 14, pp. 145–155.
12. Papadakis, N.A., and Perakis, A.N. (1989): "A nonlinear approach to the multiorigin, multidestination fleet deployment problem", *Naval Research Logistics*, 36(5), pp. 515–528.
13. Perakis, A.N., Papadakis, N., and Pagoulatos, P. (1985): *Computer-aided fleet deployment: User documentation, part I*. Report to US Maritime Administration, University Research Program, Contract #DTMA-91-83-C-30032, May.
14. Perakis, A.N., and Papadakis, N. (1985a): *Optimisation schemes for rational, computer-aided fleet deployment: Final Report, Vol. II*. Technical Report, prepared for the US Department of Transportation, Maritime Administration University Research Program, Contract #DTMA-91-83-C-30032, August.
15. Perakis, A.N., and Papadakis, N. (1985b): *Computer-aided fleet deployment: User documentation, part II*. Report to US Maritime Administration, University Research Program, Contract #DTMA-91-83-C-30032, October.

16. Perakis, A.N., and Jaramillo, D.I. (1991): "Fleet deployment optimisation for liner shipping, part I: Background problem formulation and solution approaches", *Maritime Policy and Management,* 18, pp. 183–200.
17. Jaramillo, D.I., and Perakis, A.N. (1991): "Fleet deployment optimisation for liner shipping. Part 2: Implementation and results", *Maritime Policy and Management,* 18, pp. 235–262.
18. Powell, B.J., and Perakis, A.N. (1997): "Fleet deployment optimisation for liner shipping: An integer programming model", *Maritime Policy and Management,* 24, No. 2, pp. 183–192.
19. Holmes, D. (1992): *AMPL (A Mathematical Programming Language) at the University of Michigan Documentation,* Version 2.
20. Fourer, R., Gay, D., and Kernighan, B. (1992): *AMPL A Model Language for Mathematical Programming* (San Francisco, Scientific Press).
21. Bremer, W.M., and Perakis, A.N. (1992): "An operational tanker scheduling optimisation system: model implementation, results and possible extensions", *Maritime Policy and Management,* 19(3), pp. 189–199.
22. Perakis, A.N., and Bremer, W.M. (1992): "An operational tanker scheduling optimisation system: background, current practice and model formulation", *Maritime Policy and Management,* 19 (3), pp. 177–187.
23. Cho, S.C., and Perakis, A.N. (2001): "An improved formulation for bulk cargo ship scheduling with a single loading port", *Maritime Policy and Management,* 8, No.4, pp. 339–345.
24. Ronen, D. (1986): "Short term scheduling of vessels for shipping bulk or semi-bulk commodities originating in a single area", *Operations Research,* 34, pp. 164–173.
25. Janson, J.O., and Schneerson, D.S. (1987): *Liner Shipping Economics* (London, Chapman and Hall).
26. Rana, K., and Vickson, R.G. (1988): "A model and solution algorithm for optimal routing of a time-chartered containership", *Transportation Science,* 22, pp. 83–95.
27. Rana, K., and Vickson, R.G. (1991): "Routing containerships using Lagrangean relaxation and decomposition", *Transportation Science,* 25, pp. 201–214.
28. Cho, S.C., and Perakis, A.N. (1996): "Optimal liner fleet routeing strategies", *Maritime Policy and Management,* 23, No. 3, pp. 249–259.
29. Perakis, A.N., and Papadakis, N.A. (1988): "New Models for Minimal Time Ship Weather Routing", *Transactions, The Society of Naval Architects and Marine Engineers,* 96, pp. 247–269.
30. Perakis, A.N., and Papadakis, N.A. (1989): "Minimal Time Vessel Routing in a Time-Dependent Environment", *Transportation Science,* 23, No. 4, pp. 266–277.
31. Papadakis, N.A., and Perakis, A.N. (1990): "On the Minimal-Time Ship Weather Routing Problem", *Operations Research,* 38, No. 3, pp. 426–438.
32. Xie, Xinlian, (2000): *Fleet Management and Deployment* (Renmin Jiao Tong Press, Beijing). College Textbook. ISBN-7-114-03490-3 (in Chinese).

CHAPTER 27

CONSOLIDATION, MERGERS AND ACQUISITIONS IN THE SHIPPING INDUSTRY

Photis M. Panayides and Stephen X.H. Gong
Department of Shipping and Transport Logistics, Hong Kong Polytechnic University, Hong Kong. E-mail: *stlpp@polyu.edu.hk* and *stlxhg@polyu.edu.hk*

1. INTRODUCTION

Mergers and acquisitions (M&As) have been an important phenomenon in modern economic life. As such, they have received considerable attention from the scientific community. In the economics and finance oriented studies the focus is on economic and financial outcomes whereas in the strategic management and organisation science fields, the emphasis is on non-value maximising motives and post-merger implementation processes and problems such as cultural incompatibility, competitive position games, etc.

A merger entails the coming together of companies to combine and share resources to achieve common objectives resulting in the formation of a new entity. On the other hand, an acquisition involves the purchasing of the assets or shares of a firm with the acquired firm's shareholders ceasing to be owners of that firm and may be a friendly acquisition or hostile takeover. Mergers may be horizontal (combination of competitors), vertical (combination of firms having a buyer-seller relationship) or conglomerate (combination of companies in different lines of business).

In the shipping industry, consolidation and mergers and acquisitions have been taking place in an unprecedented rate over the last few years across all major markets of the industry. This underpins the importance of studies of consolidation and mergers and acquisitions for understanding contemporary economic imperatives of the industry and the strategic direction of the participants.

This chapter is organised into seven sections in an effort to provide an understanding of the major issues in consolidation and mergers and acquisitions within the shipping industry. Section 2 provides an overview of the environmental conditions contributing towards acceleration of M&As in the shipping industry and highlights the major deals that have taken place across a number of markets in the industry. The legal and regulatory framework plays an important role in the consummation of mergers and acquisitions, particularly in the shipping industry where antitrust regulation and its application to the industry have been peculiar and contentious for a number of years. The economic principles underpinning regulation of M&As as well as the laws that govern them in the United States (US) and the European Union (EU) are reviewed in Section

3. Section 4 reviews in detail the scientific literature that deals with the underlying motives of business entities for engaging in M&As. Empirical investigations that have been carried out in a number of industries provide possible indications as to the motives of shipping companies engaged in M&As. Anecdotal evidence for the latter is also presented. Section 5 provides a framework for evaluating mergers and acquisitions. Three key issues are identified and presented. These include the short-run performance of the merged entity, the long-run post-merger performance, and problems that may occur during or after the merger. Section 6 discusses the importance of corporate governance and control in M&As, while Section 7 summarises and concludes.

2. CONSOLIDATION AND MERGER AND ACQUISITION ACTIVITY IN SHIPPING

2.1 Conditions for acceleration of M&A in shipping

The occurrence of mergers and acquisitions is not independent of broad environmental factors that may induce favourable conditions for consolidation. Changes in the economic environments may alter the domain of constraints, allowing or disallowing companies to consolidate. Technological advances, regulation (and de-regulation), excess capacity in the shipping markets, market creation and customer requirements, globalisation and trends in conglomeration are factors in the environmental domain that may induce a propensity towards consolidation.

Technological progress is directly related to the achievement of efficiency in ship operation and hence, to the achievement of the companies' objectives. Technological progress may yield economies of scale, particularly in the ocean liner-shipping sector, and such technological solutions are more accessible to bigger organisations by virtue of the greater financial power they wield. The rapid pace of technological progress suggests that small shipping companies may not be able to keep up with new technologies, and hence limit their potential to improve their competitiveness. Thus, technological progress may create favourable conditions for accelerating consolidation, through which greater market power may be achieved.

Another environmental influence on merger activity in liner shipping has been the advances in the financial markets, including a larger supply of increasingly sophisticated legal and financial advisors and the proliferation of financing techniques in the shipping industry. For instance, share offerings, the issuance of high-yield non-investment-grade bonds and, in general, the easier access to international capital markets, provide ample ground for initiation and support of a merger or acquisition strategy.

Deregulation of industries tends to relax or remove restrictions on the companies' ability to coalesce. There is evidence to suggest that consolidation and M&A activity accelerated as a result of deregulation.[1,2] Regulation and the treatment by the authorities of past merger/acquisition proposals tend to create an environment for accelerating mergers and acquisitions in shipping.

The intensity of competition between companies in various markets and excess capacity on trade routes coupled with the increasing customer requirements on a global scale have been additional contributing factors for a trend towards further consolidation and partnership-building among previously competing companies.

2.2 Growth of M&As in shipping

During the first half of the 1990s the dominant strategy in liner shipping seemed to be the formation of strategic alliances. Strategic alliances seemed to offer the benefits of bargaining power, access to a larger customer base and improvement in service quality, and more efficient use of resources. Nevertheless, the very fact that re-structuring of such alliances occurred relatively frequently with companies leaving and entering over short time spans, did seem to suggest that credible commitments have not been made by some partners rendering alliances somewhat unstable. In addition, the risk of giving away critical know-how to potential competitors has always been a deterrent to the formation of alliances, despite the potential benefits. Midoro and Pitto[3] argue that alliances in their existing form have not been workable due to lack of division of responsibilities and to the wide membership, thus culminating in alliance instability. According to a number of authors (e.g., Garette and Dussauge,[4] Killing,[5] and Weiss[6]) the consensual decision-making process in alliances increases the cost of rationalising. In consequence, reaping of long-term benefits using this strategic mode may not have reached expectations, at least for some alliance partners. In comparison, merger and acquisition has become the dominant strategic mode over the last few years, with some 40 such mergers or acquisitions having taken place and with at least one being

Table 1: Mergers and acquisitions in shipping

Date	Merger or acquisition deal	Details
March 1995	CP Ships acquires Cast	CAN$150m
January 1996	P&O Containers acquires ANL	Not Reported
January 1997	P&O Containers merges with Nedlloyd	Nedlloyd paid US$175m to P&O
February 1997	Hanjin acquires DSR-Senator Line	US$75m
July 1997	CP Ships acquires Lykes Lines	US$34m
October 1997	CP Ships acquires Contship Containerlines	US$110
November 1997	NOL acquires APL	US$825m
February 1998	P&O Nedlloyd acquires Blue Star Line	US$100–146m
May 1998	CP Ships acquires Ivarans	Not reported
July 1998	Evergreen acquires Lloyd Triestino	Not reported
August 1998	Hamburg Sud acquires Alianca	Not reported
September 1998	CP Ships acquires ANZDL	Not reported
January 1999	Maersk acquires SCL	US$240m
June 1999	Teekay acquires Bona Shipping	US$450m
July 1999	Maersk acquires Sea-Land	US$800m
January 2001	APL acquires GATX Logistics	US$210m
January 2001	V. Ships acquires Acomarit	US$30–32m

Sources: Various.

announced every six weeks.[7] Table 1 illustrates a number of important mergers and acquisitions that have occurred in the shipping industry recently. Their importance lies in the amount of the investments made, the size of the entities, and the envisaged impact on the industry.

The acquisition of Sealand by A.P. Moller-Maersk Line announced on 22 July 1999 has been the largest deal to date in the liner shipping industry. The agreement was for the A.P. Moller group to take over Sealand, the international liner business of CSX, which included 47 container vessels, 209,000 containers, 17 container terminals and certain lease obligations from CSX, among others. The merger, according to executives of the A.P. Moller group (parent company of Maersk) would culminate in benefits including rationalisation of operations and cost reductions, from bringing together administration, marketing and information technology.

The other major mergers occurred in 1997 with the integration of P&O Containers and Royal Nedlloyd Line (to form P&ONedlloyd), and the acquisition of American President Lines (APL) by Neptune Orient Lines (NOL). The formation of P&ONedlloyd Container Line was a strategy aimed towards improving the performance of the container shipping activities of the two listed companies. The partners anticipated annual cost reduction in the order of US$200m offset against an initial re-structuring cost of US$100m. The Singapore-listed NOL's acquisition of the US-listed APL, on the other hand, was aimed at achieving cost reduction in the order of US$160m offset by re-structuring costs of US$115m.

Certain liner companies have diversified interests and seem to be satisfied with such a state of affairs of not having "all eggs in one basket". For them, membership of a liner alliance may be a more logical strategy since it allows flexibility and does not preclude making substantial irreversible commitments. An example is represented by Mitsui OSK Lines which is a member of the New World Alliance whereas at the same time it has interests in bulk shipping and energy, oil and gas. With 40% of its turnover coming from the liner business, another 40% from its bulk business, and 20% from its other divisions, Mitsui OSK would not embark on a high profile merger, particularly in the uncertain climate of liner shipping.[7] It is obvious that the company seeks risk reduction rather than other benefits that mergers and acquisitions might entail. Hapag-Lloyd represents another example of a company that prefers alliances and joint service contract agreements. In this way the company has been able to serve its clients on a global basis whilst collaborating with other companies to expand into non-ocean activities. Hence, companies may pursue different strategies on the basis of their corporate objectives, reflecting differences in rationale.

The major mergers and acquisitions in the tanker sector over the past few years have been undertaken by John Fredriksen's group of companies, particularly Frontline. Frontline has had among its primary goals expansion through merger and acquisition. Realising the need for consolidation in the tanker sector, Frontline embarked on an aggressive acquisition campaign, taking over one competitor after another. Among its major acquisitions have been London & Overseas Freighters, ICB Shipping, Mosvold Shipping and Osprey Maritime.

Another notable case in the tanker sector is Teekay Shipping. The NYSE-listed company owns and operates one of the world's largest fleets of Aframax tankers through offices in 11 countries. On June 11, 1999, Teekay acquired Bona Shipping for a reported US$450 million. Bona Shipping engages in the transportation of oil products and dry-bulk commodities in the Atlantic. The acquisition gave Teekay global coverage for the first time by adding the Atlantic basin to the company's service routes and through a significant increase in its fleet size. In Spring 2001 Teekay broadened its range of global services by entering the shuttle tanker market by acquiring 98% of the Norwegian Ugland Nordic Shipping.

Consolidation through merger and acquisition has also occurred in the third-party ship management industry. The biggest deal was the acquisition of Acomarit by V. Ships to create the largest ship management company in the world with 12% market share. V. Ships has had a history of growth via acquisitions, having previously acquired Celtic Marine and Scottish Ship Management.

In the reefer trades as well, consolidation has been one of the main trends in recent years. One of the key players in this market has been Star Reefers Incorporated (SRI) of Norway. In August 2001, the Oslo-based ship owner successfully completed the acquisition of Albion Reefers, a subsidiary of the Vestey Group. This merger created an owned fleet of 26 vessels supplemented by around 18 vessels operated under various charter arrangements. Of particular strategic importance in the industry has been the 50:50 joint venture between SRI (previously Swan Reefer) and NYK to form NYK Star Reefers. The company became the third largest in the industry and more capable to compete with Lauritzen Cool and Seatrade.

A notable consolidation in the dry bulk market has been that between Italy's Coeclerici Shipping and Livanos' Ceres Hellenic Shipping Enterprises. The consolidation involved the combination of the fleets of the two enterprises under the banner of Coeclerici Ceres Bulk Carriers. The combined company will have control over 15 dry bulk carriers of 2.3m dwt and market value in excess of US$300m. The reported motives for the merger included expansion both in terms of acquisition of new ships as well as through acquisition of other companies.

3. THE LEGAL AND REGULATORY FRAMEWORK GOVERNING MERGERS AND ACQUISITIONS

3.1 Economic and political aspects in the regulation of M&As

The ability to merge with or acquire other firms is limited by antitrust legislation. The regulation of M&A is based on the premise of perfect competition. Neo-classical economic theory predicts that perfectly competitive markets will result in both allocative efficiency and productive efficiency. Under the perfect competition model, firms are "price-takers". Monopoly, on the other hand, will result in misallocation of resources and productive inefficiency as the monopolist strives to create product scarcity (in order to make excess profits) and due to the absence of incentives to reduce production costs. The monopolist is a "price-maker".

As governments seek to protect and promote consumer welfare, there is particular concern with the degree of power or control that a firm or firms exert on the market. Hence, the attention of regulators and competition law to mergers, acquisitions and other types of firm coalitions. This is because M&As may result in a monopoly or a firm having great market power that may enable it to act in a way similar to a monopolist. In addition, a high degree of concentration may lead to the problem of oligopoly where the limited number of market competitors will facilitate transparency in pricing behaviour. This mutual self-awareness may lead to a matching of pricing policies and hence, minimal price competition. In fact, oligopolists may be able to make excess profits without collusion, as they will tend to match each other's strategies and set monopolistic profit-maximising prices.

Although economic models play a role in delimiting fundamental variables for guiding antitrust policy, the formulation of competition laws and regulations is also influenced by political goals and policy objectives.[8] If the perfect competition model is to be fulfilled, then no mergers, acquisitions or coalitions between competing companies should be allowed to take place. Of course this is not the case and the latter is particularly true in the shipping industry where certain forms of cartels and coalitions like liner conferences (which are price fixing associations) are granted immunity from antitrust policy. The justifications given include the issue of protecting the continuing existence of an industry. In the United Kingdom the ultimate criterion for a merger rests on a political rather than an economic or legal assessment.

Antitrust legislation and regulation in the shipping industry regarding mergers, acquisitions and co-operative strategies have, in general, been more relaxed compared to other industries. This is evident from EU legislation that provides for the block exemption of liner conferences from competition rules and also in the US Ocean Shipping Reform Act (OSRA) 1998 with regard to the provisions made for co-operative working agreements (CWA). The latter provides for an assessment to determine the effects on competition. However, to the extent that efficiency gains are substantial then they can be enough to counter arguments of abuse of market power.

The main arguments for justifying exemption from antitrust regulation has been the special nature of the industry that culminates into practices that are otherwise considered anticompetitive, and the need to sustain an industry of strategic importance. The evidence in the shipping industry suggests that mergers and acquisitions do not, in principle, create monopoly or market power, or restrict competition.

3.2 US legislation

The US has had a major influence on competition policy, as it was the first to introduce a coherent competition system known as antitrust. US antitrust legislation is based on three key statutes, *viz.* the Sherman Act of 1890, the Clayton Act of 1914 and the Federal Trade Commission Act of 1914.

The Sherman Antitrust Act is the linchpin of all US antitrust laws. Its most important provisions include:

Section 1: Prohibits all contracts, combinations, and conspiracies in restraint of trade;

Section 2: Prohibits any attempts or conspiracies to monopolize a particular industry.

The Clayton Act served to strengthen the Sherman Act by explicitly prohibiting:

- price discrimination among customers except when it could be justified by cost economies;
- tying contracts;
- the acquisition of stock and assets in competing corporations if the effect was to lessen competition.

The Federal Trade Commission Act facilitates the effective enforcement, investigation and pursuit of antitrust violations. The Hart-Scott-Rodino Antitrust Improvements Act of 1976, enables the FTC and the Justice Department to review in advance proposed mergers and acquisitions and prohibit their consummation. The 1992 Merger Guidelines (as revised in 1997) set forth a five-step process that the enforcement authorities follow.

This entails:

(1) Assess whether the merger significantly increases concentration. This involves defining the relevant market;
(2) Assess any potential anticompetitive effects;
(3) Assess whether the potential anticompetitive effects could be mitigated by entry into the market by competitors. The existence of barriers to entry needs to be determined;
(4) Determine any offsetting efficiency gains that may result from the deal and which could offset the negative impact of the anticompetitive effects;
(5) Determine whether either party would fail or exit the market but for the merger. The negative effects are then weighted against the potential anticompetitive effects.

A more comprehensive review of the relevant merger and acquisition laws of the US can be found in Gaughan.[9]

3.3 EU legislation

Unlike the Treaty of Paris, which contains specific merger controls (European Coal and Steel Treaty, Article 66), the Treaty of Rome, which was concluded in 1957, contained no equivalent. Although Articles 81 and 82 were used for controlling concentrations that affected competition, the absence of a sufficiently coherent framework of legal rules resulted in much uncertainty. Against a background of excessive concentration affecting sound competition within the Common Market, the member states agreed and adopted the Merger Regulation (Council Regulation 4064/89). The regulation came into force on 21 September 1990 and was amended by Council Regulation 1310/97 which came into force on 1 March 1998.

The Merger Regulation covers so-called concentrations where either:
(a) two or more previously independent undertakings merge; or
(b) one or more persons, already controlling at least one undertaking or one or more undertakings, acquire, whether by purchase of securities or assets, by contract or by any other means, direct or indirect control of the whole or parts of one or more other undertakings.

Full function joint ventures are also covered by the regulation. In order to fall within the scope of the Merger Regulation, the concentration has to have a Community dimension pursuant to Article 1. Such a Community dimension will cease to exist if certain turnover threshold criteria are met. If the concentration falls within the scope of the Merger Regulation, the Commission will then investigate whether the concentration is compatible with the Common Market pursuant to Article 2 of the Merger Regulation. A concentration is deemed to be incompatible within the Common Market if:
– it creates or strengthens a dominant position; and
– as a result of which, effective competition would be significantly impeded in the Common Market or in a substantial part of it.

In reaching its decision of compatibility/incompatibility the Commission will consider the following substantive appraisal criteria:
– the structure of all the markets concerned;
– actual and potential competition from undertakings located within or outside the Common Market;
– the market position of the undertakings concerned and their economic and financial powers;
– legal and other barriers to entry, supply and demand trends;
– the alternatives available to suppliers and users and the access to supply and markets;
– the interests of intermediate and ultimate consumers; and
– the development of technical and economic progress.

In considering these criteria, the Commission will have to deal with each case of concentration on an individual basis. In addition, it will have to take a close look at the relevant product or service market and the relevant geographic market, in order to analyse the market power created or reinforced by the proposed concentration. A detailed account of EU merger regulation can be found in Cook and Kerse,[10] Morgan[11] and Rivas.[12]

The conformance of liner shipping mergers to existing anti-trust legislation is evidenced from the recent assessments of actual mergers that were undertaken by the European Commission and the subsequent granting of the relevant licences. For instance, the P&ONedlloyd merger was examined by looking at market shares in the relevant markets, the competition in those markets, and the potential for creation or strengthening of a dominant market position. It was concluded that the establishment of the merger would not appear to create or strengthen a position of dominance.

At the time of writing, the UK Competition Commission was carrying out an inquiry into the proposed merger of P&O Princess Cruises and Royal Caribbean Cruises. The issues under consideration included the appropriate definition of the economic markets affected by the proposed merger, whether the proposed merger is likely to affect competition in any of the markets identified in the UK, whether there are likely to be benefits to the public interest from the proposed merger and, in the event of the Commission finding that the proposed acquisition was expected to operate against the public interest, what remedies, behavioural or structural, would be appropriate to deal with the adverse effects identified.

4. MOTIVES FOR MERGERS AND ACQUISITIONS

Mergers and acquisitions may be initiated by motives of value maximisation and the achievement of strategic and marketing objectives. A statement by OOCL Chairman CC Tung captures some key motives for mergers and acquisitions:

"From an industry perspective, consolidation is a healthy and natural way to promote stable growth. With less fragmentation within the industry, destructive competition diminishes as does the dramatic increases in capacity. From the carrier perspective, consolidation allows carriers to build scale to broaden their global coverage, while leveraging synergies to reduce costs without the difficulties of organically building scale over what can seem an excessive period of time".[13]

4.1 Value-maximisation motives

Market consolidation and mergers and acquisitions occur as a result of the companies' quest to achieve value maximisation either through direct increases in revenues and profit or through cost reduction.

In the quest to improve competitiveness by enhancing firm efficiency and market location, companies may attempt to internalise market imperfections. Merger and acquisition constitutes internalisation as control remains in the firm and not in the marketplace. Hence, as Dunning[14] asserted, internalisation may be a powerful motive for takeovers or mergers and a valuable tool in the strategy of oligopolists.

4.1.1 Market power

Market power was defined by Shepherd[15] as: "the ability of a market participant or group of participants to influence price, quality, and the nature of the product in the market place". The sources of market power may be classified into product differentiation, barriers to entry and market share. To the extent that mergers and acquisitions create such advantages for shipping companies, they must be regarded as sources of market power.

Market power is sometimes referred to as monopoly power and is defined as the ability to set and maintain price above competitive levels. The monopoly hypothesis, or whether firms merge in order to increase their monopoly power and whether this is actually a consequence of a horizontal merger has received relatively little empirical attention. One analysis by Stillman[16] considered the value of the stock of firms in an industry when events took place that increased the probability of mergers in the industry. The results failed to support the view that firms merge in an effort to seek monopoly power. Similar results were obtained by Eckbo[17] who concluded that the gains found in mergers are not related to increases in market power but rather are motivated by factors such as efficiency gains.

The above studies use stock price data to examine the monopoly hypothesis. A more direct approach was applied by Kim and Singal[18] who utilised product price data to examine the market power effects and wealth transfers from consumers related to mergers in the airline industry. This study involved an investigation of the extent to which airline mergers have affected airfares. The results indicate that airline mergers during the 1985–1988 period led to higher prices, creating wealth transfers away from consumers. In particular, the merging firms were found to have increased airfares by an average of 9.44% relative to other routes unaffected by merger, whereas rival firms responded by raising their prices by an average of 12.17%. The price increases were positively correlated with changes in concentration and did not appear to be the result of an improvement in quality or of an industry wide contraction of air services to rectify a supply-demand imbalance. The price changes were also positively related to the distance of routes, suggesting that airlines exploit greater market power on longer routes for which substitution by other modes of transport is less likely.

Kim and Singal[18] showed that the relaxation of anti-trust policy for airline mergers during the sample period did permit greater exercise for market power, dominating efficiency gains and ultimately making the consumer worse off. In the case of liner shipping there is little evidence of the market power-related effects of horizontal mergers. Heaver *et al.* (at pp. 368–369)[19] state that "the greater market share of lines realised through mergers... may create some initial heightened market power, but this is unlikely to result in sustained high profit margins in the dynamically competitive international shipping and logistics industry". To the extent that there is no empirical evidence to support this belief, the need for further research on the issue seems to be justified.

The case of CP ships and its 1994 acquisition of CAST – a major competitor of CP Ships in the port of Montreal – provides some anecdotal evidence in this respect. After the acquisition, CP Ships controlled up to 85% of the container business in the port, something which raised questions of monopoly control and market power. In fact, it was acquisitions of this nature that enabled CP Ships to grow from a small shipping line to a company with revenues of over C$2 billion in a relatively short time period.

4.1.2 Efficiency increases

Mergers and acquisitions may increase or decrease efficiency in a number of different ways. These include the achievement of scale, scope or mix of output that is profitable. Consolidation may also change organisational focus or managerial behaviour to improve X-efficiency (managerial efficiency). Efficiency may take the form of cost efficiency, profit efficiency or market power.[20] Much of the research has been carried out in the banking sector. Many of the studies have found that expected efficiency improvements provide part of the motivation for merger and acquisitions. A substantial proportion of such merger and acquisitions involved a larger and more efficient institution taking over a smaller, less efficient institution, presumably at least in part to spread the expertise or operating policies and procedures of the more efficient institution over additional resources.[21, 22, 23] X-efficiency gains are also possible if large banks merge and reform the practices of smaller banks.[24] Case studies of US bank mergers and acquisitions support the idea that potential efficiency gains act to motivate mergers and acquisitions.[25] In a European context, studies have found that large profitable banks are acquirers and small banks targets and that more efficient banks tend to acquire less efficient banks.[26] These findings provide further evidence that mergers and acquisitions may be motivated in part by the potential for efficiency gains.

As to the consequences for such mergers and acquisitions, evidence from past empirical studies lies largely in the industries of banking, insurance and securities. In the banking sector most studies consented that there were no significant scale efficiencies to be gained and possibly some slight scale efficiency losses to be suffered from mergers and acquisitions involving large banks.[27, 28, 29] Similarly studies of cost scale efficiency in the insurance industry found most firms to be below efficient scale, but found the largest firms to be above efficient scale.[30] In the securities industry small specialised firms appeared to exhibit economies of scale, while large, diversified firms exhibited scale diseconomies.[31]

Anecdotal evidence from the shipping industry suggests that larger companies through the acquisition of smaller competitors may pursue efficiency gains. This can be seen in Frontline's acquisition of Mosvold Shipping, a minor participant in the VLCC market, operating at the time just two vintage vessels with three more on order. Frontline cited "a reduced cost structure" for both firms as a benefit of the merger which it said was "strategically based on Frontline's wishes to continue consolidation within the highly fragmented tanker industry".

Probably a good example of aiming for X-efficiency in liner shipping has been the strategy of CP Ships whose chairman moved swiftly to replace management at the newly acquired companies, thus aligning management of all associated companies with the underlying philosophy of the parent.[32] Following this strategy, the group as a whole has been achieving considerable growth and profitability. Although the post-acquisition performance has not been shown to be definitely influenced by X-efficiency, it is possible that it was a contributing factor. CP Ships has also been pursuing a strategy of acquiring companies with a good market base and assets, but which had had some form of financial problems in cash-flow or profitability. After the acquisition these companies were contributing to the growth of an efficient group, therefore the rationale that efficiency may increase when one large more efficient organisation acquires a smaller may be valid to some extent in liner shipping.

Efficiency increases resulting from rationalisation of operations have reportedly been realised by Maersk-Sealand. The combination of previously separate assets and functions resulted in less flaws in operations and greater efficiency.[33]

Cost efficiencies may be a factor of achievement of economies of scale as discussed below.

4.1.3 Operating and financial synergies

Operating synergy may arise as a result of revenue enhancements and/or cost reductions that are effected from the merger. Revenue enhancing synergies are more difficult to achieve than cost reduction synergies. The revenue enhancing opportunity has been defined by Clemente and Greenspan (at p. 46)[34] as "a newly created or strengthened product or service that is formulated by the fusion of two distinct attributes of the merger partners and which generates immediate and/or long-term revenue growth". Such a situation may arise through cross-marketing opportunities of each merger partner's products. These may include a broader product/service line, the use of a partner's brand name in a new product or the utilisation of a partner's stronger distribution network.

Cost-reducing operating synergies will arise by way of achieving economies of scale by reducing the unit costs through increase in the size or scale of a company's operations. Therefore, higher output levels may culminate in the increased specialisation of labour and management and the more efficient use of capital equipment. Of course, such an increase in scale cannot result in a continuous reduction of costs; rather, a maximum point is reached beyond which a firm may experience diseconomies of scale. Diseconomies of scale may arise as the firm experiences higher costs and other problems associated with co-ordinating a larger scale operation. In the banking sector for instance it was found that economies of scale are found at the level of smaller banks and may persist for banks with up to US$10 billion in assets.[35] Such economies cease or even become negative at the scale of very large banks (see, e.g., Hunter and Timme[36]).

The achievement of economies of scope is another reason that may be cited as a motive for merger or acquisition. Scope economies refers to the ability of a firm to utilise one set of inputs to provide a broader range of products and services. Gaughan[9] notes that scope economies may be as important as scale economies in explaining mergers and acquisitions and that the achievement of economies of scope was a major drive in the consolidation that occurred in the 1990s in the banking industry.

Financial synergy may result in a decrease in the cost of capital due to the merger of two entities that have different cash flows and investment opportunities. The advantages would arise from the lower cost of internal financing *vis-à-vis* external financing. Therefore, firms with large internal cash flows and small investment opportunities may merge with firms having low internal funds generation and large growth opportunities. The finance literature provides empirical evidence in support of this internal funds effect.[37,38]

The achievement of cost-reduction through operating synergies and resulting scale economies is probably the most often-cited reason for justifying the merger or acquisition on behalf of the entities concerned. For instance, it was stated that about three-quarters of the US$130 million savings estimated for the

NOL-APL acquisition would stem from the combined company's more efficient usage of APL's sea terminals and container freight trains as well as ships owned by the two. The deputy chief executive stated at the time that "most of these terminals and trains are more or less 80% fixed cost so when more volume is pushed through unit costs per container shipped should fall, resulting in higher profits".

Cost-reducing operating synergies will arise by way of achieving economies of scale by reducing the unit costs through increase in the size or scale of a company's operations. Such synergies have been pointed at by the management of P&O-Nedlloyd to refer to annual savings of US$200 million within a year of the merger.[39]

About one year after the Maersk acquisition of Sealand, it has been reported that evident synergies resulted that allowed the company to embark on an ambitious and impressive strategy for further growth.[33] According to the CEO operating synergies resulted from consolidation of port and transportation facilities and increased control of the supply chain and the integrated systems which make room for a flawless operation.

4.2 Strategic and marketing motives

The major strategic objectives of shipping companies may include the acquisition of market share, the expansion/entry into new markets (geographical or new service), acquisition of management skills to augment firm capabilities in relation to new growth areas and the transfer of management capabilities to acquired firms to assist rebuilding.

Studies of mergers and market shares tend to support a negative relationship. Mueller[40] in a study of mergers in the 1950s and 1960s found that the market share of acquired business lines deteriorated significantly relative to control samples of non-merging businesses, in the case of both conglomerate and horizontal mergers.

The interest of ocean liner shipping companies in inland transportation has been made abundantly evident in recent years. Recognising the changing needs of customers and the requirement for efficient door-to-door transportation, in addition to the obvious economic benefits that will accrue from involvement in inland transport and logistics, companies have diversified and expanded into this fast-growing market. Merger and acquisition has been used as a vehicle for such diversification and market entry purposes. M&A will facilitate the creation of a bigger organisation with more bargaining power and greater financial and resource muscle to facilitate easier entry into the inland transport market. Apart from the inland transport and logistics market, companies have shown increasing interest in entering new markets in terms of geographical position. From a strategic point of view, bigger liner shipping companies would also place themselves in a strong bargaining/negotiating position with respect to terminal operators, container depots and inland transportation carriers.

Marketing involves the identification and anticipation of changing customer needs and the efforts made for providing customer satisfaction under the auspices of the overriding objective, which is profitability for the entity. A liner shipping company's marketing objective would be the attraction of new and retention of current customers. It has been recognised in recent years that customer (shipper) requirements have changed. The increasing consumer demands, the increase in trade and world production and consumption have all had an impact on shippers requiring more efficient, reliable and speedier service that would be offered in terms of a total logistics package rather than as a fragmented sea and inland transport service. The horizontal integration of liner shipping companies may go a long way towards the accomplishment of the marketing objectives of ocean liner shipping companies. Mergers and acquisitions may once again contribute towards the accomplishment of marketing objectives in that they may facilitate "one-stop shopping" as required by customers.[41, 42]

No doubt the accomplishment of customer satisfaction and hence the marketing objectives of attraction and retention of customers rests on pillars of achieving better service quality. The latter would depend on setting and accomplishing operational goals that would include greater sailing frequency, reliability, responsiveness, lower costs, route rationalisation, faster transit time, flexibility and more direct ports of call.

Current thinking in the literature shows a propensity towards affirmation of the strategic and marketing benefits that accrue as a result of mergers and acquisitions. For instance, Heaver et al.[19] note that mergers may enhance service quality, increase the geographical span of services and satisfy specific needs of shippers such as using fewer lines to serve global lines. The possibility of synergistic benefits from joint marketing activities, optimisation of market shares and less capital-intensive expansion possibilities may also be realised. On the other hand, it is possible that strategic and marketing costs may be incurred. These may include losses of market shares resulting from overlapping patterns, loss of individual identity and restricted individual flexibility when it comes to making market or organisational adjustments.[43] Market share losses seem to have been experienced in the mergers of liner shipping companies. The rationale behind such losses may have been the reluctance of customers that have say 25% of their business with company A and 50% with company B, to give 75% of their business to the merged AB entity. The expectations are for a 55%–65% of business going to the merged firm, with the residual going to another carrier. The argument may be supported by evidence from the P&ONedlloyd merger. In particular, P&ONedlloyd maintained a market share of 9% in the North Europe/USEC route for the first half of 1997, compared to 7% and 5% held individually by P&O and Nedlloyd respectively in 1996, i.e. a total of 12%.[43] The reasons for this may include the overlap of shared routes of the two companies and in the type of customers targeted.

The reasons cited by the management of V. Ships for the Acomarit acquisition were related to the accomplishment of long-term strategic and marketing objectives. V. Ships president stated that "ship management has always lagged behind the rest of the shipping industry in terms of consolidation and larger, more efficient shipowners expect larger, more efficient ship managers which are able to invest in crew training, information technology, safety and environmental protection systems".[44]

In the reefer market, risk reduction and increase in the number of routes and trade areas were the main reasons cited for consolidation. The chartering manager of the consolidated NYK Star unit was quoted saying: "Overall we have a much more varied trade pattern than either of the companies did individually before. This provides a very solid trading base, as there is less exposure to a possible downturn in any particular sector. The increase in the size of the operation has enabled us to offer vessels in trades where we were not able to do so before. The sheer number of ships and the different sizes in our fleet, means we can go after more business."[45]

5. A FRAMEWORK FOR EVALUATING M&A

Not all mergers and acquisitions make economic sense, otherwise we should expect to see only a few giant corporations. Some mergers may be the result of misperceptions, miscalculations, or simply "fads". Given the tremendous impact that a merger has on the firms involved (e.g., shareholder wealth, employees' job security), it is important to have a systematic approach to evaluating the desirability of a proposed merger, and to be prepared for surprises if it is indeed consummated.

5.1 Value increases at announcement stage

A merger or acquisition is often undertaken in the belief that it will lead to increased profitability for either the acquiring firm, or the acquired, or both. Since shareholder wealth is of primary importance, the wealth effects of mergers and acquisitions as evidenced by the share price performance at the announcement of the event and post-merger are of particular interest. In an efficient market, initial stock price reaction is a good indicator or predictor of the subsequent performance of a merger. If the market prices of the common shares of acquiring and acquired companies both increase, total value will increase, reflecting the market's anticipation of value creation as a result of the M&A.[46]

Most of the past studies have found that shareholders of acquired companies enjoy substantial immediate gains. In fact, virtually every empirical study has found that target firms display statistically significant positive stock price response to the announcement of a takeover attempt.[47] Jensen and Ruback[48] provide a review of past studies and estimate an increase (over the preannouncement market price) of 20% for mergers and 30% for tender offers in the period around the takeover event. Dennis and McConnell[49] found that the average target firm's shares increased by 8.7% adjusted for market movements, on the day of bid announcement and the previous trading day. Jarrell et al.[50] in an assessment of 663 successful tender offers (period 1962–1985), found that premiums to targets averaged 19% in the 1960s, 35% in the 1970s and 30% for the period 1980–1985.

With respect to the returns to acquiring firm shareholders, results are varied as both positive and negative returns have been recorded and past studies indicate that scholars do not seem to have reached a consensus.[48,51] What most studies seem to agree on is that any price movement (positive or negative) that the bidding firm will actually experience will be generally small in percentage terms (much smaller than target firm returns). Schwert[52] found that on average the abnormal returns to bidders for the period 1975 to 1991 were not significantly different from zero. Dennis and McConnell[49] report a market-adjusted return in the equities of bidding firms of –0.12% on the day of the announcement and the previous trading day.

The findings of the change in the overall wealth of the merged firms are far less clear. While US evidences point to overall stock value gains from M&As, British merger evidence suggests that takeovers in the UK during the early 1970s had little overall impact on the combined firms' profitability; the acquiring firms in fact suffered losses that slightly more than offset the gains to the acquiring firms.[53, 54, 55] It seems, therefore, that the desirability or profitability of a merger should be judged on a case-by-case basis.

In the shipping industry context, Panayides and Gong[56] find that the share prices of both the acquiring and the acquired firms increased substantially when the strategic move was first announced. Consistent with previous studies in other industries, the acquired firm (which was also the smaller) experienced higher percentage gains than the acquiring firm (which was the larger). The empirical evidence thus suggests that M&As in shipping are positively received by the stock market, presumably because such moves are thought to add value to the companies involved, through either cost savings, increased market power, or synergies.

5.2 Long-run performance following M&A

While the immediate aftermarket reaction of the stock market is a useful indication of the perceived subsequent performance of a merger, the market can over-react or under-react in a particular case or time period (mergers come in waves). Decision-makers in the merged firm may also be unprepared for the changes that the merger causes in the firm, and therefore fail to reap the full benefits of the merger. To investigate the desirability of a merger in the first place, and to measure its performance after consummation, therefore, one must look beyond a short-term initial announcement period.

In a survey of seven studies of mergers, Jensen and Ruback[48] showed that in the one year period following the merger announcement, the average acquiring firm suffers a stock price decline of 5.5%. Magenheim and Mueller[57] report that three years following the merger announcement, the average acquiring firm's stock price falls by as much as 16%. Such evidences in part suggest that mergers and acquisitions may not necessarily improve firms' profitability or efficiency in the long run. In two studies of mergers in the UK, Firth[53, 58] presents evidence which suggests that the longer-run performance of M&As is more consistent with mergers being motivated by maximization of management utility rather than shareholder value. Agrawal and Jaffe[59] provide a comprehensive review of the post-merger performance literature and conclude that, despite some lurking methodological concerns and some mixed evidence, mergers appear to suffer under-performance in the long-run.

Few studies exist that systematically assess the long-run post-merger performance of shipping companies. However, some anecdotal evidence may be gleaned from the annual reports of the merged companies following the merger. In their 1997 Annual Reports, both NOL and P&ONedlloyd, for example, reported significant cost savings, improved efficiency and service offerings, and increased global presence and revenues following their respective integration earlier in the same year. In the subsequent years, P&ONedlloyd continued to report sustained profitability resulting from the merger, ranging from cost savings due to scale economies and efficiencies in organization, greater fleet and network efficiencies, improved value-added products and services, and volume and revenue increases. In contrast, in the years 1997 to 2000, the NOL Group seemed to have encountered various problems arising from and after the merger. These resulted in net operating loss for the Group in 1997 and 1998, plus the need to raise additional capital through an international share placement in 1999 to strengthen the balance sheet which was weakened by the acquisition of APL. In the subsequent years 1999 to 2000, it seemed that the NOL Group came to recover from the merger and improved its overall performance. However, NOL again encountered significant financial problems during 2001 culminating in the temporary suspension of shares trading from the floor of the Singapore Stock Exchange in August. The sources of the problems were traced to the US$825 million purchase of APL in 1997 which coincided with the Asian financial crisis, the sustained economic downturn that affected trade volumes and a 3–5% decline in freight rates in the first half of 2001, and the purchase of US-based GATX Logistics in February 2001 for US$210 million that produced a negative EBIT of US$9 million.

5.3 Problem areas and key to success in M&As

Mergers and acquisitions ultimately aim at value creation. The success of value creation depends to a large extent on the potential for successful integration. Hence, issues of organisational compatibility, supplementary and complementary skills and resources and the availability of general management skills are critical to the success of M&A consummation. Organisational compatibility entails congruence in corporate culture. It is essential to draw plans for managing differences in culture and to adjust to or assimilate cultural differences after the merger. Organisational complexity that may be an outcome of the formation of a bigger organisation also requires effective co-ordination. The companies need to allocate the requisite resources for successful implementation of combining the companies to achieve the potential cost savings and/or revenue enhancement. Datta[60] highlights the importance of integration and the finding that procedural integration problems are less detrimental to the performance of the acquisition than cultural integration problems associated with difference in management styles. In addition, a company's ability to transfer and effectively use the skills and resources of one partner to the competitive advantage of the other is essential. Morosini and Singh[61] draw attention to the difficulties of integrating resources across both acquiring and acquired companies, something seen as potentially detrimental to the performance of the acquisition. Talented general managers are also essential whenever value creation depends on the revitalisation of underused assets. Norburn and Schoenberg[62] identify the need for relatively specialised integration skills as follows:

(1) integration by facilitating a transfer from owner-management to professional management;
(2) integration by proactive transfer of skills to overcome a lack of integration;
(3) the need to overcome potentially conflicting national cultures.

Drucker[63] enumerated five rules for successful acquisitions. They are:

(1) the acquirer must contribute something to the acquired company;
(2) a common core of unity is required;
(3) acquirer must respect the business of the acquired company;
(4) within a year or so, acquiring company must be able to provide top management to the acquired company;
(5) within the first year of merger, management in both companies should receive promotions across the entities.

Anslinger and Copeland[64] suggest an alternative framework that would also apply to unrelated acquisitions, something that Drucker's framework seemingly neglects. They suggest certain key principles:

(1) acquire companies with track record of innovative operating strategies;
(2) capable managerial talent is most important for creating values;
(3) use strong incentive compensation programmes;
(4) link compensation incentives to future changes in cash flow;
(5) make turnarounds take place within the first two years of the takeover;
(6) develop information and feedback systems that promote continuing dynamic relationships among owners, managers and the board.

The initial difficulties that NOL seemed to have encountered immediately after its acquisition of APL are indicative of the aforesaid problems that are often associated with M&As. Schoenberg[65] presents a review of the cultural compatibility research in cross-border acquisitions and how compatibility of organizational cultures affects post-merger performance.

6. CORPORATE GOVERNANCE AND CONTROL IN MERGERS AND ACQUISITIONS

Parkinson[66] (at p. 6) defined corporate governance as "the processes of supervision and control (of governing) intended to ensure that the company's management acts in accordance with the interests of the shareholders". Traditionally, corporate governance focused on agency problems, or conflicts of interests between the shareholders (owners) and their agents (the managers).

Corporate governance has a crucial role to play in mergers and acquisitions. This role includes the avoidance of a potentially hostile takeover bid in the first place, the monitoring of acquisition decisions by the potential and actual acquirers and the assurance that the acquisition generates value for the shareholders. In fact, the failure of the merged firm to generate value for shareholders has sometimes been attributed to the failure of corporate governance. Although a number of factors may account for such failure, it is postulated that one possibility is poor corporate governance in the acquiring firms. This may lead to inadequate monitoring of the various stages of the acquisition process – pre-acquisition evaluation of the target, deal structuring and negotiation, and post-acquisition integration.

Given the centrality of shareholder wealth maximisation in corporate finance, it is essential for a number of monitoring and control mechanisms to be put in place in order to resolve agency problems. Past research dealt with a number of such control mechanisms.[67] A number of studies dealt with mergers and acquisitions as a major source of external control mechanisms and examined managerial motives and their relationship with pre- and post- acquisition performance. A review of such studies can be found in Sudarsanam.[68]

7. SUMMARY AND CONCLUSION

The recent surge in consolidation and mergers and acquisitions activity across all major shipping markets resulted in a growing interest from a practical as well as a scientific perspective. As a major activity within the modern business scene, mergers and acquisitions have long been a subject of scientific investigation from different perspectives, including management, finance, strategy and economics. This chapter provides an extensive review of the major theories and empirical studies from these different perspectives. The propensity for consolidation and mergers and acquisitions seems to be positively influenced by certain environmental conditions such as progress in the production function (including technological advances), changes in the regulatory framework, financial market development and market competition. A number of motives for mergers and acquisitions are discussed, supplemented by anecdotal evidence from the shipping industry. The main firm-specific motives for mergers and acquisitions include market power, efficiency increases, operating and financial synergies and strategic and marketing reasons. In addition, the chapter puts forward a framework for evaluating mergers and acquisitions focusing on the short-run stock market performance and on the long-run performance in both the stock market and the product market. While the acquired firms generally gain from a merger announcement, the acquiring firms either break even or lose, with virtually no gain accruing to the combined firm. In the long-run, merged firms tend to give negative wealth effects whilst senior executives of the acquiring firms often record personal gains. These evidences raise questions over the true motives of mergers in the first place and the subsequent full realization of the sought after benefits. In addition, the problems that companies may face in the implementation of a merger are discussed and the importance of corporate governance and control acknowledged. Given the rather limited scientific attention to shipping mergers and acquisitions and the needs of the professional community and the industry, the issues and frameworks discussed in this chapter provide ample opportunity for conducting further empirical research. Future research may aim to refine the methods of evaluating mergers and investigate empirically the antecedents and consequences of mergers in shipping markets.

ACKNOWLEDGEMENTS

The authors would like to thank Professor Michael Firth for his helpful comments.

ENDNOTES

1. Jayaratne, J., and Strahan, P.E. (1996): "The finance-growth nexus: evidence from bank branch deregulation", *Quarterly Journal of Economics*, 111, pp. 639–670.
2. Jayaratne, J., and Strahan, P.E. (1998): "Entry restrictions, industry evolution and dynamic efficiency: evidence from commercial banking", *Journal of Law and Economics*, 49, pp. 239–274.
3. Midoro, R., and Pitto, A. (2000): "A critical evaluation of strategic alliances in liner shipping", *Maritime Policy and Management*, 27, pp. 31–40.
4. Garette, B., and Dussauge, P. (2000): "Alliances versus acquisitions: choosing the right option", *European Management Journal*, 18, pp. 63–69.
5. Killing, J.P. (1983): *Strategies for Joint Ventures* (London, Croom Helm).
6. Weiss, S.E. (1987): "Creating the GM-Toyota joint venture: a case in complex negotiation", *Columbia Journal of World Business*, 22, pp. 23–37.
7. *Lloyd's Shipping Economist* (1999): "Shipping seeks new global rule", 21, pp. 7–10.
8. Rodger, B.J., and MacCulloch, A. (2001): *Competition Law and Policy in the EC and UK* (2nd ed.) (London, Cavendish Publishing Limited).
9. Gaughan, P.A. (1999): *Mergers, Acquisitions and Corporate Restructurings* (2nd ed.) (New York, John Wiley & Sons).
10. Cook, C.J., and Kerse, C.S. (2000): *EC Merger Control* (3rd ed.) (London, Sweet & Maxwell).
11. Morgan, E.J. (2001): "A decade of EC merger control", *International Journal of the Economics of Business*, 8, pp. 451–473.
12. Rivas, J. (1999): *The EU Merger Regulation and the Anatomy of the Merger Task Force* (London-The Hague-Boston, Kluwer Law International).
13. *Containerisation International* (March 2000): "OOCL chairman warns of danger of mergers".
14. Dunning, J.H. (1981): *International Production and the Multinational Enterprise* (London and Boston, George Allen & Unwin).
15. Shepherd, W.G. (1970): *Market Power and Economic Welfare* (New York, Random House), p. 3.
16. Stillman, R.S. (1983): "Examining antitrust policy towards horizontal mergers", *Journal of Financial Economics*, 11, pp. 225–240.
17. Eckbo, B.E. (1983): "Horizontal mergers, collusion and stockholder wealth", *Journal of Financial Economics*, 11, pp. 241–273.
18. Kim, E.H., and Singal, V. (1993): "Mergers and market power: evidence from the airline industry", *American Economic Review*, 83, pp. 549–569.
19. Heaver, T., Meersman, H., Moglia, V. and Van de Voorde, E. (2000): "Do mergers and alliances influence European shipping and port competition?", *Maritime Policy and Management*, 27, pp. 363–373.
20. Akhavein, J.D., Berger, A.N., and Humphrey, D.B. (1997): "The effects of megamergers on efficiency and prices: evidence from a bank profit function", *Review of Industrial Organisation*, 12, pp. 95–139.

21. Berger, A.N., and Humphrey, D.B. (1992): "Megamergers in banking and the use of cost efficiency as an antitrust defence", *Antitrust Bulletin*, 37, pp. 541–600.
22. Peristiani, S. (1997): "Do mergers improve the X-efficiency and scale efficiency of US banks? Evidence from the 1980s", *Journal of Money, Credit and Banking*, 29, pp. 326–337.
23. Pilloff, S.J., and Santomero, A.M. (1998): "The value effects of bank mergers and acquisitions", in Ahimud, Y., and Miller, G. (eds.) *Bank Mergers and Acquisitions* (Dordrecht, Kluwer Academic Publishers), pp. 59–78.
24. Shaffer, S. (1993): "Can mega-mergers improve bank efficiency?", *Journal of Banking and Finance*, 17, pp. 423–436.
25. Rhoades, S.A. (1998): "The efficiency effects of bank mergers: an overview of case studies of nine mergers", *Journal of Banking and Finance*, 22, pp. 273–291.
26. Vander Vennet, R. (1996): "The effect of mergers and acquisitions on the efficiency and profitability of EC credit institutions", *Journal of Banking and Finance*, 20, pp. 1531–1558.
27. Clark, J. (1996): "Economic cost, scale efficiency and competitive viability in banking", *Journal of Money, Credit and Banking*, 28, pp. 342–364.
28. Berger, A.N., Hanweck, G.A., and Humphrey, D.B. (1987): "Competitive viability in banking: scale, scope and product mix economies", *Journal of Monetary Economics*, 20, pp. 501–520.
29. Berger, A.N., and Humphrey, D.B. (1991): "The dominance of inefficiencies over scale and product mix economies in banking", *Journal of Monetary Economics*, 28, pp. 117–148.
30. Gardner, L., and Grace, M. (1993): "X-efficiency in the US life insurance industry", *Journal of Banking and Finance*, 17, pp. 497–510.
31. Goldberg, L.G., Hanweck, G.A., Keenan, M., and Young, A. (1991): "Economies of scale and scope in the securities industry", *Journal of Banking and Finance*, 15, pp. 91–107.
32. Alix, Y., Slack, B., and Comtois, C. (1999): "Alliance or acquisition? Strategies for growth in the container shipping industry, the case of CP ships", *Journal of Transport Geography*, 7, pp. 203–208.
33. Thorby, C. (2001): "Beyond the merger", *Containerisation International*, January, pp. 43–45.
34. Clemente, M.N., and Greenspan, D.S. (1998): *Winning at Mergers and Acquisitions: The Guide to Market-Focused Planning and Integration* (New York, John Wiley & Sons).
35. Peristiani, S. (1996): *Do Mergers Improve X-efficiency and Scale Efficiency of US Banks? Evidence from the 1980s* (Federal Reserve Bank of New York, Research Paper # 9623).
36. Hunter, W.C., and Timme, S.G. (1995): "Core deposits and physical capital: a re-examination of bank scale economics and efficiency with quasi-fixed assets", *Journal of Money, Credit and Banking*, 27, pp. 165–185.
37. Nickell, S.J. (1978): *The Investment Decisions of Firms* (Cambridge, Cambridge University Press).
38. Nielsen, J.F., and Melicher, R.W. (1973): "A financial analysis of acquisition and merger premiums", *Journal of Financial and Quantitative Analysis*, 8, pp. 139–162.
39. Fossey, J. (1998, "Suicidal tendencies", *Containerisation International*, May, pp. 37–41.
40. Mueller, D.C. (1985): "Mergers and market share", *Review of Economics and Statistics*, 67, pp. 259–267.
41. Frankel, E. (1999): "Intermodal integration", *Lloyd's Shipping Economist*, 21, pp. 10–11.
42. Semejin, J., and Vellenga, D.B. (1995): "International logistics and one-stop shopping", *International Journal of Physical Distribution & Logistics Management*, 25, pp. 26–44.
43. Lim, S.-M. (1998): "Economies of scale in container shipping", *Maritime Policy and Management*, 25, pp. 361–373.

44. Bray, J. (2001): "V. Ships victorious in battle of the brands", *Lloyd's List*, May 12.
45. *Lloyd's List* (2002): "Star in the ascendancy on drive for integration", February 20.
46. Weston, J.F., Chung, K.S., and Siu, J.A. (1998): *Takeovers, Restructuring, and Corporate Governance* (Upper Saddle River, NJ, Prentice Hall).
47. Roll, R. (1988): "Empirical evidence on takeover activity and shareholder wealth", in Coffee, J.C., Lowenstein, L., and Rose-Ackerman, S. (eds.) *Knights, Raiders and Targets: The Impact of the Hostile Takeover*, chap. 14, pp. 241-252 (Oxford, Oxford University Press).
48. Jensen, M.C., and Ruback, R.S. (1983): "The market for corporate control: the scientific evidence", *Journal of Financial Economics*, 11, pp. 5-50.
49. Dennis, D.K., and Mcconnell, J.J. (1986): "Corporate mergers and security returns", *Journal of Financial Economics*, 16, pp. 143-187.
50. Jarrell, G.A., Brickley, J.A., and Netter, J.M. (1988): "The market for corporate control: the empirical evidence since 1980", *Journal of Economic Perspectives*, 2, pp. 49-68.
51. Halpern, P.J. (1983): "Corporate acquisitions: A theory of special cases? A review of event studies applied to acquisitions", *Journal of Finance*, 38, pp. 297-317.
52. Schwert, G.W. (1996): "Mark-up pricing in mergers and acquisitions", *Journal of Financial Economics*, 41, pp. 153-192.
53. Firth, M. (1980): "Takeovers, shareholder returns, and the theory of the firm", *Quarterly Journal of Economics*, 94, pp. 235-260.
54. Firth, M. (1978): "Synergism in mergers: some British results", *Journal of Finance*, 33, pp. 670-672.
55. Firth, M. (1979): "The profitability of takeovers and mergers", *Economic Journal*, 89, pp. 316-328.
56. Panayides, Ph.M., and Gong, X.H. (2002): "The stock market reaction to merger and acquisition announcements in liner shipping", *International Journal of Maritime Economics*, 4, pp. 55-80.
57. Magenheim, E.B., and Mueller, D.C. (1988): "Are acquiring-firm shareholders better off after an acquisition", in Coffee, J.C., Lowenstein, L., and Rose-Ackerman (eds.) *Knights, Raiders and Targets: The Impact of the Hostile Takeover* (New York, Oxford University Press), pp. 177-193.
58. Firth, M. (1991): "Corporate takeovers, stockholder returns and executive rewards", *Managerial and Decision Economics*, 12, pp. 421-428.
59. Agrawal, A., and Jaffe, J.F. (2000): "The post merger performance puzzle", in Cooper, C., and Gregory, A. (eds.) *Advances in Mergers and Acquisitions* (London, JAI), pp. 7-41.
60. Datta, D.K. (1991): "Organisational fit and acquisition performance: effects of post-acquisition integration", *Strategic Management Journal*, 12, pp. 281-297.
61. Morosini, P., and Singh, H. (1994): "Post cross-border acquisitions: implementing national culture compatible strategies to improve performance", *European Management Journal*, 12, pp. 390-400.
62. Norburn, D., and Schoenberg, R. (1994): "European cross-border acquisition: how was it for you?", *Long Range Planning*, 27, pp. 25-34.
63. Drucker, P.F. (1981): "Five rules for successful acquisition", *The Wall Street Journal*, October 15, p. 28.
64. Anslinger, P.L., and Copeland, T.E. (1996): "Growth through acquisitions: a fresh look", *Harvard Business Review*, 74, pp. 126-135.
65. Schoenberg, R. (2000): "The influence of cultural compatibility within cross-border acquisitions: a review", in Cooper, C., and Gregory, A. (eds.) *Advances in Mergers and Acquisitions* (London, JAI), pp. 43-59.
66. Parkinson, C. (1993): *Corporate Power and Responsibility* (Oxford, Oxford University Press).
67. Agrawal, A., and Knoeber, C. (1996): "Firm performance and mechanisms to control agency problems between managers and shareholders", *Journal of Financial and Quantitative Analysis*, 31, pp. 377-397.

68. Sudarsanam, S. (2000): "Corporate governance, corporate control and takeovers", in Cooper, C., and Gregory, A. (eds.) *Advances in Mergers and Acquisitions*, Vol. 1 (Amsterdam, Jai Press), pp. 119–155.

PART NINE

SHIPPING INVESTMENT AND FINANCE

CHAPTER 28

INVESTING IN SHIPS: AN ESSAY ON CONSTRAINTS, RISK AND ATTITUDES

Helen Thanopoulou
Cardiff Business School, University of Cardiff, Cardiff, UK.
E-mail: *Thanopoulou@Cardiff.ac.uk*

1. INTRODUCTION. INVESTING IN SHIPS: A BRAVE DECISION

Shipping economics exist as a separate branch of economics for two reasons: the one is the cyclicality of the shipping markets; the other is the idiosyncratic nature of shipping investment. The two are inextricably linked: Investing in ships could be classified as an astute, a brave or an insane decision depending on the state and the prospects of the shipping markets which rarely -if ever- fulfil the promises they seem to give; although the element of risk remains inherent in all investment decisions, nowhere perhaps in the sector of services or manufacturing can the potential outcome be so wrongly estimated as in the case of investment in merchant vessels. One has to turn to the stock market or eventually some commodities to find parallels of fortunes won and lost on investment, sale and purchase decisions. Developments in the cruise sector recently[1] have proven that not only cargo ships but also passenger vessels can prove easily anything from uncertain to precarious or even suicidal investment in the context of a change in market conditions.[2]

This chapter begins with familiarising the reader with the idiosyncrasies of shipping investment in section 2 and continues with the analysis of the operational constraints that bulk and liner companies face when deciding to invest in either new or second hand-vessels in section 3. The delicate – and costly if not achieved – balance between the anticipated endurance of a vessel, cost differences and delivery lags is discussed in section 4 while section 5 focuses on what seems to be a very powerful incentive for investing in ships, i.e. asset play. The concluding part of the chapter summarises new constraints and pitfalls that await potential investors in today's modern shipping.

2. MARKET CYCLICALITY AND INVESTMENT IN COMMERCIAL VESSELS

Market cycles are common in competitive markets; competitive markets are, however, rather uncommon in the modern economy while, as discussed earlier in this volume, fluctuations in asset prices in any market can hardly be assimilated to those found in the shipping sector. The parallel effects of recessional factors on both the shipping and the shipbuilding markets[3] combined with the impact of recessions on the scrap market, create an absolute impasse for investors who can find themselves with very substantial amounts of tied-up capital and practically no alternative use for assets often valued at no more than an insignificant fraction of their acquisition price. While price fluctuations of fixed assets are common in other markets there is little comparison with the volatility of asset prices in shipping.[4]

2.1 Investing in the different shipping segments

While volatility of asset prices can vary between individual shipping markets[5] due to differences in the market structure of traditional and specialised bulk shipping markets,[6] it remains a common feature of all bulk shipping segments which make-up the majority of the world tonnage. Liner shipping is not exempt from asset price volatility either but as will be discussed later in the chapter its idiosyncrasies dictate a different approach to investment in any case.

As far as the bulk markets are concerned, volatility of both the freight markets and of asset prices should be considered as the key factors which should – or at least common sense would require so – weigh heavily on all decisions regarding investment in merchant vessels. In practice, an ex post analysis of investment decisions reveals that there is little understanding – if not the utmost ignorance – of the nature of the bulk shipping markets and their idiosyncrasies. Only the competitive nature of the largest part of world shipping can provide an explanation why investors would keep on exhibiting the same lack of prudence time after time despite the cycles markets have repeatedly experienced in modern times; the results of such lack of prudence are no different than those of plain ignorance. The history of world shipping is fraught with examples of crises that can be blamed on excessive ordering more than they can be blamed on any other factor.[7] When the competitive behaviour of investors is taken into account in the context of the competitive nature of most of the industry, the textbook ignorance of individual investors regarding the impact of their own investment decisions is put in context. What is, however, definitely intriguing is that patterns of investment may currently be changing in markets which could not justify even their designation as a market, let alone be anything near a perfectly competitive market: what could be in a broader sense called "speculative" investment, i.e. investment with no guaranteed demand, has been recently making its appearance in a market such as that of Liquefied Natural Gas (LNG) carriers where demand and supply are connected to each other to a degree that makes them indistinguishable and renders the carriage of natural gas an internalised stage of natural gas production[8] rather than a separate activity. Regardless, however, of how different in nature the different bulk shipping segments can be the inherent risks investors face are more or less common; they only differ in terms of the particular weight they can potentially hold in each individual market. Although the risks discussed below apply mostly to bulk shipping, it should be noted that the liner sector – shielded to a degree from excessively violent fluctuations – remains exposed to the potential risks of large sunk costs and of technological obsolescence.

2.2 Different markets – common risks

Uncertainty taken to the extreme
The first and foremost risk investors face when committing their money to bulk shipping comes from market volatility. All markets whether of goods or services can present fluctuations. However, most markets tend to present fluctuations more in terms of volume of sales than in terms of price levels. Competitive shipping markets such as the traditional bulk markets which constitute well over half of the world's tonnage[9] are affected by large downward volume changes resulting in rapidly declining prices in times of shipping recessions.

Problematic fitting of common investment appraisal techniques
While the risk of reduced sales or asset inactivity can be deemed common for shipping and all other markets the prospect of freight levels continuously fluctuating not only adds to the real risk of investment, it also renders all attempts for calculating this risk accurately ineffective. Indeed, most common investment appraisal techniques require some degree of assumed stability of prices or a predictable path of price changes and a reasonable chance of assets being fully employed when the investment starts yielding. In the case of bulk ships common investment appraisal techniques can prove highly misleading and their role should be limited to that of a guide about what the investment would cost and what would be the expected return.[10]

Large sunk costs
High volatility of freight rates and asset price volatility combine to create the perfect nightmare for the potential investor especially when resale values and alternative uses of the vessel themselves are considered. As already underlined, the scrap market usually shifts in parallel with the markets for shipping services and the markets for ships; that results in a barrier to exit which is difficult to surmount by a resale of the vessel for storage or other uses.[11] It is perhaps better that too many investors go ahead with their plans ignoring the worst case scenario or shipping would have become a market suffering from chronic under-investment: the knowledge of how few – if any – alternative uses and potential resale opportunities there are in a crisis should normally make the bravest of investors fret when considering the potential market depreciation of their assets.[12] While there are few sunk costs of other nature for bulk shipping companies, liner companies face an additional sunk cost as they tend to invest heavily in offices and agency networks and, increasingly, in terminals as well. The relative stability, however, of liner shipping business compared to the degree of volatility of bulk shipping markets and the nature of liner competition tend to moderate the exposure to sunk costs by limiting not their potential magnitude in absolute terms but their risk of appearing.

Technological obsolescence
Ships not only become obsolete by wear and tear they can also become obsolete through the introduction of a new type of vessel which would be deemed

superior in terms of quality of service or indeed in terms of cost for providing shipping services. Although rarely taken into account[13] or appropriately discussed, this factor can reverse completely estimates of investment returns and shorten the economic life of a vessel dramatically. Developments in recent years in both the specialised shipping markets and – most of all – in liner shipping require that the impact of what could be termed broadly technological obsolescence is taken into account. The successive generations of container vessels have rendered redundant a large part of the tonnage of a lower TEU capacity and vessel repositioning is possible only if smaller markets are developing at a pace sufficient to absorb the tonnage replaced in the main sea routes. However, it has been argued that this has not happened in liner shipping due to successive post-Panamax generations causing a chronic oversupply.[14] In bulk shipping, the replacement of traditional breakbulk reefer ships by initially modern pallet and then container friendly tonnage has finally been overtaken by the new trend of refrigerated containers replacing massively the carriage of refrigerated produce in bulk. The fading-out of an entire segment of specialised bulk shipping[15] seems inevitable as technology and economies of scale have combined to allow the carriage of cargo under controlled temperature in suitable containers at a competitive cost. These examples from both liner and bulk shipping show that there is a degree of commonality in terms of risks investors are faced with in both markets; however, it is not necessarily so in terms of constraints under which investment decisions are taken in bulk and liner shipping.

3. OPERATIONAL CONSTRAINTS OF BULK AND LINER ACQUISITIONS

Examining investment attitudes automatically leads to discussing the particular constraints companies face when proceeding to vessel acquisitions. The question of company motives for investing seems prima facie naive; a blanket statement on profit maximisation would seem to provide the rule. However, as business goals[16] can deviate from this axiom so can investment motives. In the case of shipping this will be largely dependant on the nature of the shipping company. Although a negligible minority today, state enterprises had been in the past a force to be reckoned with[17] in modern shipping and for some the source of potential threats and many – hypothetical and theoretical as it proved – worries for the future of free competition in shipping. State companies of whatever origin are likely to have different motives than the typical shipping company of private ownership when considering investment. By the same token, the profit maximisation rule is unlikely to apply to the integrated shipping divisions of non-shipping companies; the most known example of companies of this type is that of shipping divisions or subsidiaries[18] of large oil companies.[19] In the case of state companies the motive for an investment decision might be this of national security or even of national prestige[20] resulting in particular constraints under which investment decisions have to be taken; investment would for instance be decided to follow the growth of national trades that government policy would prefer to transport by state owned vessels. Table 1 summarises the different positions of each type of shipping company *vis-à-vis* the potential special constraints under which they consider new investment in tonnage. These special constraints are in addition to the usual constraints every business is faced with when taking investment decisions.

Table 1: Investment/divestment constraints in shipping[21]

Company type	Constraints
Bulk	insignificant in most cases
Liner	frequency constraints, co-operation constraints, route constraints
Non-commercial: state-owned or integrated	"share" of own transport as defined/desired by parent company or state policy

3.1 Investing in bulk shipping: no holds barred

The most significant differences in terms of investment constraints exist between liner and bulk shipping companies assuming they are both under private ownership. Bulk shipping companies, unlike liner ones, are usually exempt of limitations when programming investment or divestment in ships and hence determining company size. In most cases a bulk shipping company will invest (or divest) in whatever type or size of bulk vessel it considers profitable on the basis of the state and the prospects of the freight and ship markets. A bulk shipping company mainly active in the dry bulk sector may invest in tanker vessels or even completely shift from the dry to the liquid bulk market if the prospects of the tanker market look more promising.[22] By the same token, a bulk company can choose to diversify by investing into more than one bulk shipping segment including the specialised shipping markets. However, when it comes to the specialised bulk shipping segments absolute investment freedom might in reality prove a little more relative: specialised vessel types such as Liquefied Petroleum Gas carriers (LPG) or chemical carriers do require a significant degree of know-how and experience so entry into these markets is not automatic or barrier free. The proliferation of bulk shipping pools in the specialised shipping markets has nevertheless preserved the right of shipowners to enter with minimum investment even in these specialised shipping segments Paradoxically, shipping pools are definitely a constraint for owners when it comes to divestment from any bulk market; moreover, pools may constitute a significant constraint for engaging in asset play as will be discussed later in the chapter.

3.2. Investing in liner tonnage: operational and co-operation constraints

Liner shipping companies are without doubt under a multitude of constraints when considering their investment policy not only by comparison to bulk shipping companies but also by comparison to a large number of industries. These constraints relate not only to the specific characteristics of the routes these companies serve but also to the co-operation agreements liner companies ussually have; very few, as a rule the top 2–3 largest container companies, have historically survived successfully without resorting to the creation of alliances of one form or the other. Pools, consortia and more recently global alliances have dominated the supply of liner shipping services[23] as ways to combine capacity to serve trade routes which were becoming increasingly demanding in terms of capacity and especially in terms of desired frequency. Operational co-operation requires that operational capacity adjustments – and hence investment decisions – are planned from a common perspective otherwise under-utilisation of capacity and problems in network planning, or equipment incompatibity may lurk. It is possible that a combination of these constraints together with the eagerness of outside investors to invest in the container market has led to the current situation where a very significant part of tonnage is drawn from the container charter market.[24] Frequency constraints as well as the nature of the liner business itself, which is the provision of regular advertised and – increasingly in past years – frequent sailings of liner ships, practically preclude any drastic reduction in capacity through massive divestment as the loss of goodwill is such[25] that precludes service withdrawals without the company incurring marketing damages. In this regard the combination of co-operation agreements together with the existence of a pool of container tonnage available in the container charter market might have added to the flexibility of liner shipping companies which is in general much more restricted than this of bulk shipping companies when it comes to investment decisions.

4. NEWBUILDING v. SECOND-HAND VESSELS: BALANCING DELIVERY LAGS WITH VESSEL ENDURANCE

Shipping companies, whether bulk or liner, are faced with a number of alternative choices when they decide to proceed with new investment. Although vessels have been acquired in the second-hand market for much less, investing in vessels is definitely an expensive decision: deep-sea going vessels values, especially of newbuildings, are on average in the order of tens of millions of dollars. However, the internationalisation of the shipbuilding industry and the expansion of capacity have resulted in multiplying the choice for placing orders and prices have been kept to a lower level than they would have been without the massive rise of the shipbuilding capacity in the Far East as waves of new shipbuilding centers were added to the world shipbuilding capacity.[26]

Despite, however, the enlargement of the circle of shipbuilding competitors, aggressive competition[27] and abundant finance in the post-war period, the role of fixed cost remains critical for shipping competitiveness. In this regard the choice between investing in a new-building or in a second-hand vessel must take into account *market prospects for both the freight and – the closely related – ship markets, current price levels* as well as *price differences* between new and old tonnage.

Know thy market: New-orders v. second-hand acquisitions
Acquiring vessels is perhaps the major pillar of company strategy in an industry environment that is characterised by cyclicality of both income and asset values especially when the exit barriers already discussed are taken into account. The realisation by many firms of the importance of investment decisions in this context is perhaps at the origin of the popularity of second-hand acquisitions of vessels. Otherwise, taking into account the existence of abundant finance and – for most of the post-war period – of attractive prices, grants or of a combination of all of the above, it would seem surprising that second-hand vessels would be an investment option at all. Investing in second-hand tonnage implies not only a shorter economic life of the vessel but also assuming the risk of hidden defaults that can eventually still remain undetectable despite strict checks before the purchase of the vessel.

The reasons for the popularity of second-hand acquisitions are in essence two-fold: (a) when investing in a second-hand ship the shipping company faces a much lower capital cost[28] compared to the alternative of a newbuilding, and (b) the waiting time for the actual delivery of the ship is minimal compared to the normal 1.5–2 years in the case of new orders. Normality is, however, the exception in a competitive market entirely open and extremely vulnerable to the influence of a multitude of exogenous factors. The quick reversal of market conditions due to the oil shock of 1973 is in that sense a classic example which shows how investment in newbuildings may be even riskier than investment in second-hand vessels

During the first half of the 1970s the expected delivery lag for orders placed at the time was often much longer than the 18–24 month usual range.[29] As the case of the 1970s proved, delays can be catastrophic if vessels are to be delivered so late that they cannot catch even a glimpse of the short booms which characterise shipping.[30] Delays of that length guarantee that delivery will come after – or sometimes long after – the relatively brief period of prosperity has degenerated into a lengthly recession if not into a full-blown depression as the case was in the late 1970s and in the first six years of the 1980s.

In view of these remarks, it could seem that opting for readily available second-hand vessels while freight rates are still climbing is a much more effective strategy. The market seems to share this as price differentials between newbuildings and second-hand vessels tend to narrow as the market itself tightens.[31] This is a phenomenon that has indeed characterised modern shipping as data published in the past about the first post-WW2 years support.[32] Yet, as the most important disadvantage of a second-hand acquisition is the – normally - much shorter economic life of the ship compared to that of a new vessel it remains intriguing whether the narrowing price gap between newly-built and second-hand tonnage during market booms is a strong indication in itself that shipping cycles obey to laws particular to this specific industry and often to this industry alone. Although the short duration of shipping booms is perhaps the only certainty one can have about the bulk shipping markets, even cash-tight companies risk their liquidity on betting on second-hand vessels at the peak of the market. Although there has been little research in investment attitudes to confirm the extent of similar investment behaviour, the multitude of arrests and foreclosures at the downturn of markets serve as ex-post evidence that rationality of expectations or just plain rationality has found its way into the academic books but not in investment behaviour in shipping, at least in what constitutes over 65% of the world tonnage, i.e. bulk shipping.[33]

5. INVESTMENT STRATEGIES, RISK AND ASSET PLAY

The frequent and very ample fluctuations of second-hand ship prices which follow in general the fluctuations in the freight rates – albeit not necessarily so in the very short-run – create the *opportunity* (*not the certainty*) of large profits from speculation on ships, a strategy/activity called *asset play*. However, it should be remembered that not all *rightly timed* investment in ships falls into the asset play category as very often the aim of the purchase is simply the acquisition of additional tonnage or the replacement of vessels at low prices. Asset play has indeed compensated for lacklustre profit margins in shipping; it has, however, overshadowed the advantages of astutely timed investment in ships without necessarily the *ex-ante* intention to further sell them. In competitive cyclical markets, timing is indeed, everything. Despite, however, the association by many of investment strategies with asset play and asset play alone, there is scope for a company to formulate a general strategy of acquisitions regardless of whether the intention is to use ships for trade or trade them *per se* as sheer commodities. Besides, asset play – even if it is at the origin of the investment decision – does not preclude the commercial operation of a vessel which can be subsequently sold when selling prices are deemed of an appropriate level.

5.1 Limiting risk: a shipping averse investment strategy

The only real guarantee from cash-flow pressures and company vulnerability in cyclical markets would be to finance purchases entirely by equity. Although not necessarily a net profit maximisation strategy, as traditional loan finance may be more advantageous at times of high inflation if interest rates are slow to catch up, it is definitely a safe and most conservative approach. However, had most market participants been following a strategy with a view to avoiding risk entirely, supply of shipping services would have been considerably tighter.[34] Acquisition prices do not have to be ridiculously low to allow for a competitive fixed-cost, although this has also been recorded in the past; the use of some debt finance need not necessarily put companies at bankruptcy risk as long as their cash-flow situation is healthy and companies are aware that they operate in a cyclical market and use this knowledge as a guide to company decisions. To be competitive in terms of capital cost companies have essentially to acquire vessels at significantly lower prices than the prices competitors had to pay for their own tonnage. This can sometimes be achieved just by waiting or speeding up an investment decision by often only a few months. The investment strategy of a firm becomes thus a relative one and a continuous effort to take advantage of significant asset price shifts over time periods which may be only a tiny fraction of the entire life expectancy of the vessel. As operating costs for similar vessels are easily adjustable, variations stemming essentially from manning costs, market survival and success can easily be shown to depend to a very large extent on fixed cost – essentially capital cost in bulk shipping – and hence on investment strategies.

5.2 Fixed cost and investment strategy: the essence of competitiveness?

Shipping competitiveness is a complex issue related to market structures.[35] However, in both liner and bulk shipping markets capital cost is, as a rule, the single most important element of total cost. In addition, in markets as heavily cyclical as the main bulk markets investment strategies can make or break companies as the impact of investment related paid-out costs determines the resilience of companies in times of crises.[36] Fixed cost influences company competitiveness through differences in acquisition prices of either new-buildings or second-hand vessels, differences in the way capital is raised and in the terms of finance of vessel acquisitions. Minimising fixed cost provides a significant advance on competitors in the main bulk markets where cost leadership is still the main viable option, without taking into account the idiosyncrasies of some very specialised shipping segments or those of liner shipping where quality of service and product differentiation may have a role to play in company strategy.

Shipping has always been perceived as capital intensive and automation and the downsizing of manning requirements have contributed little in changing this; on the contrary, the labour to capital ratio seems to have declined in recent decades due to increased automation of vessels and restructuring of manning requirements.[37] However, the dream of manning a vessel "with a man and a dog",[38] seems to have reached its limits as well as encountering the limits of the real needs of vessels. Hence, as there are few margins for minimising the cost of

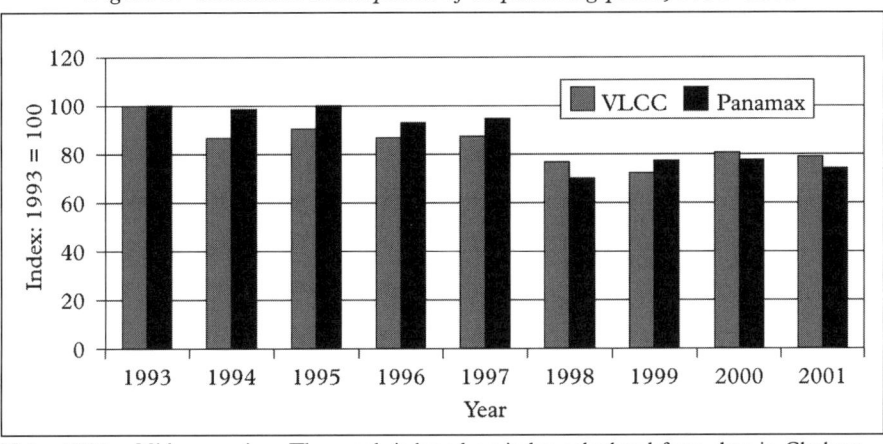

Figure 1: Indicative development of shipbuilding prices, 1993–2001

Note: 2001 = Mid-year prices. The graph is based on index calculated from data in Clarkson Research, *World Shipyard Monitor*, various dates.

main inputs such as bunkers or stores[39] the efforts for achieving an overall low cost cannot but concentrate on what constitutes on average half of the total cost of shipping services,[40] i.e., capital cost.

Minimising acquisition costs should not be mistaken as pointing necessarily to the purchase of second-hand tonnage. There are even substantial savings to be made by appropriately timing newbuilding investment although opportunities are more limited. As Figure 1 shows, however, there can occasionally be significant differences in new vessel prices over relatively short periods of time which can be translated to the difference between a low, but positive, profit margin and a limited, yet definitely negative, loss if the total cost is considered. Tankers ordered at the very high 1992 prices for example – which were above the 1993 levels included in Figure 1 – reached the market in the morose tanker markets of the mid-1990s, while orders placed at the low prices of 1998 took advantage of the millennium boom in tankers. *Timing* in shipping is indeed of essence.

Asset play: "the bulk" of bulk shipping profits?

It is a well established perception in the shipping community that the money in shipping, especially bulk shipping, is not in shipping operations but in speculation on ships. Often, this is the only justification that can be produced about why investors have kept investing in markets with such low and precarious profitability.[41] The expectation of profits as high as the ones in Table 2 is clearly a strong enough incentive for investors to be lured to bet on the turn of the market. Indeed, before the dot.com bubble there were very few legal possibilities for such rates of return.

Table 2: Indicative returns of sale and purchase

Ship type	Year built	Vessel Dwt	Bought	Price	Sold	Price	Return % year
VLCC	1976	232,616	11/85	2.6	3/86	5.45	330%
TSH	1979	56,963	9/85	4.6	4/86	6.8	82%
VLCC	1976	254,819	7/86	6.9	10/86	9.7	164%
TSH	1975	124,136	7/85	4.75	10/85	6.0	105%
VLCC	1972	254,000	6/86	6.2	11/86	7.5	50%
TSH	1972	164,545	9/87	6.1	11/87	8.0	187%
CSH	1972	19,017	7/87	0.5	6/90	2.5	133%
BC	1977	53,521	8/86	2.5	5/89	10.8	121%
BC	1972	62,535	9/87	4.3	8/89	7.8	42%
BC	1971	29,018	12/86	1.05	9/89	4.0	102%
BC	1976	23,150	10/86	1.6	10/88	5.5	122%
BC	1971	35,306	9/86	0.895	11/89	4.75	132%
TSH	1988	97,172	10/95	25.0	6/96	31.0	36%

Notes: VLCC = Very Large Crude carrier, TSH = Tanker ship, CSH = Cargo ship, BC = Bulk carrier.
Source: Thanopoulou, H., and Theotokas, J. (1997): *Pools in a Greek bulk shipping perspective: asset play vs. synergy benefits*. Occasional Paper No.46, Cardiff University, ISSN 0967-5566. Data in Theotokas, J. (1997): "Greek-Owned Shipping Companies of Piraeus: Organisational and Managerial Methods, 1970–1990", PhD thesis, University of Piraeus, 1997.

Exceptional returns as well as the achievement of a significantly lower fixed cost in relation to competitors have been based on investing against the tide or what has been called "anticyclical investment strategy".[42] Opportunities for asset play arise mainly within a full shipping cycle while the most impressive returns have been achieved at times of severe crises incorporating lengthy depressions during which distress sales become frequent.[43] Both before[44] and after World War II fortunes were made – and lost – through venturing into investment at the bottom of the market. The difficulties shipping companies with young, still not repaid, tonnage may be faced with have often resulted in even relatively new and good quality vessels being offered for sale at very low prices under the pressure of grim short-term market prospects aggravating the financial strain on the shipowning company.[45] In the worst period of the crisis of the 1970s and the 1980s tonnage could be bought at below scrap price levels as the case was with some tanker vessels bought in the early 1980s.[46] Shipping companies *able to secure funds under terms that enable them to wait for the revival of the markets or with the necessary liquidity* – possibly as a result of similar successful moves in the past or as a result of refraining from investment during market booms – have often been taking advantage of similar opportunities and exercised *anticyclical investment strategies*. In a sense, successful investment strategies are self-sustained as successful moves in the past allow the built-up of sufficient cash reserves to be invested in when the next opportunity arises; conversely, unsuccessful asset players carry the disadvantage of a precarious financial position or of no liquidity at all and perhaps of a lower ability to raise credit at times of crises as well. Banks are traditionally reluctant not only to lend to similar lenders but some to even get involved in shipping altogether when the market is depressed narrowing thus the circle of potential sources for raising capital. Banks tend to return to the shipping business along with profits and prosperity[47] but by then the real opportunities for large profits through the Sale and Purchase of vessels have lapsed. Stock markets are equally rather unlikely candidates for providing the necessary funds for such investment so, unless astute entrepreneurs manage to convince investors to contribute equity capital, asset play remains largely a self-financed and indeed self-sustained activity.[48]

5.3 Asset play: risks and attitudes

Such bold Sale and Purchase (S&P) strategies as described in the previous subsection and illustrated by Table 2 are of a high risk, as there is no time pattern for defining the point at which the market situation will turn to provide the opportunity to materialize S&P profits. "Intuition", often provided as a basis for such moves in S&P is a very poor basis for taking decisions of this type. The level of ship prices compared to the level of scrap prices seems to be a more "safe" market signal for moving into a purchase provided, of course, there is sufficient liquidity; distress sales in rock-bottom markets will tend to bring scrap and second-hand values dangerously close. The only real safe trigger for entering the market would be the sale of vessels below their scrap value.[49] Still, there are no guarantees about the success of such a move as the time horizon of the – always much awaited – revival of the markets remains uncertain under the influence of a multitude of factors, often exogenous to the shipping markets.

The term asset play is also used by researchers to describe activities related to buying and selling of new-building contracts or even of new-building options; anecdotally, returns from such activities seem to have been quite impressive with purchase and sale of such contracts taking place within relatively short periods of time.[50] The market path which could generate profits following the placement of the contract is one of a recovery of the market to higher freight rate levels which in turn would generate expectations and additional demand for quick deliveries of new-buildings driving new-building prices to significantly higher levels. Asset players can thus benefit from selling orders placed before the reversal of market conditions. Due to the necessary lags between orders and vessel delivery, this type of asset play could *eventually* prove less risky: if the market has hit low levels the reversal is likely to occur some time in the mid-term future when the order should normally have been transformed into a delivery.

Whatever form asset play activity takes, however, the most significant danger with it is that there is not really a guaranteed time or path for market reversals and as the 1980s proved market lows can be one more trough further down into a deepening depression. The only real protection from the inherent dangers of asset play is an extremely healthy cash-flow situation and the same is valid for all acquisitions in periods of crisis regardless of whether vessels are acquired with a view to a sale or to further trading. Liquidity and equity finance prove in this way the only guarantees while patience and flexibility emerge as the major attributes of the ideal asset-player.

Although speculation on ships bought during periods of low vessel prices is an extremely risky investment move, it should be reminded that the risk when investing in a booming market can definitely be – and usually is – higher[51] as investing in booming markets requires that freight rates are further sustained for a lengthy period of time at high levels. Once more, the absence of any time path for market turns[52] and the short duration in principle of shipping booms often condemns a large proportion of vessels acquired during similar periods to a chronic underperformance or even to an early death through emergency scrapping under the pressure of cash-flow problems. Very often, investors in the prosperity phase of the cycle will be the ones to feed the market with real bargains as the markets enter into a prolonged depression. The risk of moving into a booming market is perhaps the most obvious one and should be much better assessed as a move of this type requires long periods of prosperity but either through the endemic tendency to over-invest[53] or through an exogenous shock prosperity is bound to be cut short in shipping; the Reksten case in the early 70s[54] constitutes a typical example in this regard.

5.4 Asset play: a "game" with winners and losers

The review of S&P activity over the period of the crisis of the 1970s and the 1980s in shipping has proved that there are significant differences in investment attitudes not only among shipowning communities but among members of the same shipowning community. Research in the 1990s[55] has pointed that there have been marked differences in both investment attitudes and in exposure to asset play between shipping communities in Europe. The examination of data from the first half of the 1980s revealed for instance that Greek and Scandinavian owners held exactly opposite positions in terms of net acquisitions of vessels from 1980 to 1984 as the main bulk markets started their plunge into deep depression following the temporary recovery at the turn of the decade (see Figure 2). The research found this pattern of anticyclical investment to have contributed to the increased resilience of Greek shipowners to the major crisis of the 1970s and the 1980s and to the increase of the share of the Greek-owned fleet in world shipping after the revival of the markets in the late 1980s.

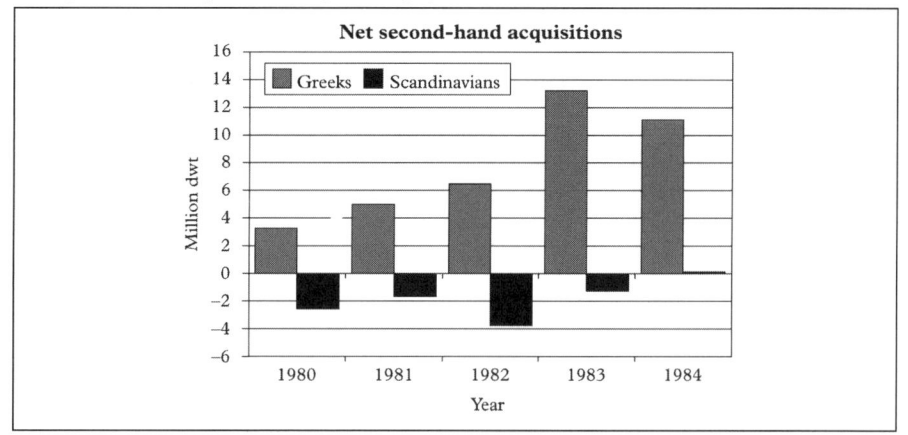

Figure 2: Net* purchases of tonnage from the second-hand market, 1980–1984

Net second-hand acquisitions

Year	Greeks	Scandinavians
1980	~3.5	~-2.5
1981	~5	~-1
1982	~6.5	~-3.5
1983	~13	~-1
1984	~11	~0

* Purchases minus sales.
Note: Graph calculated from data in Tables 2 and 3 in Thanopoulou, H. (1996), *op.cit.* Original data Lambert Brothers, *Trade Review and Outlook*, various issues.

However, an attempt to proceed with an econometric investigation of the Greek anticyclical investment pattern – within limitations due to the nature of the available data – resulted in showing that although there was a trend among Greeks to invest against the tide, the investment behaviour of many Greek shipowners at the time shows that this trend was far from uniform and definitely not a national exclusivity. Some of the most astute moves in the S&P market such as the purchases of VLCCs at below their scrap price were made by Scandinavian owners[56] pointing that although investment behaviour can be cultivated, propagated and exemplified within a shipping community, talent in shipping investment knows no boundaries and is not a geographically defined exclusive privilege.

However, most behaviours, including investment patterns, are dictated by objective constraints. Scandinavian owners traditionally invested in new-buildings while Greek owners had built a reputation for successfully managing older fleets. At a time when depression settled fast in the markets following the first oil shock in 1973, Norwegian owners found themselves with young – as well as expensively acquired – vessels with high demands in cash-flow for their repayment. As fleet age data indicate or rather reveal,[57] Greek owners could afford to be more resilient as their older tonnage was by comparison far less burdened with fixed-cost obligations since it was either bought second-hand or had been largely depreciated already, or both. However, as the face of shipping has undergone major changes in the past few years, it remains to be seen whether extending the average time of exploitation of the vessel can still be beneficial for long-run profitability and whether an older age of fleet has turned from an element of competitiveness to a clear competitive disadvantage.[58]

6. ASSET PLAY IN THE ERA OF POOLS AND QUALITY SHIPPING

World shipping is not what it used to be anymore. Prolonged periods of low freight rates have proved that market survival requires some variation on the least cost strategy even in markets where traditionally there have been no other alternatives. In markets such as tankers, untouched by such phenomena in the past – unlike the specialised markets – pooling of tonnage and consolidation are becoming a trend while the older age of vessels would most likely be classified today as a problem for the competitive ability of a company rather than as a factor of competitiveness; it remains to be seen, however, whether recent business moves and regulatory changes will indeed affect market structures and the nature of competition in the traditional bulk markets.

The commercial management of tonnage of various owners in a shipping pool as one fleet,[59] which is the essential function of pools, has its origins in the 1970s when a number of West European and Scandinavian owners realised the potential for access to large contracts and economies of scale that pools can generate together with entry to markets where know-how is important (such as the specialised shipping markets). By the 1990s the number of pools had increased rather impressively and recently the concept even penetrated markets which by definition provided limited scope for deployment optimisation and offered fewer contracts of affreightment both strong contributing factors for contemplating entering a pool.

Pools may indeed protect from market fluctuations, provide access to know-how and reduce short-run costs. Such advantages are bound to be counterbalanced by a number of disadvantages; giving up investment and especially divestment freedom is perhaps the most important price to pay for participating in a shipping pool. Pools do take advantage of their size to have access to large and long-term contracts so any sudden changes to available tonnage expose the remaining members of a pool to the vagaries of freight rate swings and the limits of tonnage available in the market to replace withdrawing vessels. Lengthy periods of notice of withdrawal are thus essential for the successful operation of a pool. In that sense, asset play and pool participation seem to be mutually exclusive and indeed the aversion of asset players to pools may be at the origin of the limited participation of Greeks to pooling agreements[60] in the past.

There can be little speculation on what the repercussions of increased pooling and consolidation in markets which have been golden fields for asset play – such as the tanker market – will be. There are few, however, doubts on what the result of increasing focus on shipping quality is likely to be. Recent safety and quality regulation has been changing the scenery in which bulk shipping companies compete. Although the old dream of many to eliminate flags of convenience has proved unrealistic with flags of convenience becoming the most significant part of the world fleet,[61] other elements of competitiveness need to be seen in a new light as well as strategies such as asset play.

Successful asset play requires a rather extended economic life of the vessel which should not only cover the length of the shipping cycle but also allow to the ultimate buyer the chance, or at least the hope, for a further profitable exploitation of an asset acquired by definition at high prices. In today's tanker shipping, tankers of more than 15 years are considered old and age has become significant to charterers even for dry bulk carriers. Although not sufficient to cover for different fixed-costs, rates for older and younger units have shown elements of differentiation.[62] More importantly, investing in older vessels is now practically constrained by regulatory requirements as recent regulation attempts seem to threaten further age limitations for existing vessels.[63] Moreover, older vessels are now subject to enhanced surveys and often to structural modifications[64] which imply added cost and loss of trading days. As the quality goalpost is being continuously moved, possibilities for impressive returns could be in inverse relation to the welcome increase of the overall quality of cargo tonnage. Although there will be always opportunities for minimising fixed-cost or even for asset-play, it seems likely that progressively these might be limited to a smaller range of tonnage age while large one-off "big money" profits through aggressive asset play may have to be replaced by less risky investment moves and more elaborate competitive strategies.

7. SUMMARY AND CONCLUSIONS

Investment strategies have been a core factor, if not the most critical one, for succeeding in shipping, especially in the volatile bulk shipping markets. Market cyclicality increases the risks for investors . The competitive nature, however, of most of bulk shipping means that there are few constraints in terms of investment and divestment. The absence of any significant constraints of this type enhances the competitive nature of the bulk markets and increases the opportunities to take advantage of speculative opportunities through asset-play on ships which is an extremely risky investment attitude but with potentially high payoffs . Changes in bulk shipping such as the rising importance of pools in some traditional markets and the increased emphasis on quality will probably affect more the scope for asset play than the fundamental characteristics of shipping investment attitudes.

ENDNOTES

1. Following the events of September 11, one the world's top cruise lines at the time, Renaissance Cruises, filed for bankruptcy protection. See *http://www.ilo.org/public/ english/dialogue/ sector/papers/factsheet/sep11 _mariti.htm#cruiseindustry*. They were not the only company doing so at the time while others had to substantially cut operations and lay-off staff. See also *Lloyd's List*, 11 March 2001. The immediate impact of the terrorist attack on the cruise sector was perhaps as hard or even more immediate than of that the first oil shock had on the tanker market.
2. The regular provision of liner services should not be confused anymore with any certainty regarding the rate of return of investments in liner ships.
3. See Chapter 10 on Shipping Market Cycles by M. Stopford earlier in this volume.
4. For example a 5-year-old tanker was in 1983 approximately worth 15% of its 1980 price and less than 10% of the respective price in 1990. Calculated on the basis of VLCC price data in Clarkson Research Limited, various publications. For more on ship prices *cf.* S. Strandenes earlier in this volume.
5. When looking at newbuilding prices for instance there are variations to the rate of change of prices. As markets turned in the second half of the 1980s the new-building price of an LPG vessel of 12,000cbm rose by less than 180% % between 1986 and 1989 while the respective increase was over 220% for a tanker of 30,000dwt. Data: ISL, *Shipping Statistics Yearbook* (ISL, Bremen). Second-hand values may also vary at different rates and it has to be reminded that in some of the specialised shipping markets, such as the LNGs, there is really no liquid second-hand market.
6. See Thanopoulou, H. (2003): *Competing in modern bulk shipping*, forthcoming, *op. cit.*, for the dynamics of the different bulk shipping segments.
7. See Thanopoulou, H. (1995): "The growth of fleets registered in the Newly-emerging maritime countries and maritime crises", *Maritime Policy and Management*, Vol. 22, No. 1, pp. 51–62, for the role individual factors – and in particular the tendency to over-invest – played in the crisis of the 1970s and the 1980s.
8. See Thanopoulou, H. (2003), forthcoming, *op. cit.*
9. According to data for the end of 2000 in Lloyd's Register (2001), *World Fleet Statistics*.
10. See the next chapters in this part of the volume for the shipping finance problems and proposed solutions.
11. There are examples, however, of successful conversion of vessels into special oil production units (FPSOs) and other uses.
12. See note 4.
13. The late Basil Metaxas was among the authors discussing the sudden depreciation of vessels due to this factor see Metaxas, B. (1988): *Principles of Maritime Economics* (Athens, Papazissis) (in Greek) and Metaxas, B. (1992): *Principles of Maritime Economics* (Athens, Papazissis) (in Greek).
14. See Gardner, B.: "EU Competition Policy and Liner Shipping Conferences", *Journal of Transport Economics and Policy*, Vol. XXX, No. 3, pp. 317–324. Although some smaller vessels will be used in feeder or smaller trades, it looks unlikely that all the successive generations can be readily absorbed.
15. See Thanopoulou, H. (2003) *op. cit.* For a detailed discussion of the container invasion into the bulk reefer market see Mehta, S.: "The Reefer Market and Changing Trends", MSc Dissertation, Cardiff, 2000.
16. For a quick overview of business objectives see Reekie, W.D., Allen, D.E., and Crook, J.N.: *The Economics of Modern Business* (2nd ed.) (Oxford, Blackwell).
17. In the heydays of the socialist bloc, the state companies of this group of countries amounted to less than 10%. See the various OECD statistics as included in the annual review *Maritime Transport*.
18. There is really no essential difference between fleets directly integrated in shipping divisions of oil companies and those belonging to controlled subsidiaries. In both

case the ultimate owner and the decision centre is the same, i.e. the oil company. More sophisticated structures created in recent years through alliances and joint ventures should not obscure the "paternity" of the investment decision.
19. Despite the significant reduction of the fleet owned by the major oil companies, they still constitute a quite significant part of the world tanker tonnage and even more so when the state oil companies are taken into account
20. For the influence of non-economic motives such as the national prestige see Haralambides, H.E (1993): *A New Future for European Shipping* (Rotterdam, Erasmus University).
21. Developed on the basis of Figure 1 in Thanopoulou, H. (1995): *Lecture notes in Special Subjects in Maritime Economics*, University of Piraeus, mimeo.
22. Freedom in shifting or diversifying has been paid, of course, dearly when the policy proved to have poorly estimated market prospects.
23. See Thanopoulou, H., Ryoo, D.K., and Lee, T.W. (1999): "Korean liner shipping in the era of global alliances", *Maritime Policy and Management*, Vol. 26, No. 3, pp. 209-229.
24. Company-owned tonnage is equally offered for hire when capacity adjustments or vessel replacements prompt so. Establishing a trend in this regard requires comparing chartered to owned tonnage over a period of years at least for the leading container companies. A *prima facie* look at current data seems to establish such a trend, however, very little can be supported by randomly examined data. For more see Min Jung Kee (2001): "Co-operation and competition in deep-sea liner shipping", MSc Dissertation, Cardiff, 2001.
25. The reader will benefit from reading Pearson, R. (1987): "Some doubts on the contestability of liner shipping markets", *Maritime Policy and Management*, Vol. 14, No.1, pp. 71-78, especially p. 77.
26. Japan's leading role in the post-war period was later challenged by South Korea while lately China claimed a non-negligible part of shipbuilding orders. Korea's ascent in world shipbuilding was so spectacular that in the late 1980s its share was almost 30% up by an equivalent figure from the 0% share it had in 1970. See Thanopoulou, H. (1994): *Greek and World Shipping* (Athens, Papazissis) (in Greek), p. 200, Table B.2.II. Data: *Lloyd's Register Annual Summary of Merchant Ships Completed* in ISL, *Shipping Statistics Yearbook 1989*, Bremen.
27. State subsidies were much more common and important in the past as were investment incentives to owners. For a review of the role of these factors on British shipping see Gardner, B., Pettit, S., and Thanopoulou, H. (1996): "Shifting challenges for British Maritime Policy", *Marine Policy*, Vol. 20, No. 6, pp. 517-524.
28. S. Strandenes pointed out that "whereas the investment is smaller when acquiring a second-hand vessel, the interest rate on the loan may exceed that offered for yard financing". I am grateful to Prof. Strandenes for this and other comments on the chapter.
29. Even in 1974, after the crisis had limited the wave of orders a delivery date in 1977 was most common. See the review of Greek orders placed world-wide in *Naftica Chronika*, 15 January 1975, pp. 92-93.
30. See chapter 10 by M. Stopford on Shipping Market Cycles earlier in this volume.
31. See chapter 9 by Prof. S. Strandenes earlier in this volume.
32. See Metaxas, B.(1972): *The economics of tramp shipping* (London, The Athlone Press).
33. Altogether, bulk ships of any kind constituted at the end of 2000, 65.2 % of the world gross tonnage. Calculated on the basis of data in L.R (2001), *World Fleet Statistics*.
34. In his classic textbook *Maritime Economics*, Martin Stopford makes a similar remark of the post-WW2 role of shipping finance in expanding shipping supply beyond what equity accumulation would have allowed. See Stopford, M. (1997): *Maritime Economics*, Chapter 6.

35. For a detailed discussion see Thanopoulou, H.: *Competing in modern bulk shipping*, forthcoming. For an introduction to the fundamentals of the traditional bulk markets see Thanopoulou, H. (1998): "What price the flag? The terms of competitiveness in shipping", *Marine Policy*, Vol. 22, No. 4–5, pp. 359–374.
36. Martin Stopford has very astutely encapsulated the importance of this factor in his book *Maritime Economics* in the title of a relevant paragraph: "Cash flow and the art of survival"; *cf.* Stopford, M., *Maritime Economics* (1st ed.) (London, Routledge), p. 93.
37. In the 1970s and 1980s the successive influences of increased vessel size and automation and then of cutbacks in manning scales resulted in the ratio declining for a number of fleets. For an econometric model of the trend towards lower demand for sea-going personnel due to economies of scale, see Haralambides, H.(1991): "An econometric Analysis of the Sea-Going labour Market", *Logistics and Transportation Review*, Vol. 27, No. 1, pp. 15–31.
38. The expression was included in an article in one of the main international shipping magazines sometime in the 1980s and was inspired by the extremely ambitious plans of some shipping circles to cut cargo crews of ocean-going vessels to about nine persons, see Thanopoulou, H. (1994), *op. cit.*
39. Efficient management can definitely contribute in minimising these costs through adequate planning of operations and knowledge of ship technical requirements and of input markets. Yet, as there are few secrets or risks in these areas results can differ little between companies.
40. Capital cost was less than 50% of the total cost at times of exceptionally high prices of bunkers such as the early 1980s. See Moreby, D. (1985): "Crew Costs", *Maritime Policy and Management*, Vol. 12, No. 1, pp. 50–60.
41. In the words of a shipowner "Independent tankers owners are not remunerated properly for the important service they provide – they should not have to rely on asset plays [s&p] to ensure their survival", *Lloyd's List*, December 1995.
42. The term is often attributed to this author. Although the investigation of the subject has indeed been undertaken by H. Thanopoulou in various publications, a similar term (countercyclical) must have been mentioned once by the late B. Metaxas in one of his teaching manuals published in Greek.
43. Less turbulent markets provide nevertheless opportunities to minimise capital cost. Fixed-cost differences between a 10-year-old Panamax bought at the lowest 1994 price and a similar vessel bought in autumn 1995 could be of the order of 25%, easily providing for a total cost differential of over 10% but also allowing asset-play profits of a respectable size. See Thanopoulou, H.A. (1997): "What price the flag? The terms of shipping competitiveness...", *op. cit.*
44. For a brief reference to Onassis' asset play in the 1930s, see Goss R. (1987): "Editorial. How to make money in shipping", *Maritime Policy and Management*, Vol. 14, No. 1, pp. 1–3.
45. See Thanopoulou, H. (1995): *Lecture Notes in Special Shipping Issues*, University of Piraeus, mimeo, pp. 247–248
46. See further in the text for details. Voyage costs for the last voyage to scrap also play a role in pushing the price below that of scrap.
47. For example, at the start of the 1980s there were 200–250 banks active in shipping finance while by the middle of the decade this number was reduced to less than 30, with banks returning massively to shipping a few years later as markets recovered. There were about 60 involved in shipping finance by the end of the 1980s and by 1997 their number had increased back to about 200. *Cf.* Thanopoulou, H. (1994): *op. cit.*, p. 190, and *Seatrade*. It is difficult, however, to compare the above figures with more recent numbers due to the wave of mergers that has swept the banking sector in the past few years. On this last point see Starbuck, S., "The shrinking world", *The Baltic*, February 2001, pp. 17–18.
48. During the 1980s depression, P. Stokes organised the raising of equity capital with a view to invest – with great success – in buying vessels which were clearly under-

valued at the time and then reselling them. See Thanopoulou, H. (1995): *Lecture notes in Special Shipping Issues*, Piraeus, mimeo, p. 252.
49. See below in the text for such incidents in the early 1980s.
50. As mentioned by Dr. J. Theotokas in his lecture notes. The author is grateful to Dr. Theotokas for enlightening discussions on this sub-category of asset play.
51. The Reksten case in the early 70s is a typical example in this category as the Norwegian shipowner was quick to pick up the tanker fleet of his compatriot Erling Dekke Naess just before the first oil shock. The Reksten bankruptcy has been recorded as the largest in Norwegian shipping history Naess had felt uneasy with the prolonged market prosperity. See Isachsen, F. (1992): *Crude Oil Shipping* (Bergen, SNF), pp. 18 20. *Cf.* Thanopoulou, H. (1995): *Lecture notes on Special Shipping Issues*, *op. cit.*, p. 251.
52. The term here means at the same time the absence of knowledge of the time path pattern and the absence of a specific pattern both concepts being intertwined. For the concept of time path in the modelling of expectations, see chapter 9 by Prof. Strandenes earlier in this volume.
53. See, on this tendency, Metaxas, B. (1971): *op. cit.*
54. See Stokes, P. (1992): *Ship finance : credit expansion and the boom-bust cycle* (London, Lloyd's of London Press), p. 35.
55. See Thanopoulou, H. (1996): "Anticyclical Investment Strategies in Shipping: The Greek case", D. Hensher and J. King (eds.) *World Transport Research* (Oxford, Elsevier), Vol. 4, pp. 209–220.
56. See Lambert Brothers, *World Trade Review and Outlook*, 1983 issues. In both cases the buyers were Norwegian despite the general perception that – as the data in Figure 2 equally suggest – Norwegian owners are not known for proceeding with purchases in times of crises.
57. See Thanopoulou, H. (1994): *Greek and World Shipping*, *op. cit.*
58. The role of older tonnage through either low acquisition cost, lengthy exploitation or a combination of both has been discussed in Thanopoulou, H. (1994): *Greek and World Shipping*, *op. cit.*, and in Thanopoulou, H. (1996): " What price ...", *op. cit.*
59. For more on pools, see Packard, W. (1989) and (1995): *Shipping Pools* (London, Lloyds of London Press), 1st and 2nd ed. respectively. Haralambides, H. (1996): "The economics of bulk shipping pools", *Maritime Policy and Management*, Vol. 23, No. 3, pp. 221–237, and Thanopoulou, H., and Theotokas, J. (1997): *Pools in a Greek bulk shipping perspective*, Occasional paper No. 46 (Cardiff University).
60. *Cf.* Thanopoulou, H., and Theotokas, J. (1997): *Pools in a Greek bulk shipping perspective*, *op. cit.* The older age of Greek tonnage was the other reason identified for this low participation.
61. As the 21st century dawned flags of convenience were close to becoming the absolute majority in the world fleet having risen to 48.5% of the total tonnage. See UNCTAD (2001), *Review of Maritime Transport 2001*.
62. For more on this subject see Tamvakis, M., and Thanopoulou, H. (2000): "Does quality pay? The case of the dry bulk market", *Transportation Research Part E: Logistics and Transportation Review*, Vol. 36, pp. 297–307.
63. Following the *Erika* incident in December 1999, pressures to limit the age of serving tanker vessels increased. As a result a new accelerated phasing-out of single-hull tankers was adopted
64. As the ones imposed on dry bulk carriers through the addition of Chapter XII to the SOLAS convention.

CHAPTER 29

VALUING MARITIME INVESTMENTS USING REAL OPTIONS ANALYSIS

Helen Bendall

Finance and Economics School, University of Technology,
Sydney, Australia. E-mail: *helen.bendall@uts.edu.au*

1. INTRODUCTION

The maritime industry is highly capital intensive. Investment in a single ship is dependent on or can lead to a commitment to a terminal and infrastructure, usually on valuable land. In turn the terminal requires mechanical handling equipment, cranes and mobiles and access to road and rail infrastructure. Any investment decision in the maritime industry is non-trivial as ships, infrastructure and equipment of landside operations run into hundreds of millions of dollars and may commit the investor for decades.

Investments are huge and cash flows are enormous but so are the risks. It is an industry whose cash flows are exposed to daily changes in international financial markets, to multi-currency risk, to multi-country sovereign risk, to pirates, to movements in oil prices, to other competitors and, above all, the trade cycle. So the decision to proceed with the acquisition of say a high speed ship or a new portainer crane can be regarded as a large scale capital evaluation problem within the context of a great number of volatile parameters. Optimisation of the firm's value is dependent on correct investment choices by management. Management thus needs sound and reliable tools to minimise the risk of poor investment decisions.

Capital budgeting, the process by which firms allocate resources among long term assets, provides the major vehicle for the realisation of management's strategic vision of the future and the ultimate value of the firm. With the scale and long term nature of maritime investments, an investment decision may prove vital to the firm's future success or failure, especially if it is not easily reversible and commits the firm for a certain long term path. Traditionally firms have relied on Discounted Cash Flow Analysis, DCF, and in particular the Net Present Value, NPV, technique for project evaluation. In the investment decision process, implicit assumptions concerning an expected scenario of cash flows, CF, are made and these are discounted at a risk adjusted rate, r, to determine the present value of the project. Projects are accepted if the discounted value of these cash flows are equal to, or exceed the capital cost of the investment, I. In this case the NPV is positive and if accepted should increase the value of the firm. In contrast, projects whose capital and start-up costs exceed the value of the discounted cash flows, i.e. when the NPV is negative, would destroy value in the firm if accepted and thus should be rejected.

$$NPV = +\sum_{n=1}^{t} \frac{cashflows^t}{(1+r)^t} - I$$

In the traditional NPV approach the investment decision is based on a single projection of future events. However, many projects require significant commitments of both capital and managerial input once the project is underway. Uncertain future developments and the firm's response to these can turn projects either into successes or dismal failures. Traditional DCF analysis fails to consider future uncertainty and strategic responses to future events.

A literature review and a discussion of the key issues of valuing investment in an uncertain world follows in Section 2. Real options analysis, ROA, is offered as an alternate paradigm as it allows managers the ability to alter/adapt the project in light of new information. The concept is developed in Section 3 by considering various applications of real options in the maritime industry and the principles of real option valuation. A specific investment in fast ship technology is used in Section 4 to demonstrate the advantages of using ROA over traditional NPV criteria for valuation. Section 5 concludes the chapter.

2. THE INVESTMENT DECISION

Conventional DCF analysis for project evaluation is taught extensively in business schools and is used by a majority of firms.[1] It appears that many academics and executives, by implementing investment decisions which have been based on traditional capital budgeting techniques and which have focused on narrowly defined problems have failed to take into account uncertainty and the flexibility to alter or adapt projects once begun. Often there is a lack of understanding of how to include strategic issues in an analysis. This is not to say that managers have not recognised that the failure to do so can lead to costly errors, but the difficulty of such planning leads many to ignore the potential costs and hope that serious problems do not arise (Teisberg[2]). Managers must be able to include uncertain future outcomes and potential strategic responses in a prospective analysis of a capital investment project. The use of traditional NPV has been called into question because of its inflexibility and the failure to take into account strategic or competitive issues. DCF criteria can undervalue investment opportunities, often leading to underinvestment and loss of competitive position.

Dissatisfaction with traditional DCF led some to propose that the problem was simply a misuse or misapplication of the underlying theory (Hodder and Riggs[3]) or that DCF was an inappropriate valuation method (Hertz[4]). Magee[5] suggested instead the use of simulation and decision trees, or Decision Tree Analysis, DTA, as a means to capture the value of future operating flexibility associated with many projects. Other academics and company executives wanting to refine DCF have turned their attention to technical questions related to the selection of the risk adjusted process without considering adequately the appropriateness of DCF for valuation of particular projects which have strategic implications. This approach does not appreciate the interdependencies between current and uncertain or contingent future decisions which make the risk-adjusted discount rate non-deterministic.

Other authors have commented that various capital budgeting techniques are often applied in practice as a set of checks rather than as the principal valuation tools (Lai and Trigeorgis[6]), or simply to justify a senior managerial decision already made. An example to illustrate this point is found in a study conducted a few years ago on investment decision making techniques and strategies in the maritime industry. The Financial Director of a major international shipping line explained that the shipping line employed graduates from all the top universities around the world. "Of course they used Discounted Cash Flow analysis for project evaluation." He explained that if the result of an NPV analysis was negative "they would be sent back to do it again!" In other words DCF was seen as a necessary justification (possibly for the board or shareholders) of a strategic investment decision already made (Bendall and Manger[7]).

Indeed in practice there appear many examples of inconsistencies between traditional theory outcomes and real world decisions. Researchers (such as Kester[25]) observed that managers/operators appear to accept investments with negative NPVs which should be rejected if standard capital budgeting theory was applied i.e. projects would be undertaken where the results of using traditional inputs in the discounted cash flow analysis indicated that if accepted, the value of the firm would be destroyed, while other projects with positive NPVs do not go ahead on the basis of "strategic fit". Special types of investments such as R&D projects, for example, generate negative cash flows with intangible benefits not accommodated for in traditional DCF valuation.

Traditional DCF is based on value maximisation under *passive* or static conditions and on implicit assumptions concerning a predetermined operating strategy in which the project would be initiated immediately and operate continuously at base case until the end of a pre-specified useful life. Ansoff[8] and Myers[9] point out that traditional capital budgeting techniques are unable to forecast the value of projects not yet in hand and that they are difficult to use in situations involving multiple objectives, substantial project interdependencies, e.g. synergies or other unique qualitative attributes (Lai and Trigeorgis[6]). The standard NPV although perfectly suitable for projects that once undertaken require no further decisions or actions by the firm, is of little assistance in the valuation of projects which offer managerial flexibility in dealing with future contingencies. In summary, DCF may be appropriate when applied to narrowly defined problems but is inadequate when uncertainty and strategic considerations are paramount (Pinches,[10] Myers,[9] amongst many). These observations point to the existence of an extra parameter which managers implicitly or explicitly factor into their investment decisions.

2.1 Expanded NPV

Despite studies indicating widespread acceptance of DCF techniques, practitioners recognise that the NPV rule and other discounted cash flow, DCF, approaches to capital budgeting are inadequate because of their failure to recognise and capture the need for flexibility over time. In the real world of uncertainty and competitive interactions, the realisation of those predetermined cash flows based on a set of assumptions will more than likely differ from what management originally expected. Management must then defer, abandon, contract, expand or in some way adapt or alter the project at different stages during its operating life.

Embedding into the capital budgeting decision tool an extra parameter which could allow the flexibility to adapt and change the investment in response to altered market conditions, expands the upside potential of an investment while limiting downside losses relative to management's initial expectations under a *passive* or pre-determined scenario. The need to adapt future income forecasts in light of new information indicates that an expanded NPV rule should be substituted which will incorporate both the direct cash flows from the traditional (passive) NPV and a real option value reflecting operating and strategic adaptability i.e. the traditional NPV analysis is expanded to include contingencies.

3. REAL OPTIONS

What is a real option?

A real option gives the right but not the obligation to undertake an action at a predetermined cost (the exercise price), for a predetermined period of time (the life of the option). The concept is similar to financial options.[11] It gives the manager the right to defer, to expand, to contract or abandon the project once more information becomes available. A *call* option is the right to buy the underlying asset at the predetermined (exercise) price As there is no obligation on the part of the holder of the option to exercise the call, the option can lapse However if the option is exercised then the profit on the option is the difference between the value of the underlying asset and its exercise price. A *put* option is the right to sell the underlying asset to receive the exercise price and thus is the opposite of a call. A *European* option can only be exercised on its maturity date where as an *American* option can be exercised at any time during its life and thus is more applicable to investment in real assets. An option is *in the money*, i.e. profitable to exercise if the price of the underlying asset is above the exercise price with a call option and below the exercise price with a put option. If not profitable to exercise it is *out of the money*.

The first recorded option occurred over 2500 years ago when Thales of Milatus, anticipating a bumper olive harvest, bought options to rent all the olive presses for a set price during the harvest season. If his predictions came true he stood to make a lot of money as he would control the supply of olive oil. If the harvest failed he had the flexibility to walk away from any deal as the option gave him the right (but not the obligation) to rent the olive presses. Aristotle reported that the harvest was excellent, Thales exercised the options and paid the owners of the olive presses the agreed rent. Because of the bumper harvest the presses were in high demand and Thales' fortune was made by charging others a much higher market price for their use (Copeland and Antikarov[12]).

Well before the development of ROA managers and strategists intuitively adjusted their investment strategies to include other factors such as future growth considerations, realising that traditional DCF criteria undervalued many investment opportunities. Kester[25] developed Myers[24] concept of thinking of discretionary investment opportunities as "growth options". These growth options embody both strategic and competitive elements. For example, shipping lines may enter a new market or trade not so much because the immediate investment generates a positive NPV, indeed it may be the opposite, but in order to keep a competitor out of the trade or to put the line in an advantageous position for valuable follow up opportunities. An investment such as this is an example of a multistage decision that involves "real" options. The decision to enter the trade has the ability to create future assets (cash flow) as a by-product of the initial investment decision. The shipping line, by undertaking the initial investment, has the option in future to expand the number of ships in the trade, or exit the trade depending on market circumstances in the future.

3.1 Real Options Analysis, ROA

Real option analysis, ROA or contingent claims analysis, CCA, enables formal analysis of these sequential investment decisions. The opportunity to put an additional ship in the trade is similar to an American call option[13] in financial markets which is the right but not the obligation to acquire a claim to the cash flow value. Similarly the right, but not the obligation, to reduce the scale of operation, say moving from two ships to one in a trade or exiting the trade altogether, is an example of a put option. ROA thus correctly values managerial flexibility by explicitly considering appropriate action at future dates on which information about the project's profitability is revealed. The project's true valuation can look more attractive when the value of this flexibility in incorporated.[14] This means that a project may have a static NPV that is negative and therefore would be rejected using traditional NPV rules but may be accepted if the value of flexibility is added

| Value of project with flexibility = Value of project without flexibility + Value of flexibility |

In other words the value of the project is equal to the traditional static NPV or base case plus a value for active management. An options approach views capital investment as an on-going process requiring active managerial involvement.

Real options are classified by their flexibility.[15] If management wants to scale up production then management needs to value an option to expand. They would need to value an American call which gives them the right but not the obligation to add additional capacity to their current project by further investment at a later date. In contrast to scale down an operation or to close an operation are examples of American put options where management has the right to sell, but not the obligation, should the operating environment worsen. An option to *contract* allows management to sell a fraction of the operation while an option to *abandon* at a fixed price leads to closure for a predetermined salvage value. Being allowed to defer the decision to invest is an option to *defer* while *switching* options are portfolios of American puts and calls which allow the flexibility to switch inputs or outputs. *Compound* options are options on options and point to the need for sequential investment decisions while *rainbow* options reflect multiple sources of uncertainty.

3.2 Maritime applications of real options

3.2.1 Option to expand

One of the most important real options is the option to accelerate the rate or expand the scale of operation by investing an additional outlay. This ability to make a discretionary investment is similar to an American call option on the increased scale of the project and with the exercise price, the additional outlay. The project then can be seen as the base scale project, or static NPV, plus a call option on the future investment, which is the value of flexibility. The option becomes profitable to exercise, if future demand turns out to be higher than expected as in the above example where a shipping line can increase the number of vessels in a trade.

A major source of value from infrastructure investments arises from the ability to enhance the upside of a project during good market conditions by making follow-on investments (Myers[24]). Ports with surplus land can build extra terminals and terminal operators can increase the number of gantry cranes on a berth. This option, which will be exercised only if future market developments turn out favourably, can make seemingly unprofitable investments (based on static NPV base-case) worth undertaking. Infrastructure investments consist of both tangible and intangible core assets on which individual operating flexibility options are based. Flexible computer based manufacturing systems, such as CAD-CAM manufacturing in the ship building industry, are evidential. Investment in training has intangible option benefits for ship and port operators if for example the management has a multi-skilled workforce to utilise.

Infrastructure investment may be encouraged by governments in developing markets when the investor is given a valuable option to expand as a "sweetener" to offset possible risk of a new venture. For example operating subsidies may be offered to commuter ferry operators to offset any negative cash flows arising from initial low demand on a new route. The operating subsidy would only be exercised if needed to make up any shortfall. Alternatively the government may offer the exclusive rights to develop terminal facilities and a shopping arcade at an inter-modal terminal. These are examples of valuable real options.

3.2.2 Growth options, strategic options, competitive options

Growth options are similar to expansion options but with more emphasis on strategic or competitive positioning. They set the path for future opportunities. Growth options are possible because of the firm's ownership of intangible assets such as patents, proprietary technologies, ownership of valuable resources, managerial capital, reputation or brand name, scale and market power which allow companies to grow through future profitable investments and to more effectively respond to unexpected adversity or opportunities in a changing technological competitive or general business environment (Trigeorgis[16]). The ownership of growth options enhances management's flexibility for future action to give the firm a sustainable competitive advantage.

Technological superiority and know-how permit further sequential (or parallel) developments ensuring competitive edge is maintained. In this way growth options such as in this example are called complex or compound options as growth comes from exercising a series of options, i.e. an option on an option. For the shipbuilding and related industries, R&D investment is essential in a competitive environment with rapid technological developments. Australian shipbuilders have been world leaders in aluminium welding techniques and design of high speed craft which ensured that they remained ahead of other competitors by continual design development. Thus the development of first generation product can create a proprietary growth option acting as a springboard for developing in the future lower cost and improved design or indeed new applications. Investment in Information Technology, IT, can be viewed as a growth option as it provides a link in the chain to interrelated projects and growth opportunities.

Similarly development of an initial market/trade which may generate a negative NPV (static base case) can open up or generate opportunities in other markets at a later stage or can pre-empt the entrance of a competitor. This investment may be viewed as a strategic investment. Strategic acquisitions such as purchase of a terminal by a shipping company gives the shipping line control over competitor access and timing to the facilities conferring on the company a competitive edge via the proprietorial option.

Once investment opportunities are properly seen as collections or a portfolio of real options, strategic planning can be more readily viewed as involving the explicit recognition, creation and management of current and future investment opportunities (Lai and Trigeorgis[6]).

3.2.3 Option to contract, option to abandon

Investors may also have embedded options to contract or abandon if a project fails to achieve the required rate of return envisaged, due to less favourable market conditions.

If market conditions are weaker than originally anticipated management can operate below capacity or even reduce the scale of operations and thus save part of planned investment outlays as well as reducing operating costs. This flexibility to lessen the loss is analogous to a put option on part of the base scale project with the exercise price being equal to the potential cost savings. The option to contract is particularly valuable in the case of entering into a new market (trade) or in choosing among technologies with different construction to maintenance cost mix. To illustrate this point management may chose initially a lower cost asset with higher maintenance expenditures in order to acquire the flexibility to contract operations by cutting down on maintenance if market conditions worsen.

3.2.4 Option to abandon for salvage

If the project suffers severe losses through a systemic market decline or for some other reason such that the firm can no longer sustain its fixed costs then the project should be shut down. Management has a valuable abandonment option if the assets and equipment can be sold at market or salvage prices. The more general purpose the capital asset i.e. lower asset specificity, the higher will be the value of the abandonment option. For example a container ship or bulk ship would be considered to have low asset specificity while a gas carrier would have high asset specificity. This real option is equivalent to an American put option. The underlying asset is the current value of the vessel where the salvage value is the exercise price.

In contrast infrastructure companies' abandonment options may be less valuable than that of shipping lines because of the sunk cost nature of the assets. This means that their exercise price is low. Once constructed a port or terminal cannot be moved to another location or may not be profitably used for another purpose, although port land can be turned over to recreational use. With low exercise prices, the options and the business that own them would be worth less than they would otherwise.

To encourage investment in infrastructure projects governments often grant real options to compensate for the sunken nature of the investment. This can be in the form of a revenue guarantee or clauses guaranteeing buy backs at given prices. Shipbuilders may offer as safety net or security to new investors/financial institutions of a buy-back of the vessel should the profitability of the venture fail. The buy-back is pre-set generally on a sliding scale, rates commensurate with depreciation and the time value of money.

3.2.5 Option to defer or waiting to invest or timing options

With uncertainty, a project with a negative NPV may become profitable if it can be deferred over a certain time period. For example although high speed ship technology is constantly improving, fuel consumption rises exponentially with increases in speed. Thus a ship operator may prefer to wait or defer an investment in a fast ferry or container ship in the anticipation that oil prices may fall in the future, making the venture profitable

Early investment implies sacrificing the option to wait. Thus the presence of the timing option requires a choice between two mutually exclusive investments; invest "now" or (maybe) invest "later". A positive NPV in the invest "now" case may not be the best profit maximising choice when we recognise that future decisions and discount rates will depend on the realisation of stochastic variables (McDonald and Seigal[17]). A company that has not yet invested has an option to invest that it exercises, i.e. gives up, when it commits itself to investing. Clearly a project that can be delayed is more valuable than one which is otherwise equivalent, but must be undertaken immediately. If the firm chooses to invest "now" rather than invest "later" the NPV must be raised to offset the loss of the timing option (Dixit and Pindyck[18,19]). This is in contrast to the expansion or growth opportunities where the option to expand makes up any shortfall in the static NPV.

A lease enables management to defer investment. If the fast ship/ferry operator had been able to obtain a time charter (an operating lease) or an option to buy (or an option on a financial lease) from the shipbuilder and was able to defer a commitment to purchase until there was more certainty regarding oil prices, or other market conditions then the ferry/ship operator would have acquired a valuable real option (to defer). Similarly a terminal may lease equipment before committing to buy, awaiting the necessary growth in throughput to make the investment profitable.

3.2.6 Option to switch (output or input), location options

Product or input flexibility is a valuable option for management. With an option to switch, management can change the output mix (product flexibility) if prices or demand change or alternately, the same output can be produced using different types of inputs (input flexibility). For instance, Kulatilaka[20] found that the value of the flexibility provided by an industrial dual-fired steam boiler that can switch between alternative energy inputs (natural gas and oil), as relative prices fluctuate, far exceeded the incremental cost of a single-fuel alternative.

In fact, because of the existence of the switch option, the firm should be willing to pay a positive premium for flexible technology over a rigid alternative that confers no or less choice. In the maritime industry there are many examples where management has opted for technology which allowed flexibility in output (product switch option) or choice of inputs (input switch option). In the 1970s a cement carrier was introduced into service on the Australian coast which could switch between diesel and compressed natural gas. In a greener world, the ability to use renewable resources to power vessels has been welcomed. The Solar Sailor can switch between wind, solar and diesel-electric power sources or can use a combination of all three, depending on weather conditions. Many ports/terminals opt for more expensive technology which allows flexibility in output (output switch), e.g. cranes with flexibility to service both panamax and post-panamax vessels. These investments may appear expensive at the time of purchase but the true valuation has included a (product or input) switch option.

Closely linked to switch options are Location Options. Multinational manufacturing firms are sensitive to changes in exchange rates and switch production inputs to choose, ex-post, the lowest input mix (input switch option) (Kugut and Kulatilaka[21]). Companies, such as Nike have moved production sites from one country to another to reduce costs and maximise profits as exchange rates, labour costs and capital incentives change. Shipping is a service industry sensitive to exchange rates. Exchange rates affect export competitiveness. The changing pattern of trade changes the demand for shipping services. However vessels can be re-routed or positioned in a new trade. Ships, in contrast to other capital intensive investments usually have low "asset specificity" (Bendall and Manger[7]) and can be switched (output switch) easily to a new trade. A vessel owner has thus acquired a valuable switch option which is nested in the initial cost of the ship.

In an earlier paper on investment evaluation in the maritime industry and financing implications, Bendall and Manger[22] developed the Fama and Jensen[23] approach of ranking projects by "asset specificity". The authors suggested that projects were not arrayed by finance providers on NPV terms, but rather in terms of "asset specificity". Debt is contractual and debt holders will exercise their rights to displace management and appoint a receiver, if the project turns sour. Whether they do so will depend on the degree to which the underlying assets of the debt contract are re-deployable, since the value of the pre-emptive claim declines as the degree of asset specificity deepens. As a consequence the terms of debt financing will be adjusted according to the differential liquidity of the investment.

3.3 Valuing real options

Early researchers (Myers,[24] Kester,[25] amongst others) suggested the existence of an extra factor, a real option, to explain valuation and investment outcome inconsistencies particularly for investments where there were strategic or competitive aspects. However the quantitative origins of real options pricing derives from the financial markets with the seminal work of Black and Scholes[26] and Merton[27] in pricing financial options. The model is complex and off-putting to many practitioners (Trigeorgis[16]). Cox, Ross and Rubinstein's[28] binomial approach presented a more simplified methodology by valuating financial options in discrete time

Although the Black Scholes' model is mathematically challenging and the assumptions necessary too restrictive for pricing of real options the principles are useful in developing an understanding of real option valuation. The basic variables in their "closed form" financial option pricing model are the value of the underlying asset; the exercise price; the time to expiration of the option; the volatility (standard deviation) of the underlying risky asset and the risk free rate of interest over the life of the option.

In the case of a real option the underlying risky asset is the value of the investment or project. If the value of the project rises so too would the value of the option. The exercise price is the amount needed to exercise the option i.e. the additional investment costs say in a multistage project. Note that in the case of a call options, as the value of the exercise price increases, the value of the option decreases but increases the value of the option in the case of a put. As the time to expiration (maturity of the option) increases so too does the value of the option. This makes intuitive sense in situations where there is a great deal of uncertainty. Obviously the longer the time there is to delay the investment decision the more information is likely to become available. The value of the option is therefore sensitive to the degree of uncertainty or riskiness (volatility) of the underlying asset. Again this makes sense if we understand that the payoff of the call option depends on the value of the underlying asset exceeding its exercise price. This is more likely to occur if volatility increases. Lastly the value of the option increases if the risk free rate rises as it increases the time value of money advantage in deferring the investment cost until more information is known.

The pricing of options was further facilitated by Cox and Ross[29] who recognised that an option can be replicated (to create a "synthetic" option) from an equivalent portfolio of traded securities. The replicating portfolio approach is based on the Law of One Price which simply states that to prevent arbitrage (riskless) profits two assets with the same payoffs ("twin security[30]" or "twin asset[31]") in every state of nature are perfect substitutes (i.e., perfectly correlated) with the underlying risky asset and therefore have the same price (value). The risk-neutral probability approach is mathematically equivalent .A hedge portfolio is created, composed of one share in the underlying risky asset and a short position in "m" shares of the option being priced. The hedge ratio m is riskless as loss on the underlying asset is offset by the gain on the option (and vice versa) – hence risk free.

Kasanen and Trigeorgis[32] maintain that real options can in principle be valued in a similar manner to financial options, even though they may not be traded, because the process of capital budgeting determines the value of the project's cash flows in the market. Copeland and Antikarov[12] point out the difficulties of finding a market based "twin asset," or "twin security" that is perfectly correlated with the underlying asset. Instead of searching for a perfectly correlated asset in the market they propose that the present value of the project itself be used as the value of the underlying asset. "What is better correlated with the project than the project itself?" The present value of the project without flexibility becomes the best unbiased estimate of the market value of the project were it a traded asset.[33]

The first step in real option valuation using the project itself as a "twin security" is to determine the NPV in the tradtional manner. The second step in the replicating portfolio approach is to model uncertainy using historical data, managerial estimates or Monte Carlo analysis to contruct an event tree. The next step is to incorporate into the analysis managerial flexibility to respond to new information, changing event trees into decsion trees. However this flexibility has altered the risk characteristics of the project, altering the cost of capital, so that the cash flows are discounted at the risk-free rate.[34] The total project is valued using algebra and spreadsheets.[35]

In summary, investment evaluation with embedded real options is independent of risk attitudes and capital market considerations. Actual probabilities are replaced by risk-neutral ones. Future cash flows (certainty equivalent payoffs) are discounted at the risk-free interest rate rather than using a weighted average cost of capital (risk adjusted discount rate). ROA does not calculate explicitly the risk-adjusted discount rate appropriate to the option component of the project's cash flows (which often is very difficult), but rather applies a no-arbitrage principle (the law of one price) which states that any two assets that yield the same cash flows in all future states of the world, must have the same price (present value). Thus, by using the techniques originally developed to value financial options, ROA properly can provide more accurate valuations

3.3.1 Real option valuation

The example, although simple, illustrates ROA valuation principles. It demonstrates how static NPV can underestimate the value of the project by not taking into account the embedded real option.

VALUING MARITIME INVESTMENTS

Assume that a firm is considering an initial investment costing $12,000. The value of the project in one year's time is dependent on the (currently unknown) demand for the product or service. If demand turns out to be high, the project will be worth $15,000; if demand turns out to be low, the project's value including the original investment would be only $10,000.[36] These high and low outcomes are equally likely, i.e., each occurs with a 50% probability (a 50:50 chance). The present value was determined by multiplying the value of the high and low outcomes by the respective probability and discounting by the risk adjusted discount rate of 12% (see Figure 1). The risk free rate is 5%. The parameters are summarised in Table 1.

Table 1: Parameters for expansion example

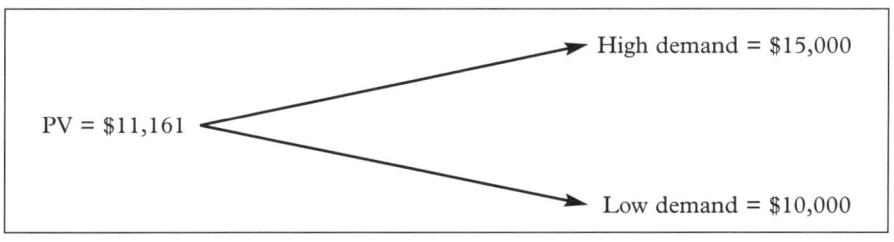

Parameter	Value
Cost of base project	$12,000
Value of base project in one year's time if demand is high	$15,000
Value of base project in one year's time if demand is low	$10,000
Probability of demand being high	50%
Cost (in one year) of expansion	$1,000
Proportional increase in base project value if expansion occurs	20%
Risk free rate of interest	5%
Risk-adjusted discount rate for base project	12%

Figure 1: Present value

```
                                    → High demand = $15,000
PV = $11,161  <
                                    → Low demand = $10,000
```

If the standard NPV analysis is applied by discounting the expected cash flows by the risk adjusted discount rate the base project's present value is $11,161.

$$PV = 0.5 \star \left(\frac{\$15,000}{1.12}\right) + 0.5 \star \left(\frac{\$15,000}{1.12}\right) = \$11,161$$

NPV = Present Value – Initial investment
    = $11 161 – $12 000
    = –$ 839 ⇨ negative. Do not invest

The NPV of –$839 is obtained by subtracting the initial capital cost of $12 000. In the absence of managerial flexibility (or real options), the DCF analysis rule leads to a rejection of the project as acceptance would destroy value in the firm. This decision ignores the ability of management to alter the investment in response to new information. Traditional NPV is unable to capture the value of embedded real options. Should demand conditions be more favourable than expected one year later, management would like the flexibility to expand (an expansion option). The traditional NPV analysis deals with this by implicitly assuming that management commits to a particular course of action (expand or not expand) at the time the project is launched, regardless of the conditions that subsequently prevail. This severely underestimates the value of the investment by ignoring the ability of management to respond to new information. ROA allows management to incorporate this flexibity into the investment valuation.

Having determined the base case NPV, the event (decision) tree is utilised to calculate the additional payoffs under both demand states should an additional investment be made in the next period. From Table 1, an additional investment of $1000 would increase the scale of operation by 20%. In high state demand the project's pay-off lifts to $18 000 ($15000*1.20), a net gain of $2 000. However, if low demand occurred the payoff would rise by the 20% to $12 000 ($10 000*1.20), a net gain of $1 000 (see Figure 2).

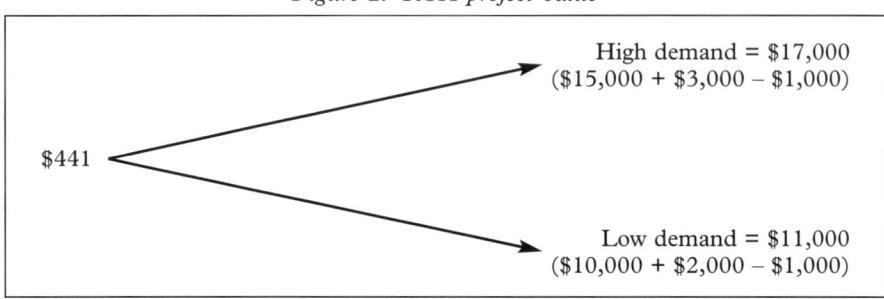

Figure 2: ROA project value

$441

High demand = $17,000
($15,000 + $3,000 − $1,000)

Low demand = $11,000
($10,000 + $2,000 − $1,000)

The next step in the ROA analyis is to identify a portfolio that exactly mimics high and low demand state-contingent payoffs. The ability to construct a "synthetic claim" or an equivalent replicating portfolio enables a solution for the present value to be independent of the actual probabilites, in this case (0.5) or the investor's risk attitudes (risk adjusted discount rate = 12%). In effect mangement can replicate the pay-off by contructing a portfolio using m units of the base case NPV and b units of the riskless bond (equivalent to financing the purchase by borrowing at the riskfree rate of 5%).

Therefore the replicating portfolio's pay-off equals

m*15 000 + b*1.05   in the high-demand state and
m*10 000 + b*1.05   in the low-demand state.

If this portfolio is to replicate the option, m and b must satisfy the two equations

15000 m + 1.05 b = $2000
10000 m + 1.05 b = $1000

The first equation says that the portfolio has the same payoff as the expansion option in the high-demand state; the second equation says that it has the same payoff as the expansion option in the low-demand state.. Solving the two linear equations with two unknown variable (*m* and *b*) gives *m* = 0.2000 and *b* = −$952.38. That is, owning a portfolio consisting of 0.2 units of the base case project and riskless borrowing of $952.38 is equivalent to holding the option to expand.

The ROA approach states that, since both have the same future payoffs, the present value of the expansion option is the same as the present value of the portfolio. Thus the ROA option value = (0.2*$11,161) − $952.38 = $1,280, and a project value of $441 (-$839 + $1,280), found by adding the real option value to the base case NPV.[37] As the value of the NPV is positive the project should be accepted. The base case NPV (value of the project without flexibility) undervalued the project by not including in the valuation the value of flexibility created by the expansion option.

Value of project with flexibility = Value of project without flexibility + Value of flexibility

The example used assumes that there are only two points in time and only two possible future states, and ignores various real-world complications. The tree only considers an expansion option.[38] However, the valuation principle can be extended to more complex and realistic situations. Although the analysis becomes more complicated, it relies on the same fundamental method; the principle that assets with the same future payoffs must have the same present value.

4. APPLICATION OF ROA TO AN INVESTMENT IN FAST CARGO SHIPS

4.1 Fast cargo ships valuation (base case)

Worldwide globalisation trends and a growing awareness of the importance of logistics management by global companies are being translated into demand for fast and reliable shipping Capital costs for operators are increasing as investments in new larger tonnage continues. This drive for economies of scale, particularly in east-west container routes, means that operators need to minimise port calls and increase the number of voyages per year to maximise productivity. Alliances have pooled their collective assets to provide cost effective vessel deployment by rationalising vessel routing. Major ports have become entrepot centres, fed by feeder ships.

The drive for seamless supply chains and the growth of perishable and high valued cargo has also led to an interest in investing in high speed vessels for a number of short sea applications. Bendall and Stent[39] developed an optimisation model to determine the profitability of a hub and spoke feeder operation based in South East Asia. The model calculated the optimum number of ships required to meet the given distribution task, the most profitable deployment of the fleet and the profitability of the service.

The regional feeder service evaluated was based on Singapore with spokes to Semerang (647 NM), Surabaya (707 NM), Penang, (395 NM), Klang (215

NM) Laem Chabang (831 NM) and Tanjong Priok (527 NM). In the study it was assumed that a finite number of TEUs per week were available at any one port and that demand to and from each port was a function of the service frequency to that port. The optimising model found that it would be most profitable to invest in one ship and to schedule the vessel for five voyages from Singapore to Klang and one multiple port visit Singapore–Penang–Klang–Singapore per week. Services to Semerang, Surabaya, Laem Chabang were found to be sub-optimal and if included, profitability would diminish.

Although the model indicated that a one ship service was optimal, the shipowner may choose to put an additional vessel into service for a number of reasons such as keeping a competitor out or perhaps to position the company to take advantage of some proposed development in the port or hinterland or even that the company has another vessel currently not in service. A "what if" analysis was conducted using this model to see the effect on the number of ports serviced if the operator employed two vessels. However, although the number of ports serviced increased, profitability fell. An NPV analysis conducted over five year horizon found at 10% cost of capital was $12.9million for the one ship operation.

4.2 Fast cargo ship ROA valuation – one vessel service[40]

The NPV calculated is equivalent to the static or inflexible NPV discussed above. Revenue was determined from implicit assumptions concerning a pre-determined operating strategy and demand. Static NPV analysis cannot take into account uncertainty and strategic considerations and so there is no allowance in the standard NPV calculation for the operator to value his/her ability to alter the project in any way should market conditions change.

If we introduce uncertainty into the model by allowing demand to be stochastically determined, that is based on a probability distribution rather than given, then the NPV falls to $7.7million

However, the ship operator still does not have the ability to alter the scale of operation in response to changing market conditions. If for instance the demand for the high speed service was less than expectations and revenue falls so that the financing costs of the ship are no longer covered and losses are being incurred, the ship operator would most likely withdraw from the service. ROA allows this flexiblity to be incorporated into the investment decisions.

Value of project with flexibility = Value of project without flexibility + Value of flexibility

When the value of the option is included the NPV for the project rises to $13.4 million. The value of the real option is $5.6million (the difference between the NPV value of the project with flexibilty and the value of the ship with stochastic demand but no flexibility to alter the scale of operation. The project is undervalued if the value of the real option is not included. This is an example of the Option to Abandon discussed in Section 3.2.3

NPV with flexibility = $13,370,745 = $7,746,195 + $5,624,640

Table 2: Valuation – one vessel service

NPV deterministic demand	NPV stochastic demand	NPV stochastic demand	Value of real option to abandon
Inflexible $12,862,337	Inflexible $7,746,105	Flexible $13,370,745	$5,624,640

4.3 Fast cargo ship ROA valuation – two vessel service

The two ship service with deterministic demand base case NPV was $1.7million. Again if we allow demand to be stochastic but give the operator no flexibility to alter the project once begun, the NPV falls to $8.5million. Note this is negative and the NPV decision rule would say do not invest as value in the company will be destroyed.

If we allow the ship operator the flexibility to withdraw from serive at any time should revenues not cover financing costs, the results are more dramatic than for the one ship service. These results demonstrate clearly how ROA is a powerful investment decision making tool. The value of the flexibility, or abandonment option, is $12.5million. The NPV is now positive, however still less than the NPV with flexibility for a one vessel service as determined by the optimising model (see Table 3).

NPV with flexibility = $4,078,709 = –$8,470,449 + $12,549,208

Table 3: Valuation – two vessel service

NPV deterministic demand	NPV stochastic demand	NPV stochastic demand	Value of real option to abandon
Inflexible $1,692,677	Inflexible –$8,470,449	Flexible $4,078,709	$12,549,208

5. CONCLUSION

Real options are persuasive and valuable and are an essential tool to value investments under uncertainty for decision makers in highly capital intensive industries, such as the maritime industry. The standard capital budgeting techniqes cannot capture the value of management flexibility to respond to changes in market conditions, forcing mangers to rely heavily on qualitative "strategic" judgment (managerial experience) when valuing investment opportunities. ROA is conceptually sound and will benefit companies in making investment decisions.

ROA was used to value the abandonment option for an investment in high speed vessels for a hub and spoke feeder service based on Singapore. The ROA analysis demonstrated that the tradtional NPV analysis failed to capture managerial flexibility in major capital investments. This problem can lead to underestimating the value of a project and perhaps to under investment and opportunity loss. The value of flexibility or real options should be included in investment decsion making under uncertainy.

ABBREVIATIONS

CCA   Contingent Claims Analysis
DCF   Discounted Cash Flow
DTA   Decision Tree Analysis
MAD   Marketed Asset Disclaimer
NPV   Net Present Value
OTC   Over the Counter
PV   Present Value
ROA   Real Options Analysis

ENDNOTES

1. Surveys of international corporate practice indicate over 90% of firm's use the NPV rule and that for most firms this is the primary method of project evaluation. See Kester, G.W., Chang, R., Echanis, E., Haikal, S., Isa, M., Skully, M., Tsui, K., and Wang, C. (1999): "Capital Budgeting Practices in the Asia-Pacific Region", *Financial Practice and Education* 9, pp. 25–33.
2. Teisberg, E.O (1995): "Methods for Evaluating Capital Investment Decsions Under Uncertainty", Trigeorgis, L. (ed.) *Real Options in Capital Investment. Models, Strategies and Applications* (London, Praeger).
3. Hodder, J., and Riggs (1985): "Pitfalls in Evaluating Risky Projects", *Harvard Business Review*, January–February, pp. 128–135.
4. Hertz, D. (1964) "Risk Analysis in Capital Investment", *Harvard Business Review*, 42:1, pp. 95–106.
5. Magee, J. (1964): "How to Use Decision Trees in Capital Investments", *Harvard Business Review*, September–October.
6. Lai, V.S., and Trigeorgis, L. (1995): "The Strategic Capital Budgeting Process: A Review of Theories and Practice", Trigeorgis, L. (ed.) *The Capital Budgeting Process Real Options in Capital Investment: Models, Strategies and Applications* (London, Praeger), pp. 69–96.
7. Bendall, H.B., and Manger, G. (1991): "Corporate Investment Decisions: What are the relevant criteria?", *Corporate Management*, 43:3, May–June, pp. 64–69.
8. Ansoff, H.I. (1965): *Corporate Strategy* (New York, Freeman Press).
9. Myers, S.C. (1987): "Finance Theory and Financial Strategy", *Midland Corporate Finance Journal*, 5:1, pp. 6–13.
10. Pinches, G.E. (1982): "Myopia, Capital Budgeting and Decision Making", *Financial Management*, 11:3, Autumn, pp. 6–19.
11. Students of financial theory will recognise the similarity with the application of financial options. An option is a financial derivative traded on exchanges or in the over the counter market, OTC. The option gives the right but not the obligation to buy or sell an underlying asset or income stream in the future. It enables the holder to benefit from upside gain while limiting downside losses to the price paid for the option, its premium.
12. Copeland, T., and Antikarov, V. (2001): *Real Options* (New York, Texere).
13. A call option is the right, but not the obligation to buy an asset. In this case the asset is the increased scale of operation. An American option can be exercised at any time before the maturity date of the option.

14. However, although the value of flexibility is always positive, the price (premium) paid for the real option may exceed the additional value added to the basic NPV. In this case the NPV would be negative and the investment would not go ahead For example a dual fired engine system may offer the ability to switch fuel inputs but the cost of the sophisticated technology may exceed the benefit of this flexibility.
15. The name of the real option simply describes its purpose however there is variation in the naming of the real options by analysts. See Section 3.2.
16. Trigeorgis, T. (2000): "Real Options and Financial Decision-Making", *Contemporary Finance Digest*, 3, pp. 5–42.
17. McDonald, R., and Siegel, D. (1985): "Investment and the Valuation of Firms When there is an Option to Shut Down", *International Economic Review*, 26:2, pp. 331–349.
18. Dixit, A., and Pindyck, R. (1994): *Investment Under Uncertainty* (Princeton, Princeton University Press).
19. Dixit, A., and Pindyck, R. (1995): "The Options Approach to Capital Investment", *Harvard Business Review*, pp. 105–115.
20. Kulatilaka, N. (1993): "The Value of Flexibility: The Case of a Dual-Fuel Industrial Steam Boiler", *Financial Management*, 22:3, pp. 271–279.
21. Kugut, B., and Kulatilaka, N. (1994): "Operating Flexibility, Global Manufacturing and the Option Value of a Multinational Network", *Management Science*, 40:1, pp. 123–140.
22. Bendall, H.B., and Manger, G. (1988): "Corporate Govenance, Capital Structure and Budgeting: Preliminary Evidence From the Maritime Industry", *Inaugural Australasian Finance and Banking Conference*, Australian Graduate School of Management, Sydney, December.
23. Fama, E., and Jensen, M. (1982): "Agency Problems and Residual Claims", *Graduate School of Business, University of Chicago Working Paper 88*.
24. Myers, S.C. (1977): "Determinants of Corporate Borrowing", *Journal of Financial Economics*, 5:2, November, pp. 147–176.
25. Kester, W.C. (1984): "Today's Options for Tomorrow's Growth", *Harvard Business Review*, March–April, pp. 153–160.
26. Black, F., and Scholes, M. (1973): "The Pricing of Options and Corporate Liabilities", *Journal of Political Economy*, 81, May–June, pp. 637–659.
27. Merton, R.C. (1973): "Theory or Rational Option Pricing", *Bell Journal of Economics and Management Science*, 4, pp. 141–183.
28. Cox, J., Ross, S., and Rubenstein, M. (1979): "Option Pricing: A Simplified Approach", *Journal of Financial Economics*, 53:1, pp. 220–263.
29. Cox, J., and Ross, S. (1976): "The Valuation of Options for Alternative Stochastic Processes", *Journal of Financial Economics*, 3:1, pp. 145–166.
30. Stock price of a similar (perfectly correlated) non-levered company with the same risk characteristics.
31. For example, the demand for oil may be used as a "twin product" when valuing options associated with tankers, if volatilities are similar.
32. Kasanen, E., and Trigeorgis, L. (1993): "A Market Utility approach to Invesmtnet Evaluation", *European Journal of Operations Research. Special Issue on Financial Modelling*, 74:2, April, pp. 294–309.
33. Copeland and Antikarov (see note 12) call this assumption that the base project can be used as the marketable asset, Marketed Asset Disclaimer, MAD.
34. Note ROA differs from Decision Tree Analysis, DTA, which discounts at the cost of capital.
35. Complex problems usually require some knowledge of stochastic calculus. However these calculations can be approximated in a simple lattice form on a spreadsheet (Copeland and Antikarov, note 12).
36. The values of the project's payoffs in year 1 are assumed for illustration purposes.
37. The risk neutral probability approach yielded the same project value of $1280. The

PV of the hedge portfolio is multiplied by the risk-free rate and set equal to the payout for the high (up) and low (down) demand state. The PV of the option is calculated using risk neutral probabilities, (pu = 0.3438, pd = 0.6563). Note these risk-neutral probabilities are not the same as the objective probabilities in Table 1. The Present Value of the option is equal to the expected payoffs multiplied by (risk neutral) probabilities to adjust them for their risk.
38. An option to abandon or an option to switch may be appropriate but are abstracted from this example.
39. Bendall, H.B., and Stent, A.F. (2001): "A Scheduling Model for High Speed Container Service: A Hub and Spoke Short Sea Application", *International Journal of Maritime Economics*, 3 September, pp. 262–277.
40. This example is adapted from Bendall, H.B., and Stent, A.F. (2002): "Investment Decision Strategies in an Uncertain World: a Real Options Approach to Investments in the Maritime Industry", *ICHCA 2002, 26th Bienniel Conference*, Yokohama, Japan, 13–15 April, pp. 197–218.

CHAPTER 30

BUSINESS RISK MEASUREMENT AND MANAGEMENT IN THE CARGO CARRYING SECTOR OF THE SHIPPING INDUSTRY

Manolis G. Kavussanos

Athens University of Economics and Business, Athens, Greece. E-mail: *mkavus@aueb.gr*

1. INTRODUCTION

Risk management in an industry which is riddled with cyclicalities in its rates and prices and which has made and destroyed millionaires over the years is extremely important. The issue has been discussed in Gray,[1,2] comparing traditional methods of hedging, as he calls the choice of contract during ship operation,[3] with the 'new' instruments that appeared in the market at the time. The latter were the futures and forward freight contracts, which were launched by Baltic Exchange in London and the International Futures Exchange in Bermuda, trading BIFFEX (Baltic International Freight Futures Exchange) and INTEX contracts for the dry bulk and tanker sectors, respectively.

A long time has gone since then without a major review of the issue. In the mean time a number of developments have occurred, including the restructuring, renaming and the eventual abandonment of the Baltic Freight Index in 2002 – the underlying commodity on which BIFFEX contracts have been trading on. The development of Over the Counter(OTC) Freight Forward Agreements(FFA) and the appearance of options and swaps can be added to these developments, all of which have major implications for the way risk is managed in the industry.

At the same time research has been published which has established formally a number of relationships not fully worked out previously empirically, and has uncovered new results on a number of important issues in the topic of risk measurement and management in the shipping industry. For instance, Kavussanos[4–8] measures for the first time the (time varying) volatility of ship prices and freight rates by sector and type of contract, allowing, thus, for formal comparison of risk levels between sectors and freight contracts at each point in time. This paper aims to provide a review of these issues in order to help the reader see where we currently stand.

Broadly speaking, the owner of the assets, ships, is faced with a number of commercial decisions. They include decisions on: (1) whether to enter the shipping industry by buying or leasing ships?, (2) what kind of ships to purchase?, (3) when to buy the ships and when to sell them?, (4) how to finance the purchase of the assets – debt, equity, shareholding, etc., (5) once owning the vessels, where to operate them and what kind of contract to seek for them?, and (6) whether to use financial instruments, such as futures and forward contracts, to manage the risk in such markets as the freight, bunker, foreign exchange and interest rate market? These are all real decisions that the shipowner is faced with in everyday decision making. They all amount to viewing ships as investments – as assets in portfolios, which generate a stream of cash flows by operating the ships and a possible capital gain by selling the assets at a price higher than what is bought. Given that commercial investments have risks attached, one can immediately see that the above issues are highly relevant for decision making.

The issues raised become more evident when examining the shipowner's balance-sheet, in Table 1. A shipowner's cash flow problem is outlined in the table, where

Cash flow = revenue – fixed costs – variable costs

Table 1: Shipowner's cash flow in spot and T/C markets

	Spot market	**Time charter market**
Revenue	Voyage hire	T/C hire
Fixed costs	less: operating costs	less: operating costs
Variable costs	less: voyage costs	–
	Operating earnings	**Operating earnings**
Fixed costs	less: fixed capital costs	less: fixed capital costs
	Capital gain	**Capital gain**
Asset play	plus: profit/loss from buying and selling the vessel	plus: profit/loss from buying and selling the vessel
	Cash flow	**Cash flow**

Notes: (1) *Operating costs* include manning, repairs and maintenance, stores and lubes, insurance, administration. (2) *Voyage costs* include broking commission, fuel costs, port charges, tugs, canal dues, etc. Fuel costs form the largest part of these, and are subject to the highest fluctuations. (3) *Capital costs* refer to debt servicing through capital repayment.

Fluctuations in revenue or costs can cause fluctuations in operating earnings. This may be due to changes in revenue, which is affected by changes in demand for freight services and by changes in freight rates, or because of changes in voyage and operating costs (e.g., changes in bunker prices, wage rates, exchange rates, etc.). Operating costs include manning, repairs and maintenance, stores and lubes, insurance, administration, and are thought to be relatively constant, rising in line with inflation. In contrast to time charter markets, operations in the spot market involve voyage cost payments by the shipowner. Thus, apart from fluctuations in the freight market, owners are exposed to fluctuations in voyage costs, the main part of which are bunker prices. This is one of the reasons, why spot markets are deemed riskier than time charter markets. The others relate to the nature of the relationship of spot and time charter rates, which leads us to expect that spot rates trade at a premium to time charters to compensate for the higher risk involved when operating the ships spot. The relationship is that, say one year time charter rates, must be the sum of a series of expected (monthly) spot rates plus a risk premium. This is discussed fully in Kavussanos and Alizadeh,[9] and also later on in the chapter.

The volatility in freight rates, also examined later in the chapter, and in Kavussanos,[4–8] could be a source of risk. From the above table though it is apparent that voyage costs – in particular bunker prices – are the source of certain volatility apparent when operating in the spot market, which does not affect the owner when operating in the time charter market. Alizadeh, Kavussanos and Menachof[10] examine ways of mitigating bunker price risks through derivatives trading. They are discussed later in the chapter. Gray[1] discusses how selection of contract type can reduce freight risks, and Kavussanos[4-8] examines the same and other issues at the empirical level. The use of freight futures contracts (BIFFEX) for freight risk management has been examined in the past by Cullinane,[11] Haralambides[12,13] and Kavussanos and Nomikos.[14-18] Finally, with the decline of interest in BIFFEX freight forward agreements, FFA's, and other financial instruments have provided the alternative for freight risk management. The issue is examined in Kavussanos and Visvikis[19,20] and in Batchelor, Kavussanos and Visvikis.[21,22] These are discussed later in the chapter.

The other source of risk for the owner apparent in the table, is the interest rate risk. This relates to the fixed capital charges associated with debt finance. They fluctuate with interest rates. The higher the debt-equity ratio in a ship, the greater is the financial leverage, and the more is at risk the residual cash flow. Thus, financial leverage compounds the risks created by operating leverage.

A further source of risk comes from the fluctuation in the value of the asset, ship. Often, owners are involved in asset play, see Stopford.[23] They see ships as assets whose prices fluctuate, and offer the possibility of a capital gain or loss. This is shown in the last part of the earlier table. Fluctuations in ship prices then influence the risk level involved in the investment. A major part of this chapter is concerned with this issue, which has been analysed in papers such as Kavussanos.[4-8]

In all the above one has to add the exchange rate risk, which is present in such an international industry. It affects the owner's cash flow through a number of routes, including payment of freight rates, voyage expenses, purchasing of the asset, etc. Interest rate and exchange rate risks fall outside the scope of this chapter. Sophisticated derivative instruments exist in the finance profession, which enable interested parties to deal with these risks.

2. RISK/RETURN TRADE-OFFS IN SHIPPING

In making commercial decisions the owner has in mind that greater rewards usually come by undertaking higher risks. Usually such risks are measured by the volatility of the variable a decision has to be made for. For example, because freight rates fluctuate widely, say from month to month, taking a position in the market in a particular month can produce substantial gains or losses depending on what happens in subsequent months. Fluctuations in freight rates around their average values over a period of time may be used typically as measures of freight risk; technically, by their variance or by its square root, the standard deviation. High (low) standard deviations reflect high (low) volatility in rates and of the risks involved.[24]

Considering shipowners as asset holders who want to maximise return and minimise risk on their portfolio of shipping assets, can they do anything to mitigate the risk involved in their shipping investments and in operations resulting from freight rate fluctuations? Say the shipowner is a specialist in the tanker sector. Then he is faced with two important decisions which can affect the risk/return position of his portfolio: (1) what size ships to invest on?, and (2)for a given investment, whether to operate the vessels in the spot or in the period (time charter) market? The issue of what size ships to invest on, if approached from the pure asset-play point of view may be answered by considering the risk-return profiles of different size vessels.

Vessel size considerations are important since the markets for each size are distinct in terms of the rewards and risks they carry, and so is positioning in the spot or time-charter market. From a different point of view, Glen[25] has shown that the industry is divided into sub-markets. Kavussanos[4-8] shows that these markets are distinct in terms of their risk return profiles. As a result, investments in different size vessels can be thought of as having the same portfolio diversifying effects as different stocks included in an investor's portfolio. To see that, consider a possible disaggregation of the cargo carrying shipping industry.

3. MARKET SEGMENTATION OF THE SHIPPING INDUSTRY

3.1 General cargo and bulk cargo movements

The *parcel size distribution* (*PSD*) of each commodity determines the shipping consignment of the cargo, see Stopford.[23] Some commodities are typically moved in larger sizes than others. For example, iron ore and grain consignments are much larger than phosphate rock or bauxite and alumna. Furthermore, the consignment size or PSD of each commodity changes over time and may be different on different routes. The PSD depends on: (1) Commodity demand and shipping supply economics (e.g., low value goods move in large consignments), (2) Transport distances (consignment is directly proportional to distance) and transport system restrictions (e.g., limited draft in ports, regulations), (3) Vessel availability. Consignments of over 2,000–3,000 tons can fill a whole ship (or hold) rather than part of a ship, and are transported in bulk. Smaller consignments, which fill only part of the ship (or hold) move as general cargo.

Bulk cargoes transport mainly raw materials and are transported on 1-ship 1-cargo basis. They are further sub-divided into liquid cargo and dry cargo. Liquid cargo includes crude oil, oil products, chemicals (e.g. caustic soda), vegetable oils and wine. Dry Cargo is broadly divided in three categories: (a) majors – that is, iron ore, coal, grain, bauxite and phosphates, (b) minors – that is, steel, steel products, cement, sugar, gypsum, non ferrous metal ores, salt, sulphur, forest products, wood chips and chemicals, (c) specialist bulk cargoes requiring specific handling or storage requirements such as heavy lift, cars, timber, refrigerated cargo. The ships involved in bulk cargo transportation are tankers, bulk carriers, combined carriers (they carry either dry or liquid bulk) and specialist bulk vessels. Bulk cargoes constitute 2/3 of seaborne trade movements, and are carried mainly by tramp ships, which constitute 3/4 of the world's merchant fleet. These are vessels which move around the world seeking employment in any place/route of the globe. Bulk ships usually carry one cargo in one ship at rates negotiated individually for the service provided.

General cargo, is also dry cargo, in general, but is not transported in bulk. A large part of general cargo is transported in containers, multipurpose and other specialised ships (RoRo, car carriers, etc.). General cargo (1/3 of seaborne trade) moves in either tramp ships or liners; the latter provide a regular, scheduled service transporting small cargo consignments at fixed tariff levels between areas of the world.

The economics of each type of transport service are different. For example, oligopolistic conditions prevail in liner markets, while conditions of perfect competition guide tramp markets.

3.2 Bulk-cargo segmentation

For analysis, dry and liquid bulk cargoes may be further subdivided according to the PSD functions of the products carried. The PSD function depends on the maximum size delivery an industry is able or willing to accept at any one time. In some industries stockpiles are around 10–15K tons, so a delivery of 50K tons is too large. Physical limitations on ship size draw a line between groups. For instance, Suez, Panamax, etc. This is because size determines the type of trade the ship will be involved in, in terms of type of cargo and route; this is a result of the different PSD's of commodities and the port and seaway restrictions for certain size ships. Design features are important. For example, cargo handling gear(cranes), pumping capacity and segregation of cargo tanks in tankers; certain ports in developing countries cannot be used, for example, from ships which do not have cargo handling gear. Also coating of tanks and ballast spaces are distinguishing factors. Table 2 and Table 3 present the sub-markets that are distinguished for dry and liquid bulk.

Capesize vessels (around 120,000 dead-weight tons(dwt)) transport iron ore mainly from South America and Australia and coal from North America and Australia. Panamax vessels (around 65,000dwt) are used primarily to carry

Table 2: Dry bulk market segmentation by vessel size

Vessel type/market	Vessel size	Cargo type
Capesize	80,000+ dwt	Iron ore, Coal
Panamax	50,000–79,999dwt	Coal, grain, bauxite and larger minor bulk parcels
Handymax	30,000–49,999dwt	Minor bulks and smaller parcels of major bulks such as grain, coal and bauxite.
Handy	10,000–29,999dwt	Minor bulks and smaller parcels of major bulks such as grain, coal and bauxite.

Minor bulks: Steel, steel products, cement, sugar, gypsum, non ferrous metal ores, salt, sugar, sulphur, forest products, wood chips and chemicals.

Table 3: Liquid bulk market segmentation by vessel size

Vessel type/market	Vessel size	Cargo type
Ultra-large crude carriers (ULCCs)	300,000 + dwt	Crude Oil
Very-large crude carriers (VLCCs)	200,000–299,999 dwt	Crude Oil
Suezmax	100,000–199,999 dwt	Crude Oil
Aframax tankers	70,000–99,999 dwt	Crude Oil
Large product tankers	50,000–69,999 dwt	Oil products Sometimes crude oil
Small product tankers (coasters)	10,000–49,999 dwt	Oil products Sometimes crude oil

grain and coal from North America and Australia. Handysize vessels (around 30,000dwt) transport grain, mainly from North America, Argentina and Australia, and minor bulk products – such as sugar, fertilisers, steel and scrap, forest products, non-ferrous metals and salt – virtually from all over the world.

Smaller vessels such as Handy and Handymax in the dry bulk sector are, in general, geared so that they can load and unload cargo in ports without sophisticated handling facilities. They can approach more ports compared to larger vessels. As ports of the world have been developed the new generation of Handymax vessels are carrying more and more of the trade the Handys carry. The same is also true in the liquid bulk sector; the very large vessels trade in only 3/4 routes as the draught restrictions in ports and the storage facilities required ashore are very large to accommodate them and their cargoes. The smaller vessels are more flexible in terms of routes and trades they are involved in.

3.3 General(dry) cargo segmentation

When general dry cargo is not moved by dry-bulk ships it is transported by liners. The following distinctions are common. Container ships, RoRo, Multi Purpose MPP(Single-deck, multi-deck, Semi-containers), Barge Carrying vessels(BCV). Other specialised vessels include Refrigerated(Reefers), Car-carriers, Cement carriers, Heavy lift, Ore carriers, Vehicle carriers, LPG tankers, etc. Within the liner trades there is a move towards containerisation at the expense of non-unitised cargo which used to be transported in MPP ships. Containerships themselves have sub-markets according to size. These are shown in Table 4.

Table 4: Container market segmentation by vessel size

Vessel type/market	Ship size, TEU	Speed in knots
Feeder	0–499	13.8
Feedermax	500–999	16.4
Handy	1000–1999	18.5
Sub-Panamax	2000–2999	20.8
Panamax	3000–3999	22.2
Post-Panamax	>4000	24

Just as with dry-bulk, each of these sub-markets has its own economic characteristics, and the risks and rewards involved for the shipowner and the charterers are different.

4. COMPARISON OF VOLATILITIES OF SECOND HAND SHIP PRICES

Since smaller vessels can approach more ports and can switch between different trades/routes they are more flexible for employment. They operate at higher unit costs compared to larger vessels requiring therefore higher freight rates. However, they are less risky than the larger vessels; the volatilities of their prices are lower. This is established in Kavussanos[4-8] who compares freight rate and ship price volatilities between different size vessels.

Having obtained data for freight rates and second hand Handysize, Panamax and Capesize vessel prices monthly returns and volatilities are calculated. Then volatilities are compared between sizes. Investments in vessels with higher volatilities are deemed riskier compared to those with lower ones. Tables 5 and 6 show the results for the dry bulk and the tanker sectors, respectively.

Table 5: F-statistics for equality of unconditional variances in dry bulk ship prices

	Cape v Panamax	Cape v Handy	Panamax v Handy
F-statistic	1.635	1.842	1.127

Notes: (1) These statistics follow the F distribution with (195, 195) degrees of freedom. (2) Critical values of the statistics at the 5% and 1% levels are 1.26 and 1.36 respectively. (3) Sample period 1979:5–1995:8. Source: Kavussanos.[7]

Table 6: F-statistics for equality of unconditional variances in tanker ship prices

	VLCC v Suezmax	VLCC v Aframax	Suezmax v Aframax
F-statistic	1.84	2.71	1.47

Notes: (1) These statistics, which are defined as $F = SD_1^2/SD_2^2 \sim F(n-1, m-1)$, where SD_1^2 and SD_2^2 are the sample variances and follow the F distribution with (n-1, m-1) degrees of freedom; in this case (166, 166). (2) Critical values of the statistics at the 5% and 1% levels are 1.29 and 1.44 respectively. (3) Sample period 1980:2–1993:12. Source: Kavussanos.[5]

Broadly speaking, for asset players who choose to have ships in their portfolio of assets they can reduce risk by investing in smaller vessels, compared to larger ones. Moreover, the results make sense as explained earlier. The smaller vessels are more flexible as assets. They have lower risk of unemployment in adverse market conditions, as they can be switched more easily between routes and trades in order to secure employment. In addition, the cargo size larger vessels carry makes them less useful for charterers requiring transportation of smaller quantities. This makes the demand for these vessels less flexible, and vessels cannot switch between sea-lanes and charterers as easily as their smaller counterparts. If anything happens (e.g., a political or economic change) in one of the routes the VLCC's operate this will have a significant impact in rates in the market, which is translated into high volatility in rates. As a consequence, the income stream from operations of smaller vessels, and their prices, as present values of the expected future income, are subject to less fluctuations in comparison to the larger vessels.

4.1 Dynamically adjusting volatilities

The two studies mentioned above, have gone a step further in the analysis of ship price volatilities. They introduce, for the first time in shipping, the class of Generalised Autoregressive Conditional Heteroskedasticity (GARCH) models of Engle[26] and Bolerslev,[27] to estimate time varying volatilities of ship prices. Thus, price volatilities are explained in terms of their past values, values of squared shocks to long-run equilibrium in each market, and possibly a set of exogenous factors. The general form of the augmented GARCH-X (p, q) model of Bollerslev[27] can be represented by the following equations

$$\Delta \ln P_t = \mu_{t-1} + \varepsilon_t \; ; \; \varepsilon_t \sim IN(0, h_t)$$

$$h_t = \alpha_0 + \sum_{i=1}^{p} \alpha_i \varepsilon^2_{t-i} + \sum_{j=1}^{q} \beta_j h_{t-j} + \delta Z_t \qquad (1)$$

$$LL = -(T/2) \ln h_t - (1/2h_t) \sum_{i=1}^{p} \alpha_i \varepsilon^2_{t-i}$$

where μ_{t-1} is the specification of the conditional mean, that is, of the change in the log of ship prices, $\Delta \ln P_t$, ε_t is a white noise error term with the usual classical properties and a time-varying variance h_t, which may include a set of exogenous factors, Z_t, and LL is the corresponding log-likelihood function after omitting the irrelevant constant. The parameters of interest are those included in μ_{t-1}, say $\phi(L)$, and the GARCH parameters α_0, α_i, β_j and δ and can be estimated by maximum likelihood methods.

The estimated time varying volatilities allow the measurement and comparison of volatilities at each point in time, rather than relying on the averages over the period examined as in Tables 5 and 6. Considering average volatilities (standard deviations) of freight rates over a period of time as indicators of risk levels provides a partial picture of the risk/return situation. This is because uncertainty in prices, is not constant over time. The patterns and relative levels of volatilities, at each point in time (market situation) can now be measured, and compared between size ships. Such estimates of time varying variances are also deemed important in the financial literature, as they may be used in the construction of dynamic portfolios of assets. These time varying volatilities for the tanker and dry bulk sub-sectors are shown in Figures 1 and 2, respectively.

This method of analysing volatilities and examining them graphically has allowed inferences for the dry bulk sector, such as that:

Volatilities, and thus risks, vary over time and across sizes; in particular, volatilities are high during and just after periods of large imbalances and shocks to the industry. These include the period of the oil crisis of the early 1980s, the recovery period of 1986-1989 and the Gulf crisis of the early 1990s. Panamax volatilities are driven by old "news", while new shocks are more important in

Figure 1: Price volatilities in the tanker sector

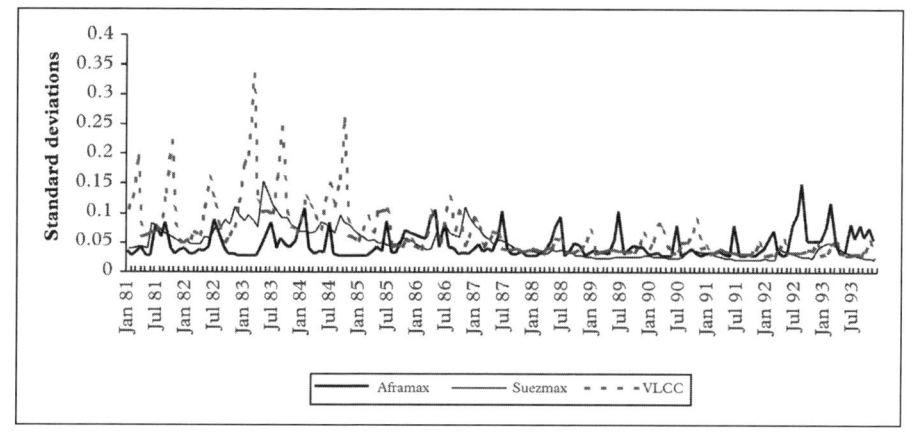

Figure 2: Price volatilities in the dry bulk sector

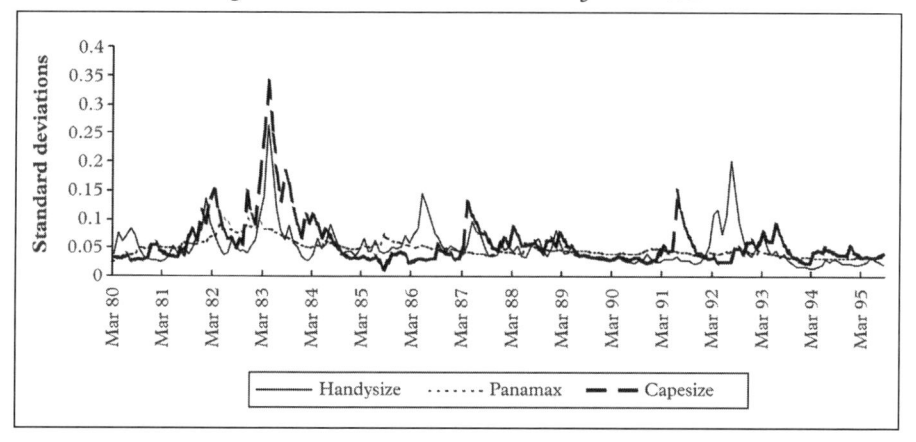

the Handy and Capesize markets. Also, conditional volatilities of Handysize and Panamax vessel prices are positively related to interest rates and Capesize volatilities to time-charter rates.

The three markets tend to respond together to external shocks, and yet quite differently, implying market segregation between different size ships. That is, there are some common driving forces of volatilities in different size markets, and yet there are idiosyncratic factors to each market that make each size-ship volatility move in its own way. These idiosyncratic factors relate to the type of trade each size ship is engaged in. Thus, volatility for Handysize and Capesize vessels has several hikes, while that for Panamax is smoother. This differing nature of volatilities over ship sizes is manifested in the GARCH alpha (news) coefficients being higher than the beta (persistence) coefficients for Capesize and Handysize vessels, while the opposite is true for Panamax.[28]

Regarding volatility levels, Capesize volatility lies in general above the volatilities of the other two sizes, except for two-three years in the mid-1980s.

Similarly, the Panamax volatility is, in general, at a level above Handysize, which, however, is exceeded at times by the hikes in the Handy volatility.

Similar results are reached by considering the time varying volatilities for the tanker sector. In addition, volatilities in the tanker sector and thus risks levels seem to be positively related to oil prices. The downward trends in volatilities observed in the dry bulk and tanker industry sub-sectors seem to indicate that risks in the shipping industry have decreased over time. It should also be mentioned that the availability of time varying volatility estimates for vessel prices, as with other assets in the financial literature, may be used as inputs in pricing derivative instruments such as options prices, etc.

5. COMPARISON OF VOLATILITIES OF SPOT AND TIME CHARTER RATES

Theoretically, ship prices are the present value of the expected stream of cash flows (profits) from their operation. The relationship has been investigated formally in Kavussanos and Alizadeh.[9] As a result of this theoretical relationship, comparison of freight rate volatilities by vessel size should reveal a similar relationship to that uncovered by examining the second hand prices. This is indeed the case. Kavussanos[6,8] shows that volatilities of spot rates and of time charter rates are smaller for smaller size vessels, compared to those of larger ones. Table 7 compares formally these volatilities in the tanker sector.

Table 7: Pairwise sample variances of time-charter (upper triangle) and spot (lower triangle) rates in tanker sub-markets

	Handymax (H)	**Aframax (A)**	**Suezmax (S)**	**VLCC (V)**
Handymax (H)		8.23*(H<A)	1.14 (H<S)	8.68*(H<V)
Aframax (A)	1.30*(H<A)		7.24*(A>S)	1.06(A<V)
Suezmax (S)	1.27*(H<S)	1.03(A>S)		7.64*(S<V)
VLCC (V)	2.68*(H<V)	2.05*(A<V)	2.11*(S<V)	

Notes: (1) 5% and 10% critical values for F (166, 166) are 1.29 and 1.22, respectively. (2) * indicates significance at the 10% level. (3) The symbol < indicates less than, while the symbol > indicates greater than. Source: Kavussanos.[6]

In both the spot and time charter markets the VLCC sector exhibits the highest volatility in rates compared to smaller sizes over the period examined. The Handymax volatilities are the lowest in both markets compared to other sizes. The Aframax and the Suezmax sectors show significantly larger volatilities in comparison to the Handymax sector and smaller ones compared to the VLCC in both the spot and the time-charter markets. However, the volatilities between the Aframax and Suezmax sectors are not statistically different between them.

The above findings, of the possible diversification effects that may be achieved by holding different size ships in a portfolio of assets have not been discussed in the literature previously. The studies by Kavussanos[4–8] have provided a formal justification of pursuing such strategies. In addition, these studies have also investigated, for the first time, empirically some well-known propositions regarding the possibility of operational risk reduction by choice of contract. Gray[1] discusses the consecutive risk reduction effects that are achieved by shipowners selecting to employ their vessels in markets such as voyage charter(spot), trip time charter, period time charter and in contracts of affreightment,[29] consecutively.

Table 8 compares, statistically, pair wise volatilities between the spot and the time-charter market for each size ship in the tanker sector. In all vessel sizes, but the Aframax, the spot rates are significantly more volatile compared to time-charters. In the Aframax size there is no significant difference between spot and time-charter volatilities. Once again the evidence seems to be consistent with a-priori expectations, in that the spot rates are much more exposed to the day-to-day market conditions in determining rates compared to time-charter rates. The latter, being theoretically the discounted stream of 12 months' expected spot rates, are smoother and this is reflected in the smaller volatilities in comparison to the one month spot rates, see Kavussanos and Alizadeh[9] for an empirical formulation of this relationship.

Table 8: Pairwise comparison of volatilities in Spot (FR) v Time-Charter (TC) rates of the tanker industry

Size	Handymax	Aframax	Suezmax	VLCC
Result	FR > TC*	FR < TC	FR > TC*	FR > TC*

Notes: * indicates statistical significance. See the notes in Table 7 for definitions.
Source: Kavussanos.[2]

It seems that the risk involved in operating tankers in the spot markets is greater than in the time-charter markets and this seems to hold irrespective of size.

5.1 Comparison of time varying freight volatilities over vessel sizes

Risks in the spot and time-charter tanker markets are a combination of industry-market risk and "idiosyncratic" risk (relating for example to the individual vessel size). As long as one is faced with more than one option over choices, then idiosyncratic risk may be diversified. The shipowner, for instance, may choose to use the spot instead of the time-charter market, or may decide on alternative size ships to invest upon. Decisions about this process takes place on a continuous basis. This is not possible by considering the averages of volatilities over a 10–15 year period. Monthly estimates of these volatilities, though, resolves the problem. The results in Kavussanos[4-8] enable this.

Consider first how the industry has been affected across markets by examining time varying risks in the spot and the time charter markets for the tanker and dry bulk sectors, as observed in Figures 3, 4, 5 and 6. A tendency for volatility clustering is observed. Volatility is high during and just after periods of large shocks and imbalances in the industry; such as during the 1980–1981 oil crises and the decline in demand for shipping services as the world economy slowed down following the second oil shock, the supply of oil restrictions imposed by the OPEC production ceiling in 1982/83, the targeting of ships in the Gulf in 1984, the sharp decline in oil prices in 1986 and the 1990–1991 period of the Gulf-war are particularly visible.

672 SHIPPING INVESTMENT AND FINANCE

Figure 3: Time charter volatilities by vessel size

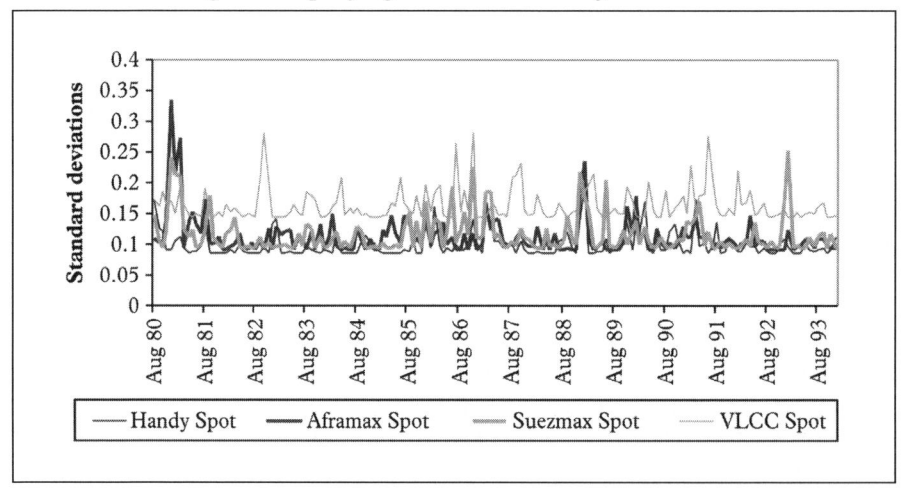

Figure 4: Spot freight rate volatilities by vessel size

The above incidents affected all markets and are manifested in patterns of risk, which, however, are specific to vessel sizes. In the tanker sector for instance, the VLCC sector seems to have the highest volatility and fluctuations are a lot sharper than any of the other sizes. The sector involves vessels trading in four routes, all lifting oil from the Gulf, which were severely disrupted in periods of crises. The Handymax volatility is the lowest in both the spot and time charter markets reflecting the steady trades this type of ships are involved in. The Suezmax and Aframax volatilities fluctuate between the Handymax and VLCC. In the spot market the levels of these volatilities are interchanged with neither being significantly above the other.

Figures 5 and 6 compare time varying volatilities of spot and of time charter freight rates between Handysize, Panamax and Capesize vessels in the dry bulk sector. Once more, risk, as manifested by volatility estimates, is in general higher in larger vessels. The reasons for the lower volatility levels in Handysize vessels as compared to the other sizes and of Panamax in comparison to Capesize have been explained before. They are that smaller ships serve many more different trades than larger ones, with less draft restrictions on certain ports because of size, and are not therefore subject to so many ups and downs in the market. On the contrary, larger size vessels may be thought of as operating in narrower markets, serving only a few major commodities and being restricted to approaching specific ports only. This has its toll on volatility levels.

Figure 5: Spot freight rate volatilities by vessel size, dry bulk sector

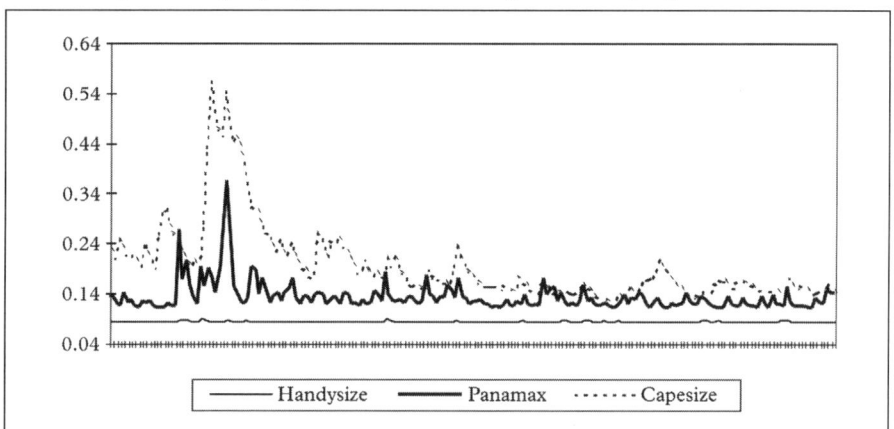

Figure 6: Time charter rate volatilities by vessel size, dry bulk sector

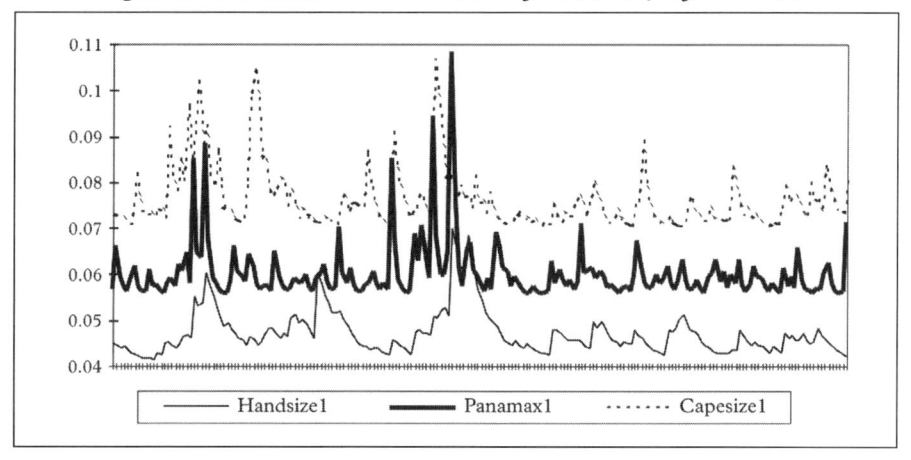

Overall, it may be said that the shipping markets tend to respond together to external shocks, and yet quite differently implying market segregation between different size ships. That is, there are some common driving forces of volatilities in different size vessels, and yet there are idiosyncratic factors to each market that make each size-ship volatility move at its own level and in its own way. These idiosyncratic factors relate to the type and number of routes each size ship is engaged in.

674   SHIPPING INVESTMENT AND FINANCE

The results suggest that operational risks in the larger sub-sectors of the tanker and dry bulk sectors of the shipping industry may be mitigated by holding smaller vessels. Hence, risk averse investors in shipping can diversify risks in their portfolios by heavier weighting towards smaller size vessels.

5.2 Comparison of time varying freight volatilities over type of contract, spot v time-charter

With respect to the choice between spot and futures markets, volatilities are compared in Figures 7, 8, 9 and 10 between time-charter and spot freight rates for each size vessel in the tanker sector. Figures 7 and 9 reveal that the volatility of spot-freight rates in the Handymax and Suezmax sectors are clearly above

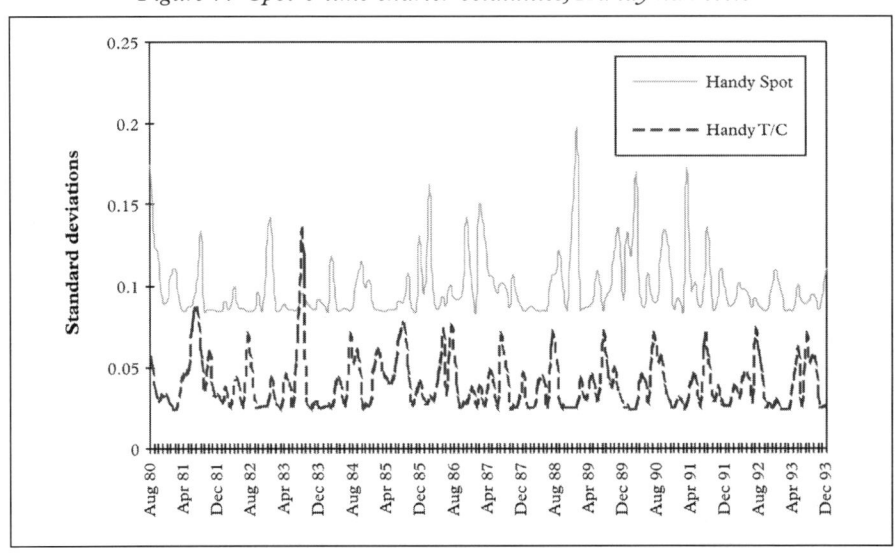

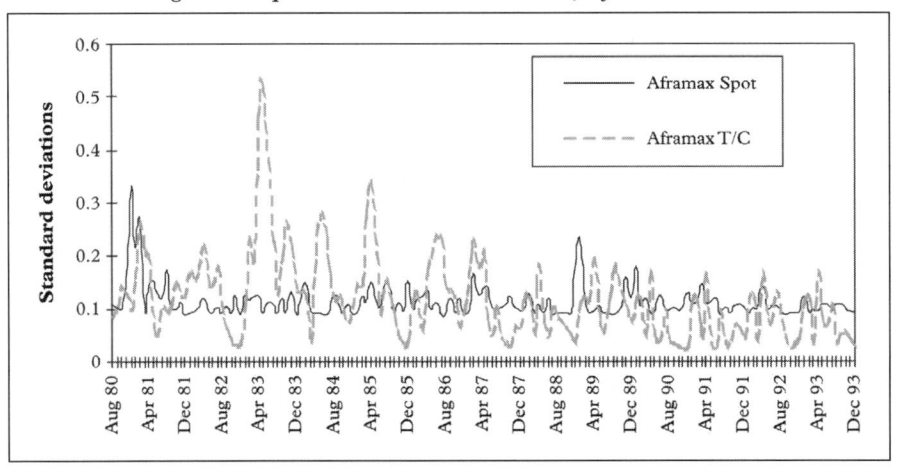

Figure 7: Spot v time charter volatilities, Handymax sector

Figure 8: Spot v time charter volatilities, Aframax sector

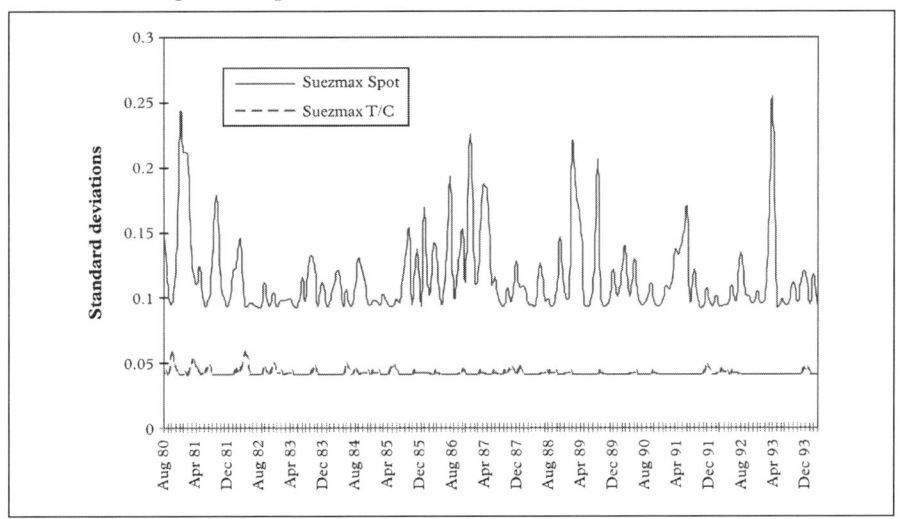

Figure 9: Spot v time charter volatilities, Suezmax sector

Figure 10: Spot v time charter volatilities, VLCC sector

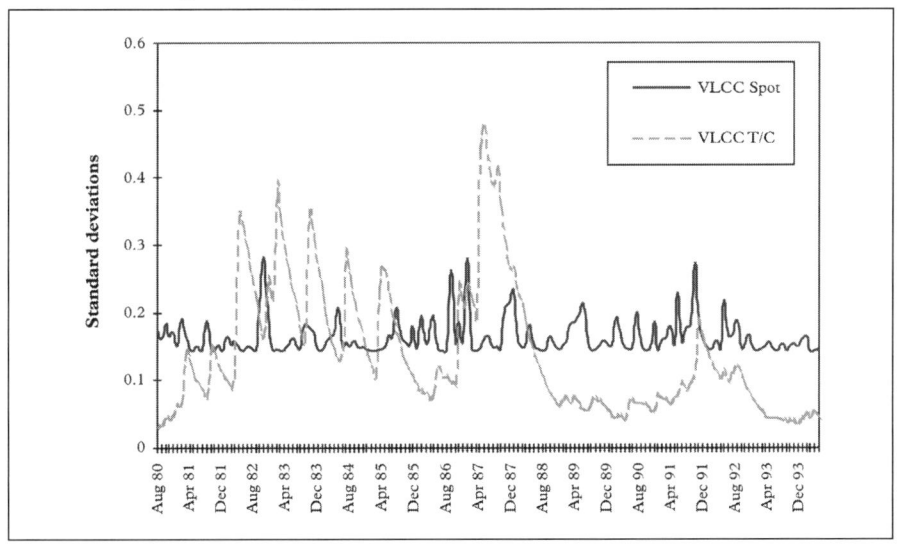

the corresponding time charter ones over the whole period. The results are not so neat for the Aframax and VLCC markets. Figure 8 shows that before 1987 the Aframax time charter volatility was mostly at a higher level than the spot one, with the reverse occurring once the market recovered. The fluctuations in the volatility of time charter rates in the early period are sharp and in wider bands as compared to the post-87 period, forcing the average in Table 8 to be, though insignificantly so, above the spot rate. The story is similar in the VLCC sector. The downward trend in time charter risk, lying constantly below the spot rate level of risk from 1988 onwards, is particularly noticeable.

Kavussanos[4] compares aggregated (over vessel sizes) spot with time-charter volatilities for the dry-bulk sector. The results there are somewhat in line with the above findings in the Aframax and VLCC sectors. That is, when the market is at its low, time charters are more volatile than spot rates. This is thought to be because time-charter rates reflect expectations of future events, which makes them more sensitive to changing perceptions of the future market. When the market is at the bottom and there is a feeling for a market upturn, charterers rush to fix vessels on time charter. This results in time charter rates moving more steeply upwards than spot rates. The opposite happens when the market is at its peak, where charterers fix in the spot market and the lack of demand for time charters results in an abrupt drop in their values.

As the data used in this last comparison of spot with time charter rates on the dry bulk sector were at the aggregate level, and did not refer to time charter rates of individual vessels, it was felt that more information could be obtained if the results were refined by vessel size. Thus, time varying volatilities of spot and of time charter rates in dry bulk have been estimated and presented for the first time in this chapter for each vessel size using GARCH models. Their plots are shown in Figures 11, 12 and 13. Spot volatilities seem to be above the one-year time charter ones for each vessel size. This takes us back to the traditional belief that spot rates are more volatile and hence riskier than time charters.

The result is justified by Kavussanos and Alizadeh,[9] identifying four types of risk which the owner is faced with, when employing the vessel in the spot as opposed to the time charter market. In a time charter the vessel is fixed, say over a year, expenses being paid by the charterer, making income from operations quite predictable over the course of the year. The alternative to the one year time charter would be, say 12, monthly spot fixtures, with expenses on the owner's side. The owner would thus be faced with the risk of not finding employment every month on the vessel; even if employment is secured the risk of having to relocate the vessel to a nearby port, thereby increasing his costs; the risk of the freight market decreasing by the time the next voyage contract is secured there-

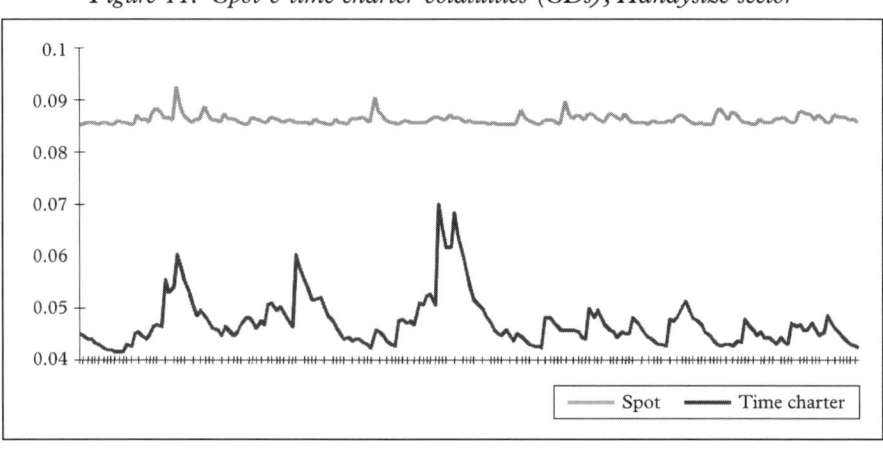

Figure 11: Spot v time charter volatilities (SDs), Handysize sector

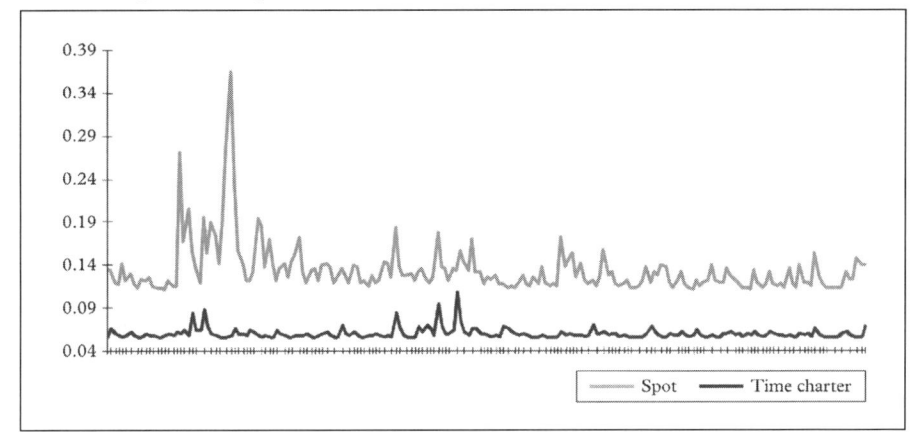

Figure 12: Spot v time charter volatilities (SDs), Panamax sector

Figure 13: Spot v time charter volatilities (SDs), Capesize sector

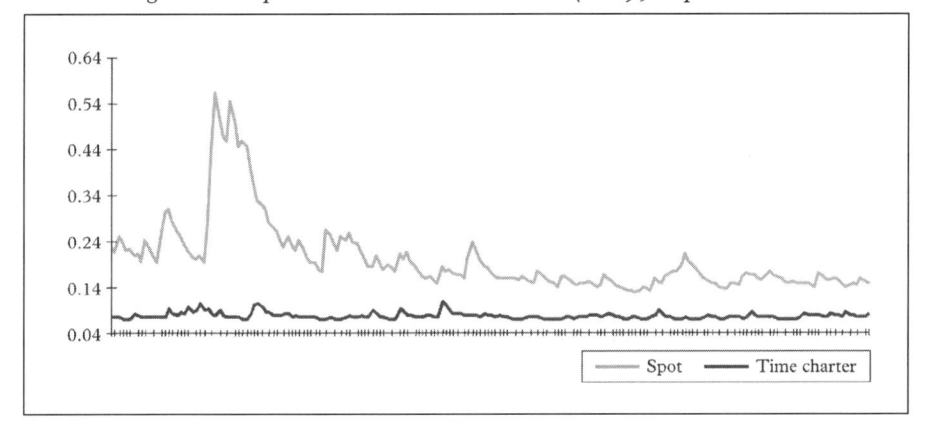

by decreasing his revenues; finally, bunker prices may move adversely for him, thereby increasing his costs. Of course, seasonal factors may also be contributing to such risks. See for example, Kavussanos and Alizadeh[30, 31] for their measurement and comparison in the dry bulk and tanker sectors under different market conditions.

On balance, one could say that policy implications for risk averse shipowners with a choice of employing ships between the spot and time charter markets, point to preferring the lower risk time charter market over the spot market, in general. However, in prolonged "bad" periods for the industry, time charter risk in some sectors, such as in the Aframax and VLCC sectors, may rise above the corresponding spot market risk.

The contribution of the analysis so far, is to point to real possibilities of risk reduction by choice of sub-sector within the dry bulk and tanker sectors of the shipping industry. In addition, the use of GARCH models to estimate time varying volatilities points to a strategy of dynamic revisions of assets which to include in a portfolio of vessels. No empirical analysis has been carried yet in the literature for the container sector, but one would expect similar conclusions regarding volatilities in rates of different vessel sizes. Once the investments (ships) have been acquired shipowners have to make similar decisions of how to maximise their return from operations, subject to the operational business risks that they face. The second contribution of the analysis so far is to point to the possibility of using period contracts as ways of reducing risks in a portfolio of "long" positions on tonnage. Caution needs to be exercised though, say in a dynamic portfolio setting, to ensure that the relationship holds true in adverse market conditions, as time charter volatility may rise above the spot one.

The strategies that the above possibilities point to are useful but may be proved to be expensive, non existent or inflexible, if not planned properly. For example, it costs to buy and sell ships and to go in or out of freight contracts. This reduces their flexibility. Long term charters may be hard for owners to find when the market is in decline. The opposite is true for the charterers when the market is improving. In addition, when the conditions turn too much against one of the parties (owner or charterer) it may be that they decide to abandon the agreement. The introduction of derivatives contracts, such as freight futures, in 1985, and of Over the Counter (OTC) forward contracts, options and swaps, has helped to alleviate these problems with respect to operational risk management. They have made operational risk management cheaper, more flexible and readily available to parties exposed to adverse movements in freight rates.

6. THE USE OF DERIVATIVES FOR OPERATIONAL RISK MANAGEMENT IN SHIPPING

Many other industries have used derivative contracts to manage risks. Say a party is "long" in a "commodity". For the shipowner this would be the freight service, for the charterer it would be the cargo he wants to transport. If freight rates are expected to decrease by the time the owner secures the next contract with a charterer, he may want to avoid taking the risk of reducing his revenue. Apart from the traditional methods of managing this risk, discussed earlier, such as entering a time charter contract, he may decide to use, amongst others, freight futures, forwards, options or swap contracts to hedge these risks.

For these to function, a market price of the underlying physical commodity is needed. For instance, if a "party" is long in coffee, a spot market price for coffee is needed – which is available in the market– and based on that, futures contracts could be issued, say one month ahead. The party that owns coffee and expects its price to be lower next month will go to the futures market and sell futures contracts in order to buy them back in a month's time at the lower price prevailing in the market (provided his expectations materialise). He will thus, make a profit from the selling and buying of the futures contracts at different periods, which will offset the loss which will occur in the physical market because of the reduction in the price of the commodity.

In a forward agreement, the two parties (owner of coffee and potential buyer of coffee) will come "directly" together. They will agree on a forward price for coffee and the producer will deliver that quantity at the agreed price. This is a practice which has been used as a hedging mechanism for years in a number of industries. Gray[2] claims that the problem with this is inflexibility and unreliability; if either party wanted to change any part of the contract (e.g., quantity delivered or price), they will not be able to do so without renegotiating the whole contract. If there is a futures market operating for the commodity both parties are flexible in terms of the possibility of being allowed to change the details of the original contract. Thus, delivery date, quantity, price and other characteristics may be altered at will.

7. THE BALTIC FREIGHT INDEX

The shipping industry did not have an underlying "commodity", which could be used to trade futures contracts. It established in 1985 the Baltic Freight Index (BFI) produced by the Baltic Exchange in London and the International Futures Exchange in Bermuda. The latter was abandoned early, so we will concentrate on the BFI, which has been used up until 2002 as the underlying "commodity" for futures BIFFEX (Baltic International Freight Futures Exchange) contracts trading for the dry bulk sector. Unlike physical goods, such as coffee, which could be delivered physically at the expiry of the futures contract, the trade of freight services amounted to delivering the cash value of the commodity. This cash settlement procedure has enabled the introduction of BIFFEX contracts, based on the BFI (Gray[1, 2]). The underlying asset, which is delivered at the settlement date, is the cash value of a freight rate index, the BFI. This makes the whole process a paper transaction with no ship or cargoes being involved.

The BFI is a weighted average index of dry-cargo freight rates, see, e.g., Gray.[2] Three major restructurings have taken place since its inception, aiming to make it more representative of the conditions prevailing in the industry, and more efficient in the functioning of the BIFFEX market. Between January 85 to 3 August 90, the BFI consisted of capesize (15% of the index composition), panamax (65% of the index) and Handysize (20%) spot freight rates. From 6 August 1990 three time-charter routes were introduced (1A, 3A and 5). The handysize routes (4, 5, 11 and 12) were excluded from the composition of the index in November 1993. In November 1999 the index was revised to keep only the seven panamax spot and time-charter routes (1, 1A, 2, 2A, 3, 3A and 9), at the same time renaming the BFI as Baltic Panamax Index (BPI). The four broad periods identified, corresponding to the major revisions in the composition of the underlying index, are shown schematically in Figure 14.

8. UNBIASEDNESS AND HEDGING EFFECTIVENESS OF FUTURES AND FORWARD MARKETS

In the theory of futures and forward markets it is claimed that there are two main economic benefits that these markets provide to market agents. These are price discovery (of future spot prices) and risk management through hedging

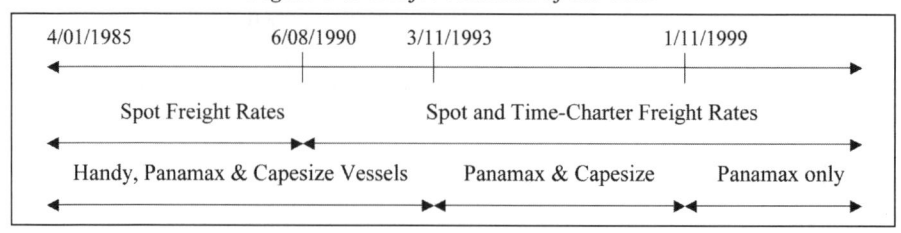

Figure 14: Major revisions of the BFI

4/01/1985	6/08/1990	3/11/1993	1/11/1999
Spot Freight Rates		Spot and Time-Charter Freight Rates	
Handy, Panamax & Capesize Vessels		Panamax & Capesize	Panamax only

(see, e.g., Garbade and Silber[32]). Price discovery is the process of revealing information about current and expected spot prices through the futures or forward markets. Risk management refers to hedgers using futures contracts to control their spot price risk. Kavussanos and Nomikos[14–18] examine these functions for BIFFEX contracts, while Kavussanos et al.,[19] Kavussanos and Visvikis,[20] Batchelor, Kavussanos and Visvikis[22] examine the same functions for the freight forward markets.

Kavussanos and Nomikos,[14] using one and two months to maturity futures contracts show that BIFFEX contracts are unbiased predictors of spot, the BFI. The evidence on the three months contract is marginal. Kavussanos et al.[19] show that FFA prices one- and two-months prior to maturity are unbiased predictors of the realised spot prices in routes 1, 1A, 2 and 2A. However, the efficiency of the FFA prices three months prior to maturity gives mixed evidence, with routes 2 and 2A being unbiased estimators, while routes 1 and 1A being seemingly biased estimators of the realised spot prices. Thus, it seems that unbiasedness depends on the market and type of contract under investigation.

The evidence on unbiasedness, uncovered by these studies, is important for market agents in that they can rely on the free information provided by the futures/forward markets as to the level the spot market will be, say two months ahead. Therefore, through the BIFFEX/FFA contracts, market agents can get an indication of the expected level of freight rates in the future. In addition, Kavussanos and Nomikos[14] show that, futures prices provide more accurate forecasts of the realised spot prices than forecasts generated from forecasting models, such as the random walk, ARIMA and the Holt-Winters exponential smoothing models.

In addition to providing a mechanism for market agents to form expectations regarding spot prices that will prevail in the future, trading in futures/forward markets also provides information regarding current spot prices. Kavussanos and Nomikos[18] show that futures prices tend to discover new information more rapidly than spot prices. Sub-period results, corresponding to revisions in the composition of the underlying index, show that the price discovery role of futures prices has strengthened as a result of the more homogeneous composition of the index in recent years. Moreover, futures prices, when formulated as a VECM, are found to produce more accurate forecasts of spot prices than VAR, ARIMA and random-walk models, over several steps ahead.

Kavussanos and Visvikis[20] investigate the lead-lag relationships between forward and spot markets, both in terms of returns and volatility. Causality tests and impulse response analysis indicate that there is a bi-directional causal relationship between spot and futures returns in all routes. The latter imply that FFA prices can be equally important as a source of information as spot prices are. A closer examination of the results suggests that causality from FFA to spot returns runs stronger than the other way in all routes. These results are in line with those for futures contracts presented in Kavussanos and Nomikos.[18]

Volatility spillovers between the spot and FFA markets are also investigated in the same study. Results from a bivariate VECM-GARCH-X model, indicate that the FFA volatility spills over to the spot market volatility in route 1. In route 1A the results indicate no volatility spillover in either market. In routes 2 and 2A there is a bi-directional relationship as each market transmits volatility in the other.

Thus, FFA prices seem to contain useful information about subsequent spot prices, beyond that already embedded in the current spot price, and therefore, can be used as price discovery vehicles. Furthermore, the FFA contracts in routes 1, 2, and 2A contribute in the volatility of the relevant spot rate, and therefore, further support the notion of price discovery. In the absence of futures contracts, following the de-listing of BIFFEX in April 2002, forward contracts seem to do an equally important job as vehicles of price discovery of spot prices.

Even if market agents are not aware of the valuable information that BIFFEX and FFA contracts incorporate for them as a source of information regarding the likely developments of the spot market, they would be keen to know how successful the use of these contracts are in mitigating their risks in freight markets. This is important as it relates to direct monetary benefits from the use of the contracts. If these are perceived important and the service offered by the existence of BIFFEX/FFA contracts is used enough by the industry it will survive to serve the players in the industry. If there is no sufficient volume generated then it is not worth for LIFFE to keep the contract.

The issue of the effectiveness of BIFFEX contracts in hedging freight risk has been investigated in Thuong and Vischer,[41] in Haralambides[12,13] and in Kavussanos and Nomikos.[15–17] Batchelor, Kavussanos and Visvikis[22] investigate the risk management function of the FFA markets. As explained earlier, hedging involves taking a position in the futures market that is opposite to the position that one already has in the spot market. The shipowner is "long" on tonnage and sells BIFFEX/FFA contracts to protect him against a decline in freight rates. The charterer is "short" on tonnage, thus buying BIFFEX/FFA contracts to protect him against a rise in freight rates. Of course for a trade to occur the views of these two "parties" to the trade must be opposite. Futures markets simply transfer risks from one willing party to another.

In hedging, the "party" interested in mitigating risk has to determine a hedge ratio, which will make the hedge as "effective" as possible. That is, he has to decide on the number of futures/forward contracts to buy or sell for each unit of spot commodity on which he bears price risk. Johnson,[42] Stein[43] and Ederington[44] apply the principles of portfolio theory to solve the problem. They show that the hedge ratio, which minimises the spot market risk equals the covariance between spot and futures/forward price changes over the variance of futures/forward price changes.

The effectiveness of the hedge is determined by the degree of variance reduction it achieves in the hedged portfolio. Alternatively, effectiveness is determined by the proportion of risk in the spot market that is eliminated through the futures/forward position (hedging). Alternative strategies in calculating hedge ratios involve a naïve one-to-one hedge, under which for each $ exposition in the spot market a $ position is opened in the futures market. Of course this is sub-optimal. Yet another strategy is to use time varying optimal hedge ratios. This would be justified if the distributions of the covariance and/or the variance entering the calculation of the optimal hedge ratio are time varying. In this case, at each point in time, a different hedge ratio would be appropriate. To make this point evident, Figure 15 plots the estimated constant and time varying hedge ratios for spot and FFA contracts for route 1. It is obvious that using the constant hedge ratio, instead of the time varying one, in observation 30 would have provided estimates, which are way off the most efficient hedge.

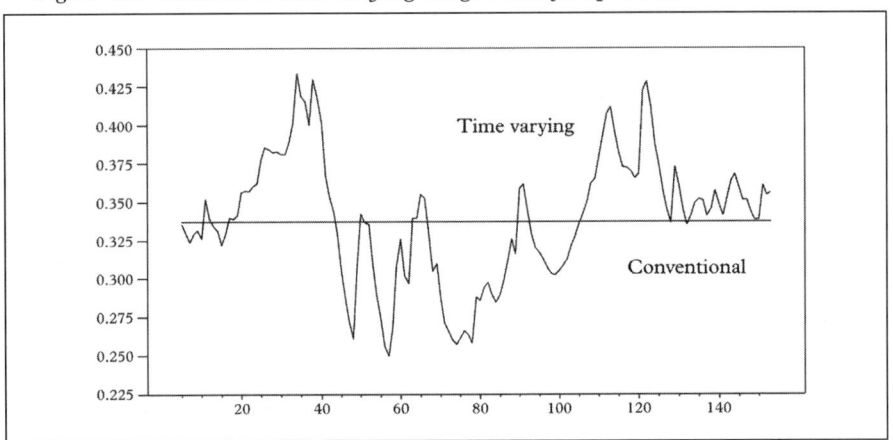

Figure 15: Constant v time-varying hedge ratios for spot and FFA in Route 1

The "technology" to calculate time varying hedge ratios for BIFFEX contracts has been introduced by Kavussanos and Nomikos[15–17] to individual routes of the BFI and in FFA contracts by Batchelor, Kavussanos and Visvikis.[22] These time varying hedge ratios, have been calculated by extracting time varying variances and covariances of spot and futures prices from the estimation of multivariate GARCH models, with a VECM specification of the mean of the variables. Alternative hedging strategies are evaluated by comparing the portfolio variance reduction from the use of a particular hedge ratio (strategy) to a benchmark portfolio; that of the unhedged position. The larger the reduction in the unhedged variance, the higher the degree of hedging effectiveness.

Whether time varying or constant ratios for BIFFEX or FFA contracts are appropriate for each individual route cannot be determined a-priori. It is a matter of empirical evidence.

Batchelor, Kavussanos and Visvikis[22] investigate the risk management function in the FFA markets. In- and out-of-sample tests indicate that in BPI voyage routes 1 and 2 constant hedge ratios are superior. In the time-charter routes 1A and 2A, time-varying hedge ratios perform better. The one to one, naïve hedge is the worst hedging strategy. Hedging effectiveness, as measured by the variance reduction, is for route 2A, 29.10% for route 1A, 32.16%, which is the highest variance reduction achieved, the lowest being that of route 1 (18.03%).

Kavussanos and Nomikos[15,17] investigate the same issue for BIFFEX contracts. Two cases are distinguished; In-sample and the more pragmatic out-of-sample hedge ratios. In the former case time varying hedge ratios are superior in routes 1, 1A, 3A, 7 and 10. Out-of-sample results indicate that time varying hedge ratios perform better in routes 1, 1A, 3A and 8. In route 3, the constant hedge ratio seems superior. The naive hedge is the worst hedging strategy in all in sample results. For out of sample, in routes 7 and 10, hedging increases the portfolio variance compared to the unhedged position, suggesting to market participants to leave their positions unhedged. Also the naive hedge in route 9 seems superior. Overall, the average variance reduction for the panamax routes is higher than that for the capesize routes across all the estimated models. This is not surprising as the panamax routes represent 70% of the total BFI composition.

Ultimately, the user of the futures contracts is interested in the variance reduction that may be achieved with the best method of hedging available. The above study shows that the highest variance reduction possible is in route 1A(23.25%) and the lowest is in route 7 (−14.86%). It seems then that for all routes a large proportion of the variability of the unhedged portfolio is not eliminated. Regarding FFA's, despite being tailor made contracts, matching forward contracts with specific routes of the index, hedging performance still remains far from that evidenced in other markets; 57.06% for the Canadian Interest rate futures (Gagnon and Lypny[45]), 69.61% and 85.69% for the corn and soybean futures(Bera et al.[46]) and 97.91% and 77.47% for the SP500 and the Canadian Stock Index futures contract, respectively (Park and Switzer[47]).

As mentioned earlier, during its history the composition of the BFI has been restructured several times(see Figure 14) to make it more representative of the industry, and to improve the hedging performance of the BIFFEX contracts. We saw how this restructuring has been shown by Kavussanos and Nomikos[14,18] to improve the price discovery function of the futures market.

Kavussanos and Nomikos,[16] investigate whether the other function of futures markets, that of hedging performance, has changed as a result of the changes in the composition of the BFI. There seems to be no evidence of statistical change in the hedging performance of BIFFEX on any route, following the inclusion of time-charter routes in the BFI. However, performance improves in route 1 following the exclusion of the handysize routes. The exclusion of the capesize routes from the index, in November 1999, making the index more homogeneous increases the in-sample hedging effectiveness for every route (except route 1) in comparison to the pre-November 1999 period. This improved variance reduction is as high as 23.03% in route 3A, with an overall average (over routes) improvement of 14.36%. For the BPI then the highest hedging effectiveness is in route 3A, reaching a figure of 39.95%.

It seems then that the increased homogeneity of the index has had a positive impact on hedging effectiveness, despite leaving the variance reduction achieved well below that evidenced in other markets in the literature. At the time of writing, Kavussanos and Nomikos[16] argued that

"the magnitude of the observed increases in hedging effectiveness is still small, and may not be sufficient to induce market agents in actively using the market for hedging purposes. This also seems to be in line with the trading preferences of participants in the shipping markets who are now increasingly using over-the-counter (OTC) forward contracts which are cash settled against the underlying shipping routes of the BPI. Because these contracts are traded against specific routes, rather than a general index, they also avoid the problem of basis risk, which is evidenced in the BIFFEX market."

Unfortunately trading volumes, seen in Figure 16, have not turned around sufficiently to justify the BIFFEX contract's existence for LIFFE. Over the period September 1992 to October 1997 the average daily trading volume has been 210 contracts per day, the equivalent of the average freight cost of transporting 220,000 tons of Grain from US Gulf to Rotterdam (that is, 4 voyages in Route 1 of the BFI). This had become minimal for the later years of the history of BIFFEX. As a consequence, LIFFE stopped trading BIFFEX in April 2002. Currently, in order to hedge freight rate risk, one has to turn to OTC financial products. Their performance is examined in a series of papers by Kavussanos and Visvikis,[20] Kavussanos, Menachof and Visvikis,[19] Batchelor, Kavussanos and Visvikis.[21,22]

9. FORWARD FREIGHT AGREEMENTS (FFAS): THE FUTURE?

As mentioned earlier, FFA's are principal-to-principal contracts, between a seller and a buyer to settle a freight or hire rate, for a specified quantity of cargo or type of vessel, for usually one, or a combination of the major trade routes of

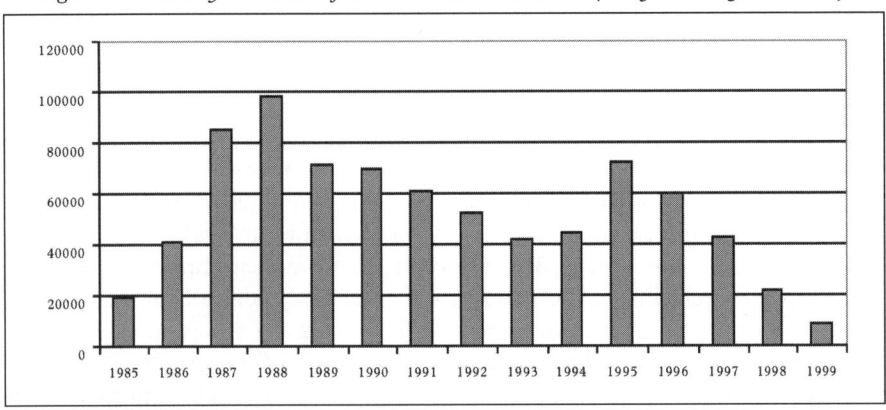

Figure 16: Yearly volumes of the BIFFEX Contract (May 1985–June 1999)

Source: LIFFE, 1999.

the dry-bulk and tanker industries. Settlement is made on the difference between the contracted price and the average price for the route selected in an index over the last seven working days. Indices are published, covering subsectors of the shipping industry (e.g., Handy Index, Panamax Index, Capesize Index, etc.), which are used as the underlying commodity on which to base the FFA's.

In an OTC derivative agreement each party accepts credit risk from the other party. Institutions, which facilitate these markets are major shipbrokers, investment banks, and other financial intermediaries in the fund management industry. The primary advantage of an OTC market is that the terms and conditions are tailored to the specific needs of the two parties. It is a private market in which the general public does not know that the transaction was done. It is considered to be flexible in the sense that the 'parties' can introduce their own contract specifications in order to cover their specific needs, saves money by not normally requiring initial, maintenance, and variation margins (common in the futures organised exchanges), and allows the market to quickly respond to changing needs and circumstances by developing new variations of old contracts.

In the dry-bulk sector, FFAs are available to match the capesize, panamax, and handymax routes. For those wishing to hedge long-term freight risk, a time-charter FFA is tradeable with settlement based on the difference between the contract price and the daily average of the time-charter routes from either the panamax (1A, 2A, 3A, 4),[48] capesize (8, 9, 10, 11) or handymax (1A, 1B, 3, 4A, 4B) indices. It is customary to divide the period into monthly settlements to establish cash-flow. These routes are regularly reviewed to ensure their relevance to the underlying physical market. The combination of time-charter routes can create the equivalent of a period time-charter trade (Clarkson Securities[49]).

Table 9 shows the growth in freight covered by FFA by the shipbroking company Clarkson Securities Ltd.

Table 9: Indications of activity growth in the FFA market

Year	Number of deals per month	Freight covered by trading FFAs($m)
1992	Average 2	0.5
1993	Average 4	48
1994	Average 10	70
1995	Average 20	203
1996	Average 27	331
1997	Average 55	852
1998	Average 90	1114

Notes: All Indications are from Clarkson Securities Ltd. They posses a market share of around 30%. Source: Clarkson Securities (1999).[49]

Figures 17, 18, 19 and 20 present the near-month FFA prices against the spot prices (underlying asset) in panamax routes 1 (US Gulf/Antwerp-Rotterdam-Amsterdam), 1A (Transatlantic round to Skaw-Gibraltar range), 2 (US Gulf/

Figure 17: FFA and spot prices in route 1, daily data (16/01/97–31/07/00)

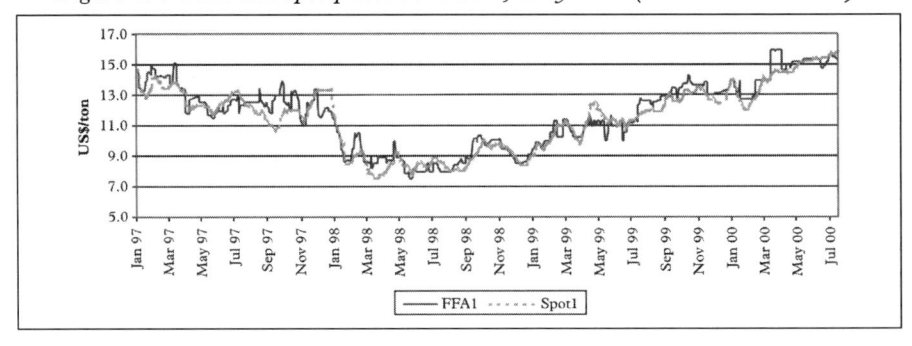

Figure 18: FFA and spot prices in route 1A, daily data (16/01/97–31/07/00)

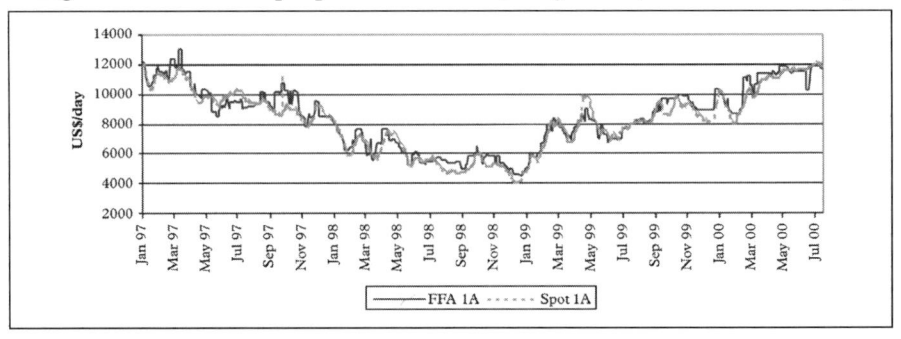

Figure 19: FFA and spot prices in route 2, daily data (16/01/97–10/08/01)

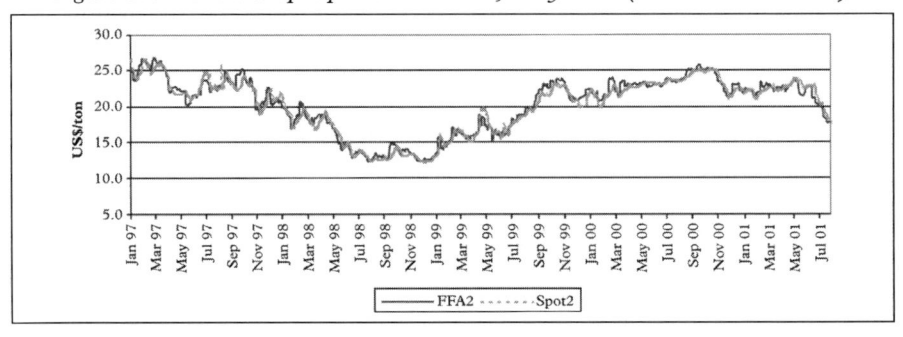

Figure 20: FFA and spot prices in route 2A, daily data (16/01/97–10/08/01)

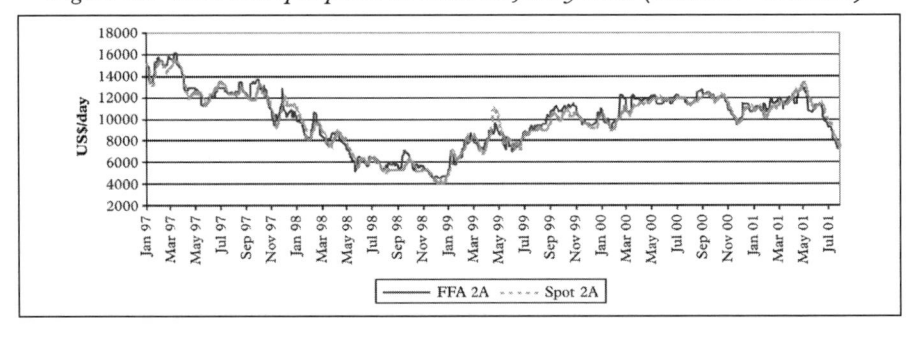

Japan) and 2A (Skaw Passero-Gibraltar/Taiwan-Japan), respectively. In every route the FFA and spot prices move closely together. This is verified by the values of the correlation coefficients of logarithmic differences of FFA prices with spot prices in routes 1, 1A, 2 and 2A. They are, respectively, 0.965, 0.972, 0.986, and 0.985.

10. THE EFFECT OF FFA TRADING ON SPOT PRICE VOLATILITY

It is often claimed that the advent of futures or forward prices can have an adverse impact on spot price volatility. Batchelor, Kavussanos and Visvikis[21] investigate the issue in the FFA market. The results suggest that the onset of FFA trading has had (i) a stabilising impact on the spot price volatility in routes 1 and 2; (ii) an impact on the asymmetry of volatility (market dynamics) in routes 2 and 2A; and (iii) substantially improved the quality and speed of information flowing in routes 1, 1A and 2. Overall, the results indicate that the introduction of FFA contracts has not had a detrimental effect on the underlying spot market. On the contrary, it appears that there has been an improvement in the way that news is transmitted into prices following the onset of FFA trading. By attracting more, and possibly better informed, participants into the market, FFA trading has assisted in the incorporation of information into spot prices more quickly. Thus, even those market agents who do not directly use the FFA market have benefited from the introduction of FFA trading.

11. STABILISING VOYAGE COSTS: HEDGING BUNKER PRICE RISK

Returning to the cash flow position of shipowners, as mentioned in section 1 and shown schematically in Table 1, the major and most volatile part of their voyage costs comes from bunker price fluctuations (amounting to 50% of voyage costs, according to Stopford[23]). Yet, there are no futures contracts to match spot prices for this commodity. Alizadeh, Kavussanos and Menachof,[10] explored the possibility of using a number of traded petroleum futures contracts as instruments for risk reduction in relation to this major operating expense for the shipowner.

Although marine bunkers are bought and sold in almost every port in the world, the world bunker market can be broadly divided into three major regional markets in which the bulk of physical bunkering activities takes place. These markets are Singapore, Rotterdam and Houston. Singapore has long flourished as a transhipment centre due to its strategic geographical location. The Singapore bunker market is by far the largest marine fuels market in the world, and is duly considered to be a prime benchmark for the industry. Singapore's turnover in marine fuel oil in 2000 has been 18.7 million tonnes. In Europe, the Amsterdam–Rotterdam–Antwerp (ARA) region sells as much as 16 million tonnes of bunker fuel annually. The heart of the ARA region is Rotterdam, which sells about 8 to 9 million tonnes of bunker oil and lubes annually, helped by a hub of oil refining and storage facilities sited in its Europort complex, which handles around 100 million tonnes of crude annually. Bunkering on the US Gulf coast is dominated by Houston, recording annual sales volume of 3 million tonnes in year 2000.

With the exception of some financial institutions,[50] offering tailor made derivatives products such as swaps and options, there is no tradable futures contract for the product.[51] In the absence of bunker futures contracts, hedging against bunker price fluctuations using futures contracts involves a cross-hedge against an existing crude or petroleum futures product.

Alizadeh et al.,[10] examine the effectiveness of hedging marine bunker price fluctuations in Rotterdam, Singapore and Houston using different crude oil and petroleum future contracts traded at the New York Mercantile Exchange (NYMEX) and the International Petroleum Exchange (IPE) in London. Using both constant and dynamic hedge ratios, it is found that in and out-of-sample hedging effectiveness is different across regional bunker markets. The most effective futures instruments for out of sample hedging of spot bunker prices in Rotterdam and Singapore are the IPE crude oil futures, while for Houston it is the gas oil futures. However, they achieve only up to 43% variance reduction when using IPE crude oil to hedge bunker prices in Rotterdam. Hedging effectiveness varies from one bunker market to the other. This is because bunker prices in markets around the world, although derived from prevailing conditions in the oil market (prices), mainly reflect the balance of supply and demand for bunker fuel in the region. It seems that bunker prices may deviate from prices for crude oil and petroleum products substantially.

For agents determined to use futures contracts to hedge bunker price risk, policy action points to using IPE crude oil contracts to hedge bunker price fluctuations when loading in Rotterdam, NYMEX gas oil contracts when loading in Singapore, and IPE gas oil futures contracts when using Houston for refuelling vessels. The maximum hedging effectiveness's are 43%, 15.9% and 14% in each case. This compares unfavourably with other futures contracts, and when coupled with the low hedging effectiveness of freight futures and forward contracts reported in Kavussanos and Nomikos[16] and Batchelor et al.,[22] they do not help in the substantial reduction of the profit fluctuation of shipowners.

12. SUMMARY AND CONCLUSION

Shipowners are faced with substantial business risks in the international environment that they operate. Some of these risks are well outlined in Table 1 when examining the balance-sheet of the shipowner. Risks emanate from fluctuations in freight rates, bunker prices, the price of the investment – ship, interest rates, exchange rates, etc. This chapter has put forward a framework for identifying and measuring these risks, and has proposed solutions of how to handle the question of risk management. In the process, a review of the literature and some new ideas about how risks can be managed in the shipping industry have been put together. At the same time it provides the state of the art of where we stand now technically in calculating instruments that can be used to hedge risks, such as the calculation of time varying hedge ratios. Also, it offers a review of where we stand research-wise in the area, and can provide a stepping-stone for further research and innovations in the area. Naturally, a lot of the details underlying the research have not been reproduced here, due to lack of space. However, these details can be found in the original papers, referenced here.

The ideas put forward in this chapter include: The sectoral disaggregation of the dry bulk, tanker and container sector of the cargo carrying shipping industry, based on distinct risk-return characteristics. As a consequence, it is suggested that shipowners can mitigate risks by holding portfolios of assets–ships– of different size; The possible risk diversification effects in ship operation by switching between contracts of different duration; The use of freight derivatives, such as futures and forward contracts to manage freight rate risks; The economic functions of price discovery and risk management of these financial instruments are discussed critically. The review looks back at BIFFEX and their role in serving the industry as hedging instruments for freight rates. It compares their performance with other financial instruments and finds it somewhat lacking. In a way, it identifies, why the industry has turned gradually to OTC products and the withdrawal of freight futures contracts after 17 years of service. The picture for hedging does not get any better, in terms of the hedging efficiency results presented for the OTC FFAs. Still, the industry has turned to them. On the bunker side, three contacts are identified in aid of risk management of this part of the cash flow equation of the owner.

ACKNOWLEDGEMENT

The author would like to thank his PhD and MSc students for valuable assistance and feedback on various parts of the research underlying this chapter. Thanks are also due to colleagues in the industry who have offered their comments on parts of this work, while presented in conferences and professional meetings around the world. Naturally, all remaining errors or omissions are the sole responsibility of the author.

ENDNOTES

1. Gray, J.W. (1986): *Financial Risk Management in the Shipping Industry* (London, Fairplay publications).
2. Gray, J. (1990): *Shipping Futures* (London, Lloyd's of London Press Ltd).
3. Contracts available to the owner/charterer include: ((1) Voyage Charters (paid as freight per ton to move good(s) from A to B, all costs paid by the shipowner), (2) Contracts of Affreightment (the shipowner carries good(s) in specified route(s) for a period of time using ships of his choice), (3) Time Charters – trip/time (the shipowner earns hire every 15 days or month. He operates the ship under instructions from the charterer who pays voyage costs), (4) Bareboat Charters (the ship is rented to another party for operation, usually for a long period of time).

4. Kavussanos, M.G. (1996a): "Comparisons of volatility in the dry-cargo ship sector. Spot versus time-charters, and smaller versus larger vessels", *Journal of Transport Economics and Policy*, January 1996, Vol. 30, No. 1, pp. 67–82.
5. Kavussanos, M.G. (1996b): "Price risk modelling of different size vessels in the tanker industry using Autoregressive Conditional Heteroskedasticity (ARCH) models", *The Logistics and Transportation Review*, June 1996, Vol. 32, No. 2, pp. 161–176.
6. Kavussanos, M.G. (1996c): "Measuring risk differences among segments of the tanker freight markets", Discussion paper No. 18, International Centre for Shipping, Trade and Finance, City University Business School, London, July 1996. Also presented at the *International Association of Maritime Economists (IAME) Conference*, June 26–28 1996, Vancouver, BC, Canada.
7. Kavussanos, M.G. (1997), "The dynamics of time-varying volatilities in different size second-hand ship prices of the dry-cargo sector", *Applied Economics*, 1997, 29, pp. 433–443.
8. Kavussanos, M.G. (1998), "Freight risks in the tanker sector", *Lloyd's Shipping Economist*, June 1998, pp. 6–9. Also, July 1998, p. 9.
9. Kavussanos, M.G., and Alizadeh, A. (2002b): "The Expectations Hypothesis of the Term Structure and Risk Premia in Dry Bulk Shipping Freight Markets; An EGARCH-M Approach", *Journal of Transport Economics and Policy*, May 2002.
10. Alizadeh, A., Kavussanos, M.G., and Menachof, D. (2001): "Hedging against bunker price fluctuations using petroleum futures contracts; constant vs time varying hedge ratios", *IAME 2001 Conference*, Hong Kong, July.
11. Cullinane, K.P.B. (1992): "A Short-Term Adaptive Forecasting Model for BIFFEX Speculation: A Box-Jenkins Approach", *Maritime Policy and Management*, 19(2), pp. 91–114.
12. Haralambides, H.E. (1992a): "A New Approach to the Measurement of Risk in Shipping Finance", *Lloyd's Shipping Economist*, April.
13. Haralambides, H.E. (1992b): "Freight Futures Trading and Shipowners Expectations", *Conference Proceedings of the 6th World Conference on Transport Research* (Lyon, France, Les Presses De L'Imprimerie Chirat), 2, pp. 1411–1422.
14. Kavussanos, M.G., and Nomikos, N. (1999): "The forward pricing function of the shipping freight futures market", *The Journal of Futures Markets*, Vol. 19:3, May, pp. 353–376.
15. Kavussanos, M.G., and Nomikos, N.K. (2000a): "Hedging in the Freight Futures Market", *Journal of Derivatives*, pp. 41–58.
16. Kavussanos, M.G., and Nomikos, N.K. (2000b): "Futures Hedging when the Composition of the Underlying Asset Changes: The Case of the BIFFEX Contract", *The Journal of Futures Markets*, 20, pp. 775–801.
17. Kavussanos, M.G., and Nomikos, N.K. (2000c): "Constant Versus Time-Varying Hedge Ratios in the BIFFEX Market", *Logistics and Transportation Review, Transportation Research Part E*, pp. 249–265.
18. Kavussanos, M.G., and Nomikos, N.K. (2001): "Price Discovery, Causality and Forecasting in the Freight Futures Market", paper presented at the *World Conference on Transport Research WCTR2001*, Seoul, Korea, July 2001.
19. Kavussanos, M.G., Menachof, D., and Visvikis, I.D. (2001): "The Unbiasedness Hypothesis in the Freight Forward Market", paper presented at the *2nd International Safety of Maritime Transport Conference*, Chios, Greece, 7–9 June.
20. Kavussanos, M.G., and Visvikis, I.D. (2002): "Market Interactions in Returns and Volatilities between Spot and Forward Markets", paper presented at *The 12th International Association of Maritime Economists (IAME) Conference*, Panama City, Panama, 13–15 November.
21. Batchelor, R., Kavussanos, M.G., and Visvikis, I.D. (2002a): "Over-The-Counter Forward Contracts and Spot Price Volatility", unpublished manuscript, Department of Accounting and Finance, Athens University of Economics and Business.

22. Batchelor, R., Kavussanos, M.G., and Visvikis, I.D. (2002b): "The Hedging Performance of the Freight Forward Market: Constant vs. Time-Varying Hedge Ratios", unpublished manuscript, Department of Accounting and Finance, Athens University of Economics and Business.
23. Stopford, M. (1997): *Maritime Economics* (2nd ed.) (London, Routledge).
24. These are known as unconditional variances as they are averages of the squared dispersions of freight rates over a period of time. Conditional variances on the other hand refer to variances, which are estimated from regression models, under which freight rates, are explained in terms of a set of explanatory variables.
25. Glen, D. (1990): "The emergence of differentiation in the oil tanker market", *Maritime Policy and Management*, Vol. 17, No. 4, pp. 289–312.
26. Engle, R.F. (1982): "Autoregressive conditional heteroskedasticity with estimates of the variance of United Kingdom inflation", *Econometrica*, 50, pp. 987–1007.
27. Bollerslev, T. (1986): "Generalized autoregressive conditional heteroskedasticitv", *Journal of Econometrics*, 31, pp. 307–327.
28. See Kavussanos (1996b, 1997) for a complete set of results, including estimated coefficients.
29. See note 3 for definitions.
30. Kavussanos, M.G., and Alizadeh, A. (2001): "Seasonality patterns in dry bulk shipping spot and time-charter freight rates", *Transportation Research Part E, Logistics and Transportation Review*, Vol. 37, No. 6, pp. 443–467.
31. Kavussanos, M.G., and Alizadeh, A. (2002a): "Seasonality patterns in tanker shipping freight markets", *Economic Modelling*, Vol. 19, Issue 5 (Nov. 2002), pp. 747–782.
32. Garbade, K., and Silber, W. (1983): "Price Movements and Price Discovery in Futures and Cash Markets", *Review of Economics and Statistics*, 65, pp. 289–297.
33. Edwards, F., and Ma, C. (1992): *Futures and Options*, International Edition, (Singapore, McGraw-Hill Book Co.).
34. Johansen, S. (1988): "Statistical Analysis of Cointegrating Vectors", *Journal of Economic Dynamics and Control*, 12, pp. 231–254.
35. Johansen, S. (1991): "Estimation and Hypothesis Testing of Cointegration Vectors in Gaussian Vector Autoregressive Models", *Econometrica*, 59, pp. 1551–1580
36. Johansen, S. (1988): "Statistical Analysis of Cointegrating Vectors", *Journal of Economic Dynamics and Control*, 12, pp. 231–254.
37. Johansen, S. (1991): "Estimation and Hypothesis Testing of Cointegration Vectors in Gaussian Vector Autoregressive Models", *Econometrica*, 59, pp. 1551–1580
38. Granger, C., and Newbold, P. (1974): "Spurious Regressions in Econometrics", *Journal of Econometrics*, 2, pp. 1045–1066.
39. Chang, Y. (1991): "Forward Pricing Function of Freight Futures Prices", unpublished PhD Thesis, Department of Maritime Studies, University of Wales.
40. Chang, Y., and Chang, H. (1996): "Predictability of the Dry Bulk Shipping Market by BIFFEX", *Maritime Policy and Management*, 23, pp. 103–114.
41. Thuong, L.T., and Visscher, S.L. (1990): "The Hedging Effectiveness of Dry Bulk Freight Rate Futures", *Transportation Journal*, 29, pp. 58–65.
42. Johnson, L. (1960): "The Theory of Hedging and Speculation in Commodity Futures", *Review of Economic Studies*, 27, pp. 139–151.
43. Stein, J. (1961): "The Simultaneous Determination of Spot and Futures Prices", *The American Economic Review*, 51, pp. 1012–1025.
44. Ederington, L.H. (1979): "The Hedging Performance of the New Futures Markets", *The Journal of Finance*, 34, pp. 157–170.
45. Gagnon, L., and Lypny, G. (1995): "Hedging Short-Term Interest Risk Under Time-Varying Distributions", *Journal of Futures Markets*, 15(7), pp. 767–783.
46. Bera, A., Garcia, P., and Roh, J. (1997): *Estimation of Time-Varying Hedge Ratios for Corn and Soybeans: BGARCH and Random Coefficients Approaches* (Office for Futures and Options Research), pp. 97–106.

47. Park, T., and Switzer, L. (1995): "Bivariate GARCH Estimation of the Optimal Hedge Ratios for Stock Index Futures: A Note", *Journal of Futures Markets*, 15, pp. 61–67.
48. As of 3 April 2000, Route 9 was renamed as Route 4.
49. Clarkson Securities (1999): *FFAs: Forward Freight Agreements* (London, Clarkson Securities Ltd), pp. 1–11.
50. For example, Barclays Capital, Morgan Stanley, Credit Leyonne, etc., offer over-the-counter bunkers derivative products.
51. Fuel oil futures were traded in Singapore Exchange during the period 1988 to 1992, however, due to the decline in trading volume and illiquidity of contracts, Singapore Exchange stopped the trade in fuel oil futures. The International Petroleum Exchange attempted to launch a bunker futures contract in January 1999. This proved unsuccessful and the contract was withdrawn after six months.

CHAPTER 31

RISK MANAGEMENT IN THE SHIPPING INDUSTRY: THEORY AND PRACTICE

Nikos K. Nomikos and Amir H. Alizadeh
City University Cass Business School, City of London, UK.
E-mail: *n.nomikos@city.ac.uk* and *a.alizadeh@city.ac.uk*

1. INTRODUCTION

Agents in the shipping industry are faced with substantial business risks in the international environment that they operate. Risks emanate from fluctuations in freight rates, bunker prices, the price of the vessels, even from fluctuations in the level of interest rates and exchange rates.[1] All these factors are determinants of the agents' cash-flows, and as such their fluctuations have a profound impact on the agents' operating profitability and consequently on their business survival. Over the years a variety of methods and instruments have been developed and used to control or eliminate the effect of adverse movements in the cost and revenue sides of the shipowners' and charterer's cash-flows. The focus of this chapter therefore is to introduce and analyse different derivative instruments, developed recently, in order to control and manage those risks.

The importance and effectiveness of risk management techniques and strategies in shipping operations has been appreciated by shipping market agents for a long time, as indicated by the development of physical hedging methods such as period time-charter contracts and Contracts of Affreightment (COA). However, it was not until the early 1980's when shipowners, charterers and other parties involved in shipping realised that risk management techniques that had been applied successfully in commodity and financial markets, such as hedging using futures, forwards and options, should also be developed and applied for the shipping industry.

It should be stressed that risk management techniques are markedly different across the liner and tramp shipping sectors. This is due to the unique characteristics of each one of those sectors. For example, while freight rates in tramp shipping are determined through the continuous interaction of supply and demand for shipping services in a nearly perfectly competitive market, freight rates in the liner sectors are determined as freight tariffs in an imperfect market and are revised periodically, e.g. every six month (see Stopford[2] and McConville[3]). As a result, liner rates are less volatile compared to rates in tramp shipping. Furthermore, liner companies use bunker adjustment factors in setting their tariffs. Such adjustments protect liner companies from adverse movements in bunker prices, in contrast to shipowners operating in the tramp market who are exposed to bunker price fluctuations.

Therefore, the aim of this chapter is to review the different risk management tools, which have been developed in recent years to control the risks associated with operating vessels internationally. In particular we focus on managing risk on the revenue and the cost sides of shipping operations, namely the freight and bunker markets, respectively. The structure of this chapter is as follows. Section 2 presents and analyses the different hedging instruments available for hedging freight rate risk. These are futures, forwards and options on individual shipping routes. Recent developments and evidence from empirical studies in the effectiveness of freight futures and forward contracts are also discussed. The risk management on the cost side of shipping operations is the subject of section 3. The most popular tools for bunker risk management – such as forwards, options, swaps and collars – are explained and the merits of each method are clearly assessed. Empirical evidence from studies on bunker price risk management is also presented. Finally, section 4 concludes this chapter.

2. FREIGHT RATE RISK MANAGEMENT

The volatility of shipping freight rates has always been an issue of great importance for shipowners and charterers involved in the transportation of cargoes by sea. Different methods have been developed and used by the agents to manage freight market risk. These are mainly hedging using physical contracts, such as period time-charters and CoA's, and hedging using derivatives, or "paper" contracts, such as freight futures, forward and options on freight rates. The mechanism of hedging freight rates using physical contracts has been discussed extensively by Gray.[4] Therefore, the following sections are devoted to the use of freight derivatives and recent studies on the performance of these instruments in hedging unexpected fluctuations in freight rates.

2.1 Historical development of shipping derivative markets

Trading in derivative contracts dates back to the mid 1860's with the introduction of commodity future contracts at the Chicago Board of Trade in the US. Since then, the trading volume as well as the variety of futures contracts available for trading has increased dramatically. Currently, there are 45 futures exchanges world-wide, trading futures contracts for more than 70 different commodities. This growth in futures trading activity is a reflection of the economic benefits that futures markets provide to market agents. These benefits are price discovery and risk management through hedging. Price discovery is the process of revealing information about current and expected spot prices through the futures markets. Risk management refers to hedgers using futures contracts to control their spot price risk. The dual roles of price discovery and hedging provide benefits that cannot be offered in the spot market alone and are often presented as the justification for futures trading (see, e.g., Garbade and Silber[5]).

The benefits of providing a futures market in freight rates had been recognised by shipping market practitioners as early as in the 1960's (Gray[4]).

However, such a market was eventually established only in 1985. The reason is that the underlying asset of the market – the service of seaborne transportation – is not a physical commodity that can be delivered at the expiry of the futures contract; by its very definition, a futures contract is an agreement to deliver a specified quantity and grade of an identified commodity, at a fixed time in the future. This obstacle was overcome with the introduction of the cash settlement procedure in 1982. When the underlying commodity is not suitable for actual physical delivery then an alternative is to deliver the cash value of the commodity at that time. The commodity which is delivered at the settlement date on the freight futures market is the cash equivalent of the general level of the freight market at that time as represented by an index. It is entirely a paper financial transaction and real ships and cargoes are not involved at all.

The Baltic Exchange commenced publication of a daily freight index – the Baltic Freight Index (BFI) – in January 1985. This index, which initially consisted of 13 voyage routes covering a variety of cargoes ranging from 14,000 metric tons (mt) of fertiliser up to 120,000 mt of coal and no time-charter routes, was developed as a settlement mechanism for the newly established BIFFEX futures contract. It quickly won worldwide acceptance as the most reliable general indicator of movements in the dry cargo freight market. Over the years, the constituent routes of that original index have been refined to meet the ever increasing and changing needs of the derivative markets. Time-charter routes were added in and, gradually, handysize and capesize routes were excluded from the index. As a result, in November 1999, the Baltic Panamax Index (BPI) superseded the BFI as the underlying asset of the BIFFEX contract. The BPI is a weighted average index of voyage and trip time-charter freight rates of seven component shipping routes for Panamax type vessels. The definitions of these routes and their weights in the composition of the BPI, as they stand on April 2002, as well as all the major changes in the composition of the BFI/BPI since its inception are presented in Table 1.

The BPI is calculated every London business day by the Baltic Exchange, from data supplied by a panel of fourteen international shipbrokers, and is reported in the market at 1 p.m. London time. The panel is composed of companies who "...*are deemed by the Baltic Exchange to be of sufficient size, reputation and integrity to be good independent arbiters of the market*" (Gray[4]). Each shipbroking company submits its view of that day's rate on each of the BPI constituent routes. These rates are based either on actual shipping fixtures concluded in the market, or in the absence of an actual fixture, reflect the panelist's expert view of what the rate would be on that day if a fixture had been concluded. As a precautionary measure to prevent any individual broker influencing the market, the highest and lowest assessments for each trade route are excluded and a simple arithmetic average is taken of those that remain. Then, the resulting route averages are used in the computation of the BPI.[6]

2.2 The freight futures market

Since their introduction, in January 1985, the shipping indices produced by the Baltic Exchange have been widely recognised by market practitioners as the

Table 1: Baltic Freight Index: major changes in its composition since its inception

	Vessel size (dwt)	Cargo	Route	4/01/85–3/11/88	4/11/88–3/08/90	6/08/90–4/02/91	5/02/91–4/02/93	5/02/93–2/11/93	3/11/93–5/05/98	6/05/98–29/10/99	From 1/11/99
1	55,000	Light Grain	US Gulf to ARA	20%	20%	10%	10%	10%	10%	10%	10%
1A	70,000	T/C	Trans-Atlantic round (duration 45–60 days)			10%	10%	10%	10%	10%	20%
2	54,000	HSS	US Gulf to South Japan	20%	20%	20%	10%	10%	10%	10%	12.5%
2A	70,000	T/C	Skaw-Gibraltar to Taiwan – Japan (50–60 days)				10%	10%	10%	10%	12.5%
3	54,000	HSS	US Pacific Coast to South Japan	15%	15%	7.50%	7.50%	7.50%	10%	10%	10%
3A	70,000	T/C	Trans-Pacific Round (35–50 days)			7.50%	7.50%	7.50%	10%	10%	20%
4	21,000	HSS	US Gulf to Venezuela	5%	5%	5%	5%	5%			
5	35,000	Barley	Antwerp to Jeddah (Saudi Arabia)	5%	5%	5%	5%	5%			
	38,000	T/C	South America to Far East								
6	120,000	Coal	Hampton Roads (US) to South Japan	5%	7.50%	7.50%	7.50%	7.50%	7.50%		
7	65,000	Coal	Hampton Roads (US) to ARA	5%	5%	5%	5%	5%	7.50%	7.50%	
	110,000	Coal	Hampton Roads (US) to ARA						7.50%		
8	130,000	Coal	Queensland (Australia) to Rotterdam	5%	5%	5%	5%	5%	7.50%		
9	55,000	Coke	Vancouver (Canada) to Rotterdam	5%	5%	5%	5%	5%			
	70,000	T/C	Japan – Korea to Skaw Passero (50–60 days)						10%	10%	15%
10	90,000	Iron Ore	Monrovia (Liberia) to Rotterdam	5%	5%	5%	5%	5%	7.50%	7.50%	
	150,000	Iron Ore	Tubarao (Brazil) to Rotterdam								
11	25,000	Pig Iron	Vitoria (Brazil) to China	5%							
	25,000	Phosphate	Casablanca (Morocco) to West Coast India		2.50%	2.50%	2.50%	2.50%			
12	20,000	Potash	Hamburg (Germany) to West Coast India	2.50%							
	14,000	Phosphate	Aqaba (Jordan) to West Coast India		5%	5%	5%	5%			
13	14,000	Phosphate	Aqaba (Jordan) to West Coast India	2.50%							
14	140,000	Iron Ore	Tubarao (Brazil) to Beilun and Baoshan (China)							7.50%	
15	140,000	Coal	Richards Bay (S. Africa) to Rotterdam							7.50%	

Notes: 1. ARA stands for Amsterdam, Rotterdam and Antwerp area. HSS stands for Heavy Grain, Soya and Sorghum; Skaw-Gibraltar is the range that extends from Cape Skaw to Gibraltar. 2. From 3 April 2001 the following route is also being published (but is not included in the calculation of the BPI): Route A1-70,000 mt of Coal from Richards Bay to Belgium – Holland. 3. Route 9 has been renamed Route 4 since 3 April 2000. 4. From 1 January 2003, routes 1A, 2A, 3A and 4 will be based on a 74,500 mt Panamax type vessel. 5. Few minor amendements are not included in the table. For a complete list of amendments see Nomikos.[11] Source: Nomikos[11] adapted using data from the Baltic exchange.

most reliable indicators of market conditions in the shipping industry. Figure 1 presents the history of the BFI over the period January 1985 to April 1998 and associates the fluctuations of the BFI with significant developments in the shipping markets and the world economy. As Gray[4] points out *"the clarity of vision [provided by the BFI] is a very useful service to the shipping industry"*. This availability of information is even more important in an industry such as shipping where physical deals are done on a private and confidential basis and hence information about physical transactions is not openly disclosed to the market. Therefore, shipping indices also provide "price transparency" in a market which has traditionally been very secretive.

Figure 1: Developments in the Dry Bulk Market and the BFI (5/01/85–30/04/98)

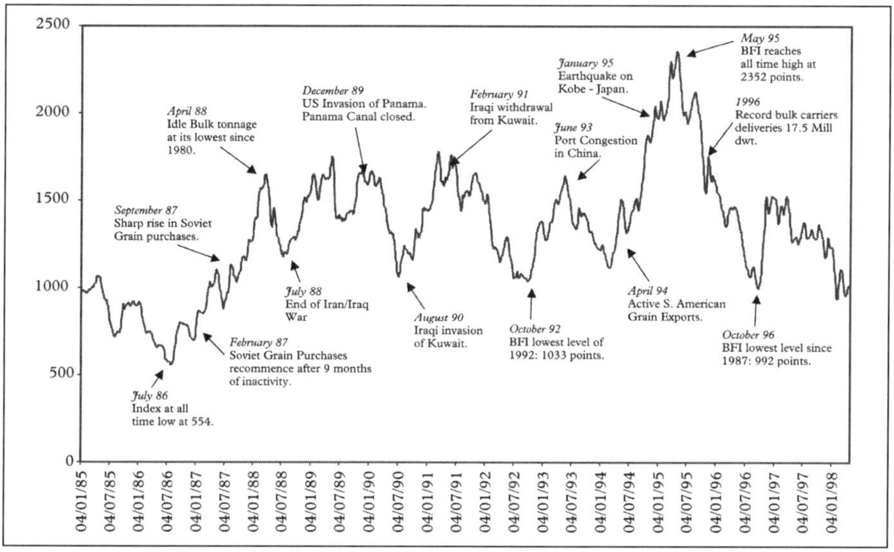

Source: Simpson, Spence and Young (SSY) Futures.

In addition to its use as the "barometer" of the shipping freight markets, on 1 May 1985 the BFI was also adopted as the underlying asset of the Baltic International Freight Futures Exchange (BIFFEX) contract.[7] The introduction of the BIFFEX contract gave the opportunity to shipping market agents to control their freight rate risk in the physical market through hedging. Additionally, through the price-discovery function, futures prices could also help reveal information about expected spot prices and hence provide valuable signals to market agents regarding the likely future direction of freight rates in the markets. The following sections provide empirical evidence on the performance of the BIFFEX contract in providing its price discovery and risk management functions.

2.2.1 The price discovery role of the freight futures market

Physical and financial asset prices are determined through the interaction of supply and demand forces in an economy. Futures markets provide a mechanism through which the supply and demand for an asset are brought into alignment, both in present and over time. Edwards and Ma[8] argue that since futures contracts are traded for the delivery of an underlying asset at various points in the future, they should reflect the current expectations of the market about the level of spot prices at those points in the future. For instance, if futures prices are higher than current spot prices then, this reflects the market's expectation that there will be an increased demand for that commodity in the future and vice versa. Therefore, through the discovery of expected spot prices, futures prices can help to smooth the supply and demand for a commodity over time, and, as a consequence, help to avoid the economic disbenefits that result from shortages in the flow of goods and services.

Spot and futures prices for financial and commodity futures markets are related through what is commonly known as the *cost-of-carry* relationship. The cost-of-carry relationship states that the price of a futures contract for delivery at some time in the future equals the current price of the underlying asset plus the total costs associated with purchasing and holding the underlying asset till the maturity of the futures contract. Any deviations from this relationship will be restored in the market through riskless arbitrage (see Kolb[9]). Therefore, the existence of arbitrage opportunities is the underlying factor that links spot and futures prices for commodities that can be stored and carried forward over time such as metals, oil, agricultural commodities and financial securities. However, the concept of carrying charges does not apply to commodities which are non-storable. One such "commodity" is shipping freight.

The BIFFEX contract trades the expected value of the service of seaborne transportation. The physical characteristics of this commodity make it impossible to store it or carry it forward in time. As a result, BPI and BIFFEX prices are not linked through arbitrage but are driven by the expectations of market agents regarding the spot prices that will prevail at the expiry of the contract. This pricing relationship is also called the unbiasedness hypothesis since it implies that futures prices are unbiased forecasts of the realised spot prices.[10]

Nomikos[11] and Kavussanos and Nomikos[12] investigate the unbiasedness hypothesis of BIFFEX prices 1, 2 and 3 months from maturity. They use a bivariate vector error-correction model (VECM), proposed by Johansen,[13,14] which provides a framework for valid statistical inference in the presence of non-stationary price series, such as BIFFEX prices.[15] Their results indicate that BIFFEX prices 1 and 2 months before maturity are unbiased predictors of the realised spot prices. On the other hand, futures prices three months from maturity provide biased estimates of the realised spot prices. This is thought to be a result of thin trading in the three-months contract and of the possible imbalance between short and long hedging demand for this contract, compared to shorter maturities.[16]

Nomikos[11] and Kavussanos and Nomikos[12] also provide a further dimension to the literature by investigating the forecasting accuracy of futures prices. After all, for futures to fulfil their price discovery role, they must also provide the most accurate forecasts of the realised spot prices. They find that BIFFEX prices across all maturities outperform alternative models for predicting the realised spot prices – such as VECM, random walk, ARIMA and exponential smoothing. This implies that market participants receive accurate signals from BIFFEX prices and can use those as indicators of the future course of BFI/BPI prices. To illustrate this, consider the following example; on 31 January 1997, the BFI stands at 1367 points and the BIFFEX contract for delivery in March 97 trades at 1455 points. This suggests that the market expects the BFI to strengthen, over the period January to March 1997, and rise above its current value of 1367 points. On 31 March 1997, the settlement date of the March 97 contract, the BFI stands at 1513 points, which is above its level on 31 January 97. Additionally, this benefit of price discovery, accrues not only to the charterers and shipowners who are involved in BIFFEX trading but also to all the market agents who have an interest in the future level of freight rates.

In addition to revealing information about expected spot prices, futures prices also provide information about the current spot prices (Edwards and Ma[8]). This issue is investigated in the BIFFEX market by Nomikos[11] and Kavussanos and Nomikos[17] who find that futures prices tend to discover new information more rapidly than contemporaneous spot prices. This is thought to reflect the fundamentals of the underlying commodity since, due to the impossibility of short-selling the underlying spot index, investors who have collected and analysed new information would prefer to trade in the futures rather than in the spot market. Sub-period results, corresponding to revisions in the composition of the underlying index (see Table 1), show that the price discovery role of futures prices has strengthened as a result of the more homogeneous composition of the index in recent years. Finally, the information incorporated in futures prices, when formulated as an error-correction model, produces more accurate forecasts of the spot prices than competing models. These findings indicate that the BIFFEX market contributes to the discovery of new information regarding both current and expected BPI prices and, as a result, the BIFFEX market performs its price discovery function efficiently.

2.2.2 The risk management function of the freight futures markets

Market agents are confronted with risks that arise from the ordinary conduct of their businesses. Derivative markets provide a way in which these risks may be transferred to other individuals who are willing to bear them, through hedging. Hedges are either short or long. A *short* or *selling* hedge involves selling futures contracts as a protection against an expected decline in freight rates. For instance a shipowner, fearing that freight rates will fall, will always be a seller of futures. A *long* or *buying* hedge, on the other hand, involves buying futures as a protection against a price increase. For instance a charterer will be a buyer of futures contracts; this will enable him to protect his forward freight requirements in case the physical market rises, thus forcing him to pay higher freight rates.

Table 2 presents a hedging example illustrating the use of BIFFEX for hedging the freight cost of a charterer.[18] It is early August 2000 and a grain trading house has concluded the sale of 54,000 tons of grain to receivers in Japan. Shipment will take place in late October and under the sale agreement, the seller of the cargo will be responsible for paying the transportation costs; the cargo will be shipped from US Gulf. The trading house is therefore worried over its exposure to freight risk since an appreciation in freight rates over the coming months will increase its transportation costs and will therefore erode the profitability of this trade. The current freight rate for 54,000 tons of heavy grains from US Gulf to Japan, that is Route 2 of the BPI (see Table 1) is 23.76 US$/tonne; had the charterer been able to charter a vessel immediately his freight expense would have been $1,283,040.

However, freight rate risk arises because by the time the charterer fixes his vessel in late October he may be forced to pay a higher freight rate. In an effort to control his freight rate costs, the charterer considers the use of a freight futures hedge, using October 2000 BIFFEX contracts; On 4 August 2000, the BPI stands at 1595 points and the October 2000 contract trades at 1600 points. This represents a premium of the futures contract relative to the spot of 0.31% (1600/1595 − 1) which reflects the market's view that freight rates may increase slightly between August and end of October. As a result, the market also expects the freight rate for route 2 to be 23.76*(1 + 0.0031) = 23.84 US$/tonne. The charterer wants to lock at this forward rate and he therefore, initiates a freight futures hedge, by buying BIFFEX contracts for delivery in October 2000; the monetary value of these contracts is 1600 * 10 $ /point = $ 16,000. In order to initiate his hedging strategy, he sets a futures position which matches exactly his exposure in the physical freight market. Therefore, he buys 1,287,360/16,000 ≈ 80 futures contracts.

By the time he fixes the vessel, on 31 October 2000, the freight rate has increased to 25.20 $/tonne. He therefore, fixes tonnage at that rate and his total freight rate expense is 25.20*54,000 = $1,360,800 which represents an increase of $73,440 over his expected position in early July. However, the increase in

Table 2: An example of hedging freight rates using the Freight Futures Market

Physical market	Futures market
4 August 2000	
BPI: 1595 Route 2 freight rate: 23.76 $/tonne Freight cost: $1,283,040 (= 54,000*23.76)	October 2000 BIFFEX price: 1600 Expected rate: 23.84 (=23.76*(1600/1595)) Expected freight: $1,287,360 (= 54,000*23.84)
Charterer **buys** 80 July 2000 contracts with a total value of: $1,280,000 (= 80*1600*10)	
31 October 2000	
BPI: 1631 Route 2 freight rate: 25.20 $/tonne Actual freight cost: $1,360,800 Loss in the physical market $1,287,360−$1,360,800 = −$73,440	October 2000 BIFFEX Settlement price: 1627 Total value: $1,301,600 (= 80*1627*10) Profit from the futures transaction $1,301,600−$1,280,000 = $21,600
Net result from hedging = −$51,840	

route 2 of the physical market (see Table 1), is accompanied by a corresponding increase in the dry bulk market in general, as represented by BPI, which implies that the settlement price of the October 2000 contract has increased accordingly. Combining the loss in the physical market with the gain in the futures market gives an overall loss of $51,840. Therefore, we can note that the use of BIFFEX for hedging has moderated the impact of the increase in freight rates.[19]

The previous example describes the mechanics of a futures hedge. More formal tests of the hedging effectiveness of the BIFFEX contract have been provided in a series of studies by Nomikos[11] and Kavussanos and Nomikos.[20-22] In order to establish a hedged position, a trader has to determine an appropriate hedge ratio, that is the ratio of the spot position which is hedged in the futures market. Ederington[23] shows that the hedge ratio that minimises the risk of a given spot position is equal to the ratio of the covariance between spot and futures price changes over the unconditional variance of futures price changes, as follows (see Appendix 1):

$$\gamma^\star = \frac{Cov(\Delta S_t, \Delta F_t)}{Var(\Delta F_t)} \quad (1)$$

This is also known as the minimum variance hedge ratio (MVHR). Thuong and Vischer[24] and Haralambides[25] apply this methodology to the BIFFEX market and find that a shipowner can achieve greater risk reduction by using the MVHR compared to a hedge ratio of 1.0.[26]

However, Kroner and Sultan[27] show that MVHR may lead to inferior hedging results due to the implicit assumption in equation (1) that the volatility in spot and futures markets is constant over time. They argue that this assumption is too restrictive and, as a result, optimal hedge ratios should be time-varying. Nomikos[11] and Kavussanos and Nomikos[20-22] estimate time-varying hedge ratios for the underlying shipping routes of the BPI. They model spot and futures returns as a VECM (Johansen[13]) with a Generalised Autoregressive Conditional Heteroskedasticity (GARCH) error structure with exogenous parameters, using what is termed a VECM-GARCH-X model (Engle,[28] Bollerslev[29] and Lee[30]); time-varying hedge ratios are then calculated from the estimated variance-covariance matrix of the model.

They then evaluate the effectiveness of these hedge ratios using both "historical" (or ex-post) hedging strategies as well as more realistic "out-of-sample" (or ex-ante) hedging strategies. They find that the hedging effectiveness of the BIFFEX contract varies from 19.2% to 4.0% across the different shipping routes which constitute the underlying index. This is well below the risk reduction evidenced in other markets, (57.06% for the Canadian Interest rate futures (Gagnon and Lypny[31]), 69.61% and 85.69% for the corn and soybean futures (Bera et al.[32]) and 97.91% and 77.47% for the SP500 and the Canadian Stock Index futures contract, respectively (Park and Switzer[33]), and reflects the fact that futures prices do not capture accurately the fluctuations on the individual routes that constitute the BPI, but rather follow the movements of the BPI itself. This is due to the fact that hedging using BIFFEX is essentially a cross-hedge. Unlike other futures markets, in which futures contracts are used as a hedge against price fluctuations in the underlying asset, in the BIFFEX market futures contracts are employed as a cross-hedge against freight rate fluctuations on the individual shipping routes which constitute the BPI. As such, there is the risk that fluctuations on these routes may not be accurately tracked by the futures prices, thus reducing the effectiveness of the contract as a hedging instrument. Cross-hedging freight rate risk using an index-based futures contract is only successful when the freight rate and the futures price move together. However, when a large number of underlying routes compose an index then the relationship between these routes and the index will not be very strong.

Therefore, BIFFEX market participants, who use the contract to hedge their freight rate risk on specific shipping routes, have minuscule gains in terms of risk reduction. This finding also explains why the BIFFEX contract is considered by the shipping industry as being a trend hedge instrument, that is an instrument that provides risk reduction against fluctuations in the general level of freight rates as these are represented by the fluctuations of the BPI. However, the contract is not very effective for market agents who want to reduce their freight rate risk on a specific cargo route since, as is evidenced by the findings of those studies, there is substantial basis risk.[34]

The poor hedging performance of the contract is also thought to be the primary reason for the low trading activity evidenced in the market. Over the period from February 1996 to June 2000, the average daily trading volume in the market was only 146 contracts. The monetary value of these contracts roughly corresponds to the average freight cost of transporting 108,000 tons of Grain from US Gulf to Japan (that is, 2 voyages in Route 2 of the BPI); market sources estimate that this level of futures trading activity corresponds to only 10% of the total physical activity in the dry-bulk shipping market.

The regulators of the BIFFEX contract, have attempted to address the issues of low hedging performance and low trading volume by altering the composition of the underlying index on a number of occasions, as shown in Table 1. Kavussanos and Nomikos[17] have shown that the price discovery role of futures prices strengthened as a result of those revisions. The impact of those revisions in the hedging performance of the contract is also addressed in the studies of Nomikos[11] and Kavussanos and Nomikos.[22] They examine the hedging effectiveness of the BIFFEX contract between sub-periods corresponding to these changes in the structure of the BPI. They find that hedging effectiveness increased as a result of the more homogeneous composition of the index over the recent years. More specifically, it seems that following those revisions in the market, the ability of the BIFFEX contract in tracking the fluctuations of the underlying shipping routes has improved. However, despite this, the magnitude of the observed increases in hedging effectiveness was still small, compared to other markets – the maximum degree of hedging effectiveness across all the routes being only 39.95%.

It seems therefore, that these changes in the composition of the underlying index have not been successful in inducing market agents to use the market for hedging purposes. As a matter of fact, the average trading volume for the period after November 1999 – when the BPI was introduced as the underlying asset of the BIFFEX – was only 17 contracts a day. This reduction in the trading activity of the BIFFEX market is also in line with the trading preferences of participants in the shipping markets who are now increasingly using over-the-counter forward contracts, called Forward Freight Agreements (FFAs), which are cash settled against the underlying shipping routes of the BPI. Because of the fact that these contracts are traded against specific routes, rather than a general index, they also avoid the problem of basis risk, evidenced in the BIFFEX market. As a result of the low trading activity in the market, LIFFE eventually decided to withdraw the BIFFEX contract from the market in April 2002. Many practitioners suggest that part of the reason that the BIFFEX contract has been delisted is because of the development and subsequent growth in the FFA market. The mechanics of the FFA contracts are described in the next section.

2.3 Forward freight agreements

A Forward Freight Agreement (FFA) is a contract between two counterparties to settle a freight rate or hire rate, for a specified quantity of cargo or type of vessel, for one of the major shipping routes in the dry-bulk or the tanker markets at a certain date in the future. The underlying asset of the FFA contracts can be any of the routes that constitute the indices produced by the Baltic Exchange. As in the case of the futures contract, FFA's are settled in cash on the difference between the contract price and an appropriate settlement price. This is usually the average rate of the route over the last seven days of a month, or the average hire-rate over a month for the time-charter routes.

FFAs first emerged in 1992 as a response to the needs of market players who were aware of the deficiencies of the BIFFEX as a hedging instrument and wanted a more precise match for their physical requirements and hence a more accurate hedging mechanism. Figure 2 presents the near month FFA and spot rates on route 2 (see Table 1 for definition). We can note that the two series move closely together, which is also confirmed by the value of their correlation coefficient (0.96).

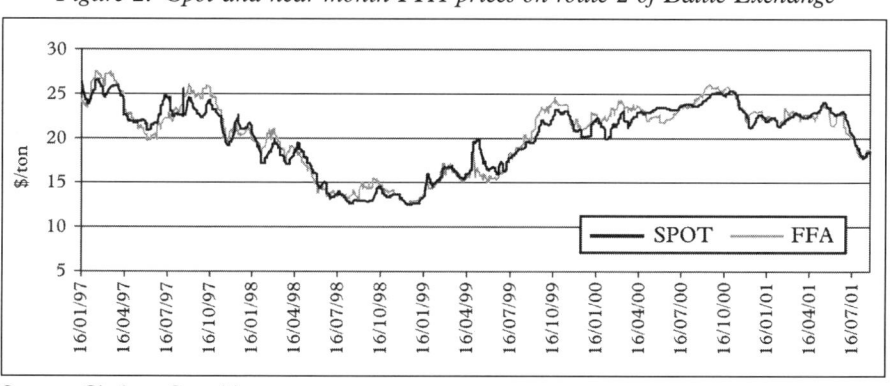

Figure 2: Spot and near month FFA prices on route 2 of Baltic Exchange

Source: Clarkson Securities.

Since the introduction of FFA contracts, the market has been growing steadily and market sources estimate that the tonal number of FFAs traded in the dry and wet shipping markets for 2001 was around 2000 contracts. The growth of transactions in the FFA market is also evidenced in Figure 3, which presents the estimated notional amount of freight which is traded in the FFA market.

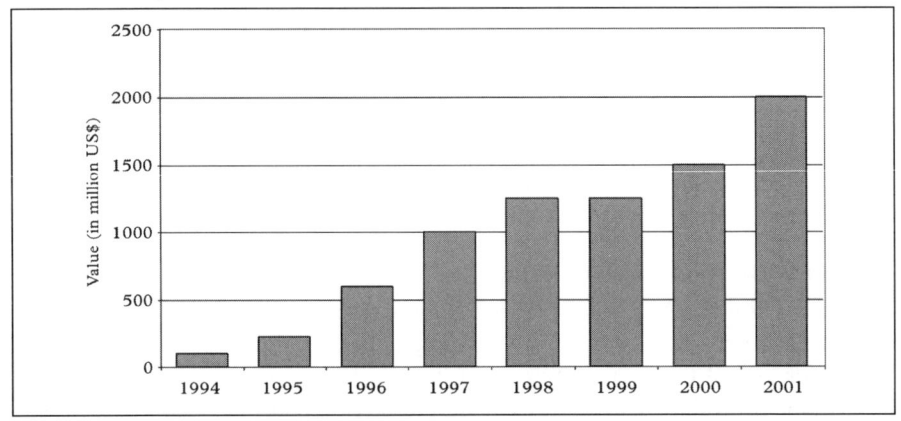

Figure 3: Estimated value of transactions in the FFA market

Source: Simpson, Spence and Young (SSY) Futures. Reported figures are market estimates. The average size of each contract is $1m, therefore, the above figures can be converted to approximate number of FFA contracts.

FFAs are traded as an over the-counter (OTC) instrument. In other words, the FFA contract are negotiated by a broker between the two counterparties (or "principals" as they are known in the shipping industry) in a manner similar to a conventional physical market negotiation. FFAs are primarily used for hedging purposes by charterers and shipowners although they can also be used for the purposes of speculating on the future direction of the freight markets. Hedging using FFAs is based on the principle that physical freight rates and FFA rate move together over time. Therefore, shipowners are sellers of FFA's - since when freight rates fall, the reduction in the freight income will be compensated through a gain in the forward position - and charterers are buyers of FFA's. The following examples illustrate the use of FFAs for hedging purposes

2.3.1 Hedging voyage freight risk using FFAs

Table 3, presents a hedging example illustrating the use of FFAs for hedging freight rate risk; the example is based on the same data that we considered for BIFFEX hedging. The charterer considers now using an FFA hedge by buying a route 2 FFA for settlement in October 2000. On 4 August 2000, Route 2 FFA is at 23.90 $/tonne which represents a premium of the forward contract relative to the spot of 0.59% (23.90/23.76 − 1); this reflects the market's view that route 2 freight rates will increase between August and end of October. As a result, expected freight cost, as implied by the FFA rates is going to be $ 1,290,600 (= 54,000 * 23.90). The charterer decides to "lock" at this rate by buying an October 2000 route 2 FFA.

By the time he fixes his vessel, on 31 October 2000, the freight rate has increased to 25.20 $/tonne. He fixes tonnage at that rate and his total freight expense is 25.20*54,000 = $1,360,800 which represents an increase of $70,200 ($1,360,800 - $1,290,600) over his expected position in early July. At the same time, the settlement price of the route 2 FFA October 2000 contract, which is calculated as the average of route 2 rates over the last seven trading days in October, has increased to 25.14 $/tonne. His FFA position therefore generates a profit of (25.14 – 23.90)*54,000 = $66,960. Combining the loss in the physical market with the gain in the futures market gives an overall loss of $3,240.

Table 3: An example of hedging freight rates using the Forward Freight Agreements

3-month hedge for the period 4 August to 31 October 2000	
Physical market	**Futures market**
4 August 2000	
Route 2 freight rate: 23.76 $/tonne Freight cost: $1,283,040 (= 54,000*23.76)	Route 2 October 2000 FFA: 23.90 $/tonne Expected freight: $1,290,600 (= 54,000 * 23.90)
Charterer **buys** October 2000 FFA contract	
31 October 2000	
Route 2 freight rate: 25.20 $/tonne 25.20 $/tonne Actual freight cost: $ 1,360,800	October 2000 FFA settlement: 25.14 $/tonne
Loss in the physical market $1,290,600–$1,360,800 = –$70,200	Profit from FFA transaction (25.14–23.90)*54,000 = $66,960
Net result from hedging = –$3,240	

We can note that through the use of forwards the hedger can achieve superior hedging results compared to BIFFEX contracts. This is due to the fact that hedging using FFAs locks in the expected value of route 2 whereas BIFFEX contracts lock in the expected value of a general index, such as the BPI, and as a result there is a mismatch. As a result, FFAs provide an almost perfect hedge. The difference between the change in the physical market and the change in the FFA market, which is $3,240, is due to the fact that the settlement rate of the FFA contract, the average rate in route over the last 7 days of October, is slightly different than the prevailing rate on the 31st October, which is the date at which the shipowner has fixed his vessel.[35]

2.3.2 Hedging timecharter freight rate risk

FFAs are also traded for trip time-charter routes from either the Panamax, Capesize or Handymax indices. Trading also takes place on the average of the timecharter routes from each of the Baltic Indices. Consider the following example. In early July 2001, a shipowner has just fixed a panamax vessel for a trip from Australia to the Atlantic which will leave the vessel open for business in the Continent around the end of August. He feels the market is likely to soft-en in the coming months, so by the time he fixes his vessel in the end of August, freight rates may be lower compared to their current levels. For that, he decides to hedge the vessel forward for a time-charter trip to the Far East by selling a Route 2A (Continent–Far East trip time-charter) FFA for settlement in August. The settlement rate will be the monthly average rate of route 2A for August and the settlement price will be calculated on the basis of a voyage duration of 60 days (see the definitions of the routes in Table 1).

The hedging example is presented in Table 4. On 2 July 2001, route 2A is at 11,158 $/day and Route 2A FFA is at 10,050 $/day. The FFA trades at a discount of 9.93% (10050/11158 – 1) compared to the physical rate which reflects the market's view that freight rates may fall between July and end of August. As a result, the expected freight rate income, implied by the FFA rates, is $ 603,000 (= 10,050 $/day * 60 days). The shipowner considers this forward rate attractive and decides to "lock" this by selling a route 2A FFA for delivery in August 2001.

By the time he fixes the vessel, on 31 August 2001, the panamax market has weakened and the hire rate has now fallen to 7,483 $/day. The shipowner, fixes his vessel at that rate and his total freight rate revenue for the duration of the voyage will be 7,483 $/day * 60 days = $ 448,980 which represents a decrease of $154,020 (= $448,980 - $603,000) over his expected position in early July. At the same time, FFA rates have also fallen; the settlement price of the FFA contract is 7,545 $/day. His FFA position therefore generates a profit of (10050 - 7545)*60 = $ 150,300. Combining the loss in the physical market with the gain in the futures market gives an overall loss of only $3,720.

It should be stressed, that in this example we have implicitly assumed that the shipowner's panamax type vessel is of an identical specification to the standard Baltic Panamax vessel (see the definition in Table 1). Of course this is a very unlikely to happen in practice and in reality one would have to assess the pre-

Table 4: An example of hedging freight rates using the Forward Freight Agreements

2-month hedge for the period 2 July 2001 to 31 August 2001	
Physical market	**FFA market**
2 July 2001	
Route 2A freight rate: 11,158 $/day Freight cost: $669,480 (= 11,158*60 days)	Route 2A August 2001 FFA: 10,050 $/day Expected freight: $603,000 (= 10,050*60 days)
Shipowner **sells** August 2001 FFA contract	
31 August 2001	
Route 2A freight rate: 7,483 $/day Actual Freight Cost: $448,980	August 2001 FFA settlement: 7,545 $/day
Loss in the physical market $448,980–$603,000 = –$154,020	Gain from FFA transaction (10,050–7,545)*60 = $150,300
Net result from hedging = –$3,720	

mium or discount his vessel would normally expect to command in relation to the Baltic standard Panamax. For some types of older vessels with higher fuel consumption, a discount of say 2,000 $/day might apply. In this case and using the example above, the owner would have been looking to protect a forward rate of less $2000 daily.

2.3.3 Empirical evidence on the FFA market

In line with the studies in the BIFFEX market, the issues of price discovery and predictability of forward freight rates, for four different routes of panamax vessels, are investigated in Kavussanos *et al.*[36] and Batchelor *et al.*[37] Kavussanos *et al.*[36] report that FFA rates one- and two-months prior to maturity are unbiased predictors of the realised spot prices in routes 1, 1A, 2 and 2A of the BPI while, for longer maturities (3-months), the results are not conclusive with the unbiasedness hypothesis being rejected in routes 1 and 1A. This could be attributed to "thin" trading on these routes for long maturities which results in the existence of a bias in prices.[38] The finding of a bias in the long maturities is also in line with the results from the BIFFEX market.[12]

The price discovery of FFAs is also investtigated in Batchelor et al.[37]; they compare the forecasting performance of different econometric models in predicting spot and forward freight rates in the same four panamax routes. Their results indicate that FFAs are to some extent predictable and it seems that multivariate models of spot and forward returns outperform univariate models in short-term forecasts (1 to 10 days ahead) while univariate models perform better for longer horizons (10 to 20 days-ahead). In addition, the forecasting performance of FFA rates, in predicting realised spot rates in the market, is compared against those from univariate and multivariate models. The results indicate that forecasts implied by FFA rates, outperform those generated from alternative models, in all routes. This is also in line with Kavussanos and Nomikos (1999)[12] and provides further evidence that the FFA market performs its price discovery function efficiently.

The FFA market has evidenced considerable growth over the recent years. This is because FFA contracts provide risk reduction against specific shipping routes; as such, they avoid the problems of cross-hedging and basis risk evidenced in the BIFFEX market and also provide more accurate match for the physical requirements of market practitioners. This implies that FFAs provide an almost perfect hedge as they lock in at the forward rate when the hedge is placed.[39] Another feature of the market, is that an FFA position has to be carried over to the maturity of the contract and cannot be closed prior to it.[40] In other words, FFA contracts cannot be bought or sold back to the counterparties prior to settlement.[41] This may put FFA traders in a disadvantageous position since they may not be able to close FFA positions if the FFA market moves against them.

2.3.4 Characteristics of the FFA contracts

Since FFA contracts are principal to principal agreements, each contract may be tailor-made to the requirements of each trade and counterparties may introduce their own variations to the contract, provided of course that they are mutually agreed. Such variations may include the trading of part cargoes – e.g., trading 27,000 tons of grain from US Gulf to Japan as opposed to a full cargo of 54,000 tons as stipulated in Route 2 – the introduction of different methods for calculating the settlement price – e.g., the settlement price being the average of a month as opposed to the average of the last seven days – as well as different settlement periods – for instance, settlement being effected in the middle of a month, as opposed to in the end of a month. This is of course in contrast to the BIFFEX market where the contracts were standardised with fixed characteristics. On the other hand, greater standardisation leads to greater liquidity and as a result, only a handful of routes, on generally accepted terms, are actively traded in the market.

Finally, since FFA contracts are traded directly between principals, the counterparties in each contract must agree to do business with each other which also means that each party is exposed to some element of credit risk in case the other party defaults. The significance of this was highlighted recently following the defaults of some of the biggest players in the market (such as Andre and Enron). Counterparties which had outstanding FFA contracts with these companies had no recourse in getting back their funds following their default. Credit (or default) risk is a feature of all the OTC markets since the contracts are not guaranteed by an independent clearing house as is the cash in the exchange traded contracts.[42] The remedies that have been suggested for the overcoming the problem of credit risk are diverse and range from full clearing of FFA contracts through the London Clearing house to the adoption and use of credit derivatives for hedging default risk.[43]

Despite these shortcoming, FFA contracts are supported by the shipping industry primarily because of their ability to track fluctuations on individual shipping routes. Their introduction also paved the way for the adoption of more exotic instruments such as options on individual freight routes. These are described next.

2.4 Options on freight rates

Option contracts as means of risk management and speculation have been established for a long time in the financial commodity markets for hedging interest rates, foreign exchange, equities and commodities. Options in the shipping industry were introduced in 1990 when trading on options on BIFFEX started. Like the BIFFEX contracts itself, however, trading on options on BIFFEX never picked-up and eventually, the contract was de-listed in April 2002. Options are also traded for the individual routes which constitute the Baltic indices. These are traded as OTC instruments, in the same fashion as standard FFAs, and over the recent years they have become more popular with shipping market practitioners.

2.4.1 A primer on options

There are two types of option contracts; call options and put options. A call option is a contract, which gives its holder (or buyer) the right, but not the obligation, to buy an underlying asset (e.g., freight rate) from the seller (or writer) of the call option at certain price, known as the strike price, and at a certain point in time, known as the expiration date or the maturity. On the other hand, a put option gives its holder the right, but not the obligation, to sell an underlying asset to the writer of the put option at a certain strike price and at the expiration date. In order to have such a right the buyer of the option pays a premium to the writer of the option on the agreement. The premium is also known as the option price. Option contracts are also classified according to the date that they can be exercised: a European option can only be exercised at the maturity of the option; an American option can be exercised at any time during the life of the option including the maturity. Options give their holder the flexibility of buying or selling an underlying asset at a certain pre-specified price during or at certain period. This is important as the holder is under no obligation to settle the contract in contrast to futures, forward and swap contracts.

There are two parties for every option contract; the buyer, or long, and the writer, or short. This also implies that the buyer's and seller's payoffs from entering into an option agreement are reverse. To see this, consider the payoff to a holder of a European call option on route A1 of the BPI (70,000 mt of Coal, from Richards Bay to North Europe) with a strike price of 6$/tonne, shown in panel (a) of Figure 4. It can be seen that if freight rates rise over the strike price, the option is exercised and, as a result, the gain to the option holder is the difference between the spot freight rate at the maturity of the option and the exercise price. On the other hand, if the spot rate is below the strike price, the option will not be exercised and expires therefore, worthless. Therefore, the value of the call option to the holder can be written mathematically as $\max(S_t-X,0)$, where S_t is the spot price at the maturity and X is the strike price.[44] Similarly, panel (b) of Figure 4 shows the payoff to the writer of the same call option. This is the inverse of the payoff to buyer of the option. Thus, the value of the option to the writer is $-\max(S_t-X,0)$.

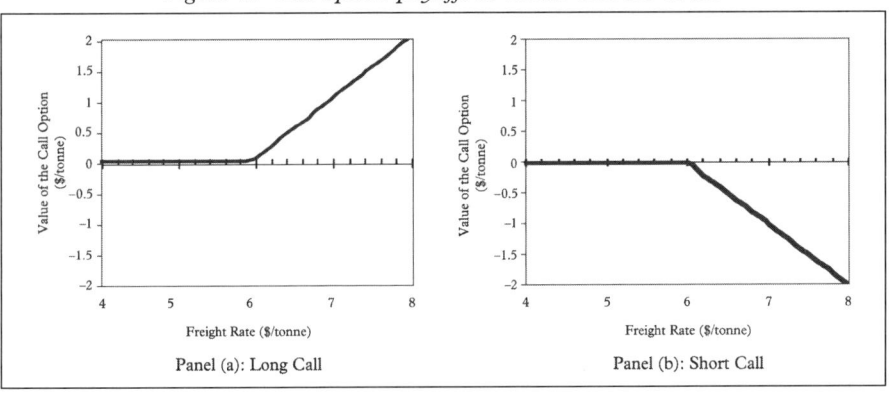

Figure 4: Call option payoffs to holder and the writer

Turning next into puts, panel (a) of Figure 5 plots the payoff of the holder of a European put option on route A1 with a strike price of 6$/tonne. It can be seen that, depending on the spot rate at the expiration of the option, the holder's payoff can vary from zero to the difference between the strike price and the spot price at the maturity. Therefore, the payoff of a put option to its holder can be written as max(X–S$_t$,0). Similarly, the payoff from a short put position is –max(X–S$_t$,0), as shown in panel (b) of Figure 5.

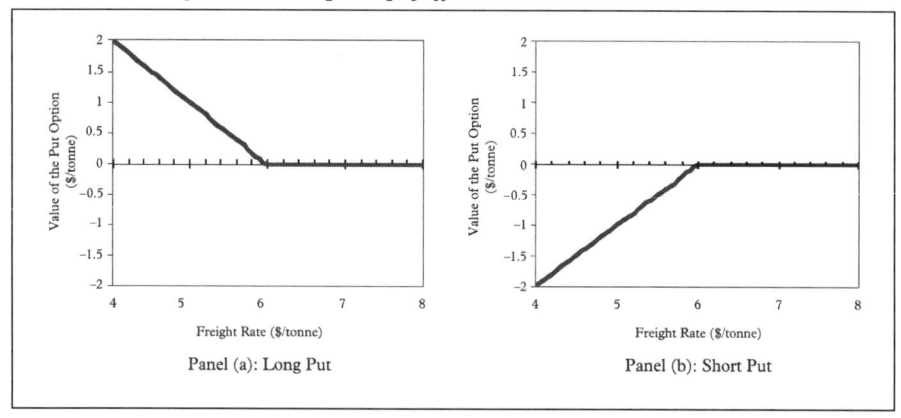

Figure 5: Put option payoff to the holder and the writer

Panel (a): Long Put

Panel (b): Short Put

2.4.2 Hedging example using options

Table 5 presents a hedging example illustrating the use of Options on FFAs. It is early April 2001 and a commodity trading house has concluded the sale of 70,000 tons of thermal coal to receivers in Europe. Shipment will take place in late October and under the sale agreement, the seller of the cargo will be responsible for paying the transportation costs; the cargo will be shipped from Richards Bay, in South Africa. The trading house is therefore worried over his exposure to freight risk since an appreciation in freight rates over the coming months will increase the transportation costs. The current rate on Route A1 of the BPI (70,000 tonnes of Coal from Richards Bay to North Europe, see Table 1) is 7.26 US$/tonne; had the charterer been able to charter a vessel immediately his freight expense would have been $508,200 (= 7.26 $/tonne*70,000 tonnes).

In an effort to control his freight rate costs, the charterer considers the use of derivatives. He could use FFAs to "lock" in a certain freight cost, however, he is concerned that such an approach is inflexible and does not enable him to take advantage of a potential fall in freight rates. For that he decides to buy an October 2001 call option for route A1 of the BPI. His broker advises him that there is a counterparty willing to "write" him an October 2001 call option with a strike price of 7.5 $/tonne at a premium of 60 cents/tonne. Therefore, the total premium that the charterer will pay to the seller of the call is 0.60 * 70,000 = $42,000.

By the time he fixes the vessel, on 31 October 2000, the freight rate has fallen to 4.86 $/tonne. The charterer therefore, fixes tonnage at that rate and his total freight rate expense is 4.86*70,000 = $ 340,200 which represents a reduction of $168,000 ($508,200 – $340,200) over his position in early April. At the same time, since the strike price is greater than the spot price at the expiration

RISK MANAGEMENT IN THE SHIPPING INDUSTRY 711

of the option (7.50 > 4.86) the option is not exercised and expires worthless. Combining the cost of the option premium with the total freight rate expense results in a total freight cost of $ 382,200 ($340,200 + $42,000).

In order to illustrate the flexibility that is provided through the use of options, consider what would have happened to the hedging position if there had been an increase in the level of freight rates. Say for instance that on 31 October, route A1 freight rate was at 9.5 $/tonne. The hedging outcome in this scenario is also presented in Table 5.

Therefore, options are a flexible hedging instrument since they enable the charterer to lock in a specific rate when freight rates increase and fix his vessels at the prevailing spot rate, when freight rates decrease. More specifically, if the spot rate is greater than the strike price at the expiration of the option then the option is exercised and, as a result, the effective freight rate for the company is the strike price plus the option premium, which is $567,000 (= (7.5 + 0.6) *70,000). Similarly, if the spot rate is lower than the strike price, the option expires worthless, and the effective freight rate is the current spot rate in the market plus the option premium. The total freight cost in this case is (4.86 + 0.6)*70,000 = $ 382,200.

Table 5: An example of hedging freight rates using freight rate options

6-month hedge for the period 2 April 2001 to 31 October 2001	
Physical market	**Options market**
2 April 2001	
Route A1 freight rate: 7.26 $/tonne Freight cost: $508,200 (= 70,000*7.26)	Option details: October 2001 Call with a strike Price of 7.5 $/tonne. Premium: 60 cents/tonne
Charterer **buys** October 2001 call at a total cost of $42,000 (= 0.60*70,000)	
31 October 2001 – falling market	
Route 2 freight rate: 4.86 $/tonne Actual freight cost: $340,200	Strike price (7.5) > spot price (4.86) Therefore option is not exercised
Gain in the physical market $168,000 = $508,200 – $340,200	Payoff from the options transaction –$42,000
Total freight cost (including option premium) = $382,200	
31 October 2001 – alternative scenario - rising market	
Route 2 freight rate: 9.5 $/tonne Actual freight cost: $665,000	Strike price (7.5) < spot price (9.5) Therefore option is exercised
Loss in the physical market –$156,800 = $508,200–$665,000	Payoff from the options transaction (9.5 – 7.5)*70,000–42,000 = $ 98,000
Total freight cost (including option premium) = $665,000–$98,000 = $567,000	

2.4.3 Other derivative instruments

In addition to the use of FFAs and Options, there are also other instruments which may occasionally be used for the purposes of freight-rate risk management. One such instrument is commodity derivatives, for instance, using oil futures to hedge tanker freight rate risk. Although this is essentially a cross-hedge and may result in significant basis risk, the use of commodity derivatives may be preferred when there are no available derivative instruments for a specific freight route or when the liquidity in those instruments is very low. Additionally, market participants occasionally use instruments such as caplets, floorlets and collars on freight rates. These are also being used widely in other areas of shipping risk management such as bunker hedging. Their uses and applications in this area are discussed in the following section in more detail.

3. MANAGING VOYAGE COSTS RISK

Voyage costs are those costs incurred in a particular voyage in which the ship is involved. These are mainly fuel costs, port charges, pilotage and canal dues. They depend on the specific voyage undertaken as well as the type and size of the vessel. For example, Suez Canal and Panama Canal tolls are based on the tonnage of the vessel.

Bunker fuel costs account for almost 50% of the total voyage costs,[45] and as a result fluctuations in bunker prices have a major impact on the operating profits in the shipping industry. In general, ships use bunker fuel for propulsion and diesel oil for manoeuvring in ports and electricity generators. Although, recent technological advances enabled ships to use lower grade bunker fuel more efficiently, high grade bunker is still used by more sophisticated ships, especially cruise ships and fast ferries.

Fuel oil is a low derivative of petroleum and its price is closely related to that of oil. Since oil prices are very volatile and depend upon many factors, including political and economic events around the world, it is possible that disturbances and shocks to the world oil market are transmitted to the bunker market causing large fluctuations in bunker prices. From the point of view of a shipowner or ship operator, fluctuations in bunker prices are undesirable as they directly affect their operating profits. Therefore, the aim of the following sections is to discuss different techniques, methods and instruments, which are available to shipowners, operators and other agents involved in the bunker market, to control their bunker risk.

3.1 The world bunker market

Although marine bunkers are bought and sold in almost every port in the world, the world bunker market can be broadly divided into three major regional markets in which the bulk of physical bunkering activities takes place. These markets are Singapore (Asia), Rotterdam (Europe) and Houston (America). Other relatively important geographical markets include New York, Fujairah, Yokohama and Hamburg.

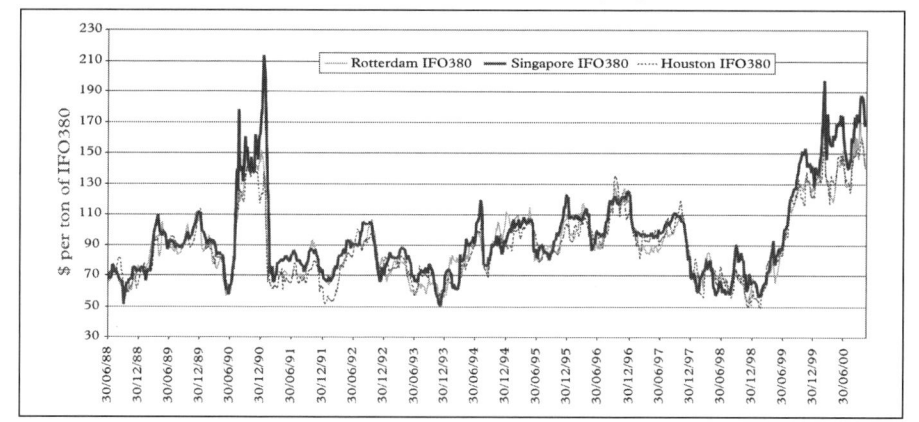

Figure 6: Plot of historical bunker prices in three major ports around the world

Source: Cockett Marine.

Figure 6 presents the historical bunker prices in three major ports; namely, Singapore, Rotterdam and Houston. Two observations can be made. First, it can be seen that although bunker prices in these three ports move together in the long run, there are short term deviations between prices. The long run co-movements of bunker prices can be attributed to the fact that bunker prices are closely related to the world oil prices as bunker fuel is a low-grade derivative of petroleum. The short run deviations between prices in different ports are mainly due to the regional supply and demand imbalances. Second, historical prices indicate large fluctuations and high volatility in bunker prices. This is also expected, because bunker prices are linked to world oil prices, therefore shocks and large swings in the world oil market can directly affect the world bunker market. As a result, bunker prices in all major ports follow oil prices very closely.

The volatile nature of the world oil and bunker markets leaves shipowners and ship operators in a very difficult position as their operating profit may be wiped off very quickly due to sudden changes in these markets. To see this point consider a panamax owner who fixes a contract of affreightment (CoA) for 150,000 tons of cargo today, which requires three shipments, one every two months, at a rate of 15$/tonne. This means that the freight contract generates $750,000 (15$/ton*50,000 ton) every two months. If the current bunker price is 100$/mt (metric ton), and the ship consumes 2500 mt of bunker per voyage, the expected profit for the shipowner from each voyage, assuming that port charges are $100,000, will be $400,000. Now consider the case where bunker prices increase by 20% to 120$/mt in two months time. This results in an overall reduction in profits of $150,000 for the entire contract. The aim of the next sections is to introduce and discuss the different instruments and techniques available to reduce such risks. These instruments include Petroleum and Petroleum product futures contracts, Forward bunker agreements, Bunker Swaps, Options on bunker prices and other tailor made derivative contracts which are designed especially to eliminate or control bunker price risk.

3.2 Hedging bunker price fluctuations using futures contracts

Fuel oil futures contract were traded in the Singapore Exchange during the period 1988 to 1992. However, trading was eventually stopped due to the low trading volume. The International Petroleum Exchange (IPE) also launched a bunker futures contract in January 1999. This also proved unsuccessful and the contract was withdrawn after six months.

In the absence of bunker futures contracts, and because of the close correlation between bunker prices and petroleum and petroleum derivatives prices, futures contracts on the latter commodities are alternative candidates for bunker price risk management. Hedging against bunker price fluctuations using futures contracts involves a cross-hedge against an existing crude or petroleum futures product. Table 6 shows the currently existing oil and oil derivative contracts which can be used for cross hedging bunker price fluctuations, and the market they are traded on.

In choosing a petroleum futures contract to cross hedge fluctuations in bunker prices, one needs to consider the futures contract which has the highest correlation with bunker prices. This is because the higher the correlation between the bunker prices and futures contract, the more effective is the performance of the hedging exercise. Alizadeh et al.[46] investigate the effectiveness of hedging bunker prices in Singapore, Rotterdam and Houston using futures contract offered in the IPE and NYMEX using constant and time-varying hedge ratios over the period 30/06/1988 to 9/11/2000. The estimated correlation coefficients indicate that historically, returns on all three spot bunkers show higher correlation with returns on the IPE gas oil futures than with any other crude and petroleum futures contracts (these are 0.4991, 0.4131 and 0.2975 for Rotterdam, Singapore and Houston, respectively), and as a result the IPE gas oil futures might be the best futures contract for risk minimisation in all three bunker markets. In- and out-of-sample test of hedging performance, indicate that the IPE gas oil futures contract offers the best hedging effectiveness, of around 25%, and the hedging performance is better in the case of the

Table 6: Actively traded petroleum futures and options contracts

Product	Size of Contract	Futures	Options
IPE (London)			
Brent Crude	1000 barrels	☑	☑
Gas Oil (ARA)	1000 barrels	☑	☑
NYMEX (New York)			
Heating Oil (#2)	1000 barrels	☑	☑
Light, Sweet Crude (Oklahoma) WTI	1000 barrels	☑	☑
NY Unleaded Gasoline	1000 barrels	☑	☑
Middle East Crude	1000 barrels	☑	☑
SGX (Singapore)			
Brent Crude	1000 barrels	☑	

Source: IPE, NYMEX and SGX.
IPE stands for International Petroleum Exchange, London. NYMEX stands for New York Mercantile Exchange. SGX stand for Singapore Exchange.
WTI stands for West Texas Intermediate.

Rotterdam market than Singapore or Houston. These results are consistent with those reported by Menachof and Dicer[47] where they compared the effectiveness of cross hedging bunker prices using gas oil futures to the bunker adjustment factors (fuel surcharge) used by liner companies. An example on bunker hedging using oil futures contracts is in Alizadeh et al.[46]

3.3 Hedging bunker prices using OTC products

Due to the poor effectiveness of cross commodity hedging in bunker risk price risk management, use of OTC instruments such as forwards, swaps and options has become increasingly popular among the agents involved in shipping operations and management. In recent years, especially following the wake of development of a variety of OTC derivative products for commodities in the late 1980s and 1990s, OTC derivatives have become quite popular in bunker price risk management too. OTC products are tailor-made and designed to suit the individual needs of agents involved in the bunker market. Nowadays many financial institutions and commodity trading houses such as Barclays Capital, Morgan Stanley, Credit Lyonnais etc., offer OTC bunker derivative products such as forward contracts, swaps and options. The most important of these are discussed in the next section.

3.3.1 Hedging bunker prices using forward contracts

A forward bunker contract is defined as an agreement between a seller and a buyer to exchange a specified quantity of bunker of certain quality, at an agreed price, at certain delivery location and time in the future. Forward contracts are usually paper contracts in the sense that settlement is made on the difference between the contracted price and the price for bunker at the delivery point, although physical deliveries are also possible.

In order to illustrate the way forward bunker contracts work, consider the case of a shipowner who has fixed a voyage charter for the end of August 1999. It is early July 1999, and the current bunker price at Houston, the loading port, is 120 $/mt. The owner will need to purchase 5000 mt of fuel oil whilst loading the cargo in Houston, and he fears that bunker prices may rise by August thus increasing his operating costs. His bunkers broker advises him that a 5000 mt forward contract for settlement in end of August 1999 currently trades at 125 $/mt. By buying the forward contract the owner locks his bunker price at 125$/mt, irrespective of the eventual bunker price in Houston in August.

On 31 August 1999, the market price for fuel oil delivered in Houston is 132$/mt. According to the forward contract, the shipowner is entitled to receive 7$/mt (132$–125$); that is, a profit of 35,000$ ($7*5,000 mt). On the other hand, in the physical market he incurs a loss of $35,000 ($7*5,000 mt), which is due to the increase in bunker price. Therefore, the shipowner's prediction was right and by buying the forward agreement he eliminates the loss of $35,000. Now consider the case where the bunker prices in Houston at the end of August rise slightly and not as much as it was expected, say 122$/mt. In this case, since the market price is lower than the forward agreement price, the shipowner has to compensate the forward seller by the difference between the market price and the forward price; that is, 3$/mt or a total of $15,000. However, the shipowner gains 3$/mt in the physical market by buying bunker for 122$/mt instead of 125$/mt, which compensates his loss in the forward market and consequently the total bunker cost will be 125$/mt. The example above can also be extended to accommodate the case of a bunker supplier. The only difference is that the supplier will be a seller of forwards with a long position in the physical market.

Table 7: Bunker hedging using a forward bunker contract

2-month forward hedge for the period 8 July 1999 to 31 August 1999	
Physical market	Futures market
8 July 1999	
Spot bunker price: 120 $/tonne Total current bunker cost: $600,000 (= 5,000*120 $/tonne)	August 31 forward bunker price: 125 $/tonne Expected total bunker cost: $625,000 (= 5,000*125 $/tonne)
Shipowner **buys** 5,000 mt of forward bunker delivery 31 August 2000 for 125 $/tonne	
31 August 1999	
Spot bunker price: 132 $/tonne Total bunker cost: $660,000 (= 5,000*132 $/tonne)	August 1999 forward bunker settlement: 125 $/tonne
Shipowner settles the difference between forward bunker price and August market price with the seller of the forward contract: $35,000 =(132–125)*5,000	
Loss in the physical market $625,000–$660,000 = –$35,000	Profit from forward bunker transaction (132–125)*5,000 = $35,000
Net result from hedging = $0	

3.3.2 Hedging bunker prices using bunker swap contracts

Swap contracts are perhaps the most popular instruments for bunker price risk management and many banks and commodity trading houses nowadays offer bunker swaps as part of their derivative products. Swaps are OTC arrangements, which involve no transfer of physical commodity, and are settled in cash at the maturity date(s). Swap contracts are normally done through a third party known as *swap facilitator* or broker. The role of the *swap facilitator* is to help the two counterparties identify each other and to settle the swap contract. Therefore, swap facilitators act as intermediaries.

A simple swap contract, sometimes called *plain vanilla swap*, is an agreement whereby a floating price for a commodity is exchanged for a fixed price for the same commodity over a specified period for a defined volume. The floating price is normally the prevailing market (spot) price for the asset and the fixed price is the price which is negotiated and agreed before the initiation of the swap contract. For example, a shipowner enters into a swap contract with a counterparty, in which the shipowner agrees to pay 129$/mt for 5,000 mt of fuel oil at the end of every month for the next 12 months after the intiation of

RISK MANAGEMENT IN THE SHIPPING INDUSTRY 717

the contract. In return the counterparty agrees to pay the floating price for 5,000 mt of bunker at a specified port (e.g., Singapore) at the end of the month for the next 12 months following the intiation of the contract. Therefore, at the end of every month during the life of the swap, the shipowner pays $645,000 (5000 x 129) to the swap counterparty and receives the market price of the bunker times 5,000. However, in practice, the parties only exchange the differences. Figure 7 presents the cash flow for the above plain vanilla swap example and Table 8 presents the cash flows between the counterparties over a 12-month period.

Figure 7: Plain vanilla swap contract between shipowner and swap counterparty

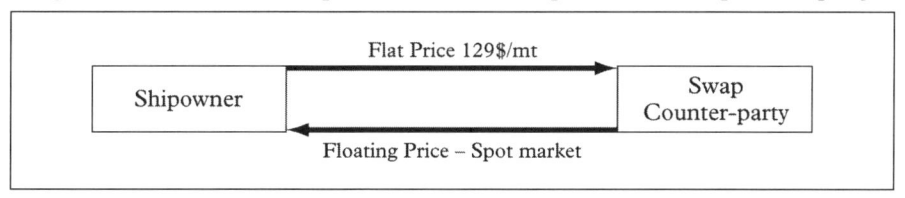

```
                    Flat Price 129$/mt
    ┌──────────┐ ──────────────────────→ ┌───────────────┐
    │ Shipowner│                          │     Swap      │
    │          │                          │ Counter-party │
    └──────────┘ ←────────────────────── └───────────────┘
                Floating Price – Spot market
```

It can be seen that although the shipowner agrees to a 5,000 mt forward contract, this does not necessarily mean that he buys the same amount of fuel in the physical market at the end of each month (e.g., beginning of the voyage) as the amount of bunker taken depends on the vessel's requirements. However, the swap contract should be fulfilled by both parties until the contract ends. Furthermore, it can be seen that the settlement varies from month to month depending on the prevailing spot bunker prices at Singapore.

Therefore using the above swap contract, the shipowner secures his bunker costs at around 129$/mt which in turn ensures a steady level of operating expenses and provides a guaranteed profit margin if freight revenue is hedged as well.

Table 8: Cash flows between counterparties in a 12 month bunker swap contract

	Bunker purchased	Spot bunker price	Bunker cost	Swap contract	Swap price	Swap result	Shipowner's cashflow
	mt	$/mt	US$	mt	$/mt	US$	US$
January	4850	128.00	620800.0	5000	129	645000	-5000
February	4950	135.63	671368.5	5000	129	645000	33150
March	5150	141.10	726665.0	5000	129	645000	60500
April	4740	123.75	586575.0	5000	129	645000	-26250
May	5200	132.00	686400.0	5000	129	645000	15000
June	4850	145.60	706160.0	5000	129	645000	83000
July	4920	133.25	655590.0	5000	129	645000	21250
August	5320	128.88	685641.6	5000	129	645000	-600
September	4820	148.50	715770.0	5000	129	645000	97500
October	4780	152.88	730766.4	5000	129	645000	119400
November	5150	142.00	731300.0	5000	129	645000	65000
December	4960	120.10	595696.0	5000	129	645000	-44500
Total	**59690**		**8112733**	**60000**		**7740000**	**418450**

So far we discussed the properties of the simplest swap contract. However, swap contracts can also be more complex in structure in order to fulfil the hedging performance and risk management requirements of the shipowners. Among these are; *Differential swap, Variable volume swap or swing, Participation swap, Double up swap* and *Extendable swap*.[48] Each contract has certain specifications, structure and payoff, which makes it more relevant to counterparties involved. More details on the payoffs and pricing of these types of swap contracts can be found in Clewlow and Strickland[49] and Hull.[50]

3.3.3 Hedging bunker prices using options

Although option contracts had been used extensively for risk management in energy markets since the early 1980s, it was not until the 1990s that options were first used as an means of hedging bunker fuel risk in shipping. Nowadays, several financial institutions and commodity trading houses offer numerous types of options on bunker fuel to shipowners and shipping companies.

The general definition, types, trading strategies and payoffs of different option contracts were discussed in section 2.4.1. The aim of this section is therefore to discuss strategies that are used to hedge bunker price fluctuations using different option contracts. Apart form American and European options, one of the most popular option contracts in the commodity markets, especially the bunker market, is the Asian option. An Asian option is similar to an European option in that it can only be exercised at maturity, but it differs from an European option in that either the exercise price or the spot price at the expiry is calculated as the average of spot prices of the underlying asset over certain period.[51] When the average market price over some period prior the maturity is used as strike price, the option is called average strike option, whereas when the average spot price over certain period prior to maturity is used as spot price, then the option is called average price option. This property of Asian options is important as sharp fluctuations and excess volatility in commodity markets, especially oil markets, increase both the premia and payoffs of European and American options. Therefore, by smoothing the strike prices in Asian options, they become cheaper and better instruments for risk management in commodity markets.

3.3.3.1 Caps and floors

A caplet is defined as a hedging position, which is the result of a long call option on an underlying asset and a short physical position on the same asset. A caplet gives its holder the opportunity to limit any possible future losses due to the increase in the price of the asset. Purchase of the call option compensates the owner in the case of a price rise and provides an upper bound on the price that the owner has to pay for bunker at expiry. A floorlet, on the other hand, is defined as a hedging position, which consists of a long put option on the underlying asset and a long physical position on the same asset. A floorlet gives its holder the opportunity to limit any possible future losses due to a price drop. Purchase of the put option compensates the bunker supplier in the case of a price fall and provides a lower bound on the selling price that the supplier receives for bunker in two months time.

RISK MANAGEMENT IN THE SHIPPING INDUSTRY

A cap is a portfolio of two or more caplets with the same exercise price but different maturity dates, while a floor is a portfolio of two or more floorlets with the same exercise price but different maturities. Therefore, both pricing and hedging techniques for cap and floors are the same as those used in the case of caplets and floorlets.

Example of a caplet option hedge

On 20 March 1999 the spot bunker price at Fujiarah is 105$/mt. The tanker Ocean Star is scheduled to load in the Persian Gulf and departs for Rotterdam on 20 June 1999. Her owner fears that bunker prices for 20 June 1999 at Fujairah, when the ship is going to take 5,000 mt of fuel oil, may rise and hence cause cash flow problems for this particular voyage. In order to avoid this, the owner decides to hedge his bunker cost; he finds that the following call option contract is available:

option premium = 3$/mt,
strike price = 110$/mt,
expiry date = 20 June 1999

If the shipowner agrees to buy the option, then by paying 3$/mt to the call writer on 20 March 1999, he buys the right, but not the obligation, to purchase 5,000 mt of bunker oil at 110$/mt on 20 June 1999 regardless of the market price of the bunker at that time.

Table 9: Hedging against bunker prices fluctuations using a cap

2-month caplet hedge for the period 20 March 1999 to 20 June 1999	
Physical market	**Options market**
20 March 1999	
Bunker price in Fujairah: 105 $/mt Bunker cost: $525,000 (= 5,000*105)	Option details: June 1999 Call with a strike price of 110 $/mt Premium 3 $/mt
Shipowner **buys** June 1999 call at a total cost of $15,000 (= 3*5,000)	
20 June 1999 – falling bunker market	
Bunker price in Fujairah: 95 $/tonne Actual Bunker Cost: $475,000	Strike price (110) > spot price (95) Therefore option is not exercised
Gain in the physical market $50,000 = $525,000 – $475,000	Payoff from the options transaction –$15,000
Total bunker cost (including option premium) = $475,000 + $15,000 = $490,000	
20 June 1999 – alternative scenario – rising bunker market	
Bunker price in Fujairah: 122.5 $/tonne Actual Bunker Cost: $612,500	Strike price (110) < spot price (122.5) Therefore option is exercised
Loss in the physical market $525,000 – $612,500 = –$87,500	Payoff from the options transaction (122.5 – 110)*5,000 – $15,000 = $47,500
Total bunker cost (including option premium) = $612,000 – $47,500 = $564,500	

The outcome of this hedging strategy is presented in Table 9. Under the first scenario, June bunker prices in Fujairah have fallen to 95$/mt and the shipowner will not exercise the option as the market price is less than the strike price. This leaves the shipowner with a loss of 3$/mt for the premium paid. In this case the total amount paid for bunkers is $490,000. However, under the second scenario, the bunker price in June has risen to 122.5 $/mt. Then, the shipowner can exercise the option, as the market price is higher than the strike price, and is entitled to receive 12.5$/mt from the writer of the option – that is, a sum of $62,500 (122.5–110)*5,000). This will compensate the owner against the rise in the physical market. However, the premium paid for buying the option should be deducted from this amount, which leaves the shipowner with $47,500 profit from the option contract. Therefore, the total bunker cost for the shipowner will be $564,500.

Panel (a) of Figure 8 shows the result of the above caplet hedge. It can be seen that by buying the call option, the shipowner has hedged the bunker cost up to a maximum of $113/t (a total of $564,500) regardless of how much bunker prices increase in June.

Panel (b) of Figure 8 shows the possible prices received by a bunker supplier once a floorlet hedge is used. This floorlet hedge is constructed by having a long position in the asset (bunker fuel) and taking a long put position with a premium of 2$/mt and strike price of 100$/mt. This hedge ensures that the bunker price received at maturity does not fall below 98$/mt.

Figure 8: Bunker price to be paid or received by a caplet and a floorlet holder

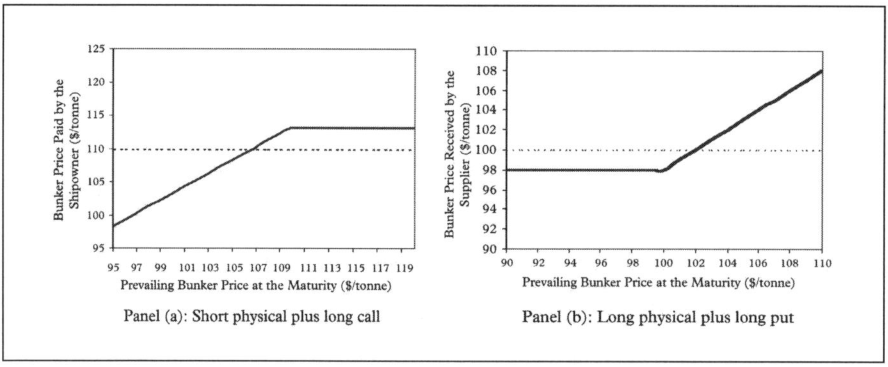

Panel (a): Short physical plus long call

Panel (b): Long physical plus long put

3.3.3.2 Collars or cylinder options

Collars are very effective risk management instruments designed to confine the gains and losses of the holder of the instrument within certain limits. They are generally a combination of caps and floors, which allow the profit/loss of the investor to be limited to a maximum (cap) and minimum (floor). A collar is the combination of a long call and short put, or vice versa, combined with a short or long physical position. For example, a shipowner who is short a certain amount of bunker in the physical market at certain time in the future can buy a call option and sell a put option for the same amount of bunker, with both options expiring at the same time as the physical market settlement to construct a collar.

RISK MANAGEMENT IN THE SHIPPING INDUSTRY

Very often collars are designed and used when hedgers do not want to incur any cost for hedging their positions and they are appropriately called as zero-cost collars. The following example explains a zero cost collar used by a shipowner to cover his exposure to bunker price fluctuations in three months time.

Example of a collar

In March 2000 a shipowner wants to hedge his bunker cost for a vessel which is going to take 5,000 mt of bunker fuel in June 2000 in Houston. The current spot price for bunkers at Houston is 110$/mt. The shipowner wants to hedge his exposure to adverse bunker price fluctuations in Houston in June 2000, but does not want to incur any upfront cost for the hedge. The best way to achieve this is to use a zero cost collar option, which limits the fluctuations of bunker costs within certain limits.

Assume the following option contracts are available to him in March 2000.

- A June 2000 call option on bunker prices at Houston with a strike price of $110 and a premium of 3$.
- A June 2000 put option on the bunker prices at Houston with a strike price of $104 and a premium of $3.

By selling the put option, the owner can raise the money to buy the call option and, therefore, there will not be any cost in participating in the options market. The overall payoff of a long call, short put and a short physical is limited between zero to $6. This means that by constructing a zero cost collar, the shipowner ensures that his bunker expenses will remain within certain limits; that is the maximum he can gain in case bunker prices drop is 6$/mt, while in the case of rise in bunker prices he will not make any losses.

Figure 9: Zero-cost collar hedged payoff to the shipowner and purchase prices after hedge against different bunker prices at the expiry

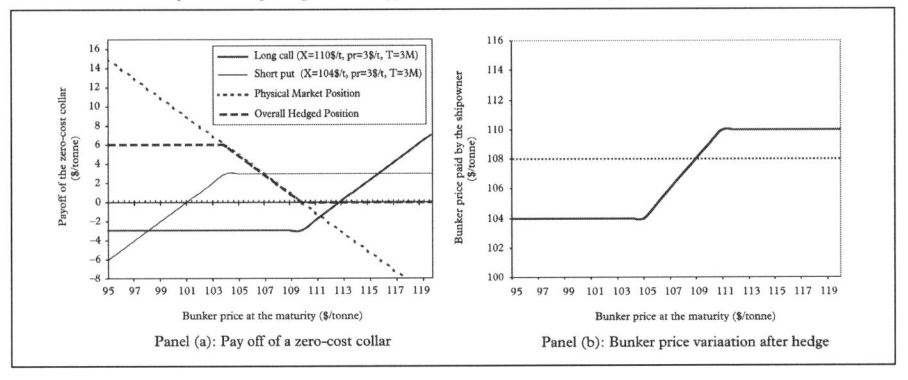

Panel (a): Pay off of a zero-cost collar

Panel (b): Bunker price variaation after hedge

Panel (a) of Figure 9 shows the payoff of a zero-cost collar against different spot bunker prices at maturity, while panel (b) of Figure 9 plots the fuel cost paid by the holder of the collar against possible spot bunker prices at the expiry. It can be seen that the the final bunker cost can only vary between 104$/mt to

110$/mt regardless of the variation in bunker prices at maturity. In other words, the holder of the collar trades off any excess loss when the bunker price increases with any excess profit when the bunker price decreases at expiry.

Table 10: The payoff of the zero cost collar hedge and overall cost of bunker for shipowner

Spot bunker price at Expiry $/mt	Call option payoff $/mt	Put option payoff $/mt	Collar payoff $/mt	Overall bunker cost for shipowner $/mt
98	(No Exe) −3	(Exe) −3	−6	104
100	(No Exe) −3	(Exe) −1	−4	104
102	(No Exe) −3	(Exe) 1	−2	104
104	(No Exe) −3	(No Exe) 3	0	104
106	(No Exe) −3	(No Exe) 3	0	106
108	(No Exe) −3	(No Exe) 3	0	108
110	(No Exe) −3	(No Exe) 3	0	110
112	(Exe) −1	(No Exe) 3	2	110
114	(Exe) +1	(No Exe) 3	4	110
116	(Exe) +3	(No Exe) 3	6	110
118	(Exe) +5	(No Exe) 3	8	110

No exe indicates that the option is not exercised and *Exe* indicates that the option is exercised.

Table 10 presents the payoffs of the shipowner's positions in the zero cost collar hedge example. The overall results indicate that the bunker cost is confined within the 104$/t to 110$/t limits regardless of any extreme swings in bunker prices at the expiry.

A similar collar hedge can also be designed for a bunker seller who is long in the physical market and therefore should sell a call option and buy a put option. This is shown in Figure 10, panel (a), which illustrates the position of the bunker supplier using a zero cost collar. The final outcome of the collar ensures that whatever the price for the bunker, the price that he receives can only fluctuate between 104$/t to 110$/t.

Due to space limitations the discussion here focuses only on the use of caps, floors and collars. In addition, there are numerous other hedging and trading

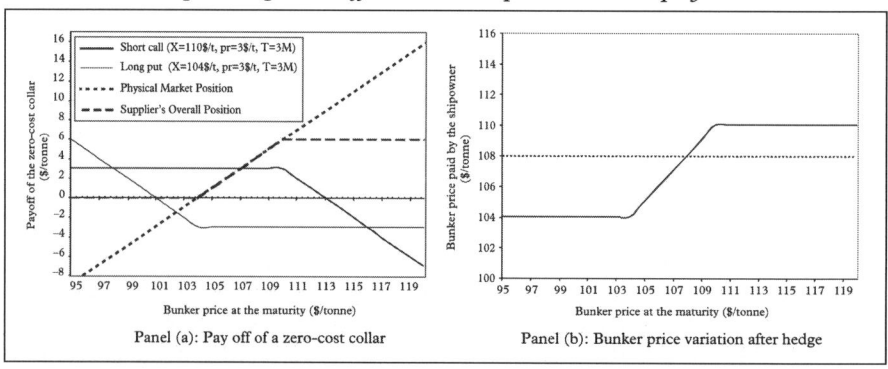

Figure 10: Zero-cost collar hedged payoff to the bunker supplier and bunker sale prices against different bunker prices at the expiry

Panel (a): Pay off of a zero-cost collar

Panel (b): Bunker price variation after hedge

strategies based on combinations of call and put options with different strike prices, expiry dates, etc. These are outside the scope of this article and the interested reader can refer to Clewlow and Strickland[49] and Hull[50] for more information.

3.3.3.3 Exotic options

In recent years the increase in the use of option contracts for hedging and trading activities lead to the development of several types of options known as exotic options as opposed to simple or plain vanilla options considered so far. The exotic options are mainly designed to suit the buyer's hedging or trading requirements and their payoffs are sometimes different and complicated.

In options pricing, certain variables such as the market price of the underlying asset, exercise price, risk free rate, volatility of the underlying asset and the time to expiry, are used to determine the price of the option. The main difference between exotic and simple options is that in the case of simple options these variables are assumed to be constant over the life of the option, whereas in the case of exotic options, these values can be changed. For example, in addition to Asian options, other types of exotic options include *Forward-start options*, *Compound options*, *Chooser options*, *Barrier options* and *Lookback options*, among others. (For more details on the payoffs and pricing of these exotic options see Rubinstein and Reiner,[52] Zhang,[53] Clewlow and Strickland[49] and Hull.[50])

4. SUMMARY AND CONCLUSIONS

The role of risk management in shipping operations has become increasingly important in recent years. This is partly because the shipping industry has become an integral part of the world economy in connecting sources of supply and demand for raw materials and manufactured goods around the globe. Therefore, fluctuations and uncertainty in the global economy, whether short term and/or long term, are expected to affect the profitability and hence the long-term survival of shipowners and ship operators. The aim of this chapter was to review and discuss different types of risk management tools and instruments available to shipping market agents to control their risks in the revenue and the cost side of the business.

In this study we identify two major sources of risk in shipping operations. These are unanticipated changes in the level of freight rates and voyage costs. Section 2 presents recent developments and studies in the area of freight rate risk management. Based on the studies in the literature, it is argued that the poor performance of the BIFFEX contract in reducing freight rate risk is due to the construction and composition of its underlying index (BPI). This is because BPI is a composite index and its movements are not correlated strongly with most of the dry bulk routes which are used to construct the index.

This has led to several revisions in the composition of the index, which have proven not to be effective and eventually the contract was withdrawn from the market in April 2002. The decision to terminate the BIFFEX contract was also attributed to the emergence of a competing OTC market for forwards (FFA), and more recently option contracts, on individual shipping routes. These OTC contracts provide a precise match against the physical requirements of market players and hence a more accurate hedging mechanism compared to BIFFEX contracts. On the other hand, being OTC instruments, there is always some element of credit risk involved in these transactions. Despite this, the OTC market has evidenced considerable growth over the recent years and for certain routes, the value of transactions in the FFA market exceeds the value of transactions in the physical market.

In the final section we discuss methods and techniques for managing bunker price risk. Bunker costs account for almost 50% of the total voyage costs and hence, any fluctuations in bunker prices significantly affect shipowners' and ship operators' profits. Different methods for hedging bunker prices - including petroleum and petroleum product futures, forward, swap and option contracts on bunker oil – are discussed and analysed. It is shown that petroleum futures are not very effective instruments for hedging bunker price fluctuations compared to OTC products on bunker oil. Despite the importance of this issue for the shipping industry, with the exception of the studies of Menachof and Dicer[47] and Alizadeh et al.,[46] there are no other studies in the literature on the costs and benefits as well as the hedging effectiveness of different derivative contracts in the bunker market. This seems to be a promising area for future developments and research from which the shipping industry will undoubtedly benefit.

APPENDIX A: DERIVATION OF MINIMUM VARIANCE HEDGE RATIO

Ederington[23] applies the principles of portfolio theory to show that the hedge ratio that minimises the risk of a given spot position is given by the ratio of the unconditional covariance between spot and futures price changes over the unconditional variance of futures price changes. To illustrate this, consider the case of a shipowner who wants to secure his freight rate income in the freight futures market. The change on the shipowner's portfolio of spot and futures positions, ΔP_t, is given by

$$\Delta P_t = \Delta S_t - \gamma \Delta F_t \tag{A.1}$$

where, $\Delta S_t = S_t - S_{t-1}$ is the change in the spot position between t–1 and t; $\Delta F_t = F_t - F_{t-1}$ is the change in the futures position between t-1 and t; and γ is the hedge ratio. Using the formula for the portfolio variance of two risky assets, the variance of the returns of the hedged portfolio is given by

$$\mathrm{Var}(\Delta P_t) = \mathrm{Var}(\Delta S_t) - 2\gamma \mathrm{Cov}(\Delta S_t, \Delta F_t) + \gamma^2 \mathrm{Var}(\Delta F_t) \tag{A.2}$$

where $\mathrm{Var}(\Delta S_t)$, $\mathrm{Var}(\Delta F_t)$ and $\mathrm{Cov}(\Delta S_t, \Delta F_t)$ are, respectively, the unconditional variance of the spot and futures price changes and their unconditional covariance. The hedger must choose the value of γ that minimises the variance of his portfolio returns i.e. $\min_{\gamma}[\mathrm{Var}(\Delta P_t)]$. Taking the partial derivative of equation (A.2) with respect to γ, setting it equal to zero and solving for γ, yields the minimum variance hedge ratio (MVHR), $\gamma^\star$

$$\gamma^\star = \frac{\mathrm{Cov}(\Delta S_t, \Delta F_t)}{\mathrm{Var}(\Delta F_t)} \tag{A.3}$$

which is equivalent to the slope coefficient, $\gamma^\star$, in the following regression

$$\Delta S_t = \gamma_0 + \gamma^\star \Delta F_t + u_t \quad ; u_t \sim \mathrm{iid}(0, \sigma^2) \tag{A.4}$$

In this model, the degree of variance reduction in the hedged portfolio achieved through hedging is given by the R^2 of the regression, since this represents the proportion of risk in the spot market that is eliminated through hedging; the higher the R^2 the greater the effectiveness of the minimum variance hedge.

APPENDIX B: BLACK-SCHOLES OPTION PRICING MODEL

Since the introduction of option contracts to the financial markets many models have been proposed for evaluating and pricing options. However, it was the pioneering work by Fisher Black, Myron Scholes and Robert Merton in 1973, which laid the foundation for pricing options. Since then their option pricing model has been widely used both by academic and practitioners.

In general, option prices depend on several observable and unobservable variables. These are the current spot price for the underlying asset, S_t, the strike price, X, the time to expiry of the option, $(T-t)$, the interest rate (risk free rate) over the time to maturity of the option, $r_{t,T}$, and finally the volatility of the underlying asset, σ. The derivation of the Black-Scholes option pricing formula requires some background on solving differential equations and therefore is outside the scope of this book.[54] The formulae for the price of a European call option, c, and the price of a European put option, p, on an asset are:

$$c = S_t N(d_1) - X e^{-(T-t)r_{t,T}} N(d_2) \tag{B.1}$$

$$p = -S_t N(-d_1) + X e^{-(T-t)r_{t,T}} N(-d_2) \tag{B.2}$$

Where $N(x)$ is the cumulative probability distribution function for a variable which follows normal distribution with mean zero and variance of 1.0, and d_1 and d_2 are given as

$$d_1 = \frac{\ln(S_t/X) + r_{t,T} + \sigma^2/2(T-t)}{\sigma^2\sqrt{T-t}} \tag{B.3}$$

and

$$d_2 = \frac{\ln(S_t/X) + r_{t,T} - \sigma^2/2(T-t)}{\sigma\sqrt{T-t}} = d_1 - \sigma\sqrt{T-t} \tag{B.4}$$

It can be seen from the formulae for d_1 and d_2 that as $T-t$ approaches zero $(T-t \to 0)$, i.e. as the option approaches its expiration, and $S_t \geq X$, then both d_1 and d_2 approach infinity $(d_1, d_2 \to \infty)$. As a result, both $N(d_1)$ and $N(d_2)$ approach one, while $N(-d_1)$ and $N(-d_2)$ approach zero. This in turn suggests that the call option value becomes $S_t - X$, while the put option value becomes zero. On the other hand, as $(T-t \to 0)$ and $S_t < X$, then both d_1 and d_2 approach negative infinity $(d_1, d_2 \to -\infty)$. As a result, both $N(d_1)$ and $N(d_2)$ approach zero, while $N(-d_1)$ and $N(-d_2)$ approach one. This in turn implies that the call option value becomes zero, while the put option value becomes $X - S_t$. These two conditions, which need to be satisfied, are known as the boundary conditions necessary for the derivation of the Black-Scholes model.

ENDNOTES

1. For instance, a shipowner is exposed to interest rate risk when his vessels are financed by debt and foreign exchange risk when the revenues of his vessel are in a currency other than the currency in which the vessel has been financed. Due to space limitations, this chapter concentrates only on the use of derivatives in freight rate and bunker risk management.
2. Stopford, M. (1997): *Maritime Economics* (London Routledge).
3. McConville, J. (1999): *Economics of Maritime Transport: Theory and Practice* (1st ed.) (Witherby).
4. Gray, J. (1990): *Shipping Futures* (London, Lloyd's of London Press).
5. Garbade, K., and Silber, W. (1983): "Price Movements and Price Discovery in Futures and Cash Markets", *Review of Economics and Statistics*, 65, pp. 289–297.
6. In addition to the BPI, the Baltic Exchange also produces a wide range of other specialised shipping indices covering different vessel sizes and different cargo types such as the Baltic Capesize Index (BCI), the Baltic Handymax Index (BHMI), the Baltic Dirty Tanker Index (BDTI) and the Baltic Clean Tanker Index (BCTI). The Baltic Exchange website (*www.balticexchange.com*) provides detailed information on the composition of these indices.
7. The BIFFEX contract is settled in cash against the BPI. The settlement price is computed as the average value of the index over the last seven trading days of each contract month; the monetary value of the settlement price is $10 per index point.
8. Edwards, F., and Ma, C. (1992): *Futures and Options* (Int'l ed.) (Singapore, McGraw-Hill Book Co.).
9. Kolb, R.W. (2001): *Futures, Options and Swaps* (3rd ed.) (London, Blackwells Business Publishers).
10. In mathematical form $F_{t;t-n} = E_{t-n}(S_t | \Omega_{t-n})$ where S_t is the spot price at time t, $F_{t;t-n}$ is the futures price at time t–n for expiry at time t and Ω_{t-n} is the information set available to market participants at period t–n. In order to test the unbiasedness hypothesis one has to make an assumption about the formation of expectations in the market. If expectations in the market are assumed to be rational (Muth, J.F. (1961): "Rational Expectations and the Theory of Price Movements", *Econometrica*, 29, pp. 315–335), then the unbiasedness hypothesis is tested empirically using the following regression model: $S_t = \beta_1 + \beta_2 F_{t;t-n} + u_t$; $u_t \sim iid(0, \sigma^2)$. The joint hypothesis of unbiasedness and rational expectations, then implies the joint parameter restriction $(\beta_1, \beta_2) = (0, 1)$.
11. Nomikos, N. (1999): "Price Discovery, Risk Management and Forecasting in the Freight Futures Market", unpublished PhD Thesis, City University Business School, London, UK.
12. Kavussanos, M., and Nomikos, N. (1999): "The Forward Pricing Function of the Shipping Freight Futures Market", *Journal of Futures Markets*, 19, pp. 353–376.
13. Johansen, S. (1988): "Statistical Analysis of Cointegrating Vectors", *Journal of Economic Dynamics and Control*, 12, pp. 231–254.
14. Johansen, S. (1991): " Estimation and Hypothesis Testing of Cointegration Vectors in Gaussian Vector Autoregressive Models", *Econometrica*, 59, pp. 1551–1580
15. Earlier studies in the BIFFEX market by Chang, Y. (1991): "Forward Pricing Function of Freight Futures Prices", unpublished PhD Thesis, Department of Maritime Studies, University of Wales and Chang, Y., and Chang, H. (1996): "Predictability of the Dry Bulk Shipping Market by BIFFEX", *Maritime Policy and Management*, 23, pp. 103–114, have been criticised on the grounds that no attempt had been made to investigate whether spot and futures prices are stationary.
16. In a related study, Haigh, M.S. (2000): "Cointegration, Unbiased Expectations, and Forecasting in the BIFFEX Freight Futures Market", *The Journal of Futures Markets*, 20, 6 (2000), pp. 545–571, also finds that BIFFEX prices one, two and three months from maturity provide unbiased forecasts of the realised spot prices.

17. Kavussanos, M., and Nomikos, N. (2001): "Price Discovery, Causality and Forecasting in the Freight Futures Market", *Conference Proceedings, European Financial Management Association Conference*, Lugano, Switzerland, June 2001.
18. The same example can be extended to accommodate the case of a shipowner; the only difference is that a shipowner is a seller of futures while a charterer is a buyer of futures.
19. It should be stressed that in this example the increase in futures prices is not sufficient to eliminate the risk in the spot position. In an ideal situation, the net result from hedging should have been zero. This is also known as "perfect" or "textbook" hedge.
20. Kavussanos, M., and Nomikos, N. (2000): "Constant vs. Time-Varying Hedge Ratios and Hedging Efficiency in the BIFFEX Market", *Transportation Research*, Vol. 36, pp. 229–248.
21. Kavussanos, M., and Nomikos, N. (2000): "Dynamic Hedging in the freight futures market", *Journal of Derivatives*, Vol. 8, No. 1, Fall 2000, pp. 41–58.
22. Kavussanos, M., and Nomikos, N. (2000): "Futures Hedging Effectiveness when the Composition of the Underlying Asset Changes; the Case of the Freight Futures Contract", *The Journal of Futures Markets*, Vol. 20, No. 6.
23. Ederington, L.H. (1979): "The Hedging Performance of the New Futures Markets", *The Journal of Finance*, 34, pp. 157–170.
24. Thuong, L.T., and Visscher, S.L. (1990): "The Hedging Effectiveness of Dry Bulk Freight Rate Futures", *Transportation Journal*, 29, pp. 58–65.
25. Haralambides, H. (1992): "Freight Futures Trading and Shipowners Expectations", *Conference Proceedings of the 6th World Conference on Transport Research* (Lyon, France), Vol. II, pp. 1411–1422.
26. A hedge ratio of 1.0 implies setting-up a futures position whose monetary value exactly matches the value of the exposure in the physical market. It is similar to the example presented in Table 2 and is also called "naïve" or "one-to-one" hedge.
27. Kroner, K., and Sultan, J. (1993): "Time-Varying Distributions and Dynamic Hedging with Foreign Currency Futures", *Journal of Financial and Quantitative Analysis*, 28, pp. 535–551.
28. Engle, R.F. (1982): "Autoregressive Conditional Heteroskedasticity with Estimates of the Variance of United Kingdom Inflation", *Econometrica*, 50, pp. 987–1008.
29. Bollerslev, T. (1986): "Generalised Autoregressive Conditional Heteroskedasticity", *Journal of Econometrics*, 31, pp. 307–327.
30. Lee, T. (1994): "Spread and Volatility in Spot and Forward Exchange Rates", *Journal of International Money and Finance*, 13, pp. 375–383.
31. Gagnon, L., and Lypny, G. (1995): "Hedging Short-Term Interest Risk Under Time-Varying Distributions", *Journal of Futures Markets*, 15, pp. 767–783.
32. Bera, A., Garcia, P., and Roh, J. (1997): "Estimation of Time-Varying Hedge Ratios for Corn and Soybeans: BGARCH and Random Coefficients Approaches", Office for Futures and Options Research, 97-06.
33. Park, T., and Switzer, L. (1995): "Bivariate GARCH Estimation of the Optimal Hedge Ratios for Stock Index Futures: A Note", *Journal of Futures Markets*, 15, pp. 61–67.
34. Basis is defined as the difference between contemporaneous spot and futures prices. The basis is a very important factor for hedging in futures markets since the hedged price depends on the basis at the time the hedge is lifted, which is not known when the hedge is placed. Basis risk is the uncertainty associated with the basis at the time a hedge is lifted.
35. The example presented here does not include broker's commission. Both principals must pay a commission of 0.5% of the fixed (or expected) freight rate to the broker. For instance, in this example, each counterparty will pay 0.5%*$1,290,600 = $6,453.
36. Kavussanos, M.G., Menachof, D., and Visvikis, I.D. (2001): "The Unbiasedness Hypothesis in the Freight Forward Market", Paper presented at the *2nd International Safety of Maritime Transport Conference*, Chios, Greece, 7–9 June.

37. Batchelor, R., Alizadeh, A., and Visvikis, I.D. (2002): "Forecasting Performance of Spot and Forward Prices in the Forward Freight Markets", unpublished manuscript, Faculty of Finance, City University Business School.
38. In fact, Clarkson Securities have stopped reporting forward rates for routes 1 and 1A of the BPI since early 2001.
39. As we show in the examples in Table 3 and Table 4, there may be a slight discrepancy between the actual rate at which the vessel is fixed and the settlement rate. This is due to the fact that the settlement rate is calculated as the avarege freight rate over a number of days prior to maturity and not the settlement date.
40. Being a principal to principal contract, the only way a participant in the FFA market can virtually "settle" an open position prior to its maturity, is to offset it by taking an opposite position in another contract for the same route and maturity. This in turn will increase the credit risk exposure and also involves additional transaction (brokerage) costs.
41. Even if settlement prior to maturity was possible, the correlation between the returns on the spot and near month FFAs on panamax routes is found to be about 28%, which translates into a very low variance reduction of the hedged portfolio. This suggest that maximum hedging effectiveness can only obtained if contracts are adhered to until maturity.
42. BIFFEX contracts for instance were guaranteed by the London Clearing House (LCH). In the event of a default, the LCH would intervene and would assume the position of the of the defaulted party.
43. For a discussion on credit derivatives see Kolb, R. W. (2001): *Futures, Options and Swaps* (3rd ed.) (London, Blackwells Business Publishers).
44. In this case we are not considering the premium paid to the writer by the option buyer.
45. See Stopford, 1997.
46. Alizadeh, A.H., Kavussanos, M.G., and Menachof, D.A. (2001) "Hedging Against Bunker Price Fluctuations Using Petroleum Futures Contracts; Constant versus Time-varying Hedge Ratios", paper presented at the International Association of Maritime Economists, 18–20 July 2001, Hong Kong.
47. Menachof and Dicer (2001): "Risk Management Methods For The Liner Shipping Industry: The Case Of The Bunker Adjustment Factor", *Maritime Policy and Management*, Vol. 28, No. 2, pp. 141–155.
48. Differential swap is a contract with which the parties agree to exchange the difference between two floating prices known as the differential, for a fixed differential price. Variable volume swap or swing is exactly the same as the plain vanilla swap, however, the volume based on which the contract is set is not known. Therefore, exchange is based on the realised volume at the exchange date or the maturity. The volume in this type of contracts is normally the reading on a meter, the amount of consumption or some similar measurement. Participation swap is also similar to the plain vanilla swap. The only difference is that the party who pays the fixed price participates fully when the floating price is higher than the fixed price, but at certain amount of the contact when the floating price is below the fixed price. In the Double-Up swap contract, the fixed price payer can get a discount on the swap contract by implicitly selling a put option on the swap (swaption) which allows the variable price swap provider to double up the volume of the swap contract when the variable swap price is below the fixed price. In this type of swap, the fixed price payer exposes himself to the risk that if the swap prices fall, the fixed price payer pays twice the original amount. The Extendable swap agreement is similar to the Double-Up swap except that the swap provider (variable price payer) has the option to extend the period of the swap for a predetermined period. This is achieved by the fixed price payer selling an implicit put swaption in the form of a discount in the fixed price to the swap provider.
49. Clewlow, L., and Strickland, C. (2000): *Energy Derivatives: Pricing and Risk Management* (Lacima Publications).

50. Hull, J. (2000): *Options, futures and other derivatives* (Prentice Hall International).
51. The payoff of an average strike Asian call to the holder is therefore
$$\max(S_T - \frac{1}{m}\sum_{k=1}^{m} S_k, 0),$$
while the payoff of an average strike Asian put to the holder is
$$\max(\frac{1}{m}\sum_{k=1}^{m} S_k - S_T, 0).$$
Similarly the payoff of an average price Asian call to the holder of the option is therefore
$$\max(\frac{1}{m}\sum_{k=1}^{m} S_k - K, 0),$$
while the payoff of an average strike Asian put to the holder is
$$\max(K - \frac{1}{m}\sum_{k=1}^{m} S_k, 0).$$
52. Rubinstein, M., and Reiner, E. (1995): "Exotic Options", Working paper, University of California at Berkeley.
53. Zhang, P.G. (1996): *Exotic Options: A guide to the second generation of options* (World Scientific Press).
54. See Hull (2000) for complete derivation of the Black-Scholes and other option pricing models.

CHAPTER 32

CREDIT RISK, ANALYSIS AND POLICY IN BANK SHIPPING FINANCE

Costas Th. Grammenos
City University Cass Business School, City of London, UK.
E-mail: c.grammenos@city.ac.uk

1. INTRODUCTION

There are three main groups of sources of shipping finance: Equity Finance, which includes retained earnings and equity offerings, either public or private[1]; Mezzanine Finance, which encompasses hybrids (warrants and convertibles), subordinated debt and preference shares[2]; and Debt Finance, which contains bank loans, export finance, subsidies, shipyard financing, private placements (traditional and 144A) and public debt issues.[3]

This chapter concentrates on bank finance – which is still the most important source of raising capital in the shipping industry – with particular reference to commercial bank loans. Bank shipping loans are granted to borrowers by a number of different financial institutions, such as: export-import banks; development banks; banks specialised in shipping; and commercial banks. These institutions deal primarily with one major risk – the credit risk (or default risk) – which is the uncertainty over the repayment of the granted loan and payment of its interest, in full, on the promised date.

Shipping Departments of a sizeable number of commercial banks, or banks specialised in shipping, have seen their profitability fluctuating substantially over the years. Increased profits strengthened the presence of commercial banks committed to shipping, and attracted newcomers. The early 1970s, late 1980s and late 1990s, are good examples of positive bank shipping profitability. However, heavy losses over periods of shipping recession or depression have also been realised and led a number of banks to the decision of abandoning the finance of shipping. Here, the mid-1980s is a representative example.[4] Loan losses may significantly reduce the return on assets (ROA) of a bank and, therefore, destroy value for the bank, or loan profits may increase the ROA and, consequently, create value for the bank.

The lending function of the bank deals with credit risk, and has four parts[5]: the first is the origination of the loan and when it is initiated, analysed and approved; the second is the funding, during which external and/or internal funds are used for the draw-down of the loan; the third is the follow-up stage when principal and interest rate payments are made; the fourth is the monitoring phase, which is carried out in parallel with the "follow up" of the loan, through collecting, processing, and analysing data and information regarding the borrower. The objective of the lending function is to create value for the bank, through granting sound loans; and sound loans are the ones which are paid off.

The rest of this chapter is organised as follows. Section 2 focuses on Credit Risk, while Section 3 discusses key issues of Credit Risk Analysis. Section 4 deals with Collateral Securities, including mortgage, assignment of revenue, assignment of insurance and guarantees. Covenants are covered in Section 5; while Section 6 presents a further discussion of Credit Analysis and issues, such as pricing of the loan, syndication and capital adequacy rules. The focus of Section 7 is Loan Monitoring; while Section 8 covers Shipping Credit Policy. In Section 9, the Conclusions are presented.

2. CREDIT RISK

A financial institution that lends funds to shipping companies for acquisitions of secondhand vessels or placements of newbuilding orders may face a number of risks – such as interest rate risk, that is to say, the probability of a change in interest rates[6] that may adversely affect the bank's profit margin; or liquidity risk which is the probability of the bank not having sufficient cash and proper borrowing capacity to match deposit withdrawals, resulting in its paying higher interest rates on borrowed funds. However, the main risk in bank shipping finance is the credit risk – or default risk. This is primarily due to the volatility of the vessel('s) income, which is the main source of the loan repayment; and the consequent fluctuations in the vessel('s) market value which is, in most cases, the main security for the loan.

The financial institutions provide loans of varying forms to shipping companies, the core of them being the term loan under which the bank lends a certain amount to the shipping company for vessel acquisition over a specific period (above one year), to be repaid normally from the income generated by the vessel(s) to be financed and, possibly, by its/their residual value. The loan is tailor-made to suit the needs of the borrower and the lender, in the particular circumstances.[7] Thus, equal or unequal instalments can be arranged; and a moratorium for one or two years can be granted, whereby capital instalments are temporarily not paid (the interest, though, is paid), to allow for poor shipping market conditions. Furthermore, a balloon can be approved for a loan – that is to say, a large amount of the loan, which reflects the residual value of the vessel (between 25 to 30% of the vessel's current market value), should be paid with the last instalment. In reality, the payment of the balloon is usually extended for one year or longer – provided the borrower has met his commitment and depending upon the amount of the balloon and the freight income of the vessel – and, in this way, the loan repayment period can be stretched further without the bank committing itself to doing so from the beginning, because the repayment period of the loan would be longer and this would increase further the uncertainty.

The interest rate is normally fluctuating and based on LIBOR (London Interbank Offered Rate), plus a margin (spread), which represents a significant part of the gross income of the bank from the loan. While the margin is fixed in advance, the LIBOR is renewed periodically, such as every three or six months, in the eurodollar interbank market, should the currency denomination be in dollars.[8] Such fluctuating interest rates prevent the shipping company from calculating, with certainty, the future interest payments. In comparison with a fixed interest rate for the entire repayment period – a rather infrequent feature in bank shipping loans nowadays – the fluctuating interest rate allows the bank to pass on the interest rate risk to the borrower, whose cost rises with increasing LIBOR or decreases with falling LIBOR.[9]

During the various parts of the lending function, the shipping departments of the banks may face problems between the bank as principal, and the borrower as agent, which could jeopardise the repayment of the loan capital and the payment of interest. The agency theory[10] explains their contractual relationships and deals with their conflicts. Asymmetry of information, moral hazard and adverse selection are the areas where the conflicts often arise. Frictions emerge due to the asymmetry of information which may exist either at the initial and/or the monitoring phase of the loan. Indeed, the borrower (as an insider) may have more accurate information than the banker, in areas such as: the financial accounts, the condition of the vessels, or the incoming freight. Another area of friction is called moral hazard. Here the borrower may deceive the banker, or change his/her behaviour – clauses in the time charters unknown to the banker, false items in the running expenses of vessels, untrue statements regarding overall net worth and liquidity of the shipping group, or transfer of income from mortgaged vessels to other companies, could fall into this category.

Finally, the problems of the adverse selection, that is to say, the approval and granting of unsound loans, may arise due to a number of reasons – such as insufficient shipping expertise of the banker, lack of judgement, and/or hurried loan decisions due to the need for quick responses to the borrower's proposals. A characteristic example of adverse selection is the shipping loan portfolio of a relatively small financial institution, at the end of the 1970s, which consisted almost exclusively of loans extended for the purchases of over-aged vessels, while charging high interest rates. In addition, many of the owners were small with only two or three vessels. When the shipping market conditions deteriorated, from 1982 onwards, the freight income devastatingly decreased and was not enough to cover the vessels' running expenses, let alone the loan repayment. At the same time, the vessel market values had declined to their scrap value, while the vessels had been purchased, at the end of the 1970s, at quite high prices. This particular institution suffered great financial losses from its shipping loans.

The financial institutions, in order to increase their value and also deal effectively with the agency problems, incur certain costs – the agency costs. These are related to – among others – the collection, processing and analysis of data for the loans granted and to be granted. However, one has to keep in mind the very special role of the financial institutions, as intermediaries between savers and users of funds. In this capacity, and due to the limited ability of the savers to obtain and analyse information regarding initial and continuing creditworthiness of the end fund users (borrowers), the financial institutions undertake this role on their behalf. Consequently, the financial institutions have a greater incentive to collect and process this information, due to the large number of savers who appoint them as their "delegated monitors".[11] In so doing, the financial institutions are also protecting the wealth of their shareholders, who are expecting to see it expanding. Therefore, the lending function should guard the interests of depositors and shareholders, and increase the value of the bank.

The question that arises now, is, how does the shipping banker minimise the credit risk?[12]

There is an array of tools that are at the banker's disposal, to minimise credit risk: credit risk analysis; collateral securities; covenants in the loan agreement and the mortgage; monitoring of the granted loans; and shipping credit policy. These are the issues that will be discussed in the following sections.

3. CREDIT RISK ANALYSIS

Grammenos[13,14] introduces the five "Cs" of Credit in Bank Shipping Finance as a sound credit risk analysis method of assessing the probability of the repayment of the loan proposals for acquisition of secondhand vessels and new-buildings, based on five key words that start with "C" – Character, Capacity, Capital, Conditions, Collateral. Later on, he added "Company" for reasons of clearer presentation. This credit analysis method has been adopted by a large number of financial institutions. Bearing in mind that the interest margin and fees are fixed and, therefore, fixed is the upside return of the loan, and the downside risk is substantial, since the loan capital and interest may not be paid as promised, the credit risk analysis of the loan has to assess the probability of their payments in full. Table 1 summarises the main elements of the credit risk analysis that a loan officer has to carry out.

3.1 Character/capacity

The first column of Table 1 concentrates on the head of the shipping company and the management team. Their expertise accumulated over years, their resourcefulness during the lower parts of the shipping cycle, and their integrity, are areas of investigation. The head and the team will specify the mission and goals of the company and the strategic plan for their materialisation. They are responsible for designing and applying the strategies to achieve the goals.

The head and team are assessed for their managerial quality as a team and their performance versus plan on strategies over a long period, for instance, the last ten years – a period that covers at least one shipping investment cycle.[15] In particular, investment and finance, chartering, insurance, technical, cost management, risk management, creditors, and human resources strategies, are looked at for their overall return to the equity; and whether they managed to decrease costs, increase revenues and profits and create efficiencies. The head's and team's "modus operandi", in comparison with their peers in the same sector, may be useful.

CREDIT RISK, ANALYSIS & POLICY 735

Table 1: Six C's of Credit Analysis

Character/Capacity	Capital	Company	Conditions	Collateral
Head of Company, and Team Capacity and Integrity	Shipowner/ Company's Head Shareholding Stake	Structure of Company	Financial Markets	Fleet's Composition
Company's Mission – goals	Financial Structure	Inflows: Forms of Employment	Interest Rate	Fleet's Condition
Strategic Plan	Analysis of Financial Statements	Choice of Charterers Quality of Charterers	World Economy Political Conditions	Vessels' Economic Life
Strategies to Achieve them	Financial Ratio Analysis	Contracts with Charterers Effective Utilisation	Seaborne Trade Specific Commodities	Securities – Mortages
In Particular: – Investment & Finance	– Gearing Ratio (Total Debt/Total Assets)	of Vessels	Manufactured goods (Structural,Cyclical Changes)	– Assignment of Income – Assignment of Insurance
– Chartering – Insurance	– Long-Term Debt/Total Capitalisation	Outflows: Operating Costs	Shipping Markets	– Personal and Corporate guarantees
– Technical – Cost Management	– Pre-Tax Interest Coverage – Pre-Tax Funds Flow	– Administrative – Technical	Present and Future Demand & Supply Analysis	
– Risk Management – Creditors	Interest Coverage – Hull to debt	– Insurance – Crew	Shipping Investment Cycle Fragmentation of Markets	
– Human resources	Cash Flow	Voyage Costs Capital Costs	Barriers to Entry	
Coherent	Cash Cushion	Markets of Operation (1)	Regulatory Framework: – Official International	
Forward Looking & Learning from the Past	Other Sources of Funds Banking Relationships Accounting Methods	Market Share (2) 1+2 = Company's Operating Position	Organization(IMO) – Flag states – Port Authorities – ISM Code – OPA 90	
			Other Organisations' Requirements – Classification Societies – Insurance companies and P&I Clubs – Major Oil Companies	

© C. Th. Grammenos.

3.2 Capital

The second column refers to Capital. A relatively large shipowner stake of shares shows higher confidence in the company, while the financial structure shows the way the company has been financed. Shipping is a capital-intensive industry, requiring substantial funds for: primarily, placement of newbuildings; and, secondarily, the purchase of secondhand vessels. All elements in this column are important, but the gearing ratio, the hull to debt ratio, the net worth and the cash flow, are of paramount importance. A high gearing ratio (debt to total assets) is a double-edge sword: in a flourishing shipping market it may cause the profits and return to equity to soar, in a declining market it may endanger the existence of the company itself.[16] Interest coverage shows how many times income covers the interest.[17] Hull to debt ratio[18] is important, not only in a declining shipping market, but also when the time charter, or contract of affreightment ends, and shows the relationship between loan and market value of the vessel.

As long as the bank knows that the real economic net worth – the difference between the market value of assets and the market value of liabilities, as opposed to book value – is positive, then it also knows that the loan is relatively secure. Cash flow is the main source for the loan repayment, while the cash cushion – the existence of accumulated cash from profits or deposited funds – is important in order to cover temporarily interest payments and capital instalments, should the freight market decline. In a falling shipping market, other sources of finance – e.g., capital markets – and strong banking relationships may be necessary.

3.3 Company

The third column refers initially to the ownership structure of the company. Very often one-vessel companies[19] registered in an open registry country, such as Panama, Liberia, Cyprus, Malta, are established and their vessels may be managed by a management company controlled by the shipowner/manager, or owned by a holding company. In the first case, the banker deals with an entity where there is no – or limited – recourse to the management company and the loan is paid by the income and secured by the mortgaged vessel, or some other form of security; while, in the second, he/she deals with a coherent structure that owns a fleet and the repayment of the loan may be only based on the cash flow of the company.

Then the column scrutinises sources of income and expenditure. It shows the chartering strategy of the company and the stability – or the vulnerability – of its income. A company with time charters, or contracts of affreightment, has more secured income in comparison with a company that operates its vessels in the spot market, the income of which fluctuates. Bankers and investors are comfortable with the former case, nervous with the second one. The chartering strategy reveals also the marketing ability of the company; the quality and efficiency of its services; the financial strengths and weaknesses of its charterers; the effective utilisation of the vessels in two, or all, legs of a voyage. This column also investigates the managerial effectiveness regarding operating and voyage costs. The competitiveness of the company depends, not only on its ability to produce income but to operate within a lean budget of costs. The capital costs are included in this column and, when they are the costs of debt financing, income stability is of paramount importance.[20] The last part of this column looks into the market(s), where the company operates, its market share, and the company's operating position against its competitors.

3.4 Conditions

The fourth column refers to the examination of the very competitive and changing international economic, financial and political environment, within which the company makes decisions and operates. The conditions in financial markets, the interest rates, the developments in the world economy, international and seaborne trade, and the conditions in commodity markets, are issues of utmost importance for shipping companies, since demand for shipping services is a derived one. As Metaxas[21] argues "Vessels carry cargoes and goods that are imports and exports of various countries, the direction and volatility of which have a direct impact on the demand for shipping. Indeed, trade cycles in advanced economies and their resultant international trade cycles affect the magnitude of demand for tramp shipping services and, for this reason, their freight rate movements tend – to a certain degree – to coincide with those of international trade." Furthermore, structural changes in the above markets, and national economies, may have a more profound and lasting impact on the company's business than cyclical ones. Examples of these structural changes could be the technological changes that affect vessel('s) efficiency, size, number of crew; or the shifts of industrial production from one country to another, which may have an effect on the pattern of seaborne trade flows and on the type and size of vessels that are employed. Scenario analysis of demand and supply of shipping market(s) where the company operates, with sensitivity analysis, is required for the discussion of their current and future conditions. Volatility in freight rates and vessel market values, that is to say the market risk, is the major parameter for the creation of the loan's credit risk that the financial institution faces.

Shipping companies operate within a shipping investment cycle, the four stages of which (recovery, boom, recession, depression) are linked with the resultant freight rate as it is established by the demand for – and supply of – vessels.[22] When freight rates are high and profits increase, an over-investment in newbuildings is noticed, which may increase the level of supply of vessels and result in an imbalance between supply and demand. In a period of expansion of supply, even a check to the rate of growth of demand will be sufficient to trigger off a downward trend in freight rates. During recession and depression, speculative ordering may take place, often due to subsidised shipbuilding. This lowers the barriers to entry for shipping companies into newbuilding markets and may also prolong the low freight rates. On the other hand, purchase of a vessel, or placing a newbuilding during this period of low market values, is excellent timing, since this shipowner may compete with vessels bought or ordered during a boom period at high prices.[23] Furthermore, the sale of this vessel during a following prosperity phase is very profitable. However, for the banker who undertakes credit risk analysis, the stable cash flow is required for the repayment of the loan and not the asset play. It is important for the lending banker to figure out the stage of the shipping cycle, during which it provides finance. Financing over-valued secondhand vessels and newbuildings, during a boom period, may result in problematic loans in a recession and depression period. The comment in note 16 is very relevant.

Within the regulatory framework, the International Maritime Organization safeguards, the international standards, safety and marine pollution of the shipping industry; flag states, where vessels are registered, impose the regulations of IMO when they have ratified its regulations; port authorities inspect vessels when they call in; the classification societies supervise the construction, safety and seaworthiness of the vessels during their life; the insurance companies and Protection and Indemnity Clubs deal with the insurance aspects of the vessels; and the major oil companies undertake their own detailed inspections of the tankers that they are going to employ. All these are major parameters for the developments in the shipping regulatory environment which, as time passes, becomes tighter. As such, new investments and their overall cost, sale and purchase market, vessels' operating expenses, and their revenue, may be seriously affected by the official and corporate regulatory environment. These demand the attention of the banker.

3.5 Collateral

The last column concentrates on the company's fleet. Its composition is important. Fleet specialisation may develop expertise, operational efficiency and better marketing. However, such a fleet may be vulnerable to market recession. The diversified one, which may offer higher income security, requires normally a larger fleet in operation. The fleet's condition and the company's maintenance and repair policy must be investigated, as the vessels are the assets which produce the (often assigned to the bank) income that repays the loan(s) and they have to be operated safely within the required standards. In addition, a mortgaged vessel(s) – the main security for the bank loan – must be kept in good condition, in case the owner is in default and the bank should decide to sell it (them) in the open market or privately.

Apart from the vessel and the mortgage on it, other forms of securities also strengthen the position of the bank: the assignment of income to the bank by which the capital instalments and the interest are paid; assignment of insurance in the case of a casualty or other specific circumstances; corporate guarantees of the holding or management company and personal guarantees of director(s) of the management company, which may cover the bank should the company default in its payment of the loan and/or payment of interest. All these forms of security are discussed in the next section.

3.6 Analysis of cashflow

Having analysed the specific areas of the six C's of credit, the bank has to make a cash flow calculation to ascertain whether the total receipts will cover the total costs of the vessel(s) to be financed, allowing for a balance (cash cushion) sufficient to cover unexpected negative financial developments. This cash flow estimate[24] should be prepared for the proposed acquisition of vessel(s); also, for the group's fleet with – and without – the proposed acquisitions.

Assessing the stability of the fixed revenue of this statement, and its quality in terms of charterers, requires understanding the legal documents of time charters and contracts of affreightments; and assessing the creditworthiness of charterers.[25] While quality of future revenue, based on assumptions, requires an emphasis on the overall creditworthiness of the borrower as revealed through the six Cs of Credit analysis; and the use of appropriate securities and documentation which is, naturally, the job for the bank's lawyers. Now, the attention will be turned to the Securities and Covenants, after the discussion of which there will be a further one on Credit Analysis.[26]

4. COLLATERAL SECURITIES[27]

In granting a shipping loan, the bank has three possible areas from which to recoup its funds. The first or "intended" way out is from cash flow generated by the financed acquisition, the second way, from the mortgage on the financed vessel (the "direct" security) and the third way, from additional securities (the "indirect" security). It must be stressed that a bank, by taking securities, does so in the expectation that a problem loan will not develop and that sufficient cash flow will be generated by the project to service the outstanding debt without requiring to enforce its rights on the securities of the loan. The decision to be taken by the financial institution, on the appropriate security or securities, depends upon the individual case of the loan and shipping company to be financed. Among the securities are, the mortgage, the assignment of revenue, the assignment of insurance, the mortgagee's interest insurance, the assignment of requisition compensation, the guarantees, the comfort letters, cash collateral security, and share security. A short analysis follows.

4.1 Mortgage

A mortgage duly registered in the country whose flag the vessel flies, and carrying conditional ownership of the acquired vessel that becomes void when the debt is repaid, is the normal method of providing bank security for vessel acquisitions. Note that the type of mortgage will depend on the legislation applicable in the vessel's country of registry.

Statutory mortgages originated in the UK and adapted in jurisdictions modelled on the UK legal system, protect the mortgagee's rights by law. UK legislation[28] gives every registered mortgagee of a UK ship "the power absolutely to dispose of the ship or share in respect of which he is registered, and to give effectual receipts for the purchase money". In addition, under UK common law, the mortgagee has the right to take possession of the mortgaged vessel whenever the owner is in default of payment of the principal or interest secured by the mortgage, or when the owner acts in a way which impairs the security of the loan. A preferred mortgage ensures the mortgagee's right by express provision in the mortgage agreement. It is usually detailed and flexible, while the statutory mortgage only stipulates general conditions.[29]

The convenience of a mortgage lies in the fact that the shipowner can run the business as a going concern, at the same time giving the mortgagee the following basic rights[30] to: take possession of the vessel and operate it or proceed to a jurisdiction for arrest; arrest the vessel; sell the vessel at auction or privately; appoint a receiver to handle the affairs of the vessel; and to assume absolute title of the vessel. All these measures aim at protecting the bank and represent an agreement between the borrower and the lender with respect to vessel maintenance, insurance and operation.

One of the major problems encountered in the area of mortgages is in establishing the vessel's market value, which represents the value of the bank's security. The market value can be regarded as the average price at which a seller could be expected to make an acceptable offer to a purchaser on the open market, and is different from a vessel's fixed insurance value[31] or the depreciating book value.[32]

In order to protect against adverse fluctuations in vessel values, banks have attached great importance to the hull-to-debt ratio:

$$HDR = \frac{MV}{D}$$

where, HDR = Hull-to-debt ratio
MV = current market value of the vessel
D = outstanding amount of the loan (debt)

The hull-to-debt ratio indicates how much the market value of the vessel and, hence, the security, may diminish and still be sufficient to cover the debt. If this ratio falls below a predetermined level – normally between 130–150% – the bank may require additional security from the borrower and, since vessel prices can fall substantially in depressed markets, the availability of additional security may cause serious problems and friction between them.

Vessels can also be subject to additional second, third, etc. mortgages. A second mortgage is defined as existing when a first mortgage already exists on a vessel. These mortgages lie behind preferred mortgages in creditor ranking and are usually offered as additional security, provided consent of the first mortgagee has been given.

4.2 Assignment of revenue

General Assignment of Revenue allows present and future revenue to be paid directly to the shipowner until an event of default occurs, and reflects the degree of confidence by the lender as to the likelihood of the debt service. An intermediate format is the Retention Account, which provides that all assigned revenue is paid into such an account held by the mortgagee, who accumulates the necessary monthly freight revenue to meet the next interest and principal payments.

Under the strict format of Specific or Legal Assignment of Revenue, all the specific rights of the borrower arising from a charterparty are assigned to the bank provided the charterer's consent has been given. Consequently, all charterparty payments are made directly to the bank, which will normally allow the shipowner to withdraw the necessary funds ensuring that the vessel remains operative in order to service the debt.

The effectiveness of the revenue assignment securities will be directly dependent upon the reliability of the revenue streams, which will in turn be determined by the relevant charterparties. Therefore, the quality, reputation, and financial condition of the charterer in terms of honouring obligations, and the quality of the charterparty itself in terms of drafting and inflation escalation or market adjustment clauses, are particularly important. Furthermore, sub standard charterparty performance by the owner is often subject to deductions from freight and, as a result, may cause a reduction or cancellation in the level of assigned revenue.

4.3 Assignment of insurance

Insurance coverage is required as an additional security should the vessel be damaged, lost, or subject to claim from third parties. Insurance protection in shipping finance primarily involves the assignment of all insurance payments due to the borrower, to be paid either directly to the bank or requiring the bank's express consent before being paid to the borrower. Different types of insurance protection are: the Hull and Machinery insurance which protects the bank by ensuring compensation when the vessel is lost or damaged, as does war cover in the case of civil war, or any hostile act by, or against, a hostile power – or strikes cover which provides protection in the case of loss or damage caused by strikers, locked out workmen, riots, or any person acting from a political motive; the Loss of Hire or Earnings insurance which protects against interruption in cash flow; and other insurance protection important for the bank to ensure cash flow and debt service, include Protection and Indemnity,[33] which covers third party risks, such as collision liability, loss of life, cargo liability; and Freight, Demurrage and Defence insurance, which provides the shipowner with legal advice and assistance, and covers expenses in pursuing claims and resisting disputes of a more operational nature.

4.4 Mortgagee's interest insurance

Mortgagee's Interest insurance is an additional one which protects the bank in the event of a policy becoming void if certain warranties are broken, for example, it covers the interest of the mortgagee in the case of a disputed claim by the underwriters on the grounds of fraud. The mortgagee's interest claim will usually be withheld, pending the conclusion of litigation. Since this can take some considerable time, and the outstanding loan plus the accruing interest are set at a default rate, the final interest claim may not cover in full the amount due. A solution to this problem is the simultaneous payments of mortgagee's interest during litigation, subject to return if underwriters are subsequently forced to pay. Alternatively, an escrow interest bearing account can receive the mortgagee's interest claim and be subject to release, should underwriters be compelled to pay.

4.5 Assignment of requisition compensation

This security consists of the borrower assigning to the bank, any compensatory payments in the event of vessel requisitioning, either in terms of absolute title, or for hire purposes during times of war, hostilities or nationalisation.

4.6 Guarantees

A guarantee is an undertaking, given to the bank by the guarantor, to be answerable for the loan and interest granted by the bank to a shipping company, upon the loan becoming defaulted. In accepting guarantees, the bank should also investigate the legal authority of the guarantor to give guarantees. Guarantees are normally personal or corporate.

Under a personal guarantee agreement, the guarantor is liable – on demand – for the discharge of all liabilities to the bank up to the stated amount or proportion, in the event of default on the part of the borrower. The personal guarantee is based on the guarantor's personal assets. However, assets may sometimes be registered in the names of other family members or "offshore" companies. Legal recourse, when necessary, against the borrower and the guarantor, who is usually the owner or major shareholder of the shipping company, is often questionable and difficult. Thus, personal guarantees are now often recognised by the banking sector as being merely an indication of good faith or moral commitment on behalf of the owner, rather than a cast iron legal security.

Corporate guarantees are usually given by the group holding company in conventional structures, or by related management shipping companies in single vessel structures. These guarantees are becoming very important in the latter case, when the security is only the mortgage and the assignment of income. Should a payment default develop, the bank has recourse to the guarantor.

4.7 Comfort letters

Comfort letters are a form of intermediate, less strict, guarantees usually containing assurances and intent.

4.8 Cash collateral security

Cash securities usually comprise a special cash collateral account, blocked by the bank, which may be established on an initial lump sum or monthly payment basis. The reason for their existence is that the bank lowers its loan exposure and also holds cash, which can be used for the payment of interest and repayment of loan instalments should the shipping company be unable to cover them in a falling freight market, during which the vessel may face temporary employment problems. Cash collateral accounts are normally interest-bearing, subject to negotiation.

4.9 Share security

The share security, which is normally taken in addition to the mortgage, consists of an owner depositing shares of the borrowing shipping company that he/she controls, with the bank, for a specific period or up to the final amortisation of the loan. This enables the lending bank, when a shipping company is in default for the loan repayment, to assume ownership of the vessel-owning company as opposed to the vessel itself, resulting in the bank becoming the new owner as opposed to a mortgagee.

A Share Pledge applies where the shares are in bearer form and, hence, the title passes – on delivery of the shares – to the bank; whilst, a Share Charge applies to shares of registered form, and delivery will need to be accompanied by executed undated transfer forms.

5. COVENANTS

Covenants are contractual obligations of the borrower to the lender, that are included in the loan agreement and those referring to the vessel in the mortgage, and refer to certain actions that the borrower should or should not undertake. They, therefore, fall into one of two groups: affirmative or negative. In a non-shipping study, where financial differences between small and large firms are discussed, Walker and Petty[34] referred to four areas that are always covered by covenants in the loan agreements. These are: liquidity, profitability, financial leverage, and dividend policy. Shipping is no exception.

According to Apilado and Millington,[35] covenants impose contractual limits on the action of the borrower and serve to reduce the risk exposure. The prime objective behind the covenants is the protection of the assets' value of the borrower. Thus, the financial institution wants to maintain the market value of the assets higher than the market value of the liabilities. In such a case, when a positive net worth exists, the shipping company has a value for the borrower and serves as security for the lender. The problems are created when the market value of the assets (vessels and other assets) decreases and, when abstracting the liabilities from the assets, the net worth becomes negative. This is the reason that the hull to debt ratio is imposed and regular valuation of the market value of the vessels, by international firms of shipbrokers, has to take place. In addition, further debt is not allowed without prior written consent of the bank and the vessel has to be well maintained and operated by the borrower.

Other covenants address: liquidity, such as the maintenance of minimum current account balances – this covenant may apply to the vessels that are financed by the bank and the accounts with the bank, or those held by other financial institutions; profitability – an example being the income of the vessel(s) to be directed to specific bank accounts; and dividend policy, such as distribution of dividends by the management to shareholders, is not allowed without – again – the prior written consent of the bank. Through these covenants, the bank oversees the liquidity and controls the cash flow of the company or the group, and watches over their further investment activities.

There is a wide variety of other covenants imposed by the loan agreement or the mortgage which is, of course, to be expected as protective measures in the lender's interest. This is because shipping companies operate in a very complex international business - and legal - environment and may be incorporated in one country; vessel(s) may fly the flag of another country (where the mortgage on the vessel will be registered); sail in various parts of the globe, often under dangerous conditions; the finance may take place by a bank in a different country and the loan agreement may be governed by the law of another country; and the crew may be nationals of other countries. Many of these diametrically different conditions and factors, which may have an effect on the repayment of the loan, should be dealt with within the covenants section.

The bank's objective in using covenants is to maintain a positive net worth of the borrowing company, to create compliance incentives for the borrower, and to establish the legal background for loan monitoring. Failure of the borrower to comply with covenants is usually an event of default, which may accelerate the repayment of the loan or allow the lender to enforce its rights. According to Myers[36] borrowers accept the added costs of restrictive covenants as part of the price of acquiring funds needed for their business operations. However, shipping banks, when imposing covenants, should maintain a balance between their need to secure the shipping company's net worth and its operating flexibility and investment expansion. This is because high restrictions may prevent a company's growth, whereas a too relaxed approach may occasionally lead to moral hazard.

6. FURTHER DISCUSSION ON CREDIT ANALYSIS

Having looked at the securities and covenants, we can further discuss some aspects of credit analysis. Table 2 shows the statistical analysis and results of a study[37] on the effect of the six "C's" of Credit, on shipping loan decisions. The study was based on a questionnaire, as well as long and detailed personal discussions with the senior shipping finance staff of fourteen international commercial banks in London, Piraeus, Hong Kong and Rotterdam.

From the bank finance viewpoint, shipping companies may fall into two broad groups: corporate shipping companies; and project shipping or single vessel companies. Under the first group, the company owns, leases, charters and operates its vessels, and may have a strong balance sheet, particularly with respect to liquidity and gearing. The paid-in capital, together with retained earnings, should provide a buffer against freight rates fluctuations. Additionally, cashflow should be relatively stable and cover debt service (interest payments and contracted amortisations) by a fair margin. Collateral securities depend on the financial standing of the shipowner as well as the repayment period. Exposure up to one year may generally be unsecured. Depending on risk class, unsecured lending can be provided up to seven years to low risk classes or, alternatively, secured financing up to a level of 80% of the market value of the vessel.

A "shipping project", or single vessel company, is an activity which can be considered separately from the activities of the sponsor (owner) of the project. In this case, the repayment of the loan is based on the cash flow of the venture, with security cover primarily on the assets of the venture, and with no (or limited) recourse to the sponsor. All such exposure are covered by collateral. In this case, the loan does not normally exceed 70% of market value at any time. Exceptions to this rule may be considered if, for example, a favourable time charter with a satisfactory charterer is in place. Loans are also considered with a tenor of up to ten or twelve years, for newbuildings to accommodate structures which are typically up to two years' pre-delivery and maximum ten years' post delivery.

Table 2: Ranking of individual factors and their effect on shipping loan decisions (6 c's of credit)

Rank	Factor	Weight (%)
1	Borrower integrity, reputation and managerial capacity	17.25
2	Creditworthiness & Loan Record	14.53
3	Securities (Collateral)	7.02
4	Project Cash Flow Projections	5.86
5	Ownership Equity Stake in the Project	5.36
6	Experience and Time Length in the Market	4.70
7	Borrower Investment Decisions	4.35
8	Project Hull-to-Debt (H/D) Ratio	3.86
9	Specific Sector Conditions (Prospects)	3.85
10	Condition of the Vessel(s) to be financed	3.79
11	H/D Ratio of the Borrower's Fleet	3.79
12	Cash Capacity of the Owner	3.43
13	Shipping Industry Conditions (Prospects)	3.12
14	Age of the Vessel(s)	2.96
15	Chartering Policy	2.37
16	World Economy Conditions (Prospects)	2.32
17	Reputation of Charterers	2.16
18	Cost Control	2.06
19	Future Default Loans	1.65
20	Financial Statements	1.57
21	Company Size	1.54
22	Company Structure	1.25
23	Engineering (Technical Team Qualifications)	1.21
	Total	100

Source: © Antoniou, A., Thanopoulos, A., and Grammenos, C. Th. (1998), *An Attempt to Quantify Individual Factors of the five C's of Credit Risk Analysis in Bank Shipping Finance*, Shipping Finance Working Paper No. 3, Department of Shipping, Trade and Finance, City University Business School, London.

In Table 2, two of the financial institutions put an emphasis on corporate financing or "near corporate financing" in the sense that the single shipping company proposals for financing are assessed as part of one larger group – above fifteen vessels – and the qualitative analysis treats both the credit risk of an individual project and that of the overall group. The other eleven financial institutions have both kinds of clients: large groups and smaller shipping companies, who own between four and ten vessels.

According to this table, character, managerial capacity and creditworthiness account for 32% of individual factors; while collateral and cash flow account for 13%. It seems, indeed, that these banks focus – or, at least, want to focus – on name lending, where managerial capacity, expertise, past investment and loan record, resourcefulness and tenacity, during a recession and depression period, are highly appreciated by the banks.

The six "C's" of Credit is an analysis which investigates the past and makes inquiries for – and projection to – the future. It requires meetings with principals of the company and key staff, analysis of financial statements, and legal chartering contracts. It also necessitates the existence of a web of contacts for obtaining information about the shipping company, such as other banks that have provided finance for its vessels, its trade creditors, and shipbrokers. In essence, the loan officer and his/her superior have to be in a position to assess the parameters of a qualitative model which, in a brief summary form, includes: the management's expertise and integrity; the debt, equity and net worth; the cash flow; the mortgaged vessels and the guarantees for the loan; and the external economic and financial environment, where the company operates. This model provides a deep knowledge of the borrower's company and its loans. The assessment should provide the probability of loan repayment or default.

Table 3: Rating scale

Rating Scale	S & P	Moody's
Highest Quality	AAA	Aaa
High Quality	AA	Aa
Upper Medium Quality	A	A
Medium Grade	BBB	Baa
Somewhat Speculative	BB	Ba
Low Grade, Speculative	B	B
Low Grade, Default Possible	CCC	Caa
Low Grade, Partial Recovery Possible	CC	Ca
Default, Recovery Unlikely	C	C

Source: Standard & Poor's and Moody's Investor Service.

Over the last decade, a number of banks have rated the shipping companies, shipping groups, and the loans offered, in a similar way the rating agencies[38] rate the bond and other debt issues. Table 3 shows the rating scale of Standard and Poor's and Moody's.[39] The financial institutions undertake their credit risk analysis (based on the six C's of Credit), and they then feed with financial information – mainly ratios – their own rating model, in order to produce the rating of the project – and/or the company – to be financed. The rating indicates the default probability. A large number of financial institutions do not use rating or other models.[40] However, there is a tendency to start to utilise them, as new proposals for Capital Adequacy 2006, will introduce similar models. This is discussed in the subsequent section on Capital Adequacy Rules.

The decision to grant the loan is, thus, based on the six C's of Credit Risk Analysis and on the rating of the company. The shipping industry, due to the volatility of freight rates has a BB, Ba rating, which places it into the "somewhat speculative" group of Table 3. There are certainly companies which belong to AA, Aa; and companies and loans whose rating is CCC, Caa as well. It is for the financial institution to target the desirable group of clients and to attract them. Should a loan, in any way, have a low rating, the provision of appropriate securities may be required. In addition, the pricing will reflect the rating, which is the topic of the next section.

6.1 Pricing of the loan

The process of assessing the probability of credit risk, or default, is also linked with the pricing of shipping loans. In general, shipping companies, which are closer to risk-free business, should compensate the banks with lower returns on shipping loans, while the ones with an increased probability of default should reimburse the banks with a higher return. The difference between the risk-free loan and the risky one is the default risk premium, the compensation of the bank for the additional risk involved.

A pricing model for shipping loans may contain four components: the marginal cost of funding the loan, which is normally the LIBOR; the bank's administrative and overhead cost structure to initiate, analyse and monitor, the shipping loan; the default risk premium of the shipping loan to be granted; and a profit margin that includes an acceptable return to shareholders. The bank, when charging the interest rate on a shipping loan, uses LIBOR, the first component, as a basis, and adds a spread (margin) which contains all the other three components.

In addition to spread, the financial institution charges fees for the provision of the loan. Two usual forms of fees are "facility fee" and "commitment fee". The facility fee is normally a flat fee, rewarding the bank for administering the proposal and granting the loan. Commitment fee is the percentage fee paid for the undrawn loan or part of it, that has been approved but not yet taken. It usually lasts for a period between six months and a year. Finally, the borrower may be asked to maintain a compensating deposit balance in the current account of the shipping company, kept with the bank. This requires that a minimum balance of the account will be maintained by the borrower, either on an average annual basis or an absolute flat amount (e.g., the minimum balance of the account will never be below $1m). Since such accounts are interest-free, or may command a lower interest rate, the effective cost of the loan increases. Furthermore, the bank controls – or follows closely – the borrower's liquidity.

When a financial institution is setting spread, fees, and compensating balances, the hard competition in the banking market for creditworthy and desirable customers is taken into account. The more competition that exists, the greater the probability that the bank will head for a leaner profit. In a competitive international banking environment, funding, administrative costs and default risk are determined by the bank's internal decisions, while the profit margin is also influenced by external competition. On the other hand, high interest rate charges may induce those who are not normally high risk borrowers to invest in risky projects, in addition to those who are already high risk borrowers; while low risk borrowers may temporarily cease investing, thus resulting in a declining quality of the bank's shipping loan portfolio and an adverse selection problem being created.

Bank Shipping Finance is, for many banks, primarily relationship banking, which refers to the provision of an existing borrower of an array of banking products – such as: cash management; derivatives; foreign exchange dealings; letters of credit; letters of guarantee; and advisory services. Here, the financial institution increases the fee income from the borrower and strengthens their relationship and mutual loyalty.

Financial institutions measure the overall profitability of the borrower and, for this reason, the following relationship can be established.[41]

$$\text{Net Before-Tax rate of return to the bank from the overall borrower's relationship during the year in question} = \frac{\text{Loan and other services income} - \text{Costs of loan and other services provided to the borrower}}{\text{Average amount of loans to the borrower} - \text{Average deposit balances}}$$

The numerator of this formula includes all sources of income in a particular year, such as the expected interest rate, loan fees, commission from foreign exchange transactions, cash management, letters of credit less all the expenses that are incurred in the same period, for the provision of the services. These expenses include – among others – salaries, utilities, rent, expenses for the initiation, analysis and monitoring of the loan, interest on this borrower's deposits, and costs of funds to lend to this borrower. The denominator includes the average loan amount of the year in question minus this borrower's average amount of deposits after subtracting the reserves that may be required by the monetary authorities. However, in the eurodollar market, deposit reserves are not required. Should the rate of return be positive, the loan proposal may proceed from the profitability viewpoint, since the required income exceeds the expenses. In case the rate of return is negative, the income and expenses items should be reconsidered.

Grammenos (1995)[42] investigates the profitability of the shipping departments of four international banks from 1988 – 1995. Table 4 shows the major components which are: interest and fees from loans; commission from foreign exchange dealings and remittances; collection of cheques and deposits; letters of credit and guarantee. It is evident that there is an increasing trend for non-interest activities, the volume of which – and therefore the profits – increase.

Table 4: Average gross income by source of four international banks

	1988	1989	1990	1991	1992	1993	1994	1995
Interest and Fees from Loans	60%	58%	57%	55%	54%	52%	52%	51%
Foreign Exchange	19%	21%	23%	23%	23%	25%	25%	26%
Commission*	21%	21%	22%	22%	23%	23%	24%	23%

*Charges on Remittances, Collection of Cheques, Deposits, Letters of Credit, Letters of Guarantee and others.
Source: Grammenos, C.Th. (1994): "Financing the International Fleet", Nautical Institute Annual Lecture, Royal Society of Arts, London.

In a recent study, Grammenos[43] discusses, again, the profitability concept as he revisits the same departments, where he identifies two fundamental changes. The first is the very intense focus on the overall return to the departments, through relationship banking. This is evidenced by their target return imposed by the head offices and the detailed sourcing of the earnings and the costs. The second is the appearance of new sources, such as derivatives and advisory services, and the intensification of banking efforts for cash management of the shipping companies. Thus, as is evident from Table 5, the main source of their income remains the loan (loan interest and fees), ranging from 45–60% of their total return from loan and services, while the borrower-related fee services account for 42–60%. These two fundamental changes are in line with the need for an increase in the capital base of the banks, which enables them to expand. It is partly a consequence of capital adequacy, a topic which is discussed in Section 6.3 of this chapter.

Table 5: Sources of income of shipping departments of four international banks, 1998–2001

	%
Loan Interest	30–40
Loan Fees including Syndication	15–20
Derivatives*	10–15
Foreign Exchange	10–15
Cash Management (Deposits – Collection of Cheques – Remittances – Float**)	20–25
Financial Guarantees; Letters of Credit	2–5

* Only two of the banks offer derivatives.
** The total of non-interest bearing deposit balances at any particular day, that is deposited overnight.
Source: Grammenos, C. Th. (2002): "Sources of Income of Shipping Departments of Four International Banks, 1998-2001", unpublished study.

6.2 Syndication

Syndication is a common method nowadays for bank shipping finance, when a loan is made by two or more financial institutions, on similar terms and conditions, using common documentation and administered by a common agent.[44] It can be very large with more than 60 participating banks but, in shipping, it is mostly the smaller form, four to eight banks, with all of them having shipping expertise and portfolio, which is called "club syndication".

In the loan interest item of Table 5, interest is included from both bilateral and syndicated loans – but it has not been possible to specify the exact percentage of each, since the ratio of bilateral to syndicated loans is quite diverse, reflecting the bank's loan syndication policy.

The reasons for the existence of syndications lie in a number of factors, the most important of which are: the need for large amounts to be financed; the spreading of risk; the increased banking return, which includes spread[45] and additional fees charged on the borrowers; and the gaining of experience and international reputation and opportunity to banks, which they do not have otherwise, to participate in the financing of leading shipping companies, who are the target clients for syndication. The main negative elements are a possible disagreement with a decided course of action and a slower decision-making process in comparison with bilateral financing, which involves only one bank.

Fees from syndication include the arrangement fee for the arranger, which is normally the leading bank of the syndication; the participation fee, which is given to each participating bank in accordance with its committed amount; the commitment fee, which is based on the undrawn amount of the loan until its full drawdown; and finally, the agency fee, which is the amount of remuneration of the agent/bank which monitors and administers the loan and handles all payments of the borrower to the syndicate.

6.3 Capital adequacy rules

Traces of the emphasis on profitability can be partly found in the Capital Adequacy Rules imposed, on 1 January 1993, by the Basle Accord on International Convergence on Capital. It was the first time that the capital of the bank, and therefore its solvency, was linked with the varying degree of credit risk of the bank's groups of assets (for example, cash, bonds, residential mortgages, commercial loans) on and off its balance sheet. Each asset group was given a different weight (e.g., cash 0%, municipal bonds 20%, loan mortgagees for residential properties 50% and commercial loans 100%) and the total capital of the bank – core capital and supplementary capital, or tiers I and II – should be a minimum, or higher, of eight per cent of the risk adjusted total assets, that is to say, the Risk Asset Ratio, the formula of which is as follows:

$$\frac{\text{Total capital (Tiers I and II)}}{\text{Risk Adjusted Assets}} \geq 8\%$$

According to the Basle regulations, shipping (and all other commercial) loans have the same risk weight (100 per cent), despite the fact that different companies and loans represent different degrees of risk – such as AAA, A, B– or CCC. However, it was argued that the 100% weight may induce bankers to concentrate on more risky loans, to boost their return on assets and increase their capital base, consequently, creating value for the banks and at the same time increasing their risk exposure which may result in escalating their loan losses and, subsequently, destroying value for the bank.

Table 6: Proposal for risk weights for a new capital adequacy framework

Claim	AAA to AA–	A+ to A–	BBB+ to BBB–	BB+ to B–	Below B–	Unrated
Corporates	20%	100%	100%	100%	150%	100%

Source: Basle Committee on Banking Supervision (2000), *A New Capital Adequacy Framework*.

There are new proposals from the Basle Committee for Capital Adequacy Rules, with a view to applying them at the end of 2006.[46] Under these, two principal options are recommended for the measurement of credit risk: the standardised approach (SA) and the internal rating based approach (IRB). Both apply to corporate exposures and many lending shipping transactions belong to this group. The SA proposes the substitution of risk weights with credit risk ratings, similar to Moody's and Standard and Poor's, while it draws on external credit assessments for determining these ratings. Table 6 shows that a wider range of weight groups is proposed to be introduced. Most of the shipping companies operating in a risky environment would fall into the groups of 100% or 150% with a corresponding 8% or 12% capital adequacy requirement.

The IRB approach, on the other hand, has two variants: foundation and advance. Under the foundation, it is proposed the banks will assess the risk of default of the borrower, but estimates of additional risk factors are derived through the application of standardised supervisory rules. A financial institution, to follow the foundation approach, has to demonstrate that it has in place the appropriate internal rating system, risk management process and ability to estimate the risk components.

The advance IRB approach is for institutions that are currently in use of a well-developed risk management system to assess both their credit risk profile and their capital adequacy. As such, a central measurable concept is the probability of default (PD) of a borrower. This is in association with the magnitude of likely loss on the exposure, the Loss Given Default (LGD), and with the amount the bank was exposed to the borrower at the time of default, the Exposure of Default (EOD). Finally the maturity of the exposure (M) is taken into account. The PD, LGD and M are estimated and used as inputs to calculate corresponding risk weights. The risk weights are multiplied by EOD and the resultant amounts are added across the portfolio of the bank. Thus, the required capital adequacy of the bank can be calculated.

In October 2001, "Object Finance" was included among other areas of finance in a Working Paper on "Internal Ratings-Based Approach to Specialised Lending Exposures", published by the Bank for International Settlements (BIS). Object finance deals with providing finance for equipment – such as ships, aircraft, trains, fleets; it is the known method in bank shipping finance of pledged vessel(s), which generate cash flow, assigned to the bank. In this case, the above discussed concepts LGD, PD and M, in order to be quantified, and Capital Adequacy to be determined, an object rating, a client rating and an integrated rating, are required. The object rating takes into account the characteristics of the vessel(s) to be financed, the financing terms and the shipping market risks. The client rating considers parameters, such as, the borrower's management capacity, track record, and financial data, that is to say, information contained in the six C's of Credit Analysis. Finally, an integrating rating will be created, which combines both object and client rating.

What can be deduced for bank shipping finance so far, from the Basle proposals? The exact methodology that will apply remains to be seen, since many more discussions and studies[47] will take place during the next two years. IRB and Object Finance differ between them in that the first deals with corporate exposures and the second, with specialised lending exposures. However, not all transactions can be clearly identified as to which group they belong. Secondly, the object finance method takes into account the collateral securities of the loan, while IRB does not. What, though, is clear is that quantitative analysis and shipping markets experts will be needed for the credit rating systems to be developed, run and implemented, in a number of financial institutions.

Another possible consequence is that the smaller shipping companies may be at a disadvantage, since the capital adequacy requirements may be higher for them than the current 8%, due to, for instance, a higher percentage of financing – over 60% – or the lack of sufficient secured income. This would result in an increase in the required adequate capital of the bank, the cost of which would be passed on to the customer. In addition, these companies, being smaller, show a lower overall profitability in their banking transactions for their lending banks. As a result, they may not be included in the desirable clients' list of these financial institutions. Therefore, tiers I and II and III shipping companies may be created based on the credit risk rating, the resulting capital adequacy requirement and the overall profitability from the relationship banking. A consequence of this may be that financial institutions will base their finance decisions on shipping projects, after comparison with other more profitable and less – or equally – risky sectors than shipping. Indeed some institutions are already so doing. Finally, financial institutions involved in bank shipping finance may consider, or reconsider, the use of derivatives and securitisation as means of transferring credit risk and releasing capital required by central bank authorities for bank shipping loans. Endnote 12 of this text is relevant.

7. LOAN MONITORING

Loan monitoring[48] is essentially the periodic evaluation of the shipping loan portfolio, by the shipping department, through the qualitative model of credit risk analysis (referred to in the section "Further Discussion on Credit Analysis") and the six C's. This may happen, for instance, twice a year or whenever there are developments in the loans that require the attention of the bank. The prime objective is for the loan officer to ensure: the borrower's compliance with the covenants and also that his/her management capacity and integrity remain at the required levels; the net worth is sufficient for the loan's overall security and/or the target hull to debt ratio remains as required; vessel(s) continue to be employed efficiently; cash flow is satisfactory for the payments of capital instalments and interest; and the financial conditions of the personal or corporate guarantors have not deteriorated. All these factors are scrutinised at the time of the periodic review of the loan and under future probable, economic, financial, and shipping conditions.

Management restructuring, splits and deaths, may have negative implications on the operation and financial condition of the shipping company. While changes in an owner's character and integrity over a depression period is not a totally exceptional event, moral hazard presents a demanding monitoring requirement, particularly in a depressed shipping market. Debt repayment and cash flow of financed vessel(s), vessel(s) financed by other banks, and overall group fleet, should be analysed for the purpose of identifying overborrowing and adverse revenue and costs developments, that may squeeze the cash flow available for the debt service.

Market movements are the main cause of decreases in freight rate revenue, although likely reasons also include aggressive chartering policy, that is to say, vessels are chartered in the spot market where income is higher for a short period, in comparison with the time charter market; unsatisfactory vessel performance in contrast to what is expected in accordance with the charterparties; default on the part of charterer; vessel inactivity from factors such as arrest, repair and blacklist. Increases in costs may arise from factors such as running costs escalation (mainly crew, technical and insurance), and adverse interest rate and currency movements.

The bank will normally monitor overall conditions in the world economy and international trade, related industry or commodities, and the shipping market, that may have implications on the repayment of its loan(s). These include: changes in economic policies (such as anti-inflationary economic policies in the early 1980s); political events (e.g., the nationalisation of the Libyan oil assets in 1971 and the Iranian political unrest in 1979); new legislation (Oil Pollution Act of 1990 that was decided unilaterally by the USA, or International Safety Management Code of the International Maritime Organisation); and vessel blacklisting. In addition, scenario analysis for the cash flow and repayment of the loan under different economic conditions and assumptions, is part of the job. The unpredictable fluctuations of income and asset value levels, make the constant reviewing of a vessel's market value and the practical effectiveness of collateral securities an essential part of the monitoring process. In terms of mortgages and vessel's value, the main cause of decreases in value are current and expected or unexpected market conditions – although vessel condition, technology, and new legislation, are also relevant. A decrease in vessel value may result in the hull to debt ratio falling below permitted levels, increasing the probability of default, since the real economic worth of the company decreases. Finally, falling freight rates and vessel market values – which may affect payments of loan instalments and securities of the loan, dry up compensating balances, postpone payments for trade creditors – are usually strong indicators of future problematic loans.

Once or twice a year, and whenever extraordinary conditions demand, a review of the shipping loan portfolio takes place, which is part of the monitoring process. Should loans be identified as having weaknesses regarding their repayment, they would be adversely classified according to the probability of loan loss.[49] This normally happens in a bad market. In this case, the bank should take immediate steps to minimise the loan loss effect.[50] However, this discussion is beyond the scope of this analysis.

Additional issues of importance for monitoring are the amount of the vessel('s) revenue assigned to the bank and the validity of insurance security in respect of paying premiums and complying with policy clauses. Finally, liquidity problems may arise from trade creditors. A sharp rise in the amount owed to trade creditors may indicate a difficulty in paying short term obligations. It may prove to be of limited use, a bank being paid promptly, if the crew or creditors – such as suppliers – have seriously outstanding debts. This could lead to arrests, disputes and non-performance of the vessel, which would affect liquidity and, in turn, the bank's loan.

8. SHIPPING CREDIT POLICY

The shipping credit policy is a package of general and specific guidelines that refers to important factors for providing bank shipping loans, allocating responsibilities, and creating a mechanism of control. It creates an internal shipping framework for the bank, within which loans are initiated, analysed, approved,

Table 7: Contents of bank shipping credit policy

Size of Loan Portfolio
Fund Apportionment and Desirable Clientele
Facilities Offered: Terms and Conditions
Legal Aspects
Loan Documentation
Type of Bank Participation
Loan Granting, Lending Authority and Responsibility
Administrative Structure, Credit Committee

Source: Grammenos, C. Th. (1983), "Bank Shipping Finance: A Spherical Approach", paper presented at Europort Congress, Amsterdam.

granted and monitored, and is a means of comparing the actual and projected performance.

The skeleton outline in Table 7 covers the fundamental areas of the content of a credit policy chart. The overall exposure of the bank to the shipping industry depends upon the decision for diversification or specialisation. The rule of thumb of portfolio theory is diversification. The extent of the bank's involvement in shipping finance, percentage-wise, versus other sectors, such as manufacturing, agriculture, energy, aviation, real estate, depends upon a number of factors, among which are the bank's geographical position (small local bank or international bank operating in large business capitals), its shipping expertise, the strength of its shipping department and credit committee, the bank's loan loss experience, the shipping loan(s) perceived risk and its/their profitability compared to other sectors, and the shipping sector's overall securities cover in comparison with that of other banks. Large international or regional commercial banks may have an exposure to shipping between 1 and 5%, although higher (such as 10%) is not unthinkable.

The financial institution may decide to allocate funds to different geographical locations and/or shipping markets and/or shipping companies diversification. Geographical diversification involves traditional or newer shipping centres, such as London, New York, Piraeus, Oslo, Hamburg, Rotterdam, Tokyo, Hong Kong, Singapore and Shanghai. Shipping market diversification includes financing companies which operate different types of vessels, for instance, dry bulk, tanker, general cargo, container, cruise, passenger, car carrier, and other types of vessels. As far as shipping companies are concerned, diversification refers to the size of the company, its ownership structure (one vessel company, or large corporation), the aggressive or conservative borrowing philosophy of the company, the type of employment of the company (such as bareboat, time charter, contract of affreightment, spot market). All these factors, individually or in combination, may affect the overall risk profile and the bank's exposure to such risk, in particular during a falling shipping market when income decreases and payment of the loan capital and interest may become problematic.

The shipping credit policy discusses all types of shipping loans that the bank is to grant, the maximum percentage of the market value of the vessel(s) to be financed, in conjunction with the securities offered or the maximum amount to be lent to a low-risk shipping company, on the basis of a stable and sufficient cash flow. In addition, the spread, maturity, amortisation schedules, interest rates and currencies, are discussed. The array of securities, their usefulness and limitations, in conjunction with properly documenting the loan, are part of credit policy. Indeed, banks have been shocked repeatedly when realising that poorly drafted loan agreements and mortgages, or lack of proper communication with insurance underwriters, have restrained or delayed them from enforcing their rights, as lenders, on the borrower's assets and other collaterals.

In the credit policy document, the bank should clarify whether shipping loans will be financed on a syndicated or individual basis. Syndication strengthens the collective financial power of the banks, while increasing their profitability through syndication fees. Individual financing by a bank, in combination with relationship banking offered services, strengthens profitability and loyalty.

Administrative aspects of loans, such as the maximum amount that can be granted by loan officers, or at a higher level and the type of decision making structure (centralised or decentralised), can be seen in a credit policy document. In the 1970s and 1980s, many European and Japanese banks tended to be more "head office" and "bureaucratic" oriented, while the American banks followed the speedy decentralisation approach. There is a distinctive improvement in the bank loan decision-making process in the past years, which is recognition of the often need for rapid reaction in the dynamic vessel sale and purchase market; the new banking generation is more oriented (and receptive) to banking competition and, at the same time, prepared for cooperation through syndication. Finally, the role of the credit committee and its composition should also be explained in a credit policy document, as a body which discusses, modifies, approves or turns down, credit proposals of the shipping department.

Table 8: Shipping credit policy of 10 international commercial banks

Year	No. of banks	Credit policy
1979	3	Quite clear
	6	Vague
	1	Absence of credit policy
1994	9	Clear credit policy
	1	The bank no longer exists

Source: Grammenos, C.Th. (1994): "Financing the International Fleet", Nautical Institute Annual Lecture, Royal Society of Arts, London.

A powerful example of the usefulness of credit policy is given in Table 8, which shows a survey on the shipping credit policy of ten international commercial banks and how it progressed between 1979 and 1994, which is also reported in Grammenos.[51] In 1979, the results of the study indicated that three of the banks had quite clear (but not as detailed as in Table 7) shipping credit policies, while six had a vague policy and one had not established a shipping policy; whereas, in 1984, the two with a clear credit policy realised small to moderate loan losses; the banks with a vague credit policy, and the third with a clear credit policy, suffered from moderate to substantial loan losses; while the losses of the one without credit policy were devastating.[52] In 1994, Grammenos re-examined the credit policy of the same banks. The results reveal that nine of these ten banks had formulated a clear shipping credit policy, while the remaining bank, which did not have a credit policy in 1979, was no longer in business.

9. CONCLUSIONS

In this chapter, credit risk minimisation in bank shipping finance, for the acquisition of vessels, has been discussed within the framework of the lending function. During parts of this function, banks are challenged by information asymmetry, adverse selection and moral hazard.

Bank Credit Policy provides the framework within which credit risk analysis – as manifested by the six C's of Credit – of shipping loan proposals takes place. Both bank credit policy and credit risk analysis are the backbone of credit risk control. Banks have also other means – not cast iron, of course – of strengthening the soundness of shipping loans, namely: securities; covenants; and monitoring. Securities, predominant of which is the mortgage – the second way out for the bank, the first being the cash flow, and the third the financial guarantees; Covenants, which pave the way for the materialisation of banking vigilance, that is to say, Monitoring, which collects, processes and analyses information regarding the loan and the shipping company, including the annual – and possibly semi-annual – loan review.

Credit risk, or credit default, may be measured by rating the loan and the shipping company. Rating is also linked with the default risk premium and, thus, with pricing. Shipping loans are a substantial part of bank shipping revenue, which is based on a wider web of services offered to shipping companies – the relationship banking. As such it may increase the gross profits of banks, and may strengthen their capital base, a necessary path for increasing their value and a contributor to sound banking expansion. Capital soundness is a requirement of the Capital Adequacy Rules; and at the end of year 2006, a new rule will be introduced, across the banking spectrum, based on rating and advanced statistical techniques. Some banks already apply these methods and there may be consequences for the finance of shipping companies.

Grammmenos 1977,[13] 1979[14] and 1983[48] states that credit risk in bank shipping finance may be minimised by the use of tools, such as, bank credit policy, credit analysis, securities, covenants and loan monitoring, all of which today remain essential.

ENDNOTES

1. There is a limited number of studies in shipping finance. In the areas of IPOs, for instance, Grammenos, C. Th., and Marcoulis, S. (1996): "Shipping Initial Public Offerings: A Cross-country Analysis", *Empirical Issues in Raising Equity Capital*, by M. Levis (ed.) (Elsevier), pp. 67–80; Grammenos, C. Th., and Arkoulis, A.G. (1999): "The Long-run Performance of Shipping Initial Public Offerings", *International Journal of Maritime Economics*, Vol. 1, pp. 34–52. While, on stock returns,

Grammenos, C. Th., and Marcoulis, S.N. (1996): "A Cross-section Analysis of Stock Returns: the Case of Shipping Firms", *Maritime Policy & Management*, Vol. 23(1), pp. 67–80; Grammenos, C. Th., and Arkoulis, A. (2002): "Macroeconomic Factors and International Shipping Stock Returns", *International Journal of Maritime Economics*, 4, pp. 81–99; Kavussanos, M.G., and Marcoulis, S.N. (1997): "The Stock Market Perception of Industry Risk and Micro-Economic Factors: the Case of the US Water Transportation Industry versus other Transport Industries", *Transportation Research*, Part E, Vol. 33 (2), pp. 147–58.

2. In the area of Mezzanine Finance, the following study is relevant, Grammenos, C. Th., and Dheere, M.J. (1990): *International and US Initial Public Offerings and Private Placements of Equity for Shipping Investments for 1987–1988*, City University Business School (Study commissioned by Pegasus Group)

3. In the area of High Yield Issues, there are only two studies: Grammenos, C. Th., and Arkoulis, A.G., "Determinants of Spread of New High Yield Bond Issues of International Shipping Industry", *Transportation Research, Part E* (forthcoming); Leggate, H.K., "A European Perspective on Bond Finance for the Maritime Industry (2000)", *Maritime Policy and Management*, 27, 4, pp. 353–362.

4. A number of international banks realised shipping loans losses, during the heavily depressed shipping market between 1983 and 1986. Among them, National Westminster Bank, Bank of America and Hill Samuel, which decreased substantially or ceased their shipping finance activities.

5. Altman, E.I. (1980): "Commercial Bank Lending: Process, Credit Scoring and Costs of Errors in Lending", *The Journal of Financial and Quantitative Analysis, Proceedings Issue*, Volume XV, No. 4. In this paper, Altman refers to the following four steps of the lending function: (i) application for a loan; (ii) credit evolution; (iii) loan review; and (iv) repayment performance.

6. This happens when a financial institution converts a deposit into a loan and does not match the deposit's period of its customer, or the deposit's period that obtains from the Interbank Market, with the period of the loan.

7. Grammenos, C. Th. (1979): *Bank Finance for Ship Purchase*, Occasional Paper in Economics, University of Wales Press, chapter 2.

8. The shipping industry uses mainly the eurodollar market, which is the largest unregulated market for deposits placed outside the United States; and eurodollar loans which are dollar denominated loans granted by banks outside the United States.

9. However, there are financial instruments such as interest rate derivatives, which can be used for hedging interest rate risk, offered by financial instutions, at a cost. For more details on how to use interest rate derivatives for hedging, see, e.g., Hull, J. (2000): *Options, Futures and other Derivatives* ((Prentice Hall International); and Kolb, R.W. (2001): *Futures, Options and Swaps* (London, Blackwell's Business Publishers).

10. For a general literature survey on asymmetric information in credit markets, see Bhattacharya, S., and Thekor, A. (1993): "Contemporary Banking Theory", *Journal of Financial Intermediation*, 3, pp. 2–50, and Van Damme, E. (1994): "Banking: A Survey of Recent Microeconomic Theory", *Oxford Review of Economic Policy*, 10, pp. 14–33.

11. Diamond, D.W. (1984): "Financial Intermediation and Delegated Monitoring", *Review of Economic Studies*, Vol. 42, Issue 3, pp. 393–414. Diamond discusses his theory of banks as delegated monitors.

12. This chapter discusses the management of credit risk by using physical instruments (e.g., collateral securities); however, in corporate finance there has been a trend to quantify such a risk and to use credit derivatives over the last decade or so – such as credit swaps, credit spread options. Up until very recently, such transactions have not taken place. However, in the summer of 2002, the NIB Capital Bank executed the first ever (synthetic) securitisation of a bank shipping loan portfolio of US$ 669.5m with the dual objective of transferring credit risk and obtaining regulatory

capital relief. This has been achieved through arrangement of credit default swaps and issuance of credit link notes.

Taking into account the requirements of the proposed capital adequacy rules, under discussion for 2006 (see section 6.3), derivatives and securitisation of bank shipping portfolios are areas that may attract the interest of relevant financial institutions. Should securitisation be employed, the lending function will change and consist of the following parts: origination, funding and selling, follow up of the loan and, possibly, monitoring. For more details on credit derivatives, see for example Hull, J. (2000): *Options Futures and other Derivatives* (Prentice Hall International); and for a discussion on the use of credit derivatives by banks to secure the risk associated with loans, see Duffee, G.R., and Zhou, C. (2001): "Credit Derivatives in Banking: Useful Tools for Managing Risk", *Journal of Monetary Economics*, 2001, Vol. 48, No. 1, pp. 25–55.

13. Grammenos, C. Th. (1977): "The Need for Credit Policy and Analysis in Bank Shipping Finance", Paper presented at Institute of European Finance, Bangor.
14. Grammenos, C. Th. (1979): *Bank Finance for Ship Purchase*, Occasional Paper in Economics, University of Wales Press. In this book, the author processed and analysed over three hundred and fifty confidential files of loans granted by five international banks, and one regional, to shipping companies mainly for secondhand purchases, but also for newbuildings. Principles for granting sound loans were established through introduction of credit analysis and credit policy.
15. See following subsection "Conditions" in text.
16. Grammenos, C. Th. (1994): *Nautical Institute Annual Lecture*, Royal Society of Arts, London. In this presentation, the author referred to one hundred problematic loans as they stood in 1984. The loans were granted between August 1979 and end 1980 to medium-size shipping companies, by international medium- to large-size banks. The striking common elements of all of them are that loans were provided when freight rates and market values of the vessels were high; the financing of the market value of the vessels was between 75 and 85%; and these vessels had to compete in a recessed or depressed shipping market from 1983–1986 with other vessels bought at much lower prices.
17. Pre-Tax Interest Coverage = Net Income (Loss) from Continuing Operations + Gross Interest Expense − Interest Capitalised + Income Tax Expense ÷ Gross Interest Expense.
    Pre-Tax Funds flow and Interest Coverage = Net Income (Loss) from continuing operations + Gross Interest Expense − Interest Capitalised + Income Tax Expense + Depreciation + Amortization ÷ Gross Interest Expense.
18. The market value of the vessel over the outstanding debt that the company incurs for the vessel's purchase. See, for further explanation, Section on Securities (Mortgages).
19. An important reason for the establishment of such companies is the "sister ship" principle, which is found in many jurisidictions, according to which a claim in rem, that is to say a claim in object, can be transferred to any other vessel, which belongs to the same beneficial owner. The creation of different shipping companies of limited liability, each one of which owns one vessel and all of these still controlled by the same owner, over-rides the "sister ship" principle. Claims which arise against a particular vessel of this fleet, for example, by a bank or trade creditors, cannot be transferred to any other vessel of the fleet.
20. Capital costs are affected by the capital structure of the company. Cost of banking loans is normally the lowest, in comparison with bond and high yield issues, while the cost of equity is the highest. The overall cost of capital including debt, preferred stock and common equity, the weighted average cost of capital (WACC) decreases initially with marginal increases in debt until the point that the company reaches its optimal capital structure. Beyond this point, an increase in debt may result in increase of WACC. One should note that these assumptions are based on a tax imposed environment.

21. Metaxas, B.N. (1971): *The Economics of Tramp Shipping* (The Athlone Press), chapter 7. In this quotation, Metaxas refers to "tramp shipping services", since his book is on Tramp Shipping. However, his quotation applies to liners as well.
22. For an analysis of fluctuations in shipping and shipping cycles, see Metaxas, B.N. (1971): *The Economics of Tramp Shipping* (The Athlone Press), chapter 3; Stopford, M. (1997): *Maritime Economics* (Routledge), chapter 2; Grammenos, C. Th. (1979): *Bank Finance for Ship Purchase*, Bangor Occasional Papers in Economics, University of Wales Press, chapter 2. In addition, see chapter 10 of this volume for a detailed analysis of shipping market cycles.
23. For a more detailed discussion on different types of shipping investment, including speculative asset play in relation to shipping cycles, see chapter 28 of this volume.
24. The cash flow calculation for vessel(s) to be financed will be based on total cash receipts minus total costs covering the period over which the loan will be repaid. Cash receipts include operating gross revenue, which could be fixed should there be contract of affreightment or time charter; while assumed revenue, should the vessel operate in the spot market, may be based on past (average over the last ten years), prevailing, and expected, conditions in the vessel('s) market. Operating expenses should be comparable to expenses of similar vessels; while projected ones should be escalated to take into account the rate of inflation. Debt service should be projected in accordance with actual loan repayment with assumed interest rates, should the interest be fluctuating. These items should be part of a scenario analysis (positive and negative), where sensitivity analysis is used.
25. In a depression phase of the shipping cycle, the charterers may be hit by the market as well. Thirty of the one hundred problematic loans referred to in note 13 of this chapter became problematic due to the financial troubles of the charterers of the vessels.
26. See Section 6 of this chapter.
27. This section draws on Grammenos, C. Th. (1979): *Bank Finance for Ship Purchase*, Bangor Occasional Papers in Economics, University of Wales Press, chapter 2, and Grammenos, C. Th., and Xilas, E.M. (1988): *Shipping Investment and Finance, Vol. II*, unpublished notes for MSc. Students in Shipping, Trade and Finance, City University Business School, London.
28. UK Merchant Shipping Act, 1894.
29. The Statutory Mortgage is normally accompanied by further terms and conditions in a separate agreement that acts as back up.
30. However, holders of maritime liens may have a priority over the claims of a mortgagee. Maritime lien is a claim against a vessel, which can be made effective by the seizure of the vessel. It is a right *in rem*, that is to say, it is attached to the vessel even after change of ownership. Among maritime liens are: salvage, seamen's and master's wages, master's disbursements, damages caused by the vessel (e.g., in collision). Possessory lien is the right of a holder of such claim, to retain possession of the vessel for any incurred expenses until the debt is paid. A typical example in this context is the ship repairer or shipyard. The possessory lien will be lost as soon as the claimant ceases possession of the vessel. Some rights of possessory liens may be created by statute, for example, the unpaid port and canal dues. The importance for the lender is that the holder of maritime, possessory and statutory liens may have – depending upon the jurisdiction – a priority over its claims.
31. The value for which a vessel is insured.
32. The value of a vessel in terms of historical cost minus accumulated depreciation.
33. Protection and Indemnity falls outside the scope of ordinary marine insurance. It is structured through membership of Protection and Indemnity Associations (often referred to as P&I Clubs), which are formed and run by shipowners.
34. Walker, E.W., and Petty, J.W. (1978): "Financial Differences Between Large and Small Firms", *Financial Management*, Winter, pp. 61–68.

35. Apilado, V.P., and Millington, J.K. (1992): "Restrictive Loan Covenants and Risk Adjustment in Small Business Lending", *Journal of Small Business Management*, Vol. 30, January, pp. 38–48.
36. Myers, S. C. (1977), Determinants of Corporate Borrowing, Journal of Financial Economics, 5, pp. 147-175.
37. Antoniou A., Thanopoulos, A., and Grammenos, C. Th. (1998): *An Attempt to Quantify Individual Factors of the 5C's of Credit Risk Analysis in Bank Shipping Finance*, Shipping Finance Working Paper, No. 3, Department of Shipping, Trade and Finance, City University Business School, London.
38. According to Moody's (1991), Global Credit Analysis, IFR, "Ratings are intended to serve as indicators or forecasts of the potential for credit loss because of failure to pay, a delay in payment, or partial payment. Credit loss may be defined in general terms as the economic difference between what the issuer has promised to pay and what is actually received."
39. The rating agencies classify the bond issues according to capacity of the company to pay interest and repay principal. The distinctive division of the scale is between two groups: the investment grade (AAB, Aaa to BBB, Baa) and the speculative grade (BB, Ba to C,C). The first group ranges from extremely strong capacity (AAA, Aaa) to adequate (BBA, Baa), to pay interest and repay principal; while the second group ranges from less near-term vulnerability (BB, Ba), to default (C,C) to bonds on which no interest is being paid .
40. In recent years, sophisticated quantitative techniques and portfolio theory have been utilised also for assessing credit risk of a bank's loan portfolio. Sinkley, J.F., Jr., *Commercial Bank Financial Management* (Prentice Hall), in chapter 11, undertakes a presentation and discussion of these methodologies, while also voicing the strong criticism of others.
41. Rose, P.S. (2002) *Commercial Bank Management* (McGraw-Hill), chapter 19.
42. Grammenos, C. Th. (1994): *Financing the International Fleet*, Nautical Institute Annual Lecture, Royal Society of Arts, London.
43. Grammenos, C. Th. (2002): "Sources of Income of Shipping Departments of Four International Banks, 1998-2001", unpublished study.
44. Horn, S. (1990): *Syndicated Loans – A Handbook for Bankers and Borrowers* (Woodhead and Faulkner).
45. Grammenos, C. Th. (2000): "An analysis of syndicated loans, granted between 1985-1999, to tanker and dry cargo shipping companies", unpublished paper, where 40 syndicated loans are analysed from collateral, covenants and spread viewpoints. Spread determinants were examined. These were: amount of the loan, tenor, balloon, and age of the vessels. Univariate and multivariate regression analysis were employed and the clearly statistically significant variable was tenor.
46. *Lloyd's List*, 11 July 2002. While the implementation of new Capital Adequacy Rules was planned for 2004, this was postponed for year-end 2006.
47. Grammenos, C. Th., is currently working on a paper for new Capital Adequacy Rules and their consequences on bank shipping finance for shipping companies. Financial institutions involved in shipping finance are also studying possible effects.
48. Grammenos, C. Th (1983): *Bank Shipping Finance: A Spherical Approach*, Europort Congress. In this paper, Grammenos discusses the lending function in bank shipping finance and the profitability of relationship banking.
49. Gramemnos, C. Th., and Xilas, E.M. (1988): *Shipping Investment and Finance, Vol. II*, unpublished notes for MSc Students in Shipping, Trade and Finance, City University Business School, London. Three categories may deal with loan losses. They are: "Loss" loans which appear uncollectable and will normally be charged to loss provisions in the financial statement of the bank; "Doubtful" loans which have considerable problems and are likely to result in losses for the bank; "Substandard" loans which have some deficiencies that may be corrected through the providing of additional security by the borrower, although there is some possibility of default.

In addition, there is a a further category, "Criticized" loans, which exist when they have smaller deficiencies (such as failure to provide financial statements) and appear to carry lower risk of borrower default. All other loans are considered to be sound.

50. The Problem Loan Treatment options available to banks is thoroughly discussed in Grammenos, C. Th., and Xilas, E.M. (1988): *Shipping Investment and Finance*, unpublished notes for MSc students in Shipping, Trade and Finance, chapter 12.
51. Grammenos, C. Th. (1994): *Financing the International Fleet*, Nautical Institute Annual Lecture, Royal Society of Arts, London.
52. One should add that the credit policy was going along, as their credit analysis (that is, from not well-established to almost non-existent in one case). Character, Capacity, was not thoroughly investigated; gearing ratio was too high, occasionally over ninety per cent; lack of secured employment was also observed in a number of cases; while loans were granted against high vessel market values. Also, clear warnings of a recession in world economy were largely ignored by some of the banks in question. These warnings came after antiflationary measures taken by industrial countries, following the second major increase in oil price in 1979.

PART TEN

PORT ECONOMICS AND MANAGEMENT

CHAPTER 33

PORT MANAGEMENT, OPERATION & COMPETITION: A FOCUS ON NORTH EUROPE

H. Meersman* and E. Van de Voorde†

*Faculty of Applied Economics, University of Antwerp, Antwerp, Belgium.
E-mail: *Hilde.Meersman@ufsia.ac.be*
†University of Antwerp (UFSIA-RUCA and ITMMA), Antwerp, Belgium.
E-mail: *eddy.vandevoorde@ua.ac.be*

1. INTRODUCTION

In the past decades, the role of port management has changed quite fundamentally. It has gradually evolved from being a supervisory and determining capacity to a more subordinate function that often consists solely in providing the required facilities for the various parties involved in port operations.

The port landscape has, after all, also altered in many respects. New technologies and strategic developments have led almost automatically to greater port competition, both at port authority level and at the level of companies operating within the various ports. All port players, from authorities to terminal operators and agents, are looking for ways to maximise profits, to maintain or increase market share, or simply to survive. These goals are not so easily achieved in an era of internationalisation of production, consumption and trade.

National and regional authorities are also monitoring these developments closely. A strong and efficiently run seaport can be an important asset for a country or region in trying to improve its economic position. For one thing, port activities generate value added and employment. Moreover, a seaport can be an important pole of attraction for a broad range of industries.

This in part explains why European ports, especially in the Hamburg–Le Havre range, are involved in such a fierce competitive struggle for attracting goods flows, shipping lines, and infrastructure and industrial investment. Economic resources are scarce, which explains the ferocity of the competitive struggle in which port authorities in particular were engaged until just a few years ago. Watching from the sidelines were a number of other "players": consignors, goods-handlers, shipping companies, etc. This situation has now changed.

The supposed strategic importance of seaports to the economy of a country (or region) has prompted quite a few national authorities to artificially protect their seaport(s), among other things through partial or full subsidising of port infrastructure and maritime access routes. This, in turn, has led to mutual accusations of (attempts at) distortion of competition. This seems quite understandable in a context where different ports within the same range have similar investment plans and are competing for the same goods flows.

The above demonstrates quite clearly that there is a connection between port management and the manner of competition. Each port management is concerned primarily with its own competitive position in the range to which it belongs. Decision-making is geared towards safeguarding or preferably improving this competitive position. Strategic moves by competing ports are monitored very closely.

In this contribution, we shall discuss this issue in some greater detail. We shall deal consecutively with evolutions in port management, the ever-changing port environment and the need for an appropriate set of analytical tools. Finally, we shall consider some recent findings in research into port competition.

2. EVOLUTIONS IN PORT MANAGEMENT

Port management used to be almost exclusively in the hands of the port authorities. However, over the years, and especially in the past decade, this situation has changed quite profoundly. The power of the port authority has clearly dwindled. It must now undergo the might of the strong(er) port players, more in particular the shipping companies and terminal operators. Still, it is interesting to consider how theory and practice of port management have changed, especially in terms of the objectives pursued and the tools applied.[1]

The objectives of a port authority are closely connected with what is considered to be the economic purpose of a seaport. In the past, these goals were restricted mainly to increasing throughput, generating value added, creating local employment, or maximising operating profits. However, today's reality is more complex and more dynamic than that, primarily because of the specific nature of the "port product".

The port product is in itself a chain of consecutive links, while the port as a whole is likewise a link in the global logistics chain. In the course of time, the relative importance of these various links has clearly changed. This was due to, among other things, significant technological developments (e.g., increasing containerisation rate, larger vessels, more speedy handling, etc.) which have increased efficiency. In other words, it no longer suffices to concentrate on one or just a few links in the chain.

However, in order to move beyond such a fragmentary approach and take full advantage of possible benefits of scale, clear insight is required into the generalised cost structure of the constituting links and of the chain as a whole. It is important to know how out-of-pocket costs and costs associated with loss, damage, and delay have an impact on the choice of port.

Within a logistics chain, the port cost usually constitutes only a fraction of the total cost. Overall demand for port services in a particular range will therefore be inelastic, especially in the absence of alternatives. On the other hand, competition between goods handlers, ports and countries within the same range is often fierce. The possibilities for substituting one port for another are often so great that the price elasticity for a specific port may be quite considerable after all.

In view of the considerable number of players in any given port (authorities, port management, consignors, shipping lines, trade unions, etc.), each of whom has different objectives, the nature of port activities is inevitably heterogeneous.

Consequently, the goals of a port authority are determined in part by the degree to which this authority is, directly or indirectly, subjected to foreign influences, external control or competition from other ports. Not surprisingly, then, these goals may differ quite considerably and indeed may change profoundly in the course of time.[2]

It is also striking in this respect that one often needs to search for a compromise between the priorities of the various important market players. As the relative strength of the different market players may change in the course of time, so might the objectives of the port authority. We shall return to this issue later on.

At the same time, evolutions in port managerial structures are also a direct consequence of technological developments and changes in the socio-economic environment. The British port sector is a very good example in this respect: it was nationalised after the Second World War and grouped in British Transport Docks Board, privatised as Associated British Ports in 1981, followed by a government decision in 1991 that the most important ports could be privatised. While the situation did not develop equally drastically in continental Europe, there was clearly a trend towards more autonomy for port authorities and a greater private stake in goods handling.

Far-reaching mechanisation and sweeping technological change have also resulted in a sharp decline in the employment of dock workers and indeed in a thorough reorganisation of the work itself. A typical example of this trend is found in container transhipment. After all, the capital-intensive nature of liner shipping demands that capacity utilisation be maximised with a view to achieving an acceptable return on investment. Ports and terminal operators are thus forced to strive constantly for a further improvement of efficiency and productivity of labour. Under this considerable pressure, an important part of port activity has become capital intensive, with a very high level of investment in infrastructure and cargo-handling equipment.[3]

It follows from this evolution that the role of government has changed. Much attention has been paid in this respect to possible financial or other support from government for port authorities and the consequences this may have on the competitive balance between companies and ports.

However, it is very hard to make sensible comparisons between ports, as they usually operate in different economic, legal, social and fiscal environments. Consequently, there are until today considerable differences in the management of European ports: the Anglo-Saxon tradition of independent port authorities, the centralising Latin tradition in France, Spain and Italy, or the municipal Hanseatic tradition in Germany, the Netherlands and Belgium.[4]

These different traditions have resulted in two important, but diametrically opposed, philosophies. First, there is the continental approach whereby "the port in the limited sense of the word is managed and operated by the port authority, the maritime access routes and the connections with the interior are more the responsibility of the central authorities, and the cargo-handling and various other services are in private hands".[5] Diametrically opposed to this continental tradition stand the ports that are run as "total organisations" (e.g., such British ports as Felixstowe), whereby the maritime access, the port and cargo-handling are the responsibility of a single organisation that supervises all port operations.

Thus, seaports possess characteristics of public utilities on the one hand and of private enterprises on the other.[6] Cargo-handling and related activities are commercial operations that, under normal circumstances, do not need subsidising. By contrast, port infrastructure has many characteristics of public good and is thus approached from a socio-economic perspective (*cf.* the application of socio-economic cost-benefit analyses to determine whether or not an investment is justified).

Is it imaginable that we may evolve towards a port landscape in which government does not fulfil a regulatory role? For the time being, it would appear that the (national) authorities had best remained an interested party, if only for strategic and safety reasons, and to prevent that monopolies are abused by port authorities, terminal operators or dock workers. Goss[7] asserts in this respect that "the conclusion must be that there are likely to be many instances of 'market failure' in seaports, e.g., in the processes of planning, controlling externalities and promoting competition if these were left wholly to the private sector: but there are also many opportunities for 'government failure', whether in port authorities or in other official bodies, including government departments supervising the port authorities".

In a fiercely competitive market such as the port business, the role of government may however continue to be hotly debated. Indeed, it may be the source of continual mutual accusations of distortion of competition. Can a European port policy resolve this issue? Is Europe able to take due account of existing differences between its ports?[8]

One of the most important points of debate remains whether port infrastructure, particularly maritime access routes to ports, has the nature of public goods. These are defined as goods that would, in all probability, not be produced in a satisfactory manner and in sufficient amounts, if at all, by a competitive industry. It concerns goods for common or non-rivalrous consumption, whereby it is impossible to exclude those who cannot pay.

Goss[9] was quite clear on this matter when he asserted that "non-rivalrous consumption occurs with all beacons, buoys and other fixed or floating navigational aids because their cost will be exactly the same no matter how many people are using them. The same is true of dredged entrance channels up to the point where they are congested. If the opportunity cost of using any of these is zero, then imposing any specific charge would have the effect of deterring the marginal user and reducing economic welfare."

The kind of port infrastructure referred to has two important characteristics: the indivisibility of the enormous investments involved and their great longevity. No private company is assured of a sufficient return over such long periods of time. The amount of infrastructure provided would therefore lie below the optimum if such investments were left to the private sector. However, one can wonder whether the discussion about the public goods nature of maritime entrance is not outdated in an era of remote transhipment centres with natural deep-water sites.

It is apparent from the foregoing that theory and practice of port management have evolved quite dramatically. The role of government, and particularly the issue of government support, remains a point of considerable controversy.

3. THE RADICALLY CHANGED PORT ENVIRONMENT

Until the 1990s, players in the port business acted very much as independent entities. Shipping companies competed for the same goods flows. Port authorities presented themselves as mainports, both to each other and to the market as a whole. Fierce competition unfolded between goods handlers operating within the same port. The hinterland modes (i.e., rail, road, inland navigation) were preoccupied with maximising their market shares.

Then a new trend emerged, as competition was unfolding increasingly at the level of logistics chains, in which port authorities, transhipment companies and the hinterland modes are the most important links. Those players who are able to contribute to the lowest generalised cost of the transport chain are most likely to be included. This also means that systematic mutual trade-offs are made between links in the transport chain. Consequently, it may still be the case that serving an inland port (e.g., Antwerp and Hamburg) is more expensive per tonne shipped, but that this higher cost is compensated for by cheaper hinterland transportation.[10]

This new market structure as such provides an incentive for establishing co-operation agreements and strategic alliances. Theoretically, the market players should after all benefit from gaining control of as large as possible a share of the logistics chain, be it for competitive purposes or for other reasons (e.g., stability).

Table 1 provides an overview of the co-operation agreements that exist within the maritime and port sectors. We shall restrict ourselves to the main actors (shipping companies, port authorities, terminal operators, hinterland transport modes).

A detailed analysis of Table 1 shows that shipping companies in particular have been taking initiatives in this respect, forging forms of partnership with each other as well as with other market players. The mutual forms of co-operation are mostly cartels of various description, but takeovers and mergers have also occurred. Through these cartel arrangements, the shipping companies hope to increase their degree of control over the total logistics chain. By means of price agreements, they also attempt to gain control over hinterland transportation and, as the case may be, goods-handling. Consider the following examples.

In 1992, the North Atlantic route was marked by a considerable surplus loading capacity in liner shipping. This led to sharp losses for shipping companies, even though there were conferences where two or more shipping companies contributed vessels and shared loading space.

The shipping companies' response came in 1992 in the shape of the Transatlantic Agreement (TAA), which became operational in 1993. With this cartel, the main shipping companies intended to acquire greater control over

Table 1: Co-operation agreements between various market players

MARKET PLAYERS	SHIPPING COMPANIES	STEVEDORES	HINTERLAND TRANSPORT	PORT AUTHORITIES
Shipping companies	⇒ Vessel sharing agreements ⇒ Joint Ventures ⇒ Conferences ⇒ Consortia ⇒ Strategic (global) alliances (e.g. Grand Alliance, New World Alliance) ⇒ Cartel agreements (e.g., TAA) ⇒ Mergers			
Stevedores	⇒ Financial stake of shipping company in stevedore (e.g., CMB in Hessenatie, Nedlloyd in ECT) ⇒ Joint ventures (e.g., MSC and Hessenatie in Antwerp) ⇒ Dedicated terminals (e.g., ECT-Maersk in Rotterdam)	⇒ Participation in capital (e.g., Hutchison Whampoa in ECT, PSA in Voltri Genova)		
Hinterland transport modes	⇒ Block trains and capacity sharing (e.g., from Rotterdam to Italy) ⇒ Alliances (e.g., CSX with DB and NS)	⇒ Joint ventures (e.g., in Antwerp between NMBS and Noordnatie for operating of a terminal)	⇒ Takeover strategy of railway companies (e.g. DB and NS cargo, NMBS and THL)	
Port authorities	⇒ Dedicated terminals (cf. land-use and concession policy)	⇒ Financial stakes port authorities (e.g., 30% ECT by Rotterdam, ECT in Trieste, Sea-ro in Zeebruges)	⇒ Antwerp in Rijn shipping terminal of Germersheim	⇒ Alliances (e.g. Rotterdam and Vlissingen, Antwerp and Zeebruges)

Source: Heaver, Meersman, Moglia and Van de Voorde.[11]

the seriously loss-making North-Atlantic shipping market by jointly determining rates, capacity supplied and the transport conditions. The consequences were clear to see: over 80% of the market was controlled in this manner, and, partly because of a shrinking capacity, rates increased sharply (by between 30 and 50% in some years).

Consignors responded fiercely, as they suddenly found it much harder to obtain loading space and were now unable to negotiate directly with shipping companies. They demanded a sufficient degree of competition, coupled with free supply and demand and the possibility of negotiating with companies separately. As the Treaty of Rome prohibits cartelisation, the TAA was outlawed because of its manipulation of tariffs, the capacity policy pursued and the fact that cartel agreements also applied to pre-carriage and on-carriage.

It speaks for itself that these kinds of cartel agreements were regarded suspiciously by ports. The possibility of higher prices may, after all, result in less maritime transport (and thus in a decline in port transhipment).

A similar reasoning is followed by ports in the case of mergers, as reorganisations and cost saving often result in fewer, but larger and stronger port users. This is illustrated quite well by the merger in 1996 of the container handlers P&O and Nedlloyd into P&O Nedlloyd Container Line. After the merger, the company had a fleet at his disposal of 112 vessels which it either owned or chartered, for 540,000 TEU containers and a turnover of USD 4 billion. Also, the merger implied that the company would be the same size as its main competitors (including Maersk, Evergreen, Sealand). This was achieved through cost saving and scale increases. Not taking into account the one-off restructuring costs, the annual cost saving was estimated at approximately USD 200 million, which amounted to about 5% of the total cost of container operations.

Within the port perimeter, the competitive struggle between terminal operators, for example, has evolved in different directions. A first possibility was that existing competition was retained, resulting in a combination of low profit margins and large volumes. Another possibility was an evolution towards a single operator, as clients were growing increasingly large and handlers needed to increase the scale of operations accordingly. Scale increases among goods-handlers is necessary in order to be considered as a fully-fledged partner by shipping companies. This is ultimately what happened in Antwerp in 2002, first with a merger between the two largest stevedores, Hessenatie and Noordnatie, into HesseNoordnatie, followed by a move in which 80% of the capital stock was taken over by Port of Singapore Authority (PSA). Thus, port transhipment companies also became subject to attempts at integration.

The above examples illustrate two important trends. First, there is a clear trend towards increasing the scale of operations by mergers, cartels and other co-operation agreements. At the same time, efforts are made to obtain greater control over larger parts of the logistics chain. Shipping companies in particular took the initiative in this respect, but other market players soon followed suit.

What is the intended purpose of such forms of co-operation? Is it connected with the market structure, i.e., is it aimed at realising economies of scale or acquiring market power? Is it aimed at management efficiency? Or do tax

Table 2: Objectives, tools and impact

MARKET PLAYERS	POSSIBLE OBJECTIVES	TOOLS	IMPACT
Shipping companies	⇒ Profit maximisation ⇒ Market share ⇒ Control over logistics chain	⇒ Tariff ⇒ Cost control (capacity, volume, time, co-operation, etc.) ⇒ Marketing ⇒ Service	⇒ Larger vessels ⇒ Rationalisation of sailing schedules ⇒ Alliances and consortia ⇒ Dedicated terminals
Stevedores	⇒ Profit maximisation ⇒ Long term customer loyalty including through logistic services and value-added activities (e.g., stuffing and stripping, storage, pre-delivery inspection, etc.)	⇒ Price setting ⇒ Technology of goods handling aimed at speed, quality, etc.	⇒ Returns to scale for terminals ⇒ Industrial logistics
Hinterland-transport modes	⇒ Profit maximisation ⇒ Market share	⇒ Tariffs ⇒ Speed ⇒ Flexibility ⇒ Capacity	⇒ Fierce modal competition
Port authorities	⇒ Contribution to cost minimisation for logistics chain (both through port dues and time costs) ⇒ Maximisation cargo handling (public company) ⇒ Maximisation of profit (private company)	⇒ Maritime access ⇒ Land and concession policy (cf. Reserve capacity of land) ⇒ Socio-economic negotiations ⇒ Price setting	⇒ Further information maritime access ⇒ Guaranteeing of social and economic stability
Shipping agents	⇒ Profit maximisation ⇒ Customer loyalty ⇒ Diversification (e.g., order picking warehouses, etc.)	⇒ Tariffs ⇒ Service	⇒ All-in-one price for door-to-door transport ⇒ Strong dependency (in both directions)
Owner of goods	⇒ Minimisation of total generalised logistics costs (incl. time cost)	⇒ Negotiating power (dependent on size)	⇒ Scale increase (positive impact on negotiating position) ⇒ Greater volatility

Source: Heaver, Meersman, Moglia and Van de Voorde.[12]

considerations come into play? Table 2 provides an overview of possible objectives and the tools used by the various market players for achieving these goals, as well as the possible consequences.

In the case of mergers between such companies as P&O and Nedlloyd, the most obvious motivation is achieving economies of scale. By merging, one intends to become an equally large market player as the main competitors and, at the same time, one aims at spreading the relatively high fixed costs over a more substantial output. However, Cowling et al.[13] observe that economies of scale are often only achieved "through an active programme of rationalisation and investment by which the constituent of scale and scope were moulded into a new entity". Be that as it may, if realising economies of scale and scope is the reason for merging, it often takes a long time before this objective is achieved.

Another rational objective besides the realisation of economies of scale may be the acquisition of greater market power, perhaps even market dominance. By merging and co-operating, players may intend to obtain control over a greater share of industrial and commercial activities.

A further objective may be to increase efficiency. In order to ascertain whether or not this is the case, one would need to test whether the initiating party is more efficient than the party that is approached and whether merging is a profit-generating activity. There may also be tax benefits to take into account, in the sense that merging can, in the first instance, sometimes have the effect of reducing the aggregate tax basis.

Finally, merging may also be regarded as a tool for achieving market entry, sometimes internationally, so that in a sense it stimulates competition. On the other hand, competition may be reduced or even replaced with a monopoly.

Now that we have identified a number of possible goals, the question arises: what are the possible consequences? Note that quite a few of the co-operation agreements presented in Table 1 have a direct impact on the internal functioning of the seaports and on the competition between ports.

Consider the example of a collaboration leading to the establishment of dedicated terminals, e.g., the co-operation between the terminal operator Hesse-Natie and the Swiss shipping company MSC (Mediterranean Shipping Company), who will jointly operate a terminal in Deurganck Dock in the port of Antwerp. Obviously, other shipping companies will not be inclined to have cargo handled at terminals that are operated by potential competitors. In other words, such dedicated terminals may result in a diversion of freight traffic. So while a port authority may have intended to improve its competitive position by providing new transhipment infrastructure, the net result in terms of throughput may in fact be negative. Moreover, the port authority in question also runs the risk that future traffic evolutions may become dependent upon the competitiveness and strategy of a limited number of shipping companies that are tied to terminal operators. The success of a port, then, may eventually be determined by the competitiveness of the shipping companies concerned.

Vertical co-operation agreements aimed at obtaining control over a larger share of the logistics chain may also have an impact on port throughput. Productive ports, with low transhipment costs and/or good hinterland connections, are at risk of being shunned as a port of call if they do not fit into the strategy of the group controlling the logistics chain. Cross-subsidising may also play a role in this respect.

In the past, there has always been relatively strong internal competition between transhipment companies in the Hamburg–Le Havre range. However, vertical mergers of logistics firms or horizontal mergers of, for example, transhipment companies may destroy this historical advantage. After all, co-operation can have the effect of suppressing competition. Indeed, this argument has often been used to justify government regulation. Stead[14] asserts in this respect that many studies "include the assumption that not only is monopoly power itself socially undesirable but so too are resources spent on competition to acquire or maintain a dominant monopolistic position".

It would appear to be advisable in the relatively short term to conduct theoretical and empirical research on the possible consequences of co-operation agreements. Relevant research questions are:

- How do market players in the logistics chain (shipping companies, transhipment companies, etc.) operate within different market structures? What is the relationship between company size and profitability on the one hand and the likely effects in terms of market concentration, market power and efficiency on the other? To what extent does government influence industrial organisation?
- What is the strategic behaviour of the above-mentioned market players? To what extent is greater efficiency related to a lower production unit cost coupled with returns to scale and greater market power through collusion on the part of certain companies in order to keep prices high?
- To what extent can other forms of alliances (e.g., licensing and cross-licensing, subcontracting, etc.) be established that imply less commitment, control and mutual dependency?
- What is the relationship between market control stemming from alliances and mergers on the one hand and pricing behaviour on the other? The existence of an oligopoly or a high level of concentration with one dominant company can result in different types of pricing mechanism: price leadership, price discrimination, limit pricing, collusion, predatory pricing, etc.

Until empirical research proves otherwise, we may assume that the unique market structure in the maritime and port business does not exist. Nonetheless, certain developments are quite clear to see, e.g., the role of government in the discernible trend towards acquiring greater control over (a larger share of) the logistics chain.

4. MANAGEMENT IN A GROWTH ENVIRONMENT

World ports operate in a growth environment. This also holds for the principal ports in the Hamburg–Le Havre range. However, growth presupposes adequate capacity and the absence of bottlenecks that may cause congestion. The accumulation of sufficient capacity in turn demands correct decision-making. In the past, one could count on unbridled government intervention, often resulting in excess capacity. This, however, is no longer the case. Today, ports bear responsibility for their own investment decisions.

From a long-term perspective, ports will be inclined to make sure that the available capacity does not present a limit to their growth potential. In order to be able to ascertain whether or not this is the case, one needs a constant supply of reliable forecasts of future goods flows.[15] However, predictions used by port authorities often consist merely in trend extrapolations of, among other things, throughput within a range under the assumption of a constant market share. If one takes general traffic forecasts as a starting point, it is equally important to acquire adequate insight into the factors determining this market share. Only on the basis of this knowledge can one arrive at correct decisions about whether or not extension of capacity is called for.

Modelling of port throughput, however, is complicated and, thus far, not always equally transparent. It requires a scientifically well-founded set of tools that allows one to simulate the consequences of policy measures and exogenous influences on the continuous struggle for goods flows and related activities (port transhipment, warehousing, distribution).

By way of illustration, we shall briefly discuss the forecasts of container traffic in the Hamburg–Le Havre range presented in Meersman, Moglia and Van de Voorde.[16] Within this range, container traffic is clearly concentrated in a limited number of ports: Rotterdam, Antwerp, Hamburg and Bremen. There are however differences between these ports, witness the fact that growing container throughput in Rotterdam in absolute terms coincided with a decline in market share. Furthermore, the position per shipping area is also different for each of these ports.

The forecasts are based on the assumption that demand for maritime container transport is derived demand. Given the great variety in goods that are transported by container, the level of container traffic is not dependent upon evolutions in one specific sector of the economy, but is rather determined by general economic activity and international trade. Thus, developments in world trade and trade flows will be reflected in levels of maritime transport. If countries grow, their economies will change and consequently so too will their trade.

In the coming years, container transport may be expected to continue to grow more quickly than global trade, for various reasons. For one thing, trade in high-value goods will increase considerably, and these kinds of commodities are transported chiefly in containers. Second, the ongoing transformation of developing countries into NICs will change the structure of their foreign trade. Furthermore, the relocation of production sites will also result in more container transport. And finally, the shift from conventional cargo to containers is still continuing.

The forecasts in tables 3 and 4 are based on estimated error-correction-models under various assumptions regarding growth of imports and exports by the EU15.[19] It is clear that the growth patterns of container traffic in the various ports diverge quite strongly. It would appear, then, that international trade does not affect container traffic to the same extent in each of these ports. Container

*Table 3: Growth forecasts of container loadings
(percentage growth with respect to 1997)*

Assumed annual growth rates of exports of the EU15	Antwerp		Rotterdam		Bremen		Hamburg	
	2005	2010	2005	2010	2005	2010	2005	2010
3%	95	178	28	65	74	134	77	148
4%	140	286	49	109	101	195	115	238
5%	196	436	73	166	132	272	162	360
Reference values for 1997 (1000 tonnes)								
	19622		32336		9648		17740	

Source: based on Meersman, Moglia and Van de Voorde.[17]

*Table 4: Growth forecasts of container unloadings
(percentage growth with respect to 1997)*

Assumed annual growth rates of exports of the EU15	Antwerp		Rotterdam		Bremen		Hamburg	
	2005	2010	2005	2010	2005	2010	2005	2010
3%	55	115	16	41	48	88	30	76
4%	88	190	32	73	69	131	55	132
5%	128	292	49	111	92	183	84	205
Reference values for 1997 (1000 tonnes)								
	13805		25946		7783		16524	

Source: based on Meersman, Moglia and Van de Voorde.[18]

traffic in Antwerp and Hamburg is more sensitive to changes in international trade than traffic in Rotterdam and Bremen. The long-term relationships provide quite an accurate picture of the general trend in loadings and unloadings of containers, but fluctuations around this long-term relationship, partly due to changes in the ports' competitive positions, are not explained equally well.

Both port management and companies located in ports require a set of tools that can help them resolve part of the uncertainty that exists in a rapidly changing environment. However, while demand forecasts based on (economic) models can provide a useful indication, they cannot explain reality in its entirety. Thus, additional explanations need to be sought, e.g., at the supply side and in cost analysis. This brings us back to such factors as available capacity, capacity utilisation, and productivity. It is after all quite clear that performance, yield and productivity of a port cannot be determined on the basis of a single measure. On the one hand, there is the complexity of port operations, while on the other there are interactions between various relevant factors (e.g., vessel configuration, shifts of workers, depth of quay walls, type of loading and unloading equipment, etc.).

The above material may constitute a useful framework for further exploration of this topic. When considering potential traffic, for example, one needs to take into account the strategic behaviour of the various market players involved, including consignors of goods and transport firms. As regards the competitive environment of ports, further attention should be paid to the choice of hinterland mode. With respect to further empirical research, a concerted effort is required to develop more and qualitatively more adequate databases.

5. SURVIVING IN A COMPETITIVE ENVIRONMENT

Throughout this contribution, we have emphasised the importance of port competition and competitiveness. Indeed, most ports are engaged in a tough competitive struggle, not only for tonnage and volume, but also for shipping lines and investment in infrastructure and industry.

This explains why more and more attention is being paid in the European transport debate to the issue of port competition, as is apparent from the recently published "Port Package". Distortion, some would say "falsification", of conditions of competition between and within ports has become an important issue on the political agenda. The debate revolves around, among other things, the granting of concessions within ports (e.g., dedicated or other container terminals), traffic diversion between ports (e.g., Antwerp v. Rotterdam and Zeebruges), (illicit) subsidising of investments in port infrastructure (Rotterdam v. Antwerp) and hinterland connections (e.g., the rail connections known as "Betuwe Line" and the "Iron Rhine", Antwerp v. Rotterdam).

In terms of tonnage, value added or employment, the European port picture is quite clear: a strong concentration of activity in a limited number of ports in the Hamburg–Le Havre range, less so in the Baltic range, and a rapidly emerging Mediterranean range (e.g., considerable investments in container capacity at Giao Tauro, Taranto and Cagliari). This situation is connected not only with structural aspects (e.g., geographical location), but also with differences in terms of costs, productivity (and speed) and technologies applied.

In the literature, one often refers to Verhoeff's definition of port competition.[20] He distinguishes between four levels of seaport competition: competition between port undertakings; competition between ports; competition between port clusters (i.e., a group of ports in each other's vicinity with common geographical characteristics); competition between ranges (i.e., ports located along the same coastline or with a largely identical hinterland).

The factors influencing competition may vary from level to level. The competitive strength of individual undertakings within a port is determined mainly by the factors of production (labour, capital, technology, and power). Competition between ports, port clusters and port ranges on the other hand is also affected by regional factors, such as the geographical location, the available infrastructure, the degree of industrialisation, government policy, the standard of performance of the port (measured in terms of proxy variables, such as the number and frequency of liner services, and the cost of transhipment, storage and hinterland transportation).

As we have already pointed out, this traditional approach to port competition must now make way for an approach based on competition between logistics chains, in which seaports (and seaport undertakings) are merely links. As the most important consideration is the overall cost of the transport chain, it is inevitable that, besides throughput, the industrial and commercial functions (including warehousing and distribution of goods) as well as hinterland transportation will come to occupy an increasingly important position.

A port and the undertakings established in it compete directly with a limited number of other ports, usually within the same range. There are few types of goods flows for which ports belonging to different ranges might compete directly (e.g., in the fixing of shipping schedules and in determining ports of call). Consequently, the crucial question in port competition is what determines the choice of port? In other words, why is one port preferred to another? Why are certain undertakings located in that port chosen? What are the preferred hinterland transport modes and routes?

Port users think predominantly in financial and economic terms. Frankel[21] asserts in this respect that "they consider the net revenue contribution of a port call which is usually defined as the difference between the added revenue generated by the port call minus the costs of making the port call". Costs are understood to include all possible items: vessel-related costs (e.g., the time factor, taking into account possible delays), port-related costs (port dues, pilotage, etc.), cargo-handling costs, cargo-storage costs, feeder costs.

Thus, the objective for management, be it of the port or of the undertakings concerned, is clear to see: to minimise the cost of transhipment and delay of vessels. For that matter, the principle of cost minimisation applies to all links in the transport chain, in the sense that the ultimate goal must be to arrive at the lowest possible cost for the chain as a whole.

The port that contributes to the cheapest logistics chain is, in theory at least, most likely to be called at. The ultimate decision process of the port user would appear, then, to be a matter of common sense: does the port considered offer advantages compared to other ports serving the same hinterland? Does the port offer sufficient advantages in order to be considered as an additional port of call for an existing or yet-to-be-established liner or indeed feeder service? The decision process of the port user concerns the transport chain, but he will also have to take due account of market factors (e.g., potential customers, competition from other shipping lines and consignors of goods, etc.).

It is important for a port authority to know who that port user is, who makes the choice of port and which factors influence this choice. However, the term "port user" covers quite a heterogeneous group that includes shipping companies, consignors of goods, owners of goods, goods handlers, etc. It is a group whose members would appear to depend on one another, but who are nevertheless often engaged in a fierce competitive struggle. Consequently, it is not always easy to determine who ultimately makes the choice of port. In addition, there is the question of which (cost) variables are most significant in the decision process (*cf.* the problem of factor assessment). In this respect, one needs to realise that the cost structure is determined by both exogenous factors (e.g., scale increases in world trade, or rapidly developing cargo-handling equipment) and endogenous factors within the port's direct sphere of influence.

Port competition has been the subject of much interdisciplinary research recently.[22] After all, the competitive position of a port is determined by strategic and legal factors besides purely economic variables. Research has shown that, in the case of the port of Antwerp, political and legal considerations rather than purely economic or geographical determinants are perceived as factors that may influence the position of the port negatively. Indeed, if a port has a fundamental weakness, this is often occasioned by a lack of clarity in terms of administrative responsibility. This lack of clarity may, for example, relate to who is the competent legislator and/or executor of an infrastructure project, and who is responsible for necessary amendments of existing legislation.[23,24]

A study by Huybrechts et al.[25] has shown that there is also an urgent need for a broader knowledge base with regard to the competitive environment in which individual ports, port clusters or port ranges operate. Research to this end should preferably be multidisciplinary in nature, grounded on a sound theoretical basis, but taking an empirical approach. In order to make such research possible, qualitatively more adequate databases are an absolute necessity. Sound scientific research into the maritime business environment requires model-based simulations of various goods flows, transported to and from different ports, in different batch sizes and at various times. The knowledge that is thus acquired may contribute to a better understanding of, and more adequate response to, factors that influence port competition and competitiveness. Or, as is suggested by the title of this section, it may provide insight into the question of how best to survive in a competitive environment.

6. CONCLUSIONS

In this contribution, we have discussed the relationship between port management and operations by that management on the one hand and port competition on the other. All are agreed that the port landscape has changed very rapidly, partly as a consequence of ever-growing port competition at different levels.

In most ports, port management has found it hard (to continue) to keep up with the pace of change. Furthermore, an important aspect of the legitimacy of a separate port management is being undermined, namely the previously often heard argument of the strategic significance of seaports to the economy of a country or region.

There is clearly a connection between port management and the manner in which players compete within or between ports. Each port management is preoccupied with protecting and/or improving its competitive position in a fierce struggle with any party that is considered a potential threat. The question arises what are the remaining tools and degrees of freedom? In the first instance, one can help prepare and outline strategies in relation to additional port infrastructure. However, financially and legally, one is still dependent upon government. Furthermore, there is the aspect of granting concessions for dedicated or other terminals. Here one encounters increasingly strong opponents, i.e., ever more powerful shipping companies (and the alliances to which they may belong).

The question is therefore: what next? Will the role of port management be restricted to correctly enforcing regulation (e.g., with respect to "Port State Control")? Or will port management be tempted to actively participate as a market player, as happened in Rotterdam recently when the Port Authority acquired a stake in the leading stevedore ECT? If one does enter into the market, there is the danger that conflicts of interest may arise and that the port community may, quite rightly, no longer consider the port management as a neutral regulator.

The present race for new port infrastructure and additional capacity suggests that port competition will become even greater in the near future. At the same time, the role and indeed the *raison d'être* of port management would appear to be becoming even more uncertain. Clearly, then, here lies largely unexplored territory for multidisciplinary research with a solid scientific basis but with empirical implementation and verification.

ACKNOWLEDGEMENTS

We appreciate comments received on this paper from an anonymous referee. All remaining errors are the authors' alone.

ENDNOTES

1. Suykens, F., and Van de Voorde, E. (1998): "A quarter of a century of port management in Europe: objectives and tools", *Maritime Policy & Management*, 25(3), pp. 251–261.
2. Suykens, F. (1986): "Ports should be efficient (even when this means that some of them are subsidized)", *Maritime Policy & Management*, 13(2), p. 108.
3. Haralambides, H., Ma, S., and Veenstra, A. (1997): "World-wide experiences of port reform", H. Meersman and E. Van de Voorde (eds.) *Transforming the Port and Transportation Business* (Leuven/Amersfoort, Acco), p. 120.
4. Suykens, F., and Van de Voorde, E. (1998): "A quarter of a century of port management in Europe: objectives and tools", *Maritime Policy & Management*, 25(3), p. 255.
5. Suykens, F. (1986): "Ports should be efficient (even when this means that some of them are subsidized)", *Maritime Policy & Management*, 13(2), p. 120.
6. De Monie, G. (1996): "Privatization of port structures", L. Bekemans and S. Beckwith (eds.) *Ports for Europe: Europe's maritime future in a changing environment* (Brussels, European Interuniversity Press), pp. 267–298.
7. Goss, R. (1990): "Economic policies and seaports: 3. Are port authorities necessary?", *Maritime Policy & Management*, 17(4), p. 269.
8. Pallis, A.A. (1997): "Towards a common ports policy? EU-proposals and the ports industry's perceptions", *Maritime Policy & Management*, 24(4), p. 375.
9. Goss, R. (1990): "Economic policies and seaports: 3. Are port authorities necessary?", *Maritime Policy & Management*, 17(4), p. 262.
10. Suykens, F., and Van de Voorde, E. (1992): "Het belang van de haven voor de uitstraling van Antwerpen. Of: een continu gevecht voor competitiviteit en marktaandelen", *Economisch en Sociaal Tijdschrift*, 46(3), p. 487.
11. Heaver, T., Meersman, H., Moglia, F., and Van de Voorde, E. 2000, "Do mergers and alliances influence European shipping and port competition?", *Maritime Policy & Management*, 27(4), p. 365.

12. Heaver, T., Meersman, H., Moglia, F., and Van de Voorde, E. (2000): "Do mergers and alliances influence European shipping and port competition?", *Maritime Policy & Management*, 27(4), p. 368.
13. Cowling, K., Stoneman, P., Cubbing, J., Cable, J., Hall, G., Comberger, S., and Dutton, P. (1980): *Mergers and economic performance* (Cambridge, Cambridge University Press).
14. Stead, R., Curwen, P,. and Lawler, K. (1996): *Industrial economics. Theory, applications and policy* (London, McGraw-Hill).
15. Meersman, H., Moglia, F., and Van de Voorde, E. (2002): "Forecasting potential throughput", Huybrechts, M., Meersman, H., Van de Voorde, E., Van Hooydonk, E., Verbeke, A., Winkelmans, W. (eds.) *Port Competitiveness. An economic and legal analysis of the factors determining the competitiveness of seaports* (Antwerp, Editions De Boeck Ltd), p. 35.
16. Meersman, H., Moglia, F., and Van de Voorde, E. 2002, *op. cit.*, pp. 55–62.
17. Meersman, H., Moglia, F., and Van de Voorde, E. 2002, *op. cit.*, p. 62.
18. Meersman, H., Moglia, F., and Van de Voorde, E. 2002, *op. cit.*, p. 62.
19. Meersman, H., Moglia, F., and Van de Voorde, E. 2002, *op. cit.*, p. 61.
20. Verhoeff, J.M. (1981): "Zeehavenconcurrentie: overheidsproduktie van havendiensten", *Vervoers- en haveneconomie: tussen actie en abstractie* (Leiden, Stenfert Kroese), pp. 181–202.
21. Frankel, E.G. (1991): "Port performance and productivity measurement", *Ports and Harbors*, pp. 11–13.
22. Huybrechts, M., Meersman, H., Van de Voorde, E., Van Hooydonk, E., Verbeke, A., Winkelmans, W. (eds.) (2002): *Port Competitiveness. An economic and legal analysis of the factors determining the competitiveness of seaports* (Antwerp, Editions De Boeck Ltd).
23. Van de Voorde, E., and Winkelmans, W. (2002): "Conclusions and policy implications", Huybrechts, M., Meersman, H., Van de Voorde, E., Van Hooydonk, E., Verbeke, A., Winkelmans, W. (eds.) *Port Competitiveness. An economic and legal analysis of the factors determining the competitiveness of seaports* (Antwerp, Editions De Boeck Ltd), p. 138.
24. Van Hooydonk, E. (2002): "Legal aspects of port competition", Huybrechts, M., Meersman, H., Van de Voorde, E., Van Hooydonk, E., Verbeke, A., Winkelmans, W. (eds.) *Port Competitiveness. An economic and legal analysis of the factors determining the competitiveness of seaports* (Antwerp, Editions De Boeck Ltd), pp. 89–131.
25. Huybrechts, M., Meersman, H., Van de Voorde, E., Van Hooydonk, E., Verbeke, A., Winkelmans, W. (eds.) (2002), *op. cit.*

CHAPTER 34

PORT PRICING*

*Hercules E. Haralambides*** *and Albert W. Veenstra*†

**Erasmus Center for Maritime Economics and Logistics, Erasmus University, Rotterdam, The Netherlands. E-mail: *haralambides@few.eur.nl*
†Centre for Contract Research and Business Support (ERBS) BV, Erasmus University, Rotterdam, The Netherlands. E-mail: *veenstra@few.eur.nl*

1. INTRODUCTION

Why is port pricing an issue in maritime economics?

In ports, as in many other industries, prices – port dues and cargo-handling charges as they are often called – can "make" or "break" a port. The right prices can lead a port to prosperity and growth; the wrong ones can guide it to extinction or to the proliferation of subsidies and inefficiency. High prices would normally deprive a port of part of its patronage (vessels and cargo owners) and thus reduce demand for port services. Since, once a port is built, it has few alternative uses if any, i.e., its investments are largely sunk,[1] excess capacity will ensue as a result, resources and infrastructure will be underutilised and investors – public or private – will be questioning the appropriateness of their decisions. Even when ports have some degree of monopoly power over their customers and demand for port services is not reduced much, high port prices would still hurt the very trade the port is supposed to serve.

Low port prices, on the other hand, may bring clientele to the port but congestion could ensue, investment costs may not be recovered in the long-run and the port's competitors may grudge about unfair competition, particularly when low prices are the result of subsidies.

In competitive industries, a producer has no influence on the price he sells his product or service; he either adjusts his costs to the externally determined price or he vanishes. A port, however, operates in an oligopolistic industry where pricing refers to "strategic pricing", i.e., the ability of the producer to influence or set prices in order to achieve certain objectives. Such objectives, many of which simultaneously pursued albeit in conflict, include profit maximisation; throughput maximisation; generation of employment and economic activity; regional development; minimisation of ship time in port; and, last but not least, the promotion of trade.

However, the pricing strategy of a port is dependent on the way the port is financed and, ultimately, on the ownership status of the port: should, thus, a publicly owned and financed port be allowed to compete on price, for the same custom, with a privately owned port that has to charge higher prices in an effort to recover its investments? What if these ports are in the same, economically interdependent,[2] geographic area? What if the effects of strategic pricing of different ports are, at the end of the day, felt by the same consumers or taxpayers? Should ports primarily engaged in commercial operations, such as container terminals, be publicly financed or should the port user pay in full for the port services he buys? Do ports need to recover infrastructure costs through pricing?

And what happens if some do and others don't while all have to compete for the same hinterland? Is there such a thing as "efficient port pricing" and is there scope for policy intervention to ensure a level playing field? These are some of the pertinent questions in port pricing that the chapter aims to address with special emphasis on container ports.

2. WHAT IS A PORT?

There is no such single thing that could be adequately described by the mere word "port" and no two ports are alike. A port could be from a small sheltered patch of sea that protects fishermen from the roughness of the sea, allowing them to moor their boats and trade their wares in safety somewhere in the south pacific, to the huge industrial complex of the city-port of Rotterdam, embracing in its expanse hundreds of companies, roads, railway lines, distribution centres, refineries and other industrial and manufacturing activity.

Regardless of how it is developed and organised, however, a port's main function is to enable, hopefully in a safe and cost effective manner, the transfer of goods from sea to shore and *vice versa*. As such, a port is an interface between sea and land; a node in a transport chain; a point where goods change mode of transport. Cargo-handling is thus a port's core business. In order to do this, a port has to organise a large array of other services, all equally important in the facilitation of cargo transfers: it has to provide (dredge) sea channels and turning basins of adequate depth (draft) to enable the approach and manoeuvres of vessels; navigational aids, breakwaters, pilots, tugs and linesmen to allow vessels to moor and unload safely; equipment to handle goods in port and move them around; warehouses to store them until they are picked up by their owners; electricity; water; security; customs; administrative offices and many more.

The paramount good a port has to provide however in order to facilitate all this is *land*. A port is a land-intensive industry. Here is the first issue where *port pricing* encounters its major stumbling block: what is the value of land? What is its opportunity cost? Under what terms should port land be made available to private port operators, stevedoring companies and others?

In many places in the world, land, particularly land close to the sea, is a scarce good with high opportunity cost and many potential claimants. Cities can use it for residential and office space; offshore industries have to be located in its proximity; tourism and recreation industries would naturally consider it as prime location; fishermen would also value it highly, while nature lovers would tend to preserve it, and its ecosystem, at all costs. This is why port management, or the supervision of port activities and expansion, is often entrusted to municipal authorities who strive to steer a balanced course and reconcile harmoniously the various interests at stake.

More important than the land itself, however, is how, and by whom, land is developed to become ready to provide the port service. Often, land has to be reclaimed from the sea, it has to be paved, reinforced, roads and rail trucks have to be constructed on it, while to extend a port, even by just a few hundred metres of quayside, would require massive investments. The way these investments are financed, i.e., publicly or privately, in other words the ownership status of a port, bears the most upon the way port services are priced. Simply, a publicly owned port infrastructure does not have to recover – through price – investment costs and thus its prices could be quite low and competitive *vis-à-vis* a privately owned port that has to recover investment costs and, other things being equal, would thus be at a competitive disadvantage had it to compete with a public port.

3. PORT COMPETITION

3.1 Infrastructure, public spending and the role of the state

In the past, particularly after WWII, the development and provision of infrastructure was largely in the hands of the State. Often, infrastructure was considered as a public good, serving the collective interest of the nation by increasing social cohesion as well as by expanding markets for inputs and output, i.e., bringing people to work and goods to consumers. This allowed for mass production, low unit costs and international competitiveness. With the exception of some developing countries, infrastructure was thus invariably developed ahead of existing demand – on the part of the industry, agriculture and commerce – in the hope that the latter activities would expand in the wake of the former (infrastructure) (Rosenstein-Rodan[3]). A notable example of this was the case of the North American railways, particularly those of Canada. Furthermore, large capital indivisibilities in infrastructure development, coupled with substantial financial requirements and long gestation periods until demand picked up, had made infrastructure development the prerogative of the public sector.

Also, the post WWII period was one of "Keynesianism" in the industrialised world and of protectionist import substitution policies in developing countries. The dire consequences of the Great Depression of 1929 had brought about President Roosevelt's New Deal policy after a painful realisation that market mechanisms alone, in spite of their merits, innovation, growth, welfare, better food, medicine, education and services that they have given us, often fail to produce the textbook efficiency they proclaim. Most importantly, markets often fail to ensure equilibrium at full employment. This latter realisation was shown very illustratively by John Maynard Keynes whose seminal book *The General Theory of Employment, Interest and Money* appeared at the same time (1936). Keynes' emphasis on fiscal policy defined the instrumental role of the government as an economic agent: a strong presence through public spending in periods of recession, but absent, as much as possible, in periods of full employment.

In the developing world, the great majority of nations were convinced that free trade could not but be detrimental to their efforts to industrialise by worsening their terms of trade and condemning them to specialise in those primary sector activities – such as agriculture and mining – that have always been sensitive to the vagaries and unpredictability of the economic cycle. Protectionist import substitution policies were thus commonplace among them. They included high tariffs, import quotas, foreign exchange controls, cargo reservation, etc. All, under the close scrutiny of a ubiquitous State, keeping to itself the control of the strategic sectors of the economy.

In the closed economies of those days, the economic inefficiency of State production was seldom an issue, particularly when the State was able to generate employment in societies where humane welfare systems were nothing more than a remote dream. On the contrary, inefficient State operations had often been welcomed by many as an effective barrier to foreign imports. For example, it had often been argued that import-competing domestic producers had strong vested interests in the existence of inefficient ports as this offered them effective protection. Evidence also exists that these producers could also be effective lobbyists and influential members of pressure groups that resisted port reform.

With regard to ports in particular, in the past, general cargo traffic was less containerisable, regional port competition was less of an issue, and ports were comprising a lot of labour intensive activities, generating considerable value-added and a multitude of direct and indirect impacts on the national economy, including of course the facilitation of international trade. They were thus seen by governments as growth-poles of regional and national development and, as a matter of fact, they were often used as instruments of regional planning. Around the world, countries have done so by steering public investment, through regional policies, towards ports, in order to encourage national development. Thus, investment costs did not have to be recovered, being financed by the taxpayer through the general government budget or similar local or municipal sources.

Ports were fairly insulated from competitive forces, each serving its own, more or less captive, hinterland. This was due to trade barriers, national borders and inadequate land transport infrastructure. No matter how inefficient the port, the ship would still have to go there. Most ports were badly run, disorganised, bureaucratic, inefficient and expensive; a shipowner's nightmare and worst enemy!

3.2 Globalisation, trade liberalisation and the new role of ports

Nowadays, however, the picture is considerably different and "conventional wisdom" is found increasingly at a loss when it comes to giving answers to the multitude of challenges emerging from the globalisation of all forms of economic activity and the increasing interdependence among nations.

Globalisation can be defined as the increase in cross-border interdependence and, more profoundly, the integration which has resulted from the greater mobility of factors of production and of goods and services. This increased mobility can be attributed to three major groups of factors:
- Telecommunications, mass media, advertising, secularism and the abolition of national barriers have all led to a substantial convergence of world cultures and consumption patterns, resulting in larger international markets and intensified competition.
- Although not as yet confirmed by factual developments, most governments are rather convinced that economic integration, promoted by the globalisation of capital markets and the virtual abolition of exchange controls in industrialised countries, will lead to more efficient resource allocation and hence stimulate growth and economic development.

– The significant advances in transport and communications technologies have increased the speed and efficiency of transport and lowered the costs of communication. These developments have lowered the barriers of time and distance and give the impression of a "shrinking world".

Globalisation and trade liberalisation, helped by the remarkable developments in transport, logistics and communication technologies, have drastically weakened the link between manufacturing and the location of factors of production and have stimulated a most noticeable shift in manufacturing activities towards countries with a comparative advantage.

Developments in international transport have been instrumental in shaping these processes. Containerisation and multimodal integrated transport have revolutionised trading arrangements of value-added goods and have given traders and global managers more control and choice over their "production-transport-distribution" chain. Furthermore, transport efficiency is necessitated by the very same nature of value-added goods whose increasing sophistication requires fast transit times from origin to destination in order to increase traders' turnover and minimise high inventory costs. Today, these costs have been brought down significantly by the use of logistical concepts and methods and also by the increased reliability and accuracy of international transport that allow manufacturing industries to adopt flexible *Just-in-Time* and *Make-to-Order* production technologies. *Inter alia*, these technologies enable companies to cope with the vagaries and unpredictability of the seasonal, business and trade cycles and plan business development in a more cost effective way.

Trade liberalisation, land infrastructure development, and new logistical concepts in the organisation of international transport of containers have had an equally profound effect on the port industry. Port hinterlands have ceased to be captive and have extended beyond national boundaries. Governments are increasingly realising that, from mere interface points between land and sea, ports have become the most dynamic link in international transport networks and, as a result, inefficient ports can easily wither gains from trade liberalisation and export performance. Convinced about this, governments have often taken drastic steps to improve the performance of their ports: new capacity and labour-saving cargo-handling equipment have replaced outdated facilities; port workers training intensified; customs procedures simplified; information technology widely adopted; and management structures commercialised.

In addition, the port industry is moving noticeably from one in which predominantly public funds were used to provide common user facilities, to one where capital – public and private – is being used to provide terminals which are designed to serve the logistical requirements of a more narrowly defined group of users. Indeed, they may be designed to serve the needs of a few or even one firm (Dedicated Container Terminals).

At the same time, economies of scale in liner shipping and the sophistication and capital-intensity of modern containerships have limited the number of ports of call to only a selected few transshipment ports or load centres. These very important ports (such as Rotterdam, Hong Kong and Singapore) have become the *foci* of international trade and goods are moved by land (road and rail) and water (barge) from inland centres and feeder ports to these global hubs. The hub-and-spoke system that has ensued in this way has made transshipment traffic lucrative business to be had at all costs.

The "mobility" of the transshipment container, however, together with intertwined land transport networks and extended hinterlands, have intensified competition among container ports immensely. Today, it makes little difference if a Hong Kong container destined for Paris will pass through the port of Rotterdam, Antwerp or Hamburg. This container has little "loyalty" to any given port and it switches between ports with relative ease. The price elasticity of demand for container handling services has thus become rather high[4] (Table 1).

Table 1: Price elasticities in selected north European container ports

Port	Elasticity
Hamburg	3.1
Bremen	4.4
Rotterdam	1.5
Antwerp	4.1
Le Havre	1.1

Source: ATENCO.

In this way, each port's development, financing and pricing decisions can have marked effects on its neighbours, nationally and – most importantly – internationally. Often, this raises strong voices for "market driven" investments, a more harmonised approach in the financing of port infrastructure, as well as pricing policies that will have to allow for full cost recovery.

These are most complex and often political issues that, as a result, have not allowed much progress to be made in terms of port policy formulation in economically interdependent areas. In all our discussions with port managers (see below), no one would question the importance of "market driven" investments and pricing for cost recovery. However, in all such discussions, there has always been an implicit "from now on" assumption and no port would seriously consider that pricing for cost recovery should reflect the costs of past (public) investment.

However, in the past, investments were not always market driven. Massive amounts of public monies have in the past been funnelled into port development, enabling many ports to consolidate such a strong market position that makes it rather easy for them, now, to advocate for the need for market driven investments. This should be kept in mind and the market-driven investments argument should not become a "limit pricing"[5] policy of incumbent ports, deterring market entry of smaller and peripheral ports who also aspire to develop and serve themselves their rapidly growing regions.

3.3 Cost recovery and limit pricing

The above point can be brought out more clearly with the following simplified example (Figure 1). Port A (incumbent) of country X has a dominant market position. This has been established over many years of public expenditure both in the port itself and its related infrastructure (roads, maritime access, etc.). As such, the port is able to meet a substantial part of the trade of country Y through transshipment. Port A is a strong proponent of cost recovery policies in port development in general but, at the same time, it is allowed to consider "bygones as bygones" and thus its prices, current and future, do not have to include the recovery of its past investments. The demand for its services is given by DD'.

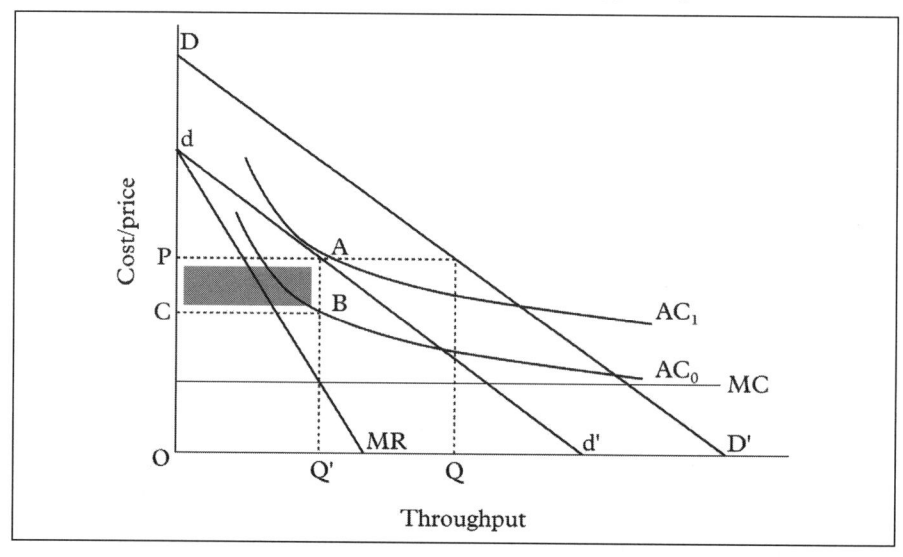

Figure 1: Cost recovery and limiting pricing

Port B (entrant) in country Y is much smaller. Although in a favourable geographic position, the port never developed its own container facilities, as a result of both lack of funds and because it was adequately served (feedered) by port A. The trade of country Y, however, is rapidly increasing and port B feels that it is now time to develop its own facilities and "claim back" its traffic – and all that comes with it – from port A. The government of Y sees the importance of such an action and it is prepared to fund the required investments.

Once developed, the demand for port B services is expected to be dd'; dMR gives its marginal revenue line. Its average cost (without recovery of infrastructure costs) and marginal cost curves are given by AC_0 and MC, respectively. The port maximises economic surplus (ABCP) by serving OQ' level of throughput at a price of OP. Only Q'Q of total traffic is now left to port A.

Naturally, port A is rather unhappy with these plans. Its port policy department mounts a very strong campaign, together with other ports in the same predicament, lobbying regulatory authorities on unfair competition from a to-be-subsidised port that, if it materialises, it would deprive it from much of its traffic. It claims that, by not charging for infrastructure costs, port B will be producing at prices below costs and thus antidumping and competition laws should be applicable.

Were port A to succeed in demanding full cost recovery pricing, port B's average cost curve would shift upwards to a new position AC_1 or even further.

At this level, there is no single price that would enable port B to break-even, let alone realise a positive surplus. In such a situation, port B wouldn't even consider expanding, leaving the whole market to port A. By insisting and achieving a policy of full cost recovery, port A has been successful in maintaining its dominant market position.

4. THE PRICING OF PORT INFRASTRUCTURE

As it was mentioned above, strategic pricing can pursue a multitude of objectives and can take various forms such as marginal cost pricing (MCP), average cost pricing (ACP), Ramsey Pricing[6] and two-way tariffs. Whatever the pricing method, or combination thereof, it is becoming more and more apparent among competing ports and those who fund them that prices should be cost-related and, in the long-run, they should allow for cost recovery, including infrastructure development costs.

There are cases however of ports that face, or pose, little competition. They serve local industries and are important centres of regional development. Often, the port is the only major economic activity and employer in the area. Such peripheral ports could still be considered as "public investment", without a need to recover infrastructure development costs. In this case, the public sector should assess, through *social cost-benefit analysis*, the relative merits from regional development impacts *vis-à-vis* the costs – and alternative uses – of public resources required to develop and maintain the port. If the former exceed the latter, prices could be set below costs in order to promote regional development. Ensuing deficits could then be seen as the "cost of regional development".

In all other cases, particularly in the case of container ports amidst intense regional competition, the setting of prices below costs, in order to attract traffic from competitors, is not an advisable strategy.

First, this would lead to a misallocation of resources (and taxpayer money). Intensified inter-port competition, combined with automated labour-saving cargo handling systems, reduces the local economic impacts of port investments and the value-added of port activities. In such a situation, the beneficial impacts of low port prices are not localised but are dissipated from the country in question to the foreign consignor/consignee. This issue causes considerable concern to governments contemplating the continuation of their public investment programmes, as it deprives them of the basic *rationale* of doing so, namely, that the port provides a public service to the benefit of the whole nation.[7] Such concerns have become noticeably "loud" nowadays when governments have to reduce in size, cut down on spending and taxes and allow for more private sector participation in some "strategic" sectors that, until recently, were jealously guarded as government prerogative.

Second, in economically interdependent regions, such as for instance the EU, such pricing would lead to complaints for unfair competition and competition law would in principle be applicable, particularly as deficits would have to be covered from public funds, often seen as State Aid.

Cost-relatedness of prices and full cost recovery are things however easier said than done. A port is a multi-product firm and prices for many of its services are often bundled in port dues. Cross-subsidisation is also common. For instance, in order to attract transshipment cargo, a port may cross-subsidise feedering operations by trunk line charges. The *joint cost* problem in economics is therefore present here too, together with the difficulty, if not inability, to allocate such costs to different port services.

The difficulty of this problem is often accentuated by our inability to accurately measure port costs, especially marginal costs. Reliable and comparable port statistics do not exist, port accounting systems diverge and, finally, the financial flows between the port and its institutional owner (municipality, State) are not always known or transparent.

Many of the above difficulties, however, are often exaggerated. What follows is an attempt to demonstrate how the consistent application of *marginal cost pricing* (MCP) in ports could eventually eliminate deficits and the need for public funding, lead to an efficient allocation of scarce resources and achieve a level playing field among competing ports.

4.1 The issue of excess capacity

As a result of substantial excess capacity, container ports are declining cost industries or, in economic terms, industries with *increasing returns to scale* (liner shipping is another good example of such and industry, familiar to the student of maritime economics). In such industries, short-run marginal cost pricing (SRMC) results in deficits, for marginal costs are always below average total costs.

Excess capacity in competing container ports has a number of causes. As a matter of fact it could be shown (Haralambides et al.[8]) that the higher the competition, the higher the need for excess capacity.

First, as already mentioned above, ports are often seen as pivots of regional development and, thus, infrastructure is built far ahead of demand in order to promote economic development. Second, managerial "ego-boosting" is often not innocent of its responsibilities for the creation of excess capacity. However, the real economic culprits of excess capacity ought to be found in capital indivisibilities (lumpiness of investments), economies of scale in port construction, and over-optimistic demand forecasts.

In competing container terminals, furthermore, excess capacity is also an "operational necessity", being the only way to provide quick turnaround times to ships and thus maintain or increase patronage. It can be easily shown through simple single-channel-multiserver queuing theory (Haralambides et al.[8]) that once a port reaches 70% capacity utilisation, congestion ensues in terms of unacceptable waiting times in today's organisation of liner shipping. With this in mind, "operational" excess capacity ought to be seen as another unavoidable cost rather than an indication of inefficiency and wastage of resources. However, in their appeals to public funding agencies, port managers have not been very convincing in bringing this point out and, as a result, governments have been reluctant to see excess capacity in this light.

The problem of "operational" excess capacity is exacerbated with the increasing deployment of ever larger containerships. As has been shown earlier (Cariou and Haralambides,[9] Cariou[10]), in general, the cost per TEU of ship-time in port is an increasing function of ship size. This has mainly to do with the limited availability of cargo-handling equipment (cranes) that can be put to work on a ship, and the problem of course intensifies at higher levels of terminal capacity utilisation (Figure 2). Still, four and sometimes five crane operations are standard today in many major ports for post-Panamax ships. One cannot envision however eight or ten cranes working a concurrent sustained operation on a 10,000 TEU vessel in Hong Kong, Singapore, Rotterdam or Los Angeles any time in the near future. (Haralambides et al.[11]). Thus, other things being equal, the utilisation of larger vessels requires more excess capacity in ports (Figure 2).

The generalised cost idea of Figure 2 illustrates the by now classical conflict of interest between ports and carriers (UNCTAD,[12] Jansson and Shneerson,[13] Musso et al.[14]), augmented in a way that also highlights the impact of ship size on excess port capacity.

Figure 2: Impact of an increase in vessel size on the generalised port cost function

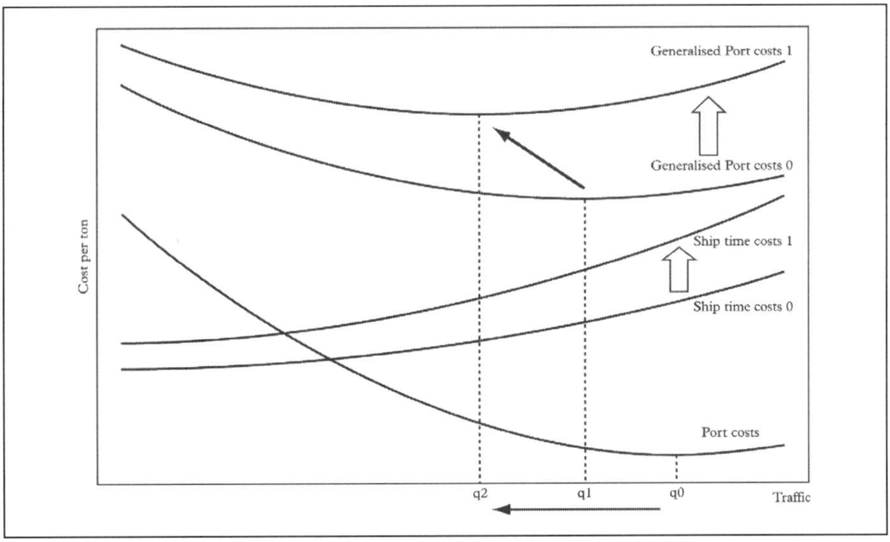

Due to high fixed costs in port production, port costs per ton decrease up to the point (q_0) where congestion starts to set in. For the carrier, after a certain point, ship-time costs per unit increase with port traffic (ship time costs 0 curve). The vertical summation of the port cost and ship-time curves gives the generalised cost curve (generalised port costs 0 curve) which determines the optimum level of port production at q_1. However, increase in ship sizes has the effect of shifting the ship-time curve upwards to a new position (ship time costs 1). The result is a new optimum level of port production at q_2, necessitating a lower level of terminal utilisation (q_1-q_2), i.e., more excess capacity.

Clearly, other things being equal, efficient servicing of larger vessels involves higher port costs, in terms of excess port capacity and availability of cargo-handling equipment. This should be kept in mind when setting port charges, negotiating concessions or dedicated terminals, as well as when considering the financing of port infrastructure, particularly when an appeal to public funding is made (Haralambides et al.[8]).

Finally, creation of excess capacity can also be seen as a form of *limit* pricing (see above) and this often explains the reluctance of both governments and regulatory authorities (e.g., the European Commission) to sanction and finance ambitious port development plans that go beyond what would normally be regarded as "realistic" demand forecasts. Here, hub-port strategies and port investments that encourage the construction of larger and larger containerships increase the sunk costs of new entrants to the competitive port arena, consolidating the incumbent ports' market power on the one hand, and making new entry unprofitable on the other.

Competition and excess capacity mix an "explosive cocktail". Competition pushes prices down to marginal costs, not allowing full cost recovery (and often survival). In liner shipping, this problem has been solved – at least so far – through self-regulation and the organisation of carriers in conferences and similar forms of cooperation (including shipping alliances).

4.2 Short- and long-run marginal costs

Let us try to see the above through the use of a simple graph (Figure 3) that will also be our vehicle for showing how MCP can have the positive effects mentioned above. In order to do this, a brief elaboration on the concepts of short- and long-run marginal costs is necessary; particularly of the latter which is a most crucial, albeit misunderstood, concept in maritime economics.

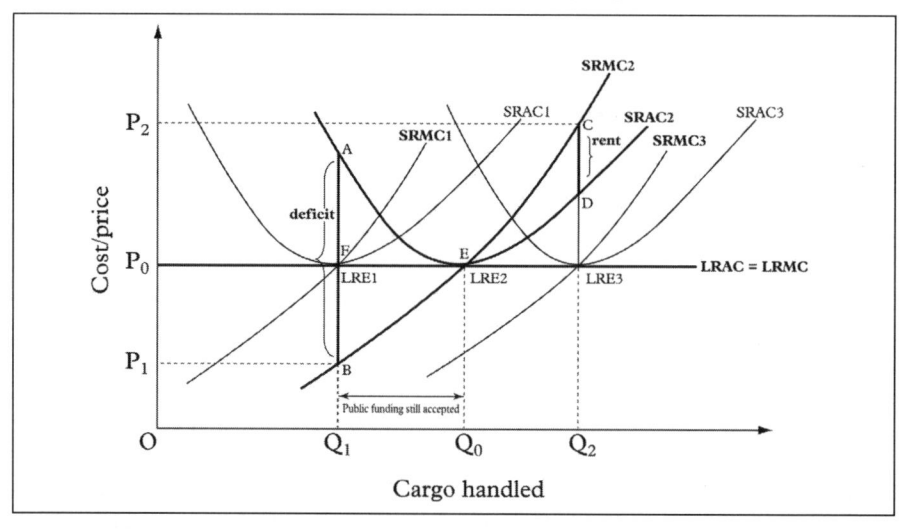

Figure 3: Marginal cost pricing in ports

In the short-run, the size of the port is considered as constant. Fixed capital assets, such as quays, yards and rest of infrastructure, are invariant to output, and variable costs mainly relate to those of cargo-handling and nautical services (e.g., pilotage). In the short-run, marginal costs (SRMC) consist of the increment in variable costs required to produce an extra unit of port service, e.g. the handling of an additional container, when all other costs are kept constant.

In the long-run, all costs are considered variable. The concept of long-run marginal cost (LRMC) is similar to before with the difference that, now, LRMC is the increment in *total* costs required to produce an extra unit of port service. By considering total costs, i.e., by including infrastructure costs as variable ones, LRMC becomes a planning concept. In principle, it gives the *long-run equilibrium* (LRE) port size, able to satisfy a given level of demand at minimum average total cost, without incurring deficits or realising *economic rent* (i.e., supernormal or monopoly profit). In the absence of rapid technological change, we often assume that LRMC = LRAC = Constant (Figure 3).

4.3 Increasing returns to scale

The above could be better grasped by looking at Figure 3. Assume that the size, organisational structure and "operational" excess capacity of our port can be adequately described by its short-run average total cost curve SRAC2. The port faces intense regional competition from neighbouring ports, its investments are publicly funded and, at present, the level of demand it has to satisfy is Q_1. Increasing returns to scale are thus present.

As a result of competition and the lack of a need to recover (publicly funded) infrastructure development costs, our port will be tempted – if not forced – to set prices equal to marginal costs, i.e., P_1. (SRMC2 is our port's short-run marginal cost curve). A deficit of the order of AB is thus created and MCP does not allow the port to recover its costs in full. Apparently, our port is too large for that level of throughput (Q_1).

Unless demand picks up considerably far beyond Q_1, such a situation is not sustainable in the long-run without continuing public support. Taxpayers, however, will become increasingly sceptical and competitors abundantly vociferous, in whichever way they can, on unfair competition. In long-run equilibrium (LRE), that level of throughput (Q_1) ought really to be produced by a much smaller port (LRE1/SRAC1) whereby SRMC pricing would allow the recovery of full costs. At that size, the port would exhibit *constant returns to scale* and it would be able to produce its services at minimum average cost.

4.4 Diminishing returns to scale

Let us now see what would happen if our port was faced with a situation where demand for its services was substantially higher, say Q_2. Here, the port exhibits *diminishing returns to scale* (diseconomies of scale) and although State coffers cannot complain in terms of revenues, congestion is a chronic problem and ship waiting times unacceptably long. Port capacity is over-utilised, accidents in cargo-handling very likely, and carriers impose surcharges on shippers. Demurrages are claimed. Such a situation, common in many ports during the pre-containerisation era, can still be found in some general cargo ports in developing countries.

Here, MCP is not only appropriate but recommended as a pricing strategy that rationalises demand and allocates scarce port capacity according to carriers' willingness to pay. Apparently, balking (carriers refusing to call at the port) and reneging (existing carriers leaving the port) are at this point the least of our port's concerns.

Setting price equal to marginal cost in this case means that our port charges a price of P_2 for the last ton of cargo it handles and this price is over and above (line CD) what on average costs the port to handle a ton of cargo when the total amount of cargo handled in a certain period of time is Q_2 tons. Now, the port realises *economic rent*, or supernormal profit, i.e., an economic surplus after all factors of production have been paid for, including entrepreneurship as well as a normal return on capital. Total economic rent accrued to the port beyond the minimum cost production level Q_0 is thus equal to the area ECD.

Here too, the situation is not sustainable in the long-run. Clearly, the port is too small for that level of throughput. Eventually it will have to expand to its long-run equilibrium position LRE3/SRAC3 where it will only earn normal profit, producing and charging at minimum average cost. The port will be helped in this by its competitors who will also invest and expand in an effort to capture part of the economic rent.

4.5 Constant returns to scale

However, port development (and contraction) are dynamic processes and rarely, or by accident, would a port be found on its LRE position. As said earlier, lumpiness of investments, economies of scale in port construction and wrong demand forecasts would see to it. This is why we stressed above that LRMC is a planning, i.e., normative, concept; a snapshot of a dynamic process. At any point in time, a port could diverge markedly from the idealised situation of LRE.

Having said that, however, if all competing ports within a certain economically interdependent geographical region were to be taken together, it would be reasonable to assume that the industry as a whole demonstrates constant returns to scale and, therefore, LRMC pricing, if ever achievable, would lead to efficient resource allocation, maximisation of social welfare and a level playing field among competing ports. This was the spirit and philosophy of the European Commission's White Paper on *fair payment for infrastructure use* which ascertained that "... *the entire infrastructure complex of the EU as a whole may not exhibit economies of scale*...". This means that, at least at an aggregate level, it should be possible to recover total costs.

4.6 Cost recovery through MCP

But let us, for the time being, return to our example of Figure 3 and to the case where our port faces the limited demand of Q_1. The port management remains optimistic that their plans and forecasts will eventually materialise and demand will pick up to the level of Q_0, if not further. However, costs have now to be recovered through port charges. If at the level of Q_1 the port charges a price of P_1, equal to its long-run average and marginal cost, there would still be a deficit but now reduced from AB to AF.

In so doing, i.e., by consistently charging at LRMC = LRAC, and as demand picks up, the port will eventually reach its LRE level of throughput where costs will be fully recovered. In the range of output Q_1 to Q_0, public funds are gradually and increasingly recovered until the deficit is phased out completely at point E.

Such public funding is and should be allowed given its digressiveness (temporary and declining) and the private sector's frequent reluctance to finance chunky investments of long gestation periods. The understanding now however is that these funds will have to be eventually recovered, irrespective of whether they are ploughed back to the public sector or used for further development by the port itself. In an era of reduced public spending, such an understanding may also help in enticing private funds to the port sector, as well as in giving an answer to the important question as to whether the pricing of port expansions should also reflect the cost of past (public) investments.

Despite the elegance and desirability of MCP, a lot of questions still remain open. Could this be done in practice? Could a port voluntarily and single-handedly charge prices higher than its competitors? Is there scope for policy intervention in pricing matters? Can we measure LRMC? Is MCP economically efficient when applied by some ports only, while the rest of the infrastructure connected to these ports (e.g., roads and railways) does not follow suit? Let us take these questions in turn.

4.7 Measuring marginal costs

With a given level of technology and organisation, fairly standard aspects in modern ports today, the measurement of long-run average or marginal costs simply boils down to forecasting future demand for port services (Figure 3). Once this is established, the LRE size of the port can be established too and the only cost element required for the measurement of LRMC is the construction cost of an additional metre of quayside and all that comes with it (aprons, yards and possibly organisational costs as a result of bigger size). Port engineers have fairly accurate data on these.

4.8 Forecasting port throughput

But can demand for port services be forecasted with any degree of confidence? This is one of the trickiest and most complex questions in maritime economics and one that can only be treated rudimentarily in an introductory chapter such as this.

In a closed economy, forecasting port demand is straightforward: observe population, agglomeration, consumption, personal income and international trade trends and translate them – mostly through regression analysis – into required port capacity; a popular exercise for students of maritime economics.

In an open and economically interdependent economy, however, things are very different. As a result of intertwined and extended hinterlands; abundant land infrastructure and short-sea feedering networks; continuously evolving liner shipping networks; and the infamous "mobility" of the container, demand is very volatile and unpredictable. Port market shares are unstable; investments in one region or country have an impact on another (e.g., a dedicated railroad line connecting Rotterdam with the Ruhr area in Germany will impact north sea German ports; new container capacity in Antwerp will take away traffic from Rotterdam; the port of Tanjung Pelepas in Malaysia has stolen Maersk from Singapore; Korea invests tremendously in order to compete, as a hub, with both Japan and China); carriers are diverting traffic to their own dedicated container terminals.

In such a "fluid" environment, how could one forecast port demand with any degree of credibility? Should ports, regions and countries compete or cooperate when it comes to infrastructure? In principle, cooperation among producers is not to the benefit of the consumer but, on the other hand, does the latter benefit when he pays taxes to develop "competing" infrastructure while knowing that he is due for reprisals in a never-ending vicious circle of public spending? Shouldn't such public spending be also liable to the same international anti-dumping laws as with other goods and services? In terms of trade policy, is there a difference between a subsidised shipyard and a subsidised port? If not, why do we shout about the former but turn a blind eye to the latter?

Answers to such questions belong to the realm of public rather than maritime economics. One could, however, start fathoming the answers by looking at the role of *public investment*; a concept that, surely, globalisation will redefine before too long. A road that connects a container terminal to the national motorway system is in principle open to all citizens and as such the road is a public good. In practice, however, the road is only used by the operator who exploits the terminal. The access channel to a port is dredged down to 15 metres. In principle, every floating craft can go through the channel but, surely, the channel wasn't dredged to that depth with the fisherman in mind! Are such investments public or private? And should their costs be paid for by the taxpayer or those who directly benefit from them?

4.9 The kinked demand for port services

Another question we posed above was whether a port would, voluntarily and single-handedly, charge a price higher than that of its competitors. The answer here is *"no, unless it has to"*, i.e., unless it has to recover costs. As we have mentioned above, ports operate in an oligopolistic market and individual upward price moves tend not to be matched by competitors who will maintain prices in an effort to benefit by capturing a larger market share. A port's demand curve is thus a *kinked* demand curve such as dD´, depicted in Figure 4.

Assume that, originally, the demand for the services of our port is given by DD'. The port is at equilibrium, charging a price of P per ton of cargo for a total throughput of Q. The port, believing that its competitors will follow suit, plans to raise prices to P_1. Knowing its price elasticity of demand, the port calculates that the increase in revenue as a result of higher prices ($ABPP_1$) will more than compensate the loss in revenue due to lower (Q_1) throughput ($BCQQ_1$); that is $ABPP_1 - BCQQ_1 > 0$.

To its bad luck, however, the competitors of our port maintain prices at the same level hoping to capture a greater market share. This does of course hap-

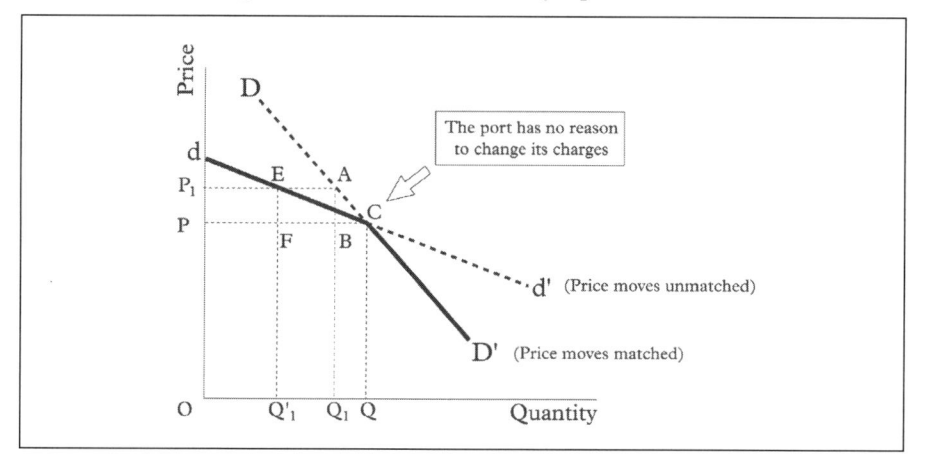

Figure 4: The kinked demand for port services

pen and our port's demand curve flattens to dd'. At the higher price of P_1, our port is only able to serve a Q'_1 level of throughput. It loses revenue much more than what it was expecting ($FBQ_1Q'_1$ more), while its extra revenue due to the price increase is only $EFPP_1$, less by $ABFE$ from what it was originally anticipating. Had our port known, as it should, that its competitors would not follow suit in raising their prices, it would have no good reason to raise its price single-handedly, as this would make it worse-off in the end. This is the more so when ports and governments are aware that LRMC pricing can lead to allocative efficiency only as long as other markets are also efficient (Pareto optimality). If the latter condition is not satisfied because of institutional restrictions, then, according to the *Theory of Second Best* (Lipsey and Lancaster[15]) "... *it is in general neither necessary nor sufficient to satisfy the remaining conditions...*"; i.e., to endorse MCP in ports when roads, railways and the rest of the infrastructure do not do the same.

In the context of the European Union, a voice is often loudly raised, by both the Commission and the port industry, arguing that MCP in ports only will make port services 'unilaterally' more expensive thus penalising the Union's efforts to check road traffic and promote short sea shipping; a most valid argument indeed. Under this light, efficient port pricing cannot be seen in isolation but only through a general equilibrium approach where the rest of the port related infrastructure and its pricing are also being considered simultaneously.

5. POLICY INTERVENTION

If ports are not, naturally, individually prepared to disadvantage themselves by charging higher prices, in order to recover costs, is there scope for *policy intervention*? Could a "pricing discipline" be imposed on competing ports in economically interdependent regions that would alleviate their own misgivings about unfair competition?

In the European Union, this was the objective of the Commission's *Green paper on ports and maritime infrastructure*.[16] The paper set out the broader context of Community port policy, with a focus on the issue of state aids and infrastructure charging. The main question was whether, and how, an efficient pricing system, leading to cost recovery, could be implemented in practice in the port sector, taking into account a variety of relevant objectives and constraints including higher market based efficiency; increased cohesion; distributive goals; the development of short sea shipping; the improvement of safety and environmental protection, etc. (Other, more recent policy documents at the European level have also addressed this issue; *cf.* Final Report by the high level group on transport infrastructure and charging concerning options for charging users directly for transport infrastructure operating costs.)

The Green Paper attracted growing industry attention on the desirability and scope of a more harmonised European seaport financing and pricing strategy. A large scale, pan-European research study for the European Commission (DG Transport and Energy), known under the acronym "ATENCO" (Analysis of the main Trans-European Network ports' COst structures), was subsequently carried out,[17] with the main goal to provide input for an in-depth reflection at the European level on (a) the design of a strategy to achieve efficient pricing and (b) the possible impacts of a cost recovery approach on the functioning of ports.

The study came up with a number of conclusions, the most important of which were: (a) The high sensitivity of demand for port services to changes in prices (Table 1). As an example, the study calculated that if the port of Hamburg were to recover the dredging costs of river Elbe from user charges, this would add Euro10 (or roughly 5%) to its terminal handling charges per TEU. According to Table 1, such a price increase would lead to a 15.3% (roughly half a million TEU) reduction in container traffic.[18] (b) No policy intervention on pricing matters would ever be acceptable by the industry, who strongly felt that pricing policies are solely for the firms themselves to decide (the argument here was that even when full cost recovery is sought as an overall objective, ports apply a variety of pricing principles simultaneously in order to achieve managerial effectiveness at the micro-level). (c) However, it was unanimously agreed, by every port management team interviewed, that *cost recovery* – regardless of how this was to be achieved by each individual port – should be pursued and, for that purpose, better port statistics, accounting systems and transparency of port accounts are required.[19]

Following the ATENCO results, the Commission came up with what has become known as its "port package" (European Commission,[20,21]). In this, the EC, convinced now about the desirability of cost recovery in ports, takes a fresh look at two most important issues: (a) the need for greater transparency in the efficient allocation (leases/concessions) of port land to service providers on an equal opportunity basis and in a way by which leases reflect better the opportunity cost of port investments; (b) the no longer indiscriminate treatment of port infrastructure investments as "public investment". Particularly with regard to the latter, although the Commission continues to remain neutral on the public or private ownership status of a port, and it does not dispute in any way the fact that public investments are the prerogative of Member States, it nevertheless attempted to have a say in whether a certain investment, that in theory is open to all users indiscriminately but in practice it is intended for a few or even one user, could, in the spirit of the Treaty, be considered as 'public investment'.

6. CONCLUSIONS

Cost recovery and the pricing of port services are complex and controversial issues, both technically and conceptually. This is so because they deal with the development and provision of infrastructure; economic development; public investment; fiscal policy and the role of the State in economic activity. Before too long, economic analysis of this type takes one into the realm of *moral philosophy*. Indeed, the type of *economics* we accept as valid reflects nothing more than our philosophical inclinations as regards the evolution of society, the desirability of equity, and the importance of production.

The issue of port pricing in maritime economics has not arisen only out of academic interest but as a response to the need felt in the port industry itself for a self-discipline mechanism that, if consistently applied, would eventually lead to the recovery of port investments and to future investments that are largely demand driven. This requirement has been the result of the recognition that, in the intensified regional port competition of today and the increasingly tightened fiscal constraints, it is no longer acceptable to indiscriminately and without a formal economic *rationale*, spend taxpayer money on port investments, often aimed at increasing market share at the expense of other ports, particularly within the same economically interdependent area.

Naturally, pricing for cost recovery looks at the "user" rather than the "taxpayer". This is just as well, given that ports (at least container terminals) are being transformed from public to private enterprises. The allocative and income distribution effects of such a switch in direction are obvious: investments are recovered, and port revenues generated, from the user of a (private) facility, who will have to somehow pass these costs on to the final consumer. The latter will in all likelihood have to pay higher prices for the goods he consumes but, at least in efficient markets, he is compensated by correspondingly paying less taxes (for infrastructure investments). Obviously, such issues are highly complex and have yet to be researched.

In principle, pricing for cost recovery should mean that depreciation of port infrastructure is included as a cost in the port's pricing system. Something like this would undoubtedly raise the level of port prices, but the overall effect of this on consumer prices and traffic diversion may not be as large as some might at first sight expect. This effect depends on the percentage of port costs in final consumer prices; the import and export elasticities of traded goods; the level of competition in transport markets (especially liner shipping) as well as all other markets along the door-to-door chain (i.e., distribution, wholesaling, etc.). It could well be argued that higher port prices are not necessarily passed on to consumers but are instead absorbed by transport operators and other market intermediaries.

But even if higher port prices are, to some extent, passed on to consumers, the overall effect on society could be ascertained by comparing the loss in consumer surplus, as a result of higher port prices, to the welfare gains had the public funds in question been invested in other sectors of the economy or led to lower taxes in general.

This chapter has argued in favour of pricing for cost recovery among competing commercial ports and it has shown how long-run marginal cost pricing can be a powerful pricing discipline that can eliminate subsidies and establish a level playing field among ports.

However, a "pricing discipline" imposed on ports through policy intervention would be unacceptable. The objectives often pursued by ports are so divergent that any uniform approach to pricing becomes meaningless and politically unfeasible. Pricing matters on the other hand, at least in a liberal economic environment, ought to be, ideally, left to the producers (ports) themselves.

The ATENCO study has demonstrated that, however controversial the issue of port pricing itself may be, there is general consensus on the importance of cost recovery. And this was an important development and step forward. Indeed, as long as this objective is respected, the specific pricing policy of the individual port becomes of secondary importance and only in so far as crowding out effects and efficient allocation of resources are concerned.

Once cost recovery is generally accepted as a guiding principle in port investment and pricing, the way forward is much simpler. It involves the compilation of better and more harmonised statistics on port costs, adoption of standardised port accounting systems, greater transparency of port accounts and of financial flows between the port and its institutional master and, perhaps, a common glossary of terms. And these are objectives not so difficult to achieve.

In conclusion, therefore, port policy is reorienting its attention from the idea of adopting uniform cost based pricing principles, towards: (a) more indirect incentives promoting cost based thinking in ports (e.g., by defining more clearly what constitutes acceptable public support in port infrastructure); and (b) rethinking how conventional competition rules (related, *inter alia*, to market access; abuse of dominant position; collusive behaviour, etc.) should be applied to the port sector.

ENDNOTES

* The chapter leans on work that has appeared earlier in the International Journal of Maritime Economics. Permission by Palgrave Macmillan, publishers of IJME, is gratefully acknowledged.
1. Students often confuse "sunk" with "fixed" costs. The former are costs that cannot be recovered once the firm decides to leave the market; a breakwater could be a good point in case here. Fixed costs, naturally, are those that do not vary with output. A sunk cost could thus well be variable, e.g., marketing and advertising expenses, while a fixed cost, such as that of a gantry crane, does not necessarily have to be sunk, as the asset could be sold to another port.

2. The concept of an economically interdependent geographic area or region, as employed here, has both a spatial and an economic dimension. It refers to a spatially delineated geographic area in which "binding" arrangements (laws) of direct economic impact are "jointly and institutionally" put in place – such as for instance competition, labour and fiscal laws – with the aim of maximising collective welfare. Apart from an individual country (with its constituencies, states, etc.) that would obviously qualify under such a definition, a good example of such an area is the European Union as well as other regional blocs depending on the strength of their institutional ties over and above trade policy.
3. Rosenstein-Rodan, P. (1943): "Problems of industrialisation of East and South-East Europe", *Economic Journal*, June-September.
4. Whether the absolute level of the elasticities in Table 1 is correct is a much less important issue than the observation of a very substantial divergence of the elasticities among the various ports. Hence, variation in prices, as a result of the adoption of alternative pricing systems, would, at least in the case of containers, lead to fundamentally different impacts on individual ports, even when engaging in similar price increases.
5. In industrial economics, "limit pricing" refers to strategic behaviour by which incumbent firms raise costs, through a multitude of ways, to a level that makes new entry unprofitable.
6. Ramsey, F. (1927): "A Contribution to the theory of taxation", *Economic Journal*, 37, pp. 47–61.
7. This was in broad terms the position of the Dutch government on the issue of Maasvlakte II terminal in Rotterdam.
8. Haralambides, H.E., Cariou, P., and Benacchio, M. (2002a): "Costs, benefits and pricing of dedicated container terminals", *International Journal of Maritime Economics*, 4, pp. 21–34.
9. Cariou, P., and Haralambides, H.E. (1999): "Capacity pools in the East/West trades", *International Association of Maritime Economists (IAME) Conference: Liner Shipping: What's Next?* Halifax, Canada, September 1999.
10. Cariou, P. (2000): "Les alliances stratégiques dans le transport maritime de lignes régulières: efficacité ou pouvoir de marché", Thèse de Doctorat, Université de Nantes.
11. Haralambides, H.E., Craig, R., Cheung Tam He, C., and Nam, K.C. (2002b): "Logistical diseconomies of scale in liner shipping: small is still beautiful", *International Journal of Maritime Economics* (forthcoming).
12. UNCTAD (1975a): *Berth throughput: systematic methods for improving general cargo operations*, TD/B/C.4/109 (New York, United Nations), p. 196. UNCTAD (1975b): *Port pricing*, TD/B/C.4/110/Rev.1 (New York, United Nations).
13. Jansson, J.O., and Shneerson, D. (1982): *Port economics* (Cambridge, MA, The MIT Press).
14. Musso, E., Ferrari, C., and Benacchio, M. (1999): "On the global optimum size of port terminals", *International Journal of Transport Economics*, 26, pp. 415–437.
15. Lipsey, R.G., and Lancaster, K. (1956): "The general theory of second best", *Review of Economic Studies*, 24, pp. 11–32.
16. H.E. Haralambides had the privilege of being member of the then EU Transport Commissioner, Neil Kinnock's group of experts that drafted the Paper. The Commissioner opened the first meeting of the group with a statement that took everyone aback: "... *if countries want to spend public money to develop their ports, so be it and there is nothing we can do about it...*". A lot has changed since then.
17. Both authors were involved in this exercise for a number of years: H.E. Haralambides was Chairman of the Academic Group of Experts and A.W. Veenstra was responsible for a major workpackage on pricing.
18. Such estimates have to be viewed with utmost caution and full understanding of the assumptions underlying them. For instance, this impressive percentage assumes that

other ports in the region would be able to absorb smoothly the extra traffic without difficulty or additional cost. It is also assumed that no changes take place in the pricing of the rest of the infrastructure (roads, etc.).

19. Surprisingly, most port authorities expected that the adoption of full cost recovery pricing would have little impact on pricing levels. It is believed here that, although in private ports such as those of the UK this may well be the case, this is far from the truth in all others, and this conviction of many port managers can only be explained by their inability to grasp in full the notion and implications of long-run marginal costs.

20. European Commission (2001a): Communication from the Commission to the European Parliament and the Council, *Reinforcing quality service in sea ports: a key for European transport*. Proposal for a Directive of the European Parliament and of the Council on market access to port services, COM(2001), p. 35.

21. European Commission (2001b): Commission Staff Working Document, *Public financing and charging practices in the Community sea port sector*, SEC (2001).

CHAPTER 35

THE PRODUCTIVITY AND EFFICIENCY OF PORTS AND TERMINALS: METHODS AND APPLICATIONS

Professor Kevin Cullinane
Department of Shipping and Transport Logistics, Hong Kong Polytechnic University, Hong Kong. E-mail: *stlkcull@polyu.edu.hk*

1. INTRODUCTION

Ports form a vital link in the supply chains of trading companies and nations worldwide. In terms of the logistics cost which they account for within any given supply chain, the level of a port's performance and/or relative efficiency will, to a large extent, determine the competitiveness of a nation and can ultimately have an influence upon industrial location decisions and the benefits derived from the economic policies of national governments. Thus, although productivity and/or efficiency ratings can be a powerful management tool for port operators themselves, they can also constitute a most important input to studies aimed at informing regional and national port planning and operation.

It is unfortunate, therefore, that in the vernacular of newspaper and television coverage of business and economic events, the terms "productivity" and "efficiency" are used interchangeably. As a result, the precise meanings of the two terms have become blurred. In the ensuing discussion of port and terminal productivity and efficiency, however, it is important to distinguish between them.

Productivity can very simply be defined as the ratio of outputs over inputs. This yields an absolute measure of performance that may be applied to all factors of production (inputs) simultaneously (as well as to all outputs) or to merely an individual factor of production. In this latter case, the outcome of such a calculation is more correctly referred to as a *partial* productivity measure. As is shown in the review contained in section 2 of this chapter, most analyses of port performance are concerned with the calculation of partial productivity measures across a range of ports and/or terminals and the comparison of such calculated measures.

In section 3 of this chapter, the theory underpinning the study of economic efficiency is presented. As will be shown, *economic efficiency* relates specifically to the economic concept of a production possibility frontier and comprises both *technical efficiency* and *allocative efficiency* combined. Fundamentally, however, the *technical efficiency* of an entity is a comparative measure of how well it processes inputs to achieve its output(s), as compared to its maximum potential for doing so – as represented by its production possibility frontier.

The production possibility frontier of an entity may change over time due to changes in the underlying technology. In the port sector, an example might be the greater reach of contemporary gantry cranes over their historic counterparts. This innovation in technology has facilitated a great improvement in partial productivity measures such as container moves per hour. Depending upon the relationship between the investment cost in such cranes and the reduction in operating cost per TEU moved, it could also mean greater output for the same level of input at all scales of production (i.e., an outward move in the production possibility frontier). If it could be established that this innovation has led directly to an improvement in the overall (total factor) productivity of the port (even where this compares favourably to that of other suitable benchmark ports), but that the new cranes like the old ones were still being optimally employed to full capacity, then a situation would exist where *technical efficiency* has remained the same (i.e., at a maximum), but there has been an improvement in *productivity* (even comparatively).

In a similar fashion, the scale of output(s) or inputs can be altered to take advantage of efficiencies due to scale. This too may mean that an entity can remain at 100% *technical efficiency* (so that output is at maximum for a given level of input) by moving along the production possibility frontier, but that its (total factor) productivity can simultaneously increase. It may be inferred from this explanation that *technical efficiency* and *productivity* also have time-scale connotations, whereby the former is much more of a long-term phenomenon, while the latter is a concept that is grounded more firmly in the short-term (see Coelli, Prasada Rao and Battese[1] for a comprehensive treatment of productivity and the different forms of efficiency).

Following the explanation of the economic theory underpinning efficiency analysis that is given in section 3, sections 4, 5 and 6 of this chapter proceed to introduce and provide detailed explanations of the two main contemporary methods for the measurement of *technical* or *productive efficiency*. Chapters 5 and 6 also provide a review of the major applications of each of the methods to the derivation of technical efficiency measures in the port and/or terminal sector.

2. REVIEW OF PORT PERFORMANCE AND PRODUCTIVITY STUDIES

The measurement of port efficiency is complicated by the large variety of factors that influence port performance.[2] The most obvious influences can be generalised as the economic input factor endowments of land, labour and capital. Dowd and Leschine[3] argue, in fact, that port and/or terminal productivity measurement is a means of quantifying efficiency in the utilisation of these three resources. However, there are other influences that are not so easily classified, nor indeed capable of being quantified, for the purpose of empirical investigation. A few examples of these influences include: the level of technology that is utilised in the operations of a port or terminal; the industrial relations environment within the port or terminal (and, hence, the risk of disruptions to the supply of labour); the extent of co-operation or integration with shipping lines and, as analysed in Cullinane and Song,[4] the nature of the ownership of the port and the impact that this may have on the way that the port is managed and/or operated.

Despite these difficulties, attempts at estimating port or terminal productivity have been legion. This is particularly the case in container handling where, as might be imputed from the plethora of studies that focus on this sector, the need for high productivity or high efficiency levels is probably greater than in port facilities that concentrate on serving other forms of shipping.

Traditionally, the performance of ports has been variously evaluated by calculating cargo-handling productivity at berth (e.g., Bendall and Stent,[5] Tabernacle,[6] and Ashar[7]), by measuring a single factor productivity (e.g., labour as in the case of De Monie[8]) or by comparing actual with optimum throughput for a specific period of time (e.g., Talley[9]).

Dowd and Leschine[10] approached the issue specifically in relation to container terminal productivity and highlight the fact that, probably because of the standard nature of the cargo that is handled in such facilities, there is an incessant demand in the industry for some form of universal standards or benchmarks for container terminal productivity. For the better terminals, there are obvious marketing advantages to be had from this. One major stumbling block in seeking to achieve such a standard is the lack of uniformity in productivity measurement across the sector. By way of exemplifying this, while some terminals will count rehandles and hatchcover removals as "moves", others do not.

A second problem exists in that each participating player has a different interest in port or terminal productivity. For the port or terminal itself, the main goal may be to reduce the cost per unit of cargo handled and, thereby, raise profitability. For the port authority, the main goal may be to maximise the throughput per unit area of land that it leases to the terminal operator, so as to maximise the benefits derived from the investments it makes. For the carrier, the goal may be to minimise the time that a ship spends in port.

In an effort to provide a more rigorous and holistic evaluation of port performance, several alternative methods have been suggested, such as the estimation of a port cost function,[11] the estimation of a total factor productivity index of a port[12] and the establishment of a port performance and efficiency model using multiple regression analysis.[13]

Chang[14] appears to have made one of the earliest efforts to estimate a production function and the productivities of inputs within the port sector. This was done for the port of Mobile in the US. In attempting to derive a port production function, the author focuses on general cargo-handling volume as a measurement of port performance and assumes that port operations follow the conventional Cobb-Douglas case as expressed by:

$$Y = AK^{\alpha}L^{\beta}e^{\gamma(T/L)}$$

...where Y is annual gross earnings (in real terms), K is the real value of net assets in the port, L is the number of labourers per year and the average number of employees per month each year, and $e^{\gamma(T/L)}$ a proxy for technological improvement in which (T/L) shows the tonnage per unit of labour. The author argues that, for the estimation of a production function of this form, the output of a port should be measured in terms of *either* total tonnage handled at the port *or* its gross earnings.

De Neufville and Tsunokawa[15] undertook an analysis of the five major container ports on the east coast of the US and derived an estimate of a container port production possibility frontier on the basis of the panel data collected. They deduced that Hampton Roads and Baltimore were consistently operating inefficiently during the period 1970–1978 and attributed this to poor management as the root cause. The findings highlight the importance of economies of scale in port/terminal productivity and, as such, the authors conclude that, because of the economic returns to be reaped, policy makers should promote and place greater investment into large load centre ports rather than into the proliferation of smaller, more regionally focused port developments.

Suykens[16] points out that the measurement of productivity and subsequent comparison between ports is extremely difficult. Quite often, this is due simply to differences in the geophysical characteristics of the ports to be compared. For instance, there will be fundamental constraints on the productivity of ports where locks are needed, or which are located up river estuaries or in the middle of a port town as opposed to at a greenfield location. Difficulties also arise where the type of cargo handled at the comparison ports differs or when one port is primarily serving its own hinterland and another is primarily a transhipment port. Under all these scenarios, it would be fundamentally unfair and possibly misleading to make productivity comparisons on a straightforward basis. It may be argued, therefore, that in order to properly evaluate the performance of a port, it is important and necessary to place it within a proper perspective by drawing comparisons with other ports that operate in a similar environment.

Tongzon and Ganesalingam[17] applied cluster analysis to compare the port performance and efficiency of ASEAN ports with counterparts overseas. The rationale for this analysis lay primarily with a purported requirement for such a comparison to be conducted only amongst ports that are similar in terms of their management or operational environment. The results suggested that the ASEAN ports, especially Singapore, were more technically efficient in terms of the utilisation of cranes, berths and storage areas, but that they were generally less efficient in terms of timeliness, labour and tug utilisation. In addition, it was deduced that port charges in ASEAN ports were significantly higher than those of their overseas counterparts falling within the same cluster (i.e., comparable ports).

Tongzon[18] elaborated upon this benchmarking concept by utilising an approach based on principal components analysis for the identification of suitable benchmark ports. Ashar[19] is critical of this approach. In particular, the need for such an analysis to be conducted at the level of the terminal is highlighted by reference to the fact that several of the ports included in Tongzon's sample were, in fact, landlord ports (as defined in Goss[20]).

Braeutigam, Daugherty and Turnquist[21] note that ports come in different sizes and face a variety of traffic mix. As such, they suggest, the use of cross-sectional, time-series or even panel data may fail to show basic differences between ports; thus leading to a misjudgement as to each port's performance. They attest, therefore, that it is crucial to estimate econometrically the structure of production in ports at the level of the single port or terminal, using appropriate data such as the panel data for a terminal. This view also receives support elsewhere.[22]

In undertaking the comparison of port productivities conducted within their study, Tongzon and Ganesalingham[23] compare ports on the basis of a basket of standard port productivity measures such as: shipcalls per port employee, net crane rate, ship rate, TEUs per crane, shipcalls per tug, TEUs per metre of berth, berth occupancy rate, TEUs per hectare of terminal area, port charges, pre-berthing time, berthing time and truck/rail turnaround time. Since the primary role of ports is to facilitate the movement of cargoes, the authors recognise that it is vital to evaluate port performance in relation to how efficient are their services from the perspective of the port user: the shipowners, shippers (importers and exporters) and the land transport owners. It is obvious, therefore, that port performance assessment cannot be based on a single measure. As is clear from the list of productivity measures employed, whilst it does contain certain operational productivity measures, it also recognises that this is only meaningful to port users when it is translated into lower costs to them.

Frankel[24] is highly critical of the productivity measures that are applied in ports when he suggests that most port performance standards are narrowly defined operational measures that are useful only for comparison with ports that have similar operations or against proposed supplier standards. He asserts that port user interest in port productivity (and the service quality that it relates to) is much more wide-ranging and it is vitally important that ports attempt to address this disparity in outlook. Port users, he asserts, are concerned with issues such as the total time and cost of ship turnarounds and (increasingly) of cargo throughput. The realignment of what a port considers to be valid performance measures is required because the commercial environment of port operations is becoming increasingly competitive as hinterlands overlap. In such a context, port users have a real choice in the selection of the ports that they want to use.

The focus which Frankel advocates, on the port users' perspective of port efficiency, is particularly interesting and important in that it shifts the need for, and usefulness of, valid port and/or terminal productivity and efficiency measures away from the fulfilment of an internally-oriented managerial (cost minimisation) objective and towards an externally-oriented marketing (revenue-maximisation) objective.

Chapon[25] specifically states that the overall cost of cargo-handling in a port is comprised of two separate components: the cost price of the actual handling and the cost price of immobilising the seagoing vessel for the period of its stay in port. In other words, this second cost is, in economic terms, the opportunity cost associated with the revenue lost or, in the terminology of logistics, the cost of lost sales. This second component has risen to even greater prominence as ships have become increasingly expensive (i.e., exhibiting high fixed to variable cost ratios), a feature that is particularly relevant to the liner trades over recent years. Several studies of productivity have adopted this perspective in undertaking productivity measurement and comparisons.[26,27]

All this points to the fact that productivity levels in ports have implications for the real cost of loading and discharging a ship. Suykens,[28] however, points to the need for caution in making such comparisons since the higher productivity in a port may be reflected in the wages it pays and/or the depreciation charges it incurs as the result of the investment in state-of-the-art equipment that has been made. Both of these influences on higher port productivity will be mirrored in the port tariff that is charged. Thus, there is a need for a balanced and joint view of both port pricing and productivity.

Ports have an interaction with other parts of the logistical chain. Indeed, the suggestion has been made that the real value of productivity improvements in ports depends upon whether this results in an improvement to the efficiency of the total logistical system or whether it merely shifts a "bottleneck" from one part of the system to another.[29] This calls for the adoption of a still wider perspective on the issue of port productivity and efficiency.

In relation to the issue of technical efficiency rather than productivity measurement and comparison, it can be deduced that by the very nature of investments in cargo handling technology and the expansion of space in ports, additions to capacity have to be large compared to the existing facilities. In other words, when investments are made, they are made primarily on an *ad hoc* basis and with a view to future expectations of expanded demand. In consequence, since available capacity cannot be fully utilised in the years immediately following the time that such investments in additional capacity come on stream, then technical inefficiency is inevitable.

In any analysis of a single port's time series of technical efficiency, therefore, the situation must be defined by numerous inefficient observations being bounded by a comparatively few observations that are deemed efficient. Because of this characteristic (i.e., that efficiency in operations cannot be assumed), De Neufville and Tsunokawa[30] point to the inadequacy of any approach that is based on a least squares regression analysis to estimate the production function for the industry. This is because any such analysis has to be based on the complementary assumptions that all observations are efficient but that any deviation of an observation from the production function is due to random effects. Without explicitly acknowledging the fact, this assertion points to the need for the adoption of contemporary approaches to the measurement of efficiency.

3. THE ECONOMIC CONCEPT OF EFFICIENCY

In simple terms, the performance of an economic unit can be determined by calculating the ratio of its outputs to its inputs; with larger values of this ratio associated with better performance or higher productivity. Because performance is a concept that is only meaningful when judged relatively, there are many bases upon which it may be assessed. For instance, a car manufacturer uses materials, labour and capital (inputs) to produce cars (outputs). Its performance in 1999 could be measured *relative to* its 1998 performance or could be measured *relative to* the performance of another producer in 1999, or could be measured *relative to* the average performance of the car industry, and so on.

The production frontier is widely used to define the relationship between inputs and outputs by depicting graphically the maximum output obtainable from the given inputs consumed. In so doing, the production frontier reflects the current status of technology available to the industry. In respect of economic efficiency, a production frontier is useful in explaining two distinctive concepts of efficiency: *productive (or technical) efficiency* and *allocative efficiency*.

In economic theory, costs can exceed their minimum feasible level for one of two reasons. One is that inputs are being used in the wrong proportions, given their prices and marginal productivity. This phenomenon is known as *allocative inefficiency*. The other reason is that there is a failure to produce the maximum amount of output from a set of given inputs. This is known as *productive (or technical) inefficiency*. Both sources of inefficiency can exist simultaneously or in isolation. These sources of inefficiency can be easily explained by using the concept of a production frontier.

An economic unit operating within an industry is considered *productively (technically) efficient* if it operates *on* the frontier, whilst the unit is regarded as *productively inefficient* if it operates *beneath* the frontier. On the other hand, when information on prices is available and a behavioural assumption (such as profit maximisation or cost minimisation) is properly established, we can then consider *allocative efficiency*. *Allocative efficiency* occurs when a selection of inputs (e.g., material, labour and capital) produce a given quantity of output at minimum cost given the prevailing input prices. An economic unit is judged *allocatively inefficient* if inputs are being used in the wrong proportions, given their prices and marginal productivity.

With respect to how to measure these different sources of (in)efficiency, let us suppose that the frontier production function of an economic unit is as depicted in Figure 1 and can be denoted by $Y = f(x_1, x_2)$, where two inputs (x_1 and x_2) are used, in some combination, to produce one output (Y). It is also assumed that the function is characterised by constant returns to scale. In this case, the isoquants Y_A and Y_B indicate all possible combinations of x_1 and x_2 that give rise to the same level of output.

Assume that the firm's efficiency is observed at point A, rather than C. This position is neither allocatively nor productively efficient. Its level of *productive efficiency* is defined as the ratio of OB/OA. Therefore, productive inefficiency is defined as 1−(OB/OA) and can be interpreted as the proportion by which the cost of producing the level of output could be reduced given the assumption that the input ratio (x_1/x_2) is held constant. Under the assumption of constant returns to scale, productive inefficiency can also be interpreted as the proportion by which output could be increased by becoming 100% productively efficient. The level of *allocative efficiency* is measured as OD/OB (or C_1/C_2). Thus allocative inefficiency is defined as 1−(OD/OB) and measures the proportional increase in costs due to allocative inefficiency.

Consider position B in Figure 1. At this point, the firm is *allocatively inefficient* since it can maintain output at Y but reduce total costs by changing the

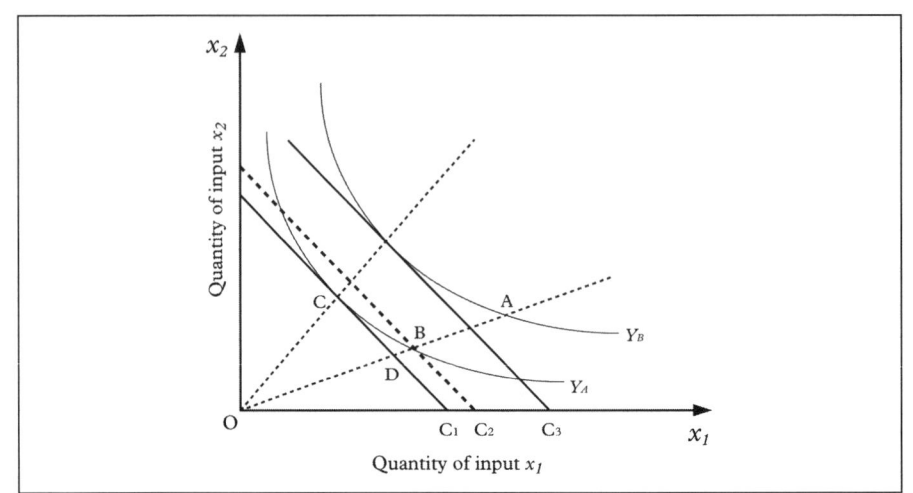

Figure 1: A firm's frontier production function

input mix to that which exists at point C. At point B, however, the firm is *productively efficient* since it cannot increase output with this input combination of x_1 and x_2 and, given a suboptimal input mix (i.e., *allocative inefficiency*), the firm has minimised the cost of producing this level of output.

4. INTRODUCTION TO MODERN METHODS OF EFFICIENCY MEASUREMENT

Over the last decade a family of methods for measuring efficiency have been proposed which revolve around utilising the economic concept of an efficient frontier. Under this concept, efficient decision making units (DMUs) are those that operate on either a (maximum) production frontier or a (minimum) cost frontier. In contrast, inefficient DMUs operate either below the frontier when considering the production frontier, or above it in the case of the cost frontier. Relative to a DMU located on a production frontier, an inefficient operator will produce less output for the same cost. Analogously, relative to any DMU located on a cost frontier, an inefficient operator will produce the same output but for greater cost.

As suggested by Bauer,[31] there are several reasons why the use of frontier models is becoming increasingly widespread:

- the notion of a frontier is consistent with the underlying economic theory of optimising behaviour;
- deviations from a frontier have a natural interpretation as a measure of the relative efficiency with which economic units pursue their technical or behavioural objectives; and
- information about the structure of the frontier and about the relative efficiency of DMUs has many policy applications.

The literature on frontier models was inaugurated in the seminal contribution of Farrell,[32] who provided a rigorous and comprehensive framework for analysing economic efficiency in terms of realised deviations from an idealised frontier isoquant. The proliferation of attempts to measure economic efficiency through the application of the frontier approach can be attributed to an interest in the structure of efficient production technology, an interest in the divergence between observed and ideal operation and also to an interest in the concept of economic efficiency itself.

Within the family of models and methods that are based on the frontier concept, a distinction exists between those methods that revolve around a parametric approach to deriving the specification of the frontier model and those that utilise non-parametric methods. Another distinction exists with respect to whether the model employed is stochastic or deterministic in nature. With the former, it is necessary to make assumptions about the stochastic properties of the data, while with the latter it is not. The non-parametric approach revolves around mathematical programming techniques that are generically referred to as Data Envelopment Analysis (DEA). The parametric approach, on the other hand, employs econometric techniques where efficiency is measured relative to a frontier production function that may be statistically estimated on the basis of an assumed distribution.

Econometric approaches have a strong policy orientation, especially in terms of assessing alternative industrial organisations and in evaluating the efficiency of government and other public agencies. Mathematical programming approaches, on the other hand, have a much greater managerial decision-making orientation.[33–35] Several studies[36–38] have compared the performance of alternative methods for measuring efficiency, focusing on the econometric method (in particular, the stochastic frontier model) and the mathematical programming method. As measured by the correlation coefficients and rank correlation coefficients between the true and estimated relative efficiencies, the results show that when the functional form of the econometric model is well specified, the stochastic frontier approach generally produces better estimates of efficiency than the approaches based on mathematical programming, especially when measuring DMU-specific efficiency where panel data are available. In addition, certain authors consider that the econometric approaches have a more solid grounding in economic theory.[39–40]

5. DATA ENVELOPMENT ANALYSIS

5.1 Method

Data Envelopment Analysis (DEA) can be broadly defined as a non-parametric method for measuring the relative efficiency of a DMU. The method caters for multiple inputs to, and multiple outputs from, the DMU. It does this by constructing a single "virtual" output that is mapped onto a single "virtual" input, without reference to a pre-defined production function.

There has been a phenomenal expansion of the theory underpinning DEA, the methodology itself and applications of the methodology over the past few decades.[41–44] A significant stimulus to this corpus of literature came with the publication of a seminal work on the topic by Charnes, Cooper and Rhodes in 1978.[45] This work espoused a model for solving the DEA linear programming problem which has subsequently become widely known by the acronym of the authors' surnames; the CCR model. The significance and influence of this paper is reflected in the fact that by 1999, it had been cited over 700 times in other papers incorporating applications of the DEA methodology or concerned with the theory or methodology of DEA.[46]

In common with other approaches based on the frontier approach, the fundamental idea in DEA is that the efficiency of an individual DMU[47] or *Unit of Assessment*[48] is compared relative to a bundle of homogeneous units. Implicit in this idea is the assumption that each individual DMU exercises some sort of corporate responsibility for controlling the process of production and making decisions at various levels of the organisation, including daily operation, short-term tactics and long-term strategy.

Figure 2 illustrates that DEA is used to measure the relative efficiency of a DMU by comparing it with other homogeneous units that transform the same group (types) of measurable positive inputs into the same group (types) of measurable positive outputs.

Figure 2: DMU and homogeneous units

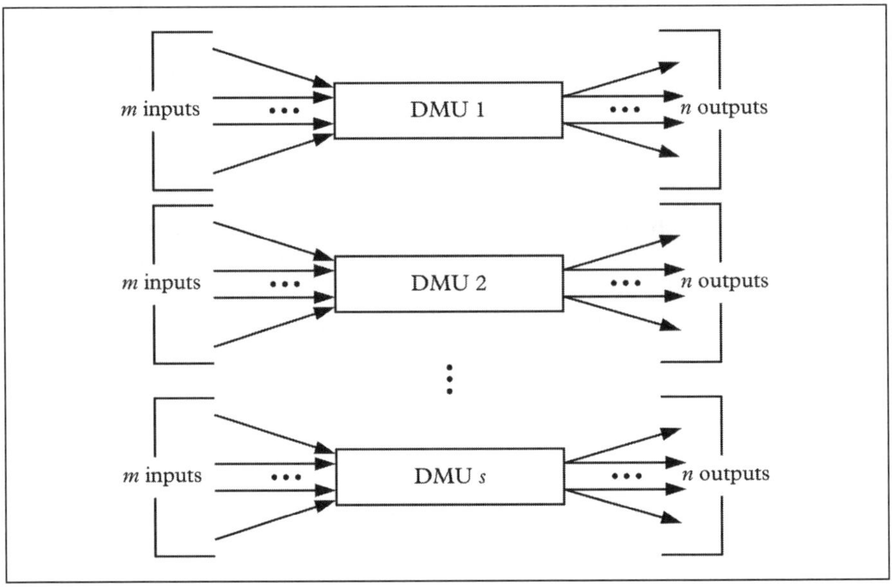

In the ports context, for example, DEA may be applied to compare the relative efficiency of a single container terminal to a set of other container terminals where the common output may be defined in terms of an annual throughput measured in TEU. Similarly, in this case, the common inputs may be the annual financial costs incurred in the provision of capital, land and labour or, alternatively, physical proxies for these factor inputs such as total length of berths, container stacking capacity, number of cranes, number of employees, total land available etc. The input and output data for Figure 2 can be expressed in terms of matrixes denoted by X and Y as shown below, where the element x_{ij} in the matrix X refers to the ith input data item of DMU j, whereas the element y_{ij} represents the ith output data item of DMU j. In X, there are m input variables and in Y, there are n output variables. In both input and output matrices, there are s DMUs considered.

$$X = \begin{pmatrix} x_{11} & x_{12} & \cdots x_{1s} \\ x_{21} & x_{22} & \cdots x_{2s} \\ \vdots \\ x_{m1} & x_{m2} & \cdots x_{ms} \end{pmatrix}$$

$$Y = \begin{pmatrix} y_{11} & y_{12} & \cdots y_{1s} \\ y_{21} & y_{22} & \cdots y_{2s} \\ \vdots \\ y_{n1} & y_{n2} & \cdots y_{ns} \end{pmatrix}$$

The basic approach to utilising DEA to measure the relative efficiencies of DMUs can be explained by the following example. Table 1 presents some basic production statistics for eight hypothetical container terminals. The "Throughput/stevedore" in Table 1 can be interpreted as a standard productivity measure. In an extremely simplistic sense that is useful for the purpose of illustrating the basic approach to DEA, this productivity measure can be employed to determine a simplistic and concise form of 'relative efficiency' by comparing all DMUs against the best in the sample.

Table 1: Example single input/single output data

Terminal	T1	T2	T3	T4	T5	T6	T7	T8
Stevedores	10	20	30	40	50	50	60	80
Throughput	10	40	30	60	80	40	60	100
Throughput/stevedore	1	2	1	1.5	1.6	0.8	1	1.25
Relative Efficiency	50%	100%	50%	75%	80%	40%	50%	62.5%

From Figure 3 it is clear that in terms of the particular relationship between inputs and outputs that we are looking at here (i.e., throughput/stevedore), *T2* is the most efficient container terminal compared with the others (as represented by the other points on the graph). The straight line from the origin that passes through *T2* can be termed an "efficient frontier" since all points along it have the maximum observed productivity measurement of one for throughput per stevedore. All the other points are inefficient compared with *T2* and are "enveloped" by the efficient frontier. Within the context of DEA, the relative efficiencies of these other container terminals, as shown in the bottom line of Table 1, are measured by comparing the productivity measure (i.e., in this case throughput/stevedore) for each of these "inefficient" container terminals with that of T2. The term "Data Envelopment Analysis" stems from the fact that the

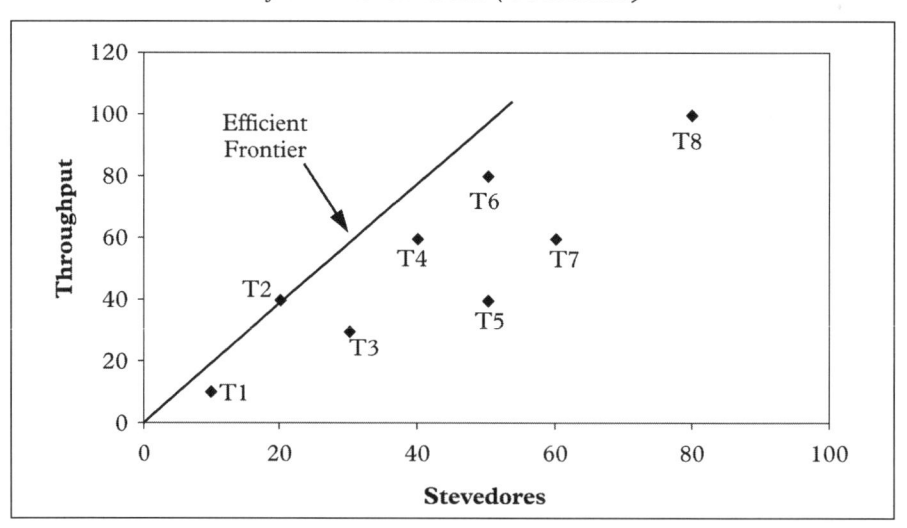

Figure 3: Theoretical comparison of efficiencies of container terminals (CCR Model)

efficient frontier "envelops" the inefficient observations and that they, in turn, are "enveloped" by the frontier.

It should be apparent that the complexity of measuring true relative efficiency (or indeed of even simply portraying the problem graphically) increases exponentially as the number of total input and output variables increase. It is this difficulty that the CCR model overcomes. This is because it was specifically devised to address the measurement of relative efficiencies of DMUs with multiple inputs and outputs.

The CCR model can be expressed as the following fractional programming problem (1)–(4):

$$(FP_0) Max = \theta = \frac{u_1 y_{1o} + u_2 y_{2o} + \ldots + u_n y_{no}}{v_1 x_{1o} + v_2 x_{2o} + \ldots + v_m x_{mo}} \quad (1)$$

Subject to:

$$\frac{u_1 y_{1j} + u_2 y_{2j} + \ldots + u_n y_{nj}}{v_1 x_{1j} + v_2 x_{2j} + \ldots + v_m x_{mj}} \leq 1 \quad (j+1, \ldots, s) \quad (2)$$

$$v_1, v_2, \ldots, v_m \geq 0 \quad (3)$$

$$u_1, u_2, \ldots, u_n \geq 0 \quad (4)$$

Given the data matrices X and Y shown earlier, the CCR model measures the maximum relative efficiency of each DMU by solving the fractional programming problem in (1) where the input weights $v_1, v_2, \ldots v_m$ and output weights $u_1, u_2, \ldots u_n$ are variables to be obtained. o in (1) varies from 1 to s in relation to the s optimisations that are required for all s DMUs. The constraint in (2) defines the fact that the ratio of "virtual output" $(u_1 y_{1o} + u_2 y_{2o} + \ldots + u_n y_{no})$ to "virtual input" ($v_1x_{1o} + v_2x_{2o} + \ldots + v_mx_{mo}$) cannot exceed unity for each DMU. This Fractional Programming (FP) problem represented in equations (1)–(4) has been proved to be equivalent to the following Linear Programming (LP) formulation shown in equations (5)–(9).[49]

$$(LP_0) Max = \theta = u_1y_{1o} + u_2y_{2o} + \ldots + u_ny_{no} \quad (5)$$

Subject to

$$v_1x_{1j} + v_2x_{2j} + \ldots + v_mx_{mj} = 1 \quad (6)$$

$$u_1y_{1j} + u_2y_{2j} + \ldots + u_ny_{nj} \leq v_1x_{1j} + v_2x_{2j} + \ldots + v_mx_{mj} \quad (7)$$

$$v_1, v_2, \ldots, v_m \geq 0 \quad (8)$$
$$u_1, u_2, \ldots, u_n \geq 0 \quad (9)$$

It is important to recognise and note that the computation of the DEA CCR model has been greatly facilitated by the transformation from its original Fractional Programming (FP) formulation into a Linear Programming (LP) form of the model. This transformation has contributed greatly to the rapid development of the DEA technique and the proliferation of DEA applications. This has occurred because the solution of LP problems has a long-established history where numerous sophisticated computational methods have been developed and where commercial software packages are widely available. As such, calculating the complicated relative efficiencies of DMUs with multiple inputs and outputs is then rendered a comparatively simple task.

One assumption that underpins the early DEA approaches, including the CCR model, is that the sample under study exhibits constant returns to scale. There is a voluminous body of evidence that suggests that this assumption is particularly inappropriate to the ports sector where, it is quite commonly asserted, economies of scale are quite significant.[50–52] In order to cater for such situations where variable returns to scale may be more the norm, the CCR model has been modified so that scale efficiencies, for example, may be separated out from the pure productive (or technical) efficiency measure that the standard CCR model yields.

The main modified forms of the CCR model that are utilised in practice are referred to as the Additive model and the BCC model, the latter being named after its creators.[53] Accordingly, the efficient frontiers that are estimated by these models are different from that of the CCR model.

Figure 4 shows a hypothetical efficient frontier for situations when either the Additive or BCC models are applied to a sample of container terminals (i.e., there is an assumption that variable returns to scale prevail). In this illustrative example, the sample observations denoted by T_1, T_2, T_6 and T_8 lie on a non-linear efficient frontier and are all defined as efficient since each observation cannot dominate any of the others given the condition of variable returns to scale. The other points that are "enveloped" by (i.e., lying below) these technically efficient points are deemed inefficient.

The Additive and BCC models are identical in terms of the efficient frontiers that they estimate. The main difference between them is the projection path to

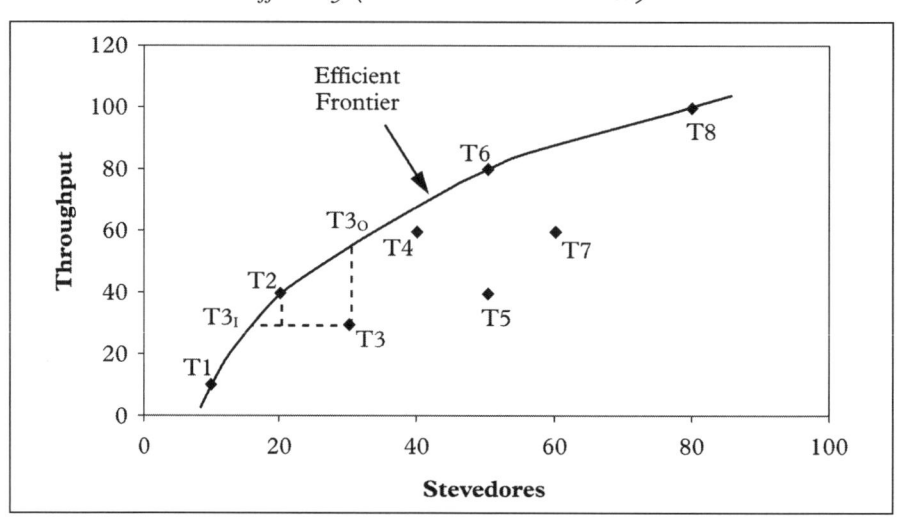

Figure 4: A comparison of container terminal efficiency (BCC and additive models)

the efficient frontier that is employed as the basis for estimating the levels of relative (in)efficiency for those DMUs in the sample that are not located on the efficient frontier. For instance, in figure 4, for the BCC estimate of inefficiency, the inefficient observation T3 can be projected either to $T3_I$ or $T3_O$ depending upon whether an input or output orientation is adopted. For the Additive model, however, T3 will be projected to T2 on the efficient frontier. This different approach to projection determines the different relative efficiencies for different inefficient DMUs. This is because the level of (in)efficiency for inefficient observations is derived from the distance it is located from the efficient frontier; a measure that is, of course, dependent upon the projection path that is utilised.

Irrespective of which model is selected for application, the main advantages of utilising a DEA approach to efficiency estimation can be summarised as follows:
(a) both multiple outputs and multiple inputs can be analysed simultaneously;
(b) more extraneous factors that have an impact on performance can be incorporated into the analysis (such as those relating to the commercial and competitive environment of the port operation, as well as other qualitative factors);
(c) the possibility of different combinations of outputs and inputs being equally efficient is recognised and taken into account;
(d) there is no necessity to pre-specify a functional form for the production function that links inputs to outputs, nor to give an *a priori* relationship (by pre-specifying the relative weights) between the different factors that the analysis accounts for;
(e) rather than in comparison to some sample average or some exogenous standard, efficiency is measured relative to the highest level of performance within the sample under study;

(f) Specific sub-groups of those DMUs identified as efficient can be ring-fenced as benchmark references for the non-efficient DMUs.

In the specific case of port efficiency, the ability to handle more than one output is a particularly appealing feature of the DEA technique. This is because there exist a number of different measures of port output that may be used in such an analysis, with the selection depending upon what aspect of port operation constitutes the main focus of the evaluation. In addition to providing relative efficiency measures and rankings for the DMUs under study, DEA also provides results on the sources of input and output inefficiency, as well as identifying the benchmark DMUs that are utilised for the efficiency comparison. This ability to identify the sources of inefficiency could be useful to port and/or terminal managers in inefficient ports so that the problem areas might be addressed. For port authorities too, they may provide a guide to focusing efforts at improving port performance.

5.2 Applications

Applications of the DEA approach to efficiency estimation in the general transport industry are now quite common and examples exist of applications to virtually all modes. For example, a comprehensive review of DEA applications and other frontier-based approaches to the railway industry was conducted by Oum et al.[54] Similarly, De Borger et al.[55] carried out just such a review for attempts to measure public transit performance. It is with the air industry, however, that the greatest proliferation of DEA applications may be found.[56-62] This is interesting because of the great similarity that exists between the air and maritime industries, particularly the analogous positions of ports and airports; a feature that would suggest that there remains great scope for further applications of the DEA approach to the port sector.

In relation to the very few applications of DEA to ports that have already been undertaken, it is particularly interesting that there has been very little correspondence between the studies as to the choice of input and output variables that are considered. As Thanassoulis[63] points out, this is significant because the identification of the inputs and the outputs in the assessment of DMUs tends to be as difficult as it is crucial. In addition, Ashar, Stopher and Appfel[64] attribute a lack of transparency to the use of the DEA technique as applied to the estimation of port and/or terminal efficiency.

Roll and Hayuth[65] were the first commentators to explicitly recommend the use of DEA for the estimation of efficiency in the port sector. By presenting a hypothetical application of the methodology to a fictional set of container terminal data, they reveal what potential the approach might hold. They point particularly to the applicability of the DEA approach to the measurement of productive efficiency in the service sector. In addition, they highlight the fact that while the DEA approach does not require a pre-specified standard against which to benchmark the performance measurements pertaining to an individual port or terminal, such standards can be incorporated into the analysis should this be desirable. This latter characteristic is particularly important in countering the argument that the weights estimated by DEA might be either misleading or, indeed, fundamentally wrong as a result of the possibility that they may be different from some prior knowledge or widely-accepted views on the relative values of the inputs or outputs.[66]

Martinez-Budria et al.[67] use DEA to analyse the relative efficiency of the Spanish Port Authorities over the period 1993–1997. The methodology as they apply it involves the classification of the different ports within the sample into three categories according to their "complexity". This classification system would appear to be highly correlated to the size and/or throughput of the ports considered in the analysis. The results of the analysis reveal that the three groupings followed three distinct evolutionary paths in terms of relative efficiency. The most "complex" ports (i.e., roughly equating to those of largest size and throughput) display the highest levels of efficiency in absolute terms and a high growth rate in efficiency over time. Ports in the medium level of "complexity" category displayed only low levels of efficiency growth over the sample period, while ports of low "complexity" actually yielded a negative trend in relative efficiency levels during the period under study. This seems to suggest that not only are there significant economies of scale to be reaped in port operation, but also that this and other factors may be contributing to a concentration of cargo throughput in larger ports. It can also be inferred that the diminishing role of the smaller ports has an adverse impact upon their relative efficiency levels that, in turn, creates a vicious circle of cargo diversion away from this group of ports. By analysing the value of the slack variables to emerge from solving the DEA Linear Programming problem, this study found that the worst source of inefficiencies were, in general, due to excess capacities.

Tongzon[68] applies DEA to deriving efficiency measurements for four Australian and twelve other international container ports. This cross-sectional efficiency analysis incorporates two output and six input variables, the data for which was collected for the year 1996. The output variables are cargo throughput and ship working rate, where the former is the total number of containers loaded and unloaded in TEUs and the latter is a measure of the number of containers moved per working hour. The input variables considered in the analysis were the number of cranes, number of container berths, number of tugs, terminal area, delay time (the difference between total berth time plus time waiting to berth and the time between the start and finish of ship working) and the number of port authority employees (as a proxy for the labour factor input).

Without precise *a priori* information or assumptions on the returns to scale of the port production function, two sets of results – for the CCR and Additive DEA models – are presented and discussed. A comparison of the results reveals that the CCR model identifies slightly more inefficient ports (6 v. 3) than the Additive model. As the author points out, this is not a surprising result as the CCR model assumes constant returns to scale, while the Additive model is based on the assumption of returns to scale that are variable. In consequence, the latter will require a larger number of ports to define the non-linear efficiency frontier.

The results of the initial analysis seemed to suggest that the model was over-specified for the sample size, i.e., that the sample data were insufficient to estimate a meaningful frontier. Since it was impossible to increase the sample size for the study, a solution was to reduce the number of output variables considered down to just one; the number of TEUs handled. The results of the DEA analysis using only one output identified Melbourne, Rotterdam, Yokohama and Osaka as inefficient with both the Additive and CCR models. Felixstowe, Sydney, Fremantle, Brisbane, Tilbury and La Spezia were identified as efficient using the Additive model, but as inefficient under the assumption of constant returns to scale that is implicit in the CCR model.

The four ports judged to be inefficient with both DEA models have opposite characteristics in terms of size and function. The port of Melbourne is quite small relative to Rotterdam. The port of Rotterdam is a hub port, while the ports of Melbourne, Yokohama and Osaka generate most of their cargo internally. The findings imply, therefore, that the technical efficiency of this sample of ports does not depend solely upon size or function. The ports of Hong Kong, Singapore, Hamburg, Keelung, Zeebrugge and Tanjung Priok are found to be efficient irrespective of the returns to scale assumption and number of outputs employed in the analysis. Similarly, this seems to indicate (at least for the sample under study) that port size or function alone is not the primary determinant of port efficiency. The enormous slack variable values deduced for the terminal area and labour inputs for the ports of Melbourne, Sydney and Fremantle confirm the particular need, according to the author, for the government of Australia to refocus its waterfront reform initiatives as an essential step towards improving port efficiency.

Valentine and Gray[69] use DEA to analyse data relating to a sample of thirty-one container ports from the top 100 container ports for the year 1998. This analysis yielded an efficiency measure for each of the ports in the sample, which the authors then compared to the port's ownership and organisational structures. It is suggested that the gap between the top three ports that are deemed to be efficient (Hong Kong, Singapore and Santos) and Houston in fourth place is quite considerable and that the reason for this may be that while the top three concentrate on the handling of container traffic, the other ports in the study seem to diversify substantially into the handling of other types of cargo.

The main objective of the study is to compare the efficiency ratings that are derived from the application of DEA to the categorisation of the sample ports into different forms of ownership and organisational structures. To this end, the study concludes that the most efficient form of organisational structure (as assigned to individual ports on the basis of the output from a cluster analysis) is the *simple structure* (as defined in Mintzberg[70]). On the other hand, the study finds that the ownership structure does not seem to have any significant influence upon efficiency; a conclusion that contradicts that of Cullinane and Song.[71] The authors also suggest that predictions can also be made on the performance of a port by examining its organisational chart to determine which of the Mintzberg categories is applicable and also its likely associated efficiency rating.

No details of the precise model form employed for the analysis are given. However, because only three ports (Hong Kong, Singapore and Santos) were found to be efficient, it is probably safe to assume that the linear CCR model was utilised. Since most studies of returns to scale in ports have found that significant scale economies are present, perhaps the utilisation of the BCC or Additive model for the analysis of this data might provide an interesting extension of the research.

6. THE STOCHASTIC FRONTIER MODEL*

6.1 Method

As has already been stated and as in the case of DEA, the econometric approach to efficiency measurement is also based on utilising the concept of an efficient frontier. The econometric approach, however, involves the specification of a parametric representation of technology. The early parametric frontier models[73–74] are deterministic in the sense that all DMUs share a common fixed and pre-determined class of frontier. This is unreasonable and ignores the real possibility that the observed performance of the DMU may be affected by exogenous (i.e., random shock) as well as endogenous (i.e. inefficiency) factors. The fact that there is no allowance for the possible influence of statistical noise is also widely regarded to be the most serious limitation of DEA.[75] To allocate all influential factors, whether favourable or unfavourable and whether under or beyond the control of the DMU (i.e., either endogenous or exogenous), into a single disturbance term and to refer to the mixture as inefficiency is clearly a dubious and imprecise generalisation.

As an alternative, the now much more widely applied stochastic frontier model is motivated by the idea that deviations from the production frontier might not be entirely under the control of the economic unit being studied.[76] Both Aigner et al.[77] and Meeusen and van den Broeck[78] independently constructed a more reasonable error structure than a purely one-sided one. They considered a linear model for the frontier production function as follows:

$$Y_{it} = f(X_{it}; \beta) \exp(\varepsilon_{it}), i = 1, 2, ..., N; t = 1, 2, ..., T \qquad (10)$$

...where Y_{it} denotes the appropriate form of output for the ith DMU at time t, X_{it} is a vector of inputs associated with the ith DMU at time t and β is a vector of input coefficients for the associated independent variables in the production function. Their disturbance term ε consists of the following two parts:

$$\varepsilon_{it} = v_{it} - u_{it} \qquad (11)$$

The component v_{it} represents a *symmetric disturbance term* permitting random variation of the production function across economic units due not only to the effects of measurement and specification error, but also due to the effects of

---

* This section represents a summary of the theoretical background to the analysis undertaken in Song, Cullinane and Roe.[72]

exogenous shock beyond the control of the economic unit (e.g., weather conditions, geography or machine performance). The other component u_{it} (≥ 0) is a *one-sided disturbance term* and represents "productive inefficiency" relative to the stochastic production function. The non-negative disturbance u_{it} reflects the fact that output lies on or below its frontier. The deviation of an observation from the deterministic kernel of the stochastic production function (equation 10) arises from two sources: (i) symmetric random variation of the deterministic kernel $f(X_{it}; \beta)$ across observations that is captured by the component v_{it}, and (ii) asymmetric variation (or productive inefficiency) captured by the component u_{it}. The term u_{it} measures productive inefficiency in the sense that it measures the shortfall of output Y_{it} from that implied by its maximum frontier given by $f(X_{it}; \beta) \exp(v_{it})$. The measure of a DMU's efficiency should be defined, therefore, by:

$$\frac{Y_{it}}{f(X_{it}; \beta) \exp(v_{it})} \qquad (12)$$

… relative to the stochastic frontier $f(X; \beta) \exp(v)$.

Nevertheless, any estimate of a DMU's efficiency level is not consistent, as it contains statistical noise as well as productive inefficiency. In addition, stochastic frontier models suffer from two other difficulties. One is the requirement of specific assumptions about the distributions underlying productive inefficiency (e.g., half-normal and exponential) and statistical noise (e.g., normal). The other is the required assumption that regressors (the input variables contained in the vector X) and productive inefficiency are independent. This may well be an unrealistic assumption since if a DMU knows its level of inefficiency, then this should affect its input choices as it attempts to address the problem. Figure

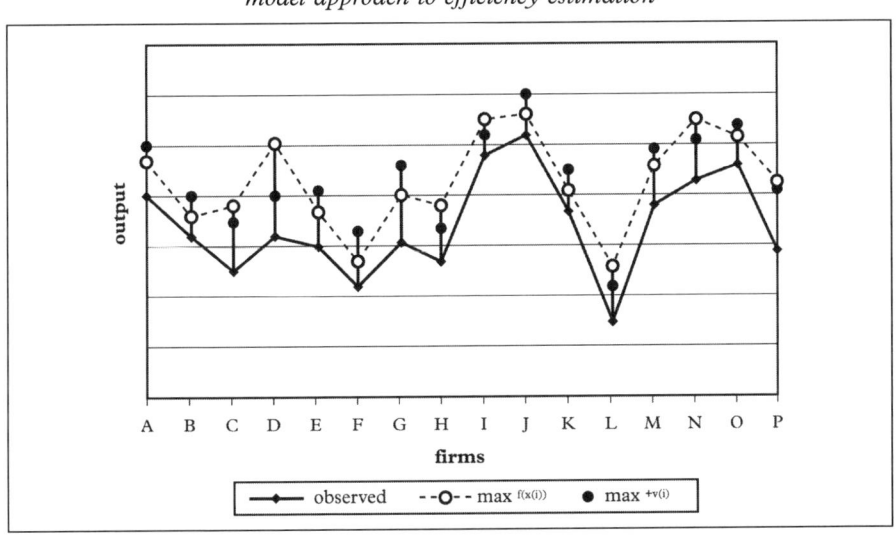

Figure 5: A conceptual representation of the stochastic frontier model approach to efficiency estimation

5 is a graphical representation of the basic idea that underpins stochastic frontier model estimates of productive (technical) efficiency.

A further development in the modelling of frontiers lies with the use of estimation techniques that involve panel data. Initially, the stochastic frontier model (10) was developed for cross-sectional data. Hausman and Taylor,[79] Baltagi[80] and Blundell[81] list a number of attractive features of using panel data, one of which is that panel data allows for the control of individual effects which may be correlated with other variables included in the specification of an economic relationship, thus making the analysis of relative efficiency on the basis of single cross-sections extremely difficult.

With respect to the frontier model, consistent estimates of the productive efficiency of a DMU can be obtained as the number of time periods tends to infinity. As a result, strong distributional assumptions are not necessary. Moreover, the parameters and the DMU's level of efficiency can be estimated without assuming that the input variables are uncorrelated with productive inefficiency. Therefore, as Schmidt and Sickles[82] note, a variety of different estimates will be considered, depending on what the analyst is willing to assume about the distribution of productive inefficiency and its potential correlation with the regressors.

Initially, it was claimed that productive efficiencies for individual DMUs could not be estimated and predicted. In an effort to explore this unresolved problem with the previous models, along with attempting to reap the benefits of the aforementioned advantages of panel data, Pitt and Lee[83] were the first to develop techniques using panel data to estimate the frontier production function. Jondrow et al.[84] presented two estimators (i.e., for half-normal and exponential cases) for the DMU-specific effect for an individual DMU under the assumption that the parameters of the frontier production function were known and cross-sectional data were available for given sample DMUs. Schmidt and Sickles[85] suggested three different estimators for individual DMU effects and productive efficiencies for panel data.

A major breakthrough in the area of panel data models was achieved by Battese and Coelli,[86] who presented a generalisation of the results of Jondrow et al.[87] on the assumption of a more general distribution for DMU effects to be applied to the stochastic frontier model. Their model is given by:

$$Y_{it} = f(X_{it}; \beta) \exp(v_{it} - u_i), i = 1, 2, \ldots, N; t = 1, 2, \ldots, T \quad (13)$$

The main difference between models (10) and (13) is the absence of the subscript t associated with u in the latter. Thus, u captures DMU-specific time-invariant variables omitted from the previous function. The symmetric terms v_{it} are assumed to be identically and independently normally distributed with mean zero and variance σ_v^2, i.e., $v_{it} \sim N(0, \sigma_v^2)$. The one-sided terms u_i (≥ 0) are assumed to be identically and independently distributed non-negative random variables which capture a DMU effect but no *time* effect.[88] In addition, the error terms v_{it} and u_i are assumed to be independently distributed of the input variables as well as of one another.

The most frequently defined distribution for the u_i is the half-normal (i.e., $u_i \sim |N(0, \sigma_u^2)|$) though other distributional assumptions for the u_i terms have been proposed by several researchers. For example, the exponential,[89] the truncated normal[90] and the gamma.[91]

As far as the productive efficiency of a DMU is concerned, Battese and Coelli[92] define it as the ratio of the DMU's mean production, given its realised DMU-specific effect, to the corresponding mean production with the DMU effect being equivalent to zero. The productive efficiency of the ith DMU (PE_i) is defined, therefore, as:

$$PE_i = \frac{E(Y_{it}|u_i, X_{it})}{E(Y_{it}^*|u_i = 0, X_{it})} \qquad (14)$$

…where Y_{it}^* represents the output of production for the ith DMU at time t, and the value of the PE_i lies between zero and one ($0 \leq PE_i \leq 1$). If a DMU's productive efficiency is calculated as 0.65, for example, then this implies that, on average, the DMU realises 65% of the production possible for a fully efficient DMU having comparable input values. From the perspective of efficiency measurement, the definition contained in equation (14) has a thread of connection with that of equation (12).

If the model (13) is transformed to a logarithm of a production function, such as:

$$\ln Y_{it} = \ln f(X_{it}; \beta) + v_{it} - u_i \qquad (15)$$

then the measure of productive efficiency for the ith DMU is defined by:

$$PE_i = \exp(-u_i) \qquad (16)$$

The measure shown in equation (16) does not depend on the level of the input variables for the DMU, while the definition provided by equation (14) for calculating the productive efficiency of a DMU clearly shows that its estimation depends significantly on inferences concerning the distribution function of the unobservable DMU effect u_i, given the sample observations.

This technique is relevant to a case where productive efficiency is time-invariant. Schmidt,[93] however, states that unchanging inefficiency over time is not a particularly attractive assumption; a criticism which is readily admitted by Battese and Coelli. With the assumption that productive efficiency does vary over time, an alternative approach has been adopted by econometricians such as Cornwell et al.[94] and Kumbhakar.[95] None of these studies succeed, however, in completely separating inefficiency from individual DMU effects[96] and, in any case, the methods proposed thus far are too complicated for empirical application.[97]

6.2 Applications

Liu[98] sets out to test the hypothesis that public sector ports are inherently less efficient than those in the private-sector. A unique set of panel data relating to the outputs and inputs of 28 commercially important UK ports over the period 1983 to 1990 is collected for analysis. Ownership is hypothesised as a potential factor input to the frontier production function and the effect of its presence on inter-port efficiency differences is investigated by applying the stochastic frontier model to derive the required efficiency estimates.

The results reveal that the efficiency difference between ports in the public versus the private sector is negligible and insignificant between trust and municipal ports on the one hand (the public sector) and private ports on the other. Capital intensity is found to have little relationship to efficiency and the impact of size is found to have a small, but significant, impact. Taken together with the scale elasticity that is estimated as part of the analysis, this is not really supportive of the expectation that substantial economies of scale exist within the sector. A peculiarity of this analysis of the UK situation is that port location was discovered to be a significant influence on efficiency, with ports on the west coast of the UK (i.e., on what many shipping commentators have described as the "wrong" side of the country) being 11% less efficient, on average, than the rest of the sample.

Notteboom, Coeck and van den Broeck[99] apply a Bayesian approach based on Monte-Carlo approximation to the estimation of a stochastic frontier model aimed at assessing the productive efficiency of a sample of 36 European container terminals located in the Hamburg–Le Havre range and in the Western Mediterranean. The data analysed relates to 1994. The robustness and validity of the estimated model is tested by comparing the results with those of four benchmark terminals in Asia (Singapore, Kaohsiung and Hong Kong's MTL and HIT terminals).

This study found that ten of the terminals, including all four Asian terminals, have efficiency levels of about 80%, with the majority of ports in the Hamburg–Le Havre range falling into the 75%–80% efficiency category. The Belgian container terminals were found to be some of the most efficient in the sample, as were the Spanish terminals included in the analysis. Container terminals in Italy were generally found to be the most inefficient. The results also suggested that small terminals do tend to be less efficient than large ones, although a more thorough secondary analysis revealed that small terminals located in large ports are, in general, more efficient than small terminals located in smaller ports.

Several relationships can be inferred from the results of this study. For instance, situations where intra-port competition is formidable (with no single terminal predominant) seem to have a positive effect upon average terminal efficiency within the port. In addition, hub ports tend to be more productively efficient than typical feeder ports. However, whether the terminal is publicly or privately owned seems to have no bearing upon the level of efficiency derived. Finally, terminals in the North of Europe were found to be generally more efficient than those in the South of Europe. All of these relationships were investigated, however, on an individual basis and no insight was gained into the potential impact of joint effects. This would appear to constitute, therefore, an interesting avenue for the extension of this research.

Coto-Millan, Banos-Pino and Rodriguez-Alvarez[100] applied a stochastic frontier model to estimate the economic efficiency of 27 Spanish ports. Panel data for the period 1985–1989 was collected and analysed using the Cobb-Douglas and translog versions of the model. The study finds that the translog version of the stochastic frontier model best represents the level of technology within the industry. Quite surprisingly, it appears *prima facie* that large ports are found to be rather more economically inefficient than their smaller counterparts, despite the fact that the analysis also reveals the simultaneous existence of significant scale economies within the sector. Indeed, in order of efficiency, the top five positions are occupied by the smallest ports, while the worst five in the efficiency rankings are relatively the largest ports with the greatest degree of autonomy. A more detailed second-stage analysis of the findings, however, reveals that it is not really size which explains the levels of economic efficiency that have resulted from the analysis. Rather, it is the degree of autonomy in management that is the critical determining factor, with those ports that are highly autonomous being less efficient than the rest. Technical progress was ascertained to be insignificant over the period covered by the analysis.

Cullinane and Song[101] assess the success achieved by Korea's port privatisation policies in increasing the productive efficiency of its container terminals. The UK container terminal sector provides a useful benchmark for comparison since privatisation and deregulation have formed an integral part of UK port reforms for nearly twenty years and the effect on efficiency, having had time to mature, is much easier to gauge. The stochastic frontier model is justified as the chosen methodology for estimating productive efficiency levels and is applied to cross-sectional data under a variety of distributional assumptions. A panel data model is also estimated. Results are consistent and suggest that: (1) the degree of private sector involvement in sample container terminals is positively related to productive efficiency, and (2) improved productive efficiency has followed the implementation of privatisation and deregulation policies within the Korean port sector. Even though not categorical, these conclusions are important because the market for container throughput is internationally competitive and if policies which promote competition between Korean container terminals lead to greater productive efficiency, this will inevitably make the sector as a whole more competitive internationally.

Cullinane, Song and Gray[102] use the "port function matrix" due to Baird[103] to analyse the administrative and ownership structures of major container ports in Asia. The relative efficiency of these ports is then assessed using the cross-sectional and panel data versions of the stochastic frontier model. The estimated efficiency measures are broadly similar for the two versions of the model tested. From the results of the analysis, it is concluded that the size of a port or terminal is closely correlated with its efficiency and that some support exists for the claim that the transformation of ownership from public to private sector improves economic efficiency. It is concluded that while this does provide some justification for the many programmes in Asian ports that aim to attract private capital into both existing and new facilities, it is also the case that the level of market deregulation is an important intervening variable that may also exert a positive influence on efficiency levels.

7. CONCLUDING REMARKS

This chapter has defined the fundamental nature of port productivity and efficiency and, in so doing, has reinforced the difference between them. It has also illustrated the development of practically-oriented research into the measurement of port and/or terminal productivity and efficiency. From this presentation, it is clear that the development of applications to the port sector has mirrored, and progressed with, the theoretical development of techniques for productivity and efficiency assessment. In particular, over the past five years or so, there has been a mushrooming of applications to ports and terminals that utilise either DEA or stochastic frontier models. It should be emphasised, however, that since both approaches have their own unique pros and cons, there can be no clear-cut "best" method for deriving efficiency estimates for the sector.

What is very clear-cut, however, is the continued critical need for efficiency estimation and partial productivity comparison into the future. The continuous monitoring of comparative measures of performance (in all relevant forms) will become pivotal to the successful management of port and terminal operations. The pressure for this will come from the relentless trend towards ever-greater competition, both in the inter-port and intra-port contexts; a characteristic of the contemporary port industry that is unlikely to cease in the short- to medium-term.

Where comprehensive information on port productivity and efficiency is available, there are also significant advantages accruing to the formulation of macroeconomic policies. At this point in time, the most relevant use to which such information may be put is to deciding on national port planning issues, including the likely effectiveness of port privatisation policies.

Finally, it is important to bear in mind that port productivity and efficiency cannot be assessed and judged in isolation. While such measures do play a major role in the evaluation of service quality, it is also the case that quality comes at a price. As such, port charges need to be evaluated within the context of the quality of service that is being offered by a port. This is increasingly becoming an inherent feature of the cargo-handling industry, particularly the container sector, as the objective of service differentiation amongst ports has been largely replaced by the desire to minimise costs. Eventually, it will displace the current vogue for focusing, to the exclusion of all other considerations, on the productivity/efficiency aspects of port operations. In this sense, the issue of balance in the price-productivity trade-off will replace the current tendency (amongst academics and industry pundits alike) for a focus solely on efficiency, in much the same way that this current fashion replaced the previous focus on port pricing which was especially prevalent at that time in the history of port development just subsequent to the implementation of the major phases in port privatisation. In the future, therefore, price-productivity trade-offs and the development of incentive-based contracts for cargo handling services in ports may well emerge as the urgent issues of the day.

ACKNOWLEDGEMENTS

The author would like to express his gratitude to the editor, Professor Costas Grammenos, for his long-running support and his patience in awaiting the delivery of this chapter. Thanks are also due to Dr Dong-Wook Song for many years of successful, stimulating and fulfilling research collaboration in the area of port privatisation and efficiency. The contribution of Wang Teng-Fei in providing valuable assistance to the author in collecting source materials should also be acknowledged.

ENDNOTES

1. Coelli, T., Prasada Rao, D.S., and Battese, G.E. (1998): *An Introduction to Efficiency and Productivity Analysis* (Boston, Kluwer Academic Publishers).
2. De Monie, G. (1987): *Measuring and Evaluating Port Performance and Productivity*, UNCTAD Monograph No. 6 on Port Management (Geneva, UNCTAD).
3. Dowd, T., and Leschine, T. (1990): "Container Terminal Productivity: A Perspective", *Maritime Policy and Management*, 17(2), pp. 107–112.
4. Cullinane, K.P.B., and Song, D.-W. (2002): "A Stochastic Frontier Model of the Productive Efficiency of Korean Container Terminals", *Applied Economics*, forthcoming.
5. Bendall, H., and Stent, A. (1987): "On Measuring Cargo Handling Productivity", *Maritime Policy and Management*, 14(4), pp. 337–343.
6. Tabernacle, J.B. (1995): "A Study of the Changes in Perfromance of Quayside Container Cranes", *Maritime Policy and Management*, 22(2) pp. 115–124.
7. Ashar, A. (1997): "Counting the Moves", *Port Development International*, November, pp. 25–29.
8. De Monie, G. (1987): *Measuring and Evaluating Port Performance and Productivity*, UNCTAD Monograph No. 6 on Port Management (Geneva, UNCTAD).
9. Talley, W. (1988): "Optimum Throughput and Performance Evaluation of Marine Terminals", *Maritime Policy and Management*, 15(4), pp. 327–331.
10. Dowd, T., and Leschine, T. (1990): "Container Terminal Productivity: A Perspective", *Maritime Policy and Management*, 17(2), pp. 107–112.
11. De Neufville, R., and Tsunokawa, K. (1981): "Productivity and Returns to Scale of Container Ports", *Maritime Policy and Management*, 8(2), pp. 121–129.
12. Kim, M., and Sachish, A. (1986): "The Structure of Production, Technical Change and Productivity in a Port", *Journal of Industrial Economics*, 35(2), pp. 209–223.
13. Tongzon, J. (1995): "Determinants of Port Performance and Efficiency", *Transportation Research*, 29A(3), pp. 245–252.
14. Chang, S. (1978): "Production Function, Productivities and Capacity Utilisation of the Port of Mobile", *Maritime Policy and Management*, 5, pp. 297–305.
15. De Neufville, R., and Tsunokawa, K. (1981): "Productivity and Returns to Scale of Container Ports", *Maritime Policy and Management*, 8(2), pp. 121–129.
16. Suykens, F. (1983): "A Few Observations on Productivity in Seaports", *Maritime Policy and Management*, 10(1), pp. 17–40.
17. Tongzon, J.L., and Ganesalingam, S. (1994): "An Evaluation of ASEAN Port Performance and Efficiency", *Asian Economic Journal*, 8(3), pp. 317–330.
18. Tongzon, J.L. (1995a): "Systematizing International benchmarking for Ports", *Maritime Policy and Management*, 22(2), pp. 171–177.
19. Ashar, A. (1997): "Counting the Moves", *Port Development International*, November, pp. 25–29.

20. Goss, R. (1990): "Economic Policies and Seaports: 2. The Diversity of Port Policies", *Maritime Policy and Management*, 17(3), pp. 221–234.
21. Braeutigam, R., Daughety, A., and Turnquist, M. (1984): "A Firm Specific Analysis of Economies of Density in the US Railroad Industry", *Journal of Industrial Economics*, 33, pp. 3–20.
22. Kim, M., and Sachish, A. (1986): "The Structure of Production, Technical Change and Productivity in a Port", *Journal of Industrial Economics*, 35(2), pp. 209–223.
23. Tongzon, J.L., and Ganesalingam, S. (1994): "An Evaluation of ASEAN Port Performance and Efficiency", *Asian Economic Journal*, 8(3), pp. 317–330.
24. Frankel, E.G. (1991): "Port Performance and Productivity Measurement", *Ports and Harbors*, October, pp. 11–13.
25. Chapon, J. (1974): *Comment Définir une Politique Portuaire* (Trieste, France).
26. Robinson, R. (1978): "Size of Vessels and Turnround Time: Further Evidence from the Port of Hong Kong", *Journal of Transport Economics and Policy*, 12(2), pp. 161–178.
27. Edmond, E.D., and Maggs, R.P. (1987): "Container Ship Turnround Time at UK Ports", *Maritime Policy and Management*, 14(1), pp. 3–19.
28. Suykens, F. (1983): "A Few Observations on Productivity in Seaports", *Maritime Policy and Management*, 10(1), pp. 17–40.
29. Dowd, T., and Leschine, T. (1990): "Container Terminal Productivity: A Perspective", *Maritime Policy and Management*, 17(2), pp. 107–112.
30. De Neufville, R., and Tsunokawa, K. (1981): "Productivity and Returns to Scale of Container Ports", *Maritime Policy and Management*, 8(2), pp. 121–129.
31. Bauer, P. (1990): "Recent Developments in the Econometric Estimation of Frontiers", *Journal of Econometrics*, 46, pp. 39–56.
32. Farrell, M. (1957): "The Measurement of Productive Efficiency", *Journal of the Royal Statistical Society*, 120(3), pp. 253–290.
33. Aigner, D., and Schmidt, P. (1980): "Specification and Estimation of Frontier Production, Profit and Cost Functions", Editors' Introduction, *Journal of Econometrics*, Supplement to the Journal of Econometrics, 13, pp. 1–3.
34. Fare, R., Grosskopf, S., and Lovell, C. (1994): *Production Frontiers* (Cambridge, Cambridge University Press).
35. Lovell, C. (1995): "Econometric Efficiency Analysis: A Policy-Oriented Review", *European Journal of Operational Research*, 80(3), pp. 452–462.
36. Gong, B.H., and Sickles, R. (1992): "Finite Sample Evidence on the Performance of Stochastic Frontiers and Data Envelopment Analysis using Panel Data", *Journal of Econometrics*, 51, pp. 259–284.
37. Yu, C. (1995): "A Comparative Study of Alternative Methods for Efficiency Measurement with Applications to Transportation Industry", unpublished Ph.D. Dissertation, University of British Columbia, BC, Canada.
38. Oum, T.H., and Waters, W. (1996): "A Survey of Recent Development in Transportation Cost Function Research", *Logistics and Transportation Review*, 32(4), pp. 423–463.
39. Forsund, F., Lovell, C., and Schmidt, P. (1980): "A Survey of Frontier Production Functions and of their Relationship to Efficiency Measurement", *Journal of Econometrics*, 13, pp. 5–25.
40. Pitt, M., and Lee, L. (1981): "The Measurement and Sources of Technical Efficiency in the Indonesian Weaving Industry", *Journal of Development Economics*, 9, pp. 43–64.
41. Seiford, L.M. (1996): "Data Envelopment Analysis: The Evolution of the State of the Art (1978–1995)", *Journal of Productivity Analysis*, Vol. 7, pp. 99–137.
42. Sarafoglou, N. (1998): "The Most Influential DEA Publications: A Comment on *Seiford*", *Journal of Productivity Analysis*, Vol. 9, pp. 279–281.
43. Charnes, A., Cooper, W.W., Lewin, A.Y., and Seiford, L.M. (1994): *Data Envelopment Analysis: Theory, Methodology and Application* (Boston, Kluwer Academic Publishers).

44. Forsund, F.R., and Sarafoglou, N. (2002): "On the Origins of Data Envelopment Analysis", *Journal of Productivity Analysis*, Vol. 17, pp. 23–40.
45. Charnes, A., Cooper, W.W., and Rhodes, E. (1978): "Measuring the Efficiency of Decision Making Units", *European Journal of Operational Research*, Vol. 2, pp. 429-444.
46. Forsund, F.R., and Sarafoglou, N. (2002): "On the Origins of Data Envelopment Analysis", *Journal of Productivity Analysis*, Vol. 17, pp. 23–40.
47. Charnes, A., Cooper, W.W., and Rhodes, E. (1978): "Measuring the Efficiency of Decision Making Units", *European Journal of Operational Research*, Vol. 2, pp. 429-444.
48. Thanassoulis, E. (2001): *Introduction to Theory and Application of Data Envelopment Analysis* (Boston, Kluwer Academic Publishers).
49. Cooper, W.W., Seiford, L.M., and Tone, K. (2000): *Data Envelopment Analysis: A Comprehensive Text with Models, Applications, References and DEA-Solver Software* (Boston, Kluwer Academic Publishers).
50. Robinson, R. (1978): "Size of Vessels and Turnround Time: Further Evidence from the Port of Hong Kong", *Journal of Transport Economics and Policy*, 12(2), pp. 161-178.
51. Tabernacle, J.B. (1995): "A Study of the Changes in Perfromance of Quayside Container Cranes", *Maritime Policy and Management*, 22(2) pp. 115-124.
52. Cullinane; K.P.B., and Khanna, M. (1999): "Economies of Scale in Large Container Ships", *Journal of Transport Economics and Policy*, 33(2), pp. 185-208.
53. Banker, R.D., Charnes, A., and Cooper, W.W. (1984): "Some Models for Estimating Technical and Scale Inefficiencies in Data Envelopment Analysis", *Management Science*, 30, pp. 1078-1092.
54. Oum, T.H., and Waters, W.G., and Yu, C.Y. (1999): "A Survey of Productivity and Efficiency Measurement in Rail Transport", *Journal of Transport Economics and Policy*, Vol. 33, No. 1, pp. 9–42.
55. De Borger, B., Kerstens, K., and Costa, A. (2002): "Public Transit Performance: What does One Learn from Frontier Studies", *Transport Reviews*, Vol. 22, No. 1, pp. 1–38.
56. Gillen, D., and Lall, A. (1997): "Developing Measures of Airport Productivity and Performance: An Application of Data Envelopment Analysis", *Transportation Research E*, Vol. 33, No. 4, pp. 261–273.
57. De La Cruz, F.S. (1999): "A DEA Approach to the Airport Production Frontier", *International Journal of Transport Economics*, Vol. 26, No. 2, pp. 255–270.
58. Sarkis, J. (2000): "An analysis of the Operational Efficiency of Major Airports in the United States", *Journal of Operations Management*, Vol. 18, pp. 335-351.
59. Adler, N., and Berechman, J. (2001): "Measuring Airport Quality from the Airlines' Viewpoint: An Application of Data Envelopment Analysis", *Transport Policy*, Vol. 8, pp. 171–181.
60. Adler, N., and Berechman, J. (2001): Airport Quality and the Hub Location Question, *Proceedings of the 9th World Conference on Transport Research*, 22–27 July, Seoul, South Korea.
61. Adler, N., and Golany, B. (2001): "Evaluation of Deregulated Airline Network Using Data Envelopment Analysis Combined with Principal Component Analysis with an Application to Western Europe", *European Journal of Operational Research*, Vol. 132, pp. 260–273.
62. Fernandes, E., and Pacheco, R.R. (2002): "Efficient Use of Airport Capacity", *Transportation Research A*, 36A(3), pp. 225–238.
63. Thanassoulis, E. (2001): *Introduction to Theory and Application of Data Envelopment Analysis* (Boston, Kluwer Academic Publishers).
64. Ashar, A., Stopher, P., and Appfel, C. (1994): "Defining Performance Measures for an Intermodal Management System", *Journal of Transportation Research Forum*, November.
65. Roll, Y., and Hayuth, Y. (1993): "Port Performance Comparison Applying Data Envelopment Analysis (DEA)", *Maritime Policy and Management*, 20(2), pp. 153–161.

66. Allen, R., Athanassopoulos, A., Dyson, R.G., and Thanassoulis, E. (1997): "Weights Restrictions and Value Judgements in Data Envelopment Analysis: Evolution, Development and Future Directions", *Annals of Operational Research*, Vol. 73, pp. 13–34.
67. Martinez-Budria, E., Diaz-Armas, R., Navarro-Ibanez, M., and Ravelo-Mesa, T. (1999): "A study of the Efficiency of Spanish port authorities using Data Envelopment Analysis", *International Journal of Transport Economics*, Vol. XXVI, No. 2, June.
68. Tongzon, J. (2001): "Efficiency Measurement of Selected Australian and other International Ports using Data Envelopment Analysis", *Transportation Research*, 35A(2), pp. 107–122.
69. Valentine, V.F., and Gray, R. (2001): The Measurement of Port Efficiency Using Data Envelopment Analysis, *Proceedings of the 9th World Conference on Transport Research*, 22-27 July, Seoul, South Korea.
70. Mintzberg, H. (1979): *The Structuring of Organizations* (Englewood Cliffs, New Jersey, Prentice-Hall).
71. Cullinane, K.P.B., and Song, D.-W. (2002): "A Stochastic Frontier Model of the Productive Efficiency of Korean Container Terminals", *Applied Economics*, forthcoming.
72. Song, D.-W., Cullinane, K.P.B., and Roe, M. (2001): *The Productive Efficiency of Container Terminals: An Application to Korea and the UK* (UK, Ashgate).
73. Afriat, S. (1972): "Efficiency Estimation of Production Functions", *International Economic Review*, 13(3), pp. 568–598.
74. Aigner, D., and Chu, S. (1968): "On Estimating the Industry Production Function", *American Economic Review*, 58(4), pp. 826–839.
75. Ray, S.C. (2002): "William W. Cooper: A Legend in His Own Times", *Journal of Productivity Analysis*, Vol. 17, pp. 7–12.
76. Greene, W. (1993): "The Econometric Approach to Efficiency Analysis", in Fried, H., Lovell, C., and Schmidt, S. (eds.), *The Measurement of Productive Efficiency: Techniques and Applications* (New York, Oxford University Press), pp. 68–119.
77. Aigner, D., Lovell, C., and Schmidt, P. (1977): "Formulation and Estimation of Stochastic Frontier Production Function Models", *Journal of Econometrics*, 6(1), pp. 21–37.
78. Meeusen, W., and van den Broeck, J. (1977): "Efficiency Estimation from Cobb-Douglas Production Functions with Composed Error", *International Economic Review*, 18(2), pp. 435–444.
79. Hausman, J., and Taylor, W. (1981): "Panel Data and Unobserved Individual Effects", *Econometrica*, 49, pp. 1377–1398.
80. Baltagi, B. (1995): *Econometric Analysis of Panel Data* (Chichester, John Wiley & Sons).
81. Blundell, R. (1996): "Microeconometrics", in Greenaway, D., Bleaney, M., and Stewart, I. (eds.), *A Guide to Modern Economics* (London, Routledge), pp.508–536.
82. Schmidt, P., and Sickles, R. (1984): "Production Frontiers and Panel Data", *Journal of Business and Economic Statistics*, 2(4), pp. 367–374.
83. Pitt, M., and Lee, L. (1981): "The Measurement and Sources of Technical Efficiency in the Indonesian Weaving Industry", *Journal of Development Economics*, 9, pp. 43–64.
84. Jondrow, J., Lovell, C., Materov, I., and Schmidt, P. (1982): "On the Estimation of Technical Inefficiency in the Stochastic Frontier Production Model", *Journal of Econometrics*, 19, pp. 233–238.
85. Schmidt, P., and Sickles, R. (1984): "Production Frontiers and Panel Data", *Journal of Business and Economic Statistics*, 2(4), pp. 367–374.
86. Battese, G., and Coelli, T. (1988): "Prediction of Firm-Level Technical Efficiencies with a Generalised Frontier Production Function and Panel Data", *Journal of Econometrics*, 38, pp. 387–399.

87. Jondrow, J., Lovell, C., Materov, I., and Schmidt, P. (1982): "On the Estimation of Technical Inefficiency in the Stochastic Frontier Production Model", *Journal of Econometrics*, 19, pp. 233–238.
88. Schmidt, P., and Sickles, R. (1984): "Production Frontiers and Panel Data", *Journal of Business and Economic Statistics*, 2(4), pp. 367–374.
89. Aigner, D., Lovell, C., and Schmidt, P. (1977): "Formulation and Estimation of Stochastic Frontier Production Function Models", *Journal of Econometrics*, 6(1), pp. 21–37.
90. Stevenson, R. (1980): "Likelihood Functions for Generalised Stochastic Frontier Estimation", *Journal of Econometrics*, 13, pp. 57–66.
91. Greene, W. (1980): "Maximum Likelihood Estimation of Econometric Frontier Functions", *Journal of Econometrics*, 13, pp. 27–56.
92. Battese, G., and Coelli, T. (1988): "Prediction of Firm-Level Technical Efficiencies with a Generalised Frontier Production Function and Panel Data", *Journal of Econometrics*, 38, pp. 387–399.
93. Schmidt, P. (1985): "Frontier Production Functions", *Econometric Reviews*, 4, pp. 289–328.
94. Cornwell, C., Schmidt, P., and Sickles, R. (1990): "Production Frontiers with Cross-Sectional and Time-Series Variation in Efficiency Levels", *Journal of Econometrics*, 46, pp. 185–200.
95. Kumbhakar, S. (1990): "Production Frontiers, Panel Data, and Time-Varying Technical Inefficiency", *Journal of Econometrics*, 46, pp. 201–211.
96. Kumbhakar, S., and Hjalmarsson, L. (1993): "Technical Efficiency and Technical Progress in Swedish Dairy Farms", in Fried, H., Lovell, C., and Schmidt, S. (eds.), *The Measurement of Productive Efficiency: Techniques and Applications* (Oxford, Oxford University Press), pp. 256–270.
97. Ferrantino, M., and Ferrier, G. (1995): "The Technical Efficiency of Vacuum-Pan Sugar Industry of India: An Application of a Stochastic Frontier Production Function Using Panel Data", *European Journal of Operational Research*, 80, pp. 639–653.
98. Liu, Z. (1995): "The Comparative Performance of Public and Private Enterprises: The Case of British Ports", *Journal of Transport Economics and Policy*, 29(3), pp. 263–274.
99. Notteboom, T., Coeck, C., and van den Broeck, J. (2000): "Measuring and Explaining the Relative Efficiency of Container Terminals by means of Bayesian Stochastic Frontier Models", *International Journal of Maritime Economics*, 2(2), pp. 83–106.
100. Coto-Millan, P., Banos-Pino, J., and Rodriguez-Alvarez, A. (2000): "Economic Efficiency in Spanish Ports: Some Empirical Evidence", *Maritime Policy and Management*, 27(2), pp. 169–174.
101. Cullinane, K.P.B., and Song, D.-W. (2002): "A Stochastic Frontier Model of the Productive Efficiency of Korean Container Terminals", *Applied Economics*, forthcoming.
102. Cullinane, K.P.B., Song, D.-W., and Gray, R. (2002): "A Stochastic Frontier Model of the Efficiency of Major Container Terminals in Asia: Assessing the Influence of Administrative and Ownership Structures", *Transportation Research A*, 36(8), pp. 743–762.
103. Baird, A. (1997): Port Privatisation: An Analytical Framework, *Proceedings of International Association of Maritime Economist Conference*, 22–24 September, City University, London.

CHAPTER 36

THE ECONOMICS OF TRANSHIPMENT

Alfred J. Baird
Napier University, Edinburgh, Scotland, UK.
E-mail: a.baird@napier.ac.uk

1. INTRODUCTION

In academic circles, and within the container shipping industry generally, the debate as to whether direct call multiport or hub and spoke (i.e., transhipment) service schedules are superior has become more prominent, primarily as a result of increases in ship size. This paper compares and analyses costs associated with alternative transhipment and multiport options in northern Europe.

As part of a separate study, interim modelled costs were presented to six major carriers and five international container terminal operators and refined accordingly.[1] That study consisted of an investigation into the feasibility of a new "offshore" transhipment terminal in northern Europe. Subsequent clarification, confirmation and refinement of key assumptions aided by industry participation serves to reinforce the reliability, and hence generalisability of the results.

Traditionally, maritime economists, ports and shipping lines have considered container transhipment to be more expensive than direct call services, mainly by virtue of the extra feeder costs and container lift charges involved. This seems contrary to ongoing industry developments, with transhipment hubs now quite common in most major regions. Here, modelled costs for transhipment have been estimated and compared with an alternative multiport service. The conclusion is that transhipment can offer substantial operating and capital cost advantages compared with multiport direct call services. The explanation for transhipment advantages relates to diseconomies both at sea and in port associated with multiport style itineraries, coupled with container handling cost and productivity advantages pertaining to pure transhipment terminals, added to enhanced feedership economies of scale. In line with a move towards hub-hub shuttles and associated feeder services, these results indicate that further developments might be expected in regard to offshore transhipment hub terminals being provided as low-cost container transfer points for very large vessels. Policy makers need to be aware of the net benefits, both ecological and economic, resulting from increased use of offshore transhipment terminals as an alternative to continued artificial development (and duplication) of big ship container terminal capacity within constrained traditional port locations, and any requirement for support thereof.

The chapter contains three main sections. Section 2 discusses the transhipment versus multiport debate from a theoretical perspective. Section 3 then describes and analyses recent industry trends in this regard, while section 4 evaluates and compares the costs of transhipment with an alternative multiport strategy in the particular context of northern Europe.

2. THEORETICAL PERSPECTIVES

2.1 Multiport direct call versus hub/spoke debate

Since the early days of containerisation, the shipping and ports industry has considered a possible change from direct call or "multiport" itineraries in which large vessels call at several ports in the same region, to hub and spoke (i.e., transhipment) services. Hub and spoke networks are widely used in the intercontinental aviation business, with the standard Boeing 747 workhorse calling at major hub airports from where an extensive array of feeder services provides onward connections. It would be very difficult to imagine 747's calling at four or five airports at each end of a route, as is (still!) current practice in intercontinental container shipping, more especially in northern Europe.

Cullinane et al.[2] highlight a number of reasons for carriers continuing to provide direct call services using large container ships, including:

- feedership costs are much higher per TEU-mile than the cost of mainline ships, and
- scale economies in liner shipping are not quite as powerful as expected and are not totally lost by multiport calling.

However, pointing to the ongoing trend towards a higher proportion of transhipped containers, Cullinane et al. suggest that direct calls by mainline vessels are being rationalised as carriers seek higher levels of return from their assets. Yet the degree of load centering which would provide a lowest cost solution tends to be route specific, and it appears difficult to generalise for all trades.

Research by UK-based consultants MDS Transmodal[3] suggested multiport schedules are preferred because relatively large volumes of cargo can be shifted and big ships can be turned around in port in under one day (i.e., through only part loading in each port). According to MDS Transmodal, the costs of making a port call are fixed and relatively small compared to the cost of transhipment, provided the size of the container exchange is significant. MDS Transmodal's study, which favoured ports situated close to the English Channel (e.g., Southampton), did nevertheless conclude that the scope for transhipment was likely to grow in future as itineraries became more concentrated.

Traditionally, the degree of load centering or "hubbing" has therefore been determined by evaluating the trade-off between feeding and extra handling costs, and the extra costs of calling at an additional port.[4,5] Even very recently, maritime economists have again restated what almost seems to have become an inevitable view, that extra feeder and handling costs must make transhipment more expensive.[6]

However, the industry, or at least major carriers, appears to be moving in the opposite direction, as they select (and in some cases build) transhipment hubs, at which ever-larger vessels call. This therefore raises the question: has the general theoretical and academic literature concerning the direct call versus transhipment strategy been sufficient?

Reflecting what may have been in effect rather crude and unsophisticated approaches to this question, most previous work appears not to consider total roundtrip voyage costs for a multiport itinerary compared with a hub/spoke alternative. Such analysis has usually only taken account of the marginal change resulting from one port in a regional itinerary being substituted by a feeder service, and the resultant cost impacts of this.

One of the more detailed academic studies investigating container ship costs[7] considered end-to-end, round-the-world, and pendulum service types, all essentially involving multiport itineraries, but did not compare any of these service types with a hub and spoke alternative. A further study concluded that the hub-feeder system could only be competitive if there was a substantial percentage of containers on the deep-sea vessel that are not feedered (i.e., about 35–45%), but remain in the mainport for onward distribution by land.[8] Without this base cargo, the latter study suggested that double handling costs involved with feeder containers and the additional transport costs would outweigh the benefits of ultra large container carriers (albeit no detailed cost breakdown was presented to justify this conclusion).

In fact, there appears to have been very limited detailed empirical work carried out to compare the relative costs of multiport and hub/spoke itineraries, and more especially the substitution of several regional port calls (i.e., a regional multiport itinerary) with a single regional hub.

2.2 Increase in ship size

One reason for increased interest in hub and spoke service networks is the trend towards bigger ships. The major world trades are now dominated by post Panamax ships of 4,000–6,000 TEU and above.

Ship size is still increasing, and early in the new millennium ships of up to 10,000 TEU are anticipated.[9] Ishikawajima-Harima Heavy Industries has designed a 25-knot 10,000 TEU vessel using existing marine engines with a small and larger propeller on a single shaft. The ship would have a length of 346.6m, beam of 49.6m, and draught of 13.5m. Fuel consumption is put at around 240 tonnes per day. Other yards, including HDW and Samsung, have similar sized vessels on the drawing board.

There has been considerable speculation regarding how big containerships may become in future. In his analysis of ships up to 15,000 TEU capacity, McLellan[10] cautioned against continued upsizing suggesting that the size of the biggest ships would be likely to plateau due to physical restrictions in ports. Yet the number of new deep-water offshore hubs that have been developed over recent years (e.g., Freeport, Salalah, Taranto, etc.) means larger vessels can now be accommodated. Investigation by O'Mahony[11] also suggested that most of the port technical barriers to handling bigger ships (e.g., crane size/productivity, quay strength, etc.) could be overcome.

In a very detailed study, Cullinane et al.[12] modelled ship costs for the major east-west trades. Findings suggested that economies of scale are enjoyed for ship sizes of above 8,000 TEU on both the Europe-Far East and trans-Pacific trades, and for ship sizes of between 5,000–6,000 TEU on the shorter trans-Atlantic trade. The study also found that continued improvements in port productivity would serve to increase even further ship size optima for all routes. However, as with Lin's earlier work, these findings reflected existing liner multiport service itineraries and were not intended to make a comparison with hub and spoke alternatives.

Based on a survey of the top-30 liner operators, Baird[13] concluded that container ships with a loading capacity of somewhere between 10,000–15,000 TEU were expected to enter service before 2010. Such vessels, according to the survey, would be primarily designed to serve "offshore" transhipment mega-hubs, avoiding many traditional liner ports. These results echo the findings of De Monie.[14] In this sense, the term "offshore" is used to imply an island (e.g., Malta, Freeport) or remote peninsula (e.g., Taranto, Salalah) location for a transhipment hub, as opposed to a traditional seaport situated in an urban area (e.g., Hamburg, New York, Tokyo, etc.).

While recognising the many constraints to handling larger ships, Wijnolst[15] maintains that the ultimate ship size will be determined by the draught limitation of the Strait of Malacca. The draught limitation in question is 21 metres, from which Wijnolst deduced that a ship size of 18,000 TEU would become the maximum size. However, the motivation behind such analysis seemed to be more to do with strengthening the potential hub function of the port of Rotterdam, rather than the result of any informed economic evaluation. Indeed, taking the depth constraint of the Strait of Malacca as the main guide to future ship size might appear to some observers to be rather crude, especially from an economic perspective.

In any event, Evergreen's intended move toward a large 20-ship fleet of hub-hub shuttle vessels based on a ship size of just 4,000 TEU appears to reflect an industry heading entirely in the opposite direction to the Malacca-max concept.[16] This dichotomy suggests that a detailed total cost analysis needs to be undertaken to fully investigate whether large container ships operating different types of itineraries, such as multiport or hub/spoke, will indeed reduce the overall transport cost.[17,18]

In this respect a study by Gilman[19] concluded that continued mainline vessel direct calls at a Benelux, German, and UK port (i.e., a multiport itinerary), irrespective of ship size, would be far cheaper than a hub and spoke operation based on calling at just one of these ports. Gilman's investigation into containership size economies concluded that ships in the 6,000–10,000 TEU range operating traditional style (i.e., multiport) services would beat ships up to 15,000 TEU on limited hub and spoke itineraries "hands down".

This was not, however, the view of regional trade organisation ESCAP, the latter suggesting that the implications of increased ship size would be an even greater focus on the hub and spoke system, in which the biggest ships would call at only a limited number of very efficient ports on the main trunk routes, with other ports (including many major traditional ports) being linked by extended feeder networks.[20]

While Gilman did consider the daily cost of ship time both in port, and at sea, for various vessel sizes, he did not consider these costs in the context of the total roundtrip voyage, and then compare multiport costs with hub and spoke costs.[21] Such analysis really needs to be looked at from a total roundtrip perspective. In addition, it is also likely that productivity improvements may be greater in a terminal at which transhipment predominates, compared with a terminal used in a typical multiport itinerary. For example, this may be due to economies of organisation through improved coordination between mother and feeder vessels.[22] Further information has been obtained which confirms such an advantage exists, and this is discussed in more detail later in the paper.

3. CONTAINER INDUSTRY TRENDS AND DEVELOPMENTS

3.1 Impact of increased vessel size on ports

One of the most important trends affecting the deep-sea container shipping industry has been the positive increase in the size of vessels employed. Over the last 10 years the capacity of the largest container vessel in service has virtually doubled from around 4,500 TEU to 8,400 TEU. Speculation now surrounds the ordering of even larger vessels of 12,000 TEU (i.e., Suezmax) and possibly eventually up to 18,000 TEU (Malaccamax).

Table 1 presents design parameters of the current and future anticipated largest container ships. Current largest ships of 8,400 TEU have a length of 348m, beam of 42.8m and draught of 14m. Adding 10% for underkeel clearance, this implies a minimum channel depth required in port and alongside the berth of at least 15.4m. The squat phenomenon is also important in that such vessels may in fact reach 16.0m when sailing in shallow water, such as port channels.[23]

Moving up to 12,000 TEU ship size (expected before 2010), channel/berth draught requirement would increase to 18.74m, and for 18,000 TEU (beyond 2010) channel/berth depth required would be 23.1m.

The introduction of bigger ships therefore places additional burdens on ports to increase the depth of water in entrance channels and alongside berths, resulting in far greater investment in infrastructure. Channel width has also needed to be increased, as have turning circles to take account of greater vessel length and beam.

Modifications on the shoreside include bigger cranes, with longer outreach, lift height, and loading capacity. Current super post-Panamax cranes can weigh over 1,300 tonnes with greater wheel loads necessitating far stronger quay structures.

Table 1: Design parameters of largest container ships in service or envisaged

	Malaccamax	Suezmax	Sovereign Maersk
Length (m)	400.00	400.00	348.00
Breadth (m)	60.00	50.00	42.80
Draught (m)	21.00	17.04	14.00
Draught + 10% clearance (m)	23.10	18.74	15.40
Depth (m)	35.00	30.00	24.10
Displacement (Tonnes)	313,371	212,194	142,500
Deadweight (tonnes)	243,600	157,935	105,000
Light Ship (Tonnes)	70,771	54,259	37,500
TEU capacity	18,154	11,989	8,400
Service speed (kn)	25.00	25.00	25.00
Engine power (kW)	116,588	91,537	61,000

Source: Based on Waals & Wijnolst, 2001.[24]

Handling larger ships also has added implications for terminal storage space, plus impact on inland transport systems. Extensive road and rail facilities are a major consumer of port land plus on-terminal rail facilities result in increased container dwell time. To fully discharge and load a big ship at a port which is largely dependent on land access for containers:

"...generates a dilemma of unimaginable proportions for the terminal operator and requires huge areas of land for train marshalling and road gate facilities."[25]

To a large extent the latter provides sufficient justification for carriers to continue with multiport schedules in Northern Europe, or at least in the absence of any "offshore" transhipment hubs in the region at which a very large vessel could easily be "tipped" (i.e., fully discharged and loaded) with virtually zero landside impacts in the event of 100% transhipment.

Although all of these pressures inevitably have to be considered, probably the most significant factor to challenge traditional ports in the context of their capability to accommodate larger ships is sea access, and in particular vessel draught.

Indeed, only five of the major container ports in Northern Europe – Rotterdam, Hamburg, Antwerp, Felixstowe and Southampton – currently offer minimum water depth of 15.0m or above alongside the berth (see Table 2). However, of these only one port, Rotterdam, offers at least this depth in the entrance channel at LAT. This means that for all containerports in Northern Europe (except Rotterdam), there is already a tidal delay faced by the largest container vessels when entering or leaving port fully laden. As ships get even bigger this tidal delay is likely to worsen, adding to carrier costs.

Research by Ocean Shipping Consultants[26] offers rather similar conclusions as to the effect today's large containerships have placed on front-rank ports by virtue of their size, for example:

- major ports repeatedly find themselves being criticised for draught limitations;
- terminals are required to provide four or more post-Panamax container gantry cranes per vessel, in order to turn them around as rapidly as vessels half their size;

Table 2: Throughput, berth and channel depth for major North European container ports, 2000

	TEU throughput	Max. berth draught	Min. channel depth
Rotterdam	6,300,000	16.6	22.0
Hamburg	4,248,247	15.0	12.5
Antwerp	4,082,334	15.3	14.0
Felixstowe	2,800,000	16.0	14.5
Bremerhaven	2,712,420	14.0	13.0
Le Havre	1,464,901	13.5	15.0
Southampton	1,063,525	15.0	12.6
Zeebrugge	965,345	14.0	13.5
Liverpool	540,000	12.7	8.5
Thamesport	528,878	13.5	11.0

Sources: *Containerisation International Yearbook*; *Fairplay World Ports Guide*; Cargo Systems *100-top container ports survey*.

- container yards need to be capable of accepting volumes of containers which are twice as large as before but in the same period of time.

Partly as a direct consequence of these physical constraints, carriers have reduced the number of port calls per service loop. This reduction in the number of port calls is dependent on the continued development of hub-and-spoke networks, based on one or two direct calls per major port range and ever-increasing use of transhipment. As transhipment effectively doubles the number of recorded moves per container, this then boosts hub port throughput to well above the rate of increase in trade.

This benefit, according to OSC, will only apply to terminals which are successful in maintaining or achieving hub status – not all ports are expected to be able to maintain their current roles in this changing competitive environment. The forecast general increase in container trade is nevertheless expected to benefit the whole spectrum of container ports, from major hub, through secondary hub, to short-sea and feeder ports.

3.2 Transhipment and dedicated terminals

The transhipment market is especially dynamic and is expected to continue to account for an increasing share of containers handled. Traditionally, this type of business was regarded as highly volatile, as transhipment operations are not necessarily tied to a particular locality to the same extent as direct import/export cargo flows. The future expected development of transhipment will be dependent on numerous interrelated factors, including:

- further increase in vessel size and moves to reduce the number of port calls in a given region;
- port and terminal accessibility for the largest classes of vessels;
- operating costs for direct call versus transhipment;
- availability of capacity for transhipment operations, as determined by the local balance of supply and demand in a particular port market;

- shipping line investment in dedicated terminals – with this effectively locking a line into a particular port;
- development of relay operations linking deep-sea services at a particular terminal;
- development of new "offshore" hubs offering attractive packages for carriers.

Transhipment pricing is determined by the balance of supply and demand at all ports competing for this business. However, the revenue per container move in transhipment – which entails both a discharge and a loading – is generally lower than achieved in the import/export sector. Thus, if there is a straight choice between these two sectors, the terminal operator will seek to maximise revenue by focusing on import/export flows at the expense of transhipment. Significantly, if there is a shortage of capacity then these pressures will intensify. However, the cost involved in developing an "offshore" transhipment hub is invariably less than providing the same scale of facility at a port which is largely dependent on land access (see below).

The ongoing process of line concentration has placed increasing bargaining power in the hands of major consortia in their dealings with ports and terminals. Today's huge scale of investment required for front-rank container handling operations also favours far closer relationships between lines and terminal operators. There has consequently been increased interest by major shipping lines in establishing dedicated – owned or joint-venture – terminals. As vessel sizes increase, the control available through integration of stevedoring with vessel scheduling becomes ever more attractive. Whilst it is far from clear that dedicated terminals are cheaper, rather they represent an integration of the service to the customer. Further, to the global carrier, a strategic hub location may simply be treated as a cost centre – its real purpose being to help minimise the costs involved in operating a global container transport network.

Over recent years a number of "offshore" container transhipment terminals have been developed in answer to the many physical and environmental constraints associated with ongoing expansion within traditional port locations. Table 3 lists some of these new ports. The main advantages at "offshore" hubs include:

- natural deep water, usually of 15m or so with minimal dredging expense;
- quick and easy access from the open sea compared to many river and city-ports;
- terminals situated on islands or remote peninsula so avoiding land transport through congested urban areas;
- plentiful and relatively inexpensive land for expansion;
- competitive labour rates compared to traditional ports;
- majority of cargo consists of transhipment, which means limited investments required in land transport infrastructure at or connecting the terminal;
- terminals owned/part-owned by carriers who are able to transfer large volumes of containers to the new hub quickly.

Table 3: Major "offshore" transhipment hub terminals and max. berth depth

Port	Max berth depth (m)	Remarks
Algeciras, Spain	16.0	Maersksealand terminal
Malta Freeport	15.5	Grand Alliance hub
Gioia Tauro, Italy	15.0	Eurogate with Maersk share
MITH, Sardinia	14.0	P&O Ports
Salalah, Oman	16.0	Maersksealand equity share
Sines, Portugal	17.0	PSA terminal
Taranto, Italy	16.0	Evergreen terminal
Port Said, Egypt	16.0	ECT/Maersksealand
Aden	16.0	PSA terminal
Manzanillo, Panama	13.0	SSA
Freeport, Bahamas	16.0	Hutchison Ports
Sepetiba, Brasil	18.5	German operator
Colombo	16.0	P&O Ports
Tanjung Pelepas, Malaysia	16.0	Maersksealand equity share
Kabil, Batam Island	17.0	Still at planning stage
Kitakyushu, Japan	15.0	PSA
Kwang Yang, South Korea	15.0	Hanjin/Hyundai

Sources: *Containerisation International Yearbook 1998; Fairplay Ports Guide 1998;* Cargo Systems *"Opportunities for container ports" Report 1998.*

In relation to the last point, and as Heaver *et al.* state,[27] larger lines are increasing their interest in dedicated terminals or obtaining a shared interest in terminals. This trend has drastically reduced the "footloose" nature of shipping companies (and transhipment traffic), placing their relationship with ports and terminals on a sounder and longer-term economic base.

On virtually a global basis, development of new style "offshore" transhipment hubs therefore appears to be the container shipping industry's answer to the changing demands posed by handling larger vessels and increased trade flows. Such a hub has yet to be built in Northern Europe, this being to a very large extent a reflection of continued state funding of port development at traditional port locations on the continent.

3.3 Industry strategy

In a competitive sense, once a line has signalled its intention to build larger ships, competitors have little choice but to follow suit as larger ships generate lower unit costs (assuming satisfactory utilisation is achieved). However, in order to fill bigger ships, lines have had to engage in a degree of service rationalisation otherwise the greater ship capacity would not be sufficiently utilised, or service frequencies would deteriorate. Carriers have therefore adopted two strategies:
  – Consolidation,
  – Transhipment.

Industry consolidation has involved the formation of alliances allowing lines to combine fleets in order to jointly offer several different service strings covering major trade routes. Table 4 indicates how this has resulted in a significant proportion of the market (i.e., 50%) on Europe-Asia and Transatlantic routes being controlled by the leading four groupings.

Table 4: *Capacity planned on major North European routes by main deep-sea alliances/carriers, first quarter 2000*

	(Annual two-way capacity – 000 TEU)			
Carriers	**Far East**	**Atlantic**	**Total**	**% share**
Grand Alliance	2395.4	310.9	2706.3	17.8
United Alliance	1391.2	296.1	1687.3	11.1
Maersk/Sea-Land	1106.5	573.6	1680.1	10.3
New world Alliance	1352.4	208.0	1560.4	11.0
Evergreen	906.1	432.1	1338.2	8.8
K-Line/Yangming	702.3	279.2	981.5	6.5
Sub total	7853.9	2099.9	9953.8	65.4
Other carriers	1345.8	3912.8	5258.6	34.6
Route totals	9199.7	6012.7	15212.4	100.0

Sources: MDS Transmodal.
Grand Alliance = Hapag Lloyd, P&O Nedlloyd, NYK, OOCL (+ MISC on Eur/FE)
New World Alliance = APL, MOL, Hyundai
United Alliance = Hanjin, Cho Yang, DSR-Senator, UASC

Carrier fleet size has also been expanding. The global MaerskSealand operation (including Safmarine) has a total fleet of some 300 ships at its disposal, while P & O Nedlloyd has 138 ships, Evergreen Group 130 ships, MSC 142 ships, COSCO 113 ships, and so on. Further consolidation would increase carrier fleet size even more.

Once an alliance has been formed, member lines then search for further economies of scale in port through combining their traffic. As a consequence, alliances require larger terminals each consisting of several berths which can accommodate all the vessels in a combined fleet. This consolidation of port activity is reflected in carriers now enjoying far greater bargaining power over port suppliers, and where carrier groupings in many instances dominate traffic flows through newly developed hub terminals.

The second strategy is a move towards greater transhipment. Increased container flows, larger ships, and carrier consolidation have combined to generate far greater transhipment volumes. This is also reflected in the development of new transhipment terminals over recent years. Approximately 25–27% of all containerised cargo now relates to transhipment,[28] and as carriers continue to alter their schedules towards hub and spoke, it is forecast that transhipment flows will more than double between 1999–2010.[29] This in turn is expected to lead to even more demand for strategically positioned and competitive transhipment terminals.

In addition to shipping line consolidation, concentration has also been evident in the container terminal operating sector.[30] Table 5 presents the market position of leading terminal operating companies in Europe (North and South Europe combined). In terms of volume throughput, a handful of operators dominate the North European container terminal scene:
  – German group Eurogate handled nearly 4.0m TEU at its facilities in Bremerhaven and Hamburg in 2000 and is considering development of a new large terminal at Wilhelmshaven;

842 PORT ECONOMICS AND MANAGEMENT

- Hong Kong's Hutchison Port Holdings (HPH) has a strategic stake of 35% in Rotterdam's ECT, whilst in the UK HPH owns and operates container terminals at Felixstowe, Thamesport and Harwich, and is planning a major new development at Bathside Bay (Harwich). HPH operates over 20 terminals worldwide and controls around 10% of world container port moves;
- P&O Ports owns 50% of Southampton Container Terminal (ABP owns the other 50%), has a 34% stake in Tilbury, and is planning to build a new terminal at the former Shellhaven site on the Thames. During 2000 P&O Ports also acquired the container activities of Seaport Terminals and ACT/MT in Antwerp, and intends to develop a new terminal in Antwerp's left bank dock complex;
- Antwerp-based Hesse Noord Natie (HNN) controls some 85% of container business in Antwerp, however, Singapore's PSA has acquired the majority of HNN to give it a foothold in the North European market. HNN also operates a terminal in Zeebrugge and is planning a new terminal on the River Scheldt at Flushing.

*Table 5: Market position of leading container terminal operators in Europe, 1999**

Operator	Market share	Remarks
Hutchison Port Holding, China	9%	-
ECT, Rotterdam	13%	HPH has 35% stake (limited by EU)
Eurogate, Germany	17%	Maersk stake at B'Havn + G.Tauro
Hessenatie, Belgium	7%	PSA acquiring 51% of Hessenatie[†]
HHLA, Germany	7%	Hamburg port authority owned
P&O Ports, Australia	5%	-
PSA Corp	2%	-
Other operators	40%	-
Total	**100%**	

Sources: Notteboom, T., & Winkelmans, W. (2001).
* Includes both north and south European container throughput totalling 37.8m TEU in 1999 (Baltic excluded).
† PSA's stake in HNN is now 80%

4. TRANSHIPMENT COST MODELLING APPROACH

4.1 Methodology

This section presents modelled results relating to the economics of transhipment in northern Europe based on a single hub facility as compared with alternative multiport direct service strategies at existing north European hub ports (i.e., current practice). In the modelling exercise, a new north European container transhipment hub at Scapa Flow in the Orkney Islands (Scotland) is considered. That is, large container vessels would call at Orkney as a substitute for multiple direct call services at existing north European ports. The results presented here form part of previously unpublished research carried out on behalf of entities proposing development of a major container transhipment hub in Orkney.[31] The cost model used in illustrated in Figure 1.

THE ECONOMICS OF TRANSHIPMENT

Scapa Flow is the UK's largest sheltered deep-water harbour, providing a natural deep-water location (26 metre deep channel), which already functions as an oil transhipment center handling the largest vessels. It has a long history as both a commercial trading center and as harbour for vast fleets of naval vessels. As long ago as 1263 Orkney acted as pivot for the Viking fleet of King Hakon in its excursions around the coasts of Great Britain, Ireland and further afield. In the nineteenth century Scapa Flow was used to marshal convoys of ships heading for North America and the New World, and the famous Hudson Bay Company concentrated its activities in Orkney. During both World Wars, Scapa Flow was the Royal Navy's premier northern anchorage, and is still used today in NATO exercises.

This analysis considers the effects resulting from altering an Asia-Europe-US East Coast pendulum service offering multiple direct port calls in northern Europe, to a scenario where only one northern European port (i.e., Orkney) receives a direct call. A pendulum service itinerary involves vessels taking in two trade lanes rather than one as in a typical end-to-end service. The exercise begins with analysis of relevant port location deviation times, and related feeder distances and costs, followed by estimated port productivity and terminal costs. Deviation costs are then summed together with transhipment costs and feeder costs and the lowest cost option is identified. Finally, the financial implications resulting from mainline fleet and service network changes due to transhipment are considered.

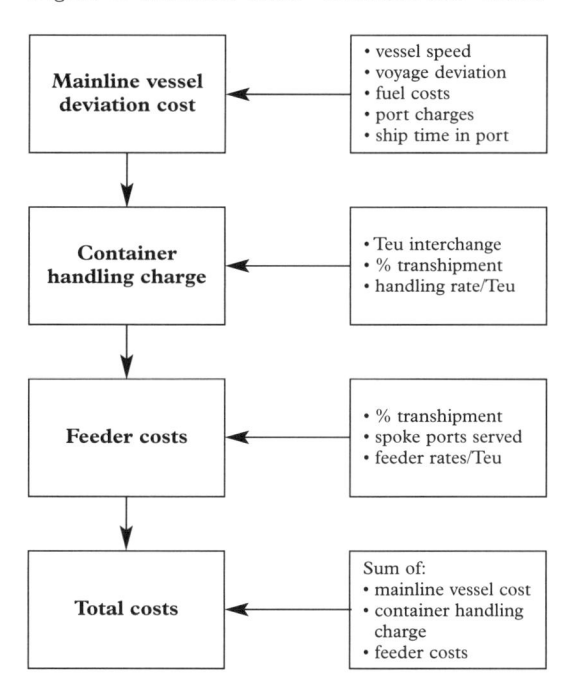

Figure 1: Mainline vessel "deviation cost" model

Cost assumptions used in the modelling have been presented to most of the major container lines and to several container terminal operators, and refined according to comments received. That is, most of the sources of costs applied in the model are the lines themselves. Cost estimates are therefore believed to be a fairly accurate representation of reality, although certain costs will of course change over time (e.g., vessel charter costs, fuel costs).

4.2 Mainline ship deviation, feeder distances and costs

The ability of Orkney, or any other offshore hub for that matter, to attract and retain transhipment traffic, will be determined by the shipping line economics of serving northern Europe as a whole. Different service and network patterns carry different costs, which means that the aim of carriers will naturally be to select the port (or ports) which delivers the lowest cost solution consistent with maintaining service requirements.

Deviation costs are a function of location relative to the main east-west routes. Any ship having to steam from the Atlantic through the English Channel, Straits of Dover and then into the North Sea, returning to the Atlantic the same way, will obviously incur a significant deviation relative to a port location that permitted such a long transit to be avoided.

For the purpose of this analysis, Brest in north-west France is taken as the deviation position to/from Asia as it from this point that vessels entering northern Europe from Asia would divert, either eastwards towards the English Channel/Dover Strait/North Sea, or alternatively northwards to Orkney.

As Table 6 illustrates, with voyage deviation starting from a position 50 nm west of Brest, and with a typical port call rotation of Felixstowe–Rotterdam–Hamburg–Le Havre, for a mainline vessel this represents a deviation of 1,643 nm. This is equivalent to 3 days steaming time at sea, which, for a 5,500 Teu vessel with all-up running costs of $59,000 per day (carrier estimates), involves an expense of more than $175,000. The deviation position as the large vessel then heads from Europe to the USEC in the second part of the pendulum voyage is taken as Bishop Rock Lighthouse, at the south-western extremity of the British Isles.

The alternative of using Orkney as transhipment hub involves a deviation from the stated position west of Brest of 756 nm, which is equivalent to 1.3 days steaming time. From Bishop Rock Lighthouse it is virtually the same distance to the USEC as it is from Orkney, which means an Orkney call does not incur any further deviation penalty in respect of a pendulum service. A hub located in Orkney therefore offers an advantageous position for mainline vessels compared with existing north European hubs.

So, whether a vessel is inbound from, or outbound to the USEC or Asia from northern Europe, the direct call deviation for a mainline vessel using existing north European hub ports is substantial. Moreover, this deviation is further extended by the common practice of mainline vessels calling at typically four ports in relative close proximity to one another, thereby significantly adding to ship time spent in port.

THE ECONOMICS OF TRANSHIPMENT

Table 6: Deviation distance in North Europe for Asia-Europe-USEC pendulum service

Port	Deviation (nm)
TRANSHIPMENT	
Brest–Orkney	756
DIRECT CALL	
Brest–Felixstowe*	458
Felixstowe–Rotterdam	121
Rotterdam–Hamburg	305
Hamburg–Le Havre	500
Le Havre–Bishop Rock**	259
Total multiport deviation	**1,643**

*Deviation taken from a point 50 nm west of Brest as vessel arrives from Asia.
**Vessel then heads across Atlantic to complete the pendulum (Bishop Rock–USEC same distance as Orkney–USEC).

Table 7 estimates the deviation costs of multiple calls for a mainline ship at the typical north European port range compared with transhipment at a single hub in Orkney. In addition to costing the deviation (in terms of the cost of ship's time and fuel), the example also reflects the likely variation in port time and port productivity. The results show that mainline ship costs via Orkney are reduced by about two-thirds compared with the direct call multiport option.

The main assumptions applied in the model at this point are:

– Ship size 5,500 Teu
– All up vessel running cost of $58,905 per day
– Fuel consumption of 165 tonnes per day and fuel cost of $140 per tonne
– Average service speed 23 knots

A key weakness of multiple direct calls by mainline ships serving the same trading region is that a vessel repeatedly incurs port entry/exit time penalties, in this example on four occasions (i.e., four port calls in rotation). As port entry/exit (i.e., from pilot till vessel starts being worked by gantries) averages out at 4 hours each way for the ports considered, this equates to 0.33 days (8 hours) for each and every port visit. In other words, 32 hours is spent by a mainline ship simply entering and exiting (4) ports during each port rotation in northern Europe. Other factors that tend to limit productivity in a multiport direct call itinerary during each port call include having to remove lashing and then re-lashing, re-opening and closing hatch covers, and restowage of containers. Conversely, in the event of mainline vessels using a single hub for the region, these activities would only need to be carried out once, not four times, resulting in considerable mainline ship time savings. It is assumed, therefore, that 1 day is spent in port for each direct call, and this also corresponds with carrier and port estimates.

The net result is that a mainline vessel would be expected to spend only 1.25 days in port when using a single transhipment hub in northern Europe, compared with 4.0 days given the present arrangement where there are four direct port calls involved. By adding ship time in port together with deviation time, a large vessel serving Orkney would spend only 2.6 days in northern Europe whereas each multiportship spends 7.0 days. Additional information regarding port productivity levels used in the cost model is given in section 4.3.

Port charges are assumed to be lower in Orkney compared with existing multiport terminals. Due to the natural deep-water channel there is virtually zero dredging expense relative to current direct call ports, and no need for extensive road and rail access. Reclamation costs are also limited due to the possibility of development on what is a flat island (the island of "Flotta", which in Norse means "flat"). Towage and Pilotage rates are expected to be more competitive than at traditional direct call ports, reflecting benefits brought about through greater concentration of traffic (at a single location) thereby generating operating economies of scale and scope, aided by Orkney's faster port entry/exit time.

Table 7: Estimated mainline vessel deviation costs (US$)

Port	Deviation time (days)*	Time in port (days)	Vessel deviation time cost ($)**	Fuel cost ($)***	Port access charges ($)	Cost of time in port ($)	Total marginal cost ($)
TRANSHIPMENT							
Orkney	1.37	1.25	80,674	31,637	36,000	73,631	221,942
DIRECT CALL							
Brest–Felixstowe	0.83	1.00	48,874	19,166	55,000	58,905	181,945
Rotterdam	0.22	1.00	12,912	5,064	55,000	58,905	131,881
Hamburg	0.55	1.00	32,547	12,764	55,000	58,905	159,216
Le Havre	0.91	1.00	53,356	20,924	55,000	58,905	188,185
Le Havre–Bish. Rock	0.47	0.00	27,638	10,839	0.00	–	38,477
Multiport Total	2.98	4.00	175,328	68,756	220,000	235,620	**699,704**

* 23 knots average speed.
** $59,000 per day for 5,500 TEU vessel.
*** Fuel consumption 165 tpd @ $140 per tonne.

Multiport services are clearly more expensive in terms of mainline vessel deviation compared with hub/spoke via Orkney, which is largely a reflection of direct call port locations being quite distant from the Atlantic Ocean, although there are also inefficiencies in port resulting from multiport calls in the same region to consider. Given that a major carrier may make several calls per week at its hub port, the potential annual cost saving can be substantial. For example, if 104 calls per annum were assumed (i.e., a weekly Asia-N.Europe-USEC pendulum service, in each direction), Orkney could represent a saving of almost $50 million. Looking at this another way, depending on the length of round voyage involved, the time saving could help to reduce the total number of mainline ships deployed (this issue is explored further in Section 4.5). However, it must be remembered that offset against these savings would be the additional feeder costs necessary, and this is considered in Section 4.4.

Table 8 aims to place into context the relative locations of the key hub ports in the region in relation to existing feeder markets. As well as showing mainline vessel deviation, it also provides feeder distances to typical feeder ports in each of the key north European feeder sectors (i.e., UK/Ireland and Scandinavia/

THE ECONOMICS OF TRANSHIPMENT

Table 8: Comparison of mainline deviation and feeder distances (nm)

Hub	Mainline vessel deviation	Spoke port distances UK/Ireland Liverpool	G'mouth	Dublin	G'borg	Baltic/Scan Helsinki	Bergen	Total spoke port dist's	Average spoke port dist.	Average spoke plus mainline
Orkney	756	466	225	436	505	1,162	286	3,080	513	1,269
Felixstowe		624	360	559	523	1,180	544	3,790	632	
Rotterdam		693	401	628	501	1,158	536	3,917	653	
Hamburg		946	506	881	326	721	487	3,867	645	
Le Havre		501	523	436	691	1,348	698	4,197	700	
Multiport total	1,643								657	2,300

Baltic). Besides the total of these feeder distances, the average feeder distance is also given. This has then been added to the mainline vessel deviation to give an indication of the "centrality" of the location of each type of service. Whilst this is to some extent a simplistic approach, it is still an effective way to illustrate the locational advantages of transhipment versus direct calls, as well as indicating the potential for reduced ship movement.

What is immediately apparent is that the combined mainline deviation and average spoke port distance for Orkney is considerably lower (i.e., about half) than the direct call option. Average feeder distance is also very competitive for Orkney compared with existing hubs. However, one factor which inevitably complicates this is that existing hub ports also generate local cargo in their own right, which means that if they are not hub ports they could well be spoke ports. Section 4.4 explores this in more detail.

4.3 Port productivity and terminal costs

For the shipping line, what really matters is how long it takes to turn a ship around – from arrival at the pilot station to dropping off the pilot on departure. However, it is important to note that there will be differences in the level of terminal productivity achievable in typical direct call ports compared with transhipment facilities. Carriers expect and generally receive improved levels of productivity, and hence faster ship turnaround, at ports where transhipment predominates (e.g., Singapore, Freeport, Algeciras, etc.). An explanation for such productivity advantages is given below.

A container-handling rate of 175 moves per berth/hour has been modelled for Orkney (Table 9), which is similar to productivity levels regularly achieved

Table 9: Comparison of container handling performance

Port	Gross moves per hour/crane	Number of Cranes	Moves per Hour
Orkney	35	5	175
Felixstowe	23	3.5	80.5
Rotterdam	23	3.5	80.5
Hamburg	23	3.5	80.5
Le Havre	23	3.5	80.5
Multiport average	23	3.5	80.5

at a number of transhipment terminals (although detailed modelling has indicated that this can be further improved upon). Indeed, if an indented berth were provided as a possible alternative to a straight quay, with cranes working both sides of a ship, this could increase productivity levels to around 300 moves per hour.[32] For existing direct call ports in northern Europe productivity levels as stated by carriers and other sources are modelled. This typically equates to about 80 moves per hour at the established north European ports.

The model assumes that throughput at the Orkney terminal comprises 100% transhipment. Existing direct-call container ports in northern Europe have a transhipment throughput level well below this, and typically under 30%, which means Orkney is a quite different concept more in keeping with the reality of transhipment hubs being developed in other regions of the world.

A particular problem experienced at existing direct call ports involves the bunching of vessels (a consequence of tight multiport schedules), and this leads to added pressure on berth space and crane allocation. Moreover, where the mainline vessel is part loading a relatively small percentage of its overall capacity at each port (in itself a direct result of multiple calls within the same region), it cannot be simultaneously worked by very many cranes; for example, due to the relatively limited container interchange involved, often only a few hatches are needing to be worked at the same time.

Specific productivity advantages favouring transhipment terminals over regional multiport direct call facilities include:

- yard equipment at a hub mainly supports quay cranes, with a limited requirement to load/unload trains and road trailers, leading to enhanced quayside productivity;
- moving large blocks of boxes at the one time means more quay cranes can be utilised for longer periods;
- a greater container interchange means dual cycling is more common, with cranes lifting boxes on and off a ship in the same cycle;
- there are less restows, with the number of restows reducing as the number of intra-regional port calls decrease;
- more "dynamic transhipments" can be performed, with boxes moved directly along the quay between mainline and feeder ship.

Prospects for more effective berth utilisation are also likely to be improved at a transhipment terminal compared with direct call multiport options. In the direct call scenario, very large vessels take up valuable berth and access channel space at four ports during a regional rotation, and each time for a relatively limited container interchange. Conversely, in the transhipment scenario the large vessel requires berth space at just one terminal in the region, and for a far larger interchange which also benefits from superior productivity levels. This implies that spoke ports need allocate only sufficient berth space to handle shorter feeder vessels, with feeder ship size more accurately reflecting local demand. An important effect of transhipment at an offshore hub in northern Europe will therefore be to reduce pressure to expand quay length at traditional direct call port locations.

Table 10: Comparison of container transhipment tariffs

	Average per TEU cycle ($)
Orkney	39
Felixstowe	78
Rotterdam	78
Hamburg	78
Le Havre	78
Multiport average	78

Source: Based on carrier information.

These efficiency improvements, coupled with greater traffic concentration, would permit a handling price advantage for a transhipment terminal compared with present multiport direct call facilities (Table 10). In the cost modelling, therefore, a transhipment handling rate of $65 per container cycle (i.e., discharge and load) is used in the case of Orkney, compared with the current rate of $130 for each direct call port, which are the same rates suggested by industry actors. With a ratio of 1.66 for the 20'/40' container split, this equates to a rate of $39/Teu for Orkney and $78/Teu for direct call ports.

4.4 Lowest cost options

In simple terms, location is a key determinant of the competitiveness of a region's transhipment ports. The extent of the deviation from the east-west shipping routes for mainline vessels, plus the distance from each hub port to the various spoke ports will play an important role. In this sense, rather than "centrality" being important as it formerly was in the case of traditional ports, the notion of a terminals "intermediacy" becomes significant,[33] with carriers themselves influencing this decision.

With regard to the volume of cargo for each particular part of the region, existing north European hub ports are different from Orkney in the sense that a far greater proportion of their traffic is not transhipment but relates to their own hinterland, however defined. This tends to have a positive influence on their *perceived* attractiveness as transhipment hubs. It also means they have sufficient "local" cargo to justify being spoke ports if they are not hubs themselves.

Inevitably, not all carriers will have the same requirements and a combination of the use of varying hubs on different strings may well be the most cost-effective hub and spoke option, although this will not always allow the full network advantages to be realised (e.g., reducing the number of mainline ships and/or upgrading mainline vessel size). A network change (e.g., linking separate services at a common hub) can result in a saving in terms of the total number of ships required. Orkney has a location suitable for this, being well positioned for vessels serving both Asia and the USEC, whilst existing hubs are not well positioned, as the earlier deviation analysis showed. In this regard, perhaps the most significant aspect about Orkney is that its "new" location (relative to the established ports in the region) allows carriers to consider a network change that previously was not an option.

Feeder costs are one of the most important factors in the overall equation when determining the relative attractiveness of alternative hub port options. Table 11 provides indicative feeder rates between the main hubs and selected spoke ports. In the case of Orkney, four current mainline ports have been included as spoke ports, these being Rotterdam, Hamburg, Felixstowe and Le Havre.

Feeder cost estimates in respect of existing spoke ports are calculated based on current rates of $0.25 per Teu/mile, or a minimum charge of $100 per Teu. The larger volumes moving between Orkney and the four current mainline ports, aided by employment of larger feeder vessels (i.e., around 1,000 Teu or above), would enjoy a reduced rate of $70 per Teu. The latter is similar to feeder rates stated by carriers using major transhipment terminals in other regions (i.e., about $0.13 per Teu/mile).

Feeder connections would therefore need to be introduced between Orkney and UK/Ireland and Scandinavia/Baltic, as well as to existing mainline hubs. One option is for carriers/alliances to employ their own feeders, this perhaps being more realistic when serving current mainline direct call ports at which proportionately larger volumes (and hence larger feeder vessels) are likely. Existing feeder ports are more likely to be supplied by third party feeder operators.

Table 11: Estimated feeder costs matrix

Spoke port	L'pool	G'mouth	Dublin	G'borg	Helsinki	Bergen	F'Stowe	R'dam	H'burg	Le Havre
TRANSHIPMENT										
Orkney	117	100	109	126	291	100	70	70	70	70
DIRECT CALL										
Felixstowe	156	100	140	131	295	136				
Rotterdam	173	100	157	125	290	136				
Hamburg	237	127	220	100	180	122				
Le Havre	125	131	109	173	337	175				

($/per laden TEU)

Note: Based on current feeders @ $0.25 per Teu/mile ($100/Teu minimum) and $70/Teu for ex direct call ports.

Carriers could, in addition, use an Orkney hub for interlining mainline services. For example, traffic discharged from a large hub-hub vessel arriving inbound from Asia could be picked up by a more moderate-sized end-to-end service vessel calling northern Europe inbound from the USEC and en-route for north continent ports. The inbound vessel from USEC would be discharging traffic at Orkney anyway, and therefore have space to load cargo destined for north continent ports. The same procedure could also be carried out in reverse, with a vessel sailing from north Europe to the USEC dropping off Asian destined containers on its return to the Atlantic, and then picking up UK boxes for USEC. To a large extent this would avoid the need to deploy additional feeders to serve existing hubs. Interlining in such a way would clearly result in improved utilisation of mainline ship time and capacity.

Indicative feeder rates are believed to be achievable and competitive, reflecting the considerable buying power of mainline carriers and alliances. In the modelled example, the assumption is for a 5,500 Teu vessel operating an Asia–Europe–USEC pendulum service, and a total cargo interchange of 6,600 Teu (i.e., 60% of ship capacity, 3,300 Teu discharged, 3,300 Teu loaded) in northern Europe. In such a pendulum service the vessel would also be carrying traffic to/from other hubs (e.g., USEC-Med/Mid East etc.) so cannot be worked to full capacity in the north Europe sector of the voyage.

With existing direct call multiport arrangements, on average approximately 28% of cargo (i.e., 1,848 Teu) is already assumed to comprise transhipment (Table 12). In the event of Orkney being used as a hub, 100% of cargo (i.e., 6,600 Teu) would be transhipment. The model ignores the possibility for interlining services as suggested above, although this represents an additional low cost option for carriers to consider relaying cargo between mainline vessels thereby avoiding some feeder expense.

Table 12: Estimated mainport transhipment cargo

Main Port	Teu per Port	Assumed % Transhipment	Teu Transhipped
Orkney	6,600	100%	6,600
Felixstowe	1,320	28%	370
Rotterdam	2,310	28%	647
Hamburg	1,650	28%	462
Le Havre	1,320	28%	370
Total	6,600	28%	1,848

Table 13 further breaks down the expected cargo split for each spoke port assuming current arrangements. Former hub ports therefore become major spokes in the new system. The final spoke port split for feeder traffic moving via Orkney is shown in Table 14.

Table 13: Feederport transhipment cargo

Spoke port	Assumed % of total	Teu transhipped
Liverpool	20%	370
Grangemouth	15%	277
Dublin	20%	370
Gothenburg	15%	277
Helsinki	15%	277
Bergen	15%	277
	100%	1,848

Table 14: Feederport plus former mainport transhipment cargo

Spoke port	Assumed % of total	Teu transhipped
Felixstowe	14%	950
Rotterdam	25%	1,663
Hamburg	18%	1,188
Le Havre	14%	950
Feederports	28%	1,848
	100%	6,600

Table 15 presents estimated costs for the direct call service (inclusive of current transhipment levels) compared with hub & spoke transhipment via Orkney. Mainline vessel deviation costs have been taken from Table 7, and transhipment costs have been calculated on the basis of the data in Table 10. Feeder costs are then factored in for each hub port, and these are aggregated together in the case of the four direct call ports served in the multiport itinerary.

When the mainline ship deviation costs and transhipment costs are summed together with the feeder cost, Orkney appears as the lowest cost option, generating a saving of 7%, or $83,000 per weekly call. This is equivalent to $4.33 million per annum assuming 52 calls. However, each pendulum service involves two ship calls per week (i.e., one eastbound, one westbound, and 104 per annum), which means that a weekly pendulum service would generate operating cost savings of approximately $8.6 million per annum using transhipment via Orkney, compared to the direct call multiport option.

What is evident from this analysis is that a carrier or alliance changing its network and using Orkney as a transhipment hub for northern Europe does not incur any cost penalty; on the contrary, the network change should actually result in cost savings, and this is before overall mainline fleet savings are factored in (see Section 4.5 below).

This last point is perhaps best illustrated when looking at the changing carrier cost structure due to a shift from direct call to hub and spoke in northern Europe (Table 16). With direct call services, 61% of costs incurred calling in northern Europe relate to mainline vessel deviation, placing the financial burden very heavily on carriers to provide more expensive mainline ships (in order to directly call at four different ports, part loading in each, within the same trading region). Conversely, in the hub and spoke transhipment option via Orkney, mainline vessel deviation accounts for just 21% of the cost of calling in northern Europe, with the bulk of costs taken up by transhipment (24%) and feeder costs (55%).

Altering the network from multiple direct calls to hub and spoke transfers the majority of costs (incurred serving north European markets) away from mainline vessels towards terminal and feeder costs, with the added potential for carriers to reduce total costs, as well as significantly lessen mainline vessel capital commitments. Added network benefits are likely to accrue due to what would inevitably be improved management and consolidation of mainline vessels and feeder cargo at a single regional hub, giving further scope to drive down feeder rates, plus easier coordination of regional mainline vessel calls.

Table 16: Cost breakdown for direct call and transhipment ($)

	Direct call		Transhipment	
Deviation Cost	699,704	61%	221,942	21%
Transhipment Cost	144,202	13%	257,503	24%
Feeder Cost	305,759	27%	586,948	55%
Total Cost	1,149,664		1,066,393	
One way saving per weekly pendulum		83,271 (7%)		
Saving per Teu		12.6		

Table 15: Estimated comparative costs of wayport hub & spoke transhipment at N. European ports

Hub port	Mainline vessel deviation cost ($)	Transhipment Teu	Transhipment Cost ($)	L'pool	G'mouth	Dublin	G'borg	Helsinki	Bergen	F'stowe	R'dam	H'Burg	Le Havre	Feeder Cost ($)	Total Cost ($)
TRANSHIPMENT															
Orkney	221,942	6,600	257,503	43,058	27,720	40,286	34,997	80,527	27,720	66,528	116,424	83,160	66,528	586,948	1,066,393
DIRECT CALL															
Felixstowe		370	28,840	11,532	5,544	10,330	7,249	16,355	7,540						
Rotterdam		647	50,471	22,412	9,726	20,310	12,152	28,087	13,195						
Hamburg		462	36,050	21,853	8,766	20,351	6,930	12,491	8,437						
Le Havre		370	28,840	9,258	7,249	8,057	9,577	18,683	9,674						
Total multiport	699,704	1,848	144,202	65,054	31,285	59,048	35,908	75,617	38,846					305,759	1,149,664

4.5 Mainline fleet changes and cost savings

Calculations have been made to estimate the effect of network changes due to a shift from direct call via existing ports in northern Europe to a hub and spoke system using Orkney, and the impact this has on a carrier's/alliance's overall mainhaul fleet composition. Calculations are based on an Asia–MidEast–S.Europe–N. Europe–USEC hub/spoke pendulum service calling only at an Orkney hub in northern Europe, and then comparing the outcome of this with the same service maintained via direct calls at four ports in northern Europe (i.e., multiport service).

The specific example used for a hub/spoke pendulum itinerary is presented in Table 17. Ports selected are purely for illustrative purposes; carriers will inevitably have their own views as to which ports in other regions are optimal in terms of cargo generation as well as other important factors (e.g., port productivity, costs, terminal availability, land access, etc.). However, many of the ports in the itinerary already function primarily as transhipment centres, so Orkney would be little different in this sense.

With Orkney as north European hub, the pendulum itinerary as modelled involves 10 port calls, and a single voyage distance of 15,424 nm. The trip can be completed in 39.2 days (inclusive of port time) at an average service speed of 23 knots (i.e., 25.5 knots less sea margin).

The alternative service offering direct calls at four ports in northern Europe extends the mainline ship distance by over 700 nm and, inclusive of extra port time incurred, a single trip for this itinerary is achieved in 43.2 days. Effectively, with direct calls, every mainline vessel stays in northern Europe for four days more than would be the case using transhipment via Orkney, and a total of eight days based on a weekly service in each direction.

Table 17: Asia-Europe-USEC pendulum service mainline vessel charter cost by transhipment and direct call in N. Europe

Itinerary:	Shanghai–Hong Kong–Singapore–Aden–Gioia Tauro–Algeciras–Orkney *or* (Felixstowe/R'Dam/B'Haven/Le Havre)–New York–Charleston–Freeport	
	Transhipment (N. Europe)	**Direct call (N. Europe)**
Ports of call	10	13
Single trip distance (nm)	15,424	16,130
Ship speed	23	23
Ship time at sea (days)	28.9	30.2
Ship time in port (days)	10.3	13.0
Total time single trip (days)	39.2	43.2
No. ships – weekly service	11	12
Ship size (Teu)	5,500	5,500
Charter cost/day/Teu	$5	$5
String cost/year	$112,420,000	$123,891,429
Annual saving	$11,471,429	

Notes: N. Europe port time (4 ports) for direct call is 4.0 days, and 1.3 days for Orkney. All other ports are 1 day. Service speed 25.5 knots less sea margin = 23 knots. Suez transit of 1 day included in time at sea.

With transhipment via Orkney, to maintain an each-way weekly schedule on the multi-trade pendulum itinerary requires a string of 11 vessels. Based on a ship size of 5,500 Teu, this represents a total annual charter cost of $112.4 million. The alternative multiport service offering four direct calls in northern Europe requires 12 mainline vessels and involves annual charter costs of $123.9 million. Shipment via Orkney therefore provides carriers with a potential fleet saving equivalent to one large vessel and $11.5 million per annum for each service string deployed. That is, if two service strings were deployed (i.e., a twice-weekly service frequency in each direction), the potential saving would double to $23.0 million, and so on for each service string introduced.

In addition to cost savings, there are significant operational advantages to be gained from a pendulum hub/spoke service as modelled. In order to increase service frequency (e.g., from weekly to twice weekly), carriers' would need fewer mainline vessels than for individual end-to-end services, or for pendulum services offering multiple direct calls in northern Europe. The management process is also simpler in that carrier's need only coordinate one extra mainline vessel port berthing slot in northern Europe as opposed to four with direct calls.

5. SUMMARY AND CONCLUSIONS

Findings presented here suggest there would be no cost penalty incurred from adopting a more comprehensive approach to hub/spoke transhipment in northern Europe. This is particularly so when the hub in question offers a strategic location that significantly reduces mainline vessel deviation time and costs. Indeed, there should be worthwhile cost savings from such a change.

Nevertheless, to be competitive, transhipment on such a scale will depend on:
- Lower terminal construction costs at "offshore" site
- Higher productivity levels (at transhipment terminal)
- Lower container handling rates
- Reduced port charges
- Attractive feeder rates and comprehensive spoke port coverage

Offshore hubs appear to offer significant scope for meeting these essential conditions, whereas the same efficiencies are unlikely to be achieved within current multiport direct call strategies. Moreover, it is well established that carriers cannot change to a single hub strategy using an existing north European port (e.g., Rotterdam) even if they wanted to because of the massive landside delays that would ensue. Conversely, "tipping" a large vessel at an offshore terminal, as in Orkney, does not present any landside difficulties.

Findings from this analysis suggest that a move towards hub/spoke pendulum services in northern Europe, with Orkney acting as offshore hub, would reduce carrier costs by about 7%. For a single weekly each-way pendulum service string this equates to a cost saving of $8.6 million per annum, based on 5,500 Teu ship size (Table 18). Operating cost savings would be even greater than this if carriers were able to interline mainline services at Orkney, thereby avoiding an element of feeder costs.

Table 18: Total annual cost saving

Weekly pendulum service string via Orkney (5,500 Teu ship)	
Mainline fleet saving	$11,471,429
Operating cost saving	$8,660,141
Total saving per string	$20,131,570
Saving with 3 strings/week	$60,394,709

Further cost savings can be achieved by carriers/alliances through reductions in mainline fleet commitments as a result of a shift towards hub/spoke pendulum services. Compared with a weekly direct call multiport (pendulum) service employing ships of 5,500 Teu, a change to using Orkney as north European hub terminal would reduce mainline fleet expense by about $11.5 million per annum, a saving of 10% for each weekly service string. Essentially, transhipment allows the same weekly service frequency to be maintained with one less mainline vessel than is necessary for direct calls.

Thus, the combined operating and ship capital/charter cost savings from a shift to transhipment and using Orkney as hub terminal for northern Europe would amount to approximately $20 million per annum for each weekly service string calling at the port.

Transhipment would inevitably result in a need to increase feeder capacity in the region. While mainline carriers/alliances could provide some of this extra feeder capacity (which has been fully costed in the modelling results), it is also likely that third party feeder operators would seek to expand their services to accommodate additional traffic. Interlining in Orkney offers carriers added opportunities to reduce costs even further.

A further advantage of hub/spoke transhipment in northern Europe is that it would be easier and less expensive for carriers/alliances to increase service frequency, or to introduce new service strings; each hub/spoke pendulum service string requires fewer mainline ships compared with direct call multiport itineraries, and with one main hub in northern Europe, this makes port scheduling arrangements for mainline vessels far simpler to manage and control, thereby improving overall service reliability.

Importantly, hub/spoke pendulum services would substantially alter carrier/alliance operating cost structure when serving the north European region, with a shift away from the current concentration on mainline ship costs. In addition to a net cost saving, the new carrier cost structure would focus to a greater extent on transhipment and feeder costs, with many elements of these investments being met by entities other than carriers. This would be attractive for mainline carriers.

The foregoing analysis demonstrates that there is a strong economic argument in favour of increased hub/spoke transhipment in northern Europe, and in selection of strategically located "offshore" hubs by carriers/alliances employing pendulum liner services. Such an outcome corresponds closely with general global container shipping industry trends and developments in most major trading regions.

A shift by carriers/alliances towards a regional hub port transhipment strategy in northern Europe would therefore mirror what has already happened in many other regions of the world (e.g., Caribbean, southern Europe, Mid-East, Asia, etc.). Indeed, it seems anachronistic that today's very large container ships still call at four or more ports in close proximity to each other in the same trading region, and with overlapping hinterlands.

Traditional seaports in northern Europe have exacerbated this practice through being permitted to expand capacity at historic port locations, mostly helped by state aids used to artificially create new port infrastructure (e.g., dredged channels, reclaimed land, etc.). In the absence of a European seaport policy, established ports (and indeed member states, city states, municipalities, etc.) appear willing and able to continue this practice,[34,35] in spite of the fact that natural deep-water transhipment hub alternatives offer a more sensible, sustainable and far less expensive option to tackle the combined challenge of handling ever-larger vessels and increased cargo flows.

The European Commission has previously assisted "offshore" hub developments in southern Europe (e.g., Gioia Tauro),[36] while curiously also granting aid to help artificially create new deep-water terminals and breakwaters (!) elsewhere (e.g., Le Havre). While some argue against state aids,[37] it is already evident that the market is distorted to a significant extent, and this makes it very difficult for new hubs in natural deep-water locations to develop. State aid in some form will therefore most probably be necessary to assist development of any new offshore transhipment hub(s) in northern Europe, although individual circumstances may differ.

Today, the reality is that all northern Europe can offer (unlike southern Europe) to handle the megaships is a cluster of dredged (i.e., artificial) harbours accessed via shallow and sensitive estuaries in the most congested areas of the Community. This is hardly sustainable and should not be allowed to continue. It does not need to continue given the availability of natural deep-water sites. In order to move away from this unfortunate position it will be necessary to identify, selectively assist, and promote more sustainable transhipment terminals at strategic "offshore" natural deep-water locations.

ACKNOWLEDGEMENTS

I wish to thank the anonymous referee for his/her remarks on the paper and for suggested improvements, almost all of which have been taken on board.

ENDNOTES

1. Napier University, (2000): "Orkney Container Terminal Study", unpublished report for Orkney Islands Council, Halifax Port Authority and Highlands & Islands Enterprise (Edinburgh, Napier University).
2. Cullinane, K., Khanna, M., and Song, D.W. (1999a): "How Big is Beautiful: Economies

of scale and the optimal size of containership", *Published proceedings of the IAME Conference Liner Shipping: What's Next?* (Halifax, 13–14 September), pp. 108–140.
3. MDS Transmodal (1994): "The future of Southampton Docks: Dibden Bay port development", unpublished report for Hampshire County Council. May.
4. RSPB & MDS Transmodal (1997): *Port Development & Nature Conservation: Supply & Demand in the GB Ports Industry* (Bedfordshire, Royal Society for the Protection of Birds (RSPB)).
5. Cullinane, K., and Khanna, M. (1999b): "Economies of Scale in Large Container Ships", *Journal of Transport Economics and Policy*, (33)2, pp. 185–208.
6. Stopford, M. (2001): "A new revolution", *Containerisation International*, January, pp. 46–48.
7. Lim, S.M. (1996): "Round-the-world service: The rise of Evergreen and the fall of US Lines", *Maritime Policy & Management*, (23)2, pp. 119–144.
8. Wijnolst, N. (2000): *Ships, Larger and Larger: Containerships of 18,000 TEU – impacts on operators and ports*, Dynamar Liner Shipping 2020 Workshop, London, 19 May (Rotterdam, Dynamar), pp. 13–29.
9. Flynn, M. (2001a): "IHI breaks barrier to speed giant boxships", *Lloyds List*, 6 February, p. 1.
10. McLellan, R.G. (1997): "Bigger vessels: How big is too big?", *Maritime Policy and Management*, (24)2, pp. 193–211.
11. O'Mahony, H. (1998): *Opportunities for Container Ports: A Cargo Systems Report* (London, IIR Publications).
12. Cullinane, K., and Khanna, M. (1999b), *op. cit.*
13. Baird, A.J. (1999): Container Vessels in the New Millennium: Implications for Seaports. *Published proceedings of the IAME Conference Liner Shipping: What's Next?* Halifax, 13–14 September, pp. 141–173.
14. De Monie, G. (1997): The global economy, very large containerships and the funding of mega hubs. *Published proceedings of the Cargo Systems Port Financing Conference*, London, 27 June.
15. Wijnolst, N. (2000), *op. cit.*
16. Flynn, M. (2001b): "Evergreen mulls plan for 20 fast boxships", *Lloyds List*, 9 February.
17. Lim, S.M. (1994): "Economies of container ship size: a new evaluation", *Maritime Policy and Management*, 21(2), pp. 149–160.
18. Rijsenbrij, J.C. (2000): The Infrastructure for Tomorrow's Ships. *Published proceedings of Dynamar Liner Shipping 2020 Workshop*, London, 19 May, (Rotterdam, Dynamar), pp. 13–29.
19. Gilman, S. (1999): "The Size Economies and Network Efficiency of Large Containerships", *International Journal of Maritime Economics*, (1)1, July–September, pp. 39–59.
20. ESCAP (2001): "Regional Shipping and Port Development: Strategies under a Changing Maritime Environment", *Journal of Ports & Harbors*, (45)10, pp. 16–21.
21. Gilman, S. (1999), *op. cit.*
22. Haralambides, H., Cariou, P., and Bennachio, M. (2000): "Costs, Benefits and Pricing of Dedicated Container Terminals", *International Journal of Maritime Economics*, 4(1), pp. 21–34.
23. IAPH (2001): "Trends in ship size", unpublished report of the IAPH (International Association of Ports & Harbors) Committee for Port Industry Research and Analysis. *Proceedings of the 22nd IAPH Biennial Conference*, Montreal, 19–26 May. (Tokyo, IAPH Secretariat).
24. Waals, F., and Wijnolst, N. (2001): Malacca-Max: Container shipping network economy. *Published Proceedings of the International Association of Maritime Economists (IAME) Annual Conference*, Hong Kong, 18–21 July.
25. Nye, T. (1999): "Mega-terminals, Trends and Issues", *Port Technology International*, pp. 197–200.

26. Ocean Shipping Consultants (2000): *The Global Containerport Market to 2015* (Chertsey, UK, Ocean Shipping Consultants).
27. Heaver, T., Meersman, H., and Van de Voorde, E. (2001): "Co-operation and competition in international container transport: strategies for ports", *Maritime Policy and Management*, 28(3), pp. 293–305.
28. Drewry Shipping Consultants (2000): *The Drewry Container Market Quarterly* (London, Drewry Shipping Consultants), April.
29. Sjetnan, K.C. (1999): *The future of the container shipping industry* (London, Cargo Systems).
30. Notteboom, T., and Winkelmans, W. (2001): Consolidation and Contestability in the European Container Handling Industry. *Published Proceedings of the International Association of Maritime Economists (IAME) Conference*, Hong Kong, July.
31. Napier University (2000): *Orkney Container Terminal Study, op. cit.*
32. Beddow, M. (2000): "Amsterdam ambition", *Containerisation International*, October, pp. 82–83.
33. Hayuth, Y., and Fleming, D. (1994): "Concepts of strategic commercial location: the case of container ports", *Maritime Policy and Management*, (21)3, pp. 187–193.
34. Stevens, H. (1999): *The Institutional Position of Seaports* (Dordrecht, The Netherlands, Kluwer Academic Publishers).
35. Baird, A.J. (1996): "Containerisation and the decline of the upstream urban port in Europe", *Maritime Policy and Management*, (23)2, pp. 145–156.
36. Winkelmans, W. (2002): "Strategic Seaport Planning", *Journal of Ports & Harbors*, 47(3), April, pp. 17–21.
37. Wiegmans, B.W., Ubbels, B., Rietveld, P., & Nijkamp, P. (2002): "Investments in Container Terminals: Public Private Partnerships in Europe", *International Journal of Maritime Economics*, 4(1), March, pp. 1–20.

PART ELEVEN

ASPECTS OF INTERNATIONAL LOGISTICS

CHAPTER 37

INTERNATIONAL LOGISTICS AND MODAL CHOICE

Kunio Miyashita

Graduate Business School of Business Administration, Kobe University,
Kobe, Japan. E-mail: k-miyashita@joy.hi-ho.ne.jp

1. INTRODUCTION

The container shipping mode of transportation has in large part cooperated with but has also competed against the air transportation mode. The concepts of both total distribution costs and the opportunity cost support a division of labor by the two modes (air and sea) and explain the existence of a competitive grey zone. However, traditional theory is not sufficient enough to explain a recent trend towards air-oriented cargo flows. The modal choice problem is not in the sole domain of the transport field, but has a new dynamic dimension, which involves integration with both logistics strategy and the supply chain management of shippers. This paper brings insight into the current economic phenomenon of modal choice and denotes the frontiers of innovation indicating topics for future research.

The interaction between the shipping and air modes of transportation has been dominated by a trend towards air-oriented transport,[1] if observed from the point of view of the value of trade volumes. Needless to say, in terms of total volume as measured by weight-ton, sea shipments are responsible for more than 99% of total international physical distribution. Hence, the shipping industry plays a core status role in the international transport industry. However, in terms of value of the goods shipped, the share of industrial goods transported by air has increased significantly.[2]

Traditionally, the principle of total cost[3] based on the difference in the service quality between the two modes of transportation has explained modal choice. This view is important even today. However, a point has been reached where it has become necessary for a new analytical angle based on logistics theory to be combined with the aforementioned traditional argument. In other words, there is a need for a greater level of entrepreneurial spirit in the shipping industry, especially in relation to container shipping and air transportation, which supports the logistics activities of the shipper. In this paper, we discuss a hypothesis in which structural change in both shipping and air transportation modes will be derived according to the international logistics strategy of shippers. The core problem of modal choice will a be closely related to a shippers' logistics strategy, under which international direct investment, the product cycle and the stability of international transactions will generate a rational causal relationship with modal choice. In accordance with a shipper's logistics strategy, international physical distribution markets will be composed of both sea and air-based logistics systems. Both of these types of logistics systems will either compete or cooperate, so that the modal choice problem of transport is gradually absorbed into the logistics system.

2. COMPETITION AND COOPERATION OF CONTAINER SHIPPING AND AIR TRANSPORTATION

2.1 Total distribution cost as the criterion of modal choice

The higher the value of goods is, the faster the speed of the transport mode that will be selected. This is the reason why inventory costs will fluctuate in proportion to both the price of goods and the transportation period. Hence, it is preferable to transport high value goods by the speedier air-based mode in order to reduce the transportation period (inventory period), if the saving rate of the inventory cost is higher than the increased rate in the transportation cost. The sum of these two costs is referred to as the total distribution cost. In this case, the total distribution costs relating to high value goods will be decreased if a high-speed mode is utilised. The establishment of the concept of total distribution cost is very important in terms of determining modal choice between container shipping and air transportation. It is the concept of distribution costs that has led to the transport of high value goods by air since the 1960s.

According to the concept of total distribution costs, the value of goods is negatively correlated with the transport period. As is commonly known, if we select the transport period as the measure of the horizontal axis and total distribution costs as the measure of the vertical axis, a downward convex total

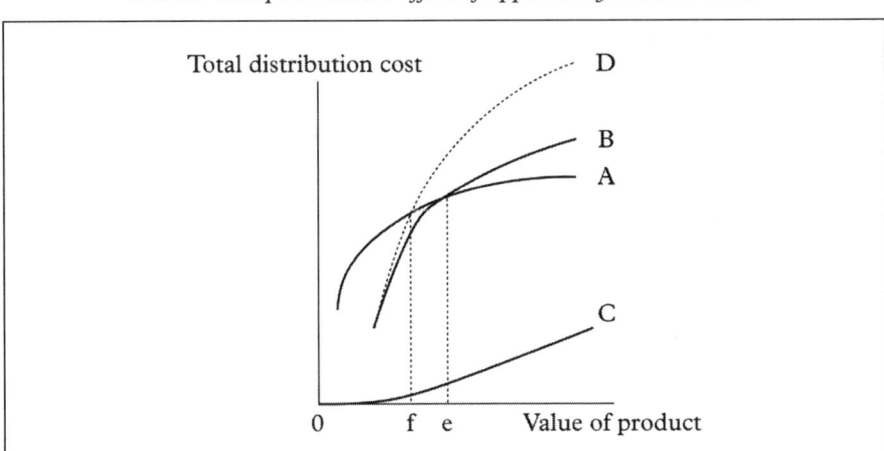

Figure 1: Comparison of total distribution cost between container shipping and air transport and the effect of opportunity costs on them

Note: A = Total distribution cost of air transportation
 B = Total distribution cost of container shipping
 C = Opportunity cost of container shipping
 D = Modified total distribution cost of container shipping (= B + C)

distribution curve can be generated. On the contrary, if we select the value of the goods instead of the transport period as the measure of the horizontal axis, an upward convex total distribution curve will be generated as shown in Figure 1.

In Figure 1, the total distribution cost curve for container shipping intersects with the cost curve for air transportation at the value of the product e. If the value of the product is greater (more expensive) than e, it will be advantageous to transport a particular product by air, and vise versa. Hence, it can be hypothesised that a division of labor between the two modes can be confirmed at e. In addition, the higher the value of the product, the higher the opportunity cost will be for products transported by container shipping. If a seasonal product, such as a currently fashionable good, is transported by the sea mode, large scale, temporary opportunity costs will be generated. In this case, the opportunity cost will increase in a greater proportion to the value of product as indicated by curve? If we add opportunity costs to the total distribution cost of container shipping, a new interactive point (intersection) indicating the total distribution costs of air transport can be realised at f, which is located to the left of the existing point e.

Thus, it is possible to discriminate between three kinds of value ranges for a particular product:
(1) shipment by container is the logical modal choice if the value range of a particular product is lower than f,
(2) air transportation is the logical modal choice if the value range of a particular product is greater than f, and
(3) a value range between e and f indicates a "grey zone", where modal choice is extremely competitive.

The relationship in terms of modal choice between container shipping and air transportation is in principle complementary but if it is considered from a total distribution cost point of view, it will be competitive.

2.2 Turning point in modal choice

According to Japanese export trade volume data between 1969 and 1992, in terms of value, there exists a parallel relationship between the export share of goods transported by container shipping and the share of goods transported by air transportation. The share of goods shipped by air transportation increased steadily as new markets were exploited, while container shipping continued to maintain its share of the conventional liner shipping business. However, after reaching a plateau in 1992, container shipping gradually began to lose share relating to export transport. Since 1992, modal share has fluctuated in the reverse direction. In 1992, container shipping was responsible for 52% of all export shipments. In 1998, the share decreased to 47%. On the contrary, in 1992, the modal share for air transportation was 18%. This increased to 29% by 1998.

Thus, it appears that 1992 can be considered to be the turning point in the share fluctuation between the two modes in the case of exports from Japan. It should be noted that it is the shipper that has changed international physical distribution strategy. In addition, the modal choice problem has structurally changed since 1992 in Japan. Generally speaking, it is necessary to generate a different model of modal choice for the period before 1990 as opposed to model considered representative of the 1990s.

2.3 Modal choice model prior to 1990

Before 1990, the principle of total distribution costs dominated the modal choice behavior of shippers. Following, the principal and basic complementary relationship between two modes will be determined. As shown in Figure 1, opportunity costs will generate a competitive grey zone. In this case, it can be hypothesized that while air transport service is not a superior good, container-shipping service cannot be considered to be an inferior good. If this is indeed the case, the question of which type of modal service will be preferred by shippers remains to be answered, especially if the income (revenue, profit) of a shipper determines modal choice.

Accordingly, the modal choice activity function will be noted as follows.

$$(ETA_i/ETS_i) = f((TCA_i/TCS_i); GDP_i; OPC_i; TAS_i) \qquad (1)$$

where ETA = value of export trade volumes by air transportation,
 ETS = value of export trade volumes by container shipping,
 TCA = total distribution costs by air transport,
 TCC = total distribution costs by container shipping,
 GDP = gross domestic product of export country,
 OPC = opportunity cost of container shipping,
 TAS = preference by shippers for freighter, and
 i = specific time point.

The data for the variables *ETA*, *ETS*, *GDP* and *TAS* are readily available in each of the countries under study. An approximation of total distribution costs can be determined hypothetically by calculating the reciprocal of freight share as measured by *commodity price/freight rate*.

In equation (1), the dependent variable (the ratio trade volumes between air transportation and container shipping) will fluctuate in a reverse direction as compared to the ratio of the total distribution cost between the two modes, if their respective transport services are both substitutive and competitive. In this case, the sign of the ratio representing total distribution costs will be negative. On the other hand, if the trade volume ratio fluctuates in the same direction as the total distribution cost ratio, both transport modes will possess a complementary relationship. In this case, the sign of the total distribution cost ratio will be positive as per our hypothesis.

Next, we assume that as the GDP of an export country increases, its trade volume ratio will increase. Thus, the sign of the GDP ratio will be positive. In this case, an increase in the GDP of a particular country will lead to an increase in air transport volumes, which represents the numerator in the trade volume ratio. Hence, air transportation service can be classified as a superior good with container shipping service representing an inferior good. On the contrary if the sign of GDP ratio is negative, air transportation service can be classified as neither a superior or inferior good.

In general, the opportunity cost of container shipping will have a positive sign. This is because the total distribution cost of air transportation will lead to cost advantages over container shipping. The preference by shippers for freighter will likely increase the share of trade volume flows by the air transportation mode, so it can be assumed that its sign will be positive.

For Japan, the signs of the variables in equation (1) and the estimated results of the equation are summarized in Table 1. Equation (1) is specified in the logarithmic form and is estimated by the least square method.

Table 1: Conditions of the signs in Equation (1)

Main determinant factors \ Causality	Complementary causality	Substitution causality	Estimated result
Total distribution cost ratio of air transport to container shipping	Positive	Negative	0.433^a
GDP of export country	Negative*	Positive**	-1.077^b
Opportunity cost of container shipping	Positive	Positive	1.996^b
Preference for freighter	Positive	Positive	0.599^c

Note:
*Air transport services are neither superior goods nor inferior ones.
** Air transport service is the superior goods.
Statistical Indicator of Estimated Result: RB2 = 0.733, SE = 0.127, DW = 1.58. Constant = 2.063. Estimated Period: 1963–1983. RB2 denotes the coefficient of determination adjusted by the degree of freedom, SE the standard error of estimate, and DW the Durbin-Watson Statistics. a, b and c show the t- statistics and respectively represent significance at 5%, 10% and 20% levels.

The estimated results with respect to the sign of the coefficient indicate a complementary relationship between air transport and container shipping. The coefficients of both the total distribution cost ratio of air transport to container shipping and the GDP of the export country (Japan) are statistically significant and demonstrate a complementary causality. At the same time, the basic relationship is influenced by both the opportunity cost of container shipping and the preference for the shipper to freighter, which leads to the existence of a competitive zone, which we refer to as a grey zone.

2.4 Increase in substitution causality in the 1990s

Next, we increase the estimated period to cover the years 1980–1996. In the 1990s, in addition to the total distribution cost ratio of air transport to container shipping, the function of the logistics network is also a determinant factor. Such network effects, as represented by foreign direct investment, will absorb the traditional function of opportunity cost, income and preference on a shipper's modal choice behavior. Direct investment will determine the shipper's international logistics strategy to the extent that the existing simple modal choice mechanism will no longer be appropriate due to the structural change in the network effects. The function is thus adjusted as follows.

$(ETAi/ETSi) = f((TCAi/TCSi); DIUi; DIEi; DIAi)$ (2)

where DIU = direct Japanese investment in US,
DIE = direct Japanese investment in EU, and
DIA = direct Japanese investment in Asia.

Equation (2) is specified in the logarithmic form and is estimated by least square method as in equation (1). The estimated results are detailed in Table 2.

Table 2: The effect of total cost and networking on modal choice

Total distribution cost ratio of sea and air	Direct investment in US	Direct investment in EU	Direct investment in Asia
0.307[b]	-0.078	-0.228[a]	0.688[a]

Note: RB2 = 0.962, SE = 0.05, DW = 2.12. Constant = –4.69.
Estimated Period: 1980–1996. a = 1%, b = 5%.

The estimated results of the total distribution cost ratio as detailed in Table 2 suggest a fundamental complementary relationship between air transportation and shipping. On the other hand, the effects of direct investment on modal choice vary considerably. The sign representing the coefficient of direct investment in Asia is positive, indicating that the shipper regards air transport service as the superior good. In the Asian region, the substitutive nature of air and sea service is clearly indicated. However, direct investment in the EU strongly indicates the complementary nature of the services. Finally, the coefficient representing direct investment in the US is not statistically significant. Thus, the network function as related to air transportation and shipping services is neither complementary nor substitutive. In the Pacific region, the effect of service quality on modal choice is neutral.

It is important to keep in mind that the estimation period of equation (2) includes data for the 1980s. During that period, the competitive zone is only limited to the aforementioned grey zone. Hence, the estimated results of equation (2) do not necessarily reflect the characteristics of a shipper's logistics strategy and its network operations. However, it is possible to recognize a trend towards the utilisation of an air-based logistics system in the global economy. In particular, it is necessary to consider closely the economic circumstances behind the investment behavioral patterns of the three regions. For example, why is it possible to discriminate between modal choice behavior in the three regions? The answer is that the modal choice in a specific region will be affected by a logistics strategy, which is based on the competitive advantage of a specific product. In next section, we try to access this problem.

3. LOGISTICS STRATEGY AND MODAL CHOICE

3.1 Determinant factors supporting the shippers' behaviour

From the previous section, it is clear that shippers of Japanese exports base modal choice on the level of direct investment in a particular region. In this section, we attempt to construct a more sophisticated modal choice model, which represents export logistics systems.

The basic determinants of modal choice from the shippers' point of view are the following two factors which are based on the analysis in Section 2 and logistics concepts in general:
(1) The total logistics cost ratio of air-based logistics systems to sea-based logistics systems to different destinations from Japan.
(2) The level of direct investment by shippers in different regions of the world.

The total logistics cost ratio is the main factor determining basic modal choice between an air-based logistics system and a sea-based logistics system. Carriers such as airlines and container lines act as logistics service providers striving to realise an advantage in terms of reducing total logistics costs. In the current logistics era, forwarders also act as logistics service providers.

Certainly from a historical point of view of the transport service provider, air forwarders have maintained an advantage in terms of the network available for cargo booking over air carrier. In contrast to this, container-shipping carriers have dominated booking activity for cargo flows over sea borne forwarders. At this stage of development, it is possible to classify both the carrier and forwarder as transportation service providers. Based on their background, it is possible to find different advantages in terms of booking power between the carrier and the forwarder in different markets.

In the transition period, during which the transportation service provider gradually developed into a logistics service provider, shippers have strived to combine successively and cross-functionally value added logistics services with their procurement (physical supply), production support and sales marketing (physical distribution) activity. Based on the Bowersox concept, a logistics system is composed of both a value-added inventory flow as mentioned above and other required information relating to market forecasts, order analysis, production planning, and procurement planning.[5]

During the process of logistics development, the product cycle became shorter and shorter and industrial shippers preferred "speedier" logistics systems. In addition, there was a considerable increase in foreign investment in global markets at the same time. Currently, debates revolve around where the optimum location for assembly and parts production is. It has become necessary for parts production and assembly to be relocated in a timely fashion, in response to cross-functional logistics system analysis. Courier transport has been developing at a tremendously high growth rate with companies such as FedEx and UPS being representative. These companies have taken advantage of a preferential environment in which information technology has been utilized to exploit a new frontier of logistics system integration amongst different firms. Supply chain management (SCM)[6] responsive strategy has become a common component of logistics systems.

Under a SCM strategy, international express service companies are playing a leading role as an integrated carrier. FedEx utilises a SCM responsive strategy in terms of its integration with Dell Computer, Hewlett Packard, Laura Ashley,

Rosh, and American Express.[7] The integrated carrier plays the dual role of the logistics system builder and the logistics operator. Enterprising forwarders also commonly utilise this type of strategy. The role played by the integrated carrier is often referred to as third party logistics (3PL).[8]

International express services as well as enterprising air forwarder services have been developing as part of the package of services provided by the logistics system provider. This has had the effect of increasing the preference for the air mode. If this is indeed the case, it's becomes necessary to select the following as determinant factors of modal choice:

(3) international air express services,

(4) enterprising air forwarder services.

These two factors function in the incremental zone of modal choice. Needless to say, there has been a trend towards the greater utilisation of SCM in the development process of logistics. Under a SCM strategy, partnership among SCM members is the key factor leading to sustainability. The international logistics industry should insist on maintaining an equal partnership as a core member of a strategy utilising SCM. As a result, it is necessary to reflect on the level of customer satisfaction amongst member shippers in an SCM responsive logistics system. Under SCM, it is necessary to achieve cooperation amongst the final assembly company and the parts and accessory manufacturing companies. The main issue facing each member of SCM thus becomes the product cycle of the industrial goods manufactured and traded in a specific SCM system.

The product cycle has certainly been the most important factor not only during the period of the transport service provider but also currently with the logistics service provider. The role of the product cycle becomes even more important for the logistics system provider under SCM. Thus, it is necessary to add this factor as a key environmental component of modal choice in international logistics:

(5) At each stage in the logistics system, the product cycle in each region (US, EU and Asia) is distinct from each other.

There are basically five factors determining modal choice for a shipper, which are represented by the circles in Figure 2. The circles with the dotted lines represent the environment factors, which were detailed previously. The arrow indicates a causal relationship between a basic logistics strategy, the different types of providers, the five direct determinant factors and modal choice behaviour.

3.2 Product cycle theory and modal choice hypothesizing

As is well known, product cycle theory as proposed by Raymond Vernon can explain the relationship between investment behavior and cargo flows between specified countries.[9] Vernon introduced three phases – innovation, maturity and simple standardisation – which occur during the developing stages of the product cycle. Mark Casson then modified Vernon's research slightly and added a new original third stage referred to as standardised differentiation, which falls between the maturity and simple standardised stages.[10] Thus, the Vernon-Casson model depicts the total dynamics of the product cycle as follows.

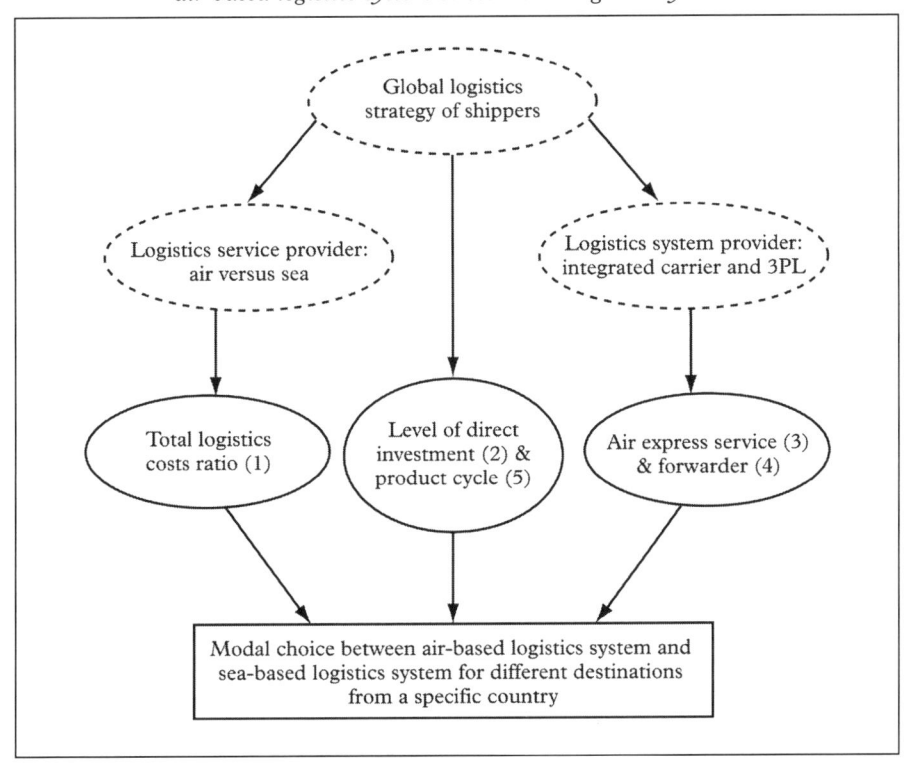

Figure 2: Modal choice flow chart of logistics system – air-based logistics system or sea-based logistics system?

During the initial stage of the life cycle, innovative products including parts and accessories are manufactured solely in the country of origin and then exported to other industrial countries. Technical advancements are directed towards reductions in labour costs. These advancements tend to be repeated to keep pace with consumer demand. As information exchanges between production and sales arms increase, it becomes more conducive to relocate the production center closer to the market. However, it is too early in the cycle to establish the know-how necessary to utilise this technique. Only a few industrial countries are able to continue such innovative market research, production and marketing in their home countries. Direct investment is restricted to establishing and expanding sales centers as foreign subsidiaries. As it is only finished goods, which flow between the parent company and the foreign subsidiary, a horizontal physical distribution flow is dominant among industrial countries in the innovative stage.

In the second stage, the transfer of manufacturing technology to foreign subsidiaries located in industrial countries is instigated by the introduction of a technological manual used for manufacturing. In this scenario, the promotion of import-oriented production is increased. Foreign subsidiaries begin to produce and assemble almost all of the necessary parts. The parent company concentrates on producing the key components of the product, in such a way that a vertical type of physical distribution appears among industrial countries. On the contrary, horizontal physical distribution is common between developed and developing countries.

The third stage of the production cycle is referred to as standardised differentiation, where a rational production method is introduced involving the division of labour among foreign subsidiaries. Under the concept of selection and concentration, each subsidiary is ordered to produce specific components if an inherent comparative advantage exists. Such a production system will promote both a refined division of labour as well as lead to a reduction in production costs. New products can be introduced by utilising different combinations of components even though the components themselves are standardised. Such an exchange system of components allows products to remain fresh and maintain differentiation. In this sense, the third stage of the product cycle determines whether or not the cycle will survive over a period of time. As a result, subsidiaries in developing countries and economies are able to produce the general components necessary for assembly, although even in this stage, a limited amount of the key components necessary to produce a given good are manufactured by the parent company. The main flow of physical distribution is horizontal with components moving from developing countries and economies to industrialised countries.

As we move towards the end of the product cycle, goods become perfectly standardised and gradually begin to lose market status. At this stage, new innovative products will begin to appear in the market.

According to product cycle theory, it is possible to construct a modal choice hypothesis pertaining to export shippers in an international logistics system.

(1) During the first stage, export shippers prefer to utilise an air-based logistics system. This is due to the highly value-added nature of innovative products, which leads to high inventory costs over time. In order to minimise total logistics costs, the share of this product shipped by air in terms of total product shipped will grow rapidly as opposed to a reduced share for a sea-based logistics system.

(2) At the second stage, as the product's life cycle begins to mature, a sea-based logistics system will be developed in parallel with an air based logistics system. The assembly line is relocated gradually to other developed industrial countries. Exports of both components from the parent company and finished goods from the subsidiary lead to a trade off relationship between air-based and sea-based logistics systems. At this point, the second stage reaches peak levels.

(3) During the third stage, the share of product moved by a sea-based logistics system increases to a greater level than the share of product moved by an air-based logistics system. Standardised differentiation promotes the utilisation of a sea-based logistics system for goods moving from emerging countries and economies to countries worldwide. On the other hand, the share of the core components shipped from the parent country is decreasing.

(4) Finally, at some point, a simple standardized product loses market share due to the appearance of new innovative products. In this final stage, the volumes of goods shipped not only by air-based but also by sea-based logistics systems will decrease simultaneously.

Based on the above hypothesis, it is possible to construct Figure 3, where the vertical axes represents the share of product shipped by an air-based logistics system on a specific export route from a specific country and the horizontal axes the share of the same product shipped by a sea-based logistics system. A product cycle with a circular line of the same orientation much like the hand of watch is generated.

Figure 3: Product cycle and the modal choice for a logistics system for export trade in a specific destination: hypothetical case

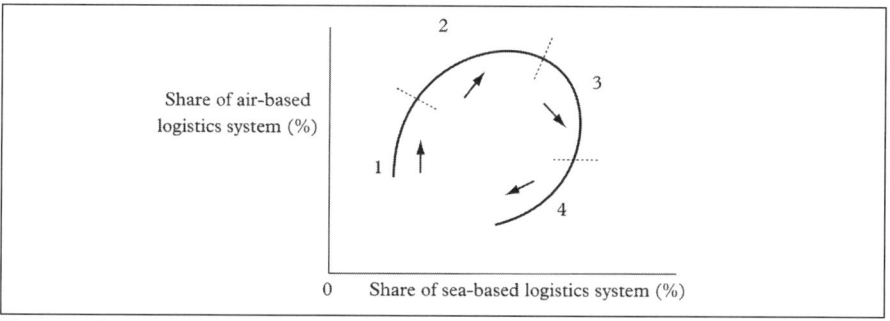

Note: 1 = Innovative stage; 2 = Matured stage; 3 = Standardise differentiation stage; 4 = Simple standardisation stage.

In order to generalise this hypothesis, we formulate the share of product shipped by an air-based and sea-based logistics system:

where S = share of products shipped by a sea-based logistics system (%),
A = share of products shipped by an air-based logistics system (%),
i = destination of products shipped from the export country (for example; 1 = US, 2 = EU, 3 = Asia), and
j = specific year (for example, j = 1998),

thus,

$$\Sigma S_{i,j} + \Sigma A_{i,j} = 100.$$

By observing the time series path of both $S_{i,j}$ and $A_{i,j}$, it is possible to drawn three theoretically generated circular lines based on the three destinations of the goods exported (i). If we input data for Japanese exports to the US, EU and Asia into the set of $S_{i,j}$ and $A_{i,j}$, it is possible in practice to trace a full circle as shown in Figure 3 and its successive half circle, which will demonstrate the modal choice of the logistics systems in each destination between 1983–1998. It is clear that a modal choice hypothesis based on the dynamic product cycle as shown in Figure 3 coincides with the current export logistics systems utilised in Japan. The main characteristic of such a system is the increase in the share of volume being shipped by an air-based logistics system. This tends to cause the central point of the circle to shift in a northwest direction.

4. MODAL CHOICE PERSPECTIVE AND DETERMINANT FACTORS OF AIR-BASED LOGISTICS SYSTEM

It is necessary to gain insight into the air-based export logistics system in a specific country in order to understand the modal choice problem from the viewpoint of international logistics. This is because it is common to construct an export logistics system based solely on air service as was concluded in the previous section. In the model, the air cargo volume of a specific product is the dependent variable. It will be determined mainly by the total distribution cost of an air-based logistics system (assumed to have a negative sign) and a sea-based logistics system (negative sign in a complementary relationship with air-based system or positive in substitutive relationship), foreign direct investment flowing from export countries to import countries in a specific industry (positive sign), the GDP of the import country (positive sign), the foreign exchange rate ratio of the export country to the import country (positive sign) and the function of the forwarder (positive sign).

In the case of an air-based logistics system, the forwarder plays a dominant role in terms of cargo booking. In other words, the air carrier initially outsources this business to the forwarder. In contrast to a sea-based logistics system, the air forwarder plays a key role as the 3PL for export shippers in order to promote their logistics activity.

In addition, the foreign exchange rate ratio of the export country to the import country represents whether the transaction of a specific product will be determined by market functions or by a long-term contract, which includes intrafirm transactions. If the transaction is market-oriented, the theoretically appropriated sign of the factor will be positive. But if intrafirm transactions are dominant, the factor will have either a negative sign or there will be no effect on the determinant.

Based on an econometric analysis of three kinds of high value export goods (automatic data processing machines, electric circuits and integrated circuits – all to six countries) which were shipped by air from Japan to the US, Germany, UK, Korea, Taiwan, Singapore, Hong Kong and Malaysia, it is possible to propose the causality of the six determinants mentioned previously and to generate an overall flow chart.

Initially, export shippers will analyse the foreign exchange rate ratio between the export and the import country. If the exporter is dealing with a market-based transaction, the foreign exchange market environment will play a significant role. Based on our analysis of the movement of automatic data processing machines and electric circuits to each of the six import countries, these types of transactions can be considered as market-oriented transactions. Integrated Circuits, on the other hand, consist of intrafirm-based transactions with exports to Korea being the only exception.

Next, we focus on the level of industrial foreign direct investment pertaining to specific products of an export country. If this factor promotes an air-based physical distribution system, as indicated by a positive sign, foreign direct investment in the industry under study indicates that the product has reached the innovative stage of product cycle. If this is not the case, then the product will be at the maturity or standardised differentiation stage of the cycle. Based on our analysis, a positive sign for the coefficient is common for the three kinds of export products shipped to the eighteen countries under study. This demonstrates that the products have reached the innovative product stage of the life cycle.

Thirdly, the GDP of the import country will represent a measure of the stability of a particular transaction. If this factor has the positive sign, the transaction will develop on a long-term basis. In our analysis, about two-thirds (10 cases out of a total of 16) of the results indicated a positive sign. But there were exceptions in six of the cases, of which three of the cases are related to exports to Germany. The three remaining cases involved exports of automatic data processing machines to Taiwan, electric circuits to Korea, and integrated circuits to Malaysia. It is possible to conclude that highly technological components exported from Japan are extremely competitive with the components of Germany and maintain a slight competitive advantage over other Asian countries.

Fourth, the function of the forwarder will promote and stimulate stability in the frequency of physical distribution. The order in rank of the import countries based on this fourth factor tends to robustly coincide with not only the order of rank based on the results of the second factor (the current stage of the product cycle) and the third factor (stability of a transaction) but also the fifth factor (total distribution cost of an air-based logistics system) which will be described in the following paragraph. This indicates that an air-based logistics system is a rational result in a multi-dimensional logistics service world. It is the operations of the forwarder that support this system and generates an effective logistics network.

The fifth determinant factor is the total distribution cost of an air-based logistics system, which operates almost uniformly to or in other words indifferently from other countries or regions.

Finally, the sixth determinant factor is the total distribution cost of a sea-based logistics system. This factor measures the level of independence of an air-based logistics system from a sea-based logistics system. Based on the estimated results, a complementary relationship exists between the two types of logistics systems, which deal with automatic data processing machines, while a substitutive relationship exists in a system dealing with electric circuits. However, the effect of this factor is similar to effect generated by the fifth determinant factor as indicated above.

In summary, shippers tend to focus on their logistics network, in which they strive to discriminate their logistics strategy between different export counties in accordance with differences in the transaction method, the product cycle, long-term transaction stability and stability in the frequency of distribution. We assume that the dynamic development of their logistics system is based on the concept of 3PL. On the contrary, shippers accept the differences in total distribution costs when compared between a sea-based logistics system and an air-based one. This generates either a complementary or substitutive relationship between the two modes. This traditional concept is generally recognized as the basis of logistics infrastructure. If we are able to consider the modal choice problem from the perspective of the logistics network strategy of shippers, it will become possible to access not only the multidimensional but also the coordinated aspects of international logistics. This is an important topic for further research.

ENDNOTES

1. Sletmo, G.K. (1984): *Demand for Air Cargo: An Econometric Approach* (Bergen, Institute for Shipping Research, Norwegian School of Economics and Business Administration).
2. Miyashita, K. (1994): "On the Fusion of International Transport Market", *Annals of the Graduate School of Business Administration*, Kobe University, p. 38.
3. Lambert, D.M., Stock, J.R., and Lisa, L.M. (1998): *Fundamentals of Logistics Management* (Boston Bur Ridge, Irwin/McGraw-Hill). Mckinnon, A.C. (1989): *Physical Distribution System* (London and New York, Routledge). Wood, D.F., Barone, A., Murphy, P., and Wardlow, D.L. (1995): *International Logistics* (New York, Chapman & Hall). Gourdin, K.N. (2001): *Global Logistics Management* (Oxford, UK, Blackwell).
4. Sletmo, G.K., and Williams, Jr. (1981): *Liner Conferences in the Container Age* (New York, Macmillan).
5. Bowersox, D.J., Closs, D.J., and Helfrich, O.K. (1986): *Logistical Management* (New York, Macmillan). Bowersox, D.J., and Closs, D.J. (1996): *Logistical Management* (New York, McGraw-Hill).
6. Younger, K. (1997): *Logistics Trends in European Consumer Goods: Challenge For Suppliers, Retailers and Logistics Companies* (London, *Financial Times*). Christopher, M. (1998): *Logistics and Supply Chain Management* (2nd ed.) (London, *Financial Times*). Committee on Supply Chain Integration (2000): *Surviving Supply Chain Integration* (Washington, DC, National Academy Press).
7. Taylor, D. (ed.) (1997): *Global Cases in Logistics and Supply Chain Management* (London and Boston, International Thomson Business Press). Dornier, P.-P., Ernst, R., Fender, M., and Kouvelis, P. (1998): *Global Operations and Logistics* (New York, John Wiley & Sons).
8. OECD (1996): *Integrated Advanced Logistics for Freight Transport*, report prepared by an OECD Scientific Group (Paris, OECD).
9. Vernon, R. (1966): "International Investment and International Trade in the Product Cycle", *Quarterly Journal of Economics*, LXXX.
10. Casson, M. (1986): *Multinational and World Trade* (London, Allen & Unwin).

CHAPTER 38

THE ECONOMICS OF INTERNATIONAL TRADE LOGISTICS AND SHIPPING TRANSACTIONS

Ernst G. Frankel

Massachusetts Institute of Technology, Massachusetts, USA.
E-mail: *Efrankel@mit.edu*

1. INTRODUCTION

International trade, and in particular trade in break bulk goods, has grown rapidly in recent years. This is to an extent the result of an increased use of global outsourcing which, in some industries such as the automobile industry, now accounts for over 20% of the total costs of that industry. International trade logistics which includes all physical and non-physical services and transactions required to move international trade are now estimated to exceed one trillion dollars per year, a cost which is growing at 6–8% per year as outsourcing, globalization of trade, and more recently e-commerce continue to grow. The rapid expansion of these trades introduces new challenges. Most important among them is control of logistics and particularly shipping costs and service quality.

A major issue has been the underestimation of non-transport logistics costs. Logistics costs are usually assumed to consist largely of transport costs, while in reality, the cost of transport itself often contributes less than 50% and sometimes as little as 30% of total door-to-door logistics costs. This problem is particularly acute in container and trailer ocean and land transport, where new technology, larger ship size, double-trailer combinations, double-stack unit trains, and more have resulted in major economies of sea, road, rail, and inland water unitized cargo transport. Yet these same improvements in transport efficiency often contribute to major new increases in intermodal, port and other interface investment and operating costs. For example, the increase in and introduction of large numbers of post-panamax containerships has resulted in the ratio of TEU containers handled by ports to TEU actually transported by transocean vessels to grow from 2.2 to 3.8 between 1990 and 1999. In other words, 55% of all transocean containers moved are now transshipped at least once.

This trend is expected to continue with as many as 50% of all transocean containers transshipped (twice) at transshipment ports at each end of their trade route. This may drive up the number of times containers are handled at ports (transferred to or from ships) to nearly five by 2010. This trend may cause port or terminal, as well as transactional, costs to rise even more in both absolute as well as relative terms.

2. LOGISTICS AND SHIPPING TRANSACTIONS

Shipping, and particularly container shipping, has become an integral part of intermodal logistics chains and its management as a result must be fully integrated into total logistic supply chain management. This in turn demands integration of information management, approval, inspection, and other transactional services.

Shown in Table 1 is the multitude of participants in trade logistics and shipping information flows. These in turn use various transactions, approvals, and operational management decisions such as money transfers or payments, customs clearance, bills of lading or other documentary issuance, escrow account deposits, space bookings, cargo routing, insurance estimates, and many more. In fact, today it is quite common to require in excess of 50 different documents in international door-to-door trade of containerised break bulk cargo.

Table 1: Participants in supply chain and shipping information flows

• Port and terminal operators	• Rate bureaus/agencies
• Freight forwarders	• General shipping agents
• Cargo consolidators	• Warehousing companies
• Customs/clearance agents	• Stevedoring companies
• Cargo bureaus (valuators)	• Shippers' representatives
• Customs authorities	• Tax agents/agencies
• Environmental protection agencies	• Classification agencies
• Agricultural inspectors	• Government import/export
• Health and safety inspectors	(commerce) agencies
• Freight/cargo brokers	• Trade financing institutions
• Cargo traders	(banks)
• Cargo insurers	• Others

These procedures are not only expensive but such paper-based systems are prone to many errors, are difficult to transact and store, and cause innumerable delays. Modern electronic management information systems offer the opportunity to eliminate paper-based information recording, transfer, and approval processes.

In this chapter the economies of international trade logistics and shipping transactions are discussed and approaches towards a completely paperless transactional system are advanced. These advances would be designed to not only reduce the inordinately high costs of traditional transaction management, but also eliminates most of the inherent time losses and inaccuracies of the currently used systems.

Typical documentation flows in international freight transportation are shown in Table 2 that lists over 30 documents. Many of these must be submitted to more than one recipient and/or originate from more than one source. Overall, there is an 80% overlap in the information registered on these documents. Recent studies by US Customs indicate that by adding about 20% more information to existing forms, the number of universal forms required could be reduced to five or fewer. Currently document responsibility rests with the following:

(1) *Shippers and their agents (freight forwarders, brokers, etc.)* are responsible for preparing: bills of lading (ocean, inland/domestic, dock receipts, delivery documents, export declarations, consular invoices, commercial invoices, certificates of origin, insurance certificates, etc.)
(2) *Shipping and transport companies* prepare cargo plans, loading/unloading plans, arrival notices, etc.
(3) *Consignees, their agents, customs brokers, etc.*, prepare letters of credit, customs entries, carrier certificates, inland/domestic bills of lading, delivery orders, etc.

Increases in both foreign and domestic governmental controls, and inspection and recording requirements have affected an inundation of documentary and information requirements to satisfy imposed restrictions and regulations. This deluge of paper requirements is today a major drag on efficient logistics operations, particularly in foreign trade.

Table 2: *Typical documentation requirements and agents*

Shippers agents	**Shippers**	**Rail carriers**
Booking documents	Instructions receipt,	
Space charters	Acknowledge	**Ports/terminals**
	Customs declaration	Inland depots
	Export declarations	
Customs	Shipment trace documents	**Truckers**
Declaration review	Lighterage documents	
Declaration approvals	Cargo consolidation documents	**Banks and**
	Delivery permits	**financial**
Consular offices	Shipper advisories	**institutions**
	Carrier bookings	Escrow agents
Shipping companies	Consular documents – invoices	
Dock receipts	Bills of lading	**Government &**
Customs receipts	Dock delivery documents	**trade**
	Dock receipts	**facilitators**
Insurance underwriters	Customs declaration	Export and import
Cargo bureaus	Packing lists	
Cargo inspectors	Commercial invoices	**Security agents**
Agents/brokers	Insurance declarations	
Shipping/cargo	Risk specifications	
	Insurance certificates	
	Billing documents	
	Invoices	
	Consular invoices	
	Bills of charges	
	Cargo plans	
	Stacking/storage plans	
	Staffing plans	
	Receipts	
	Transfers	
	Bills of charge	
	Consignees	

2.1 Determination of logistics and transactional costs of international trade

Logistics costs are difficult to derive not only because of the number of parties involved in supplying services in a supply or intermodal transport chain, but also because many of the parties involved have diverse or overlapping interests. For example, major container shipping lines such as APL and others are usually also engaged in bulk, tanker, and other shipping, as well as logistic and IT services. They may similarly also own or operate unit trains, trucking, and terminals. Therefore to determine their container liner operating revenues, revenues from other activities must be backed out. This was done using annual reports of the major publicly traded companies. The results were used to estimate those of other container liner operators, assuming on average similar revenues in proportion to fleet size and composition. Using revenues for oil and dry bulk carrier, general cargo, and other shipping operators obtained from reports of publicly-traded companies, reports, revenues for the world fleet of these vessels were obtained as shown in Table 3.

Obviously this kind of scaling assumes that all operators are equally effective in the use of their fleet capacity. Tanker and dry bulk carrier revenues were also adjusted for age as charter rates are usually affected by the age of the vessel, particularly in the case of tankers. To verify the results global fleet data assembled by size and age distribution and by percentage of fleet utilisation and prevailing charter rates were used to verify the results. Obviously, these revenue estimates are approximate as other factors such as local demands, imbalances in supply, oil price, and more affect owner revenues. Yet, we feel that the results are reasonably accurate.

Table 3: World ocean shipping revenues container carrier revenues ($ Billions)

	1987	1989	1991	1993	1995	1997	1999
14 major carriers*	26.6	27.9	35.6	39.7	43.5	46.5	52.0
Other liner operators	8.8	9.1	9.3	9.7	10.2	10.5	11.2
Total	35.4	37.0	44.9	49.7	53.7	56.6	63.2
Operating Profit (major 14)	–0.7	0.6	0.4	0.6	0.5	0.7	0.9
Other types of shipping revenues ($ Billions)							
	1987	1989	1991	1993	1995	1995	1999
Oil and dry bulk carriers							
Estimated Revenues	28.4	30.1	32.3	35.4	37.8	39.8	42.6
General cargo carriers							
Estimated Revenues	9.2	9.4	10.1	10.7	11.6	12.3	13.1
Other shipping (short sea, etc.)							
Estimated revenues	6.8	7.2	7.4	7.9	8.2	8.5	9.1
Total shipping							
Estimated revenues	79.8	83.7	94.7	103.7	111.3	117.2	128.0

Source: Containerisation International and others.
* Sealand, NYK, MOL, Nedlloyd, OOCL, Zim, APL/NOL, HMM, NYK, KL, Hapag Lloyd, CGM, Maersk. Estimated.
Comments: It should be noted that major container shipping companies such as NOL, Maersk, etc., also operate other shipping as well as other services and operations.

ECONOMICS OF INTERNATIONAL TRADE LOGISTICS

Table 4: International trade – 1999

Seaborne international trade		
Capacity:	Tankers	DWT 311 m
	Dry bulk	DWT 281 m
	Containerships	DWT 58 m
	General cargo	*DWT 98 m*
	Total	DWT 748 m
Volume Container 49.2 m TEU (Port throughput 190.2 m TEU) (1694 crude, 608 prod)		
Seaborne trade volume		
Volume:	Liquid bulk (1694 m tons crude, 608 mtons product)	2302 m tons
	Dry Bulk	1980 m tons
	General Cargo	441 m tons
	Containerised Cargo (49.2 m TEU, Port Throughput 190.2 m TEU)	*499 m tons*
	Total Seaborne	5222 m tons
Non-ocean international trade (North America Canada/US/Mexico, Intra Europe, Intra Asia, etc.)		
Volume:	Container (trailer)	318 m tons
	Liquid bulk	1620 m tons
	Dry bulk	880 m tons
	General cargo	*322 m tons*
	Total	3130 m tons
Total volume international trade (1999):		8,352 m tons

Seaborne trade volume and ship supply capacities are shown in Table 4 were obtained from sources such as UNCTAD, Container International, IMO, and various other sources. Non-ocean international trade was obtained from OECD and various trade organisations. Land and non-liner water feeder transport, including inland water transport, was estimated for both seaborne and non-seaborne international trade using

- feeder service ocean port data,
- international trade carried by inland water transport to/from international sea ports,
- inland feeder rail or truck traffic serving ports.

Similarly, for non-seaborne international trade border crossing or national trade statistics were used. For example, US/Canadian trade by truck and rail, etc. To compute estimated revenues, volumes were multiplied by published tariffs where available or estimated. The results for both seaborne or all-inland international trade, land and water, feeder or inland transport are summarised in Table 5.

Port, terminal, inland depot, warehousing, tank farm, rental and similar costs (Table 6) were computed from sample charges. For seaborne containerised trades for example port charges were obtained by multiplying say the 1999 port throughput of 190.3 m TEU by the average port charges per TEU for loading/unloading plus wharfage, tonnage, pilotage, storage, etc., costs which were estimated at $182/TEU. The resulting container terminal charges of $34.6b were added to estimate inland depot, warehousing, and handling charges onto or off inland transport to reach the total cost of $80.0 b. Similarly, average tank farm, warehousing, and transfer costs were used to estimate these costs for seaborne international trade bulk commodities and general cargo.

Table 5: Land and water feeder transport in international trade (1999 $billions)

Year	1987	1989	1991	1993	1995	1997	1999
Containership Feeders	4.3	4.9	5.3	5.9	6.7	7.9	9.2
Tanker Lightering and Feeding	3.1	3.4	3.9	4.2	4.8	5.4	5.9
Inland Water	6.4	7.2	7.8	8.3	9.2	10.1	10.6
Rail	19.2	20.8	22.3	23.9	25.3	27.1	28.8
Truck	76.7	82.3	89.2	95.4	102.9	111.8	122.7
Pipeline	11.2	12.8	14.2	15.3	16.2	17.4	18.8
Total	120.9	131.4	142.7	153.0	165.1	179.7	196.0

Table 6: Port, terminal, and inland depot/warehouse revenues (1999 $billions)

	Bulk	General cargo	Container
Ocean Terminals and Ports*	18.2	30.6	104.0
Inland Depots and Ports	12.8	14.4	42.8
Warehouses	7.4	21.0	30.2
Tank Farms/Stockpiles	18.6	B	–
Total	57.0	66.0	177.0
Grand total			**300.0**

*Container terminal throughput 190.2m TEU.

Interestingly it was found that non-seaborne international trade was usually transported over significantly longer land transport distances than seaborne trade which used ports closely located with respect to origin or final destination. As a result though, seaborne international containerised cargo trade is somewhat smaller than seaborne trade, transport and depot, warehousing, handling, and related costs were found to be higher on both average and in total.

Finally, the most difficult problem was to estimate transaction costs by which we imply costs of all non-physical services associated with the logistics chain. These include administration, information management, brokerage, agency, commission, insurance, bank fees, costs of discounts, inspection, marketing, representation, and more. These were found to dominate in containerised or trailer trades which came as something of a surprise. Another surprise was the high cost of container, trailer, and tanker repositioning. In seaborne container trades just ocean repositioning costs of containers in international trade are estimated to account for $11.8 billion in 1999 or nearly 20% of total container shipping costs. Adding handling, port, land transport, and related repositioning costs more than triples that number. This truly is an incentive for better coordination of empty repositioning among operators and containers lessors. We faced a similar problem with empty trailers in non-seaborne international trade though data is difficult to obtain.

Total estimated costs of international trade logistics are summarised in Table 7, which shows the dominance of transaction or non-physical management and service costs. It is here where the greatest opportunities for both cost savings and performance improvements exist. In recent years we concentrated most of our efforts on improving efficiencies of transport modes, larger and more efficient ships, unit trains, feeders, trucks, barges, etc. It appears that we are reaching a state of diminishing returns in that area and that other cost components in complex logistic chains offer greater opportunities for cost savings and performance improvements.

The data assembled here obviously represents gross estimates and is by no means an accurate statement of actual costs. It was compiled from general sources and may include significant errors. The purpose of this work was to get orders of magnitude and gross relative costs and was driven by the recognition that pure transport (ton mile, slot mile, etc.) costs constitute a very small percentage of total door-to-door costs, particularly in international trade. Another issue was the amounts internally spend by shippers and consignees on transaction-type costs such as response inventory, delay, documentation, communication, credit/escrow, and other costs that do not appear in computations of logistics costs. These may constitute 5–15% of total logistics costs. These costs were included in our estimates.

Table 7: Summary table – costs of international trade logistics (1999 $billions)

Transocean Trade — 5.22 billion tons
Non-transocean (all inland including inland water) — 3.13 billion tons
Total 8.35 billion tons

	Bulk commodities			General break bulk cargo			Containerised cargo			Total		
	Total	Seaborne	Inland	Total	Seaborne	Inland	Total	Seaborne	Inland	Total	Seaborne trade	Land trade
Shipping*	42.6	42.6	–	13.1	13.1	–	72.37	63.6	9.2	128.0	119.3	9.1*
Land transport inland water, pipe, road, rail, etc.	49.1	20.0	29.0	21.0	6.0	15.0	126.0	38.0	88.0	196.0	64.0	132.0
Port, inland depot, depot, tankfarms, warehousing, rentals, etc.	57.0	19.0	38.0	66.0	24.0	42.0	177.0	80.0	117.0	300.0	123.0	187.0
IT, transaction, brokers fees, cargo, insurance, leasing, etc.	40.0	12.8	27.2	52.0	21.2	30.8	196.0	78.0	118.0	286.0	112.0	174.0
Total	188.6	94.4	94.2	152.1	64.3	87.8	571.3	209.6	332.2	910.0	409.9	502.1

* Ocean positioning costs of empty containers by container shipping are estimated to be $11.8b in 1999, excluding port handling, trucking, and lost opportunity costs (Drewry 2000).

In other words, about 34% of the total (door-to-door) logistics costs of international containerised trade are consumed by IT, transactions, documentation, and related costs. This is obviously extraordinary in an age of technological breakthroughs in electronic information and communications technology.

3. OPPORTUNITIES FOR IMPROVEMENTS AND IMPACT OF THE NEW MARKET TECHNOLOGY

It appears that the major advances in transport technology and electronics have not produced the economic bonanza in logistics costs and performance over the short run. Post-panamax containerships, double-stack unit trains, and fast post-panamax container gantries have marginally reduced the unit costs of operations, but often as in the case of large ships at the cost of added needs for costly transshipment.

On the other hand, E-commerce firms, particularly in B–to–C commerce which expected electronics to provide major economies and added market attractions, found the economies lacking and market responses to be indifferent. It now appears that major mistakes were made in both the introduction of physical and electronic technology into logistics enterprises and a reevaluation is urgently needed to assure that the technological advances really provide improvements in logistics performance and costs.

Most importantly, transaction management must be vastly improved and many transactional steps eliminated. It is curious that while we use advance electronic communications in most transactional steps, the rationale or even need for many of these steps, particularly in money transactions, verification, authorization, control, and more, are seldom questioned. It is essential to eliminate as many intermediaries and intermediate transactions or operations as possible, assure near seamlessness of all operations, reduce intermodal delays and inventories, and integration everything into paperless real time managed operations.

New electronic IT and communications technology provide the tools for the seamless integration of all logistics operations, particularly all physical transfer and transport operations with few if any transaction links and real time information flow, control, and monetary transactions or transfers, eliminating all transactional paper requirements and transferring and storing all documentation electronically for real time or delayed accounting or approvals. Currently e-commerce uses old economy methods or transactions. Just using electronic technology does not significantly enough improve these old economy approaches to have a significant impact and justify the large investments in e-commerce. New economy transactional approaches must be developed and used to assure the hoped-for savings from e-commerce. This is true in international trade and e-commerce in general as well as e-logistics which, to accrue real advantages must redesign associated transactions in a truly new economy form.

As noted, transactional costs consist largely of marketing, administration, inspection, verification, billing, collection, tracking, etc. A larger sample of container moves by simple truck–ship–truck logistic chains which include intermodal inventory and storage costs show that on average 26% of total logistics costs are spent on transport, with about 34% for terminal, interface, inventory storage, etc., and the rest for transaction costs. On long intercontinenal moves, the breakdown is usually 35%, 35%, and 30%, while on shorter intra-continental multi-modal moves which involve at least three sequential modal carriers it averages 30%, 35%, and 35%.

Great improvements have been achieved in road, sea, and rail transport efficiency and costs, but much more must be done in improving intermodal terminal or transfer efficiency and costs as well as in reducing major non-transport or transactional costs. The latter is highly information, technology, and use dependent and new IT developments offer opportunities to greatly reduce and often eliminate unnecessary transactional costs. For example, automated electronic funds transfer for logistic services rendered when the service is performed or has been completed versus hard copy billing and collection often lowers transactional cost by 10% or more, while improving logistic chain efficiency, and obviously cash flow. Some intermodal logistic service providers such as the Port of Singapore do exactly that and have become completely paperless operations with total cost savings in excess of 25%, as well as vast improvements in terminal capacity utilissation, user responsiveness, and cash flow.

The major logistic systems functions and cost elements for typical supply chains are listed in Table 8 and can be divided into seven major functions as shown. The logistic system provides the network of the physical transfer/transport, inventory, flow, transactional, and marketing system functions required, including the management of all the procurement, outsourcing, and delivery functions. The objective is to combine logistic systems management efficiency with flexibility which permits near real time, seamless, adjustment of the logistics function network to respond to changing market, product demand, technology, material procurement, outsource availability and cost, and manufacturing requirements and conditions.

It should be noted that the non-physical elements of the logistic system requirements (Items 4–7) are all information intensive activities. These were in the past largely performed using low-speed communications, hard copy, and rather cumbersome approval, inspection or verification processes. Their costs as a result exceeded the cost and time required for the performance of the physical transport or transfer. Similarly, the cost and time spend on intermodal, pre/post modal or consolidation/deconsolidation transfer and associated handling often exceeds that of the actual transport and transfer required by logistics management. Here mismatch in size of modal vehicles such as ships and trucks, for example, lack of seamlessness, and ineffective intermodal transfer management and technology use are often to blame.

4. E-LOGISTICS SOLUTIONS

Logistic systems can be broken down into physical logistics functions such as transportation, intra- and intermodal handling, and buffer/storage handling and inventorizing/warehousing, packaging, consolidation/deconsolidation on one hand and management, transactional, and marketing functions or services on the other hand. While some of the latter such as inspection, clearance, and marketing/delivery may involve some physical processes, by and large they require information handling, storage, review, approval, etc., much of which can today be done much more efficiently, seamlessly, cheaply, and in near real time by the effective choice and use of modern information, computing, and communications technology. The purpose is usually to not only streamline but also consolidate the total supply chain from source of supply through the whole logistics, manufacturing, assembly, to marketing and even maintenance chain activities, making everything as seamless, self-correcting, and integrated as possible by the use of integrated electronically managed, paperless trransactions, and management. The main objective is to eliminate many of the transactional activities and thereby the need for many of the middlemen, brokers, forwarders, warehousers, and much of the intermediate logistics and financing transaction facilitators and related hard copy activities. This results in a radical change in the structure of logistics systems and trade by making it a truly seamless business-to-business transaction without any intermediaries and delays.

A major reason for the high transaction and management costs of logistic systems is that information generated by the various physical logistics functions as

Table 8: Major logistic systems cost elements

Item	Logistics system function	Major components
1.	Transportation	Land transport – road/rail/pipe, etc.
	Sea transport	
2.	Inter- and intra-modal handling	Consolidation
		Deconsolidation
		Packaging
		Loading
		Unloading
		Transfer
3.	Buffer storage handling and inventory	Inventory – lot size build up
		Buffer accumulation
		Regulatory approval storage
4.	Logistics operations management (standard operations)	Modal choice and sequencing
		Scheduling
		Routing
		Tracking
		Receipt/delivery management
5.	Supply chain management (customised requirements)	Material and parts procurement
		Vendor/supplier outsource selection and management
		Order entries
		Receiving management
		Quality management
		Delivery management
6.	Transaction management	Documentation
		Clearance – Customs, excise, customer, etc.
		Inspection - quality control
		Title registration
		Delivery approval guarantee
		Audit trail B validation
		Billing B invoicing
		Payment guarantees
		Insurance - use of futures/derivatives and risk management tools
		Security control
		Money transfers - exchange costs
		Exchange control
		Transaction financing
		Outsource specification and documentation
7.	Marketing	Customer identification and sale channels
		Customer and market preferences
		Product identification and technological change
		Product delivery channels and alternatives
		Sales

well as for the various externally imposed regulatory, inspection, and other requirements is seldom ever effectively coordinated, standardised or integrated. As a result, huge amounts of uncoordinated data flows usually accompany or more often follow the logistic chain. This in turn causes wastage of effort or costs and time in trying to consolidate and verify information and often introduces serious errors which in turn cause delays, added costs, wrong deliveries, and consequential problems in manufacturers and order delivery.

Table 9: Intermodal transport information flow

Shipper			
Content, weight, special handling requirements	Internet requirements		Transport requirements
Clearance – customs inspection requirements	Commerce server	Web server	Transport link, route schedule alternatives
	Data base matching capacity with demand		Transport providers
	Credit clearing	Auction of excess capacity and services	Transport integration
	Special terms		
Transport and contract terms			
Contract approvals and terms of payment			
Service provision			
Order receipt			
Consignee			

Table 10: Decisions and information flow

	Change in decision
	Information requirements
Form & format of information	Sources of information Information collection, manipulation and storage
Conversion of information to use	Transmission of information Receipt of information
	Information use
	New decision
	Generation of new information resulting from new decision
	Transmission of new information to other affected functions B decisions

We need a completely integrated logistics management information system which performs the functions of all the dispersed functions as listed in Table 9 which are now largely managed by their own specialised information systems if any. To achieve this the various responsible internal and external parties or agencies must agree on standardised terms, measures, recordings, information content, validity checks, and more. For example, just considering a single shipper-to-consignee transport chain, the information flow generated and used to manage that chain is highly complex as performed now (Table 10). This is particularly worrisome as it is usually handled as a stand-alone information system without effective information exchange with external parties who may affect or be affected by these operations.

The intermodal transport listed requires on average over 50 separate documents and several hundred items of information, many of which are time varying and dependent on external developments such as fuel costs, port or terminal occupancy, interest or exchange rates. The transport information flow management is often handled in complete isolation of manufacturing, procurement, and marketing information flow. As a result, major inconsistencies creep in which in turn cause extra delays, costs, and often misdeliveries and customer dissatisfaction. Each of the action items listed in Table 2 usually involves and/or generates a fair number of data or information items. Nowadays these are usually handled as stand-alone information and only used to meet the needs of subsequent decision requirements. For example, content and special handling requirements information will be used in rate and service but not necessarily in inspection, financial, and special term decisions. Similarly, this information may not be coordinated with non-transport information generated or required. The most urgent need is therefore the complete integration and standardisation of information in all logistic systems functions.

Although the various logistic system functions are interdependent, they are usually handled separately in terms of related information management. Adjustments are only made periodically which cause a lot of revaluations and reassignment. These in turn are the major causes for large transactional and other non-transport logistics costs. While it is often practical to design a separate management information and control system for each of the major logistics functions listed in Table 1, it is essential to design effective real time information links which assure continuous near real time updating of all the functions. For example, information on a change in origin of a major delivery would obviously affect demand for and scheduling of transport capacity, inter- and intramodal handling, and much more. Therefore, near real time information links must be available between all interdependent functions so as to permit effective change management. Each decision in the logistic system and the supply chain requires up-to-date information and generates new information which affects other decisions and resulting performance of logistic functions. Table 9 is a simple list showing the information flow.

While much of this results in a long paper trail, the inter-, intra-, and ethernet give us the tools to perform information transfer updating and use by paperless and in future completely wireless operations in near real time. The Internet's ability to handle data, audio, and video gives us an ability to streamline all non-transport and particularly transactional functions, makes them not only more efficient, but also more accurate and effective. Our ability to translate audio into text and data or *vice versa* and transmit accurate video allows us to integrated most of the management and transactional functions and requirements of complex logistic systems.

6. WHERE DO WE GO FROM HERE?

With the imminent availability of Internet 2 with higher band width networks, more efficient protocols for the transfer of data, communications speeds of up to 2.4 Gigabyte/sec, and the more ready availability of capable portable wireless devices, most if not all wired communication based and often paperbound transactional services, associated traditionally with logistics systems, will soon be replaced resulting in major cost reductions in getting the product to the buyer. Logistic services add value by transporting or transferring products from lower to higher value locations. Transactional and other non-transport services usually add little, if any, value to the product and their costs must be reduced or eliminated. The Web offers unique new potentials to B–to–B e-commerce and Web enabled logistic services provide both access to real time market places and manufacturing capacity and more efficient, faster, and cheaper movement of products.

E-logistic exchanges are now under development and should provide for vastly improved and much lower cost supply chains for parts and material procurement e-commerce enterprises such as COVISINT. Use of e-logistics solutions abound and the effective use of the Internet in improving transactional and other non-transport logistic services or functions is developing rapidly. Recent developments include:

(1) Standardisation of logistic measures such as volume, weight, density, containment, frequency of service, schedule, etc.
(2) Standardisation of measures of logistic services such as cost and time of origin to destination transport, etc.
(3) Standardisation of unit costs for transport, transfer, and storage or warehousing services
(4) Standardisation of receipt and delivery documents and acceptance (legality) of electronic documentation such as bills of lading, manifests, etc.
(5) Standardisation of clearance and inspection requirements and acceptance of electronic clearance and certification
(6) Standardisation of financial transaction documents, clearances, approvals, and transfers

Many regulatory and customs authorities (such as US Customs) are converting their clearance, approval or licensing requirements to electronic systems. Similarly, many of the modal transport operators, such as shipping, air, and road transport companies, are moving rapidly towards Internet-based electronic data transfer and operations management for cargo load planning to scheduling, manifest transmittal/approval/clearance to space marketing and feeder or other modal interface management. As a result, we are rapidly developing largely e-based transport management and control systems. It is now necessary to integrate the traditional transactional and other non-transport services in the logistics system or eliminate them to achieve the major cost reductions in getting the product to the buyer which can be as large as 50% of current logistics costs. E-logistics is not a dream but an achievable reality and an essential development to assure the full benefits of globalisation.

The amount of hard copy documentation used is still huge, independent of the fact that most port and shipping operators made large investments in information, communication, and computing technology that permit large-scale reduction and/or elimination of hard copy recording, documentation, etc. Also many of the regulatory, inspection or tax collecting agencies from customs to classification societies, immigration, and more are in many countries today fully computerized. Therefore, most if not all the traditional hand-type transactional operations could be eliminated while still providing all the required information. There are opportunities not only for major cost savings in reducing and/or eliminating many of the transactions but such a move would similarly permit the streamlining of the total door-to-door supply chain by eliminating many of the delays caused by the unavailability of documentation or information when required to proceed with operations or transport. Recent transactional developments in e-logistics (Table 11) provide effective tools for the introduction of e-paper or all electronic logistic information, documentation, and control or management systems in logistics operations.

Table 11: Transactional developments in e-logistics

Internet 2	high band width – efficient protocols for data transfer – high communication speeds – multi-function hand-held wireless devices
Integration	order entry – operational, inspection/approval – financial – order receipt - marketing functions
Standardisation	data formats – entry – reporting – performance measures – control receipt
Coordination	financial – operational marketing – outsourcing – manufacturing B delivery – exchanges with E-commerce
Web-enabled logistic systems	

There is a whole array of E-logistics programs available, some as part of large integral service systems such as Singapore's PORTNET which was moved onto the Internet and provides various E-commerce suites such as EZ-Ship, Boxchange, SlotMax, and eOrdering, designed to help port users such as shipping companies with their transshipment management, empty box management, and in the trade of empty vessel slots among shipping lines. Other E-solutions such as CITOS are designed to improve port operations by using real time, wireless data communication to manage port activities, while GEMS is a global equipment management system designed largely to help manage empty container inventories. In addition, there are a number of broader based marine E-commerce sites such as Asiaship.com which offers capacity marketing and other services including bunkers, supply services, ship repair, and more. There are similarly Internet portals offering ship repair, bunkers, crew hiring, and other services. While some are designed as E-commerce sites and major operators such as APL have become leaders in E-logistics, Cargo Exchange-Net and others again concentrate on selling excess capacity. Major interest is growing in auction marketing of marine services where excess ship (slot, tanker, bulk carrier, etc.) capacity is auctioned to users who cannot afford to ship at full freight. Similarly, ports may in future consider auctioning off unused capacity and time at their facilities and equipment.

While these are very useful, we will soon see the development of completely integrated E-port and E-shipping management where the Internet and wireless broad band communications are used to:

- market and book cargo including auctioning of excess capacity as well as containers
- reserve cargo space, containers, feeder transport for just-in-time pickup/delivery, minimise empty space and containers
- coordinate all cargo flows
- schedule of transport links
- develop cargo plans including loading/unloading plans
- generate electronically all required E-documents
- licenses, E-customs, forms, etc.
- generate and file E-bills of lading
- assure timely clearance, funds transfers or credit authorisations
- track all cargo, information, and E-clearances/documentation
- integrate all intermodal flows
- schedule and route ships and assign cargo capacity
- manage shipboard personnel, ship supplies, bunkers, ship surveys, ship repairs, inspection, etc., and assure up-to-date certification
- assure effective customer service by real time customer access to all information
- monitor all cargo, ship, and other vehicle flows
- provide real time information and feedback to all organisations as well as customers
- assure effective integration of network with ports, inland depots, various modal carriers, and major customers

In other words, we are rapidly moving to a state where bridge-controlled ships manned by 11–14 crew will be managed via the Internet centrally by a skeleton of experts with all cargo booking, space or vehicle assignment, transport coordination, delivery of crew bunkers and ship supplies, and in fact all the management of the ships and the shipping companies done using the Internet and related technology.

In ports, we will similarly use the Internet and wireless communication-based systems to:

- market port services and port capacity, including the auctioning of excess capacity
- assign facilities, space, and equipment to various users and uses
- control equipment and facility operations
- manage intermodal cargo and vehicle flow in and out of the port
- introduce electronic cargo flow control, clearance, release, acceptance, etc.

- collect all data and provide necessary information, documentation, on cargo and ship traffic, etc.
- assure E-fund transfer, cargo flow communications, etc.
- schedule equipment surveys, repair, supplies, replacement, etc.
- manage power, water, communications, and other services in the port and to port users
- manage port personnel assignment, use, payroll, hiring/firing, etc.
- manage safety and environmental requirements of port and port equipment

Similarly, these e-logistic systems will manage all inspections, controls, verifications, and regulatory activities, inform respective agencies, trigger releases or retentions and arrange for storage, transfer, notification, and ultimately pick-up and delivery by land transport.

Such developments are expected to not only significantly reduce transaction costs of land transport, ports and shipping, but also to reduce or eliminate time losses. The potential direct monetary savings should be of the order of 30% of total logistics costs, but higher ship and port utilisation of unused capacity and better in time operations could also add to profitability by greatly increasing revenues. To support efficient information flow, interactive web sites using vertical and horizontal portals should be used to record and store information and connect the various parties concerned.

6.1 The role of wireless communications and the Internet in logistics management

Wireless communications have exploded with the advance of wireless technology and applications. There are over 100 million wireless subscribers in the U.S. and over 650 million worldwide now. Similarly, the costs of wireless communications have gone down by 50% over the last decade. Wireless Internet access is also now a reality. We now have web access on pagers, cell phones, hand-held

Table 12: Wireless communications for enterprise resource planning in logistics

Wireless Gateway XML based Conversion	Wireless Devices Wireless Networks Internet Link Middleware Servers: Applications Synchronisation Transformation of Data and Information *Enterprise Resource Planning* *E-Logistics* *Supply Chain Management Systems*	Wireless Server WAP etc.

computers, etc. In two years, wireless Internet users will exceed PC Internet users. While there are still problems with technical standards, GSM, CDMA (Asia), these should be resolved on a global level soon. The U.S. is behind Europe and particularly Asia in wireless Internet use at this time, but rapidly catching up. We expect that in three years, 300 million out of 900 million wireless phones will be Internet-ready, but to make this a meaningful advance, the speed of wireless Internet connections must improve. While new technology formats such as WAP (wireless access protocol) and iModeDoCoMo/Japan (not WAP compatible) among others are already available, they still have major shortcomings in terms of speed and mobility. Out of 400 million Internet subscribers in year 2000, only about 28 million or 8% were mobile Internet subscribers. Wireless is increasingly accepted as the foundation of global E-commerce and E-logistics, but such technology must scale globally (Table 12).

Search engines, for example, are largely tied to the English language only and often cannot handle double byte character sets as used in many Asian languages. An important issue in wireless Internet communication is not just data compression in communication but also in presentation. While on a computer screen web pages contain as many as 250 words, cell phone and similar hand-held devices often accommodate only 20–40 words.

Wireless communication has been used by ships for decades, but not ports are starting to recognize its value in managing and controlling spread-out port operations from actual equipment control, gate control, to cargo sequencing, recording, and many other functions. Recently a major shortcoming in wireless short-range communications has been overcome. Bluetooth (Ericcson, Sweden), a low power technology (Freq 2.4 Ghz band) allows laptops, cell phones, hand-held devices, etc. to communicate over short distances (with much less radiation). Bluetooth technology users short range radio frequencies to transmit voice and data over ranges as short as 30' (10m) enabling a personal area network to be established over short distances or in confined spaces. It connects to the Internet as well as links mobile phones, PCs, and other devices and therefore provides a unique capability for efficient intra-port communications for management and control. It gives us new tools for effective remote control and many new unmanned operations. The need for crane, transtainer, straddle carrier operators working their equipment for high up on the equipment will be gone, and be replaced by remote and/or preprogrammed operations with real time feedback, update, etc.

Bluetooth can be used in public or private spaces and use WAP or comparative protocols over Bluetooth servers. The new Intel personal wireless USB adapter is already designed to allow notebook and other hand-held devices to connect wirelessly via Bluetooth. Wireless communications therefore will impact on ports both in their communications with users such as Qualcom's Omni Tracs (satellite tracking and management systems) used for example in China for land and inland water transport tracking and various long distance wireless communications systems, with increasing bandwidth as well as narrow local area wireless to actually manage and control port operations themselves and assure near real time feedback, feed forward, recording, and accounting.

6.2 The new logistic environment

Major parties in international traded logistics, such as ports as well as shipping companies, will continue to merge or form strategic alliances as well as on-line partnerships. The increasing viability and use of E-commerce will contribute to the benefits of integration of port and intermodal transport operations. The increasingly large supply chain/B–to–B networks will not only connect ports and shipping companies with their customers but also enable smoother communication flow throughout the whole supply chain. Similarly, the integration of all links in the supply chain and ever larger logistics entities will permit effective integration of information transaction and operations management requirements and use of the Internet to greatly simplify and reduce the costs of logistics information and transaction management. E-logistics will become a truly revolutionary development.

Ultimately the aim is to develop regional or global wireless networks to provide real time logistics transaction facilitation by linking the various E-commerce and E-logistics exchanges so as to improve door-to-door logistics operating efficiency. The electronic revolution, largely triggered by the Internet, is rapidly catching on in the inland transport shipping and port community, and its use will reduce information and transaction costs significantly and enhance revenues to improve and ensure profitability for shipping, ports, and land transport in truly integrated intermodal supply chain logistics or transport systems.

Most of the larger intermodal transport companies and most large container shipping companies have become intermodal and run or operate trucking, rail, and inland depot/ warehousing operations, have also developed or acquired logistics management entities. In addition, there are many logistics B-to-B, e-commerce service providers to third parties such as:

- LevelSeas.com which buys, sells, and manages bulk ocean transport
- Tradiant.com which links shippers, carriers, and forwarders of containerized freight
- PrimeSupplier.Ltd, a ship supplier and Internet marine procurement system which also aims at managing ship cost control
- Freightdesk.com, forwarder/logistics solutions
- OptimumLogistics.com, an Internet based open bulk commodity logistics system
- APL Global Container Transport and Logistics
- Asiaship.com, a freight logistics management system

There are in addition to about 40 such maritime/logistics B-to-B, e-commerce services many portals such as Bulknet, Fuel trading net, Oceanconnect .com, Bolero.net, bunkerworld.com, Marex.com, freightquote.com, and many more offering an array of data bases, quotes or services. The Internet and wireless long distance and local area communications have opened the door to wholly electronic transaction and operations management which can perform in near real time and be very secure.

In fact, security, which is becoming an increasing concern in international trade logistics, can be significantly enhanced by eliminating paper-based transactions. Electronic systems security has achieved a degree of sophistication and invulnerability not attainable in paper-based systems. Global electronic banking and similar systems have shown its capability. Integrated electronic logistics paperless management can be readily developed using existing technology and networks. Integrated logistics management facilitates slot sharing on ship, train, and terminals, and thereby assures greater capacity utilisation and revenues.

6.3 Economic implications

The new world of electronic transactions offers tremendous economic opportunities for integrated intermodal transport and logistics operations, not only by eliminating and/or transforming most paper-based operations, but also by eliminating most delays, improving transactional accuracy and assuring greater security. The major reasons for mistakes in logistics operations and management are human error, and most of these occur with multiple human involvement in paper-based transactional transfers. Considering typical container liner operations, direct and indirect ship operations and management costs usually account for 50–60% of total, with management, sales/marketing, IT, public relations, real estate, and other costs accounting for the rest (Table 13).

Table 13: *Typical shipping company costs*

		% Total cost
Direct and indirect ship operations and ship management costs	Ship finance costs	13.0–15.0
	Ship crewing costs	5.5–8.0
	Insurance costs	1.5–2.0
	Ship administration, eng. and crew mgmt.	3.0–4.0
	Chartering costs	7.0–8.5
	Bunker costs	11.0–14.0
	Repair & maintenance costs	1.5–2.0
	Ship supplies	1.0–1.5
	Port costs & dues	2.0–4.0
	Inspection, etc. costs	0.5–1.0
Subtotal	50.0–60.0	
Shipping company management costs	Company administration and management	7.0–9.0
	Sales and marketing	14.0–16.0
	Information systems and communications	10.0–13.0
	Public relations, legal, etc.	1.0–2.0
	Rental, real property, etc.	10.0–12.0
	Other	1.0–2.0
Subtotal		40.0–50.0
Total annual costs	Average	100%

Considering costs in more detail, it is interesting to compute typical slot costs, say on a transatlantic crossing. A typical containership (5200 TEU) for example costs about $65m and therefore about $18,000/day in interest (8.5%) and depreciation costs. Crew costs, M&R, supplies, bunkers, insurance, ship management, etc. will add another $46,000/day for a daily operating cost at sea of about $64,000/day or $12.31/day/TEU slot. Assuming 60% effective slot utilisation (after subtracting unused slots and slots filled with non-revenue (empty) containers, the daily slot (TEU) cost underway is about $20.52 or about $215/TEU per slot (TEU) on a typical transatlantic voyage of 10 days. The actual total costs, excluding port, intermodal, trucking, and other non-shipping company costs, are more than twice that number or about $450/TEU.

The costs of marketing, sales, rentals for marketing and sales, administration, accounting, ship management, etc. are about 56% of total or about $500/TEU. Many of these costs are transaction costs such as marketing and sales, documentation, accounting, collection, clearance, etc., whose costs could be vastly reduced and/or eliminated by the use of the Internet, electronic transactions, and more. In addition, these transactions would then be performed in real time with many additional savings or operational improvements from time savings or elimination of delays.

Considering port operations and management, we find similar inefficiencies in many ports which are largely caused by administrative, documentary, inspection, clearance, accounting, and other transactional activities, most of which can be eliminated or replaced by Internet and electronic transactions. As in shipping, many even among major ports employ more people in offices, administration, and marketing than in the actual operations of the port. A few ports and terminals have started to reverse this trend and moved towards the Apaperless@ port concept. Singapore, among these, developed a paperless port management system as well as PORTNET which provides information workflow on all services required by port users and their customers. There are other examples of transactional inefficiencies in ports and other logistics operations.

Using a simple example of say a container gantry crane with a capital cost of $8 million, financial, insurance, maintenance, electric power, spares, etc. costs are about $5000/day. Adding manpower costs and the cost of the supporting berth structure (75 m of berths/crane), we obtain a total cost of about $12,000/day or $500/hr. With a utilisation of say 12 hrs/day and 25 moves/hr, the resulting direct gantry crane costs per move would be $40 which is obviously much less than normally charged. The added costs are stevedoring (including tractor/trailer, etc.), administrative, documentation, and more which ultimately raise the cost per move to $100–150. There are many other examples in ports, as in shipping, where indirect costs outweigh direct costs. Obviously, many of the indirect costs are for essential services and may be reduced but not eliminated. Others though can often be eliminated or replaced by technology. There are similar examples all along the logistics supply chain and particularly in international container trade shipping.

Electronic transaction management has many additional economic benefits. For example, electronic funds transfer not only reduces costs of billing but also the payment period from 30–60 days to real time. In other words, services are paid for when rendered. This can increase cash flow of a typical logistics or integrated shipping firm by 5–10% and increase its profit margins by as much as 30%. There are obviously losers in the process such as cargo brokers, freight forwarders, customs agents, and so forth who usually work on a commission or percentage basis, very much like travel agents. But as the latter have in recent years been largely replaced by on-line usually real-time services, the trend in logistics transaction management can be organized within an integrated logistics company or provided by specialized electronic transaction management providers.

7. CONCLUSIONS

A major reason for the high transaction and management costs of logistic systems is that information generated by the various physical and operational management logistics functions as well as for the various externally imposed regulatory, inspection, and other requirements are seldom if ever effectively coordinated, standardised or integrated. As a result they are mostly performed by traditional paper-based procedures. As a result huge amounts of uncoordinated data flows usually accompany or more often follow the logistic chain and impose large unnecessary, ill coordinated information and communications requirements. Recent investigations indicate that information and communication requirements of essential transactions and controls in international trade logistics can be simplified and readily managed by an Internet-based system which controls all moves and transactions while providing effective and secure access to all authorised decision makers and recording, filing, and transmitting all relevant information in near real time to all who require access to some or all the information.

Many of the procedures used in international trade logistics and shipping are based on tradition more than actual need in todays environment. The costs in economic terms of holding onto these traditions though have become unbearable. In one new global trading environment new methods of transaction management must be introduced if we are to reap the real benefits of globalisation.

REFERENCES

Frankel, E.G. (2000): "E-Logistics Solutions: A Key to Major Cost Reduction in Getting the Product to the Buyer", *2nd Global Automotive Trades and Logistics Conference*, Bremen, Germany, September.

Frankel, E.G. (2000): "Capitalizing on IT/E-commerce in Singapore's Development as a World Class Port", *4th MPA International Advisory Group Conference*, Singapore, August 2000.

Frankel, E.G. (2001): "Where the Money Goes: Economics of International Trade Logistics – Opportunities for Improvements and Cost Savings", *TOC Asia*, Hong Kong, June.

Frankel, E.G. (2001): "Profitability Through Connectivity B The E-Port Terminal Operations in the Internet Age", *TOC Europe*, Amsterdam.

CHAPTER 39

IT IN LOGISTICS AND MARITIME BUSINESS

Lauri Ojala* and David Menachof†

*Turku School of Economics and Business Administration, Turku, Finland.
E-mail: *Lauri.ojala@tukkk.fi*
†City University Cass Business School, City of London, UK.
E-mail: *d.menachof@city.ac.uk*

1. INTRODUCTION

This chapter deals with contemporary information technology (IT) solutions and applications in logistics, and focuses on their usage in maritime business. The chapter discusses some of the underlying reasons for the pervasive use of IT, and exemplifies some existing solutions on various levels in shipping. More specifically, the chapter is organised under the following sections:

(i) intra-company systems, applications and uses of IT (operational systems in capacity allocation, tracking & tracing, ERP/ES-based on management level etc.)
(ii) inter-company systems between business operators (exchange of operational data on cargo, shipments, payments etc. on a system-to-system basis using EDI, XML, etc., and relying either on shared software or dedicated (proprietary) systems)
(iii) company-public authority exchange of data (such as to/from trade and transport authorities – port agencies, customs, border/coast guard etc.)

The list is not exclusive, and for example various public sector systems, either within or between public bodies is left outside the presentation. One should also realize that these categories are simplified, and that many of the systems will have overlap into the other sections, but are classified as to their main section. The interesting linkages of IT to Vessel Traffic Service or Management Systems (VTS /VTMIS), to safety at sea,[1] or regional development[2] are beyond the scope of this chapter.

The text tries to avoid excessive technical detail and acronyms that are ubiquitous in this field.

Freeman and Soefe[3] argue that the fifth so-called long wave of technological development emerged in the 1990s, which could be called the age of microelectronics and computer networks. Consequently, the main fields of transport and communications affected are the so-called information highways and digital networks. The previous long wave started in the 1940s, dubbed as the age of mass production (typically of cars and synthetic materials). During this period, the main transport innovations were the motor highways and airlines, and to a certain extend also container shipping. TV and radio made their breakthrough in the field of communications.

As far as various sectors of maritime business are concerned, liner shipping is perhaps most affected by IT development.[4,5] In liner shipping, the service offered has become a commodity, which is transacted in very high quantities with relatively little negotiation between the parties. The increasing logistics or supply chain management (SCM) needs of shippers also underline the need of efficient information management along the whole supply chain.

In industrial shipping, the number of transactions is typically much smaller than in liner shipping, but the operations often require more negotiation between the trading partners, or parties involved in transport operations. Industrial shipping solutions tend to be dedicated and more long-term arrangements with multiple parties. For this reason, they may be used as an illustrative case to highlight the complexity of information flows between stationary parties (see *Illustrative Case in Industrial Shipping and IT* on page 906).

The maritime business includes a large number of operators both at the seaside and the landside that are or that could be involved. This chapter deals mainly with shipping companies within liner and industrial shipping, and port communities. For IT and information flows in (industrial) bulk shipping, see, e.g., Hull.[6]

2. IT IN LOGISTICS AND SUPPLY CHAIN MANAGEMENT

SCM enables the coordinated management of material and information flows throughout the chain from your sources to your customers.[7] The Global Supply Chain Forum defines SCM as "the integration of business processes from end-user through original suppliers that provides products, services, and information that add value for customers".[8]

The supply chain is both a *network* and a *system*. The network component involves the connections needed in the flow of products and information. The systemic properties are the interdependence of activities, organisations and processes. As one example, transportation transit times influence the amount of inventory held within the system. Generally said, actions in one part of the system affect other parts.[9]

Mentzer[10] defines a supply chain as a set of three or more companies directly linked by one or more of the upstream and downstream flows of products, services, finances and information. To be supply-chain oriented means that the company consciously develops the strategic system approach to enhance the processes and activities involved in managing the various flows in a supply chain. Supply chain management can envisage almost all of the company's main functions, or at least those functions like sales, marketing, R&D and forecasting can be handled within a supply chain context. To sum it up, SCM means a systemic coordination of the traditional business functions within a particular company and across businesses within the chain.

Enterprise resource planning is one of the most essential functions in a modern manufacturing company and it also has a very strong supply chain implication. The old MRP-originated model, nowadays running at the core of the most sophisticated ERP systems: "What do I need, what do I have, what do I need to get and when" is right at the backbone of the integrated supply chain. The requirements are taken from a customer or from internal forecasts.[11] This has also had a profound effect on the way in which major companies now operate their global manufacturing and supply chains.

"Innovative supply chain management structures are rapidly emerging. These incorporate expanded access to 'e-sources' of supply, which use web-based exchanges and hubs, interactive trading mechanisms and advanced optimisation and matching algorithms to link customers with suppliers for individual transactions."[12]

Many industries have embarked on reengineering efforts to improve the efficiency of their supply chains. The goal of these programs is to better match supply with demand so as to reduce the costs of inventory and stockouts, where potential savings can be enormous. One key initiative is information sharing between partners in a supply chain. Sharing sales information has been viewed as a major strategy to counter the so-called "bullwhip effect", which is essentially the phenomenon of demand variability amplification along a supply chain. It can create problems for suppliers, such as grossly inaccurate demand forecasts, low capacity utilisation, excessive inventory, and poor customer service.[13]

The result for many companies is an expanded role of global sourcing of supply, and global reach in the search for customers. This, in turn, signifies an increasingly important role for liner shipping companies in making supply chains more efficient.

3. LOGISTICS IN TRANSOCEAN TRANSPORT

Trade and transport operations invariably involve numerous partners both in the public and the private sector, such as banking and insurance agents, in addition to various logistics service providers. Likewise, the trading partners (buyers and sellers or consignors and consignees) evaluate the practicalities often on a case-by-case basis.

This is illustrated in Figure 1, which exemplifies a typical transocean transport movement from an inland point-of-origin to an inland point-of-destination (for example, from East Asia to Europe or the US). Each point along the curve indicates separate cargo handling operations. At each point, the handling time or cost may deviate from the expected levels.

The number of business parties, logistics providers and officials taking part in a transocean transport for each individual shipment is very large. Thus, it is very difficult to control the overall information flow along the route. In order to stay competitive in the global logistics markets, practically all major liner shipping operators now offer extensive door-to-door tracking and tracing services (see, e.g., Heaver[15] and the websites of Maersk Sealand, P&O Nedlloyd and APL).

It is noteworthy that the direct cost (i.e., unit freight) especially in container liner shipping has decreased over the past decades in real terms – and often also in absolute terms – in practically all major routes. At the same time, the aver-

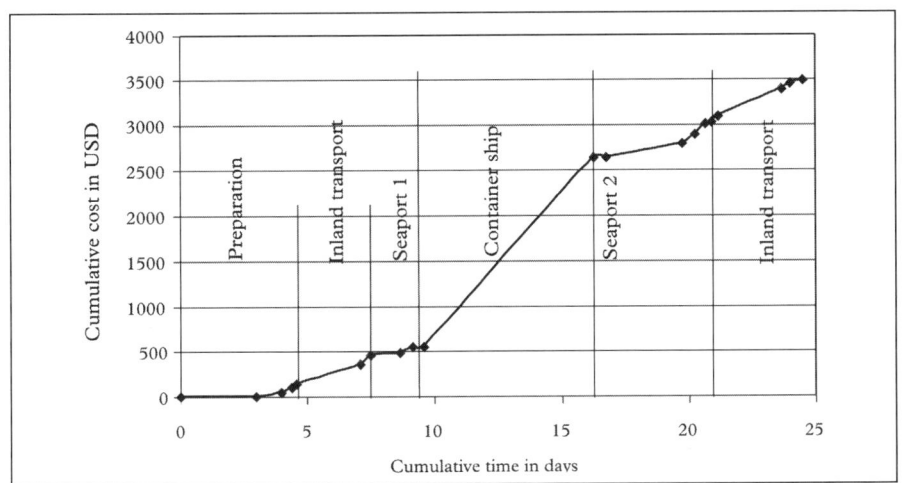

Figure 1: Cumulative time (days) and cost (USD) between inland and transocean inland points for a ISO container

Source: Frankel, E.G.[14]

age value of goods has increased and the overall attention to logistics has risen. As a consequence, the cost of time and the value of transport-related information has surged (see, e.g., Mason-Jones and Towill[16]).

4. INTRA-COMPANY INFORMATION FLOWS

It is not possible to describe all the possible uses of IT for intra-company information purposes, and many of these intra-company systems integrate with inter-company systems. What we will attempt to do is describe some of the sys-

Table 1: Base functions of ERP programmes

Manufacturing and logistics	Finance and accounting	Human resources and payroll
Operations (production) planning	General ledger	Human resources administration
Engineering	Accounts receivable	Payroll
Shop floor control	Accounts payable	Benefits
Procurement management	Fixed assets	Self-service HR
Order entry and processing	Cash management	
Sales, marketing, and after sales	Budgeting	
Warehouse (inventory) management	Treasury management	
Distribution (transportation) management	Cost control	
Project management	Financial consolidation	
Plant maintenance		
Customer service management		
Extended supply chain management		

tems in place and highlight the key issues that are related to these systems. It should also be noted that the logistics functions must still take place whether or not there is an IT solution available. For example, before ERP programs, accounting data was still maintained, Bills of Materials were still created, sales orders were still processed, but much less efficiently as today.

Enterprise Resource Planning programmes are the foundation for many firms' IT capabilities. Companies like SAP, J.D. Edwards, PeopleSoft, Baan, and Oracle are the major companies in this multi-billion dollar industry. All ERP providers are looking to extend the capabilities of their products by adding additional functionality to their product. The three major functional areas of ERP are: Manufacturing & Logistics, Finance & Accounting, and Human Resources & Payroll (see Table 1 for more detail).

Jakovljevic[17] identifies some of the key reasons why ERP systems have become so popular and are essential to the modern firm. These are Strategic, Tactical and Technical.

Strategic reasons include:

- Enable new business strategies
- Enable globalisation
- Enable growth strategies
- Extend supply/demand chain
- Increase customer responsiveness

Tactical reasons include:

- Reduce cost/improve productivity
- Increase flexibility
- Integrate business processes
- Integrate acquisitions
- Standardise business processes
- Improve specific business processes/performances

Finally, technical reasons include:

- Standardise system/platform
- Improve quality and visibility of information
- Enhance technology infrastructure to handle the immense amount of data

Programmes that "plug-in" to ERP systems are gaining popularity, as enhanced functionality not offered by the base ERP system is required to gain competitive advantage.

Customer Relationship Management (CRM) software is designed to keep track of more than just customer orders. Delivery preferences, and past ordering profiles are among some of the information captured by CRM systems. An interesting but increasingly standard function of CRM is used by the CSX railroad. When customers call into their customer service centre, the telephone system is integrated into the CRM system, and assuming caller ID is working, the caller's details are flashed on the screen before the representative answers the phone, saving time and assisting in anticipating the caller's needs.

After a day of sales orders being generated and shipments organised, companies that have their own delivery fleets must send those vehicles out on the road to deliver to their customers. This is the job of routing and scheduling software, provided by firms such as ILOG, Radical, and Swisslog. Simple routing and scheduling problems can be solved by Linear Programming (LP) but as the number of constraints grows, the ability to obtain an optimal solution decreases. This is where the complex algorithms used by these specialised programmes come into their own.

In routing problems, the objective is generally to minimise cost subject to constraints such as road distance between deliveries, waiting time at each stop, and driver work regulations. Costs are assigned to each type of constraint, and the programme searches for a feasible solution. PCmiler (ALK associates) is just one version of this type of software programme.

Scheduling is a much more complex task, as it must incorporate many more requirements. Routing software generally doesn't check to see if the total quantities you are trying to ship exceed the capacity of the vehicle. Scheduling looks at total capacities and also looks at additional constraints such as delivery windows. Many companies working with just-in-time production facilities require strict delivery times. They cannot take delivery early or later than specified periods, and thus a vehicle that could deliver to all the customers in terms of capacity constraints might be unable to deliver those goods within the time parameters set by the customers. The costs and distance travelled using scheduling constraints is generally higher than when "routing only" issues are required. ILOG Solver software allows a user to integrate shipment data from their ERP system by consolidating all the shipments for a given time period, then using the available fleet information along with the information for all of the shipments, to generate a set of shipping plans to assist in the order of deliveries for each vehicle required to meet all of the constraints. If no feasible solution is found, the user is notified, and will have to make management decisions as to which shipments will be unable to be delivered within their time windows, or must attempt to find additional vehicles that enable a feasible solution to be found.

Warehouse Management Systems are another popular "plug-in" adding enhanced capabilities for inventory control. While ERP systems have some ability to keep inventory storage location data, it is not nearly enough for complex warehouse operations. For example, newer automated warehouses may have Automated Storage and Retrieval Systems (AS/RS). These systems need to know where the inventory is stored, which the ERP system can provide, but the ability to schedule and run the automated forklifts requires additional computing power, provided by WMS. Warehouses today can be some of the most simple of operations just keeping the inventory dry, but have also become some of the most IT intensive aspects of the supply chain.

Because they have been around for so long, one may not think of a barcode as much of an IT solution, but that little printed symbol can help a warehouse run smoothly. At Wal-Mart's distribution centres, automated conveyor belts scan the barcodes on packages at several locations, redirecting them to specific conveyor belts assigned to each store's destination.

Many traditional warehouses that use forklift trucks are being upgraded to use Radio Frequency technology (RF) to save time and reduce errors. Picking and Storage information is sent directly to a screen on the forklift, giving the driver instructions on where to go for their next movement. Once the driver gets to the location, using a handheld scanner, he/she scans the barcode for that location to verify he/she is in the right place, and then picks or stores the correct quantity. Once completed, he/she sends a signal that he/she is ready for the next movement. There is no need to come back to the office to collect the next movement order. The driver can stay on their forklift, being more productive than previously.

In many operations, firms do not have their own fleet to deliver the shipments, and use commercial carriers. There are now systems that take information for each shipment, and based on the weight/volume, destination, and time constraints, calculate the best carrier to use, and print the specific waybill required for that carrier, thus minimising shipment costs. For example, a firm may have the choice of using the Royal Mail, or UPS, or DHL to deliver the shipment. Checking each tariff manually to find the lowest cost would be prohibitively time consuming for high volume businesses.

5. INTER-COMPANY INFORMATION FLOWS

There have been many recent developments in inter-company information flows. One of the more recent initiatives has been CPFR (Collaborative Planning, Forecasting, and Replenishment). The process of implementing CPFR involves the sharing of information in order to better provide for end-customer requirements. As in any collaborative process, the key is the commitment from the firms involved. Theoretically, CPFR could take place without IT systems, but as the number of SKUs (Stock Keeping Units) increases, the ability to track the information manually becomes infeasible. In general, CPFR involves three stages and is summarised in Figure 2. The Planning Stage, involves an initial front-end agreement regarding what information is going to be shared, how it is to be shared, when, and other details. Then there is a quarterly planning session which looks at the wider strategic issues of the collaboration.

The Forecasting Stage involves several steps. Typically, each firm will create a sales forecast for the upcoming period, and once that has been done, the information is centralised. Step two is to compare the forecasts and identify the exceptions. The initial agreement might state that when both forecasts differ by more than 20%, for example, flag this record as an exception. The third step is for both parties to meet and resolve the exceptions. Typically, one firm will host the database on their computer system and allow the other remote access to their data, now easily possible via the internet, and password protected.

The Replenishment Stage follows the steps of the Forecasting Stage, but this time looks at existing inventories along with the forecasts to determine how much to supply for the upcoming period. Once this stage is completed, the actual order is processed and submitted into each firms' ERP system.

IT IN LOGISTICS AND MARITIME BUSINESS   905

The Process then continually repeats itself, with the end goal of enhanced inventory management, resulting in better customer satisfaction.

Figure 2: The CPFR process

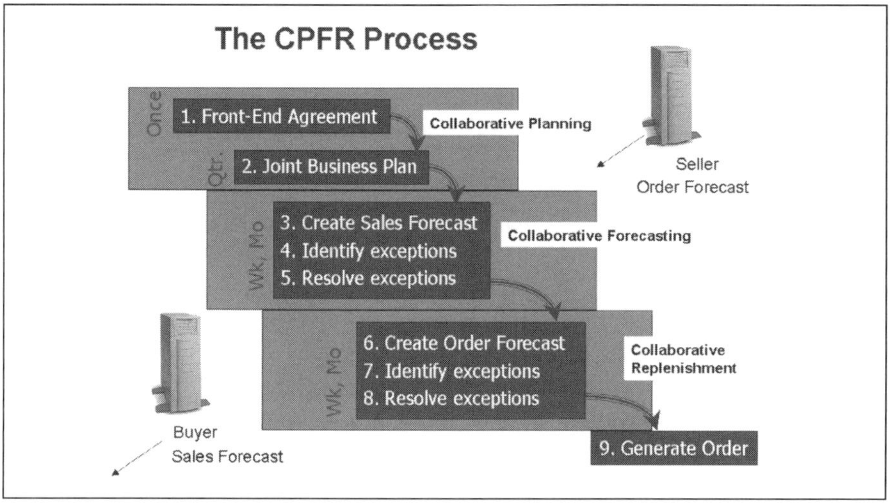

The CPFR Process

1. Front-End Agreement — Collaborative Planning
2. Joint Business Plan → Seller Order Forecast
3. Create Sales Forecast
4. Identify exceptions
5. Resolve exceptions — Collaborative Forecasting
6. Create Order Forecast
7. Identify exceptions
8. Resolve exceptions — Collaborative Replenishment
Buyer Sales Forecast
9. Generate Order

Source: Bob Cowdrick, Manager of Business Consulting, Logility Inc.

Another example of where intra-company information can be exchanged is by firms using VMI (Vendor Managed Inventory). "VMI has been around for some time, but it is becoming increasingly accessible and relevant now as data communications systems improve."[18] EPOS (Electronic Point of Sales) data is automatically transferred to the vendor, who will be responsible for replenishment of the stock based on agreed service standards and inventory levels. "The control of his customer delivery and visibility on customer needs, which VMI gives to the vendor, enables him to plan production and supply more reliably."[19]

Although there is much that can be done electronically, the paperless supply chain is not yet here. One major issue that international logistics faces is documentary requirements by government agencies world-wide. Electronic Bills-of-Lading, although technically possible, are still not accepted for customs clearance world-wide. Likewise, people still like the security of a physical document, even though electronic PODs (Proof of Deliveries) are being used by major delivery companies on a regular basis.[20]

Business to Business procurement websites have come and gone. B2B procurement will be, if it is not already, an important tool for many companies. B2B is not new, and was the basis for the use of EDI. It was a direct relationship between one company and its supplier. It was expensive, but for large companies that could afford it, offered competitive advantage over smaller competitors.

Figure 3 identifies the general type of e-procurement concepts. On the vertical scale, the nature of the transactions is measured, while the horizontal looks at the infrastructure and access to the system. Looking at the bottom right quadrant, with open access to the public, and a direct relationship between buyer and seller, general e-commerce is transacted here. As we move to many buyers and sellers getting together, we move to the e-marketplaces, with hubs designed to bring those parties together. Some are private, while others are open to anyone. Conceptually, they are appealing to the buyer, with more choice and enhanced price competition. However, for the seller, the proposition is less than appealing at the moment. Sellers have been staying away as price is the only selling point, and things like reputation and quality are hard to factor in at this point in time.

B2B exchanges come in several general models with vertical and horizontal hubs. Vertical hubs are generally industry/commodity based, attempting to bring together all players in the steel industry, for example. Other vertical hubs exist in plastics, chemicals, energy, telecoms, and even flowers.

Horizontal hubs attempt to look at specific functions, that are used across industries. Logistics hubs fit into this area. elogistics is a London-based firm that attempts to match companies excess transport capacity with firms who are looking for capacity. According to Richard Hunt, former CEO of elogistics, more than 30% of road haulage vehicle miles are run either empty or under capacity. There is significant scope for improved efficiency.

Although there is significant consolidation taking place in the industry currently, as firms figure out how to become profitable providing online procurement services, it is evident that the desire for the services are needed. The keys to success in this quick developing arena include integration with participating firms' back end systems (ERP), value creation for all parties, and the critical mass needed to bring the initial fixed costs of these IT investments down to reasonable per transaction costs.

Illustrative case in industrial shipping

To illustrate the flow of information in industrial shipping, a supply chain project for the Finnish paper industry called the Intelligent Supply Chain (ISC)

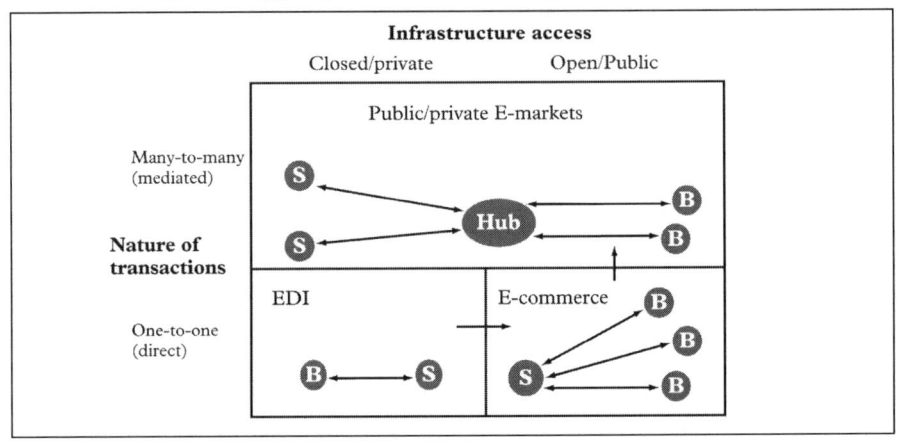

Figure 3: Types of business to business procurement models

concept is shown. The ISC example reflects the current customer requirement to identify packages at each stage in the supply chain, starting from the producer (paper mill) and ending at the final customer. The hinterland transports (railways and trucks), port operators and the shipping line are included in the concept. The cargo volume handled through this concept is several million tonnes per annum.

The ISC-concept relies on four major elements. First, the parties need to have a commonly agreed way of working, which is valid only if all partners commit themselves to the common rules. In a dedicated industrial shipping (or logistics) context this can, in principle, be achieved. Second, the supply chain from the mill to the final client can be seen as an extended warehouse where the cargo is moving from one stock position to another. Along the chain, the goods can either be in a static or dynamic status, i.e. stationary, or in transit. Third, data integrity means that at any point the party despatching the goods is responsible for the physical flow of goods and the respective set of data to be equal and due, by timeliness and accuracy. Additionally, a forecasting element is part of the concept.

The ISC-concept relies on joint planning and on joint operations for the supply chain partners whereas operations are carried out by individual partners. The planning tools are agreed jointly. The main functional activities are described below.

Order management (order receiving/confirmation, changes etc.) is the basis for ISC-concept. The preplanning of the supply chain starts in the order management.

Despatch planning is synchronised with the production planning of the mill. The despatch planning means that the loading from the mill is planned in advance.

Loading at the mill (freight waybills). The loading at the mill is normally confirmed by a freight waybill, which confirms what has been loaded. The freight waybills are transmitted electronically to the cargo receiver.

Truck and railway transport the goods including tracking services and estimates of arrival times. The transport companies provide delivery information to the partners who are entitled to receive it.

The activities of the port operator. These have several sub-activities (cargo receiving, cargo unitising, and loading to vessel). All sub-activities produce agreed preplanning information and performance reporting to the partners who need it.

The activities of the shipping line include, for example, vessel time schedule, cargo location in vessel (i.e., stowage plan), cargo manifest and estimated time of discharge.

The activities of the port operator normally have several sub-activities such as vessel discharging reporting, cargo locations in warehouse. Performance reporting is given to the partners who need it.

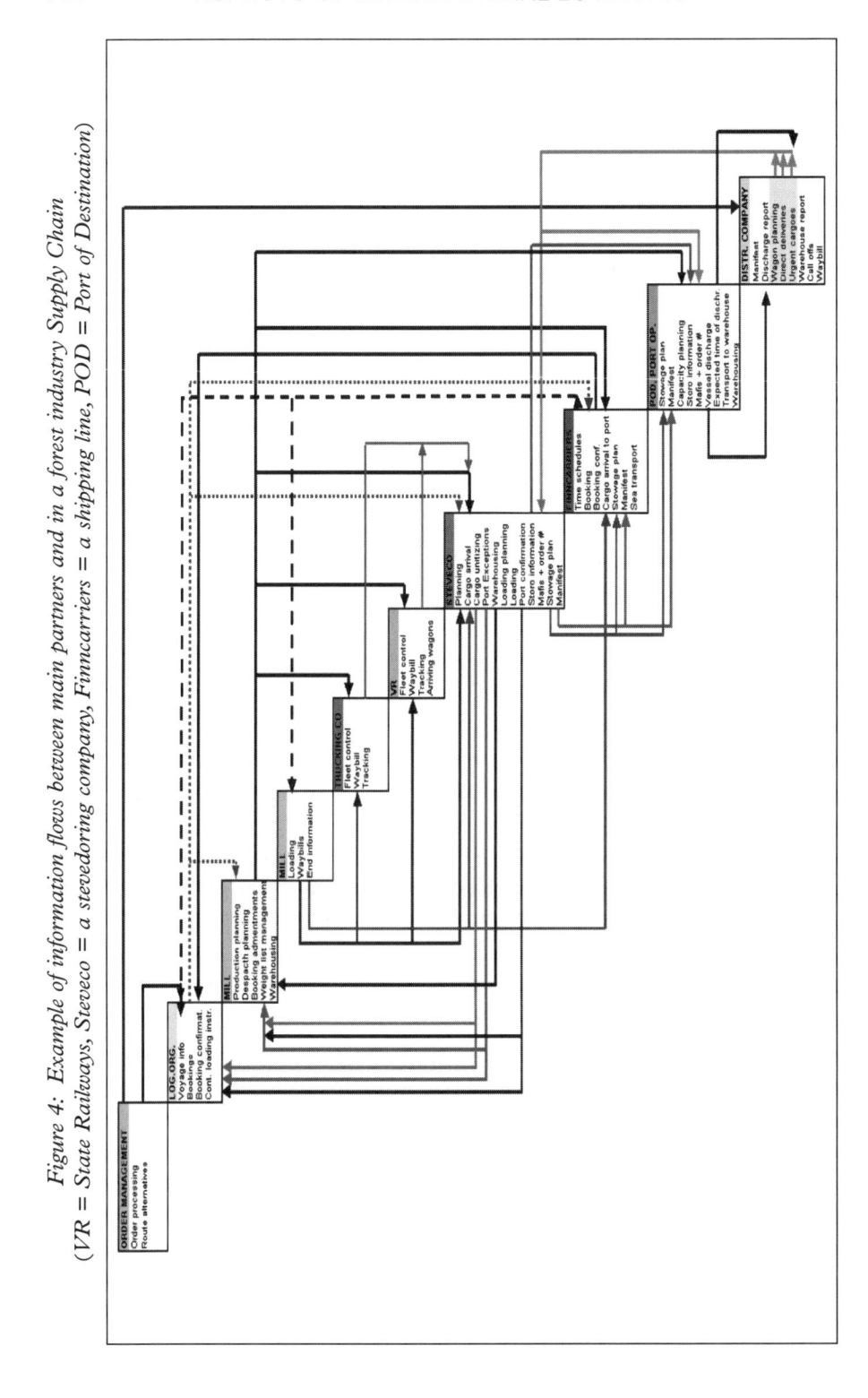

Figure 4: Example of information flows between main partners and in a forest industry Supply Chain
(VR = State Railways, Steveco = a stevedoring company, Finncarriers = a shipping line, POD = Port of Destination)

The basic functional elements of the concept include the following: unit identification, planning and performance reporting, transparency of operations, integration of the data communication rules, and uniform functional processes. The working processes of the parties are shown on a rough level in Figure 4.

Unit identification is a rapidly developing area, where a number of commercial solutions already exist, such as radio frequency tags (RFID) and GPS-based tracking solutions.[21,22] As security issues around the world have become a much more critical issue, the need for online real-time tracing for critical commodities is real. Similar to the use of RF communications in a warehouse, standardised tagging of shipments is a growing priority to firms and governments. Many years ago, US railroads implemented a barcode style scanning system for all carriages used on their systems. The problem was that if the train was going too fast, or the barcodes got dirty, the system didn't work properly. RFID eliminates those problems, and is rapidly being adopted on a global basis.

6. COMPANY-PUBLIC AUTHORITY EXCHANGE OF DATA

Port community systems (PCS) have been developed to assist the rapid flow of information between all of the firms involved in moving goods in/out of a port. Since many of them were developed before clear standards were created, they were generally independent from each other. Port of Charleston has the Orion system, Felixstowe has its own system, and as illustrated below, Finnish ports use the *Port@Net* system. The general concepts of PCSs are the same, although the systems and interfaces may be different at each port. One of the major benefits is the reduction in time needed to transmit information. For example, a container vessel's load plan may have been upwards of 60 pages, sent by fax or telex. Once received by the port, a computer operator would enter the data into their system, with many chances for errors occurring. These systems eliminate that need for re-keying of data, maintaining the accuracy and integrity of the information.[23]

Illustrative case: A Finnish port community system: *Port@Net*

The *Port@Net* is a national port community system that offers a single administrative desk for all the declarations required with vessel's arrival and departure to major ports and authorities in Finland.[24] It is used by shipping lines, ship agents, a number of ports, the Customs, and Maritime Administration. It has over 1000 users in Finland. The *Port@Net* extranet application was implemented in 2000 when it replaced the previous application in use since 1994.

The shipping line or its agent can send the advance notice of vessel's arrival and departure, the dangerous goods notification and the cargo declaration either by using the *Port@Net* website or by sending EDI or XML[25] files. The cargo declaration can be given as a manifest whereby the cargo can be cleared for Customs purposes in advance. This means in practise that for example the same dangerous goods information is used by the Customs office as well as by the Port Authority and by the Finnish Maritime Administration (FMA). The following diagram illustrates the *Port@Net* system in general.

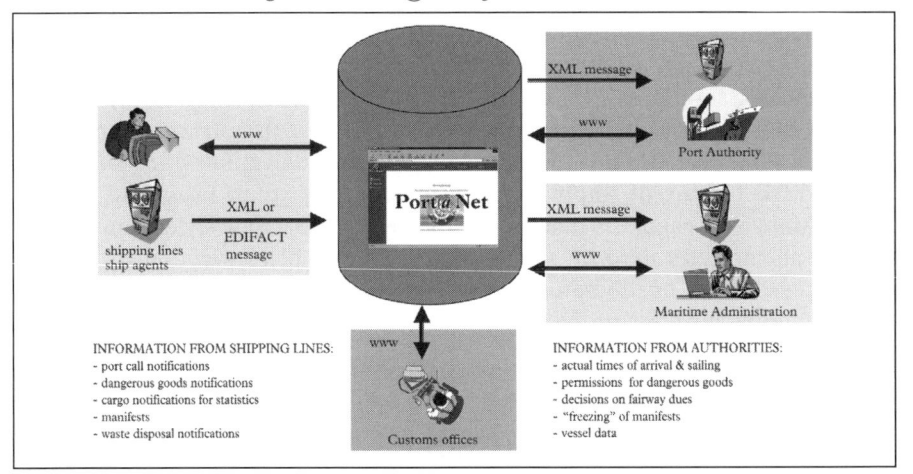

Figure 5: Port@Net *system illustration*

By courtesy of the Port@Net community and the Finnish Maritime Administration.

The procedures for vessels entering or leaving the port are in principle mirror images. For illustration purposes, the procedure for vessels leaving the port are highlighted below. When using the Web interface, the reporting principles similar, but instead of EDIFACT messages, XML-based messages are used. The following screen exemplifies the web pages available.

Before the vessel arrives, information of the vessel and its voyage has to be transferred to the Customs 24 hours before. If this cannot be achieved, the exceptions must be agreed with the Customs office of the port of call. From the agent's side the procedure is the following:

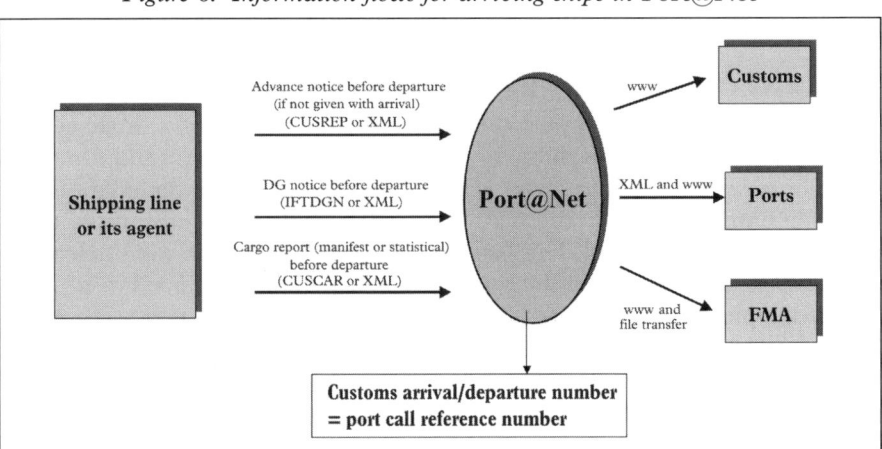

Figure 6: Information flows for arriving ships in Port@Net

By courtesy of the Port@Net community and the Finnish Maritime Administration.

- the agent sends the Customs Report (CUSREP) message informing about the vessel and its voyage, the Customs arrival/departure reference number can be generated automatically in the agent's IT system. This reference number functions as a port call reference number relating to all the succeeding messages of the same voyage;
- the advance notice can cover either arrival or departure information or combined;
- if the vessel or voyage data changes, a replacing message can be sent.

If the vessel carries dangerous goods, the agent has to report those goods to the port of call 24 hours before the arrival. The EDI message used is called the IFTDGN message. When sending this message the reference is made to the Customs arrival/departure reference number thereby linking the dangerous goods notification to the advance notice.

There exists two different type of cargo reports: one giving cargo information on manifest level and the other one on statistical level. The cargo report on manifest level functions as a report to the Customs, too. The procedure for the agent if giving cargo report on manifest level is the following

- before the vessel's arrival the cargo report is transmitted using the CUSCAR message;
- several cargo reports can be sent per one advance notice (supplementary B/L's);
- the cargo report(s) refer to the same Customs' arrival/departure reference number;
- cargo information can be updated or modified before the arrival of the vessel;
- after the vessel has arrived, the agent can send updated cargo reports BUT then the changed information has to be faxed to the local Customs office;
- the agent will fill in the information of the general Customs declaration, sign it, attach a copy of the manifest to it and deliver the papers to the Customs office;
- the Customs office accepts the general declaration and gives permission for discharging;
- the port operator unloads the cargo and delivers the list of discharged cargo to the Customs.

If the cargo report is given on statistical level, this message can be transmitted after the vessel's arrival. For the port authorities the manifest information is the basis for port cargo dues and for the Maritime Administration it is the basis for cargo statistics. Figure 6 shows the data flows with vessel's arrival.

EPILOGUE

Despite the profound change the development of IT has brought about in many fields, including the maritime business, it could be argued that the age of digital networks is only starting to take shape. One of the developments that would profoundly change the international logistics and shipping operations and business is the possibility to track, trace and control individual parcels and shipments wirelessly, and virtually in real time. Many of the technological breakthroughs required for that to happen have already been made, and their cost is likely to approach the level of commercial exploitation fairly soon. This type of technology could even change the nature of maritime business, or at least the liner shipping part of it beyond recognition.

As Churchill might have said[26]: "This is not the end. It is not even the beginning of the end. But it is, perhaps, the end of the beginning."

ENDNOTES

1. Goulielmos, A., and Tzannatos, E. (1997): "Management information system for the promotion of safety in shipping", *An International Journal of Disaster Prevention and Management*, 6, 4, pp. 252–262.
2. Sletmo, G. (1999): "Port Life Cycles: Policy and Strategy in the Global Economy", *International Journal of Maritime Economics*, 1,1, pp. 11–38; and Airriess, C.A. (2001): "Regional production, information-communication technology, and the developmental state: the rise of Singapore as a global container hub", *Geoforum*, 32, 2, pp. 235-254.
3. Freeman, C., and Soefe, L. (1997): *The Economics of Industrial Innovation* (3rd ed.) (MIT Press).
4. Frankel, E.G. (1999): "The Economics of Total Trans-ocean Supply Chain Management", *International Journal of Maritime Economics*, 1, 1, pp. 61–69.
5. Stopford, Martin (2002): "E-commerce implications, opportunities and threats for the maritime business", *International Journal of Transport Management*, 1,1, pp. 55–67.
6. Hull, Bradley (2002): "A structure for supply-chain information flows and its application to the Alaskan crude oil supply chain", *Logistics Information Management*, 15, 1, pp. 8–23.
7. Boubekri, Nourredine (2001): "Technology enablers for supply chain management, Integrated Manufacturing Systems", Vol. 12, No. 6, pp. 394–399.
8. Alvarado, Y. Ursula, and Kotzab, Herbert (2001): "Supply Chain Management: The Integration of Logistics in Marketing", *Industrial Marketing Management*, Vol. 30, pp. 183–198.
9. Schary, Philip B., and Skjott-Larsen, Tage (2001): *Managing the Global Supply Chain* (2nd ed.) (Copenhagen Business School Press).
10. Mentzer, John T. (2001): *Supply Chain Management* (London, Sage Publications Inc.).
11. Ptak, Carol A., and Schragenheim, Eli (eds.) (2000): *ERP: Tools, Techniques and Applications for Integrating the Supply Chain* (St Lucie Press).
12. Agarwal, V., and Cohen, M. (2001): "Long live the revolution", *Understanding SCM, The Financial Times*, Autumn, pp. 4–5.
13. Lee, Hau L., So, Kut C., and Tang, Christopher S. (2000): "The Value of Information Sharing in a Two-Level Supply Chain", *Management Science*, 46, 5, pp. 626–643.
14. Frankel, E.G. (1999): "The Economics of Total Trans-ocean Supply Chain Management", *International Journal of Maritime Economics*, 1, 1, pp. 61–69.
15. Heaver, Trevor (2002): "Supply chain and logistics management: Implications for liner shipping", see this volume, *Maritime Business and Economics*, chapter 17.
16. Mason-Jones, Rachel, and Towill, Denis R. (1999): "Total cycle time compression and the agile supply chain", *International Journal of Production Economics*, 62, pp. 61–73.

17. Jakovljevic, P.J. (2000): "Essential ERP – Its Functional Scope," March 10th, at *www.technologyevaluation.com*
18. Wallis, R. (2002): "Elements in value chain design", *Manufacturing and Logistics IT*, April, p. 35.
19. Wallis, R. (2002): "Elements in value chain design", *Manufacturing and Logistics IT*, April, p. 35.
20. Packington, R. (2001): "The paperless supply chain? Perhaps not yet", *e.logistics*, Vol. 1, No. 11, May, p. 16.
21. Kärkkäinen, M., Ala-Risku, T., and Kiianlinna, P. (2001): *Item Identification Applications and Technologies* (Helsinki University of Technology, TAI Research Center).
22. van Dorp, Kees-Jan (2002): "Tracking and tracing: a structure for development and contemporary practices", *Logistics Information Management*, 15, 1, pp. 24-33.
23. Garstone, S. (1995): "Electronic Data Interchange (EDI) in Port Operations", *Logistics Information Management*, Vol. 8, No. 2, pp. 30–33.
24. Based on material of the PortNet community, hosted by the Finnish Maritime Administration.
25. XML = Extensible Mark-Up Language; used for making *www-sites*.
26. Referring to Winston Churchill's speech on the Battle of Egypt, 10 November 1942.

Related Titles of Interest

● Lloyd's Law Reports Editor-in-Chief: Mavis D'Souza, Barrister

Lloyd's Law Reports is the most authoritative and comprehensive collection of maritime and commercial case decisions available. As the leading maritime and commercial law reports since 1919, Lloyd's Law Reports is the recognised citation in this area.
ISSN: 0224-5488   Fortnightly Reports, Alert Service, Bound Volumes and Citator

To subscribe or for more information, please visit www.informalaw.com/llr

● Lloyd's Maritime Law Newsletter Editor: Michael Daiches, Barrister

Since 1979 Lloyd's Maritime Law Newsletter has provided its readers with comprehensive and authoritative coverage of the latest court decisions, judgments as well as exclusive access to London Maritime Arbitrations through an agreement with the L.M.A.A.
ISSN: 0268-0696   Fortnighty Newsletter, also available online at lmln.com

To subscribe or for more information, please visit www.informalaw.com/lmln

● Lloyd's Maritime and Commercial Law Quarterly General Editor: Professor Francis Rose

A detailed authoritative analysis of the most topical issues that surround shipping and maritime law, international trade, commercial law and associated areas.
ISSN: 0306-2945   Quarterly Journal with Annual Bound Volume

To subscribe or for more information, please visit www.informalaw.com/lmclq

PUBLISHING IN NOVEMBER 2002
● The Law of Tug and Tow, Second Edition By: Simon Rainey QC

This book provides a detailed and comprehensive analysis of English law specifically relating to the operations of tug and tow and the increasingly important related activities in the field of the offshore service and supply industry.
ISBN: 1843111691   Hardcover/350pp

To order your copy or for more information, please visit www.informalaw.com/legalcatalogue

PUBLISHING IN NOVEMBER 2002
● The Law of Shipbuilding Contracts, Third Edition By: Simon Curtis, Partner, Curtis Davis Garrard

The Law of Shipbuilding Contracts, 3rd Edition provides a comprehensive update of legislation and developments that have affected the law of shipbuilding and conversion contracts since the last edition, six years ago.
ISBN: 1843111683   Hardcover/350pp

To order your copy or for more information, please visit www.informalaw.com/legalcatalogue

For further information on these or any other Informa Law titles please call Customer Services on +44 (0) 1206 772 223 or email professional.enquiries@informa.com

Informa Law publishes a vast portfolio of market-lading publications, internationally recognised as essential resource for all those involved in the legal aspects of Insurance and Banking, Intellectual Property, Maritime, Construction, Commercial and Healthcare. With over 60 information-led newsletters, magazines and directories and 200 specialist books you can receive the very latest, up-to-date business information direct to your desk, in formats designed to suit your needs.
For further information please view our Legal Catalogue online http://www.informalaw.com/legalcatalogue

On ordering please quote your reference: AHLR196A

Informa Law - keeping you up to date with
the very latest legal developments in Maritime Law

informa
L A W

All information supplied true at time of printing
Lloyd's and the Lloyd's Crest are the trademarks of the Society incorporated by the
Lloyd's Act 1871 by the name of Lloyd's"

INDEX

Accident analysis
  maritime safety and, 426–442. *See also* Maritime safety
Air transport
  air cargo carriers, top ten 2000, 99
  container shipping, competition and co-operation, 864–868
  threat to ocean trade, 97–99
  total distribution cost, container compared with, 864

Baltic Freight Index (BFI), 679
  developments in Dry Bulk Market and 5/01/85–30/04/98, 697
  major changes since inception, 696
Banking
  credit risk in shipping finance, 731–761. *See also* Shipping finance
Brazil
  shipbuilding industry, 534
Brent Crude
  oil pricing, and, 125–130. *See also* Oil
British
  impact on international ocean trade, 68–69
  shipping companies, 18–22
    largest, 20
Bulk carriers. *See also* Bulk shipping; Dry bulk carriers
  deletions, 187
  deliveries, 187
  freight rates, 1990s, 193
  market
    cycles, 205
    values, 1990s, 193
  ships, investing in, 623–641. *See also* Investing in ships
  sold for scrapping, 1991–2000, 196
Bulk commodity trades, 2000, 69–78. *See also* Bulk shipping
  coal, 73–74
    major trade routes, 2000, 74
  combining, feasibility of, 78–80
  composite picture of, 76–78
  crude oil, 71–72
    major trade routes, 2000, 72

Bulk commodity trades, 2000—*cont*
  dry bulk market, 227–250. *See also* Dry bulk market
  fleet deployment, more realistic models, 582–588
  grain, 74–76
    major trade routes, 2000, 75
  iron ore, 72–73
    major trade routes, 2000, 73
  market locations, 70–71
Bulk shipping
  Baltic Freight Index, 679
    major revisions, 680
  bulk cargo
    market segmentation, 665–666
      dry bulk by vessel size, 665
      liquid bulk by vessel size, 666
    movements, 664–665
  bunker price risk, hedging, 687–688
  business risk assessment and analysis, 661–692
  forward freight agreements (FFA)
    effect on spot price volatility, 687
    future?, 684–687
  futures and forward markets
    hedging effectiveness, 679–684
    lack of bias, 679–684
  general (dry) cargo
    market segmentation, 666
      container market, by vessel size, 666
    movements, 664–665
  market segmentation, 664–667
  risk/return trade-offs, 663–664
  risk management, use of derivatives for, 678–679
  secondhand ship prices, comparison of volatilities, 667–670
  shipowner's cash flow in spot and T/C markets, 662
  spot and time charter rates, volatilities, 670–678
  time varying freight volatilities
    over type of contract, 674–678
    over vessel sizes, 671–674
  voyage costs, stabilising, 687–688

915

916 INDEX

Bunker prices, 712–721. *See also* Risk management

Canada
 modal splits, 96–97
 national shipping policies, 485–487
Caribbean
 maritime business
  clustering, and, 48–50
China
 changes in economy, 544–545
 national shipping policy, 487–489
 shipbuilding industry, 534, 544–547
Coal, 73–74, 134–145
 consumption, 141
 demand charcteristics, 140–142
 major trade routes, 2000, 74
 marketing, 142–145
 physical characteristics, 134–135
 production, 137, 138–140
  anthracite, 140
  bituminous, 139
  lignite, 140
 reserves, 138–140
 shares, 139
 supply characteristics, 135–140
 trade, 142–145
  coking coal and steel, 142
  international hard coal, 143
   exporters, 144
   importers, 145
Competition policy
 maritime economics, 6
Container services. *See also* General cargo trades; International logistics; Liner shipping
 competition and co-operation with air transport, 864–868
 growth in world, 161
 industry trends and developments, 836–842
 movements in major liner routes, 2000, 479
 port
  management, 765–781. *See also* Port management
  pricing, 782–802. *See also* Port pricing
  productivity and efficiency, 803–831. *See also* Port productivity and efficiency
 ships, 168–169
  sizes, 169
 time and cost between inland and transocean inland points, 901
 transhipment, economics of, 832–859. *See also* Transhipment
 transpacific, demand and supply 1996–2001, 175
 world,
  fleet 2000, 169
  growth in 161
Credit risk
 shipping finance, in, 731–761. *See also* Shipping finance

Crude oil, 71–72, 115–120. *See also* Oil
Cruise vessels, 167

Derivatives
 shipping derivative markets, historical development, 694–695
 use of in shipping risk management, 693–730. *See also* Risk management
 bulk shipping, 678–679
Discrimination
 seafarers, 456–461
Dry bulk carriers, 170–173. *See also* Bulk shipping
 development in size and tonnage, 172
 newbuilding market, efficiency of, for, 245–247
 secondhand market, efficiency of, for, 245–247
 ships, investing in, 623–641. *See also* Investing in ships
 type variations, 172–173
Dry bulk market, 227–250
 competition, 234
 conditions in, 231–234
 developments in, and BFI,5/01/85–30/04/98, 697
 efficient
  information dissemination, 233–234
  market hypothesis, 240–243
 freight rates
  levels and volatilities
   spillover effects, 243–245
  seasonal behaviour of, 234–240
   changes in
    spot rates, 236
    TC rates, 236
    3-year, 237
   under different market conditions, 238
   elasticity of supply curve, 239
 homogeneity of services, 233
 mobility of ships, 234
 newbuilding market, efficiency of, for dry bulk carriers, 245–247
 no barriers to entry and exit, 232–233
 number of participants, 233
 secondhand market, efficiency of, for dry bulk carriers, 245–247
 segmentation, 228–231
Dry bulk trades, 161–163. *See also* Bulk commodity trades; Dry bulk market

Economics
 economic regulation
  liner shipping, of, 327–345
 economic theory
  trade and transport, in, 38–42. *See also* International trade
 energy and trade, 105–146. *See also* Energy
 international trade logistics and shipping transactions, of, 877–897. *See also* International logistics

INDEX

Economics—*cont*
  liner shipping, economic regulation of, 327–345
  mainstream, and transport, 41–42
  marine environment, relationship with, 416–418
  maritime safety and environment regulations, of, 399–425. *See also* Maritime safety
  market for ships, 186–202. *See also* Ships
  port management, 765–781. *See also* Port management
  seafaring labour market, of, 443–468. *See also* Labour market
  shipping freight markets, of, 157–185. *See also* Shipping freight markets
  ships, investing in, 623–641. *See also* Investing in ships
  shortsea shipping, of, 280–304. *See also* Shortsea shipping
  trade and energy, 105–146
  transhipment, of, 832–859. *See also* Transhipment
Employment
  victim of globalisation?, 54–58
Energy
  coal, 134–145. *See also* Coal
  consumption
    industrial, 107–108
      production in OECD, and, 106
    residential, 106–107
    transport, 108
      US passenger car efficiency, 108
  demand for, 105–109
  economics and trade, 105–146
  natural gas, 130–133. *See also* Natural gas
  oil, 111–120. *See also* Oil
  supply, 109–110
    long-run average cost curve, 110
    world primary production, 106
Environment regulations
  maritime safety, and, economics of, 399–425. *See also* Maritime safety
Environmental factors
  shipping, and, 175–176
Europe
  feeder service schedule, 178
  gas use in, 132
  northern, port management, 765–781. *See also* Port management
  shipbuilding industry, 533–534
  shortsea shipping policies, 296–299
  trade flows
    establishment of, 147–154
    foreign, integration of, 148–149
    shipping, 148–149
    land/sea trade data, 147–148
    origin/destination matrices
      compilation process, 150–151
      Germany, 150
      pilot study on interregional, 149–151
        choice of route, 149

Europe—*cont*
  trade flows—*cont*
    "road to sea" split functions, assessment, 151–153
      modelling approach, 151
      results, 152
        mode choice, 153
        theoretical modal split function, 152
    traffic flows data, 147–148
European sailing vessels
  ocean routes of, 66
European Union
  competition rules, 335–336
  economic regulation of liner shipping in, 335–338. *See also* Liner shipping
  legislation for regulating shipping industry, 604–606
Exports
  world manufactured, by product 2000, 92

Far East
  crude oil market, 129
Finance
  credit risk in shipping, 731–761. *See also* Shipping finance
Finland
  port community system, Port@Net, 909–911
Flags
  choice of, 524–525
  importance of, 524–525
  of convenience
    maritime economics, 6–7
  ships and taxes, 512–529. *See also* Ships
Fleet operations
  deployment, 580–597
    bulk shipping, more realistic models, 582–588
      cargo carried per year, 584
      constraints, 583–587
      objective function, 583–587
      total cost per ton, 586
      total operating cost per year, 585
    liner shipping models, 588–594
      integer programming problem formulation, 589–594
        constraints, 590–591
          lay-up time, 590
          non-negativity, 591
          service frequency, 590
          ship availability, 590
          ship/route incompatability, 590
        decision variables, 589
        objective function, 590
        software application, 591–594
          optimisation examples, 591
            comparison of frequencies, 594
            current ship allocation, 591
            integer programming allocation, 593
            linear programming allocation, 592
            resultant ship allocation, 592

Fleet operations—*cont*
  deployment—*cont*
    multi-origin, multi-destination problem, 587
    simple problem, 581–582
    optimisation, 580–597
Forward freight agreements (FFA), 703–708. *See also* Risk management
Freight costs
  as factor in demand, 163–164
  as percentage of import values, 164
Freight futures market, 695–703. *See also* Risk management
Freight markets. *See also* Shipping freight markets
  green, 183
Freight rate, 694–712, *See also* Risk management
Fuel emissions, 179

General cargo trades, 2000, 81–86
  directional imbalances, 85
  container services
    global inter-core container trade, 83
    growth in world, 161
    inter-core route container traffic, 2000, 84
    pendulum services, 84
    RTW services, 84
    shuttle services, 84
  growth in, 161
  ships, 168–169
  network strategies, 81–82
  northern latitudes, 82–83
  shipping freight markets, economics of, 157–185. *See also* Shipping freight markets
  trade flows, Europe, establishment of, 147–154. *See also* Europe
  transhipment, economics of, 832–859. *See also* Transhipment
Germany
  trade flows, 150
Global supply chain, 46–50. *See also* Globalisation; International logistics
Globalisation, 35–62
  employment, victim?, 54–58
  global
    supply chain, 46–50
      management, 46–47
    trade, 36–38. *See also* International trade
      how it is being moved, 36–38
  globalised business in globalised economy, 35–36
  maritime business, relevance for, 46–58
    outlook, 58
  maritime transport, relevance for, 36–46
    outlook, 45–46
  national shipping policies, and, 471–472
  policy issues, 51–54
  safety, victim of?, 54–58
  shipping policy, and, 495–511. *See also* Shipping policy

Goods. *See* Manufactured goods
Government
  policies and shipbuilding industry, 530–549. *See also* Shipbuilding industry
Grain, 74–76
  major trade routes, 2000, 75
Greek shipping companies, 25–27
  largest, 28

Information technology (IT)
  logistics and maritime business, in, 898–912. *See also* International logistics
International logistics. *See also* Liner shipping
  container shipping
    competition and co-operation with air transport, 864–868
  costs
    typical shipping company, 895
    determination of, and transactional costs, 880–883
  documentation requirements and agents, 879
  e-logistics
    economic implications, 895–897
    solutions, 885–888
    transactional developments in, 890
  improvements, opportunities for, 883–885
  information flow, 887
  information technology (IT) in
    and maritime business, 898–913, *see also* e-logistics, *above*
    and supply chain management, 899–900
    information flows
      company-public authority exchange of data, 909–911
        Finnish port community system, 909–911
      industrial shipping, 906–909
      inter-company, 904–909
        between main partners, forest industry supply chain, 908
        business to business procurement models, 906
        CPFR process, 905
      intra-company, 901–904
        ERP programs, 901
      transocean transport, 900–901
        time and cost between inland and transocean inland points for container, 901
  international trade
    1999, 881
    land and water feeder transport in, 1999, 882
  management, wireless and internet in, 892–893
  modal choice
    and, 863–876
    determinant factors
      air-based logistics system, 874–876
      supporting shippers' behaviour, 868–870

INDEX

International logistics—*cont*
  modal choice—*cont*
    flow chart of logistics system, 871
    hypothesising, product cycle theory and, 870–873
    logistics strategy and, 868
    model prior to 1990, 866
    perspective, air-based logistics system, and, 874–876
    product cycle and, 873
      theory and hypothesising, 870
    substitution causality, increase in 1990s, 866–868
    total distribution cost
      as criterion, 864–865
      comparison with air transport, 864
      effect of, and networking, on, 868
      turning point in, 865–866
  new
    environment, 894–895
    market technology, impact of, 883–885
  port, terminal and inland depot/warehouse revenues, 1999, 882
  shipping
    company costs, typical, 895
    information flows participants, 878
    transactions, and, 878–883
      economics of, 877–897
  supply chain participants, 878
  systems, major, cost elements, 886
  transactional costs, determination of logistics and, 880–883
  world ocean shipping container carrying revenues, 880
International ocean trade. *See* International seaborne trade
International seaborne trade. *See also* International trade
  air transport threat, 97–99
  British impact on, 68–69
  bulk commodity trades, 2000, 69–78. *See also* Bulk commodity trades
  container traffic, growth in world, 161
  general cargo trades, 2000, 81–86. *See also* General cargo trades
  international trade
    1999, 881
    land and water feeder transport in, 1999, 882
  patterns of, 65–89
    in major commodities, 229
    prospects, 86–87
  port
    management, 765–781. *See also* Port management
    pricing, 782–802. *See also* Port pricing
    productivity and efficiency, 803–831. *See also* Port productivity and efficiency
  regulations in international shipping, 473
  sail, under, 65–68
    ocean routes of European vessels, 66

International seaborne trade—*cont*
  sail, under—*cont*
    world wind systems (January), 66
  shipping freight markets, economics of, 157–185. *See also* Shipping freight markets
  world seaborne trade,
    1840–2000, 160
    1985–2000, 91
International trade, 36–38. *See also* International seaborne trade; Trade
  1840–2000, 160
  1999, 881
  cargoes and routes, different size vessels, 230
  container traffic, growth in world, 161
  economic growth, and, 38–41
  land and water feeder transport in, 1999, 882
  Latin American countries, modal split, 2000, 39
  logistics and shipping transactions, economics of, 877–897. *See also* International logistics
  manufactured goods, in, 90–104
    air cargo carriers, top ten 2000, 99
    air transport threat, 97–99
    exports by product 2000, 92
    how carried?, 95–97
    modal splits
      Canada, 96–97
      Latin America, 2000, 39
    key goods traded globally, 90–93
    top ten trade flows 2000, 94
    trader's view, 100–101
  patterns of,
    in major commodities, 229
  routes and cargoes, different size vessels, 230
  shipping freight markets, economics of, 157–185. *See also* Shipping freight markets
  transport
    economics, and, 41–42
    mode of, by, 37
    mutual relationship, 42–45
    outlook, 45–46
    type of, by, forecast 2002, 38
  how it is being moved, 36–38
Investing in ships, 623–641
  asset play
    bulk of shipping profits?, 632
    game with winners and losers, 634–636
    in era of pools and quality shipping, 636–637
    investment strategies risk and, 630–636
    risks and attitudes, 633–634
  bulk shipping, 627
  common risks, 625–626
    large sunk costs, 625
    limiting, 630–631
    problematic investment appraisal techniques, 625

920 INDEX

Investing in ships—*cont*
  common risks—*cont*
    technological obsolescence, 625
    uncertainty, 625
  constraints
    co-operation, liner tonnage, 627–628
    operational
      bulk and liner acquisitions, 626–627
      investment/divestment constraints, 627
    delivery lags, balancing with vessel endurance, 628–630
  different shipping segments, 624
  investment
    strategies
      fixed cost and, 631–633
      indicative
        development of shipbuilding prices 1993–2001, 631
        returns of sale and purchase, 632
      limiting risk, 630–631
      risk and asset play, 630–636
      valuing using real options analysis, 642–660. *See also* Maritime investment
  liner tonnage, 627–628
  market cyclicality, 623–626
  newbuilding *v.* secondhand, 628–630
    know the market, 629–630
    net purchases of tonnage from secondhand market, 1980–84, 635
  port
    management, 765–781. *See also* Port management
    pricing, 782–802. *See also* Port pricing
    productivity and efficiency, 803–831. *See also* Port productivity and efficiency
  risk
    investment strategies, and asset play, 630–636
    limiting, 630–631
Iron ore, 72–73
  major trade routes, 2000, 73

Japan
  gas use in, 132
  shipbuilding industry, 533, 541–543
Japanese shipping companies, 27–30

Korea
  financial crisis
    impact of, on Korean companies, 358–374
    overcoming, 358–360
  liner shipping companies, challenges for, 360–364
  reforms in economy, 359
  selected economic indicators, 360
  shipbuilding industry, 533, 538–541, 543–544

Labour market
  labour economics, theory of, 444–450

Labour market—*cont*
  seafaring
    discrimination, 456–461
      monopsony, 457–459
        discriminating, 458–459
        pricing, 458
      wage
        monthly, comparison, 460
        officer, 461
    economics of, 443–468
    labour
      markets, 448–450
      supply of, 445–448
        top 10 countries, 450
    laws relating to health and welfare, 454
    migration, 450–452
    mobility, 450–452
    segmentation, 452–456
      cultural, 455–456
      legislative separation, 452–455
    trade unions, 462–465
      collective agreements, 463
      effect on, 462
      non-nationals as members?, 464
  seafarers
    demand for, 444–445
      discrimination, 456–461
    education and training investment, 446
    foreign, restrictions, 453
    labour markets, 448–450
    migration, 450–452
    mobility, 450–452
    supply of, 445–448
    trade unions, 462–465
Latin America
  foreign trade, modal split, 2000, 39
  intra-Latin American trade, cost determinants, 44
  maritime business
    clustering, and, 48–50
Life
  loss of, at sea, 56
Liner shipping, 307–326. *See also* Container services
  agreements
    alternative models of, 309–317
    introductory, 309
  alliances, definitions of, 346–347
  cartel enforcement, 312–313
  collusion, models of, 312–314
  competition
    destructive, 314
    measuring, 309–312
    rules (EU), 335–336
  competitive business strategies, 347
  conclusion, 321–343
  conference practices, 317–321
  container shipping
    cost leadership in, 348
    differentiation as strategy, 348
    focus strategy, 348

Liner shipping—*cont*
  container shipping—*cont*
    globalisation strategy, 349
    movements in major liner routes 2000, 480
  contestable markets, 313–314
  co-operation
    business strategy, and, 346–374
      forms in terms of, 369
      importance of, 370
    forms of, 347
    motives for forming, 366
    nature of, 365
    research
      analysis, 351–358
      business strategy
        motives
          categorisation of, 354
          comparison of, 352–353
        cost reduction strategy, 355
        focused on, 356
        hypotheses, 350
        market
          development strategy, 356–358
          stabilisation strategy, 355
        methodology, 350–351
        role of co-operation in business strategy, 353–358
        service differentiation strategy, 355
    types of, 365
  customer needs
    challenges and opportunities, 377–380
  challenges and opportunities, 379–380
  economic regulation of, 327–345
  European Union
    competition rules, 335–336
      applying them to transport, 336
      economic regulation in, 335–338
      regulations, 337
        scope and effect of, 337–338
  fleet deployment models, 588–594
  historical origins, 308–309
  horizontal restructuring of, 382–383
  intermodal services, involvement in, 385–
  Korea
    liner shipping companies, challenges for, 360–364
    financial crisis
      impact of on Korean companies, 358–374
      overcoming, 358–360
      reforms in economy, 359
      selected economic indicators, 360
  liner freight market
    over-capacity in, 174–175
  lines, horizontal and vertical restructuring, 382–388
  logistics. *See also* International logistics
    changes in industry, 380–382
    developments, 377
    evolving conditions, 376–382

Liner shipping—*cont*
  logistics—*cont*
    just-in-time and postponement, 378
    management, 375–396
      definition, 376–377
    services
      function, importance of, 391
      involvement in, 385–388
      nature of, 390–391
      organisation structure, 390–393
      process performance, effectiveness of, 391–393
    sourcing in low-cost locations, 377
    supply chain visibility, 379
  loyalty contracts, 318–319
  markets, measuring, 309–312
  modelling competition and collusion, 307–326
  organisational structure
    assessment of, 388–393
  predatory pricing, 317–318
  price discrimination, 319–321
  restructuring of, 382–388
  ships, investing in, 623–641. *See also* Investing in ships
  strategies
    business, 353–358
    competitive business, 347
    container shipping, 348–350
    cost reduction, 355–356
    generic, 348
      beyond classic, 349–350
    market development, 350, 356–358
    market stabilisation, 355
    as, 349
    service differentiation, 355
  supply chain, 375–396
    evolving conditions, 376–382
    management
      definition, 376–377
      responses of lines to, 393–394
    visibility, 379
  terminal management, involvement in, 383–385
  transhipment, economics of, 832–859. *See also* Transhipment
  United States
    antitrust laws, 328–329
    economic regulation
      Advisory Commission on Conferences in Ocean Shipping, 333
      Ocean Shipping Reform Act 1998, 334–335
        impact of, 339–342
      pressure for change in 1990s, 333–334
      Public Law 87-346 ("1961 amendments"), 330
      Shipping Act, 1916
        after, 330
        before, 329–330
      Shipping Act 1984, 331–333

922 INDEX

Liner shipping—*cont*
  vertical restructuring of, 383–388
Logistics. *See also* International logistics
  information technology (IT), and maritime business, in, 898–912
  international
    modal choice, and, 863–876
    trade, and shipping transactions, 877–897

Manufactured goods
  international trade in, 90–104. *See* International trade
Marine environment
  relationship with economics, 416–418. *See also* Maritime safety
Maritime business. *See also* Maritime investment
  bulk shipping, business risk assessment and analysis, 661–692
  credit risk, shipping finance, in, 731–761. *See also* Shipping finance
  globalisation, relevance for, 46–58
  information technology (IT), logistics and, in, 898–912. *See also* International logistics
  investments, valuing using real options analysis, 642–660
  marketing strategies, 553–579
  new order, rise of, 52–54
  port
    management, 765–781. *See also* Port management
    pricing, 782–802. *See also* Port pricing
    productivity and efficiency, 803–831. *See also* Port productivity and efficiency
  ship registration trends, 53
  ships, investing in, 623–641. *See also* Investing in ships
  specialisation in, 47–48
    clustering, and, 48–50
      Latin America and Caribbean, 48–50
    traditional maritime nations, decline of, 51–52
    engagement of, end 2000, 52
  twentieth century, 9–34
    continuity and change, 30
    introductory, 9
    largest fleets, 11
    shipping companies, 17–31
      British, 18–22
        largest, 20
      Greek, 25–27
        largest, 28
      Japanese, 27–30
      Norwegian, 22–25
    shipping markets, 15–17
      1870s–1970s, 14
      1970s–2000s, 16
  world shipping developments, 9
Maritime economics. *See also* Economics
  competition policy, 6
  flags of convenience, 6–7
  future of, 3–8

Maritime economics—*cont*
  investments, valuing using real options analysis, 642–660
  policies generally, and, 5–7
  port pricing, 782–802. *See also* Port pricing
  protectionism, 5–6
  safety, 3–5
  seaport economics, 7
  ship design, 3–5
Maritime investment. *See also* Investing in ships
  credit risk, shipping finance, in, 731–761. *See also* Shipping finance
  valuing using real options analysis, 642–660
    conclusion, 657–658
    introductory, 642–643
    investment decision, 643–645
      expanded NPV, 644–645
    real options, 645–
      analysis (ROA), 646–647
        application to investment in fast cargo ships, 655–657
      valuation
        base case, 655–656
        ROA
          one vessel service, 656–657
          two-vessel service, 657
      competitive options, 647–648
      growth options, 647–648
      location options, 650–651
      maritime applications of, 647–651
      option to
        abandon, 648
        for salvage, 649
        contract, 648
        defer or waiting to invest, 649–650
        expand, 647
        switch (output or input), 650
      strategic options, 647–648
      timing options, 649–650
      valuation, 652–653
      valuing, 651–652
      what is, 645–646
Maritime nations
  decline of traditional, 51–52
Maritime safety, 175–176
  accident
    analysis, and, 426–442
    ship
      causes, 431–433
      costs
        classifying, 433–434
        property damage, determinants, 434–438
        fatalities and injuries, determinants, 438–439
      seaworthiness, determinants, 439–440
      statistics, 429–431
  concerns, 427–429
  economic analysis and formulation of, 420–422

# INDEX

Maritime safety—*cont*
  economics, 3–5, 399–425
    relationship with, 416–418
  environment, and
    benefits and costs, evaluation, 418–420
    economic issue, 400–401
    economics of, 399–425
      special features of, 401–404
    marine environment
      relationship with economics, 416–418
    overview, 400–406
    regulate, alternative ways to, 411–413
    regulations, and, 404–406
      aims of, 406–407
      cost and benefit, measuring, 414–422
        valuation methods
          overview, 414–416
          revealed preference (RPM), 414–415
          stated preference (SPM), 415–416
      cost-benefit analysis for optimal, 407–409
      variations of, and complementary methods to, 409–411
      economic analysis
        and formulation of, 420–422
        options, and, 406–413
  loss of life and vessels at sea, 56
  management of, 176–177
  maritime safety, and, 175-176
  sea, at, 54–56
  seafarers, and, 56–58
  victim of globalisation?, 54–58
Maritime transport. *See also* Transport
  relevance for globalisation, 36–46
  port
    management, 765–781. *See also* Port management
    pricing, 782–802. *See also* Port pricing
    productivity and efficiency, 803–831. *See also* Port productivity and efficiency
Marketing strategies, 553–579. *See also* Shipping marketing strategies
Markets
  competitive, effect of externality, 403
  crude oil, 128–129. *See also* Oil
  cycles in shipping market, 203–224. *See also* Shipping markets
  dry bulk, 227–250. *See also* Dry bulk market
  forward freight agreements (FFA), 703–708. *See also* Risk management
  freight. *See* Shipping freight markets
  freight futures, 695–703. *See also* Risk management
  labour. *See* Labour market
  liner shipping, 307–326. *See also* Liner shipping
  shipping derivative, historical development, 694–695
  ships, for, economics of, 186–202. *See also* Ships

Markets—*cont*
  shortsea shipping, 280–304. *See also* Shortsea shipping
  tanker, 169–170, 251–279. *See also* Tanker market
Mediterranean, 128-129
  crude oil market, 128–129
Middle East
  crude oil market, 128–129
  oil, and, 116–117
Modal
  choice
    international logistics and, 863–876. *See also* International logistics
  splits
    Canada, 96–97
    Latin America, 2000, 39
    theoretical function, 152

National shipping policies
  came into being, when?, 476–478
    rooted in antiquity, 476
  Canada, 485–487
    core fleet or reliance on world market?, 486–487
    exporters, role of, 486
    national defence argument, 486
    policy or not?, 485–486
  China, 487–489
    bilateral cargo rights exclude cross-traders, 488
    expansionist policy, 487–488
    future maritime superpower, 489
  continued support for, 477–478
  differences
    by region, 479–480
    by type of service, 478–479
  economic regulation
    versus safety and environmental regulation, 482–483
  globalisation, and, 471–472
  institutions involved in, 482
  key
    agencies, 483–485
    players, 480–485
  liner service versus charter, 478–479
  maritime policy
    what is?, 472–474
  maritime power, 476–477
  merchant fleets, top 12, 1 October 2001, 481
  policy and circumstance, 485
  private versus state intervention, 480–482
  regulations in international shipping, 473
  regulatory levels, 482
  rise and fall of, 471–494
  West Africa, 489–491
    Cotonou (June 1997), 490–491
    creeping realism, 490–491
    failed policy, 490
    policy making, slow, 491
  where use most prevalent, 478–480

Natural gas, 130–133
  proven resources, 121
  trade in, 132–134
  use
    Europe, 132
    Japan, 132
    United States, 131
    World, 133
Newbuilding
  market, 188–189, 194–195
    efficiency of, for dry bulk carriers, 245–247
  v. secondhand, 628–630
North Sea crude oil market, 127
Norwegian shipping companies, 22–25

Ocean routes
  European sailing vessels, 66
OECD
  energy consumption and industrial production, 106
Oil, 111–120. *See also* Energy
  Brent Crude
    oil pricing, and, 125–130
    price
      quotations, 126
      reporting, 125–127
  consumption, 253–254
    economic drivers of, 254–258
    end of twentieth century, 163
    patterns, 123–124, 254
    regional, 123
      patterns, 2000, 254
    total world 1965–2000, 243
  crude, 115–120
    Brent, 125–130
    consumption
      patterns, 123–124
    exports 1999, 120
    markets
      Far East, 129
      Mediterranean, 128–129
      Middle East, 128–129
      North Sea, 127
      United States, 127–128
      West Africa, 128
    price quotations, 126
    production, world, 162
    trade in, 115–120
      1975–1999, 123
      switch to, 116
  geology, 111–114
  exploration programme
    time plan, 113
  exports 1999, 120
  extraction, 111–114
  major trade routes, 2000, 72
  physical characteristics, 114
  production trends, world, 258–259
    consumption patterns, 2000, 258
    regional
      flows of oil, 2000, 259

Oil—*cont*
  production trends, world—*cont*
    regional—*cont*
      production patterns, 258–259
  products, 121–125
    consumption
      patterns, 123–124
      2000, 258
    regional, 123
    exports 1999, 120
    futures, 129
    markets, 129–130
    regional production patterns, 258–259
  refining, 121–123
    capacity
      throughputs, and, 122
      world, 122
  regional flows of, 2000, 259
  reserves, 114–115
    proven, 111
    seismic survey, 112
  tankers. *See* Tankers
  trade in
    crude, 115–120
    current situation, 120
    exports 1999, 120
    Middle East, and, 116–117
    turbulent years, 117–118
    OPEC, and, 118–120
    products, 115
  transportation demand trends, 1990–2000, 261
Options
  freight rates, on, 708–712. *See also* Risk management

Poland
  shipbuilding industry, 534
Policies
  government, and shipbuilding industry, 530–549. *See also* Shipbuilding industry
  national shipping, rise and fall of, 471–494. *See also* National shipping policies
Port management
  northern Europe, 765–781
    co-operation agreements, 770
    competitive environment, surviving in, 777–779
    evolution in, 766–769
    growth
      environment, in, 774–777
      forecasts of container
        loadings, 776
        unloadings, 776
    objectives, tools and impacts, 772
    port environment, radically changed, 769–774
  port, terminal and inland depot/warehouse revenues, 1999, 882
Port pricing, 782–802

INDEX

Port pricing—*cont*
  cost recovery
    limit pricing, and, 787–789
    through MCP, 794–795
  excess capacity, 790–792
  infrastructure
    pricing of port, 789–797
    public spending and the role of the state, 784–785
  issue in maritime economics, why?, 782–783
  marginal costs
    measuring, 795
    pricing, 792
    short and long-run, 792–793
  policy intervention, 797–799
  port
    competition, 784–789
    cost function, impact of vessel size on, 791
    new role of, 785–787
    services, kinked demand for, 796–797
    terminal and inland depot/warehouse revenues, 1999, 882
    throughput, forecasting, 795–796
    what is?, 783–784
  price elasticities in northern Europe container ports, 787
  returns
    constant, to scale, 794
    diminishing, to scale, 793–794
    increasing, to scale, 793
  trade liberalisation, and new role of ports, 785–787
Port productivity and efficiency, 803–831
  data envelopment analysis, 811–820
    applications, 817–820
    DMU and homogeneous units, 812
    efficiencies of container terminals, 814, 816
    method, 811–817
    single input/single output data, 813
  efficiency
    economic concept of, 808–810
    measurement, modern methods of, 810–811
  firm's frontier production function, 810
  port
    performance, review of, 804–808
    terminal and inland depot/warehouse revenues, 1999, 882
  productivity studies, review of, 804–808
  stochastic frontier model, 820–825
    applications, 823–825
    approach to efficiency estimation, 821
    method, 820–823
Protectionism
  maritime economics, 5–6

Regional integration
  transport, and, 45
Risk management
  derivatives
    other, 712

Risk management—*cont*
  derivatives—*cont*
    use of in shipping risk management, 693–730
    bulk shipping, 678–679
  freight rate, 694–712
    forward freight agreements (FFA), 703–708
      contracts, characteristics of, 707–708
      empirical evidence on, 707
      estimated value of transactions, 704
      hedging
        timecharter freight risk, 705
        voyage freight risk, 704
      spot and near month FFA prices on Baltic Exchange, 703
    freight futures market, 695–703
      Baltic Freight Index, major changes since inception, 696
      developments in Dry Bulk Market and 5/01/85–30/04/98, 697
      hedging freight rates using, 700
      price discovery role of, 697–699
      risk management function of, 699–703
    options on, 708–712
      call options payoffs, 709
      hedging example using, 710–711
      primer, 708–710
      put option payoff, 710
    other derivative instruments, 712
    shipping derivative markets, historical development, 694–695
  voyage costs risk, 712–723
    bunker prices
    hedging
      using futures contracts, 714–715
      actively traded contracts and options, 714
      using options, 718–723
        caplet option hedge, 719
        caps and floors, 718–719
        price to be paid or received, 720
        using cap, 719
        collars or cylinder options, 720–721
        collar, 721–723
        exotic, 723
      using OTC products, 715
        bunker swap contracts, 716–718
        cash flows, 717
        plain vanilla, 717
        forward contracts, 715–716
    world bunker market, 712–713

Safety. *See* Maritime safety
Scrapping
  market, 189–190, 196–197
Seafarers. *See* Labour market
Seafaring labour market, economics of, 443–468. *See also* Labour market
Seaport economics, 7

INDEX

Secondhand ships
  market, 190, 197–198
    efficiency of, for dry bulk carriers, 245–247
  newbuilding *v.*, 628–630
  prices, comparison of volatilities, 667–670
Shipbuilding industry
  Brazil, 534
  China, 534, 544–547
    changes
      in economy, 544–545
      in shipbuilding industry, 545–546
    State Shipbuilding Corporation, role, 546
    volume of newbuilding
      completions, 546
      orders, 545
  demand and ship cycles, 534–535
  global shift of, 532–535
  government
    intervention, impact on, 532
    policies and, 530–549
    role of and policies, 536–541
  indicative development of shipbuilding
    prices 1993–2001, 631
  Japan, 533, 541–543
  Korea, 533, 538–541, 543–544
    changes in composition of builders, 542
  naval shipbuilding, 537–538
  Poland, 534
  shipbuilding
    enterprises, 530–532
    national economic development, and, 538
  ships, investing in, 623–641. *See also*
    Investing in ships
    changes in volume of orders, 543
    volume of new completions, 544
  state subsidies, 536–537
  structural change
    major shipbuilding countries, 541–547
    world, 532–535
  Western Europe, 533–534
Shipping. *See also* Shipping industry; Ships
  bulk. *See* Bulk shipping
  companies, 17–31
    British, 18–22
    largest, 20
    Greek, 25–27
    largest, 28
    Japanese, 27–30
    Norwegian, 22–25
  derivative markets, historical development, 694–695
  finance, credit risk in, 731–761. *See also*
    Shipping finance
  fleet operations, 580–597. *See also* Fleet
    operations
  industry. *See* Shipping industry
  international, regulations in, 473
  liner, 307–326. *See also* Liner shipping
  marketing strategies, 553–579. *See also*
    Shipping marketing strategies
  markets. *See* Markets; Shipping freight markets

Shipping—*cont*
  port
    management, 765–781. *See also* Port management
    pricing, 782–802. *See also* Port pricing
    productivity and efficiency, 803–831. *See also* Port productivity and efficiency
  ships, investing in, 623–641. *See also*
    Investing in ships
  shortsea. *See* Shortsea shipping
  supply, 166–167
  transactions, international trade logistics
    and, economics of, 877–897. *See also*
    International logistics
Shipping derivative markets
  historical development, 694–695
Shipping finance
  credit risk, in, 731–761
    collateral securities, 739–743
      assignment
        of insurance, 741
        of requisition compensation, 741
        of revenue, 740–741
      cash, 742
      comfort letters, 742
      guarantees, 742
      mortgage, 739–740
      mortagee's interest insurance, 741
      shares, 742–743
    covenants, 743–744
    credit policy, 753–756
      banks', 755
      contents of, 754
    credit risk, 732–734
      analysis, 734
      banks' income, 748, 749
      capital adequacy rules, 750–752
      cash flow, of, 739
      further discussion, 744–752
      loan
        pricing of, 746–749
        ranking and effect on decision, 745
        syndication, 749
      rating scale, 746
      six Cs of, 735
        capital, 736
        character/capacity, 734–735
        collateral, 738–739
        company, 736–737
        conditions, 737–738
    loan monitoring, 752–753
Shipping freight markets. *See also* Bulk commodity trades; Dry bulk market
  1870s–1970s, 14
  1970s–2000s, 16
  changes in, 160–183
    impact on political economy, 165
  competition, 177–178
  container
    fleet, world, 2000, 169
    ships, 168–169

Shipping freight markets—*cont*
  container—*cont*
    ships—*cont*
      sizes, 169
      traffic, growth in world, 161
    costs, 177–178
      comparative
        external, modelling, 183
        tonne-mile, 165
    cruise vessels, 167
    cycles in, 203–224
      affect freight rates?, 221
      asset price, 206
      bulk carrier, 205
      causes of, 217–220
      characteristics of, 204–206
      demand factors, 217–219
      dynamics of, 220–221
      four periods of, 207
      generic, 204
      laid-up tonnage, 215
      length of, 215–216
      mechanisms, 217–220
      predictable?, 222–223
      revenues, 206
      role of, in shipping economics, 204–206
      secular trends, 220
      shipping fundamental trends, 221
      structural factors, 220
      summary, 223–224
      supply/demand model, 217
      supply factors, 219–220
      tanker, 205
      volatility, 215–216
    demand factors, 164–165
    dry bulk
      carriers, 170–173. *See also* Dry bulk carriers
      market, 227–250. *See also* Dry bulk market
      trades, 161–163. *See also* Bulk commodity trades
    economics of, 157–185
    environmental factors, and, 175–176, 183
    feeder service schedule, 178
    fleet operations, 580–597. *See also* Fleet operations
    forward freight agreements (FFA), 703–708. *See also* Risk management
    freight costs
      as factor in demand, 163–164
      as percentage of import values, 164
    freight futures, 695–703. *See also* Risk management
    fuel emissions, 179
    general cargo
      growth in, 161
      ships, 168–169
    liner shipping, 307–326. *See also* Liner shipping
    main, post 1970s, 161–183
    maritime safety, and, 175-176
      management of, 176–177

Shipping freight markets—*cont*
  shipping, supply, 166–167
  shortsea shipping, 280–304. *See also* Shortsea shipping
  serious accidents, 181–183
  structure, 158–159
  supply and demand, 170, 173
    capacity *v.* volume, 173
  tanker, 169–170, 251–279. *See also* Tanker market
  theoretical framework, 159–160
  twentieth century 15–17
  waste, disposal of, 179
  world
    crude oil production, 162
    drybulk trades, 162
    shipping tonnage, growth of, 166
    trade
      1840–2000, 160
      growth in seaborne, 160
      v. cptm, 163
Shipping industry
  acquisitions in, 598–620, *see also* mergers and acquisitions, *below*
  consolidations in, 598–620, *see also* mergers and acquisitions, *below*
  mergers and acquisitions in, 598–620
    activity, 599–602
    conclusion, 616–617
    conditions for acceleration, 599–600
    corporate governance and control, 615–616
    framework for evaluating, 612–615
      increase in value at announcement, 612–613
      long-run performance following, 613–614
    growth of, 600–602
    keys to success, 614–615
    legal and regulatory framework, 602–606
      economic and political aspects, 602–603
      EU legislation, 604–606
      US legislation, 603–604
    motives for, 606–612
      efficiency increases, 607–609
      market power, 606–607
      marketing, 610–612
      operating and financial synergies, 609–610
      strategic, 610–612
      value maximisation, 606–610
    problem areas, 614–615
  port
    management, 765–781. *See also* Port management
    pricing, 782–802. *See also* Port pricing
    productivity and efficiency, 803–831. *See also* Port productivity and efficiency
  ships, investing in, 623–641. *See also* Investing in ships
Shipping marketing strategies, 553–579

INDEX

Shipping marketing strategies—*cont*
  competition, dealing with, 556–562
  competitive
    marketing strategies, 562–570
    position of transportation, 560
    strategies, 558–562
    maritime industry, for, 564
  cost leadership strategy, 564–566
  differentiation strategies, 566
  environmentally friendly transport
    promotion of, 562, 568–569
  maritime industry
    competitive
      marketing strategies, and, 562–570
      strategies, for, 564
    environmental analysis of, 562–564
    external macro and micro environment for, 563
  market
    logistics and dealing with competition, 556–562
    orientation, 554–555
  marketing public relations, 561, 568–570
  promotion targeting
    service providers, 570
    service users, 570
  relationship marketing, 560–561
    applications, 567–568
  service quality, 559–560
    maintaining, 566–567
  strategic planning
    market oriented, 555–556
      model, 557
    marketing and, 553–556
  strategy and planning, 554
Shipping markets. *See* Shipping freight markets; Ships
Shipping policy
  contexts, 503–507
  factors that drive, 497–502
  globalisation era, in, 495–511
  interest groups, 502
  international, 495–511
  making, context for, 500
  national, 495–511
    rise and fall of, 471–494. *See also* National shipping policies
  research,
    spatial perspective, 496–497
  supra-national, 495–511
Ships
  accident statistics, 429–431. *See also* Maritime safety
  design
    economics, 3–5
    parameters of largest container ships, 837
  different size, cargoes and routes, 230
  economic life of, 200–201
  flags,
    choice of, 524–525
    flagging out, response to, 525–527

Ships—*cont*
  flags—*cont*
    importance of, 524–525
    taxes, and, 512–529, *see also* taxes, *below*
  fleet operations, 580–597. *See also* Fleet operations
  fuel emissions, 179
  future income, expectations on, 199–200
  investment
    in, 623–641. *See also* Investing in ships
    incentives, 513–516
  leasing, 192–193
  loss of, at sea, 56
  market for, economics of, 186–202
    auxiliary markets, 187
    bulk carriers
      deletions, 187
      deliveries, 187
      freight rates, 1990s, 193
      market values, 1990s, 193
    competition, 193–198
    different vessel types
      characteristics specific for, 191–192
    economic life of vessel, 200–201
    future income, expectations on, 199–200
    leasing, 192–193
    main characteristics, 186–191
    newbuilding market
      characteristics specific for, 188–189
      order book as percentage of existing tonnage of main vessel types, 189
      structure, 194–195
    polluting emissions, 292
    pricing, 198–201
    real markets, 187
    renting, 192–193
    scrapping market
      characteristics specific for, 189–190
      structure, 196–197
    secondhand market
      characteristics specific for, 190–191
      tankers, values, 191
      structure, 197–198
    ship values, 198–201
    structure, 193–198
  pricing, 198–201
    behaviour, 268–270
    tankers, 268–270, 275–276
  registration, trends, 53
  renting, 192–193
  taxes, flags and, 512–529, *see also* flags, *above*
    investment incentives, 513–516
    methodology, 516–517
    model, 521–523
    tax positions, 517
      full tax, 518
      new entry, 518–520
      no tax, 518
      timing of capital allowances, 519
  values, 198–201
  valuing using real options analysis, 642–660

Ships—*cont*
  waste, disposal of, 179
Shortsea shipping
  cargoes, 282–284
  competitiveness
    factors influencing, 290–291
  definition, 280–282
  development of
    geographic and economic conditions for, 286–290
      critical thresholds, 286–290
      generalised costs, 290
      rationale, 286
  economics of, 280–304
  field of analysis, 282
  fleets, overview, 282–285
  implementing, pros and cons, 291–293
  market organisation, 282–284
  modal split, and, 285
  policies
    commercial actions, 294–295
    Europe, 296–299
    infrastructure, 294
    law and regulation, 294
    organisational actions and, 295
    possible, 293–296
    pricing, 295
    technological actions, 296
  purpose, 280
  traffic
    flows, trends, 284–285
    overview, 282–285
South Korea. *See* Korea

Tanker market, 169–170, 251–279. *See also* Tankers
  cargo, 163
  current structure, 251–279
  cycles, 205
  demand, 259–262
    and supply approach, 270–276
    cyclical features, 261
    derived, 259–260
    measurement, 260–261
    trends, 261
  economic analysis, 251–279
  economics of, 268–276
  environmental standards, 180–181
  freight rate
    behaviour, 268–270
    explaining, 271–273
    profitability, and, by tanker size, 273–274
  oil
    consumption, 253–254. *See also* Oil
      economic drivers of, 254–258
    production trends, world, 258–259
      consumption patterns, 2000, 258
      regional production patterns, 258–259
    regional flows of, 2000, 259
    transportation demand trends, 1990–2000, 261

Tanker market—*cont*
  profitability, freight rates and, by tanker size, 273–274
  shaping of present, 251–253
  ship price, 275–276
    behaviour, 268–270
  supply, 262–268
    and demand, 170
    approach, 270–276
    short-run, 271, 272
    composition, 262
    curve, short-run, 271
    external regulation, and, 266–268
    fleet
      development, 262–263
      structure, 263–265
    tanker ownership structures, 265
    term structure relations, 274–275
    timecharter rates, 1996 onwards, 262
Tankers. *See also* Ships; Tanker market
  cargo, 163
    oil consumption, end of twentieth century, 163
  demand, 259–262
  environmental standards, 180–181
  fleets
    development, 262–263
    market, 169–170, 251–279
    cycles, 205
    ownership structures, 265
  secondhand values, 191
  serious accidents, 181–183
  ship price, 268–270, 275–276
    behaviour, 268–270
  ships, investing in, 623–641. *See also* Investing in ships
  supply, 262–268
    and demand, 170
Taxes
  ships, flags, and, 512–529. *See also* Ships
Trade. *See also* International seaborne trade; International trade
  energy economics and, 105–146. *See also* Energy
  flows, European, establishment of, 147–154. *See also* Europe
  leading traders of manufactured goods 2000, 93
  outlook, 45–46
  transport, and, in economic theory, 38–42
  world, 1840–2000, 160
    growth in seaborne, 160
Trade unions
  seafarers', 462–465. *See also* Labour market
Traders
  leading,
    manufactured goods, of, 2000, 93
    who are?, 93
  view, 100–101
Transhipment
  capacity on north European routes, 841

Transhipment—*cont*
 container industry
  strategy, 840–842
  trends and developments, 836–842
 cost modelling approach, 842–855
  deviation distance in north Europe, 845
  lowest cost options, 849–853
   cost breakdowns for direct call and transhipment, 852
   estimated
    comparative costs of wayport hub and spoke transhipment, 853
    feeder costs matrix, 850
   feederport
    transhipment cargo, 851
    plus mainport, 851
   mainport transhipment cargo, 851
  mainline
   fleet changes and cost savings, 854–855
   ship deviation
    cost
     estimated mainline, 846
     model, 843
    feeder distances
     and costs, 844–847
     comparison of mainline, 847
   vessel charter cost, 854
  methodology, 842–844
  port productivity and terminal costs, 847–849
   comparison of
    container
     handling performance, 847
     transhipment tariffs, 849
 economics of, 832–859
 increase in ship size, 834–836
  design parameters of largest container ships, 837
  impact on ports, 836–838
 multiport direct call *v.* hub/spoke, 833–834
 terminals
  dedicated, and, 838–840
  major off shore hub, 840
  max berth depth, 840
  market position of leading operators, 842
  throughput berth and channel depth, 838
 theoretical perspectives, 833–836
Transport
 comparative tonne-mile costs, 165
 energy consumption, 108
 international maritime, costs
  determinants, 42–45
   intra-Latin American trade, 44
  mainstream economics, and, 41–42
  outlook, 45–46
  rediscovering, 42
  regional integration, and, 45
  trade, and, 42–45. *See also* International trade
   economic theory, in, 38–42
 traffic flows, European, establishment of, 147–154. *See also* Europe

Twentieth century
 shipping markets, 15–17
 maritime business, 9–34

United States
 Advisory Commission on Conferences in Ocean Shipping, 333
 antitrust laws, 328–329
 crude oil market, 127–128
 gas use in, 131
 legislation for regulating shipping industry, 603–604
 liner shipping, regulatory regime, 327–345. *See also* Liner shipping
 Ocean Shipping Reform Act 1998, 334–335
 passenger car efficiency development, 108
 Public Law 87-346 ("1961 amendments"), 330
 Shipping Act 1916, 329–330
 Shipping Act 1984, 331–333

Vessels. *See* Ships
Voyage costs risk, 712–723. *See also* Risk management

Waste
 disposal of, 179
West Africa
 crude oil market, 128
 shipping policies, 489–491
World
 bunker market, 712–713
 container traffic
  fleet 2000, 169
  growth, 161
 crude oil production, 162
 fleet, 1 October 2001, 479
 dry bulk trades, 162
 gas usage, 133
 manufactured exports by product 2000, 92
 merchant fleets, top 12, 1 October 2001, 481
 ocean shipping container carrying revenues, 880
 oil refining capacity, 122
 primary energy production, 106
 seaborne trade, 1985–2000, 91
 ship losses
  1992–1998, 430
   bulk vessel, 431
   tanker, 430
 shipbuilding, structural change, 532–535
 shipping developments, twentieth century, 9
 shipping tonnage, growth of, 166
 trade. *See also* International trade
  1840–2000, 160
   growth in seaborne, 160
  v. cptm, 163
 wind systems (January), 66